W9-BAK-386

COMPANION TO LITERARY MYTHS, HEROES AND ARCHETYPES

COMPANION TO LITERARY MYTHS, HEROES AND ARCHETYPES

Edited by
PIERRE BRUNEL

Translated from the French by
WENDY ALLATSON
JUDITH HAYWARD
TRISTA SELOUS

LONDON AND NEW YORK

First published in French as *Dictionnaire des Myths Littéraires*
by Éditions du Rocher, Jean-Paul Bertrand Editeur, Paris, in 1988

This edition first published in 1992
by Routledge
11 New Fetter Lane, London EC4P 4EE

Simultaneously published in the USA and Canada
by Routledge
29 West 35th Street, New York, NY 10001

Typeset in 10/12pt Ehrhardt, Linotron 300
by Intype Ltd, London
Printed in England by Clays Ltd, St Ives plc
∞ Paper manufactured in accordance with the proposed ANSI/N150
Z 39.48–199X and ANSI Z 39.48–1984

British Library Cataloguing in Publication Data
A catalogue record for this book is available from the British Library.

Library of Congress Cataloging in Publication Data
A catalog record for this book is available on request.

ISBN 0–415–06460–0

Contents

List of Entries

Preface

To the best of my knowledge there is no equivalent to this book available in print anywhere in the world. There are dictionaries of myths, notably the outstanding *Dictionnaire des Mythologies* published by Flammarion in 1981 under the aegis of Yves Bonnefoy. But that book made only occasional, incidental references to the treatment of myths in literature. Noting this limitation in its perspective, I had the idea some time later of bringing together a team capable of creating a different and quite distinct compendium of myths.

There were also, of course, the two dictionaries compiled in Germany by Elisabeth Frenzel, *Stoffe der Weltliteratur* and *Motive der Weltliteratur*. While the latter has a fairly pronounced thematic emphasis, the former has more in common with the present work. Indeed, even *Motive* overlaps with our study in certain areas: the inclusion of 'Doppelgänger' amongst its motifs is echoed by our use of 'Doubles and counterparts' as the title for one of our entries. This is the first indication of an imprecision in the use of terminology that can probably never be entirely resolved, especially as, in the context of a book, it is difficult to separate a myth from the book's theme or subject, and it may sometimes even be possible to talk of mythical themes. In terms of its approach, the present work is very different from those of Elisabeth Frenzel. While we have certainly tackled fewer subjects, we have usually studied them at greater length. Above all we have repeatedly drawn attention to a topic that is barely touched on by the *Stoff-geschichte*, namely the concept of the myth.

I shall take this as my starting point, since I am acutely aware that it is impossible to embark on a study of literary myth without first considering what the word myth implies. However, this does not mean that literary myths are merely myths in literature. I shall try to define the difference between the two terms, and to suggest the extent of the field of study that is opened up to us by analogy, though, of course, it was quite impossible for us to explore it fully. We had to make choices, and I shall conclude by trying to justify some of them.

In an issue of *Esprit*, Michel Panoff argued that the word 'myth' had become 'irritating', adding that 'hardly any other word today is loaded with more resonance and less meaning'. Like other imprecise terms it is used as an all-purpose word, particularly by the media, to such an extent that it would be quite possible to add another chapter to Roland Barthes's *Mythologies* entitled 'The mythology of myth' or 'The myth of myth'. The very fact that one can duplicate the term in this way is confirmation that there has been a shift of meaning. As Henri Meschonnic has pointed out, it has become 'laden with a pejorative, petty significance' and has come to mean 'advertent or inadvertent collective deception'.

To avoid this pitfall, I feel that it is wise to define myth in terms of its functions, following the example of Mircea Eliade, a religious historian who also helped to shape religious terminology. In *Aspects du mythe* he suggests the following definition of myth, which he regards as 'the least imperfect, because it is the widest':

> Myth recounts a sacred story; it relates an event that took place in primordial times, during the legendary era when things began.

Myth narrates. Myth is a story. In Plato's dialogues this is the respect in which it differs from simple discussion. Of course when it is recounted by Socrates, the mythical story is refined (and thanks to Plato's artistry, it already becomes an example of literary myth). The tales told orally by the shamans are much less linear, and attempts have been made to get back to the nebulous mythical forms that underlie any given linear story and are merely shaped by it. Whether these forms exist or not, myth is animated by the dynamism of the story. This fact gave rise to the comprehensive, though complicated, definition of myth proposed by Gilbert Durand in *Les Structures Anthropologiques de l'Imaginaire*:

> By myth we understand a dynamic system of symbols, archetypes and schemas, a dynamic system that tends, when prompted by a schema, to take the form of a story.

There are no doubt occasions when the story is condensed, and then all that remains is an image, such as that painted on a Greek vase or rising to the surface of a literary text (for example, 'Andromache, I think of you'). But it seems to me that the whole story is implicit in the illustration or the name alone.

Myth explains. That is its second function. The event that André Jolles in his book *Formes simples* regards as the 'verbal act' of myth is, according to Mircea Eliade 'an event that took place in primordial time, the fabulous time when things began.' And he adds:

> In other words, myth tells how, through the exploits of supernatural beings, a reality came to be, whether it is total reality, the Cosmos, or only a fragment of reality: an island, a species of plant, a form of human behaviour, an institution. Thus it is always the story of a 'creation': we are told how something was produced, started to exist.

Jolles is in complete agreement with Eliade in this respect. He uses the story of Genesis as his first example, the myth par excellence. The 'simple form' of the myth is shaped by the interplay of question and answer. Hardly has the question been asked than it is answered, 'and that answer is such that it becomes impossible to ask another question, that the question is cancelled just as it is being framed; the answer is decisive'. And this leads to a new definition of myth that is certainly the narrowest, but also the most concrete:

> Myth is the place where an object is created from a question and its answer . . . myth is the place where, starting from its innermost nature, an object becomes creation.

Thus mythological analysis implies a return to the beginning, to the archetype, and for both Jolles and Eliade, creation is perhaps the only archetype. Myth explains, it explains the causes, it is aetiological – unless it is spuriously aetiological, as Claude Lévi-Strauss pointed out in the context of the myth of Daphne.

The third function of myth is that it reveals. Eliade uses this verb in another of his books, *Mythes, Rêves et Mystères*, and points out that 'all mythology is a manifestation of being'. Myth reveals existence, and it reveals god. It is because of this that it can be presented as a 'sacred story'. In these circumstances, we can understand why in the *Phaedra* or *The Symposium* the mythical story can be told only by a visionary: namely Socrates, who is or claims – in the second of these dialogues – to be no more than the spokesman of the priestess of Mantinea.

There is thus a religious concept of myth, and even a pious concept, found, for example, in Milosz's the *Cantique de la Connaissance*. On the other hand, there is also a sceptical concept involving a refusal to believe in the language of the gods and exemplified by Claude Lévi-Strauss in *Le Cru et le Cuit* when he writes:

> Myths have no author: as soon as they are perceived as myths, whatever their actual origin may have been, they exist only embodied in a tradition. When a myth is told, individual listeners receive a message that properly speaking comes from nowhere; that is why supernatural origins are attributed to myth.

Will this scepticism eventually become part of a contemporary movement towards 'mythoclasm'? At least it leaves the living character of myth intact and recognizes the strength of a tradition that is in turn a source of inspiration for literature.

This is a tradition that can, in the first place, appropriately be termed mythology. But perhaps we should consider here what is meant by the very notion of mythology. Etymologically, the word means a discourse on myth. However, in a more practical context it can be understood as designating a codified body of myths, and in fact is generally used in this sense, being applied especially to the body of Greek and Roman myths. When, in 1801, François Noël set out in his *Dictionnaire de la Fable* to deal with 'Greek, Roman, Egyptian, Celtic, Persian, Syrian, Indian, Chinese, Scandinavian, African, American and iconological mythology', he made a point of stating in his preface that 'any comparison that can be made between these different mythologies is . . . entirely to the advantage of Greek mythology'. Almost at the same time, however, Chateaubriand launched his great attack on mythology, which he saw as belittling nature, thereby fomenting a new dispute between the 'Ancients' and the 'Moderns', between the supporters and detractors of myth.

This quarrel has probably not been resolved. On the one hand, there are those who tend to see mythology as debased, and will comment ironically, like Bloch in *A la recherche du temps perdu*, on the reference to 'the daughter of Minos and Pasiphaë' without understanding that that line actually contains within it the whole tragedy of Phaedra. On the other hand, there are those, such as Antonin Artaud, who are aware of the living strength and magic power of myth – though he admittedly sought it out not in conventionally accepted masterpieces, which he regarded as outdated, but in Balinese theatre or the rituals of the Tarahumara Indians.

Some Moderns are even firmly of the belief that literature is inimical to myth, not on the old grounds that literature is enfeebled by being overloaded with mythology, but because literature debases myth. Denis de Rougement comes close to adopting this position when, in *L'Amour et l'Occident*, he picks out two points at which myth was profaned: its birth in literature and its decline into sub-literature. And even Claude Lévi-Strauss seems so fascinated by the purity and strength of the structural oppositions that he identifies in myth (as in his famous analysis of the Oedipus myth, or Marcel Détienne's analysis of the Adonis myth), that he tends to denounce literature as involving shredding and dilution, as 'the last murmur of a dying structure', as a process of degradation and dislocation.

In my opinion this is unfair to literature. 'If *muthos* does indeed mean "word, or handed down story" ', Régis Boyer comments, 'is not all myth literary, to the extent that it inevitably requires a means of being handed down, which in the final analysis, especially in our day, implies that must be recorded in written form?' At the beginning of *Mythe et Epopée*, Georges Dumézil is on the verge of conceding that we know myths only through literature. Let us, therefore, accept that literature is the true repository of myths. What would we know of Ulysses but for Homer, of Antigone but for Sophocles, of Arjuna but for the *Mahabharata*? Like prehistoric research, pre-literary research merely wanders at random. And just as it is necessary to study history in order to understand prehistory, so it is only from the starting-point of literary texts or traditions that we can move on to hypotheses concerning what preceded them.

It follows from this that myth reaches us completely swathed in literature and is already literary, whether we like it or not. It also follows that literary analysis will inevitably at some point come up against myth. Recent attempts at 'myth-analysis' or 'mytho-criticism' have in fact demonstrated that they constitute a fruitful approach to the interpretation of texts.

However, literary historians and theorists have also taken an interest in literary myth in its own right. Rather than studying it in relation to a single text (for example Prometheus in *Le Temps retrouvé*) or a single author (for example Orpheus in Nerval), they have confronted it head on, seeing it as a unified mass, and unravelling it throughout its linguistic evolution. A work of the type that Raymond Trousson has undertaken on Prometheus gives a good idea of this type of approach, which sets out to build up a comprehensive view. On a lesser scale, the articles in this encyclopedia will also attempt to give some idea of the uniqueness of each literary myth, freed of its context and considered on its own merits.

This type of research has long been known as the 'study of themes'; and it is probably on the basis of subject or theme that we should start to try to define the literary myth. In his essay on methodology *Les Etudes de Thèmes*, written in 1965, Raymond Trousson did not use the word myth, but saw a theme as occurring,

> when a motif that seems like a concept, a mental image, becomes fixed, limited and defined in one or several characters acting in a particular situation, and when those characters and that situation give rise to a literary tradition.

Prometheus and Epimetheus, Eteocles and Polyneices, Abel and Cain, Oedipus and Medea were thus all considered as themes, illustrating fraternal strife, incestuous love or the betrayal of woman. It is not entirely by chance that in a second edition of his essay in 1981 the author gave it the new title *Thèmes et Mythes*. Even if he criticized the word 'myth' and the expression 'literary myth', and even if he finally elected not to use them, Raymond Trousson could not ignore – and, indeed, did not want to ignore – striking developments in the terminology of contemporary comparative studies.

It would be impossible to exaggerate the part played by Pierre Albouy and his remarkable essay, *Mythes et Mythologies dans la Littérature française* (1969) in fostering these developments. In broad terms, he suggests calling what Raymond Trousson had called a 'theme' a 'literary myth', but at the same time he makes a distinction between the 'literary myth' and the 'theme'. For him, the literary myth consists of the story implied by the myth – a story 'that the author can treat and alter with great liberty' – and of the new meanings that are then added to it. If there is no extra meaning added to what has been handed down by tradition, there is no literary myth, just a theme or subject. 'No literary myth arises unless there is a regeneration that conjures the myth back to life at a given period, demonstrating its capacity to express pertinently the problems of that age.'

I am in favour of this approach; I do not see it as being a facile acceptance of the fashion of the day. But the distinction drawn by Pierre Albouy between literary myth and theme does not seem very clear to me, nor, in the final analysis, very relevant. Is it really conceivable that a theme could be reworked without the addition of some new elements? And, in any case, is it not a basic principle of the study of literary myth that what Jean Rousset calls the 'constants', the nucleus of the myth itself, should be revealed?

To start with, therefore, and I must obviously be tentative in my approach, I shall reserve the term 'theme' for a concept. But I accept that a literary myth may illustrate a theme: the mythical figure of Antigone, for example, represents rebellion against the law of the *polis* when that law ignores blood ties and the demands of religion. That particular literary myth is based on fixed elements that can be used to formulate a mythical plot: the conflict between the heroine and the tyrant, his refusal to allow the burial of one of her brothers, the breaking of this prohibition, her betrothal to the tyrant's son, her condemnation and death. But, given these fixed elements, there are still many possible variations, which actually indicate the freedom and vitality present in literature.

However, this does not resolve every difficulty, for one should also try to define the idea of literary myth in relation to the idea of myth itself. In an article entitled 'Qu'est-ce qu'un mythe littéraire?' published in *Littérature* in 1984 Philippe Sellier very successfully did exactly this. The thread of his argument is as follows. He first defines ethno-religious myth as a primary, anonymous and collective story that submerges the present in the past and is accepted as true; the logic of the story is that of the world of imagination, and when analysed it reveals powerful structural oppositions. He then points out that during the passage from myth to literary myth the first three characteristics disappear: literary myth is not primary – it no longer initiates anything; works that contain it are normally signed; and literary myth is of course not accepted as true. But 'language – as so often – has implied a real relationship by using the same noun to designate religious myth and literary myth'. Their shared characteristics are saturation with symbols, compact organization (more compact than so far identified in the case of literary myth), and metaphysical illumination.

The other contribution made by Philippe Sellier's brilliant article is to show that literary myth does not merely represent the survival of ethno-religious myth in literature. Versions of stories with mythical origins that now form part of the western cultural heritage represent a large proportion of the works considered here. These emanate from the famous 'dyad' of sources represented by Athens and Jerusalem: on the one hand, there are the plethora of variant Greek myths and, on the other, the narrowly defined body of holy writ. However, there are other varieties of myth that also merit consideration in the context of literary myths. First there are 'recent literary myths', such as those few marvellous literary stories that have been produced in the West during modern times: Tristan and Isolde, Faust, Don Juan. Here it is possible to feel that myth actually derives from literature, for example that the imagination of the priest-playwright Tirso da Molina was essential to the creation of Don Juan. These myths are, in a sense, doubly literary, and it is not difficult to recognize the mythical elements in their plots: the love philtre, as in the myth of Medea; the pact with the Devil; the stone statue.

Philippe Sellier is more cautious about the other groups of 'literary myths' that he identifies. Those that fall into the category that Michel Butor regards as evoking 'the spirit of a place' – for example Venice – no doubt appeal to the imagination and allow the use of repetitive images, but they do not embody a situation that develops into a story. Politico-heroic myths (Alexander, Caesar, Louis XIV, Napoleon) do introduce stories, but they are dragged out interminably: here myth involves the glorification of a personality or a group using the process characteristic of epic. Finally, some myths that are para-biblical rather than truly biblical (Lilith, the wandering Jew, the Golem) owe their existence less to holy writ than to the exceptional success of a single work with an expertly devised plot.

As we can see, the range has already widened considerably. It will become wider still if we accept a different definition of myth and of literary myth. I am thinking of the definition put forward by André Dabezies, for example, in his *Visages de Faust au XX*^e^ siècle: 'a fascinating, symbolic illustration of a human situation that is exemplary for a particular community'. In an article entitled 'Des mythes primitifs aux mythes littéraires' the same writer first recalls Eliade's definition and then notes that both in modern times and in the past sociologists and political economists have exploited powerful images (Progress, Race, the Machine etc.) that exercised a collective fascination not dissimilar to that of primitive myths. This takes account of an essential factor that, it must be admitted, to some extent confuses the picture. Its mythical name, coined by Mallarmé, is the Demon of analogy. If for example we consider a particular great historical person as a myth, this is because we see him or her as a mythical hero, a new Achilles or Hector. In some cases, he may, like Caesar, have actually sought to establish himself as a god. On occasion, too, literature has made a myth of an historical person; as Jean Tulard has shown (*Le Mythe de Napoléon*, 1971), Napoleon has been turned into either an ogre or a Prometheus. Sometimes the process whereby a person is transformed into a myth takes place in the collective consciousness, and literature simply records it; but there are also cases where literature takes the initiative. And this gives us a large new category of literary myths, encompassing everything that literature has transformed into myth.

Clearly, when we embarked on this work there were substantial theoretical questions to be answered. At first, we thought of grouping the articles devoted to them in a separate section of the encyclopedia. However, we realized that theoretical discussion would very quickly become invasive, and it seemed preferable to include just a few of the most important essays and insert them in their proper place in the alphabetical order of entries. For example an article such as 'Historical and mythical figures' is included under the 'Historical' heading and develops the points recently discussed above, thereby justifying the presence in the encyclopedia of such figures as Joan of Arc and Louis XIV.

In the same vein, we felt that it was appropriate to make room for articles comparing literary myth with closely related genres. To some extent this meant dealing with a 'grey area', but it was justified by our desire to avoid the types of confusion that only too frequently arise: I am thinking of entries such as 'Tales and myths' or 'Utopia and myth'.

As we were aware that we could not cover everything, we also decided in some cases to study groups of myths: 'African myths', 'Germanic myths', 'Japanese myths', etc. However, this approach does not always preclude the individual treatment of a particular subject that falls into one of these categories: 'Shaka' or 'Sundiata' make indispensable contributions to the overall picture of African myth. The groups are not necessarily confined to a single geographical or linguistic area. Links are established, as for example in the article on 'Manlike women', which ranges from the Amazons to the Valkyries. There are even occasions when we have to transcend the divisions between different cultural zones, as happens in the article on 'Mythical bestiary'.

In the majority of cases the entry is based on the name of a character or a mythical hero. This does not imply that a myth always hinges on a single individual. In this respect, the name serves as an indicator, though there is no doubt that much of the focus is on it. The names Antigone and Oedipus, members of the Labdacid family, conjure up the history of a tragic *genos* at the same time as evoking the dilemmas that the two figures faced as individuals. People may be surprised by some of the things that we have omitted – and by some that we have included. We have placed less emphasis on providing an exhaustive collection than on providing a varied one. There is geographical variety of course: Amerindian myths take their place alongside Greek myths. But above all there is variety in the examples chosen: as well as mythical figures, there are also historical and literary figures who have become literary myths.

One final word about the project. This book is the product of work on literary myths carried out by a research team at the Centre de Recherche en Littérature comparée at the university of Paris IV. It has involved not only a great many work sessions, but also much friendship, co-operation and goodwill. No doubt in some ways it is still experimental. It represents a 'work in progress', and it should therefore be possible to add to and improve on it in subsequent editions.

Pierre Brunel

Abraham

Only one episode in the biblical account of the patriarch Abraham has attracted literary and artistic attention, namely the 'sacrifice of Isaac'. And what a subject it is: a deity compelling a father to kill his beloved son! Even if the god in question seemed alien and remote, like Diana requesting the immolation of Iphigenia, we would still shed tears for the defenceless child condemned to its fate, in the same way as the audiences watching the tragedies by Euripides and Racine; but the god who orders the sacrifice in the Bible is the very touchstone of the believer's faith. On the lofty summit of Moriah the air that we breathe is rarefied; inevitably we react with fear and trembling, or with horror.

THE SOURCE OF THE MYTH: GENESIS 32. 1–19

The story appears rugged and dry, but pure and harsh. It combines simplicity and complexity, brevity and interminable length, and offers the maximum of fact with the minimum of detail. Everything about it remains unexpressed; what is not stated is indispensable for its true understanding. The density of the gestures and objects and the way in which they are thrown into relief signify their exact opposite. According to Eric Auerbach, two phrases adequately sum up the unusual qualities of this text: 'bereft of background' and 'crying out for interpretation'.

At first sight, its structure seems like that of a biblical saga, a genre that is close to the folk tale. From the very first verse the emphasis is on the 'setting of a test': 'After these things God tested Abraham.' After God's 'command', in verse 3 we find Abraham 'obeying', 'deciding' and 'embarking on the test'. ('So Abraham rose early in the morning and saddled his ass.') His perfect obedience is thus highlighted.

If the usual terms 'combat' and 'victory' are not actually used explicitly, they are nonetheless implied in the second verse by the mention of the 'son . . . whom you love' and 'offer . . . as a burnt offering'. By avoiding mention of 'confrontation', the author achieves two things: on the one hand, he draws attention to the divine command and its prompt execution, and, on the other, he spreads the 'struggle' right through the story, inviting us to perceive it as internal. The hero is faced with a dilemma: either he obeys God's command and denies his role as a father, or he saves his son and denies his role as the servant of the Lord – a perfect illustration of the definition of myth suggested by Greimas: 'the conjunction of contradictions, of choices that are equally impossible and unsatisfactory'. The fact that this is a conflict between man and God further enhances the mythical status of the story, which is indicated by topographical and chronological codes.

The journey of Abraham and his son in fact follows a circular route. Starting and ending at Beer-sheba (the family's dwelling-place), it includes the ascent of a holy mountain, where the vision, or theophony, occurs. ('And Abraham called the name of that place The Lord will provide, as it is said unto this day, "On the mount of the Lord it shall be provided" ' [verse 14].) The course of the action is bound up with the space that it covers; it is a god who instigates the journey and who is there at its end, while the hero of the test returns from the journey transformed: the deity now knows that he 'fears God'. Thus the journey clearly constitutes a rite of passage, and this is confirmed by its chronology. First, the divine command was imparted 'in a dream' when the hero rose 'early in the morning', and this is the usual means by which mystical instructions are given. Then there is the duration of the expedition: 'On the third day Abraham . . . saw the place afar off'. This calls to mind the three days spent by John in the belly of the whale, or the three days during which Jesus lay in the tomb.

In sum, though it appears soberly realistic and utterly devoid of any overt mythology, the story of the 'testing of Abraham' can still justifiably called mythical in the profoundest sense of the term. It is a 'condensed human drama, symbolizing a real situation': a model for the relationship between God and man, and one that has been imitated countless times.

The Traditional Paraphrase

From the medieval mystery plays to the lyrical dramas of the late eighteenth century a whole series of works that draw their inspiration from chapter 22 of Genesis show similar characteristics. In the first place, they are all theatrical pieces. Israelite saga was intrinsically suited to dramatization: the sober backdrops and the intense action involving two or three people invited the reader to endow the characters involved with voices and gestures. It is thus unsurprising that medieval clerics set actors representing Abraham and Isaac on the stage. The 'Story of Isaac' figured in various English mystery plays, and, 'Le Sacrifice d'Isaac' formed part of the collection *Le Mystère du Viel Testament*; while the Spanish *autos*, whether written anonymously or by a genius such as Calderón, continued the spirit of the Middle Ages on into the sixteenth and seventeenth centuries.

In contrast to the biblical story itself, adaptations of it for the stage thrive on conflict, accentuating and multiplying its sources: there is conflict between God and Abraham, between Abraham and his son, between Abraham and Sarah, and inside the characters themselves, with monologues to show how they are torn by irreconcilable loyalties. In Abraham, the father is at war with the believer, and in God Himself, Misericord fights with Justice, in the form of personified allegories.

Another characteristic of these pieces is that they enrich the original material by placing it in context, between the events that precede it and follow it in the original biblical text. Usually the play opens with a tableau of happiness and peace that serves to accentuate the horror of the drama that subsequently unfolds. The parents offer thanks to God for the child that He has given to them; after this the inescapable demand for its sacrifice will be felt all the more cruelly. Finally, in all of these works it is made clear that the sacrifice of Isaac 'prefigures the Passion of Christ'; its theological significance is fused with its human, realistic dimension.

Whereas the anonymous Spanish *auto* is a lively, even trivial, affair, Calderón's version neglects the human drama to concentrate solely on the underlying ideas; in one case, the tragic aspect of the original text is dissipated in banal comic detail, while in the other, it is rendered sterile in the cut and thrust of a theological debate.

During the Renaissance the naive genre of the mystery play was embellished by the influence of classical drama and Aristotelian theory. A spate of works on the subject of Abraham and Isaac appeared throughout Europe, written in every conceivable language and mostly scholarly rather than popular. This fashion lasted throughout the Classical period, with a sprinkling of masterpieces such as *Abraham sacrifiant* by Théodore de Bèze, *Isaaco, Figura del Redentore* by Mestastasio and *Abraham und Isaak* by Lavater.

As well as the plays there were numerous poems, such as those by Du Bartas, but all the works of the Classical period have the same characteristics: each verse in chapter 22 of Genesis is developed, details are exploited exhaustively, the psychological analysis is handled without probing, there is greater stress on heartbreak than on the divine plan – in sum, the story is amplified simply by being expanded. These paraphrases aim merely to reproduce the ancient text, almost never abridging it, but tending rather to embroider it. They faithfully preserve, or set out to preserve, the religious message of the writer in the Bible. The words of the Bible are interpreted in a tradition going right back to the first compilers of the Pentateuch and handed down through the rabbis to the Fathers of the Christian Church who added a new element to the Jewish interpretation by representing Isaac as prefiguring the Redeemer. Moreover, in a Christian culture the text is not dead, but peculiarly alive. Those who read it or see it acted out can look upon it as their own; they share the same faith as the hero, and they can relive his experiences and apply them to themselves. From the medieval clerics to the Protestant Théodore de Bèze, from the Catholic Calderón to the Pietist Lavater, those copying the story showed a uniformity of approach that was not destined to continue.

The Paraphrase Renewed

This traditional approach was challenged by Kierkegaard in his book *Fear and Trembling*. In four consecutive paraphrases he sets out to show how the story is interpreted by a man whose faith is uncertain, and who was prosecuted for disputing accepted views and for voicing thoughts quite naturally aroused by the extraordinary events described. The extreme lyricism of the text, its mildly emphatic tone and its omission of religious elements all attest to his intentions. Yet at the end of the paraphrases, the Danish philosopher contradicts the conclusions apparently to be inferred from them and offers a 'eulogy of Abraham' – far from being a monster, he was a good and sensitive man:

> Either we have to score right through the story of Abraham, or we have to learn the terror of the dreadful paradox that gives meaning to his life, in order to understand that our age too can be happy like any other, provided it has faith.

Topical Relevance

Wilfred Owen no longer viewed Abraham as the first believer, but as the adult of 1914 who sacrificed his son on the altar of nationalism, a son representing 'half the seed of Europe'. He used the ancient story to reinforce an eternal lesson: human beings should not kill the innocent, even using the pretext of war, which is no more than the expression of national pride. His poem extends the application of the biblical text from the individual to the community, but makes no reference to the pledge given to God.

The same allegorical technique is used to the same effect in Leonard Cohen's song, 'Story of Isaac', in the context of the war that the Americans were waging in Vietnam in 1970. Two verses put into Isaac's mouth denounce adults who kill children and force them to wear uniforms to protect themselves. These adults do not have the excuse of the patriarch in the Bible; they have not been put to the test 'by the devil or a god'. This vague allusion projects the story into a mythical universe where there is no clear-cut distinction between the Lord of Lords (Elohim) of Genesis and Satan.

Josip Brodsky's poem *Isaac et Abraham*, which is over 600 lines long, expresses the feelings of a Russian Jew who is both a cabalist expert in the symbolism of numbers and a man suffering the heartbreak of exile far from his native land. He is concerned only with the meaning of Abraham's experience for a Russian – first himself, and secondly the rest of his people. The victim burning on the pyre is actually the poet, and his sufferings are interminable; the bush on Moriah is changed into an altar, and then into a cross. These ideas are close to those of religious writers who think that the original sacrifice, anticipating, as it does, that of Christ, must be the fate of every Christian, indeed of all humanity.

Demythicization

In his *Tales of Jacob (Die Geschichten Jakobs)*, Thomas Mann reconstructs the customs and outlook of the men of Abraham's day like a well-informed archaeologist, but he gives his heroes, Jacob and Joseph, completely modern souls. He makes a distinction between Abraham, the believer, a figure from the past, and those who came after him and were incapable of belief. The Moriah episode is experienced by an anti-hero and ends in his apparent defeat when he refuses to sacrifice his son. It is not clear, though, whether the novelist really sees this as a defeat; he suggests that it is more of a victory for humanity, which has become more rational. While proclaiming the myth, Thomas Mann in fact destroys it; for him it has ceased to be 'the outer garb of the vital mystery'. If it can be enjoyed at an aesthetic level, then it can be believed.

In his approach to the story of Abraham offering up his sacrifice, Laurence Housman sets out to rob it of its universality, to *demythologize* it, to use Bultman's term. In the play *Abraham and Isaac* that he based on Genesis 22, the English poet eliminated all the miraculous aspects: gone are the summons in a dream and the voice of the angel – there is no miracle, and therefore no divine voice ordering or staying the execution of a beloved son. But this does not mean that the supernatural has been suppressed, it has merely been internalized: man seeks God, and God answers him, but this exchange takes place within their hearts. It seems that Housman is representing the journey to Moriah as prompted by Abraham's own distress, as a self-inflicted punishment for loving his son too much; and in this respect his interpretation is in line with that of a Freudian critic. The play is, in fact, imbued with a deep internal religious feeling that favours obedience at the expense of conscience. While it may not be faithful to the original text in a literal sense, it is faithful to the spirit behind it, to its highest objective, which is to encourage a sacrifice 'in spirit and in truth'.

The Projection of the Unconscious

Hegel must have been the first person before Freud to see the Elohim to whom Abraham had pledged his faith as 'the image of his own nature'; to him the Hebrew patriarch was a cruel, selfish creature, proud and domineering, a being apart, who, in his contempt for humanity went as far as rejecting the deepest emotion that can exist, love for one's own child. According to this interpretation, the story in Genesis is the account of a personal crisis experienced in the unconscious by a man who loves his son too much; his super-ego condemns his (too) natural instincts and, by means of a dream, orders him to suppress them. Just as its command is about to be carried out, the super-ego rewards the individual's obedience by magnanimously revoking it:

the child will not be killed, on the contrary, the controlling super-ego voices the universal principle forbidding killing.

This interpretation might also apply to the passage in which Marcel Proust conjures up the episode from Genesis; to him God is none other than the father, and that father is an executioner who separates the son from his mother:

> He still stood there in front of us, tall in his white nightshirt with his head swathed in the purple and pink Indian cashmere shawl which he had tied round it ever since he had suffered from neuralgia, making the same gesture as Abraham in the print based on Benozzo Gozzoli that M. Swann had given me, telling Sarah that she must leave Isaac's side.

Behind the Bible story, the novelist sees the archetypal relationship between father, mother and son; as is often the case, Jewish legend rather than Greek fable provides him with a vehicle for expressing his own fantasies and endowing a personal experience with sacred overtones. The myth illustrates a situation that arises very early in childhood, and therefore has an exemplary vitality and value, though it does not retain any vestige of religiosity.

Belief in the God of Abraham

In his *Jacob*, Pierre Emmanuel pushes Abraham into the background and lets Isaac speak – making him the personification of the willing victim, the slave of God, a silent, submissive creature forever bearing the marks of his childhood. His God, perceived as a cruel tyrant who transfixes him with his eye, his God, 'concentrated on the tip of the dagger', is not dissimilar to the original father figure outlined by Freud in *Moses and Monotheism*. However, if there is a whiff of blasphemy, reverence still wins the day; the god of the Bible has two aspects, commanding 'fear' and 'worship', being an implacable Judge and a kind Benefactor.

The same applies to a crucial passage in Alfred Döblin's novel *Berlin-Alexanderplatz*: the hero, Frank Biberkopf, is foreshadowed by Isaac and, like him, must consent to his own suffering, and so become a new man. The lesson is the same as in the Bible: God will be obeyed in all he asks. However, after dragging the reader into the depths of despair, the novelist celebrates the act of divine intervention with a series of alleluias: 'Alleluia! . . . You obeyed me, alleluia! You will live, alleluia! Listen to me: throw the cutlass into the gorge. Alleluia!'

Alfred Döblin and Pierre Emmanuel, who were both religious believers, let us hear the voice of Isaac or of Abraham, the human voice riven by the fear of death; in *L'Acte du Bélier*, another poet, Claude Vigée, represents Abraham as the symbol of the Jewish people, whose task it is to bring the ram out of the thicket, in other words, to reveal the god hidden in the undergrowth of our complexes. The ram is the allegory both of the victim, the Jewish people, and of their god: in the conflagration of the burnt offering, the poet glimpses the glow of the ovens in which Jews massacred by the Nazis were cremated during the Second World War; but the thicket on Moriah also conjures up the Burning Bush, where God manifested himself to Moses. There is a lesson of hope: the 'tears of blood' will be transformed into tears of joy; God will give life to his people.

In formal terms, the sacrifice of Isaac is similar to all the sacrifices of new-born babies attested in the ancient East, the significance of which is readily understood. Some writers (Hegel, Proust, Thomas Mann) concentrate on this aspect of the story, and see it simply as involving a group of neurotic characters. Others strip the biblical text of its religious character and use it merely as an empty form to carry a social or political message, as in the case of Owen and Cohen, or the echoes of a more personal experience of suffering, as in the case of Brodsky.

However, both in traditional paraphrases of the story and in most contemporary versions there is another dimension, relating to religious experience. Abraham is seen as the champion of faith, that is of the freedom to commit oneself to a completely separate individual. In the Elohim of Genesis, the writers of such works recognize their own personal god. For them, the mythology is alive; true, it is decked out in miraculous trappings, but what matters is the genuineness of its kernel of faith and hope. While death in all its horror lurks at the heart of this experience, in the end it is routed; as in a famous painting by Rembrandt, it is celestial light that eventually triumphs, and with it life, the overflowing life desired by the god of the Bible, the 'god not of the dead but of the living'.

Robert Couffignal

Adonis

Ever since it was first introduced into Greece the myth of Adonis has been associated with poetry, as it was inseparably linked to a cult with a ritual consisting mainly of songs, which were apparently commissioned from famous poets of the day. While the story itself may be short, it contains major themes that have inspired writers of outstanding quality from antiquity until the present day.

The Legend

The account that follows is based on the oldest known version of the myth (Panyassis of Halicarnassus, fifth century BC) augmented by several variants that have been thoroughly integrated into the conventional version (Bion, Ovid).

Adonis was born as a result of incest between King Cinyras and his daughter Myrrha, whom the King pursued as soon as he realized that he had been duped. When she was about to be caught, Myrrha called upon the gods, who transformed her into a myrrh tree, the aromatic substance itself being produced by her tears. The trunk split open giving birth to a fine child, whose beauty moved Aphrodite so much that she concealed him in a chest, which she entrusted to Persephone, who subsequently refused to return the boy to her. Zeus settled the dispute between the two goddesses, decreeing that the youth should spend a third of the year with each of them, and choose for himself where to spend the remaining third: not surprisingly, he chose to spend it with Aphrodite.

Adonis was a passionate huntsman and while Aphrodite was away he was gored by a monstrous boar and died of his wounds. The goddess returned only in time to lament him. A flower, the anemone, sprang from his blood.

The original story stopped at this point. But due to the influence of the annual cult celebrating Adonis's reunion with Aphrodite and lamenting his loss when he returned to Hades, the idea of alternating homes, on the earth and below it, seems to have been transformed into a story of a permanent return.

The Greek mind with its inclination to seek reasons for everything could not accept the idea of a simple accident. In some versions, Adonis is guilty of neglecting the goddess's warnings; in others he is the victim of the vengeance of some other deity – Artemis, Ares, Apollo, etc.

The story has a number of variants, and though these differ in antiquity and importance, none of them can be completely disregarded. An isolated variant may be readopted or reinvented by a modern poet – proof that it is more central to the myth than might have been thought.

Origins and Development

Further details of the myth are provided in W. Atallah's scholarly study, *Adonis dans la Littérature et l'Art grecs* (1966). The emphasis here will be on its subsequent treatment in literature.

Adonis is of oriental origin: the root of his name is Semitic (*Adon* = Lord). However, there is no certain information as to his origins. From the late classical period (Origen) he was identified with Tammuz, a Babylonian god later found also in Phoenicia, whose legend and cult are strikingly similar to his own. In both cases, the hero, held against his will by the goddess of the underworld, is set free by a beneficent earthly goddess (in the case of Tammuz, Ishtar). But is it the same story in both instances, or are the two myths merely related? In early versions of the Adonis story, his father was the King of Assyria, then of Phoenicia and Arabia, though the accepted version places his kingdom in Cyprus. For a long time Cyprus was accepted by poets as the setting of the legend, but later it was shifted back to Byblos and the heights of Lebanon, which exercise a powerful attraction over modern writers.

The legend and the cult must have travelled via the islands to Greece at a very early period. They figure fully developed in fragments attributed to Sappho of Lesbos. In Athens in the fifth and fourth centuries BC the cult of Adonis, as celebrated by women in particular, inspired the humour of comic poets, while its funerary aspect is described by Plutarch. After Alexander's conquests it became more widespread in the Hellenized world. According to Theocritus, it was particularly popular in Alexandria in the third century BC. Apparently it then spread back towards its country of origin, and it was a ritual re-imported from Alexandria that Lucian of Samosata observed in Byblos (*De dea Syria*). Finally, during the Roman imperial times the cult reached the outermost limits of the empire.

The cult ritual occupied two days, one given over to mourning for the death of Adonis, the other to hymns of joy at his return and reunion with the Aphrodite; the sequence, however, varied from place to place. The young god was offered the fruits of the earth, and one element of the ritual, known as the 'Gardens of Adonis', has been written about at length. This involved sowing various plants in vases or baskets shortly before the festival, and observing how the sun made them grow quickly, but made them wither quickly too. When the day of mourning was over the plants were thrown in the water. This rite lent itself to symbolic interpretations, and the word 'gardens' was misconstrued, so that poets were sometimes inspired by faulty perceptions.

By the early centuries AD, the young god was no longer the dewy adolescent lamented by Sappho. Gradually he had been contaminated by association with comparable mythical characters and new gods, and finally by a religious syncretism that tended to result in confusion over his identity. Which concept of Adonis has appealed most to poets?

The Family of Adonis

It is immediately apparent that the story of Adonis is a combination of three families of myth. The first involves youths whose beauty attracts the love of one of the immortals, and *who die as a result of this*, either because their lover is thoughtless, or because of the enmity of another god. Examples include Hyacinthus, Daphne and Semele. Other shared traits are the role of the hero as huntsman or shepherd, and a link with the plant world (the final metamorphosis). The second group of myths concern heroes who confront monsters, particularly wild boar (Calydon, Erymanthus); while the third family relates to heroes who descend into the underworld and return alive, though Adonis's *periodic* return is exceptional.

At a later period, Adonis became part of a very different family of deities: those who rise permanently from the dead. By this time, the youth, who started off by being human and then became a demi-god, has finally attained the status of the one and only god, recognizable in a variety of guises. According to an epigram by Ausonius (fourth century AD) he is called Osiris in one place, Dionysus in another, and so on. He is a god 'with many names', according to *Orphic Hymns* 56, and sometimes even an androgynous figure, so that female manifestations (Selene) can be integrated into the myth.

Nevertheless it should be noted that over the centuries the distinctive features of the person and cult of Adonis were retained or restored.

Interpretations

It must be emphasized in this context that we are not looking for a single 'true' interpretation of the myth of Adonis, nor should we necessarily believe that the oldest interpretation is the correct one. All the interpretations inherent in the myth (legend and cult) are true, at least for one period or one type of mind.

However it is remarkable how early interpretations of the myth occur and how unvarying they remain. From the first few centuries AD a symbolism of natural cycles began to be developed, in two related forms: the plant cycle, and the astral cycle. These interpretations recur in the writing of almost all modern mythologists and are inspired either by the influence of schools of philosophy or by mystic sects. The plant exegesis is the earlier: Adonis is assimilated to the produce of the earth, particularly corn, which is seen as dying, then coming to life again (Porphyrius; various Fathers of the Church). Later, when syncretism based on the sun was dominant in the Roman Empire,

Adonis was identified with the sun detained, beneath the earth in winter (Macrobius, fifth century AD).

Poets of the Renaissance and Baroque periods gained their knowledge of myths and fables from collections compiled by classical scholars, and from direct reading of the classical poets (especially Ovid).

Speculation concerning myths revived in the eighteenth century, though only those mythologists with a particular interest in Adonis who inspired poets to write about him are relevant here. Some of these scholars were actually poets themselves, an example being Friedrich Creuzer (*Symbolik*, 1810–12, 1. IV). He uses both interpretations of the Adonis myth, seeing them as a single explanation on two levels, astral and terrestrial. However, he also supports a third, spiritual interpretation, connected with mystery religions that regard the trials successfully endured by their gods as a guarantee of salvation. He gives the impression of being attracted mainly by the death of Adonis and the dark poetry of the funeral rite.

No-one is more sensitive to that poetry or expresses it better than Renan. He pursues his study (*Mission de Phénicie*, 1864) in the guise of a somewhat disappointed archaeologist, but is captivated by a vision of nature in which tormented grandeur goes hand in hand with springlike grace, and obsessed by a personal experience that has something of the character of a descent into the underworld. Both he and his sister are struck down by the same illness, but he alone emerges from a period of lethargy, during which the sacred river is transformed in his dreams into Lethe. Henriette is for ever at rest in the land of Adonis; Ernest wakes up haunted by a nostalgic feeling of loss that he attributes to the followers of Adonis – and that is certainly experienced by the poets who write about the deity. 'A dangerous attraction where you let yourself go and fall asleep. Religious feelings float within it hovering between voluptuousness, sleep and tears.'

The magic of Lebanon and the fascination of death also affect Charles Vellay (*Le Culte et les Fêtes d'Adonis Thammouz dans l'Orient antique*, 1910), but he succumbs to a tendency prevalent at the end of the nineteenth century to trace all religions back to sun worship (Mallarmé, *Les Dieux antiques*, 1880). For Vellay, Adonis is the supreme god, under a variety of names; he embodies all creative and destructive powers; as an adrogynous figure, he is both Sun and Earth, as well as being Moloch the devourer. This highly imaginative book had some impact on other writers, more because its conviction is almost contagious than because it had any substantial factual basis.

For James G. Frazer (*Adonis, Attis, Osiris*, 1906) Adonis was simply one of several related divinities associated with vegetation. His basic hypothesis is that *the rite preceded the story and gave birth to it*, the aim being to encourage a natural process by re-enacting it; the process is dramatized and becomes the story of two divine partners embodying the powers of fertility. Frazer accepts the identification of Adonis with various plants: he may have been a tree, browsed grass, or harvested corn. In any event he *had to* die. But Frazer also felt the lure of Byblos and of Renan's writing. He forgives Renan for colouring the myth with his own personal feelings and even suggests that it may be necessary to take account of love in considering how myths arise.

Two books worth considering have been written too recently to have had an influence yet on other works of literature. One, already mentioned, is by W. Attalah and is more wide-ranging than its title suggests; in seeking to understand the myth of Adonis, the author makes the rare and wise decision to seek out features that make it resemble other myths, but ones that distinguish it from them. The second work, *Les Jardins d'Adonis. La Mythologie des Aromates dans le Monde grec* (1972), by Marcel Detienne, applies a Structuralist schema to the Adonis myth. It is clever, complex and systematic, but, in my opinion, it gives a signally distorted view of the hero and his legend.

Adonis in the Poetry of Classical Antiquity

The Greek literary works inspired by Adonis are strictly related to his cult. The surviving texts give at least some echo of the ritual songs, evoking both emotional poles of the legend: the marriage with the goddess, and the hero's death.

The first of these two events is celebrated in Theocritus *Idylls XV*, which was composed in Alexandria (274–70 BC) and vividly evokes the splendid festivals of Adonis organized by Queen Arsinoë. The poet first describes their lavish ceremonial, then makes a famous female artiste perform the epithalamion (hymn of the bridal chamber). The atmosphere is of joy and tender affection for the young demi-god and of faith in the divine protection being afforded him. A mention of the ceremony the following day, when the statue of Adonis was taken down to the sea, perhaps symbolizing Hades, is softened by an expression of hope for the demi-god's return.

The second event is illustrated by the *Lament for Adonis*, very probably by Bion (third century BC), which must have been composed *in conformity with* the cult. Woven into it are appeals to the sleeping goddess and lamentations interrupted by the cries of the weeping women. Among the latter are the words 'Beautiful Adonis is dead!', a riveting refrain, which has the force of an incantation and expands into the splended lament of Cypris. All the themes of the myth are already present: the mourning of the creatures of the forests and the powerlessness of the goddess either to keep her beloved or to follow him. The poem offers no consolation: Adonis seems to be Persephone's prisoner for ever. The poetic impact of this piece was evidently extremely powerful: Ronsard, Marino, La Fontaine, Shelley and D'Annunzio were all haunted by it.

In the work of Ovid (*Metamorphoses* X, first century BC) there is a change of tone and the ritual element disappears. Ovid is a story-teller and what interests him in the legend is its narrative qualities: he spends longer on Myrrha's guilty passion than on the short story of Adonis himself. A few graceful passages concerning his amorous adventures do not compensate for the disappearance, not of the *miraculous*, but of the truly *mythical* elements. There is no dual life, above and below the earth, death is simply a hunting accident; the hero is a pallid creature – Venus is more alive, though she is handled somewhat irreverently.

A completely different Adonis is portrayed in the second century AD in a Greek text that is both a religious document and a literary work. *Orphic Hymns* 56 is a paean and prayer addressed to a young god reminiscent of the one honoured in Alexandria five centures earlier in his gentleness and kindness and the tender affection that he inspires in those weeping over him. However, this Adonis is no longer so human; the shifting outlines of his body enable him to be simultaneously boy and girl, the child of both Cypris and Persephone. His beauty is expressed in plant metaphors related both to the young shoots whose growth he stimulates and to the mature fruit that he bears. This obscure work exercises a particular fascination, felt much later by mythologists and poets.

Adonis in the Hands of Modern Poets

The development of the myth of Adonis has followed a curved route. This has taken it through a period of humanization, even secularization, back much closer to its origins and symbolic values, thanks to the work of mythologists and also to a change of outlook. At the same time, there has also been a resurgence of interest in the cult, and, in particular, the funeral rite, which was re-enacted on the stage for the first time by Gabriele D'Annunzio. Of course, the curve has not been constant – for example the religious aura persisted in English poetry at a time when it was disappearing elsewhere.

A brief review of the elements of the myth reveals the absence of the story of Myrrha from treatments of it by modern writers (she is hardly mentioned by Marino). The contest betwen the two goddesses has also disappeared, as has Persephone herself. The poetically evocative descent into Hades is hinted at only by D'Annunzio, and the story of Adonis in the underworld has clearly been eclipsed by that of Orpheus. Nevertheless his stay in an unearthly abode reappears in different forms: underground captivity in the power of a romantic sorceress in Marino and a sojourn in a realm of peace in Spenser, Milton and Keats. Keats is the only one to have retained the idea of the *periodic* return of Adonis; other poets (Spenser, Milton, D'Annunzio) describe his recovery, or permanent revival.

The theme that recurs with remarkable persistence is the dramatic one of love between an immortal goddess and a fragile youth subject to the vagaries of Time, a theme that incorporates the concept of Beauty and its fearful powers.

THE RENAISSANCE AND BAROQUE PERIODS

Whilst the return to favour of Adonis was associated with the rediscovery of the poets of classical antiquity, it was also encouraged by the contamination of the legend by the pastoral convention. In the process, Adonis acquired two new guises. In the first, he is a shepherd-poet, in the second a child of the forest (to borrow the expression used by Siegfried), a countrified youth who adores hunting and is wary of the overtures of others; sometimes like Hippolytus he is faithful to Diana and disdainful of love.

The pastoral convention also provided a new literary form, the first example of which is Virgil *Eclogues* V, which is a funerary eclogue in two parts, one dark and one light, recalling the two days of the festival of Adonis.

In the works discussed below as typical examples of their kind, the supernatural element disappears; the story becomes human, more fiction than myth, and Adonis's links with the plant kingdom are used purely for their poetic grace. However, in one exceptional instance Adonis appears in a supremely symbolic work, the *Dream of Poliphilo (Hypnerotomachia Polophili*, Venice, 1499). The scene is enacted on Cythera, where Venus has just blessed the marriage of two lovers. The nymphs take them on a pilgrimage to the tomb of Adonis where bas-reliefs recount his varying fortunes. Besides the ashes of the young huntsman, the tomb contains the blood and tears of the goddess, and these relics are venerated at a spring commemoration ceremony in which red roses, coloured by the blood of the goddess, play a prominent part. This graceful episode seems to be intended to complete the lovers' initiation.

Ronsard (P. de), 'Adonis', 1563. Repeated in *Elégies*, 1567, 369 lines

In this instance, the story is derived from Bion and Ovid and has taken on a very human aspect despite the element of divine revenge: Adonis is just an innocent victim. His striking attribute is his freshness – not identified with young plant growth,but implied by surroundings that all evoke the spring. He is not a prince, but a shepherd lad; at his side Venus becomes a shepherdess, a motif used by Ovid, and their rustic life is portrayed in a very concrete fashion. The poor 'shepherd lad' loves, sings and dies as simply as a bird, but the true heroine of the story is Venus. It is her passion and despair that overflow in an unusually full and eloquent lament (144 lines), though this comes to a shockingly abrupt end, when she is immediately unfaithful. For Adonis there is neither a metamorphosis nor a happy return. He does not become a god. Venus's readiness to forget consigns him to oblivion.

Lope de Vega, *Adonis y Venus* (1597–1603) and Calderón

Lope de Vega was responsible for one of the few interesting attempts to transfer the legend to the stage. The subject is handled at a distance, and extraneous episodes are added to it; the construction is loose, but the work is memorable for its very real charm – the pastoral atmosphere, the characters of the shepherds, and the Arcadian setting. Adonis, who is the personification of the child of the forest, is shy of women and loves only the woods; he is simple, naive and inclined to be boastful; and though he lets himself be seduced, he is suspicious of the experience. As in other versions of the story, he is the victim of Venus's machinations: Apollo arouses Tisiphone to fight him, in the shape of a wild boar, and, as in Ronsard's work, the goddess is quick to find consolation. There are some attractive scenes, the play is witty, the stanzas are musical and there are also some songs.

Even though it deals still more arbitrarily with the myth, another theatrical work by a great poet also deserves mention – *La Purpura de la Rosa* by Calderón de la Barca (Don Pedro) (Zarzuela, 1659). Though written at about the same time as La Fontaine's *Adonis*, it is quite different in character. Mounted in honour of the marriage 'of the most Serene Infanta Maria-Theresa and the very Christian King Louis XIV', it is a spectacular musical play involving apparatus, transformations on stage and all the stage magic of the Baroque period. There are appearances by peasants, soldiers and allegorical characters, and the play includes a variety of pastoral and martial music. Adonis is again portrayed very much as a child of the forest. He is chivalrous and brave in coming to the aid of Venus in the guise of a huntress pursued by a wild boar, but he speaks to her brusquely: 'I run away from beauty, not from wild animals.' Inevitably, he yields to love, and though he falls victim to Mars, the play ends happily with his apotheosis. The rose stained red by Adonis's blood (not Venus's as in the traditional version) features prominently.

The play is written in a 'cultivated' style, full of metaphors, antitheses, witty sallies, and repeated choruses that must have raised the hackles of the French audience in 1659 – if they understood it. Later generations are more appreciative, finding the work highly imaginative and very poetic.

Marino (G.B.), *Adone*, Paris, 1623

This work is a huge narrative poem (5,123 stanzas) written in France and dedicated to Marie de Médicis, the queen mother. It was well received when it first appeared, but was then unfairly denigrated by Classical taste – though it is now regarded as a monument to Baroque genius, since metamorphoses and disguises, verbal virtuosity, a taste for pomp and circumstance, and for purple passages and parody, are all better appreciated today. Marino himself had a quick, open, inquisitive mind, and the poem includes references to the discoveries and problems of his day. In addition, he had a very subtle musical ear and the true spirit of a poet.

At first sight, nothing could appear more composite than this work; it is mythological, pastoral, chivalrous, erotic, scientific and initiatory. In it one finds fairyland, magic, combats, tournaments – and even the legend of Adonis.

The poet is unwilling to forgo any of this store of riches, but he fails to arrange them into a coherent plot, so that the meaning of the work is not immediately clear. Nonetheless, the poem does have a meaning, and it can be discerned.

The story is set in a pastoral Eden, the island of Cyprus, and a description of Adonis being taken to the abode of Venus gives the poet an opportunity to expatiate on architecture and gardens. The youth passes through the gardens of the Five Senses, receiving a slow initiation of the flesh, before reaching the centre of the building where the supreme revelation of love awaits him.

However, even after this, his education is continued by means of a journey through the planets towards Mercury, the star of the arts and sciences, and then on to Venus where beauty dwells. And on the way back he undergoes a further series of novel adventures. Threatened by the jealousy of Mars, he takes refuge in an underground hiding-place – a manifestation of the underworld. Here a powerful female magician, who is in fact the daughter of the gods of the Lower Regions, vainly tries to win him away from Venus, first by seduction, then by harsh imprisonment, keeping him confined through the winter as in the original myth. However, by now the myth has been left far behind and the story has entered a realm of witchcraft more fantastic than the world of Apuleius. Transformed into a bird, then disguised as a girl, Adonis embarks upon a cycle of tragi-comic warlike adventures that leave *Orlando furioso* in the shade.

Eventually, the hero returns to his goddess, and after a magnificent coronation in Cyprus (used purely as a pretext for a display of poetic virtuosity) the traditional version of the story is resumed exactly where it was left. Venus is away and Adonis the huntsman is obstinate. The monstrous bear, seduced by his beauty, tries to embrace him and in so doing crushes him to death (an Alexandrian motif). Though warned of Adonis's impending death by a dream, Venus delays her return over a triviality: even the gods cannot escape Fate. She is in despair, but her lover dies as a huntsman and his dignified farewell enhances his stature. He has a splendid funeral, but for this Adonis there is no coming back.

In this version of the story, the hero is depicted as the plaything of the gods, and particularly of a dire fate decreed in the stars; but he is also the victim of his own fecklessness. He is a shy child who lets himself be seduced or guided easily. When faced with misfortune he is transformed into the Perfect Lover, according to the precepts of Urfé's *L'Astrée*, submitting to the whims of his mistress, and remaining faithful throughout a graduated series of tests, and even when betrayed by her. But Adonis reappears in mythical guise in the final phase of the drama, when the dead youth, embalmed in aromatic substances, seems to return to the arms of nature with which he has always maintained a secret bond; here the poet reacts intuitively, compelled by the underlying logic of the myth.

Though *Adone* is primarily a love story, portraying all the stages in the passion of love, it is also about education and possibly initiation. Despite the lasciviousness of some episodes and his constant pursuit of the 'marvellous', Marino was very concerned to give his work a moral meaning. Mercury plays the ambiguous role of go-between, schoolmaster and mystic sage. He instructs Adonis in all the fields of science known at that time, from anatomy to celestial mechanics, presenting them with an optimism that is still redolent of the spirit of the Renaissance. Nor is that all – Adonis is portrayed as following first one and then another initiatory route, leading in opposite directions. The first journey takes him from the most spiritual of the senses, sight, to the most sensual, touch. However, the delightful abode of Love turns out to be a trap – it is impossible to find the way out – and the bed chambers at its centre are compared to tombs. The lessons of this initiation are first corrected by an exposition of Neoplatonic metaphysics, then contradicted by the increasing difficulty of the series of tests that Adonis has to overcome. He emerges with increased stature, but he is still a naive child, incapable of appreciating the threats of a disastrous horoscope or the dangers inherent in intimacy with the gods. There is no lack of warning (in the form of the stories of Psyche and Actaeon), but once he is reunited with Venus and reassured by her, he is back to exactly where he started off. The educational significance of the long story is lost on him – but not, Marino must have hoped, on the reader.

La Fontaine (Jean de), 'Adonis', 1658, published in 1669

This famous poem was commented on by Valéry, but not in connection with its relationship to the myth. When it appeared in 1669, its author modestly described it as an 'idyll', but he actually saw it more as an 'heroic poem', and the central episode, the hunt, has epic overtones, with a suggestion of parody. Nonetheless, the work as a whole is pastoral in inspiration, finishing as an elegy.

The author makes no claim to originality and acknowledges his many predecessors, but still strikes a very personal note; he is constantly concerned with propriety and moderation, and is suspicious of the supernatural. The atmosphere is hardly mythical. Rather than resembling a goddess, Venus is more like a queen, smitten by love for a young country squire; both in confessing her love and in her despair she retains the dignity of her rank. Adonis is a romantic hero, combining good looks, love and gallantry. We are told nothing of his origins, or of his posthumous fate. La Fontaine is the only poet to make him win his contest with the boar, though he dies in victory; and this is the one episode in which the logic of the myth seems to carry the poet along – for a brief moment Adonis regains his connections with the sun, confronting the forces of darkness.

The poem also reflects another aspect of the myth. As Shakespeare realized, the story of Adonis is concerned with the fleeting nature of time, and La

Fontaine's poem suggests a very personal awareness of time, a way of seizing and savouring it, of feeling it as it escapes. This enjoyment of time is embodied in the word 'moment', which is given an immense emotional charge in a few incomparable lines.

AN ISLAND ADONIS

It is now necessary to backtrack a little so that the English treatment of the Adonis myth can be studied as a single distinct literary tradition; for, writers in England from the Renaissance to the Romantic movement, despite the diversity of their gifts, handled the story in a certain peculiarly English way.

Spenser (Edmund), *Faerie Queene*, 1590

In Spenser we find three different versions of the myth, which underlie the three different ways in which it is viewed in English poetry.

The first of these (*Faerie Queene* III. I. 34–8) is the most traditional. It involves a description of tapestries illustrating the legend, and the images are inspired by Ovid, though more graceful and poetic.

The second passage, which is much more important (*Faerie Queene* III. VI. 29–49), is a long episode known as the 'Garden of Adonis'. It has been widely annotated and discussed, and is disconcerting in the way in which it shifts from the physical world to philosophical allegory. Its fascination lies in its beauty and its enigmas, and it introduces into the mythical story an element that will be taken up again. This is a garden of delight, halfway between earth and the underworld, where Venus is free to enjoy the love of Adonis, who has been removed forever from the grasp of death. The garden itself extends far beyond the grove in which the lovers meet, and assumes the proportions of Virgil's Elysian fields (*Aeneid* VI). It is a place where the substance of all mortal beings returned to take root again and re-emerge in new forms in a thousand years. Adonis himself hesitates, grows and becomes the god 'of many names' mentioned in *Orphic Hymns* 56 (which Spenser had been able to track down in a learned work, compiled in 1581 by Natalis Comitis: *Mythologiae, sive explicationum fabularum, Libri X*). As such, he is eternal in his mutability, the father of all life as Venus is its mother. This merging of the Orphic aspect of Adonis with the forces of nature recurs in Shelley's 'Adonais'.

The myth makes its third appearance when it is used allegorically in a funerary eclogue in praise of a famous soldier and poet who, like Adonis, had died young: Philip Sidney, lamented here under the name 'Astrophel' that he himself had chosen. The eclogue is not one of Spenser's greatest poems, but it is another landmark on the route leading eventually to the masterpiece by Shelley.

Shakespeare (W.), 'Adonis and Venus', 1593

At first sight this seems to be a licentious poem about a totally human love affair. Venus is not in the least like a goddess; she is a lecherous hussy who spends 140 stanzas vainly attempting to overcome the resistance of a shy, unschooled adolescent. Nor, on the face of it, does he appear to have any supernatural qualities either. However, there are other dimensions to the story. Adonis personifies the child of the forest, a truly magnificent figure. In addition, he is an incarnation of pure Beauty, ephemeral and fragile, threatened by time and the jealousy of the gods, and, in this case, above all by covetousness, a destructive force that is the opposite of love. A Neoplatonic doctrine lies below the surface of the poem, and will become explicit in the 'Sonnets'.

Turning aside from Shakespeare, Milton alludes to the Adonis myth several times, and is inspired by it in his eclogue *Lycidas*. A brief episode at the end of *Comus* (1634), which probably has a religious significance, also merits attention. As in Spenser's work, and later in that of Keats, Adonis does not go down to the underworld; instead, he is taken to a semi-paradise, in this case the garden of the Hesperides, where he recovers from his wound watched over by the goddess, while Psyche, reunited with Cupid after her trials, is already in Paradise itself.

Keats (J.), *Endymion* II, 1818

This is a myth within a myth. The poet has retained only one crucial motif, the cyclical dual life of Adonis, thus staying closer to the Greek tradition than any of his predecessors. The poetic fragment evokes two images, the winter sleep, and the spring awakening, and its theme is handled in keeping with the poet's own peculiar genius: there is no violent death, no descent into the underworld. Instead, after being wounded and cured, Adonis is at rest in the Virgilian myrtle forest, which Venus provides for him while he sleeps. As in Spenser and Milton, this is a place of delight, half-rustic and half-sophisticated, with an atmosphere almost redolent of Baudelaire. For Keats, Adonis is the very incarnation of Beauty, a wonderful figure that Venus brings to life. There is an admirable contrast between the poem's two images, the first imbued with calm voluptuousness, the second sparkling with light. However, the impression of a slow, almost painful return to life reveals the poet's preference for frozen perfection – or perhaps his longing for death.

Shelley (P.B.), 'Adonais. An Elegy on the Death of John Keats', 1821

This great poem extends the classical tradition revived during the Renaissance of using a funerary ecologue as a device to extol a man of outstanding distinction who has died young, addressing him as if he were a shepherd-poet. As we have already seen, Spenser has exploited this technique to endow Sidney with the attributes of Adonis; while Shelley himself had translated Bion's Adonis elegy.

Shelley chose the figure of Adonis to extol John Keats no doubt partly as a tribute to the episode in *Endymion*, but also because, as a poet, he perceived similarities between the two characters. In Shelley's view, Keats's premature death had been caused by a moral wound, in the form of an anonymous and treacherous critical review. Thus like Adonis he had become the victim of a monster. But that is not all. Though Shelley retains the form of the ecologue, he stretches it. All the traditional themes – the mourning, the laments and the appeals – recur, but they are transfigured: the mourning flocks become the poet's dreams; the mourning of the shepherds become his fellow poets; and the mourning Venus becomes Urania, Plato's celestial Aphrodite, mother of bards, the most wonderful of apparitions. Though the apotheosis starts traditionally with a violent rejection of mourning and the snatching of the poet from the earth, it is essentially original.

There are two major aspects to its interpretation, relating to the poetic vocation and to the mystery of death. The first is more relevant to Adonis than might be thought, since beauty and genius are both divine and awesome. Like Adonis, Keats figures as a combatant, and like him he is defeated – but might he be a victim with redemptive powers? He certainly does not survive as a god brought back from the dead; Shelley emphatically rejects the physical reawakening that Keats had proclaimed. But, recalling Cicero's *Somnium Scipionis* (*Dream of Scipio*), Shelley imagines that poets may enjoy immortality in the stars, each providing a missing note in the celestial chorus. This heaven is reserved for universal Poetry. Immortality of a different kind awaits Adonis; he returns, body and soul, to nature, thus rejoining the Adonis of the Orphic poems as a vegetation deity. His spirit is reunited with Power whose love sustains and ignites the world and imposes form on matter.

Does the poem imply reunion with Adonis? The final stanza of this superb masterpiece, representing a mysterious embarkation on the Sea of Darkness, hints at a personal revelation that it would be almost sacrilegious to describe.

A 'DECADENT' ADONIS

Towards the middle of the nineteenth century writers began to take renewed interest in Adonis, but by this time they had lost their innocence – the mythologists had been at work. There was a desire to respect the original source, and to find a single explanation of the myth. The focus of attention moved back to the East, and Byblos became more important than Greece. At the same time, paradoxically, Adonis was once again identified with the god 'with many names' of late Antiquity, losing his individuality and merging with other divine figures; in short, he was surrounded by a confused aura of mysticism. The Greek demi-god, condemned to an alternating existence in conformity with a cyclical concept of time, gave way to a figure of suffering, destined for a glorious resurrection. At the same time an unsavoury attraction to bruised and battered flesh ensured that the cult prevailed over the legend. Nerval, Flaubert, D'Annunzio and Barrès were all haunted by the bleeding figure surrounded by weeping women. In the process, the graceful love story completely lost its human character and became a purely sacred union.

A short dense passage by Nerval (*Le Temple d'Isis*, 1845, repeated in *Les Filles du Feu, Isis* VII, 1854) summarizes what was to follow. Nerval, like Renan soon afterwards, sees Lebanon as the source of all forms of worship. The god whose birth is celebrated, whose wounds are venerated and whose resurrection is fêted 'is called Osiris in one place, Adonis in another, Attis in yet another' – and Christ as well. In the same way, all the women or goddesses lamenting him become one and the same person. The piece is very beautifully written, with its suggestion of prophetic mystery.

In *La Tentation de saint Antoine*, Flaubert turns the funeral rite of the Adonia into a vision shown to St Anthony by the Devil, along with visions of other cults whose mixture of affinities with Christianity and impure practices is intended to disorient the poor hermit. Flaubert, who is an artist rather than a mystic, retains an awareness of the original details. The vision of the dead body of Adonis – which is revealed to be a mere wax figure only at the end of the piece – is a fine dramatic device. The women's lament is full of a macabre sensuality, while the truly poetic song of the goddess reveals the meaning that Flaubert ascribes to the myth: for him, it represents the marriage of the Sun with the Earth in the morning.

D'Annunzio (G.), *Le Martyre de saint Sébastien*, 1911

Notwithstanding its title, Adonis plays as large a role in this work as Sebastian himself. The play, which is the only one of its kind, represents the followers of Adonis celebrating the festival of the Adonia. It is set in a Roman Empire that has degenerated into a mythical state of decadence, involving a confusion of cults and a breakdown of religion presided over by an emperor who is himself a mythical figure. In the background lies Asia, which is represented as a scorched place, full of aromatic spices and a multitude of strange rites, a continent where mysticim and sensuality are inextricably linked. And this atmosphere is vividly reflected by Debussy's brilliant music.

The true subject of the play is the efforts of incipient Christianity, in the person of Sebastian, to break free from this confusion; and in the play, the cult of Adonis is destined to drag it back. However, the strangely enticing figure of the saint creates ambiguity. Smitten by his beauty, the emperor wants to deify him, identifying him with Adonis. If Sebastian attempts to conjure up his Lord, the hymn of the worshippers of Adonis is immediately heard: Christ too . . . Sebastian's only means of escape will be death, and, even then, the worshippers of Adonis seize his body pierced by arrows; only his soul goes to Paradise – and the music frees us with him.

The atmosphere in this work is perhaps the most stifling ever to have been created by the European Decadent movement. Nevertheless, as a true artist, D'Annunzio respected the legacy of Bion: the songs of the participants in the Adonia have great purity of line, and the lavish, overloaded show came as near to the ancient Adonia as it was possible to come in 1911.

Barrès (Maurice), *Une Enquête au Pays du Levant*, 1923 (concerning a journey made in the spring of 1914)

Before discussing this work, it must be emphasized that the rite described by Barrès has no basis of historical, or even poetic, truth. Nevertheless, the piece is interesting because of what it reveals about Barrès's emotional responses and the period that they reflect.

Barrès states that he was prompted to undertake this study (which was political rather than archaeological) by a powerful attraction to Asia, which he perceived at times through the eyes of Renan and D'Annunzio (both of whom he mentions), and at times through those of Vellay. He also maintains that he went there in search of a cure for his chronic dehydration. 'I perceived it in a mist of heat, rustling with dreams and inchoate forces.'

Like others before him, he feels the enchantment of Lebanon, but the young huntsman and his legend are of no interest to him. What fascinate him are the orgiastic cults that he associates with Asia and, on the basis of a few cautious suggestions made by Renan, who was a conscientious scholar, he imagines a huge procession winding up the dangerous gorge to the temple of Afaka. It is a hallucinatory image, constructed from bits and pieces of different cults, and particularly from the *Bacchae* of Euripides. With a perfect disregard for history, he describes these supposed Adoniasts as Bacchants. Flagellants, people who have deliberately mutilated themselves, and priests cut each other to pieces, rolling down precipices in their frenzy: there is blood, voluptuous pleasure and death. None of these things was ever part of the Adonia, but the author of *La Colline inspirée* gloats over them at great length, before using them to draw a lesson about the wisdom of the Church . . . Nonetheless, there is magic in Barrès's writing, which is apparent in the passages that precede and follow this episode, especially in the account of his peaceful journey back towards the sea.

Inevitably, it has not been possible to discuss lesser-known works of literature, or the treatment of Adonis in musical theatre. Readers wishing to discover more can easily pursue their own research, by following up the various lines of enquiry suggested here, relating to the changes undergone by the figure of Adonis according to the intellectual climates of different periods, or simply to his relationship with beauty, time and death. This is an 'open' myth and, though it has not resurfaced since 1911, it may once again capture the imagination of a poet through its sheer vitality. This arises from a consistent core lying at the heart of the myth in all its varied forms – like the Sun with which Adonis was assimilated.

Hélène Tuzet

African Myths

The work of ethnologists and Africanists stresses the importance of myth in traditional black African societies, which are characterized by a close link between the social and the sacred. Myths establish origins, provide the foundations of beliefs, explain and legitimate social institutions, give meaning to everyday realities and constitute a fund of useful knowledge for members of the ethnic community. In black African societies with an exclusively oral tradition, knowledge and the spoken word have acquired their own mystique. Myths belong to the esoteric domain of ritual and initiation ceremonies, and this explains why they are seldom disclosed. For even in highly Islamicized or Christianized regions, initiation is still a flouishing institution. As a consequence any non-initiates old enough to undergo the ceremony can still have the great secret of the origins of things revealed to them through cosmogonies and founding stories featuring members of the pantheon and mythical ancestors.

Throughout sub-Saharan Africa, myths bear the direct stamp of animist beliefs. Despite the development of so-called cultural zones, due to historical events and to the fact that different environments (savannah or forest) favour different activities (hunting, herding or farming), animism is still the unifying spiritual foundation of black-African thought and the basis for the beliefs of the great majority of Africans. Indeed, a belief in the existence of an insubstantial principle, of a 'soul' that is present in all being and all things, is to be found in almost all traditional African religions.

Given this conception of the world, the notion of a vital force lies at the very root of black African metaphysics and ontology, while the idea of a single, invisible and immortal god, who created the world, often merges with it. He it is who, through the power of his saliva or of his speech, brought the world out of chaos or the primeval void. This divinity, who is essentially a sky-god represented in the form of a spiral, but who may sometimes be assimilated to the primordial womb, is the first vibration, which gives life to the world (note the 'turning' of Amma in Dogon cosmology).

Every force emanates the supreme being, and below him is a hierarchy of lesser beings: the richest in vital force are the spirits, supernatural creatures delegated by God to organize the universe; then come dead ancestors, followed by living people and lastly the inferior spirits that inhabit the animal, vegetable and mineral world. In addition, African symbolism also establishes a system of correspondence between all the different realms of creation, with peopole seen as a microcosm obeying the laws that govern the universe as a whole.

This dynamic vision of the world forms the framework for a system of morality in which anything that may increase or strengthen vital force is regarded as good and anything that may weaken it as bad. Magical practices and initiation rites, such as worship of the spirits that organize the world or of ancestors who continue to influence the living, are the logical result of these values. Moreover, in societies structured on the basis of age, it is only after undergoing initiatory tests that a person becomes complete.

Each ethnic group has cosmogonic stories recounting the different stages of the creation of the universe and human beings by God and his spirits (see 'The Dogon Myth'), and these stories form the basis of education, which is regarded as a gradual unveiling of the mysteries of Creation.

Because they refer to primordial times, myths provide essential knowledge for the initiate; they are compendia of indisputable primal truths, knowledge of which is indispensable for the harmonious integration of all members of the community. The cosmogonic story explains, clarifies and orders the secrets of life, death and evil; it uncovers symbols and reveals the links that were established in the beginning between the human and supernatural orders. In so doing, it responds to mankind's existential anguish and reassures human beings by giving them an appointed place in the universe.

Myths of origin describe an entire coherent metaphysical system portraying the spirits going about their task of constructing the world, establishing the human realm with its strengths and weakenesses, initiating the first people into various skills and encouraging them to develop the first social institutions (such as funeral rites, the wearing of masks or the practice of circumcision). This coherent system creates a series of analogies between the cosmic and human orders and combines cosmology and sociology in a vision of the universe that is both dynamic and harmonic. Thus, it is always with a certain nostalgia that contemporary African writers refer to the mythical accounts of the genesis of the world, whether they are simply transcribing ancient legends (as in the case of Birago Diop or Bernard Dadie) or creating modern fables (as in the case of Sony Labou Tansi).

Initiatory stories are intended to be didactic, edifying and exemplary. They are structured around a symbolic journey undertaken by a man who, after many trials and many meetings with supernatural figures, eventually attains knowledge, and they reflect human aspirations towards a better way of being, towards perfection and wisdom. The traditionalist Malian writer Amadou Hampate Ba has recorded several of these narratives, which form part of the traditional teachings of the Peul people of the loop of the Niger. These include the most popular tale, 'Kaydara' (see also 'Koumen'), which is the name of the supernatural being to whose call postulants for initiation respond.

Kaydara is polymorphous, but appears most frequently to human beings in the form of a deformed little old man or a beggar. (His unimpressive appearance is intended to discourage the curious and superficial, who do not deserve access to nature's secrets.) In the Peul pantheon he is the god of gold and knowledge. The actual myth 'Kaydara' aims to show that material wealth is nothing without moral wealth and wisdom. In the story, some friends make a subterranean journey into the 'twilight land', hoping to meet with the god. Their descent passes through eleven levels, corresponding to eleven trials and eleven symbols. (Peul cosmogony has eleven forces, the first being stone, source of the other ten.) Kaydara gives each of the friends three oxen laden with gold, but only the third, Hammadi, uses his treasure wisely and proves himself worthy of ordination by the god.

While the first friend decides to use his wealth to acquire power and the second prosperity, Hammadi, who is unconcerned with material things, seeks to conquer knowledge and sacrifices his gold to this end. The first two men die, but Hammadi continues with his initiation. After his return to his village, where he becomes king, he receives a beggar at his table who is none other than Kaydara himself. The god is touched by Hammadi's kindness and reveals to him the secret meaning of the eleven mysteries that he encountered in the land of the dwarfs. Having thus reached the highest level of initiation, Hammadi can in turn pass his knowledge on to his descendants. The sequel to this story is recorded in *Laaytere Koodal ou L'Eclat de la Grande Etoile* by Amadou Hampate Ba. This tale, about initiation into power, is presented as a treatise on political morality delivered to Hammadi's grandson, the young prince Diom-Dieri by old Bagoumawel, who is a *silatigi* (religious leader) embodying the forces of good in the struggle against those of evil, and also a magician.

Leaving aside its didactic aspect, the initiatory story also provides an immense reservoir of symbols referring to the whole Peul cosmogony. Of interest in this connection, is Werewere Liking's interpretation of *Kaydara* in terms of the five-pointed star and the numerology of Thot, whose symbolism is used in certain initiatory rituals. (The star represents the initiate as a perfect microcosm sparkling from its five points: body, emotions, thought, will and conscience.)

The number three (three travellers, three sacrifical stones, three loads of gold, three pieces of advice) refers symbolically to the Peul triad, in which there are three kinds of herdsmen (those of goats, sheep and cattle). Secret Peul teachings represent three as the product of incest between 'him and his flesh', for the number is hermaphrodite and copulates with itself to reproduce. Eleven is the most sacred number.

At the structural level, all initiatory stories describe a period of transition in the form of a journey at the end of which people are tranfigured and reach maturity (collective initiation by age group), power or wisdom (individual initiations). The ladder always symbolizes progress towards knowledge; climbing it signifies the search to understand the world of appearances; descending it, as in 'Kaydara', signifies the search for occult wisdom.

The theme of the journey appears frequently in the modern African novel, which can thus be regarded as an avatar of the traditional initiatory story.

Between 1953 and 1968, the problems dealt with in many African novels of the *Bildungsroman* type concerned the transformation of the African who comes into contact with Western values either through a journey to Europe (as in *L'Enfant noir* by Camara Laye, *L'Aventure ambiguë* by Sheik Hamidou Kane, *Kocoumbo L'Etudiant noir* by Ake Loba, *Un nègre à Paris* by Bernard Dadie and *Chemin d'Europe* by Ferdinand Oyono), or as the result of moving from village to city (as in *Ville cruelle* by Ezo Boto, *Maïmouna* by Abdoulaye Sadji or *Afrika Baa* by Rémy Medou Mvomo). The quest of the 'hero' is for knowledge (penetrating the secrets of the West by going there to study), prosperity or simply modernity; it is motivated by desire, curiosity, ambition and above all the fascination exerted over young minds of the myth of a wise, rich and happy Europe, where everything seems easy. The journeys described in the novels take up the theme of encounters with initiators or mediators, but the trials that the hero undergoes often prove too hard. The experience portrayed is more one of disillusion or painful failure than of success. In a foreign world, the sometimes tragic journey takes on the character of an initiation that has failed (see *L'Aventure ambiguë*, the most representative example of a novel dealing with the drama of cultural integration, but also *Ville cruelle, Afrika Baa* or *Maïmouna*) because of the incompatibility between traditional African values and those of the West. Culture shock thus produces a sense of tragedy, sometimes held at bay by humour and irony, as in the case of Dadie or Oyono.

However these novels make absolutely no direct allusions to the ancient myths, as Professor J.L. Gore stressed at the Afro-comparatist conference held in Limoges in May 1977. They are part of a secularized body of literature concerned with describing everyday reality, which avoids or renders banal any references to the supernatural world and thus never alludes to cosmogonies. Nevertheless, after 1968, a certain 'return to the myths' does apparently become discernible.

Thus in his novel *L'Etrange destin de Wangrin*, Amadou Hampate Ba presents us with a 'hero' who is entirely defined by his spiritual alliance with the 'god of opposites', Gongoloma-Snooke, whom he chooses as his guardian. The author begins the book with a mythical tale about the origins of the village in which his central character was born. However, after this point, references to the Bambara pantheon disappear and the mythical substratum dissolves into the eventful story of a particular individual, in the manner of a countermoral.

To the extent that the central character accepts the mythological elements in their entirety and with a complete absence of ridicule, the book represents an attempt to create a kind of 'mythical novel', illustrating traditional belief in predestination within a modern framework.

More generally, it is by re-using traditional symbols that contemporary African novelists seek to revive, if not the structures and substance of the myths, at least their language, as demonstrated by the works of Alioum Fantoure, Tierno Monenembo, Tchicaya U Tam'si or Williams Sassine.

Myths concerning the establishment of particular communities, under the direction of one outstanding individual, are particularlay numerous. These create an heroic mystique and arise from the tradition of ancestor worship. Their subject matter is drawn from the history of migrations and they explain the formation of tribal groupings and the birth of the first states.

The myth of the hero's birth is widely illustrated by tales about the creation of ancient kingdoms and empires (see 'Sundiata', 'Shaka'). Sickly or illegitimate at birth, the future hero is exceptional in having a superior vital force, passed on to him by his legendary ancestors (see 'Sundiata') or acquired through initiation into the occult forces (see 'Shaka'). His ordination by the powers of heaven or of the underworld (in the case of the dead ancestors) destines him for glory, and his rise to fame is marked by exploits that reveal his supernatural aspects.

Foundation myths are both epic and heroic and are highly eulogistic; they extol the high moral qualities incarnated by the hero, such as courage or a sense of sacrifice, and are the vehicle for expressing traditional values. An example is the legend of Queen Pokou recorded by Bernard Dadie. This myth about the migrations describes the creation of the Baoulé people and their establishment in the Ivory Coast as a result of the difficult sacrifice that Abra Pokou was willing to make. To save her fleeing clan from extermination, she offered her only son to the water spirit of the flooding river Cormoe, thereby enabling her people to cross it, and then went on to establish a realm in the Bouake region, though she came originally from Koumassi (an Ashanti kingdom).

The Yoruba myth (from Nigeria) tells of the deification of King Shango, who is subsequently assimilated to thunder and revered as such, and is also the brother of Ogun, the god of iron and war. The myth is rooted in historical legend and explains the establishment of sacrifices and ecstatic dances linked to the Yoruba cult of the orisha. Shango is said to inhabit or 'ride' the faithful who have invoked him, and, when possessed by him, the worshipper behaves like an archetype of the god, whose terrestrial avatar he becomes for as long as possession lasts. The myth thus provides a 'foundation story' for the rite and institutionalizes the celebration of the god-king. The cult of Shango is still practised in Nigeria, and was spread during the black diaspora to places such as Haïti, Cuba and Brazil, where it forms part of the voodoo religion.

Pierre Verger has recorded many versions of the Shango myth. Shango is said to be the Yoruba's fourth king, and to have put their enemies to flight with flames that came out of his mouth. He was endowed with magic powers and is said to have set fire to his palace while trying to make the lightning strike his enemies. Having brought about his own downfall, he is then supposed to have abdicated and hanged himself from a *karite* tree, while his wife Oya threw herself into the river. But in popular belief, Shango did not die, he burrowed into the ground using a great iron chain and became an *orisha*, able to manifest his anger by unleashing terrible storms. His worship was instituted on the site of his 'disappearance'. Revered and feared, Shango is also seen as a tyrannical and cruel king who was begged by chiefs and people to abdicate because of his excesses and then killed himself.

In *La Tragèdie du Roi Christophe* by Aimé Cesaire, allusion is made to the mythical Yoruba king when the Haïtian ruler invokes Shango and identifies himself with him. This is partly a literary motif indicating a quest for authenticity characteristic of the poets of Blackness, but the reference also suggests a mystical authority for kingship arising from a conception of power inherited from the African tradition, where the political and the sacred constantly influence each other.

The adaptation of the Yoruba legend by the Nigerian playwright Ola Balogun in his piece *Shango* (1968) invites the audience to witness the birth of the myth in the popular imagination. Through the mystery surrounding his death, the revered warrior and feared chief becomes the object of worship. This is an instance of modern theatre, itself a form of ritual, celebrating the heroes of the past; but by explaining the ancient myth and bringing it up to date, the play secularizes it in openly critical dialogues which, as in Cesaire's work, deal with the problem of tyranny.

In conclusion, since the granting of independence to various states in Africa in the 1960s, a dramatic form of literature has evolved in the region, drawing its subject matter largely from historical myths (see 'Sundiata', 'Shaka'). New African theatre extols the exploits of the founding heroes of ancient Africa partly as a means of recovering a history that was hidden by the European colonizers, but also to celebrate the martyrs who resisted colonial penetration (as in *Les Derniers jours de Lat Dior* by Amadou Cisse Dia, *L'Exil d'Albouri* by Sheik N'Dao, *Les Sofas* by Bernard Zadi-Zaourou and *Béatrice du Congo* by Bernard Dadie) and the architects of decolonization (*Simon Kimbangou le Messie noir* by Philippe Elebe). As a result, its message is primarily nationalistic, embodied by heroes of promethean stature such as those of Aimé Cesaire (*Et les chiens se taisaient, Une Saison au Congo*). Though it sometimes excessively didactic, this theatre is making a contribution to the perpetuation of the heroic myth in societies where ancestor worship remains an essential duty.

Nicole Goisbeault

Ah Q/Ah Q ism

Ah Q is the hero of *The True Story of Ah Q*, the longest and most famous of the stories by Lu Xun (Zhou Shuren, 1881–1936) and one of the first literary texts written in modern Chinese ('bai hua') after the triumph of the political, ideological, literary and linguistic revolution of 1919 ('May Fourth Movement'). The story first appeared in 'serial' form in nine episodes, between 4 December 1921 and 12 February 1922, in the *Supplement* of the Beijing (Peking) daily paper *Chenbao*, under the pseudonym 'Baren'. Lu Xun subsequently included it in a volume entitled *Nah-han* (*Call to Arms*), published in Beijing in 1923 ('Xinchaoshe' Editions), and it also appears in the first volume of all editions of his complete works, *Quanji*.

The True Story of Ah Q is a biography in the tradition reserved for great figures, but is narrated in the pedantic style of the young westernized scholars. The name Ah Q is a grotesque juxtaposition of the colloquial prefix 'Ah' of popular parlance and the Western letter 'Q' which, as well as being the Latin initial of an unidentified Chinese character, is also reminiscent of the awful 'queue' or pigtail imposed on the Chinese by the Manchus, as an indication of their race.

With biting humour, the story recounts the pitiful adventures of a miserable wretch who is half peasant and half vagabond, who has nowhere to live, no family, no work and ultimately no name. The story is set around the time of the 'failed Revolution' of 1911, which put an end to the Manchu dynasty, but left in office, albeit under the flag of the Republic, the same urban and provincial authorities with their greed for power and wealth. Attracted by the idea of revenge, which he confuses with the concept of the Revolution, Ah Q passes from the old to the new regime but is not offered the chance of escaping from his poverty. On the contrary, he is excluded from the 'Party of Freedom' – which consists of landowners, scholars and members of the bourgeoisie from both the old and the new regimes – by the party's own vigilante group and is finally executed as a thief for trying to educate the masses. He meets his end without ever having stolen and without understanding what is happening to him. Just as he is about to die, he becomes aware with sudden terror of the 'burning curiosity' in the eyes of the crowd that has come to watch the 'performance' represented by his insignficant death, a performance that fails miserably because he is unable to sing the customary light-hearted operatic aria. Except in his final moments, he manages to keep intact the good opinion that he has of himself, to maintain the image that he feels that he should present in order to gain recognition, and to sustain, without any significant setbacks, his secret conviction that he is 'the best', despite the misfortune, injustice and despair that he has had to endure.

Many of his contemporary or later *Essays* confirm that Lu Xun believed that the repeated humiliations of the Chinese nation (the most recent being the signing of the Treaty of Versailles in 1919, which had provoked the 'May Fourth Movement'), and the terrible sufferings that threatened the very existence of the masses were adequately explained by a habit instilled into the Chinese people over the years. This was the tendency to 'save face' at all costs – by adopting a policy of 'laissez-faire' and stoical endurance; by a smiling and lofty denial of reality; and by keeping up appearances and deceiving others by first of all deceiving themselves. When, contrary to expectation, Ah Q once again becomes a victim of repression, this time concealed behind a façade of modernism and liberalism, it is because the new regime – like the old – draws its basic strength from the 'consent' (unconscious ideology) of the victims themselves, who willingly serve their masters and persecutors. Ah Q is the symbol of these victims.

The ideology referred to by Lu Xun has a name. *The True Story of Ah Q* was written during the aftermath of the 'May Fourth Movement', whose instigators and supporters had launched a violent attack on the beliefs of Confucianism. Lu Xun is particularly vehement in denouncing two aspects of Ah Q's almost unlimited ability to 'rationalize' even the cruelest of defeats and humiliations as 'spiritual victories' (a process whose only advantage is to enable him to continue stoically to endure more suffering). The first is his personal belief in traditional morality, reinforced by twenty-five centuries of observance and veneration of the Confucian *Classics*; the second is the blind, arrogant faith that he demonstrates in relation to practices and superstitions that are in fact extremely harmful to his own condition as a member of a sub-proletariat, which is being exploited to death.

There is no doubt that this was the meaning of the 'call' issued by Lu Xun when he wrote *The True Story of Ah Q*. He himself said, several years later, in his preface to the Russian translation of the story, that he considered it an extremely difficult task to 'rouse the impenetrable and silent spirit of the people of ancient China'. But however strong the historical and national connotations of the peculiar method of 'winning victories' to which Ah Q gave his name, it is not limited to the philosophy of a single nation (a philosophy that at a certain point became suicidal). Nor, as has sometimes been maintained, does it specifically reflect the 'Chinese nature' that Lu Xun is supposed to have embodied as an 'eternal' characteristic. Nor, indeed, is it the reduction of sacrosanct traditional thought to a caricature of itself that is both naive and pathetic, hateful and amusing, that occurs when it is simplified to the point of absurdity and projected into the most uneducated minds at the lowest level of the social scale. *The True Story of Ah Q* is in fact a work that is so perfectly executed that it defies any attempt to produce a simplified interpretation. As a result, the opinions expressed about it vary widely.

At the most basic level, *The True Story of Ah Q* can be read as a realistic description of the condition of the poorest of the poor in the Chinese peasant class. Though Lu Xun pities Ah Q and feels indignation towards his executioners, his assessment of him is extremely critical. Ah Q is portrayed as an essentially weak person who mistreats those weaker than himself, and as a revolutionary who dreams of revenge – an image that Chinese critics after 1949 tended to modify in order to present him as an honourable peasant, and an authentic revolutionary who merely lacked the right opportunity.

The True Story of Ah Q is also very obviously a political tract – so much so, that certain readers of the serial saw it as employing the open aggression of a 'roman à clef'. It is a desperate patriotic call to arms, but not so desperate that it ceases to be a 'call' intended to 'rouse'. Through the thoughts of the anti-hero Ah Q, it presents a catalogue of the accepted ideas inherited from the past. 'Ah Q ism' is presented as an accumulation of preconceived values and behaviour that relates to all aspects of human existence, from the obligatory length of shallot stalks to the most serious questions concerning life and the after-life, for example attitudes towards power, rules governing social relations, religious practices and superstitious precautions, family duty, the feminine ideal, and male superiority. Although all these concepts do indeed carry the hallmark of oriental cultures, they also bear a marked resemblance to the 'old-fashioned' ideas of the West.

Finally, and above all, *The True Story of Ah Q* is a sort of apology for philosophy, which is general enough to rise above the Chinese and oriental context. It is a sort of theoretical working-drawing based on the analysis of a borderline case, and, as such, it exposes the role of ideology in the regeneration of oppression, one of the main tenets of Lu Xun's thought. The philosophy developed by Ah Q, and of which he is so proud, has the power to control the cries of pain and despair and the needs and desires of his body, and to suppress all the rebellious feelings aroused in him by poverty and injustice, which should impel him to defend himself. 'Ah Q ism' is a deadly and well-oiled mechanism that enables the oppressors, whoever they are, to economize on violence and to defend an order that has been so firmly established for so long that one wonders how it can possibly be destroyed. *The True Story of Ah Q* represents the dismantling of this infernal machinery, which stands in the way of the liberation of all human society. In this respect, the work reaches far beyond the specific circumstances of a particular period or a particular nation, and assumes a universal significance.

Michelle Loi

Ancient Apollo: Darkness and Light

In her *Nouvelle Mythologie de la Jeunesse* written during the reign of Charles X in the 1820s for French schoolchildren, Madame Tardieu-Denesle said that Jupiter made Apollo responsible for spreading light in the universe, and that every morning the god climbed into the sun-chariot for a race that finished with nightfall. The children were thus led by their own teachers into the lamentable error of confusing Helius and Apollo! In fact, there is ample excuse for Madame Tardieu-Denesle's mistake as the confusion had already been prevalent for a long time. If we examine its associations, the name 'Apollo' conjures up such words as 'light', 'harmony' or 'balance'. He is associated with Periclean Athens, with the rays of the sun setting over the Acropolis, with *sophrosune* – wisdom tempered by moderation, the precepts of which were engraved on the pediment of his temple at Delphi. We tend to contrast Apollo's serenity with the uncouth drunkenness of Dionysus (and Nietzsche himself played no small part in reinforcing this antithesis). The notion of a god of light and harmony became established in very early times, and yet it most certainly does not correspond with the original image of a god who had a great many dark aspects: a disturbing, complex god of contrasts, a sun god and a god of the underworld, a bringer of life and of death.

THE PROBLEM OF APOLLO'S ORIGINS

The difficulty of identifying Apollo's origins and personality becomes obvious from a simple examination of the names used to describe him. He is called *Lukeios*, an adjective that scholars long thought was associated with *luke*, light – and sometimes still do. This etymology fits in well with Apollo's best known title, *Phoibos*, the 'light', 'bright' or 'pure' one, which can be found in the first lines of works by Homer and Hesiod (*Iliad* I. 43: *Theogony* 14). It paves the way for the assimilation of Helius with Apollo, which was already beginning in the *Homeric Hymn to Apollo* written in the seventh and sixth centuries BC ('Then Apollo, the Lord Archer, rose up from the ship, *in the guise of a star that shines in the daytime*': 400f.) and that was reinforced during the first half of the fifth century BC in Aeschylus's *Bassarides*, where Orpheus declares that the Sun is also called Apollo. In a similar way Aeschylus also identified Selene, the Moon, with Artemis, the daughter of Leto and sister of Apollo, in his play *Xantriae*.

And yet Apollo the bright is also known as *Loxias*, the oblique or obscure. The *Etymologicum Magnum* (642) informs us that this title is linked with the name Loxo, belonging to the daughter of Boreas who brought up the young god as a child. But even if this were so, and even if Apollo's Delphic oracles were renowned for their clarity rather than their lack of it, writers more concerned with dramatic effect than with the truth would still have given the impression that Apollo spoke ambiguously, making human beings risk misinterpreting his predictions, perhaps with catastrophic results: 'Yet I can speak the language of Greece. So does Loxias: but his oracles are obscure' (Aeschylus, *Agamemnon* 1254f.). There are many stories in Herodotus showing how poor humans were misled. Examples include Croesus who had no idea that the great empire that he was about to destroy was his own, or that the 'mule' he should distrust was Cyrus, born of a mother who was a Mede and father who was a Persian.

The dark side of Apollo is also to be found in his ambivalent relations with the chthonic world. He is the slayer of a female dragon (*Homeric Hymn to Apollo* 300) that guarded the very ancient oracle of Gaia, the Earth, at Delphi, and there is a famous statue of him as a *sauroctonus*, or slayer of lizards. Meanwhile, he is also known as *Smintheus*, the destroyer of rats (*Iliad* I. 39). Yet at Epidaurus, in the sanctuary of Apollo's son Asclepius, the god of healing (whose sacred animal was the mole, another creature from the underworld), serpents crawled among the consultant physicans as they practised the rite of incubation. There is a serpent entwined around Asclepius's staff and he himself sometimes takes on the appearance of a snake (Pausanias II. 10. 3), as does another of Apollo's sons, Trophonius, who had an underground oracle at Lebadeia. But Apollo the rat-killer may originally have been a rat-god who healed the sick, as is suggested the striking common features linking him to the Indian god Rudra: the bow, illness, the mole, the rat, obliqueness and poetry.

Thus it is far from satisfactory to translate the epithet *Lukeios* as 'luminous'. Indeed, ancient classical writers put forward a different explanation: Apollo *Lukeios* was said to be the killer of wolves (*lukos*): 'And you, the god who destroys wolves, destroy the army of our enemies' (Aeschylus, *The Seven against Thebes* 145f.); 'Yonder is the market-place, Lycean they call it, from the god who killed the wolf' (Sophocles, *Electra* 6f).

It is by no means absurd to represent the god in this way, because there are many links between Apollo and the wolf. It was because he sent a wolf to attack a herd that Danaus became ruler of Argos. And, significantly, the new king built a sanctuary to Apollo *Lukios* (Pausanias II. 19. 3–7). At Argos sacrifices of wolves were offered to the god, while the Lyceum at Athens, which was dedicated to Apollo, was named after a hero called Lukos (Pausanias I. 19. 3). On coins the god was also associated with wolves. He is ruler of the beasts, like his sister Artemis. But was he a destroyer of wolves, a protector of wolves or even a wolf himself, as Zeus *Lukaios* may have been? It was in the shape of a wolf that Apollo approached the nymph Cyrene (Servius, on Virgil, *Aeneid* IV. 377). But there is a risk that the theory of theriomorphism may distort the true explanation and even a danger of drifting into 'polytheriomorphism' – after all, why not suggest that Delphian Apollo was originally a dolphin-god, since he is described as leaping over a Cretan ship 'in the guise of a dolphin' in the *Homeric Hymn to Apollo* (400f., 493–6)?

There is a third possible explanation of the title *Lukeios*, and it is certainly the most convincing. Apollo may originally have come from Lycia, in Asia Minor, since he is described as *Lukegenes*, apparently meaning 'born in Lycia'. It is true that the word is sometimes translated as 'born of the wolf', as, according to one tradition (Aristotle, *Historia Animalium* VI. 35), before making love to Zeus, Apollo's mother transformed herself into a she-wolf to escape from the jealousy of Zeus's wife Hera. And it is also true that the suggested translation does not fit in with the most widely accepted tradition, according to which Apollo was born on Delos. Eager to reconcile the irreconcilable, Antoninus Liberalis (*Metamorphoses* XXXV) suggested that Apollo spent some time in Lycia after being born on Delos, and that Leto called the country Lycia because wolves guided her to it. What is certainly true is that there are many sanctuaries to Apollo in Asia Minor; that the god fought on the side of the Trojans and not the Achaeans in the *Iliad*; and finally that the palm tree on Delos at the base of which Leto gave birth (*Homeric Hymn to Apollo* 115ff.) is an oriental tree.

The different interpretations of the word *Lukeios* by no means represents all the various hypotheses put forward regarding Apollo's origins. According to one viewpoint, he is an Indo-European god: we have already noted that some have compared him to the Indian god Rudra, while certain others, who agree that he is of Indo-European origin, maintain that he comes from the North and emphasize his connection with the Hyperboreans. In this context, we are reminded that the first Greeks were nomads and herdsmen. And there is a striking resemblance between the word *apella* ('gathering of the people', but also 'sheep pen' according the lexicographer Hesychius of Alexandria) and *Apellon*, which is the form of the god's name used by the Dorians. Here, the myth seems to support the etymology: Apollo did have flocks and worked as a shepherd for Laomedon and Admetus. Moreover, Dumézil recognizes the three features characteristic of Indo-European societies in Apollo's speech to the goddesses (*Homeric Hymn to Apollo* 131ff.). The first (magico-religious sovereignty) can be seen in the allusion to the oracles and the lyre that accompanies the singing and dancing at the cult feast, the second (war) in the mention of the bow, and the third (wealth, fertility) in the gold cover over Delos, a promise of prosperity to come.

However, other scholars believe that Apollo was originally called *Pelun*, and that he was the ancestoral hero of the Pelasgians. And the *Homeric Hymn* points in yet another direction, towards the Aegean world, more specifically Crete. Delphian Apollo entrusted Cretans from Knossos with the duty of guarding his temple, while it was a Cretan who purified Apollo and Artemis after the dragon was slain, and a Cretan who won the first victory at the Pythian Games (Pausanias X. 7. 2).

As in a description by Robbe-Grillet, each successive interpretation effaces the one before. We are led to the conclusion that Apollo does not have a single origin; as far as the historical era is concerned, his personality is formed from a conglomeration of gods from a variety of countries, representing a sequence of strata. Nor should we be too hopeful that the other titles by which he was invoked will shed more light on the issue. Is Apollo called *Puthios* (Pythian) because he left the corpse of the dragon to rot (*puthein*) (*Homeric Hymn to Apollo* 371ff.), or because as the god of an oracle he informs (*puthesthai*) those who consult him (Strabo IX. 419)? Should *Paian, Paieon* or *Paion*, all names by which he was invoked, be associated with healing (as traditionally supposed) or with the song of victory?

THE AMBIVALENT GOD

While the mystery shrouding Apollo's origins is disconerting for scholars, it has at least had the advantage of allowing free rein to the imagination of creative artists, as the outlines of the god's original character have been lost. They have been able to present the image of a god of light, or of a god of darkness and death – as they pleased. Nevertheless, even in the most clear-cut portraits of Apollo, there is still complexity. He is never a completely just, good god; nor does he ever range himself on the side of totally evil forces.

To judge from the beginning of the *Iliad*, Homer opted for the terrible aspect of the god; when he is angry with Agamemnon's troops, Apollo strikes the army with a deadly scourge (*nousos* or *loimos*), the plague:

> A terrible sound came from the silver bow. He vented his anger first on the mules and swift dogs. Then he aimed at the men, loosing his sharp arrows on them; and the funeral pyres burned unceasingly in their hundreds.
>
> (*Iliad*, I. 49–52.)

As a fierce enemy of the Greeks it was he who directed all the rivers of Mount Ida against the Achaean wall (*Iliad*, XII. 24ff.), he who struck Patroclus in the back, shaking off his armour and exposing him to Hector's spear (*Iliad*, XVI. 788ff.). Yet this terrible god could also bring death without suffering, and then his cruel arrows become 'gentle darts' (*Iliad* XXIV. 759). In addition, the corollary of his hostility towards the Achaeans is the protection that he unfailingly affords to the Trojans. Aeneas, Glaucus and Hector each in turn benefit from his help. He unceasingly supports, comforts, encourages or saves them. If his shots can bring death, they can also deflect evil. Apollo is the Protector (*hekaergos, Iliad* I. 439). Across the centuries, the various epithets by which he was invoked (*alexikakos, apotropaios, epikourios*) show the constancy of this characteristic.

On the other hand, while the *Homeric Hymn* is evidently devoted to glorifying the eternally young and handsome conquering god, it does not conceal his 'overweening pride' (1. 67) and shows him being ridiculed by Telephus. Here, young Apollo has neither the moderation referred to on the pediment of his temple among the precepts of Delphic wisdom ('know thyself', 'nothing to excess') nor the omniscience of his father Zeus.

However, Pindar, writing at the beginning of the Greek Classical era (fifth century BC) does endow him with omniscience:

> You who know the inevitable outcome of all things and the ways they will follow; you who can count the leaves that the earth will put forth in the spring, the grains of sand tossed by the waves in the sea or the rivers, and the gusts of the wind; you who can see the future and its origins clearly.
>
> (*Pythian Odes* IX. 44ff.)

He is portrayed as generous, offering mankind his benefactions and causing peace to reign:

> It is he who supplies both men and women with the remedies that cure their cruel illnesses; he has given us the cithara; the Muse inspires those he favours; he fills hearts with a love of harmony and a horror of war. He rules over the prophetic shrine.
>
> (*Pythian Odes* V. 63ff.).

As the son of Zeus, Apollo tends, like him, to become the very incarnation of the divine, the unnamed *theos* (god) celebrated in the *Pythian Odes* II (49ff.). Even so, Pindar does not go so far as to remove every trace of his other aspect, as a cruel, destructive god. He avenges himself on Coronis for her infidelity by sending Artemis, an implacable and blind agent, to inflict sudden death on the young woman, as well as on many other people whose only crime was to live near her (*Pythian Odes* III. 36f.).

Aeschylus was a contemporary of Pindar, but his Apollo marks a halt in the development of the god's personality, or even a retrograde step. In his tragedies, we find the sanguinary god who massacres all Niobe's sons with his arrows. His hatred is implacable. Laius disobeys his oracle, so the god Septimus brings about the fraticidal murder of his grandsons Eteocles and Polyneices at the seventh gate of his city (*The Seven against Thebes* 800). Cassandra does not keep her promises, so she is mocked, taken captive and killed. Yet the god himself fails to keep his promises far more than Cassandra. After assuring Thetis that the gods will watch lovingly over her entire destiny, he kills her son Achilles (*Judgement of Arms* fr. 284 Mette). He is a terrifying deity: *Phoibos* is associated with *phobos*, fear or rout (*The Persians* 206), *Apollo* with *apollon*, the one who destroys (*Agamemnon* 1081). The justice that he metes out is the archaic justice of the vendetta: a killer must himself be killed. He is on a par with the Furies whom he fights in the *Eumenides*: he shares the same violence, the same bad faith, the same contradictions.

And yet this fearsome god is invoked by the Argive herald as a saviour and healer (*Agamemnon* 512). This imperfect god is the representative of Zeus, a fact repeatedly emphasized at the beginning of the *Eumenides*. This conquering god peacefully takes his seat on the ancient Delphic throne: the killing of the dragon is never mentioned (*Eumenides* 1 ff.). The god with areas of darkness retains some aspects of the god of light.

Apollo's regression in the plays of Aeschylus was due to the convulsive forces at work in a world in the process of taking shape: the Greek city state was born amidst social and political tensions that were reflected in the way in which thinkers perceived the cosmos. Similarly, Apollo's regression in the works of Euripides can be explained by the convulsions of a world in the process of breaking up. The City states were tearing each other apart, beliefs were undermined, the gods fell from their pedestals and stooped to human level. Thus, in *Electra* (1302) the Dioscuri absolve Orestes of Clytemnestra's death. The person responsible was Apollo, who had given an 'imprudent order'. The god is vindictive and does not forgive offences. When Pyrrhus comes to offer amends he treacherously wreaks vengeance on him in his own shrine, crushing him beneath the blows of thousands of men:

> This is how the Lord who gives oracles to others, the arbiter of what is right for the whole human race, treated Achilles' son when he offered reparation! Like a wicked human, he remembered old old grievances. How can he be called virtuous?
>
> (*Andromache* 1161–5.)

Nor was the god who lay with Creusa very virtuous:

> Ah! do not behaved like this; practise virtue, if you have the power to do so! For all who are wicked are punished by the gods. How can we bear it if you who make the laws for human beings are yourselves guilty of breaking those laws?
>
> (*Ion* 439–43).

And yet Euripides' Apollo can be as luminous and resplendent as the god of the *Homeric Hymn* and of Pindar;

> How beautiful the children of Leto are, to whom she gave birth in the fertile valleys of the island of Delos – the god with his golden hair who plays the lyre so skilfully, and the goddess proud of her prowess with the bow and arrow!
>
> (*Iphigenia in Tauris*, 1234–9.)

The bloodthirsty god can preach peace: 'Be on your way, and let the most beautiful of divinities, Peace, be honoured among you' (*Orestes*, 1682f.). And however critical the *Ion* may be of the god's behaviour, the poet still praises the luminous, cosmic beauty of Delphi, which would never have had such grandeur had it not been touched by his grace:

> Here is the shining chariot with its quadruple harness: Helius is already lighting up the earth. And the stars flee from the ether catching fire in the sacred night. The inviolate peaks of Mount Parnassus, flooded with light, welcome the disk of day on behalf of men.
>
> (Ion, 82–8.)

The god's ambivalence, arising from his varied origins, is just as apparent in the works of those who view him askance as it is in those of his respectful admirers.

TOWARDS DIVINE PERFECTION

With the works of Plato, the god came to be perceived in a completely different way. The philosopher no longer saw Apollo as one Olympian among many; instead, he made him into *the* god. The development started by Pindar was brought to its conclusion. Apollo, who was closely associated with Helius (an association that verged on assimilation), became the supreme god, the only god, the *divine essence* of which other gods were only manifestations. Because the Platonic doctrine was expressed symbolically through the figure of Apollo, we should pay heed to the etymologies in *Cratylus* 404eff., for all their playfulness (see 'Apollo, the mythical sun'). He is the god who cleanses, *Apolouon*, representing physical and spiritual purification (*Phaedo*); as *Aploun* he reveals the link between unity and truth (*Parmenides* and *Philebus*); as *Aei ballon* (he who always attains), he is infallibility, perfection. And as *Homopolon*, simultaneous movement, he is harmony: not just musical harmony, but celestial harmony too, the harmony of the spheres, or the stars (see the *Temaeus* or the story of Er at the end of the *Republic*). This respectful attitude towards the Delphic religion is not a submissive acceptance of tradition by someone wedded to the past; piety is the prop of metaphysics. In these circumstances, we can understand Plato's vehement rejection of a lying, vindictive, bloodthirsty Apollo of the kind described by Thetis in the fragment of Aeschylus's *Judgement of Arms* mentioned above – which has actually been preserved because of Plato's denunciation of it (*Republic* II. 383b).

Apollo's elevated position as the embodiment of divine unity, first alluded to by Pindar, was firmly assured by Plato and thereafter accepted without question. This Apollo is far removed from the killer of Achilles, Coronis or Cassandra. From Plato's time on moral perfection went hand in hand with power. Unity had replaced multiplicity. It was in this light that the god was perceived by Plutarch; after discussing the various interpretations of the mysterious E inscribed in Apollo's temple at Delphi, he finally decided that it meant 'Thou art'.

ROMAN APOLLO: POLITICS AND RELIGION

Horace's famous verse, 'Greece in defeat has vanquished its uncouth conqueror' (*Epistles* II. 1. 156), is well know, and the story of the Greek god Apollo in Rome illustrates the truth of it. Of course, various factors modified and filtered the Delphic religious, adapting it to the mental outlook of the Romans: these include the sibyl at Cumae, associated with an ancient chthonic goddess, and the cultures of the Etruscans and the Falisci. Nonetheless the stages of the god's progress can be followed. At the beginning of the fifth century BC, Tarquinius Superbus sent two of his sons to consult the Pythian oracle; in 433 BC a temple was dedicated to Apollo on the Campus Martius; in 212 BC the first *ludi Apollinares* were held; and on 2 September 31 BC, in full view of the temple of Apollo on the promontory overlooking the entrance to the Gulf of Ambracia, Octavius inflicted a crushing defeat on the fleet of Antony and Cleopatra at the battle of Actium.

That event really marked the beginning of Apollo's appearance in Latin literature (earlier mentions by Ennius, Naevius and Lucilius had been relatively fleeting). Octavius, soon to call himself Augustus, was a skilful orchestrator of propaganda, and the rumour was spread that his mother Atia had been impregnated by the god. The victory became the 'miracle of Actium' and in 28 BC a temple on the Palatine Hill was dedicated to Actian Apollo, close to the site of the palace that Augustus was having built for himself. On the cuirass of the statue of Augustus found at Prima Porta, Apollo is depicted astride a griffin and playing his lyre, with his sister Diana opposite him, mounted on a stag and carrying a quiver. After ensuring the victory at Actium, Apollo was next associated with the promotion of peace, the *Pax Augusta*, in his guise as the god of harmony.

Writers played their role in Augustus's efforts to exploit his alleged connection with the god. Writing in 40 BC, even before Actium, Virgil foretold the rule of Apollo in his *Eclogues* (IV. 10); while in the *Aeneid* Apollo plays an all-important role: he orders Aeneas and his companions to go back to the land of their ancestors (III. 94ff.), and he is Aeneas's protector (III. 395). He is as handsome as he was in the works of the Greek poets: 'the god walks on the slopes of Mount Cynthus, his flowing hair gently pressed down by leaves and encircled by a band of gold; and his arrows clatter at his shoulder' (IV. 147–9). He has regained all his ancient attributes: he is a prophet, a musician, an archer and a doctor (XII. 391ff.) He is 'the greatest among the gods' (XI. 785).

Similarly, Horace opened his *Carmen Saeculare*, sung on 3 June 17 BC, on the occasion of the secular games organized by Augustus, with an invocation to the two children of Leto: 'Phoebus, and you Diana, queen of the forests, luminous ornaments of the sky, both always adorable and always adored.'

In the episode relating to Daphne in *Metamorphoses I*, Ovid treated the god with a tinge of disrespect. He is overcome by the child Cupid whom he had despised. Smitten by passion for Daphne, he hopes to be united with her, the 'dupe of his own oracles'. He makes a very eloquent speech, to which the nymph, continuing on wayward course, does not listen, and, just as he is about to achieve his objective, Daphne is transformed into a laurel tree and so escapes his attentions for ever. Nonethless, if we look carefully at the way in which Ovid treats the gods throughout the *Metamorphoses* it is evident that Phoebus Apollo has been given pride of place. The other deities are not portrayed with the dignity befitting their rank; they are concerned with virtually nothing but love affairs and quarrels. In contrast, Ovid's Apollo, like Virgil's, retains all his ancient associations with divination, medicine, and music, and, in addition, is credited the magical power of metamorphosis, which he raises to the level of a science. He is the god of harmony and light. His identification with the sun, which, over the centuries, was sometimes emphasized and sometimes neglected is expressed without reserve in the speech that Ovid puts into the mouth of Pythagoras (XV. 191ff.).

As a result of Augustus's veneration of Apollo, the god began to be represented largely as a sub-deity, to the exclusion of his other attributes; and this tendency was developed by Augustus's successors. The Lycian and the wolf had long been forgotten. Apollo had become the luminous, harmonious, perfect figure that has been impressed ever since on our cultural unconscious.

Alain Moreau

Androgynes

THREE FOUNDATION MYTHS

All cultures have numerous myths featuring androgynous divinities. These stories ascribe the origins of the world to primordial chaos or to a primordial egg containing a combination of male and female principles and portray the ancestors of humankind as bisexual. The discussion that follows concerns three foundation myths, which exhibit common influences: the myth of an androgynous Adam; that of Plato's androgynes; and that of Hermaphroditus and Salmacis as recorded by Ovid in the *Metamorphoses*. All three have a cosmogonic aspect (although this is not clearly apparent in the last), all three are aetiological, that is they explain sufferings or aspirations that would be inexplicable without them, and all three have been censored or distorted in the course of transmission, as though their revelations were found to be too shocking. Lastly all three have an extremely long history in Western literature.

The latent idea of an andrognyous creator producing an androgynous creature is apparent in the first account of the creation in Genesis, which is much less often commented upon and illustrated than the second: 'So God created man in his own image, in the image of God he created him; male and female he created them.' These words imply the bisexuality of God and, in their image of Adam and Eve as forming a dual entity before the Fall, suggest the harmonious combination of male and female. Though suppressed by Judeo-Christian exegesis, the bisexuality of God and of human beings before the Fall was preserved as a living tradition in some rabbinical commentaries, notably the *Zohar*, which teaches the existence of an Adam Cadmon, whose androgyny is said to be a faithful reflection of the bipolarity of God. According to Abravanel Judah, author of *Dialoghi d'Amore (Dialogues of Love*, 1536), the two contradictory versions of the creation of human beings in the Bible carry an esoteric meaning: that a perfect androgyne was formed in the first creation and that Original Sin led to the subsequent separation of the sexes.

The androgyne myth told by Plato in the *Symposium* is put into the mouth of his enemy Aristophanes, perhaps as a way of distancing himself from a vision that he finds dangerously sacrilegious, and it may have a quite different status from that of the myths that he uses allegorically to express his philosophical ideas as a follower of Socrates. Jean Libis echoes Abravanel Judah's opinion that the myth was borrowed from the text of Genesis while some specialists think that Plato was referring to an Orphic-Babylonian tradition, which they see as the common source of both the biblical and Greek androgyne myths. Both traditions follow the same model: the original perfection of two elements in union, a transgression inspired by human pride, mutilation performed by an enraged divinity, the tragic wanderings of the severed human halves and the hope that the suffering caused by their separation will end with time and that they will be reunited. It should be noted that, far from being based on human experience or on the observation of people with physical abnormalities, the myth carries a scandalous message that runs counter to the lessons of life. In a single act, mankind trangresses the social norms encouraging the differentiation of the sexes and breaks off a relationship of submissive dependence upon the divinity.

The Platonic myth is often told in a partial way. In accordance with Greek philosophy, it is said to be about prmitive androgynes, whereas the text in fact portrays three sorts of ancestors for humankind: the first with entirely masculine characteristics, the second with entirely feminine ones, and only the third with a combination of both. The aetiological function of the myth is clear: to explain the suffering of separated lovers, whether homosexual or heterosexual. According to Mircea Eliade, in depicting these primordial beings as endowed with exceptional strength and a spherical form, Plato reveals the myth's cosmogonic nature, which connects it to accounts of the origins of the universe involving an egg or an anthropocosmic giant. The cosmogonic nature of the myth is also shown by the parentage of the three types of beings: the males are the childrem of the Sun and the females are descendants of the Earth, while the androgynes are children of the Moon, the celestial body that is halfway between the Sun and the Earth. This can be seen as an echo of the ideas of Hesiod, who does explicitly refer to a bisexed divinity, but recounts a cosmogony with an indisputably androgynous content. In his *Theogony*, the Earth engenders the Sky unaided, and then unites with it: this means that the Earth at first contained a masculine principle within its feminity, from which it separated and with which it then united – an archetypal model of dual unity shattered and then restored.

How did the abstract and general notion of the androgyne with which ancient thinking became familiar (particularly when it was reinforced by the introduction of Eastern divinities such as Cybele) lead to the existence in Ovid's time of Hermaphroditus, a god who acquired the characteristic of both sexes in the course of his history?

A particular aesthetic outlook helped to prepare the ground for this transformation, since especially in the Hellenistic period, Greek artists sought to represent masculine and feminine beauty in a single effigy. But above all it is clear that it was ritual practices that created the myth. In Sparta, Cyprus, Cos and Argos (the original home of the Greek colonists of Caria, where Hermaphroditus's metamorphosis was said to have occurred) intersexual exchanges of costumes and customs often formed an initiatory prelude to marriage or constituted propitiatory practices intended to encourage fertility. Meanwhile, at Athens and Halicarnassus, the city of Caria neighbouring the spring of Salmacis, Aphrodite and Hermes were originally associated in worship simply as gods whose task was to protect sexual union.

It was against this background that the utopian myth of the androgynes was succeeded by the story involving a single bisexual being, Hermaphroditus, in book four of the *Metamorphoses* – about whose originality Ovid boasts. This story is linked to a place, Caria, to an element, water, and to a nymph, Salmacis, with her own story, to which that of Hermaphroditus is more or less inextricably linked. The poet's tale has often been regarded as a simple erotic curiosity and has rarely been taken seriously – perhaps because, like the two myths discussed earlier, it has had its significance partially obscured. In fact, like the other two myths it deserves to be seen as a scandalous revelation providing an archetypal model of human behaviour.

It is only late in the tale (IV. 383) that Ovid actually uses the name Hermaphroditus; before this he calls the character Atlantius, a name that he also gives to Hermes, his father (I. 682; II. 704, 834; VII. 627). On this point Ovid is followed by Hyginus, who regards Hermaphroditus simply as a nickname. This all suggests a desire to identify father with child and to show that the child obeys the laws of heredity: the tendency towards feminization already apparent in Hermes recurs in his child. However, it is more interesting to note that Atlas, the ancestor to whom Hermaphroditus's other name refers, belongs to the generation of gods before the Olympians, taking us back to the time of Chaos and of bisexual confusion. According to some traditions, Hermes' grandfather, Atlas, is also the father of Dione and thus grandfather of Aphrodite. If this is accepted, the common ancestry of Hermes and Aphrodite may then be a prelude to their total union in the figure of Hermaphroditus. Thus the name Atlantius is related more obscurely but more profoundly to bisexuality and incest than the name Hermaphroditus. It can be seen as combining both the paternal and maternal lineage, recalling the feminization of the first and the masculinization of the second (a bearded Aphrodite was worshipped on Cyprus). Furthermore, in the tradition according to which Dione was Aphrodite's mother, this same Dione, daughter of Uraneus (the Sky), may be the sister of Salmacis, as we shall see.

Thus, though Ovid himself does not establish a genealogy for Hermaphroditus, the name Alantius recalls a dignified cosmogonic background. This cosmogonic element is also to be found in the name of Salmacis. While Ovid tells us nothing about the nymph's parents, Pompeius Festus presents her as the daughter of the Sky and the Earth. He also seems to link the word Salmacis to the root *sal*, the sea, since he explains that Salacia is a water goddess, thus named because she causes the sea to move. When Ovid uses the periphrase *Nymphae salaces* to refer to water, he is doubtless thinking of the same etymology, and, in his eyes Salmacis is certainly an aquatic divinity. Thus Salmacis may embody the old conceptions of Hesiod's *Theogony*, in which the Earth, an androgynous element, engenders the Sky, and then, by uniting with her son-husband, gives birth to the Ocean. The connotations of the names Atlantius/Hermaphroditus and Salmacis thus imply that the transgression of sexual differences can involve the transgression of the taboo on incest. Geographical details lead to a similar conclusion. It is in Caria, Ovid tells us, that the union of Salmacis and Hermaphroditus takes place. But it is there too that the same poet places another story involving an explicit desire for incest between brother and sister: that of Byblis and Caunos. In addition, when discussing the properties of the spring Salmacis, Vitruvius, Strabo and Pompeius Festus all recall that it is close to Halicarnassus, the city once governed by Mausolus, who married his sister Artemisia.

The mythographers say nothing about Salmacis's youth, but the few lines that Ovid devotes to Hermaphroditus's childhood are interesting: 'A child that Mercury had had by the goddess of Cythera was raised by the Naiads in the caverns of Ida' (*Metamorphoses* IV. 289 t.) It is the Phrygian Ida that is meant here, but there was, no doubt, a homonymic link between the chain of mountains in Asia Minor and the Mount Ida of Crete, birthplace of Zeus. In addition, his education in the mountains, the presence of initiatory caverns and the substitution of guardian nymphs for parents all emphasize the similarity between Hermaphrodites's upbringing and that of the master of Olympus. Though no details are given – and the silence of the text in this context may be eloquent – Hermaphroditus is presented as a rejected child, condemned to wander far from family and friends and destined by his exilt to an exceptional fate. Moreover, his banishment seems to be necessary to ensure the peace and happiness of Hermes and Aphrodite, just as, for Plato, the authority of Zeus threatened by the strength of an androgynous humankind.

Before his metamorphosis, Hermaphroditus's bisexuality is apparent in the contours of his body. When Ovid comments 'In his features one could easily recognize his mother and father' (IV. 290 f.) this is surely more than a conventional allusion to a child's resemblance to his parents.

The most important theme in the myth is that of the union of Hermaphroditus and Salmacis. Here water, as the prime element of dissolution, fully assumes its role of erasing differences. Although Ovid speaks of a pool – unlike Vitruvinus and Strabo, for whom Salmacis is a spring – the poet removes all the malignant vegetation usually associated with stagnant water. The story bathes in a euphoric atmosphere of elemental reverie: the nymph letting down her hair is herself an integral part of the aquatic scene.

Ovid's text provides full explanation of the conduct of Salmacis. Before she even meets Hermaphroditus her whole attitude already inplies transgression. She refuses to go hunting like her companions. She proclaims that a 'right to laziness', or rather to 'eros' is the only form of civilization. These transgressions pave the way for the one to which the myth itself is leading up: the reunion of the sexes. Doubtless older and more experienced, she makes the same speech to her fifteen-year-old partner as Odysseus makes to Nausicaa. Salmacis initiates three activities: speech, lovemaking and lastly prayer, which fixes and eternalizes the union of the sexes. In contrast, Hermaphroditus adopts the passive role traditionally attributed to the woman: he refuses her embrace then indirectly accepts it by succumbing to the delicious temptation to plunge into the water.

Like all great mythical tales, this story is ambiguous, since the final union is experienced differently by Hermaphroditus and Salmacis. Strangely, however, commentators have generally censored the latter's feelings and only concerned themselves with those of Hermaphroditus. The hero experiences the metamorphosis as non-sexuality, an erasing of the sexes: he feels himself becoming a half-man and internalizes the taboos regarding his monstrous and freakish condition. He is saved from shame only by the granting of his prayer to his parents that his disgrace should be shared by all who bathe in the pool. In this way, the myth dissolves almost as soon as it has formed: Hermaphroditus gives way to hermaphrodites. But while the man is frustrated, the woman is satisfied. Salmacis experiences a metamophosis that is a victory over nature and that, by giving her both sexes in superabundance, increases her vitality. Following her own logic, she pushes her transgression to the limit.

The message of Ovid's myth is apparently the opposite of that of the androgyne myths of the Bible and of Plato analysed above. For the latter dual unity is the beginning of paradise, while for Ovid it is an unhappy outcome (at least from Hermaphroditus's point of view). However Ovid's story highlights a similar problem to those raised by its counterparts. The three myths concern the time when things began: the first two explicitly, the third indirectly through the presence of water and through the cosmogonies alluded to by the names Atlantius and Salmacis. The three myths portray the interaction of the human and the divine, suggesting that possession of both sexes is a fearsome reflection of the latter and that when human beings have this privilege it can bring them into conflict with the demiurge. The situation is doubly tragic because human beings are exposed, in turn or at the same time, to the battle of the sexes and to conflict with God. The latter seems to be absent from Ovid's tale: Salmacis and Hermaphroditus each persuade the gods to fulfill their wishes. But the unexplained abandonment of Hermaphroditus, who was given over to the care of the Naiads at birth, turns him into an accursed brother of Oedipus and indicates the difficulty of maintaining harmony between God and human beings when the latter acquire divine androgyny. Often humans choose neither to exult in triumph like Salmacis nor to wander tragically like the multilated Adam, nor to regain their primordial unity like Plato's spherical being that was split in two. Instead, they adopt the sado-masochistic attitude of Hermaphroditus, morosely enduring their difference and wishing the same monstrous fate on others.

Thus in the sequence of androgyne myths leading from the Bible to Ovid by way of Plato, the bisexed being may be a source of scandal or a model of perfection, which in turn, may be either acquired for the first time or rediscovered. Between these two approaches, there is the myth emphasizing human suffering and the equivocal model. The characters in the former can live on as mutilated creatures without denying their sexual bipolarity; they may also feel definitively excluded from primordial wholeness. In any case, they experience lack. Those in the latter take action that they know to be presumptuous by uniting that which should remain asunder. These, then, are directions in which we find the literary myths of androgyny moving, and they are sometimes less divergent than one might think.

FROM SCANDALOUS MONSTER TO LIBERTINE

Ovid's half-man and the unfavourable interpretations of the myth of Hermaphroditus given by Pompeius Festus and by Strabo, who speaks in this *Geography* (XIV. 2. 16) of the weakening effects of the Salmacis fountain, spawned a whole literary tradition featuring an effeminate, monstrous being, a mechanism of desire entirely devoted to pleasure. The author of the fourteenth century poem *Ovide moralisé*, provides a fairly faithful translation of the story in the *Metamophoses*, but turns Salmacis into a courtesan and makes her responsible for corrupting the man who unites himself with her to such an extent that they end up with only one body. The writer also produces two other allegorical interpretations of Ovid's myth, one of which will be analysed below. Ovid had not described the monster's future: his narrative told only of the scandal of its appearance; and this idea of scandal became inextricably attached to the word 'hermaphrodite'. Describing the stylistic device of ambiguity, which was then considered heretical and satanic, Boileau, the literary theorist and writer of an anti-baroque polemic, began the diatribe in his *Satire* XII (1705) with the words: Du langage francais bizarre hermaphrodite,/De quel genre te faire, equivoque maudite,/ou maudit? (Bizarre hermaphrodite of the French language, what gender should we make you, cursed [feminine] or cursed [masculine] ambiguity?) For at that time, the gender of the word hermaphrodite had not yet been grammatically fixed. In France in the seventeenth and eighteenth centuries the hermaphrodite was often considered to be a male homosexual, so much so that at this time the two words were sometimes synonymous. Bayle in his *Dictionnaire historique et critique* (1697), recalls that for Plato the word 'androgyne' was a term of disgrace in its everyday usage and adds: 'He is right, for besides the fact that whether or not hermaphrodites are monsters is a matter for dispute, this name is also given to the most wicked libertines.' This association with libertinous activity forms the background to the pamphlet *L'Ile des Hermaphrodites (Island of the hermaphrodites* (1605)), which Thomas Arthus aimed at the three young men regarded as favourites of King Henri III. The many reprintings of this pamphlet until as late as 1726 show that it reflected the fantasies and taboos of seventeenth and eighteenth century readers. In the *Encyclopédie*, Joucourt wrote a medically researched article on actual hermaphrodites studied at the time and considered to be monsters, again using Ovid's story as an aetiological myth.

When Flaubert introduced a hermaphrodite into the first version of *The*

Temptation of Saint Anthony (1849), making it speak after the pig and before the pygmies and dog-faced baboons, it was to act as an incarnation of perverse and unsatisfied desire. Like the famous ancient sculpture to which Bernini added a mattress, Flaubert's reclining hermaphrodite is perhaps seeking to conceal its physical form. It looks at its reflection in the water and its outline (if not its face) displeases it; and like its precursor in Ovid's poem, it wants to see its disgrace multiplied. It wants to spread the 'unknown happinesses that keep [it] in anguish'.

The Decadent movement adopted this perverse figure. A female androgyne is portrayed by Albert Samain in *Le Chariot d'Or* (posthumous edition, 1901). With her 'grinding spasms' she becomes a kind of Antichrist preaching inhuman pleasure. Her cruel appearance and taste for jewels are inspired by Gustave Moreau's paintings, which are revered by Joris-Karl Huysmans' hero Des Esseintes: 'And the Androgyne with great green phosphorescent eyes,/ Blooms in the golden charnel house of a rotting world.'

While the quest of pleasure links this androgyne to the Decadent movement, the pride that makes it confront God recalls its Platonic model.

By a euphemistic process, monstrosity becomes a libertine game in *The Unbearable Lightness of Being* by the Czech author Milan Kundera, which makes explicit reference to Plato's androgyne myth. Teresa dreams that she and her husband are transformed into hermaphrodites. Other women, whom she herself has washed and bathed, are erotic playthings for both of them. The source of these libidinous desires connected with water can be found in Ovid's story and in the interpretations of it by Vitruvius and Strabo. This text falls halfway between the lascivious and shocking fantasies to which the Decadents were inclined and a surrealist eroticism that seeks to bring opposites together through the imagination alone.

A SUFFERING HUMAN BEING

When the hermaphrodite does not provoke a scandal, it arouses pity. A fine poem by Tristan L'Hermite called 'La Fortune de l'Hermaphrodite' (*La Lyre*, 1641), which represents a personal adaptation of an epigramme by the fourteenth century New Latin poet Pulci, is a meditation on the hero's tragedy. Three oracles given by Jupiter, Venus and Mercury make him heir not to two but to three natures. This is probably an updating of the Platonic myth and recalls its two other primitive species of beings, usually forgotten in favour of the androgyne. But it is the hermaphrodite's end, predicted by Saturn, Mars and Diana, that gives L'Hermite the greatest scope for reflection. A triple death follows his triple birth. The poet returns to Ovid's setting, inverting the charm and making it malevolent: the limpid waters become 'troubled water', 'deep, black water', and the surrounding vegetation becomes a murderous trap. The inclusion of Diana, who's named last, reminds us that Plato's androgyne is the child of the Moon. 'Battered, hanged, drowned', this hermaphrodite is indeed a suffering being; and he paves the way for the character celebrated by Lautréamont in the second canto (verse 7) of the *Chants de Maldoror* (1869).

The latter also has a particular connection with the Moon: but in this case his descent from her has become a mythical device. His adolescent state and past history (long years of solitary wanderings far from his parents and a stay in the mountains) link him to Ovid's hero. But there is also a Salmacis side to him: his hair is eroticized, like that of the nymph. The material reverie underlying the text gives earth and air their place, reminding us of the nymph's parents, the Earth and the Sky. Needless to say, Lautréamont's character does not have to endure the disgrace of being asexual. He has all the sexuality and emotional life of a man and a woman: in him 'virile energy' and 'grace' come together. Far from being castrated, he has dual erotic possibilities; his unhappiness arises from his loneliness, which he cannot accept, and from the feeling that he is monstrous, not in his own eyes, but in the eyes of others. More generous than his model in Ovid's poem, he turns his bitterness against himself alone, feels no hostility towards his fellow human beings or Providence.

Thus in the hermaphrodites of Tristan l'Hermite and Lautréamont we find a 'super-humanity' that makes the inhumanity to which they themselves fall victim seem all the more unjust. However, the hermaphrodite is sometimes depicted as suffering for exactly the opposite reason: instead of being a creature with a superabundance of emotional and erotic energy springing from the potencies of both sexes, it may feel that it is somehow wanting. Gautier's heroine in the novel that bears her name, *Mademoiselle de Maupin* (1835–6), glimpses wonderful adventures of adopting the roles of both sexes: 'continually absorbing and radiating, being sometimes the moon, sometimes the sun, seeing the whole world and all of creation in a single being [. . .] redoubling oneself in giving oneself'. However this glimpsed ideal merely serves to make the feelings of division that she suffers when disguised as Théodore all the more painful. These feelings spread to those who have sexual relations with her, Rosette, and in particular d'Albert. Mlle de Maupin first experiences them as an internal rift: 'It often happens that the sex of the soul is not the same as that of the body.' She has to make do with a shape that 'fits badly with the mind it houses' and declares at the end of her adventures that 'I belong to a separate third sex that does not yet have a name: [. . .] I have the body and soul of a woman, the mind and strength of a man, and I have too much or not enough of both to be able to mate with either.' Divided in herself like the Plato's half-beings to whom the text refers, she cannot hope to meet a man or woman who will make it possible for her to recover her unity. Of the men into whose company she has willingly slipped she declares that they 'are fit for a thousand things, all excepting the single thing for which they were created, which is to serve as male to the animal called woman, with whom they have not the slighest rapport, be it physical or moral'. The novel portrays three failed efforts to achieve union: with Rosette, d'Albert and the young page in disguise, Isnabel. Physical union – desired and attempted with Rosette and once consummated with d'Albert – seems to bring about the welding together of two beings in the Hermaphroditus myth. (Indeed four references, two of which are extended, show that Ovid's tale was influential in this context.) But the more total the physical union, the more it tragically leaves the souls aside. It is d'Albert's understanding of this that leads to his relationship with Rosette and so to the frustration experienced by the principal heroine: 'Like ancient Salmacis, lover of the young Hermaphroditus, I sought to melt her body into mine; [. . .] the more our bodies entwined and the more intimate out embraces became, the less I loved her. My soul, sadly sitting apart, watched this deplorable marriage to which it was not invited with an air of pity.' And yet d'Albert had done his best to reproduce the ancient setting; his mistress was in the bath and he himself tried to act 'the Triton as best [he] could': but in vain. The reason for his failure is the same as in the case of Mlle de Maupin: the struggle that he experiences between those fraternal enemies, his body and soul, can be found in all couples, whether licit or illicit, who are condemned to live 'in a state of permanent war'. Faced with the impossibility of transforming himself into an androgyne, d'Albert dreams of the multiple existence of Tiresias, or of those lived out by the monstrous gods of India through their avatars. Theatre is then used as a derisory substitute for successive incarnations: by acting in Shakespeare's *As You Like It*, the novel's trio can enjoy exchanging 'hermaphrodite speeches'. Rosalind-Ganymede played by Mlle de Maupin fulfils the desires of both Rosette and d'Albert. But, as P. Albouy notes, the 'fantasy hermaphrodite' cannot long obscure the 'unhappy hermaphrodite'.

The motif of the multiple death endured by the hermaphrodite, which so moved Tristan l'Hermite, can be used in a conventional human context. In *L'Androgyne* (1890) Péladan sought to portray a person who is at first entirely satisfied by bisexuality but whose entry into adult masculinity brings tragedy. However, despite its promising title, only the last pages of the novel appear to draw inspiration from myth. Up to this point the hero, Samas, is merely a youth prey to the feelings shared by many young men of his time living in a Jesuit school. It is when he teaches the crisis of puberty that two 'gynanders' decide, like Salmacis, to reveal femininity to him. According to the title of the last part and final chapter, this is 'the death of the androgyne'. Turning Ovid's story on its head, the literary myth expresses a nostalgia for the wholeness of Adam and the scandalized horror of the adolescent as he feels his borgeoning virility tearing him apart: 'They suffer, she because she understands nothing, except that she is not loved, and he because he feels the androgyne dying, because he is becoming a horrible, sexual man'.

The catastrophic death of the androgyne at puberty is also a major theme in the novels of Dominique Fernandex, particularly *Porporino or the Secrets of Naples* (1974). This writer continually looks back to the 'circular happiness' that, according to Plato, was enjoyed by primitive beings. He makes women responsible for awakening Adam from the paradisiacal sleep of sexual non-differentiation. Without women, human beings 'would be both sexes at once, of indeterminate age, with no career to make'. This carries echoes of the right to laziness asserted by Salmacis. The Platonic model is present, but it, again, is turned upside down. The brutal division of male and female ordered by Zeus has its equivalent in the novel: a surgeon is required to perform a castration as the only way to halt mutilating development towards a single sex. Fernandez links his nostalgia to the ancient cosmogonies of primeval chaos: 'gigantic egg, where there was neither shadow nor light, wet nor dry, hot nor cold, left nor right.' Only the Italian opera with its castrati can revive this archetype of human fantasy, but in a 'counterfeit', 'humiliated' form as part of a 'scandalous exhibition'.

One of the darkest pieces of contemporary theatre, Giraudoux's *Sodom et Gomorrhe* (1943), is on the subject of the death of the androgyne, followed by the end of the human race and the destruction of harmony with the cosmos. This dramatist remained influenced by the thought of Abravanel Judah after his univeristy studies, and the more his earlier plays fantasize about recovering the lost unity of the sexes by means of the belts of flesh that Ondine wants to attach to her lover, the more bitter the dislocation of the couple appears. In Giraudoux's eyes the perfection of the primitive androgyne has been perpetuated by love until modern times. The Fall did not happen in the distant past, but is happening before our very eyes. His conception of the Creation is close to that expressed in the first account in Genesis: God created 'two twin bodies united by ties of flesh', then he cut these ties, replacing them with affection. The human couple is in harmony with all forms of life and its breakdown causes the dislocation of the animal world: some animals follow man, others woman. There is nothing to suggest that it may be possible to reunite what has broken apart.

The problem posed by Musil in his novel *The Man Without Qualities* (1930–3; posthumous fragments, 1950) is similar to that posed by Giraudoux. Here the dream of union between man and woman is simply a mask for the impossible union of androgyne and cosmos. The mythical image of the androgyne reflects an old concern in Musil's work. In 1923 he wrote a poem on the theme of the exchange of identities and the fusion of Isis and Osiris, which paved the way for the treatment of brotherly love in the novel. In the latter, the hero's reunion with his forgotten sister marks the beginning of an adventure that fulfils the quest that is the central element in the work; a quest for a wholeness that it is impossible to attain in this increasingly fragmented world. The meeting of brother and sister signifies a mutual recognition that they are lost halves of the same whole. Agatha proclaims that their role in the world is simply to be together, inactive and bathing in the beatitude of being both one and two. The androgyne is the prime symbol of the sought-for wholeness, the fusion of opposites. Thus Musil does not regard it only as a myth representing paradox of the sexes, but also as one representing the impossible resolution of all contradictions. The brotherly passion of *The Man Without Qualities* is rooted in the concept of original unity and twinhood: for both heroes, its dissolution of the principle of separation represents a protest against the world at large. Thus the love of the brother and sister symbolizes the difficulties that they experience in their relations with the world. The mythical image also represents a bond that one can merely glimpse even in a state of ecstacy: 'a closeness without measure', in the hero's words, an ambiguous condition in which the couple are 'neither separate nor united'.

The utopia of androgyny and the spherical whole is thus just a passing element in the incestuous story. In fact, Musil thinks that mythical images bear within them a 'partial truth about the world and human experience' and that they represent a combination of the rational and the irrational, the two conflicting elements that, according to him, have destroyed the unity of the subject. The myth is thus, above all, the expression of something lacking.

AN AMBIGUOUS MODEL

While many works on the theme of androgyny concentrated on either the ordeal of being split apart or the urge to achieve wholeness, another approach occurs in Italian literature from Dante to Marino. Here, the androgyne becomes an ambiguous image symbolizing a literary undertaking.

In Dante's work we find a most unusual allusion to the androgyne myth: in the last circle of Purgatory, where the souls of those guilty of sexual indulgence are serving their time of penitence, Dante meets two groups of sinners moving in the opposite direction. The first are the Sodomites, while the second are people who say that their sin was to be hermaphrodite (*Purgatory* XXVI. 82). Because of the clear contrast between the two groups, commentators usually interpret the reference to hermaphrodites as a metaphor for normal sexuality carried to excess. However, one element in the account casts doubts: as an illustration of their sin, these 'hermaphrodites' cite Pasiphaë, a symbol of bestial sexual practicies and thus hardly a symbol of normality. It seems more satisfactory to link Dante's metaphor to the allegorical tradition and to see it as a symbol of the union of body and soul – or more precisely of the divine aspect of mankind (symbolized by Hermes, as the god of intellect and guide of dead souls, and Pasiphaë as the daughter of the Sun) with the animal part (instincts and desires). (In this context it is worth noting that The Minotaur, born from the sexual union of Pasiphaë and the bull, resembles Hermaphroditus to the extent that both are hybrid monsters, one half man, half woman, the other half man, half animal.) In addition, the 'hermaphrodite' souls in Purgatory are poets, and are recognized by Dante as his masters – the troubadors of the *dolce stil nuovo*. It seems that they are excluded from Paradise because their poetry seeks to reconcile profane and sacred love, and this constitutes a crime of presumption against God comparable with that of the alchemist. Thus, the metaphor of the hermaphrodite seems intended to represent poetry as a domain of tension and duality, and poets as those who believe it possible to bring together two opposing forces that should be kept apart: the aspiration towards higher things and the aspiration towards baseness. Likewise in a different interpretation of the myth from the one discussed above, the fourteenth-century author of *Ovide moralisé* sees in Hermaphroditus the monk who turns away from his contemplative life in an attempt to reconcile life in the world with the love of God.

This metaphrocial use of the myth becomes particularly pronounced later in literature, where the treatment of the fusion of the sexes as a mythical experience becomes a frequent novelistic device, involving cross-dressing and substitutions. The most euphoric example of this secularized descendant of the myth – which constrasts starkly with the version in *Mademoiselle de Maupin* – occurs in canto XXV of Ariosto's *Orlando Furioso*. This involves Bradamante, a latter-day Amazon who leads the life of a knight and is always dressed as a man, but is no less a woman in her love for Ruggiero. She has an identical twin brother with whom she is confused, and who appears in the tale merely to take on the masculine role that Bradamante cannot play with another woman. Bradamante inspires the young princess Fiordespina with such a violent passion that the latter begs heaven to turn her into a real man. The twin brother, who is in love with the princess, siezes the opportunity to substitute himself for his sister and, dressed as a woman during the day, fulfils his male role with his lover at night. This story is an exaggerated reworking of the fable in Ovid's *Metamorphoses* (IX) concerning Iphis, a girl who is brought up as a boy, and is really turned into a man on her wedding day. In addition, there is probably also an allusion to Tiresias, who experienced the pleasures of both sexes alternately. In Ariosto's work, Bradamante's twin portrays his faked metamorphosis as genuine, much to the wonderment of his lover. Thus, the mythical metamorphosis becomes a novelistic trick, but its symbolism is maintained through the inclusion of a mythical tale within the main story, even though the tale is portrayed as a lie. The myth informs the literary work and, by becoming secularized, loses some of its symbolic charge in favour of a more literary work. In this context, substitution represents not so much the reunification of the heramphrodite's two parts as the doubling of a single whole.

In the Marinist poetry of the seventeenth century, the myth again exerts an active but diffuse influence. There are some direct allusions, which are mainly of an iconographic type, reducing the fusion of Salmacis and Hermaphroditus to an erotic image, but its impact is mainly apparent in the form of a web of relationships between several mythical figures. Thus Hermaphroditus plays an important, but latent, role, in Marino's *Adonis* (1623), for it is Adonis himself who appears as an androgynous figure. In accordance with the traditional code of the madrigal, he is described with feminine attributes; his colouring is that of the lily and the rose and his beauty is that of the dawn. Similarly, his passivity in response to Venus's bold advances is that of a virgin.

Furthermore, Hermes and Aphrodite both act as initiators (as his spiritual father and mother) and the entire poem shows that the male and female principles are not opposed, but merged. Like Dante, Marino defines poetry as an attempt to unite opposites though he views the process from a completely different perspective. He represents it through the metaphor of alchemy and thus as a fundamentally ambiguous activity.

A PATH TO PERFECTION

In antiquity the derogatory comments of Strabo and Pompeius Festus concerning the properties of the spring of Salmacis contrasted with the remarks of Vitruvius (II. 8), who gave his own allegorical interpretation of them. According to this, the fountain was justly famous. Its encouragement of an enriching union of masculine and feminine had softened the souls of the barbarians, enabling them to accept the charms of civilization. Later, when the author of *Ovide moralisé* was condemning Salmacis, a whole mystical movement involved in experiments with alchemy returned to the sources of the androgyne myth and pronounced Ovid's account to be the finest. The alchemist Nicolas Valois (1475–1541) discerned a cosmological aspect to the *Metamophoses* that seemed to him to prefigure the search for the philospher's stone, since the alchemical process was designed to engender a microcosmic creation, fusing sulphur and mercury and recreating the egg of the world in the sacred vase in which it took place. This is a reminder of the bisexual nature of the primordial egg emphasized by the authors of cosmogonies.

Taking up the medieval tradition in his *Dictionnaire mytho-hermétique* (1758) Dom Pernety gives an alchemical meaning to the union of Salmacis and Hermaphrodite, seeing it as equivalent to combining sulphur and mercury. Citing the alchemist D'Espagnet (1550–1630), for whom 'water is the menstrual fluid containing the seed of things, which carries them into the earth', Dom Pernety revives the reverie on water apparent in Ovid's text: 'the mercurial water of the philosophers is one with the bodies bathed in it.' The idea of a philosophical form of incest between royal lovers may also be a revival of a myth theme that seems implicit in Ovid's fable.

This mystical current may have been responsible for the rehabilitation of Salmacis in a quite extraordinary context. In his *Discours poétique à Messieurs de la Religion prétendue réformée* (1607) Filière sees the myth as the Roman church inviting the Protestants to return to its bosom!

In *Les Etats et empires du Soleil* (published posthumously in 1661), Cyrano de Bergerac abandoned the satirical vein of *Les Etats et Empires de la Lune*, and produced one of the most euphoric and imaginative retellings of the myth of Hermaphroditus and Salmacis. A guide to the Empire of the Sun shows the narrator two twin apple trees striving for unity. These trees were produced by the metamorphosis of Orestes and Pylades and their fruits make a love potion as magical as the one that united Tristan and Isolde. Chewing the twin fruits brings about the rebirth of lovers from the ancient epics: 'Achilleses and Patrochluses, Nisuses and Euryaluses' appear in ever increasing numbers, but an incestuous couple, Cinyre and Mirra, are also present. The juice of the two apples overcomes the most pronounced differences: between a girl and a bull, an adolescent youth and a plane tree and a man and marble (Pygmalion and his statue). The sculptor has only to eat one of the apples and to moisten his unfinished work with its juice and the two of them will form an inseparable couple.

Amidst all these stories about the lifting of taboos and the removal of differences, the union of Hermaphroditus and Salmacis is represented as taking place in an idyllic, paradise setting. Hermaphroditus is a shepherd bound by an adolescent friendship to a local girl, Salmacis. He wins a race and she a beauty contest: the magic twin apples are their reward. Like Eve, to whom Cyrano de Bergerac is surely comparing her, Salmacis is the more eager to eat the fruit, and immediately falls in love. Only after the intervention of Hermaphroditus's parents, who regard the union of their son and the nymph as advantageous, do both young people distill and drink the juice of Orestes' and Pylades' fruit. By giving an active role to the parents, the seventeenth-century writer seeks to respect the proprieties of his time and to make the nymph innocent, while still giving her a passionate desire for the fusion of the sexes, as in earlier versions of the myth. This is a rare instance in which fusion if presented as equally happy for both man and woman, who are, at the same time, both united and fertile. 'This double something or other nevertheless kept its unity; it engendered and conceived, without being either man or woman.'

This text vindicates an observation made earlier on the basis of Salmacis's connection with Caria and confirms Jean Libis's conclusion that 'androgyny, incest and twinhood may constitute the reversible elements of the samc mythogenic family'. He adds: 'Each of these elements transgresses an order in one way or another, opposing the status quo, turning into phantasmagoria. Each of them abolishes a distance and to some extent erases a duality. Each restores a lost intimacy.' Twinhood is depicted as the work of the magic fruit. Incest is not only the subject of a story by Cyrano involving the androgyne, it may also lie at the heart of the story of Pylades and Orestes' since the two cousins desire each other through Electra who comes between them. In any case, their at least intent homosexual and semi-incestuous desire is presented by Cyrano as the fertilizing source of the desire of Hermaphroditus and Salmacis. Furthermore, underlying this version of the myth is an animist refrain, the idea of a fertile intermingling of the kingdom of nature. The happy fusion of the sexes is relocated in a vision of a world in which, antitipating Diderot's *Le Rêve de d'Alembert (D'Alembert's Dream)*, 'every animal is more or less a plant'.

In the literary myth presented by Cyrano, the fusion of beings is followed by blissful happiness. In contrast, Gabriel de Foigny's utopian work, *La Terre australe connue* (1676), depicts human beings still in a primordial state of androgyny. Just as the author of *Les Etats et Empires du Soleil* represents this condition as something to be won, so Foigny represents it as something to be defended. He places his utopia on an island using the setting and, according to Libis, the idea of androgyny as a visible symbol of introversion and self-sufficiency. Cyrano's mythical source is the account in Ovid which he has reworked to show Salmacis in a more sympathetic light; Foigny's is Plato's myth, merged with the account in Genesis, 1. The Australian androgynyes, like Plato's, have an excess of life and vigour. In their eyes, it is the single-sexed Europeans who are half human. Like Cyrano's Hermaphroditus and Salmacis, they are fertile and self-generating, but unlike them, they do not experience desire. They reproduce by laying eggs (which, three years after Foigny, Antoinette Bourignon describes as the method used by Adam before the arrival of sin). Between the corrupt, single-sexed Europeans and the bisexed Australians, the author places an intermediary, the narrator Sadeur, who is physically endowed with both sexes, but does not have the privilege of emotional and sexual self-control. A prisoner of his instincts, he is only on the path of perfection; his mission is to discover the androgynes of Australia and to reveal their ideal life to his compatriots.

For Foigny, as a rationalist author, the emotional tranquility of the Australians is a precondition of their happiness. By emphasizing the perfection of these people in the form their continuing wholeness, he aims to show that the myth of the Fall is not universal. In the article on Sadeur in his *Dictionnaire historique et critique*, Bayle demonstrates that *La Terre australe* follows the biblical image of an earthly Paradise. The function of the androgyne myth in this philosophical work confirms observations made earlier concerning its use in other writings on the same theme: it serves specifically to dissipate the anxiety that gives rise to the battle of the sexes and not merely to soften the contrasts between man and woman. It is presented as reducing the differences between the sexes in three respects. First, the conventional Christian antithesis between soul and body is resolved by the concept of a body that is unified and glorious: the Australians do not eat meat, produce hardly any excrement and do not menstruate. Similarly, the antagonism between the individual and the group that is found in Western societies is assuaged by relations between individual Australians and their community that are brotherly and, according to Pierre Ronzeaud, almost those of twins. Finally the gap between time and eternity, which has always been most tragic for the human race, is also lessened: the burnt remains of each Australian return to the whole from which they sprang. Thus hermaphroditism induces other forms of fusion, besides the obvious one between masculine and feminine.

The tales of Cyrano and Foigny are vivid embodiments of their philosophical ideas. However, when Balzac wrote *Séraphita* (1835), he was only partially successful in telling the story of an androgyne and had difficulty in breathing life into his characters, Wilfrid, Minna and Séraphita. Nonetheless, an effort to portray the relationship of man to the cosmos, and a genuine atmosphere of elemental reverie prevent his work from sinking into abstraction. His three central characters are based on Plato's three original types of human being, while his choice of Norway as the setting for the action reflects his desire to recreate a primitive climate. As primordial beings of the kind described by Plato the three heroes are endowed with immense strength: Minna and Séraphitus (as she is called at first) have climbed the Falberg, an exploit hitherto regarded as impossible. The strange circular shape ascribed to the androgynes by the Greek philosopher, is transposed in the case of Séraphite: she is the 'radiating centre of a circular'; 'whoever entered it submitted to the power of a whirlwind of lights'. Like the Platonic androgynes, who are children of the Moon, Balzac's androgyne has a particular connection with moonlight. The details of Séraphite's real birth are less important than her fantasy origins. She seems to have been 'brought forth by the union of ice and sun'. Her glances are sometimes filled with 'fluid light', an 'almost phosphoric body'. In moral terms, she again has lunar attributes for she is a 'mirror in which moral nature is reflected, with its causes and effects'. When she disappears, leaving nothing but 'a voice in the sunbeams', 'a celestial spirit in the new flowers', she completes the synthesis of Sun and Earth embodied in the Platonic androgynes. In a spiritual context she has the strengths of both sexes, and her aspirations to reach heaven place her beyond desire. Séraphita's whole being is a reflection of an imagination obsessed with fusion: fusion of the sexes, the meeting of earth and sky, and the meeting of Wilfrid and Minna, the two people in whom she has aroused desire. In the latter connection, her good fortune makes her the antithesis of Mlle de Maupin, who never succeeds in uniting the two sexes in herself, nor in bringing together the man and woman whom she has caused to fall in love with her.

The happy tranquility achieved by Foigny's Australians and desired by Séraphita is also ascribed by Gide, in his *Traité du Narcisse* (1892), to the androgynous Adam before his fall into sexual disunity. Feelings of desire, subjection to the tryanny of time, and the ever-disappointed hope of recreating a primeval state of perfection through physical reproduction are certainly signs of exclusion from Paradise. In the blissful Beginning, Gide's Adam, like Foigny's characters, was at one with a cosmos whose unity was represented by the logarithmic table and which, like the primordial egg in the cosmogonies, combined Earth and Sky in a protective night. 'Everything strives after its lost form', and Paradise can be recreated by a poet-Narcissus who, like Adam before the Fall, rejects desire in favour of tranquil contemplation and reabsorbs all differences with just his gaze.

Thus Foigny, Balzac and Gide are unanimous in praising the androgyne's non-sexuality and resulting emotional self-control. An interest in hermaphroditism (suggested *en abyme* by Elstir's paintings, which are similar to those of Gustave Moreau) lends the novelist Proust also to portray it as the path to salvation. Proust's ideas show curious similarities to those of the eighteenth-century philosopher Saint-Martin, and, like him, he lays emphasis on physical cases of bisexuality. These, he argues, attest to the persistence of the legacy of the golden age of hermaphroditism in people of his own day. Thus nature is already the world's time regained, 'a beginning of art'. Again like the philosopher, in his novel *In Remembrance of Things Past* (1913–27) Proust seeks to show that androgyny can be restored through artistic creation: the latter is represented as true parthenogenesis reflecting the artist's powers of self-fertilization, and thus his or her mental bisexuality.

Consequently, the androgyny's self-control is not synonymous with sterility in the eyes of Foigny, Balzac, Gide or Proust; on the contrary, it goes hand in hand with a fertility that the last three writers regard as being of an essentially spiritual nature.

Séraphita and *In Rememberance of Things Past*, are novels of initiation and Gustave Meyrink's work *The Golem* (1915) is similar in this respect. In it, the author strives to reconcile the realistic framework of a narrative recounted by the book's hero, a writer stopping briefly in Prague, with a novel consisting of the hero's dreams. The main character in the dream novel, Athanasius Pernath, who is seeking his own identity and a spiritual awakening, is confronted with his malevolent double, the Golem, who, according to rabbinical tradition, is born from a clod of earth and periodically reincarnated. The Golem represents Pernath's inner demon, the brutal drives of the id that lead him to desire the death of the husband of the temptress Angelina. When he rids himself of the demon, he is able to heal his inner rift and to unite with the feminine part of his soul, represented by Mirjam, who is destined to be his companion for all time. At Christmas, the double reappears. However, it is no longer the Golem, but the hermaphrodite of light, who can be recognized by his attributes, the white coat and crown. At the end of the novel, the character writing in the first person identifies the exuberant vegetation of an eternal spring as a Garden of Eden watched over by a servant of the androgyne, and recognizes himself as the hero in his dream. The garden of Eden revives the Talmudic tradition of an androgynous Adam, while the white light recalls the mythical lunar origins of Plato's bisexual beings.

According to Meyrink, during this life the two partners can only begin the reconstitution of the androgyne divided at the time of the Fall. However, André Breton, in *Arcane 17* (1945) maintains that total reconstitution can take place before our very eyes and portrays a very physical androgyne, with a superabundance of masculinity and feminity. Since he is the son of the moon, like his Platonic archetype: 'The old pool is no more. All the water has regained its full breathing beneath the crook of the moon.' Breton thinks in terms of an active union taking place between two mutually attracted sexes (a theory already present in *L'Astrée*). An androgyne pre-exists them and they reconstitute it by virtue of a law that 'says that every human being was thrown into life seeking a single being of the other sex who matches him in every respect'. Marc Eigeldinger, the leader of the Surrealist movement, regarded erotic fusion as also having a poetic meaning. In his view, alchemical symbolism underlies the androgyne of *Arcane 17*: this 'signifies the substance of the philosopher's stone' and 'performs the synthesis of opposites, through which monism conquers the split consciousness of dualism'. Breton's narrative and that of Cyrano discussed above both bear witness to a similar type of imagination. To tell the story of the reduction of the differences between the sexes, both authors use several myths intended to suggest a process of mediation. Breton portrays Mélusine as mediating between man and nature, and the oppositions between man and woman and death and life represented by Osiris and Isis as being resolved by incest between brother and sister. He also depicts the myth of Osiris and Isis as expressing a capacity of regeneration. Finally, the woman in *Arcane 17* who spills out the contents of a golden urn with her right hand and empties a silver urn on to the earth, with her left is intended to recall the myths of Ovid and Plato – Plato's myth because of the presence of the earth, sun and moon, which according to it, gave rise to the three original types of human being, Ovid's because of the aquatic setting and the initiatory role played by a woman. Bayle had earlier dared to write a single article on this myth, entitled 'Salmacis', in which he expressed a timid sympathy for initiative taken by the woman in the reuniting of the sexes: this initiative was unreservedly applauded by the Surrealists.

Among the most recent and successful descendants of the androgyne myth is the one that breathes life into Michel Tournier's novel *Gemini* (1975). The novel returns to one of the earliest forms of the myth in an attempt to draw inspiration from the ancient cosmogonies and to describe the adventures of unusual characters. Tournier makes the rabbinical tradition according to which God created man in his image 'both male and female, hermaphrodite' his own. Meanwhile, from Plato, he borrows the theme of violent separation, speaking of 'the tearing, the axe blow that severed us, the horrible amputation'. However, for him, the primitive androgyne still survives in the microscopic cell whose endlessly repeated oval form recalls the spherical beings in the myth. However feminity apparently has no place in the 'oval loves' of the twins Paul and Jean. In fact, their cell carries within it both male and female elements: one of the twins, Paul, is maternal and interoverted; the other, Jean, is extrovert, and has aspirations to conquer the world . . . and women. The ultimate failure of their personal relationship when Jean tears himself apart from his twin does not signal the end of the novel. Amputated from his brother and from half of his own body, since he loses an arm and a leg trying to unite the divided twin halves of the city of Berlin Jean himself represents the final mutilation with which, according to Plato, Zeus threatened human beings if they persisted in their pride even after being cut in two: 'if . . . their impudence continues . . . I shall once again cut them in two, in such a way as to make them walk by hopping on one leg.'

However, the twin micro-cell, which is impossible to reconstruct, is replaced by the macro-cell that Paul reconstitutes with the universe and, in particular, with its airy, pneumatic, meteoric part. While the right half of his body is paralysed and irremediably bound to the earth, representing the feminine element that he has always incarnated, the left half is 'spread out over the sea like a great sensitive wing'. Like Salmacis, Paul becomes the son of the Sky and the Earth. Tournier reconciles the old cosmogonies of the bisexual primordial egg with a third Testament announcing the diffusion of the Holy Spirit after Pentecost.

This article has drawn attention to the idea of dangerous transgression that surfaces in the original myths concerning androgyny. In fact all three warn of the risk inherent in any attempt to overcome the dread spectre of separation in all its forms: between man and woman, creature and creator, man and cosmos and time and eternity. While similar sentiments are most clearly perceptible in the more tragic literary versions of the myth, they are not entirely absent from the more euphoric versions. These often belong to a marginal current of thought: alchemical researches are experienced as heterodox even by those who pursue them. There is a boldness disguised as utopia in Foigny's clearly deist fictions or Cyrano's atheist ones, both of which deny the Fall. Even at a time when political censorship and social condemnation of the unorthodox are waning, a certain lyrical aggression can be found in the work of André Breton or Michel Tournier, the high priest of scatological themes. The price of taking the path of androgynous perfection is mutilation, loneliness and divine or human disapproval: even when it is represented as exultant, this path is still threatened by the dangers apparent in the earliest tales of androgyny.

Marie Miguet

Andromeda

THE CLASSICAL MYTH

The story of Andromeda, which has become a myth in its own right, originally formed part of the cycle of exploits that grew up around the legendary hero Perseus, slayer of the Gorgons.

Perseus was the fruit of one of the many amorous liaisons between Zeus and mortal women, in this case the beautiful Danae. Her father, Acrisius, had been told by an oracle that he would be killed by his own grandson, so to escape this fatal prediction he imprisoned his daughter in a large room that was open to the sky but otherwise inaccessible. However, although this precaution proved effective against other mortals, the ruler of the gods managed to unite with Danae in the form of a golden shower of rain.

Greek mythology celebrates many of the young hero's splendid deeds, but thc crowning glory of his reputation was the slaying of the fearful Medusa, the only one of the three Gorgons who was not immortal. Bearing the bloody head of his victim, whose hideous features provides a striking contrast to his own masculine beauty, the victorious Perseus presents a striking image, captured in the marble sculpture by Cellini.

Persus's encounter with Andromeda took place as he sailed along the coast of Philistia (Palestine). In the distance he caught sight of a beautiful woman, naked except for a few pieces of jewellery, chained to a rock at the water's edge. This was Andromeda, daughter of Cepheus and Cassiopeia. Her mother had boasted that she and Andromeda were more beautiful than the Nereids and these sea nymphs had complained to Poseidon. To punish the pride of Cassiopeia, he sent a sea monster to the borders of the kingdom and told Cepheus that he must sacrifice his own daughter to the creature, which fed on human flesh. Cepheus tried desperately to be released from this terrible duty, but was forced to surrender Andromeda to the monster by his subjects, who feared that they might be compelled to sacrifice their own children. His daughter accepted her fate with the courage that her name, a woman 'with the mind of a man', implies.

Perseus fell in love with the beautiful victim and offered to protect her on condition that she agreed to marry him and return with him to Greece. He killed the monster and the marriage took place, in spite of reservations on the part of Andromeda's parents who had promised her hand to a certain Agenor. The rival interrupted the ceremony to claim his rightful bride, but Perseus was able to use the head of Medusa to turn him and his companions into stone. But despite the happy outcome of this early adventure, the prediction of the oracle remained inexorable, and much later Perseus accidentally killed his grandfather, Acrisius.

This reconstruction of the collection of interwoven legends that still survive makes it possible to identify the constituent parts of the myth of Andromeda: 1) it is set against a maritime background where the waves break against the rocky shore; 2) a beautiful, naked woman, chained to a rock at the water's edge, awaits her fate with painful resignation; 3) a monster, whose terrifying bulk is just breaking the surface of the water, is about to emerge from the sea; 4) an intrepid hero flies through the air, and attacks and kills the monster; 5) a wedding takes place between the hero and the prize of his victory, the victim herself. Other versions of the myth associate Perseus with the fabulous winged horse, Pegasus, born of the body of Medusa, or describe him as having winged feet – spectacular attributes that were emphasized in later adaptations of the myth.

The portrayal of Andromeda constitutes, as it were, the second panel of a diptych. Facing the hero, who is full of confidence and brandishes his trophy in his hand, is the moving image of a female victim, vulnerable in her nakedness, tied to the rocky ground, her lovely body condemned to be torn apart. This disturbing sensuality, combined with the apparent injustice of the terrible and undeserved sacrifice, create a curiously ambiguous effect. What is the significance of this fettered body that is unclothed, but still adorned with a few pieces of jewellery? And why is the victim condemned to be mutilated in this horrific way? It seems, in fact, that there was an earlier version of the myth in which the victim was actually guilty and so deserving of punishment. In the Palestinian version of the legend, the young woman is associated with the figure of Aphrodite, Ishtar and Astarte, and was thus probably originally represented as an object of physical desire. The early counterpart of Perseus was Marduk, the sun god, who killed a sea monster while mounted on a white horse. But in this case, the monster was actually an evil manifestation of Woman, and he chained its true female form to a rock to prevent her from committing further wickedness. The myth seems to illustrate the ambiguous male view of the eternal female principle. On the one hand, there is the hypnotic image of the immodest nakedness of a sensuous and beautiful woman who is unable to escape from her plight without calling for male assistance. On the other, there is the monstrous embodiment of the power of physical desire, which threatens to destroy the hero's vocation with its seductive image of nuptial bliss. The nakedness of Andromeda and the terrible fate that awaits her seem, therefore, to be explained by this early version of her story. In the later version, she is transformed from an evil temptress into a submissive maiden, although she is still naked and wears jewels, recalling her earlier role as a symbol of temptation. Meanwhile, her sin has been transferred to her mother, who is guilty of arrogance.

Before considering the modern versions of this particular myth, it is interesting to note that the same pattern is repeated in other classical myths, such as the rescue of Hesione by Heracles, Jason's slaying of the hundred-eyed dragon that was used to threaten Medea, and the story of Cadmus and Harmonia. There is also a particularly interesting early version of the myth of the Labyrinth, in which Ariadne is actually inside the maze and at the mercy of the Minotaur, which is killed by the timely intervention of Theseus. These various episodes confirm the richness of the archetypal model, which will be discussed later, and of which the story of Andromeda provides a particularly evocative example.

THE MYTH OF ANDROMEDA: AT THE TIME OF CORNEILLE

The playwrights of Antiquity took advantage of the excellent theatrical properties of the myth of Andromeda, although the only example of their work to survive is a fragment of the *Andromeda* by Euripides. The most complete account of the story from classical times occurs in Ovid's *Metamorphoses* IV and V, which constituted the main source for the various subsequent adaptations of the myth, the most famous of which was by Pierre Corneille. Versions of the myth were also produced by two major Spanish dramatists, Lope de Vega (*El Perseo*, 1621) and Calderón (*Las Fortunas de Perseo y Andromeda*, 1653), the latter being inspired by Corneille's work.

The spectacular 'tragédie à machines' by the author of *Le Cid*, produced in January 1650 with music by d'Assouci and scenic effects by Torelli, was a great and lasting success. But to appreciate the full significance of this production, which stands out so strikingly from the conventional theatre of the time, it has to be viewed in a wider context. In the first place, Corneille's play about Andromeda was not the only French version of the myth to have been set before the public. In addition, the story of Andromeda and her rescue had for a long time been part of the Italian operatic tradition and continued to provide inspiration for fashionable librettists until the end of the eighteenth century. As a result, Corneille's *Andromède*, which was already a semi-operatic piece because of its many songs, must be considered in a wider Franco-Italian perspective. An opera entitled *Andromeda* was performed in Italy as early as 1587 and, closer to the time at which Corneille was writing, versions of the same myth, again in operatic form, were produced in Venice in 1637, and in Ferrara in 1639. The subject, often embellished with events from the life of Perseus, provided inspiration for other operas during the seventeenth century, and records from the eighteenth century show that there were no fewer than seventeen Italian operas based on the same theme.

Most of these productions were soon forgotten, but occasionally famous composers were involved. Examples include Monteverdi who composed his own *Andromeda* in 1617 and Michael Haydn, brother of the famous composer Joseph and a composer of some importance in his own right, who wrote the music for another opera entitled *Andromeda* in 1797. The international appeal of the myth and the infuence exerted on it by opera were also reinforced by translations into Dutch (four between 1699 and 1739) and a German version in 1679. Meanwhile, Corneille's play was translated into Dutch in 1699.

It is important to establish the degree to which Corneille was influenced by the Italians. He was perhaps familiar with the versions of *Andromeda* produced in 1637 and 1639, while the two operas in Italian verse, *La Finta Pazza* and *Orfeo*, presented in Paris in 1635 and 1647 respectively, may have inspired him to produce a French version of the myth in operatic form. It is known that the scenery for *Orfeo* was used in Corneille's play. However, Corneille was not the first French playwright to produce a version of Andromeda in his own language. According to Dubuisson-Aubenay, a play entitled *Andromède et Persée la délivrant* was performed by the actors of the Marais Theatre in 1647–8. The play, which was by an anonymous author and is now lost, was probably presented in an attempt to compete with Corneille's own forthcoming play, which was to be performed by the King's own troupe, the Comédiens du Roi. In any event, the Marais company was unable to forestall the success of Corneille's play, which was mounted in a series of productions until 1660. Even later, towards the end of Corneille's life, *Andromède* was used as a weapon in the rivalry between two theatres. In 1682, with the vogue for opera at its height, Quinault had the idea of adapting Corneille's play as a libretto and giving it the title *Persée.* The music was written by the great composer Lully, whose Royal Academy of Music had been installed at the Palais-Royal since 1673. The Comédie-Française, founded in 1680, was trying to recover from a somewhat shaky start and wanted to counter this dangerous competition – Quinault and Lully had had the temerity to use a real horse to play the part of Pegasus – with a new production of Corneille's original version of *Andromède.* The attempt does not appear to have met with the same success as *Persée*, which enjoyed thirty-three successive performances, and a total of forty-five, a remarkable figure for the period.

THE MYTH OF ANDROMEDA ACCORDING TO CORNEILLE

As the basis for his tragedy, Corneille used the version of the myth by Ovid and, as was his wont, listed all the changes that he had made to his source, in his 'Examen' of 1661. First, for the sake of propriety, the heroine was no longer naked, a detail that he attributed, in any case, to a purely pictorial tradition. In making this change, he unintentionally broke the last link with the early erotic myth. Next, in Corneille, Perseus is reunited with his legendary mount, whereas Ovid had given him his own wings. The identity of the hero is also initially concealed; he is a mysterious character whose name is only disclosed after his arrival, in a revelation that is characteristic of the heroic archetype. Again, Corneille gives Perseus an adversary, Phineus, whose mythological predecessor is Agenor and who is a representation of evil. His death makes it possible for the other characters to be united in a harmonious dénouement; he is the expiatory victim, effectively replacing Andromeda herself. It is well-known that Corneille had a high regard for this 'dual' intrigue in which good was rewarded and evil punished.

Having reduced the details borrowed from his mythological source virtually to the single image of a young woman waiting chained at the water's edge, Corneille not only felt obliged to extend the list of characters but also to embellish the action. As a result, in the first scene, Venus is represented as demanding a single sacrificial victim, rather than a potentially unlimited number of acts of atonement. At the same time she announces the amorous rivalry between the mysterious stranger (Perseus) and Phineus. Andromeda does not learn that she has been chosen as the victim until Act II, and the focal point of the myth is not dealt with until Act III. Andromeda condemned (and clothed), resolutely awaits death, but Perseus, astride Pegasus, saves her by killing the monster. To maintain the interest of the audience, the act finishes with a new motif. Neptune is furious that Perseus, a son of Jupiter, should defy him in his maritime kingdom and threatens to disrupt the wedding ceremony.

At this juncture, Phineus maddened by jealousy, tries to kill Perseus, who escapes by using the head of Medusa to turn him to stone. With Phineus dead, the action draws to its close in the apotheosis of the play's characters among the stars. Jupiter, Juno, Perseus, an appeased Neptune, Cassiopeia and Andromeda will shine in the heavens for eternity. A joyful song celebrates this reconciliation between the gods, as well as between the heavens and the world of mortals.

We must now consider the revision and adaptation of Corneile's *Andromède* by Quinault. While retaining the basic framework of the play, its later adaptors introduced additional elements typical of opera, for example by including many minor parts to extend the list of characters. In terms of the plot, they created a new balance between the main characters by creating the role of Merope, a young woman promised to Perseus in marriage. This gives rise to an imbroglio that complicates the relationship between two central male and two central female figures. Andromeda loves Perseus and he returns her love. The rival of Perseus, Phineus, pays court to the heroine, while the rival of Andromeda, Merope, claims the love of Perseus. Quinalt also embellished the plot by staging episodes that, strictly speaking, belong to the early version of the myth of Andromeda, for example the offence committed by Cassiopeia (Act I, Scene 1) and the beheading of Medusa in the cave of the Gorgons. (In this context, he perhaps felt that the play's title *Persée*, allowed him to incorporate extra episodes from the life of the hero.) Act IV is the counterpart of Act III in Corneille's play; Andromeda, the chosen victim, is exposed to danger, threatened and saved. Meanwhile, Act V culminates in the obligatory heavenly apotheosis; with the rivals safely out of the way, after Merope dies and Phineus is turned into stone, Perseus and Andromea are raised to the heavens along with the gods. A joyful dance brings the opera to its close.

THE MYTH OF ANDROMEDA REVISED AND ADAPTED BY JULES LAFORGUE

Outside the theatre, there is little trace of the myth of Andromeda. However, towards the end of the nineteenth century, Jules Laforgue used the central theme of the myth as the basis for a remarkable satirical adaptation. In 'Adromède et Persée', one of the finest pieces in his *Moralités légendaires* (1886–8), we find the traditional mythical elements: the heroine wearing only her jewellery, the rocky shore washed by the waves, a monster in the form of a dragon and the winged hero bearing the legendary head of Medusa. But, although Laforgue pays homage to the components of the myth, it is only so that he can parody them with cynical irony, and use them to create a completely different type of fable.

In Laforgue's version, Andromeda is a frail young girl who has just reached puberty. The mature and resigned heroine is replaced by a neurotic adolescent who is forever on the move, whether writhing on the sand or running frantically up and down the steep slopes of her island. She is prey to an unknown desire, which is both vague and suppressed. She begs a migratory bird to come and 'take away the burning source of her pain' ('pain' replacing the word 'sexuality' in the original version): an obvious reference to the myth of Leda, who was seduced by Zeus in the form of a swan.

Although the physical appearance and the character of Andromeda are downgraded in this way, the monster, on the other hand, is elevated to the role of a wise and gentle protector. It remains quietly in its cave, calling Andromeda 'baby' and treating her with the deepest respect; and even makes her a necklace, which she throws petulantly into the sea. In spite of Andromeda's erratic and selfish nature, they live together in complete harmony and appear always to have done so.

At this point the hero, Perseus, appears on the scene, reduced to the level of a ridiculous, self-opinionated and cynical womanizer with appallingly bad taste – his arm tattooed with a heart pierced by an arrow. Determined to make off with Andromeda, he profers the gallant invitation: 'Come on, up you get! We're off to Cythera.' He kills the poor monster, which offers only a token resistance, and then continues to stab its body relentlessly. Overwhelmed by this senseless killing, Andromeda dismisses her 'liberator', who does not appear the slightest bit disappointed and flies away on Pegasus yodelling. Andromeda is left to weep bitterly over the loss of her monster, but, to her great surprise, the beast is revived by her caresses and – a second miracle – changes into a handsome young man. The night that follows is to all intents and purposes a wedding night for this beast-turned-prince-charming and his beauty, and the myth has taken on a quite different identity.

To reinforce the partly mythical, partly realistic tone of the story, Laforgue includes numerous explicit references to mythology, for example to Pyramus and Thisbe, and Prometheus and Cythera, as well as thinly veiled allusions.

The latter include the allusion to Leda already mentioned, while Laforgue's description of Andromeda admiring herself lovingly in a rock pool clearly recalls the myth of Narcissus. But, at every turn, he undermines these lyrical evocations with clichés and deliberate platitudes. Perseus utters the most awful and inspid gallantries: 'Love you? I adore you! My life without you would be unbearable and plunged in darkness'. And, not long afterwards, Andromeda exclaims to the slayer of the Gorgons: 'Clear off! You've come to the wrong place'.

In summary, Laforgue brings about a curious transformation of the myth, by combining irony, lyricism and fantasy. In so doing, he to some degree anticipates the great irreverent mythological works of twentieth-century fiction.

THE ARCHETYPAL MODEL

According to the German scholar Hudo Hetzner, there are numerous myths, sagas, legends and tales that recount the exploits of a young hero who rescues a maiden from a dragon. In the version of the story discussed above, Andromeda is exposed on a rocky shore, as a sacrifice to a sea monster, and Perseus arrives just in time to kill the dragon and marry her. Alternatively, the tale may involve a dragon terrorizing an entire country and holding the young maiden prisoner in a cave. Again, the hero appears, defeats the dragon and frees the maiden. Thus, the story of Andromeda is merely one particular version of a much larger tradition. In fact, it is easy to extend the archetypal framework of the myth, since it is only one step from dragon to giant or from the half-human monster to the human with monstrous tendencies. Whether it is the maritime lair of Andromeda's sea monster, the dragon's cave, Dracula's crumbling castle or the very ordinary house of the 'villain' of modern melodrama, we are faced with the same archetypal setting. The myth of Andromeda is basically similar to a whole range of traditional folk tales and legends, such as the story of Saint George and the dragon and the legends of the chivalric tradition. A whole succession of knights have saved their lady by single-handed combat against an evil enemy, a dragon or something similar. Popular cinema proves that this is a particularly fertile area for the human imagination. *Dragonslayer*, a recent film now on general release, follows in the true fairy-tale tradition, and presents the entire sequence of events that we have observed to a greater or lesser extent in the myth of Andromeda. The ruler of a vaguely mythical kingdom that is being terrorized by a flying monster has to pay the monster a regular tribute in the form of a young maiden chosen by the drawing of lots. It so happens that the king's daughter is chosen as the next victim, and the radiant and beautiful young woman, her head crowned with garlands of flowers and her body barely concealed by a flimsy white gown, is chained to a rock in an infernal cave. A terrible bellowing echoes from the gaping depths of a nearby chasm. A young hero challenges the monster and, after many setbacks, manages to kill it. The king gives his daughter to the victor in marriage and the entire kingdom sings the praises of its liberator.

The works discussed above illustrate the possibility of producing a whole range of variations on a general mythical framework that undoubtedly plumbs the depths of the human psyche. The myth of Andromeda is only one example, but it is an example that is particularly rich and evocative, to judge by the number of adaptations consciously based on it since ancient times.

Harold C. Knutson

Antigone

It was Bertolt Brecht who stressed that the myth of Antigone tells an entirely human story. No miraculous elements appear in the plot, and, it can thus easily be adapted to modern sensibilities and ideologies.

The character of Antigone belongs to the legend of Thebes. Her death brings to an end the lineage of the Labdacid, in other words that of Oedipus. The details of her family tree were emphasized by Aristotle in his *Art of Rhetoric* in the context of the setting in which a tragedy takes place, and displayed below.

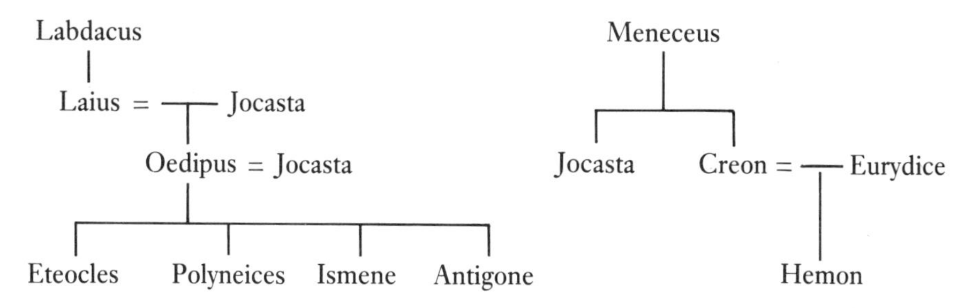

The story of Antigone has been preserved by four Athenian tragedies of the fifth century BC: the *Seven Against Thebes* by Aeschylus (467 BC), the *Antigone* by Sophocles (441 BC), *The Phoenician Women* (*Phoenissae*) by Euripides (409 BC) and the *Oedipus at Colonus* by Sophocles (407 BC) Meanwhile, a few centuries later, the Roman Statius reworked the whole legend in his long epic poem *The Thebaid* (90 AD).

Sophocles' two tragedies effectively created the myth, though, strangely, they are not in sequence. The theme of the tragedy of 407 BC runs as follows. Having learned that he has unwittingly committed patricide and incest, King Oedipus blinds himself and leaves Thebes, leaning on his daughter Antigone's arm. He dies in the woods of Colonus. The king's sons, Eteocles and Polyneices, fight over the succession, while Creon temporarily holds power. It is at this point that the earlier tragedy of 441 BC begins. The two brothers have killed each other, and Creon refuses to bury Polyneices, who has attacked Thebes. However, Antigone is intent on following the precepts of religious law and gives him his funeral rites. Despite warnings from the priest Tiresias, Creon condemns the girl to starve to death walled up in a cave. She commits suicide, whereupon Hemon and Eurydice, Creon's son and wife, also kill themselves.

Here we have two tragedies, two roles and ultimately two Antigones. The myth develops along two different paths. The earlier version shows Antigone as a paragon of family virtues, while the later one portrays her as a symbol of resistance, who refuses to accept established authority and dies rather than obey an unjust order. It was initially the first image of Antigone, as the daughter who devotes herself to her blind old father, that attracted the attention of later writers.

ANTIGONE OR PIETY

In the Middle Ages, the main source for the Theban myths was Statius's *Thebaid* in Latin. Thus, in *Le Roman de Thèbes* (1150), as in Dante's *Divine Comedy* (1472), Antigone and Ismene play only a minor role. It was not until the sixteenth century that the myth of Antigone herself began to be revitalized, as a result of the discovery of Sophocles' tragedies. *Antigone* was translated into Italian by Alamanni (1533) and into French by Baïf (1573). In 1580, Robert Garnier made the story into a play with the significant title: *Antigone ou la Piété*. This was a poem of 2,700 lines, which it was impossible to stage unchanged, and which was mounted by Thierry Maulnier in 1944 only at the price of a great many cuts. It is the one work that presents the whole of the story of Antigone on stage. The girl is a paragon of devotion to her family. Torn between worry over her feuding brothers, anxiety about her mother who is trying to kill herself and the need to help her aged and infirm father, she does her best to give each of them her care and attention. She is so edifying a figure that Jocasta, the Chorus and Creon himself all predict immortal glory for her. In fact, a girl who was attached to her sick father was, for a long time, referred to as 'an Antigone'. In this sense, Garnier follows the spirit of *Oedipus at Colonus*. But he has already changed the myth, by discreetly christianizing it. It is not the name of Zeus that is invoked, but 'the great God who formed Heaven and Earth'. Religious and family piety are covered by the same word.

A similar concern to adapt ancient vocabulary to a Christian society appears in Rotrou's *Antigone* (1637). The heroine has a lofty view of her family obligations, and sees her civic duties as organized according to a fundamentally religious hierarchy: one must obey the orders of the gods, but not necessarily those of mortals. Creon is guilty of not respecting the decrees of 'heaven', a useful word that seventeenth-century playwrights employed to refer to supreme being without having to use pagan language.

The latent or acknowledged tendency to christianize the myth, which prevailed in many plays and operas staged in France and Italy in the eighteenth century, blossomed in the epic narrative *Antigone* written by Ballanche in 1814. The work is dedicated to the duchess of Angoulême, daughter of Louis XVI of France, who, it is suggested, may have provided the model for its heroine. Ballache's approach is worthy of some attention, for, without actually using the word, he quite deliberately turned the ancient fable into a modern 'myth' with universal scope. 'I took my subject from ancient times and transported it whole into modern beliefs; I appropriated it by changing sphere, making it undergo a kind of palingenesis' (Preface of 1830). His Antigone overcomes all her ordeals with angelic gentleness. She is a religious soul, a saint, and her dying father extracts from her a vow of eternal chastity. 'All she needs is a linen band to be a Carmelite virgin', said Barchou de Penhoen. The author carefully removed all episodes that might contradict Christian teachings. There is no 'scene of the laws' since, otherwise, the heroine might have taken on the too-unfeminine appearance of a rebel; there is no suicide, which is forbidden by the Church. Jocasta, Antigone and Hemon die from the weight of their sufferings. Ballanche's human beings do not raise their heads, they can only remain pious to the point of sacrifice in this vale of tears. This devotion is a form of expiation and Antigone redeems the sins of the Labdacids. Her example thus as a general significance: 'Man, that dethroned king, goes through exile, always accompanied by the Antigone that heaven has sent him' (Epilogue, 1814).

Ballanche's contemporaries applauded this spiritual interpretation of the ancient fable. Thus, although the model seemed to him to be 'despairingly' perfect, Charles Nodier observed in 1830 that 'the story of Antigone needed a God and M. Ballanche has given it one'.

In France, during the nineteenth century, most Hellenists supported this christianization treatment of the myth. The words 'My way is to share my love, not share my hate' given by Sophocles to his heroine in line 523, were constantly mentioned; and Antigone was frequently compared to Joan of Arc: for Paul de Saint-Victor and Charles Péguy, both women had the same vocation of sacarifice. Meanwhile, under the influence of Monsignor Dupanloup, who was eager to spread the Greco-Latin humanities, Sophocles' play was staged in small seminaries. In the twentieth century, there has also been no lack of mystic interpretations. Simone Weil had a special regard for Antigone, as long as she was seen in a Christian light: 'The unwritten law that she obeys is none other than the extreme, absurd love that drove Christ to the Cross' (*Ecrits de Londres*, 1942). The heroic figure of Antigone acquired a particular significance during the 1939–45 war: on the 8 May 1945, Paul Zumthor saw in Sophocles' play both a symbolic image of biblical texts and a prefiguration of the victory of the French people (*Antigone et l'espérance*).

Thus Antigone was seen successively as the epitome of the pious and helpful girl, as the nun who sacrifices herself for the sins of this world, as a martyr comparable to Joan of Arc and as an emulator of Christ.

POLITICIZATION OF THE MYTH

Despite the picture given above, during the nineteenth century other interpretations of the myth were also gradualy developing. In the 'scene of the laws'

Sophocles made a seminal distinction, for Antigone countered Creon's decrees with what she called the unwritten, unchanging laws that date not from today, nor yesterday, but are eternal and whose first appearance no one can trace. A century later, when Aristotle sought to define the laws common to all peoples, he referred specifically to this line from Sophocles: the law invoked by Antigone was a 'natural law' (*Art of Rhetoric*). This concept passed from Aristotle to Roman law, then to Saint Thomas Aquinas, Rousseau, Kant, the upholders of human rights and, in our day, to the neo-Thomists inspired by Jacques Maritain. The *Antigone* became a focus of political debate.

It is interesting to consider when writers first perceived this new dimension to tragedy. One of the first dramatists to do so was Alfieri, who was an ardent revolutionary and who put on a violently antimonarchist play entitled *Antigone* in Rome in 1776, in which he criticized the prime argument used by tyrants to support their actions: that they are necessary for reasons of state. In Germany and France, the debate was opened by the staging of Sophocles' *Antigone* in 1841 in Potsdam and in 1844 at the Odéon in Paris. This was the first time that audiences had been confronted by the original version of the tragedy, without the classical proprieties and insipid love stories with which it had been encumbered during the eighteenth century, and with the 'scene of the laws' back in its rightful place at the start of the drama. But, for public opinion, still infused with the values of Christianity, natural law merged with divine law, and Antigone remained a pagan saint and martyr. Only Gérard de Nerval understood the true significance of the work. He saluted *Antigone* as a fine narrative 'of ancient or modern resistance', and added, 'The scene of the laws presents the invariably sublime struggle against force and the questionable wisdom of the powerful' (*L'Artiste*, 26 May 1844). With his stress on resistance and challenge, Nerval places himself in the tradition of the French Revolution, while also using what were to become key words for the youth of his country a century later.

In Germany, the work of A.W. Schlegel had also drawn attention to the original text of Sophocles' play, but had drawn different conclusions from it. In 1821 Hegel, who was one of the greatest admirers of ancient tragedy, maintained that the two opposed characters at the centre of the play were each claiming an equally valid justification for their actions. There was neither a guilty nor an innocent party. 'Antigone honours the bond of kinship, the gods of the underworld, while Creon honours Zeus alone, the dominating power over public life and social welfare' (Hegel 1975: 1213). Each makes the mistake of asserting that his or her law is exclusively right, instead of trying to harmonize the moral powers that they represent through 'a tragic reconciliation' (Hegel 1975: 1216). In Sophocles' play the conflict is resolved by the death of the two adversaries, thus manifesting their essential accord and equal worth. This new interpretation, which led to the rehabilitation of Creon, was adopted by the Hellenist Müller and by many German critics (except Goethe). The result was a controversy between German and French writers, which was exacerbated by the war of 1870. Hegel's Antigone was called 'Prussian' by Jules Girard (*Revue des deux mondes*, January 1877), while in France, Antigone, in her guise as the heroine of universal morality, gradually found her place among the great national figures.

It is not surprising, therefore, that her name should have been invoked when France was shaken by a crisis of authority. In 1893 and 1894 the Comédie-Française presented the *Oedipus Rex* and *Antigone* in Paris and Orange, making a profound impression on intellectuals and students. Some months later the Dreyfus affair began and, not unnaturally, those alleging that the judiciary had made a mistake depicted the authorities in the image of Creon and identified themselves with Antigone, who disobeyed the authorities of the day in the name of justice and truth. This, for example, was Péguy's position. That of Barrès was more subtle, though he too was moved by the 'immortal dialogue'. His first impulse was to enlist Antigone, 'the burier', in his crusade for the earth and the dead. But in relation to the Dreyfus affair, he sensed a danger: 'If I give way to Antigone's prestige, it is the end of society . . . Following her, each of us can please ourselves, invoking the unwritten laws' (*Le Voyage de Sparte*, 1906). Here, heroism is seen as a public menace, and for Barrès, as for Hegel, the conflict between Creon and Antigone is 'immoral'. The prophet Tiresias is merely a venal agitator who exploits the body of Polyneices for political gain. This is an ingenious interpretation, which it is interesting to compare with that of Maurras. One might have thought that the latter, following the logic of his political ideals, would have sided with Creon, the established authority. Far from it. For him, Creon is the anarchist who has 'violated the tradition of the Altars, Homes and Tombs, whose origin no one knows' (*Antigone vierge-mère e l'Ordre*, 1948). It is Antigone who represents the legitimate authority. Lastly, in 1915, Romain Rolland draws a final lesson from Sophocles: he addresses a vibrant appeal to the 'eternal Antigone', who, with the voice of all the women of Europe, is to bring living peace in the midst of war (*Les Précurseurs*, 1919). The ancient myth thus seems to have become an integral element in all the West's moral and civic conflicts.

RESISTANCE WORKER OR ANARCHIST?

The postwar period brought about a breakdown of values with profound repercussions for the image of Antigone. Her prestige was great enough for her to lend her name to rebels of all kinds, including anarchists and those who openly espoused amorality. In 1922 Cocteau set the tone (*Antigone*, L'Atelier). Like Ballanche a century earlier, he was aware that he was rejuvenating the myth: 'I clear the way, I concentrate and remove the dead matter that was covering the living substance of an immortal drama.' His 'contracted' tragedy (which reduced Sophocles' text by half) was intended to be provocative. The production, worked on by avant-garde figures of the time including

Picasso, Honegger, Dullin, Antonin Artaud and Chanel, conflicted violently with classical taste. Yet it was still not immediately clear where Cocteau was going. Through his contraction of the play, he gave Antigone his own taste for anarchy. Indeed, he admitted as much to Jacques Maritain, saying: 'Instinct always drives me to counter the law. That is the secret reason why I translated *Antigone*' (Letter to Jacques Maritain, 1926).

This literary anarchism was not a danger to society. However, when, twenty years later, the French had to choose to support or oppose the 'legal' government imposed by the Germans, the Resistance gave the story of Antigone back its contemporary relevance. The events of this period provide an excellent example of how even a myth as heavily commented on as this, could still prove ambiguous. For in 1941 Léon Chancerel tried to use a production of *Antigone* staged in Marshal Pétain's youth workshops to extol the values of the 'National Revolution', until his young audience inverted its message by seeing Oedipus's daughter as embodying the just struggle against France's Nazi invaders. Equally paradoxical was the staging of Anouilh's *Antigone* at the Atelier in February 1944. This was not a translation but an original work – the first on the subject produced in France since the Revolution. In it, there were two significant omissions: the character of Tiresias and the 'scene of the laws'. The result was a secularization of the myth and a reduction of Antigone's stature. Creon is not a tyrant, but a statesman who has chosen to keep a firm hand on the tiller when faced with extreme danger to his country, even if this means getting his hands dirty. For those reading between the lines, this rehabilitation of the king of Thebes was a justification of Pétain and the Vichy regime, both still in place at the time at which the play was staged. And yet the spectators had eyes only for Antigone. The author's intentions were misunderstood. It was the resistance that was applauded, so proving the strength and tenacity of the myth.

Without either author or spectators being aware of it, Anouilh's work was the precursor of a new generation of plays based on Sophocles' tragedy. In them, Antigone becomes the one who says 'no'. This is a sign of courage, for it is hard to say 'no' when one is alone against all the rest. But her 'no' extends beyond the conflict in which she is directly involved. She is saying no to society, to adults, perhaps to marriage, to what the young were soon to call 'the system'. She expresses the conflict between the generations that shook America and Europe in the 1960s, when demonstrators carried banners saying 'No to tomorrow'.

In Germany Antigone became the one who said 'no' to bourgeois and capitalist society, in the plays inspired by socialism or Marxism written by Hasenclever and subsequently by Bertolt Brech. The heroine of Hasenclever's *Antigone* (1916) is not an anarchist. Nor is she alone in 'fighting the good fight'. At her side are the people, whom she wins over to her cause – in the process, becoming a defender of the poorest in society. Brecht's *Antigone* (1948), partly translated from Hölderlin, is openly Marxist in conception. In their war against Argos, whose iron mines they covet, the people of Thebes are led into the abyss by a bloody despot who resembles Hitler. (Indeed the author daringly replaces Hölderlin's *Mein König* with *Mein Führer.*) Aristocratic Antigone is unmoved when her brother Polyneices is brought down by Creon's blows. Her rebellion comes too late and precipitates the defeat of her people. Thus 'the great figure of Resistance in ancient drama does not symbolize the fighters of the German Resistance' (*Antigone Modell 1948*, 1949).

By going against the interpretations of Antigone current at the time, Brecht sought to emphasize the distance between the actor and spectator that was so important to him. However, his efforts were to no avail: in the case of his work as in the case of Anouilh's the audience persisted in its admiration for Antigone, whose role seemed so well adapted to the tragedy of the 1940s.

Indeed, it was Brecht's play that was staged by Judith Malina and Julian Beck in their Living Theatre. The two were involved in civil disobedience campaigns in the United States, and Brecht's book *Antigone Modell 1948* filled them with enthusiasm. They transformed the Marxist reading of the *Antigone* into a celebration of anarchy (Paris, 1967) in which the audience is constantly attacked and transfixed by the aggressive production. A ritual of violence unfolds around Polyneices' corpse, the show's magnetic pole, at the end of which Antigone and Hemon triumphantly raise up the victim's body and place it over Creon, who has fallen on his back. Rebellion has triumphed over the state; the deserter glows with new glory above the old world that he has destroyed. The negation of humanist values and the dissolution of the state can surely be taken no further.

The French public would find it hard to see signs of religious anarchy in Antigone or to condemn her for the hubris that makes human beings rise up against the gods. However, philosophers from other countries who have studied Sophocles' text in detail have been more severe with her. Following Hegel, the Danish philosopher Kierkegaard, one of the Theban heroine's greatest admirers, judges her both innocent and guilty, but regards this contradiction as being precisely what constitutes the tragic character (*Either/Or*, 1843). Hölderlin had gone even further in his *Remarks* of 1804. He perceived a sublime presumption in Antigone's conduct and saw her speech as bold and blasphemous; so much so that he regarded her as a manifestation of the 'Antitheos', on the grounds that she listened only to her own advice and thus appropriated to herself the role of the gods. It was this that explained her bitter solitude and the profound despair that emanates from the farewell scene (*Remarks on Antigone*, 1804). The German philosopher Heidegger returned to Hölderlin's analysis and took it to its ultimate extreme: for him, Antigone provides an example of transgression. In this she is the embodiment of humankind – not a wonder of nature, as proclaimed by Sophocles' Chorus, but an unstable, dislocated creature, disturbing and always close to exclusion (*An Introduction to Metaphysics*, 1952).

These very different interpretations from political and metaphysical standpoints can all be summed up in one sentence: Antigone is the one who disrupts things; she disrupts the established order and upsets notions of good and evil.

Since the Second World War the myth of Antigone has gone from strength to strength. After 1944, Antigone touched the emotions of more people than she had done since Sophocles first presented her drama on the slopes of the Acropolis in 441 BC. The Athenian tragedy was re-staged by great national theatres and small provincial companies or youth groups alike. Anouilh's play toured the world. It was produced in Berlin, Moscow, New York and South Korea. Living Theatre's *Antigone* went all over Europe and America, while cinema and television also took up the theme. There are several hundred versions of the play and even some editions in samizdat form.

The 'scene of the laws' lies at the heart of Western political thinking. It constantly challenges fundamental legal notions concerning the basis of the law and possible justifications for disobeying it. Antigone's name has also been a password for Western journalists. They have invoked it during the Algerian war, in the name of the Irish or the Libyans and indeed every time that resistance fighters have confronted the domination of the state or foreign occupation. Philosophers often use Antigone as a symbol of their ideas: for the German Ernst Bloch she represents the rights of the mother (*Natural Law and Human dignity*, 1961) and for Jacques Maritain she is a heroine of natural law (*Les Droits de l'homme et la loi naturelle*, 1942); while Marguerite Yourcenar has hailed her with the words: 'Antigone's heart is the pendulum of the world' (*Fires*, 1967). There is no mythical hero with whom modern sentiments, particularly in France, have been more easily identified.

Simone Fraisse

Aphrodite

There is more than one myth, or, rather, traditional story, in which Aphrodite plays a prominent role. Without listing them in any particular order, these include: the goddess's love for Anchises as described in the *Homeric Hymn to Aphrodite*; her passion for Adonis; her affair with Ares recounted by Homer in *Odyssey* VIII; her role in the story of Psyche; and the rivalry between her, Hera and Athena in the beauty contest judged by Paris that resulted in the Trojan war. In addition, she was also responsible for the death of Hippolytus, on the one hand, and the good fortune of Aeneas, on the other.

All these tales date from different periods, and it is not always possible to pinpoint accurately when they first appeared. What is certain, however, is that there is no possibility of placing them in strict sequence within the life of the goddess. No matter how keen textbooks on mythology may be to agree on a standard account of any given subject, none appears ever to have attempted to establish a chronological life of Aphrodite.

A significant question that arises in this contxt is whether, behind all these tales, there is a single constant figure common to them all. When the goddess's name occurs in a work of literature, does it conjure up anything beyond this jumble of stories? It would seem, at first glance, that the answer is 'yes': Aphrodite is the goddess of love. However, there is something disquieting about this response, for it removes any suggestion of myth. The proper name gives way to an abstraction and can be used simply as a metonym. 'He knew both aspects of Venus', Ovid says of Tiresias (*Metamorphoses*, III. 323), by which he apparently means that, having been first a man and than a woman, he had experienced love from the perspectives of both sexes. This is equivalent to suggesting that one could talk about a masculine Venus – and, if that is so, why spell it with a capital letter and make it a proper name?

Nonetheless, however forced Ovid's use of Venus as a metonym may seem, it is scrupulously correct. It carries to the extreme a process that involves explaining myths and using them as allegories to such a point that any concrete or visual element disappears. Aphrodite was the ideal victim for such treatment, since criticism of the traditional stories surrounding her inevitably tended to concentrate on those that were deemed immoral. People did not want to accept that Homer had described a goddess committing adultery; and the episode in the *Odyssey* is considered as apocryphal as the porter's scene in *Macbeth*.

One method of getting rid of the immoral elements in the myths was to reject certain traditions and play on their ambiguities and contradictions. This is what Pausanias does in Plato's *Symposium* (180 d). He points out that, while Hesiod states that Aphrodite was born from the sea into which the sperm of Uranus had fallen when he was castrated by his son, Zeus, Homer is unaware of the story and makes Aphrodite the daughter of Zeus and Dione. This difference can be interpreted as involving two different and contrasting versions of the goddess: a Uranian (celestial) Aphrodite and an Aphrodite Pandemus (perhaps common to all people – though this may be a mistranslation). It has then to be conceded that the celestial Aphrodite is not only earlier but also more dignified; she engenders or represents spiritual Love, while the people's Aphrodite is concerned with affairs of the flesh.

This opposition is important only if it is repeated in Eros, and he too has a celestial and a popular version. Aphrodite would thus represent no more than a stage in the evolution of this old and yet young deity with the evocative name, whom the Romans were to call 'Amor', or Love. The vital, brutal Eros – 'Erod falling on the flocks' as Sophocles describes him in a famous chorus from *Antigone* – should not be confused with the purified Eros who shows the path to wisdom and knowledge. The former is a symbol of rutting, while the latter is the son of Urania. And Hesiod tells us that Urania is also the name of a Muse. Needless to say, in the context of the *Symposium*, it is the celestial Eros that is drawn to handsome youths, and only the popular Eros that is interested in women.

Even though Plato puts this mythological flight of fancy into the mouth of one of his lesser characters, and thus seems to question its literal truth, more than one Greek was inclined to accept it, and it went on to produce far-reaching echoes. The first reason for this is that the interpretation has what might be called a 'nationalistic' aspect, though to use the term in this connection may seem an anachronism. Rightly or wrongly, Aphrodite was regarded as an oriental goddess; and the mythological epithets commonly applied to her – such as Cypris, Cytherea, Paphian and Amathusian – alluded to cult places in the eastern Mediterranean, for example on Cythera and Cyprus. The Orient was regarded as barbarous and effeminate; and people there practised strange religions, some of which even encouraged sacred prostitution. Aphrodite symbolized indolence and frenzied desire. The music appropriate to her was Phrygian music, Asian and lax.

Turning Aphrodite into an allegory and subordinating her to an increasingly abstract Eros also satisfied the misogynist tendency characteristic of classical Greece. The idealization of Diotima at the end of the *Symposium* or that of Athena in civic cults must be set against the wild speeches that Euripides puts in the mouths of some of his characters: Hippolytus's violent words are aimed, through Phaedra and her nurse, at the goddess of love herself.

The Western intellectual tradition has not ignored any of the three tendencies described above. The spiritualization of love became even more pronounced at a much later date, when Christianity rejected Eros and tended to equate Amor with Caritas. This had the predictable result that physical love came to be regarded as despicable and even dangerous; *contemptus mundi* turned into *contemptus feminae*, and women were regarded almost as devils. Paganism too was often described in terms borrowed from the Greek tradition, as exemplified by the discourse on the Barbarians, which represents it as an unleashing of all the appetites, absolute licence and a negation of effort.

Indeed Venus herself would have been completely denigrated if the Romans had not come to her rescue. As it was, the assimilation of the Italian Venus to the Greek Aphrodite was effected effortlessly. However, one crucial detail must not be forgotten in this context: Venus was the mythical ancestress of the Romans in general and the imperial family in particular. As such, she occupies a prominent position in their national poem, the *Aeneid*; while Ovid's *Metamorphoses* end with the grand vision of an apotheosis in which Caesar becomes a god at the intercession of an august Venus. Perhaps it is thanks to these two widely known works, which have been studied in schools uninterruptedly from classical times up to the present day, that the goddess of love, as we tend too glibly to call her, has been able to remain an imaginary character rather than dwindling into a mere figure of speech.

Long before the time of Virgil, Venus was treated with equal veneration in another famous work of Latin literature, the *De Rerum Natura* by Lucretius. In its superb prelude she is described as the 'mother of Aeneas and his race, delight of men and gods', and is said to rule over nature. These lines certainly come very close to being allegorical, so that it is not easy to distinguish the deity being invoked from the abstract concept of nature, a concept that would be taken up by an entire philosophical tradition. Indeed, in book III of the poem Nature is personified and made to address the reader in a prosopopoeia. Here, rhetoric is clearly at work, subordinating concrete figures to abstract ideas that are regarded as more seemly. Even so, being the poet that he is, Lucretius evokes images that are more than simple pedagogical devices:

> The winds flee before you, oh goddess, the clouds of the sky
> Flee at your approach; beneath your feet the earth
> Lays sweet flowers, and the sea smiles for you.

Fiften centuries later, Botticelli would paint the picture conjured up by these words.

Thus even when the study of Greek was in abeyance in the West, the ancient words of Hesiod lived on:

> It is there [in Cyprus] that the revered and beautiful goddess came to earth, causing the grass to grow around her beneath her light feet . . . The things that have been assigned to her . . . are the prattle of little girls, smiles and cheepings, gentle pleasure, tenderness and sweetness.
>
> (*Theogony* 194 ff.; after Maxon's translation.)

To modern ears this sounds rather precious and seems to underlie a whole tradition of boudoir 'poetry'. It recalls periods at which it was fashionable to write Alexandrine verse, and also a certain current of decadence in the nineteenth century, when the novel *Aphrodite* by Pierre Louÿs paved the way for *Monsieur Vénus* by Rachilde. Suggested too are the graceful, slightly roguish, scenes of *Les Déguisements de Vénus*, 'tableaus copied from the Greek', which brought Parny fleeting fame a century earlier; while the mood also evokes the decorative arts: pier glasses, miniatures and fans give a moment's immortality to chubby little Cupids and the unveiled charms of their mother.

The poems apocryphally ascribed to Anacreon were reread and imitated; Renaissance poetry is full of such conceits. They crop up in the work of Scève, Ronsard, Spenser, Gongora and Tristan l'Hermite, and are scattered throughout neo-Latin poetry modelled on Ovid, Catullus or the Latin elegists.

In all the resultant portraits of Venus as pretty, complaisant woman, the figure of the goddess and her unique qualities disappear. She is used as a pretext by poets and painters alike; and the story in Parny's poem is typical in this respect. In it, a shepherd has many encounters with women, some human and some immortal, all of whom look kindly on him; on his deathbed he learns that, behind all these different faces, was the one and only Venus, capitivated by him as she had been by Adonis. This amounts in the end to yet another rhetorical game where 'a Venus' is used to mean 'a beautiful woman'.

These trivial entertainments might encourage us to pass a similarly damning judgement on Hesiod's verses, or even one of the few surviving odes by Sappho: 'Aphrodite, daughter of God / Immortal weaver on your gleaming throne' (after Brasillach's translation). But this would be wrong; these very early poems record a society in which women were neither shut away nor occupied with servile tasks and trivial activities. Admittedly a childish image of Aphrodite is depicted in Homer; after being 'scratched' by the spear of Diomedes during a fight, she goes to complain to Zeus who reminds her: 'Matters of war, my daughter, are not your business. Devote your energies to the tender concerns of love and marriage' (*Iliad* V. 428 ff.,; after Mazon's translation).

However, the commentaries prompted by this passage merit study in their own right. The very word 'scratch', used by more than one translator, does not in fact tally with the description in Homer's text; the wound suffered by the goddess was far from slight. And why should we censure her for fleeing when her conduct, under the circumstances, would probably seem quite normal to everyone in this most unbombastic epic. Aphrodite is not the only person to retire from the battlefield after being hurt.

There is little to suggest that Homer regarded warlike attitudes and peaceful activities as incompatible. Paris, like Aphrodite, is certainly more drawn to dancing than to fighting, and he is reproached for it. But it would be hard to find any indication that Paris was fundamentally cowardly because he was a barbarian. What Zeus describes as 'matters of war' and the 'sweet concerns of love and marriage' are complementary rather than contradictory. The time had not yet come when heroes would be forced to choose between them.

To understand Homer's Aphrodite we must look beyond the story of her wound or what is said about the girdle borrowed by Hera and remember the account of the meeting between the goddess and Helen. Aphrodite is disguised as an old woman, but Helen recognizes her, perceives her beauty and trembles. The word used by Homer has religious connotations, and implies the sacred terror, combining wonder and panic, that grips any mortal who comes face to face with a god. Aphrodite's beauty is no mere cosmetic beauty: it strikes, confounds and overwhelms.

It is significant that the authenticity of this passage has been called into question by grammarians. They enquire how it was possible for Helen to recognize 'the beauty of the goddess's neck, her lovely breast, her luminous eyes' (*Iliad* III. 396; after Mazon's translation) when she was so thoroughly disguised. However, this short-sighted concern for realism blinds them to the most crucial element in the story, namely the transfiguration. Aphrodite is not just a wonderfully beautiful woman; first and foremost, she is the one whose beauty can suddenly be revealed as even more luminous and imposing than before.

This idea emerges clearly when we compare the lines from the *Iliad* with the *Homeric Hymn to Aphrodite*, in which an unknown bard describes the goddess's love for Anchises, which resulted in the birth of Aeneas. The poem is extraordinarily ambiguous. It starts by describing Zeus's plan to exact revenge on Aphrodite on the grounds that, since both gods and mortals are subject to her goad, she herself should experience the pain that it inflicts. This opening passage apparently portrays the young male gods avenging themselves on an old fertility goddess, and what follows seems to confirm this interpretation. Aphrodite goes through the forests and all the animals are overtaken by amorous frenzy; but when the Mistress of the Beasts reaches the shepherd Anchises she wears the innocent guise of his fiancée. After they have made love the goddess gets up, her head touches the ceiling and her face is bathed in light. Anchises is seized by fear.

A similar and much more famous episode can be found in *Aeneid* I. There, the young huntress who has just told Aeneas the story of Dido turns away and a light shines on her neck. 'Et vera incessu patuit dea'; her gait reveals her as the goddess.

Of course other gods disguise themselves too; for example, Athena appears in the most varied of guises in the *Odyssey*. But transfiguration seems to be peculiar to Aphrodite; the divine radiance that it produces is similar to a smile lighting up a face, and Aphrodite is the smiling goddess.

And yet Aphrodite can also be terrible and frightening. The story of Psyche, as told by Apuleius and later by Corneille, Molière and La Fontaine, portrays her as a jealous, spiteful woman ferociously pursuing her rival in beauty: 'The ridiculous excess of foolish obstinacy / Means I have a little girl as a rival!' She comments scornfully in Molière's *Psyché*.

The terror felt by Anchises in the *Homeric Hymn* is not caused by the petulance of a rejected flirt. Aphrodite does not need to become angry to instil fear into mortals: anyone who touches her risks death or complete powerlessness. She is like a flash of lightning. Euripides reduces her stature in the prologue of the *Hippolytus* when he makes her give reasons for her conduct particularly as these reasons are extremely petty. With exceptional wisdom, Racine offers no explanations. O haine de Vénus! ô fatale colère!'

It can doubtless be argued that the mythologists themselves were familiar with the idea of Aphrodite's divine anger. After Helius had told Hephaestus about his wife Aphrodite's amorous misdemeanours (again in *Odyssey* VIII) the goddess wrought terrible vengeance on his descendants, including Pasiphaë and Phaedra. Nonetheless, however much Racine may have enjoyed adorning his text with cryptic allusions, the reference just cited does not seem to be one of them. The word 'colère' is fairly weak compared with the 'fureur' that the goddess's anger gives rise to and the terrible events that follow. The perhaps irrational anger of the goddess and the unbearable passion that devours her victim are called by the same name. And, considering Racine's wide knowledge of the classics, it is hard to regard the famous line 'I recognized Venus and her fearsome fire' as purely metaphorical.

It is not surprising that some medieval authors regarded Venus as a she-devil, or that the story of Tannhäuser on which Wagner's opera is based was invented during the age of witch hunts.

Nonetheless medieval poetry was generally inclined to treat the goddess kindly. This is because she frequently appears as a mere adjunct of 'Amour' or Cupid, who emerges almost as a new character despite his classical name. The 'Amour' addressed by the troubadours is a human figure, not just an idea. Anyone who has ever read Ovid imagines Cupid with a bow shooting his arrows into the hearts of the young: golden arrows bringing the sweet pangs of love, and leaden arrows making those struck by them cold and disdainful. But Cupid the archer of the *Metamorphoses* (I. 456) is a child laughed at by Apollo, whereas Amour in the *Roman de la Rose* is a young prince to whom respectful homage is due. Cupid as a little rascal seems almost forgotten. The poet writes serenely of the young god: 'He seemed like an angel / Straight from heaven.' (*Rose* 902)

The resemblance between the angelic Cupid/Amour and the god Aengus of Irish legend inevitably poses certain questions, including where do all the birds that fly around the handsome prince come from? The idea of the radiant lord who makes his servants suffer in order to inflame their passion also occurs in Dante:

> when suddenly Cupid appeard to me
> in the form which memory makes me dread.

He seemed cheerful to me as he held
my heart in his hand.'

(*Vita Nuova* III; after Pézard's translation.)

Perhaps inadvertently, the Florentine poet suggests the same terrifying radiance as is described by the anonymous author of the *Homeric Hymn*.

The medieval Venus is the mother of this prince Cupid, as Dante reminds us when explaining why the third heaven bears the goddess's name (*Banquet* II. V). Guillaume de Lorris had anticipated him, saying of Venus:

She is the mother of the god of Love
Who has helped many a lover.
She holds a flaming torch
In her right hand, the flame of which
Has heated many a lady.
So elegant and well dressed
That she resembles a goddess or a fairy.

(*Rose* 3404)

The torch has replaced the arrows. As for the elegance, this should not be interpreted as a coquettish love of finery: taking care of one's personal appearance was a hallmark of quality and courtliness. Venus had become a Lady, just as her son was a Lord; and she protected those who paid homage to her.

This majestic image can be better understood through German poetry. French writers did not dare draw attention to the fact that their word for 'love' was feminine, and so they retained the Latin god. In the poetry of Walther von der Vogelweide or Gottfried von Strassburg, 'Frau Minne' (Lady Love) is a powerful goddess, awe-inspiring yet gentle. And this vision is recalled by Wagner:

Do you not know Lady Minne?
The power of her magic?
Queen of extreme daring,
Sovereign of the future,
Life and death are in her thrall,
Woven by her from joy and pain.

(*Tristan* II. 1)

However, references to Minne in poems in German in the *Carmina Burana* collection seem already to have been influencing works by Latin writers, often inspired by Ovid. The scene of homage to a sovereign lady is evoked by the following lines: 'Venus amoris dea / me tibi subicio / auxilio / egens tuo' (*Carmina Burana* 168).

Transformed into a Lady, Venus could inspire prowess and valour, referred to as 'melhuramen' in the Occitan langage of southern France. Not surprisingly Guillaume de Machaut interpreted the story of the judgement of Paris in his own way: according to him, Juno represented wealth, Pallas the clergy or knowledge, and Venus chivalry (*La Fontaine amoureuse* 2132 ff).

For all this, Venus was too closely associated with lasciviousness and thus with the most hated of pagan practices for her to attract the widespread attention of medieval scholars. While the Renaissance brought a renewed interest in the Classics, this principally involved a return to Platonism, which provided a noble concept of Love to contrast with Cupid, and abandoned Venus to frolics and frivolities. Shakespeare compares Cleopatra to Venus, but only to describe her immediately afterwards as a 'royal wench' (*Antony and Cleopatra* Act II. Scene 2). At most the goddess was invoked along with other deities to look favourably on royal marriages; she had her place in an artificial style of poetry that accompanied ceremonies and performances at court, such as ballets, processions or operas. Her footsteps were dogged more than ever by allegory, as in Musset's poem 'Rola' which opens with the words:

> Do you yearn for the time when heaven walked on the earth
> Inhabiated by a race of gods;
> When Veus Astarte, born from the bitter waves
> And still a virgin, stirred up her mother's tears,
> And made the world fertile by twisting her hair?

This was not the first Romantic work to restore Venus to her lost grandeur; it would be easy to find a similar tone in Schiller or Foscolo, for example. What is particularly interesting here is the emphasis on the goddess's oriental associations, for Astarte is an Asiatic divinity. It is probabably because she is depicted in a pantheist context stressing the bountifulness of Nature, that the ancient figure of the Mistress of the Beasts tends to reappear.

'Let old Plato frown austerely.' Baudelaire's 'Lesbos' is also a hymn to Venus, as are several poems by Hugo, Banville, Swinburne '('Laus Veneris') and Ruben Dario. Even Malarmé, who is disinclined to turn his poems into a collection of mythological allusions, still uses 'Venus' to rhyme with 'ingénus' in 'L'Après-Midi d'un Faune' and makes his hero recall Anchises by saying: 'I have the queen in my arms. Punishment is inevitable!' It is clear too whom Rimbaud had in mind when he entitled an early poem 'Credo in unam'. As in Musset, the goddess is called Astarte – and also Cybele.

So is it the oriental aspect of the goddess that finally prevails? Flaubert's Tanit is also clearly recognizable as a Venus figure, and in his novel *Salammbô* the heroine discovers Aphrodite Pandemus behind Uranian Aphrodite. Finally, it was near the ruins of Carthage that al-Chabbi, in his poem 'Prière dans le temple de l'amour' (*Chants de la Vie*) written in 1931, asked the mysterious being who had haunted him through forests and rocks: 'Es-tue Vénus?'

Jean-Louis Backès

Apocalypse

When asked 'What is the Apocalypse?' most people today have no hesitation in answering that it is the violent end of the world. A few refer briefly to the last book of the New Testament, but again only before stressing the end of the world that it foretells. And yet the Apocalypse is above all Revelation.

Nonetheless, by emphasizing the content of the book of Revelation – even if only in a truncated and distorted form – people today are unwittingly alluding to the original meaning of the word Apocalypse. This was first used to describe actual visions, and only later became a generic term for books containing material revealed by visions. As a title, it does not appear until the first or second century AD, with *The Book of the Apocalypse of Baruch, Son of Nerias* (*II Baruch*) (certainly written between 70 and 135 AD) or The Revelation to John dated around 70 or 90 AD). It was still rare at this period, but became more common later, being applied to Christian, christianized Jewish or gnostic works. However, by extension, the term is now applied to books of the same type written between 200 BC and 150 AD, and is even used of fragments of earlier works, such as *The Apocalypse of Isaiah* (fifth to third century BC). In the popular mind, however, the word's associations with visions dominate its associations with books, and not surprisingly, since most of these Apopcalypses are apocryphal texts.

This article will attempt to explore the convergence between these two aspects of the term, since discussing the myth of the Apocalypse does not mean studying apocalyptic literature. The latter is a body of literature with clearly defined historical, philosophical, theological and literary characteristics, that lie beyond the scope of this work. Furthermore, apocalyptic literature also influences many other myths, such as creation myths and the myth of the fallen angels, Adam or Satan. However, a discussion of the myth of the Apocalypse does not simply include the myths of the End of the World either. For the latter can take various forms: there are slow deaths, where the cosmos gradually freezes, dries or turns to stone through the effects of decrepitude, weariness or illness, as it is undermined by human sin; and there are violent deaths, brutually ending the degradation of the world and of humankind with fire or water (Tuzet 1965). Some deaths are total, some limited; some occur in a single act and some are multiple; some are followed by a rebirth or new creation and some are permanent; some are in the past and some are yet to come. In this vast panorama, the vision presented by Judeo-Christianity is resolutely original, and the term Apocalypse, which is usually reserved for it, bears witness to its uniqueness.

STRUCTURE AND MEANING OF THE MYTH

1 Unlike prophecies that portray salvation in the context of continous time and the historical destiny of the chosen people, the Apocalypse is based on faith in a future salvation outside history. It therefore assumes a radical break between the present era, in all its evil, and the age of the Triumph of God that is to come. Babylon and Jerusalem are the symbols of this particular dualistic outlook: all the good to come is in Jerusalem and all the present evil in Babylon, Nineveh or Tyre; on one side, there are the Bride, the Mother and the Son of Man, on the other the Harlot, the Beasts and the Dragon.

This inevitable break between the two ages of the world is dramatically expressed through the themes of violence and death and in the scenario of the Last Judgement:

- First there is cosmic violence and disorder: the sky blackens and the moons are red (Isaiah 13.10 and 24.23; Revelation 6.13 and 8.12; IV Ezra 5.15); the stars fall like lighted torches (Isaiah 34.4; Revelation 6.14; *Sybilline Oracles* 1.64–5), turning the seas to blood; the earth shakes and the sky disappears (Isaiah 24.19 and 34.4; Revelation 6.13–14).
- However, there is also human violence and immorality; people kill each other, blaspheme, lie or prostitute themselves (Daniel 12.1; Isaiah 22.3; Revelation 16.11 and 17; *Ethiopian Enoch* 7.56; *Sybilline Oracles* 1.39), their cities fall and their ships sink (Isaiah 25.2; Revelation 16 and 18; *II Baruch* 1.4).
- Finally, 'natural' disasters, such as storms hurling hail or insects down from the sky, and droughts or epidemics, become so frequent and extensive that they are just as damaging as the more obviously supernatural misfortunes: 'And blood flowed from the wine press, as high as a horse's bridle, for one thousand six hundred stadia' (Revelation 14.20).

The figure of the Antichrist, the fallen angel, monster or dragon, symbolically combines all these different fears: his reign represents the total reversal of all social, moral and religious values in a paroxysm of evil:

- After the annihilation of the world, the Last Judgement sets the eternal seal on the break between two ages and two realities: 'That of present history, in which the consequences of sin are unfolded and thwart the realization of the aim of salvation, and that of an absolute future in which God will accomplish this aim in full' (Grelot 1977). It is the dividing line, but it is also more than this: unlike in the ancient myths that describe the total regeneration of the world, here the Last Judgement ensures that the Kingdom will only be open to those who are considered worthy. In this 'absolute future', the effects of the process of selection and exclusion are like an unhappy memory of the dualist break between the two ages of the world. Satan will be vanquished, but he will not be saved (Isaiah 27.1;

Daniel 7.10–12; Revelation 20.10–12; *IV Ezra* 7.33–7; *II Baruch* 4.39; *Ethiopian Enoch* 54.1–2 and 90.20).

With the eternal torment of the 'wicked', the Apocalypses contrast the blessings of eternal life in a new world enjoyed by the 'good': 'Then I saw a new heaven and a new earth; for the first heaven and the first earth had passed away, and the sea was no more' (Revelation 21.1). At the centre of this new world are the new temple or the new city celebrating the union of Man and God in the perfection of God's measures or His forms and in the purity of materials (Isaiah 48.31–5 and 60.1–2; Zechariah 2.5–6; Revelation 21.9–27 and 22).

2 Yet this paradise is certainly not something totally new: rather than representing a break with the past, it really represents an inversion, for Paradise is always seen as a reversal of previous realities. Sickness and infirmity will disapear, 'neither shall there be mourning nor crying nor pain' (Revelation 21.4); and there will be no more death (Isaiah 30.19, 35.3 and 65.19; Zechariah 14.11; *Ethiopian Enoch* 69.29).

Indeed, since the rule of Satan represented a radical reversal of values, the establishment Paradise is really a process of restoration. Thus the tree with twelve crops and the river of life recall the original Garden of Eden (Genesis 2.9 and 3.22; Ezekiel 47; Zechariah 14.8; Revelation 33; *Ethiopian Enoch* 48, 1). Perhaps this is a return to the Golden Age.

The convulsive disappearance of the world also recalls myths involving a return to Chaos: there are the same extraordinary cosmic phenomena, similar monsters and similar battles (Delcor 1977). Thus the apocalypses might seem simply to offer another version of the Eternal Return?

3 However, the continuity between the images in oriental mythology and in the apocalypses cannot conceal a radical discontinuity in meaning. For 'Judeo-Christianity presents a most important innovation: the End of the World is unique, as the cosmogony was unique' (Eliade 1966: 83). The catastrophes happen only once: this is the end of History; the coming of the Kingdom of God is final. Time is no longer conceived as circular, as in the case of the Eternal Return, but as linear and irreversible, directed by God to 'realize his aim'. Unlike the old cosmologies, which use a cyclical theory to explain the world's progressive and inevitable decline, Judeo-Christianity proclaims that Yahweh is the sole master of history: the dualist emphasis is diluted. History is rehabilitated because this conception of the universe makes it possible to decode the eschatalogical meaning of the here and now. The climax of disasters represents a point of no return: the end of the world is nigh and its imminence is signalled by grave warnings in the form of conflicts and ordeals. 'The time is near' (Revelation 13): the apocalyptic message is urgent, for it associates the End of the World with the hope for a Messiah. The sufferings of today are actually birth pangs (Isaiah 66.5; *II Baruch* 4.24; *IV Ezra* 4–5).

4 Consideration of its form and function is as essential in understanding the meaning of the Revelation as study of its content ('what must soon happen'). Just as there is an apocalyptic scenario, there is also a language and a tone appropriate to the Apocalypse and necessary to the survival of the myth. The prophet is an inspired visionary: 'I was in the Spirit on the Lord's day, and I heard behind me a loud voice like a trumpet saying "Write what you see in a book" ', (Revelation 1.10–11). There follows a series of fantastical images, and to explain their meaning the author uses comparison, symbolism and the most unexpected analogies. For the vision always ends with an order such as 'go', 'write' or 'tell the nations'. To see and hear God is not only to understand His plan for History and the end of Time: it is to enter and participate in History itself, by bringing about 'intelligence' and the conversion of nations. And yet, the understanding of these visions remains a rare privilege: the message, with its allegories, coded allusions, mysterious proclamations or cryptic explanations, is confidential. This increases the prophet's stature immeasurably – something that poets will remember.

BIRTH OF THE MYTH

Its Judaic and Christian Origins

According to many commentators the book of Ezekiel (*c.* 590–570 BC) prefigures the Apocalypses in its visionary power, its language and its all-pervading concern with the end of the universe. However, a reading of Isaiah suggests that it is the very distant ancestor of apocalyptic literature and the first work to broach the subject of the final crisis in history. In the eighth century BC, the very existence of the Kingdom of Israel was threatened by the Aramaic wars and by the growing power of the Assyrians; and it was in this context that the first Isaiah foretold the ruin of Israel and Judah as a punishment for faithlessness (Isaiah 5.8–30), while still maintaining that God's promises would be fulfilled after this punishment had been carried out. About two centuries later, the second Isaiah extended and modified this historical perspective: writing after the exile, the fall of Jerusalem and the disappearance of the kingdom of Judah, at a time when God's promise was belied by events, he reinterpreted that promise in eschatological terms. Salvation is no longer envisaged in an historical context, but as something beyond history, a definitive form of redemption involving the establishment of the Kingdom of God. However, before God's kingdom could come there must be a break, for the present remained dominated by evil – hence the dramatic scenario at the End of the World, which was taken up and developed at will in later centuries, as in the *Ethiopian Enoch*. Joel (*c.* 400 BC) paints an impressive picture of Yahweh's judgement of the nations while Zechariah (*c.* 520 and early fourth century BC) sets Babylon against Jerusalem and Satan against God. It is in this work that the images of horsemen, horns and the Harlot and the symbolic use of colours first appear – all of which were subsequently copied with enthusiasm.

However, it was the book of Daniel (between 167 and 164 BC) and one of the many sections of the apocyrphal *Book of Enoch* that inspired the apocalyptic genre of writing first hinted at in *Isaiah*. Intended to maintain the faith and hope of the Jews during their persecution by Antiochus IV, these books look beyond the annihilation of Israel. Visions of the past and future mingle in their timeless evocation of the total destruction of evil and the coming of God's Kingdom. To express this hope in the face of the evidence of history, Daniel returns to myth. 'The traditions of Genesis concerning origins, particularly those of the Golden Age and the Fall, almost eclipsed by history in the biblical tradition, become essential in the apocalyptic representation of history and make possible an original expression of the theology of salvation and suffering' (Delcor 1977: 57). The myth saves Israel from having to accept the evidence of its history; in conformity with the message of the Old Testament, everything is still going according to the plan of the one God.

After Daniel, no apocalyptic writing was allowed into the Jewish canon of Scriptures. The most widely accepted explanation of this, especially since the discovery of the Dead Sea Scrolls at Qumran, involves regarding the second part of the book of Daniel as a Hassidic text. In contrast, most later apocalypses are of Essenian origin, which would also explain the areas of continuity and discontinuity between the various narratives. Daniel's influence is evident in *The Apocalypses of Baruch* (the Syriac *Apocalypse* or *II Baruch* after 70 AD; and the *Greek Apocalypse* or *IV Baruch* of around the second and third centuries AD) as well as in *IV Ezra* (*c.* 81–96 AD). The events of 587 BC influenced the writers' interpretation of those of 70 AD: one destruction is absorbed by the other and the books of *Baruch* and *Ezra* once again challenge history by offering a message of hope. Christianity was born in the apocalyptic atmosphere of later Judaism, and today we are again aware of the importance of eschatalogical and apocalyptic influences on early Christian thought.

Disillusioned by the tardiness of the Second Coming and in an effort to counter the oppression to which they were being subjected, the Judeo-Christians adopted the apocryphal apocalypses. Some they reworked – such as the case of *The Ascension of Isaiah* (first half of the first century AD), *The Testaments of the Twelve Patriarchs*, certain *Sibylline Oracles* emanating from Jewish circles in Alexandria, and the Greek *Apocalypse of Baruch* – and some they used as sources of inspiration. In his Revelation, John claims to unveil the secrets of the End of Time whose coming is near; and to express his visions, he uses a great number of images borrowed from the Old Testament, the apocryphal apocalypses and the myths and legends of Asia Minor. Yet the work is highly original in its powerful seven-part composition (developing the sevenfold revelation of the *Proto-Zechariah*), in its prodigious imagination and in its Christian interpretation of history, according to which the new age, awaited in Jewish apocalyptic literature, has been inaugurated by the Resurrection of Christ.

And yet the presence of John's text in the Christian canon is due entirely to its – doubtless erroneous – attribution to the 'disciple whom Jesus loved'. The official Church very soon became suspicious of apocalyptic outbursts and the millenarian interpretations to which such works gave rise. The Christian apocalypses (of Peter, Paul, Thomas, Mary and Zechariah) came most frequently from the fringes of Christianity – in particular those influenced by Manichaean thought – and remain apocryphal.

Commentators and intermediaries

After the third century AD, the apocalyptic current was gradually stemmed by the attacks of Origen, Demetrius of Alexandria and, above all, Saint Augustine, in *The City of God*. Thereafter it could only draw sustenance from the existing texts, primarily *The Revelation to John*. It persisted on the fringes of official religion, as in the popular movements of the Middle Ages studied in depth by Cohn (1957), haunting the minds of the oppressed, exploited or uprooted, feeding the Cathar and Bogomil heresies (*La Cène secrète*), and even arousing the curiosity of certain clerics (Sironneau 1984: 3). Three texts aroused considerable interest in the Middle Ages: *La Description des Derniers Temps* by Psuedo-Methodius, the treatise *Sur la Naissance et l'Époque de l'Antichrist* by Adson de Montier en Der and *L'Oracle de la Sibylle Tiburtine*. All of them proclaim the arrival of the Emperor of the Last Days, the fall of tyrants, the Last Judgement and the triumph of Christianity. Their speculations had nothing abstract about them: people of the period were awaiting the Antichrist with ever more feverish anticipation, watching out for the signs that, according to the prophets, would announce and accompany the end of time, such as wars, famines, epidemics or comets. Each new day might usher in the Apocalypse.

However, at this time, apocalyptic texts were often only paraphrases of *The Revelation to John* or commentaries on it – sometimes of disproportionate length (for example, *Beatus*). There was much interpretation, but nothing creative; the Apocalypse was presented as a symbolic 'grid' for understanding the world, or as a battle engine against the powers of evil.

At the end of the twelfth century, Joachim of Fiore completely updated these speculations by attempting a synthesis of the two opposing currents in the Latin church, the dominant, pessimistic movement, which hoped only for the Last Judgement, and the underground, but lively, millenarian movement, which he modified by giving it a spiritual emphasis. His most famous work is the *Liber introductorius in expositionem in Apocalypsim*, but the book that radicalized his thought was written by a disciple, di Borgo san Donnino, with the title *Liber introductorius ad Evangelium Aeternum*. Joachim of Fiore's theory of the ages of the world represented a return to the ideas of the Apocalypse. 'It is not simply a question of a smooth, continuous historical development, brought about by divine pedagogy, but an eschatological inversion of historical and social roles: the first will be the last, time has broken its bounds, the world is turned upside down; we are in the presence of apocalyptic subversion and no longer of the peaceful unfolding of the history of salvation' (Sironneau 1984: 6). He exercised a profound and lasting influence on poets, philosophers and social reformers (including Lessing, Leroux, Ballanche, Sand and Merej-kowski). But his work was merely derived from the myth of the Apocalypse and from a by-product or sub-set of it: the myth of the Millenium. For the latter myth was based on the Apocalypses and their commentaries, which were often more enthusiastic than critical. Thus Boehme's 'mystical speculations', Swedenborg's illuminist commentaries and visions, and the interpretations of the members of the Cabbalist sect all stimulated the imaginations of the poets. As Bénichou (1977) has emphasized, illuminism allied religious speculation to the interpretation of contemporary events and the prediction of the near future. And the Apocalypse was central to these activities.

Many writers have also borrowed elements from John's text, as well as from the other biblical revelations.

In Dante's *Divine Comedy* there are numerous images, allusions and lines adapted from apocalyptic works. Similarly, the theme of *Paradise Lost* – the fall of Satan, the temptation of Man and the combat of the angels – also recalls an apocryphal apocalypse, though this work was certainly unknown to Milton.

However, it can scarcely be maintained that these works gave rise to a genuine Apocalypse myth; and, in any event, this was not their aim. Biblical inspiration and deliberate borrowings are not enough to imply the contrary.

The works of Dante and Milton (including their illustrations) served as intermediaries between the sacred texts and profane authors in the same way as the occult and official commentaries – and perhaps to an even greater extent.

LITERARY INTERPRETATIONS OF THE MYTH

Historical Apocalypses

Agrippa d'Aubigné deserves special attention in this context, since for him, as for his predecessors, the Apocalypse was a weapon. In it he found a fervent tone, striking images and a dualist conception of the world appropriate to the vigour of his language and his Protestant convictions. But *Les Tragiques* (1616) is not merely a politico-religious pamphlet, any more than it is just a brilliant paraphrase. His visions are his alone: the Apocalypse inspires the Christian in him and frees the poet. The division of the work into seven parts based on The Revelation to John makes it possible to integrate historical events, and passages of condemnation and satire not only into God's higher plan but also into that of the poet. Here the myth involves the future of history.

A few centuries later, the view of history in this myth would be read and 'would be listened to through doors'. During the period of the French Revolution, it was totally misinterpreted to imply that the events of 1789 prefigured the Last Judgement. Whether they were for or against the Revolution, everyone liked to see it as the handiwork of God: it was a necessary punishment for the fallen monarchy and a fallen Christianity (Saint Martin, de Maistre); it was an ordeal to be endured, from which a new society and a new spirit of poetry would arise (Ballanche); or it was the first awakening of a new freedom, a burst of energy against all kinds of oppression.

In giving the subtitle 'A Prophecy' to the poems that he was inspired to write by the war with America (*America, a Prophecy*, 1793) and the upheavals in Europe (*Europe, a Prophecy*, 1794), William Blake deliberately placed himself under the patronage of John: the events have passed but, when projected into the future, they demonstrate all the better the urgency and meaning of the present. Faced by narrow rationalism, the triumph of materialism and the tyranny of ideologies, religions or economic constraints, faced by sleep and death, Blake celebrates painful dreams, terrible births, breaks and upheavals. 'The tygers of wrath are wiser than the horses of instruction' (Blake 1977: 184).

The projected seven-part structure of Blake's vast unfinished poem called *The French Revolution, a poem in seven books* (1791) clearly has apocalyptic associations. But the images alone clearly demonstrate the vitality of the myth: cataclysmic forces that shake Blake's universe are indeed those of the Apocalypse, such as the fire-red dragon, the Beasts, or the Harlot:

> The sun was black & the moon roll'd a useless globe thro' Britain!
>
> (Blake 1966: 699)

> Blood issu'd out in mighty volumes pouring in whirlpools fierce
> From the flood gates of the Sky
>
> (Blake 1966: 359)

> . . . then the Pestilence began in streaks of red
> Across the limbs of Albion's Guardian; the spotted plague smote Bristol's
> And the Leprosy London's Spirit . . .
>
> (Blake 1966: 202)

But there are also the new Jerusalem, the Lamb, the redeemed and the Son of Man:

> . . . his feet become like brass,
> His knees and thighs like silver, & his breast and head like gold.
>
> (Blake 1966: 199)

The same burning images and the same litanies appear again and again in the poems with the passing of time: 'Sound! Sound! my loud war trumpets' (Blake 1966: 199) or 'Mark well my words, they are of your Salvation' (Blake 1966: 489). As in the Apocalypses, his prophetic books unfurl their visions in different settings simultaneously, in earth and in the heavens, in Time or in

Eternity. And again the aim is to connect human experience and mythical action in an apocalyptic interpretation of the history of the world. Tyre, Rome or Babylon, Versailles, London or Verulamium are all one in Blake's imagination. And against this background, the poet gives himself the same role as that of Saint John on Patmos or Ezekiel on the banks of the Kebbar, setting himself up as a prophet of the imminent Day of Judgement. 'In answer to the revolution and its scourges (I would add to its hopes also) there must be a poetry of the time of trials, daughter of the prophets' (Bénichou 1977: 137).

Following Blake's example, in *La Ville des Expiations* (1831) Ballanche cried out that he was the solitary man of Patmos, and in the *Chant lyrique du Judgement Dernier* (1827) Lamartine wrote:

> Oh come! open the source of miracles to me once more,
> Angel who inspired the oracles of Patmos,
> Angel whose glance, turned towards the future,
> Sees, like a day past, the day that is to come.
> . . . He grants my prayer! And I have seen!

When a historical outlook on the excesses and weaknesses of governments and revolutions led Hugo to despair, the myth of the Apocalypse maintained his faith in a future of hope. His projected trilogy encapsulating the 'progressive', the 'relative' and the 'aboslute' (*La Légende des siècles, La Fin de Satan, Dieu*) was intended to be the humanitarian epic dreamed of by the poet and his century. Though it remained unfinished we can already see its seeds in the movement of *Châtiments* (1853) from *Nox* to *Lux*; or in the crowning passages of the first cycle of *La Légende des Siècles* (1859), in *Plein Ciel* and in the vision beyond time and number that opens up around *La Trompette du Jugement*. We can also see them in his view of the grumblings and obscurities of history: like seals, the seven books of *Châtiments* mark out the unfolding of the scourges. But the seventh ironically inverts the signs: 'the saviours will save themselves'. After the last trumpets have sounded and the last horrors have been undergone, the day of *Lux* crowns the collection beyond the seven books of Time, beyond contemporary history:

> (future times! Sublime vision!
> . . .
> And the Earth is like a wife
> And man is like a betrothed!)

The revolutionary myth at the heart of *Les Misérables* (1862) is clearly inspired by the Apocalypse, as the following sentence proves: 'We need not speak of the exile in Patmos, who mightily assailed the world as it was with a protest in the name of the ideal world' (Hugo 1982: 888).

Such references give book X (part IV), '5 June 1832', a meaning that goes beyond its entirely historical description of the riot. In any case, the original version ends beyond history with the following vision: 'there is an element of apocalypse in civil war, all the mists of the unknown mingling with fierce bursts of flame'. All the events are reinterpreted and characters revisited: for example, Enjolras is the Angel of the Apocalypse as well as, in the original, the 'lion of the tribe of Judah' (Hugo 1985: 940). His vision of the future combines faith in social, scientific and political progress with the spread of light and the harmony of the new Jerusalem: 'One might almost say, indeed, that there will be no more events' (Hugo 1982: 1006). Does this imply Eternity?

The Apocalypse myth gives a particular dimension to the myth of Progress, which is then seen as a Second Coming. In Zola's work, the miners' strike at the end of *Germinal* (1885) and particularly the bloody confrontations between the Commune and Sedan at the end of *The Debacle* (1892) are presented in the millenarian context of a Jerusalem that has to be brought into being. After the horrors of defeat and death, Etienne and Jean go off 'walking into the future'. *The Debacle* closes with the apocalyptic vision of a sunset transfiguring the skyline of a town in flames: 'And yet, beyond the still roaring furnace, undying hope was reviving up in that great calm sky, so supremely limpid' (Zola 1972: 508).

The Russian revolutionaries of 1917 were borne along by the same hopes. Mircea Eliade notes the frequency with which the Apocalypse myth appears in the most clearly secular of politico-social doctrines. Communism (and Nazism) proclaimed the end of the world and the beginning of an era of abundance. However, the concept of the last battle and the dawn of a new age were no longer much in evidence in the European imagination: the horrors of war inspired a lively apocalyptic vein in the writings of poets and novelists, but although the imagery of the Apocalypse was still helping in the portrayal of history, it was no longer being used to transcend it. With a title borrowed from The Revelation to John, Duhamel's *Les Sept dernières Plaies* (1928) invites the reader to go beyond the poignant account of everyday horrors; while the title of Blasco-Iñez' *Los cuatros jinetes del Apocalipsis* (1916) and its epic conclusion, where war is symbolized by horsemen announcing the reign of the Antichrist, bring the vision and spirit of the myth to this naturalist novel. However, the future is black in the wartime tales. In them history opens only on to eschatology.

The two world wars, the new fears arising from technological developments and, above all the feeling that God was 'dead' seemed to demand a change of myth. And yet, the term apocalypse reappears again and again like an obsession, though no longer with its connotations of hope. Science fiction stories create what Frye would no doubt call 'panoramic apocalypses' (Frye 1981), designed to be viewed passively. In its early days, science fiction reflected the nineteenth-century faith in the power of science. Its initial utopian outlook was based only on the concept of an earthly Jerusalem, borrowed from the millenarian readings of The Revelation to John: there would be no more battles, continuous progress, and thus no more Apocalypses. But when disillusionment set in, the genre swung over to the opposite extreme. It became encased in the anxiety and fears of today, glancing pessimistically at the months to come. For urgency is no stranger to science fiction, but most frequently it is the urgency of desperation. The catastrophes often spare a community (as in Merle's *Malville* or Barjavel's *Ravage*), so that it becomes a profane version of the Bible's Chosen Few. The meaning of the myth is also turned upside down: in place of towns and a society based on technology, the few escapees of *Ravage* (1943) recreate an original paradise, recalling the agricultural and patriarchal roots of humankind. This is Eden, not the Jerusalem of the Apocalypses. It represents a movement backwards, on earth and through time. Before the infernal machine appeared, it was understood that everything must start again; and, indeed, everything does start again, human beings will invent new machines to save time, turn it upside down and move backwards through it. The tragically ironic title of the first part of the book, 'The New Times', alludes to the vision of a cyclical destiny that follows and deals a mortal blow to the messianic optimism of the eighteenth century. All the themes of the apocalyptic myth are there: the Horsemen, the Dragon and the Harlot, cosmic disorder and the ideal society; but the myth is that of the Eternal Return, despite Blanche's rose.

This is also one of the messages of the returns to the past intended for, significantly, the seventh chapter of Cendrars's novel-poem-screenplay *La Fin du monde filmée par l'ange Notre-Dame* (1919). In chapter 6 the End of the World is identified with primordial chaos and perhaps with nothingness. 'But a fuse is blown – a spring goes – and the film runs giddily backwards.' The world is imprisoned in an infernal circle. The screenplay closes symbolically with a series of dots and the word 'etc.'.

But eschatological hope is not always absent from science fiction. It is a sentiment felt by *Le Jour des Voies* by Higon (1977), and the novel plays on its many aspects. The Day of Ways, which starts off as an enormous exercise in mystification, escapes from the control of its instigators, and the End of the World takes place in an apocalyptic setting: the lie is a sign. Once 'the iron bridge in the middle of the sky, perhaps in nothingness' has been crossed, the characters seem to sense a promise of happiness in their feelings of well-being and forgetfulness. But the novel ends a few lines later with a passage involving carnivorous flora and the prostitute of the Universe-Aden, 'a trap for mad poets and naïve girls who eternally wanders along the ways seeking Eden.' All the signs are false. The Apocalypse is only . . . a myth!

Inner Apocalypses

The myth of the Apocalypse can be a 'response' to the assaults of the world and of history, a collective response, which involves humankind. But there is a 'pneumatic', mystical tradition that interprets the myth, not in terms of a messianic vision of social or political progress, but as a personal illumination, an inner experience. In this context, the luminary replaces the prophet, the individual replaces society and inner contemplation replaces commitment to the outside world. The idea of the vision from outside, imposed from on high, is inverted: 'Every man has his own Patmos within him' (Hugo 1985: 331). It is a dream, or madness.

The German Romantic movement forms part of this tradition in its search for the path to the unknown regions of the soul, in an effort to find 'the secret of all that extends us beyond ourselves in time and space and makes our current existence a simple point on the line of an infinite destiny' (Béguin 1965). The quest of Jean-Paul or Novalis is to find the lost unity of the world and the individual and to attain true life. The poetry draws on inner springs to rise up towards the infinite. 'The poetic meaning is closely related to the prophetic and religious meaning and to all forms of seeing' (Beguin 1965: 207). But for Novalis, revelation does not require destruction, or the end of the world and of time: it includes death, assimilates it and adapts to it.

Jean-Paul's imagery, on the other hand, is filled with a lingering fear of dead worlds, oceans of blood and catastrophes. But his visions of death and resurrection are all inner visions. In *Die Mondfinsternis*, images of flaming swords, black suns and snakes are combined with the neo-Platonic myth of the fall of souls to provide a fantastic allegory of the eternal return of the ages of misfortune. And yet there is still a judgement, although it has to conform with the cycle: 'and the sword of judgement waved again'. The poet is 'working' to save the cosmos from the coils of the snake. The Dream and the Poem are preparations for the final work: Death. It is in the depths of the night that the Revelation appears. Paradises flooded with light and peopled with benevolent angels sweep away the terrifying images of collapsing buildings and of fire, hail or ashes pouring down from the sky, and banish the ghastly apparitions of Death (*Traum über das All – Die Vernichtung*). Jean-Paul's dreams express the 'cry of one imprisoned within temporal bounds, who longs for Eternity' (Beguin 1965): 'Alas! and if I die, everything will die!' said Gérard de Nerval's Christ in the olive grove (Nerval 1972: 185).

Dreams and madness are inner apocalypses; the visions of the myth penetrate and order the quest in *Aurélia* (finished in 1854). 'Dreams are a second life' (Nerval 1972: 3) and sleep, like death, is a passage. The Revelation of the Apocalypse makes it possible to escape from the infernal cycle of impoverishment and degeneration that afflicts races, nations and cosmic forces, to conquer death and to enter Eternity:

> Oh death, where is your victory, since the conquering Messiah was riding between us? His sulphurated robe was the colour of hyacinths and his wrists and the ankles of his feet sparkled with diamonds and rubies. When his light holly staff touched the pearly gate of the new Jerusalem, we were all three drenched in light.
>
> (Nerval 1972: 91f.)

The haunting spectre of dying worlds 'is only' the phantasmagorical projection of a very personal obsession – an obsession with the extinction of a purely inner fire. This is how we should interpret the symbolic fight between the two spirits on the mountain, the black sun, the mad moons and the charnel house of history. But the certainties imparted in apocalyptic dreams or trances are valid for everyone: 'The revelation of Jesus Christ, which God gave him to show to his servants what must soon take place' (Revelation 1. 1). Like John or Christ, Nerval maintains that he came down among men to proclaim the good news to them.

The implication is that inner apocalypses open out onto the world and history, completing or transfiguring historical apocalypses.

The two apocalyptic perspectives coexist in Hugo's work, but without really coming together. His original plan for the *Contemplations* (1856) was identical to that for *Châtiments*. In a note to Hetzel in 1852, he wrote: '*The Contemplations* . . . will be in two volumes; first volume: *Autrefois*, pure poetry. Second volume: *Aujourd'hui*, flagellation of all rascals and the chief rascal.' But when he decided to end his collection with *Solitudines Coeli*, Hugo changed his approach: 'First some light, happy, bright things . . . then some criticism, some mockery, then gaiety! The book will grow darker. I shall put in my daughter's death, then exile, then *I shall leave this world and enter extra-human life*, the book will begin with childish things and will extend as far as God' (Hugo 1972: 631). The suppression of *Solitudines Coeli* meant that the work left Hugo on the edge of 'the monstrous gulf' of the final revelations. The last book, *Au bord de l'Infini*, is an echo of the silent heart of the work, where the shadow of exile mingles with the shadow of the tomb. But the poet hears the apocalypse from the Mouth of Shadow: it is no longer an historical revelation, but a metaphysical one involving the Fall, evil, the end of the world and the resurrection. History is just a time of Being.

After his initial concern with historical apocalypses in *America* and *Europe* Blake moved on, in *Vala* (1795 and 1804) and *Jerusalem* (1804–20), to an expression of the inner apocalypse that shaped his understanding of the Bible and of Art. Around 1800, the English poet distanced himself from the historical and revolutionary interpretation of the myth of the apocalypse. For him, millenarianism had become little more than a variant expression of the idea of eternal return. Salvation should not be sought only in history, which was always subject to repetition, but in Eternity, through works of art. History promised only ephemeral apocalypses or unfinished revelations. 'Art is the tree of life' (Blake 1966: 777) whose task is to transfigure them. Blake's poems always draw on the apocalyptic tradition for their images and structures, and it was at this time that Blake produced the superb illustrations to The Revelation to John. However, his work of this period is no longer an invitation to play an active part in history, but an invitation to contemplation and to a life in Art:

> If the spectator could Enter into these Images in his Imagination . . . then would he arise from his Grave, then would he meet the Lord in the Air & then would he be happy
>
> (Blake 1966: 611)

The Last Judgement is the ever-repeatable time of illumination:

> There is a Moment in each Day that Satan cannot find
> . . . but the Industrious find
> This Moment & it multiply & when it once is found
> It renovates every Moment of the Day.
>
> (Blake 1966: 526)

This is the apocalyptic point where history is reread, transcended and transfigured.

In fact, the internal apocalyptic revelation does not often remain divorced from an historical context. In *The Brothers Karamazov*, after emerging from a period of isolation, Alyosha Karamazov tries to live out his vision of the ultimate in the everyday world. For Dostoyevsky the resurrection in chapter 20 of The Revelation to John is a resurrection in this world and, as in The Revelation, its coming will not take place without death. This explains the presence of the legend of the Grand Inquisitor, the insidious embodiment of the Antichrist, at the heart of *The Brothers Karamazov*. However, Alyosha does not turn the world upside down: he decodes the signs of his resurrection. Apocalypse and transfiguration . . .

Palimpsests

With the decline of religious faith and the questioning of the idea of progress, the myth of the Apocalypse loses its eschatological dimension and its historical urgency. What is left? The message of the signs of 'what must soon take place' is forgotten in favour (at last?) of the memory that any Apocalypse is a tissue of alien symbols, be they Aramaic, Syriac, Greek or Ethiopian: it is a text. This realization ushers in a period during which the emphasis is on creating variations of these different symbols.

In Cendrars's often black humour all symbols are emptied of their original meaning. In *La Fin du monde filmée par l'ange Notre-Dame*, God is merely an American busnessman whose task is to accomplish, for the Grigri's Communion Trust Co. Ltd, the apocalyptic prophecies of John and Ezekiel. His great book is his ledger and churches are a big attraction. But the central element is the film of the end of time. Cendrars is aware that John's revelations form a total and everlasting spectacle: 'Come up hither and I will show you . . . And I saw'. He is conscious of a silence like that in a theatre before the curtain goes up, following the traditional knocks: 'When the Lamb opened the seventh seal there was silence in heaven for about half an hour' (Revelation 8. 1) – this was followed by the 'show'. In the book, the film is this show.

But the writer goes further, since the screenplay portrays a film within a film: and he makes his audience giddy when the film is shown once more, backwards. This, of course, represents a pessimistic cycle inspired by the war, but it is also an excellent metaphor for the way in which symbols fit into each other or are rolled up in each other. The Lamb opens a sealed scroll (Revelation 6), and Cendrars lets the film unroll once more.

In giving his 'presentation' of The Revelation to John the title *Le Grand Théâtre* (1961), Giono returns to the same idea, making it part of his meditation on matter and time. His undertaking justifies a brief digression: when Giono produced a huge calligraphic version of *Le Grand Théâtre* on parchment, which occupied seven painters and seven writers for a full three years, his aim was to create a monument to the glory of John's text. The work was exhibited in the Museum of Modern Art: to exist, the Apocalypse needs to be looked at.

Le Grand Théâtre indeed represents the raising of a curtain. But what do the symbols signify? The apocalyptic excess of John III's first words is misleading: 'You will hear talk of many other wars . . . the heavens will not fold up, they will curl up . . . Leviathan will be a fruit fly and Behemoth the mite that crackles in the bindings of Books' (Giono 1974: 1069).

However, the Apocalypse is not to be found here. It lies in everyday putrefaction, in the gradual isolation and entirely internal imprisonment of Eugène. Transcending all tangible signs, it lurks within us all: 'There are beginnings of the Apocalypse within me, within your mother and within yourself, or at least points from which, when the moment comes, it will spread' (Giono 1974: 1071). But the signs are always ambiguous and misleading: for Eugène, the Apocalypse is the shrinking of his external universe, but it is also an entirely internal expansion or deepening.

Alternatively, the signs may be dead: 'If in Patmos they had pointed to that star and if they had said [to John], "What is that?" he would have replied, "It is a star." When at that time it was already nothing' (Giono 1974: 1081). In other words, the End of the Universe may have happened thousands of years ago, since the stars that we see at night were extinguished millennia ago. Thus the future does not exist. Everything is past, the present is only an ephemeral point. This is a dizzying reversal of prophetic activity: 'We can be threatened only with the past'.

Yet again, the signs may be empty: 'One thing is certain: numbers are the expression of that which does not exist' (Giono 1974: 1078) and mathematical signs merely express the activity of our intelligence, they do not explain anything beyond it.

However, even if there is nothing beyond this world and beyond the signs but emptiness or the past, both this world and the signs still remain, like an 'invitation'. The Apocalypse is a show, and people will never allow a show to be left without spectators, even if it kills them. Yet: 'If it kills [them], what is the point of the show?' (Giono 1979: 1083). The answer is given as a kind of apology at the end of the narrative: 'He talked without stopping in silence . . . into the void . . . in total solitude. . . . He spoke not to pass on his thoughts, but simply because thought takes shape in speech' (Giono 1974: 1075).

The Apocalypse is the symbol of this work and of all works. Eugène is another Saint John, like John III who speaks and John IV who 'tries' to transcribe his words fifty years later. The myth of the Apocalypse is paradoxically a myth of literary creation.

Umberto Eco's novel *The Name of the Rose* (1980) is presented as a detective story. However, in the millenarian Europe of the fourteenth century, the apocalyptic connotations of the mysterious crimes that strike the abbey is obvious to everyone; while the seven-part structure of the novel, marked by the seven murders and the canonical seven hours, reinforces this apocalyptic interpretation. Apocalyptic themes and images proliferate.

But all these signposts are false, designed to deceive enquirers and to lead them astray. The Apocalypse is a pretext or, even worse, a false trail, an empty structure; it seems full of meaning, but it explains nothing. The detective work and the decoding of the signs of the End of the World lead no more to the murderer than they do to the expected Apocalypse.

And yet, we do encounter the Antichrist who instigated the terrible events, and the abbey collapses in a gigantic fire. It is explained that, although the model used to interpret the culprit's actions was false, the culprit nonetheless acted in accordance with it. The false leads to the true and the symbol creates, or recreates, the creature. The key to the enigma and the keystone of the whole work is the labyrinthine library, where the alphabetical signs combine in different ways to direct progress or to disorient, to perplex and to lead to the truth. In this, they are, like the murder inquiry itself, like the Apocalypse and indeed like the book. 'For', the note to readers states, 'it is a tale of books not of everyday worries' (Eco 1984: 5). A story of signs and not of events, of images and not of things; a myth or a parable whose value is only heuristic.

> I prepare to leave on this parchment my testimony as to the wondrous and terrible events that I happened to observe in my youth, now repeating verbatim all I saw and heard, without venturing to seek a design, as if to leave to those who will come after (if the Antichrist has not come first) signs of signs so that the prayer of deciphering may be exercised on them.
>
> (Eco 1984: 11)

This is the role of Saint John.

Adso's novel is put together using charred pages saved from the fire and for its inspiration the writer draws symbolically on the scattered notes that he made on a lost translation of the mythical book at the centre of the mystery – a book recalling the second book of Aristotle's *Poetics*, which was 'found' and lost forever. Every book is an impression or a symbol of another.

The Apocalypse influences Eco's book not as a myth of the end of time, but as a myth of revelation, and as a book to be deciphered.

> On sober reflection, I find few reasons for publishing my Italian version of an obscure, neo-gothic French version of a seventeenth century Latin edition of a work written in Latin by a German monk toward the end of the fourteenth century.
>
> (Eco 1984: 4)

Beneath the humour of this statement, there perhaps lies a comment on the destiny of 'literary myths'.

Apocalypses are sealed books, to be broken open so that the Revelation can appear and they can be exposed to the questioning of human beings.

> And I warn everyone who hears the words of the prophecy of this book: if any one adds to them, God will add to him the plagues described in this book, and if any one takes away from the words of the book of this prophecy, God will take away his share in the tree of life and in the holy city, which are described in this book.
>
> (Revelation 22. 18f.)

Was John aware, when he finished his Revelation, that he had opened the Bible to the breath – and the risk – of the imagination?

Danièle Chauvin

Apollo, the Mythical Sun

'Of all the gods of poetry it is Apollo who has been most disguised by fables and by etymologies based on his name' (Pontus de Tyard 1552). Though Apollo is depicted in Western literature as one of the most conventional of mythical figures, he was regarded by ancient mythographers as one of the most complex, and had a variety of names and qualities attributed to him. He was first of all a universal archetype of the Divine and, as such, he is referred to in literary sources by three main names – Apollo, Phoebus and the Sun – which are used in alternation and apparently indiscriminately. In the course of time, the solar aspect of the god seems to have taken on an increasingly symbolic character, less intimately associated with his mythological adventures. As a result Apollo the sun god became more important in relation to poetry itself than in terms of his association with specific myths (with the exception of the story of Daphne).

NAMES OF THE SUN

Followers of the Platonic tradition and scholars right up until the Renaissance invented a number of etymological theories providing derivations for the god's names. Their most significant feature is probably their very diversity, since they indicate the different functions attributed to the sun god. The name Apollo was interpreted as combining the idea of destruction with that of deliverance (from the verb *luo*, to untie), and was also connected with purification (on the basis of the verb *louo*, to wash). These contrasting associations were explained in terms of the drying effects of the sun, which can be harmful or beneficial. They doubtless indicate the survival of the ambivalent characteristics of the ancient god.

The interpretations of the god's name given in the *Cratylus* (see 'Ancient Apollo: darkness and light') help to identify the four main activities with which he was associated, namely medicine and divination (both forms of purification), music and archery. The name Phoebus is linked by Isidore of Seville with the eternal youth of the ephebe (e-Phoebus), and by Cartari (1556) with the light of life (*phos*, light, and *bios*, life). Pluto interprets the Greek word for the Sun (*helios* as meaning the one who 'shades' colours (deriving it from *aïoleïn*). However, all later commentators associate its Latin equivalent (*sol*) with the adjective *solus* (alone), which is perpetuated in all neo-Latin languages. 'He is called sun (*soleil*) as being the only eye (*seul oeil*) in the sky' (P. de Tyard). Following Plotinus and Macrobius, Cartari finds a Greek etymology of the name Apollo that conforms with this interpretation. He translates it as meaning 'he who is not multiple' (*a*, deprived of, + *polu*, many), and thereby lays considerable emphasis on the identification of the sun with oneness.

MAIN ATTRIBUTIONS

Renaissance mythographers did valuable work in synthesizing what had been written about Apollo. As a result, they provide a virtually definitive account of the various interpretations of his myth, culled from ancient, medieval and oriental sources. In his *Images des Dieux* (1556), Cartari breaks the sun myth down into a series of themes linked together by an allegorically based interpretation:

- First and foremost, in the diversity and universality of its effects the sun represents an archetype of Divinity. Thus the Assyrians assimilated it to Jupiter as the world's soul (it is he alone who is always evoked through all other gods), while Macrobius in his *Saturnalia* (I) took the view that all theology could be traced back to sun worship.
- Apollo is the symbol of eternal youth, on analogy with the day which is always new and constantly reborn. Thus he is always shown without a beard (except by the Assyrians) and is associated with Dionysus.
- Because of its central position in the Universe, the sun is called 'heart of the sky'; and, as such, it performs the same vital 'pulsating' function as the human heart. The sun, from which life emanates, instigates the movement of the stars. That is why it sits in the middle of the nine Muses, who are allegories of the nine celestial spheres, and forms with them the configuration of Harmony and the Universe, a sign of 'symmetry and concordance' (Tyard). Thus the Music of the Spheres, which R. Lully was to represent by the Great Lyre of the Universe, lies behind the attribution to the sun god of Music and Poetry (which was originally Song).
- The rays of the sun represented by the arrows carried by Apollo (and his sister Artemis) have the ability to penetrate to the very heart of the earth. That is why there was an ancient tradition according to which Apollo was also a god of the underworld. (In this role he could be called by the female name Hecate, as the primitive deities were sexless.)
- It is because of the drying and purgative qualities of the sun's rays that Apollo is also the god of medicine. Mythographers link the story of his killing of the serpent Python soon after his birth, to this power, assimilating Python to the Flood, a humid and pestilential phenomenon that encircled the earth.
- Similarly, Apollo's association with the laurel and the story of Daphne are explained by the properties of the laurel itself. Being evergreen and not subject to decay, it is seen by the mythographers as the emblem of Health. It too is connected with the alchemical symbolism of humidity, for it was

as a result of the intervention of the river Peneius, her father, that Daphne was transformed into a laurel tree.

- Finally Apollo is the god of divination, because he is the eye of the sky, which sees everything and reveals secrets. (That is the meaning of the mythological episode in which he exposes Aphrodite's adulterous affair with Ares.) In the context of the universe he occupies the same place and performs the same function as the human eye, acting as 'the mind's spy', 'censor' or 'guide'. Moreover, his pre-eminent position is a sign of omnipotence: Cartari describes an Egyptian hieroglyph denoting the sun by means of a sceptre with an eye above it, and so identifying it with the concept of royalty.

The type of synthesis outlined above, which defines and interweaves the main mythological themes relating to the sun god served as the basis for all later poetry. Du Bartas provides an important example of this in his *Sepmaine ou Création du Monde* (1578). Here, the sun has ceased to be a god and become a simple 'ornament in the sky', but it is still referred to by a series of names encompassing all the mythological associations of the sun god in his cosmic role: golden-haired Phoebus; fair-haired Titan (referring to the original sun deity); Latonian Torch (associating him with Artemis, as the son of Latona, or Leto); the Archer; soul-inspiring Apollo; Fountain of Heat; Life of the Universe; Bringer of Honours; King of the Sky; Eye of the Day; Censor; and even (in an allusion to his main ancient sanctuaries) Delian Torch and Delphic Flare that 'rejuvenates the face of the world'. At the same time, Cartari began the process of codifying the various aspects of the god, with the result that he was progressively simplified to the point of becoming the patron deity of Poetry and no more. In this role, he was portrayed as crowned with bay leaves and sun rays, sitting with the Muses on Mount Parnassus. His lyre was always with him (indeed, the lyre alone was sufficient to symbolize the god); and he distilled poetic inspiration from the Hippocrene spring (created by a blow from the hoof of Pegasus) – which Ronsard was to describe as 'the fountain of verse'.

THE PHILOSOPHERS' SUN

In the alchemical tradition, the god of Poetry was seen as the symbol of philosopher's gold reconciling the opposed principles of fire and water, dryness and wetness. In Orphism and Pythagoreanism he symbolized the divine creative spirit; while in Neoplatonic literature, in which Apollo with his lyre is always associated with his mortal counterpart, Orpheus, he is the very image of all creation. During the Renaissance, Apollo was the god who inspired the Poetic Frenzy essential for producing lyrical verse; under his influence the spirit 'penetrates the secrets of the skies' and the soul 'is elevated among the gods' (Ronsard, 'Hymne de l'Automne'). It was in Apollo that the soul rediscovered its celestial origins through the workings of divine enthusiasm (from the Greek word *theos*, god); and this was the Orphic origin of poetry. For Ronsard and other poets in the Pléiade, the inspired Poet was a 'prophet' and 'priest of Apollo' (hence the tremendous recognition according to the Sibyls and the oracles by the poets of the sixteenth century).

This Neoplatonic interpretation of the myth of Apollo, which confused the two principal activities associated with him, namely prophecy and lyricism, in fact became the main vehicle for transmitting the image of the god to later generations. It was based on Marsilio Ficino's commentaries on the *Symposium*, in which he defined four types of divine frenzy or passion, which he associated with four tutelary deities. The first and most elevated of these is poetic frenzy, which emanates from the Muses. The second is the frenzy associated with mysticism or priesthood, which emanates from Dionysus; while the third is prophetic frenzy, which comes from Apollo, and the fourth is love, which comes from Aphrodite. Despite the clear distinction made here between Apollo and the Muses, poets happily invoked either the god (understood as a universal principle) or his Muses (allegorical figures each representing a different type of poetry). It should be noted that Neoplatonism does not represent Apollo as being opposed to Dionysus – instead, their functions are seen as complementary. The god of divination, or penetration into divine secrets, is connected so closely with the god of initiation into the divine Mysteries, that Pontus de Tyard describes them as 'brothers'. In the process, he mistakenly derives the name 'Delphian Apollo' from the Greek word *adelphos* (brother) 'because of the brotherhood thought to exist between Dionysus and Apollo'. To the extent that Neoplatonists regarded Apollo as one of the poles in the duality of the world, they saw him as One-ness, a universal principle – as opposed to Artemis, who embodied Nature, or Multiplicity. According to Plotinus, whose ideas were taken up again by Giordano Bruno (*Eroici Furori*, 1585), Nature (Artemis) is the mirror of God (Apollo). The latter is absolute light, whose essential property is to be hidden, which can blind and can be seen only in its reflections. A variant interpretation developed by Leone Ebreo (1535) represented Apollo as the 'simulacrum of divine intelligence' and the Moon as the 'simulacrum of the soul of the World', serving as an intermediary between the divine plan (the world of the mind) and the physical plane (the world of the senses). This idea had an especially powerful impact on later literature. In particular, it led to an extremely strong emphasis on seeing, whereby the physical power of vision was identified with mental vision, on the grounds that the spiritual qualities of light enable us not only to distinguish beauty from ugliness but also good from evil. This supremacy of the eye over the other senses was to be developed extensively in various poetic and metaphorical contexts throughout the sixteenth and seventeenth centuries. Even in anatomical descriptions by Baroque poets, the eye is perceived as an intermediary between the world of the senses and the world of the intellect, a counterpart to the Sun whose light illuminates mind as well as matter.

THE MYSTICAL SUN

In the Renaissance, the sun began to be regarded as a royal emblem, and this tendency became considerably more pronounced in the Baroque period. This iconologically based interpretation is first attested in panegyrics ('Henry, the Apollo who inspires me'; Ronsard, 'Elégie' I), and then in actual emblems, with the royal crown being depicted as a crown of rays. While Tyard regarded the image of the sun, the 'Prince and ruler of the sky', in positive terms, the Baroque poet Drelincourt, writing in 1677, compared it to 'a proud King, shining in his Court, Crowned by rays . . .' but then went on to accuse it of being no more than a simulacrum of God, a 'weak painting'. In the same vein, Du Bartas drew an explicit distinction between the true God and the false pagan god, even when calling Him by the latter's name: 'The world is a cloud through which divine Phoebus, not the archer son of beautiful Latona, shines . . .' ('Premier Jour', 143–6). It is significant that when Drelincourt adopted a critical, secular approach to the subject, depriving the sun of its mythical name and function he was writing at the court of Louis XIV. At this time, the king was being portrayed as the ideological embodiment of the solar allegories found in literature (notably in Campanella's *City of the Sun* and the *Dream of Poliphilo*), and was having himself represented as Apollo at Versailles, 'the residence of the Sun', implying a reversal of the natural order, whereby the sun was brought down to earth. Drelincourt's sonnet 'Sur le Soleil', reduced to 'the portrait of the First Cause', concludes: 'your brightness is just a Shadow, and you are no longer the Sun'. The mythical Sun is a false sun. But it is replaced in the metaphorical heavens by the true mystical Sun, Christ, sometimes depicted by Renaissance painters in the guise of Apollo. As a reflection of the true God, an interpreter and vehicle of his light, Christ is a sun figure; his death is the sun setting and poets used this type of metaphor to describe his eclipse at Calvary. This identification between Christ and the Sun, which was quite conventional in mystical Baroque poetry, sometimes even encompassed certain episodes from the legend of Apollo (notably those involving Clytia and Hyacinthus) – though this was unusual.

THE SUN OF THE INTELLECT

Though the mystical sun only rose to prominence as the mythical sun declined, in a paradox that left its mark on all poetic interpretations of Apollo, it nonetheless harks back to an old idea, the concept of Deus Pictor. If god is a painter and the Universe is his picture, then the Sun (according to poets from the Hellenistic period onwards) must clearly be his paintbrush. In Baroque versions of the sun myth, which was used frequently, though more often metaphorically than allegorically, this concept was developed in a rather abstract direction. Its treatment is related to two myth themes. On the one hand, the Sun, as a divine principle and instrument of creation, becomes the mythical counterpart of the poet, who now dares to identify himself not merely with Orpheus but with Apollo himself. On the other, the daily journey of the solar eye becomes a metaphor for writing. There are numerous instances in French Baroque literature where a word-play between 'rayon' (ray) and 'crayon' (pencil) is used to describe the Creator's role as a painter and writer. Similarly, it was common to punctuate a long poem with descriptions of sunrises and sunsets treated in such a way that they create a mythically inspired analogy between the rhythm of the days and that of the poem itself.

This device occurs in 'Adone' by G. B. Marino; at the end of the poem the Muse is summoned by Apollo 'to finish the weaving of this long canvas', while the end of the last day of the story is described in terms of a written text: 'The sky is paper, the darkness ink and the ray a pen / With which the sun wipes out the closing day to write in brilliant golden letters / In the west the end of its long journey' (Canto XX). Apollo is present in 'Adone' in various guises. He can also be recognized in metaphorical form in the figure of the hero, Adonis, who is just a spectator passing through the sights of the world (the heavens, the earth and the world of culture). Indeed, he is often compared to Apollo because of his youthful good looks. Just as the sun is the eye that lights up the world, revealing it and enabling it to exist, the first creative gaze to fall on the poem is that of the poet himself; but there is another gaze, like that of the human eye that reads and interprets the great Book of Nature. In Marino's poem Adonis plays this role of reader, the counterpart of the creature from whom the secrets of creation are hidden. Thus he too is a 'false sun', and, as such, is depicted as a passive hero who, throughout the whole course of the poem, understands nothing of what he sees. The result is an inverted image of the philosopher's sun of the Renaissance. The sun symbolizes the human soul, but only in terms of appearance; the latter takes itself to be the sun because it is an image of it. Marino's Adonis is a solitary eye to which the gods (Venus and Hermes) reveal secrets, but the only world that his gaze lights up is that of the book, of which Apollo, 'he who enlightens the wise of mind', is the true author. This 'enlightener' represents the god of Poetry in his final manifestation, as the representative of the divine Intellect. He makes the mind brilliant and penetrating, in other words, capable of invention and divination. Here, the solar symbolism is discarded, and the emphasis is placed on human Intellect, particularly individual understanding. The god no longer 'inspires', but perhaps performs an even more important function by 'lighting up' the work.

Thus Apollo seems to become ever more heavily disguised, to the point at which he even loses his name, is forced to make way for substitutes and is not even referred to as a god. However, as a mythical symbol, he regains a great deal of coherence, since the use of the Sun as a metaphor for the eye of God preserves the clear outlines of his mythical nature. Indeed, the connotations attached to the sun merely represent the transposition onto a metaphorical plane of the myth-themes associated with the ancient god. The very frequency with which the sun is evoked in the sixteenth and seventeenth centuries indicates the almost ritual status still accorded to it at a time when literature was distancing itself from the actual myth of Apollo.

It seems that the figure of the tutelary god of poetry was gradually abandoned as soon as poetry ceased to use the myth of inspiration as a prop. Though writers continued to invoke the Muses up until the nineteenth century, they did so only occasionally or from force of habit. In addition, the words Apollo, Muses or Lyre could also be used on their own as metonyms for the concept of poetry, without suggesting any particular mythological theme.

HYPERION

With the advent of Romanticism, Apollo once again came to be thought of as an archer: the poet's divine inspiration was not seen so much as a flash of illumination and revelation, but more as a blow that stupefied and took possession of its target. Poets such as Hölderlin were 'struck by Apollo' (Letter 240, Pléiade editionk p. 1009), and after being brought face to face with the god could no longer be understood by men. The poetic vocation was thus likened to a curse and a cause of suffering (or of passion). In Hölderlin's work Apollo is confused with both Jupiter, who strikes with a blinding flash of lightning, 'shatters and enlivens' (*Hyperion*, above edn, p. 209), and with Dionysus; before finally being condensed into the figure of Christ. He is also identified with the Titan Hyperion, who, according to Hesiod, was his father. Like Hyperion – whose name he bears in Hölderlin's allegorical novel (*Hyperion*, 1797–9) – the poet is a fallen, exiled Titan whose (pre-Apollonian) attempts at rebellion are doomed to failure, but who retains a confused memory of his solar origins and his mission, while at the same time being destined, like the sun, to solitude. In this context, solitude has both a positive, inspiring aspect and a negative aspect, which turns the poet into someone accursed or mad. Apollo and Dionysus are again united, in the Romantic idea of madness as a sign of being chosen by the gods, and of mystical intoxication. The concept of Apollo's fundamental ambiguity recurs in this dual image of poetic inspiration, as both a state of grace and a state of exile from the conventional world.

The Romantics viewed this duality in terms of its emotional impact on the individual, and no longer merely in coneptual terms, as in Renaissance times.

It is worth looking in some detail at the exceptional treatment of Apollo in one final work of literature, a treatment that is strangely reminiscent of Hölderlin's interpretation of the god. Only in the nineteenth century does

Apollo appear as the *subject* and main hero of a literary work: in Keats's (unfinished) poem, also entitled *Hyperion* (1819). This short epic in Miltonian style describes the casting out of the Titans by the New Gods, and the accession to divine status of Apollo after his initiation by Mnemosyne. In Keats, as in Hölderlin, Apollo is seen as symbolizing 'new beauty', and as the tutelary god and incarnation of New Poetry. In the work of both writers the emphasis is on the process by which Apollo *becomes a god*: in Keats, Apollo only attains divine status when he is made aware of his divinity by Mnemosyne (who, according to mythological tradition, was the mother of the Muses). This acquisition of knowledge is painful – before striking poets Apollo himself suffered 'a pang as hot as death is chill' and 'shriek'd' at the moment of his epiphany (*Hyperion* III, final lines). In Hölderlin's work, antonomasia ('your brother, the Hyperion of the sky, lives in you', p. 195 of the edition quoted above) is used to make the name Hyperion symbolize the heartbreak of the book's hero, who looks towards the old gods, whose interpreter he feels himself to be, and is destined to start the renewal of the Sun Youth by means of a New Poetic Religion. The poet speaking here is not yet born, and Hyperion represents the mythical prehistory of someone who will become divine, as a pure and solitary spirit ('The Hermit of Greece') freed of heroic temptations, only after the events recounted in the novel. In a similar vein, Keats abruptly breaks off his poem at the moment when Poetry is born.

Françoise Graziani

Archetypes

This term is among those widely debased by modern criticism, and particularly by those with pretensions to a familiarity with psychoanalysis. The most lowly writer has only to trot out some glib story about the eternal triangle of the murderer, victim and avenger for everyone to go into ecstasies over this archetypical situation. The worst poet is an heir to Orpheus, and critics fall over each other to scratch away the surfaces of the so-called palimpsests offered by contemporary events and find the archetypal manuscripts beneath. Or should this be prototypical? Or, why not stereotypical!

Myths in literature do indeed constitute exemplary stories, which are themselves usually crystallized into a prestigious and dynamic form because they condense or sum up the most profound spirit of a culture. But any tale or image worthy of literary expression can ultimately be linked to one or more archetypes. Eve lies behind every woman, since every woman is, by definition, a *femme fatale;* an initiation rite underlies every adventure story; there is a ritual drama related to sacred mime in every theatrical form; and, finally, as Kierkegaard has shown, without expressly speaking of archetypes, Don Juan, Ahasverus or Faust are present in every search for and assertion of self intended to bring the salvation of transcendence. It is not so long since we were regaled with the 'great universal types' of world literature. Ethnologists and anthropologists, and particularly those of a structuralist bent, aim to prove that, because of this relationship and, as Montaigne would have said, for whatever place, time or circumstances, we merely annotate each other. This claim to find the same patterns of motivation gravitating around the same magnetic poles in every conceivable context is likely to irritate those who believe in freedom. (There is always a Sigurdr to kill the dragon, take communion with its blood, and so cross the natural boundaries to gain an understanding of the language of the titmice; the Father or Patriarch always lays down the Law and watches over his Order; the Mother or the Great Goddess indefinitely protects the caprice, absurd proliferation and charm – *carmen* – of Life; and which should we place first in our unformulated consciousness? Which should we place first in the innocent language that conveys that consciousness, in all our dual languages (which have only one personal pronoun to express the idea 'you and me')? For it is from these that we derive the idea of our primordial dual nature or the fascinating concept of the androgyne, which has continually haunted our amorous, existential and indeed metaphysical reveries. Unless it is the languages themselves that are a reflection of a true primeval duality. However, while we are free shortsightedly to deplore our single, common state, there is nothing to prevent us from exulting in the infinite diversity of colour with which we have always been able to embellish it. Since the dawn of time, all the magic of all religions has sought to remove the dividing line between life and death, sometimes to the point of denying its existence. So too has all speech – particularly of the measured kind; though the distinction is perhaps unnecessary. After all, is not the latter simply a less crude, more subtly orchestrated attempt to return its purity to the yearned for One, beneath its numerous manifestations?

All this implies that the archetype is invariably to be found at the end of any investigation of literary myths. However, it is still important to identify the connotations of a term that is too often misused.

Three connotations spring to mind, and though, in practice, they overlap completely, and can be superimposed, by looking at them individually, we may be able to shed more light on this complex notion.

a) First we should understand an archetype as being the *prototype* of something, the first real example of it. This does not imply a value judgement, any more than the terms archetypal or imaginary manuscript do in the context of the historical study of texts. There is a primordial and fundamental battle at the origin of any mythical or mythological story, a complex situation involving naturally conflicting elements. When these elements are unleashed by something inherent in the human condition, they introduce Evil or Temporality and their consequences into the history of mankind. The situation depicted in terms of the centaurs and Lapiths of William Golding's *Lord of the Flies* in the Scandinavian *Völuspá*, or in Rabelais' caricature, Picrochole's war, deserves to be classed as an archetype. Amphion founding the city by playing his lyre or Romulus with his sacred furrow can also be seen in this light, just as much as Cronos devouring his children. These are ancient (more properly archaic) figures – primal figures that, it seems will never cease to give birth to new versions of themselves, since the characteristic of any true literary myth is to be contagious.

No doubt this is how we should also understand the Platonic Ideas that Maurois described as 'mother fictions of all human thought'. To the extent that they are initiatory and, in that sense, paradigmatic, they are certainly archetypes, since all things are based upon them. It was Chateaubriand who described them precisely when, in speaking of the Trinity, he correctly interpreted it as 'the archetype of the universe or, put another way, its divine framework'. He developed this concept with the same meticulous precision in his choice of words, when suggesting that behind 'the external and material form' taken by the Trinity through the diversity of our cultures there is an 'inner and spiritual arch which supports it'.

The sensualists, Locke, Condillac, and Berkeley (who regarded the distinction between the spiritual and material worlds to be vain), and Malebranche, who expressly speaks of the archetype as the 'eternal model', certainly stressed its primal as well as atemporal aspect. The archetype is atemporal to the extent that it is part of its nature not only to have existed first, but also to have given rise to the temporality that explains its successors. This is what the Hindus understood so well, this is what some languages still convey – particularly the Germanic ones which sometimes seem so awkward in their handling of past tenses. The famous German prefix *ur-* (primeval, originally; *Urheimat, Urvolk, Urgeschicte*) implies a, no doubt diffuse, awareness of the *Urbild*, the primal image, whose elements humankind tries constantly to reconstruct.

To find more modern and detailed expressions of the notion of a fundamental symbol that acts as a kind of matrix for repeated representations of itself, we need only turn to the experts on religious and anthropological phenomena (Micrea Eliade, Van der Leeuw), since the concept has attracted considerable attention in recent times. This is not the place to expand on the archetypal principles that Mauss points to behind the gift, the offering or the exchange. However, it is clear that, for example, the Tree of Life, the Tree of Knowledge, the Tree of Jesse or the Tree of the World, *Axis Mundi, Universalis Columna* – and particularly the Scandinavian Yggdrasill or the Vedic Skambha – provide an exhaustive *Weltanschauung.* Their images are like an inexhaustible ideogram that is infinitely suggestive and ever-renewable in ways that depend on the imagination and sensibilities of the individual. A Prometheus who steals fire is always needed to give legitimacy to our will to survive. Conversely Pandora has once and for all 'explained' our earthly misfortunes: earthly indeed, just as the Snake, the emblem and archetype of all Evil, is a creature of the underworld.

Cassirer sees the human being as a symbol-producing animal: and it is quite evident that these symbols always originate in a primordial, archetypal image or idea. It is significant that in Greek the word 'symbol' (from the verb *sumballein*, to assemble) first referred to a token of recognition (re-cognition) consisting of an object, coin or medal, broken into two pieces so that only those who possessed them could put them back together. This postulates the existence of an original state, *in illo tempore*, when no split had yet occurred.

b) Secondly, the word archetype can be used in the sense of *ideal model*, as already suggested by the passage from Malebranche quoted above. The shift in meaning is only slight, but the essential distinction is that here the term is coloured by a value judgement, no doubt to the detriment of its original simple, paradigmatic quality. Any hero or warrior worthy of remembrance gains his status from measuring up to the yardsticks provided by Heracles, Gilgamesh, Beowulf, Cucuchlain or Kullervo, all of whom, by definition have a heuristic power. In their own agonistic domain, they reveal not only that there are more qualities in human beings to admire than to despise, but that we can never exhaust the resources of our own intelligence. Robinson Crusoe merely perpetuates the immemorial act of all discoverers and colonizers, from those of the Land of Canaan to the conquistadors, by way of Icelandic pioneers of the 'Books of Colonization'. The difference is that he is at first alone, like all the divine creators in our various mythologies and religions, and that, unlike them, he is already rich with acquired knowledge, like all primitive giants. He is thus not absolutely archetypal in the first sense of the word. He does not create the world, he recreates it in the image of the one that he carries within him (which is only his secondarily – hence the distinction). This also applies to the protagonists of all our futuristic novels and of some works of science fiction.

Going further, we may ask, with good reason, what is archetypal about the strange sort of 'hero' who appears in all the Germanic legends and whose exemplary status is undisputed. For this is a 'hero' who has done nothing heroic in the sense that, given its conventional associations with figures such as Achilles, Aeneas or the Knights of the Round Table, we would usually ascribe to this epithet. Although he kills the dragon Fafnir, Sigurdr accomplishes this exploit without 'glory'; although he manages to go through the wall of flames behind which the Valkyrie sleeps her magic sleep, it is entirely thanks to his horse Grani, the gift of Odin. Nor does he even meet a noble end; on the contrary, he is murdered in a wood or even, in some versions, treacherously killed in his bed! So why is he unanimously hailed as an ideal model, while 'real' heroes such as Starkadr or Beowulf, who have vanquished not just one, but several, dragons are not? A moment's reflection is sufficient to provide the answer. Sigurdr goes to his death aware of his destiny, he does nothing to prevent the fatal blow because he is bound by sacred oaths of sworn brotherhood; from beginning to end, he remains open, honest, obliging and generous. Now these are the virtues that the old Germanic and Scandinavian texts constantly and explicitly praise. As a consequence, Sirgurdr-Siegfried is, indeed, the epitome of the hero. In his person he combines all the values for which his followers agree to live and die. He is the first hero, not in the sense of being the original one, but in the sense of being superior to all others.

It is surely in this sense too that Rabelais presents Homenaz as 'the archetype of a pope': he is not the first pope (or the first church leader), but the one who offers us the most complete image of the qualities and virtues that we should like to see in someone holding his office. As such, he represents a model image, an antecedent who has nothing necessarily primordial about him, but to whom we may refer implicitly, or explicitly whenever we wish, emphasizing whatever aspect seems most relevant at any particular time. Without going into the complex details of the functional attributes of the sacred king, it is clear that a paragon or archetype is essential to legitimate our reverence for any leader whatever his or her title: raj, rex, konungr, Führer, duce, ayatollah, tsar (in other words caesar), basileus, or indeed General Secretary of a communist party or trade union. Depending on one's ethical outlook, they either deserve to be utterly overthrown or unreservedly admired. David or Ghengis Khan, Pericles or Tamburlaine, Louis XIV or Stalin, Napoleon or Hitler – there is something in the edifice that gives them their stature that cannot be dismantled. They all hark back, not to a symbol, but to another concept mentioned in passing a moment ago, namely a mother fiction. This archetype (used in the first sense of the word) provides for its current anecdotal and episodic manifestations an archaic basis without its influence being uppermost in our minds. In this context history – the history of events and facts, the history explored by science – plays a primary role. The example that should not be overlooked, and which stands out prominently in the three interrelated senses of the term archetype proposed here, is that of Christ: who was, who is and who is to come. As we shall soon see he is archetypal because he is of a supreme type, but he is also archetypal because he is integrated into history. It is precisely this that gives him an advantage over Adonis, Baal, Ormuzd, Baldr and all the other paragons of perfection, who are not represented as men but as gods or occasionally men and gods. His image is an absolute archetype precisely because it is relatively verifiable. Because of this our intellect can legitimate our emotions and our flights of imagination more easily than in the other cases.

Conversely, it can easily be argued that, in the modern mind, Hitler is the 'historicized' archetypal image of the Devil, who occurs in all religions in at least some of his manifestations. He is a model, whatever its status may be – a located and identifiable point and the object of a process of transference. Behind the capricious nature of the events that the present may throw up, there is always a possible reference point, below or above. The appearance of a particular archetype depends on one's viewpoint and knowledge. Despite the historical reality that lies behind it, which is easily traced and well documented, the image of the 'Viking' fluctuated in our imaginations for a thousand years, like the lines on a fever chart. He has been the scourge of God come to punish the softened West; the romantic knight; Nietzsche's superman; and the bawdy brute paradoxically equipped with the most subtle technological devices of his age – in sum, the irresistible Superman come from the Cold!

c) A third interpretation of the archetype, which transcends all temporal or ethical dimensions and is thus truly metaphysical, seems to me to be the most important. According to this definition, the archetype is the *supreme type*, the absolute, the perfect image that transcends particular circumstances because it goes straight to the essential point wherever one chooses to tap it whether the context is religious, mythical or fictional. As such, it encapsulates one of the most fertile sources of all literature, and also one of the most difficult to define. Among its best formulations is the one produced by Meister Eckhart. Eckhart posits the existence of an ideal world where only archetypes can develop; the divine Creator makes them move from that universe to the physical universe, where they are incarnated in people and concrete objects. Thus all creatures have a spiritual double that connects them to God the creator and gives them an underlying nobility and dignity. There are few systems of thought that have not in some way paid tribute to this vision – even if only in a fury of denial. At its heart is the implicit certainty that we are neither alone, nor absurd, and that a transcendental ideal justifies our existence – in short, that there is always an archetype that will ultimately welcome us in our wanderings or put an end to our exile.

The simple act of writing, in itself, can surely have no other reason for existing: the spoken and written word have no meaning except in terms of the communication that they are intended to establish and, beyond this, in terms of the sensed, expected or ardently desired communion that they re-establish. The choice of the word re-establish, as opposed to establish, is deliberate since speech and writing presuppose the existence of a transcendent reality. If we are talking of people, we may call this the supreme type. An example of it is the 'angel', whom men have always been seen in any woman they love or the civilizing hero who attracts her imperious admiration, since the heroic culture is something with which none of us can fail to connect. Alternatively, if we are referring only to the actual narrative – what the Greeks so aptly called poetry, poiesis; a (re)creative act or, rather identification – we may call this the perfect tale or architext.

In fact, however disinherited we may be or may think ourselves to be, we are all the Trista to some Isolde (or vice versa). It is surely true too that when our love is crystallized in its archetype its quality is linked to the clear awareness of our failure to match up to this double, or to the desperate hope of doing so. No one sensed this better than Swedenborg, and Seraphitus–Seraphita – so called because the explorer of the *Heavenly Arcana* judiciously combined the sexual signs to reflect their inevitable complementarity – bewitched both Balzac and Nerval (see 'Androgynes'). But the Gnostics had long felt 'its' presence, and, indeed, it doubless pre-existed the idea that we have always had of the soul, from the Egyptians to the Rhennish nuns such as Hildegarde of Bingen. It lies behind the Amandus and Amanda of Stagnelius and Byron's quest for adelphic loves: they all reinvented Jakob Boehmes venerable 'union of the outside and the inside', in an act that is identical to alchemy. And, in the wake of Swedenborg, it would amount to a gross act of mutilation if one reduced Baudelaire's equation in 'Correspondances' or Rimbaud's in 'Voyelles' to a simple register of the senses.

Jung, who is the ultimate authority on the subject of archetypes, based his study upon a conscious perception of the anima-animus couple, and this may represent the current state of our knowledge.

It is worth reminding ourselves of the nature of the phenomenon that Jung called 'the transcendental imagination' and that we usually call the 'collective unconscious'. In one sense, it is a vast spiritual reservoir, accesible to all those of a particular culture – and, to a certain extent, to any human being. From it we obtain, involuntarily rather than consciously, the dreams, delusions, myths, literary images and symbols on which every religion and literary tradition draws. In the context of the Indo-European world, Georges Dumézil's brilliant work, *Mythe et Epopée*, can be seen, in a sense, as an inventory of our collective unconscious, whose structures he has revealed. The same image of the life force appears from one end of the Euro-Asiatic continent to the other, with Varuna-Zeus-Ju(piter)-Týr representing the elements of magic and sovereignty, those of Mitra-Mars-Ares-Thórr representing its martial aspects, and Nasatayja-Quirinus-Freyr/Freyja evoking its powerful fertility. Again, the single eye of all esoteric knowledge, the unstoppable thunderbolt and the phallus erectus arc the archetypal images of the three functions we assign to our pantheons, as a consequence of our own desire for immortality.

Commenting on Plato and regarding 'archetypal ideas' as always remaining 'at the bottom of our minds', Voltaire internalized them. In contrast, Jung regarded them as external but accessible – permanent infrastructures that a community could use to organize the vision of the world by which it lives. In this context, he did not see humanity as differentiated, and though anthropologists have constantly sought diversity the end result is often the rediscovery of fundamental invariables – all in all, the black Orpheus differs from Eurydice's lover only in the details of his story; his underlying quest and the sacred transgressions that his love dictates are in essence identical. In Jung's view, there is thus a whole treasury of organic, pre-existing mental elements, which we call instincts. We are the collective vehicle for the original 'types' of representations which are shared spontaneously by individual unconsciouses, even though we are often unaware of this. It is worth remembering what studies by folklore specialists and the analyses carried out by Bettelheim rediscovered behind the most apparently innocent of our so-called fairy stories.

Of course this theory masks a grave danger which amounts to nothing less than a denial of our freedom. Jung spent a long time studying concepts such as the archetype of the Father and the Mother. In doing so, he went far beyond Freud's short therapies, which provided too limited interpretations of the old myths with their proven literary echoes. (For Freud, Oedipus represents the murder of the Father and rape of the Mother: coversely, Narcissus stands for imprisonment within the self and Circe for dehumanization – not to mention his ideas on the universal castration of the Child through a reflex self-defence mechanism. What works can ultimately escape from being rapidly decoded with this crude key?) Jung's analysis undoubtedly runs the risk of reducing all our behaviour and, particularly, all our literature to a reflection of a known and recognizable (archetypal) element in the collective psyche. Job on his dungheap primarily represents the lamenting Son bullied by his cruel Father; one step further and here is Satan moving from tears to rebellion, then to usurpation (Trismegistus); and, finally, here is Nietzche's Zarathustra denying himself by denying God, in other words by exulting in his death. All that is left then are the invariable, or almost invariable, elements. Generation after generation, pitiful humanity exhausts itself by reformulating them, and unlike the poet, wears itself into the ground by writing new lines based on ancient thoughts. Once these elements have been identified, there are almost no literary myths that cannot be decoded unambiguously at any given place or time. It is no coincidence that all our great works are cyclical, or that all our religions can be fitted into a mandala.

But Jung saw the danger, and not enough heed is paid to it in what is supposed to be our present orgy of technocracy, determinism and materialism. The Holy Grail, the Golden Fleece, the philosopher's stone and anti-matter are doubtless of us and within us, but they demand both that we return to the sources and that we go beyond them. At this juncture we are brought back to the animus and anima; just as their supposed opposition cannot be resolved in an androgyne, so we can find complete happiness only in the pursuit of what Teilhard de Chardin called the Omega Point. This certainly lies beyond them, but not in the way that the magnetic pole is separate from the skiffs that it attracts. It is like a burning sun towards which all our heliotropic souls are fatally attracted because, concealed in their depths, they hold the very essence of its heat. It is another case of Pascal's 'you would not seek me if you had found me'.

So, whichever term we use, the archetype or supreme type is an expression of the fundamental fascination that the thinking, writing human being seems always to have feared or cherished: that of *amor fati*. In literature, it was probably Proust who went the furthest in pursuing it. He is, perhaps, the modern figure who has been most successful in supplying the images of men and women demanded by our irrepressible, unconstrainable need; in offering them to our saving hope of loving in ourselves the archetype of Time that both finishes and completes us.

Régis Boyer

Ariadne

Originally, Ariadne was probably a Cretan goddess who was worshipped in Cnossus, Delos and Argos and was closely associated with Aphrodite. According to Greek mythology, she was the daughter of Minos and Pasiphaë and fell violently in love with Theseus, who had come to Crete to confront the Minotaur, as one of the seven youths sent to King Minos each year as tribute by the Athenians. To enable him to find his way through the Labyrinth, Ariadne gave him a ball of thread provided by Daedalus or, according to another version of the myth, a luminous crown made by Hephaestus, following which she eloped with him to avoid the wrath of her father. The story of how she was abandoned by Theseus when he put ashore on Naxos is well known, but in most accounts, the tale does not end there. Theseus's vessel had scarcely put out to sea when Dionysus arrived in his chariot, which is sometimes represented as drawn by panthers, accompanied by his retinue. Captivated by the young woman, Dionysus persuaded her to marry him and carried her off to Olympus where he made her a gift of a golden crown. The crown subsequently became the constellation named after Ariadne, who bore Dionysus several children.

The story of Adriadne begins when she falls in love with Theseus, but during the course of it she takes on three distinct roles in turn: the guide of the hero, the abandoned lover, and the mortal woman married by a god. These combine to provide an ideal illustration of Woman, or specifically of Woman in love. Ariadne is the Lover whose secret conceals depths of knowledge, an inexpressible suffering and a divine transcendency. In the inherently female nature of her passion, there is a hidden core that will always be inaccessible to Man.

In Greek literature, Ariadne is dealt with very summarily. She appears in the *Iliad* alongside Daedalus (and probably the Labyrinth) in connection with the *choros* (dancing floor?) designed by Hephaestus, which is said to be 'like that which once in the wide spaces of Cnossus, Daedalus built for Ariadne of the lovely tresses' (XVIII. 590–3). This provides mythologists with an extremely important clue as to the initial nature of the Labyrinth and the origins of the ritual for which it eventually became the setting', but the poem only refers to the ancient myth in passing. Ariadne is treated in much the same way in the *Odyssey* where she appears with Phaedra as one of the many princesses that Odysseus encounters in the underworld. Here Homer also echoes a version of the myth according to which Ariadne did not fall in love with either Theseus or Dionysus. The latter apparently took his revenge by telling Artemis that Ariadne was guilty of sacrilege, so that Artemis pierced her with arrows (if lines 321–5 of book XI are not a later addition). In the *Theogony*, Hesiod gives a completely different version of the myth, according to which Dionysus married Ariadne and made her immortal (947). However, in Greek literature of the Classical period even passing references to Ariadne are few and far between, and it was only in the *Argonautica* (III. 1074–1108) by Apollonius of Rhodes (second century BC) that the story of her fate was developed in more depth.

Excluding the lost Alexandrine verse that may have inspired it, by Catullus, was the first work by a Roman poet to mention Ariadne, the 'Marriage of Peleus and Thetis'. The poem is dedicated to the nymph Thetis, who has chosen to marry the mortal Peleus, and gives a description of the wedding gifts that the couple receive. These include a length of sumptuous purple cloth intended to cover the marriage bed and decorated with scenes from the story of Ariadne. As if to stress the pain that she feels, Ariadne never takes her eyes from Theseus's ship as it sails away, the story tells of the past, the future and other dimensions. In its suffering, Ariadne's soul tries to escape the present by launching itself into space, but stays tied to the source of its pain. Alternatively, it is Ariadne who remains motionless, as if eternal, while time moves on. This image of Ariadne watching Theseus's departing ship reappears in the *Elegies* of Propertius (I. 3. 1–2; c. 20 BC). However, it was Ovid who showed a particular interest in the abandonment of Ariadne, writing about it several times in his earlier works, before going on to tell the full story of the Labyrinth in his *Metamorphoses*. Thus, while the fourth letter in his *Heroides* (20–15 BC) contains Phaedra's confession to Hippolytus, the tenth is from Ariadne to Theseus. Her complaint is reminiscent of the one imagined by Catullus, but is characterized by a much greater degree of sensuality. The motif of the abandonment of Ariadne reappears in a simile in the *Amores* I.70 15–16; 18 BC) and is extended to include the image of her being carried off by Bacchus riding in a chariot drawn by tigers and accompanied by satyra in the *Ars Amatoria* (1. BC – 2 AD). Even if the story of Ariadne on Naxos is not exclusive to Ovid, his image of Ariadne as the tearful lover was so haunting that, for a long time, it was preferred to the image of Ariadne as the guide of Theseus.

Finally, writing in Greek during the fifth century AD, Nonnus of Panoplis described the wooing of Ariadne by Dionysus and the joyful celebration of their marriage in the 47th and final book of his *Dionysiaca* (265–481). By developing this dénouement, already suggested by Catullus and Ovid, the poem tends to create an impression of fantasy and myth, rather than of psychological reality. As well as providing the only version of the story of Ariadne in ancient Greek, it shows great qualities of strength and vividness in developing a theme that was to enjoy considerable success in the future: the marriage of Ariadne and Bacchus.

Apart from a few allusions to her cruel fate, and some comparisons of stars with the constellation that bears her name (for example, in Dante's *Inferno* XII. 20 and *Paradiso*, XII. 13), Ariadne was hardly mentioned in medieval literature. The adventures of the 'Duke of Athens' left little room for the Cretan maiden. However, in fourteenth-century Italy, during what is generally agreed to be the 'first' Renaissance, Boccaccio repeatedly referred to her abandonment by Theseus in favour of Phaedra (*Il Filocolo* II. 17 and *Amorosa Visione* XXII. 4–33), while, in his Latin works, he echoed the curious version of the story, according to which Theseus abandoned her because she was drunk and fast asleep (*De casibus virorum illustrium* I. X. 14). Meanwhile, in Petrarch's *I Triomphi* (1352), Ariadne accompanies Theseus in the lovers' procession, after he has been punished for betraying her. Finally, the heroine features prominently and very appealingly in Chaucer's *The Legend of Good Women* (1386). Telling the story of Ariadne in his own picturesque and simple manner, Chaucer made his own highly personal contribution to the literary development of the myth. Condemned by Cupid to sing the praises of nine faithful women, the poet chooses to recount the tale of Ariadne after those of Cleopatra, Thisbe and Dido. Theseus left Ariadne asleep on the deserted island 'For that her sister fairer was than she'. When she awoke, she saw his ship far out at sea, and though she waved her handkerchief tied to the end of a stick, it was to no avail. The poet-narrator considers Theseus extremely ungrateful, but excuses himself from repeating all that Ariadne had to say on the subject on the grounds that this would take too long and that 'In her epistle telleth al' – a reference to Ovid's *Heroides*. This is the most attractive version of the legend written during the Middle Ages, and in it the character of Ariadne is portrayed with a great deal of charm. Chaucer's friend, Gower, imitated the work in his *Confessio Amantis* (1390), but without managing to recapture the same youthful spontaneity.

During the Renaissance proper, the theme of the abandonment of Ariadne did not inspire any great literary works. Leaving aside brief references to the story elsewhere, it lies behind the misogynous and generally unconvincing poem by Thomas Underdowne, *The Excellente Historye of Theseus and Ariadna* (1566), in which the author maintains that Ariadne became involved in something that did not concern her and thus fully deserved to be abandoned. Though equally unsatisfactory from a poetic point of view, the complaint by Cartwright, *Ariadne deserted by Theseus*, was closer to the classical tradition, being based on the versions of the myth by Catullus and Ovid, and during the seventeenth century it was used as the libretto for an opera by Lawes. Like this work, the Spanish poem by Juan de la Cueva, *Romance como Ariadna fué dejada en la Isla de Quios por Teseo, y lo que sucedió mas* (1558), appears by modern standards to follow the ancient story far too closely. On the other hand, the theme of Ariadne's marriage to Bacchus, neglected since the time of Nonnus of Panopolis, made a brilliant reappearance in the *Trionfo di Bacco e Arianna*. Written towards the end of the fifteenth century this is the most famous of the carnival songs by Lorenzo de' Medici, and it is significant that the theme was treated in a satirical vein, animated by the euphoric carnival atmosphere. The song urges us to taste the pleasures of life and love without delay, inviting us to be merry, play music and dance, while the refrain expresses regret for the passing of time and a fear of death. The evocation of pleasure is all the more intense because it is developed against this counterpoint of suppressed anxiety. (The verses describing the triumphant chariot are transcient while the refrain remains.) The literary and popular success of this song meant that the theme of the abandonment of Ariadne was neglected during the rest of the Renaissance in favour of the theme of her marriage. However, it was chiefly series of masterpieces by famous artists that made the latter such an evocative element in the Western cultural tradition. These included an etching by Botticelli(?), decorations on chests by Cima da Conegliano and Piero di Cosimo(?), a painting by Titian and frescos by Tintoretto. However, the dual theme of Ariadne was to achieve its greatest expression only in the seventeenth and eighteenth centuries, when it was painting, once again, and the newly developed art of opera that were to play the dominant role in ensuring its success.

During the Spanish Golden Age mythological poetry continued to be very much in vogue and the poem *Ariadna* written in 1642 by Salcedo Coronel, was highly praised by Lope de Vega for its solemnity and harmony, while the poems 'Teseo y Ariadna' and 'Llanto de Ariadna' are among the most important in the collections in which they occur: *Varias Rimas* published by Colodrero Villalobos in 1692, and *Rimas*, published by the Marquis de San Felices in 1636, respectively. However, during the Classical period, it was in theatre and its immediate relative, opera, that the dual destiny of Ariadne was most eloquently developed.

The first theatrical work on the theme of the Theseus's inconstancy and desertion of Ariadne was probably scripted by the major Dutch writer Pieter Cornelisz Hooft as early as 1601. In 1610, Alexandre Hardy also used the theme in his *Ariadne ravie*, where Act IV consists of a monologue by the heroine of almost 300 lines long, at the end of which she throws herself from a cliff. Fortunately, she only loses consciousness and soon awakes in the arms of Bacchus, who offers her celestial immortality. In the play by Lope de Vega, *El Laberinto de Creta* (1621), Ariadne does not appear overly distressed at her abandonment and is extremely willing to be comforted. This complicated and easy-going tragi-comedy is not a great work of literature, although Ariadne's imaginative and enterprising nature have a certain dramatic appeal. By this time Aradne was becoming a well-known theatrical figure, as is shown by the passage in Shakespeare's *Two Gentlemen of Verona* (1623) in which Julia tells how, during the pageants of Pentecost, she played the part of Aradne so movingly that it made her poor mistress weep (IV. 4. 156–70). It was during this period that Ivan Gundulic, the great poet from Ragusa (Dubrovnik), presented his version of the story of Aradne (1628), and that Calderón stressed her rivalry with Phaedra in the second act of *Los Tres Mayores Prodigios* (1636). Interest in the subject reached its height in 1672 with Thomas Corneille's *Ariane*, which is known to have been one of the most warmly received of all the French plays of the Classical period. Although the elegance of Theseus is somewhat affected, Ariadne has real strength of character. She is passionately in love and, when she realizes that she has been betrayed, she swears to kill her rival (who is in fact her sister) and marry Oenarus. However, the departure of Phaedra and Theseus thwarts her planned revenge and she becomes imprisoned in her own grief. The rivalry between the two sisters was too sensitive a subject to be tackled explicitly. Thus the emphasis is on Ariadne as a figure in the depths of tragic despair, shaken to the very core of her being and completely distraught. In the same year, Donneau de Visé echoed the tragedy by his older friend Corneille with his own play *Le Mariage de Bacchus et d'Ariane*. This is a character comedy in which deprivation gives rise to a desire that subsides as soon as it is requited or even seems about to be requited. The naive jealousy of Theseus is treated in a lively manner, and there is more than a hint of burlesque travesty. But perhaps the most important aspect of the play is that the women intervene in the tragic process to which they are condemned. In a reversal of traditional roles it is they who take the initiative, making full use of comic licence to explore the delights of freedom, under the watchful eye of Bacchus. The two plays, the tragedy and the 'heroic comedy', illustrate two distinct approaches to the classical myth of Ariadne. While the poetic clarity of the two most famous lines by Racine (*Phèdre* I. 3. 253–4) condemn her to a tragic destiny, the story retains all the diversity and contradictions of the original myth in its attempt to discover, if not the whole truth, at least part of the truth about women.

During the Classical period it was probably opera that was most instrumental in making the character of Ariadne as important as that of Phaedra or even more important. During the seventeenth and eighteenth centuries, about forty operas were devoted to the stories of Ariadne's abandoning or consolation. The earliest of these used *Arianna a Nasso*, a short tragedy by Ottavio Rinuccini, as its libretto. Indeed, the main interest of the original play lies in the fact that it was set to music by Monteverdi for the marriage of the Prince of Mantua and Margaret of Savoy and, as a result became one of the first 'real' operas (1608). The only music that survives is the 'lamento' of Ariadne, and even this has been altered, so that all that remains of the play is the famous passage, 'Lasciatemi Morire'. This truly wonderful piece was extremely popular during the seventeenth century and provided the inspiration for the 'renaissance' of the myth of Ariadne, involving its conversion into operatic form. Music by Lawes, Bonacossi and Benedetto, in turn, gave new resonance to the story. A year after the triumph of Thomas Corneille's *Ariane*, Robert Cambert, who had left France for London because of Lully's newly obtained 'opera privilege', presented his last operatic piece, *Adriane* (1673), based on a libretto by the Abbé Perrin. In some works the theme of Ariadne's marriage to Bacchus takes precedence, as for example in the libretto by Postel, *Die schöne und getreue Ariadne* (1691), which was set to music by Conradi and later by Keiser, and which ends with the entire island of Naxos being transformed into a delightful setting for the wedding. Meanwhile, in the libretto *Adriane et Bacchus* (1696) by Saint-Jean, set to music by Marais, Bacchus, wearing a crown of vine leaves, personifies a very conventional kind of happiness. However, the greatest number of works on the theme were produced in the eighteenth century. For unknown reasons, the libretto by Pariati appeared in a succession of different adaptations, set to music by Porpora (1714), Leo (1721), Abos (1728), Sarti (1756) and Scarlatti (1760). But there was also music, based on other librettos, by Mouret (1717), Marcello (1727), Feo (1728), Handel (1733) and Pasqui (1764). Gerstenberg had scarcely completed his poem, *Ariadne auf Naxos*, than it became a cantata (1765), was extended into a 'melodrama' by Brandes (1774) and, with the music of Benda, became an opera, considered by Mozart to be 'truly excellent'.

By the end of the eighteenth century, the myth had become so popular that it was often parodied and satirized, as for example in *Theseus und Ariadne* by Schiebeler in 1767, *Die Travestierte Ariadne auf Naxos* by Satzenhofer in 1799 and *Ariadne auf Naxos* by Kotzebue in 1803. Artistis also contributed greatly to developing the theme. Most of them, including Guido, Jordaens, Tiepolo, and the weavers of Beauvais and Flanders, made the excellent choice of portraying the marriage to Bacchus. In addition some of the poetry written at the end of the century also anticipated the development of the Dionysian element of the myth. Although the poem by Willamov, *Bacchus und Ariadne* (1766), which tells the story of the marriage of Ariadne and Bacchus in the form of a Bacchanalian song, has been forgotten, the lines by Chénier are remembered: 'Come, oh divine Bacchus, oh young Tyoneus Oh Dionysus, Evander, Iacchus and Lenaeus' (*Bucoliques*).

The mythical Greek names unfurl for Ariadne with the brilliance of a galaxy of stars.

The extent of cultural awareness of the myth of Ariadne during the nineteenth century is clearly indicated by the fact that the names Ariadne, Theseus and Bacchus were used with the indefinite article (in France by Sandeau, Baudelaire and Berlioz) to describe the archetypes of the abandoned woman, the unfaithful lover and the consoler respectively. Opera, which had made such extensive use of the twofold drama of the story over the centuries, continued to exploit it frequently, as a source of evocative argument. Examples of works on the theme range from *Arianna e Teseo* by Benvenuti based on a libretto by Niccolini (1810), to *L'Abandon d'Ariane* by Milhaud based on a libretto by Hoppenot (1927), by way of *Ariane* (1906) by Massenet and Catulle Mendès and, of course, *Ariadne auf Naxos* by Strauss and von Hofmannsthal (1910). However, with the advent of Romanticism, and particularly that of Symbolism, there was a movement on two axes to make the character of Ariadne deeper, and more complex interest in the marriage to Bacchus lead to the recognition of the heroine's Dionysian element; while the episode involving the Labyrinth and the thread, which had previously tended to be neglected, began to attract renewed attention, giving rise to questions involving the nature of time and consciousness.

The wonderful and much-reproduced marble group by Dennecker, *Ariadne auf dem Panther* (1814), which portrays Ariadne reclining elegantly on the back of a panther, probably represents the first hint of the concept of a deep-seated link between the heroine and Bacchus-Dionysus. Meanwhile a poem of the same period by Leigh Hunt, *Bacchus and Ariadne* (1819), is surprising in its joyful fluency and its lavish description of the marriage. Less surprising is Nietzsche's decision in his 'Klage der Ariadne' (*Dionysos Dithyramben*, 1888–95) to give the last word to Dionysus, in spite of Ariadne's uncertainty. 'I am your Labyrinth . . .' the god concludes imperiously, again raising the question of the Dionysian aspect of Ariadne. In *Trophées* (1893), the sonnet dedicated to Ariadne by Hérédia is particularly reminiscent of the German sculpture mentioned above. Ariadne is lying naked on the back of a huge tiger as she waits the approaching Iacchus-Bacchus. The beast is described as 'roaring with desire and biting the flowers on its bridle'. Meanwhile, in 'Dans une vigne vendangée', one of the poems in *Jeux rustiques et divins* (1897) by de Régnier, Ariadne is mythically associated with autumn because of her fertile melancholy. However, it is probably the three-act morality play by the Belgian writer André Ruyters (1901), that provides the first in-depth consideration of the heroine's relationship with Bacchus. In it Bacchus goes to Naxos with Silenus with the intention of persuading Ariadne to resign herself to her misfortune, but instead, he himself is smitten by her and offers her a different kind of love, telling her to forget Theseus. Ariadne refuses, on the grounds of her unhappiness, which she sees as her sole 'raison d'être', and dies alone, grief-stricken. Although the play lacks dramatic intensity, it does at least treat the myth in a new way. In the excellent *Ariane* by Marina Cvetaeva (1924), Ariadne is portrayed as the favourite of Aphrodite and perhaps represents the true manifestation of the goddess, who sends her to give Theseus the 'thread and the sword' and to persuade him to use weapons to fight the Minotaur, when he is supposed to fight barehanded. Ariadne succeeds in her mission, but, just as Theseus is easily convinced to do as she says on this occasion, so too he is easily convinced to do as Bacchus says, on Naxos, when he is told that Ariadne has been promised to a god for all eternity and that he must relinquish her. The Cretan maiden is the only female character in this tragedy and provides the one glimmer of light in its gloom. But although she constantly foresees what is going to happen, she is unable to avoid it. She is a prophetess in love, self-effacing and lucid, the priestess of Aphrodite who seems to hold the spindle of fate, from which she unwinds one of those obscure threads linking love and death. *Qui n'a pas son*

Minotaure? by Marguerite Yourcenar, begun in about 1932 but not published until 1963, also gives Ariadne a more prominent role. Theseus is seduced by Phaedra and allows the other Athenian hostages to be taken into the Labyrinth while he sleeps. However, he is given a second chance by Ariadne, who helps him to enter the lair of the Minotaur and save his fellow youths. Attached to her by the thread 'like a newly born baby to its mother', Theseus is given the opportunity to confront his true self and emerge a better person. But Araidne has misjudged him. Her 'ideal' man is only concerned with his own social advancement and it is only with Phaedra, not with her, that he will feel fulfilled. Ariadne refuses to be as compliant as Phaedra; on Naxos she thinks that she has 'seen the light' and tells Theseus to leave. In doing so, she places moral values and asserts her spiritual dimension above purely social considerations. Shortly afterwards, she is visited by Bacchus who, as in the writings of Nietzsche, is also the Minotaur. He offers her 'conscious immortality' and, as she hesitates and considers his proposal, he assumes the form of Nature and then of the cosmos, into which Ariadne's island is finally raised to become a constellation.

The tendency mentioned above for the story of Ariadne to be reinegrated into the story of the labyrinth is already apparent in the lyric drama *Ariadne libera* (1802) by Herder in which the separation of Ariadne and Theseus is represented as being due to her offence against Minos. Increasingly insistent questions began to be asked about the significance of Ariadne's thread, and a highly influential interpretation of it was developed by Hugo. Although in *Notre-Dame de paris* (1831) the thread is no more than the symbol of Gringoire's wisdom, in the preface to *La Légende des Siècles* (1859) it becomes 'the great and mysterious thread of the human labyrinth, Progress'. Thereafter, the thread came to be regarded as a symbol of the progress produced by human reason. In 'Thésée' by Baissette, written for *Cahiers du Sud* in 1939 the Labyrinth is called 'Absolum' and represents the 'path of Human Progress', while Ariadne's thread represents 'pure reason'. The thread can also be linked to the concept of time and identity. In Théophile Gautier's 'castle of memory', Memory is described standing at the side of the road leading to the castle and, like Ariadne, holding a ball of thread (*Emaux et Camées*, 1852). The beautiful poem by Vyacheslav Ivanov, 'Time' (1917), also reflects on the nature of memory, using the image of Theseus's desertion of his lover. In works that focus on the episode of the Labyrinth, Ariadne and her thread are reconsidered in depth. In Gide's *Thésée* (1946), the thread was made by Daedalus out of an 'unknown material', a contradiction that runs through the greater part of the text. It simultaneously represents the bonds that make it possible to construct the future and the 'fil à la patte', those that tie us down and hold us back. Theseus's only chance of success is to tie himself to Ariadne's thread, but he must also know how to free himself from it, in other words free himself from Ariadne's invasive and ultimately importunate love. Knowing how to break emotional ties is one of the most important methods of achieving freedom. In the lyrical and evocative play by Julio Cortazar *Los reyes* (1947), Ariadne is on the side of the Minotaur, her illegitimate half-brother, imprisoned by Minos. The thread that she gives to Theseus is both a sign of her gratitude and the means of reaching her and attaining freedom. In *Thésée* by Kazantzakis (1949), Ariadne is sent by her father to prevent Theseus from confronting the Minotaur, but the hero persuades her to accompany him into the Labyrinth with her flute and the 'magical skein' of her mind. The melody played by Ariadne transforms the confrontation into an exchange of embraces and leads to the liberation of the god whom Theseus then takes away with him, forsaking Ariadne and the old world.

The reintroduction of the story of the Labyrinth, and the realization that the myth could be used as a basis for interpreting the world were not obvious developments. The myth of Theseus and Ariadne is among those that the narrator of *Emploi du Temps* by Butor (1956) uses to illustrate his own personal predicaments and is represented as being depicted on the eighteen panels of an eighteenth-century tapestry. When he sees the image of Araidne, the narrator thinks of Ann, who sold him a map of the town, Ann whom he possibly loves and who, as he writes, soon becomes Ann-Ariane. At this point the story appears to follow the myth quite closely, because it is with Rose, Ann's sister, that the narrator really falls in love though he does not know how to tell her or how to win the heart of Phaedra-Rose, as she is now called. However, this is where the similarity with the traditional story ends, because Rose falls in love with the narrator's friend, Lucien, who was initially associated with Pirithous and with whom, in the fifteenth panel, the narrator had gone down into the underworld. This Lucien thus cannot be the Dionysus of the twelfth panel who consoled Ann-Ariadne, the abandoned lover, as is made quite evident when she announces her engagement to James! There is little point in going into greater detail; the myth does not represent destiny, nor is it an early version of the literary tapestry, which can be expected to provide a direct explanation of the events in the book. It is only of use indirectly and temporarily, to be questioned and developed and reflected in the distorting mirror of the literary work. The questioning is less insistent and the mirror less inventive in *La Côte Sauvage* by Huguenin (1960). However, one of the most symbolic episodes in the novel involves a visit by its central characters to the labyrinthine hall of mirrors at the fun fair in Brest. The mystery and suffering surrounding Olivier are linked to his affection for his sister, Anne, from whom even 'the blond young Ariadne' cannot distract him, so convinced is he that, deep down, his preference is for the shadow rather than the reality. In *The Magus* by Fowles (1966), the narrator is drawn into a labyrinth devised by a magician-conjurer and at one point believes that he is being lead by the real Ariadne. But the young woman changes into diabolic twins, who even have false names. In this way, the myth reappears pervaded by mystery, in the form of a 'baroque' novel.

Thus, the historical development of the myth can be briefly summarized as follows. Having practically disappeared from Classical Greek literature, Ariadne reappeared in the works of the Latin authors as the symbol of the abandoned lover. Subsequently, her tearful figure remained one of the most popular mythological devices for representing the suffering of Woman in love. However, during the Renaissance, the carnival song of Lorenzo de' Medici inspired extensive development of the theme of her marriage to Bacchus, first in art and subsequently in the theatre and opera. In the seventeenth and eighteenth centuries, the myth was one of the most persistent images in the cultural consciousness of the West. Whether suffering or being consoled, being sacrificed or being deified, Ariadne was represented as hesitating between her two destinies. Following from this, a number of modern works have used an in-depth comparison of these two aspects of the myth to develop an emotionally charged study of the nature of love and of the woman of the future. No doubt as part of the same process, Ariadne's central role in the myth of the Labyrinth began to attract renewed literary interest, making her once again the 'provider of the thread'. Since then, she has often appeared in this role, as an entrancing figure and a compelling example of magical thought.

André Peyronie

Artemis

It is not easy for the religious historian to define the essential character of Artemis as a mythological figure: it seems to slip the grasp and be multiplied into a variety of often contradictory aspects. The poetic tradition, particularly as codified by Latin writers, who deliberately contrived to identify Artemis with Diana, might give the impression of a certain uniformity. The goddess, evoked in a couple of lines, is easily recognizable. Arts too played a part in creating this illusion: whether in statues or in paintings, all that was needed to identify her was a bow and some arrows, a crescent moon on the forehead and a short tunic.

Indeed, poetry should perhaps have made such details, for there is little in the way of narrative material to go on. Perhaps only the episode involving Actaeon has real sustance, and even that does not lend itself to expansion. Meanwhile, in the other stories in which Artemis plays a part, her role is extremely limited: she is behind Iphigenia's misfortunes; by rousing a monstrous wild boar, she provokes the great events at Calydon leading to Meleager's downfall; it is because he has served her too single-mindedly that Hippolytus meets his death; and, finally, it is Callisto because he has been unfaithful who meets a similar fate. Artemis sets intrigues in motion, or sometimes resolves them; but she is hardly involved in the events that mark their progress. In both *Iphigénie* and *Phèdre*, Racine mentions her in passing, almost absent-mindedly. Yet this relative neglect does not distort the tales that he recounts.

As more of a mythological figure than a mythological character, Artemis might be expected to have only a few, emblematic features. But this is not so. Though during the past twenty-five centuries poets have done little more than quote her name, when we leaf through their work we realize that she has more than one face and that each mention of her, with its associations and contrasts, is the stuff of dreams. A number of imaginative processes are at work, and the proliferation of the goddess's identities extends the domain of study farther than might have been thought.

In a hymn that could be regarded as a prime source because of its description of the goddess, the Alexandrian poet Callimachus starts off by asserting her 'polyonomy' yet pays no heed to the assimilation of Artemis to Hecate or Selene, which we will consider later. Without even mentioning the moon he lists her various more unusual epithets, most of which are associated with cult places, since Zeus had promised his daughter that she would be worshipped alone in thirty cities and worshipped along with other gods in many more.

Homer's poems rarely feature Artemis, and never in an important role. On the other hand, they shower her with fine-sounding epithets, sometimes with obscure meanings. Thus she is 'the killer of stags' (*elaphebolos*), 'the one who shoots her arrows far' (*hekatebolos*), 'the one who shoots arrows' (*iokheaira*), 'the one who has golden arrows (or a golden distaff)' (*khruselakatos*), etc. However, Odysseus chooses a simple genealogical epithet when he says to Nausicaa: 'Goddess, among the gods who rule the skies you must be Artemis, the daughter of great Zeus: you have her stature, beauty and grace' (*Odyssey*. VI. 160; after translation by V. Bérard). This is an illuminating comparison. Nausicaa had left the town with a small group of young women, and Odysseus had met her near a wood beside the sea. The picture conjured up might relate to Artemis herself for it evokes a particular setting and a particular type of retenue: a wild landscape and young girls at play dominated by the goddess because of her height. It is significant that a little later Odysseus compares Nausicaa to the palm-tree on Delos. This again emphasizes her height, but also links her with the plant world, and the island sacred to Artemis's brother, Apollo.

The appealing image created by the fleeting comparison between Nausicaa and Artemis should not be dismissed. The poetic tradition always portrayed Artemis as an attractive young woman – indeed, she appears in this guise in the hymn by Callimachus mentioned above. Moreover, even if dark stories of human sacrifice and pitiless revenge remind us that there is an Artemis who is decidedly less attractive than Nausicaa, it would be wrong to suppose that these two pictures of the goddess are completely incompatible. While the images are psychologically at odds, they have a shared characteristic in imaginative terms: Artemis is a remote deity, who stays far from towns and farmlands, in the realm of virgin nature. The epithet *hekatebolos* certainly conveys the idea of the goddess shooting arrows but it perhaps gives particular emphasis to the distance over which she shoots them. Artemis is a being that one does not get near to. And it is certainly not just empty politeness that makes Odysseus say he is afraid of Nausicaa and does not dare touch her. He did not choose the comparison with Artemis at random.

This same element of distance can be observed in more than one anecdote involving Artemis. The goddess avenges some injury done to her in her absence. She hears *from afar* that she has been treated disrespectfully. Niobe has boasted about her children, Agamemnon has killed a sacred animal or has claimed to be the most skilled of all hunters, Actaeon, in the earliest version of the legend (Euripides, *Bacchae*, 337) is guilty of the same boast. The insult is cruelly punished, but *not directly*: a scourge is sent, a monster suddenly appears. Even the bow used against Niobe is not a weapon for fighting at close quarters.

Of course, Artemis is not the only deity to act in this a way. Indeed her brother Apollo shares the dread epithet *hekatebolos*. But it does seem to be particularly characteristic of her; and it is this characteristic that poets have seized on. In the process, they have neglected the occasional allusions to Artemis as the protectress of cities that occur in Anacreon's work or in the *Homeric Hymn to Aphrodite*; and it should be noted in this context that, even in a town, the area sacred to Artemis was a wood, as indicated by Callimachus, for example.

It is also Callimachus who makes Zeua say to Artemis: 'And you will be guardian of the roads, and guardian of the harbours.' This may be seen as alluding to the identification of Artemis with the goddess Hecate who was already referred to as a protector of travellers in Hesiod's *Theogony*. However, in Aeschylus's *The Suppliants* (675) it is in her role as the protector of women in childbirth that Artemis is assimilated to Hecate, while the assimilation may also be due to a play on words, since Hecate means 'distant'.

In his play *Medea*, Euripides makes the famous sorceress invoke Hecate as her mistress and helper in the performing of magic (397), but by the time of Theocritus, Hecate has been put on an equal footing with Selene and Artemis (*Idyll* II). This evidence is crucial. For one thing, it implies that, at least from this point on, Artemis may have been associated with witchcraft. Since she was said to be capable of cruelty, and even ferocity, and particularly since witchcraft was practised in wild remote places this would come as no surprise. In addition there may be a connection between the exoticism of the classic sorceresses Circe and Medea and the strange alien nature sometimes apparent in Artemis, for example in *Iphigenia in Tauris*.

As regards Artemis's assimilation to Selen, the Moon, traces of this can already be found in Euripides (*Phoenissae* 175). This was an ambiguous association; taken with Artemis's links to Hecate it could be used to emphasize the terrifying side of her nature; alternatively, taken alone, it could be employed to the opposite effect, to exalt her luminous qualities. As time passed, poets played more and more with allegorical explanations of mythology, and showed an interest in astral interpretations. Just as Apollo tended to be increasingly closely associated with the Sun, so his sister Artemis became assimilated to the main body in the night sky, the Moon. So she comes to dominate the stars, just as, when portrayed as a young girl, she had stood head-and-shoulders above her companions. As the Moon, she inherits an ancient legend associated with Selene already recounted by Sappho: the story of Endymion. The result is that the inaccessible virgin goddess now has a lover – though this dream lover, bathed in a milky light, 'the sleeper on Latmos', is again a figure rather than a person, and it took considerable imagination on the part of Ketas to turn the anecdote into a story.

Even if we confine ourselves to allusions made to her by the poets, it is clear that the ancient Greek view of the personality of Artemis was unusually complex.

Latin writers simplified matters somewhat; their Diana was a goddess of the moon, and they had no difficulty in merging her at a single stroke with Artemis and with Hecate, who was also the Roman goddess Trivia. Catullus's short poem (34) brings together all the goddess's Latin names, including Latonia, Lucina and Luna, while his allusion to Delos, the goddess's birth place, forms a link with the Greek tradition. At the same time as being the goddess of the forests and the mountains, in other words, of wild places in general, as an astral body, Diana was in charge of a regulated calendar, and was therefore the protectress of agriculture.

While Catullus seems content to juxtapose the different manifestations of the goddess, other writers, such as Virgil, provide extra elements that allow them to be synthesized. In the *Aeneid* (IV. 511), when Dido invokes Hecate of the three forms, Diana the maiden of the triple countenance, she must be alluding to the fact that Trivia, or Hecate, is the goddess of crossroads. But, at the same time, she implies that Diana has three aspects according to where she resides: as Hecate, she is terrible and belongs to the underworld, as Diana, she is terrestrial and belongs to the woods, and as Phoebe she is celestial and luminous. Significantly, this last name, meaning 'luminous', does not occur in the surviving works of any ancient Greek poet. This suggests that the process of synthesis and rationalization embarked on by the Roman poets caused Artemis and her brother Apollo, whom Homer had already called Phoibos (Phoebus in Latin) to be seen as perfect parallels. Thus Artemis, who had become the Roman Diana, whilst retaining her old Greek names, such as Dictynna, was also given new names that reflected those of Apollo: for instance, Cynthia, or Delia.

In intellectual terms, the result seems to be a perfect definition of her nature, and a perfect balance of her attributes. However, this harmonious state of affairs does not actually exist outside textbooks on mythology. If we look at poetry, things become more complicated, for the name Hecate, or an allusion to the triple form of Diana, immediately conjures up associations with the dead, with subterranean powers and perhaps even with chaos. Magical invocations became a literary convention exploited by Virgil, Ovid, and Seneca, and Horace, and later by Ronsard and Shakespeare, not to mention countless writers of librettos for opera. Though Diana's identity as a terrestrial goddess had been fixed, whilst, at the same time, she had been discreetly associated with Phoebe by the inclusion of a crescent moon in her diadem, some doubts still lingered regarding the sweetness of her light. As Ovid put it, 'The form of the night-time Diana cannot be like herself.'

Astrological rationalization inevitably created some unease. Goethe was well aware of this when he made one of the scenes in his classic portrayal of Walpurgis Night begin with an invocation to Luna (*Faust II* Act II) 'Even if in the horror of the night/Sorceresses of Thessaly/In earlier times drew you down here, what a wicked act . . . /Favour our enterprise, fair Luna.' The 'even if' clause serves to remind us that nothing is simple. The 'favouring' moon is also involved in casting spells. And the scene takes place in Thessaly.

This classical Walpurgus Night is the counterpart of another entirely medieval one in *Faust* , and Goethe is reminding us that, despite its pure reputation, classical antiquity also had its sorcerers and monsters.

It is curious that in the Middle Ages Diana was often invoked in connection with wild animal hunts or night-time processions of witches, said to be led by Herodias, 'Dame Abonde' or Diana. In his history of the kings of Britain, adapted from the work of Geoffrey of Monmouth, Wace has his hero consult: 'Diana, a soothsayer:/A devil who deceived/The people by enchantment;/She took on female form/By which she deceived the people./She had herself called Diana/And the goddess of the woods.' (*Brut* 636 ff.)

Here the woodland motif seems to have been reinterpreted: the wild places are those where Christianity has made least inroads. Admittedly, Brut is thought to have lived before Christ, but it is no accident that the story uses a cult that takes place in the woods as a model for pagan worship.

The romance *Lancelot* calls the lake near which the hero's father dies the lake of Diana, adding that Diana was a queen of Sicily who lived at the time of 'the fine author Virgil', who had a passion for hunting and who was taken for a goddess by the pagans. Indeed, it is on the lake of Diana that the fairy who kidnaps Lancelot to take care of his education has his home. We may thus wonder whether there is a link between the name Diana and the Vivien or Niniane who, in some traditions, is the Lady of the Lake. However, this may not be the most significant aspect of the reference to the goddess; clerics educated in the scholarly tradition tended to introduce the textbook version of Diana into fairy stories that they wanted to make more plausible. A profound imaginative shift was at work: Diana was once again she who is far away.

If Diana reigned over the lake where Lancelot spent his childhood, she also reigned over several other literary realms: domains of purity set apart from the world. In *L'Astrée*, the Forez district, which forms the book's setting, is said to have been haunted by the goddess, who stipulated when she left the region that it must always be governed by a woman. Thus the exclusively female society that surrounded the goddess in the woods resurfaces, with a few minor adjustments. It is surely also significant that one of the most famous pastoral romances of the sixteenth century, written a few decades earlier than *L'Astrée*, is entitled *Diana*. Admittedly, the name is that of the heroine, but it seems probable that the author, Montemayor, did not choose it by chance.

The popularity of the story of Actaeon in the sixteenth century may owe something to its association with fairy stories, for meeting fairies could have dangerous, even fatal, consequences. Fairies also steal children; it is interesting that Shakespeare named the queen of the fairies Titania, a title applied to Diana by Ovid. In addition, fairies take human lovers, and the story of Endymion was revived by Lyly before it inspired Keats.

If fairy stories were still current at this period so too, of course, were stories about witches. Reading Ronsard, we are struck by the vibrant immediacy of his evocations of the goddess: for him Hecate was more than just a name in a book. We should remember this when we find recurrences of the triple aspect of the goddess emphasized by the Romans, for example in Maurice Scève's work: 'Like Hecate you will make me wander/Both alive and dead for a hundred years among the Shades' (*Délie* XXII). Through the name Délie, or Delia, which is one of Diana's names, Scève recreates the feeling of the goddess's distance or unattainable nearness. He develops extraordinary variations on every possible aspect of a legend that cannot itself be pinned down. When someone says, 'Lady, either your Lover is forgetful,/Or he takes the name Délie from the Moon/To Show that you are changeable, like her', he is answered with the admission, 'For behind that admirable name I hide you/So that you may light up the dark night in me' (LIX).

It is precisely because the legend is so immense and varied – whatever Scève may say – because it unfolds like a huge oxymoron between the cruelty of Hecate and the sweet smoothness of Selene, that poets, from Ronsard to Petrarch, from Agrippa d'Aubigné to Desportes or Herrera, have been able to exploit the associations of the goddess's many names. What is involved is not the systematic rhetorical development of an organized tradition, nor could it be; everything is a matter of rare and fleeting allusion. And on every occasion an infinite variety of perspectives is opened up to the reader.

It is remarkable that the myth has withstood every learned attempt to turn it into allegory. Of course, the expression 'Diana's labours' is employed to mean hunting, just as the name of the goddess can be used merely to signify the moon. But these glib and pedantic metaphors did not prevent Goethe or D'Annunzio from conjuring up a diffuse light around the name of Endymion ('An Luna'; 'Sera su i colli d'Alba'); nor did they prevent Hugo from writing:

> Oh fearful nature! oh tremendous bond
> Of the wood that grows with the ideal
> contemplated!
> The goddess bathes in the starlit gulf!
> Wild nudity of the dark Diana
> Who, seen from afar and through the darkness,
> Causes monstrous trees to grow on the brow
> of the rocks!
> Oh forest!
>
> ('Le Satyre'.)

The 'potnia theron' or Mistress of Beasts talked of in the *Iliad* (XXI. 470) reappears in Rimbaud's *Illuminations*: 'Up there, with their hooves in the waterfall and among the brambles, the deer are suckled by Diana' (*Villes* I).

The 'Erstwhile Diana of alabaster', as Gottfried Benn describes her ('Acheron'), may have become a statue but she has not become a clearly defined figure. Even though she is afar off, Rilke feels the life pulsing through her in his 'Kretische Artemis'. And, as anticipating the Symbolist movement, Afanasy Fet's poem describes *Diana* as a goddess that one almost expects actually to come to life. The subject of the poem is revealed to be a statue, but the suppleness of Russian syntax enables the poet to end the last line with the word 'inaccessible'.

Some Celtic enthusiasts in the Romantic movement thought they had discovered that 'Diana' was a Breton word, since a quite sensible etymological analysis enabled it to be translated as 'un-knowable'. Perhaps they were thinking of the Irish Dana. Alternatively, the idea may have been to re-establish the male nature of the ancient deity invoked by Brut or Brutus in the medieval poem by Layamon – Brutus, of course, being the ancestor of the Britons.

By a strange coincidence, Artemis reappeared at almost the same time in the work of Nerval as a very distant figure, associated with the dead and consigned to the abyss with the other gods of bygone times: 'The Thirteenth comes back . . . She is still the first;/And she is always the only one.'

Jean-Louis Backès

Arthur

If King Arthur actually existed, which is possible, but by no means certain, he was a leader of the Britons who fought against the Saxon invaders of Britain at the beginning of the sixth century AD. Although he appears a great deal in much later Celtic literature, he owes his glorious reputation and pre-eminent position in the literature and imagination of the Middle Ages to authors writing in Latin, and subsequently, particularly to the French writers of romances. The French Arthurian romances were read, translated and copied throughout Europe and it is well known that Paolo and Francesca da Rimini were plunged into Dante's inferno because of a passage from *Lancelot.* Ironically, though, in modern times, it is the Anglo-Saxons, the old enemies of the semi-historical figure, who have most faithfully preserved the memory of King Arthur and his knights. Even the name Arthur is more widely used in England than on the continent, while the name Perceval, which is not uncommon in England, is not used either in France or Italy. Conversely, in these countries the more enduring reputation of another epic explains why so many children are called Roland. In the 1930s, the Ford motor company brought out a model called the 'Excalibur' (named after King Arthur's sword), but the name would have meant nothing in France, where batteries were being sold under the 'Durandal' trade mark (called after Roland's sword). In spite of all this, and however vague it may be, the memory of King Arthur and thc Breton adventures exerts the same fascination everywhere, for writers and film producers and, indeed, in the popular imagination.

FROM THE EARLY ACCOUNTS TO GEOFFREY OF MONMOUTH

When, around 545 AD, Gildas wrote his *De excidio et conquestu Britanniae* and narrated the victory of the Britons over the Saxons at Mons Badonicus, which, according to him, took place in the year of his birth (i.e. *c.* 500 AD), he made no mention of Arthur, even though the latter was described in later works as the victor of that battle. Similarly the *Historia ecclesiastica gentis Anglorum* by the Venerable Bede, completed in 731, did not mention Arthur either, although it provided details which were unknown to Gildas, such as the name of the British king, Vortigern, who was destined for a brilliant future, along with those of the Saxon leaders, Hengist and Horsa. Indeed, Arthur appeared for the first time only in the *Historia Britonum*, attributed to Nennius, of which the original version, which appears to contain the lines referring to him, dates around 800. Chapter LVI of this work describes how the Kent kings fought the Saxon leader Octha, son of Hengist, who had attacked them, and continues: 'It was, then, at that time that Arthur fought against (the Saxons) with the Briton kings, but he himself was a war lord.' ('Tunc Arthur pugnabat contra illos in illis diebus cum regibus Brittonum, sed ipse erat dux bellorum.') The author goes on to list twelve of Arthur's victories. The eighth was that of Guinnion castle, where he wore a portrait of the Virgin on his shoulders; the twelfth, and most dazzling, was that of Mons Badonicus, where he alone killed 960 of the enemy.

Around 950, the *Annales Cambriae* confirmed these details with minor variations, giving 516 AD as the year of the battle of Mons Badonicus where 'Arthur carried the cross of Our Lord Jesus Christ on his shoulders for three days and three nights, and the Britons were victorious', and 537 as the date of the battle of Camlann where Arthur and Medraut died. This is the first mention of what would later come to be known as the last battle between Arthur and Mordred, although it is impossible to tell whether the author of the *Annales Cambriae* thought that the two men were enemies and killed each other, as in the version of the story that was told by Geoffrey of Monmouth and which became canonical thereafter.

At this point, we should consider the first accounts of Arthur's activities in more detail and assess the significance of the absence of any reference to him in the earliest texts. The sentence from the *Historia Britonum* quoted above can be interpreted in two ways. The author may have meant that Arthur was one of the kings in league against the Saxons and that his peers had entrusted him with the military command. Alternatively, the word 'sed' may have a restrictive value – as implied by an eleventh-century manuscript – modifying the sentence to make it clearer. If so, the passage means that Arthur was not himself a king, but someone of a lower rank, a professional warrior, who had been put in charge of the troops (as 'dux bellorum'). Thus, when Arthur is mentioned for the first time there is some doubt as to whether he is 'King' Arthur at all. Indeed, even the origins of the name itself, which makes its first appearance in the *Historia Britonum*, are uncertain. The most likely suggestion, which is well supported by other sources, is that it derives from the Latin name Artorius. It has also been argued that it is a derivative of the Indo-european root 'ar' (to work), or a formation based on the Celtic word 'artos' (bear), or combination of the prefix 'ar– ' and the Welsh 'uthr' (frightening, amazing), or, indeed, an extension of the stem 'art' from the Gallic Mercurius Artaios. However, none of these theories has been shown to have any solid foundation.

Another mystery is why Gildas omitted to name the victor of Mons Badonicus, when he evidently attached considerable, indeed exaggerated, importance to the actual battle. Some scholars suggest that he did believe Arthur to be the victor but deliberately left out any reference to him. Among them is Kenneth Hurlstone Jackson, who argues that Arthur was not named because

Gildas was writing a sermon criticizing his contemporaries, rather than a genuine historical account, and that, generally speaking, he was avoiding the use of specific names. He adds: 'After all, what English bishop condemning his contemporaries' vices in around 1860 would have been so inept as to refer to the Battle of Waterloo, *which was won by the Duke of Wellington*?' (Loomis 1959; 3). The argument is more amusing than convincing, since the actual identity of the victor of Mons Badonicus in Gildas's text is virtually beyond dispute. He as Ambrosius Aurelianus, a member of the Roman aristocracy to whom the Britons, in their powerlessness to resist the Saxon invasion, had entrustd their fate. Signficantly, Bede, who agreed with this identification, interpreted Gildas's account in this way.

Is there, then, no hope of finding any trace of Arthur prior to the work of Nennius? There have been attempts to shatter the 'silence of the centuries' surrounding Arthur, as there have been in the case of Roland. It was discovered that the two names Oliver and Roland most closely associated with the *Chanson de Roland* suddenly became fashionable in the century preceding the composition of the poem. And, similarly, at the end of the sixth and the beginning of the seventh century, four, or possibly five, people in the regions of the British Isles with a predominantly Celtic population are known to have been called Arthur, even though the name was previously unknown and subsequently very rare. It is tempting to see this as evidence that Arthur's claim to 'greatness' began in this period. Around the same date (i.e. *c.* 600) the Welsh elegy *Gododdin*, attributed to Aneirin, claims that the valour of a certain warrior was second only to that of Arthur; this evidence would be decisive if the poem were not littered with later interpolations. Finally, a very minor observation also hints at the existence of a tradition associated with Arthur before the time of Nennius. It is based on the same sentence from the *Historia Britonum* already quoted above: 'Tunc Arthur pugnabat . . . etc'. Nennius does not present Arthur in the same way as the other figure in his story; he deems it necessary only to name him. On the other hand, he strongly emphasizes the circumstances ('Tunc . . . in illis diebus') that led to Arthur's involvement in the wars between the Britons and the Saxons, and endeavours to define, in confused terms, Arthur's position in relation to the Briton kings. The impression given by this sentence is that the author is introducing a figure well known in another context into events with which he was not originally connected. Moreover, it has been maintained, on the basis of linguistic observations, that Nennius may have been using a Welsh source. However, despite all these efforts to establish Arthur's historical existence, no convincing proof of it has ever been found. The excavations carried out on the borders of Wales and Cornwall have produced some interesting information relating to the period in question, but nothing on Arthur himself. Nonetheless, it still seems reasonable to believe that the figure was known before the *Historia Britonum*.

Subsequently, and especially from the eleventh century onwards, an increasing number of stories and legends were recounted about him. The *Historia Britonum* itself – includes among the marvels of Brittany a 'cairn' whose top stone bears a paw print left by Arthur's dog, Cabal, when he was chasing the boar, Troit, as well as the tomb of Amr, the son of the warrior Arthur ('filius Arthuri militis') – though, admittedly, these references occur in a passage that could also be an eleventh-century addition. The first of the two marvels should be seen in relation to the Mabinogion of *Culhwch and Olwen*, which tells, amongst other stories, the tale of Arthur's hunting of Troit. Significantly, several 'lives' of Welsh saints written in Latin towards the end of the eleventh century – 'The Life of Saint Padarn', 'The Life of Saint Cadoc' and 'The Life of Saint Carannog' – also mention Arthur, whom they associate with Bedivere (Beduier) and Kay. In them he plays the traditional role of the king whose arrogance and baser instincts eventually succumb to the saint's power.

It appears too that, about the same time, the belief began to circulate that Arthur was not dead and would one day return to rule over the Britons. Thus, in an anecdote that forms part of his account of a series of quests that took place in England in the spring of 1113, Herman de Tournai wrote: 'According to the custom of the Britons of arguing with the French about King Arthur, this man picked a quarrel with one of our men . . . claiming that Arthur was still alive.' However, as Faral has shown he can only have written this passage at a much later date, after the publication of Geoffrey of Monmouth's work. In contrast, the evidence provided by an account written by William of Malmesbury in the first edition of the *Gesta requm Anglorum* (1125) is irrefutable. To begin with, he tells how the last Roman ruler, Ambrosius, the successor of Vortigern, appealed to the 'valiant warrior Arthur', the victor of Mons Badonicus, for his help in driving out the Saxons, and adds: 'This Arthur is the man about whom the Britons still invent ridiculous stories' (Faral). Next, when speaking of the tomb of Walwyn, Arthur's nephew on his mother's side, he notes that 'Arthur's tomb has never been seen anywhere and this is why the old legends say that he will return.' Gawain is referred to for the first time here, too, probably as a result of the influence of Welsh oral sources. It is also worth noting that, in 1120 or 1130, an Arthurian scene was depicted on the archivolt of Modena Cathedral. It features the episode during which Arthur and his knights (Ider and Gawain) free Winlogee (Guinevere), who has been taken prisoner by Melwas (Méléagant from the *Chevalier de la Charrette* by Chrétien de Troyes; and since the names of the figures are carved quite clearly, there is no doubt as to their identities. The story may have been brought to Italy by the Norman entourage of the Countess Mathilda of Tuscany.

The literary stage was now set for Arthur's grand entrance, in the work of Geoffrey of Monmouth. However, it should first be mentioned that Arthur also appears in several Welsh poems that Celtic scholars believe to date back to an earlier period. Unfortunately, these poems are only preserved in recent manuscripts (from between the end of the thirteenth and the sixteenth centuries), so that it is difficult to distinguish their early content from later modifications made under the influence of the Latin historians and French writers. Nonetheless, they constitute an important source of evidence. They are preserved in *The Book of Taliesin* (*c.* 1275), *The Red Book of Hergest* (*c.* 1400), *The White Book of Rhydderch* and *The Black Book of Camarthen*, and it appears that one of the earliest tells the story of a disastrous campaign led by Arthur against a mysterious city, which seems to represent the other world. In addition, some mabinogi, such as *Culhwch and Olwen*, which probably date from the twelfth century, seem to record an original Arthurian tradition, though others (*Geraint*, *Owein* and *Peredur*), are, in their present state, partially indebted to Chrétian de Troyes, while *The Dream of Rhonobwy* projects the Arthurian legends into a distant, inaccessible world.

The *Historia requm Britanniae* by Geoffrey of Monmouth, devoted to the history of the Britons from their origins to the eighth century AD, appeared in 1136 and provided the real basis for the extensive treatment of King Arthur in later literature. Born in Monmouth, and himself a Briton, Geoffrey appears to have been closely associated with Walter, the archdeacon of Oxford, for most of his life. He was appointed bishop of St Asaph in his homeland of South Wales and died in 1151. As well as the *Historia requm Britanniae*, Geoffrey was the author of the *Prophecies of Merlin* (*c.* 1134), which he incorporated into the Historia, and also of a *Vita Merlini* (1148). The Merlin that appears in the second work is quite different from the Merlin of the *Historia* and much closer to the one of the Celtic texts – as always, in the later form in which we know them – which represent him in various guises. Geoffrey claimed to have used an ancient Welsh text as the source of his *Historia* but, although this is impossible, it cannot be verified.

The *Historia* devoted a considerable amount of space to Arthur – more, indeed, than to any other figure; in the manuscripts in which the work is divided into books, more than two out of twelve are dedicated to his exploits. Whereas in previous writings, he had been accorded only a few scattered lines, whose content even raised doubts as to whether he had always been considered a king, at this point he suddenly became the central figure in Briton history. Geoffrey was the first to give an account of his birth, which is reminiscent of that of Heracles, since King Uther, with the help of Merlin's sorcery, assumed the appearance of the Duke of Cornwall in order to make love to the Duchess Igerna. Geoffrey's book divides Arthur's glorious reign into five main episodes: the unification of Great Britain through the victory over the Saxons and his marriage to Guinevere; the conquest of the neighbouring islands and of Gaul; the coronation festivities that mark the height of his rule; the challenge from the emperor of Rome and the victorious campaign that Arthur wages against him in Gaul; his betrayal by his nephew, Mordred (who during this time seizes power and marries the queen), culminating in the final battle, during which the uncle kills the nephew; and the departure of the wounded Arthur for the island of Avalon. From this time on, the world of Arthurian legend, and the identities or many of its protagonists, were firmly established. During the course of the next century, the monks of Glastonbury exploited the interest that Geoffrey's work had aroused, by maintaining that the site of their abbey was in fact the island of Avalon, and by pointing out the alleged location of King Arthur's tomb.

KING ARTHUR AND FRENCH LITERATURE IN THE MIDDLE AGES

The success of the *Historia requm Britanniae*, is amply attested by the number of manuscripts of the book that have survived. Around 1155 it was translated into French verse by Wace – a cleric from Caen, born in Jersey. His work was entitled the *Roman de Brut* (Brutus) and, according to Layamon, who wrote an English *Brut* at the end of the twelfth century, was dedicated to Eleanor of Aquitaine, the wife of King Henry II, Plantagenet. Brutus, the great-grandson of Aeneas, was described, not only by Geoffrey, but also in the *Historia Britonum*, as the eponymous hero of the Britons and the ancestor of their kings. However, the *Roman de Brut* is dominated by the figure of Arthur even more than the *Historia* had been before it. The story of his reign alone takes up 4,000 of the 15,000 lines of the romance, while the stories of the three kings Aurelius (Aurelius Ambrosianus), Uther and Arthur together take up more than 7,000. Wace gave his poem a pre-courtly flavour lacking in Geoffrey's work, but also introduced some features that were previously unknown. He is thus the first to refer to the Round Table, around which King Arthur's knights gathered to maintain their equality; but he treats it as though it were a well-known Briton legend: '. . . la Reonde Table/Dont Breton dient mainte fable' (the Round Table/Of which Britons tell many a tale, 11. 9751 f.).

After Wace, the history of the Arthurian legend merges with that of French and then European literature. But however great the significance that Wace attributed to Arthur, he did not make him the sole hero of his poem. His ambition, like that of his predecessor Geoffrey, was to recount the collective history of the Britons after the arrival of Brutus in Brittany. Indeed, at the request of King Henry, Wace later wrote a *Roman de Rou* (Rollon) which extended the *Brut* and traced the line of the English monarchy back to its Norman origins. In addition, between 1155 and 1170, the first French romances were produced at the court of the Plantagenets, adapting works of classical antiquity. All were connected with the story of Troy in such a way that, taken together, they traced the origins of the Briton kings right back to their alleged Trojan ancestors – thereby continuing a process that had begun with the *Brut*. The works involved were: the *Roman de Thèbes*, based on Statius' *Thebaid* and covering events that were considered to antedate the Trojan War because of the role played by Jason; the *Roman d'Enéas*, based on the *Aeneid*; and the *Roman de Troie*, based on the compilation by Dares Phrygius. This group of romances was followed by the *Roman de Rou* and the *Chronique des Ducs de Normandie* by Banoît de Sainte-Maure, the author of the *Roman de Troie*, which dealt with the same subject; and together they presented a vast dynastic fresco extending from the Argonauts to Henry II, Plantagenet. Arthur appears merely as one figure, although certainly a particularly prestigious one, among many others. To fulfil his literary destiny, the poets had not only to focus their attention on Arthur himself, but also to renounce their historical aspirations. They had to set their sights on a truth outside the realm of reported facts and to apply themselves, in each romance, to the portrayal of an individual destiny rather than a collective history. Arthurian legend leant itself particularly easily to this sort of development because no one had ever had a very high opinion of the historical veracity of the writings of Geoffrey of Monmouth. Historian colleagues, such as William of Newburgh, had accused him of fabrication, and Wace himself had been sceptical. The transition from the purportedly historical accounts of Arthur's life to the romances based on his story was achieved by Chrétien de Troyes.

Probably a little earlier, or at about the same time as he was producing his first writings, the Anglo-Norman poetess Marie de France wrote a set of lays – short narrative poems inspired by the Breton *lais*, evoking an adventure or legend and intended to be sung – and the action of one of these, *Lanval*, unfolds at Arthur's court. Other anonymous poems of this sort have also been preserved, but only a few tell the story of King Arthur.

Between about 1170 and 1185, Chrétien de Troyes wrote five romances, under the patronage of the Countess Marie de Champagne, and then of Philip of Alsace, Count of Flanders. These were all set within the Arthurian context and were entitled *Erec et Enide*, *Cliqès*, *Le Chevalier au Lion* (Yvain), *Le Chevalier de la Charrette* (Lancelot) and *Le Conte du Graal* (Perceval). All five followed a similar pattern, which soon became canonical for all romances, whatever their themes. In this scheme, a young knight reveals his character both to himself and to others and then discovers the direction that his destiny is to take. This is usually achieved during wanderings symbolizing his inner development and through experiences in adventure and love. In these romances, Arthur occupied the position that, except in a few unusual instances, he would retain from then on. He played an unobtrusive and indispensable role as the arbiter and guarantor of courtly and knightly values against which the hero must judge himself. At the same time, each romance was presented as a fragment of the vast, universally familiar, Arthurian legend. King Arthur himself achieved a curious position of prominence: his behaviour, his way of life, the nature and origins of the ceremonies at his court and even the characters and past lives of those who frequented it, were all presented as if they were well known, while at the same time being surrounded by an aura of mystery. This was because the reader of the romance was discovering only one episode in a vast legend, the underlying coherence of which was never disclosed. The abundance of symbols suggesting an enigmatic and ominpresent meaning, and the pretence that everything was too familiar to require explanation, merely ensured that the underlying significance of the work was constantly sought and guessed at, but to no avail. The method introduced by Chrétian was used in many Arthurian verse romances until the end of the thirteenth century, although never with as great success.

The last romance by Chrétien de Troyes, the unfinished *Conte du Graal*, exerted such a fascination that it opened up a rich new vein of imagery to be explored not only in the context of Arthurian legend, but also, to an extent, in that of French literature as a whole. Several poets tried to complete the interrupted work by writing endless continuations to it, while two others, disturbed by the fact that it began 'in medias res', sought to add a prologue. Far more importantly, the story of the Grail, reworked and developed on the basis of the incomplete account given by Chrétien, caused the Arthurian legend to be clothed in new literary forms,and gave it a quite new significance. At the turn of the thirteenth century, Robert de Boron, a knight from Franche-Comté, wrote an extensive trilogy retracing the history of the Grail to the time of Christ, whose blood was supposed to have been collected in it. The holy chalice, which had been entrusted to the descendants of Joseph of Arimathea, was said to have been brought by them to Brittany. Robert de Boron thus gave the Grail a purely religious significance and lent an air of mysticism to Perceval's quest. His work was soon rewritten in prose, and it was perhaps no coincidence that the first French prose romances, which appeared at the beginning of the thirteenth century, were on the subject of the Grail. As argued earlier by Isidoro de Sevilla, prose was felt to be less frivolous, less elaborate and less tortuous than verse, as well as more realistic. French prose, which imitated Latin prose, the language of the Bible and the language of God, seemed to be the only worthy vehicle for a subject as holy as this. Other Grail romances in prose followed, such as the *Perlesvaus* – a strange, self-contained romance that is difficult to date, in which Perceval was still the hero, along with Gawain and Lancelot, and which sought to substantiate the Glastonbury version of Arthurian legend. The most important of these was the vast *Lancelot-Graal* cycle of around 1225–30. Two initial parts – the *Estoire du Graal* and *Merlin* – were probably later additions and were partially based on the work of Robert de Boron while its remaining three elements are: *Lancelot*, the *Queste del saint Graal* and the *Mort le roi Artu*. The originality of this collection of romances is twofold. First, it gives the principal role not to Perceval, but to Lancelot, and then to his son Galahad; and, secondly, their own development mirrors the transition from the courtly tradition to one of ascetic mysticism. In one sense, Lancelot is the best knight in the world because of his love for Guinevere, who enhances his worth; but he fails in his quest for the Grail because his adulterous love for Guinevere means that, in another sense, he is not the best knight in the world. The mysteries of the Grail are revealed to his son, Galahad, to whom Lancelot's first cousin, Bors, and Perceval are also linked.

The increasing importance given to the story of the Grail meant that King Arthur himself was viewed in a different light. His glory, prophesied and prepared by Merlin, lay in being the man during whose reign the Grail would be revealed, to the accompaniement of the burgeoning and subsequent decline of the Brittany marvels. According to Robert de Boron, the Round Table is the replica and symbol of the table employed at the Last Supper and of the table around which Joseph of Arimathea and his twelve companions used to sit. The Grail appears in its centre at the beginning of the *Quête du Graal*, while the knights seated around it receive supernatural nourishment. At the same time, however, Arthur does not represent the culmination of his dynasty, which now extends further back than Brutus to Joseph of Arimathea. The chosen descendant, related by blood to the Fisher King and to the lineage of the guardians of the Grail, is Perceval or Lancelot–Galahad. On the other hand, the King Arthur of the *Lancelot-Graal* is by turns a dangerous and pitiful character, vindictive, sensuous, and blinded by his passions, as in the episodes with the sorceress Camille and the false Guinevere. However, his greatness lies in his weakness, and the *Mort le roi Artu*, which is probably written by a different author from the other stories, uses vivid colours to depict the Arthurian twilight. The vast cycle does not end, as might be expected, with the *Quête du Graal*, because the writer of this work deemed it necessary to follow King Arthur to the filfilment of his own destiny, which involved discovering the meaning of the collective history that he embodied. The disclosure of the hidden sins that had for a long time undermined the Arthurian world causes it to collapse. Although his sister, Morgan le Fay, has shown him the room on the walls of which Lancelot has painted scenes of his love affair with Guinevere, and in spite of increasingly insistent denunciations, for a long time Arthur refuses to believe that Lancelot is 'disgracing him with the queen'. But when the lovers are discovered 'in flagrant delicto', a savage passion explodes, shattering the oldest and strongest bonds. The king demands that the queen should be burnt at the stake, Lancelot rescues her, but kills one of Gawain's brothers in the skirmish. This in turn gives rise to an implacable hatred between the two former friends, who eventually kill each other in single combat in Gaul, the new theatre of war after Lancelot has returned the queen to Arthur. But it is the consequences of another longstanding and secret sin that complete the catastrophe – a sin committed by King Arthur himself. His nephew Mordred, to whom he had entrusted his kingdom and the queen before travelling to Gaul in pursuit of Lancelot, is in fact his son, born of his incestuous love for his sister, in the same way that Roland, according to the *Vie de Saint Gilles*, was the son of Charlemagne. Mordred rebels and besieges the Tower of London, where Guinevere has taken refuge. As in the works of Geoffrey and Wace, the final battle takes place on Salisbury Plain and leads to the deaths of all the Knights of the Round Table. Arthur kills his son, but is himself fatally wounded. He is carried off in a ship by Morgan le Fay, before the very eyes of his squire,

Girflet, the sole survivor of the battle, who has earlier followed Arthur's orders by throwing the King's sword into a lake, from which a hand emerged to receive it. Later, Arthur's tomb appears in Glastonbury, while the alignment of the megaliths at Stonehenge is seen as a monument to the battle of Salisbury. Thus, King Arthur meets a worthy end, which places him, for the first time, at the centre of the action of the narrative. The author of the *Mort le roi Artu* followed the same sequence of events as Geoffrey of Monmouth and Wace, but he replaced their simple political and military account with a description of the forces working inexorably to produce a gloomy personal tragedy: the blows dealt by fate; the passions of love, jealousy and revenge; the broken friendships; the irreconcilable duties; the impossible loyalties; the shameful secrets; and the tissue of sin.

This rise and fall from glory did not mark the end of King Arthur's literary destiny. As early as 1170–5, Béroul's poem linked him with the legend of Tristan, involving him in the episodes of 'The Flour on the Floor' and particularly 'The Vindication of Yseut'. Similarly, around 1226–30, Gerbert's continuation of *Perceval* describes Tristan taking refuge at Arthur's court, then returning to King Mark in disguise, accompanied by his friends, the Knights of the Round Table. A little later, the syncretism of the stories of Arthur and Tristan was taken much further by the prose work *Tristan*. Indeed, by the end of the Middle Ages, it was the driving force behind reformulations of these works that were compiled when new manuscripts were produced (e.g. the Michaud Gonnot manuscript; ms. Paris Bibl. Nat. fr. 112) and that subsequently became classics. At this time, the attraction of the world of Arthurian legend was based on a fascination with the past. For one thing, the age of King Arthur was considered to be quite ancient, since the chronology in the romances matched accounts given by early historians that situated it at the beginning of the sixth century. More importantly the Arthurian literary tradition had already lasted sufficiently long for the language and poetry used to express it to have had time to develop, with the result that the romances written in the twelfth century had begun to be difficult to read by the fifteenth. King Arthur had become merely the guarantor of threatened – and by now obsolete – knightly values that were justified by being traced back to the past. He himself was portrayed as elderly in certain romances that had passed on from his exploits to those of later generations – for example *Isaïe le Triste*, whose heroes are Tristan's son and grandson. At the same time, there was a proliferation of courtly festivals and tournaments based on Arthurian themes, which were in turn obligingly celebrated by literature. Thus, an interaction developed between literature and contemporary life, each claiming to be inspired by the past and to be reflected by the other. An example both of this exaggerated feeling for the past and of the complacent tendency merely to reflect contemporary knightly activities is provided by the romance *Perceforest*, which deals with events from before the time of Arthur. The loss of all awareness of the deeper meaning of the Arthurian legend is obvious in

Froissart's *Méliador* which, in the 1380s, revived the verse tradition of the Arthurian romance neglected for over a century. The 'quête' that King Arthur proposes to the Knights of the Round Table is nothing more than competition for suitors in the form of a championship based on points. The *Chevalier du Papeqau, a short fifteenth-century prose romance whose similarity to the thirteenth-century German romance Wiqalois* has often been remarked on, tells the story of an adventure that King Arthur himself had during his youth. But it restricts itself to tales of successes in combat and sport, the sole function of which is to pave the way for success in love – which, in turn, is limited to the warrior's short period of rest. The hero of both these romances could be anyone and the identification with King Arthur is merely an attempt to disguise a lack of real meaning with grandiose echoes of the past. The world of Arthurian legend was dying, along with the tales of chivalry.

KING ARTHUR IN EUROPEAN LITERATURE OF THE MIDDLE AGES

From the end of the twelfth century onwards, the Arthurian romances, like all works of French literature, were copied throughout the rest of Europe, and particularly in Germany. Thus Hartmann von Aue was the author both of an Erek (*c.* 1190) and several years later of an *Iwein*. Although these were adapted from the romances of Chrétien de Troyes, they were not lacking in originality and revealed the writer's interest in the problems of the chivalric code. Between 1200 and 1212, Wolfram von Eschenbach wrote his *Parzifal*, in which he acknowledged his debt to Chrétien de Troyes, but criticized him for not having adhered to historical fact, which he himself claimed to have reinstated by following the authentic version of the legend, by 'maître Kyot le Provençal'. The arguments provoked by this enigmatic passage have been widely aired. About the same time, a priest from Thurgau named Ulrich von Zatzikhoven wrote a *Lanzelet*, which he presented as a translation of a French book that he had received from Hugo de Morville, one of the hostages sent by Richard the Lionheart to Duke Leopold VI of Austria in 1194. *Lanzelet* gives an account of Lancelot's childhood that is similar in some respects to the prose *Lancelot*, but it is still a very different work from the French romance. Other German Arthurian romances written during the thirteenth century were *Wigalois*, by the Franconian Wirnt von Gravenberg (*c.* 1210), *Diu Kröne* by the Austrian Heinrich von dem Türlin, *Daniel vom blühenden Tal*, by Stricker (*c.* 1215) and *Wiqamur* (*c.* 1250). The list could be extended to include some of the Tristan romances, since the earliest, by Eilhart von Oberge, introduces the Arthurian theme, as does the very similar one by Béroul.

In Spain and Portugal, books I and III of Geoffrey of Monmouth's work were translated around 1260 in the *Estoria General* by King Alfonso X of Castille; while the *Joseph d'Arimathie* by Robert de Boron was translated into Portuguese in 1313, and a *Storia del San Graal* in Catalan dates from 1380.

The end of the Middle Ages witnessed the appearance of several translations of French Arthurian romances, in particular the ones contained in the *Lancelot-Graal*, as well as the prose *Tristan*. Finally, at the end of the fifteenth and the beginning of the sixteenth century, the new wave of Spanish tales of chivalry – *Amadis*, *Tirant* and *Palmerin* – were so successful that Don Quixote suffered as a result.

In Italy, the Modena sculptures referred to above attest to an early interest in Arthurian legend, while literature also brought the theme to prominence, inspiring two works written between 1272 and 1279: the compilation by Rusticiano of Pisa entitled *Il Milione* and the *Prophecies of Merlin*, which created a considerable stir. Dante too refers several times to *Lancelot* and the *Mort le roi Artu* in both the *Divine Comedy* and the *De Vulgari eloquentia*' while, more generally, Arthurian legend acted primarily as a source of literary allusions in Italian poetry as well as furnishing the subject matter for several fourteenth-century 'cantari'.

From the second half of the twelfth century onwards, the langue d'oc troubadours also frequently alluded to the Arthurian tradition. Indeed there is even one Arthurian romance in this language. This is the *Jaufre*, which probably dates from the thirteenth century rather than being the model for the *Conte du Graal* by Chrétien, as sometimes claimed. Among the Arthurian romances translated into Dutch are: *Joseph d'Arimathie* and *Merlin* by Robert de Boroni; the *Lancelot-Graal* and the rare verse romances; the *Conte du Graal* by Chrétien; and the *Vengeance*, *Raguidel* and *Fergus*. There are also some romances that appear originally to have been written in other languages but now are known only in Dutch: for example *De Ridder metter Mouwen*, *Walewein ende Keye* and *Torrez*. Two of these – *Moriaen* and *Walewein* – seem to be works of some originality.

Translations of Arthurian texts into Norse appeared from the beginning of the thirteenth century onwards. The earliest of these is the *Merlinusspa* (Merlin's Prophecy), a work by the Icelandic monk Gunnlaug Leifsson (d. 1218) based on book VII of the *Historia requm Britanniae* by Geoffrey of Monmouth. This was followed by a translation of the remainder of the *Historia*, summaries or free adaptations of Chrétien's *Yvain*, *Erec* and *Perceval*, a version of the *Mantel mautaillé* and translations of *Lanval* and *Chèvrefeuille* by Marie de France. On the fringes of Arthurian literature, there was also a condensed Norwegian version of the story of Tristan and a later Icelandic work on the subject by Thomas. This tendency to translate and adapt the Arthurian tales lasted until the beginning of the fourteenth century.

Excluding French literature, it was naturally English literature that was the richest in Arthurian legends. We have already mentioned the Celtic texts, as well as Layamon's *Brut*, which really marks the start of the literary tradition. No less than twenty-three romances in rhymed verse or prose are known from between the end of the thirteenth century and the sixteenth century. These range from *Arthur and Merlin* (1250–1300) to *Joseph of Arimathea* in prose and

The Boy and the Mantle (sixteenth century), by way of: *Sir Tristram* (*c.* 1300); *Libeaus Desconus*, *Sir Perceval of Galles*, *Sir Launfall* (all three before 1340); the *Morthe Arthur* in verse (*c.* 1400); *The Carl of Carlisle* (*c.* 1400); the *Holy Grail* and the *Merlin* by Lovelich (*c.* 1430); *The Wedding of Sir Gawain* (*c.* 1450); *Lancelot of the Laik* (1482–1500); *King Arthur's Death* (*c.* 1500); etc. – not to mention Chaucer's tale of *The Wife of Bath* (1392–4). The majority of the texts were inspired by – indeed, translated from – French romances. However, between 1200 and 1400, the north and north-west of England also produced some alliterative, unrhymed romances. These include a *Joseph of Arimathea*, of which a fragment of 709 lines has survived, and a *Morte Arthure*, but the real masterpiece is a short romance called *Sir Gawain and the Green Knight* (between 1360 and 1400).

Finally, mention must of course be made of the works of Sir Thomas Malory, a rebel knight who was born early in the fifteenth century and died on 14 March 1471 after many convictions and periods in prison between 1443 and 1460. Indeed, it was apparently whilst in prison that he wrote *Le Morte Darthur*, a huge compilation based on both French and English romances. He drew his inspiration for *The Tale of King Arthur and the Emperor Lucius* primarily from the English alliterative work *Morte Arthure* and then based *The Tale of King Arthur* on the French *Suite du Merlin*, and *The Noble Tale of Sir Lancelot of the Lake* on the original *Lancelot*. His source for *The Book of Gareth* is unknown, but he used the prose *Tristan* as his inspiration for *Sir Tristram de Lyones*, before returning to the Arthurian cycle, where *La Quête du Graal* and the *Mort le roi Artu* provided the subject matter for *The Tale of the Sankgreal*, *The Book of Sir Lancelot and Queen Guinevere* and *The Tale of the Death of King Arthur*. The *Morte Darthur* is a work of the highest order, which is far superior to the French romances of the end of the Middle Ages. It has continued to enjoy great popularity right up to the present day, and probably largely accounts for the survival of the Arthurian tradition in the Anglo-Saxon world.

THE RETURN OF KING ARTHUR: CONCLUSION

Interest in King Arthur naturally declined when the values of the Middle Ages fell into disrepute during the Classical period, although certain romances have always continued to be read. Moreover, his rediscovery at the end of the eighteenth century, and during the Romantic period, seems to have occurred later than that of the epic. When Arthurian legend did eventually become fashionable once more, this was a result of two events: first, the great upsurge of Romance research during the 1860s and 70s; and secondly, the composition of Wagner's *Parzifal*, which is said to have been inspired by Wolfram. At the time, the Symbolists were also attracted by the Breton adventures, which were shrouded in mystery and readily incorporated into fairy tales. The tales were soon subsumed into children's literature, as illustrated in the inter-war period by the delightful *Quand les fées vivaient en France* by Yvonne Ostroga with a preface by Paul Bourget (1923). There is no need to re-emphasize the importance of Arthurian themes, and especially of the figure of Merlin, in the work of Apollinaire. But Lancelot and Guinevere never acquired a status to rival Tristan and Isolde, in spite of several poems by Aragon, in particular *Les Yeux d'Elsa*, that reveal a certain knowledge of the Breton romances. Once again, the world of Arthurian legend was a more familiar theme in English literature than in literature in other languages; for example, only an Anglo-Saxon readership could appreciate *A Connecticut Yankee at King Arthur's Court* by Mark Twain (1889). Whilst English and American Arthurian literature was prolific during the first half of the twentieth century, the theme has not been neglected in France in recent years. Recent French works on Arthurian themes range from the *Roi Pêcheur* by Julien Gracq, based on German sources, to the Graal Théâtre, by Jacques Roubaud and Florence Delay, based on the *Lancelot-Graal* cycle, while the allusive and secretive poetry of Yves Bonnefoy, is also scattered with Arthurian references. Many recent films too have dealt with Arthurian themes, and have done so more ambigiously than, for example, *The Knights of the Round Table* by Richard Thorpe (1955). They include *Lancelot* by Robert Bresson (1974), *Perceval le Gallois* by Eric Rohmer (1978), *Excalibur* by John Boorman (1981), and even – in a completely different vein – Monty Python's *Holy Grail* (1975).

In the final analysis, few figures have a greater right to take their place among the great myths of literature than King Arthur. He is a myth because he himself, and the stories that have grown up around him, have been situated in the distant past and used to explain the origins of the chivalric order and its values, and so justify its existence. The 'marvels' that marked his reign were ultimately made to centre around the mysteries of the Grail, which became the ultimate Christian revelation, to the benefit and greater glory of chivalry. But King Arthur is not a mythological figure as such, he is barely an historical figure, and his folkloric origins are uncertain. In fact, he is almost entirely a figment of the literary imagination.

Michel Zink

The Aryan Myth

The Aryan myth first appeared in Europe in the course of the nineteenth century when many people in Germany, France and, to a lesser extent, Britain saw it as a myth about origins that could be advantageously substituted for the biblical myths of Adam and Noah, or superimposed on them, as well as on secondary myths that were more specifically related to particular nations. The course of events suggest that a civilization in the throes of profound structural change was looking to the Aryan myth for a more satisfactory explanation of its roots and ultimate direction.

At this period, Christian mythology had been weakened considerably by the pressures created by European expansion throughout the world, by scientific advances and by socio-economic change . During the period between the discovery of the Americas and the growth of European colonialism, the teaching in the myth of Adam that all men are brothers descended from a common ancestor and equal before God had been increasingly undermined by the sense of racial superiority felt by the victorious white man. The conquerors were reluctant to see the peoples that they were subjugating as in any way kindred to them, as this would have removed all moral justification for their activities. From the eighteenth century on, the emerging discipline of anthropology seldom proved able to dissociate scientific research from racial prejudice. For all their relative moderation, Blumenbach, the founder of physcial anthropology , and Christophe Meiners, sometimes regarded as the pioneer of social anthropology , cannot help extolling the virtues of white race; while some other writers put the black man at the bottom of a tacitly accepted scale, close to animals. However, it was linguistics that eventually crystallized this vague, collective image of a superior race that was the sole custodian of Civilization. When Jones, writing in 1788 , underlined the relationship between Latin and Greek and Sanskrit – a thesis later confirmed and extended to the Germanic languages by Franz Bopp – and when Anquetil du Peyron borrowed the term Aryans from Herodotus to describe a particular linguistic group, both contributed to the development of a theory endowing the Europeans with new origins, for the assumption was soon made that the linguistic relationship implied a racial one. Friedrich Schlegel was the first to describe the inexorable westward advance of the barbarian hordes, and before long emphasis was being placed on their role in transforming the foreign tradition of Judaism into the noblest expression of religious faith: Christianity. The idea of Providence was abandoned, and race became one of the driving forces of history . At the same time, the Europeans experienced the negative consequence of the intellectual achievements and geographical conquests of which they were so proud. The old socio-political structures were obsolete: the Revolution in France deprived the country of a monarch who ruled by Divine Right; while Germany's attempts to achieve political unity were based on nationalistic zeal that had very little to do with the Christianity of the Holy Roman Empire. The result was gradual emergence of an era in which the Course of History tended to supplant the Christian God in providing a final explanation for human existence.

In combination, these factors provided the Aryan myth with most of its strength and distinctive characteristics. Writers such as T. Arnold and A. R. Wallace in England, F. Schlegel, Schelling and Carus, in Germany, and Gobineau in France, as well as the musician Richard Wagner and his son-in-law H. S. Chamberlain , again in Germany, made it the focus of their visions of the world. But the influence of the myth is also apparent, to varying degrees, in the thinking of many of the other luminaries of the period, including Renan, Schopenhauer, Marx, Nietzsche and Darwin.

In its most developed form, it is based on a mystical belief that gives rise to a particular view of man and of his historic destiny, and that defines a moral code and a vision of Utopia. The white race has been specially chosen by a most unorthodox version of the Christian deity, and it alone is capable of fully developing the essence of humanity imprinted in its ethnic nature, within the context of History. Unlike the Christian myth, the Aryan myth generally does not encourage a feeling of overwhelming humility in the face of God. As a typical German idealist, Schelling identified Man as the Soul of the world; while, for Carl Gustav Carus, he represented the perfect material expression of the Idea. Meanwhile, both Gobineau, in his *Essai sur l'Inégalité des Races humaines*, and Richard Wagner made reference to the old Germanic pantheon. Its gods were stirred by very human passions and were constantly threatened by ambitious heroes anxious to achieve divine status. Thus the mystical elements in the Aryan philosophy hark back to a pre-Christian form of religion in which the concepts of Nature, humanity and divinity were extremely confused. Nonetheless, the Aryan people were seen as being uniquely endowed with spirituality. In contrast to coloured people, who were naturally superstitious, amoral and degenerate, they had an innate moral sense, a resolute will and weak sensual urges that they could easily control. Indeed, some writers, including Gobineau and G. Klemmy , turned to the symbolism of masculine and feminine to express these differences. The Aryan was both the quintessence of humanity and the revealer of the Western intellectual tradition. Originally this paragon of humankind had made its home in the harsh isolation of the high plateaux of Asia, where it had lived to perfect social conventions. However, in the course of time, it had spread across the world bringing Civilization in its train. All great societies, from prehistoric Assyria to the modern United States of America, and including Egypt and China, were the handiwork of this glorious race, which was inherently capable of the highest forms of culture and social organization, but constantly under threat from cross-breeding.

In addition to defining the orgins of the Aryan race, the myth also expressed the concept of an End to History, which was always conceived as the resolution of a racial conflict. 'Optimists' saw the domination of the world by the white race as inevitable and as representing the apotheosis of mankind's progress. Thus, Jones, Wallace and Schelling regarded the coloured races as an instrument or primary matter of Destiny whose fate it was eventually to disappear from History. However, Courtet de l'Isle, a follower of Saint-Simon and the probable – though unacknowledged – source of Gobineau's ideas, saw the future as a choice between two alternatives: either cross-breeding would prevail bringing equality and disorder in its wake, or the white race would impose order and thereby restrict freedom. For Gobineau, it was cross-breeding that was inevitable. This would foster increasing decadence and lead ultimately to the end of the world: there would be a return to nothingness, sincc Direction would disappear alongside racial purity.

The conceptualization of the vague feeling of superiority current in European society at a time when its own spiritual tradition was uncertain, gave rise to a disastrous train of thought. When carried through to their final logical conclusion these ideas proved capable of unleashing demonic forces. In combination with the Darwinian theory of a 'struggle for existence', which appeared at about the same period, the myth led almost inevitably to political experiments in eugenics and eventually to genocide. For Hitlerism represented a monstrous and tragic attempt to mould History into conformity with its message.

Though psychoanalysis and socio-psychoanalysis evidently can never justify the myth, they can at least attempt to explain it. Whether the analysis is applied to Gobineau's *Essai sur l'inégalité des races humaines* , the nineteenth-century mania for things Indian , or, indeed, to Nazism , the results are strangely similar. From the nineteenth century onwards, the individual and collective subconscious seems to have replaced the traditional parental model of the world, defining the values governing human activity, morality and reason, the domination of natural forces and the legitimacy of power, with a (psychically) more archaic tutelary image. Far from completely contradicting the traditional maternal image (involving passivity, desire and pleasure, irrationality, acceptance of nature, and despotism), this image adopted certain aspects of it. Thus, while championing moral law, the Aryan also presented himself as uniquely endowed with peremptory instincts that could justify his every act. The result was a fascination for the earliest times when the white race had all its pristine strength and beauty, and an eager striving to recapture them. This, in turn, led to a fear of anything out of the ordinary, and a childish megalomania that authorized the most extreme violence and encouraged a totalitarian mentality. The psychological analysis just attempted undoubtedly leads to a better understanding of a myth that came into being as a result of a crisis in Western, Christian civilization and that had unparalleled apocalyptic consequences.

Sylvie André

Atlantis

The myth of Atlantis is referred to at some length in the works of Plato, who ascribes the details of the story to an ancient tradition brought back from Egypt by the Greek statesman Solon about 600 BC. No one has ever found any traces of a poem on the subject by Solon or of the annals to which his informant the Egyptian priest apparently alluded. Thus the tale must belong exclusively to the oral tradition, or simply have been invented by Plato himself. Almost all commentators subscribe to the latter view, according to which Plato's explanation that Solon told the story to an ancestor of Critias, whom he then invited to recount it, is simply intended to lend the tale some authenticity.

The myth is recounted in fragmented form in two distinct passages; it constitutes the preamble to the *Timaeus* and takes up the whole of the unfinished *Critias*. The first text outlines the historical events involved: the invasion of the Mediterranean basin by the armies of Atlantis; the Athenians' victory over them; and the catclysm that buried the island beneath the sea off the Pillars of Hercules. The narrator explains that his compatriots have always been ignorant of this momentous event and recalls the tradition in Egypt relating to the cyclical return of floods. He maintans that, in Greece at least, these floods spare only the illiterate, who are incapable of recording memorable events. The second fragmentary passage seems to belong to a detailed development of the heroic story but, because it is unfinished, it is limited to the description of the two enemy powers. Nonetheless, it is this section that has attracted greater attention over the centuries, because of its length and because it provides a great deal of information about the vanished civilization.

The impression of great antiquity produced by this memory embedded in the human consciousness is heightened by the fact that the whole myth is presented in an inverted chronological setting. The conversation with which *Timaeus* opens takes place in Plato's own time, around the fourth century BC, but then the reader is taken back through the centuries to the dim prehistoric period, nine thousand years before Solon's journey, when the Greeks are said to have defeated the forces of Atlantis. The *Critias* harks back to an even more distant past – 'in illo tempore' to use Mircea Eliade's words – the time when the gods shared out the world among themselves and founded the two cities. This strange journey back into the mists of time is mirrored by a change in the treatment of the narrative. The tale of the war, which is hardly started in the first dialogue, becomes a double tableau in the second, where the topography and institutions of the two nations are used to contrast the political perfection of the one with the megalomania of the other. The outline of an epic is replaced by an unfinished utopia.

Significantly, the ancient Athens portrayed in the *Timaeus* and *Critias* recalls the organization of the ideal city described in *The Republic*. In it we find the same separation of the social classes, the same communal ownership of property and sharing of women and children and the same importance attached to the guardians of the state. The inhabitants have been educated by their divine protectors, Hephaestus and Athena, and are self-sufficient, disdaining gold and trade. They are farmers or warriors and are all 'autochtonous' – in other words, born on their own land and thus concerned with the wise use and protection of Mother Earth. In stark contrast to the austerity of Attica, there is the opulence of Atlantis, an enormous island split into ten kingdoms, each further sub-divided into thousands of districts. This domain has been allotted to Poseidon and is both a military state and a land of merchants, with several ports and a huge networks of canals. Its natural products, described in a truly hyperbolic style, are as limitless as its countryside is varied and its armed forces are numerous. The whole island is dominated by a splendid capital, and above all by Poseidon's sanctuary, the walls and statues of which are covered in ivory and gold and that strange substance orichalcum, with its fiery lights.

The author starts by emphasizing the moral grandeur of the land-based republic as opposed to the entirely material grandeur of the maritime empire. Thus unity, which is a philosophical and political principle dear to Plato, is represented here by the single rampart surrounding the Athenian Acropolis, the single spring that irrigates the country and the entirely divine origins of the Greeks. By contrast, the structure of Atlantis consists of a multiplicity or patchwork of different elements: canal systems alternate with earthworks, there are two springs, and the people are of mixed stock, since they trace their ancestry back to the union of a god with the mortal Clito. Every detail stresses heterogeneity, right down to the uneven interval separating the meetings between the kings who, 'every fifth year, and then alternately every sixth year' mutually splash each other with the blood of a bull to seal a non-agression pact (*Critias* 119d). Plato seems to be saying that Atlantis sank because its inhabitants harboured aspirations towards 'dissimilarity', an abstract concept that the author had already used in the *Politicus*, (273d) to describe the return of humankind to a state of chaos.

All in all, this account of the total destruction of a warlike nation is simply a more dramatic version of another myth, that of the ideal City. Plato was merely trying to make his message more persuasive by claiming that it has an historical basis and that his utopian model had been derived from the little-known past of his Athenian ancestors. Indeed, most commentators suggest that the heroic episode in the *Timaeus* may be based on the Persian wars, in which the Greek armies triumphed over a barbarian foe. However, when the two dialogues were written, the glorious era was well and truly over and the reforming author was a bitter and powerless witness to the moral, political and economic collapse of his country. The myth's manichaean ambiguity gives it an ironic edge: Plato flatters his fellow citizens while simultaneously humiliating them; by praising the Athenians of yesteryear he shows his contemporaries that they themselves are no different from the inhabitants of the sunken island. The comparison is expressed particularly effectively in a fine metaphorical passage in which the narrator contrasts the flourishing Attica of the past, covered by alluvial soil, with the peninsula of his own day, so ravaged and shattered by floods that it resembled the 'skeleton of a sick man, all the fat and soft earth having wasted away' (*Critias* 111b). The subtle device of combining the story of the fate of Atlantis with an idealized vision of Greece, is linked, paradoxically, with a depiction of the fallen civilization that is in some ways 'utopian'. There is no doubt that Plato's audience was seduced by the image of this naturally abundant island, fully irrigated and wisely governed for as long as Atlas, the first king, and his descendents knew how to manage their riches without being dominated by them. That Atlantis is a counter-utopia is clear from the way in which it contrasts with Athens, from its defeat and from its disappearance; but, in a supreme paradox, the barbarian paradise of the *Critias* is set in the Golden Age.

Its ambiguities give Plato's account its literary richness. The author pretends to be exalting the earliest era of human existence, since this period symbolizes primitive human happiness, but at the same time he is afraid of it, because it also represents regression and the forgetting of 'science that is hoary with age' (Timaeus 22b). Plato was deeply concerned with this theme, particularly at the end of his life, when he wrote the two dialogues and book III of the *Laws*. That is why he put his faith in the persuasive qualities of a myth, which allowed him to integrate a moral discourse on the dangers of imperialism into a dramatic vision of the succesive death and rebirths of the universe. Thus the myth's undoubted success is based on a series of paradoxes that are bound up with the didactic aims of the philosopher, but also with the literary genre of the Platonic myth itself. Despite its intensely serious aims, the device recalls works of fiction because it plays tricks with truth and falsehood and mixes irony with a tone of edification. Since it is 'passing strange' but 'wholly true' (*Timaeus* 20d), the story of Atlantis is also convincing, moving and amusing. The date of the events is unbelievable, the disappearance of all traces of the civilizations is suspect and the dimensions and wonders of the island are exorbitant. And yet how can the word of an Egyptian priest and his mouthpiece Solon be doubted? Nor is their testimony totally incredible, for realistic features are mingled with the more obscure aspects of the myth to lend them authenticity. The details most often invoked to give substance to the myth include the port complex of Piraeus and the memory of the Cretan thalassocracy. Meanwhile, the mythical Atlantis itself is portrayed as being situated on the boundary between the utopian islands (Homer's Scheria) and real countries (Herodotus's Orient).

This strange tale provided later generations with both a scientific enigma and an imaginary theme. Because its details were not wholly unbelievable, it prompted geographers and scholars to search for the vanished continent; while the unfinished story itself offered a framework rich in poetic symbols and epic or romantic deeds. From the earliest times until the present day, the literary myth has straddled the line between science and fiction, two domains that are not contradictory or in competition, but that are complementary and sometimes even confused. The literary representations of Atlantis result from the impossibility of identifying the actual island, as though the constant questioning of the 'legend' in the name of 'truth' can give rise only to fictional reconstructions and images. The latter have generally borne little resemblance to the Platonic vision. Scientists and writers have mainly presented an idealized view of Atlantis, presumably because the sheer fact that it cannot be found makes it seem all the more marvellous. Though the *Critias* actually describes the decadence of a great empire, it has left behind the confused memory of an ancient and superior civilization. This strange inversion of the original emphasis in the Platonic account dates to the era of the discovery of America, for this event was a crucial landmark in the process by which Atlantis came to stimulate the imaginations of enlightened eighteenth-century reformers, certain poets and, above all, countless nineteenth-century and twentieth-century novelists.

The story of the sunken island actually aroused little interest in Antiquity. Strabo and Pliny the Elder mention it when describing the earth and its geological changes, but they appear sceptical of its veracity. Those who took it more seriously used it to prove a point. They included Tertullian, in his Christian *Apologeticus*, and the neo-Platonic philosphers – notably Proclus, who published a voluminous commentary on the *Timaeus* in the fifth century AD.

When scientific and literary works on the subject did start slowly to emerge this was as a result of advances in scientific knowledge and of polemics written about Plato's two texts. The latter were first republished in Italy in the fifteenth century, under the influence of the humanist Marsilio Ficino, and then in France, where the first translation of the *Timaeus* by Loys le Roy appeared in 1551. However, true breakthrough occurred when the chroniclers discovered a real *terra incognita* in the form of America. Thus, in *La Historia general de las Indias occidentales*, published in 1552, Lopez de Gomara suggested that Christopher Columbus might have been guided by the passage in which Plato says that beyond the island of Atlantis lies 'the continent over against them which encompasses that veritable ocean' (*Timaeus* 25a). Gamboa too maintained that America was the vast remains of a sunken continent. However, in

1580, Montaigne, in his famous chapter on cannibals (*Essays* 1. 31), denied that the fable had any truth in it at all.

Whatever the validity of any comparisons, the link established between Atlantis and the New World had two consequences. First, it raised once again the general issue of how much truth was preserved in legends, and secondly, it conferred undisputed prestige on the engulfed island. The commentators generally regarded it as a 'fortunate island', like the other paradisiac lands that ancient writers and the cosmographers of the Middle Ages had situated in the mysterious western sea. From this point on the Platonic myth seems to have been revealed in all its richness as an inexhaustible source of material for scientists as much as for writers.

An Italian doctor, Girolamo Fracastoro, heralded the era of its literary exploitation with a strange poem entitled *Syphilis sive morbus gallicus*. In the exotic setting of Haiti, the survivors of the catastrophe of Atlantis tell the Spanish conquerors how they were punished for failing to honour their gods by having their land engulfed and by being afflicted with the appalling disease syphilis. Here, the Greek literary tradition is used to embellish a glorious description of the Columbian expedition. However, the main aim of this medical work is to reveal that the disease in question can be healed by an American tree, the gaiac. It was nearly a century later that the legend first became the subject of a true work of fiction: Francis Bacon's *New Atlantis*, a utopia written in 1621, but published in 1627, after the Lord Chancellor's death. Revised and adapted by Bacon, the ancient tale became a story of the wars waged by the New World (the 'Great Atlantis') against the little island of Bensalem (the 'New Atlantis'). The framework of the legend allowed him to contrast the barbarian culture of the Indians with an ideal state governed by a community of learned men, who founded a magnificent laboratory for experimental science. Emphasis is laid on the sacred mission of these 'seekers of light', who were initiated by the Holy Apostles and are now working on the systematic classification of the various branches of knowledge. From a philosophical point of view, the work prefigures the thinking of the eighteenth-century encyclopaedists. However, it is important to stress that although its author transforms the original myth to suit his purpose, he still respects its didactic function and utopian tone.

The period from the sixteenth to the eighteenth centuries was, in fact, an era of transition. The myth did not inspire many literary works at this time, but following the impetus given to it by Bacon, it was enriched with new associations by the burgeoning hypotheses concerning the location of the catastrophe. The site of Atlantis moved from the Azores and Canaries, which most experts agreed were its remains, to the Svalbard, where Jean-Sylvian Bailly located it in a work addressed to Voltaire called *Lettres sur l'Atlantide de Platon* (1779). The many sites proposed reflected entirely subjective interpretations of the myth. Following those commentators who identified the mythical country with Palestine, Friedrich C. Baër linked the fate of its vanished people to the history of the Hebrews in his critical and historical essay on the 'Atlantics' published in 1762. Other scholars proffered nationalistic interpretations of the myth, so that the island's total disappearance seemed to entitle anyone anywhere to claim it as a lost motherland. In 1674 the Swede Olaüs Rudbeck drew on the mythology of the *Edda* to describe a Scandinavian Atlantis in his *Atlantica;* while the Italian Giovanni R. Carli made Janus one of the first rulers of the legendary empire in his *Lettere americane*, published between 1784 and 1794.

These works exploited the old source for ideological ends. As a consequence, their authors had to rewrite the original tale, so that they were effectively reinventing Atlantis rather than examining its historical basis. This makes them of considerable interest in the context of the development of the literary myth, since they presented a vision of the vanished civilization that was invariably positive. In their eyes, it embodied the Golden Age, the pristine world that constituted the original and absolute source of all knowledge and traditions. Indeed, the polemics on Atlantis reflect the major philosophical concerns of seventeenth-century and eighteenth-century Europe. In their cult of progress, the thinkers of the time were fascinated by the vision of an enlightened race that had escaped from natural disasters and wars and taught the other peoples of the world their arts, skills and beliefs. Voltaire accorded this privileged status to the Hindus, but, after Bacon, many other authorities referred to the mentors of humankind as 'Atlanters'. By reinventing the old fable to serve their ends, they prepared the way for countless literary works of later periods.

The nineteenth century formed an important stage in the development of the literary myth. The Greek tradition, which until then had been confined to European countries, spread to America, where it proved very attractive. As a result, works on the subject proliferated and became more diversified, particularly when the intensification of archaeological research shed new light on the mysterious Atlantis itself. The scientist Kurt Benesch rightly stresses that the many modern challenges to Plato's account arise from advances in knowledge, the main effect of which is a constant 'pushing back of the time of reference' (Benesch 1979: 11). The discovery of the sites at Sumer, Troy and Knossos probably played a decisive part in this process while, even at the end of the twentieth century, there is an increasingly strong belief that we still have not discovered all the secrets of the ancient times.

As a consequence, without losing sight of the theme of a highly advanced civilization, authors have tended to adapt the myth to reflect their own aesthetic preoccupations, the ideologies of the times or contemporary political events. Some have emphasized its poetic elements, choosing to see the engulfed island as a symbolic landscape rather than a scientific enigma. Many more have exploited the potential of the unfinished *Critias* as the subject for a novel by rewriting the story of the war and the cataclysm.

Before novelists began to represent it as a real continent, Atlantis long remained an entirely imaginary, indeed fantastical, place. For example, in E. T. A. Hoffmann's *Der Goldene Topf*, written in 1814, it is a magical land inhabited by supernatural creatures who tear the student Anselm away from everyday reality and initiate him into a higher life. Transfigured by his union with Serpentina, he acquires the true knowledge that allows the Poet to pierce Nature's mysteries. As in the work of Novalis, who briefly described it in *Heinrich von Ofterdingen* in 1802, the Atlantis of *Der Goldene Topt* is a super-terrestrial sphere, a kind of original Paradise to which only art can reveal the path.

This symbolic interpretaion seldom inspired actual poets either in the Romantic period or later. When they did exploit Plato's myth they were sensitive to the unfinished tale's principal motif: heroic action. The result is a few epics based on the tale , such as Népomucène Lemercier's *L'Atlantide*, published in 1812, and *La Atlantida* by Jacinto Verdaguer, published in Barcelona in 1878. Lemercier wanted to be the Hesiod of a 'Newtonian theory', and, to this end, he invented a new Olympus peopled with allegorical forces, signifying the superiority of a world governed by the laws of physics over the blind universe of superstition. The dogmatic tones of this piece contrast with the flamboyant images use by Verdaguer to exalt the renaissance of Catalan nationalism. While he alters the story of the cataclysm and introduces Hercules and the Hesperides, the author's chief concern is to describe the wonders of the land that saw Christopher Columbus leave for a new world. His poem is not without a lyrical beauty, and Manuel de Falla recalled it in his scenic cantata *Atlantida* (1928–46).

These works are highly significant in literary terms, but they do not represent the sort of writing that made the myth popular, no doubt because they offer too abstract an image of the vanished continent. In 1870, Jules Verne lent some authenticity to the story of Atlantis when he made the heroes of *Twenty Thousand Leagues Under the Sea* discover its remains. But this, like other passages in the *Voyages extraordinaires*, is merely an allusion intended for the general edification of his young readers. So it was only when adventure stories and stories about the future came into vogue that the sunken island began to be exploited in novels, both as a setting and as a subject in its own right.

The imaginary quest for Atlantis takes many forms. Among the most memorable and successful works on the subject was Pierre Benoit's novel *Atlantide*, which was published in 1920 and made into afilm in 1932 by G. W. Pabst. Set in the context of the colonial policy of the time, this story of love and death brings French officers in the Sahara into conflict with Antinea, the sole descendant of Neptune. Seen as the continuation of the *Critias*, the work has a strange but not extravagant tone, for the author remains close to his Platonic source, which he illuminates using the theories of Etienne Felix Berlioux (*Les Atlantes, Histoire d'Atlantis et de l'Atlas primitif*, 1883). Antinea is cruel, as the tyrant Nod was later to be in Georges Bordonove's historical novel *Les Atlantes* (1965): whereas *Les Portes de bronze* by Jean Gattefossé (1946) and Noël Roger's *Le Soleil enseveli* (1928) describe a civilization that is both materially and spiritually superior to that of the modern West.

While French authors have adapted the story of Atlantis in various ways and some have revived the emphasis on its decadence, most others have idealized the island. In any case the writers of popular literature have sought not so much to reproduce the *Timaeus* and *Critias* as to illustrate the pseudo-scientific views of commentators on the dialogues. The American Ignatius Donnelly played an important part in popularizing this approach, with his *Atlantis, the Antediluvian World* which offered the reading public of 1882 the image of an amazing intercontinental bridge forming the cradle of all races and cultures. Also relevant is the influence exerted by the theosophists, who integrated Plato's myth into their vast cosmologies, as illustrated by the long *Story of Atlantis*, written in 1896 by W. Scott Elliott. Obviously it was also an interest in the esoteric that led certain novelists to describe another forgotten world that was not lost but was only accessible by means of telepathy. Some of them combined the idea of the reincarnation of the Atlanters with motifs and structures favoured by writers of science fiction, as Alexei Tolstoy did in 1922 when he depicted an Atlantis situated on Mars (Aélita). The occult approach to the myth has enjoyed most success in the Anglo-saxon countries, as illustrated by the tales of Stanton A. Coblentz (*The Sunken World*, 1928) and Arthur Conon Doyle (*The Maracot Deep*, 1929), which are only two examples among many.

So with a few exceptions, most modern works have tended to treat Atlantis as a utopia. From the undersea expedition invented by André Laurie in 1895 (*Atlantis*) to recent interplanetary adventures, writers have produced ever increasing numbers of variations on a similar theme: the repeated migrations of a people that no cataclysm has been able to destroy. The salvation of the illiterate, mentioned by Plato (*Timaeus* 22d), has been replaced in more recent works by the survival of the Wise.

What elements survive from the first 'fiction' about Atlantis? Not much, it would seem, since historical reconstructions of the lost empire have seldom attracted poets or novelists. True, the original tale actually lends itself to all sorts of manipulation, partly because it is unfinished and because of its ambiguities, but also because of Plato's exhortation that although it is a legend, it should still be believed. In addition, while modern writers have replaced Plato's account of the fall of the ancient civilization with descriptions of its salvation, like Plato himself, they have emphasized the idea that knowledge of the past sheds light on the present.

Because most of the novels on the subject were written between the carnage of 1914 and the Cold War period, they mainly have a pacifist message. In them, though Atlantis is all-powerful, it is a fragile utopia, constantly threatened by wars and natural disasters. In this sense, it is both the reflection and the inverted image of the West. On the one hand, the fictional representation of the disasters is a metaphor for the violence of the West itself and for anxiety about the danger represented by, for example, its nuclear weapons. On the other hand, unlike our self-destructive societies, Atlantis survives. This makes it a symbol and model for the contemporary world just as in the works of Plato and Bacon a vision of the ideal city of the past was intended to guide future humanity.

The idea of the survival of this mythical society has inspired settings, characters and plots that give the twentieth century novels on the subject a sometimes unexpected tone. While many have not been noticed by the critics, some have generated substantial interest, particularly Gerhart Hauptmann's *Atlantis*, published in Berlin in 1912. In it we find a sick and disillusioned doctor for whom the memory of the vanished continent becomes an obsession when he miraculously escapes a shipwreck. As this is an initiatory quest ultimately leading to rebirth into 'real life', the setting of the disaster can be compared to an inner landscape, of the type found in the work of Hoffmann or Novalis, a realm of dreams and the imagination. However, Atlantis also symbolizes the moral decline of a hero and, through it, the malaise of a generation that is questioning slavish materialism. This particular work provides a good example of the various ways in which authors have sought to evoke images of an original world populated by superior ancestors as if, by doing so, they could regenerate our own threatened universe.

The story of Atlantis is 'passing strange', as the Egyptian priest commented to Solon, but it should not be forgotten because memory and writing protect societies against regression. To retain their exemplary function, myths must be passed on; and the literary adaptations of the story of Atlantis strangely mimic the process of repetition, since they all rely on a device used by Plato himself, that of the indirect narrative. Unlike Solon, who never wrote anything from memory (*Timaeus* 21e), novelists transcribe accounts passed down from the mists of time. They translate clay tablets, publish ships' logs and describe hallucinations. The form of the literary myth is in harmony with its fundamental motif: it is an embedded story, a *mise en abyme*. In *L'Eternel Adam*, published posthumously in 1910, Jules Verne dramatizes this kind of structure. The plot concerns a scientist of the future who decodes a very old document in which the last Atlanter describes the decline of his own civilization just before he dies. Despite their infinite variations, the successors of the *Critias* all constitute a similar message from beyond the grave, a message that convinced Verne's narrator of 'the eternal re-beginning of things'. As a paradoxical utopia, Atlantis exercises a particular fascination because it evokes both original chaos and the Golden Age. From the era of Plato to the twentieth century, the myth has taken on many different meanings. Although in Bacon's time it was used to express faith in progress, later on it attracted much darker interpretations:

the romantic nostalgia for a lost paradise was supplanted by the collective fear of universal destruction.

Chantal Foucrier

Black Tezcatlipoca, Sower of Discord

In awarding the 1967 Nobel Prize for Literature to the Guatemalan Miguel Angel Asturias, the Swedish Academy followed its tradition by crowning the whole of a writer's work, which in this case was varied and embraced almost all genres: novels, short stories, plays, poetry and countless journalistic articles on the most diverse subjects. Probably best known to the jury, however, was Asturias' first novel, *The President.* Although this is a deeply American novel, and we shall see why, it was paradoxically written in Paris, between 1923 and 1930. Perhaps not enough attention has been paid to Asturias' original plan to write a novel entitled *Tohil.* It would seem that the only vestige of this first intention is a short sequence in chapter 37, which is called 'Tohil's Dance', which a conventional reading would judge artificial and as structurally 'inexplicable' to the reader as the vision is 'inexplicable' to Angel Face, who is its beneficiary in this sequence. Its inclusion inevitably seems artificial since it refers to the mythical universe of *Popol-Vuh* in which *Legends of Guatemala,* for example, is bathed, but from which the context of social and political criticism of *The President* seems to distance itself. And yet:

> There is the novel, literarily speaking, there is political criticism, but underneath all that there is, there lives, in the shape of a President of the Latin-American republic, a conception of ancestral, magical force, and only of our time in appearance ... Our political literature should be studied. This study would embrace the myths that predate the Spanish conquest, the myths of the pre-Columbian peoples ... It would be interesting, in the chapter concerned with the political analysis of the myths of the pre-Columbian age, to show that at that time there were already two very precise forces in the art of manipulating peoples and individuals. That of the bloody Aztec god Huitzilopochtli, or 'Warrior who points his arrow towards the south' (Tohil to the Maya-Quechuas), who demanded human sacrifices ... and that, represented by Quetzalcoatl or Kukuclan to the Mayas, who rejected them ... I opened up this perspective in my novel which, until now, has always been studied from the literary and political points of view, but which should also be studied in relation to this mythical vision or cosmovision.
>
> (Asturias, 1972)

To sum up, what Asturias is asking us to understand is that between the first title, *Tohil,* and the definitive title, *The President,* one could and should write an equals sign, for the bloody president is merely the novel's incarnation of the 'ancestral forces' which ruled the American world through religion before the Spanish conquest. Thus Angel Face's vision appears during a stormy and difficult interview with the President, as though on the fictional level the fantasized ritual sacrifice was the projection of the tyrant's dark plans and, more generally, the metaphor for the events (political murders, torture, imprisonment and all kinds of vexations) created in the narrative to illustrate the political programme of Tohil/the President: 'On men who are hunters of men I shall build by government'.

Tohil is still present as a myth. In the novel, Asurias calls him 'Giver of Fire', following the traditions of the *Popol-Vuh*, according to which the tribes accept the human sacrifices required by the god in exchange for the return of fire which they have lost. Asturias makes Tohil the Maya equivalent of the Aztec god Huitzilopochtli, the tribal god of the ancient Mexicans, a warrior god symbolizing the rising sun and the expansionist dynamism of the Aztec nation. His cult certainly required 'the flowery war', a periodic ritual war whose aim was to capture victims to sacrifice to the god. But his rivalry with the peaceful Quetzalcoatl was above all a problem of philosophico-political choice which concerned the clergy and was grafted on to the internal struggles of the religious hierarchy, who used the dominance of the cult of one or other god as an instrument of power. It was not Huitzilopochtli whom the myths presented as Quetzalcoatl's 'conceptual' enemy, or at any rate not in the form of Huitzilopochtli the rising sun, but in that of the twilight and nocturnal sun, Tezcatlipoca, the 'Smoking Mirror' or 'Shining Mirror'. In the Aztec pantheon Tezcatlipoca had above him only Ometeotl, Two God, who was a principle both masculine and feminine, but had been a single god for the Toltecs. The Aztecs, who regarded themselves as heirs to the Toltecs, preserved Ometeotl's memory as a metaphysical concept.

Ometeotl was a god for intellectuals, for the religious élite who were capable of appreciating the beauty of the principle 'of what is near and what is far' as Ometeotl was also called. Other names given to him were 'Night and Wind', because he was similarly impalpable and invisible, and 'Lord who thinks of and invents himself'. For ordinary people, the artisans, traders and farmers, there was nothing to be had from so abstract a god: to solve everyday problems they preferred to turn to Tezcatlipoca. The latter's importance can be grasped in the many names with which he was addressed in prayer, each corresponding to one of his functions.

As ever, *Historia general de las cosas de Neuve España* by the Franciscan Bernardino de Sahagun (1975) is an unavoidable source of knowledge, but one could also cite *Historica de las Indias de Neuva España e Islas de la Tierra Firme* by the Dominican Fray Diego de Duran (1967), both written in the sixteenth century, in other words almost contemporaneously with the conquest, and thus first-hand documents whose information was gathered in the field. In Sahagun's work we find how Tezcatlipoca used magic tricks to make Quetzalcoatl leave Tula, the Toltec capital, thus bringing about its downfall. We also read on what date and in what form the ceremonies took place and even what position the supplicant should adopt to speak to the god. But above all we learn that Tezcatlipoca was the all-powerful creator of heaven and earth, that he was omniscient and omnipresent and that, on earth, he stirred up wars and hated, exhorting people to discord, hence his name Nevoc Yaotl, meaning 'Sower of Discord'. The god alone could dispense and withdraw prosperity and wealth, depending on his whim; he was feared and honoured, particularly by the sick, who begged him to rid them of the illnesses he had inflicted upon them. At these times he was called Moyocoyatzin because he did only what he pleased and no other power could prevent him. He had the power to heal or to let someone die, he could even destroy heaven and earth and bring about the end of all living things. When he appeared it was as a shadow, but he usually remained invisible, like air and darkness. On the codices his body is painted black and his head crowned with quail feathers. His idol was also black, carved in an obsidian that resembles jet. His attribute is the *tlachialoni*, a kind of gold disc, polished like a mirror and with a hole in its centre through which, it was believed, Tezcatlipoca watched all that happened on earth and in human hearts. It is probably this *tlachialoni* which earned him the name of 'He-who-has-a-yellow-face'. His 'doubles' were the jaguar and the sacrificial knife.

In fact Tezcatlipoca and not Huitzilopochtli is the equivalent to the Maya's Tohil, whom Asturias refers to in *The Président*, a text which caused a great stir and profoundly marked Hispanic-American literature. Asturias recounts the novel's beginnings in the following way:

> In 1923 I met several Latin American writers in Paris, where we met almost every evening at the café 'La Rotonde'. During these conversations each of us would tell anecdotes, some picturesque, some piquant, some tragic, about our countries. Unawares, as though reacting against the picturesque America so beloved of Europeans, we stressed the darker sides of our stories to the point where we were competing with stories to make the flesh creep, stories of the imprisonments, persecution, barbarism and vandalism of Latin American dictatorships. For this macabre exercise, in contrast to such spectacular tyrants as Juan Vicente Gomez, I described my own, and it was thus that, as in an empty picture, on a black background, there gradually appeared, written in the white chalk of memory, anecdotes that I had experienced as a child, tales told in lowered voices when the door was firmly shut.... In the beginning, the text was not written but spoken. Spelt out. It was the time of the renewal of speech as a means of expression and magical action.... Later came the problem of the spoken language: when it was spoken it was fine, it was my language, but would it express what I wanted to say once it was written down? In the Spanish language there is a very Castillian way of saying things, just as there is a Mexican or an Argentinian way, and what I was looking for was the Guatemalan way, without writing criolla literature. Knowing the literary past of my country, I consulted the most famous authors. How did they manage to remain faithful to the Guatemalan style without breaking up the language? At that time I was studying the pre-Columbian religions and this kept alive my capacity for mixing up two realities, reality and dreams, because while the Indians were realistic in

> the details, they plunged this realism into a kind of dream-imagination which made two forms of time accessible to them: historical time and the time of myths, in other words a time with a different pace from historical time, oneiric time. The result was the integration of what we could call a mythological integration into the text.
>
> (Asturias 1972)

Astonishing as it may seem, Asturias' declarations have had hardly any repercussions in studies on, *The President*, so true is it that the deafest person is the one who will not read. Hispanism wanted its great political novel and imagined that this integration of a mythological attitude diminished its ideological worth. The importance of this plunge down to the deepest roots of the American continent was so little understood that academics themselves, who are not always wide awake, adopted the credo that Asturias was dominated by the Spanish model, in this case the novel *Tirano Banderas* by Ramón del Valle Inclan (1980). To think this is truly to ignore the text and Asturias' unchanging position as a fierce partisan, one could even say pioneer, of an American culture freed from European models. What need was there for a European model (for *The President* does have a model) when the prime American model was to hand, another bestseller, *Amalia* by the Argentinian José Marmol (1980):

> We should mention José Marmol, the author of one of the most widely-read novels in America, *Amalia*. The pages of this book moved through our fevered, sweaty fingers when we felt in our own flesh the harshness of the dictators who ravaged Central America. . . . Across time, *Amalia* and José Marmol's imprecations still shake readers to the point of constituting, for many of them, an act of faith.
>
> (Asturias 1972)

In brief, in two sentences (our last two quotations) Asturias gives us the generating forces behind *The President:*

- a nineteenth century novel of a historical and satirical nature;
- pre-Columbian myths.

Let us examine the process by which a historical figure is transformed into a romantic character, by which the Argentinian dictator Juan Manuel de Rosas became the character Juan Manuel de Rosas in the fictional work *Amalia*, and then a literary myth as a result of his fusion with a myth itself.

When on the 8 December 1829 the federal Juan Manuel de Rosas, saluted by the President of the Junta as 'the Restorer of Laws', officially received the position of Governor of Buenos Aires from the hands of the Junta of Representatives of the Provinces of Argentina, for a period of three years and with expectional powers, it was the start of a dictatorship that was to last for twenty-three years. The country, which had gained independence from Spain in 1810, had since that time been torn between the ambitions of the unitarians, who supported a constitution that would give the political power to Buenos

Aires, and those of the federalists, who wanted supremacy to lie with the provinces. Rosas, who was a federalist, at first sought support from the Guachos, whom Sarmiento defined as 'colonial and barbarian peasants', and the lower classes, the Indians, blacks and people of mixed race. In short, Rosas' men were the complete opposite of the unitarians, who consisted of intellectuals and cosmopolitan aristocrats and who thought themselves, not without cause, to be the salt of the Argentinian earth.

When Rosas came to power many unitarians soon chose exile rather than tyranny and went to live in Montevideo, on the eastern bank of the Rio de la Plata. Among these exiles was the family of José Marmol. Born in 1818, Marmol was only eleven years old when Rosas came to power and fourteen when he went into exile, which in his case lasted five years. In 1837 he returned to Buenos Aires and enrolled at the university, but at the end of 1839 he spent a few days in prison because of his political activities. It was a brief stay, but sufficient to convince him that it was in his interests to go back into exile. He returned to Montevideo early in 1840. This, one of the darkest, most bloody years of the Rosist regime, is precisely the time in which the plot of *Amalia* takes place.

From 1851 onwards in Montevideo, opposition to the Rosas intensified. Marmol founded a newspaper, *La Semana*, to support the anti-Rosist campaign of General Urquiza (who became president of the republic after the tyrant fell). Drawing his inspiration from what Emile de Girardin had done in France during the 1830s, Marmol used serials to increase the newspaper's circulation and, in order to keep the spirit of war alive in the Argentinian colony, he designed it as a true pamphlet. The episodes of *Amalia* appeared in a literary supplement to *La Semana* until 9 February 1852, the date when Rosas fell and Urquiza triumphed. Marmol then returned to Buenos Aires, stopping both the paper's existence and the episodes of the novel dead. *Amalia* remained unfinished until 1855, when the missing chapters of the fourth part and the entire fifth part finally appeared. The public, who had praised *Amalia* to the skies from the earliest episodes, demanded a sequel to the love story of Eduardo Belgrano and his lovely Tucuman. Although in the reality of 1852 it was all over, the tyrant had fallen, the dark year of 1840 which the fiction brought back to life had been too tragic to allow the end of the novel to be other than tragic. If the readers were hoping to weep, they were unlikely to be disappointed.

So the substance of *Amalia* is thus to some extent the history of Buenos Aires in 1840, under the dictatorship of Juan Manuel de Rosas, a history which was strictly contemporaneous for the writer, who portrayed characters most of whom were still alive in 1855, the date of the final draft. We should therefore emphasize that, although *Amalia* falls into the category of nineteenth century romantic historical novels, its originality lies in the fact that the text was designed as a tool in the struggle, a means of denouncing the tyranny and protesting against its crimes. We are thus closer, not in genre but in ideological aim, to Victor Hugo's *Châtiments*, written in 1853 during his exile in Jersey, than to great romantic designs in the manner of Walter Scott or Alexandre Dumas, which are nevertheless still recognizable and acknowledged as models. Because of the pamphlet-like vehemence of the text, Marmol's contemporaries doubted its historical worth. However, for more than a century, in moments of crisis in Latin America people have turned to this novel, which is ceaselessly questioned and interpreted, as witnessed by the many editions and critical studies which have been and are continually published in most Latin American countries.

To identify the literary descendence of the 'black man' in *Amalia* and *The President*, it is not necessary to quote Asturias, we need only read and compare:

> He wore trousers of black cloth . . . a black tie . . . and a straw hat whose wide brim covered his face. (*Amalia*)
>
> The President was dresses as usual in deepest mourning: black shoes, black suit, black tie and the black hat which he never took off. (*The President*)
>
> One never knew exactly where he was. He pretended to settle somewhere for the night and half an hour later the place was empty with a soldier on guard . . . He changed places so that no one would know where he was. (*Amalia*)
>
> No one knew where his home was because he lived outside the city in several houses at once, nor how he slept, because it was said that it was near the telephone with a whip in his hand, nor when because his friends asserted that he never slept. (*The President*)

The same comparative reading would bring to light other similarities, for example that of the tyrants' respective secretaries and their scapegoats:

> A little old man of seventy to seventy-two, with a wizened, colourless face over which fell locks of his disorderly and almost entirely white hair. (*Amalia*)
>
> His teeth projected between his tight lips like those of a comb, combining with his hollow cheeks and his anguished expression to give him the air of a man condemned to death. (*The President*)

It is not just the period of Rosas' rule as Marmol's novel portrays it but the whole implicit context, historical details which are not mentioned in the Argentinian text that are recognizable as the origins of some of Asturias' situations or characters: thus the name of the protagonist, Camilla – for which several hypotheses have been advanced which are plausible but lack meaning for the novel – which might have been inspired by the tragic and true story of Camila O'Gorman. Camila O'Gorman and the man who had seduced and carried her off died victims to cholera and Rosas' vengeance for having loved each other without his consent. Perhaps, like the couple who are Asturias' protagonists, they were simply guilty of loving each other at a time when only hate and evil were allowed. The fact that Camila O'Gorman's seducer was a defrocked priest was not an aggravating circumstance, far from it, in the eyes of a tyrant whose biography demonstrates the little respect he had for religion and his still lesser respect for the clergy. An unlucky love, then, in worlds of hate and fear (chapter 17 of *The President* is precisely entitled *Amor urdemales*), but in literary terms it is a romantic love, born at first sight, whole and unalterable, of the mutual and revelatory contemplation of beauty by the characters as the laws of the fiction determined them in themselves. Before meeting Camila, Angel Face, as the protagonist is called, is 'as handsome and wicked as Satan'. This unbearable dichotomy is corrected when love gives him a heart. Angel Face then seeks some good deed to do: he becomes part of the opposition since only bad deeds flatter the President and 'a citizen's most complete support for the President' has a murder as its signature. Beauty and Goodness are banished.

Since a fictional character exists only in writing, his field of action and way of being are strictly bound up with the capacity of expression of the narrative discourse. The conflicting words 'as handsome and wicked as Satan' thus determine the character Angel Face's make-up until his meeting with Camila. The details of his physique and dress are not just features revealing something, they are all elements in which the text's functioning can be perceived. I shall quote Angel Face's first appearance in the text, in chapter 6 which is entitled 'Angel Face', as he is seen by (we are in a fictional world and by convention the characters are supposed to be people) a woodcutter whose amazement should not allow the reader, who is outside the fiction, to forget that everything depends on the perfection of the narrative mechanism:

> The man who had spoken was an angel: a complexion of golden marble, fair hair, a small mouth and an almost feminine appearance, in strong contrast with the manly expression of his black eyes. He was wearing grey. In the fading light he seemed to be dressed in cloud. . . . 'An angel!' The woodcutter couldn't take his eyes from him. 'An angel' he repeated, 'an angel!'
>
> Asturias (1972)

Angel or demon? Between the cloud clothing and black eyes the writing lets us glimpse the possibility of a double nature. In the first chapters the black side wins out, as is understandable in 'the man who had the President's complete confidence' and who, as a creature, displays the colour before submitting to its lethal symbolism: the black of his eyes is echoed by the aestheticism of the black scarf which half conceals the favourite's face. Significantly the last occurrence of 'his black velvet eyes' comes in chapter 37, 'Tohil's Dance', when Angel Face, sitting opposite the President, falls into the trap of his black soul by believing in the possibility of the trip abroad which the President dangles in front of him to make its loss more cruel and above all, to frustrate him the more. In the last chapter the blackness of the eyes of Angel Face, who is now the anonymous prisoner of cell 17, is that of 'near blindness'. In narrative terms, the detail of the colour of Angel Face's eyes recalls the master's indelible mark upon his creature and foretells the triumph of Evil. On the other hand the scarf is a narrative accessory which disappears from the story as soon as the character becomes an angel and loses his blackness.

As we have seen, Asturias found his model for the black man in Juan Manuel de Rosas. But although Marmol's hero is drawn from an objective model taken from Argentinian history, he remains above all a literary figure constructed according to the stereotypical pattern of the romantic figure. He is a solitary rebel, enemy of society and bearer of a dark curse which keeps him on the fringers. To avenge himself, he destroys the system which rejects him and replaces the law with his law. With his implacable will, cynicism and violence upheld by means which are, if not superhuman, at least exceptional, Rosas, like Hernani, is 'a moving force', 'a soul of misery made of shadows'. Shadowy he certainly is (and a widower too, like Nerval's Desdichado), preferring to work in darkness, hiding his thoughts and even his face. He is the incarnation of evil and also follows the pattern of romances and particularly of serials by engendering its opposite, Good, in other words Beauty, in other words Daniel Bello. *Bello y malo como Satan*, Angel Face is also a double who becomes an opposite and the adjective which stereotypes his beauty perhaps refers to the beautiful Amalia's romantic cousin, Daniel Bello. One could discuss the traits that make up Rosas' literary character and apply them pertinently to the President, particularly his hatred for a social system which caused him to be born marginalized as a poor man of mixed race, hence his desire for vengeance against his fellow citizens, who are witnesses to his humiliating past. But just as the romantic dimension of *Amalia* and its descendence from European models in no way detract from its speficially American ideological scope, so the romantic facets of Asturias' President have in no way hindered his influence as a symbol, a literary symbol through the originality of the writing and a political symbol through the fiction's external references.

The black man, all-powerful lord of the life and death of his subjects, omnipresent ('he lived outside the city in several houses at once'), omniscient ('the President knows everything', he reminds Angel Face, and the anonymous informers he favours give him information every day), invisible to common mortals ('no one knew where his home was', how he slept or even if he slept and when he appeared high on the balcony once a year, it was always in profile, never face on), this black man is certainly a romantic figure out of a political serial, but he is also, more than an 'ultimately secondary political expression, the manifestation of a primitive force and the survival, in the contemporary world, of the mentalities of the most archaic societies'. For this reason *The President* is a deeply American novel, which owes much more to its indigenous roots than just a figure in a novel, even one so spectacular and representative of contemporary Latin American reality. I use the word 'deeply' in the sense that Asturias himself, referring to the 'deep fathers' of Paul Valéry's *Cimetière marin*, understood 'the deep ancestor' (*Maladron*), whom Golden Skin in *Legends of Guatemala*, who has become changed into a tree, seeks with his roots through the layers of emotional and cultural archaeology and that the narrator of *Tres de cuatro soles* claims as the last and the true face: 'the mask of whitened bones'.

It matters little that Asturias calls the dark, destructive god, Quetzalcoatl's enemy, Huitzilopochlti and not Tezcatlipoca: he has always refused to act the ethnologist and anthropologist; he wants only to be a poet, using his material freely (close reading of *Tres de cuatro soles* reveals, despite everything, a perfect analysis of the dialectic of Quetzalchhuatl/Tezcatlipoca, the Feathered Serpent/Smoking Mirror: 'fire turned into smoke . . . smoke turned into cloud . . . cloud turned into feather . . . feathered serpent in the highest point of heaven'). What matters is to recognize the myth behind the literary myth, the inheritance of the men of maize in which the man of maize that Asturias was found a natural means of expression throughout his work. In fact it is Night Wind/ Tezcatlipoca who is recalled to Tazol (*Mulata*), the invisible devil who dispenses wealth, or Cashtoc, the worker of miracles and the worst practical jokes (Tezcatlipoca was, among other things, the patron of magicians). We find him again behind the fabulous Alhajados, dressed entirely in black, who are never seen, who never die but simply 'disappear' (*El Alhajadito*). In a feminine version, the 'Immense Widows' of primal night in *Clarivigilia primaveral* and 'The Great Night' in the 'Second Sun' in *Tres de cuatro soles*, are avatars, if distant ones, of a motif whose traces we find in almost all Asturias' fiction and in the metamorphoses that the writing dizzily exalts in every image that can possibly be invented for the concept 'black'.

Carlos Fuentes, in *Terra nostra* (1978), makes the black god, whom the myth describes as limping because when he was born the monstrous mother earth ate one of his feet (or legs), the limping 'double' of the fair and luminous Quetzalcoatl/Polo Febo, who has one arm. Haunted by the theme of twins (omnipresent in Mesoamerican culture), and a great leader of Lacan, the Mexican writer interprets the struggle between these brothers, who are born enemies and complementary to each other, as a metaphor for the antagonistic forces which rend and enrich our personalities.

We can rightly recall that, although *The President* acts as a model with the quality of its writing, the character of the dictator as a literary theme was in vogue at the time, proof being that after Joseph Conrad's *Nostromo* in 1904 there appeared in the same year of 1926 both Francis de Miomandre's *Le Dictateur* and *Tirano de Banderas* by Ramón del Valle Inclan. A quarter of a century later the literary dictators returned in force, since *El Secuestro del general* by the Ecuadorian Demetrio Aguillera Malta (1973), *Reasons of State* by the Cuban Alejo Carpentier and *I the Supreme* by the Paraguayan Augusto Roa Bastos (1974) and *The Autumn of the Patriarch* by the Colombian Gabriel García Marquez all appeared in the space of three years.

None of these authors belong to the cultural space ruled by the black Tezcatlipoca, but they all knew *Amalia* and particularly *The President*, since all had been friends, some very dear, of Asturias. It is thus by literary descent rather than direct cultural inheritance that we can explain the presence of salient features which allow us to identify the figure of the black god in all the novels cited. Let me repeat that in the beginning came the creation of José Marmol, who borrowed from both the wardrobe of nineteenth-century man and that, equally conventional, of the romantic hero the dark clothing characteristic of Rosas. Here too let me stress this detail, for one might make the common-sense objection that in Rosas' time all men of the world dressed in this way. This is true, but I would counter it by returning to the problem of the character who is dressed not in clothing but in writing. In this case Marmol selected a number of elements whose aim was not sartorial realism but the aesthetic of blackness. So much so that, in the description of Rosas cited above, the text lays stress on the hat which covers the dicator's head, a detail which is interesting because it is unusual as the scene takes place in Rosas' lair, thus indoors and furthermore in the middle of the night. The hat makes it possible to omit from the portrait something which would not square either aesthetically or ethically with the author's project, the fact, noted by historians, that Rosas was blond with blue eyes and pale skin. A taste for secrecy and the precautions which must be taken by one who knows his life is always more or less under threat, is a trait shared by most tyrants in reality. Marmol uses writing to make it a peculiarity of Rosas. Asturias in turn returns to these features and singles them out, this time in such a way as to bring into relief their similiarity with the properties of the black god. Thus it is that either through direct inheritance from Marmol (Valle Inclan, Asturias) or through the intermediary of Asturias, sartorial and moral blackness makes its appearance:

– in Francia in *I the Supreme*, the black cape lined with red: 'I see a man dressed in black with a scarlet cape on his shoulders: a black adolescent was waiting on him with folded arms, near the horse . . . The stranger's face was dark and his black eyes very penetrating.'

– General Banderas in *Tirano Banderas*, stylized in the profile of a night bird.

We should add that, in every case, in the blackness of his eyes, hair and sometimes his moustache the dictator, who is either of mixed race or an Indian, presents ethnic features which serve the ideological intentions of the writing. Asturias accentuates them to an extreme degree, to the point of caricature, saying that the President's nails were in mourning.

The 'nocturnal' character of the will to power has as its corollary a taste for solitude (García Marquez' Patriarch is a 'solitary despot', 'the most solitary man on earth') which is appropriate for the creation of the kind of invisiblity which is a determining factor for the myth: 'none of us had ever seen him' says the narrator. 'Corporeal person/impersonal figure', 'no one will even see you, no one will see or hear you' sighs Doctor Francia about himself. These words are all the more ironic because the character is in fact a fantasy since the narrative voice which dictates memoirs and edicts throughout the fiction is that of the posthumous dictator.

Strangest of all is the detail which refers to the *tlachialoni* or *itlachiayan*, through the central hole of which Tezcatlipoca saw all that was happening in the world. To refer to this curious object without having to use the native word, which was difficult to pronounce, the Spanish chroniclers gave it the Spanish ame *catalejo*, meaning a spy-glass. Now the spyglass is precisely the favourite tool of the characters Tirano Banderas and Doctor Francia, both of whom are astronomy fanatics. Thanks to informers the 'spyglass' as a metaphore for omniscience (let us recall the threatening words: 'the President knows everything') is textually present in *Amalia* and *The President*.

Many other elements contribute to bring out with even greater clarity the Tezcatlipoca-like literary figure of the Latin American dictator, but to list them would require work on the texts which would go behind the scope of the present article. I shall however give one last example, the theme of the double, the *alter ego* that allows the god the great number of metamorphoses, disguises and tricks which are so many images of his duplicity. These metamorphoses explain why Tezcatlipoca was invoked as the god of magicians and acrobats. Their duplicity was not moreover a pejorative attribute, on the contrary it was an extra quality for the god. Thus the literary manifestations of the Tezcatlipoca-like 'double' are the double in *The Autumn of the Patriarch*, the favourite in *Amalia* and *The President* and the scapegoat secretary in *I the Supreme*.

Dorita Nouhaud

Cain

The stories about the origins of the world that served as myths in the context of Judaism and Christianity revolve around two central themes: the greatness of Creation and Man's narcissistic rebellion. Just as there are three versions of the cosmogony – of which the third, involving the Flood, appears most vividly to our imagination – so Man's rebellion and fall are presented in three forms. One of these is the story of Cain, which is often associated with that of the Tower of Babel, and which symbolizes the disastrous nature of transgression much better than the tame theft of an apple. The hatred of a brother, the spilling of blood, the anguish and wandering of the culprit and the proliferation of violence create a striking parable that has never ceased to haunt Western literature.

THE DEATH WISH AND CIVILIZATION

The whole story of Cain and his descendants is contained in the twenty-six verses of chapter 4 of Genesis. It is placed at the heart of a group of tales about the origins of the world that occupy the first eleven chapters of the book, before the beginning of the saga of the patriarchs (Abraham, Isaac, Jacob and Joseph). The author is commonly called 'Yahwist' because he uses the name 'Yahweh' for God, and the book must have been written in Jerusalem, probably during the reign of Solomon (*c.* 970–31 BC). The presence of a 'genealogical mould', which is barely perceptible in the first part of the chapter, devoted to Cain himself (vv. 1–16), becomes clear when the descendants of Cain are introduced (vv. 17–24).

Unlike in the case of the stories of the Creation and Flood, no sources have yet been discovered from which the writer may have worked. From the biblical text, it seems that Eve chose the name 'Cain' (in Hebrew *Qayin*) to create one of those plays on words in which Genesis abounds: 'I have gotten [*ganiti*] a man with the help of the Lord.' However, it should be pointed out that in Arabic the word means 'blacksmith', which may help to explain the fact that one of Cain's descendants, Tubal-cain, was presented as a 'forger of all instruments of bronze and iron' (v. 22). It has also been suggested that Cain might be the eponymous ancestor of the clan of Kenites who eventually entered the tribe of Judah. In this context, the 'mark' that God put on Cain (v. 15) could correspond to a tattoo used by the Kenites to distinguish themselves from members of other clans. As for the name Abel, it has been associated with the Hebrew *Hebel*, meaning a puff of wind or something empty. However, it has also been linked to the root *ybl* (a leader of flocks in Syriac), which would underline the antithesis developed in Genesis between the nomadic life of herdsmen and the sedentary life of farmers, which is found so often in archaic tales.

We do not know the location of 'the land of Nod, east of Eden' (v. 16) in which we are told that Cain dwelt after murdering Abel. However, again, the name may have originated from a simple play on words, whereby Cain takes flight (*nad*) to the land of Nod. In any case, the chapter is set against the background of the cultural developments and background discoveries of the Neolithic Age: agriculture and urban life appeared in Palestine towards the end of the eighth millennium BC; while copper and ancient bronze were in widespread use from 2600 bc. We are thus dealing with a popular and picturesque representation of the origins of civilization, following immediately on the two cosmogonies with which Genesis starts. The study of proper names is revealing in this context: Enoch means 'inauguration' (of a town); while Lamech, who was the first polygamist, may have taken his name from Lamga, the carpenter god of the Sumerians. Lamech's three sons also have a role to play in this small-scale *Discours sur les sciences et les arts* (to borrow the title of the work by Rousseau): Jabal is the 'father of those . . . who have cattle'; Hubal is the player of the horn (*yobel*); and Tubal shares his name with a metal-working site in Asia Minor.

One of the most significant aspects of the story of the descendants of Cain is that it outlines a sort of 'theology of culture', providing a religious meditation on the *ambiguity* of science and technology. On the one hand, there are weapons, invented by the offspring of a murderer, Cain, and of a proponent of the principle of limitless revenge, Lamech. On the other there are tools, and above all musical instruments. Nevertheless it is suspicion of technology that predominates: technology was only developed after the Fall – it was not needed in Eden, a land of harmony and plenty. Similarly, towns too aroused the suspicion of the Israelites who never completely forgot that they had pledged their allegiance to the one God during their long sojourn in the Desert.

However, the best-known message of the story is spelt out in the first part of the chapter, which describes the murder of Abel. All men live under the size of a God who is both exacting (in that he forbids homicide) and forgiving (in that he does not abandon the murderer). Wrongdoing is a matter of free will, and the temptation to do harm can always be overcome. Thus, in verse 7, when Cain is threatened by a hostile Power personifying Sin he is exhorted to resist and overcome it. In choosing violence we set in train an infernal spiral of reprisals: diametrically opposed to Lamech's bloodthirsty frenzy is Christ's exhortation that we should forgive not 'seven times, but seventy times seven' (Matthew 18. 22).

A STORY WITH GAPS

The account in chapter 4 of Genesis rushes along at breakneck speed. The writer is so absorbed in the pursuit of his religious objective that he ignores inconsistencies that he can hardly have failed to notice. Cain takes his brother out 'to the fields' and is frightened of being killed by those he meets; but as the son of Adam whom could he have met? Who would live in the same town as him?

The silence of the text on important points provides a crucial explanation for the countless reworkings of the story. Four of these 'gaps' inspired flights of imagination throughout the millennia that followed.

Why did God have regard for Abel's offering, but not for Cain's? There is plenty of room for conjecture. If we look at the Bible as a whole, it is easy to notice the recurring theme of God's preference for the youngest son (Jacob, Joseph) and for the weak (David). There is also the leitmotif of the prophets: God looks into the hearts of those making an offering, not just at the material value of the sacrifice itself. It is this prophetic view that surfaces in the New Testament: 'By faith Abel offered to God a more acceptable sacrifice than Cain, through which he received approval as righteous' (Hebrews 11.4). The 'way of Cain' (1 John 3. 12; Jude 11) is denounced as being counter to the Gospel (Matthew 23. 35; John 8: 44).

The events surrounding the murder of Abel are no less enigmatic. The account simply talks of 'the voice of your brother's blood . . . crying . . . from the ground' (v. 10), in reflecting the Jewish belief that human blood that has been spilt and not covered with earth cries out to heaven (Isaiah 26. 21; Job 16. 18 etc.). the apostle John envisages Abel as having had his throat slit, no doubt because he is a forerunner of Christ, the true paschal lamb. But the *Zohar*, the main work in the Jewish Cabbala, which contains mystical commentaries on the Pentateuch and portrays Cain as the son of Eve by the Serpent, maintains that the murderer bit Abel like a reptile. Other writers have imagined him being bludgeoned to death (Gessner 1758) or have seen Cain using a symbolic panoply of weapons anticipating the universal rule of War, the Gibbet and Prison. Indeed, this sinister triad articulates the structure of a huge poem by Hugo (*La Fin de Satan*): 'When Cain, the ancestor of dark beings, / Had floored his smoothbrowed brother, Abel, / He struck him first with a bronze nail, / Then with a stick, then with a stone.'

The *mark* that God made on Cain to protect him has often been wrongly interpreted as the sign of a curse. The rabbis have come up with innumerable theories as to its form, seeing it variously as a kind of permanent grimace, a perpetual tremor, a tattoo, or even a horn (with Cain being seen as a unicorn). Mythologists have been less bold, merely pointing out that many mythical blacksmiths suffer from some physical defect: Odin is blind in one eye, the Cyclops have only a single eye, Hephaestus is lame . . .

Finally the wandering of Cain – alluded to in the Bible in a simple play on words that represents him as *na' wa'nad*, a 'fugitive and wanderer' – has inspired works such as Coleridge's poem 'The Wanderings of Cain' (1798) and R. Hamerling's epic 'Ahasver in Rom' (1867).

CAIN AS AN OUTCAST

From the time when the biblical account was written until Byron published his 'Cain' in 1821, there was almost unanimous disapproval of the first murderer. The very earliest 'news-item', the slaying of Abel, seemed to encapsulate the horror of all those that would follow. Cain was inevitably seen as a cruel unrepentant monster, set apart from other men, and Jewish and commentators found it hard to envisage that such a person might be pardoned. Those that represent him as being forgiven seemed to feel obliged to compensate for this by making him die when his own house collapsed on him or be killed by Lamech, who supposedly took him for a wild animal. But for many Cain remained an unmitigated reprobate, and it was one of his descendants that necessitated the Flood. This was the view held by Philo Judaeus of Alexandria (d. 45 AD), who wrote eight treatises on Cain, and particularly by Flavius Josephus (*Jewish Antiquities*, 94 AD).

Christian writers superimposed a Christ-centred interpretation of the Scriptures onto this Jewish attitude of disapproval. Abel, the innocent and persecuted shepherd who had offered up a sacrifice and unjustly been put to death became a symbol of the righteous, and particularly of the righteous Man par excellence, Christ. Over the centuries, a constant flow of commentaries and paraphrases was produced by writers ranging from famous theologians to humble village priests. Most of these, including *Of Cain and Abel* (*c.* 375) by St Ambrose of Milan appeal to virtue, true sacrifice and repentance. However, the dominant work during the thousand years separating Origen and St Bernard, which constitute the patristic age in the broad sense of the term, was undoubtedly St Augustine's *The City of God* (413–27 AD). In this grand vision Cain's wickedness and Abel's saintliness form a parable describing the route that every human being must travel: everyone starts off as Cain, but the objective is to become and remain Abel. The opposition between the two brothers permeates the entire theological view of history: 'Two cities have been formed by two loves: the earthly by the love of self, even to the contempt of God; the heavenly by the love of God, even to the contempt of self' (*De civitate Dei* XIV. 28). One city stands for Cain, the other for Abel. Men are divided between two invisible cities: Babylon, which means 'unquiet town' and Jerusalem, 'the city of peace'. Most earthly cities have lived under the shadow of Cain, who was the founder of towns. These include the historical Babel, in the form of Sodom and Gomorrah, and particularly Rome, the town of wolves, the foundations of which were sprinkled with the blood of a brother – Romulus's compulsive homage to his true father, Cain. St Augustine's vision was to leave its mark on all Western culture. Its literary brilliance fascinated even the agnostic novelist Michel Butor, whom it inspired to write a superb 'Cainian' meditation, *L'Emploi du Temps* (1956).

From the thirteenth century onwards an increasing number of dramatic or epic versions of Genesis 4 were produced. The *Historia scolastica* by Petrus Comestor (1172–3) deals with the subject of Cain in an essay that was to inspire many medieval works. German versions stayed closed to their source material. They portrayed Cain as being essentially a trickster (*Altsächsische Genesis, Wiener Genesis*); as someone inspired by the devil (Lutwins, *Adam und Eva*, thirteenth century); or as a miserly reprobate who offered God damaged corn (Arnold Immessens, *Sûndenfall*, *c.* 1460). The literature produced in France during this period was dominated by two more original works, *Le Mystère d'Adam* (*Ordo representacionis Adae*, end of twelfth century) which devoted 154 lines to the murder of Abel, and *Le Mystère du Vieil Testament* (fifteenth century), a heterogeneous piece 50,000 lines long, with about 3,000 lines expanding the accounts in Genesis 4 (11. 1883–4969). The latter invents wives for the two brothers in the form of sisters called Calmana and Delbora. In England, too, literary works elaborated on the biblical material (*Story of Genesis and Exodus, Cursor Mundi*) even to the extent of giving Cain some comic aspects (*Towneley Plays*).

In the sixteenth century the story began to be freed from its religious context, despite the controversy aroused by the Protestant Reformation. Luther himself saw Cain as a man who lacked faith; and soon both Catholics and Protestants started to identify each other with him. This evidence occurs in the play *Kinderzucht* (1591) by A. Quitting, and also in *Les Tragiques* (published in 1616, but written from 1577) by Agrippa d'Aubigné, who anticipated Hugo by dwelling on Cain's interminable wanderings and the outcast's remorse. The splendid lines written by another French Calvinist, Du Bartas, typify the process whereby the story virtually took on a new life of its own. In his *Seconde Semaine* (1584) he presents an amazing picture of Cain busy taming a wild horse while Tubal contemplates the flow of molten metal and Jubal ponders on the sound of hammers and invents the lute.

A similar development can be traced in the literature of the German-speaking countries. Alongside plays that are still completely religious (Valten Voith, *Ein schön lieblich Spiel* . . . , 1538; *Luzerner Osterspiel*, 1571; *Freiburger Fronleichnamspiel*, 1599) we find the first dramas in which Cain the pariah is superseded by a hesitant, doubt-wracked figure (Macropedius, *Adamus*, 1552; J. Stricker, *Ein geistlich Spiel* . . . , 1570). At the same time various attempts were being made to remedy the lack of substance in the biblical story. These ranged from J. Ruof's *Adam und Eva* (1550) to Z. Zahn's *Tragedia Fratericidii* (1590), and from H. Knaus's *Tragedia von Verordnung der Stende* (1539) to H. Sachs's *Comedie von den ungleichen Kindern Evä* (1553).

At the height of the Baroque period in the seventeenth century writers placed a strong emphasis the contrasts in the story, as H. Zieglers had already done in 1559 in his play *Abel justus*. Brute force triumphs over weakness, the prototype of the tyrant tortures the first martyr: that is how the tale is seen in plays by Lope de Vega (*La Creación del mundo*, 1624), M. Johansen (*Von Kain dem Brudermöder*, 1652), C. Dedekind (*Erster Märterer Abel*, 1676), C. Postel (*Cain und Abel*, 1689), C. Weises (*Cains Brudermord an dem unschuldigen Abel*, 1704) and even in the neo-Latin play by the Jesuit A. Claus written as late as the middle of the eighteenth century (*Caedes Abelis*, 1750).

The secularization of Cain became more pronounced with the approach of the Romantic period, notably in *Der Tod Abels* (1732), an oratorio composed by Metastasio for Emperor Charles VI, or *Der Tod Adams* (1756) by Klopstock. One of the most famous works from this period is *Der Tod Abels* (1758) by the Swiss writer Salomon Gessner, a prose poem in five cantos. The first human beings celebrate God in an idyllic atmosphere, and Cain kills Abel only in a fit of anger after a nightmare, before giving way to tears of repentance. This milk-and-water version of the story brought tears to people's eyes throughout Europe; and in the nineteenth century it was a popular text at boarding-schools. Patzke in 1771 (*Der Tod Abels*), Alfieri in 1790 (*Abele*) and Legouvé in 1792 (*La Mort d'Abel*) were tainted by the same sentimentality.

Meanwhile, the Sturm und Drang movement was mainly interested in portraying the troubled soul of the murderer, both in poetry (F. Graf zu Stolberg, 'Kain am Ufer des Meeres', 1774) and on the stage (J.C. Zabuesnig, *Kain und Abel*, 1779). The poet Maler Müller, who wrote fragments of a life of Faust (1776–8), also devoted two works to Cain, *Der erschlagene Abel* (1775) in which Cain is represented more as rebelling against his father than as bearing a grudge towards his brother, and *Adams erstes Erwachen . . .* (1778).

THE TRIUMPH OF THE CAINITES

In the nineteenth century, the work of some writers showed a radical switch of values: 'We will give the *holy* writ the name it deserves, namely the *accursed* writ' (Nietzsche, *Law against Christianity*). Cain became a hero, in an astonishing echo of the beliefs of an obscure Gnostic sect, the Cainites, that had existed in the second century AD. According to its teachings, the cruel Yahweh of the Old Testament was no more than a demiurge rebelling against the supreme God, who was benevolent and a friend to mankind. The sect's adherents therefore admired all those who opposed the usurper: the Sodomites, Esau, Korah, Judas and especially Cain, who had been the custodian of secret knowledge since the world began.

The rehabilitation of the rebel was started in 1821 in a 'mystery' by Byron, translated into French prose the following year by Amédée Pichot, then into verse by Fabre d'Olivet, who also refuted it in 1823. Inspired by various passages in Bayle's *Dictionnaire*, Byron put terrible accusations against God into the mouths of Satan and Cain: it was he who had created evil, and the snare of Eden. Cain bemoaned that Eve had not picked the fruit of the Tree of Life as well as that of the Tree of the Knowledge of Good and Evil, denounced Abel's bloody sacrifices and killed him to free their sister Aclinia who loved Cain and not him.

When the Romatic writers portrayed good angels, the result was often bad literature. Conversely, they were rather more successful in dealing with evil. Endowed with the richly evocative qualities of Prometheus and Satan, the figure of Cain experienced a fantastic new lease of life in the course of a single century. Poems, novels and plays in his honour proliferated; and often the shadow of the Reprobate hovered over entire works, such as *Conrad Wallenrod* by Mickiewicz (1827), *Les Chants de Maldoror* by Lautréamont (1869), and *Le Désespéré* by L. Bloy (1886), where the main character is called Caïn Marchenoir.

The flourishing interest in Cain between 1820 and 1920 is epitomized by six brilliant works devoted to him. After inspiring a series of Byronesque rebels his next major appearance was in Nerval's admirable *Voyage en Orient* (1851). The best known part of this work, 'The story of the queen of the morning and Suleiman prince of the spirits', celebrates Adoniram and his ancestors Kaïn and Tubal-Kaïn. Nerval draws not only on the Bible but on Arab texts and esoteric doctrines, especially Masonic ones. He goes back to occult traditions according to which Kaïn was the child of Eve and Eblis (Satan) so that he and his descendants are sons of the light, sons of the fire, in contrast to ordinary men moulded from clay.

Though it was written in 1846, Leconte de Lisle's 'Qaïn' was not published until 1869 when it appeared in *Le Parnasse contemporain*, before featuring as the first poem in the collection *Poèmes barbares* (1872). Its hero pushes the case made against the Almighty in the Book of Job to its extreme and refuses to submit to a sadistic God who recognizes only cowardice as a virtue: 'My breath, oh kneader of the ancient clay, / Will one day raise your victim alive. / You will tell him: Worship! He will answer: No!'

Sacher-Masoch and Hugo were more ambitious; both undertook a huge review of the human condition in the name of Cain, and in both cases the project remained unfinished. About 1866, the Austrian novelist had the idea of producing a vast group of stories entitled *The Legacy of Cain* figuring Love (the unrelenting battle of the sexes), Property, the State, War, Work and Death. The prologue, 'The Wanderer', states the propositions that: 'Man is a ferocious animal' and 'the world is flawed'. The epilogue would have celebrated the man of Nazareth, with no experience of sexual love, no possessions, no native land, no weapons and no work. The most famous part of the *Legacy of Cain*, 'Venus im Pelz' (1870), unfortunately ensured that Masoch's complex undertaking was remembered only in terms of the word 'masochism'.

In *La Fin de Satan*, Hugo alternates 'extraterrestrial' episodes in the domain of Satan with events that take place in the human world in the penumbra surrounding Cain, who was born from the word 'Death', which the rebellious archangel called out during his interminable fall. The figure of the Outcast provides a dominant theme in all Hugo's work, perhaps finding its most intense expression in the poem 'La Conscience' (1852–5) published in *La Légende des Siècles*. In this work the poet is obsessed by certain images and events, by the disfigured forehead and the ruined tower (Cain and Babel), by the pursuit into hell and the exile, but also by the final redemption of Cain. Perhaps the fact that Hugo was called Victor and had a brother called Abel explains this fascination.

The Romantic concept, enriched with some Nietzschean ideas about the super-man isolated at the heart of a gregarious society, has probably never been more powerfully expressed than in Hermann Hesse's novel *Demian* (1919). According to its main character, the whole story of Cain originated from his 'mark'. There was a bold race whose faces shone with an intelligence that frightened the mediocre, who invented the story in Genesis to quell their unease. The sons of Cain still exist today: they cannot stay long grazing with the herd, and after solitary wandering they join the select circle of initiates – Moses, Buddha, Caesar, Jesus, Loyola, Napoleon, Nietzsche . . . They and they alone are truly 'awake'.

RIVALRY BETWEEN BROTHERS

Gradually as the twentieth century has progressed both the 'dark' legend of Cain (representing him as an outcast) and the 'light' legend (portraying him as a magnificently rebellious Titan) have disappeared, despite the success of works such as *Demian* or *L'Emploi du Temps* (1956). The latter was written by Butor, who drew inspiration from both St Augustine and Nerval for his reflections on accursed cities and industrial pollution, in which Manchester became *Bleston, Babelstown*, the city of Cain.

Under the influence of psychology, the story from Genesis has taken on a more human emphasis. The psycho-analytical approach to the tale of the two brothers has followed one of two patterns. The intention in one case is to isolate a 'Cain complex' (Charles Baudouin); but, much more frequently, the aim is to interpret the terrible, heart-breaking events in the light of the Oedipus complex. Thus in *Le Motif de l'Inceste* (1912) Otto Rank discusses Otto Borngräber's play *Die ersten Menschen* (1908) in which Cain and Abel fight over the love of their mother.

However, the rivalry between the brothers generally arises from less profound sources of conflict, such as when both fall in love with the same girl. This was not a new theme, but it became a central element in works entitled *Kain* by G. Kastropp (an epic poem, 1880), L. Weber (a play, 1896) and P. Heyse (a 'mystery play', 1904). It also inspired John Steinbeck's novel, *East of Eden* (1952), which was turned into a film by Elia Kazan in 1955, with James Dean in the role of Cai, the rejected teenager. Finally, in 1980 this psychological interpretation of the myth influenced novels by José-André Lacour, *Le Rire de Caïn*, and Vladimir Volkoff, *Les Humeurs de la Mer I. Olduvaï*.

Since the Second World War the story of Cain has attracted writers haunted by the proliferation of evil or the approach of the Apocalypse. They include Alexander Trocchi in the United States with *Cain's Book*, a 'handbook for junkies and other polyps', and Pierre Emmanuel in France with *Babel* or *Le grand Oeuvre-Cosmogonie* (1984), which includes a 'Book of Cain'.

LITERARY GENRES AND DREAMS

The story of Cain has appealed to many playwrights, but it has mainly inspired dramas and mystery plays. Though the tight-knit family setting seems to make it ideally suited to tragedy, given the emphasis in Aristotle's *Poetics* on the link between the family and tragic events, Cain's freedom of choice and his personal responsibility for what happens, are at odds with a sense of fatality. Since the original Bible story is sketchy and is narrated at a gallop, adapting it for the stage involves a huge amount of amplification, which explains the invention of additional characters, such as the two sisters mentioned earlier. Nonetheless the theatrical pieces named after Abel and Cain are generally static works in which poetry and music make up for the story's lack of movement. That is why the theme inspired so many eighteenth-century and nineteenth-century oratorios (for example, by G. Stolzel, W. Sutor, F. Morlacchi, G. Perry, F. Spindler and F. Weingärtner), as well as operas such as *La Mort d'Abel* by Rodolphe Kreutzer (1766–1831) or *Abel* by Enrico Sansone (b. 1905).

The presence of a 'genealogical mould' throughout the biblical text suggests that it could easily be adapted to form strings of episodes like those characteristic of epic poems, and St Augustine did, in fact, sketch out a kind of *Anti-Legend of the Centuries*. In Hugo's work, too, the rise of humanity is achieved despite back-sliding towards crime, involving figures such as Cain, Nimrod and Canute. The superhuman figure of the murderer has fired the imagination of many would-be epic poets, including Du Bartas and Agrippa d'Aubigne. However, a greater insight into the psychology of the characters was developed, the epic poem gave way to the novel (Steinbeck), and, quite fittingly, even to the detective novel (Butor).

The story of Cain has proved an amazingly fertile source for works of imagination. Its elements include rebellion against the Father, rivalry between hostile brothers and desire for the mother (as illustrated on the thirteenth-century capital in Tarragon cathedral where Cain is shown snatching Abel from the arms of Eve who is suckling him). In addition there are its mysterious features and the vagueness about Cain's wanderings. According to René Girard (*La Violence et le Sacré*, 1972) the latter turned Cain into a *pharmakos*, on a par with Oedipus; just as, when Oedipus was driven from his city he became a source of blessings, so Cain, the Jewish Oedipus, brought technology to mankind. To begin with Cain belongs to the plant world, but his punishment condemns him to the coldness of the mineral world, where he becomes a man of stone and metal. As such, he is the ancestor of the many 'mythical blacksmiths' that our imagination turns into powerful giants who are sometimes hostile towards the gods; or else he is a representative of the bronze race described by Hesiod in *Works and Days*. As a man of fire struck on the forehead by a thunderbolt, or a hero often connected with the moon, Cain also shines in his role as the father of artists (Nerval, Butor). His story has inspired countless painters, sculptors, glassmakers and illuminators . . . while the novelist Butor has made amazing use of the qualities of stained glass in a literary context. Like Hugo, we should perhaps be ready to forgive the first murderer a great deal – after all, according to Michel Leiris in *Biffures* (1948) he had a hard name to bear:

> Troubles never come singly: the wrong-doing of the parents was soon followed by that of their eldest son Cain, with a name that foretold his destiny, since it seems that all his wickedness, his baleful character, his aggressive, adamantine hardness as opposed to the gentleness of good, handsome Abel are contained within the short, sharp 'Cain'; [in French] Caïn is shorter than 'caillou' [stone], with the final *a-ïn* grating angrily – a solid object with sharp, spiky edges rubbing against another solid object that also has sharp, spiky edges – while the word 'caillou' though it may start roughly finishes with a liquid, polished almost gentle sound, like the pebble that has been polished and repolished by the water of the stream that carries it along.
>
> In 'Caïn' the diaeresis over the *i* is equivalent to a sort of grimace, drawing the lips back to reveal two sharp canine teeth protruding beyond the other teeth.

Philippe Sellier

Carmen

Most mythologies contain numerous figures symbolizing a formidable type of feminity associated with darkness and the night. In the Greek and Roman myths this role is performed by Artemis and Circe who, as the embodiments of a disturbing inevitability, exercise an evil power over men. During the nineteenth century the image of Woman as half angelic and half evil became more prevalent, and she was represented on the one hand as the terrifying old hag, the witch or the shrew, or on the other, the devil's daughter concealing her wickedness behind an enchanting facade. The sexual constraints and misogyny characteristic of the period contributed to the popularity of the image of woman as both seductive and dangerous.

In his short story, *Carmen*, Prosper Mérimée gave the central female character the attributes associated with this imge of the 'femme fatale'. To suit the purposes of the tale, Carmen was a gypsy of dubious morality who seduced a nobleman with an exemplary respect for traditional values, and thereby caused his downfall. She had to be a woman of easy virtue who unleashed the man's passion and drove him to commit an uncharacteristic crime. As such, she is the perfect scapegoat and she pays with her life, sacrificed in the name of morality and propriety as the victim of Don José's ardour. However, recent artistic versions of the story have renewed the image of Carmen as a 'femme fatale' and freed it from the negative connotations with which it was invested by nineteenth-century society and culture. As a result the complex and multifaceted nature of Woman has been rediscovered.

THE ARCHETYPE OF THE 'FEMME FATALE'

In the context of the literature of the period, Carmen was merely another version of the archetype of the 'femme fatale'. Physically, she embodies all the symbols associated with the night by those who see it as something sinister. Her beautiful black hair has 'the blue glints of the raven's wing', she has the dark, penetrating 'gaze of the wolf' and the copper-coloured skin of a Moorish woman. The dominance of black evidently evokes the darkness and obscurity of night, and Carmen lives in a world that is diametrically opposed to the world of light. In Mérimée's story, the narrator first encounters her as she emerges from a shadowy half-light, returning from the river, a forbidden world coveted by men, a place where women indulge in the pleasure of bathing. She appears in the 'shadowy light of the stars'. Her beauty and grace, devoid of all purity, are both fascinating and intriguing. Everything seems to condemn her – she is impure and dishonest – while the nocturnal setting reinforces the idea of something forbidden. Carmen lives at night. She makes her living from illegal practices such as smuggling and theft; she uses her charms and resorts to magic and witchcraft. She endangers men in the sense that she seals and unseals their fate without them being able to control what happens. In Peter Brook's *The Tragedy of Carmen*, Carmen sits enveloped in a blanket on the bare ground like an old fortune teller and decides the fate of Don José. She holds up the Gemini tarot card representing love of the sun. Then, placing the card on the ground, she arranges various items in a circle around it: a double cord, symbolizing a bond and human destiny, and other magical objects, such as a feather and a piece of lead. She uses the powers of evil to ensnare and cast spells, and love is born under bad omens. Repeated references are made to the blackness of Carmen's soul. She is treated as a devil, and she herself claims to be the devil. She represents the evil woman, the witch who is the bearer of misfortune, the female version of the scapegoat. She is enveloped and inhabited by black, as she is by death. Carmen is the witch of fate and destiny.

Carmen is not only characterized by blackness, but also by constant movement and noise. Half woman and half animal, she is never still 'as is usual for women and cats'. She combines the feminine with the animal: 'she rolled her eyes ike a chameleon'; 'one of her crocodile laughs'; 'no monkey ever capered more than she, nor made such mischief'. In act IV of his operatic film, Francesco Rosi makes a perceptive comparison between Carmen and the bull in the ring, emphasizing that both represent the final sacrifice and associating them both with Cronos and Thanatos – the passing of time and death.

The colour red, which is often associated with black, also features prominently in the imagery of the 'femme fatale'. It symbolizes extroversion tending towards aggression and provocativeness. It is a flamboyant, gaudy, crimson associated with daylight and with conquest. 'She wore a very short red shirt . . . dainty red leather shoes tied with flame-coloured ribbons'.

Another shade of red is associated with impurity and the blood which will be spilt on behalf of Carmen. Don José kills Carmen's husband and lovers, and then Carmen herself. 'I am tired of killing your lovers – you are the one I will kill.'

THE OUTLINE OF THE DOWNFALL

The downfall of Don José is expressed in terms of his being 'possessed by evil'. Carmen, the emodiment of human wickedness and sin, unleashes his passion, jealousy and violence. Moral decline is represented in female terms: 'A pretty girl makes you lose your head. You fight for her, something terrible happens . . . and you become a thief before you know where you are'. This decline is suggested already during the first meeting between Carmen and

Don José on the 'calle de Candilejo'. Carmen's voracious appetite amounts to greed and, as such, is severely criticized by Don José. 'When she had eaten sweets like a six-year-old child, she took more by the handful . . . There is no limit to her tricks and stupid pranks'. The stomach, with its sexual and digestive functions, is both a symbol and a portent of the final downfall.

The departure to the mountains is the beginning of Don José's descent into hell. He confronts the world with his sword or 'maquila' in an attempt to re-establish moral good, to control his own destiny and to avoid the death that awaits him.

On several occasions, Don José wants to believe that Carmen has been converted into a virtuous and well-behaved young woman, and that good has finally triumphed over evil. 'It was the first time she had approached me with the reserve of a decent woman and I was naive enough to think that she had renounced her former ways'.

However, Carmen is different from other 'femme fatales' in the sense that, unlike Manon Lescaut, she does not see fidelity in terms of inconstancy. She does not expect love to bring about redemption.

THE THEME OF THE MOTHER: THE ANTITHESIS OF THE 'FEMME FATALE'

In his conflict-ridden thoughts, in his need to confront and distinguish himself from other rivals, Don José is also a figure on the heroic scale. Meanwhile, in Bizet's opera, the introduction of the character of Micaela reinforces the concept of the two opposing aspects of Woman.

In contrast to Carmen's 'blackness', Don José praises the purity, 'whiteness' and gentleness of Micaela, an ideal companion comparable to the Virgin Mother. She fosters an image of peace and tenderness that is identified with one's homeland and Mother Earth. She represents the beneficent woman of the mystical constellations of the night sky, and she wears blue, which is devoid of any suggestion of sexuality. It is due to Micaela's presence that Don José is carried off by a dreamlike vision of his homeland encircled with a halo of light, and it is Micaela who acts as a shield to protect him from the charms of Carmen.

In *The Tragedy of Carmen*, Peter Brook decides to oppose the two women in the very first scene, which marks the beginning of the conflict between them. Don José's understanding of women involves judging them in relation to the maternal ideal, an ideal that excludes all other forms of femininity.

THE THEME OF 'OTHERNESS'

Mérimée's short story presents a conflict between two cultures. On the one hand, there is Don José who represents a military and even religious order, since it is stated that he was once a seminarist. He can be defined in terms of his 'attachment' to the values established by society, namely honour and respect for the social hierarchy. On the other hand, there is the gypsy Carmen, who belongs to a group on the margins of society, who transcends the established order and who acts 'according to her pleasure'. Although Spain provided an ideal setting for the scenes of confrontation, passion and violence, it may be wondered whether it was actually *necessary* for Carmen to be Spanish. Her mantilla and castanets are certainly not necessary, and, in the artistic cinematic representations of the story that have followed the literary and operatic versions, local colour has been relegated to the background. The title of Jean-Luc Godard's film *Prénom Carmen*, uses the first name symbolically to refer to a type of woman rather than to a woman of a specific nationality. Similarly, Otto Preminger presents a black Carmen who is always referred to as 'the Carmen'; while in modern versions of the opera *Carmen*, the sober and sparse décor tends to emphasize the inner emotions of the main characters.

Don José and Love According to the Concept of 'Being'

For Don José, Carmen will always be a stranger – she will always be an indomitable part of the darkness that lies repressed within him. His first reaction is thus one of a fear of the evil in others. 'What is more, the Andalusian girls frightened me with their continual mockery'. Although Don José is fascinated by Carmen's spirit, his glimpse of the wrold of eroticism accentuates his lack of understanding of both the Other and himself, and this in turn breeds fear. For this obscure force, this passion that takes hold of him and devours his whole being surely reveals a fear of change and, ultimately, of chaos. The sorceress personified by Carmen becomes a creature of his subconscious. Finding himself unable either to control his emotions or to abandon the rational principles that he has hitherto defended, Don José's second reaction is to try to appropriate the Other. His desire is one of conquest. Paradoxically, he sets out to control the uncontrollable Carmen in his desire to prove to himself that he is capable of subjugating the perfidious femininity that she represents. Male power is achieved through combat, so, for example, in the duel with Carmen's husband Garcia, Don José feels inspired by an invincible force and rediscovers the grandeur of his race. 'I set about it in Navarran fashion . . . I felt stronger than a giant'.

He reaches a stage where he wants not only to keep his relationship exclusively for himself but also to give it a hierarchical form. 'Smugglers on horseback, carrying their blunderbusses, with their mistresses behind them . . . I already saw myself riding through mountains and valleys with the sweet gypsy girl behind me.' 'If I keep you in the mountains I can be sure of you'.

It seems, therefore, that the idea of a 'fatal passion' should be understood in terms of Don José's desire to conquer, which leads him first to the destruction of others and ultimately to self-destruction. His confrontational and dualistic attitude is bound to end in failure. He is a victim not so much of fatal passion as of his 'pride in his own existence'.

Carmen and Love According to the Concept of 'Having'

For Carmen, love implies the casting off of all attachments and constraints and the right to do as she pleases. She scorns Don José's subservience and obedience to rules. ' "At the barracks," she said, "are you a negro slave to be ordered about with a stick? You are a canary, by nature as well as with all your fine plumage".' Carmen's rejection of the ring, a symbol of union and fidelity, which she throws at Don José's feet, will ultimately cost her her life. Unlike Don José, Carmen always remains in control of herself and is steadfast in her determination. Thus, her devastating laugh is a sign of self-assertion both towards the world and in defiance of it. Her attitude is symbolized by a response to any attempt to control her that recurs in all versions of the story: 'I do not want to be plagued or, above all, ordered about. I want to be free and able to do as I please'. She is determined to protect her freedom, whatever the cost. She escapes from prison, and although Don José is imprisoned in her place, she offers him the means to escape. She claims her freedom even in death: ' "I can see you want to kill me" she said, "it was inevitable, but you will not make me give in . . . Carmen will always be free" '. Her desire for freedom is expressed in the evocative image of the mountain; her nocturnal domain of 'over the mountains' represents an invitation to peace and intimacy in a privileged place free from all forms of law and authority. The mountain is for Carmen what the Basque village of his homeland is for Don José. 'The open sky, the gypsy life . . . and above all the intoxication of: freedom! freedom!'. However, Carmen is not rebelling against the social order. As a woman who feels free to love as she wishes, she has been quite wrongly used as a feminist symbol. Conversely, she has been described as a frivolous woman of easy virtue, and considered to be immoral. In fact, she is amoral and merely wishes to preserve her individuality. In his study of the image of the Sorceress in *La Sorcière*, Michelet points out that if Woman is feared and hated it is because she demonstrates a spirit of individuality and freedom that is in direct conflict with the values of traditional religion. This is certainly true in Carmen's case. She seems closer than men to primitive nature. She lives life in its most immediate and ephemeral form. Instinctive by nature, 'uncivilized' and halfway between child and animal, she responds only to her immediate needs. She enjoys the little epicurean pleasures and treats money, pleasure and love as commodities that are all part of the game.

THE THEME OF THE WOMAN OF DARKNESS

In the seduction scene, the Habanera, Carmen sways her hips in a fascinating and insistent rhythmic gyration, symbolizing physical desire and sexual union.

For Carmen, music and sexuality combine in a perfect synthesis. In the prelude to seduction her approach is subtle and measured. Carmen's body has the undulating suppleness of a snake, and is vibrant with sexuality. She accompanies her dance with a tambourine, the symbol of fertility and creation. A hummed tune and the rattle of castanets are far more suggestive than words. Carmen knows how to speak through her body. Her whole being is animated by an inner vitality and sensuality, and the sensuality becomes a law unto itself. Carmen experiences her femininity to the full, while still remaining in complete control of herself. Her personality contains certain qualities that are also characteristic of Hermes. She develops a strategy for negotiation, and resorts to trickery and the manipulation of language. In the scene in which she deceives an English lord, she leads him on with wonderful panache. As a businesswoman and a woman of action she is indispensable to men. She moves easily through the underworld of smuggling, changing her role at will. She is the link between the visible and the invisible world. Through her expertise in magic and with tarot cards, she re-establishes contact with the forces that animate the world. Because she is able to see into the future, she knows that death awaits her, but she remains calm and composed until the fatal blow is delivered. In Peter Brook's *The Tragedy of Carmen*, Carmen and the toreador Escamillo are linked by the same tragic fate. Death occurs brutally, with the same intensity and violence that pulsated through their lives. Both characters symbolize creative and undisciplined energies that are unleashed in contexts of sport and celebration, such as the fiesta or the bullring. At the beginning of Act IV of the opera, Carmen appears in a sumptuous shining costume like that of the toreador. As a female devotee of Dionysus she searches avidly for new experiences and is willing to live out the drama of death rather than submit to a life devoid of excitement. She chooses death in preference to mediocrity. 'I may be yours in death, but I will no longer live with you.' Only death can stop Carmen in her tracks.

Recent artistic versions of *Carmen* have re-emphasized the multifaceted quality of the mythical figure. She remains a woman of paradox, 'of obscure light'. As a woman of daylight, her presence is fascinating and radiant. As a woman of darkness, she is regenerated in the recurring theme of love. Although she is accused of lying, stealing and deception, she is also capable of performing deeds of kindness. She protests Man from danger, cures him and even goes as far as to save his life. Like a black sun, Carmen shines with a vital fire that is obscured by a lack of male understanding. Today, Carmen's fate has led to a renewed awareness of Woman in all her sensuality and individuality, and an awareness that she still continues to be sacrified as long as she lives.

Corinne Booker-Mesana

Celtic Myths

Since a myth is always a religious phenomenon, studying the myths that underpin the Celtic civilization is tantamount to studying the religious beliefs of all peoples of Europe between the seventh–sixth centuries BC and the sixth–seventh centuries AD. In fact, the Celtic religion did not disappear as an organized system of thought and social practices until about the thirteenth century – and even then not entirely. True, it seems clear that the Catholic Church played a major part in ensuring its decline from about the sixth century AD, notably through the establishment of the cult of the Virgin Mary, of the ritual year, etc. But it was only in the thirteenth century, with the activities of Saint Bernard of Clairvaux, that Christian beliefs became prevalent throughout the Celtic world, penetrating even the rural areas that had earlier been the preserve of paganism (derived from the Latin word *pagus* meaning 'village' which is also the root of the word 'peasant'. These rural societies had previously been extremely hostile to all alien forms of religious thought, which they regarded as ideas imported by the Roman colonizers, and their conversion would scarcely have been possible but for the systematic use of 'religious syncretism'.

When one religion is usurping another, the proponents of the new beliefs will adopt any elements in the old religion that may facilitate their task, reprocessing them theologically and ideologically as required. This ensures that the followers of the old cults will be less disorientated by the demands of the new form of worship. The process is known as 'syncretism' and its effects are particularly apparent in the use of religious myths, regardless of whether or not they are actually written down. Normally, a myth forms part of an oral tradition and does not lend itself readily to the written form. This was probably more true of the Celtic myths than of their Christian counterparts, but the vitality of the Celtic myths in the collective Celtic imagination meant that Christians were forced to make use of them. This meant transforming them to their advantage, but the changes had to be kept to a minimum so that the Celts still felt themselves to be part of a living tradition.

The study of Celtic myths requires some sort of definition of the geographical outline of the Celtic world, based on the development of these myths during the course of history. This introduces the concept of a 'cultural zone', which is inherent in the very concept of religion and society. Myth, which shapes political as well as religious aspects of society, must ultimately be defined in relation to space and time.

Because myths form the framework of any human society, or more exactly, because a community defines itself through its myths, there is no doubt that the most fundamental myths can be grouped into two categories: as 'political', or 'literary'.

The survival of the Celtic myths is due, on the one hand, to their adaptation by means of the syncretic process just described and, on the other, to the political and literary form that they assumed during the thirteenth century in particular. However, our understanding of them is based to large extent on another type of myth: the 'folk tale'.

The folk tale is a narrative in the oral tradition, which usually has no connection with writing. The view held here is that a tale is merely a mechan-mism used by any initiatory religion to disseminate the substance of its religious myths among masses of uninitiated believers, who are not entitled to know the full details of the myths themselves. Telling a story was therefore equivalent to reciting a 'catechism' and served to spread the basic theological knowledge essential to the spiritual life of the population. It is thus possible to trace the development of any myth by deciphering the folk tales that have been handed down to us.

In Europe, there is a very sizeable core of recorded tales that enable us to trace the development of original myths in this way. However, it can obviously only be clearly defined in terms of the concept of the cultural zone referred to above. This makes it possible to identify, for example, which elements of the material in question were produced by the Celts and which must be attributed to the Germanic civilization. This makes it essential for the researcher to adopt an almost archaeological approach to religion. However, even when the material has been divided in this way, there still remains an extensive body of recorded tales to be studied.

The tale, like the myth, with which is must always be linked if its 'anthropo-logical' value is to be preserved, is always a composite narrative. It represents the co-ordination or subordination of a certain number of more basic 'narrative elements' (called, depending on the author, the 'function' or 'theme'). These produce a relatively rigid 'structure' in which imagination has virtually no place, except in terms of particular features of the narrative such as the language used. The tale is thus a 'fixed form' narrative.

It is particularly difficult to study Celtic myths exhaustively. The discussion that follows can only be understood in relation to the method used to collect the research material, since no Celtic myths have been handed down to us in the form of first-hand accounts. The Celtic priests, or Druids, always refused to commit any account of their religion to writing. They regarded writing merely as a convenient secular technique, but considered it an unsuitable vehicle for reporting any form of intercourse between Man and the divine or between Man and Knowledge. For this reason, the versions of myths that we can reconstruct by cross-checking with the sources described above are all relatively late. In fact, it was not until the thirteenth century that written material became quite abundant, and we only have this now because the

Christian religion was then in direct competition with the old ancestral religion of the Celts: in short, it is a product of religious syncretism. Our sources are basically as follows:

- First, there is the 'Arthurian' legend, either in its courtly form, in the romances by Chrétien de Troyes, or in other versions from the same tradition. The latter include Robert de Boron's *Roman du Graal*, as well as works of an earlier date than those just mentioned, the earliest certain versions of which date mainly from the eighth or ninth centuries (Geoffrey of Monmouth, Wace, Nennius, etc.). This legend flourished chiefly from the twelfth and thirteenth centuries onwards.
- *La Légende dorée* is also an important source of information, whether in its established literary form by de Voragine (Iacopo da Varazze) who refers constantly to the thoughts of Saint Bernard, or in its more popular form represented by the countless 'Lives of the Saints'.
- Next there are the 'penitentials', lists of sins revealed by penitents during confession and of the penances allocated to them. These contain a series of statements concerning official religious dogma and pagan beliefs in the areas concerned, made in response to questions from priests.
- And, finally, there are the folk tales, described above.

From a comparison of these different sources, it is possible to detect a general structure forming the basis of the Celtic religion and involving a 'great underlying myth' to which the Christian religion endeavoured to adapt itself as much as possible. The main features of this myth are summarized below.

ELEMENTS OF THE GREAT CELTIC MYTH

> Mercury is the most honoured of all gods and many images of him are to be found. He is considered as the inventor of all the arts, the guide of travellers and of merchants, and the most powerful god in matters of commerce and gain. After him, the Gauls honour Apollo, Mars, Jupiter and Minerva. Of these gods they hold almost the same opinions as other peoples do: Apollo drives away diseases, Minerva promotes handicrafts, Jupiter rules the heavens and Mars controls wars.

Like the material in other parts of the work, the remarkably detailed information in this much-quoted passage from Caesar's *The Gallic War* (VI. 17), must apparently be taken at face value. Though its validity has been questioned, for the purposes of the present study, we shall treat it as entirely accurate. The order of precedence of the most important gods in the Celtic pantheon is exactly as stated.

Mercury, Apollo, and Mars were the gods of the kingdom of This World, Jupiter was the ruling god of the kingdom of the Otherworld, while Minerva was the Mother Goddess. Also, as in Greek and Roman mythology, Apollo and Mars were brothers; and there are even occasional hints that they may have been regarded as twins. However, it seems that ultimately they were not, although they do appear to have been the Celtic form of the Dioscuri. As regards 'Jupiter', he seems to have been the deity referred to elsewhere as 'Dis Pater'. In addition to being the supreme deity of the Otherworld, he was also the ruler of all the gods, who drew their authority from him, whether they were from This World or the Otherworld. This meant that the Celtic pantheon was remarkably restricted. Finally the Great Goddess appeared by turns in both kingdoms and ruled with her consort.

1 The immediate conclusion to be drawn from the information given above is that the Celtic universe consisted of two kingdoms that were complementary and often in conflict. Mortals were only familiar with one of these, the kingdom of This World, where they lived. However, they were also subject to the various influences exerted on it by the Otherworld, in the same way that they knew that actions performed in This World inevitably had repercussions there. Contrary to the belief prevalent since the birth of Christianity, the Otherworld was not merely the kingdom of the Dead. Rather, it was the location of another dimension of life, though among its many areas devoted to different activities, there was also a specific domain reserved for their eternal sojourn. As in Egyptian mythology this domain was located at the most westerly point of the world, which explains why the folk tales of the European 'ends of the earth' (Land's End, Finistère, Finisterre) place such a strong emphasis on death and ghosts. In this context, it should be remembered that the main reason why such themes occur in the folklore of these places is that the boundary between land and sea constituted the frontier between the two kingdoms. It was from this very coastline that the dead began their journey to their domain in the Otherworld, while it was also across this frontier that ghosts returned to This World. Thus mortals made the same journey in death as their great god made throughout his life (see below).

2 The first characteristic of Celtic mythology to emerge from the present study is therefore that the gods were subject to the usual natural cycle of life and death: they were born, grew old and died, exactly like human beings. Consequently, the myths that describe the adventures of individual gods portray them at various stages of their lives – which created the impression that there were many more divinities than there actually were. Instead of forming continuous narratives, the stories connected with the three male gods and the Great Goddess tended to take the form of a series of episodes. One adventure occurs during the deities' early youth, another when they have reached sexual maturity and yet another when they are about to lose their power and their life. The gods experienced eternity in a particularly interesting way: they died merely to be restored to life and to repeat a life cycle similar, or even identical, to the previous one. The fundamental Celtic myth is thus characterized by the theory of the Eternal Return, according to which, in the infinite Time and Space formed by the two worlds, time progresses in a cyclical manner, so that events recur in an identical form in those that the

original cycle follow. The divine adventure and human life begin again and again exactly as they did the first time. In *La Légende dorée*, the cycle of the Eternal Return seems to be one of 372 or 377 years, and if this is indeed the timespan that the Celts envisaged, this has considerable importance in relation to the ritual calendar. The significant concepts underlying the Celtic calendar are the subject of a continuing controversy between specialists and will be considered later.

3 A further conclusion that can be drawn from the first two points made above is that the Celtic myths are 'oriented' according to the points of the compass. The space that they defined – the Celtic 'templum', so to speak – had the following characteristics. The inhabitants of the kingdom of This World were perpetually drawn to the West, which was the point of departure for their journey to a region in the mysterious kingdom of the Otherworld. They had a strong desire to penetrate the mystery of death, while they also wanted to discover mysterious routes that their great god took when he left for the Otherworld to experience the Passion that would regenerate him. In addition they were eager to know more about the great periods of the Eternal Return and, possibly, to find out when the era referred to by the Romans of the Augustan period as the 'Golden Age', would come back. That the 'doctrine' of the Golden Age appeared or reappeared during the Augustan era may in itself be highly significant, since it surely implies that the political and religious thinkers of the new Roman Empire were strongly influenced by Celtic mysticism. This is extremely likely, since the Roman army under Caesar had come into direct contact with pristine Celtic culture only a few decades earlier, and knowledge of the theory of the Eternal Return must have been widely disseminated among the population. This is borne out by the fact that the same idea suddenly reappeared as a veritable article of faith during the early stages of the establishment of Christianity in Gaul, in the form of the millenarian belief. Thus, it seems that same system of belief recurred twice in parallel cultures.

For Celts living in the East, the very act of departing on a long journey towards the western ocean meant that the traveller was beginning a journey to the Otherworld that would bring him into contact with the mysterious subjects of the other kingdom. Perhaps this urge to move west was one of the unknown forces motivating the great invasions that took place from the Magdalenian period onwards, and perhaps even before. It should be noted in this context that this is precisely the voyage made by Odysseus's companions in the *Odyssey*.

However, it seems that, in the case of certain gods, the original route towards the western ocean was deflected towards the north-west, as seen from the Italian peninsula, though the reasons for this are difficult to understand. Thus, the gods whom, for the sake of simplicity, we have called 'the Dioscuri', became separated on their journey towards the West. After landing in Italy at Monte Gargano, the great sun god, whom the Christians later called Saint Michael, continued his journey towards the north-west and settled on the Mont Saint-Michel and at Stonehenge, among other places. His brother, whom Caesar called Mars, because of his characteristics and those of his cult, arrived in Italy virtually at the foot of Mount Vesuvius, probably in the vicinity of Amalfi, and continued his journey more directly towards the west, until he came to the other major European 'ends of the earth' with all their religious associations. The Christians changed this god, with his characteristic cult of the bull (still recognizable in the 'corridas' of Spain and south-west France), into Saint James, who was so devoutly worshipped at Santiago de Compostela.

The goddess also found her embodiment in the West. She alighted on the earth very near Marseilles, at Saintes-Maries-de-la-Mer' and then took a more northerly route than her companions, passing along the Rhône valley. Finally, she settled in a sacred area between thc confluence of the Rhône and the Saône, and the sources of the Seine and the Meuse, where she still continues to exist as a figure in French folklorc. However, the Christians also made her into a highly revered 'deity' whose sanctuary was in Vézelay and who was given the name, among others, of Saint Mary Magdalene.

When the gods were well and truly established in the West, on the boundaries of the two Celtic worlds, they may have wanted to return to their eastern origins to reinvigorate themselves. Thus, for the peoples living in the extreme West, the East came to represent the other boundary between the two Celtic worlds. The kingdom of This World and its subjects were, so to speak, displaced, which obviously did little to simplify the religious vision and setting of the myth. This process illustrates the concept of the geographical evolution of religion mentioned earlier.

In the world of the extreme West, the myths were those orientated according to the points of the compass and each of the deities became, to some extent, the 'owner' of the 'line of force' that he or she chose at any moment of his or her earthly life. Thus, the Great Goddess moved along a series of parallel lines – and also a series of parallels! – running from north to south. One of these has already been mentioned. Another runs from the Orkney Islands in the extreme north of the Celtic world to Lourdes, and probably extends even further south. Along this route we, of course, find her most famous avatar in folklore – Melusina. Apollo, the great Sun God, but also the healer, is found everywhere in northern and western Europe, except where later invasions have completely erased his earlier traces. However, if there is a region that is particularly sacred to this deity, it centres on the two furthest points on his journey referred to above: the Mont Saint-Michel and Stonehenge. Many of the places where he appeared as a healing deity (the famous Apollo Borvo), still exist in the area of the Mont Saint-Michel and in particular on the Cotentin peninsula. It is also possible that the sanctuary and the sacred spring that were focuses for worship well before the construction of Chartres Cathedral were dedicated to this great god.

On the other hand, it seems that the cult of his brother belongs more to the Celtic-Iberian and Celtic-Ligurian Midi, where its traces can be found from the Vallée des Merveilles to Mont Bégo and as far as Santiago de Compostela, mentioned above – and also probably in the great sanctuaries of the Pyrenees.

It is obvious that, in a religion where the Great God of the kingdom of This World is a later manifestation of the Sun, the two points of the compass at which that star enters and leaves our world every day cannot help but be regarded as sacred.

4 Geographical hypotheses about the development of a religion such as those outlined above should be proved by archaeological research, as well as by a comparative study of religions and any other relevant disciplines. One possible outcome of such research could be to show that this form of religious system was not the exclusive preserve of the Celts. If this theory were accepted – which is still far from being the case – it would imply the existence of a characteristic Indo-European religion modified over the centuries of man's history and inherited by the Celts, whatever their geographical origins. Indeed, the Celts seem to have adopted this heritage as their own, reusing even the religious trappings of their predecessors in a successsful process of syncretism. They did not build the megaliths of Cro-Magnon man, but they systematically made use of them for their own religious practices. There was perhaps an important reason for this. As a small minority in the Western population, they may have been obliged to adapt to the prevailing religious circumstances. All in all, they must have found themselves in much the same position as their successors did during the sixth to thirteenth centuries AD. Unable to impose their religion by converting the indigenous population, they had to practise syncretism as best they could. That is precisely what the western Christians did centuries later.

5 The time of myth, which is also the time of folk tale, is the Time of Origins. What is told is the god's actual story, the one that served as a model for believers in the recurring cycle of religious practices. This sacred story can only have been developed during the earliest period of the god's existence, when he experienced his adventures for the first time; and this period marks the starting point of History. Because in Celtic thought time is cyclical – except in human representations of the divine adventure, which convert it into a ritual – the Sacred Story was constantly renewed through a new manifestation of the god, as already explained above. This meant that time on a human level was regarded as extremely sacred, because at each moment in Man's life the god could decide to honour History by reappearing in a new incarnation. There was no distinction between the two worlds that constituted reality. The gods lived among men in an unpredictable and unexpected manner and enabled societies to convert human lives into acts of an exclusively religious nature. The human being was surrounded by the divine and drew

the justification for his life and his historical continuity from the very nature of his gods. History was thus constantly regenerated and restored to the purity of its Origins. This was certainly what gave the western Celtic civilization its unique character, since it lived not only surrounded by its gods and through them, but also for them. Faith must play an omnipresent role in the daily activities as well as the 'historical' acts of both communities and individuals. This is surely the explanation of the apparent inability of the Celts to organize themselves into empires like that of the Romans. Nothing should have been able to harm this society because it was in the hands of the god. No power could be given to a human, elected king, because he could only gain his true power from the god, in whose image he was created. A flesh-and-blood king could only have real power if he was the embodiment of the Great God, who had returned by manifesting himself through him – a truly miraculous event in the case of man. It is therefore possible that Vercingetorix's failure to establish a system of supreme kingship that might have enabled him to resist Caesar successfully was due as much to religious factors as to sinister political rivalries. It was because he was not acknowledged as being the incarnation of the God-King as he wanted to be, and because his contemporaries were probably not aware of the signs of his divine election. The tremendous hopes that could be raised by the divine election of the king are apparent in literature. In the Arthurian legends, Arthur's personal adventure is of little importance. What does matter is that his kingship symbolizes, in mythical terms, the dual investiture that French monarchs later sought to establish with their coronations. He was initially chosen by the gods and subsequently by his human subjects. He was therefore the God-King who was expected to restore the ideal society. Arthur's venture failed, since he did not succeed in transforming mankind and society as expected. Though he was, indeed, essentially divine, he fell victim to the merciless conflict between the deities from the kingdoms of This World and the Otherworld before he could fulfil his mission.

6 The basis of the fundamental Celtic myth lies in an endless and ubiquitous conflict between the monarchies of the two kingdoms. The only way to become king in This World was for the aspirant to intervene in the Otherworld; while only the brother of the Great God of the kingdom of This World could become king of the Otherworld gaining sovereignty over it by force and cunning. Incessant *conflict* was the very driving force behind the theology of the two kingdoms – conflict and violence. A true Passion was enacted by these three male divinities when they became Kings of the two realms. It was the destiny of the god who was the elder of the 'Dioscuri' to become king of the kingdom of This World, and the destiny of his younger brother later to become the god of the Otherworld, but neither of them could take up their kingship without first seizing the previous ruler's symbols of office. The latter lost his life and his kingdom because he was drained and exhausted by his reign, since a king, whether human or divine, had to bring prosperity and

fertility to the community of which he was the religious leader. This act of giving gradually used up all his energy, which he meted out by the very act of reigning. This is what also happens to the Sun, which is apparently exhausted by its fertilization of the Earth during the springtime of its youth. By the end of the summer, the impregnated Mother Earth has brought forth her offspring and become infertile, while the male god is equally incapable of fertilizing her again. The seasonal cycle is thus the visual representation of this great divine adventure. But if, in astronomical terms, the solar cycle is annual, it seems that the same is not true of the religious cycle.

7 This brings us to another hypothesis that has yet to be corroborated conclusively, namely that the Celtic ritual cycle was perhaps not annual, like its Christian counterpart. It is known that the Christians condensed the divine time scale in order to accommodate all their rituals within the exact period of a solar year. Thus, every year, Christ is born in the winter solstice and dies around the time of the spring equinox. This has an extremely strange result. The entire annual chronology of his life is accelerated. In fact, not only are the thirty-three years of his historical life scaled down so they can be incorporated within the twelve-month framework that constitutes the timespan of the ritual calendar, but the rational structure of all life has also been accelerated. The emphasis is placed entirely on the god's birth and death. These are linked by a holy period of three months, and the interval that separates them is effectively reserved for the narrative of the Passion that precedes this death. In other words, it is necessary to remove from the 'holy period' any stories that deal with the rest of the god's life, in particular anything to do with his 'public life', his teaching, etc. Christians have thus apparently refused to stress the god's humanity, and put an almost exclusive emphasis on the doctrine of Redemption by the Passion, which itself was made possible by the unique event of the Incarnation. If Christ's life is supposed to be a model for humanity, theologians do not seem to be interested in its more 'everyday' aspects.

For the Celts, on the other hand, the entire life of their god was of theological interest. This was because it effectively provided the model for all other individual lives, or, more precisely, because the individual had virtually no intrinsic value, and it was the collective life of the community that would be fully invigorated, from within, by the god's life. God alone could be the spiritual and physical leader of the human society, and the leader, if he were well chosen, could only be one of the god's avatars. This meant that the social group lived in eternal hope that the next leader that it selected would embody the confirmation of the god's actual return, in other words, be his reincarnation; for it was unthinkable that the divine entity could abandon the human beings that he had created and who were nothing without him.

Of considerable interest in this context is a strange but well-known document dating from the second century AD, known as *Le Calendrier de Coligny* (the Coligny calendar), after the town in the Jura where it was found at the beginning of this century. This calendar, which is indisputably of Celtic origin, has a number of distinctive characteristics, though there is not sufficient space to study it here in detail. The calendar is composed of a sequence of sixty-two months. However, there is no allusion to an annual cycle, which precludes the possibility of referring to a '*five-year*' calendar; even though the period of sixty months that is covered is more or less equivalent to five of our years. The calendar is also apparently lunar, and so cannot simply be designed to make up the time difference inherent in a solar calendar, a time difference of which the Celts of this period were certainly aware, since they had already been in contact with their Roman colonizers for some time. Two intercalary months – which bear specific names in the document that we possess – have been added to the sixty basic months. The first of these occurs at the beginning of the calendar and the second occurs thirty months later. This deliberate break makes the caldenric cycle a complete entity divided into halves, each lasting thirty-one months. The resulting system is perfectly cyclical, and the festivals belonging to each solstice come at the beginning of each period. One, the winter solstice, was devoted to the celebration of the birth of the new god of This World in the Otherworld – a hostile world in which he was surrounded by dangers. The other intercalary month was in all probability devoted to the celebration of the same god's seizure of power in the kingdom of This World when he had come of age at the time of the summer solstice, in other words, when he was fifteen, which for the Celts was the age at which an individual became an adult and could, for example, get married.

If this view is correct, then it is evident that the reduction of real time to make it conform with ritual is not nearly as drastic as in the case of the Christian calendar. In this case, the temporal reduction respects the chronological development of life.

These observations suggest that Celtic ritual time was based on a sacred period of five years at the end of which, in ritual terms, everything began again; and though this is only partially correct when presented boldly in this way, it is extremely significant.

Thus, the timespans of the various elements of the Celtic myth discussed so far are generally based on a five-year period. Close examination of Robert de Boron's *Roman du Graal*, reveals that its three parts chiefly cover a period of five years or a multiple of five years. The same is true of the story of Merlin's birth, from his conception to the date when he started his active life. It is also the period that has to elapse between the union of Arthur's parents, Uther Pendragon and Igerna, and the birth of Arthur himself. And there are other examples. However, the total length of time covered by the myth is much longer than these five years, because generally the story depicts the divine adventure over several generations. Indeed, its *four generations* appear to make it the archetype of the ancient Indo-European family. This is not only illustrated by the Arthurian legend transcribed by Robert de Boron in the *Roman du Graal*, but also by the *Légendes sur les Nartes*, compiled by Dumézil among the Ossets. This five-year period only seems to have applied to male deities, though: the situation was entirely different in the case of the Great Goddess. Regenerated from generation to generation, this mother goddess usually created a triple female lineage. She was called the Triple Goddess, or the Triple Brigit, for example, by the Welsh and the Irish. The goddess's three daughters – who occasionally seem to be triplets – were born in the Otherword and all share the same characteristics. The eldest would become the Virgin Mother and would succeed her own mother, the second would be the Sacred Whore and would ultimately become the queen of the kingdom of the Otherworld, while the third and last would be the eternal infertile Virgin, whose task it was to watch over and protect the vast family treasures in the depths of the earth. When one of the goddess's daughters gave birth only to boys, it was because she had lost her divine powers. She might, for example, have married a man and though he might have attained kingship as a result, he was still only a man and could not under any circumstances accede to divine sovereignty. An example of this 'decline of the goddess' or, at any rate, of her 'degeneration' can be found in *Mélusine* by Jean d'Arras. In this instance, the myth has to some extent been divested of its sanctity and has taken the form of a myth of foundation. Thus the goddess's divine power could be embodied in another of her avatars, if, for example, the one who usually received it was no longer worthy of it because of one of her adventures – as in the case of Mélusina just cited.

OUTLINES OF THE GREAT MYTH

It is worth giving a brief summary of some of the main theological characteristics of the various gods mentioned above.

Adventures from the Time of Youth

a) *'Mercury'*

The god whom Caesar called Mercury is in fact the one who has left the greatest number of perceptible traces. The memory of his divine adventures is still preserved in the stories of his later embodiments who appear under various names, including: Merlin, Tom Thumb, Cernunnos, Cú Chulainn and Connor, Riquet à la houppe (Riquet with the Tuft) and, in the Christian world, Saint Andrew, Saint Christopher, etc. Although this is by no means an exhaustive list, its length already demonstrates the importance of this multifaceted divinity.

This god made use of magic and was above all the 'Multiple Craftsman'. Thus, it was not unusual for shamanism to feature in his various adventures, and, indeed, he employed this art during his youth to accomplish his initiatory journey to the Otherworld. Although, like Tom Thumb, he left for the

Otherworld at Samain to complete his initiation, he did not go there to find a woman who would invest him with sovereign status, but to learn how to master all the magical powers that he had inherited from the outset. He was the first Druid and was given the task of protecting the great Sun God and his brother when they arrived in This World to conquer their kingdom.

As illustrated by Robert de Boron's text, for example, the god was the son of the god of the Otherworld and a maiden from the kingdom of This World, whom that god had raped and he was conceived expressly to help his father in his struggle against the god of the kingdom of This World. Other versions of the same myth suggest that his conception actually resulted from adultery between the consort of the god of the kingdom of This World and the god of the Otherworld. It is difficult to know whether the adulterous act was forced upon the woman by rape, or whether she was a willing party to it, since both versions appear in the mythical tradition.

What is certain is that the mother spent her pregnancy imprisoned on an island, often represented by a tower. The child was so remarkable that the gestation period was extremely long, and when he was finally born, he was as remarkable for his ugliness as for his extraordinary abilities. He was, in fact, a seer, who could look into the past as well as the future, and he revealed his chthonic blood – inherited from his mother – by controlling dragons. At the same time, he was also the deity particularly revered at Shrovetide and, because he was as much of the kingdom of This World as he was of the Otherworld, he was the object of a cult that inverted the customary values of this world. He was already the ferryman-god and it was his resonsibility to expedite the Great God's journey into the kingdom of This World.

b) '*Apollo*'

Apollo was the youngest child of a family of three boys. In folk tales, he was always presented as the one least likely to obtain the supreme sovereignty as, for example, in Perrault's story *Le Chat botté* (Puss-in-Boots), which precisely mirrors this aspect of the myth. The same situation arises at the beginning of the story of *Mélusine* and in the story of Uther Pendragon in the Arthurian legend, where the youngest of the three sons marries the eldest of the mother goddess's daughters.

The young god lived the early part of his life in the Otherworld and only returned to the kingdom of This World with his brother, who helped him to conquer his kingdom. However, the most important element in this part of his epic story is his marriage, which only took place when the hero was *chosen* by his consort. The hero himself played no active role in this part of the adventure; he was at the mercy of external forces embodied in the female deity. The marriage was only possible after the young god had undergone the most advanced type of initiation in the form of a journey. This is why his usual companion is the ferryman-god mentioned above – the latter had already preceded him in his conquest of magical power in the Otherworld and was the master of requisite 'shamanist techniques'.

The hero was impelled to make the initiatory journey by the goddess, who had chosen him from the Otherworld; and this impulse was provided by a magic hunt, in which the hunter became the prey of his own quarry. The event took place at Samain, where the hero's personality underwent an extremely interesting split, a phenomenon which also occurs among peoples renowned for 'shamanism', for example, in Siberia. Returning to the story presently under consideration, during the course of the hunt the hero fell into a trance, which led to exhaustion and illness. In the Otherworld, the regenerated Great Goddess allowed herself to be seen by the man that she had chosen and he became sick with love. His choice of consort was therefore controlled by the woman herself and, in return, she made it possible for him to attain sovereignty and become its joint guardian along with her. He himself was under the impression that it was he who was choosing his consort by arranging a competition, and did not realize that all the elements in the competition were in fact controlled by the Great Goddess. The marriage made the young couple the divine rulers of the kingdom of This World and, for the inhabitants of that kingdom, the ceremony represented the beginning of an era of prosperity and happiness referred to elsewhere as 'the Golden Age'.

c) *'Mars'*

Mars was the brother of Apollo and while, in Christian terms, the latter was represented, for example, by Saint John and Saint Michael as well as by Christ, 'Mars' was represented by Saint James. He was the second of the Dioscuri, even if this title is somewhat inaccurate.

The god arrived in the kingdom of This World before his brother, to pave the way for him. In the Arthurian epic, he was represented by King Pendragon, who reigned for only a short time, and he should thus be older than 'Apollo'. He helped his brother to conquer the kingdom of This World and when the latter had taken possession of it – before his marriage – he left it for great adventures in the Otherworld. There, he eventually became the Great God of the kingdom since it was his destiny to conquer the Otherworld and take it from its ageing ruler.

So that he could achieve this, his brother had to intervene just after his marriage, and 'Apollo', therefore, made a short expedition into the Otherworld before returning triumphant. A brief account of this event can be found in the *Sleeping Beauty*, for example, although the story there is generally considered to be told from the standpoint of the Great Goddess and not from that of her consort. Mars could only attain the sovereignty to which he aspired through his marriage to another of the Great Goddess's daughters. To achieve this, he violently abducted the wife of the ruling king of the Otherworld, and it was because of this act of adultery that 'Apollo' was forced to come to his brother's aid.

Adventures from the End of the Reign

d) *'Jupiter'*

Jupiter was another manifestation of the god 'Mars', representing him when he was established as the great god of the Otherworld, reigning uncontested over his kingdom. Because he was the elder brother of the god of the kingdom of This World and because he gave up his kingdom to the latter, he was effectively more important than him and appears to be the ruler of the gods. He was the ruler of water, especially the sea, where he was often to be found roaming his watery kingdom on his swift horses.

When he came of age, he fell in love with his sister-in-law, the queen of the kingdom of This World, and abducted her against her will, locking her in a tower-island in his kingdom. It would be helpful to know whether the rape occurred when the goddess was pregnant or whether she became pregnant as a result of the rape. What is certain, though, is that she spent her pregnancy locked up in her prison. The abduction to the Otherworld took place during Shrovetide and the child was born at the time of the winter solstice.

Not long before this adventure, in the course of three rapes, only one of which produced offspring, Jupiter had sired the new ferryman-god referred to earlier. The rape of the three young sisters, all virgins, took place at the time of the autumn equinox, and the new ferryman-god was born around mid-July, this time probably in the kingdom of This World. In this instance, too, the mother and the child were imprisoned in a tower-island, probably the one that the Welsh and the Irish refer to as the 'Land of Women'. The god committed this triple rape not because he was in love with the three virgins, but because he wanted to counter the invasion plans of the god of the kingdom of This World, which threatened his position as king of the Otherworld. His aim was to prevent the new generation from deposing him, but his efforts were to no avail. After the period at the beginning of their reigns when there was complete harmony between the two kings and the two kingdoms, there came a time of intense conflict, undoubtedly caused by the god of the Otherworld's rape and abduction of his sister-in-law.

e) *The Ageing 'Apollo'*

Deserted by his spouse, the ruler of the kingdom of This World went virtually mad with grief. The period of the Sun God's madness occurred at the end of the summer and the god began to burn up the entire kingdom of This World. Since the queen was no longer with him and he had become infertile, he was dispossessed of his sovereignty. In an effort to regain it, he determined to remarry with a young, and therefore nubile, Mother-goddess. The only possible candidate was his daughter and he was therefore prepared to commit incest, although there is some doubt as to whether or not he achieved his aim. In any event, his plan caused the young regenerated goddess to leave for the Otherworld from whence she captivated the succeeding king of the kingdom of This World. (The entire adventure can be found in the fairy tale, *Donkey Skin*.) Thus, as a result of his madness the king of the kingdom of This World was deposed, and the cycle of divine adventures began again. The basic driving force of the cycle can therefore be seen as the conflict caused between the two kingdoms by a goddess.

f) *The Great Goddess*

The goddess in question was the one that Caesar called 'Minerva'. Although the name may not take full account of the figure's complexity, it was not altogether inappropriate. For one thing, all the characters in the divine epic of the two kingdoms were involved in a family affair. For another, the goddess gave an effective display of the remarkable wisdom that was the exclusive attribute of Minerva, who was also the 'daughter of Jupiter–Dis Pater'.

The Great Goddess sometimes appeared as a Triple Goddess, and sometimes as a single goddess, according to the role that she had to play in the epic. When she was about to become the mother of the god 'Mercury' she appeared as the Triple Brigit. Similarly, in *La Légende dorée* she bears the triple name of Marguerite, Marie-Madeleine and Marthe, and it is significant that the Celtic festivals of the triple goddess were celebrated at the end of July, just as were those of her Christian descendants. However, when the goddess appeared as the wife who gave sovereignty to the Great God of the kingdom of This World, she was portrayed as an only daughter. Her father also committed incest with her, but she was regenerated in the Otherworld, from whence she returned only when she had decided to marry the man that she had chosen at the future king of the kingdom of This World.

As the victim of abduction by the god of the Otherworld, the goddess was both the queen of This World in her youth and the queen of the Otherworld when she was older. And, despite everything, it is she who appeared as the central, if not the most important, figure in Celtic religion. She was also undoubtedly the most ancient deity in the pantheon, and there is more than a hint of matriarchy in her epic story, especially in the way in which she alone could choose the consort on whom she would bestow sovereignty. She enjoyed this right because she was the true holder of power and divine authority; the male gods needed her not only in order to be regenerated but also to be able to accede to their divine status, which was only accorded to them when she chose them. The only exception to this rule appears to be the ferryman-god who, as we have seen, did not undertake his initiatory journey in order to win a consort, but only to attain supreme knowledge. The course of his divine life does not seem to have been overly influenced by female power, and it was probably only during its final stages that it was affected by the intervention of the Great Goddess, with whom he was also in conflict.

It is virtually undeniable that the Great Goddess is omnipresent in Celtic theology and popular belief, and practically all the major tales in European folklore deal with her adventures. A number have already been mentioned, but *Little Red Riding Hood, Snow White, Patient Griselda* and *Blue Beard* could also be added to the list. This handful of stories all provide an account of the Earth Mother's adventures with the god of the Otherworld – especially, of course, *Little Red Riding Hood, Snow White* and *Blue Beard*.

The Great Goddess was a chthonian deity, associated with the running water of the spring that emerges from the Otherworld through the bowels of the earth. However, she was also represented by the full moon; whilst in this context, the Triple Goddess mentioned earlier was associated with the moon's other phases. It seems that this deity had extremely ancient origins and was retained in the Celtic pantheon because of the size of her following and the faith that she inspired in all generations of the peoples of Europe. Whilst being a lunar deity, she was still the ruler of chthonian dragons and also the consort of the Lord of the Animals.

CELTIC MYTH AND ITS RE-USE

It is relevant to consider, very briefly, the protean way in which Celtic myth has been re-fused in the context of later European society. We have already seen that it formed the source of the oral tradition our ancestors and, as such, underlies traditional European folk tales. It is difficult, or even impossible, to reagard these tales as mere products of the imagination, and much more convincing to consider them as a very efficient method of disseminating the content of sacred texts (which should really have been the secret preserve of the priestly class) throughout a society in which everything was seen in terms of a religion. Indeed, it is precisely because they were of a strictly religious nature that they had to be taken very seriously by any new religion seeking to superimpose itself on the existing faith. The result was the syncretism discussed earlier.

1. It is clear that the Christian religion did not produce many folk tales, though there were, of course, some which existed in various guises: the *Fioretti*, the legend of Saint Francis, is one of the most elaborate, while the 'Lives of the Saints' provide another example. However, there were only a few stories in either written or oral form that were intended to spread sacred knowledge among the masses. This is because the Christian religion has never, strictly speaking, been an initiatory one since the mythology that underlies it is available to all. The Bible is only inaccessible to those who cannot read, and the clergy is obliged to disseminate the very text of the myth in its teaching. Indeed, the dissemination of its message to the people was one of the main concerns of the medieval church. To supplement the written word, it used images carved on capitals and the luminous pictures on stained glass windows as additional ways of transmitting knowledge.

2. Although Christianity has produced relatively few folk tales, it has, in contrast, re-used a great deal of pre-existing oral material to its advantage. This practice seems to have been inspired by Saint Bernard of Clairvaux,

under whose influence the Christian religion was enriched by the 'doctrine' of courtly love, applied initially to the relationship between the worshipper and the Virgin Mary, before being secularized in thirteenth-century literature. This 'doctrine' can probably be fully understood only in relation to the pagan cult of the Great Goddess that flourished in the rural areas of Europe. If so, it is another example of the process of syncretism involving the two religions that succeeded each other in the Celtic world. Furthermore, this development surely did not start simply with the activities of Saint Bernard. The introduction of the cult of the Virgin into the western hemisphere from the sixth century onwards should be seen as representing the almost enforced recognition of the importance of the cult of the Great Mother in the Celtic world. The exclusive contribution of Saint Bernard himself was the systematization of the process of syncretism in order to bring about the end of paganism once and for all. This point is illustrated by several works that were contemporary with those of the saint: firstly, *La Légende dorée*, then the *Quête du Graal*, and finally the *Roman du Graal.*

The work by de Voragine (Iacopo da Varazze), Archbishop of Genoa, justifies its very existence on the basis of the premises of Saint Bernard's philosophy. Although the author did not belong to the Cistercian order, he expressed his sympathy with Saint Bernard's line of thought throughout the book. In addition, the fact that the Roman martyrology in the book covers only 197 of the 365 days of the year immediately raises the important question of why the remaining weekdays were not used. One possible answer is that the author included only days that corresponded to the major festivals in both the new religion and the one that it was replacing. This is the simple principle that we endeavoured to employ to reconstruct the Celtic ritual calendar. Finally, it seems that the writers of the *Quête du Graal* and the *Roman du Graal* also set out to re-use material from an earlier tradition to vindicate the new religion.

This plausible suggestion may also apply to the romances by Chrétien de Troyes. In any event, in the case of all these works, this possible attempt to use traditional subject matter as a means of 'theological vindication' may be accompanied by an attempt to use it also to justify secular institutions. If so, the Celtic myth has developed from a religious force shaping an ancient society into a means of political justification for a new social order or a new dynasty, in which case, it has effectively become a traditional foundation myth.

3. Except in the thirteenth century, the fashion for returning to 'national' roots persisted in French literature.

In this context, a special study should be made of the entire output of Rabelais, since his work uses figures in the Celtic pantheon to revive certain elements of Celtic myth (see Gaignebet, *Gargantua*). However, the inspiration of traditional stories is particularly evident in works from the following century onwards. It is also entertaining to note that, thanks to Perrault, the Celtic folk tale appeared in the forefront of the political and literary conflict that became known as the dispute between the 'Ancients' and 'Moderns'. Interestingly, on this occasion, the Celtic was exploited by the 'Modern' faction, a tendency that persisted in subsequent French literature. While others of equivalent social standing were composing 'pastorals', Mme d'Aulnoy and Mme. de Beaumont collected and published folk tales, thereby helping to preserve several stories that might otherwise have been lost.

During the nineteenth century, Charles Nodier was also inspired by folk tales, as were Grimm and Andersen. However, this was the period during which texts compiled from folk memory started to be incorporated in original works of fiction. Andersen's *Tales, Told for Children* represents just such a combination of the author's original writing with transcriptions of Germanic literature, as well as other stories that also occur in a Celtic context. Even before the nineteenth century, when Macpherson's crucial discovery of the Ossianic texts was one of the main factors contributing to the birth of the Romantic Movement, the scope of the Celtic world had been extended by 'regionalist literature', notably in the work of George Sand. Virtually all her 'regionalist' novels are permeated by reminders of Celtic folklore. The same applies to the collections of Breton stories that flooded the French literary scene on the heels of the work by De la Villemarqué and that inspired the separatist movement of the beginning of the twentieth century. The history of this extremist movement, which culminated tragically in its contribution to the pan-European designs of Hitler's Third Reich during the Second World War, is now well known.

During the twentieth century, the momentum of Celtic traditionalism has been maintained. In fact, Celtic studies have been fashionable since the second half of the nineteenth century, when, as already pointed out, the Celtic tradition helped to sustain the initial wave of European Romanticism. However, since works concerned with or inspired by folklore have featured more prominently than ever at the forefront of modern literary output, especially during the second half of this century, it is impossible to provide a complete overview of such publications. Folklore books of varying quality and specialist journals of the highest intellectual calibre, such as *Les Etudes celtiques* and *Gallia*, are ranged side by side in the bookshops, while folk tales have become secularized, have lost their value as a collective expression of a society's system of faith, and have been transformed by many authors into children's stories, which they were not originally intended to be. Alongside this relentless process of bastardization, Celtic culture has continued to provide the inspiration for several, arguably major, works. Amongst the most notable are *La Vouivre* by Marcel Aymé, the works by Vincenot, and especially Henri Pourrat's monumental work *Le Trésor des Contes*.

Finally, the fact that the Celtic religion was based on a 'scientific' vision of the universe and that it also provided a 'rational' and coherent explanation of the natural world, has encouraged the development of esoteric doctrines that claim to be based on rationalism. The religion of the Druids was based on a significant body of astronomical knowledge, which necessarily implies that it was also based on important astrological beliefs. As a religion that also considered mystery and secrecy to be inherently necessary, it has undoubtedly been responsible for engendering a number of misguided theories about the universe that have enjoyed considerable success, if only among devotees of astrology. After all, does not astrology also purport to provide a 'scientific' explanation of the entire universe?

Paul Verdier

Centaurs

The battle between the centaurs and the Lapiths features prominently among the sculptured scenes that tourists and pilgrims could admire on the metopes of the Parthenon and in the pediments of the temple of Zeus at Olympia. Their appearance on two such renowned buildings at two such renowned places provides a clear indication of the importance of the centaurs as a motif in representations of Greek art. Indeed, they occur frequently in all branches of classical art, not only as large-scale sculptures but also as statuettes, on pottery, and in paintings such as those from Pompeii, several of which depict Nessus and Deianeira. This profusion of images clearly implies that the centaur was a familiar figure for the Ancients and that it occupied a prominent position in the classical imagination. As a result, one naturally expects also to encounter these cloud-born sons of Ixion on frequent occasions in works of classical literature.

Paradoxically, this is not the case, as one soon discovers when attempting to find references to them in the works of Greek and Roman authors. True, there are occasional allusions to the various mythical events associated with the centaurs, the most famous being the marriage of Pirithous described in Homer's *Odyssey* (XXI. 295–304), Hesiod's *The Shield (of Heracles)* (178–90) and Virgil's *Georgics* (II. 454–7). There are also references to their ambivalent nature: their liking for violence and their brutal lust contrasting with the wisdom of individual centaurs, such as Chiron or Pholus. But there are no texts in which the centaur appears in its own right. For example, whereas the monstrous creatures, such as Laestrygonian, Cyclopes and Sirens, that battle with Odysseus in the *Odyssey*, have been easily incorporated into the narrative and given an essential role to play within it, the centaur was never accorded this type of role in the extensive field of classical literature, whether in works of fiction or elsewhere. Although it did eventually appear in this capacity, this was not until much later and in the context of a different literary tradition. Through a succession of reinterpretations and reappearances, the centaur never ceased to be a familiar figure to readers, audiences and art enthusiasts of subsequent eras. Thus, to restrict ourselves to the twentieth century, it is well known that Picasso included centaurs in his imaginary bestiary and that César sculpted a huge statue of a centaur in homage to Picasso.

Philippe Heuzé

THE CENTAUR: A MODERN AND 'MODERNIST' FIGURE

The mythical figure of the centaur came to prominence in nineteenth-century French literature, initially in the writings of Maurice de Guérin and then in those of the Parnassians. However, its success in this context was subsequently equalled in works by the Modernist generation in Latin America. This movement consisted of young poets who endeavoured to create a personal, inner world that was remote and inaccessible, where they could take refuge from the realities of a world which was not conducive to creativity. In their bid to free themselves from the literary influence of Spain, they turned to foreign literature and, in particular, to that of France. Although they continued to admire Victor Hugo, they favoured the works of Baudelaire and Verlaine, and appreciated the artistic writings of the de Goncourt brothers. They were interested, too, in Renan's critical essays and the novels of Huysmans and Villiers de l'Isle-Adam, as well as being captivated by the purity of form of the poetry by Leconte de Lisle and José Maria de Heredia. In their search for 'another world' as well as a past that they did not possess, they found that they could satisfy their need to escape by reading the works of the nineteenth-century French poets, who constantly paid tribute to the culture of ancient Greece, a culture made accessible by their great erudition. In their turn, the Latin American poets re-used the ancient myths, not as mere decorative motifs, but as a fertile source of inspiration, usually presenting them in personal terms. Among these myths was that of the centaur.

In the context of the Americas, the myth of the centaur was doubly 'imported' – first, because of its connection with the ancient world and secondly because of its association with the horse, introduced into America by the Spanish conquistadors. That the Modernists chose this myth in preference to other myths of lasting and universal significance, seems, initially, to be another indication of their desire to distance themselves from anything specifically related to their own culture. However, the mythical figure of the centaur, which features to varying degrees in different works throughout the 'Modernismo' movement, was often used to communicate the poets' own feelings and personalities.

The centaur first appeared in the work of Rubén Darío, who chose it in preference to the other figures of ancient mythology. Between 1887 and 1908, at various significant stages of his literary career, he dedicated four verse and prose works to it, of which the most important and the best known is the *Coloquio de los Centauros*. The centaur also appears in sonnets belonging to the 'aesthetic', modernist poetry of South America, as represented by the works of the young poet, José Juan Tablada (*El Centauro*, 1894), and by the more sober style of his compatriot, Luis Urbina (*El baño del Centauro*, 1905). It plays a prominent role, too, in the long philosophical poem by the Colombian writer, Guillermo Valencia (*San Antonio y el Centauro*, 1898), and is one of the Hellenic themes used by the Argentinian Leopoldo Díaz, whose literary career began and ended with the Parnassians. Similarly, it recurs in the *Cantilenas* of the Peruvian writer Ventura Garcia Calderón, whose writing retained the basic features of Modernism, even though he was only a late adherent of the movement.

The Modernists were avid readers of both ancient and modern works, whether in their original languages or in translation, and were able to draw on sources other than the Greek and Latin texts. These sources were mystical writings and prominent among them were Saint Jerome's 'Lives of the Saints', in which the centaur appears as a monster and represents paganism confronting Christianity. Contemporary literature supplied another interpretation of this mythical figure. The centaur in the work of that name by Maurice de Guérin is represented by the young Macarée, whose dual nature is contrasted with the wisdom of Chiron in his peaceful old age. With his love of wild gallops combined with a propensity for meditation, Macarée is the vehicle for expressing the problems and anxieties of the author's inner life. Following Guérin's example, Leconte de Lisle also attenuated the wild and bestial side of the centaur's nature. His 'Khiron' in the *Poèmes antiques* combines the characteristics of Guérin's two centaurs: the wisdom and erudition of the one and the unbridled strength of the other. For both poets, the centaur is the mythical figure that represents the conflict and synthesis between a vital strength that aspires to be boundless and a wisdom that is serenely contemplative.

Finally, José Maria de Heredia accentuated the duality of man and animal in his *Hercule et les Centaures*. The centaur of *Les Trophées* represents a transitional state, the metamorphosis of animal into Man, whereby the advent of Man, symbolized by Heracles, seals the fate of the centaur. 'Nessus' poses the problem of the coexistence, within one creature, of a sexual passion that is purely bestial and of a higher aspiration that raises it to the level of humanity, namely love, an emotion associated with anxiety and of which the female centaur is also aware. The centaurs' confrontation with the human race reveals that they prefer to belong to the animal kingdom ('Centaures et Lapiths'); and, on the eve of their extinction, their bestiality is all that remains of their dual nature ('Fuite des Centaures').

The Modernists put this wealth of literary sources, supplemented by pictorial sources illustrating dictionaries of mythology, to different uses. In their poems, centaurs appear both individually and collectively. When treated as a representative of its species, and thus as an exemplar, a centaur is designated by the name of the species preceded by the definite article, and is also referred to as Hippofos or 'son of Greece' (Valencia) or given an identity such as 'Neso', 'Quirón', 'Folo', 'Hipea', 'Rito', or 'Abantes' – names that clearly indicate their classical origin. The centaur is described 'near myrtles, under laurel tres', in *La Isla de Oro*, written with Darío's characteristic inner richness. Meanwhile, in other works it is portrayed in the 'dark and nuptial recess' (Tablada), crossing the burning Egyptian desert (Valencia), in the wild setting of the seashore (Díaz), or in the middle of a Mexican lake (Urbina). It moves among among its fellow creatures, encounters nymphs and satyrs, or confronts Saint Anthony. Its strange silhouette is described in a way that creates startling visual effects, and/or endowed with a symbolic significance. When they are portrayed as a group, the Modernist centaurs blend into one great cavalcade (Darío's *Palimpsesto*) or stand out from an anonymous mass (*Coloquio de los Centauros*). When they are described individually, their differences emerge from the poet's pen as if under a sculptor's chisel:

> One advances with rhythmic step,
> Another vigorously arches his neck,
> As if part of an elegant bas-relief
> Carved by Scopas' enchanted chisel.
> Another raises his white hands in the air,
> While the sun's warm glow
> Burnishes his slender rump.
> Another, jumping over rocks and fallen trees,
> Utters joyous cries as resonant
> As the conch's clarion call.
>
> (Darío, *Palimpsesto*)

The dual nature of the centaur is again conveyed in sculptural terms in the following line from the *Coloquio de los Centauros*: 'His legs bind him to the earth; his head rears, uncurbed, against the sky.' Here the use of antithetical verbs gives his outline a simultaneously visual and symbolic dimension. The centaur is no longer the monster bound to the earth by his legs. He rears his head against the sky, in a movement of freedom. The same symbol recurs in the words of Macarée: 'One half of myself, submerged, was constantly active in order to stay afloat, while the other half rose serenely above the surface, and I held my idle arms clear of the waves.' Meanwhile, it also reappears in Luis Urbina's description of the centaur, in which only the human head and torso are allowed to emerge from the water (*El baño del Centauro*).

One description involves an evocation of youthful pleasure, the other, an autobiographical recollection in which the author transfers the nymphs' bathing scene to the lush natural surroundings of Mexico and substitutes the theme of the awakening of carnal desire in the sensual native girl who is bathing in the Chapala lake for the usual abduction.

> A smiling nymph with firm brown flesh, sleek hair and primitive features, is bathing; the water, like a sash, encircles her waist; and she has no sense of shame . . . and her breast quivers with the desire to surrender, voluptuous and wild, to the swarthy Centaur's rough embrace.

The centaur as the object of female desire – in this instance, little more than a straighforward sexual impulse – had already appeared with different connotations in one of Darío's early stories, *La Ninfa*. In this 'Parisian' tale in the tradition of Catulle Mendès and Armand Silvestre, which reveals the poet's 'sensual excitement', Darío highlights the pleasure experienced by the 'femme fatale' in deceiving men and sending them to their ruin, a theme which was dear to the Decadents.

Although strength, seen as an elemental impulse, is the main trait of the Modernist centaurs, it manifests itself in different ways. Associated with agility, it enables Díaz's Neso to carry Deianeira on his shoulders and the young centaur in *Palimpsesto*, who is possibly Pholus, swiftly to carry off Diana's female companion. As a violent impulse, it is the driving force behind the battles between the centaurs themselves (Díaz's *Combate de Centauros*), or between centaurs and men, as they fight 'heroically and simply' in natural surroundings (Urbina).

The centaur experiences two opposed inner forces: 'Two conflicting forces struggle deep within me, an inner god [sometimes] revels and at other times groans', soliloquizes Díaz's Chiron, who ultimately succumbs to the temptation of combat (*Soliloquio del Centauro*). Finally, strength is seen as a 'joyous force' in the context of old Hippofos, whose 'powerful arm can comb the nymph's hair and strangle the bear', and who regards his dual nature as a strange symbol (*San Antonio y el Centauro*).

However, the centaurs' strength is not invincible, and they can be defeated either by heroes and gods, or by Christianity. The Modernists did not create images as beautiful as those produced by Henri de Régnier in *Le Centaure blessé*, or arouse emotion as intense as the visual imagery of Bourdelle's sculptures. Instead, they tended to describe the fatal wound inflicted on Nessus and the pain caused by the avenging arrows of Diana or Heracles with more restraint (see 'Deyanira' in Díaz's *Palimpsest*). As for the 'joyous strength' possessed by the 'last of the centaurs', it is powerless against Saint Anthony's words in praise of Christ. The centaur disappears in the same way that the memory of early paganism would fade in the collective memory of mankind (*San Antonio y el Centauro*).

The powerful physical activity and strength embodied by the centaurs can be kept in check. In the *Coloquio de los Centauros*, they have their fiery nature under control and, unlike Leconte de Lisle's 'Khiron' and Maurice de Guérin's 'Macarée', do not give free rein to their impetuosity. They are no longer instinctive creatures, prey to obscure, inner forces. They are free and conscious of their own vitality.

Rubén Darío's originality lies in the fact that, while reworking the mythological sources, he invested the centaurs of the *Coloquio de los Centauros* with human characteristics. In this erudite discussion of such philosophical subjects as the principle of the World, the problem of Evil, and the nature of Woman and Death, they not only possess the ability to think, meditate and philosophize but are also able to subjugate their strength to the laws of concord and harmony. They use their vital inner strength to sing of 'the awesome mystery of things' and to extol a Nature that has been sanctified and invested with dignity, in an ardent profession of pantheistic faith.

The centaurs represented the struggle of the poets, who were constantly speaking out against the philosophers, materialists and positivists, in favour of 'the soul of things' – a soul that had just been discovered at the end of the nineteenth century.

They discovered harmony in a world consisting of forms, colours and the interplay of light and shadow, and devoted their creative powers to the service of Art. The 'monster' was therefore saved by beauty, by dedicating itself totally to Art.

However, the sensitivity with which the centaurs of the *Coloquio de los Centauros* are endowed also means that they experience human emotions. The female centaur, Hipea, is deeply and violently jealous of her human rival. Neso recalls nostalgically the brief moment when he held the beautiful Deianeira in his arms, and is unable to forget her.

Other writers, after Darío, invested the centaurs with the same feeling of nostalgia. Díaz's young centaurs are nostalgic for 'another world', while Ventura Garcia Calderón expresses his own nostalgia for a boyhood that had been followed by a life of wandering. A product of two cultures, Calderón loved Versailles and had always been affected by the tyranny of his past life. He confides to the centaur, his brother and the companion of his solitude:

> . . . (you) who pass through the earthly valley, beneath the glory of the fiery dawn: I want to tell you of the sad sweetness of the venom and the anxious wandering which will have been my life. ('Dije al centauro joven'.)

In its guise as a mythological creature with a dual nature, the centaur inspired Modernists other than Rubén Darío, though many of them are now forgotten. It represents, in various ways, the vital impulses of those young poets who were the first to use a very pure plastic form of imagery in erotic poetry. The sonnet by José Juan Tablada gives an example of their work:

The Centaur

The dark hair unbound
in its dorsal reptilian waves
– quivering ebony – tapers
in a funereal fall of lust.

Over his shapely haunches, light
splinters as over polished marble,
the golden twilight radiance bars
the curved zebrine rump.

She steals the whiteness and the fire
from the Arabian mares in her desire:
and in the dark and nuptual recess,
where the last of Phoebus's dying rays
embroiders the mahogany coat with gold,
the fiery union of the Centaur!

For those who believe in the immortality of poetry, the centaur also represents the synthesis of strength and thought, of impulse and reason, of instinct and emotion – as well as the conflicts to which they give rise.

The recurrence of the mythical figure of the centaur in Modernist poetry cannot be explained merely by a desire to follow a literary trend. As a hybrid creature, the centaur apparently represented the ideal symbol through which the movement's young poets could communicate their own duality and the, often painful, contradictions that accompanied it. This duality was linked to their origins, to their role as American writers using European sources, to their carnal appetite and their need for spirituality. In this respect Rubén Darío's situation was typical. Through its glorification 'of the perpetual ascent of Psyche' the *Coloquio de los Centauros* clearly illustrates the extent to which Darío was familiar with spiritual longing. Yet this longing was almost invariably smothered by the demands of his dominant sensuality. The symbolism of Darian Desire permeates an entire range of works. Its manifestations extend from Henri de Régnier's 'monsters of Desire, monsters of the Flesh' which reappear as the centaurs in *Palimpsesto*, where their erotic impulses drive them to throw themselves on the nymphs to satisfy their need for possession, to Quiron in the *Coloquio de los Centauros*, whose eyes caress the curving bodies of the nymphs and whose animal instincts have assumed a more human dimension.

This feeling of duality experienced by the poets was also shared by nearly all Modernist writers, who were divided between their Spanish Christian heritage and the pagan love of life for which the unspoilt natural environment of the New World provided the ideal setting. In this natural environment, the myth of the centaur, the creature that was half horse and half man and that had no physiological existence, became a psychological reality.

Christiane Séris

THE AMERICAN CENTAURS: FROM CONQUISTADORS TO COWBOY BOOTS

Although modern Europeans interpret myths as sacred stories impinging on social institutions, the ancient Mexicans regarded them as the history of the world, and they 'knew' that this history was 'true'. Indeed, it was so 'true' that, when a group of adventurers landed in Mexico in 1519, the hitherto warlike and all-conquering Aztecs lost their control over their own territory and that of their neighbours in the space of a few months, simply because the omens had predicted that Quetzalcóatl, the Feathered Serpent, the civilizing priest-god and fabled king of Tula, might return in that year. The myth's promise that peace and progress would one day be restored was, in fact, accurate, but the Aztecs' identification of progress with Cortes and his soldiers proved to be a fatal mistake, with incalculable consequences, for the New World as much as for the Old.

The new arrivals also had their myths, as well as a substantial number of devils, which – according to the expert opinion of Friar Bartolomé de las Casas – were effectively incarnated by the very people whom they should have sought to protect from the devil with baptism and the blood of Christ. Above all, they had a single, jealous God. When they disembarked, it was with both weapons and baggage – in fact with more weapons than baggage, since, in the final analysis, their only baggage may have been their horses and their swords and of the two again according to las Casas, it was the horse that was the more terrible as far as the Indians were concerned. Gifts from the New World to the Old included cocoa, tomatoes, beans and tobacco, but not the 'mustang', which some people wrongly regard as synonymous with the wild expanses of the American landscape. The horse, in its domesticated form, was not introduced into America until the sixteenth century by the Spaniards, who raised their eyes to heaven ('to the depths of the ocean', according to the poet) and located the constellation Centaurus close to the Southern Cross. For their part, the Indians could not believe their eyes when they saw, on earth, the embodiment of a mythical figure dreamed up by other men whose existence they did not even suspect: the Greeks had invented the centaur, the American Indians encountered it. It is hard to imagine which of the creature's two halves, the animal or the human, was more disturbing for these people whose ethnic characteristics were quite different from those of the newcomers. All in all, as will be seen later, it was the four legs that seemed less alien than the black or red beards and the white skins of these hitherto unknown beings.

A new era had dawned. The West Indies were beginning to experience the horrors of colonialism, and the myths that had explained the Cosmos for so long were no longer of any use in a devastated world whose chaotic state they were unable to explain. Although denounced by the Christian religion and marginalized by the culture of the conquerors, these myths were still adapted to suit a foreign narrative and linguistic tradition and reappeared in national literature when the Americas were liberated in the nineteenth century. Coatlicue, Tezcatlipoca and Quetzalcóatl found a rich sanctuary in contemporary fiction, while, through the intermingling of cultures, new myths were also created on American soil. Eldorado (i.e. El Dorado: the Golden One), was either an individual or a land that the conquerors sought frantically from the Peruvian lakes to the eastern slopes of the Andes, a quest that is inextricably associated with the insane figure of Aguirre. Finally, other, genuinely European myths, such as the myth of the centaur, were given a new and original lease of life in the New World.

When the centaur invaded the New World for the second time, it was in literary terms, as the vehicle for the 'American' dream of the Modernists. The nineteenth century was drawing to a close and little of historical importance had happened since Cortés and his horsemen had landed in the Gulf of Mexico in 1519. The 'centaurs' of Veracruz were certainly not mythical, but even for the Indians, who were not aware of this, and in the absence of a narrative to explain their coming, similar to the myths that predicted and consequently determined the conditions of Quetzalcóatl's return, the new phenomenon was no longer fantastic but merely alien. It would have taken time, a great deal of time, for the story of its appearance to be incorporated into an oral tradition, and time was the one thing that was not available. Inevitably, a Spaniard dismounted, destroying the image of the centaur and creating two separate entities that were just as enigmatic for the Indians. The action of separating himself from his mount, which is so ordinary for the rider, negated the impression of a man-horse and gave rise to another, specifically American myth, the myth of the man-on-horseback, whose 'raison d'être' was neither as a man nor as a horse but as a synthesis of the two. This was a myth that allowed its central figure to be depicted in a dual role, at times as the sexually motivated abductor and at others as the highly intellectual educator. Whereas the myth of the centaur had initially stressed the emotional instability of this complex figure, it now demonstrated the figure's inescapable unity by imposing a choice between aspiring to higher things or stooping to baser actions but, paradoxically, ensuring that, whichever choice was made, it was made wholeheartedly each time. When the Spaniard dismounted this was a tragic act, in that it simultaneously brought relief at the ending of what had ceased to be and the wish to revert to it forever. This action dramatized the man-horse link by simultaneously negating it and making it a symbolic focus of desire.

This was the birth of the American centaur myth, which can be explained as follows. The initial amazement that greeted the supposed man-horse was due partly to its strange appearance and partly to its size. (No American animal was as large as this, since even the Peruvian llama was no rival for the horse; while the alien ethnic features of the Spaniards have already been emphasized.) In contrast, dimorphism of the man-horse held nothing disturbing for the Indian imagination. The mythology of the region abounded in such dual dieties as Ometeotl, the male and female Dual-Deity, and Quetzalcóatl and his twin Xolotl, as well as endowing every individual with a 'nahuatl'. This was an animal double, another self so closely identified with the first, that the two forms, animal and human, were interchangeable – a concept used by Miguel Angel Asturias in the narrative of *Hombres de Maíz* (*Man of Maize*). But it soon became apparent not only that was there no basic reciprocity between the man and the horse, but also that the bestial element actually resided in the human upper half, despite its superior position, since it was transformed by ignorance, greed and cruelty. Thus, the terms 'bestial' and 'bestiality' recur frequently in Bartolomé de las Casas' descriptions of the Spaniards in *Brevísima relación de la destrucción de las Indias*. As a consequence, it was inevitable that the status of the apparently lower half should be reassessed. This process was all the more spontaneous because it conformed with the deep-rooted cultural practices of Meso-American societies in which majesty, both human and divine, was conveyed by the 'elevation' in spatial terms. This could be achieved by the pyramidal structure that served as a base for the temple and the sacficial altar, by a plinth or by a simple rug. How it was done did not matter. The important issue was not the hierarchical organization of the supports used but the fulfilment of an idea, that of 'heightening'. Space thus had a crucial religious significance, and the horse was seen as a twofold, and so complete, expression of the concept, in that it heightened (vertically) like the pyramid or stilts (the Tree), as well as covering distances (horizontally) at great speed. This last aspect is certainly one of the most interesting when considered in the context of nations that had a deity – the double of the sun god Huitzilopochtli – called Paynal ('He who Hastens'), and that referred to the present personified by Xolotl, Lord of Movement, as 'Sun (era) of Movement'. In the Codices, Xolotl, whose double (as has already been mentioned) was Quetzalcóatl, assumes the form of a coyote, the American wild dog, one of the signs of the Nahuan calendar. And there is nothing surprising in the identification of the horse and the dog. In the Peruvian rituals that accompany the foundation of a house or property, the apotropaic role is performed by terra-cotta figurines filled with 'chicha' (maize liquor). Although these supposedly represent a bull (as a result of Spanish influence), they are extremely reminiscent of the jaguar, an animal with a rich symbolic significance in the pre-Incan period. According to Dumézil, the centaur is associated with the themes of abduction, fire, descent into the land of the dead, and carnivalesque fancy dress. This is significant in the context of a myth involving Xolotl, the Lord of Movement. In it, he helps to create the Fifth Sun (which requires the death of a victim by fire) by descending with Quetzalcóatl into the kingdom of the Lord of the Dead, and helping him to steal the bones that will be used to create a new race of men. During this adventure the god escapes sacrifice by dressing up, first as corn with two heads when he is called 'xolotl', then as maguey when he is called 'maxolotl', and finally as a fish when he is called 'axolotl'. Xolotl is a representation of vital energy and the daily resurrection of light as it leaves the nocturnal world, a figure symbolizing the return. For these reasons the coyote is the double of the postman in the novel *Hombres de Maíz*. In addition, he is the companion and double of Quetzalcóatl. Thus, Xolotl had inevitably conferred his prestige upon the swift creature that served as a plinth for the bearded 'god' briefly identified with Quetzalcóatl. (In the Museum of Anthropology in Mexico, there is a statue of Quetzalcóatl, carrying on his back the young sun, his double, his twin Xolotl, in the form of a child's head.)

The 'man-horse' link was mentioned earlier as being a symbolic focus of desire. If the white man on the divine horse was able to attain divinity, then it was certainly possible for the native to attain it as well. It is not known how long it took for the Indo-European myths, with which we are now so familiar, to develop. The issue is confused in the case of America by the fact that the

Europeans were involved in their development from the relatively recent time when the first Spaniard on horseback set foot on American soil until the day when the first Indian, riding bareback and with a bow in his hand, became the symbol of Sagittarius. If we accept that the Indo-European myths can, in their own way, describe the repression of a civilization, why should the situation be any different in the context of other cultures? From the moment that the first Spaniard dismounted from his horse, an Indian longed to mount the horse and so become what had just ceased to be. An entire continent of mixed racial origins viewed the man-on-horseback as the incarnation of glory, power and revenge. Since myth is a narrative, the record of the various stages of this deeply libidinous process is preserved in Latin American literature. As regards the deification of the plinth, there is an interesting tradition preserved in legends collected by Miguel Angel Asturias in *El Caballo del Trueno*, an unfinished work that has unfortunately never been published. This concerns a horse that Cortés entrusted to the natives of a village before leaving on an expedition to the Honduras, because the creature was lame from a leg injury. The village was threatened with terrible reprisals if the horse was not cured by the time that Cortés returned, but, in fact, threats were not needed to make the natives treat the creature in the same way in which they treated their deities. They offered the animal sumptuous dishes served in bowls made from jade, precious stones, gold and silver, but the horse had no appetite, and the Indians were desperate. When the horse died of hunger, they sculpted a stone horse and offered it in good faith to Cortés, as much to escape the conqueror's wrath by trying to deceive him as through a deep belief in the consubstantiality of the living deity and its representation.

In a continent where the native inhabitants were set to work by the conqueror and generically referred to as 'peons' (those who go on foot) – mere pawns who had to respect the layout of the chessboard, in contrast to the knight with its privileged moves – it was inevitable that the horse should have become an obscure object of desire. Those who were on horseback were those in command: the masters and the military. The sexuality of the Indo-European 'centaur' lay in his 'macho' (male, virile) image, with the horse as the external symbol of his virility. Significantly, too, women in the Americas had to walk wherever they wanted to travel, as illustrated by the wonderful images in the Mexican film *Enamorada*, by Fernandez, where Man, the Hero of the Revolution, leaves for war on horseback with the women following on foot. This gave rise to the literary image of the female centaurs rebelling against male dominance. The former include such figures as Doña Bárbara, in the novel of the same name by the Venezuelan writer, Romulo Gallegos, and Doña Flora in *El Papa Verde* (*The Green Pope*) by Miguel Angel Asturias. Both are claiming, by means of their equestrian activities that make them 'open their legs like a man', their right to social advancement through the exercise of power. However, when the artist Diego Rivera painted Emiliano Zapata, the champion of an agricultural reform promoting equality between masters and peons, he placed him at the front of a crowd of peasants, standing beside his legendary white horse and holding it by the bridle. In countries such as Venezuela and Argentina that are famous for their livestock and where horses have bred for a long time in complete freedom on vast tracts of unspoilt land, the capture and breaking of a stallion has assumed the value of an initiatory rite, a test of virility. Thus, in *Doña Bábara*, when a young landowner returns home from Caracas, where he is studying law, he is mistrusted by his peons as an intellectual until he succeeds in mounting an unbroken colt and bringing it back, finally broken, after a wild gallop across the savannah. The Venezuelan *llanero* maintains that 'in matters of love, [his] horse comes first'. But, in spite of a legendary tradition that occupies a prominent place in literature and describes the life of the *llanero* in terms of the rituals of work and play, involving breaking in, branding, rodeos, etc., it is the gaucho from the regions of the River Plate who has assumed the dimensions of a mythical figure. This process was facilitated by the economic developments of the end of the nineteenth century which led to the disappearance of the real figure on which the myth was based. The gaucho, who would challenge this, represents the most faithful image of the man-on-horseback, and the Argentinian gaucho is now, just as indisputably, a myth. According to Faustino Domingo Sarmiento, this American centaur is a descendant of the brutish barbarians. But José Hernández's wonderful work, *Martín Fierro*, restores his original duality, and in the same way that there were good and bad centaurs, there are 'buenos' and 'malos' gauchos.

It would be unfair to curtail the image of the centaur by ignoring the Hollywood descendant of the American man-on-horseback. The myths of the 'silver screen' have revived the classical centaurs in their dual role, either as Indians armed with bows, who abduct women, eat raw meat and generally live up to the image of 'barbarians', or as the swaggering Yankees in their uniforms, with their biblical culture and their 'civilized' puritanism. It is this New World, which Europeans, as inhabitants of another – perhaps ageing – world, continue to find exciting, that has given rise to the final incarnation of the centaur, an incarnation that, although it may not yet be a true myth, has an undeniably ritualistic quality. If the centaur was an image of inclusion, then the rodeo is a ritual of exclusion in which both rider and mount know that their functon is to be separated. Repetition is an essential part of ritual. Every time the rider falls he remounts, and thus the rodeo is the most successful embodiment of the Fifth Sun, which the pre-Colombian races called Movement.

Dorita Nouhaud

Chinese Legends and Mythology

Like all other ethnic communities throughout the world during their early histories, the early Chinese produced some wonderful legends. From the twenty-first to the fifth century BC, the myths of this slave-based society were constantly modified and embellished and passed on in the oral tradition without ever being written down. The first traces of written versions were found from the feudal period onwards, (i.e. after the fourth century BC) either in philosophical works, such as the *Zhuang Zi* and the *Huai Nan Zi*, or in accounts of journeys, such as the *Shan Hai Jing* (the *Classic of the Mountains and Seas*). It is therefore impossible for modern students of this literature to study it in its complete form, that is assuming that a complete original version did, in fact, ever exist.

In the myths, it is possible to identify a natural or social phenomenon that has been remoulded into an artistic form by the human imagination. Mythology, by virtue of its very origins, is the result of a naive attempt on the part of our ancestors to interpret the forces of nature – which for them were unpredictable – as well as an indication of their desire to control them. In its later manifestations, it also reflected social phenomena and conflicts such as tribal wars, but it was usually concerned with both nature and society. Although apparently fanciful, and sometimes even ludicrous, the legends were by no means pure figments of the imagination. They were born of the work and conflicts experienced by the people of ancient China.

Many legends provide a miraculous explanation of the origins of heaven, the earth and man, or of the sun, moon, stars, landscape and vegetation.

The three Chinese legends that follow are relatively complete. They describe Nüwa, the Fashioning Deity, who repaired the vault of heaven, Houyi, who destroyed scourges, and Yu, who controlled the flood.

NÜWA

Nüwa was a goddess with a human head and either a serpent's or a dragon's body. She 'created men by patting yellow earth together'. These were the first men. After working for a long time, she felt tired and had the idea of 'drag[ging] a string through the mud' to enable her to work more quickly and to create a greater number of human beings; and thus '. . . the rich and the noble are those men of yellow earth, whereas the poor and the lowly – all ordinary people – are those cord-made men'.

The most interesting episode in the story concerns the repairing of the vault of heaven, which is described as follows in the *Huai Nan Zi*:

> In very ancient times, the four pillars [at the compass points] were broken down, the nine provinces [of the habitable world] were split apart, heaven did not wholly cover [earth], and earth did not completely support [heaven]. Fires flamed without being extinguished, waters inundated without being stopped, fierce beasts ate the people, and birds of prey seized the old and the weak in their claws. Thereupon Nü-kua (Nüwa) fused together stones of the five colours, with which she patched together azure heaven. She cut off the feet of a turtle, with which she set up the four pillars. She slaughtered the Black Dragon in order to save the province of Chi (Ji) [the present Hopei (Hebai) and Shansi (Shanxi) in North China]. She collected the ashes of reeds, with which to check the wild waters.

The text goes on to say that the vault of heaven was repaired and was once more supported by four solid pillars, that the waters were checked, that the wild beasts were destroyed, that universal harmony was restored and that the people of China were finally able to live in peace.

HOUYI

Houyi was a Herculean hero in ancient Chinese mythology and also appears in the *Huai Nan Zi*:

> In ancient times, during the reign of the tribal chief Yao, ten suns rose simultaneously, burning up the harvests and drying up the grass and the trees. Famine was rife throughout the land. All sorts of monsters appeared and attacked the people: Yagu the centaur, Zuochi the ogre with long teeth, Quiying the monster that kills with water and fire, Dafeng the giant bird which unleashes the wind, Fengxi, the giant boar and Xisushe the giant serpent. On the orders of Yao, Houyi, the famous archer, killed the ogre Zuochi on the wild southern plain, the monster Quiying near the northern river Xiongshui, and pierced the giant bird Dafeng with an arrow above an eastern lake. He shot down nine suns so that only one remained, killed Yagu the centaur in the same manner, cut the giant serpent in two on the shores of the lake Dongting, and finally captured the giant boar at Shuanglin. The people, overjoyed, proclaimed Yao the universal emperor. These exploits also made a significant contribution to the improved knowledge of the geography and all the regions of the country.

In this legend, Houyi accomplishes a total of seven exploits, including the one involving the shooting down of nine suns. According to ancient Chinese folklore, there used to be ten suns, which all perched on a huge tree called the 'fusang' at Yanggu. The suns each had the form of a crow, and every day the sun god Xihe harnessed them in turn to his chariot. But on the occasion in question, the ten suns all rose simultaneously, burning the earth so fiercely that it became unbearable for all living creatures. Thus Houyi was forced to act ruthlessly. He shot down the giant bird Dafeng to punish the god of the wind who, according to the legend, was a bird or a bird with a stag's head, and he also destroyed other scourges, cannibalistic monsters who were half human and half animal. These few examples illustrate the extent of the difficulties and ordeals that Houyi had to overcome in order to free the world of these banes.

YU

According to the *Shan Hai Jing*, a flood spread throughout the earth, threatening the very survival of the human race. In order to save the world, Gun stole the 'swelling mould' (*xi rang*), a sort of magical soil that had the property of continually swelling in size, from the Lord on High (Shangdi) to build dams to hold back the flood waters. The Lord on High was furious and killed him. His remains, which did not decompose in spite of being exposed to the elements for three years, engendered Yu the Great, who continued the struggle against the flood. He travelled far and wide throughout the land, cleaving mountains, digging holes in the earth, dredging waterways and re-routing rivers so that they ran into the sea. He enlisted the help of a winged dragon, which indicated the direction to be taken by the waters with its tail. During this work, Yu assumed the form of a bear to split Mount Huanyuan, which was blocking the course of the Yellow River. He had agreed with his wife, Lady Tushan, that as soon as she heard the drum, she would bring his meals. But as he leapt about at the top of the mountain, Yu loosened some stones, which rolled down into the valley and accidentally hit the drum. As she arrived, Lady Tushan saw her husband changing into a bear and she departed in shame. When she reached the foot of Mount Songgas, she was turned into stone. Yu cried out to her: 'give me my son!' and the stone split open and gave birth to Qi, the son of Yu.

According to other traditional sources, although Yu clearly heard the cries of the newly-born Qi, he nevertheless hurried off to check the flood waters and did not have time to admire his baby son. The story attests to the diligence and devotion of Yu the Great.

As a result of his exploits, Yu was proclaimed emperor and, on his death, his son was chosen to succeed him. Yu became the first emperor of the Xia dynasty and, according to mythology, lived during the twenty-first century BC.

Less complete legends also illustrate the incredible determination of the early Chinese in their struggle against the forces of nature. The *Shan Hai Jing*, for example, tells how the daughter of the emperor known as Yandi (fiery, blazing) was drowned in the Eastern Ocean while out walking. She changed into a bird, the 'jingwei', which haunted the western mountains in its search for stones and branches from trees with which to fill in the sea. Another legend describes how the giant Kuafu set off in pursuit of the sun and finally caught up with it at Yugu, in the furthest regions of the West. But he was so thirsty after his chase that the combined waters of the Yellow River and the Weihe River were not enough to slake his thirst. As a consequence, he set off for a northern lake, but he died of thirst on the way, leaving behind a staff, which changed into a grove of leafy peach trees.

Other myths recall social conflicts. They are the reflection of historical realities that, over the centuries, produced wonderful tales and legends and became a rich source of imagery. A good example is provided by the adventures of the Yellow Emperor and Gonggong.

One of the most extraordinary deeds of the legendary Yellow Emperor was the war that he waged against the fearsome Chiyou.

Chiyou and his eight-one brothers had bronze heads and the bodies of animals, spoke the language of men but fed on sand and stones. They knew the secret of maming all kinds of weapons, with which they deliberately massacred the population. Although they had for a long time been under the rule of the Emperor Yandi, they started a military campaign against him and pursued him as far as Zhuolu, where he took up position in the bottom of a valley. At the decisive moment of the battle, the Emperor Yandi asked for the help of the Yellow Emperor, who sent reinforcements in the form of bears, tigers and other wild animals. Then Chiyou, who had been carefully forging a great many weapons, launched an attack against the Yellow Emperor. The latter summoned the dragon Ying – which had the power to gather clouds to raise storms – and enjoined him to go and fight Chiyou on the plain of Hebei. Chiyou, for his part, summoned the Count of the Wind and the Lord of the Rain, whose magical powers were greater than those of Ying-the-dragon. The Yellow Emperor then invoked the goddess of drought, who scattered her strife so widely that the Lord of the Rain had to admit defeat and the storm abated. To counter a thick fog spread by Chiyou, the Yellow Emperor invented a chariot with a compass that could find its way in the worst conditions, and so the Yellow Emperor won the victory.

The story of this battle, recounted in many classical Chinese works, is echoed by that of another conflict, which, according to mythology, took place between Gonggong and Chuanxu.

The *Huai Nan Zi* gives the following account:

> Many years ago, Gonggong and Chuanxu were quarrelling over the throne. In his rage, Gonggong blundered against Mount Buzhou, which happened to be one of the pillars supporting the sky, thereby causing the pillar of heaven and the cord of the earth to break off at that point. The sky became higher in the north-east and the sun, moon and stars all moved in that direction. The earth sank lower in the south-east and the waters moved in that direction.

The struggle for the throne recounted by the legend probably reflects a tribal conflict. But, with daring imagination, the legend also attempts to provide an explanation for the geography of China, whose waterways mostly flow towards the lower, south-eastern regions of the country.

The legend of Xingtian, the hero who dared to persist in his struggle against the Lord on High, is even more imaginative. According to the *Shan Hai Jing*, a quarrel broke out between these two figures, and, in his fury, the Lord on High decapitated Xingtian and buried his head beneath Mount Changyang. However, the headless Xingtian used his nipples as eyes, while his naval became his mouth. Holding his shield in one hand and a hatchet in the other, he declared his determination to continue the combat. This is the reflection of the unyielding struggle between the ancient Chinese and the slave masters.

The fragments of legends discovered in classical Chinese works reveal that the mythology of ancient China was extremely rich and colourful, though this slave-based society has left very few documents, with the exceptions of oracles inscribed on tortoise shells.

The legends of ancient China nonetheless preserve their specific characteristics. Many mythological figures are intransigent heroes. Far from remaining inactive when confronted with natural disasters or formidable enemies, they demonstrate an extraordinary energy in overcoming them. The examples of Nüwa, Houyi, Gun, Yu and the Yellow Emperor are proof of this. It is not the Lord on High, but their own determination that shapes their destiny. Instead of being subservient to a divine will, they find themselves in direct opposition to it.

The mythology of ancient China has greatly influenced the art and literature of later periods. Bronze objects belonging to the period from the sixteenth to the ninth century BC bear the *taotie* and *kui* (dragon) motifs that were directly inspired by certain legends. These legends are also echoed in paintings and sculptures from between the fifth and third centuries BC. The motif of the painting on the silk banner excavated in 1972 in a Han tomb at Mawangdui near Changsha in the Hunan province, is inspired by the 'myth of the ten suns'. Meanwhile, in 1969, a clay tree was discovered in a tomb from the second century BC in the Jiyuan district of the Henan province. This tree was an exact replica of the mythological *fusang* and symbolized the general rejoicing after Houyi had slain the nine monsters.

Chinese poems and essays written after the fifth century BC were also often inspired by myths. Qu Yuan, the great poet of the fourth century BC, based a great deal of his work on mythology, and his daring imagination enabled him to produce some wonderful pieces. Other poets, such as Li Bai (701–62 AD) and Li He (790–816 AD), also used mythology to enhance their work. The origins of the Chinese novel, too, lie in ancient mythology. *The History of Mu, the Son of Heaven* (third century BC), which recounts the legendary voyages of King Mu (1001–947 BC), is one of the first narratives in this genre. The fantastical novels from the third to the fifth centuries also contain legends, while the famous fifteenth-century novel, *The Journey to the West*, which retraces the struggle between the Monkey King and the evil spirits, is in many respects inspired by mythology.

It is also possible to observe the influence of mythology in modern Chinese works of art and literature. Lu Xun (1881–1936), Guo Moruo (1892–1978) and many other modern writers are often inspired by myths. With his *Old Tales Retold*, Lu Xun introduced the genre of the historical narrative into modern Chinese literature. His eight colourful tales, which include those of Nüwa, Houyi and Yu the Great, offer the reader a pleasant introduction to Chinese mythology, history and thought.

Mythology is one of the earliest sources of inspiration for Chinese literature and art, and the style and characteristics of the Chinese arts are already apparent, in outline, in the ancient legends.

Li Shengheng

The Cid

The only one of the great Spanish literary myths to be based upon an historical character is that of the Cid. Nonetheless, it is difficult to separate proven, or even plausible, facts from the mythology surrounding the Cid that proliferated between the twelfth and the seventeenth centuries. Rodrigo (Ruy) Díaz was born around 1040 at Vivar near Burgos into the minor aristocracy, and between 1066 and 1071 his name appeared at the foot of documents signed by the King of Castile, Sancho II. Acting against the will and testament of his father, Ferdinand I, Sancho II had seized Galicia, his brother García's rightful inheritance, and then invaded León, the kingdom of his brother Alfonso. Sancho was killed during the siege of Zamora in 1072, leaving no heirs, and Alfonso, who was wary of restoring Garciá to the throne, became king and united the three kingdoms. The implication seems to be that Rodrigo had been involved – on the wrong side – in the fraternal feud. His name, however, continued to appear at the foot of royal decrees between 1072 and 1079, while, in 1074, he even married one of Alfonso VI's nieces, Jimena Díaz. He disappeared from public view between 1076 and 1079 and probably spent time on his land, away from court, but in 1080 he countersigned a royal document in Burgos. There then followed another long period, between 1080 and 1087, during which there is no mention of him, and several chronicles agree that Rodrigo was banished from the kingdom by Alfonso though they differ over the reasons for this. The chronicles describe Rodrigo fighting in the pay of the Muslim king of Saragossa against the Aragonese and the Catalans during this period, but the years 1087–8 marked his return to favour. The arrival of the powerful Almoravid armies in Spain and the decisive defeat of the Castilians at Sagrajas led the sovereign to decide upon reconciliation. At the time, Rodrigo was in charge of maintaining the Muslim kingdom of Valencia under the dependence of Castile. In order to protect the area from the expansionist desires of the surrounding principalities, both Christian and Muslim, he established a type of protectorate in this buffer zone, which separated Castile from the Almoravid invaders. In 1089, Rodrigo was unable to go to the aid of the besieged city of Aledo whence he had been summoned by Alfonso and once again there was a break in relations. His Castilian possessions were confiscated and his wife and children were taken prisoner. Left to his own devices and acting on his own initiative, the disinherited knight took it upon himself to establish peace in the area on the eastern coast of Spain that had been unsettled by the Almoravid successes. Rodrigo maintained a strong presence in Valencia, holding the city and its surrounding areas to ransom against such aspirants – of both long-standing and recent status – to its capture as the Count of Barcelona (whom he defeated at Tebar in 1090), the King of Saragossa and the Almoravids.

When, in 1092, the King of Castile in turn attempted to conquer the area, Ruy Díaz withdrew, allowing events to take their course. However, Alfonso's defeat and the establishment of a pro-Almoravid group in power in the city prompted him to conquer Valencia once and for all and, after a siege, it surrendered in 1094. The conditions of the surrender, which were initially lenient, were revoked following a revolt inspired by the hope of a revival in Almoravid fortunes. While the Castilian armies, defeated at Consuegra and at Cuenca in 1097, were retreating on all sides before the forces of Islam, Rodrigo consolidated and extended his domain, notably by taking Murviedro (Sagonte) in 1098. As regards the question of whether the conquest of Valencia restored the Cid permanently to royal favour, there is documentary evidence of Jimena's presence in the city at her husband's side. The Cid, the undisputed master of Valencia, died in 1099, and, in 1102, in spite of help from Alfonso VI, Jimena was forced to leave the city in the hands of the Almoravids. Rodrigo's only son had been killed at Consuegra, but his eldest daughter Cristina married an illegitimate descendant of the Navarran dynasty, and from this union a king, García Ramirez, was born. Meanwhile, his youngest daughter, Maria, married the Count of Barcelona, Ramón Berenguer III. Thus, by an accident of marriage, the blood of Ruy Díaz soon flowed through the veins of all the royal dynasties of mainland Spain, as well as through those of the most aristocratic families. Consequently, it was as much the nobility of the Cid's descendants as his somewhat short-lived personal adventure that contributed to the creation and development of the myth.

The earliest literature relating to the Cid is of Muslim origin, and consists of well-documented historiographical works dating from about 1110. The information contained in them is provided by first-hand accounts, although, unfortunately, these are generally restricted to matters relating to Valencia. Rodrigo is presented very much as the product of his banishment, in other words, as a marginal warlord faced with the reluctance of the Christian princes and the ulterior motives of his Muslim allies. He is shown using his courage and ingenuity to get the best out of his forces and to turn the divisions within the ranks of the enemy to his advantage. He emerges as the clever and intransigent tyrant of Valencia, who at times showed himself to be ruthless. Although these chroniclers may have provided an accurate historical account of the Cid's activities, they were also responsible for bringing history closer to myth. By exaggerating Rodrigo's cunning and cruelty, they made every effort to emphasize the disappointments that the Moorish princes of Spain experienced when asking the Christians for a military guarantee of their independence. Under the pretext of recording past events, the chroniclers advocated a policy of submission, for the time being, to the Almoravids.

In spite of Ruy Díaz's association with the East, demonstrated by his policy with regard to marriage, there is no doubt that the first Cidian narrative was produced in Christian Castile. In the second or third decade of the twelfth century, following the return of Rodrigo's relatives and those close to him – including Jimena, Jerome, the Bishop of Valencia and several of his lieutenants – the Castilian royal family decided that it would be advantageous to make the Cid a hero, since the princes of eastern Spain, who were relatives of the Cid and were themselves supported by several of his former companions, had begun to claim that they were his true successors. The dissension between Rodrigo and Alfonso VI, who died in 1109, was only too well known, but great attempts were made to efface the memory of it, or at least to ensure that it was not seen as a dispute with the Crown of Castile itself. According to the legend, the Cid was the closest colleague of Alfonso's predecessor, Sancho II. In single combat and through personal acts of bravery on the battlefield, he had served the cause of Castilian hegemony over the Iberian peninsula, working alongside a king who had made him the supreme commander of his armies. It was precisely this success, based upon an exemplary loyalty, that had earned Rodrigo the enmity of Alfonso, who vehemently distrusted the right-hand man of his enemy and brother. The Castilian Crown thus resurrected a hero whom it had rejected during his own lifetime. In the process, it wove the first strands of his laurel wreath and denied his associations with the Moors by presenting them as due to the indiscretions of a youth in fact devoted entirely to its service.

This first Castilian narrative, on which the *Legend of the Siege of Zamora* was based, is similar to works written around 1140 that constitute the first evidence of the development of the legend of the Cid. This particular legend certainly owes much to the redefinition of the Spanish political landscape as a result of the dismemberment and temporary alienation of the Aragonese Crown on the death of Alfonso I (Alfonso the Warrior). The secession of Navarre, the invasion of the territory of Saragossa by Castile and the relinquishing of sovereignty to the Count of Barcelona meant that there were new powers all seeking to establish their legitimacy through the figure of the Cid. In Navarre the nobility placed on the throne one García Ramirez, an illegitimate descendant of the old royal dynasty. After being condemned by the Pope and threatened with removal by the neighbouring princes, the 'Restorer' invented a royal ancestral line for Ruy Díaz, his maternal grandfather, according to which he traced his origins to the elected Judge, Laín Calvo, whose colleague, Nuño Rasura, was said to be the ancestral founder of the Castilian dynasty. He had as much right to rule as Alfonso VII of Castile or Ramón Berenguer IV, Count of Barcelona and Prince of Aragon, the son of Ruy Díaz's second son-in-law. This imaginary Cidian genealogy was established by the *Legend of the Judges* designed to restore the Navarran dynasty and passed down over the centuries unchanged. At about the same time, the *Carmen Campiodoctris*, a Latin poem composed in Catalonia, of which sadly only a small fragment remains, used the relationship between the Cid and the Count of Barcelona as its central theme, placing great emphasis on their first military encounter. For a long time this relationship was one of conflict. However, it is reasonable to assume that the *Carmen* ended with a glorious reconciliation, sealed by a marriage. Thus Ramón Berenguer IV used the reputation of his illustrious relative to support his claim to the Crown of Aragon, which was being contested by García Ramirez. In addition, he also employed it to help maintain Catalan influence over the Levant (the eastern coast of Spain), a cause to which he devoted most of his diplomatic and military activity from 1140 onwards. The Cid was not in fact his ancestor, for the count was the product of Ramón Berenguer III's second marriage. Around 1145, the *Historia Roderici* dismissed both the Navarran and the Catalan theories. In spite of several errors and, above all, certain important omissions, this Latin chronicle undeniably constituted an attempt to return to the historiographical and documentary sources of the story of the Cid. Its version of Rodrigo closely resembled the one that appeared in the Muslim writings, to the extent that he was portrayed as a brave warrior who made his living by offering his services as a mercenary, by plundering and by extorting ransoms. He is also described as a man who was clever at taking advantage of a complex and changing political situation. However, it is the relationship between Ruy Díaz and the Christian princes that forms the centre-piece of the narrative, and the ancestry of the counts of Barcelona is among the main subjects discussed. Ramón Berenguer II and Ramón Berenguer III appear as ridiculous characters whose conceit is equal only to their cowardice. Meanwhile, the Navarrans are not presented in a much better light. Their descendants appear as the constantly luckless hereditary enemies of the knights of Vivar. In particular, the genealogy that favoured the claims of García Ramirez was discredited by the ousting of Laín Calvo's double, Nuño Rasura, the ancestor of the kings of Castile, and by passing over the authority for the legend in silence. On the other hand, the Castilian royalty (and to a lesser degree the lineage of the Aragonese kings prior to the Catalan alliance) are shown in a good light. The disagreements between the Cid and Alfonso VI are presented as the result of a misunderstanding that, throughout his life, the Cid does his best to resolve. For his part, Alfonso carefully avoids becoming involved in leagues conspiring against Rodrigo. In addition, he also helps Jimena after the death of her husband and finally has the body of his vassal taken to Castile for burial. There is a divergence of opinion over where the *Historia Roderici* was composed. However, the general orientation of the work makes the theory that it was written in Castile seem the most probable. Faced by neighbouring powers claiming to be the genealogical descendants of an independent hero, the Crown of Castile simply claimed the political heritage of a loyal vassal. This was a more shrewd move, since, at the time, Alfonso VII, the Emperor, was endeavouring to impose his suzerainty on all the Christian kingdoms in Spain, by demanding the allegiance of the King of Navarre in particular, and also that of the Count of Barcelona for the purpose of securing possession of Saragossa.

The writings of the first half of the twelfth century show the heroic figure of the Cid recognizing the legitimacy of the Spanish sovereignty. However, it must be asked whether they in fact contribute to the development of the myth. They do if judged in terms of the largely imaginary nature of their sources, the uniqueness of their references to heroic deeds and their intention of using past events to provide a basis for the present order. They do not, though, if one considers the incongruity of the messages expressed in them and especially the superficial nature of the issues that they record. The defence of a right of sovereignty is the stuff from which legends are created, while the task of myth is to provide a firm basis for social order. In this sense, it was the *Cantar* (or Poema) *de mío Cid* that truly initiated the myth of the Cid.

Composed in Castilian verse between the middle of the twelfth and the beginning of the thirteenth century, the *Cantar* opens with the banishment of Ruy Díaz, the confiscation of his wealth and the imprisonment of his family by the Crown. However, by obtaining a loan, more or less fraudulently, from the Burgos Jews, plundering and holding to ransom several small Moorish villages and gaining a victory over the Count of Barcelona at Tebar, the hero is able to maintain a large and well-equipped force that soon dominates the Levant. The seizure of Valencia transforms the highwayman into a rich nobleman who arouses the covetous attentions of the Castilians. The Cid obtains the liberation of his family and a pardon from the king. However, by order of the king, he is also forced to agree to a marriage of convenience between his daughters and the sons of a favoured noble family. Having made their fortunes effortlessly and believing that they have married beneath them, the sons-in-law mistreat and abandon their wives. The Cid appeals to royal justice. Before a judicial assembly solemnly convened by Alfonso, he obtains redress and is accorded the highest honour – a request for the hands of his daughters in a second marriage, this time with the Infantes of the royal houses of Navarre and Aragon.

With the exception of a few historical facts relating to Ruy Díaz that form its basis, the *Cantar* is mostly fictional. It was probably responsible for inventing the name the 'Cid' (from the Arabic 'sidi' meaning 'lord'), which was subsequently used in preference to his real name, and for linking it inseparably with his traditional name 'Campidoctor', which then became 'Campeador' (Champion). Meanwhile, its narrative combines and accentuates the striking events of Rodrigo's career, which it embellishes with an abundance of new dramatic material. As a result, the story is raised to a level of symbolic meaning that operates both by connotation and implication and that is appropriate to a creative work. The *Cantor* centres on two important elements: banishment, followed by reinstatement. These two changes of fortune do not simply cancel each other out and produce a return to the status quo. The narrative involves the progressive rehabilitation of the hero and the organization of the microcosms of society constituted by his household and by the Valencian aristocracy. It records the Cid's edifying speeches and the terms in which he denounces his enemies – all of which pave the way and provide the reason for his final, triumphant reinstatement. It is an illustration of the values of the medieval community: the moral emphasis on work and merit; the institutional emphasis on frankness and social mobility; and particularly the economic emphasis on a financial hierarchy. There is, however, an obvious paradox, since the political orientation of the *Cantar* is primarily feudal. Thus the custom whereby vassals, such as the Cid, his family and household, pay homage to their overlord is of central significance. In contrast to a fundamentally territorial definition of royal power, based on the Romano-Gothic tradition, Rodrigo seems to embody the principle of personal allegiance, which was a better guarantee of the rights of inheritance. He also offers a contrast to a monarch surrounded by a court consisting exclusively of feudal barons, a political replica of the empire of León, by embodying a more just and dynamic system of contractual bonds based on an exchange of services. This dual ideology could imply that the work was written in two main stages, as is also suggested by certain philosophical evidence. However, it is necessary to take account of the fact that the two messages are deeply interwoven throughout the entire work. The crucial point is thus that the twelfth century witnessed the simultaneous establishment in Castile of two systems of relations and values. The legal redefinition of urban space, involving negotiations that gave rise to an increased number of local 'coalitions' and municipal charters known as *fueros*, was accompanied by the exploitation, by a monarchy faced with the political disintegration of Christian Spain, of a new alliance agreement, which allowed a more effective resistance to Almoravid and subsequently Almohad pressure. In this way, the profound economic and social change taking place in the cities was accompanied by the establishment of a political superstructure based on the feudal system. The gains made by Christianity were achieved through feudal coalitions supported by the growing power of municipal militiae. The aristocracy's appetite for land, the middle classes' desire to open up new roads and the concern of Royalty to gain the united support of all social and political forces, meant that there was strong common interest. The contract sealed by Christian oath must have appeared to all parties to be the most flexible and efficient system of organization and also the best means of ensuring a balance of power. The first great Cidian myth, based on the *Cantar de mío Cid*, thus favoured social and political restructuring. According to its view, the initial status of chaos justified the collapse of the seignorial order of the empire, and the subsequent restoration of stability heralded the emergence of a feudal monarchy based on the new feudal order of the bourgeoisie.

In parallel with the dominant tradition of the Cid, centred around the reign of Alfonso VI, the legendary connection of Ruy Díaz with the story of Alfonso's predecessor, Sancho II, underwent important developments throughout the twelfth and thirteenth centuries. At the centre of these stories lies the drama of an ambitious and quick-tempered king, who, following the partition of the kingdom of León-Castile by Ferdinand I, deposed his brothers before being murdered outside the walls of Zamora. The Cid plays an increasingly important role, the significance of which varies according to the historical context. After the new partition of the kingdom by Alfonso VII in 1157, the Cluniac writer of the *Crónica Najerense* (1160) attempted to warn the new sovereigns of the dangers of a fractricidal conflict. Similarly, when the union had been permanently established and the ateliers of Alfonso X (Alfonso the Wise) embarked upon the composition of the *Primera Crónica General* (*Estoria de España*) in 1260, the companion of Sancho of Castile provided an illustration of the basic principles of the political order of the monarchy. These included the need for harmony between the royalty and nobility in the general conduct of affairs, and, above all, the need for the nobility to show the nobility unfailing loyalty due to the royal house even in circumstances where there was a total lack of agreement or where the nobility felt that the Crown was making a gross error of judgement. The myth of the Cid thus became subordinated to the ideology of the monarchy – to the extent that even the *Cantar de mío Cid* was subjected to a pious and lacklustre revision in the *Crónica general*. The result was to provoke a mythological reaction. At the very end of the thirteenth century a new narrative inspired by the chivalric tradition became the source of a second great myth of the Cid destined to dominate the latter part of the Middle Ages and the Classical period. The reigns of Alfonso VI and Sancho II had little more to offer, so that the *Mocedades de Rodrigo* drew its inspiration for the story of Rodrigo's youth from the reign of their father Ferdinand I (1035–65), founder of the royal line of Castile.

During the course of a duel, Rodrigo kills the Count Gómez de Gormaz, and the Count's daughter, Jimena, pleads with the king for justice. However, Rodrigo is excused from paying redress and, instead, the two young people marry, although Rodrigo swears that he will only consummate the marriage after having won five battles. In rapid succession, he puts a band of Muslim thieves to flight, emerges victorious from a single combat, the prize for which is the annexation of the city of Calahorra to Castile, crushes the armies of five Moorish kings, stifles in its early stage a plot being hatched by Castilian counts and, having been made commander of the royal armies, defeats the army of the Moorish Empire, freeing the Castilians from the excesive duties-that the Moors were attempting to levy on them. In fact, the long narrative structure of the work gives rise to lengthy and divergent interpretations of it in later texts. Official historiographical works, such as the *Crónica de Castilla* (1300) and the Portuguese *Crónica de 1344* – which is also known as the *Secunda Crónica General* and which was a plagiaristic version of the *Primera Crónica General* – portrayed the brilliant career of a young aristocrat whose loyalty to the royal house was quite exemplary. A contrasting view was presented by the *Crónica Rimada*, a poetic text of which the only known edition is dated, with certain reservations, to the second half of the fourteenth century. In it, Rodrigo is a quick-tempered knight who is a fanatical defender of chivalry and its values. As such, he is a relentless opponent of any sovereignty that has not proved itself worthy of respect, but is the last resort of a king weakened by the incompetence and disloyalty of his highest-ranking nobles. However, these two versions share certain characteristics for which it is possible to identify a common source. Thus both follow a reassessment of the Cidian genealogy suggested by the *Legend of the Judges*. This presents Laín Calvo as the ancestor of the great old families of Haro and Castro and also, surprisingly, of the small house of the knights of Mendoza, and asserts that Rodrigo was only connected with him through a younger branch of the family. In addition to this demeaning of the Cid's status, several secondary elements, as well as some of the main structural points in the narrative, suggest a figure belonging to the second level of the nobility. The former include the unfortunate choice of steed made by the young hero, the fact that several of the main characters are younger members of the family, the illegitimacy of Rodrigo's relatives, and the fact that access to the paternal name is dependent upon exploits achieved. Meanwhile, the oath to carry out five victories before marrying the daughter of a count is an example of the latter. Royal chronicles simply toned down the fervour of the Cid's aspirations, while the *Crónica Rimada*, which contains accounts of the activities of elite groups on the fringes of society accumulated during the course of a long oral tradition, stressed the stigma of social disadvantage by extending its cast of characters to include urban oligarchy. Once again, it is history that contains the substratum of the literary myth of the Cid. Dynastic struggles and plots by royal minorities caused upheaval in the higher ranks of the Castilian nobililty during the first half of the fourteenth century and thereby fostered the establishment, in the shadow of the Crown, of a minor aristocracy on whom the continuity of power was dependent. Subsequently, during the second half of the century, the traditional nobility gradually became extinct through natural causes or bloodshed, while the dynasty itself was split by the defeat of Peter I by his illegitimate brother Enrique de Trastámara, behind whom the nobility gradually regrouped. The result was a climate in which knights and the younger sons of the great families, which at one point were threatened with decline, could rise to the upper echelons of the aristocracy. However, having learned the lessons of history, the Trastámara family did not entrust power to this new nobility, preferring instead to surround itself by loyal and devoted knights. And this provided a further source of inspiration for the myth. The dream of a rise in rank, symbolized by the striking example of the Mendoza family, appears in the *Mocedades*, which uses Rodrigo as a model in which the parvenu could contemplate the reflection of his own success and on which the aspirant could build his hopes of advancement. The legend of the Cid, which was conceived by the *Cantar* in terms of profound social and political change, has been replaced by the legend of Rodrigo, merely glorifying the ambition of a new elite.

The change in the chivalric orders, which became the theme of most Castilian heroic works during the fourteenth century, inspired a new variety of poetry that was to dominate the history of the mythology of Castile during the fifteenth century and for several centuries afterwards: the *romancero* or Spanish ballad. The break with the traditional rules and aims of the historical narrative was complete. The ballads were short sung poems that focused on fragmentary incidents, isolating the intracies of a short powerful scene and using them to symbolize the most diverse conficts. In the *romancero*, the Cid is contrasted with a king and court uncertain of their own criteria, and is shown fiercely championing values and codes with which all members of the secular elite could identify: independence, honour and patriotism. Cidian mythology ceased to interpret history and became instead a poetic weapon used in all kinds of battles. When, around 1520, the cities of Castile, led by the knights and initially supported by the nobility, rose up against Charles of Ghent – a foreign sovereign who had no respect for national traditions – they must undoubtedly have felt that their aspirations were echoed in the ballads. The episode in which the severe and haughty Cid demanded in the name of Castile that Alfonso should swear that he had not been involved in the murder of his predecessor before he would acknowledge his legitimacy, must have called to mind the painful oaths that the future Charles V had himself to make to the Spanish Cortes. Similarly, the marriage scene with Jimena, transformed into a violent break between Rodrigo and the king in the name of national aristocratic traditions, undoubtedly constituted a veritable call to insurrection. The imperial poets were not caught out for, once the insurrection had been crushed, they composed counter ballads, which reinstated the obedient Rodrigo of the *Primera Crónica General*. However, these didactic writings were weighed down by the prose of the sources from which they were drawn and lacked the symbolic force of their rivals, with the result that they did not survive to the end of the oral tradition. The early form of *romancero*, which persisted until the sixteenth century, inspired numerous imitations illustrating the ancestral merits and the political independence of a nobility dispossessed of its power by Charles V and Philip II. Having achieved its aims under Philip III, the nobility preferred to see itself reflected in a court *romancero* in which an amorous and civilized Cid was the embodiment of the perfect courtier. Thus, at the beginning of the seventeenth century, the literary mythology of the Cid created an impression of irreconcilable division. However, this does not appear to have concerned the compilers. The collections of ballads by Escobar entitled the *Romancero General* (1600) and the *Romancero del Cid* (1605) presented a picture in which the rebellious knight, the faithful servant of the king, the haughty noble and the affected courtier all coexisted in apparent chaos. Indeed, this very state of chaos provides a good illustration of the diversity and even the contradictory nature of the values of the elite of the time. This monstrous body of work marks the apogee of the Cidian myth in Spanish literature, just as the first theatrical version of the myth marks the beginning of its decline.

Around 1618, Guillén de Castro completed a *comedia* which owed its title and narrative structure – copied from the *Mocedades de Rodrigo* – to the Cidian traditions. Its characters were taken partly from the *Mocedades* and partly from the *Legend of the Siege of Zamora*, while several speeches either reproduced or adapted certain well-known ballads, although the ballads chosen were invariably the most recent. The traditional figures were exaggerated into caricatures and made to seem trite, by being represented in accordance with the norms and speech of contemporary times. The focus of the narrative was moved from heroism to passion, and the narrative structure and its points of emphasis were drastically changed. However, Guillén, who was often said to be the first writer to present a drama of love confronted by honour, did not reduce the myth to a new type of amorous discourse. The crucial point was that the traditionally political content of the myth was pared down to a minimum. For a long time, the image of Rodrigo had illustrated the values of those aspiring to rise up the social scale, before being broken up to reflect the ideas of a dominant class. At this period when the defeat of the nation and its elite was self-evident, he was used in the service of a group of royal favourites. The myth was no longer one of conquest but of compensation. It was no longer social, or even truly political, but almost 'politicking'. The play opens with the challenge issued by the Count to the elderly Diego Laínez and closes with the marriage of Rodrigo and Jimena. Apart from Rodrigo's military exploits – a battle against the Moors and his single combat for the prize of annexing Calahorra – the action takes place entirely within the palace. In the presence of a king who is respected in spite of his weakness, the noble advisers represent values that are supposed to triumph: the honour of lineage, service of the State and loyalty. Above all, they are proud of their noble status. No attempt is made to challenge or change the ruling order that, constituted by an aristocracy that controls most of the power, is linked to royalty by the complexities of blood, is certain of its own permanence and unanimously admires Rodrigo as a paragon of its own greatness. This was theatre designed for the court of Philip III, the theatre of privilege, of the great, of eldest sons and royal favourites. The interwoven themes of love and honour were primarily symbols of this deep-rooted harmony between the masters of Spain – in spite of the vehement evocations of honour, which reflect the anguish of a nation in real decline, and in spite of the apparent glorification of the sudden upsurge of national pride inspired by the arrogant Duke of Osuna. Osuna was Guillén's patron and the rival of the Duke of Lerma, whose pacifist diplomacy he criticized, proposing instead the re-establishment of a military presence in Flanders, Italy and Savoy. As well as being the year of Lerma's fall, 1618 also marked the end of the Cidian myth's role in dubious battles for ascendancy between the various factions and families of the Spanish aristocracy. It was now the era of the anti-hero. The shining star of the Cid was overshadowed by the black sun of Don Quixote and Don Juan.

However, perhaps under the inspiration of the small Spanish settlement in Rouen, and in particular of a certain Rodrigue de Chalon, it was at this point that Corneille introduced the Cid to France. In his 1648 edition of the story, he listed his sources as Mariana's *Historia de España*, Loys de Mayerne Turquet's *Histoire Générale* and above all Guillén de Castro's *Comedia*; and the scenario of Corneille's work follows that of Castro quite closely. However, the French poet also omitted a large number of elements. These included the hatred felt by Don Sanche (Don Sancho), the king's eldest son, towards his sister and brothers because an astrologer had predicted that he would be assassinated by a member of his family, and the episode involving the leper who, in Castro's play, was greeted by Rodrigo on his return from Santiago de Compostela.

Anxious to respect the three 'Unities' as far as possible, and the unity of time in particular, Corneille has obviously simplified and shortened the action. The diversity and liveliness of the Spanish work is replaced by a scheme that is more linear and more coldly logical. However, the result was that the myth was transformed and assumed a completely different meaning.

Rodrigue (Rodrigo) no longer appears as the Christian knight; perhaps out of a sense of propriety and to avoid presenting the sacred in the theatre of the profane, Corneille eradicated all religious references from his work. The political aspect was also changed. Court life with its divisions and even hatreds is almost absent from this version of the story. Likewise the Infanta has a less obtrusive role. Her significance is more ideological and poetic than strictly dramatic – more like that of the hero's sister or ideal wife. In fact, the play has frequently been staged without this character. The king, however, who is weak and inactive in the Spanish play, displays a certain efficacity and majesty in spite of his discretion. From a world of quarrelsome and presumptuous royal favourites, Corneille takes us into a new setting: the period of French civilization between 1630 and 1660. The death of the count represents the death of feudalism. Rodrigue is bound to honour his father, but is even more bound to honour his king; and, by sending him to fight the Moors, his father demonstrates his own support for this shift of allegiance. The young man who has proved his valour and, through his duel, has become the equal of a count, is elevated to even greater heights by defeating the Moors and saving Spain. *Le Cid* is therefore a reflection of social change. The nobility must renounce the blustering and haughty individualism of the associates and contemporaries of Maria de' Medici. Service to king and country is its most important obligation. For these reasons, although the killing of the count was an obvious mark of the youthful valour of Rodrigo, it was ultimately a crime – a crime that only the rout of the Moors could erase.

This represents a veritable reversal of ethical values. Apparently de-Christianized (or perhaps merely endowed with the faith of French Classicism, rather than that of the Spanish crusades), Rodrigue covers the entire history of nobility in the course of the play. He becomes a hero because he is unafraid of death and because he kills. However, this heroism is insufficient and even wrong, in terms of the true morality demanded by the absolute monarch and by the state of war. Richelieu demanded obedience from the nobility, and the war against Spain made the salvation of the State the supreme law. Thus it was possible for Rodrigue's crime to be forgotten and – later – for Horace to be acquitted.

However, the Cid did not become a myth in France as a result of the political significance with which Corneille invested his play. The poet himself pointed out in his *Examen* that, when Rodrigue appeared before Chimène (Jimena) 'a shiver ran through the audience, which was the sign of a wonderful curiosity and an increased attention to what they had to say to each other in such pitiable circumstances'. Although Corneille did not invent the story of the love between the count's daughter and the son of Don Diègue (Don Diego), but rather obtained it from Guillén de Castro's *Comedia*, he developed the theme into one that was much richer and more impressive.

Love has its place in the play's moral argument. Rodrigue sacrifices his passion in order to avenge his father, but this sacrifice only serves the cause of his love and allows him to prove himself worthy of Chimène. In his service to the king he finds both glory and love. He is worthy of both his father and the woman he loves.

In the play, Rodrigue becomes a young man who is virtuous, courageous and in love. He moves us because he tries to reconcile what he owes to his father with what he owes to the woman he loves. It is satisfying to find that Chimène shares the same qualities and sentiments, and moving again to see these young people confessing that they have never ceased loving each other, even though they have to act as though they hate each other. By uniting them at the end of the play, the king not only demonstrates that royal authority can resolve apparently irreconcilable contradictions, but also indicates that those who do their duty and are ready to sacrifice their personal feelings will ultimately achieve both glory and happiness. In other words, 'he who loses his life, regains it' – the most painful sacrifices will always be rewarded and, after the ordeal of suffering, what has been sacrificed will be restored.

The 'Querelle du Cid' developed around the concept of 'bienséance' (propriety). The love between Chimène and Rodrigue, their imminent marriage at the end of the play and the young man's visit to the young girl's home were all potentially shocking. In the event, however, these paradoxical situations ensured the play's success and renown. The public established a parallel between *Le Cid* and *Romeo and Juliet* and *Tristan and Isolde*, comparing its young lovers with the other perfect couples separated by social conflict unless their superhuman vows of fidelity enable them to reunite and transcend anything that can harm them.

During the seventeenth century, Chevreau (*La Suite et Le Mariage du Cid*, 1638), Desfontaines (*La Vraie Suite du Cid*, 1638) and Thymothée de Chillac (*L'Ombre du Comte de Gomès et la Mort du Cid*, 1639), attempted to exploit the success of Corneille's work. However, their three plays received little acclaim. Though the three poets portrayed Rodrigue as persecuted by the

Infante, imprisoned by the king and saved by the people, King Ferdinand falling in love with Chiméne, and the son of Don Gomez avenging his father and killing the Cid, this does not alter the influence or significance of Corneille's hero.

Two nineteenth-century plays – Le Brun's *Le Cid d'Andalousie* (1825) and Casimir Delavigne's *La Fille du Cid* (1840) – made an attempt to return to the original Spanish setting and sources. By contrast, in *Le Nouveau Cid*, Gabriel Hugelmann portrayed an impossible love affair between a French officer and a young Austrian girl at the time of Magenta and Solferino, and, in the process, demonstrated that the myth had not changed inherently, even though the modern hero sacrifices his passion for mankind, not for his father's honour. Finally, Massenet's *Le Cid* tried to remain faithful to the play by Corneille.

The work produced by the poets of this period was more interesting than that of the playwrights, and they usually attempted to return to the Spanish tradition. In *España*, Théophile Gautier describes the monastery where the hero has been laid to rest and, in accordance with the legend, portrays the Cid's funerary statue as coming to life to frighten a Jew who has dared to mock it. Meanwhile, Barbey d'Aurevilly depicts the compassionate Cid of the *Romancero*, who takes pity on a leper. Victor Hugo imagines Rodrigo before the Caliph of Granada as he receives the young king Don Sancho, suffering the pain both of the monarch's ingratitude and of his own exile – although, to tell the truth, he sacrifices the character of the hero to an historical and even philosophical panorama. In a different vein, Leconte de Lisle and José Maria de Heredia attempt to move away from Corneille's Classicism and to revive the ancient cruelty of the Spanish myth. They have no hesitation in describing the bloody head of the count, which the young man offers to his offended father. Although *Le Soulier de Satin* is much more obviously reminiscent of Lope de Vega and Calderón (and Shakespeare) than of Corneille, the hero is nevertheless called Rodrigue.

Nineteenth and even the twentieth century French writers often preferred to return to the figure of the Cid associated with Spanish legends and churches. However, Victor Hugo's historical reflections, and Heredia's and Leconte de Lisle's gory scenes did not really change anything fundamentally. Corneille's *Le Cid*, which continues to be studied in schools and performed at the Comédie-Française and the Odéon, remains easily the most popular version of the legend. For a modern French audience, Rodrigue remains the perfect son and lover who saves Spain and thus fully deserves to marry the woman he loves. Although thirty years ago Gérard Philipe's Romanticism presented a new poetic image of Corneille's hero, this did little to affect the perception of the figure of the Cid in France.

The literary myth of the Cid is essentially historical. Despite acting as a vehicle for expression of social and political issues in both Spain and France, the story has only rarely served to establish a particular order by giving an account of its origins. Its main significance has been to reflect changes in the status quo that have taken place over a period of time. Two great epochs give the myth its structure. The first, a state of chaos, does not represent the primordial chaos of the beginning of things, but merely the breakdown of the order that existed before the Cid embarked on his exploits. The second is the dawn of a new order that the myth sets out to glorify. The transition between the two does not change the structure of the traditional political regime. What does change, however, is the social elite and the elitist values on which the same centralized power continues to be based. The new elite may consist of a class in the process of expansion, or it may merely comprise newcomers, parvenus from a social stratum inferior to that of the traditional dominant group. The myth of the Cid has never been revolutionary, but it has always been profoundly reformist.

G. Martin and A. Niderst

Coatlicue, the Mother Goddess

In his *Historia general de las cosas de Nueva España*, Brother Bernardino de Sahagun, the sixteenth-century Spanish Franciscan monk who may rightly be regarded as the first Americanist, cites the myth, told to him by his indigenous 'informers', of the woman called Coatlicue (from *coatl*, meaning snake and *cueitl*, meaning skirt). One day, when engaged in sweeping (which in the Mesoamerican cultures was a ritual act rather than a mere household task, Coatlicue felt a ball of feathers fall on her. In order not to interrupt her work, which was effectively an act of worship, Coatlicue slipped the ball of feathers under her clothes, against her belly, but when her work was over and she tried to examine the curious object, it had disappeared and she herself had become miraculously pregnant. Irritated by this secret pregnancy, which they regarded as an affront to the family honour, Coatlicue's sons, the Centzonhuitznahua (from *centzon*, meaning four hundred, in other words countless, and *huitznahua*, the term for the southern divinities who are the cosmogonic representations of the constellations visible from the Mexican high plateau) and her daughter Coyaulxauhqui (from *coyaulli*, meaning little bells, and *zauhqui*, meaning painted or decorated) plotted their mother's death. However, the child that she was carrying comforted her and preserved her from external dangers until he was born, with a shield in his hand, 'holding a spear and a blue rod, his face painted, his left leg slender and feathered, his thighs and arms painted blue'. This child was the god Huitzilopochtli, and two of his names are He-who-was-born-on-the-shield and Warrior-of-the-South because his first act was to fight his brothers and send them 'to the southern region', while he also, cut off his sister's head and sliced her body to pieces. Huitzilopochtli (from *huitzilin*, meaning hummingbird, and *opochtli*, meaning left, or perhaps southern) was the tribal god of the Aztecs and, as such, he was both the rising sun and the sun at its zenith, which was the embodiment of the nahua civilization at the height of its prosperity.

In her analysis of the myth Laurette Séjourné explains that the dark Coatlicue had to disappear in order to give birth to the luminous creature inside her. Aztec iconography commemorates this dialectical death in statues of the goddess that always represented her as decapitated. The myth complicates the story with different versions, in which Coatlicue's daughter, the god's sister, merges with Coatlicue herself, who then becomes Huitzilopochtli's first victim: 'He began with her when he killed her down there . . . down there he ate her heart.' Heart-of-the-Earth is moreover one of Coatlicue's many names; she was also called Obsidian Butterfly, White Flower or Yellow Flower in her manifestations as goddess of vegetation and harvest. But as Mother-of-the-gods, Our-Ancestor, Coatlicue is also the Warrior because like the sun, the earth feeds on blood and demands the hearts of warriors sacrified in her honour. As the Warrior, Coatlicue is naturally also the goddess of hunting and appears in the form of a stag, as in the myth of the stag with two heads, the protagonists of which are Mimix and Xiuhnel, who are descended from the northern god Mixcoatl, Cloud-Snake.

During a hunt, Mimix and Xiuhnel see a two-headed stag, which changes into two women. 'Come and drink, come and eat' cry the women to the hunters, who are at first surprised and then enthusiastic. 'And Xiuhnel drank blood and slept with her and when he had laid her on the ground he laid himself on top of her and he bit and pierced her, then he said to Mimix, "I am going, I have eaten what was due to me." And the other woman got up and called him . . . and Mimix did not call her but he made two bits of wood leap from the fire, then he damped down the fire and when he had damped it down he ran into it and the woman behind him. She stayed with him for a whole night and half of the next day.' Then, the myth continues, the divine cauldron came down from the sky and the woman fell into it and her body fell into pieces. First green flint, then white, then yellow then red burst from it. And Mixcoatl siezed the white flint, wrapped it up and worshipped it as a god and, taking it with him, set off to conquer new lands.

Psychoanalysis could make much of the unambiguously sexual significance of drinking and eating – indeed the verb 'to eat' has retained the same sexual connotations in the slang of some Latin American countries. These activities open up strange paths of penetration to the terrible Aztec gods, who are always hungry and thirsty. The pieces of Huitzilopochtli's sister's body and the fragmented body of Mimix's companion both have the same significance, as is suggested by the 'Song to the Mother of the gods', in the first line, 'Oh, the yellow flower has opened its corolla' and the last two, 'Oh, turned into a stag Xiuhniel and Mimich saw you in the desert'. Many very fine pre-Cortesian poems provide explanations of the mother goddess's name, of which the preferred form is Cihuacoatl, Snake-Woman, which shares the element *coatl* with Coatlicue and thus literally means She-who-wears-the-snake-skirt – death's heads and snakes being the attributes of the mother goddess. Laurette Séjourné, the great specialist on Latin American cultures, was struck by the omnipresent representations of snakes at all the region's archaeological sites. These take many different forms, from the Greek scalare to the S-shaped design composed of two interlaced bodies. The latter is particularly interesting in that it forms the glyph for 'movement', the sign of our era, the Fifth Sun that myth condemns to disappear in seismic cataclysms. The snake itself represents matter, which is creative and renews itself endlessly in different forms. Thus the 'monster of the earth' is a snake with its mouth wide open, in the depths of which one can just see a human head.

One day, like the great god Pan, Coatlicue died – or at least that was the rumour that spread across the lands that the newly arrived Spanish had called New Spain. But with the Spaniards arrived printing – in other words books, works of fiction, modern myths. Thus, various embodiments of Coatlicue, the goddess of the Mesoamerican culture, can still be found in the literature of the Central American countries. The Guatemala of Miguel Angel Asturias and the Mexico of Carlos Fuentes evoke her memory in stories in which all her names and all the symbols of her myths are brought to life one by one.

Thus, in 'The Deer of the Seventh Fire', the third part of *Men of Maize* by Miguel Angel Astuias, Mama Tecun, beloved 'nana' of the Tecun sons, suffers from terrible hiccups. The curer has of course been consulted, but how can he precribe a remedy when he is ignorant of the root of the trouble? The immediate cause of the problem is no real mystery: it is obvious that the poor woman has a cricket in her belly. So there is the curer, standing mediative and oracular on the threshold of the room where the patient is hiccuping. With one ear listening to her and with the other listening to the darkness outside, he can be sure beyond all possible doubt that his patient's 'hics' are merely answers to the thousand little hiccups of the crickets in the night. The real difficulty is to discover the true nature of the malevolent force that has managed to insert a cricket through Mama Tecun's navel and so cause her deadly spasms.

In the universe of the 'men and maize' into which the story transports us, disease is an element in an unrelenting conflict between opposing wills and interests. In this conflict sickness represents, at most, a temporary and partial seizure of power, the temporary victory of one element over the others. Sickness is a sign of foreign interference in a system that it is trying to take over for reasons and by means that are never accidental, let alone objective, and that seem to be utterly irrational. *Men of Maize* is a work of fiction, but its descriptions of these primitive beliefs has a sound anthropological basis. Moreover, it is the survival of such beliefs in modern Indian communities that underlies what is otherwise an entirely secular plot: the story of the struggles of Guatamalan peasants dispossessed of their land against the arbitrary actions of local authorities working in cahoots with greedy traffickers. Thus in a sense there is no need for any diagnosis by the curer. Leaving aside its purely narrative elements, the whole logic of story points to the guilty parties from the very beginning. These are the Zacatons, who are said to be in league with the maize growers and the 'ladinos' of Pisigüilto, and are therefore hostile to the Tecuns, who are their natural enemies in narrative terms and have joined the guerillas fighting with the Cacique Indian Gasper Ilom. (The same situation recurs in *The Green Pope*, where Doña Flora's association with George Maker Thompson leads Mayari to say, 'I can't look at my mother any more because she reminds me of the Malinche.' Doña Flora does not know who the malinche was, but her partner is able to explain: 'The Malinche helped Cortes against the Indians during the conquest of Mexico, and since you're helping me . . .' (Asturias 1971: 47).)

It seems simple and logical to interpret the story as a politico-rural drama recounting the settling of scores between families from rival ethnic groups. However, simplicity and logic are not the most prominent features of Asturias's writing, while placing the greatest emphasis on novelistic logic and thus viewing the narrative element as enshrining the first degree of meaning involves dismissing the ideological aspects of the work. What is true is that the metaphorical splendour of the writing, which is sometimes almost deliriously rich, paradoxically conceals the very thing that it is trying to convey: the ideological importance of what is written. It is, indeed, ironic that the distinguishing feature of Asturias's writing and the element that he has always deliberately sought to emphasize is hard to appreciate. This is an 'intertextual' approach whereby the contemporary story acts as a vehicle for a message involving more profound ancient myths, which were used by the Mayans as the chief means of disseminating their cultural traditions. In the view of Asturias, a writer must strive after brilliance not just for his or her own aesthetic pleasure, but as a matter of duty in order to be effective; for if speech is to be 'sonorous' and to be listened to, it most be decorated with unexpected devices. Without going into a detailed discussion of Asturias's intertextual approach, it is worth recalling that *Men of Maize* is introduced by an epigraph taken from the last two lines of a pre-Columbian poem (*Canto del Atamalcualoyan*) which provides the substance for the entire book: 'Here, the woman. I, the sleeper.' (The full text of these lines reads 'Dormido, dormido, duerme./Con la mano he arrollado *aqui a la mujer, yo el dormido*', the words in italics being those used in the actual epigraph.)

The figure of the sleeper brings us close to that of the curer, who is preparing to give a potion – which it is magic rather than purely medicinal – not to the still hiccuping mother but to her son, Calistro. The dialectical relationship between mother and child, emphasized by the myth of Huitzilopochtli and Coatlicue, is one of the constant features of Asturias's depictions of maternal figures and explains the ambiguity of the character of Doña Flora in *The Green Pope*. This ambiguity disappears as soon as we consider the dialectical relationships between the mother and daughter, Doña Flora and Mayari. In *Man of Maize*, Calistro falls into a deep sleep and speaks with the curer from 'the other side': 'Urged by the curer, Calistro spoke, spoke in his sleep: "My Nanita was done wrong by the Zacatons, and to cure her we must cut the heads off every one of them" ' (Asturias 1988: 52). The implication seems to be that the story is really about the settling of scores between the Tecus and the Zacatons. However, this is not so: that the feud is only a secondary element is shown by the fact that when Maria Zacaton escapes from the massacre and becomes the main protagonist she is able innocently to usurp the patronym of Maria Tecun without any particularly dramatic consequences. It is not immediately clear what is going on here. However, the aim, in fact, is to set the stage for the entrance of Speech, the 'true' speech – for the epiphany of a 'known knowledge' that is the basis for an act of justice that goes far beyond a guerilla battle, however politically justified the latter may be.

The important thing is not that the guilty are called Zacaton (which is simply a narrative detail). What matters is that, above the voice of the people, which is always fallible, we should hear the voice of the god in the words of Calistro the madman, and that this voice orders the severing of heads. At this point the story suddenly enters the realm of myth, implicitly evoking archetypal themes such as that portrayed on the bas-relief of the pelota court in Palenque. There the beaten player's severed head is shown sending out seven jets of blood ending in seven snakes' heads, the snake being the emblem of the earth. For the game of pelota itself was a cosmogonic rite, commemorating the sun's journey through the sky between the two equinoxes and its daily decapitation on the horizon. As such it also symbolized the process by which maize grows to its mature height before falling once more in the form of seed to germinate in the soil during the night.

Similarly, the first chapter of *Men of Maize*, gives a mystical account of the effects of drunkenness – which is seen as another path to the 'known knowledge'. In it the inebriated Indian Gasper Ilom is emotionally encircled by 'a serpent of six hundred thousand coils of mud, moon, forests, rainstorms, mountains, birds and echoes' (Asturias 1988: 1) and feels his head fall to the ground at the very moment when his masculine seed, 'a handful of sunflower seeds', impregnates his wife. Every work by Asturias pays its tribute of severed heads: the mythical heads of the Seven Hunaphu in *Popol-Vuh*, with their intertextual associations; that of the first Sun in *Tres de cuatro soles*; that of Saint John the Baptist in *Mulata*; that of the circus leader in *El Alhajadito*; that of Cuculcan in *Leyendas de Guatamala*; and, lastly, that of Calistro, since when the poor boy becomes the tool of the true Speech, he loses his reason. Calistro believes he has nine heads, his own and that of the eight Zacatons. Yet is it madness to know the ritual value of the number nine, which is related to mysterious, noctural, germinative, uterine things (just as the numbers seven and five introduce the names and deeds of the agrarian gods, the guardians of the fertility of the earth and of human beings – seven being found in the curer's name, in other words in the name of his 'nahual' or double, the Deer of the Seventh Fire)?

The character of Mama Tecun functions in an intertextual fashion, since she is associated with the figure of Ixmucane in *Popol-vuh*. In the Quechua text the letter has contrasting and complementary functions as mother of the sun gods. She is the nocturnal, generative sun in the adventure of the Seven Hunahpu decapicated at Xibalba and the diurnal, creative sun through the figures of her sons, the twins Hunahpu and Ixbalanque, who are musicians, dancers, blowpipe users and wonder-workers – artists and archetypes of the civilized man in terms of the Mayan culture. 'Big Mama' Ixmucane reigns over the masculine world of her family, all of whom are devoted to her; and it does not even occur to her daughter-in-law Ixquic to compete with her. It is the same in the Tecun family: Mama Tecun, who has given birth to twelve male children, rules the domestic world of her married sons, the inner world where woman finds her place and her importance: 'Some have a kid on their backs. Others are pot-bellied, hoping for family. Their tresses like snakes writhing on their heads.'

The graphic impact of the image of the snake-tresses emphasizes the female symbolism of the snake. It is the emblem of the mother goddess, who is known as Cihuacoatl, snake-woman, when she is associated with the fertility of the earth. The adjective 'pot-bellied' also has a mythical significance, recalling the young Ixquic, who is driven out of Xibalba by her father when the size of her belly makes it obvious that she is pregnant and who is then taken in by her mother-in-law. Ixquic's tasks are to sweep and fetch water at the fountain, and, in addition to the ritual significance of sweeping already mentioned, these two jobs have strong cultural connotations. In literature and iconography women and the moon are constantly portrayed as dispensers of water, the former of water for the household and the latter of the rains, which are indispensable for growing maize. The belly of the jar that the moon spills onto the earth grows empty, just as the disc of the moon gets smaller until it becomes a crescent and as the rounded belly of the pregnant woman goes flat after she has given birth. Thus Asturias speaks of 'pot-bellied' women just as in the *Leyendas* he describes the 'pot-bellied clouds' that bear the spring rains. From one book to another, these recurrent images reveal the influence of a mythical model. Who are these Tecun women? The sons' wives, according to the logic of the story, for the narrative restricts their area of activity, referring to them collectively and anonymously as 'the women of the family'.

A detailed study of the symbolic function of the couples portrayed by Asturias would lead us away from our original aim of examining the literary role of the mother goddess. Let us therefore accept that on all occasions in the narrative the relationship of man to woman is viewed as reflecting the archetypal relationship between the sun and moon. The premise (or perhaps the consequence) of this view is that there is no difference between man and woman, man being woman plus the 'activities of the day' (*Leyendas*). When reading Asturias's books one must never forget the mythical aspect and interpret women's household tasks as merely mundane activities, since to do so would render the phrase from *Leyendas* completely absurd. Although in social terms Woman is portrayed as a charming chatterer with a tongue as agile as her hands who peddles her tittle-tattle while making tortillas and is confined to *tortear periqueando*, her deeper, true nature gives her a role of far greater importance. As *Mulata* suggests, Woman is the cloak of dreams in which the earth is dressed. Woman's role is fundamentally and paradoxically passive, oneiric and germinative. It is nocturnal and lunar, in contrast to the solar, diurnal and active role of man. In fact, at the risk of making the most execrable pun, in mythological terms the only specifically masculine activity is that of rising.

Indeed, this pun is not wholly inappropriate since the myth of the feathered serpent, which underlies all American accounts of the creation of maize, is basically phallic. So too is the image of the growing plant and the sun at its zenith; the vertical element in both cases symbolizes the process of thought, which is ultimately the most exalting human experience. In an episode in chapter six of *Men of Maize*, the guerilla action that the Tecun sons carry out at night has a deeper meaning in relation to their usual daytime activities, in which Man's phallic role is fulfilled. This is because the pleasure principle is replaced by that of death, as a result of the crimes that the maize growers commit. Machetes and guns deal death when the hands that wield them have abandoned their true function of sowing maize, when the penis is no longer used to give life. In contrast to Horizon Floods, who, in *Leyendas de Guatemala* 'takes off his battledress to cover his penis', the Tecun sons are obliged to take off their penises to put on their battledress.

This is why, in this episode, Woman, the witness to what Lacan calls 'the Truth of Man', appears only in the character of Mama Tecun, seen as the mother goddess of the earth, the warrior, and the one who by giving life has the right to deal death. Mama Tecun lives with her daughters-in-law according to the family tradition established by Ixmucane and Ixquic in *Popol-Vuh*. Like Ixmucane, mother of dead men (the decapitated Seven Hunahpu) and of living men (their twin brothers Hun Batz and Hun Chuen, their twin sons Hunahpu and Ixbalanque), Mama Tecun also has five living sons and seven others in the cemetery. She can thus claim a place 'on both sides', on the basis of her character as a loving mother in the novel and of her role as the mythical symbol of the mother goddess, since 'it is the weight of the dead which makes the earth turn at night and, during the day, the weight of the living' (*The President*). And here we can add the tragic dimensions and iconography of Coatlicue to the model of *Popol-vuh*: as soon as Calistro has uttered the sentence against the Zacaton, his brothers go off to carry out their duty, and come back to present their tribute to their mother in the form of a sinister bouquet of eight freshly severed heads. For the reader this revolting proof of filial piety calls up the image of Coatlicue,

> square, decapitated, with her garland of death's heads, her skirt of snakes, her hands open and lacerated [who] seeks to be impenetrable: monolithic . . . Coatlicue admits of no crack: she is the perfect monolith, a totality of intensity, self-contained and all-containing. Significantly she has no head, she has renounced anthropomorphism, she is a goddess, not a person, and a goddess cut off from temptations, hesitations, needs and human freedoms.

Carlos Fuentes, from whom this quotation is taken, is describing a famous statue in the Mexican National Museum of Anthropology. The Mexican writer is meditating on the iconographic features that make this statue into an exact image of what is symbolizes.

Although the context of our discussion of Asturias's book is quite different from that of Fuentes's description, both are linked by the concept of impermeability. By introducing a cricket into Mama Tecun's body, in other words a seed into the earth, the Zacatons have assaulted and cracked her in a most untimely way. Their deed simulates the act of fertilization and it is against nature because the woman is long past childbearing age and because it reproduces thc guilty activities of the maize growers who, season after season and driven by the desire for money, exhaust Ilom's land with intensive sowing without giving it time to rest and 'sleep'.

It is clear now how everything is played out in terms of heads: the absent head of Coatlicue is balanced by Calistro's absent head, Calistro's head by the Zacatons' heads, the head of the Deer of the Seventh Fire by Calistro's head, and lastly the head of the curer by that of Coatlicue/Mama Tecun, since the curer is the Deer's double. We can also observe that both the mythical element and the narrative proper suggest that death gives birth to the living. In the first context, the head of the decapitated Seven Hunahpu impregnated Ixqui after being stuck on a tree; Gasper Ilom feels his head fall at the very moment he impregnates his wife. The consequences, in both the myth of Ixmucane and the actual stories, is the existence of mothers who are 'widows' (Mama Tecun, Doña Flora. The image of the cricket and the hiccup also has a particular significance, because in Asturias's work cries and seed have an identical meaning. This explanation sets in train a long story, the first episode of which is played out in *Leyendas Le Guatemala*. In this book Golden Skin who is alone in the forest without a companion and thus sexless, dances on one foot trying to split into two to the rhythm of the vowels a-e-i-u-o/u-o-i-e-a, a cry emphasized by the cry of the crickets. Asturias was living in France when he wrote *Leyendas de Guatemala*, and this explains his use of the French language in developing this acoustic image to suit his literary aim. The cricket's song is onomatopoeic, and forms a syllable that, in French, is also a word sounding exactly like what it is intended to signify: a cry.

Asturias returned to this charming linguistic device in 1962 in *Clariviglia primaveral*, speaking of 'syllables and onomatopoeia, seeds of the infinite cry, poetry'. Just as the seed engenders the maize cob, so the syllable engenders the word and the word the poem. Consideration of the oral nature of both language and food, the identity between the oral and the genital, and the interdependency between the development of agriculture and that of population enables us to understand that in Asturias's writing a cricket's cry and a handful of sunflower seeds have the same meaning, that eating is speaking and speaking is writing – in other words that all involve creation. Another passage in *Leyendas* defines this idea more clearly: 'Five times my mother's belly opened . . . and with me my mother's belly closed for ever . . . In opening for the last time, your mother's belly was a conch with two lips which let out a word with the destiny of a mollusc.'

The navel, too, can act as a natural opening for penetrating the body, whether in a mythical or a fictional context. Thus, in *Mulata*, it is through

Catalina Zabala's navel that the devil Tazol is introduced into her belly and impregnates her, as the ball of feathers does Coatlicue.

The latent model of Coatlicue carrying the god Huitzilopochtli's fire within her and disappearing after being killed by him when he is born is perpetuated in an agricultural context by the belief in the divine and solar origins of maize expressed metaphorically by myths that call the sun the 'tooth of maize' and the 'hummingbird's eye'. Calistro, who sacrifices himself for his mother, represents a mirror image of this relationship. As a 'man of maize', he contains the sun's fire: 'Calistro's laughter interrupted the coming and goings of the curer. It sizzled between his teeth and he spat it out like the fire that was burning him inside' (Asturias 1988: 53).

This mother/son/fire relationship once again alludes to the myth of the earth mother, whose body is fragmented by the fire that heats the celestial cauldron.

In the context of the scene with the curo in *Men of Maize*, it may be wondered how effective a severed head is as a remedy for hiccups. The reader may easily judge the sight of her sons coming in with the bleeding heads of the Zacatons not only took away Mama Tecun's breath, but also cured her hiccups once and for all.

The mythical aspect of Mama Tecun as the giver of life, even in death, stands out all the more clearly because the story provides her with a foil in the shape of Vaca Manuela, the sterile woman whom nature has rightly deprived of the power to reproduce. According to the myth, children represent true wealth and are the luxury of the couples that have them, but Vaca Manuela prefers the illusory wealth of gold. By associating with the Ladinos and the whites, she agrees to profit from maize, which is tantamount to saying that she has sold farmers her children, her children of maize. In *The Green Pope*, the pernicious role of the maize farmers is given to the salesman from the Yankee banana company, George Maker Thompson. And yet, although Doña Flora is in league with the Americans, who strip the Indian peasants of their lands to expand the banana plantations, she cannot be confused with Vaca Manuela. This is because, half sincerely, half craftily, she says that progress demands it and that, without being a Cortés, George Maker has a duty to bring civilization as the 'blond high priest of progress', as she likes to call her future son-in-law. She understands, or thinks she understands, that the times have changed, that fire, which in Spanish hands had consumed the painted wood of the Indians, their manuscripts written on amate bark, their idols and their insignia, is now, four centuries later, devouring 'christs, virgin-maries, saintanthonies, holycrosses, prayer books and novena books, rosaries, relics and medals, reducing them to smoke and sparks . . . Another god [is] coming: the Dollar, and another religion, that of the "big stick".'

Despite the error of her ways, this complex character is disturbing because of her ambiguity. One senses the presence in her of several specific features of the mother goddess – and, indeed, Doña Flora is a mother of two. One of the more interesting of these is the mother–daughter relationship. This functions in a similar way to the relationship between Mama Tecun and Calistro in *Men of Maize*, but its mythical dimension lies above all in its echo of the two interchangeable figures of Coatlicue and her daughter, who are the propiatory victims of Huitzilopochtli's birth and act as models for the dyad of Doña Flora and Mayari.

The name Flora obviously refers to the vegetal manifestations of the mother goddess, Yellow Flower and White Flower, to whom annual offerings of the first flowers were made. Thus Doña Flora is a tropical flower, passionate and 'still desirable', with her tanned breasts poised to burst out of her blouse at the first deep sigh. At the same time, though, she is also the Warrior, a woman who has 'exchanged face powder for gunpowder' and who rides a horse like a man with her legs apart, 'dreaming with a cleaver in her hands'. The vehemence of her desire for George Maker feeds the image of a prey that, far from fleeing from the hunter, actually provokes him ('what a pleasure to feel oneself pursued'). Her sexual drive recreates the atmosphere of the hunter Xiuhnel's amorous adventure ('let him catch me, let him take me by the waist, take me off my horse, lay me down, roll me over . . .'). He is Mixcoatl, the conquering god of the north, 'dynamic, metallic, cruel', before whom 'the several women that were spread out in her – mother, partner, mother-in-law – must have joined together into the woman that this man hoped to find in her person'.

Contrary to what her mother believes, Mayari is a worthy daughter to this warrior, for she fights at the head of the peasants who are in revolt against the injustices of the banana company. Unlike Doña Flora, she does not accept the role of the flint splintered in George Maker's fire and become the tool of his power. (After Doña Flora's death, George Maker, her husband and legitimate heir, extends the Company's property by incorporating his wife's lands.) Mayari's suicide and marriage to the River Motagua are intended to prevent her marriage to George Maker and to render impossible the appalling prospect of her bearing his children. Her lunar character is reminiscent of Yai in *Leyandas*, for after spending the night with Cuculcan, the latter is torn from the nuptial bed 'by the rivers' hands', so that there will be no descendants, for there can be no descendants of the couple of the Sun and Moon. Similarly those who exploit Maya lands cannot be allowed to have descendants and Mayari sacrifices herself so that she will not be a mother. Thus it is through Bobby, born to Doña Flora's second daughter and George Maker, that the latter receives his punishment. Bobby is the heir to the banana empire but dies at the time when his grandfather is also dying of a throat cancer that prevents him even dictating his orders to check the Wall Street prices, and when the Company's workers finally call a general strike (*The Eyes of the Interred*).

Although it seems very different from Asturias's work in terms of its style, its narrative system, its geographical setting and the cultural tradition to which it belongs, the Venezuelan novel *Doña Bárbara* by the writer Romulo Gallego contains some similar elements. Once again we meet the figure of a deity whose two fundamental facets as earth and mother are revealed through the now familiar emblem of the snake and through her dialectical relationship with her child. Like that between Coatlicue and her daughter, the relationship between Doña Bárbara and Marisela is one of exclusion, but it differs in that it is the mother who hates the daughter and plans to kill her. As with Doña Flora and Mayari, mother and daughter merge, in accordance with the myth, in their desire for the same man, and again the mythical outcome is reversed to ensure that the daughter triumphs over her mother. The text stresses that Woman and earth are the same by playing on the name Bárbara, which is used with its adjectival meaning 'barbarous' to refer both to the Venezuelan landscape and to Doña Bárbara herself. The plain is 'barbarous but beautiful', and the woman is 'at once wild, beautiful and terrible' – indeed both women are, for Marisela, who is 'as simple as nature', is 'sometimes disturbing also like nature's monstrosities', and, like her mother, is 'a mixture of pleasant and dreadful things, interesting, certainly, like all nature's monstrosities'. Doña Bárbara is a devourer, since she is referred to as 'the devourer of men'. One episode in particular stresses her tragic aspect as Coatlicue, when the idiot Jean Primito has visions of fantastic birds, 'a materialization of Doña Bárbara's evil instincts', and says that he quenches their thirst by putting pots filled with blood on the roof. Most significantly, however, is the splendid episode in which Doña Bárbara meditatively watches the death of a heifer as an anaconda sucks it into its mouth and drags it to the bottom of the swamp. The snake, symbol of earth and water, is a reminder that 'the devourer of men' is also 'daughter of the rivers': 'a fruit engendered by the violence of the white adventurer and the dark sensuality of the Indian, her origins were lost in the dramatic mystery of virgin lands'. The river that brought her is the same as the one on which she leaves and disappears, yielding to 'the fascination of the fluvial landscape, the untimely attraction of the msyterious rivers where her story began'. The waters of the yellow Orinoco, the red Atabapo and the black Guainia merge before they reach the ocean, just as two bloods mix in her veins. Her tragic dimension lies as much in the difficulties caused by her mixed racial origins as in the fact that she herself was raped when barely an adolescent; she is a violated, fissured land, assaulted in her sacred virginity.

Romulo Gallegos's ideological outlook leads him to suggest, perhaps involuntarily, that being of mixed race and being raped are both degrading and mark body and soul with an indelible stigma in the context of a particular moral and social climate. In contrast, while the mixing of the races experienced by the Mexicans, both collectively (even if they are white) and culturally, is also seen as tragic, this is not because it implies that in the beginning a woman was defiled and degraded. Indeed, the mythology of Mexico to some extent refuses this interpretation through the figure of the goddess Tlazoteotl, protector against all defilement and guardian of carnal love. Instead, the tragedy arises from the fact that this woman was treacherous, that she put foreign interests above those of her own race. And henceforward all people of mixed race, all Mexicans, are living reminders of her treason. In *El laberinto de la soledad* the Mexican poet Octavio Paz gives a perfect analysis of the inexorable consequences of being the son of the Malinche. However, it is Carlos Fuentes in his play *Todos los gatos son pardos* who gives the most subtle and powerful exposition of the pain and grandeur of this sudden and shocking meeting of the races using the triple figure of Malinche, Marina or Malintzin – goddess, concubine and mother of the first mixed race child.

Before her appearance in *Todos los gatos son pardos*, the mother goddess played a dominant role in Fuentes's first work of fiction, *La región más transparente* in the form of Teodula Moctezuma, a dark divinity thirsty for victims. Her son Ixca Cienfuegos, whose name has an obvious solar symbolism, depicts her as being 'made of stone, of snakes', while she condemns him to 'an appalling game, no less, a game of forgotten rites and dead words'. Another mother goddess, this time lit up by the glow of 'sunlight' appropriate to a screen idol, is Claudia Nervo (a character inspired by the mythical Mexican actress Maria Felix), who celebrates the cult of her own perpetual glory and beauty in *Zona sagrada*. The cult's first victim is her son Mito, whose name is the diminutive of the diminuitive Guillermito but has additional connotations as the noun meaning 'myth'. Claudia is the phallic, castrating mother and the psychoanalytical plot revolves around the relationship between a thirty-year-old son, 'reduced to a reflection of himself', and a mother who has and will always have 'the brilliance of twenty-five', as, indeed, she does in the many portraits that immortalize 'her famous face' and 'convert her body into a perpetual metamorphosis of bird and ash, flame and dragon'.

Yet none of these devouring or generously fertile Coatlicues who haunt Fuentes's earlier work attains the perfection of the character of Doña Marina in *Todos los gatos son pardos*. Fuentes had always been obsessed by the theme of the double, the twin and the Other, and in this book he found an historical subject that measured up to his fantasies. Its plot concerns the face-to-face encounter between two men born in totally different parts of the world and separated by language, social position, education and religion who had both overcome the most incredible obstacles: the Spanish adventurer Hernán Cortés and Montezuma, the last Aztec *tlatoani*. Theirs is a relationship of fascination and rejection and long before they actually meet each thinks only of the other, the Spaniard feeling an implacable desire to reach Montezuma, the Aztec full of anguished doubt about the significance of the meeting. Between the two men is a woman, Doña Marina. She belongs to the Spaniard as his concubine and to the Aztec because she is a member of his race and he is her ruler; but she escapes each through the other. Yet, at the same time, it is through her that they communicate, since she is their interpreter, speaking both their languages.

As Lacan rightly points out, she embodies the Truth of Man, bearing witness as much to Montezuma's truth as to that of Cortés. Two scenes portray her performing this double function. At the beginning of the play a timeless Marina defines her role as being to act as a 'midwife to history' because she has experienced it under the three names that are the keys to her destiny: goddess, Malintzin; whore, Marina; mother, Malinche'. The setting then moves to a room in Montezuma's palace where 'a man, wearing only a G-string, is slowly sweeping; it is Montezuma'. We have mentioned the ritual connotations of sweeping and its particular significance for the character of Coatlicue, representing sweetness, humility and devotion, as does Marina, and as does Montezuma. All is thus ready for the intervention of a god, but there still remains the question of what form this intervention will take. Montezuma knows no better than Coatlicue with her ball of feathers whether he is dealing with Huitzilopochtli or Quetzalcoatl. Marina, the 'midwife to history', will give the answer, which is valid for both herself and for Coatlicue: in order for the luminous being that they carry within them to be born, they must both disappear. This will be accomplished through the agency of Cortés: Montezuma will be killed and Marina abandoned to one of the conqueror's soldiers.

Who is Cortés? He could have been Quetzalcoatl the bringer of civilization, as the augurs foretold. In fact, though, he was Huitzilopochtli the Warrior, born to Doña Marina. This is the meaning of the passage in the second scene mentioned above, in which Marina asks Cortés, 'And you, my lord, who are you?' This is not a request for an introduction, she has been his concubine for weeks and she is bearing his child, so there are few things that she still does not know about him. The point is not that she wants to know more about Cortés, but that she wants Cortés to know himself to the full. Similarly, her second question, 'Are you not a prince in your own country?' is not the fantasy of a foolish young girl. It is the barest expression of surprise that elsewhere Cortés is not what he can and must become here. This is a difficult birth, for Cortés resists, sometimes making quips about his turbulent past as an impoverished student and sometimes lapsing into nostalgic reminiscences about a distant country that he cannot forget. But despite his jokey answers the certainty that his birth was predestined gradually emerges ('when I was born, there was an eclipse of the sun and it was a year of epidemics and torrential rains'). And when he asks, in his turn, 'Do you think if I had a hundred thousand ducats, a private residence in Madrid . . . that I would have got involved in this business?' the calm, firm answer that so astounds him that he asks for it to be repeated is, 'Yes, I believe you would be here in spite of everything'. She believes, she believes in him. He understands and accepts this belief, since the dialogue ends with another declaration of faith: 'I have come to multiply the promises of the New World for a new man'. In short, Marina's real act of betrayal was not that of a mother who gave birth to a son of mixed race, but that of a goddess who acted as a midwife to the father, and was thus the first, true *hijo de la chingada* in Mexican history. And in

Mexico the expression 'son of a whore' has had bitter cultural connotations ever since.

Dorita Nouhaud

Cosmogonic Myths

Many ancient explanations of the origins and workings of the universe are based on cosmogonic myths. These myths have abounded since the earliest times in literary texts of a philosophical, scientific, religious and esoteric nature. Indeed, it would be surprising if this were not so, since such myths are, by nature, connected to science, to the sacred and to the idea of a revelation concerning how the world was formed. The creation of the universe is an unimaginable and extraordinary subject, beyond normal human understanding. As a consequence, it entails problems for the imagination, which serves principally to rationalize and to visulaize what seems to be inconceivable, by means of images, narratives and myths. The aim of this process is to clarify what is assumed to have been the impetus, force or divine power that brought about the birth and organization of the cosmos, and, in this sense, cosmogonic myths offer an imagery of our origins.

Despite its limited scope, this article also enables us to identify and discuss some of the myths that have sprung from the original cosmogonies. After this we shall proceed to a chronological study of some major literary manifestations of cosmogonic imagery; this is a complex subject, for a myth about origins can inspire many different visions. Indeed, it is important to stress just how fertile cosmogonic myths are; they provide explanations for the order of the world that sometimes interpenetrate each other and themselves become pretexts for new mythical schemes. Meanwhile, the latter perpetuate and complicate themselves, surviving through numerous transformations.

In a literary context, it seems best to limit the field of inquiry to those cosmogonic beliefs that lie at the roots of Western civilization: the Vedic texts, the writings of the Greeks and the Hebrew tradition.

The *Vedas*, some of which, such as the *Rig Veda*, date from the second millenium BC, give a special place to myths of this kind. The texts of the *Vedas*, the *Upanishads* and later the *Purana*, in which a poetic quality underpins the depth of philosophical thought, develop a 'mythology' whose aim is to facilitate an understanding of the universe. Although the correlation drawn in the *Vedas* between the cosmos on the one hand and human beings on the other finally leads to the definitive assertion that the universal soul (brahma) and the soul of the individual (atman) are one, its prime function is to show how the machine of the macrocosm arose as the result of a plan, a form of organization and a demiurgic will. The Vedic writings give expression to a tradition that uses myth to explain the mysteries of the origins of the world and also provides a description of the paths that the soul must take to reach salvation, deliverance and karma.

Among the numerous cosmogonic myths of the *Vedas*, those of the sacred mountain and the egg of the world deserve particular attention. The first demonstrates the crucial role of Mount Meru, home of the divine creators and axis of the world, around which the planets and heavens revolve (*Padmaporana* 1. III. 26–48; 3. III. 26–48). The second, mentioned on many occasions, represents one of the most significant literary descriptions of the cosmic egg, Brahma's egg, in other words, the world. (According to one of the Vedic texts:

> In the beginning this universe was water, it was only a wave. The water expressed a desire: how can I reproduce myself? It mortified itself, it raised the ascetic heat. When it had raised the ascetic heat, a golden egg appeared. There were as yet no years at this time. The golden egg floated for as long as a year takes.
>
> At the end of the year a male creature appeared, Prajapati . . . He broke the golden egg, but there was no anchorage: so the golden egg floated for as long as a year takes, carrying him.
>
> (*Satapathabrahmana* XI. I. 6. 1–11)

This is a myth of the water mother, the supreme myth of fertility, which persists throughout the centuries in various civilizations (we need only think of the Egyptian tradition and the Babylonian poem *Enuma Elish*) and is the dominant type of cosmogonic myth.

Arising from a different geographical and cultural perspective the Greek cosmogonic myths made a decisive contribution to Western culture and literature. The story of the creation of the world by the gods was a noble subject favoured by poets and philosophers who devoted hymns, treatises and pseudo-scientific or allegorical discourses to it. Texts containing cosmogonic myths proliferated; besides those dealing directly with the mystery of the creation of the world, there are an extraordinary profusion of allegorical commentaries based on literary works – generally poems – of which the cosmogonic aspects are not immediately evident. Thus Theagenes of Rhegium presented the quarrel of the gods in *Iliad* XX as a lesson in physics, while Porphyrus, amongst others, developed allegorical interpretations of a cosmogonic type. Hesiod's *Theogony* is the major work in this context, being the 'first' true poem with a mythical, cosmogonic element. However, there are ambiguities here, for in establishing the genealogy of the gods, Hesiod touched on questions concerning creation itself only incidentally and in a rather obscure way. He mentions the birth of the earth (line 117), of the heavens (line 126), of the sea (line 131), of the rivers (line 337) and of the stars (line 382). According to his scheme, in the beginning were the children of Abyss: Erebe and Night. Ether and Light of Day were born of Night (line 125), while the heavens and sea sprang from the earth. Then after descriptions of a series of combinations and couplings, the children of the earth and the heavens are mentioned (lines 133–53) along with those of the earth and sea (lines 233–6). Otherwise, the cosmogonic aspect of the poem is eclipsed by its epic vein, the description of battles and struggles between the gods, from which Zeus emerges as the victor. Much the same picture emerges from the Homeric and Orphic hymns and, following these, from the works of Plato and the Neo-platonists, which established a fundamental link between the architecture of the world and mathematical principles (*Timaeus*) and between water and the emergence of life. It is significance that in the *Cratylus* and the *Theaetetus* Plato recalled Homer by quoting the lines from the *Iliad* (XIV. 201) that refer to Ocean as the origin of the Gods and Thetis as their mother.

These different cosmogonic accounts and their attendant imagery have been taken up regularly over the centuries. This was particularly so during the Middle Ages and the Renaissance when the literary genre of genealogies of the gods included works such as Boccacio's between 1350 and 1375, and later those of Giraldi (*Historia deis Gentium*, 1548), Conti (*Mythologia*, 1551) and Cartari (*Le Imagini de I dei de gli antichi*, 1556) while allegorical interpretations of Platonic texts or texts influenced by Platonism also flourished unabated. Latin writers, poets and philosophers also readily adopted and developed ideas from Attica. Lucretius (*De Rerum Natura* II. 596–641) and Ovid (*Metamorphoses* I. 5–75 and 313–415), reveal how the power and fascination of the cosmogonic myth persist, even though the philosopher–poet is not taken in by the fable that he is using.

In Hebrew culture the myth of the primordial cosmogonic couple was challenged and superseded by the concept of the single creative word. The narrative of Genesis, which constitutes out earliest source, offers a remarkable vision of the power conferred upon this word, an idea that profoundly marked the minds of writers such as Philo or Clement of Alexandria and which the later authors of the *Talmud* and the *Zohar* did not wish to abandon entirely. Thus in his commentaries on the creation of the world, Philo of Alexandria drew on Platonic theories and on the numerological concepts popular in ancient times as a basis for his notes on Genesis. In so doing, he sought to reveal the hidden meanings of the sacred text, whose every detail he interpreted allegorically (*Legum Allegoriae*). For Philo, who, in this respect, adhered closely to the Platonic scheme, the world was created by God according to a model, which was the intelligible world formed by God in his mind (*On the Creation of the World* 4). For him, as for the authors of the *Talmud*, God was naturally the great artisan, the architect and supreme geometer of the universe.

Beyond the archetypal narrative and the explanation of the cosmos that it gives, the Hebrew tradition also involves the mysterious use of words and language. Thus the creation narrative begins with the letter *beth* (the first letter of 'Berakha', meaning blessing) and not with *aleph* (the first letter of 'Arina', meaning 'curse'). The Hebrew word for the heavens, 'chamayim', is formed by a cross-combination: 'cham'/'mayim' signifies place of the waters and 'ech'/'mayim' means water and fire. Equally interesting is the tradition that within the temple of the world there is a 'foundation stone' (which can be linked to the Vedic myth of mount Meru, the axis of the world), so called because the world rests upon it and because it marks the navel around which the world was created. Strengthened by Judeo-Christianity, the Hebrew tradition also attached unrivalled importance to the study of angels: the hierarchies of angels, who provide divine support for the planets, ensure the birth, maintenance and renewal of all life. This was a theme popular during the Middle Ages and the sixteenth century with writers ranging from Saint Thomas Aquinas to Henri Corneille Agrippa (*La Philosphie occulte* III. 14 and 15), and from Dante (*Paradise* XXVIII. 98–135) to Jean-Edouard du Monin (*Le Quaresme*, 1584: 41) or Thomas Heywood (*The Hierarchie of the blessed Angells, their Names, Orders, and Offices*, 1635). This current is also illustrated by the development in the fifteenth, sixteenth and seventeenth centuries of Christian or Christianized astrological systems (George of Venice, *De harmonia mundi* I. 8. 18; Du Bartas, *Seconde semaine, Second jour, Quatrième Partie, Les Colonnes* 499–528; Valentin Weigel, *Astrologia Theologizata*, 1580?; Drexel, *Zodiacus Christianus* 1632; William Lilly, *Christian Astrology* 1647; R. P. Carlo Giaconia, *Zodiaco Eucaristico*, 1655; J. B. Morin de Villefranche, *Astrologia Gallica*, 1661; William Derham, *Astro-Theology* 1715). The cosmogonic myths linked to religious, philosophical and literary traditions from Antiquity to the flowering of Christianity, may not originally have been a major source of inspiration for poets, but later they provided them with indispensable material and with an unrivalled mechanism for combining wisdom and beauty. Because cosmogonic myths had a particular aura of sanctity, they apparently claimed greater aesthetic attention than other themes and were employed in an elevated form, in accordance with the noble treatment that they demanded.

The frequent use of cosmogonic myths in the course of literary history reflects a link between a vision of the world and the writing that aimed to reproduce that vision. Thus it is important to consider some of the most representative stages in the literary use of these myths and the authors responsible for the works concerned.

In the Middle Ages the Greco-Latin inheritance was of crucial importance. As well as being based on the Bible, the literary and philosophical use of myths concerning the world, its creation and functioning was also inspired, directly or indirectly, by Homer, Hesoid, Ovid and Virgil. The interpretation by Fulgence Placiade, of *The Aeneid* and Virgil's role among the 'authorities' – as illustrated in *The Divine Comedy* – demonstrate the importance of the ancient literary inheritance and the studies to which it gave rise. While the Chartres school magnified the powers of creative light, Albert le Grand and Saint Thomas Aquinas preserved the dominance of the Word. At the same time as the myths were being interpreted and sometime distorted, they also lost their quality as myths, as can be seen in medieval texts discussing the 'cosmic egg', in which the myth is too often reduced to no more than a stock literary theme:

> The Ancients gave an example, saying that the world is like an egg. The outside shell of the egg signifies the firmament. After the shell is a little white skin . . . which is cold and dry and signifies the earth, for the earth is by nature cold and dry. And beneath this skin is the white, which is cold and wet and signifies the water which is on the earth, which is cold and wet. And after the white is a little skin and this other skin and the yolk are understood in terms of the order of the world, for the yolk signifies the air, which is hot, clear and wet – and so is the air hot, clear and wet – and the skin signifies the fire, which is above everything, which is hot and dry. And inside the egg is the germ. Thus all creatures live in the elements and all living things take sustenance from the four elements.
>
> (*Placides et Timeo ou Li secrés as philosophes* 118)

The myth has become degraded: it no longer illustrates the imagery of the earth's origins, but simply represents its organization. It took all Dante's genius to start from this limited perspective and build up a theological and poetic picture of the universe. In book XXVIII of *Paradise*, the point and the circles of light are used in two ways: to represent the mysteries of the Divinity and of the foundation of the hierarchy of celestial intelligences that guarantee the order of the world; and, in a more literal fashion (lines 16–45), to describe the universe and its confines. In the same book (lines 97–139) Beatrice gives Dante vital explanations of the symbolism and role of the celestial hierarchies taken from Gregory the Great and pseudo-Dionysius. Dante's theological perspective adapts and develops the Greco-Latin tradition according to which the celestial intelligences govern the planets and determine the rhythm of the cycles of nature.

The members of the Platonic Academy of Florence, established in 1462, and the Neoplatonic movement of the Quattrocento helped to prolong the life of the cosmogonic myths, as demonstrated notably by Ficino and Politian. It was because of their enthusiasm for Plato and the writings attributed to Hermes Trismegistus that the European Renaissance benefited from a new renewed interest in cosmogony. This is particularly evident in scientific, didactic and metaphysical poetry. To different degrees, poets calling themselves the 'disciples' or 'secretaries' of Urania drew on ancient myths to describe the world and its functioning hoping that they would provide an insight into an original truth: that of the first age of the cosmos. Guy Le Fèvre de la Boderie (*L'Encyclie des Secrets de l'Eternité*, 1570) and Jean-Edouard du Monin (*L'Uranologie, ou le ciel*, 1583), to name only two, sought to create a form of poetry in which the myths were in complete harmony with the expression of their highest meaning. True, in his *Sepmaine, ou Création du Monde* (1578) Du Bartas used cosmogonic clichés, notably that of the egg:

> For the Heavens are not at all bound together. As the lower are encircled by

> the higher, so the roundness of their bellies is more confined, depending on how close they are to the centre: like the skin of eggs beneath the shell, and in order. The white beneath the skin, the yolk beneath the white.
>
> (*Première semaine, Quatrième jour*, 297–302)

However, he also tried to find a more appropriate expression to lead his reader on to the sources of the myth's meaning, as in these lines on the theme of the harmony of the universe:

> All this great universe is like an instrument, well put together, well regulated, skillfully tuned. And whose admirably sweet symphony sounds the laws of God, who beats time with his thumb . . . But as man is the principle string of the Lute of the Universe, when he is too stretched he puts all the other nerves out of tune: and after this, instead of playing an enchanting air he makes such a rumble that Enyo is surprised. Enyo the cruel who starts up the old debates on chaos once more.
>
> (*Seconde Semaine, Premier Jour, Troisième Partie, Les Furies*, 19–22 and 45–50)

With more elegance than Du Bartas, the great poet Ronsard had already tackled this noble poetic theme in *Les Hymnes* (1555 and 1556), which were intended to reveal the 'secrets' of the universe. By this time, it was no longer simply a matter of turning myth into poetry: the myth must be questioned and enriched, the better to penetrate its meanings. Although theological concerns predominate in 'The Christian Hercules' (*Seconde Livre des Hymnes*, 1556), the hymns dealing with the seasons tend to employ true cosmogonic myths. Among the most representative is the 'Hymn to Autumn', in which Ronsard depicts the palace of Nature and the activity within it (*Second Livre des Hymnes*, 'Hymne de l'Automne' 327–356). Ronsard also took up the myth of the cosmic egg in an unexpected fashion, using it in a way that is quite unrelated to the cosmogony of the *Hymnes*:

> I give you eggs. The egg in its round form is like the sky, which can hold all in its arms, the fire, the air and the earth, and the humour of the sea and, without being held, holds everything in the world. The skin is like the air, and the fertile white is like the sea, which makes all things sprout; the yolk is like the fire which can bring everything to life, the shell is heavy like the abundant earth. And the sky and eggs are covered in whiteness. In giving you an egg I give you the whole Universe: the gift is divine, if it pleases you. But although it is perfect, it cannot equal Your perfection, which nothing resembles, about which only the Gods are worthy to speak.
>
> (Sonnet from *Amours diverses*, 1578)

Many more references to cosmogonical themes occur in the works of the metaphysical poets who, from Donne to Vaughan or Crashaw, contemplated the universe and its infinite spectacle with amazement or fear. In 'Eternity' (2. 466–72) Vaughan 'saw Eternity the other night/Like a great Ring of pure and endless Light/Calm and brilliant;/And beneath it, Time, hours, days, years,/lead on by the spheres/A vast shadow spun, carrying off in its movement/ the world and its cortège'. Myths of creation were also employed in a different tone and with only a secondary concern for their poetic expression by many authors of works of 'high philosophy' – Fludd, Maier, Kircher and even Kepler (*Harmonices Mundi*, 1619) – who adapted them and degraded them as their arguments required. It is remarkable that despite the discoveries and theories of Copernicus, Galileo, Tycho Brahe and Kepler, the cosmogonic epic survived as a literary genre in the works of the successors and close or distant imitators of Du Bartas, such as Il Tasso (*Il Mondo Creato*, 1607), Murtola (*Della Creazione del Mondo, poemo sacro*, 1608), Saulnier (*Cosmologie du monde tant céleste que terrestre*, 1618), Milton (*Paradise Lost*, 1667), Sir Richard Blackmore (*Creation*, 1712), Henry Brooke (*Universal Beauty*, 1735), Moses Browne (*Essay on the Universe*, 1753) and indeed, albeit in a completely different tone, in those of Quinet (*La Création*, 1870) and Queneau (*Petite cosmogonie portative*, 1950). The abandonment of an anthropocentric view of the universe led to an at least partial decline in the popularity of cosmogonic myths, for they could no longer explain the mystery of the universe's origins. However, since poets are relatively detached from scientific developments, they could still indulge in the pleasures of the imagination, producing reveries, and imaginary worlds and mythologies. William Blake knew this better than anyone:

> To see a World in a Grain of Sand
> And a Heaven in a Wild Flower
> Hold Infinity in the palm of your hand
> And Eternity in an hour
>
> ('Auguries of Innocence' 1–4)

Thus his poetic frescoes like *The Book of Thel* (1789), *Urizen* (1794), *The Book of Los, The Book of Ahania* and *The Song of Los* (1795) demonstrate the way in which he constructed his own personal cosmogony.

Closer to our own time, Swedenborg, Saint-Martin, Ballanche and Soumet (*La Divine Epopée*, 1842) also preserved the vitality of the cosmogonic myths and their philosophical and literary influence. As well as featuring prominently in the works of Hugo (*Les Contemplations, La Fin de Satan*) and de Nerval (*Aurélia, Le Voyage en Orient*) such myths were also extraordinarily popular in German literature, from Brentano to Wagner and from Hölderlin to Novalis. Thus, in *Heinrich von Ofterdingen*, Novalis used a symbolic tale to return to 'the fabulous epic of the origins, where every seed was still sleeping concentrated upon itself and, in its inviolate solitude, aspired in vain to open out the secret plenitude of its inexhaustible being' (chapter 5). Nature, the 'magic petrified town' of the kingdom of Arcturus, would only be brought to life when Freya, the galvanic force, had seen Eros again; the world would know new hope, communion, 'the fountain all frozen and stiff in the flowerbeds' would come to life.

In the twentieth century, the tradition has not died out. Surprising though it may seem, cosmogonic myths appear to have recovered some of their seductive power. Whether they are derived from the Latin American civilization (as in the case of D. H. Lawrence, *The Plumed Serpent*, 1926, or Paz, *Sunstone*, 1957) or are more traditional stories derived from Classical or Judeo-Christian sources (as in the case of Rilke, *Duino Elegies* and *Sonnets to Orpheus*, 1923; Milosz, *Ars Magna*, 1924, and *Arcana*, 1926; Supervielle, *Gravitations*, 1925, and *La Fable du monde*, 1938; and, more recently, Jabes, *Le Livre des questions*, 1963–5), they contribute to the rebirth of a poetic mission with a precisely defined aim that is absolute in itself: to overcome the trap of words and so overcome that of the cosmos and its mirrors. The poets' objective is no longer to reveal great arcana, or to give sumptuous expression to a scientific theory; their project, at once both humble and ambitious, is to follow the teaching of the ancient poets, for whom the world was a book and the starry heavens an alphabet.

Understood in this way, cosmogonic myths continue to provide a powerful impetus for poetic escape. They thus form a constant element in what might be seen as a particular structure underlying the imaginative approach to understanding the mystery of the origins of the universe. This is except when they constitute the most complete expression of a faith and set of beliefs, as in Claudel's *Cinq Grandes Odes* (1904–8).

Cosmogonic myths are used mainly in works written on sacred topics and characterized by a high degree of literary inspiration. In these, the quest for perfect asethetic expression is united with great depth of thought. It is because of their content (explaining the formation of the cosmos and its functioning) that these myths have constantly been revived. They act as elements in an intellectual process and provide imagery for expressing ideas about the origins of the universe. In doing so, they go beyond their traditional literal meaning and still offer an explanation for the harmony of the world. It is no coincidence that George of Venice's *De harmonia mundi* was translated by the philosopher and poet Guy Le Fèvre de La Boderie and that it influenced the scientific poets in a deep and lasting way. The influence of the cosmogonic myths naturally extends further than their literay expression, since they concern reality, the past and the beginning of everything; and yet they remain literary, for their written expression is a perpetual source of questions about speech, beauty and knowledge. Should what is most sacred not be what is also most beautiful, something from the pen of a poet inspired by the mystery of our origins and the omnipotence of the Creator, or illuminated by the dark rays of the black sun of imaginary creations?

James Dauphiné

Cronos

The specific characteristic of a literary myth is that it brings to life for a particular age, and within the fragile framework of a particular style, the various elements of an archetype. In the process, it maintains the archetype's general structure, even though one of the main themes may take precedence as a result of circumstances that focus attention on some aspect of the basic myth. By heightening the colours of one particular archetypal image at the expense of the others, this new perspective gives a specific emphasis to the story without compromising its overall unity. In this way, changes occur during the course of time that enable the myth to survive.

The myth of Cronos, inherited from the Orient and introduced into Greek literature by Hesiod, is an illustration of this process. In the space of only a few centuries, the story of this ancient god was used successively in cosmogonical and eschatological contexts before becoming the subject of a philosophical analysis that exploited all its potentialities to the full. The changes to the myth were all the more spectacular because Cronos appeared in such diverse settings: the Greek lyric poetry of Hesiod and Pindar, as well as the philosophical prose of Plato.

The myth of Cronos is the myth of divine royalty. When Hesiod made Cronos the first ruler of the gods in his *Theogony*, he probably drew his inspiration from a Hurrian myth entitled 'Royalty in Heaven', which tells the story of the conflicts for sovereignty between the ancient gods. Certainly Cronos has inherited the same violent and sombre characteristics as the Hurrian deities. In fact, the essential elements of the mythical drama date back to the Hurrian prototype of Cronos, Kumarbi, who represents the god of heaven deposed by his son. These are: the emasculation of the heavenly divinity by the young conqueror, the use of the 'sickle of ancient times', and finally the removal of the previous champion by one of his descendants. As soon as Kumarbi-Cronos had been defeated by Teshub-Zeus, a new order appeared in the world, which relegated the ancient gods to oblivion. But even when the latter had been supplanted by younger gods, they still retained their place in mythology because they played a vital role in the field of cosmogonical tradition. Cronos, the son of Uranus and father of Zeus, stands on the threshold between two eras, the one that began with Chaos and the one introduced by Zeus.

His remarkable position inspired Hesiod to make his reign the point at which the 'golden race' appeared on earth. The origins of this first 'race' created by the Immortals are also recounted in a myth that originated in the

Orient, and which describes the various attempts by the gods to produce human beings not subject to deterioration. By placing the first – and most perfect – race under the protection of an 'ancient god', Hesiod established an association that led ultimately to the god of the 'golden race' being invested with a peaceful function. In fact, Hesiod's synthesis produced a Cronos with two sides to his nature: fearsome in the *Theogony*, which tells the story of the dynastic conflicts, and reassuring in *Works and Days*, where he watches over the 'golden race' from heaven.

The second of these two aspects of Cronos was stressed by the Orphico-Pythagorean tradition, which presents a version of the myth of Cronos unknown to Hesiod, according to which the 'ancient god', pardoned by Zeus, is released from Tartarus and installed as the ruler of the Islands of the Blest. Pindar's eleventh *Olympian Ode* (fifth century BC) consecrated Cronos's 'divine royalty' by giving the myth a new eschatological emphasis, as opposed to its earlier cosmogonic one. The myth at the centre of the ode describes the three dwelling places occupied by souls after death. The first, where pain is unknown, is reserved for the 'good', the second, where there is nothing but suffering, is reserved for the 'wicked', while the third, the 'castle of Cronos', represents the state of eternal bliss granted to souls that have been freed from reincarnation. It is situated on the Islands of the Blest, on the shores of Ocean, in the same area that Hesiod had already chosen for the afterlife of heroes with exceptional destinies. In this paradise where freshness and light produce a spectacular vegetation, the Blest enjoy a divine existence, totally removed from the cycles of destiny. The 'castle' is the symbol of Cronos's royalty. As ruler of the Blest, he occupies a privileged position in accordance with his status as an 'ancient god', and has Rhadamanthus, the judge of the dead, as his assessor. His prestige is due to his ancient standing, and his authority does not compete with that of Zeus. The paradises of Homer and Hesiod, interpreted to form the Orphico-Pythagorean 'heaven', had been spiritualized as far as possible, and the myth was ready for its final metamorphosis, which was carried out by Plato.

The philosopher remained entirely faithful to Hesiod. His contribution, in the *Politicus* (the *Statesman*), was to improve the coherence of the myth by strengthening the connection between the 'golden race' and Cronos. His presentation of the myth of the Golden Age depicts the ideal way of life as lived by mortals under the direct rule of the god (*Politicus* 271d–2d). The Pythagorean version of the myth, which had finally eradicated the sombre aspect of Cronos by placing him at the end of the spiritual development of the 'pure', enabled Plato to present this ancient god as the guarantor of the world's original standard of perfection. The presence of the god among mortals is the source and explanation of their happiness (see 'The Golden Age).

In the *Laws*, where Plato puts forward a utopian version of the myth presented in the *Politicus*, Cronos is portrayed as the wise legislator. To avoid the despotism that is a potential temptation to all men in positions of power, he decides to entrust the management of the cities to 'beings of a superior and more divine race, the demons' (*Laws* 4. 713 c–d). This policy results in peace, justice and plenty.

In terms of its Platonic treatment, the 'myth of Cronos' is the myth of divine government, understood in the sense of government born of wisdom and likely to achieve 'the happiness of the human race' (*Laws* 4. 713 e). And that is where the story of the great myth of Cronos, the ancient god, comes to an end. Euhemeristic theory, which reduced gods to the level of ancient royal benefactors of humanity definied by the gratitude of men, dated the story of Cronos back to the initial dynastic conflicts, and, unfortunately, this impoverished version of the story proved extremely popular during the Hellenistic period and was retained by Roman mythographers and adopted by Ennius. The memory of an archiac god who ruled over heaven and earth in a state of joy and plenty before the age of social order and social hierarchies was preserved only in the popular tradition, by the 'Cronia', the festival of Cronos. For its duration, class differences were abolished, the activities of the courts were suspended, disputes and conflicts were made illegal and all work ceased, as if the forgotten Golden Age had returned . . . The festival, which served as a model for the reform of the Saturnalia in Rome in 217 BC (see 'Saturn'), was more successful than any work of literature in ensuring the survival of the myth of Cronos.

Marie-Josette Bénéjam-Bontems

Daedalus

The story of Daedalus unfolded in three distinct locations, the first of which was Athens, as Daedalus was an Athenian of royal descent. His mother was Alcippe, granddaughter of Cecrops, and his father was either Metion or Eupalamus, both descendants of Erechtheus, which made him the cousin of Theseus. In Athens, Daedalus was considered to be the father of sculpture as well as an imaginative inventor who was responsible for such discoveries as the plumbline, birdlime and the gimlet. His nephew, Talus, was also an ingenious inventor and claimed that it was he, and not his uncle, who had invented the saw. Daedalus became envious and flung Talus off the Acropolis, as a result of which he was exiled by the council of the Areopagus. He sought refuge in Crete at the court of King Minos, where he constructed a wooden heifer covered in hide for Queen Pasiphaë, thus enabling her to consummate her passion for the bull sent by Poseidon. At the request of Minos, he later turned his hand to architecture and constructed the Labyrinth, in which to conceal the Minotaur, born of the queen's union with the bull. When Ariadne wanted to help Theseus to find his way through the Labyrinth, it was Daedalus who provided the thread to guide him. This earned him the wrath of Minos, who imprisoned him inside the Labyrinth with his son, Icarus. Daedalus constructed wings to enable them both to escape from their prison, but Icarus flew too near the sun, the wax on his wings melted and he fell into the sea. Daedalus spent the last years of his life alone in Camicus, in Sicily, at the court of King Cocalus, where he worked not only as an architect but also as an engineer. However, Minos had set out to look for him and everywhere that he went he asked if there was anyone who could pass a thread through a snail shell. When he arrived at the court of King Cocalus, he was told that there was someone who could tell him how to do it, and Minos guessed that this must be where Daedalus was hiding. However, before he could lay hands on Daedalus, the latter had him scalded to death in his bath by the king's daughters.

Daedalus is not so much the hero of a single cosmological myth as the focal point of a composite group of legends made up of individual myths. His very name conjurers up images of craftsmanship and artistic creation. He was an imaginative and resourceful inventor and a creative artist for whom the pleasures of design and creation outweighed moral considerations. For the most part, the literary tradition has reduced the story of Daedalus to the Cretan episode and has focused on only three of his many inventions, which have enjoyed varying degrees of popularity over the centuries. Daedalus is sometimes remembered for having built the wooden heifer for Pasiphae, but more often as the architect of the Labyrinth in which the Minotaur was imprisoned, or as the designer of the wings that enabled him to take to the air and so escape from the Labyrinth he had constructed. In each of these three cases, his invention resulted in some form of disaster, and there is a tendency to pity him, probably because he symbolizes the inventor persecuted by his own creation.

In the context of Greek literature, a whole series of terms have been found in the works of Homer and Hesiod that are etymologically related to the name Daedalus and that make it possible to determine the types of activities ascribed to him during the pre-Classical era. However, the disappearance of these terms during the Classical age was in no way balanced by the appearance of Daedalus as a figure in literature. Although there is a reference to him in one of Plato's dialogues as the creator of walking statues that take to their heels if they are not tied down (*Menon* 97 d) – in other words, perhaps as the first sculptor to have represented the human form in the attitude of walking – not a single surviving epic or other poem glorifies the life and works of the father of sculpture. True, Sophocles and Aristophanes do appear to have had an interest in Daedalus. It seems that Sophocles wrote two tragedies based on the Sicilian episode, but only the titles, *Daedalus* and *Camicus*, and a few fragments remain; while the same is true of the comedies, *Daedalus* and *Cocalus*, by Aristophanes. In addition it is also possible that Daedalus appeared in *Theseus*, part of a lost trilogy by Euripides. Apart from this, though, he does not feature in Greek literature. Nonetheless, in the context of the visual arts, a black-figure vase of the seventh or sixth century BC known as the 'Rayet skyphos' shows that the Athenian was a popular figure in ancient times.

In a literary context Daedalus first began to come to prominence in Latin literature. However, he did not long remain the simple craftsman and sculptor of the pre-Classical era to whom Cicero referred in his *Brutus* (71) in 46 BC. At the beginning of *Aeneid* VI (18 BC), when Aeneas pauses for a moment on his way to the underworld to look at the temple door on which Daedalus has sculpted his own story, it is the artist's skill that is emphasized, inspiring his admiration as he begins to reflect upon the work and its cruelty. Nonetheless, the accent was already beginning to be placed on Daedalus's presumptuousness in taking to the air on 'swooping wings' and on the tragedy of Icarus. Thus when, in letter XVIII of Ovid's *Heroides* (c. 15 BC), the lover Leander wants to cross the sea, he asks Daedalus to make him some 'audacious wings'. However, it was the *Ars Amatoria* (II. 15–96) and the *Metamorphoses* (VIII. 185–235), of around 2 BC and 3 AD respectively, that established the image of Daedalus as the man who could fly and of his son Icarus as a foolhardy show-off. In these two passages, factual details are combined with the dream of flying to form a sort of idealized image. Daedalus therefore became, first and foremost, the man who could fly like a bird and, as a result, the symbol of the inventive genius of Man. After Ovid, the poets Horace, Juvenal and Martial saw him more as the man who 'took to the emptiness of the air on wings which had been denied to man' than as architect of the Labyrinth (*Odes* I. 3. 34–5 and IV. 2. 12–4; *Satires* III. 25; *Epigrams* IV. 49). However, in Petronius's *Satyricon*, Trimalchio nicknames his cook Daedalus because of his skill in transforming meat into unrecognizable dishes (70). As well as probably indicating that Daedalus still remained a symbol of the ingenious inventor, this also clearly reveals that Trimalchio did not have a great knowledge of the poets – an ignorance evident elsewhere (52) when he states that it was Daedalus who had shut Niobe into the Trojan horse.

During the Middle Ages, Daedalus appeared most frequently in the guise of the man who made wings for himself and for Icarus. This story is supposed to have been told, among many others, in the *Roman de Flamenca* (twelfth century) at the marriage of the heroine (695–8), and is referred to again in Jean de Meun's continuation of the *Roman de la Rose* (5225–8). Similarly, when Dante allows himself to be carried down into the depths of the Circles of Fraud by Geryon, he says that his fear is no less than that of Icarus and his father when they both noticed that the wax on Icarus's wings was beginning to melt (*Inferno* XVII. 109–11). Later (XXIX. 115–8), Dante meets Griffolino d'Arezzo, who has been condemned by Alberto, Bishop of Siena, to be burnt at the stake for having failed to his promise to 'make him Daedalus' and teach him to fly. Meanwhile, in *Paradiso*, there is a reference to '. . . that sire / Whose winged flight cost him his son Icarus' (VIII. 125–6). Boccaccio also mentions Daedalus in relation to his escape from the Labyrinth with Icarus in *Il Filocolo* (IV. 108) and in *Amorosa Visione* (XXXV. 36–47). But, on a more down-to-earth level, Daedalus seems also to have retained his status as the patron of architects and the keeper of a complicated and almost esoteric body of knowledge. The beginning of the inscription next to the Labyrinth sculpted on the doorway of the twelfth-century Lucca cathedral reads: 'Hic quem Creticus edit Daedalus est laberinthus' ('This is the Labyrinth built by the Cretan Daedalus'). In the centre of the ruined labyrinth of Amiens Cathedral, were depicted, by way of signatures, the figures the bishop who had sponsored its construction and the three architects responsible for the cathedral design, while, in a fourteenth-century document, the labyrinth is described as the 'house of Daedalus'. Likewise, the first garden labyrinths, which were probably arbours rather than the hedge mazes found later, were also known in fourteenth-century France as 'houses of Daedalus'. In the prose version of *Berinus* (fourteenth century), Daedalus is described as a 'very subtle engineer' whose sculptures of three scorpions and two dragons at a bridge entrance seemed so ready to devour passers-by that people wondered if they weren't real (130).

During the Renaissance, the theme of the winged flight captured the imagination of several poets. The Italian poets Sannazaro and Tansillo and the

French poets of the Pléiade sometimes used the figure of Icarus to symbolize poetic aspiration or, as in the case of Desportes, to represent the sublimation of love. But Daedalus was never far away and, in Desportes' *Amours de Diane* (Droz, I. 67), he even became confused with his own son. However, Du Bellay referred to him independently of Icarus as the 'audacious artisan' who 'Dared to assault the once empty air' (O. P., III. 126). As well as inspiring a passage by Ronsard praising a poet for having restored the wings to romantic poetry (O. C., XVII. 254–5), Daedalus was also, in a less obvious but complementary manner, the inventive architect that Rabelais had in mind when describing the fantastical fountain in his *Cinquième Livre* (XLII), and the builder of the Labyrinth that Jamyn refers to in a simile (O. P., p. 165). Thus, despite his role as the winged man, Daedalus was not associated with the sun in the same way as Icarus, but tended still to be seen as the ingenious architect.

It is possible to trace the figure of Daedalus during the Classical period, starting in the mid-seventeenth century, with Hieronimo Barrionuevo's *Fabula de Icaro* and ending in the late eighteenth century with the 'Ode sur l'enthousiasme' by Ecouchard Le Brun. However, with the exception of a beautiful line in a poem written in 1762 by William Falconer (*Shipwreck* II. 208) in which he is described as 'In mazes self-invented long immured', it should be emphasized that the figure of Daedalus is virtually absent from 'classic' literature. It was not until the end of the eighteenth century, with one of the first major groups sculpted by Canova (*Daedalus and Icarus*, c. 1779) and the burgeoning dreams and utopian visions of flight, that the winged man began to occupy a more promient position in the collective imagination. This is borne out by the title of the *Nouveau Dédale* (of uncertain authorship), published in 1742, and the alternative title of the work by Restif de la Bretonne, *La Découverte australe par un homme volant, ou le Dédale français* (1781).

During the nineteenth century, and independently of the increased popularity of the poetic theme of Icarus, there were also signs of a revival of interest in Daedalus. Hugo looked beyond the image of the winged man and rediscovered the sculptor and architect of the original Greek myth. He is a 'vertiginous' architect in the *Orientales* ('Reverie', 1829), the keeper of great architectural secrets in *Les Rayons et les Ombres* (XXXV, 1840), and is later compared with Hermes in *Toute la Lyre* III. 3 and III. 46). Likewise in *Les Contemplations* (1856) he symbolizes the supreme form of architecture (III. 30. 2), while in *La Légende des Siècles* (1859–63) he is the ideal sculptor, whose statues, like those described by Plato, astonishingly come to life, and in *Dieu* (1891) he is considered on an equal footing with the Titans (19th Fragment). He combines the qualities of the skilled technicians with those of the constructor of the impossible. He is one of the figures used by Hugo to question the creative act and, on occasions, to evoke the misfortunes of fatherhood. In England, Falkener chose the emblematic title *Daedalus* for a substantial work on 'the causes and principles of the excellence of Greek sculpture' (1860). Meanwhile in the twenty-third letter of his *Fors clavigera* (1871–4), Ruskin pursued his parallel between the story of 'the House that jack built' and the story of the Labyrinth, and saw Daedalus as symbolizing the highest level of skill and expertise that a human being could possibly achieve in seeking to rival the gods.

During the twentieth century, the image of Daedalus as the winged man has often been superseded by that of Icarus. This is particularly true in the realm of poetry. For example, in the 'Ditirambo IV' of the *Laudi* (1904–12) by d'Annunzio the young Icarus tells his story in a long narrative poem in which he appears to be more imspired by the idea and the desire to fly than his father is. He persuades the latter to take part in the project, although he is resolved from the very outset not to follow his advice. In Apollinaire's 'L'ignorance' (*Il y a*, 1925), Icarus admits, 'My father taught me the way through the Labyrinth', but it is Icarus alone who takes to the skies and burns his body on the sun's rays, which here symbolizes the light of knowledge. Similarly, it is Icarus, rather than Daedalus, who can be recognized in Char's 'Hymne à voix basse' (*Le Poème pulvérisé*, 1947) as he sets out on 'the nuptial flight of man, at last free to discover himself and to perish like a bird'.

However, restored to his tole of architect and inventor, Daedalus has once more become an important symbolic figure in modern literature. This is already apparent in the play by Herbert Eulenberg, *Ikarus und Daidalos* (1912), while the ingenious Athenian is also the focal point of several novels, such as *Dedalo* (1932) by Juan José Domenchina, and *Ich und die Könige* (1958) by Ernst Schnabel. Daedalus is to some extent the forerunner of all creative geniuses whose creations sometimes escape their control, and thus is not all that far removed from the character of the mad scientist or the sorcerer's apprentice. By way of a warning, the heroine of the *Dream Master* (1966) by Roger Zelasny tells the dream maker and creator of the universe the story of the snail shell that enabled Minos to find Daedalus. However, the image of Daedalus is essentially positive. After dedicating an ode to him entitled 'Au père des artistes' (1938), Anghelos Sikelianos made him the freedom fighter in his tragedy *Dédale en Crète* (1943), where as an initiate, a politician and a poet, Daedalus helps Pasiphaë and Theseus to overthrow the tyrant Minos. The British author Michael Ayrton first dedicated a small collection of drawings, poems and prose writings to the ancient craftsmen in *The Testament of Daedalus* (1962), and later a statue, a film and a novel in the form of an autobiography. In the latter, *The Maze-Maker* (1968), Daedalus represents the rational principle of leading a creative life, as opposed to the heroic principle represented by Icarus. Towards the end of his life, having witnessed a volcanic eruption and encountered the Minotaur, the hero manages to transcend this opposition and begins to see its ambivalence.

Finally, and most importantly, as an imaginative inventor and the architect of the Labyrinth, Daedalus is most frequently evoked as the archetype of the artist. He appears in this role in Joyce's *Portrait of the Artist as a Young Man* (1917), where Stephen's unusual surname is both the name that he inherited from his father and that of the distant and mysterious legendary figure. To suit his name, Stephen must become a master of words. Thus, on five occasions (one in each chapter), he has to confront the words of others; and these five conversations represent five labyrinths from which he has to find a way out. Not only does Stephen have to provide immediate answers but, in order to control the experience, he must also invent the words to express it. In writing the *Portrait*, Stephen constructs a labyrinth of words that is both the symbolic equivalent of the labyrinth of the world and, at the same time, enables him to control it. The novel of apprenticeship is also the novel of the artist, since artistic creation brings independence and self-determination. Furthermore, these ideas are not so very far removed from the symbolism of alchemy, and Daedalus is closely associated with another winged man, Thoth, the Egyptian god of writing who became Hermes-Trismegistus, the father of alchemy. All narrators who imprison themselves in the labyrinth of writing to achieve a symbolic representation of reality are Stephen's sons and grandsons. 'Finally, I identified with Daedalus', wrote Friedrich Dürrenmatt in *Stoffe* (1981) as he pursued his 'theatre of the labyrinth'. In this respect, Daedalus is the modern hero of the Labyrinth to a much greater extent than Theseus. But his position is not without its risks. Nabokov, in his usual ironic and parodistic manner, describes grandfather Dedalus Veen (*Ada*, 1969) looking up at the sky as he runs, and 'falling into the drinking trough'.

Thus the theme of Daedalus, which was virtually absent from Greek literature, enjoyed a remarkable degree of success in Latin literature, where it also underwent a shift of emphasis. Particularly in the works of Ovid, the craftsman and sculptor was pushed into the background by the image of the man with wings symbolizing Man's dream of flight. Until the nineteenth century, Daedalus continued to be seen primarily in this guise, though the writers of the Renaissance and the nineteenth century often preferred to use Icarus as the fascinating symbol of the winged man. Nonetheless even in his more spectacular role, Daedalus retained his status as the inventive craftsman and keeper of the secret knowledge of architects, albeit fairly unobtrusively. He was finally reinstated by the poetry of Hugo, and twentieth-century writers began to treat him as the symbol of the artist. The writer was no longer simply someone inspired and transported by genius, but also a creator dealing with the tools and techniques of his trade and endeavouring to achieve freedom. As well as prisons, palaces and passageways, literary labyrinths are also ingenious constructions, albeit made of words. If they imitate the world and render it more enchanting, this is their way of making it inhabitable for us, and it is this that makes Daedalus the architect of freedom.

André Peyronie

Daphne

The different versions of the tale of Daphne are all based on a highly consistent narrative sequence with a 'dramatic' form of structure involving a build up of tension finally leading to catastrophe. The events progress logically towards an 'exemplary' type of denouement and the story runs basically as follows. A young nymph devotes herself to Diana, vowing to renounce love and marriage, but Apollo falls in love with her and vainly tries to convince her to give herself to him. She flees: he pursues and threatens her. She is then changed into a laurel tree, and the distressed and repentant god incorporates the plant into his cult.

This sequence of events is remarkably simple and balanced in two respects: first in its pattern of development, which the episodic or accessory elements added to it often do not alter; and secondly in its 'plasticity', which makes possible a great variety of interpretations of the myth.

The myth has frequently been portrayed by artists, and was also popular in works of literature. With the myth of Orpheus (to which it is to some extent related), the story of Daphne is the great ancient myth of a love that is tragic but can be transcended.

The tale of Daphne first appeared in Greece in the second half of the third century BC, but its origins are probably oriental (Indo-European) and far more ancient. Thus the Eastern solar myths include the story of Dahana (meaning 'the burning one' in Sanskrit), the Dawn, who flees the rising sun and disappears the moment that he reaches her. The Greek name for the laurel (Daphne), which is comparable to the Sanskrit word for dawn, may have caused the story to be modified and explain the form of Daphne's metamorphosis. The latter is probably linked to the cult of trees that was so widespread around the Mediterranean. Three local versions of the mythical story are known:

1. The Arcadian version, which is the oldest, portrays Daphne as the daughter of Earth and of the river Lādon. Her metamorphosis on the river bank is effected by the power of her mother. This account stresses the union of the elements of earth and water necessary for the laurel to grow, and so suggests a naturalistic interpretation of the myth. We find this account in Palaephatus, in the ancient commentaries on *The Iliad* and also in later texts (Pausanias, second century AD; Aphthonius and Libanius, fourth century AD).

2. The Laconian version makes Daphne the daughter of the Spartan king Amyclas and the sister of Hyacinthus, who was also loved by Apollo. She has devoted herself to Diana, but is loved by the prince Leucippus. On the banks

of the Eurotas, Leucippus disguises himself as a woman to try to approach Daphne, but he is unmasked and put to death by her companions. Apollo, Leucippus's rival then also tries to attack the girl, whose metamorphosis is brought about by Jupiter. In this case, the explanation of the legend seems to be euhemeristic. This version of the myth was less widespread than the others, being recorded by Parthenius of Nicaea (first century BC) and Plutarch (first century AD).

3. The most famous version of the story originated in Thessaly and became the 'vulgate' account. In it, Daphne is the daughter of the river Peneus (between Ossa and Olympus, in the vale of Tempe) who is pursued by Apollo and changed into a laurel by her father. The entire region was consecrated to Apollo (whose principal sanctuary is at Delphi), and the victor's crown in the Pythian Games was made of laurel. The myth may thus be aetiological, explaining the existence of Apollo's cult. It was used by many authors, from Nicander of Colophon (late third and early second centuries BC) to the most notable of all, Ovid.

4. Lastly, a later, Syrian version locates the story on the banks of the Orontes near Antioch. This is a foundation legend, linked to the establishment of the city and of Daphne's temple. It occurs in *The Life of Apollonius* by Philostratus (first century AD), in Eumathius's *Ismene and Ismine* and in the *Dionysiaca* of Nonnus of Panopolis (c. 450 AD).

What is clear in every case is that the fable is linked to a river – and perhaps also to a particular type of vegetation, the laurel forest – situated in an area where Apollo is worshipped. Indeed, the latter's cult perhaps replaced the more ancient worship of trees reflecting beliefs in living beings hidden beneath the bark. Nor is there much difference between the versions; on the contrary, they show a remarkable consistency (which does not exist, for example, in the tradition relating to Orpheus) and even direct connections implying successive transmission.

Though ancient writers often used the myth it is not the chief element in any of their works: instead it is usually only alluded to or mentioned in passing in an appropriate context. The most significant references to it include those in the works of Virgil (*Aeneid* II and III: Eclogues III, IV and VII), Statius (*Silvae* 1 and 2: *Thebaid* I, III, IV and VU) or Lucian (*True History*). Meanwhile, it is also mentioned by scholiasts (Servius), mythographers (Hyginus, Libanius, Fulgentius, Lactantius) and novelists (Nonnus, Achilles Tatius).

However, it is to Ovid that Daphne owes her renown since his *Metamorphoses* c. 3 AD) provide the most developed and complete narrative (I. 417–567). Ovid was an artist who enjoyed carving out moving, strange and fascinating tales, and his collection of fabulous stories reflects his vision of a shifting world, where everything is transformed and influenced by the natural forces at work throughout it. Metamorphoses into plants provide a particularly rich theme: these changes are quick, striking people in their youth, and mark a passage from one beautiful shape to another that is equally beautiful. There is something touching and grave about Daphne's fate. Empedocles thought that for a human being of great virtue there were only two suitable fates after death: to be changed into a laurel or a lion.

Ovid established the standard version of the myth of Daphne: a narrative sequence that organizes the action into clear stages. In the 'prologue', Apollo defeats the monstrous snake Python (while the 'epilogue' portrays his own defeat by purity and beauty). In the 'first act' Apollo mockingly challenges Love, who decides on revenge. Apollo is struck by a golden arrow, which awakens his desire, while Daphne is hit by a lead arrow, which makes her unaware of it and indifferent to it. Thus a tragic element is introduced, in the form of 'predestination' for the two protagonists. Furthermore, the contrast between gold and lead (hot/cold; desire/indifference; Sun/Saturn) was to lend itself to many interpretations, ranging from ones based on Platonic idealism to ones associated with alchemy. The 'second act' introduces Daphne, described her vow to Diana, her activity as a fierce hunter and her beauty. Apollo sees her and falls madly in love with her. He addresses a long harangue to her and plays her his lyre, but to no avail. In the 'third act', Apollo pursues Daphne as she is undressing. This episode, which is similar to many others in the *Metamorphoses* (involving Io, Syrinx, Callisto, Dryope, Arethusa, Lotis), serves to highlight the emotional relations between the protagonists while also constituting the story's most dramatic event, which is soon followed by the pathos of the metamorphosis. When she is just about to be caught and raped, Daphne begs her protecting gods to intervene. She is transformed into a laurel and Apollo gives vent to his grief. In the 'epilogue', Apollo makes the laurel an emblem of his own divinity and worship. This denouement creates two victorious victims: Daphne loses her human shape and preserves her purity, while Apollo, whose love is disappointed, manages to transcend it. Thus the omnipotence of love is not absolute, and the myth creates a vision that is as much tragic as optimistic (for example in line 458 the rivers wonder whether they should congratulate or commiserate with Daphne's father).

Ovid's contribution to the development of the myth was considerable. First, he dramatized the story and provided a sense of structure, both of which were obviously useful to later writers on the subject. In addition he placed it at the beginning of his work, in the earliest period of the universe's existence so that the myths that immediately precede it are those of Chaos, the four ages of the world, the giants, Lyacon, the flood, Deucalion and Pyrrha, and Python). It is thus the first story depicting the feeling of love. Ovid links it to the Python episode, to create a contrast between the monster and the nymph, victory and defeat, and provides motivation for the drama in the challenge made to the omnipotence of Love (line 453: 'It was not blind chance that brought this about, but Cupid'). He inserts the tale into a series of stories recounting the fates of nymphs loved by the gods, the next being that of Io who was loved by Jupiter. He allows Apollo to make a plea of generous length on his own behalf and slips in a few voluptuous touches, for example when the wind lifts Daphne's clothing as she flees, the better revealing her charms to her pursuer. And finally his description of the actual metamorphosis is far more than a mere account: it is the most perfect tableau in this whole fantastical passage and no other passage in the *Metamorphoses* achieves such suggestive density and conveys such vibrant emotion. It is also worth noting that Ovid used the conclusion to the story as a means of flattering Augustus, who particularly venerated the laurel.

Without seeking to compete with Ovid as a storyteller, other ancient writers (particularly in later Antiquity) suggested rather timid interpretations of the myth, whereas Ovid himself had not suggested any. Some followed the approach developed by Euhemerus, suggesting that myths represent distortions of historical events, while others adopted a philosophical perspective portraying Daphne as the mistress of her passion and desires, and thus as the embodiment of Sophrosune, the true Wisdom. However, the most frequent aim was to illustrate the physical properties of the laurel (the absence of fruit in some species or the crackling of the burning leaves) or else its various uses. The latter included the practice of dephnemancy or divination using the laurel, the chewing of laurel leaves, and the practice of oneirology in which laurel leaves were placed under a pillow to ensure that dreams told the truth. The myth's significance as a theogony is rarely mentioned in these commentaries. Instead, while not actually emphasizing this aspect, they suggest a psychological interpretation of the story, in terms of the incompleteness of the passion of love, which never attains total possession, and the lack of satisfaction and unhappiness of loving.

The success of the myth of Daphne in the Middle Ages was linked to the diffusion of Ovid's work during this period since from the eleventh century onwards he was one of the nine writers on whose texts the study of the liberal arts was based. However, it was primarily due to the fact that the myth had been appropriated for Christianity by the early Fathers of the Church. This determined the way in which the myth was interpreted by profoundly modifying its very nature and scope. The aim was to get to the *integumentum*, the deeper meaning assumed to lie hidden in this kind of fabulous story. One approach was allegorical and involved 'decoding' biblical episodes or obscurely argued doctrinal points in mythological narratives. Another was tropological and sought to find an ethical dimension in myths, while yet another was anagogical and drew out a spiritual and mystical element from the ancient tales. Thus, in their efforts to diminish the influence of paganism by integrating it into Christian doctrine, Fulgentius (*Mythologiae* I. 13–14; end of V), Lactantius (*Divinae Institutiones* II. 9; end of III), Eusebius of Caesarea (*Evangelica praeparatio*, 340 AD) and Cyril (*Contra Julianarum*, 444 AD) proposed a 'moralizing' interpretation of the story of Daphne, which was one of those that best lent itself to this sort of treatment. This represented it as exalting the figure of a girl who, by her virtuous efforts, succeeded in preserving her virginity at the cost of her life; as a virgin, a martyr and almost a saint, Peneus's daughter could be used as a model to the young Christian girl.

From this period until the sixteenth century, the narrative element of the myth was subordinated to a moralizing approach, which was often developed at great length and in an increasingly subtle way. Arnoul d'Orleans (*Allegoriae super Metamophosin*, end of the twelfth century) made Daphne a symbol of the Christian virtue of virginity. For Jean de Garlande (*Integumenta c.* 1234) she was the virginal symbol of that glory which the Sage loves and pursues. However, the most famous work of this sort is undoubtedly *Ovide moralisé* (late thirteenth and early fourteenth centuries), which is attributed to Chrétien Legouais de Sainte-More. More than seven hundred lines of this poem are devoted to the story of Daphne which is first recounted according to the version in Ovid, though with some amplifications, and then interpreted from various viewpoints. The latter comprise the naturalist approach, euhemerist approach (according to which Daphne is a chaste girl who dies of exhaustion after being pursued by a man full of brutal desire), the moralist perspective (praising chastity) and the Christian outlook. Finally, Daphne is identified with the Virgin Mary, the Sun of the world and beloved of God. If Apollo crowns himself with laurel, it is because God took flesh from the Virgin, enclosing himself in her body. The abridged reworking of the poem presented in *Ovide moralisé en prose* (*c.* 1466–7) reveals the persistent nature of such interpretations, which Erasmus, Luther and Rabelais were to mock with some indignation. The most 'luxuriant' of these moralizing accounts occurs in Pierre Bersuire's *Reductorium morale* (*c.* 1337–40). Book 15 of this compedium contains the *De reductione fabularum*, also known as *Ovidius moralizatus*, which was later adapted in French with the title *Bible des Poètes de Metamorphose* (1484 and 1493). In this work Daphne is the pure Christian soul threatened by Apollo, the demon who comes to tempt her and fails. Alternatively she is human nature, which Apollo (this time representing Christ, the god of Wisdom) desires to draw to himself; at first she flees and rejects him but, once he has caught her, she changes shape to become one with him. There are other interpretations too: Apollo symbolizes those who seek the empty glory of the world rather than true wisdom; Daphne represents the Synagogue that rejects the Messiah; Laurel is the tree used to make the cross; Daphne is Mary, whom God loves and who remains virgin. Other commentators were to have difficulty in finding new moralizing explanations of the story: for Giovanni del Virgilio (1322–3) Daphne represented modesty; according to Giovanni dei Buonsignori (*Allegory, c.* 1370–5) she is that virtue sought by the truly wise, that Prudence which attracts the 'modest and chaste person' of Apollo. Meanwhile, in the work of Boccacio, the naturalist interpretation is overlaid with a symbolic one in which Daphne becomes the emblem of the glory that rewards poets (*Genealogica deorum, c.* 1363–72), or the symbol of poetic activity (*Trattatello in laude di Dante*, 1351–55).

At this time, the first translations of Ovid were also appearing (*c.* 1210, by

Albrecht von Halberstadt; *c.* 1339, by Arrigo Simintendi), and alongside the moralizing texts and commentaries, original works of literature began to use the myth of Daphne. Thus, in his *Ninfale Fiesolano (c.* 1335) Boccacio rewrote the story around the tragic love of Africao and Mensola in connection with the legend of the foundation of Fiesole. The delicacy of his descriptions of nature and the elegiac tone in which he depicts the lovers' feelings make this epyllion one of the first great modern works inspired by the myth. However, Boccacio introduced an important change: in his poem the girl is raped by her pursuer; he, in pain and despair at losing all trace of her, kills himself; and Mensola first gives birth to a son and then turns into a river. *L'Espinette amoureuse* by Jean Froissart (*c.* 1370) is an autobiographical novel in verse about the loves of the poet's youth. Sick with love and despair because his lady is to marry another, the hero composes a long lament in which he compares himself to Apollo in love with Daphne. This provides the opportunity to retell the story, applying it to the hero's own situation. However, the lament ends with the lady softening her heart and promising to be true to her faithful lover. Froissant slips further allusions to the myth into his *Joli Buisson de Jonece* (1373–4). Similarly, John Gower's *Confessio Amantis (c.* 1386–1400) also alludes to it in the context of education in chivalry and courtly love, which treats the inevitability of destiny with a kind of optimistic fatalism. Finally, Christine de Pisan devoted the eighty-seventh story of her *Epître d'Othéa (c.* 1402) to the myth, in an arrangement prefiguring the formula of the 'emblems triplex': a gnomic lesson ('Through great diligence one reaches perfection') is illustrated by a story, first presented in the form of a miniature, then in a series of commentaries. Thus, the myth is retold, and then interpreted: a woman who is pursued and caught under a laurel tree gives in to the young knight who has pleaded his love for her; the laurel crown, the sign of victory, is the knight's just reward and indicates his nobility of soul. After this, an allegorical explanation is offered based on Christianity: Apollo's desire actually represents a wish to reach the blessedness of Paradise; his pursuit of Daphne is thus entirely praiseworthy.

The myth of Daphne was given a decisive new impetus when Petrarch, who was in love with a woman named Laura, established a whole network of comparisons between his own situation and that of Apollo. As well as identifying Laura poetically with the laurel and with Daphne, he represented the ancient myth as a prefiguration or model of his own fate (*Canzoniere*, sonnets 5, 6, 29, 35, 37, 44, 49, 50, 159, 168, 221, 227, 229, sextines 1 and 2, canzone 1, etc.). Laura slips away, like Daphne, but the lover remains constant in his love. Laura attracts Petrarch and makes him suffer, but in doing so she forces him to surpass himself and ultimately she becomes the symbol of Perfection and Beauty. From this time on, and particularly in the European current of Petrarchan lyric poetry, the myth was used to illustrate the themes of the pain of love, of love beyond reach, of the ceaseless quest, of transfiguration through love and of the idealization of emotion. However it was also the myth of the poet: again, in the third eclogue of his *Bucolicum Carmen*, Petrarch reworked the subject by adapting it to his personal experience. Stupeus is in love with Daphne, who at first rejects him. But after Stupeus has made an ardent plea and asserted his faithfulness and constancy, she finally accepts his love, leads him to Olympus and offers him a laurel branch. Here Daphne evidently represents the glory of poetry, which enables the chosen one to enter the realm of the divine.

Also playing on a similarity of names, Laurent de Medici (the Magnificent) used his own experience of his love for Lucrezia Donati to create a new version of the myth in *Rime*. Here, Daphne, the laurel, is Laurent himself, who will waste away if he is no longer lit up by his sun, and the poet even imagines his own metamorphosis. In the poem *L'Ambra* Laurent adheres more closely to the ancient story, recounting the pursuit of Ambra by Ombron and attributing her metamorphosis to Diana.

It is not surprising that we find frequent references to the myth of Daphne in the *trattatisti d'amore* of the Cinquecento (Bembo, *Azolains*, 1505; Abravanel, *The Philosophy of Love*, 1535). According to Ficini, Daphne tends to be criticized in their work because of her rejection of Apollo, since Apollo's love is 'a certain desire to have fruition of Beauty'. In the same way, the Petrarchan poets (such as Varchi, Tasso and Ariosto) often identify the attitude of an insensitive mistress with that of the nymph, stressing the unhappy outcome that it will bring.

This was the era of the great mythographers (Giraldi, Conti, Cartari) of the great verse translators whose works were almost new creations in their own right (Dolce, 1553; dell'Anguillara, 1561) and also of the last great 'moralizer', Raphaël Regius (1490). In their work we find numerous syntheses relating to the myth and its meangings. During this time, neo-Latin poetry was continuing the elegiac tradition of the myth (Pontanus, *Urania*, 1505), while the famous *Hypnerotomachia Polophili* (1467, published 1499) by Francesco Colonna incorporated Daphne in a naturalist allegory and condemned her for rebelling against a natural order from which Eros cannot be absent.

Whereas writers during the Middle Ages favoured allegorical interpretations of the myth, those of the Renaissance preferred to use it as an analogy for their own personal circumstances and so brought it back into the world of human feelings. The myth became a symbol of unsatisfied love, the tragic illustration of an inaccessible love. Sometimes it was used as an invitation to overcome earthly passion; at others, it was used to condemn the rejection of love. The relationship between the two protagonists became a model sadly evoked by the lovelorn poet: 'You flee Apollonian ardour, Daphne' said Scève to his Delia (1544), bemoaning the bitterness of his fate, which he compared to the bitter leaves of the laurel. Similarly, in his love poems addressed to a lady called Genèvre, Ronsard recalled the words that Ovid put into the mouth of Apollo, while he also wrote a poetic tale involving a metamorphosis into a tree (*Le Houx*).

One of the most interesting treatments of the myth, and one of its most seductive variants, is the story in *La Saulsaie*. This involves not one nymph, but several, not one god, but a whole troop of satyrs. Far from fleeing into the woods, the nymphs at first accept the satyrs' company. However, when the latter reveal their brutal desires they take fright and run off to the banks of a river, where they are changed into willows the moment that they are caught. This tale forms the subject of several works, including Sannazaro's *Salices* (1526) and Giraldi's *Eglé* (1545). In the *Fable du Faulx Cuyder* by Marguerite de Navarre (1543), it is turned into a kind of parable condemning vain presumption and submission to uncontrolled desires. Meanwhile, in *La Saulsaye ou Eglogue de la Vie solitaire* by Scève (1547) it is treated as a decorative episode. As in Belleau's *La Bergerie* (1565), the story is interpreted as representing the foolish pursuit of chasity by desire.

The most elaborate work on the theme of Daphne produced by a writer of the French Renaissance is a poem of 470 lines by de Baïff called *Le Laurier* (1573). In it Baïff amplifies Ovid's narrative by slipping in ornamental devices, little nature tableaux, details of the nymph's charms, mentions of the properties of the laurel and a passage in praise of poetry. By contrast, in another poem called *Le Laurier* by Guillaume Du Maine (1556), the writer's chief concern is to extol humanist studies. At the beginning of the sixteenth century *Le Grant Olympe* provided an alchemical interpretation of the myth (1532), while translators of Ovid's text strove to add their own comments to it (Marot, *c.* 1531; Fr. Habert, 1557; Du Bartas, *Olimpe*, 1597; de Massac, 1603). As symbols, Daphne and the laurel did not feature prominently. However, they were used occasionally to represent a clean conscience (Sambucus), intact virtue (Camerarius), poetic activity (De Soto), imprudent love (Aneau), and, indeed, truth, unless the implication is that one should transcend the perishable and attach oneself to that which lasts.

The only Renaissance drama based on the myth was *Die Daphne eins Königs Tochter* (1558) by Hans Sachs. This is a very static 'tragedy', despite its brevity, and consists of speeches paraphrasing Ovid. More than half the play is devoted to the combat with Python and the challenge made to Love. Apollo is portrayed as an unctuous lover, and Daphne finds the time to say goodbye to her father during her metamorphosis. The whole work soon takes on a moral tone: a man should never be sure of having what he desires; ladies should beware of admirers who are too keen and they should preserve their virtue and chastity until their wedding day. The audience addressed by the play was made up of the middle-class traders of Nuremberg.

In a sense, the seventeenth century marks the point at which the myth came to fruition. Not only was it frequently mentioned or retold, often in an unoriginal way, but, more importantly, it was also given quite striking treatment in a number of major literary works. At the same time the study of mythology came to be considered as a form of criticism. The works of Vossius (*De theologia gentilis*, 1641) and Samuel Bochart (*Geographia sacra*, 1646) prepared the ground for the great treatises of the following century, including *La Mythologie et les fables expliquées par l'Histoire* (1738–40) by the Abbé Banier. In addition, they were used by Desmarets de Saint-Sorlin in his strange euhemerist novel *La Vérité des fables* (1648), which mixes the imaginary adventures of Prince Apollo and Princess Daphne with the stories of the principal gods of Olympus. This baroque allegorical novel depicts Apollo pursuing Daphne on a floating island that takes him round the world. It remained unfinished and reflects its author's encyclopaedic knowledge and deranged imagination.

The seventeenth century was also the era of the great translators of Ovid: Renouard (1606), Du Ryer (1655), Thomas Corneille (1669), Marolles (1670), Bellegarde (1701) and Banier (1732) in France, Sandrart (1698) in Germany, Sandys (1626) in England, Van Mander (1604), Vondel (1671) and Valentijn (1678) in the Netherlands. Their versions of the text were often accompanied by notes or commentaries that employed and amplified current interpretations and occasionally contained more original insights. A form of hostility towards the myths is increasingly apparent in their work, reflecting Christian denunciations of what were seen as absurd pagan beliefs or else efforts to provide rational explanations for the mysterious events described – a trend that resulted in a vogue for historial or naturalist interpretations of the stories.

Baroque poets were particularly attracted by the concept of metamorphosis, the dynamics of the passage from one shape to another and the fantastical way in which they were interwoven. The 'metamorphosis' virtually became a genre, made fashionable in the salons by Voitre and illustrated by the works of Saint-Amant (*Métamorphose de Lyrian et de Sylvie*) and of Lemoyne. The seventeenth-century Baroque, *précieux* and society poets (such as, d'Audiguier, Lingendes, Expilly, Desmarests, Scudéry and Mme Deshoulières) made frequent references to the daughter of Peneus. In his *Métamorphoses d'Ovide en rondeaux* (1676) Benserade portrays the story of Daphne in two rondeaux that typify the elegance and blandness of the artistic current popular in high society. In 1696 the provincial writer Julien published a dialogue in verse entitled *La Pudeur triomphante ou la métamorphoses de Daphné*, which had a certain charm but was basically outdated. However, it was the Italian Marino who seems to have been most attracted to the myth, featuring it in several of his works: a pastoral eclogue; a madrigal; a sonnet; the poem the 'Speech of Apollo pursuing Daphne' in the collection *La Lira*; the sixth magical idyll of *La Sampogna*; and lastly a description of Guido Reni's painting in *La Galleria*. All of these works are masterpieces produced in the concettist spirit by a sharp artistic mind that shows ingenuity and inventiveness in adding refinements to a fairly conventional treatment of the actual myth itself.

The burlesque poets adopted a different type of approach. They seized on Daphne and portrayed her as a ruddy peasant hounded by a wicked satyr, making their characters talk like petty criminals and fishwives. Bracciolini's *Le Scherno degli Dei* (1618) is still in good taste; Quevedo's sonnet *A Dafne huyendo de Apolo* is simple mockery. True burlesque is to be found in the work of Polo de Medina (1634) or Dassoucy (*L'Ovide en belle humeur*, 1653) and, in a freer form, in that of Vion Dalibray, the author of *Métamorphose de Morille*, which is a double parody of Ovid.

During this period the Spanish poets developed a 'speciality' rarely found elsewhere. This was the mythological fable, a medium-length narrative poem ostensibly with a moral message, exemplified by (Silvestre's *Fábula de Dafnes y Apolo* (1592) and Quevedo's *De Dafne y Apolo Fábula* (1605) as well as works by Pérez (1602) de Faria y Sousa (1624) Acosta (1624) Villamediana (1629) Sánchez (1688) and others. These strophic epyllions incorporated lyrical passages created by the inclusion of characteristic elements from romantic tradition. Their emphasis on the story's denouement was intended to communicate emotion and they all cheerfully echoed the same message: since love is all-powerful, what point is there in resisting it?

It was in the domain of theatrical productions that the story of Daphne enjoyed particular popularity during the seventeenth and eighteenth centuries. True there are only a small number of relatively minor plays on the subject: two Italian pastorals, Enrico Magi's *La Dafne overo la Verginità trionfante* (1649) and Antonio Fachinelli's *La Dafne* (1690); and a few Spanish *comédias*, including Lopez de Vega's *El Amor enamorado* (1637), published posthumously), from which Calderón drew his inspiration for *Zarzuela, El Laurel de Apolo* (1658).

However musical productions on the theme, such as ballets, interludes and operas, were extemely numerous. Indeed, by a quirk of fate the story featured prominently in the development of opera in many countries. In 1486 mention was made of an interlude by Della Viola entitled *Festa del lauro* (but also called *Rappresentazione di Dafne*) played at the court of Mantua, while only the name of the musical *favola pastorale*, composed by Beccari around 1560, now survives. In addition it is known that many ballets devoted one or more entrées to the myth. In 1594 the Florentine Camerata of Bardi and Corsi sought to revive ancient musical drama and the poet Ottavio Rinuccini wrote a libretto that was set to music by Jacopo Peri. This was the first opera, and it is known originally to have been staged in 1597 before being published in 1600. The score is lost, but the dramatic poem provides a very fine libretto with its mixture of elegance and seriousness. It describes Apollo's fight against Python, the challenge to Love and the pursuit of Daphne in recitative verse intercut with couplets of *canzonette* and chorus. The metamorphosis is described by a messenger in a long dramatic narrative – a formula destined to enjoy great success and used again by Rinuccini and Peri in their masterpiece, the account of the death of Eurydice in the opera of the same name. There then follows a *lamento* from Apollo and a final chorus.

In 1607 Marco da Gagliano reset the libretto for Rinuccini's work on Daphne to music, while in 1627 the German poet Martin Opitz and the musician Heinrich Schütz collaborated on the first German opera. This was entitled *Dafne* and was produced at Dresden, though its score is also lost. The libretto was based on that of Rinuccini, but was developed into five, more balanced, acts. Around 1640 the librettist Busenello and the musician Cavalli staged *Gli d'Apollo e di Dafne*, a grand opera of typically Baroque splendour, in Venice. Meanwhile, mention is also made of an unattributed *Dafne* produced in 1647 in Bologna. In 1650 the French poet and musician Dassoucy published the first French musical comedy, though it is not known if he managed actually to stage it. Its score is lost, but it was entitled *Les Amours d'Apollon et de Daphné* and combined Italian influences with Baroque tastes. Works based on the myth of Daphne became more numerous between 1650 and 1700, with operas by Ferrari (1651) Valentini (1654), Epibenio (1660), Bontempi and Peranda (1671), Danielli (1684), Ariosti (1685), Pollarolo (1694), Aldrovandini (1696), Jean-Baptiste Lully (a *divertissement*, 1698) and an anonymous Italian (1699) as well as court ballets by Benserade. Their success continued over the next century with further operas by Astorga (1705), Sabadini, (1705 and perhaps 1690), Fago (1714), Galliard (*c.* 1718), Caldara and Biave (1719), Porta (*c.* 1730), Pasquini and Reuter (1734), Monsigny (a *pasticcio, c.* 1740), Conti (1747), Pigné and Boismortier (1748), Burnet (1771), Pitra and Mayer (1782), and Hensel (1799); as well as cantata by Campra (1708), Handel (1708) and Paisiello (*c.* 1802). Excluded from this impressive list is La Fontaine's failed opera *Daphné* (1674, published 1682), which was written for Lully, who refused to set it to music and chose verse by Quinault instead. In this opera, La Fontaine delays the action with a great number of *divertissements* (choral interludes and dances), subsidiary episodes (such as the consultation of an oracle) and even a passage emphasizing the rivalry between Leucippus (the lover) and Apollo (the admirer). Though some parts of the work are superior to the rest, they cannot save it from mediocrity. In the nineteenth century, the vogue for mythological subjects declined significantly and far fewer operas were based on the story of Daphne: (Ferron 1855); de Giosa, 1864; Gilson, 1865; and Bird, 1897. In 1938 Richard Strauss composed a one-act opera with a libretto by Josef Gregor that took the form of a rather sombre 'bucolic tragedy' emphasizing the tragic nature of love. In it, Leuccipus is killed by Apollo, and Daphne, overwhelmed with grief and pain, is changed into a laurel on the request of Apollo himself.

One can speculate as to why the story of Daphne met with such differing degrees of success in the domains of conventional drama and opera respectively. For one thing, a mythological subject involving appearances by the gods and various magical elements is no doubt little suited to tragedy, although it may suit pastoral drama. In addition the tale of Daphne is too linear, with few twists and turns, and thus lacks suspense unless a secondary plot is added or extra emphasis is placed on the rivalry between nymph's lovers. On the other hand, the story's simplicity and its lyrical and pathetic character can be well exploited by opera; while the plot acutally involves the god of music and offers interesting possibilities in the form of of echoes, hunting scenes, accounts laden with pathos, laments and so on.

In the eighteenth century the myth of Daphne lost its attraction and fascination; like most ancient myths, it only occasionally appeared in literature. Mythology was demystified by writers such as Fontenelle (*De l'origine des Fables*, 1724), Banier (1732) and Ramsay (*Voyages de Cyrus*, 1727). It was given a saucy treatment by Demoustier, (*Lettres à Emilie*, 1786) and an ironic treatment by Fontenelle, La Morlière, and Diderot in his *Pensées détachées sur la Peinture* (1775). And few writers shared the sentiments of Chenier, who felt a sacred shiver at the mysterious presence of the gods. In his novel *Agathon* (1795) Wieland presented several pantomimes based on the tale, in his *Principes de la Philosophie de l'Histoire* (1725), allowing the guests at a banquet to make philosophical comments. By this time Vico had already attempted to interpret the myth as an allegory of human progress. There Apollo is the god who brings the enlightenment of social organization and who pursues Daphne, the symbol of still wondering humankind, with the aim of introducing her to a sedentary life and so to civilization. We do not really know what place the myth would have occupied in Vigny's unfinished *Daphné* (*c.* 1835), but the pages that survive do not follow the traditional account. Daphne was hardly mentioned at all during the ninetcenth century before her appearance in Emmanuel Signoret's collection of symbolist poems (*Daphné*, 1894). After this, a few literary stragglers devoted the occasional verse to her (Paul Feuillâtre, 1911; Henri de Fégnier, 1924; Albert Giraud, 1924); but only the Swiss writer Jacques Chenevière attempted to give the myth new life by using it figuratively and bringing it up to date with a narrative in the first person, in his short story *Daphné* (1926).

Though, like other well-known myths, the story of Daphne has inspired no first-rate works of literature, it still remains embedded in the collective memory of western culture. It has also enjoyed some periods of success: in the Middle Ages with their enthusiasm for allegory; during the Petrarchan and Neoplatonist Renaissance; and in the seventeenth century with its musical extravaganzas. Such magical tales certainly have some seductive qualities in their own right; but the interpretations based on them are more fascinating still. Three of these relating to Daphne seem to be of central importance:

(1) The belief that the myth represents of the tragedy of human existence in its pursuit of a good that always slips away. Ovid said: *Nitimur in vetitum semper cupimusque negata.* ('We strive for what is forbidden and always desire what we cannot have'). Similarly the Flemish mystic Ruysbroeck spoke of the irresistible human desire 'continually to strive to grasp the ungraspable'; while the bitter result of these attempts is described by Aragon with the words 'and when he thinks he is clasping his happiness, he destroys it . . .'

(2) The notion that the story is a 'parable' for the metamorphosis of desire. According to this theory, desire is represented as moving away from tangible, material forms, imperfect external beauty and the sensual attraction that it

arouses, and as focusing on an insubstantial, ideal essence, on absolute and perfect Beauty. As a consequence, it becomes spiritualized and sublimated, and is led from the earthly to the divine, from the contingent to the boundless (Petrarch, sonnets 227–9).

(3) Lastly, the idea that the myth presents an image of a form of artistic creation that transmutes what it takes hold of and for which the reward is eternal glory.

Yves Giraud

David, or the Journey

In a sense there was a *need* for a figure such as David. The Zohar suggests that he was planned from the very beginning. Adam, the first man, is supposed to have given up seventy years of his life so that David would have sufficient time for an existence equal to the seventy years foreseen for him. This shows that the need for David as a person was felt before he was born, but still tells us nothing about his nature.

The first thing to consider is the description of his emergence and the famous formula, 'Here is David'. To do this we need to have an idea of its context, at least in outline. The highly ambivalent Book of Judges ends with the remark, already made earlier: 'In those days there was no King in Israel; every man did what was right in his own eyes.' The subject of kingship is first mentioned – variously as being desirable, permitted, or forbidden – in the books of the Torah, or the Pentateuch. But it was only when some action started to be taken that its full implications were revealed.

When the prophet Samuel grew old, the people asked for a king, which displeased the prophet, who referred the matter to God. The Lord gave a very bleak answer: 'Hearken to the voice of the people in all that they say to you; for they have not rejected you, but they have rejected me from being king over them.' Since the exodus from Egypt this rejection had been constant. The Lord's kingship had been devalued in favour of substitutes and 'other gods'. In spite of being warned of what having a king would entail, the people insisted, and it was at that point that the figure of Saul dramatically emerged. It was to counterbalance the tragedy of Saul that David himself would arise in an attempt at reparation forming a complicated network of meanings that we shall try at least to sketch out. David soothed Saul's suffering in his madness by playing the lyre, and the strange relationship involving a mixture of love and hate was, in a sense, transferred from Saul onto David. As a result, the oil that the Lord had used to anoint Saul 'to be prince over his heritage' ceased to protect his fragile hold on kingship – itself essentially a fragile institution. The concept of divine kingship, which had been compromised by Saul's vulnerability, resurfaced in the strange, complex and fascinating personality of David.

From one point of view, the interest of the story of David as a mythological theme stems from the ambiguity of kingship and the fascination that it exercises over people. Sometimes the king is an idol, sometimes he has to be beheaded. Awareness of this ambiguity, which has already been mentioned in the context of Saul, is essential to understanding both the contradictory aspects of David's personality and his considerable significance as a 'pillar of history'. The central problem, which is returned to in I Samuel 10. 18 in particular, is always the same: God *himself* had brought Israel out of Egypt, delivering its sons 'from the hand of the Egyptians and from the hand of all the kingdoms that were oppressing' them. Yet here were the Israelites rejecting the very God who had helped them in 'all [their] calamities and . . . distresses', and asking for a king! When Saul came to power, he was inspired – momentarily – by 'the spirit of God'. But Samuel was not deceived. And after Saul's first victories over the Philistines the king committed his first offence: he took it upon himself to offer a burnt offering – a fatal initiative. Saul had not shown due humility, and Samuel warned him 'now your kingdom shall not continue. The situation went from bad to worse. Samuel was angry and 'cried to the Lord all night', but to no avail. The outcome became increasingly clear: Saul's kingship was finished.

As a consequence, the Lord ordered the prophet Samuel to seek the King's successor among the sons of Jesse. But it was not to be Eliab, or Abinadab, or Shammah, or any of the seven sons that Jesse presented to him. Their physical stature was not important: for 'man looks on the outward appearance, but the Lord looks on the heart'. Jesse had just one more son, the youngest, who was tending the sheep. Here again, we have the figure of the shepherd, an image deeply anchored in the heart of mankind which recurs throughout literary history. The young boy appeared: 'Arise, anoint him; for this is he.' Up to this point we are not even told his name. But if the Lord 'repented that he had made Saul king over Israel', the spirit of the Lord that descended on David did not cease to influence his actions from that day forward. The need for David was linked to the need to make repairs (Tikkun) to the ambiguous element in human kingship – a process that remained essentially incomplete, as we shall see. The relative perfection, or perfectibility, of David the shepherd was shown by his care for his sheep. It is said in the Haggadah that 'God chose himself a righteous man', for David inspected his whole flock. He tended each lamb according to its needs and size, and, as a shepherd, behaved towards his flock as Jacob had done towards his people. It was in connection with a lost ram that David came face to face with God, just as in the case of Moses before him. Since figures such as Jacob and Moses were also shepherds, the shepherd seems to have within him the potential to rehabilitate kingship and power.

And yet what richness there is in David's personality! He takes on power because it has been entrusted to him. He takes it on when confronted with a test that makes him worthy of it. Afflicted by madness, Saul wants to kill him and twice falls into David's hands. But, in spite of being urged by his men to take advantage of this, David refuses to do so. Instead, he tries to reason with Saul and show him by his deference and compassion that he still respects him as his symbolic Father, the anointed of the Lord – though, in fact, in the eyes of the Lord, Saul has forfeited this position.

David found favour with Saul, driving out the evil spirit that had taken possession of him by playing the lyre. But the confrontation between the two men soon became more violent and their rivalry more bitter. However, all the bitterness was on Saul's side, as he was the tragic figure, none was felt by David, who continued to respect Saul even after his death. In Oedipal terms Saul is a very dubious father, while David is a model son. Saul tried to dissuade David before his encounter with Goliath the Philistine, saying: 'You are not able to go against this Philistine to fight with him; for you are but a youth, and he has been a man of war from his youth.' David replied humbly but pragmatically:

> Your servant used to keep sheep for his father; and when there came a lion, or a bear, and took a lamb from the flock, I went after him and smote him and delivered it out of his mouth . . . Your servant has killed both lions and bears; and this uncircumcised Philistine shall be one among them, seeing he has defied the armies of the living God.

A clear theme is emerging, and it is spelt out by David when hecontronts Goliath: 'You come to me with a sword and with a spear and with a javelin; but I come to you in the name of the Lord of hosts, the God of the armies of Israel, whom you have defied.' We all know the outcome of their confrontation, but everything depended on David's *adherence* (DVeKuth, in Hebrew) to the values that underpinned and safeguarded his kingship. A son would be born to him who would be the builder of the Temple. But does this mean that David was pure and free of sin?

On the contrary, it is his extreme and fallible humanity that makes David such a powerful symbol and of such great interest to writers of all eras – even though at times he may seem almost superhuman, for example in his indulgence towards Saul, his potential murderer. In literary terms, the power of a theme lies in the very fact that it cannot *be stated* until the end. The source of what is said is what cannot be said. The Greek thematic concept, summarized in Parmenides' statement, 'what can be thought is at the same time that which gives rise to thought', stands in sharp contrast to the Jewish one. The latter places its emphasis on the fact that the source of all thought, God, whose name is beyond expression, cannot under any circumstances be comprehended or described. And, curiously, some similar notion comes to apply to David.

In the commentary on David's reign, which carries far more layers of implications than are suggested here, we find the following statements regarding three series of events:

- Something can be said about the events involving Reuben (maase Reuven), but the story cannot be translated.
- Something can be said about the events involving Tamar and Yehudah, and something can be conveyed in translation.

- The story of David cannot be said or translated.

Since it is not something that can be enunciated, David's story escapes any and every commentary. We know that on the one hand it involved David and Amnon, and on the other David's love for Bathsheba and what follows from it – the indirect, but premeditated, murder of Uriah. The commentary feebly says that Bathsheba had been destined for David from all time, and that he simply lacked patience. There was a precedent, a 'rehearsal' for this story in David's meeting with Abigail and the conveniently timed death of Nabal. He only had to wait! The Zohar provides us with an extraordinary dialogue between Satan and God. God turns a deaf ear when 'Douma' (Satan) asks for the sinner to be handed over to him. God pleads David's cause. Meanwhile the time of repentance and Pardon, and the poetry of the Psalms, intervene. 'We are born with the Psalms in our entrails', Chouraqui wrote in his first translation of them. The poetry of the Psalms wells up so naturally that again it cannot be said or expressed. The 'events involving David' (maase David), which can be neither enunciated nor translated and which are passed over in silence in the Haggadah, consist both of the absolute crime and the absolute love that wipes out that crime – provided that it really is love and is accompanied by the values inherent in love, awareness of one's wrongdoing, and repentance of it.

The episode concerned is more than just an episode: it occupies the central, pivotal place in David's journey through life. Considered in isolation, the 'maase David' merits the penalty of death, and the prophet Nathan came to remind David of this. David had despised the word of the Lord and misfortune would inevitably befall him. With great frankness David said to Nathan: 'I have sinned against the Lord', and Nathan replied, 'The Lord also has put away your sin.' But the child conceived in sin had to die. Nonetheless, David had proved to Bathsheba that he loved her by consoling her for the death of her husband; and he would console her again, in spite of his own sorrow, for the death of their child. And when their second son, Solomon, was finally born, the Bible says with overwhelming simplicity: 'And the Lord loved him.'

The central theme, which 'cannot be talked about', takes the form of a journey, the importance of which can never be exaggerated. David is *emergence, the man who is simultaneously overcome by and contained in his weaknesses*. He is a victorious warrior, but he will not be able to build the temple dedicated to the Lord precisely because he has waged war, even though that war was just. It is Solomon, his son, who will build the house of the Lord on the consecrated spot that is still today called the Mount of the House, Har Habait. David travels towards peace, but he wages war. David travels towards a single love, even if several women play a role in his life. Standing between Saul's daugher Michal, who is too proud, and cannot bear to see her husband, the king, dance before the Ark, and Abigail, who is too humble and ready to wash the feet of her royal consort, Bathsheba cuts a different, regal figure. When David is dying she safeguards the kingship of her son.

Nor should we forget Jonathan's overwhelming love for David. Jonathan was first struck by David's humility towards his own father, Saul: and 'the soul of Jonathan was knit to the soul of David, and he loved him as his own soul'. There can scarcely be a better definition of homophilia and this is what particularly struck the writer Coccioli. David, however, was touched by what he saw merely as innocent brotherly love, and the only ambiguous words spoken by him on this subject were uttered after Jonathan's death: 'your love to me was wonderful, passing the love of women'. Jonathan died along with Saul and his brothers, and the very manner of their deaths illustrated what it was about them that attracted death. David brought their names together in a single lament: 'Saul and Jonathan, beloved and lovely! In life and death they were not divided.' The bitter conflicts between Saul and Jonathan, and between Saul and David, had been erased, as had the ambiguity of the relationship between Jonathan and David. David was again travelling along his own road, the road of action and love, the road of unavoidable war and of peace, the peace alluded in the first name of his son Solomon, Chlomo – CHLoMO, based on the root *shalom*.

Later, when Solomon wrote the Song of Songs – and, in this context, it is irrelevant whether or not the work was just attributed to him – the same symbolism persisted. It is spelt out by his beloved in chapter 8, when she says, 'Might I be for Him the way towards peace'. Chlomoh (Solomon) finds in the CHuLaMit – based again on the same root – the essence of the peace to come. This peace would not have come to Solomon, the Prince of Peace, but for the journey followed by his father David, who was both belligerent and compassionate, the conqueror of the Philistines and the Jebusites, and, at the same time, a peacemaker.

David's end is a time of glory for Bathsheba, who safeguards both the royal heritage and the divine promise. David, 'advanced in years', was dying. Even the young maiden brought to warm him did not make him warm. She 'ministered to him; but the king knew her not'. What was at stake was who would succeed him, and 'Solomon sat upon the throne of David his father; and his kingdom was firmly established'.

The question that remains is how we should conclude this study. If we had started from the literary works and gone back to the sources, we would never have got anywhere. The source is so profuse, the text so inexhaustible, that all that we can do is point to the various paths that later writers and poets were to follow in drawing their inspiration from it, often basing their works on a partial and intuitive understanding of its significance. It is not possible to define biblical heroes totally; each contains an infinity of meaning which, to borrow Levinas's words, is always beyond the verse. The text of the Bible is absolute in itself, as J. L. Borges wrote. Its organic nature continually resists any attempts to break it up into fragments to facilitate its interpretation; but only refracted parts of it are found in works of literature. Nonetheless, its original incandescent qualities still give life to these imperfect perceptions of it. The very fact that it is incomplete, that biblical figures in general, and David in particular, are incomplete in such a human and heartbreaking way, provides an image of the actual creative process – at a human level, and perhaps, insofar as we can appreciate it, at a divine level too. According to Bergson the life force creates a gradually emergent meaning that lasts for an instant – the duration of a human life – and raises it above itself. The descent back into death and the finite nature of the story will never exhaust the sap that flows in it. This feeds the text and all other works that draw a certain perception of humanity from its fullness. Because of his contradictions and the courage with which he faces up to them, because of his sincerity and qualities of spirit and also because of his clear-sightedness, David, the man who travels through life and who was necessary from the very beginning, is a figure of whom 'nothing can be said' because we always say too much yet not enough.

NB With thanks to David Ben Ezra and Michaël Avital who helped me to locate the references to the Haggadah and the Talmud quickly.

E. Amado Levy-Valensi

The Dictator

The twentieth century is yet another age of dictatorships, the nature of which historians and students of politics will probably continue to debate for some time. Passing from crisis to revolution, and from revolutionary coup to counter-revolutionary reaction, the century since 1918 has been dominated by a constant extension of authoritarianism in politics. The establishment between the two World Wars of new authoritarian regimes in Europe, some revolutionary, some reactionary, but all 'totalitarian', marked only the beginning of an extremely widespread secular phenomenon. In *Les Dictateurs du XXe siècle* Conte lists no fewer than 132 dictatorships in a total of 169 states in the world in 1984. Thus the collapse of the fascist and Nazi regimes in 1945 by no means put an end to dictatorship. 'Totalitarianism' has continued to spread ever since, under a multiplicity of titles, in almost all countries, on every continent. In the process, the concept of dictatorship has been rehabilitated in the name of doctrines and ideologies of all sorts. Whether they have been met with admiration or censure, these political experiments have inevitably left their mark on the collective memory.

The meteoric careers of such people as Mussolini, Franco and Hitler in Europe, Stalin in the Soviet Union, Mao Tse-tung in China, Perón and Vargas in South America, or Sékou Touré and Idi Amin in Africa have created an impressive mythology. In these dark times violence rules the world. Picked out by destiny and bathed in a mysterious 'aura', new 'saviours' keep cropping up, motivated by a secret wish for godlike status. They are ready to withstand adversity, dominate chaos and save their people – or so they say. The concept of power has been reconsecrated. In the new political treatises dictatorship has become the ultimate explanation for the unfolding of events.

An immeasurable craving for power, the 'will to power' that Nietzsche predicted would arise in this century, seems to be at work everywhere. Dictators are the living incarnation of it. Like other idols and divine rulers, they have emerged – or claim to have emerged – from nothing to act out the obscure designs of a mysterious providence. Are we dealing with trickery? With irrational belief? With a distortion of the meaning of the sacred, as suggested in essays by Crossman ('The God of Darkness') and Lévy ('La Barbarie à visage humain')? It would be wrong to represent the history of totalitarian dictatorships merely as a commonplace process involving the personalization of power, or to see the dictatorships themselves just as political attempts at mystification. As we come to the end of the twentieth century, it is hard to measure the hold of the myth of the dictator and the prestige exerted by these totalitarian leaders at their hour of triumph. A growing number of historians and sociologists see these fascist, communist and totalitarian regimes as political manifestations of a veritable explosion of new materialist religions that are 'modern', 'profane' and 'secular'. The power of dictators rests on a mysterious act of faith. As a consequence, the dictator is a 'figure' with an indeterminate and extremely ambiguous mythical nature, standing on the boundary between the religious, the spiritual and the political domains. This figure exercises a great fascination for writers and the great historical dictators have been tremendously well served by literature. Such controversial personalities as Hitler and Stalin have inspired dozens of films, hundreds of books and thousands of written articles, pamphlets and lampoons. Whether hallowed or unhallowed, whether based on false mysteries and imposture or on a more banal footing, the figure of the dictator has the further quality of being exceptionally malleable. The question that springs to mind is how we should interpret the explosion of forms of mythical expression, some religious and mythological, others historical and political, yet others secular and mundane, inspired by this figure.

FICTIONAL REPRESENTATIONS OF RELIGIOUS DICTATORS

The links between dictatorship and religion are murky. We find a multiplicity of false prophets in literature, vying with God by breaking idols, restoring ancient cults, or founding new sects. As early as 1900, a posthumously published essay by Nietzsche entitled 'Der Wille zur Macht' heralded a tremendous shift in traditional values of which the contemporary onset of religious nihilism is perhaps a symptom. There are disturbing prophets in *The Plumed Serpent* by D. H. Lawrence, *A Dance to the Music of Time* by Anthony Powell and *Les Puissances des Ténèbres* by Anthony Burgess, to cite only a few works by English writers. Fascinated by the absolute and searching for a purer form of spirituality, these people experience life in an extraordinary way. They are manifestations of a higher divine principle, reincarnating forgotten, perhaps archetypal, deities who are often cruel. They are gods, or living myths, figures embodying the absolute and transcendent. Their words are oracles, their decisions the decrees of fate. In the context of Latin America, in Marquez's *Cien Años de soledad* and *El otono del patriarca*, Carpentier's *El recurso del metodo*, and Asturias's *El senor Presidente*, the 'will to power' is represented as a divine demand and dressed up in a deliberately fantastic and grandiose 'aura'. The reformers portrayed in these books must rebel against the Christian God in order to change the course of history and save the world. By contrast, in Kingsley Amis's *The Alteration* they only just manage to establish a theocracy in an imaginary England. Perhaps this vision of a messianic calling and the glorification of rebellion and pride convey a tragic need for damnation, as suggested by Camus's account in *La Chute*. In books ranging from Ernst

Jünger's *Auf den Marmorklippen* in Germany to Gracq's *Rivage des Syrtes* in France, lack of moderation leads only to catastrophe.

The same is true more recently of the 'messianic leaders' who feature in novels about Africa, such as Grainville's *Les Flamboyants* or Sony Lab'ou Tansi's *La Vie et Demie*. Thus the figure of the dictator can be camouflaged beneath countless mythological figures, both old and new. They may be totemic, as in Lawrence's *The Plumed Serpent*, classical and Celtic, as in C. S. Lewis's *That Hideous Strength*, Vedic, as in Julien Green's *Varouna*, or completely imaginary, as in Wyndham Lewis's *The Human Age*. The gods lose all individual identity. There is a single mystery, a single primordial, obscure, omnipotent deity who, according to Lawrence in *The Plumed Serpent*, had expressed his nature since the beginning of time through divinities as diverse as Thor, Teutatés, Wotan, Mithras, Quetzacoatl and Dionysus. Any worn-out myth, any forgotten symbol, any primitive religious tradition can play its part in evoking the birth and disappearance of an absolute authority. And perhaps even the camouflaged return of these gods may herald the death of God. The same writers denounce the apostles of these deities as dangerous seducers, eaten up by ambition and skilled at exploiting others. The degree to which they are identified with the deity varies, but the apparent divinity of these false prophets has always been usurped. Don Ramon Carrasco in Lawrence's *The Plumed Serpent* is also an 'Antichrist'. Thus the influence of the Christian tradition is always present, either within the mythological allusions themselves or outside them.

If the myths are all equivalent to one another and all interchangeable, they are also all inimical to Christianity. Thus this syncretist tendency raises another crucial point: mythical sanctity is independent of the Christian religion so that any attempt to idealize the 'will to power' is immediately negated. At most these portrayals of the figure of the dictator create the illusion, inadvertently or quite deliberately, that it belongs to a superhuman universe, outside the twentieth century and outside history.

FICTIONAL REPRESENTATIONS OF HISTORICAL DICTATORS

Historical and political representations of dictatorship seem to obscure its religious aspects. In this context, myth takes on a different role. The cult of power in Europe between the World Wars gave rise to veritable 'secular' religions in places where authoritarian regimes were in control. Dictators were living gods, new demiurges of history. An immense mythology of dictatorship was gruadually built up, and sociologists and political scientists including Caillois, Sauvy and Sabais strove to define the essence of its originality. It made authoritarian regimes seem to be a sacred inevitability in their contemporary political contexts, thereby sanctifying the 'fascist phenomenon', the preeminence of the 'Stalinist phenomenon' and, more recently, the explosion on every continent of what since 1930 to 1950 has been called the 'totalitarian phenomenon'. Fascism made an immediate impact on European literature. As early as 1922, D. H. Lawrence's novel *Aaron's Rod* described the seductive charms of Mussolini's rule in Italy. And subsequently, this first manifestation of the Fascist illusion also influenced the play *Le Dictateur* by the French dramatist Jules Romains and the novels *Point Counter Point* and *The autocracy of Mr Parham* by the English authors Aldous Huxley and H. G. Wells respectively. However, after 1933, this first fascist myth inspired by Mussolini was quickly eclipsed by the extraordinary popularity of the figure of Adolf Hitler and the 'Hitler myths'. They featured in thousands of books and personal accounts inspired by the Spanish Civil War and the Second World War, expressing views in favour of or against the 'brown god'. The discovery of the extermination camps in 1945 discredited Fascism and National Socialism for a while. However, despite general disapproval of Nazism, echoes of what Rosenberg in a controversial essay written in 1930 called 'The Myth of the Twentieth Century' have kept being heard since the 1960s. They are found in extremely disturbing books ranging from Grass's *Die Blechtrommel* in Germany and Rachline's *Bonheur Nazi ou la mort des autres* in France to Chessex's *L'Ogre* in Switzerland and Steiner's *The Portage to San Cristobal of A. H.* in England.

The spate of literary works reflecting the 'Stalinist phenomenon' was not interrupted in the same way. A whole generation of intellectuals known as 'fellow travellers', ranging from R. Wright to I. Silone, and including Brecht, Gide, Barbusse and Stephen Spender, succumbed to the fascination of the Russian Revolution during the 'pink decade' between 1920 and 1930. It seemed inevitable that the story started in 1917 would be finished. Virtually everywhere communist and pro-communist authors, and others with communist sympathies played a part in disseminating 'Soviet myths' and the hope of a universal, egalitarian revolution. Only after the Spanish Civil War in 1936 and the Moscow trials in 1937 did the first accounts by Soviet exiles, such as Serge, Koestler and Sperber, begin to reveal the hidden face of Stalinism. The 'dictatorship of the proletariat' was like any other dictatorship. Joseph Stalin, the 'red god', the 'demiurge of history', the 'leader of mankind', who embodied the miracle of a successful revolution was just another 'god of darkness'. Following the start of the process of de-Stalinization Pasternak's *Doctor Zhivago*, Solzhenitsyn's *The Gulag Archipelago* and Ginzburg's *Into the Whirlwind* brought confirmation 'from the inside', so to speak, of what the 'Stalinist phenomenon' and the 'cult of the personality' had really meant in the Soviet Union from 1924 to 1953.

It is worth considering whether Stalinism, Nazism and totalitarianism in general are just accidents of history. From Zamyatin's *We* to Doris Lessing's *Shikasta*, the prevalent feeling is that these successive transformations of the face of power only foreshadow terrifying things to come. The enslavement of the masses under even more absolute dictators who are accorded an equally divine status is made complete in George Orwell's *1984*, Anthony Burgess's

1985 and G. Dalos's *1985*. The figure of the dictator seems to become still more horrifying in literature set in the future – in all the 'utopias', 'atopias', 'dystopias' and 'cacatopias' based on Aldous Huxley's *Brave New World*. This book depicts the worst of all possible societies in a future that may already be here without us realizing it – as suggested in Le Clézio's *Les Géants*.

FICTIONAL REPRESENTATIONS OF SECULAR DICTATORS

Whatever we may think of it, authoritarianism is commonplace in everyday life and there is hardly a literary work that fails to touch on some aspect of it, in however tenuous a fashion. Works of literature ranging from *Adrienne Mesurat* by Julien Green to *The Ballad and the Source* by Rosamond Lehmann contain an abundance of dominant characters, who are quick to abuse some form of power over others, without having any political or religious pretext to justify their behaviour. The mythical manifestations of the 'will to power' seem to have vanished. However, these ordinary, secular representations of it may be more profoundly based on a layman's religious intuition, even if this may seem to be a contradiction in terms. When there is nothing to explain or excuse the domination exercised by one person over another, in whatever situation, the arbitrary has become absolute, and the superiority conferred on the dominant figure comes very close to that attributed to the gods. The legitimacy of the authority that is exercised is derived only from itself, and in the restricted circle of the community concerned the dictator is like an all-powerful god. These petty dictators are just anonymous deities. The sacred emphasis has shifted, but the dream at the heart of the myth persists, and the dictator figure keeps on recurring. Thus a great many novels, dramas and plays are actually no more than insistent, insidious myths stripped of their sacred connotations, continually telling the single, eternally repeated story of the petty dictator.

In some cases the true natures of the camouflaged mythological figures are clearly indicated. This is true in the case of *Moïra* by Julien Green and *Genitrix* by François Mauriac. On the other hand, the references in William Golding's *The Lord of the Flies* and Avril's *Les Gens de Misar* are less clear. And elsewhere there are none at all, as in Iris Murdoch's novels, the series of novels by Ivy Compton-Burnett and C. P. Snow, and the sagas by Anthony Powell, Jules Romain and Georges Duhamel. Perhaps these works discover – or rediscover – the unrecognized, unconscious sources of the desire for power. At any rate, they certainly describe commonplace, undisguised forms of this desire in every type of setting and in every kind of person, whether colourless and insignificant or individualistic and forceful. And, in the world that they depict, authoritarianism arises from the constant disturbances caused by emotions and impulses. Hatred gives rise to violence, and violence gives rise to hatred. The instinct to dominate is omnipresent, as is the will to submit, encouraged by the constant violation of the taboos that should contain or repress them. And if the 'sacred' is indeed that which is 'separate, forbidden and different', as opposed to what is 'secular, commonplace, permitted and normal', the continual crossing of sacred boundaries in the intimacy of the day-to-day existence of each and every individual may be the main crucible in which the 'will to power' and its most spectacular mythical expressions come into being. We should be under no illusion, as Bernanos's remarkable analysis of the subject in *M. Ouine* has shown: the relative colourlessness of the figure of the dictator, the unexpected nature of the ways in which he is represented and the impression of transparency given by some portrayals of acts of domination in no way mean that the myth of the dictator is withering away. The drive for power may have been inverted in some kind of way, so that it is seen inside out, but the archetype remains. And, for all we know, these secular forms of expression may touch on the essential mythical reality behind the concept of the dictator.

At what point do mythical representations of the figure of the dictator start and end in the context of contemporary literature? The subject is inexhaustible and the slightest attempt at analysis provokes more questions than it provides answers. Where does the reality of the myth reside in each individual work? Where does the figure of the dictator actually come to the surface in these various forms of literary enterprise, be they novels, short stories, chronicles, fables, parables, essays, narratives or eye-witness accounts? Where, in all these countless mythological, historical and secular portrayals of it, can the underlying features, the subconscious bases and the genuine manifestations of the myth be identified with certainty? Are its insidious, suppressed forms of expression always less meaningful that their showy, flamboyant counterparts? This tremendous literary output suggests the emergence of a new and original mythology, but, even so, are we actually dealing with 'literary myths'? Perhaps what we are really concerned with is a multiplicity of variants of religious and political myths that are infinitely more vast, as presented in literary works of various types. It therefore follows that literature is only the preferred medium for expressing, and perhaps investigating, the mythical concept of the dictator. In these literary works mentioned above this concept undergoes unceasing development through the processes of repetition, borrowing, allusion, amalgamation and contrast. Through their behaviour, the dictators, whether real or imaginary, seem to reincarnate in a primitive, primordial 'archetypal' figure: Eliade's 'dieu lieur', Dumézil's 'Souverain Terrible' or Jung's ' "mana" personality'. This implies that such a figure lies at the root of all the modern myths, which are thus based on a nucleus of archaic religious beliefs. Consequently, a whole area of contemporary literature seems simply to be a manifestation of a sort of very ancient mythical 'testament' concealed behind innumerable disguises.

Is the figure of the dictator universal and eternal? Western literature concentrates mainly on developments in Europe. In this context, Russia, the home of revolution in 1917, becomes a quite different land of darkness in 1924, and Germany between 1933 and 1945 is transformed into a place of terror, while, in 1945, Britain and the United States figure as the last bastions of freedom.

The forms of control exercised by one person over others are limitless, and the concept of omnipotence is not the same in Europe, Africa, Asia and Latin America, as the new works of literature emerging from the last three regions attest. The dissemination of the dictator figure through world literature has been on a vast scale, and one might question whether it is still worth trying to elucidate its mysteries now that it is so difficult to explore. Particularly in futuristic novels, writers are less concerned with the nature of the mythical basis of dictatorship than with its moral and metaphysical significance. What are dictatorships a sign of? Where is this intoxication with power leading to? What is its ultimate secret? There is no work that succeeds in answering these questions fully, but since 1945 literature has become apocalyptic. The myth is still active. 'Everyone is capable of anything, literally anything', Aldous Huxley reminds us in *Temps Futurs*. Human beings have acquired the power to destroy themselves, and the last and most powerful dictator will perhaps be the one who triggers a universal disaster, becoming, at the moment of the apocalypse, a sort of terrifying god of destruction. Our most recent causes for concern coincide with the apprehensions expressed in the most ancient myths; and, unless it implodes on itself, the figure of the dictator will inevitably continue to haunt our imagination.

Alain Vuillemin

Dionysus of the Ancients: the Indefinable One

Of all the gods of Olympus, Dionysus is the one whose essential nature is the hardest to define. Whether we examine his origins, the episodes of his childhood, his physical appearance, his character, his place in society, the symbolic use he has been put to over the course of history or the interpretations of the mythologists, he continually evades us. Rich, complex and fleeting, he is the god of metamorphoses, the indefinable.

ORIGINS: AN ANCIENT AND RECENT GOD

The impossibility of placing Dionysus in one particular setting becomes apparent as soon as one starts to study him. Research into his origins is disconcerting. And yet there is no doubt that Dionysus is a most ancient god. He is called Dendrites, tree god, and is even represented with branches springing from his chest. This links him to the oldest deities of vegetation and fertility, the ancient mother goddesses, such as the Greek Demeter: 'Everything that blesses Demeter also blesses Dionysus', states Callimachus (*Hymn to Demeter* 70) while Pindar calls him Demeter's companion (*Isthmian Odes* VII. 3–4). He is also linked to Cybele, as in Euripides' *Bacchae* (79); and these connections extend beyond Cybele: to the Syrian goddess Kubaba; to Zemelo, the Phrygian mother goddess, whose name is strangely like that of Semel, the mother of Dionysus; and to all the gods who were worshipped in Asia Minor, in Thrace, in the Aegean world and in Crete. In Athens, festivals of very ancient origins, – the Anthesteria, Apatouria and Oschophoria – were wholly or partially dedicated to him, and, in this context, Tiresias was right to speak of 'the traditions of our fathers from time immemorial' (*Bacchae* 201–2). It is thus very likely that the cult of Dionysus dates back to the pre-Hellenic period. That he was worshipped in the Mycenean period, in the middle of the second millenium BC, is proved by two tablets from Pylos inscribed in linear B, on which his name occurs in the genitive form, *diwonusoyo. The Bacchae* provides another indication of the antiquity of the god and his cult. Beneath the story of the death of Pentheus for impiety, we can glimpse a second layer of meaning, which may not have been apparent even to the playwright, but has been noted by mythologists and ethnologists. This refers to a ritual of human sacrifice and implies that the tragedy is based on a primitive rite.

But, despite all this, the historian Herodotus states that the name Dionysus was the last to be learned by the inhabitants of Greece (*The Histories* II. 52), while Pentheus calls him 'the new god' (*Bacchae* 219), as does the seer Tiresias (*Bacchae* 272). Dionysus was new because he was foreign. He was said to have come to Greece from Thrace or from Asia Minor, and ancient writers link his name to a magical country, which they located in widely differing places but always beyond the Greek world. These included Caucasia, India, Ethiopia, Arabia, Egypt and Libya. Many myths tell of the difficulties that were encountered in establishing the cult of Dionysus in Greece, and particularly in Boeotia, the home of the god's mother Semele, the daughter of Cadmus the founder of Thebes. Even later mythologists adopted this mistaken view and, until recently, most of them thought that Dionysus was a late-comer, an imported god.

This contradiction doubtless arises from the unique nature of the cult of Dionysus, involving possession, orgiastic rites and wild dashes through the mountains. As we shall see, these features made him a god apart, a god of the people rather than the aristocracy. Consequently, for a long period, he enjoyed less prestige than the other inhabitants of Olympus, scarcely appearing in the work of Homer, for example. Later, however, he exacted his revenge. The process seems to have been as follows: after the eighth century BC, the god underwent a kind of revival, a reawakening. The cult was spread by women, and religious currents from Phyrgia, Lydia, the islands and Thrace encouraged this renewal, putting new vigour into the cult's ancient forms and heightening its orgiastic aspect. The movement accelerated with the rise of Eastern cults in Athens towards the end of the fifth century BC. This external element explains the feeling, widespread among the Greeks, that Dionysus was a recent, foreign god. In any case, the history of his cult helps to emphasize what seems to be one of the god's fundamental characteristics: the indefinable nature of his personality.

A TURBULENT CHILDHOOD: BIRTH AND REBIRTH

The various childhoods of Dionysus all share the same quality of strangeness. He is a god who is always being born and dying, before escaping those who are hounding him and definitively establishing his authority. This is illustrated by the following accounts.

- On the malevolent advice of the jealous Hera, Semele asks her lover Zeus, the king of the gods and husband of Hera, to manifest himself to her in all the brilliance of his glory. Zeus has promised to grant Semele any wish and is thus obliged to appear to her accompanied by thunder and lighting. This kills the unfortunate Semele, who is six-months pregnant with the baby Dionysus, and Zeus therefore pulls the foetus from its mother's womb and encloses it in his thigh. When the full nine months are over, Zeus opens his thigh and little Dionysus is born, perfectly formed. This is the source of one of the etymologies of the latter's name: the twice-born god.

- At Zeus's command, the god Hermes gives the infant Dionysus to Athamas, king of Orchomenus, and his wife Ino. The child is dressed in girl's clothing so that the jealous Hera will not recognize him. But Zeus's wife is not decieved and strikes the foster parents with madness. Zeus then moves the child to Nysa and gives him to local nymphs, at which point he is said to have been changed into a kid. In Homer's account (*Iliad* VI. 130 ff) Nysa is replaced by the 'divine Nyseion'. This is generally taken to refer to a mountain in Thrace, where King Lycurgus ruled, though according to Jeanmaire, it might equally well refer to the country of the 'Nysai', the nymphs – in other words, fairyland. Lycurgus drives the child's nursemaids away and pricks them with his goad. The nursemaids throw down their thyrsi. The young Dionysus is terrified and dives into the sea, where he is taken in by Thetis.
- In the Cretan story of Dionysus-Zagreus, which is given in later texts but is in fact very old since the name Zagreus appeared in the sixth century BC in the *Alcmaeonid* and in the first half of the fifth century BC in Aeschylus's, *Sisyphus the Fugitive*, Dionysus is provided with different foster parents, the Curetes. However, while these inattentive carers dance around the child clashing their shells, the titans slip up to him unnoticed and lure him away with toys (knucklebones, a ball, a top, apples, a musical instrument, a mirror and a fleece). They then kill him and dismember him, before boiling the pieces in a pot (except for the heart, which is saved by Athene) and then roasting and eating them. But Zeus strikes the Titans with a thunderbolt and, using the heart which is still alive, revives the young god.

THE PROTEAN GOD

The appearance of a god whose origins were so hard to identify and who could cross the frontier between life and death with such apparent ease was evidently hard to define. Sculptors oscillated between three standard representations: that of a child, often in the arms of Hermes or of a satyr; that of an imposingly stocky, bearded adult (which was the most usual during the Archaic period); and that of an effeminate adolescent, making a graceful gesture with his arm (which became most frequent after the fourth century BC). Similarly, his worshippers were unsure what to call him: Dionysus, Bakchos, Bakcheus, Iakchos, Sabazios, Bromios, Zagreus and so on. Wentzel enumerates more than 130 names.

In the same way, it was difficult describe a god who spent his time in disguise or changing his shape. He was a lion when facing the giant Rhetus (Horace, *Odes* II. 19. 21–4), a goat when fleeing Typhon (Antoninus Liberalis, *Metamorphoses* 28; Ovid, *Metamorphoses* V. 329), a kid at Nysa (Apollodorus, *The Library* III. 4.3) and a lion and a bear in the presence of the terrified eyes of the Tyrrhenian pirates in the *Homeric Hymn*. He became a ghost and a bull when confronting Pentheus and a bull, a panther and a lion before the daughters of Minyas (Antonius Liberalis, *Metamorphoses* 10). He moves from one shape to another, becomes a ghost, a reflection or even two people, since the mirror in which the child looks at himself while the Titans are preparing to slit his throat has a symbolic significance. In the *Bacchae*, a tragic double of Dionysus gradually appears before the eyes of the spectators: like Dionysus, Pentheus is young and beardless; like him, he has fine blond hair. At the beginning of the play these similarities serve to highlight the contrasts betwen the two characters: Dionysus is effeminate and lets his blond curls float around his shoulders; Pentheus, on the other hand, as Jean Rous writes, 'wears his long hair plaited and wound around his head, in the manner of an aristocrat who practices sport and combat'. The king of Thebes is virile and scorns the foreigner with scented hair, whose eyes are filled with the charm of Aphrodite and whose appearance is effeminate (lines 235–6, 353); but to drive him more surely to his downfall, Dionysus changes Pentheus into a different version of himself. Yielding to his request to spy on the Baccants, he undoes his plaits, dresses him up as a woman, in a long pleated robe and the skin of a dappled fawn, and puts a thyrsus in his hand. In this new guise, Pentheus becomes deluded and imagines himself cradled in his mother's arms (lines 968–9), as the young Dionysus was cradled by his foster mother Ino when he was dressed as a girl. Pentheus's identification with the god signifies his downfall: in line 1192 the word *agreus* recalls Zagreus. The fate of Dionysus-Zagreus is the fate that is in store for Pentheus: death and dismemberment. But there is no resurrection. The ambiguous process of identification reaches a supreme ironic climax in the passage in which Agave imagines that she is carrying the head of a lion (one of the shapes most frequently adopted by the god) when in fact it is the head of her son (line 1173 ff). Once again, in this play about doubles, Dionysus emerges as the indefinable victor.

A COMPLEX PERSONALITY

In the stories of his childhood, Dionysus is presented as a fragile, defenceless creature. He flees in terror from the hatred of Hera and Lycurgus and is naive enough to fall into the Titan's trap. As an adult, on the other hand, it is he who ensnares the opinionated people who refuse to recognize his divine powers, and takes his revenge with the most appalling cruelty. Seized with mystical madness the daughters of Minyas, take Hippasus, the son of Leucippe who is one of their own number, and cut him to pieces thinking that he is a young fawn. Pentheus is hurled from the top of a pine tree and torn limb from limb by the Bacchants (including his aunts and his own mother Agave). And, as for Lycurgus, poets and writers of myth have competed to give the most ingenious description of his suffering. In Aeschylus's *Lykourgeia* Dionysus plunges him into madness so that he kills his son Dryas with an axe thinking that he is a vine stock. According to Hyginus he also kills his wife and tries to rape his mother, following which Dionysus exposes him on Mount Rhodope, where he is torn to pieces by panthers. According to Homer, Zeus blinds him, while in Apollodorous's version of the story, he is tied down and killed on Mount Pangaeus, and then eaten by horses. Finally, in the account given by Diodorus of Siculus, Dionysus puts his eyes out, tortures him at length and crucifies him.

But this bloody god who brings tragedy can also change into a god of comic tales. It was he who managed to bring Hephaesus back to Olympus to save Hera, who was stuck on the magic throne. He got him drunk, made him straddle a mule and led him back to the company of the Olympian gods, as shown in the scenes painted on the François Vase (early sixth century BC). The mule and, more particularly, the donkey are associated with the procession of Dionysus. The donkey carries either the god hmself or the round-paunched Silenus, staggering beneath the latter's weight. It is an ithyphallic animal, and paniers are sometimes hung from its genitals. An elderly satyr approaches it, ready to rape it. Here we are in the context of grand farce, of carnival. It is, therefore, not surprising to find Dionysus in Aristophanes' comedy *The Frogs* along with an allusion to the donkey (line 159). Throughout the first part of the play, the god is depicted as a cowardly buffoon, given to farting.

But the buffoon may also turn into a god in love. Dionysus was the lover of Ariadne, with whom, in the oldest versions of the myth, he was united in a sacred marriage – and, significantly, Ariadne herself was an ancient goddess of vegetation. In later versions, the hero Theseus is introduced into the story and Dionysus either acts as the comforter of Ariadne when Theseus abandons her on Naxos (a subject treated magnificently by Catullus in the digression in poem 64), or else takes on the role of an abandoned and jealous lover who has his unfaithful mistress killed by the arrows of Artemis (*Odyssey* XI. 325 ff).

However even in his loves, Dionysus remains indefinable. In a strange story, found in its most developed form in Clement of Alexandria's *Exhortation to the Greeks* (II. 34. 3–5), the heterosexual lover of Ariadne becomes the object of the homosexual attentions on Prosymnus. Dionysus obtains directions from Prosymnus to guide his descent into the underworld on condition that he will grant the latter his favours when he comes back. But when the god returns he finds that Prosymnus is dead. He therefore goes to Prosymnus's tomb, cuts a fig branch at random, shapes it into a male member and uses it to fulfill his promise to the dead man. According to Clement, it is to recall the mystery of this dead that phalluses are dedicated to Dionysus in the cities of the classical world.

Thus Dionysus is both a naive child and Machiavellian adult, both a cruel god and a buffoon, both heterosexual and homosexual; his personality is no easier to define than his physical appearance.

THE CULT OF DIONYSUS: OUTSIDE AND INSIDE THE CITY

A god such as Dionysus seems to have no place in the city: Séchan and Lévèque tell us that 'the basic element in the cult, which is both joyful and fierce, is the thiasus, in other words, a group of devotees of either sex who are independent of any civic or familial organization'. Judging from the iconography and the descriptions of it in Euripides all the features of the cult seem to be completely at variance with the rational organization of a state. The rites are held in the setting of the countryside, thickets and mountains (*oribasia*), and at night (*pannuchis*). The participants have their hair unkempt or crowned with ivy or laurel. Their 'chitons', or tunics, are often replaced by a fawn skin and they use snakes as belts. They hold the thyrsus in one hand and sometimes a small animal, a hare or young fawn, in the other, and occasionally have the skin of a young leopard hanging from their waists. The music is strange, played on dulcimers, castanets and flutes, and the ceremony itself has an erratic rhythm, involving violent, convulsive dances and wild chases. During the sacrifice animals are torn limb from limb and their flesh is eaten raw (*omophagia*). There were thiasuses of men, but the most famous and widespread were thiasuses of women, who were variously called Maenads, Baccants, Thyiades, Bassarids and other names. The wild behaviour of these women, who were usually cloistered in the women's quarters of their homes, helped to give the cult of Dionysus a unique position on the margins of the city's official ceremonies, whose conventions it shattered. In the same way, because the mysteries of Dionysus united men and women, citizens and slaves, they undermined the social hierarchy.

And yet Dionysus, the destroyer of the city's order, occupied a place of honour at Delphi, in the sanctuary of the most Greek of all gods, Apollo – as the Pythia recalls:

> I revere the nymphs who keep the Corycian rock's deep hollows, loving haunt of birds where the spirits drift and hover. And Great Dionysus rules the land. I never forget that day he marshalled his wild women in arms – he was all god, he ripped Pentheus down like a hare in the nets of doom.
>
> (Aeschylus, *Eumenides* 22–6)

Every year, during the three winter months, while Apollo was in retreat in the land of the Hyperboreans, Dionysus supplanted him. And every two years the Thyiades of Delphi and the Bacchants of Athens worshipped Semele's son by torchlight on the slopes of Mount Parnassus. His tomb was said to be in the adytum of Apollo's temple, and the poets sometimes even swapped the names and attributes of the two gods: 'Apollo of the ivy, bacchant and seer' cried Aeschylus in the *Bassarides*, while in *Likymnios* Euripides replied, 'Lord Bakchos, friend of the laurel, Paean Apollo of the fine lyre!' The Nietzschean contrast between the god of the harmonious mean and the god of wild drunkenness is thus far from reflecting the complete truth.

Dionysus was also at home in the city of Athens, being worshipped not only at festivals such as the Apatouria, the Anthesteria and the Oschophoria mentioned above, but at the rural Dionysia, the Lenea and above all the Great Dionysia, during which there were competitions for dithyrambs, tragedies and comedies, to which spectators flocked from all over Greece. Indeed, the word tragedy is generally interpreted as meaning the song of the goat (*tragou óde*), the animal sacrificed in honour of Dionysus. On the first day of the Great Dionysia, the statue of the god was taken to the centre of the theatrical *orchestra*, in other words to the very heart of the celebrating city, while during the competitions, the place of honour was reserved for his priest. Thus the marginal deity won his place among both men and gods: 'Dionysus is the equal of any of the gods!' (*Bacchae* 777).

At the very heart of Dionysian disorder there is a superior order, a *eukosmia*, or discipline (*Bacchae* 693). Pentheus, the young tyrant full of hubris, remained unaware of this, but it was recognized by the wise leaders of Athens. These leaders were more tolerant than the Roman senators who, in 186 BC, pitilessly suppressed participants in the Bacchanalia.

DIONYSUS IN THE SERVICE OF POLITICAL AND RELIGIOUS DOCTRINES: DIFFERENT USES

Multifaceted, complex, contradictory and protean, Dionysus was a highly malleable deity, ripe for exploitation by all kinds of political and religious thinkers. The oriental epic of Dionysus and that of Alexander had influenced each other reciprocally. Alexander himself and his soldiers and hsitorians were all familiar with the god's missionary journey to the East which Euripides makes Dionysus describe as follows:

> I left behind the gold-bearing acres of the Lydians and Phrygians, passed through the sun-beaten plains of the Persians, and Bactrian walled cities, and that windy land of the Medes, and prosperous Arabia, and all Asia which along the salt sea lies . . .
>
> (*Bacchae* 13 ff)

Alexander led his army in the very footsteps of Dionysus, and this provided a fine opportunity to place his expedition under the patronage of the god and to celebrate its leader as a 'new Dionysus' a title later adopted by the rulers of Alexandria. These associations were given particular relevance when the army came upon a place named Nysa, situated near Mount Meros (a homonym of the Greek word meaning 'thigh'), whose prince claimed to be the heir to colonizers installed by Dionysus himself. India is not mentioned in the account in the *Bacchae*, but after Alexander's exploits, Dionysus became the conqueror of India too. The theme of the Indian war, which was unknown to Euripides, became a popular subject for poets, painters and sculptors, attaining colossal dimensions in the fifth century AD in Nonnos's *Dionysiaca*. This is an epic in forty-eight books, of which books 13–40 are dedicated to the Indian adventure.

Despite the reservations of some recent commentators, it is possible that Caesar and Augustus may have made political use of the prestige of Dionysus, who was worshipped throughout the eastern part of the Roman empire and in Rome itself – both among the eastern Greek population of the city and by members of the Roman elite who had come to admire Greek culture. Dionysus had long been assimilated to Liber Pater, the god of Latium, and despite sometimes vigorous resistance to it, as in the case of the repression of 186 BC, his cult was widespread. This success cannot have been a matter of indifference to Roman politicians. Caesar 'was the first to bring the mysteries of Liber Pater to Rome', says Servius in his commentary on the following lines by Virgil: 'Daphnis? He was the first to succeed in harnessing a chariot with the tigers of Armenia, to introduce the thiasuses of Bacchus and to cover flexible shafts in soft leaves' (*Eclogues* V. 29–31). Behind the triumphs of Daphnis we can discern those of Dionysus, Alexander, and Caesar, whose heir Augustus considered himself to be.

This favourable policy towards Dionysus reached its highest expression in the second and third centuries AD, beginning with the reign of Hadrian, the philhellene emperor who called himself the 'new Dionysus' as Alexander and the Hellenistic rulers had done. It was promoted by Gallienus, who was fighting on two fronts, against both Barbarians and Christians, and wanted to return to the Greek tradition; and earlier, in a more unorthodox fashion, by Elagabalus (Heliogabalus) who drove a chariot harnessed with lions and tigers.

Philosophical and religious movements also exploited Dionysus. These included the Orphics, who laid particular emphasis on the myth of the god's murder by the Titans. As Marcel Detienne points out, 'the myth of Dionysus directly illustrated the principal teaching of Orpheus: that people should abstain from murder, in the two senses of not eating meat and putting an end to the killing of human beings'. In addition, Dionysus's resurrection recalled the doctrine of palingenesis taught by the disciples of Orpheus.

It is understandable too that Christian writers, such as Clement of Alexandria and Firmicus Maternus, concentrated their attacks on a myth that seemed to them to be a caricature of the beliefs and sacraments of their own religion. Common to both Christianity and the cult of Dionysus were the concepts of the passion and the resurrection: indeed Gregory of Nazianzus even used three hundred lines from the *Bacchae* in his *Christus Patiens*. Meanwhile, other shared elements included the eucharist and even the notion of original sin, since, according to Dio Chrysostomos (XXX. 55), human beings were born of the Titans' ashes mixed with earth and were thus associated both with the Titans' crime and with the divinity of Dionysus, who was eaten by the Titans. Christian attacks were all the fiercer because, through the medium of the myth, Orphism gave the cult of Dionysus the theology that it lacked: in the Dionysiac mysteries ritual practices were more important than dogma.

THE DIVERSITY OF INTERPRETATIONS

The figure of Dionysus is so complex and fluid that it is impossible to provide a single interpretation of it. The god was a focus of religious beliefs and practices from the third millenium BC until the collapse of the Roman Empire, and his image was constantly reshaped by various societies, rulers and peoples. The interpretations offered by scholars of mythology enable us to enrich our understanding of the deity, but cannot claim to give an exhaustive explanation of his nature. Thus all that we can do is to provide some pointers towards the most illuminating insights.

Despite the excesses occasionally perpetrated by scholars at the turn of the twentieth century, the interpretations of Dionysus offered by Frazer, Farnell and Miss Harrison have undoubtedly retained most of their validity. Dionysus is first and foremost a chthonian god of vegetation and fertility, and many of the ceremonies in his honour are rituals celebrating renewal. The emblems of this god of vegetation are the thyrsus, the branch and the reed; he is crowned with a wreath of ivy or vine leaves, or by a pine cone – all of which belong to plants that play an important part in both his rituals and myth, even if, after the seventh century BC, the god himself came to be associated primarily with the vine and wine. Dionysus is the lord of trees. He is linked, as we have seen, to the mother goddesses of the East and of the Aegean world. He marries Ariadne, who had the status of a human being in Classical times, but who had previously been an Aegean goddess of vegetation. He is the master of animal and human fertility, and his companions and animal associates – satyrs, goats, donkeys and bulls – are all endowed with impressive phalluses. He went down to the underworld to look for his mother Semele, and he presides over the Anthesteria, which include a feast of the dead. Zagreus is the son of Persephone and Zeus or Hades, and is sometimes even identified with Hades himself. This chthonian aspect of Dionysus was developed in the mysteries connected with his cult: the aim of the initiation rites, the purification rituals and learning of sacred phrases was to enable the initiates to escape from the dangers of the voyage into the other world after their death and to find happiness in Hades.

The phenomenon of drunkenness in Bacchic ritual, and the possession experienced by the Maenads have also inspired numerous psychological, psychological, psychoanalytical and ethnological commentaries. The ecstatic dances of the Bacchantes have been compared to the ritual dances of the whirling dervishes, the American Shakers, the Jewish Hasidim and Siberian shamans. It has been shown that such practices were widespread throughout almost the entire perimeter of the ancient Mediterranean and that they still exist in parts of Africa.

> In many features, the delirium of the Bacchantes, with convulsive, spasmodic movements, the bending of the body over backwards, the bending and shaking

> of the neck, recalls neuropathic ilnesses, well documented today, which involve a feeling of depersonalization, the invasion of the self by someone else.
>
> (Séchan and Lévêque 1966)

Psychoanalysts observe resemblances between the mechanisms at work in Dionysiac possession and certain concepts used in the psychoanalysis of children, and see a therapeutic quality in the rituals practised in the god's honour. We discussed Dionysus-Hades above, and now we have discovered a Dionysus-Asclepius.

An important insight is also provided by the theory of the scapegoat (*pharmakos*) popularized by Frazer and then by René Girard in his interpretation of the *Bacchae*. Euripides' tragedy is first presented as a bacchanalian ritual. Differences are swept away: old men, young people, women and slaves all join in the celebration. But then things turn nasty and violence erupts. Ordinary differences are supplanted by a reversal of roles: women start acting like warriors, men dress up as women. The animal and human worlds interpentrate each other: the Bacchantes tear a herd of cows limb from limb thinking that they are men, Pentheus harnesses a bull that he takes for Dionysus, Agave kills Pentheus whom she thinks is a lion. Pentheus, dressed as a woman, is a carnival prince, a temporary king, 'both a scapegoat bearing the wrongs of the past year and an expiatory victim offered to the new year' (Roux 1970: 17). The symbolism is underlined by the pine tree that Pentheus climbs dressed as a woman. Bather points out that 'in Russia, on the Thursday after Whitsunday, the villagers cut a young pine, dress it as a woman and bring it with rejoicing into the vilage: three days after, on Trinity Sunday, they drag it out and throw it into the water' (1894:250). At the end of the celebrations, the pine is uprooted, the king is killed and torn apart: Pentheus suffers dismemberment at the hands of his mother and aunts, themselves further scapegoats who will be expelled from the country. A new order is to reign in Thebes: Dionysus is 'the god of decisive mob action' (Girard 1977:134). However, as we have seen, Pentheus is a double of Dionysus. Like his adversary and reflection, the god too is subjected to dismemberment, in the myth of the Titans. There is also an identification between the uprooted pine and Dionysus Dendrites, the god of trees. In the ceremony of the scapegoat, the god who organizes the events in Euripides' play was perhaps once the victim.

Lastly, we should not forget the many similarities linking Dionysus to the *kouroi*, novices who have to go through initiatory ordeals. Pausanias (III. 24. 3) tells how Cadmus had Semele and the young Dionysus placed in a chest that was thrown into the sea and finally washed ashore at Brasiai (or Prasiai), a port in Laconia. Overcoming an ordeal entitles one to an exceptional destiny, as illustrated by the stories of Perseus, Moses and Romulus. Like the initiates of the highest three castes in ancient India (*dvija*), Dionysus was born twice. As in the case of Achilles, Heracles and Jason, who were brought up by a horse-man, the centaur Chiron, beast-men also featured in the childhood of Dionysus: goat-men, satyrs and sileni; Lycurgus, 'he who acts the wolf' (*lukos*, meaning wolf and *ergon* meaning acton); and Athamas, who is connected with wolves (Apollodorus, *The Library*. 9. 2). Like Achilles and the companions of Theseus, who were dressed as girls, like Theseus himself, whom the masons teased because of his robe and plaited hair, like Heracles who also wore female clothes and spun at Omphale's feet, Dionysus too dresses as a woman. Like Achilles, Melicertes, Heracles, Pelops and Jason, he has gone through the ordeal of the cauldron. Killed, dismembered and boiled, he has experienced resurrection: his is 'a myth of a clearly initiatory nature, explaining and interpreting the dangers facing children and adolescents and thus tied to the most ancient practices' (Jeanmaire 19. 5: 390). As in African initiation trials, the rhombus plays a part in this ordeal of death and resurrection. Like Pelops, whose homosexual affair with Poseidon bears disturbing similarities to the initiation rites of young Cretans, Dionysus is the hero of an adventure of an initiatory type aided by the mysterious Prosymnus. Like Odysseus, Heracles, Orpheus, Theseus, Aeneas and Jason, he goes down to hell – though Jason's descent takes a purely symbolic form. Like Theseus and Gilgamesh he dives into the sea – indeed, he does so twice, once to escape Lycurgus and once to look for his mother in Hades. All these ordeals are initiatory trials, necessary rites of passage to enable the adolescent to leave the world of his childhood and be accepted into the company of adults.

Thus, despite the efforts of critics to proved an exhaustive definition of the personality of Dionysus that takes account of all his complexity and diversity, the god still eludes us; he shatters the definitions with which we seek to enchain him. He will remain indefinable to the end, and we can conclude only by quoting some lines of poetry that stress what is perhaps his fundamental characteristic, his nature as a 'loosener' or 'untier' (Eleuthereus, Luaios, Lusios):

> But him the fetters held not, and the withes fell far from his hands and feet.
> (*Homeric Hymn to Dionysus* I. 13–14)

> 'But how were you set free, after your encounter with that unholy man?'
> 'Myself I rescued myself, easily, without effort.'
> 'But did he not tie your hands in captive knots?'
> 'This was just the ignominy I did him, that he thought he was binding me,
> but neither touched nor laid hands on me but fed on empty hopes.'
> (*Bacchae* 613–617)

Alain Moreau

Dionysus: the Development of the Literary Myth

The prevalent image of Dionysus left by the ancient Greeks is of a young god – often an adolescent, sometimes almost a child – and, perhaps for this reason, his name has been seen as a Phrygian equivalent of the Greek Dioskouros, boy of Zeus. In fact, it seems more plausible to derive it from Nysa, the name of the god's nurse and homeland, but this is of little consequence. What really matters is that both these interpretations endow the god with foreign origins; yet we know these to be mythical since the discovery of Mycenaean archives attesting to the very early establishment of his cult in Greece.

The question that thus arises is why Dionysus should have been represented as a foreign deity. This may have been partly because it was important that he should be seen a 'god who comes'; but it was primarily to provide a fictitious explanation of his strange and disturbing nature.

THE BIRTHS AND REBIRTHS OF DIONYSUS

Dionysus's mother Semele, was a mortal woman loved by Zeus, who died as a victim of Hera's jealousy: when, at the latter's suggestions, she asked her divine lover to appear to her in all his glory, his thunder and lightning struck her dead. Zeus then took from her womb the child that she had conceived with him, and sewed it into his thigh, where it finished its period of gestation. Dionysus thus went through two births and his cult bears the traces of this tradition. This is particularly apparent in the rite of the *liknites* (child in the cradle), during which women called and searched for the infant god who disappeared every year to reappear the next.

The Passion of Dionysus

The myths of Dionysus's childhood and wanderings present him as a persecuted god: he is cut to pieces, cooked and eaten by the Titans, though Demeter brings him back to life; the vengeful Hera strikes his first nurse, Semele's sister Ino, with madness; and pirates abduct the child to sell him. In the *Iliad* (VI. 128–40), Homer recounts a dramatic story in which Lycurgus pursues Dionysus and his nursemaids the nymphs, armed with a murderous axe, and the terrified child throws himself into the sea, where he is taken in by Thetis.

The passion of Dionysus, who suffers and dies, but is always reborn, is symbolic of the annual process of renewal undergone by plants. Thus it is no coincidence that the four great Dionysian festivals all took place between the end of December and the beginning of April, the winter solstice and the start of spring.

Ivy and Vine

The legend of Dionysus illustrates his links with other plant gods: Cybele and Rhea, two manifestations of the great Earth Mother, who save him from Hera; the rustic nymphs who surround him; Ariadne, the Minoan goddess of vegetation, whose lover he is; and, above all, Demeter, to whom he is linked by the mysteries of Eleusis and whom Pinder regards as his companion. According to Euripides the name Bacchus comes from *bacchos*, meaning 'branch', and as Bacchus, the god who is 'ploutodotes' (the giver of riches), Dionysus gives plants vigour and growth. Among his many vegetal attributes most important are the ivy, which forms his crown, and the vine, which is his gift.

In the myths relating to the god, these plants both have a salvational role: an ivy saves Semele's child from the lightning of Zeus; intertwined tendrils of ivy and vine suddenly encircle the mast of the pirate ship, frightening the abducting pirates; and a hounded nymph suddenly turns into a vine stock and suffocates Lycurgus. Yet the contrast between the two plants – the coldness and sterility of the ivy, and the warmth and generosity of the vine – casts the god in an ambiguous light.

Finally, Dionysus was the god of wine, and it was wine that symbolized his presence at festivals. In the Lenaea (January–February) new wine was offered to the deity, who was represented by a mask decorated with branches. According to Euripides (*Baccae* 280–1) the lot of Dionysus, the *polygethes* (joyful), is 'laughing as the flute plays and putting an end to cares'.

Fertility and Fecundity

Yet this god, who is a friend of the nymphs and feels at home with Thetis at the bottom of the sea, whose statue is ritually immersed in water at Halae, and who enters Athens on a chariot in the form of a ship, has too many affinities with water, the universal element of fertility, for his powers or fecundity to be confined to plants. This is clearly demonstrated by the composition of his retinue, which includes donkeys, goats and bulls, which are often portrayed as ithyphallic, as well as satyrs and sileni, whose lubricity counterpoints the chastity of the maenads. Meanwhile, during the festival of the Anthesteria (February-March), Dionysus himself guaranteed the city of Athens a fertile year through his carnal union with the Basilinna.

Phalloria provide another example of the exaltation of virility in the god's cult, but it was Dionysus's role to present a complete image of fertility, both masculine and feminine. He was thus surrounded by women in his myths and in his cult. Aeschylus calls him 'the effeminate', alluding to his juvenile appearance and his frequent practice of wearing a woman's robe. Some authors and artists make him an androgyne, and the very ambiguity of his sex recalls the sexuality of that ideally fertile being, the hermaphrodite. Baudelaire went so far as to portray the thyrsus – the long stick decorated with leaves that was brandished by the god's worshippers – as symbolizing a combination of the two sexes: the male element was represented by the straight line of the shafts, the female by the sinuosity of the branches ('Le Thyrse', *Petits poèmes en prose*).

Yet while Dionysus is certainly *polygethes* and *ploutodotes*, to reduce him to this role is to neglect the nocturnal side of his power, for he is also the one whom Homer calls *mainomenos* (the mad), a god who upsets, and, indeed, overturns, the order of things.

THE DERANGED GOD

Sensuality and Cruelty

In *The Birth of Tragedy*, Nietzsche links the words sensuality and cruelty to form a definition of Dionysiac religion, and they do, indeed, represent the two facets of drunkenness and of the god's magic. Dionysus can make milk, honey and wine flow to increase human prosperity, but he can also use the same powers to cause anguish. Thus, when he punishes the daughters of Minyas for having refused to leave their husbands and follow him, he makes milk and wine flow from the ceiling of their room to terrify them.

Those women who follow Dionysus become Maenads or Bacchantes. Rendered invulnerable by the effects of 'mania' or divine possession, they are endowed with extraordinary strength and filled with a murderous delusion that drives them to tear apart young beasts that they have themselves suckled, and sometimes even their own children. The bacchic *orgia* (rite) unfolds in three stages. The first is the *oribasia*, during which women run wildly through the mountains. The second is the *diasparagmos*, or sacrifice by tearing limb from limb, which is illustrated in Euripides' *Baccae* (405 BC by the murder of Pentheus by his mother Agave:

> But she, discharging foam from her mouth and rolling her eyes all round, her mind not as it should be, was possessed by the Bacchic god . . . Grasping his left arm below the elbow and setting her foot against the unhappy man's ribs, she tore his shoulder out, not by her normal strength, but the god gave a special ease to her hands'.
>
> (*Bacchae* 1121–9)

Finally, the third stage is the *omophagia*, during which the flesh that has just been torn apart is devoured raw and barely dead.

This ritual cruelty is also reflected in the cult of Dionysus: women are flagellated in Arcadia, while the Boetia they are pursued by the priest of Dionysus armed with a sword; and, as a substitute for a human victim, a young calf with buskins on its hooves, representing a child, is burnt to death in the god's honour.

Thus through the medium of *mania*, Dionysus makes his followers undergo the same cruelty to which he himself fell victim, when he was chased by Lycurgus, and torn apart and eaten by the Titans. This perhaps explains the sensuality that accompanies the cruelty of the Baccants: while satisfying their darker instincts they can relive the passion of the god who possesses them.

Between Life and Death: Contradictions

The ambivalence of Dionysian drunkenness, which may bring joy or frenzy, life or death, is reflected in the animals that form part of the god's retinue: on the one hand, there are the goat, the donkey and the bull, representing fertility; on the other, the lion, the lynx and the panther, representing murderous ferocity. This paradox is also symbolized by what Nietzsche calls the 'mortally silent din' (*Dithyrambs of Dionysyus*) of a god who is called Bromios (the roaring one) and whose companions play thunderous music with tambourines, flutes and cymbals to encourage the Maenads' convulsive dance, but who can also impose a silence that leaves the same Maenads petrified.

Even Dionysus's origins are rooted in this contradiction, since his birth itself was marked by the meeting of life and death. This perhaps explains the importance of the dead in the god's myth and cult. Horace recounts the story of how he went down to hell to seek his mother, while in Aristophanes' parody *The Frogs* (405 BC), he is portrayed as looking for Euripides. The third day of the Anthesteria, the Chystres, was sacred to the dead, who returned to haunt the living, and Dionysus's affinities with death allowed Heraclitus to assimilate him to Hades, who was also portrayed as a dispenser of wealth (Plouton).

The different versions of the story of the love affair between Dionysus and Ariadne also bear witness to this oscillation between life and death: sometimes Dionysus is seen as Ariadne's comforter after Theseus has abandoned her, sometimes, as in Homer's *Odyssey* (XI. 325), as a jealous lover, who sends his mistress to her death through the agency of Artemis.

The contradictions of the Dionysiac religion and, above all, its irrepressible cruelty, made it hard for it to find an accepted place within any conventional political system and explain the cult's subversive role in Greek society.

Undermining the Social and Political Order

The depiction of Dionysus as a foreign god, worshipped during his actual epiphanies, creates a sense of exoticism that seems to reflect the strangeness of a deity without a fixed abode, whose cult is chiefly celebrated in undesignated settings rather than temples. Similarly the thissus, the gathering of worshippers on which the Dionysiac religion was based, deliberately eschewed social conventions, including men and women, rich and poor, citizens, metics and slaves without distinction.

In addition, Dionysus himself displayed a feminine, subversive, nocturnal form of power that was the antithesis of the diurnal, organized, masculine power of Apollo. This god, who tears women away from their looms to chase them through the mountains, clearly challenges the stability of the family and hence the political order. The process of disruption reaches a climax in the Bacchae, when the social and then the political dislocation of Thebes is crowned by the collapse of the palace, the symbol of royal power.

The very order of human values was undermined by the fact that Dionysus, the only god to be born of a mortal woman, remained close to human beings and allowed them to assimilate themselves to him. Unlike the cults of all the other Greek gods, the Dionysian religion broke down the barrier between the human and the divine.

Thus, in ancient Greece, the cult of Dionysyus had a cathartic function: it temporarily delivered people from their civic traditions and at the same time freed them of their cruel instincts. When it was imported to Rome the *orgia* degenerated into a licentious festival and was banned. Rome honoured Bacchus more in art than in religious observance, stressing his image as the god of wine and as the joyful musician of the bacchanalia. It was this blander image of the god that became dear to European painters of the Classical period and that predominated until his rediscovery by the philosophers and poets of the late nineteenth century and the twentieth century.

MODERN APPROACHES TO DIONYSUS: THEATRE AND DRUNKENNESS

Nietzsche: *The Birth of Tragedy*

As already mentioned, during blending of the wine at the Lenaea, the presence of Dionysus was symbolized by a mask. Meanwhile, it was also through the god's magic that the theatrical mask was given life. Greek theatre began with the invocation of Dionysus: it was to him that the chorus in the dithyramb competition addressed itself, and it was he who inspired the poets who entered the drama competitions held during the rural Dionysia (December–January), the Lenaea and above all the Greater Dionysia (March–April). On the seats of the theatre, as in the thiasus, the different sexes and social classes were able to mingle, at least in theory; while, on stage, the imaginary triumphed over reality, and madness reigned.

Rather than comedy or satyrical drama, it was tragedy that consecrated the Dionysian spirit. In *The Birth of Tragedy* (1872), Nietzsche emphasized the correspondences between the genre of Greek tragedy and the cult of the god. Underlying all the dramatic portrayals there is a metamorphosis, a sort of enchantment, that recalls Dionysian possession. The tragic chorus, which is both a spectator amidst the action and at the same time its hero, is a symbol of the crowd preyed upon by Dionysus. And, finally, tragedy brings the same forgetfulness of the past, the same deliverance, the same catharsis as Bacchic drunkenness.

Following the tradition according to which the word tragedy comes from *tragos*, the Greek for 'goat' – an animal sacred to Dionysus which was supposed to have been sacrificed before dramatic competitions – Nietzsche accepted the theory that the passion of Dionysus himself was the first subject portrayed in tragic drama. In any case, it is clear that the cruelty inherent in Greek tragedy is the same as that to which the god inspires the Bacchantes. Madness, murder and the tearing apart of bodies are all represented – or recounted – on the tragic stage, as in the myth of Dionysus himself.

Nietzsche concluded his work by announcing a rebirth of tragedy, which, he argued, had been diverted from its Dionysian aim by the influence of Aristotelian theory. And, later, Artaud called for the same renewal of theatre in his manifesto *The Theatre and its Double* (1938). Without naming Dionysus, this argues that tragedy should return to its original source of inspiration: cruelty. Freed of its psychological deviations it should become metaphysical once more, acting like a plague and bringing a liberating catharsis. To Artaud, the theatre is an evil, because it represents the supreme balance, which cannot be attained without destruction. It invites the spirit to partake in a delirium that exalts the energies. This latter idea is particularly suggestive of Bacchic *mania*; but Artaud preferred to refer to Balinese theatre, seeing Dionysian delirium as an anarchic force, rather than a calculated one.

Nevertheless, for Artaud, the theatre is politically subversive: in showing the dark and hidden power of groups of people, drama is undoubtedly Dionysian; it is nocturnal and dangerous like a bacchanalian orgy.

Bacchic Delirium and Contemporary Poetry

All of Nietzsche's works invoke Dionysus, and to use his own words, it was a 'Dionysian demon' that he glorified in *Thus Spoke Zarathustra* (1885). In addition to making numerous allusions to the god's attributes (honey and wine, the donkey, lion and snake), the poem chiefly exalts two aspects of Dionysiac: dancing and a form of drunkenness that manifests itself in laughter.

> Lift up your hearts, my brothers, high! higher! And do not forget your legs! Lift up your legs, too, you fine dancers: and better still, stand on your heads!
>
> . . .
>
> This laughter's crown, this rose-wreath crown: to you, my brothers, do I throw this crown! I have canonized laughter; you Higher Men, *learn* – to laugh!
>
> (Nietzsche 1961: 305 and 306)

It is noticeable that Nietzsche is more enthusiastic about the abolition of barriers between the human and the divine which makes possible the existence of 'higher men', than about those between human beings themselves, even though the latter is equally fundamental to the cult of Dionysus.

In this respect, the evocation of 'holy drunkenness' given, before Nietzsche, by Rimbaud in 'Matinée d'ivresse' (*Illuminations*, 1872–3) is quite different. Rimbaud retains an emphasis on the ambivalent qualities of Bacchic delirium, the meeting of pleasure and pain: 'Terrible fanfare in which I do not stumble! Fairy rack! Hurrah for extraordinary work and the marvellous body . . .' Pain involves a promise of sanctity; although Dionysus is not named, the theme of a drunkenness that is painful, but that brings salvation, is inspired by him: 'Oh we who are now so worthy of these tortures! Let us fervently gather up this superhuman promise . . . this promise! This madness!' The 'superhuman promise' may be that of enthusiasm, of identification with the god. As in a bacchanaliam ceremony, children, slaves and virgins all join in the nocturnal rite, the 'wake'. Meanwhile, the poem's last words, 'This is the time of Murderers' perhaps link the heralded 'madness' and 'violence' to the bloody cruelty of the Bacchantes themselves.

In 'Les Muses', the first of his *Cinq grandes odes* (1908), Claudel updates the ancient image of the delirious maenad, adapting the syncopated rhythm of his verse to her convulsive dance:

> A drunkenness like that of red wine and a heap of roses! of the grape that spurts beneath the foot, of great flowers all sticky with honey!
>
> The Maenad maddened by the drum! to the piercing cry of the fife, the Bacchante stiffens in the thundering god.
>
> All burning, dying, languishing!

The Bacchant's ecstasy is described in terms that recall the dying ecstasy of Semele, since 'the thundering god' refers to Zeus and the last verse alludes to the convergence of sexual desire and death. Semele was said to have been seized by an irresistible urge to dance when she was pregnant, and here Claudel presents a vision of her as the first Maenad, a victim of Dionysus even before he was born.

But for Claudel the musical element in the Bacchic frenzy also symbolizes poetic inspiration: 'Oh, I am drunk! oh, I am given up to the god! I hear a voice within me and the beat growing faster'.

Poet and text are taken over, possessed by the divine force ('La Muse qui est la Grâce').

Finally, the concept of possession is extended, and viewed on the scale of the 'whole world of things', by Saint-John Perse. In *Vents* (1946), he sees it, and those subjected to it, as among the great subversive forces that are sweeping away the worn-out conventions and institutions of the twentieth century:

> Unforeseeable men. Men assaulted by the god. Men fed on new wine and seemingly pierced by lightning.
>
> Our salvation is with them in wisdom and intemperance.

Assimilated to lightning, as in Claude's work, *mania* here retains its original ambiguity, reflected in the linking of the opposed concepts of wisdom and intemperance. This is because the Dionysiac religion represents both destruction and balance: while it may lead to anarchy, it is not anarchic in itself, as Artaud believed. Instead, it is governed by what Rimbaud calls a 'method' which may correspond to the three stages of the *orgia*. However, in this context, balance does not mean stability, nor serenity; on the contrary, the Dionysiac religion represents a balance only to the extent that it is the necessary counterweight to the moderation of the 'normal' world, to Apollonian order.

Conclusion

'Do not be too confident that sovereignty is what rules men,' the seer Tiresias says to Pentheus, 'nor, if you hold an opinion, but your judgement is sick, take that opinion for good sense' (*Bacchae*, 310–2). So the wisdom of a king who refuses to give madness its rightful place is illusory. 'Those who live without madness are not as wise as they think', wrote La Rochefoucauld. The paradox of wise insanity does not, however, imply that the needs of madness can be satisfied by a few festivals, a few temporary outbursts. True wisdom consists in knowing that madness and cruelty are inevitable. True insanity would involve turning the cult of this god who breaks the norms into an accepted institution and systematically revering those he possesses, whom Nietzsche calls 'supermen'. The result would be a dictatorship that would lead to the total denial of Bacchic freedom and to the death of Dionysus himself – an outcome that we have perhaps already experienced.

Ann-Déborah Lévy

Discoveries

A belief in the existence of an unknown land lying beyond the supposed limits of the accessible world has formed a constant theme in the mythical and philosophical works of the imagination. Thus pioneering navigators and their biographers quite naturally associated the great journeys of discovery with famous early texts such as the *Odyssey*, the *Argonautica* and the *Aeneid*.

In ancient times, it was thought that the world was basically bounded by two main barriers. The first was the great ocean that was thought to girdle the earth; and the second, in the context of the Mediterranean area, was the Pillars of Heracles, which Heracles had built between Spain and Africa and which he alone had been authorized to pass beyond, sailing in the 'goblet of Helius' on his way to the island of Erytheia to seize the cattle of Geryon. Beyond the ocean that could not be crossed, lay Thule, variously located in the extreme West or the far North and marking the end of all land. In his *Geography*, Ptolemy described three 'known' continents, and a fourth constituting 'terra incognita' which formed a mysterious uncharted area on all representations of the world until the fifteenth century AD. Gradually ancient place names were applied to newly discovered locations; the Islands of the Blest were confused with the Canaries, and later the historian Oviedo (1535) identified the Hesperides and Atlantis with the New World, which was called America from 1507 onwards.

During the Renaissance the limits of the known world expanded in both geographical and cultural terms. This expansion was accompanied by an increase in scientific knowledge, but also by an extension of the scope of mythology, so that late Renaissance Italian mythographers were able to draw additional inspiration from mythological traditions of China and pre-Columbian America. The enlargement of the known world around the small circle of the Mediterranean was still represented in a symbolic circular form. Indeed, it was his vision of this shape that inspired the voyage of Christopher Columbus, for it was to map out an ideal spherical world that he travelled west. When he crossed the boundaries of the ancient world his aim was not to discover a different world, but to explore the continuation of a single world, the two ends of which met somewhere in the great ocean.

TYPOLOGY OF THE NEW WORLD

Ever since the composition of the *Odyssey* the crossing of the seas has represented a symbolic adventure which is characterized by a whole nexus of attributes that still determine the structures of most modern literary works dealing with real or imaginary journeys.

The Topic of Navigation

This consists of four great themes, and hinges on two great symbolic concepts that were accorded extensive study at the time of the Renaissance: the 'ship of the sun' and the 'journey of the soul'. The four mythical themes are: the figure of the hero as a discoverer, inventor or conqueror; the hubris that drives men to seek out the unknown; the role of Fortune or Nemesis in this quest; and the seach for gold, which is used symbolically to encapsulate the various objectives of the journey.

The figure of the hero is fundamental: every great navigator is compared more or less explicitly to the mythical first navigator, Tiphys, the helmsman of the *Argo*, to whom Athena revealed the art of navigating a sailing ship and who showed the others the way. The present-day captain combines the functions of helmsman and pilot, hero and conqueror, discoverer and inventor. The novelty of what he reveals to the world through the voice of the poet is twofold: it lies in the novelty of the discoveries themselves – new lands and new empires; but it also lies in the opening up of new routes, new paths, a new space for the imagination. Meanwhile, poets who celebrate discoveries are implicitly assimilated to Orpheus, the bard who travelled with the Argonauts. In the resultant epic, the fame of the hero is not personal; it is used to establish the image of a nation chosen by the gods: it was the destiny of the Ligurian (Colombus) and the Lusitanian (Vasco da Gama) to raise their countries to the status Athens and Rome. Just as in the age of Augustus the Roman Empire saw Aeneas as its founder, so too the royal dynasty of Portugal would pride itself on an empire founded by its navigators.

In ancient times the ability to invent was regarded as an attribute of gods or heroes raising mankind to a superhuman status and was often portrayed as being accompanied by pride. As a result, because the navigator was consciously revealing 'the secrets of nature', he was often compared to the great hubristic figures of ancient mythology such as Prometheus, Icarus and Phaethon (*Lusiads* IV. 94–104). The audacity of the first person who dared to 'put a sail hoisted on a plank into the sea' was a challenge to the gods. Similarly the urge to answer the call of the unknown, and the spirit of conquest that goes with it, are always condemned in epics in a speech put into the mouth of an old man, who deplores the misfortunes and deaths brought about by the excessive boldness of the navigators.

Fortune, traditionally depicted on her ship, is the motivating force in these poems. She determines the fate of the heroes, leading them through the 'accidents' and dangers of discovery to an often tragic end; for whether he is celebrated or unknown in his native country, the hero–discoverer is cursed – like Prometheus; or like Tiphys, who died before the end of the voyage of the *Argo*; or like Columbus who was brought back to Spain in chains and in disgrace. In the epic, Fortune often takes the form of rivalry between two gods, with Aphrodite ranged against Poseidon, Athena or Bacchus.

It is also an aspect of Fortune that presides over the supreme discovery, representing the actual objective or the figurative apotheosis of an expedition: the discovery of gold. The symbolism of gold is very powerful in tales of navigation. From the search for the Golden Fleece to the search for the Land of Gold (Eldorado), the pursuit of the unknown has been seen as a descent into the depths, into the buried secrets of the mines, because it involves bringing into the light what was previously invisible. Following the symbolism of alchemy, it provides an image of Knowledge (the philosopher's gold), and represents a return to a primitive Golden Age (the Foutain of Youth). Thus imaginary journeys to the South Pole, the Southern Land that remained a mystery for much longer than the Far East, were often portrayed as passing through the centre of the earth, the mythical crucible where gold was produced.

There is an allegorical tradition that represents the journey of the sun, 'which governs the universe', by means of a ship carrying the stars; while the symbol of the 'ship of the world' is used to enrich some allegorical works in which life is portrayed as a 'perilous sea' and a 'journey of the soul'. A 'morality play' by Lope de Vega entitled *El Viaje del alma* (1604) has the Soul as one of its characters. As it is about to set out with Memory and Will towards the celestial Jerusalem, the Soul is at first led astray by the demon sailor, who promises it 'the New World', the 'great riches of the Indies' and 'the islands of gold'. However, thanks to the intervention of Reason, it leaves the boat bound for perdition and boards the Ship of Penitence with Christ at its helm.

Allegory of the New World

Because the rising sun had positive, fruitful connotations, the West, conversely, was linked with images of night and death, in a tradition that persisted until the period of the great sea voyages. Ancient writers located the entrance to the underworld there, while the Islands of the Blest were the dwelling-place of the most fortunate of the dead heroes, or the realm of Persephone. In the Middle Ages, an Irish Christian epic entitled *St Brendan's Voyage* described a quest for earthly Paradise that included a crossing of the Ocean and a visit to the island of Hell. The West is thus the domain of Night, the Other World, and poems celebrating discoveries always allude to it in a doubly symbolic way, in terms of a return to the night of time. In 1620 Tassoni made a draft of a Columbian Odyssey entitled *Oceano*, in which he portrayed as the domain of the 'king of darkness' who summoned up storms to defend the inviolability of his kingdom. For others, including Columbus himself, in his own writings, the New World was the celestial Jerusalem, or earthly paradise finally regained.

It was a new region that had emerged from the domain of Chaos represented by the pre-Colombian gods (Claudel, *Le Livre de Christophe Colomb*). Atlantis had resurfaced complete with traces of pre-Christian civilizations that were destined to be forgotten once the Sun of Christ had exposed their deficiencies. At the same time, it was also regarded as the Empire of the Sun, the place where the mythical Sun was most vehemently worshipped, for details of the religious practices of the Incas and Aztecs, started to emerge from the beginning of the sixteenth century onwards through the works of Las Casas and Sahagun. And, finally, it was the place where Thomas More and Tommaso Campanella (*La città del Sole*) located their Utopias. From this New World, which was universally described as an enchanted garden, a *locus amoenus*, came the myth of the 'noble savage' representing Adam before the Fall. The subject was first tackled by Montaigne and remained popular until the end of the eighteen century.

In *La Vérité des Fables* (1648) Desmartes adopts a synthetic approach to this allegory, conbining it with the themes of the ship of the sun and the search for gold. His work describes the 'marvellous journey' of Prince Apollo, who travels to the New World on the floating island of Delos. There he explores the Rivers of Silver, the virgin forests, and there Lands of Gold, before founding an empire. In this euhemeristic, parodic interpretation of the myth, its relation to reality is turned upside down: the hero is no longer compared to a god; instead the gods are merely deified heroes.

MYTH AND EPIC: *THE LUSIADS*

Discoveries were primarily a subject for epic poetry, since the great captain, who is also an inventor, has the status of a hero. *The Lusiads* (1572) by the Portuguese writer Luis de Camoens is an updating of the *Aeneid*, and in it the deification of the hero is justified in accordance with the euhemeristic tradition by the argument that the old gods of the pagans were 'only simple human beings whom their genius and valour had rendered divine' (IX. 89–93). As strange and wonderful events were a literary convention in epic, pagan myths and Christian miracles overlap and are blended together, while, ironically, it is real events that engender the mythical tale. Vasco da Gama himself recounts the story of his own adventures, as Odysseus did to Alcinous, and can thus make a distinction between truth and falsehood:

> Do you believe that Aeneas, or eloquent Ulysses travelled as far? Is there anyone, however many lines may have been written in his praise, who has dared travel over the eighth part of what I have seen on the ocean deep? . . . However perfectly the poets may write these lying tales which show such imagination, the truth I tell, simple and unadorned, is greater than any pompous fiction.
>
> (V. 86–9)

Vasco da Gama discovers not a new world, but a new navigation route and

Camoens turns this triumphant figure into a Heraclean hero, associating his mission to bring Asia under Portuguese influence with the Labours of Heracles. Portugal, predestined by its geographical position on the limits of the Old World to open up new horizons, is portrayed in the guise of a new Rome, a mythical land destined to dominate the world. It is the poet's role to glorify the hero and the chosen nation, as Virgil did in the case of Aeneas and Rome, and with this in mind, Camoens uses conventional mythical themes to help to transform the voyage into an epic.

Camoens uses onomastics as the basis for the deification of his heroes. Thus the Lusitanians are the descendants of Lusus, the mythical companion of Bacchus during his conquest of India (an allusion to Nonnos of Panopolis, *Dionysiaca*). Moreover the rivers Indus and Ganges appear to their king in a dream as an omen of their destiny. The Lusitanians are regarded as rivals by Bacchus because they threaten his glory by actually *enacting* his epic adventure, but, like Aeneas, they are protected by Venus. When visiting the island of Love on his way home, the hero da Gama marries the sea, Thetis, and is thus assimilated with Apollo. On this floating island, which now allegorically symbolizes Glory (IX. 89) rather than Fortune, the goddess reveals the future destiny of the Lusitanians by showing the hero 'the great machine of the world' in the form of a map on two crystal hemispheres.

However, as an epic poem based on the Christian faith, the *Lusiads* always turns myths into allegories, making the false gods subject to the True God, just as the pagan world is subject to the chosen country. Venus is sometimes assimilated with the Virgin who protects sailors, 'she who calms the storms', and sometimes with Providence, a Christianized version of Nemesis. Similarly, Bacchus personifies the devil, who tries to impede the progress of the Christian heroes. Finally, the passage relating to the revelation of the map of the world on the island of Love includes Thetis's account of how the Gospel was taken to India and of the miracles worked by the apostle Thomas.

HISTORY AND TRAGEDY

Seen from the point of view of the New World, Discovery is Conquest: an act of violence, a human sacrifice offered up by the conquering 'hero'. Thus the play by the Mexican writer Carlos Fuentes *Todos los gatos son pardos* (1970) opens with a quotation from Brecht: 'Unhappy the land that needs heroes!' According to the author's own analysis of the play in his preface, it is a 'ritual' representing the meeting of two symbolic forces: Montezuma, 'the power of fatality', and Cortés, 'the power of the will' – in other words, tragedy and history. The new race born from the meeting of these opposing forces and represented by the 'first Mexican', the child of Cortés and the Indian woman Marina, 'joins the two spheres together', uniting the two worlds and transforming them into 'destiny'. In the context of the tragedy Montezuma is identified with his god Quetzalcoatl, in the sense that human history has taken over from myth: 'the very day when the cyclical time for the return of the god had been foretold, the plumed serpent drew back, its identity was usurped by men, by new cruel, rapacious, violent men.'

CHRISTOPHER COLUMBUS

In heroic terms, Columbus is not a Conqueror, but rather a Discoverer, subject to an inexorable fate. He himself is torn by contradictions, but his role is essentially predestined. Thus the epic treatment of his character in works such as Stigliani's *Mondo nuovo* (1628) which follows Tasso's *Gerusalemme librerata* in portraying him as a new Crusader by assimilating the New World to a new Jerusalem, has been criticized by other poets, such as Alessandro Tasoni. For Tassoni, Columbus's adventures are more akin to the 'wanderings of Ulysses' than the military feats of the *Iliad*, and he describes the hero as the 'tamer of the Ocean'. In most of the works written in praise of him, Columbus's name is endowed with cosmological associations. Tasso sees him as the 'rival of the sun' who 'measures the circle of the Universe', even if the Eulogy spoken by fortune aboard her ship also describes him as 'worthy of poems and fables', like Bacchus and Heracles (*Gerusaleme Liberata*, XV. 30–32). As a second Tiphys, Columbus is the archetypal Discoverer, and his status as a Christian hero adds a theological dimension to this role. His name can be interpreted as doubly predestining him for his mission: Christopher meaning the bearer of Christ, and Columbus, the dove, the messenger of God. 'I have guided the dove [colomba] of the Spirit of God to places where it had never previously flown' wrote G.-B. Marino ('Christoforo Colombo', *La Galeria*).

This onomastic approach also underlies Claudel's 'musical mystery play', *Le Livre de Christophe Colomb* (1927) in which the dove has a double role as a prophet and a redeemer in the first context, 'it is the dove, symbol of the Holy Spirit, that crosses the sea and delivers its vibrant message into the hands of a child in Genoa'; while, in the second, 'death approaches and the dove at last escapes as in the days of the Flood and brings a twig picked in the world that has newly emerged from the breast of the Pantocrator, and lays it down' (Foreword, 1935 edition). Claudel sees Columbus as having a mystical vocation: 'for you the New World as been the donor to the Eternal World!' (II. 7: 'Au paradis de l'Idée'). Meanwhile, the element of predestination contained in his name again makes him archetypal: 'this took place not just in time, but in Eternity. For it is not he alone but all men who hear the call of the Other World and that far shore which God's grace may enable us to reach' (I. 2: 'Priére').

In his *Book of Prophecies*, Columbus himself argued that his exploits were predestined, quoting both the biblical Prophets and these lines from Seneca:

> A time will come in the final years of the world when the Ocean will unloose

> the bonds holding things together. A huge land will be revealed, and a second Tiphys will discover a new world. And Thule will no longer be at the ends of the earth.
>
> (*Medea 375–80)*

The glorification of Columbus in the sixteenth century was due as much to the belief that he had realized this prophecy as to the significance of his actual discoveries. Moreover, at the end of that century his status was amplified in a slightly bizarre way as a result of the interpretation of his role presented by the philosopher Giordano Bruno. The latter introduced a third element into the analogy equating Columbus with Tiphys: that of the Philosopher. If Columbus is greater than Tiphys, Bruno muses, 'what place should be accorded to a person who has discovered the means of rising to the heavens, widening the sphere of the stars, stepping beyond the limits of the Universe?' (*Cena de le Ceneri* Dialogue I, 1584). Bruno is regarded as the first philosopher to have grasped the infinite nature of the Universe, and thus it is himself that he is comparing to the Discoverer. His intellectual exploration had enabled him to push back the limits not of the terrestrial world, but of the celestial one, and, with a daring comparable to that of the navigators, to pass beyond the bounds supposedly formed by the 'fixed stars', whose existence even Copernicus had not dared to question. A few years later a new Discoverer would emerge, who would again fulfil this prophetic vision; the discoverer of the skies, Galileo.

GALILEO, THE REVEALER OF THE SKIES

Galileo's contemporaries honoured him as a hero, according his discoveries – particularly the telescope – the status of modern day myths. Their glorification of him was based on the analogy made by Giordano Bruno, which thus provided a new eulogistic theme. After comparing Galileo to Tiphys and Columbus, G.-B. Marino concludes his sonnet with the following lines:

> But greater than both of them you have dared to explore the secret, inaccessible fields of the World of the Stars. And gaining access into these unknown areas you have found in the heart of that world new spheres, new stars and new systems.
>
> ('Galileo Galilei', *La Galeria*)

In Canto X of his long poem *Adone*, Marino puts the same prophetic eulogy into the mouth of Mercury, developing it at length and focusing on the mythical status on the telescope. Galileo is seen as a 'new Endymion' for he can 'gaze at the moon in her nakedness', and the poet claims for the telescope the right to a place among the constellations, alongside the vessel *Argo*. Thus astronomical observation became an accepted analogy for the journey to the Other World, which the ancient imagination had located on the earth itself. As a result, Galileo, even more than Columbus, was a 'rival of the sun'. By inventing a means of 'rising to the heavens', other than simply through the imagination, he had emulated the main properties of the Sun, its ability to see everything and travel everywhere. However, Galileo's exploits differed from those of the navigators in one notable respect, on which the writers of panegyrics laid considerable emphasis: his discovery of the skies involved 'no risk, no war', so that the astronomer was not guilty of temerity. As a consequence he was not a true 'hero' (Brecht, *Leben des Galilei*), but the embodiment of a new form of modernity that would give rise to a future culture based on peace and not on feats of war.

Françoise Graziani

The Dogon Myth of Creation

The Dogon people are for the most part farmers. Today they live in lands on the border between Mali and Burkina-Faso, but they originally came from Mande, where the Malinke empire and the Keita dynasty were established in the thirteenth century. Their migration, between the tenth and thirteenth centuries, was due to their refusal to convert to Islam.

A certain cultural unity can be observed among the peoples of West Africa who have settled along the course of the Niger. The sorcerer-musicians all recount the same myth of the creation of the world by a single god, who then delegated his powers to spirits, whom he charged with organizing the universe and setting down the bases for human society. The texts relating to this myth are recited in *sigui*, the ritual language taught to the dignitaries of the Society of Masks, when they are ordained during the ceremony of the Sigui, enacted every sixty years.

Two versions of the myth have been recorded.

FIRST VERSION

In 1948 Griaules' book *Dieu d'eau: entretiens avec Ogotemmeli* provided a record of the account given by an old, blind Dogon hunter, whose version of the story established a direct link between the cosmogony and the appearance of the first human skills, such as pottery, weaving, agriculture and ironworking.

Amma, the divine creator, made the sun from a white hot pot, around which a spiral of red copper was wound eight times. The moon was made in the same way, but is heated only by quarters and its copper is white. The god made the earth in the same way as he had the stars, fashioning it from a roll of clay, which he threw into space. As it opened out, the substance took on the shape of a woman's body, with an anthill as the genitals and a termite hill as the clitoris. But the god was lonely and wanted to mate with the earth. To do this he had to 'knock down' the termite hill. The product of this first rape was a single creature, the jackal, instead of the intended twins. However, a clitoridectomy performed on the 'earth-woman' purified the blighted union and twins were then born. These were two spirits, called Nommo (or Nummo), who set in motion the regular cycle of the birth of twins, which represents ideal unity. They were androgyne creatures, and half-man, half-reptile, conceived in the womb of the earth. As the two homogeneous products of the God they carry the vital force of the world, which is assimilated to water and to the divine word, the chief organizing principle.

The earth was 'naked and speechless', and the Nommo pair was instructed by the god to carry it to him in the twisted fibres of celestial plants. This clothing of the earth was the first act of universal ordering. But the jackal, the God's disappointed eldest son, introduced disorder into Creation: he wanted to possess speech and put his hand on the clothing of his mother the earth, which contained it. He was thus guilty of the first act of incest, and achieved only the 'first speech', which was incomplete and still inarticulate, but which he was later to use to speak to seers through the medium of the divining table.

Also linked to this incestuous act was the appearance of menstrual blood, sign of the impurity of the earth, from whom the god then turned away, creating other living beings directly. Thus he fashioned the first human couple, providing both the man and woman with two souls of different sexes, to retain the principle of twin birth. Their eight descendants, who were to be the ancestors of the Dogon people, were regenerated by the Nommo pair in the earth's womb (the anthill) and themselves changed into Nommo.

As the number seven, the sum of femininity and masculinity, is the perfect number, the seventh ancestor was made aware of a clearer form of speech, which was destined for all human beings. He thus surpassed the God's wicked son the jackal, who had only the power of first speech, and bestowed the power of second speech upon mankind, using the ant, an avatar of the earth, as an intermediary. He 'wove' this speech in cotton threads, crossing and uncrossing them with his teeth, just as the Great Nommo had done. The ant, which had accumulated a store of cotton fibres, then spun them, pulling the threads before the humans as the spirit had done, thereby divulging words, which the people repeated.

Thus the seventh ancestor passed on his powers of speech using a technique that demonstrated the necessity for a harmonious interplay between material acts and spiritual forces.

After being changed into Nommo, the eight ancestors went back up to heaven, whence they later came down to bring all the things that were useful to human beings and necessary to the development of civilization.

Their descent was the result of the breaking of a prohibition: they did not follow their instructions to live separately, each feeding on one of the eight seeds given to them by Amma. As a consequence, they became impure and had to leave the heavenly regions. To come down to earth they were given a large woven basket, which was inverted, so that its bottom formed a square roof or 'terrace' and its upper opening a circular base. This basket symbolized the entire system of the world, whose monitors they were to be. The base of the edifice represented the sun, while its square terrace recalled the sky, with a circle in its centre representing the moon; and inside were four stairways oriented towards the four cardinal points and each supporting a category of beings linked to the constellations. The whole structure was designed to resemble an anthill with eight compartments, each containing one of the eight grains given by the God and recalling the eight organs of the first Nommo. The ancestors' basket is called the 'grain store of the master of the pure earth', and the image of the system and functioning of the world that it represented was to provide the model for all earthly grain stores.

The human beings in this primordial grain store were the Bozo, the earliest inhabitants of the Niger region.

The first of the eight ancestors was also the first smith, who escaped down a rainbow after stealing fire from the Great Nommo's heavenly smithy, using a curved stick called the 'thief's stick'. He gave iron to humans in the form of a hoe, thus signalling the beginning of agriculture. It was he, too, who marked out the first field: a square with sides 80 cubits long, divided into eighty sets of eighty one-cubit squares, which were shared out among the eight families descended from the first ancestors. He purified the soil, which had been contaminated by the sinful behaviour of the jackal, by setting the heavenly torch to it. From then on all agricultural work would lessen the earth's impurity. This was the civilizing contribution of the smith ancestor.

Since he had given up some of his powers to impart them to the soil, the ancestor depleted his own vital energy, and this explains the social status of smiths. They are men apart, who do not cultivate the earth and have to practise their craft to retrieve the force that has passed into it.

On a symbolic level, the smith's hammer is the webbed hand of the water spirit, the male Great Nommo of the sky, while the anvil represents his female. When the hammer strikes the anvil, the couple mate.

The wife of the smith ancestor had her own role, as the first potter, and the mat on which she worked was that of the first human couple. In kneading the clay she imitated the work of the god.

Once the first ancestor had come down to earth, the others followed, the most notable being the ancestors of shoemakers and of the sorcerer-musicians. However at this point an important incident occurred: the eighth ancestor broke the order of precedence and came down before the seventh, who was the master of speech. The latter was very angry and arrived on earth in the form of a great snake, which rushed to the grain store to take the seeds. The smith ancestor then advised men to kill the snake, eat it and give him the head. He then dug a hole and buried the head, covering it with the seat that he used when beating iron. This is why, today, people say that the smith sits on the snake's head.

At this point, there were eight families living on earth, descended from the eight ancestors, and the oldest person, Lebe, belonged to the eighth family. Before mankind could learn the third speech, the form that was articulate, complete and definitive, Lebe had to 'die' and pass into the same world as the Nommo seventh ancestor, who had the power of this speech. When the sound of the first forge was heard, the seventh ancestor took the shape of a spirit that was half human and half reptile and 'swam' to Lebe's tomb. There it swallowed him, revived him in its womb and transformed his bones into *dougue* stones, which are called wedding stones. In the process, it took what was good from the old speech and inserted it into the eight stones that would later be carried by the totemic priests. These stones recall the eight grains in the heavenly grain store, and that men eat the victim each year at the time of the great sacrifice in honour of Lebe represents the seventh *nommo* ancestor and Lebe combined, thus marking the indissoluble link between human and heavenly nature. When Lebe was sacrificed, the Nommo also spat out his nails in the form of cowries: eight for the hands and eight for the feet. This is why, when trade was invented, cowries were always counted in eights (eight times ten fingers times eight).

To pass the third speech on to human beings, the seventh *nommo* made the first drum by a technique similar to weaving, using his fingers to manipulate strings that formed the war and weft. Then, using his tongue, he threaded through the strings a kind of chain made from a thin band of copper and bent into a helix. At the same time he talked about a new type of speech, while the copper conducted the sound. The drum was destined to bind human beings to the *nommo* and teach them the 'complete, clear and profound' speech of modern times. Thus each head of the eight families then in existence made a drum appropriate to his group, according to the specifications of the seventh Nommo.

Since the mythical revelation of speech was linked to weaving, clothing has great importance to the Dogon: 'to be naked' and 'to be speechless' are equivalent expressions. Similarly, because, in symbolic terms, clothing represents the seventh Nommo himself, to dress oneself means to cover oneself with his words. Speech is the supreme fertilizing element: it comes from the liver, which is the most prestigious organ, situated in the most secret part of the human anatomy, which the officiator alone may eat at the time of sacrifices.

When this revelation occurred, death did not exist; at the ends of their physical lives, people changed into Nommo spirits and continued their earthly existences in the form of a large snake. The appearance of death was linked to the breaking of a prohibition by an ancestor. Although he had changed into a snake he addressed human beings in their third speech when he should have used the first speech, which was the language reserved for spirts. In so doing, he cut himself off from the superhuman world and, as he could not return to the world of men either, he died. His spiritual elements were released and found shelter in the child born by a pregnant woman. This ancestor's death formed the prelude to human death, and with it came the obligation to provide all the dead who followed with a home for their freed spiritual forces. This is the origin of funeral rites and of the institution of the 'Great Mask', an ambulatory rite called 'Sigui', which takes place every sixty years in memory of the first death.

SECOND VERSION

Le Renard pâle by Marcel Griaule and Germaine Dieterlen which was published in 1956, gives a rather different version of the Dogon myth, particularly as regards the creation of the world.

In the beginning was the primordial Egg, which is called 'Amma's Egg', after Amma, the divine creator who gave the first impulse to the existence of things. This egg is compared to a termite hill and divided into four parts called 'Amma's collar bones', which prefigure the four elements. The centre of the egg, called 'Amma's Seat', is the original womb and placenta where all beings are formed, and it has a spiral shape, connoting vital force and the inner movement of life. It was with his 'speech' that Amma formed and fertilized the original placenta.

Before creating the world, Amma imagined it and drew it in space using 266 signs, collectively called 'invisible Amma'. These comprised two signs for Amma himself and 264 others, divided into twenty-two categories of twelve, which summed up his thought and were later to be associated with the sharing out of totems.

The first thing to be created was the *sene* (acacia) seed, formed simply by the superimposition of the four elements. However, Amma was not pleased with his work and returned to it, this time stirring the four elements together. The result was the *po* (fonio) seed, in which he placed his seven words. The number seven encapsulates the principle of twinhood, which is the image of perfection. The god thus created eight seeds, with the haricot bean seed, called 'Amma's food', forms the symbol of fertility.

Amma's labour of creation is associated with a spinning movement, and it this 'dance' of god that the mask-wearer reproduces.

The second stage of Creation involved the appearance of the first animate creatures. The original calabash-shaped placenta split in two, signifying the division of time into night and day, as well as the sun and the moon, and the fundamental duality of human beings. This led to the birth of the silurid called 'Nommo anagonno', which is double, in the image of completeness and future fecundity, and is thus immortal like its creator. The god gave it eyes, the four corners of which represent oriented space and it thus forms 'Amma's eye', overseeing the workings of the universe.

Amma then went on to multiply his creatures. His aim was to create four mixed pairs of twins who, by a process of successive doublings, were to give birth to beings as perfect as themselves, but this undertaking was blocked by the action of the fourth Nommo, Ogo. Impatient for his female 'twin' and wanting to penetrate Amma's secret, Ogo emerged prematurely from the placenta, tearing a piece from it, which became 'Ogo's Ark.' In addition, he also stole the first seed. Amma intervened in this 'disorder' and made the earth from the piece of placenta, whereupon Ogo decided to fertilize it to make himself the equal of the god. However, in penetrating it, he mated with his mother, thereby performing the first act of incest. This had serious results, and only incomplete beings were born from their union. After this failure, Ogo wanted to return to heaven, but Amma ordered the second Nommo to transform the stolen placenta into a burning fire: this was the sun, which is called *nay* ('four'), recalling the placenta's femininity. At this point, Ogo thought he could take possession of the universe. He stole the eight male seeds that had also been created by Amma and hid them in a second ark, before redescending to earth and piercing a hole in the primordial egg, which Amma made into the moon. Amma instructed the ant to recover the seeds and the second Nommo to crush the piece of placenta, because, as it rotted, it was introducing the seeds of destruction and death into creation. As a punishment, Amma circumcised Ogo, cut out his tongue and turned him into a fox, *yurugu*. Deprived of speech, Ogo could communicate with human beings only with his paws, leaving their prints on the divining table. He remained the permanent agent of disorder in the universe and his ark, made of impure earth, is the symbol of the uncultivated bush, which was henceforth his domain.

To purify the world of the results of the fourth Nommo's rebellion and to be able to return to his creative work, Amma sacrificed the third Nommo, from whom he took back the 'seats of speech' with which he had endowed him. At the time of the sacrifice, he also removed the victim's 'four body souls', adding to them 'four sex souls'. Creatures formed after this were to have different sexes and no longer to be androgynous, with the result that sexual intercourse would be necessary for procreation. In addition, he took out the Nommo's teeth, using them to preserve articulate speech in the form of eight little pearls or wedding stones matching the original eight seeds. Then he extracted the sperm containing male and female water, and the image of the two silurids, which formed the first couple, prefiguring man in the foetal state. Lastly, he removed the Nommo's eight principal organs and divided his body into sixty pieces, which he made into seven piles, from which there arose a constellation of seven stars. He then made the pieces into four piles, which he threw in the direction of the four cardinal points in order to purify space.

After sacrificing the third Nommo, Amma revived him in the form of a mixed pair of human twins, shaped in the very centre of the original placenta. These twins received eight souls (four body souls and four sex souls), as well as Amma's vital force and the eight seeds from the collar-bones. This second creation was carried out in five stages, corresponding to the Dogon week of five days.

From the blood of the sacrificial victim came the stars and planets, whose movement bears witness to the reorganization of the universe; the stars that came from Amma's breast are called 'the Nommo's adornments'.

The male water from the sacrificed Nommo's penis fell to earth as the rain that forms the freshwater channels, while the female water formed the seas.

The revived Nommo pair then became monitors of the universe and fathers of mankind, guarding people's spiritual elements, dispensing rain and controlling water in general. After descending to earth, they returned to their original silurid form and took up their abode in the water to reveal speech to human beings. The twenty-two joints in their bodies correspond to the twenty-two categories of Amma's thought in the primordial egg.

Amma then returned to his work of creation and, using the substance of the original placenta, he shaped within himself the eight first ancestors of humanity (belonging to the second mythical generation), who formed four couples, the 'sons' of the sacrificed Nommo. Each couple was associated with one of the fundamental elements: Amma Sèrou and his female twin, Amma's witness, with the air; Lebe Serou, the witness to Amma's message, with the earth; Binou Serou with water; and Dyongou Serou, Ogo's witness, with fire. In addition, they were also associated with the eight seeds whose symbol the revived Nommo carried in his collar-bones and which represented parts of his body. The revived Nommo himself was the head, Amma Serou his chest, Lebe Serou his abdomen, Binou Serou his still living arms and Dyongou Serou his navel and penis.

As well as the eight ancestors, who were to come down to earth with the Nommo's ark, Amma created the smith and the sorcerer-musician, who descended separately. The smith, made from the umbilical cord of the sacrificed Nommo, is regarded as the latter's twin. To come down to earth, he received the victim's penis, his empty scrotum and his severed arm, which was changed into a hammer containing the eight cereal seeds. The penis became the forge's twyer and the scrotum its bellows. According to popular belief, the smith, like the Nommo, can turn himself into all kinds of living things at will.

The sorcerer-musician, who was created from the placenta, and the blood from the sacrificial victim's throat, is associated with speech, which was granted to human beings by the third ancestor (Binou Serou) at the time of the first *Sigui*. When he descended to earth with his female conterpart, the sorcerer-musician brought with him the victim's skull, from which he made the first drum. Rather than having eight seeds in his collar bones, he had eight words, symbolizing the power of speech that he is charged with preserving and spreading on earth.

The Nommo's ark, which came to earth with the eight ancestors, is linked to the organization of the world: its lower deck is the Old World, while its upper deck represents the New World. It has sixty compartments – corresponding to the number of holes dug in the earth by the fox – is made of pure earth and, in contrast to Ogo's ark, became the symbol of cultivated soil. On the Nommo's ark were the Mossi, Bambara, Bozo, Peul and Yebem peoples, while it also contained animals and plants, sand dunes, metals and the stars and planets. The ark rocked backwards and forwards for eight 'periods', in a helicoidal movement representing the movement of life, and the shock of its contact with the ground gave the earth its uneven appearance.

When he got out of the ark, the Nommo left the print of his copper sandal on the fox's 'field', as a sign that he had taken possession of it. Then came the first sunrise. All the living creatures emerged from the ark, and Amma pulled in his chain and 'closed up' the sky again, returning to his original shape as the Egg. The Nommo took on the shape of a horse and dragged the ark to the hollow formed by Lake Debo, which filled up with the first rain. The ark floated in this first 'pool' and on entering the element of water, which forms his domain on earth the Nommo returned to his original form as a silurid. Ever since he has been called the 'pool Nommo'. As such, he is the Master of Water, always present in springs, streams and rivers, while his female counterpart resides in the sea. For the Dogon, as for the Malinke, Bambara and Bozo, the Nommo is represented by the course of the Niger from its source in Lake Debo.

On earth, the four ancestor couples have well-defined functions. The oldest, Amma Serou, is the head of the family, the patriarch and the representative of Amma; it is he who makes the decisions about agricultural work. Binou Serou is the first totemic priest, while Lebe Serou embodies the earth and the forces of vegetation. It was the latter who was to sow the first communal field. However, he broke a prohibition and was sacrificed and resuscitated as the Nommo to purify the earth. Finally, Dyongo Serou incarnates anger and violence and is the hunter, though he is also the healer and initiator into the Society of Masks. He dies in an impure state and passes death on to human beings, while his wife supervises births and eases deliveries.

The myth stresses the idea that human beings were created speechless. The descent of the ancestors symbolizes their true birth, since they only became complete people when the Nommo made them the gift of speech, out of goodwill towards humankind and in order to make progress possible. From the 'pool' where he resides he revealed to them the technique of weaving, though only Binou Serou could appreciate it straight away, because he had divine intuition. He was so struck by it that he had a fit similar to the trance-like seizure that makes modern priests struck by inspiration start to 'tremble'. 'Speech came like a wind, entered his ear, went down into his liver, sat down, came out through his mouth. The form of speech received by Binou was still rudimentary; in fact it consisted of only one word: *so*, meaning 'speak'. However, this word contained the potential for all the future vocabulary of the six Dogon dialects and the six foreign languages (Bambara, Kouroumba, Tuareg, Songhay, Bella; and the Bobo group: Peul, Bozo, Mossi). When Binou acquired speech, he felt his lungs expand. He repeated the first word, and an echo answered him: this was the first drum, which sent this word to the other ancestors, who also began to speak. Later in conversations with the Nommo, Binou received all the other words of the vocabulary.

IMPLICATIONS OF THE DOGON MYTH

These two versions of the Dogon myth complement each other and reveal a metaphysical system and a conception of the human being grounded in a 'mythology of speech' and a 'mythology of seeds' befitting a chiefly agricultural people. It is Amma's 'speech' that brings the world into being, a fertilizing speech that gives life to creatures and things. The conception of humanity is established through the mythical story of the infancy of mankind and the birth of the world from the first eight seeds.

The human foetus is a replica of the first living creatures, created in the form of fish. For the Dogon, the human being consists of a body, a composite vital force that takes the form of a fluid circulating in the blood, and eight souls (four 'body' souls and four 'sex' souls like those of the first ancestors). Meanwhile in their collar-bones humans also have a symbolic representation of the eight primordial seeds of Creation. Like the first pairs of twins, humans are sexually ambivalent until circumcision or clitoridectomy. When they die, their 'vital force' (*nyama*) escapes and becomes an active entity that needs to be guided by funeral rites; these freed spiritual elements later take up residence in one of their descendants.

Social organization, essential techniques (such as cultivation, pottery, weaving and metalworking), some daily activities and, above all, ritual practices are explained and justified by a system of analogies referring to mythical events. The symbolic interpretation of numbers plays a particularly important role in this context.

The four Dogon tribes correspond to the four mythical lineages originating with the first ancestors who came down in the Nommo's ark or the 'heavenly grain store'. Meanwhile, the totemic system that forms the framework for Dogon society is linked to the story of the sacrificed Nommo and based on the principle of one clan, one totem, one prohibition. Each of the twenty-two totems corresponds to one of the twenty-two joints of the Nommo's body, which also reflect the twenty-two categories of Amma's thought, and so establish a close tie between the divinity and humankind.

All religious practices are directed primarily towards the god Amma and towards his agents the Nommo:

- The worship of Binou, which is highly complex, is directed towards the sacrificed Nommo as the holder and protector of mankind's spiritual principles and of seeds.
- The object of the worship of Lebe is the ancestor Lebe Serou, who is the protector of cultivated land. The Hogon, the religious leader of this cult, also has authority on the Council of Patriarchs, while the highest-ranking Hogon is regarded as the direct representative of Amma.
- The Society of Masks, to which all circumcised men belong, worships the ancestor Dyongou Serou.
- The ceremonies of the Sigui commemorate the revelation of speech, and

the spiral created by the dancers who perform in them recalls the spiral of life within the first seed in Amma's breast.

Like that of sanctuaries, the structure of the family house is based on mythical events in a highly symbolic way: the facade, with eight rows of ten niches, represents the eight ancestors and their descendants (of whom there are ten, just as a human being has ten digits) and the square terrace echoes that of the heavenly grain store. Meanwhile, seeds intended for sowing are placed beneath the conjugal bed in an analogy between agricultural activities and the act of procreation.

In the context of particular crafts, the activities of weavers, smiths and potters all have strong sacred connotations. The weaver, for example, is regarded as consecrating a personal altar to the divine creator, for the band that he weaves is the physical manifestation of the divine speech that it contains. The special status of leather-workers, smiths and sorcerer-musicians also has a mythological basis.

All this bears witness to the pervasive nature of the Dogon myth and to its decisive influence on traditions and works of art connected with the different crafts and on their place in Dogon society.

Nicole Goisbeault

Don Juan

According to Jean Massin, the clarity of the image presented by the figure of Don Quixote results from the fact that it remained unchanged. In contrast, the character of Don Juan has undergone many transformations since the writing of Tirso de Molina's comedia, *El burlador de Sevilla*, around 1630. Indeed, Byron considered Don Juan to be the classic example of adaptability.

> I want a hero: an uncommon want,
> When every year and month sends forth a new one,
> . . .
> Of such as these I should not care to vaunt,
> I'll therefore take our ancient friend Don Juan
>
> (*Don Juan* I. 1)

The treatment of the literary myth of Don Juan has therefore been remarkably free of constraint. Although it has primarily featured in theatrical works, it is also the subject of long poems (Byron's *Don Juan*, 1819–24), short poems (Rilke's *Don Juans Kindheit* and *Don Juans Auswahl*, and Baudelaire's *Don Juan aux Enfers), tales (Hoffmann's Don Juan, Eine fabelhafte Begebenheit, die sich mit einem reisenden Enthusiasten zugertragen*, 1813, and Mérimées's *Les Ames du Purgatoire*, 1834), and even novels (Roger Fairelle's *La Vie voluptueuse de Don Juan*, 1973, and Carlos Fuentes's *Terra nostra*, 1977). Some writers have focused on only a part of the hero's life as, for example, Pushkin in *The Negro of Peter the Great* (1827–8), while others, such as Byron, have covered it in its entirety, actually adding episodes, even at the cost of indulging in flights of fancy.

However, this freedom may have its limits. Even Byron, who used Don Juan as he would have used any other figure, to say whatever he personally wanted to say, was conscious that he had seen him represented as one who had been 'sent to the devil somewhat ere his time'. The meeting with Peter's guest is an event that cannot be omitted, since it constitutes the very heart of the myth, and Don Juan's own significance lies in his mythical status. 'I will remain what I am,' says Grabbe's hero. 'I am Don Juan. I would be nothing if I became another. It is better to be what I am in the sulphurous flames of hell than to be a saint in the light of paradise' (*Don Juan und Faust*, 1829). Thus the 'mobility' of the character does not preclude a certain amount of monotony in its portrayal. However, the history of the literary myth is long and varied, and provides an excellent example of the processess of development involved.

THE 'MOBILITY' OF DON JUAN

Don Juan is the 'flying' seducer, who, at the beginning of *El burlador de Sevilla*, jumps from the balcony of the palace of the Viceroy of Naples and disappears as effortlessly as Chérubin. However, he is bound by various social and emotional ties and his flight is hindered by the weight of the Statue, which drags him down to Hell with its hand of stone. Whether he becomes a stone mask, as at the end of Montherlant's *La Mort qui fait le trottoir* (1958), a snowman, as in Odön von Horvath's *Don Juan kommt aus dem Krieg* (1952) or simply a corpse, as at the end of Roger Vaillant's *Monsieur Jean* (1959), he invariably succumbs to its weight. He falls like a discarded child's toy and, lacking Icarus's magic powers, is unable to regain height.

Don Juan creates the illusion of change through his mobility. In *El burlador de Sevilla*, he is described by his valet Catalinon as an Egyptian locust (*langosta*). We see him travelling from Naples to Tarragona, from Tarragona to Seville, from Seville to the village of Dos Hermanos. No sooner has he arrived for the village wedding than he asks Catalinon to prepare and saddle the horses so that they can make their getaway as soon as he has seduced the young bride, Aminta. Indeed, in his production of Mozart's *Don Giovanni*, Louis Erlo decided to place the horses permanently at the back of the set. However, Don Giovanni actually has little need of his horse. On stage he is never still. The aria in Act I ('Fin ch'han dal vino') illustrates the amount of energy that he expends in frivolous activity. He organizes a ball, sets an unending succession of minuets, allemandes and quadrilles swirling around him, and introduces a group of young girls to another form of dance drawing them into his whirlpool of movement until they surrender to his amorous advances in his *casinetto*. This is all part of his nature, a form of *scherzo* that is his way of living. It is even with too brusque a movement that he kills the Commendatore who is 'skewered on his blade like a chicken' (Max Frisch, *Don Juan oder die Liebe zur Geometrie*, 1953). His mobility seems to transcend the confines of the stage. Don Juan needs the space of the epic (as in the odyssey of Byron's Don Juan, who is borne away by the waves of the Mediterranean, and with the help of pirates, arrives at a harem), or else the space of the novel. It takes very little for him to become a cloak and dagger hero, a role that he fulfils as one of Zévaco's characters in *Don Juan* and *Le Roi amoureux* (1916).

Don Juan also creates the illusion of change by his readiness to put on a mask. He is a man of many disguises. The lord bedecked with gold who is admired by Mathurine and Charlotte in Molière's *Dom Juan* (1665) can just as well make do with his valet's clothes, as in Mozart's and Da Ponte's version of the story, which involves the classic theme of mistaken identity. In Byron's poem he disguises himself as a woman, and so is able to enter the Sultana Gulbeyaz's apartments (Canto V). In the process he becomes a type of Doña Juana, in spite of his dislike of effeminate clothes. Even worse, he is able to change faces, as when he feigns repentance, love for his father and piety in

Act V of Molière's *Dom Juan*. Sganarelle, like Dom Louis, is momentarily deceived and congratulates the new convert. Don Juan takes care to disillusion him:

> No, no, I am completely unchanged and my feelings are still the same.
>
> (*Dom Juan* V. 2)

Finally, Don juan creates an illusion of change by his very inconsistency, which he readily confesses in his first scene with Sganarelle in Molière's *Dom Juan* (Act I. Scene 2). He is utterly incapable of being satisfied with one object of desire because he is continually attracted to another, and he has such a strong aversion to marriage that he is constantly parodying it. Certainly his marriage to Elvira does not restrict him in any way. This is partly because Don Juan escapes from the actual bonds of marriage despite being pursued and discovered by Elvira's brothers, but chiefly because the marriage is not in fact a real marraige at all. Molière's Elvire and Mozart's and Da Ponte's Elvira claim to be Don Juan's *épouse* and *sposa* respectively. However, the 'compulsive suitor' has only married them in the same way as all his other women, for example Aminta. Sganarelle takes care to point this out to Gusman, Elvira's loyal servant:

> You tell me that he has married your mistress. Believe me, he would have done more for his passion, and with her he would have married you, her dog and her cat into the bargain. A marriage costs him nothing to contract; he uses no other method to trap the fair sex, and he is a compulsive suitor.

This provides valuable evidence that Don Juan is not opposed to marriage, as has sometimes been claimed. On the contrary, he is passionately interested in it and continually multiplies the threads of his marriage ties until he becomes entangled in their web. At the end of Lenau's *Don Juan* (1844), Don Juan's 'list' becomes a procession of accusing victims who are all seeking revenge.

THE MONOTONY OF DON JUAN

It could be said that the only thing that does not change about Don Juan is his appetite for change. Indeed, this trait could even be described as monotonous, and nowhere is it more noticeable than in *El burlador de Sevilla*. Although Don Juan changes his choice of location and his victims (Isabella, Tisbea, Aminta, Anna, Aminta) he does not change his refrain: 'Que largo me lo fiais!' ('Your day of reckoning is a long way off'). Nor does he change his gestures – the same invitation, 'give me your hand', is issued to Zerlina in the famous duet in *Don Giovanni* – or his mocking manner (*burla*), which constitutes the most mechanical and crudest form of the scherzo. That is why dramatic portrayals of the story have to take such a repetitive form. Thus the second act of *Don Giovanni*, the banquet scene, is effectively a repetition of the first, the ball: the celebrations begin all over again. In *El burlador de Sevilla*, Tirso de Molina adopted an even more repetitive 'double parallel' structure. There are two plots involving noblemen, and two plots involving commoners, but there is no difference between them in terms of the *burla*. Instead, the result is a levelling of the social orders in a single play about the sins of the flesh.

The montony is also explained by the deep resemblances between all the women in Don Juan's life, as well as by a strange and little-observed consistency in the character of the original Don Juan. Brother Gabriel Tellez, otherwise known as Tirso de Molina, actually presented Don Juan, the would-be non-believer, as a man whose convictions were too strong. For Tirso, Don Juan's sin was really his excess of faith. This is demonstrated by the fact that he went to the trouble of producing a play with the opposite scenario: *El condenado por desconfiado* (Damned through Lack of Faith). Don Juan believes that he is the scourge of God and that God has entrusted him with a mission of revenge: to punish women for the ease with which they surrender their bodies. Isabella, who does so in the shadows of the royal palace of Naples, Tisbea, who rebels against marriage, Anna, who is having an affair with the libertinous Marquis de la Mota, and Aminta, who is prepared to commit a carnal sin even on her wedding night, all give themselves out of wedlock – and immediately – to the man who has seduced them. Don Juan's cry is not the lover's cry of satisfied desire. It is the triumphant cry of a man who can use the new name on his list of conquests as further proof of the easy virtue of women.

It has sometimes been suggested that Don Juan was a sad figure. Indeed, Pierre Jean Jouve observes this sadness even in the duet between Don Giovanni and Zerlina: 'What is remarkable about the 'Andiam' duet, a sort of lullaby in which the melody changes completely within a short interval, is its sadness.' This must be the sadness of knowing in advance what is going to happen, of knowing for certain that this time will be like all the others, and just as disappointing. It must come from the feeling that after this woman, there is yet another already waiting to be seduced. At the very moment when he is using all his wiles to win the ultimate victory over Zerlina, Don Giovanni announces that ten names must be added to his list by the following morning. He is caught up in the intoxication of quantity, and the quantity is never enough. This aspiration to infinity condemns Don Juan to Horvath's snowfields and to the desert in which Camus chose to place him. However, Camus does not agree that Don Juan is sad. For him, Don Juan's gaiety does not turn into dreadful gloom, in spite of the fact that he considers Don Juan to be a man without hope: 'that laugh, the triumphant insolence, his constant activity, and his appetite for the theatrical – all this is bright and joyful. All healthy beings tends to duplicate themselves' (*Le Mythe de Sisyphe*, 1942). In this context, 'duplicate' should not be misconstrued as meaning fathering illegitimate children (as in the case of Don Felipe Acacer in Montherlant's play) or even having a hoard of children to feed (as at the end of Lenau's *Don Juan*). Instead, it should be interpreted as referring to a duplication of the self. Because his life involves constantly projecting an image, and because the image that he projects is always of himself, and always the same, Don Juan is responsible for creating his own doubles.

Otto Rank's study of Don Juan has come to be regarded as a classic work on the subject, although the French edition rather misrepresents it by calling it *Don Juan et le Double*, and thereby juxtaposing the titles of two articles written and published in German at different times (*The Double* in 1914 and *The Legend of Don Juan* in 1922). In fact, Rank considers that the structure based on the concept of the double antedates the myth of Don Juan and is reinforced by it. Having established that Don Juan engenders his own doubles (so that he is ultimately the only real Don Juan), Rank suggests that there is a split within his personality between two conflicting images of himself. In fact, however, the opposite view may be more accurate, namely that Don Juan is a monolithic character who engenders impersonators. Some of these impersonators are well known. One example, in the context of the theatre, is Leporello; jealous of his master or perhaps 'indulging in some of his master's poetry' (Flaubert's draft of *Une Nuit de Don Juan*) he takes delight in this multiplicity – and can even imitate it – which explains why he reads the list in such detail. Meanwhile, an actual historical example is provided by Miguel Mañara. He cannot have provided the inspiration for Don Juan, as has sometimes been suggested, since he was three years old when Tirso's *comedia* appears to have been staged for the first time – instead he seems deliberately to have modelled himself on the fictional character, at least in the early stages of his career. Yet another example is the actor, José van Dam, who plays Leporello in Joseph Losey's film *Don Giovanni*, but is able to sing the role of Don Juan in other performances.

However, the most remarkable instance of the 'proliferation' of Don Juan occurs in Carlos Fuentes's novel, *Terra nostra*, in which there are several Don Juan figures. These include Juan Agrippa and the castaway, as well as the lord dressed in black (Philip II) and his father, the former lord, who readily exercises his *ius primae noctis*. The idea of Philip II in the role of Don Juan appears paradoxical, to say the least. However, the paradox becomes less marked if one bears in mind that Fuentes's intention was to present Don Juan as a dream counteracting the asceticism of the period of the Escorial. It is thus an erotic fantasy in an age of austerity, which creates this compensatory image only to bring about its violent destruction. For 'there is compensation for everything in this world'.

CHRONOLOGY OF THE LITERARY MYTH

Nothing is known of Don Juan before Tirso's *comedia* of 1630. Attempts have been made to find historical models for the character, but these have proved to be either imaginary (Don Juan Tenorio) or inadequate (the Count of Villamediana who, according to Gregorio Marañon, was in fact Don Juan of Tasis). Efforts have also been made to identify mythological prototypes (Theseus or even Zeus himself according to the theory of Gendarme de Bévotte's). Though in *Terra nostra* Fuentes portrays the origins of Don Juan in the Spain of Philip II, the book is also a novel of the year 2000 when all that remains of Latin America is a landscape ravaged by advertising or genocide and a few refugees bearing witness to the past culture of the continent. Is this why Don Juan annihilates himself in his own multiplicity? Is it decadence? Is it demystification? This new question leads us on to consider the process of change not in the context of Don Juan himself, as he is not really a figure of change and actually changes very little, but rather in terms of the history of his literary myth.

Broadly speaking, it is possible to identify three major periods in the myth's development. During the Classical period Don Juan appeared primarily as an entertaining figure, whether one considers the *burla* in *El burlador de Sevilla*), his mockery and defiance in Molière's *Dom Juan*, or the scherzo in the versions of *Don Giovanni* by Da Ponte and Mozart. The most remarkable feature of works of this period is their rigorous use of the principle of reversibility, which basically represents another means of duplication. Not only does Don Juan constantly repeat the same adventure, but the adventure ultimately rebounds upon him. He lights the fire of Tisbea's passion and is subsequently burnt by it. He asks his victims for their hands, and the Statue of the Comendador in turn asks him for his, which it then grasps in a terrifying grip. Don Juan did not allow the Comendador/Commendatore time to confess before he killed him, and the Statue later drags Don Juan himself, unrepentant, down to hell. This represents the enforcement of the principle of demanding an eye for an eye, which is expressed in its crudest form by Catalinon in Tirso's *comedia*.

During the Romantic period, Hoffman's tale, *Don Juan, Eine fabelhafte Begebenheit, die sich mit einem reisenden Enthusiasten zugertragen*, introduced an important innovation. For the first time there was a proper dialogue between Don Juan and one of his lovers. Like Don Juan, Donna Anna has been blessed with a 'desire for infinity, a thirst for the unattainable'. Like him, she has a lofty and demanding character with aspirations of the highest order. However, when Don Juan meets her it is too late for both of them. To attain his level, Donna Anna must plumb the same depths. Thus, when she sings a last 'non mi dir' after his death it is no longer intended for the insignificant Ottavio but for Don Juan himself, whom she chooses to follow to hell. In contrast other women were represented as putting him on the road to redemption. With the Romantics, the Manara tradition (or the Marana tradition, as it is sometimes called) merged with the Tenorio tradition (Mérimée) or dominated it (Zorrilla, *Don Juan Tenorio*, 1844; Alexandre Dumas père, *Don Juan de Marana ou la Chute d'un Ange*, 1836). If the drama of Don Juan unfolded in a different way, this was because it was shaped by the great Romantic theme of redemption and by a structure that led to deliverance.

Byron's Romanticism also marked the birth of modern ironic literature, and in modern times this irony has been directed against Don Juan. In its purest form it involves the combined representation of Don Juan himself and his reflection in miniature. This technique was used in Michel de Ghelderode's *Don Juan* (1928), and even more markedly in the musical production by Michel Butor and Jean-Yves Bosseur at the Théâtre Oblique, where a miniature orchestra and miniature instruments were placed next to their normal-sized counterparts.

The modern era is one of demystification, or rather it attempts to be. Thus the symbolic episode involving the Statue is downgraded into a mere deception. Byron had already had the idea that a slightly mad, old duchess could be disguised as a ghost in an attempt to seduce Don Juan, while in Max Frisch's play, *Don Juan oder Liebe zur Geometrie*, it is Celestina (the procuress) who is disguised, on the orders of the Bishop of Cordoba and the Duchess of Ronda. She wishes to marry Don Juan and, in fact, eventually holds him captive. Meanwhile, producers are tempted to treat the Statue in a derisory fashion or to exclude it altogether. This demystification ultimately becomes a 'demythification', since the slighting of the role of the Statue represents the destruction of the sacred element that turns the story of Don Juan into a myth. For it is not royal or divine anger that precipitates the catastrophe. Instead, it results from the violation of an interdiction and the non-observance of a taboo relating to the dead and death, and recalls the *lithinos thanatos* ('stony death') referred to by Pindar.

The process of demystification or demythification has not, however, ended interest in the figure of Don Juan. The clearest proof of this can be found in Roger Vailland's play, *Monsieur Jean*. In spite of the fact that Don Juan has become the Managing Director of an aviation company, that the Statue has become the portrait of his former assistant manager, Monsieur Commandeur, killed during a test flight, and that Leporello has become Leporella, the theme of the vengeance of the dead man is very much in evidence. It is not the laws of physics alone (a cord that is too short and a painting that is too heavy) that explain why the portrait breaks the neck of Monsieur Jean.

Although the treatment of the adventure of Don Juan reflects changes of ideology between different eras, Don Juan himself hardly changes at all. He remains the same even in the context of his strange power of proliferation. Fuentes wrote a nine-hundred-page novel on the subject, but a few lines are enough to re-evoke his story. A young nun tells it to Celestina:

> He killed my father on account of his love for me. I loved my father's murderer. My love for the living man was stronger than my love for the dead man. He did not take advantage of me at all, but he took advantage of my father, who is buried here in this very convent. He came to mock the grave, and challenged

> the statue of my father by inviting it to dine that evening at the inn. He refused to take me with him even though I begged him to, declaring that he had only a few days to devote to each woman he loved: one day to fall in love with her, one day to seduce her, a third to abandon her, a fourth to replace her and an hour to forget her. I begged him, but he refused. My brothers arrived and challenged him to a duel. He laughed, and seized hold of me, not through love but in order to defy my brothers. As he jumped over the wall of the convent, we fell. I fainted and he was killed.

This fall clearly recalls the impact of the stone.

Pierre Brunel

Doubles and Counterparts

Many expressions have been used to convey the idea of the double or counterpart. One of the first was the Latin term alter ego, while the French words *sosie* and *ménechme*, used to refer to two people who are so strikingly similar in appearance that one can be mistaken for the other, are also of Latin origin, being derived from the names Sosia and the Menaechmi belonging to characters in comedies by Plautus. The expressions twin souls, Siamese twins and kindred spirits carry connotations of a related nature, but it was the German term *Doppelgänger*, which can be translated as double or second self, that was hallowed by the Romantic Movement after being coined by Jean-Paul Richter in 1796. It literally means 'someone walking beside you, a travelling companion', but here it will be used in accordance with the definition actually provided by Richter: 'this is the name used by those who see themselves'. The implication is that what is involved is a primarily subjective experience. Finally, other expressions used in various works of literature have also enjoyed a certain vogue, for example 'je est un autre' ('I is someone else', Rimbaud) or 'el otro' ('the other', Borges).

According to J.-P. Vernant in 'Mythe et tragédie en Grèce ancienne', Oedipus is the paradigm of the double man. In the *Oedipus Rex*, Sophocles raises the question of the extent to which Man can be entirely accountable for his actions since because of his human aspect he is here, while, at the same time, because of his superhuman aspect he is elsewhere. In this case, the theme of duality is only apparent from detailed analysis of the text. However, such analysis will not be carried out in the present study; instead, we shall limit our attention to works that tackle the subject explicitly, by using terms such as 'double', 'I – another – he', 'I – two-in-one', or 'I – the same', by exploiting homonymy or resemblance, or by suggesting a strange closeness between the narrator and another figure, thereby raising the question of identity, or identicalness. All the works studied have at their core this strange sense of another presence.

Only Western literature will be considered, since the double is one of the great myths of the West. In addition, the theme is particularly suited to one particular literary genre: fantasy and, later, science fiction. The myth of the double is also well represented in the arts – for example, in medieval art with its two-headed creatures, in Mannerism and in Surrealism – as well as in the cinema. The double constitutes an ancestral image that experienced its apotheosis in the literature of the nineteenth century in the wake of the

Romantic Movement, though its myth has continued to provide inspiration for twentieth-century writers too.

The theme seems to be particularly well suited to the novella, as a form of literature used to relate a sudden and strange event (Goethe). Theatrical treatments of the subject, in which the double can be represented on stage by a second character, were prevalent mainly before and after the Romantic era. It was also popular in the introspective context of lyric poetry, while its treatment in the Romantic ballad is redolent of folklore. Finally, by contrast, the myth features rather less frequently in the novel.

THE LEGENDARY AND SYMBOLIC MYTHICAL ASPECT

Though the myth of the double was particularly popular during the Romantic period, its origins go back to far earlier times. Ancient Nordic and Germanic legends describe meetings with a double, and the release of the double is portrayed as an ominous event that often heralds death. In this context, the alter ego is sometimes represented in the form of a restless soul that leaves a person's body during sleep and takes on the appearance of an animal or a shadow, while the double is also a person's *Schutzgeist*, or guardian spirit.

Pre-Columbian divinities were thought of as double, both in terms of their sex and of their potential for good or evil. The foremost god in the Mexican pantheon is Ometeotl, Gods-two, who features prominently in *Popol-vuh*, a book used by the council of the Maya Quechua Indians of Guatemala.

These ideas were taken up by Miguel Angel Asturias, particularly in his book *Leyendas de Guatemala* (1929). This recounts the legend of the tatuana, in which the Master Almond-tree can adopt either a human or a plant form. As a rule, the double is the 'nahual', an animal form that is interchangeable with the human one and this concept preserves the memory of a symbiotic relationship between animals and humans. Significant too, is the fact that according to the Mayan ethical tradition, it was the twins Hun Batz and Hun Chuen who were the prototypes of civilized man.

In ancient Egypt, a manifestation of the individual's life force known as the Ka was also a double. This entity led an existence independent of the body with which it was created and survived its death, thus to go to one's Ka meant to die. A positive view of doubleness and twinhood is also presented in Plato's *Symposium* in the mythical tale told by Aristophanes. The double man, double woman or androgynous being represented an original state of perfection and union, which human beings brought to an end by threatening the gods. Division is the punishment meted out by the gods, and implies that each person is now only half a human being. This point has important repercussions for the use of the myth in literature, as it implies that people are malleable, and that their destiny involves a quest, the search for one's double. This quest is an ambiguous one, with both beneficent and maleficent associations. It represents a form of passage, a crossing of the confines of what is human, and recalls a punishment symbolized by the divisive cut. As a consequence, the myth is related to other stories of men acting rebelliously towards the gods, such as those of Prometheus and Icarus.

In Genesis also, Man was originally one being until God cut it in two, and again, as in the myth in the *Symposium*, division makes humankind weaker. In all these myths Man is portrayed as having a double nature, containing, in particular, both male and female elements. Thus the structure of the inner man is based on the union of two separate entities: a concept apparent in the distinction made by traditional religions between body and soul.

The idea of the duality of the human individual – whether expressed in terms of male and female, man and animal, spirit and flesh, or life and death – reflects a belief in metamorphosis, or even metempsychosis, and implies a feeling that Man is responsible for his own destiny. Mythology emphasizes the double aspect of the power for good or evil inherent in living persons, a dichotomy that recurs in symbolic religious figures (for example the devil and the guardian angel in Christianity). Meanwhile, the occult, with its symbolism of death and rebirth, also influences literary works in which the double appears.

Most of the studies of the double undertaken in the twentieth century concentrate on its psychological aspect. The first is Rank's psycho-analytical interpretation of the concept (1914), which combines an examination of the various aspects of the treatment of the double in literature with an analysis of the personalities of the authors concerned and a study of myths (Narcissus) and mythological traditions. He concludes that heroes who have a double show a tendency to be in love with their own egos and suffer from an inability to love others. It is psychic conflict that creates the double, which is merely a projection of inner disturbance, and the cost of deliverance is the fear of meeting one's other self. According to Rank's second proposition, the concept of the double is related to the problem of death and the desire for survival, since love of self and the fear of death are linked. Seen in these terms, the double is a personification of the immortal soul, which becomes the soul of the dead person, an idea that the ego uses to protect itself from annihilation. However, by the same token, the double is also perceived as a 'frightening harbinger of death', hence the ambivalent feelings towards it (ranging from passionate interest to terror). It is simultaneously the protecting principle and the threatening one.

Rank's analysis develops from one based on a purely Freudian notion, the repression of sexual desire, towards one based on a Jungian concept. Following Jung's vision he sees the ego's feeling of guilt as resulting in the desire for death, with the aim of being reborn to a different existence. The study by Rogers is based on an analaysis of the Freudian unconscious and its infantile associations, and distinguishes between the objective double (two people) and the subjective double (the divided self). Similarly, Tymms makes a distinction between doubles created by division and those created by multiplication.

There are shrewd commentaries on the works listed in the Further Reading section at the end of this book, and it is to this that readers seeking further information are referred.

Keppler (1972) devotes his attention solely to the study of doubles in literature, commenting on numerous Anglo-Saxon examples. In doing so, he provides a more rigorous definition of the term than those offered by his predecessors. For him the double is simultaneously identical to and different from – indeed, even opposite to – the original. It is always a source of fascination to the person who possesses it, because of the paradox that it represents (being simultaneously internal and external, here and there, opposite and complementary). In addition, it arouses extreme emotional reactions in the form of attraction or repulsion. The relationship between the two entities is one of dynamic tension and the meeting between them takes place when the ego of the original is particularly vulnerable. Nonetheless, Keppler's definition based on an analysis of the concept of the double in literature is still not narrow enough. As a result it leads him to discuss works such Melville's *Bartelby* and Hugo's *Les Misérables* that do not feature doubles in the sense in which the term is used here.

Keppler lists seven different manifestations of the double: the pursuer; twins; the beloved; the tempter; the nightmare vision; the saviour; and the double from another age. However, others could also be added to the list. In addition, he notes the connection between the double and the *Bildungsroman*. In this context the double acts as the catalyst for a profound change within the self and consequently is profoundly ambiguous, embracing evil and good, the subjective and the objective. Basing his ideas on the psychology of Jung ('the integration of the personality') he describes the double as an unrealized part of the personality, or one excluded by the ego's self-image. This explains its closeness and its antagonism, since what are involved are two complementary sides of the same being.

Approaching the question from the same Jungian perspective, Arenberg links confrontation with the double with the Shamanist concept of rites of passage. In their works, the Romantics portrayed this confrontation as leading to a process of death and rebirth, and she thus sees them as seeking a new mythology, also based on initiation. In contrast, using a purely literary approach, Krauss develops the idea that a longing for the infinite results in a painful split in the individual. What satisfies such a desire is diametrically opposed to what thwarts its fulfilment in an irreversible form of dualism. This recalls the platitude of the romantic who lives in 'two worlds'.

In the West, the myth of the double is closely associated with the idea of subjectivity. In the seventeenth century this resulted in the formulation of the binary relationship between subject and object, where previously the tendency had been to emphasize unit. This opposition between a unitary concept of the world and a dialectic concept of the world is reflected in a change of direction in the literary myth of the double. From classical antiquity until the end of the sixteenth century this myth had symbolized homogeneity and identicalness. The physical resemblance between two people was used to allow one to be substitued for the other usurping his or her identity: the hero's living image, exact double or twin was mistaken for the actual hero and vice versa, but each retained an individual identity. This tendency to stress unity was particularly apparent when one actor played the roles of both characters.

From the end of the sixteenth century, the double began to represent heterogeneity: in the nineteenth century the division of the self reaching exploding point; and in the twentieth century, the 'I' became capable of infinite division. This development reflected a change in the idea of Man's place in nature notably in relation to God. According to the tenets of monotheist religions, Man is made in the image of God, and thus has an objective double. However, the affirmation of the independence of the ego from God in the seventeenth century led to the 'death' of God. The free exercise of reason dates from the time when Descartes examined his ego and founded the principles of metaphysics and moral philosophy that had previously been deduced from God on his maxim 'cogito ergo sum' ('I think, therefore I am'; second *Méditation métaphysique*). This marked the beginning of a philosophical tradition that portrayed the subject as the centre of the world (Kant). Its final outcome was an excessive emphasis on subjectivity (Fichte, Schelling) that explains thc feeling of alienation represented by the double self of the Romantics.

Twentieth-century psychoanalysts are still embroiled in the troubled area of heterogeneity, while (pragmatic) philosophers place the subject in a ternary relationship involving subject–language–object. Thus the myth of the double still has topical relevance and the figure of the double is frequently employed as a symbol of heterogeneity.

I THE DOUBLE AS A HOMOGENEOUS FIGURE

1 The twin double and the usurpation of roles in comedies based on mistaken identity

In legends, the hero who is a twin is someone who has succeeded in making his double visible in this world. Thus in literature the twin is the first form of double.

A feature-for-feature resemblance between two people that is so strong that it leads those around them to mistake one for the other supplies the plot of comedies dating back to the time of Plautus, who was himself influenced by Greek writers. In the *Menaechmi*, first staged in 206 BC, identical twin brothers, both with the same name but who do not know each other, come by chance to the same place, giving rise to a spate of misunderstandings. The plot revolves entirely around the family; the twin who arrives at Epidamnus unintentionally usurps his brother's identity, causing such confusion that the brother has to counter the belief that he is mad. The twins are caught up in a painful and inevitable train of events, which concludes only with the recognition scene, when the dumbfounded onlookers become aware that there are two identical living people whom they are unable to tell apart.

The plot based on the resemblance between two people recurs in Shakespeare's *Comedy of Errors* (1592–3). Here, the dramatist gives the twin brothers twin servants, thereby multiplying the opportunities for confusion. In the process, he creates a comic counterpoint to the question of identity, with the servants naively expressing a sense of the loss of their own selves as a result of the series of misapprehensions. The confusion is resolved in the final scene, in which everybody is recognized by everybody else. The same idea was exploited by Régnard in *Les Ménechmes* (1705), Goldoni in *I due gemelli veneziani* (1748), Tristan Bernard in *Les Jumeaux de Brighton* (1939) and Sacha Guitry in *Mon Double et ma moitié* (1931).

Starting with Cardinal Bibbiena's play *La Calandra* (1513), Italian comedy also gave rise to a popular new theme. Bibbiena's work features a twin boy and girl who have been separated and are brought together again in Rome. Confusion arises because the girl has disguised herself as a boy and become a replica of her brother. This plot provided the inspiration for *Gli Ingannati* (anonymous, 1531) in which the twins Fabrizio and Lelia are separated and Lelia craftily exploits her disguise as a man to rekindle the passion that her lover Flaminio no longer feels towards her. The return of her brother to Modena and the appearance of her double reunites the couples and brings about a happy ending. Lope de Rueda used the same plot in *Los Engañados* (1556), which he based on the Italian comedy.

Secchi's *Gli Inganni* (1562) also features a similar situation. A twin boy and girl are sold as slaves in Naples, and the girl, dressed as a man, arouses the love of another woman. This would cause problems, but for the appearance of her brother. Shakespeare's *Twelfth Night* (1602), inspired by a play similarly entitled *Gli Inganni* (1592), by Gonzaga, shows originality in its ingenious management of two plots. The themes of the reunion of the twins and the confusion of identity are used only to provide a means of escape from a situation that has become excessively complicated because of the vagaries of human emotions. The main plot is based on the identical twins Viola and Sebastian who share the same spirit of adventure.

2 The double and the deliberate usurpation of identity

In the story *Ami et Amile* (1090), written in Latin by Radulfus Tortarius, substitution is used as a proof of friendship. Ami takes Amile's place in an ordeal, and is in turn saved by Amile. Meanwhile, in *Titus et Gisippus* (twelfth century) by Alfonso, Gisippus allows his friend and 'spitting image', who is much more in love with his wife than he is himself, to take his place beside her. Because of their resemblance, she does not notice the difference.

The theme of the usurpation of power through the exploitation of the resemblance between a king or dignitary and a peasant featured frequently in Spanish Renaissance theatre. Thus, in *El Rey por semejanza* (1600) by Grajales, the queen has her lover murder the tyrannical king, and puts a peasant with an uncanny resemblance to her dead husband on the throne in his place to conceal her crime. The peasant becomes a model ruler, and the replacement of the true king by his double turns out to be beneficial for the country.

The same idea is used by Tirso da Molina in *La Ventura con el nombre* (1630). Ventura, the shepherd who is the hero of the story, is not only a beneficent substitute king who goes off to fight successfully against the Saxons, but is also, in fact, the half-brother of the murdered ruler. Accepted as the true king the false king proves his own worth, and so confirms his parenthood. The theme of using a double to save a country from a power vacuum recurs in *A un tiempo rey y vasallo* (anonymous, seventeenth century) and *Sulpitia* (1672) by Draghis.

In the comedy *El palacio confuso* (1630) by Lope de Vega, the queen replaces her husband who has died in the wars with a new king, who starts to banish the nobles and to give power to the people. However, while the new ruler is asleep the queen employs a double to countermand his orders and, as a result, he comes to believe that he is mad. As far as the nobility is concerned, the king embodies evil, but he is gradually rendered powerless by the use of his double; while, in a final twist at the end of the play, we discover that the new king and his double are the twin sons of the dead king. Corneille used the same plot in *Dom Sanche d'Aragon* (1649); in it, a tyrannical husband is rendered harmless by his twin brother who has been brought up as a peasant.

The theme of usurpation of identity by a claimant to the throne features in *El Imperador fingido* (1650) by de Bocangel, *La Crueldad por el honor* (1623) by de Alarcón y Mendoza, and *El pastelero de Madrigal* (1660) by de Cuéllar, in which a pastry cook who is identical in appearance to the King of Portugal is executed by the Spanish.

In all these plays the resemblance that allows one person to be substituted for another is used both to aid in the unfolding of the drama and as a device in plots involving political manoeuvres affecting the nature of government.

Usurpation of identity may be based on simple disguise, with the same person playing two different roles to ensure a happy conclusion to some amorous liaisons, as in *Miles Gloriosus* (*c.* 206 BC) and *Don Gil de la calzas verdes* (1617) by Tirso da Molina. In the latter, four different Don Gils appear at the same time, resulting in countless misunderstandings (see also *El hombre pobre todo es trazas* by Calderón and *El semejante a si mismo* (1630) by de Alarcón y Mendoza). The use of disguise as means of propelling the plot and the love story was also a feature of Marivaux's comedies. In *Le jeu de l'amour et du hasard* (1730) the switch with a double in the form of a valet or maidservant draws attention to the nature of social relations, through contrasts in clothing and in the use of language. By contrast, in *Die Verkleidungen des französischen Hofmeisters und seines deutschen Zöglings* (1835) Arnim uses the device of disguise mainly to highlight the duality that exists within every human being and the instability of reality, employing the double as a symbol of heterogeneity.

3 The supernatural double

Plays involving a magic double are derived from heroic legends telling of the amorous encounters between gods and mortal women. These represent mystical union between heaven and earth, which is supposed to result in the birth of a hero and saviour, and feature in Indian mythology and in the cycle of Theban legends relating to Zeus's metamorphosis into a bull to mate with Europa, a swan to mate with Leda, a shower of gold to mate with Danaë, etc. In his *Amphitruo* (201–7 BC), the Roman playwright Plautus transformed legend into a miraculous yet domestic tragi-comedy. In it the gods come down to earth and Plautus humanizes them by making them undergo metamorphoses and by giving them personalities. Jupiter assumes Amphitryon's features in order to enjoy the favours of Alcmene, while Mercury takes on the form of the slave Sosia. The central element is the story of the birth of Heracles. As a mortal, Amphitryon fathers a mortal son, Iphicles; while, as a god, Zeus begets the hero himself, who is one night older than his twin brother.

The comic element arises from the confrontation between the real Sosia and the false Sosia (Mercury), at the end of which the real Sosia is robbed of his identity after being convinced that his double is really him. At the end of the play itself, Jupiter reveals the deception, managing at the same time to retain his Olympian majesty.

In 1636 Rotrou based a comedy entitled *Les Sosies* on the Latin play, while Molière also employed the same fashionable theme in his *Amphitryon* (1668), transforming the heroic legend into a comic marital misadventure in which the deceptive elements include ones based on appearances. He gives the plot an echo by making the servant couple Sosie and Cléanthis express similar feelings to those of their employers, but in suitably adapted forms. The climax of the drama is the revelation of the double imposture, which leads to the denouement. Unlike the play by Plautus, which had a religious and redemptive theme in the form of the birth of Heracles, who would slay the monsters threatening mankind, Molierès work merely involves a commonplace extramarital misdemeanour, and it is Sosie with his down-to-earth reasoning who sets its overall tone. Kleist drew on Molière in his play *Amphitrion* (1806), while Giraudoux took up the same plot in his *Amphitryon 38* (1929).

Many works describe the momentary metamorphosis of a god into the form of an individual human being, whose identity he then usurps. Thus, in *Historia regum Britanniae* (1132–5) by Geoffrey of Monmouth, Uther Pendragon spends a night of love with Queen Igraine by masquerading as her husband. Meanwhile in the Indian holy book the *Mahabharata* (fifth–fourth century BC), the episode of 'Nala and Damayanti' (book III) recounts how four gods took on the appearance of Nala and so finally helped Damayanti to regain the real Nala.

People who meet their magic doubles invariably suffer as a result. Even when the ploy is used for comic purposes, this sudden confrontation with the enigma of their identicalness makes them end up thinking that they must be mad. The epic story of Gilgamesh, which occurs in Assyrian literature dating from the end of the third millennium and forms a cycle of poems written in Sumerian, recounts the trials and tribulations of Gilgamesh, the king of Uruk who has become a burden to his people. In answer to their prayers the goddess Aruru creates Enkidu, a replica of Gilgamesh. At first they fight, but subsequently they become friends and accomplish a whole series of heroic feats. Eventually, Enkidu dies in the arms of Gilgamesh, and the latter travels the world looking for the secret of eternal life.

In contrast to Gilgamesh, who is completely absorbed by physical battles in the outside world, Enkidu is concerned with matters of the spirit, and is thus his counterpart. After entering the kingdom of darkness Enkidu continues to help Gilgamesh, who up until then had been unaware that the underworld even existed. Enkidu shows him that Man needs to have dealings with the invisible world through worshipping the spirits. However, Gilgamesh, the external man, is brought to understand his internal existence (Enkidu) only when Enkidu, as a replica of himself, has returned to the kingdom of darkness. It is his confrontation with a mortal double that teaches him about man's destiny and his metaphysical dimension.

In all the works considered so far, the identity of the person who sees his or her double is not placed in doubt. The double is only temporarily substituted for the original, after which the latter regains all its rights and prerogatives. In the denouement the oneness of the person is reaffirmed. People can also be tempted to make magical use of alter egos for their own advantage, for example to enjoy a love that would be forbidden to them if they retained their original identities, as in *Avatar* (1857) by Gauthier. However, both human magic and occult knowledge are powerless to effect a perfect exchange of personalities. The ageing Casanova takes on the identity of a younger, beloved double to enjoy a last night of love in *Casanovas Heimfahrt* (1917) by Schnitzler. Similarly, the dream of achieving everlasting life through reincarnation in the form of a younger double provides the theme of Bulwer-Lytton's 'Strange story' (1862) and H. G. Wells's 'The story of the late Mr Elvesham' (1897).

Through the myth of the double, Man gradually arrogated to himself the prerogative of the gods, the ability to pass through various transformations and so to be reborn.

II FROM HOMOGENEITY TO HETEROGENEITY

Advances in knowledge of the inner workings of the human mind that started in the seventeenth century gradually forced the abandonment of the belief that human consciousness was a unity, and that each individual had a unique and clearly defined identity.

Thus, Miguel de Cervantes's *Don Quijote de la Mancha* (1605–15) was written at the turning-point between two eras, at a period when attitudes towards the concept of the double underwent a radical shift. In his role as a would-be hero, Don Quixote sets out to copy and actually embody the heroes of the chivalric romances, and is thus a real-life imitator of what are only products of the imagination. He sets out to imitate Roland and Amadis of Gaul, and proclaims 'I am mad, and mad I must remain'. Exact imitation is his way of living and he defines his own identity in terms of analogies with literary doubles. He has equipped himself with borrowed clothing and a borrowed name; when he becomes Don Quixote of La Mancha he discards the life history of the fifty-year-old Don Quixano, a selfish, lonely provincial gentleman of limited means.

He elects to become dead to the world and to be reborn in the form of a 'righter of wrongs', who establishes new identies for Rosinate and Dulcinea. This is the choice of true life, the bringing into being of another world within the one we all know.

But though the person who has become his own double gives himself the illusion of affecting things that are outside him, all he is really doing is making the drama inside himself objective. His awareness of the pointlessness of 'real' life leads to his rebirth into a heroic life of the mind. Because he lives in the world of chivalric romances, Don Quixote will have dealings only with people who are masked or disguised, false knights, false princes or false squires.

Reality has fiction as its double, and the former is influenced by the latter, even if only in mocking it. The sphere in which Don Quixote and the other characters develop is split in two; he conjures up the imaginary within the real, and the real, in turn, is in some way influenced by the imaginary. He seeks to abolish time by faithfully mimicking the knightly code, but in the process he is denying the dual nature of reality and of its representation in fiction and art, as illustrated by the puppet scene. He embodies the lack of substance in literature by claiming to live in the real world. Turning himself into a living myth, he sets Sancho Panza to work on the menial tasks of reality, and it is onto reality that he sloughs off the flesh that encumbers him (Robert, *L'Ancien et le Nouveau*).

But who is whose double? When Sancho Panza diverts him from his objective, Don Quixote is just as much Panza's tempter as his victim. The affection binding them together turns their original duality into a deep unity, the unity of what can be felt and what can be understood. Because he has so little hold on the world, Don Quixote is a hero who reflects the modern concept of the double, and his attempt to combine the ideal with reality fails. Through bringing together two people who are not alike, but complementary, the author gradually creates a portrait of a man split in two.

The character of Don Juan, first depicted in 1620 in the play *El Burlador de Sevilla y convidado da piedra*, illustrates the transition from the earlier view of the double to the later. In the context of this work, it is the wrongdoer who comes up against the representative of the law (the Commendatore). Thus, in his study on Don Juan, Rank discerns the outlines of a conflict between two entities, the unbridled individual ego and the social ego and, from the same perspective, Don Luis (Molière's *Dom Juan*) can be seen as the part of his own soul that Don Juan rejects.

However, Don Juan is himself split. Thus Tirso makes him into a Protean figure who uses multiple false identities to achieve his amorous 'conquests'. With a purloined identity he delights in the pleasures of a night of love-making in place of the expected lover, and promises marriage. Meanwhile, in Molière's play he is someone who splits words.

The deceiver of women would also like to deceive God, but fails in that task. Hoffmann (1813) uses his figure to conjure up the conflict between divine and demoniac powers, portraying the desire to achieve infinity on earth through the possession of a woman as being prompted by the devil. However, it is in *Don Giovanni* by Da Ponte and Mozart (1787) that the structural influence of the theme of the double is most clearly apparent. Here, Leoporello is a menial Don Giovanni, and disguises himself as his master, while Don Juan pretends to be Leporello in the company of Leporello's wife. Don Giovanni is the heroic part, while Leporello is the buffoon; and Don Giovanni's seductive charm is reflected in Leporello's lewdness.

Don Giovanni uses his dual identity as a ploy to escape punishment, naming his double as the guilty party. He owes his continued existence and his ability to make fools of the authorities to this confusion, and Leporello identifies with him. (Indeed, in the years leading up to the French Revolution, the relationship between the master and the servant was reversed.) Don Juan thus represents the life instinct, as opposed to the social instinct. By precipitating an encounter with the forces of the law, he provokes his own meeting with himself, with what he will become: a stone statue. As such, the purloiner of identities will be frozen in a single form. It is the fascination exerted by this confrontation between the living and the dead, and the strange nature of this enchanter of women, who is himself fascinated by evil, that make this work such an important landmark in the representation of the double.

Faust is the hostile brother of Don Juan, with whom he is associated in Western culture (Grabbe). He combines inside him elements that were dissociated in the case of Don Juan, and thereby represents the possible conjunction between the instinct for life, desire, and considered action. Goethe's *Faust* is in two parts. *Faust* I (1806) depicts a man driven to desperation by the co-existence within him of two souls, one of which is firmly anchored to the earth, while the other aspires to free itself in order to rise to the divine mystery (V. 870–6). Mephistopheles misunderstands his desire, which is conveyed metaphorically by the use of the word *Streben* (a desire to unite learning and personal knowledge through experience).

Faust's duality lies in the fact that, as a subjective being, he aspires to contact with the objective world. This implies transcending the contradictions in his own character by means of action that has an impact on the world. The necessary synthesis of thought and action can be achieved only in the context of a small community, while the juxtaposition of Mephisto, who excites Faust like evil itself, emphasizes the bipolarity associated with the figure of death and rebirth.

In his split personality, Goethe's Faust represents the ultimate show-down between conscience and evil. Faust is kept going by his vision of the moment of fulfilment, an unattainable ideal that would repair the rift in his very nature. Goethe makes him the prototype of humanity, engaged in a continual struggle involving enthusiastic impulse, setback and partial success. It is Faust's split personality and the placing beside him of the spirit of evil, with whom he fights like an enemy, that give the play its dynamism. Confrontation with evil including the evil within oneself is a stage that has to be negotiated; the dual nature of the tragedy of Faust is based on the constant relationship between events and character. Far from being a weakening factor, it is the split in one's personality that establishes an active relationship with the world, the dialectic condition of the individual: being torn in two is the condition of Man's freedom. Thus *Faust* II (1831) brings about a synthesis between subjectivity and the objective world, through the idea of polarity as a union of opposites: 'Wir sind geeinte Zwienatur' ('we are two natures in one').

The conflicts portrayed are those of a soul in search of itself. Here, the myth of the double becomes the metaphor or symbol of a search for identity that leads inwards – even if, in the outside world, the original protagonist is also brought face to face with an objective double. We have moved from the external to the internal. The essential conflict becomes the struggle for a better self, involving the choice between good and evil, and it is the human soul that is at the centre of the debate. It may be prepared to accept without question the objective existence of the double (as in *Wilhelm Meisters Lehrjahre*, 1795–6), or prepared to accept the mirages of art at the expense of reality (*Der Triumph der Empfindsamkeit*, 1777).

In the Age of Enlightenment the unmasking of the double came to symbolize the triumph of reason over obscurity, as in Chamisso's poem 'Die Erscheinung' (1826), and his philosophical fairy tale *Peter Schlemihls wundersame Geschichte* (1814). In the latter, Schlemihl sells his shadow to the grey man (the devil) to acquire wealth and prestige, but, in doing so, he loses his right to a social identity, and becomes an object of scandal. The double, the shadow, has an allegorical meaning, and becomes something that can be separated from the body like a coat. The exchange of the immaterial shadow for a constant supply of money is a fool's bargain since the shadow is the symbol of appearance, and not even a rich man can do without it. Schlemihl has attempted to acquire social status by giving up the only possession that is essential to him.

Chamisso depicts a society that confuses appearance (the shadow) with reality (Fink (1982) *Recherches germaniques* 12). It inverts values by regarding the man who takes Schlemihl's place beside Minna as honest, when he is in fact a thief. Meanwhile, money is useless if the signs of money (the shadow) are absent. A year after selling his shadow, Schlemihl is offered it back in exchange for his soul but he refuses. The external double, the shadow that represents social image, is contrasted with the soul, which equals real identity. Schlemihl is opposed to the inversion of values in society, to people's acceptance of the shadow. In the end, he accepts his condition as a man without a shadow and lives apart from society, renouncing his false double and keeping his soul intact. Chamisso's story of the loss of the shadow left its mark on later works. Ewers was inspired by it in his film *L'Etudiant de Prague*, and so, much earlier, was Hoffmann in his book *Die Abenteuer der Sylvesternacht* (1815). In the latter the double reflection symbolizes the indestructible nature of the physical desire that prevents the protagonist from regaining middle-class respectability. The theme recurs too in Hans Christian Andersen's tale 'The Shadow' (1846) where regaining your lost shadow is equated with condemning yourself to being no more than a shadow of a shadow, and so with dying). Finally, it also features in Hofmannsthal's libretto for Strauss's opera *Die Frau ohne Schatten* (1919). Here, the loss of the shadow symbolizes sterility, and renunciation of it represents a triumph of the moral individual. Accepting the loss of the decoy-double means coming through a test strengthened.

A related image occurs in the 'Wunderbare Geschichte von Bogs dem Uhrmacher' (1807) by Brentano and Görres, where the severance of a second face that starts to appear beneath his hair enables the hero to be fully himself.

III FIGURES REPRESENTING HETEROGENEITY

1 The strange self, the dissipation of the self

When the feeling of a genuine otherness, a Romantic vision of the self, finally emerged, it was influenced by political and historical factors (notably the French Revolution) and by idealistic philosophy (Fichte, *Über den Bergriff der Wissenschaftslehre*, 1794). In a period of political turmoil when established hierarchies were under attack and the authority of the State and the Church were being questioned, the problems of personal identity became of crucial importance, and, against this background, philosophical idealism acted as a metaphysical prop for the theory of the double self.

The vision that emerged was of a world that is double, in which everything is just appearance, while true reality is to be found elsewhere. Everything that seems objective is in fact subjective, and the world is no more than a figment created by a dialogue within the mind itself. Convinced of the truth of this view, the heroes of the works by Jean-Paul (the pen name of Johann Paul Friedrich Richter) experiment with the way in which a familiar body seen in the mirror or seen only partially is transformed into something obscure and unfamiliar to the conscious mind. This introduced the myth of the double, which forms a recurrent theme in Jean-Paul's books.

In *Siebenkäs* (1796–7), a novel about character development, the eponymous hero is a poor man's lawyer who feels stifled by the narrow world of Kuhschnappel and by his marriage. He therefore exchanges names with his soulmate, double and counterpart, Leibgeber. However, this arangement does not suit the latter, and to escape from his new identity the false Siebenkäs makes people believe that he is dead and resumes Leibgeber's identity. This allows him to marry Nathalie, the woman whom the false Leibgeber loves but has renounced to travel the world as a 'waltzer through life', living out the multiple identities that are the curse of the human condition.

Leibgeber is a symbol of idealistic philosophy, and suffers from the divisible nature of the feeling of self that arises from its multiple manifestations. He and Siebenkäs together represent the ideal of the 'noble man', a reuniting the two complementary halves of the human being referred to in the Platonic myth. They are soulmates, twins . . . a double man composed of two natures. When Leibgeber disappears, Siebenkäs becomes himself *and* his friend, for good.

It is the tragic side of the double man separated from his other self that Jean-Paul explores in *Titan* (1801–3). This continues the story of the two characters in his earlier book, but Siebenkäs alias Leibgeber is now called Schoppe, and is the tutor of Albano, the ideal hero who struggles against the disease of subjectivism. Leibgeber is obsessed by the enigma of identity, and, as a humorist, he represents the split between a self that acts and a self that looks on. He observes his own body, overwhelmed by the idea of the separation and reunion of a finite principle (the body) and an infinite principle (the soul). This sense of estrangement leads him into schizophrenia and he is haunted by the idea of meeting himself in a visible form. Behind the obsession with doubleness is the dissolution of the objective reality within the subjective framework of the consciousness, and his fear of mirrors illustrates the philosophical basis of his anguish: he is both the subject that is conscious and the object of which he is conscious. When he meets his friend and double Siebenkäs, he thinks that he is seeing his own self, and collapses repeating the words spoken by Swift on his deathbed, 'I am I'. This split in consciousness leads to madness and death. It prevents us from coinciding with ourselves, since the conscious state which is possible only with and through this division will not allow us to reach substantial reality. Everything that is perceived outside the self is still the self – an idea also expressed in Kleist's essay 'Über das Marionettentheater' (1810).

Becoming double, or acquiring consciousness, is synonymous with losing the innocence associated with the lack of consciousness that meant that Man was at one with nature. Human consciousness with its ability to become double and its powers of imagination turns into a source of terror. Jean-Paul's book *Titan* (1800–1), which is a novel about education, depicts the dangers of subjectivity turning in on itself. The loss of the substance of the self goes hand in hand with an alienating sort of concretization. The self is petrified into the form of a double, creating an anguish that deprives the world of its reality and makes people develop an aversion towards their own bodies.

In *Hesperus* (1795), also by Jean-Paul, the hero Victor agrees to allow a waxwork model of himself to be made to please to curate. This wax doll represents an attempt to fossilize his soul in an alienating form and reproduction as an effigy is thus used to illustrate the anguish caused by encountering the strangeness of one's own body. Confrontation with something that seeks to embody you raises the problem of existence: where is the infinite located within this form? In thc case of Schoppe, the identity crisis that empties the self of its substance is marked by the repetition of the same act: he removes one mask, but beneath this he is wearing another mask, and so on – the self is merely the mask for an infinite number of other selves. (The same anguish at being brought face to face with one's own reflection is expressed in an episode in Fouqué's novel, *Der Zauberring*, 1813.)

The split personalities of Jean-Paul's characters express a discontinuity within the individual, a perversion of reality that arises because the reflection is made to deviate from its original function, which was to ensure the coherence of the self. Their illness leads Jean-Paul's heroes, and Tieck's hero William Lovell in the novel of the same name (1795–6), to madness and crime. The instability of the self is sometimes conveyed through the existence of actual living doubles, as in *Die unsichtbare Loge* (1793) and *Siebenkäs*, and sometimes through the figures of dummies, puppets and robots. Man is surrounded by physical images of himself that make him lose touch with his identity because it has been irrevocably altered, as in the case of Schoppe and the wax figures.

In the works discussed above, the loss of the substance of the self was expressed in terms of an alienating concretization of subjectivity, represented by a meeting with one's double. However, pseudo-scientific theories, such as that of animal magnetism, developed by Franz Anton Messmer (1734–1815), were based on a belief in the existence of a fluid permeating every aspect of nature. This created a state of hypersensitivity, explaining the occurrence of phenomena such as second sight, telepathy, hypnosis or premonitory dreams, and constituted a spiritual principle acting as a link between man and nature. This pseudo-discovery encouraged belief in the possibility of a remote magnetic union, which the Romantics used as the basis for their theories about the unconscious and about dreams. There is a continuity linking the amorphous and the living, and the double becomes a metaphor for a person's relationship with the world.

2 The Bond Between the Living Person and the Artificial Image

In *Isabella von Ägypten* (1812) by Arnim, the golem Bella represents a simplified form of the double, the sensual self as opposed to the spiritual self. However, the treatment of the mannequin double in *Mellück Maria Blainville* (1809) also by Arnim is more subtle. In it, the count wears a coat as a pledge of his faithfulness to his betrothed from whom he is separated, but the Eastern sorceress Mellück contrives to place it on the shoulders of a dummy, and the dummy, whom she has made resemble the count, comes to life. Thus, when the count's friend destroys the dummy as he holds the count's wife in his arms, he feels that he has committed murder by proxy. The dummy is the count's double in several ways: in his role as Mellúck's lover; because it wears the coat as a symbol of betrayal; and also in physical terms, since the count has lost his heart to Mellúck. Magic is just a way of dressing up a psychological reality, and the double is the outer manifestation of inner mayhem. Mellúck is able to take possession of the count's heart from afar by means of a glance and to use it to bring the dummy to life only because the count is in the thrall of passion, though he fights against it. Thus, it is the soul or psyche that is the central element in the story.

The artificial man ceases to be mere matter and becomes a living being through the agency of the hero. It is a creation of his subjectivity, even if it needs someone else to make it (for example, Spalanzani and Coppelius, who make the dolls in Hoffman's 'Der Sandmann', 1816). Nathanaël and the automaton Olimpia are portrayed as a couple, and Olimpia has a social existence. Nathanaël is a new Pygmalion, who gives Olimpia life through his gaze, for she represents his inner self. It is himself that he loves in her; as in the case of Narcissus she is his reflection and counterpart, his only means of relating to the world; yet Olimpia is also the symbol of his alienation. He has made this entity derived from himself into a physical subject, as compensation for his failure to be a writer. Artistic creativity could be the road to salvation for someone who responds more to fiction than to life. The dismantling of the doll before his very eyes gives physical expression to the schizoid fear of disintegration that repeatedly threatens Nathanaël himself through the image of the sandman who tears out children's eyes. This event goads him into madness, and, after a respite, into suicide. At the same time, Olimpia is also an allegorical version of Nathanaëls flesh-and-blood fiancée, Klara.

For the German Romantics, the double in the form of an automaton became a symbol of Man's degeneracy, as in 'Die Nactwachen des Bonaventura' (anonymous 1805) or 'Die Automate' (1819) by Hoffman. The artificial figures, mistaken for their living counterparts, represent an emotional illness leading to madness, murder and suicide. By contrast the Golem in Meyrink's novel *The Golem* (1915) has the power to enable the human heart to see into itself. It is an empty form that forces the hero to seek his own fundamental identity. He becomes aware of his inner being (a process represented by means of a journey into a room with no way out) and is reborn psychically (a reflection of beliefs).

Hoffmann presents the meeting with a real or imagined double as the means whereby the hero can find his true self. However, some characters, such as Nathanaël, fail in their search for it through surrendering to the omnipotence of thought and failing to recognize the dual nature of feeling and understanding. The hero's narcissistic desire to bring to life a doll that will fulfil his nostalgic longing for the ideal – represented by the 'court of Arthur', the 'pledge', and the 'choice of a bride' – ends in madness and death, which is portrayed in terms of the petrification of the hero inside his own dream. The double represents a paradox whereby the imaginary takes on a human form with which the hero wants to achievc physical union. The artificial form of life comes to be idolized at the expense of the instinctive living person (the philistine), so that the values of life and death are inverted.

To recognize oneself in counterfeit objects, such as automata and portraits (as in 'Das öde Haus' by Hoffmann, or 'Die Jesuitenkirche', 1813) or statues that come to life as in Arnim's 'Raphaël und seine nachbarinnen', Eichendorff's 'Das Marmorbild', 1819, and Mérimées 'La Vénus d'Ille', 1837, or to find one's counterpart in them, is to be lost (see Erckmann-Chartrian's *L'oeil invisible*, 1858).

In 'The Oval Portrait' (1842) Poe demonstrates the relentless process of transference that takes place from life into art, a theme that was reflected in the story's original title, 'Life in Death'. The artist creates a living portrait of his wife, and, as a result, she dies. The artist's act in creating a double feeds parasitically on the vital sources of womanhood, and thus involves a process of pictorial assassination. In a strange form of osmosis, art thrives and flourishes on the blood taken from life, but as it takes life, it also gives it back. In the mind of the hero who sees his double, there is a continuity between the living and the inanimate, so that to put one's portrait to death is to die oneself. Thanatos is the double of Eros.

This theme persisted into the post-Romantic era, when the danger of inverting the values of life and death was demonstrated in *The Picture of Dorian Gray* (1891) by Oscar Wilde. Looking at his portrait, Dorian discovers how handsome he is and vows always to match this likeness. In the process, he interchanges the animate and the inanimate, the external and the internal. Dorian has become his effigy, the object of his own worship. He escapes the human condition of ageing (through having an ideal double), while the portrait becomes the emblem of his inner self (the image of conscience). Dorian discovers a second double in the story of the Parisian who has experienced all the pleasures of the flesh and is in despair because he has lost his looks. The perverted dandy, Lord Henry's friend, who places himself above the level of ordinary mortals by adhering to the principle that 'everything is permitted', sees in the portrait a mirror of his soul. By putting a dagger through his likeness he commits suicide, and in his death the superficial and the intimate are inverted. Dorian becomes petrified in an external image without achieving self-awareness. The warning function of the increasing ugliness of the double is not perceived and he fights to the very end against the internalization of consciousness.

In popular superstition, a strikingly expressive and accurate portrait may be regarded as a work of witchcraft. Meanwhile, the fear aroused by an image that is too lifelike is also associated with the fear that it may expose a hidden vice. Thus in 'Prophetic Picture' (1837) by Hawthorn, the painter who is making the portrait of the engaged couple depicts a fixed expression of fear on the face of Elinor, and a strange, perverse animation in the features of Walther, thereby prophesying the bloody fit of madness that is to come. The shame that a confrontation with his double represents for the hero lies in the fact that it reveals what is hidden. At the same time, however, this unmasking can provide an opportunity for furthering one's knowledge of one's self and even changing it.

3 The Symbol of the Search for Identity

In *Die Elixiere des Teufels* (1815–6) Hoffmann tells the story of the doomed descendants of the painter Francesko. The latter had married the devil, who had taken on the appearance of Venus, and was condemned to return to earth until his family should be saved by the living doubles Médard and Aurélie. Médard is the son of an unknown father and is condemned to multiple identity. When he meets his living double, his half-brother Victor, whom he does not know, and borrows the latter's identity, this precipitates his feeling of depersonalization. His uneasy awareness of his own faults causes him to project the sensual and criminal instincts that represent the facet of his nature that he does not wish to acknowledge, onto a double.

His living double, Victor, represents abandonment to the brutality of instinct and the temptations of madness, while his dream double, Francesko, the ghostly father, is a redemptive figure who awakens the voice of conscience. There are two tendencies at war within Médard. He aspires to virtue, and when he recovers from a period of unconsciousness following the final attack by his double, who leaps on his shoulders in a fantastic chase through the forest, this leads him to be 'reborn' and choose the quiet, secluded life of the monastery. At the same time, he seeks the immediate satisfaction of his impious desire to possess Auréklie, and so profane all that is sacred.

The metaphysical dimension represented by the concept of inherited sin, the idea that the sins of the fathers seethe in the blood of their sons, is counterbalanced by the psychological dimension. Médard is a sensualist who aspires towards the ideal. Though he is tied to the earth, he looks towards heaven. Torn in two directions, he has to fight with his double, his own sensuality, which goes as far as murder in its search for satisfaction.

Hoffmann portrays a man riven apart who reacts by projecting his antisocial impulses onto a third party. In Freudian terms, the imaginary double is his repressed self, whereas the living double is the reminder of his hereditary burden. Thus the vertigo that the latter inflicts on him symbolizes the compulsion to go on repeating what has gone before. By giving shape to his impulses Médard the visionary is protecting himself against murder and madness.

In other works by Hoffmann artistic endeavour serves as a means of transcending the split existence that is the common lot of humankind; here it is by finally accepting his identity in the solitude of religion that Médard will be able to assume it. Dreams about infinity, about the other reality that must be sought outside permitted channels through acts of transgression, create a sense of menace and it is from this that consciousness of an original sin arises. Identical portrayals of the double recur in Hoffmann's *Kater Murr* (1819). Here, the central character is a musician named Kreisler, who suffers from a feeling of alienation. He doubts that it is possible to achieve self-knowledge and identifies with the mad painter Ettlinger. Meanwhile, Ettlinger himself has become a new Pygmalion, by falling madly in love with the portrait of Princess Hedwiga that he painted as a young man. Kreisler becomes aware that the artist's love takes the form of a gaze that can see internal reality, without any desire to possess it. The concept of the double also affects the structure of the work, and enables it to give a complete picture of Kreisler. It forms a composition in which the tragic life story of the musician alternates with the cheerful autobiography of the cat mentioned in the title, which is also in search of its identity. A humorous style is used for the cat's story, which is told in the first person, and an imaginative style for the episodes involving Kreisler, whose character is based on 'Kresleriana'. In the process, the figure of the double provides a highly effective vehicle for relationship between the artist and the world.

4 The Emblem of the Surreal

The artist is the supreme dual character, who is able to understand that hidden behind the life's appearances there lies another reality, who appreciates that the world is double. In Hoffmann's 'Der goldene Topf' (1814), Anselme experiences the dilemma of the Romantic artist situated between two poles. In everyday life he is the happy middle-class citizen, yet at the same time he is the artist who renounces superficial happiness to reach the other reality. This reality is represented by the myth of the 'return of the Golden Age', and also that of Atlantis, which is rendered accessible to initiates by a mentor with a double personality, the archivist-magician Lindhorst. The resultant journey inside the self breaks the narrow framework of appearances represented by a mirror and a golden vase with the help of magic instruments. By opening up a third eye it turns the universe into poetry and 'romanticizes' it (Novalis), bringing about a transformation that can be achieved only by those who 'shut themselves off' from everyday life. Meanwhile, hostile forces (fairies, magicians, etc.) resist this process of initiation. In the same way, in 'Prinzessin Brambilla' (1820), the struggle between the hero Giglio, who suffers from a chronic form of split personality, and his double Prince Cornelio Chiappari is resolved by the myth of the hero's redemption. Here the metaphor of the double serves to update a theme that was constantly to recur at the beginning of the twentieth century: that of the antagonism between the artist and the middle classes (Thomas Mann). In Hoffmann's story this conflict is resolved only the synthesis of spirituality and sensuality (a wonderful tale, a utopia).

The myth of the double features repeatedly in Hoffmann's work, in all its varied forms. In 'Die Doppelgänger' (1821) Doedatus and George are so similar that other people take one for the other. Though each sets out with a clear sense of his own identity, their experience of the confusion that they arouse in others leads them to ponder the difficulty of knowing which is the self. An amusing theatrical variation on the theme of the double occurs in *Signor Formica*. Here, Pasquale Capuzzi is confronted on stage by a double who does things that he does not want to do, and becomes involved in a heated argument with himself. In 'Meister Floh' (1822), Man's double nature is portrayed in terms of two individuals, while 'Klein Zaches' (1819) describes a society of theists deceived into believing that everything done by anybody else is the work of a horrible freak. Adopting a rather different approach, 'Das Fraülein von Scudéry' (1820) portrays the double personality of a well-respected middle-class jeweller who becomes a murderer through his fetish-istic love for one of his own creations, while 'Das steinerne Herz' (1817) portrays doubles acting as proxies. In the latter, two young people fulfill the destiny of their parents, who had been unable to make a life together because of the blind pessimism of the hero (symbolized by the heart of stone of the title). The hero of Hoffmann's 'Don Juan' (1813) is depicted as someone who projects onto women the beauty that he senses in himself, making them into his dolls. As a result, the contrast between the women's real appearances and the image that he dreams of fills him with bitter disappointment. Finally it is the image of the diabolical double that features in 'Ignaz Denner' (1816).

For German Romantics, duplication not only expressed the attitude of the self towards the world, but also represented a means of reaching beyond normal reality to a higher reality. Thus the first-born heir in 'Die Majoratsher-ren' (1820) by Arnim sees double, and has visions involving a dialogue between the self and reality. In this context, the double symbolizes access to hidden reality, an apothesis.

This was the idea that Nerval had in mind when he spoke of 'old Germany, mother to all of us, Teutonia'. His reference to 'the spreading of the dream into the real world' portrays duplication as second sight, and this concept forms a recurrent theme in his stories, as well as in the poem 'el desdichado' (*Les Chimères*, 1853). The motif of lost happiness gives rise to the image of the self as a palimpsest, whereby the present self is seen as the denial of past selves. Thus in 'Sylvie' (1853), the young Parisian lives in a present peopled by ghosts. God has ceased to exist, and the combination of the image of the dead god and the experience of the loss of one's own being gives rise to the sense of duality. The only love that Nerval expresses is split between two paradoxical female figures, Sylvie and Adrienne, who are complentary opposites. In the eyes of the narrator, Aurélie is a reincarnation of Adrienne, but the irreversible passage of time makes oneness impossible. Thus Aurélie does not identify himself with Adrienne and denies being the divinity that he sees her as being. The double that acts as a focus of desire is just an empty shell. The self is cured of its split only on exceptional occasions when time ceases to exist, as when Sylvie and Gérard conjure up the wedding of their uncle and aunt during an eternal minute that brings recognition of the eternal self. This raises the question of how we can live permanently in a state in which the ideal and the real are fused. In *Aurelia* (1854) Nerval describes a journey through the city of Paris as if it is a waking dream, and, from the Romantic period onwards, the theme of travel or wandering was constantly used in association with the myth of the double. This is because the latter involves the search for one's better self, and, in Nerval's case, for one's happy self. In *Aurelia* the descent into the underworld is a descent into the self. On his initiatory jouney various tests await the traveller, the most fomidable being a confrontation with the frightening phantom of his double, which he encounters in a state of consciousness between dream and reality (chapter IX). He sees his double become an actor to usurp his place, and then being led away by guards. This 'other self', which takes advantage of its resemblance to him and deceives his friends, including even Aurelia, will accomplish the objective of the journey beyond the grave by finding the dead woman again and celebrating the mystical marriage.

The tragic personal adventure becomes a symbol of the opposition between hostile principles that prevents the cosmogonic couple whose union is ordained by Providence from actually coming together (see 'Histoire du calife Hakem' inserted in *Le voyage en Orient*, 1835). The figure of the double represents the moral choice between god and evil, and is thus related to the central question of salvation: 'Am I chosen or cursed?' Aurelia is lost in the argument with the self, while the 'other' is the evil genius. The appearance of the double is linked with the theme of wrong-doing: the selfish thought that the woman he loves belongs to him more in death than in life; the deification of love; and the insult to the Creator. Meanwhile, Nerval's account re-emphasizes an idea that runs like a leitmotif throughout the works of German literature relating to doubles: that to see one's double is to be mad.

The story of a meeting with a double in *Nadja* (1928) by Breton follows in the tradition of the works of Nerval. Through the motif of a journey across Paris with a female counterpart, Nadja, Breton conjures up a mental landscape involving contrasts between the subjective (the narrator) and the objective (the 'other': Nadja), dreaming and waking, reason and madness, the present and the past relived. The world is double, a porous cloth that enables contact between the self and others. Wandering through the streets at random, the characters have a series of encounters with the world of impulses and the unconscious. Meeting the 'other' becomes a way of getting inside oneself.

The process of initiation and the quest for a better self that is in harmony with the world portrayed in stories concerning the double are inevitably doomed to failure. The meeting with the double constitutes an important landmark in the quest, but, paradoxically, the double represents both what would make the attainment of its goal possible and what makes the self flawed and imperfect. The *Au Château d'Argol* (1932) by Julien Gracq centres on a young hero in seach of knowledge: Albert or 'Dr Faust'. He is portrayed on the road leading to an enchanted castle, lost in the forest and battered by waves, where he experiences (or imagines that he experiences) a meeting with Herminien, his double and his oppoosite, the dark angel. The latter represents the sensual part of his spirit, which will divert him from his spiritual quest by taking him to the castle of Heide, a creature with two contradictory sides to her nature – a holy side symbolizing the Grail and Christ, and an impure side representing a play on her name (Heide = *Heidin*, pagan). As a result, the spiritual quest changes into a sensual one, symbolized by the rape of Heide. The impossible union of which Albert dreams involves the merging of three entities into a single body, recalling the myth of the Trinity. He seeks to combine the intellectual, the sensual and the feminine principle, love and fraternal feelings of affection, but the actual outcome is the murder of the female and male double. Nonetheless, even if the quest for a better self does inevitably end in failure, the theme of the meeting with one's double symbolizes the longing for a meeting with the 'other', the aspiration of a reasoning self to become a dreaming self that experiences passion. It thus represents fusion beyond the limitations of personality, and the desire for communion.

5 A myth of love

The duplication of a lover in the form of a false double (as in the fragment of *Tristan* by Thomas the Rhymer of Erceldoune) does not consign true love to oblivion, or reduce the desire for a bond of love that will last for ever. Indeed, this is the idea that underlies stories involving living doubles or dead women who were loved passionately during their lifetimes. Poe returned frequently to the theme of women who survived their own deaths in the form of doubles. In 'Ligeia' (1837) the double was the woman's rival, while in 'Morella' (1839) it was her daughter, and in 'Eleonora' (1835) it was someone who took over her place. The dead woman's immortality in the form of a double permits her to reconstitute a unit with the narrator, treating a union of twin souls that in real life is constantly threatened by death.

This is why Poe's story 'The Fall of the House of Usher' (1839) serves both as a model for these love stories and, at the same time, as a metaphor of them. In it, the family home of the twins Roderick and Madeline is split by a fissure, so that it symbolizes both oneness and doubleness, while this image is also conveyed by the house's reflection in the tarn and 'the strange and equivocal appellation of the house of Usher'. The latter can be divided into the words 'us' and 'her', representing a dualistic combination of the protagonist and the narrator 'us' as opposed to the single 'her'. In this way, the split is always present despite the illusion of union.

The actual return of a dead woman symbolizes the omnipotence of thought, as in the case of 'Véra' (1874) by Villiers de l'Isle-Adam, where the reappearance of Véra is brought about by the mystical power of love. However, the creation of the double through the hero's desire, engenders a feeling of guilt leading to punishment by death and thereby creating a circular pattern exemplified by Poe's story 'Berenice' (1835). For the lover, meeting his own double symbolizes the loss of the woman he loves, and results in a bitter solitude leading to a longing for death. In *Das Buch der Lieder* (1817–21) by Heine the theme of the double, in the guise of the pale companion, recurs in 'Junge Leiden', nos. 2 and 3, 'Die Heimkehr' (1823) nos. 13, 20 and 33, and 'Lyrisches Intgermezzo' (1822–3), no. 38. Heine concludes the 'Heimkehr' cycle with a farewell to the Romantic perception of life (no. 44), using irony to dissociate himself from the suffering self.

The same painful perception of life is expressed in the vision of a 'stranger dressed in black who resembled me like a brother' in 'La Nuit de décembre' (1835) by Musset. This figure is a travelling comlpanion and a ghost, a witness of sorrows whose presence represents absence and aloneness with oneself, and is a prelude to death. The stranger dressed in black has not yet acquired an image tainted by indescribable vice. Thus, in *Lorenzaccio* (1834), the dream of another self (Marie's hallucination) is used to contrast the pure double with the corrupt hero. In this context, becoming double can be used as part of a defence strategy aimed at denying the painful self.

6 Internal monsters or a private hell

As the nineteenth century progressed one approach to the theme of the double already outlined by the Romantic writers became increasingly prominent. This was the depiction of a split within the self that included an examination of its pathological aspects. Ontological analysis still underlay the psychological approach, but the latter was now to the fore. Thus the Freudian concept of the split personality appeared in literature before the actual theory itself was proposed. One aspect of heterogeneity is represented by the duality of the individual. This involves a conflict between the desired self, and the actual personality, in the form of the image imposed by society.

The antagonism between the wished-for self and the social self, the image of conformity demanded of anyone with social ambitions, has given rise to three variations on the theme of the double, all of which end tragically in the destruction of the self through madness or death. In the story of 'William Wilson' (1839) by Poe the hero is a young Titan who wants to exercise his striving for power in complete freedom. As a consequence, he resents his twin brother's continual championing of morality, and crosses Europe in an attempt to escape from this hated double. The story ends with the latter's murder, which is merely a form of suicide. A gasping conversation with the image in the mirror seals Wilson's illusion; to the very end he refuses to understand that he has tried to kill his own conscience, but that it has finally proved stronger than him.

In this context, the double is perceived as a persecutor because it has the qualities demanded by society while the original is an outsider, or sees himself as one. This theme recurs in Dostoyevsky's story 'The Double' (1846). In contrast to Wilson, its central character, Golyadkin, is a timorous man defined solely by his position as an 'appointed councillor'. As he tries to advance his career, the only thing that matters in his life is the way in which he is regarded by his bosses, 'his fathers'. This masochistic Golyadkin 'senior' finds himself accompanied by a Golyadkin 'junior', a sadistic and hated double with whom he secretly connives. The patronym reveals the parasitic nature of the double; it alludes to Goliath, but at the same time expresses in Russian the idea of being down-and-out, or indigent. It thus highlights the dilemma of the person who wants to move up the social ladder, but has come to share the pejorative judgement of himself that he attributes to his superiors. If he were to accept that Golyadkin 'junior' was a part of himself, this would mean having to admit to being ambitious, pleasure-seeking and eager for luxury and honours. Instead, he lives in perpetual denial of his own individuality and finally goes mad, assailed by the vision of a multiplying number of Golyadkins, a metaphor for the army of ambitious petty bureaucrats awaiting promotion.

An image of respectability that is at odds with the egotism of the deeper self, represents an opposition between the mask and the individaul that is all the more pernicious when the person who is split in this way has a judicial role and thus leads others to their doom. In 'Mr Justice Harbottle' (1851) by Le Fanu, the evil judge is pursued by the double of the accused and is condemned to death by his own double, Lord Twofold, in a phantasmagorical court hearing that mirrors the real trial in an inverted form and reveals the wickedness of the judge himself.

Stevenson's *The Strange Case of Dr Jekyll and Mr Hyde* (1885) is the most famous of all the stories relating to doubles, but the theme made its first appearance in Stevenson's work in 'Markheim' (1885). This depicts a man who refuses to see himself as he actually is, and believes that he is having a conversation with a maleficent double (compare the 'Tale of Tod Lapraik', 1893). In the story of Jekyll and Hyde Stevenson went further. Jekyll knows that he has a double nature and, as a scientist, he sets out to rid himself of this unwelcome part of his character that does conform with his social ambitions. By inventing a special substance, he tries to separate off the part of himself that represents desire. The latter is described in euphemistical terms suited to the rigid moral climate of the Victorian era, as being a certain proclivity towards gaiety, so that it is unclear whether it involves simple sensuality or actual perversion. Jekyll hopes that once he has been freed from this defective part of his character he will totally embody the part that remains, becoming the epitome of the virtuous and austere scholar who knows nothing beyond the simple pleasures of masculine friendship. The first narrator of the story, Jekyll's friend the lawyer Mr Utterson, is the double and embodiment of this persona. However, once the evil side of Jekyll's nature has been released, in the form of a kind of repugnant dwarf called Hyde (or 'hide'), it acts robustly, and feeds on its pale shadow the virtuous Dr Jekyll, like a parasite. The two sides of Jekyll's character were not equal in strength: indeed, the virtuous aspect symbolized by the title of 'doctor' is revealed as being very weak. Using Freudian terms, one might say that the ego (Jekyll) is flattened between the id (Hyde) and the super-ego (Doctor).

The message that emergees from the story is that it is dangerous to allow evil to express itself. Gradually Hyde takes over from Jekyll; evil, in the form of Hyde, is stronger than Jekyll, the pallid figure representing honour who ironically set the brute free. When Hyde agrees to resume the appearance of Jekyll, it is purely through his instinct for self-preservation; the hellish alter ego of the respectable Dr Jekyll has freed himself of all moral restraints, and Jekyll is his hostage. Even in the form of Jekyll, Hyde is still alive and active; Jekyll protects Hyde, for he is only concerned with keeping up appearances. In the end, death reveals what Jekyll really was: the huddled mortal remains are ghastly and hideous. The moral ending to the story seems to imply that pleasure leads to crime, but looked at from a different perspective the story demonstraters the failure of repression. Jekyll wanted to shelter from evil by enclosing it in an apparition external to himself, but it was then that it hit back with redoubled power. The story represents a development in the treatment of the figure of the double in comparison with its treatment by Dostoyevsky. Whereas the existence of Golyadkin's double was still ambiguous, here Hyde exists physically, and is seen by everyone.

As an image of the hell that exists within the human heart and mind, the double, of course, represents the devil, and it is in this guise that it appears in Hogg's *The Confessions of a Justified Sinner* (1824). This is the story of a paragon of religious dedication, who is devoted to preserving a good conscience and fulfilling his own destiny, but who ends up committing suicide when he realizes that the tempter, or devil, in the form of his external double Gil Martin, who is guilty of extortion and other crimes, is actually within him, and that he thus has two souls, which possess him in alternation. The story is structured in the form of an objective account followed by the diary of a man possessed, so that its increasingly introverted progress reflects the growing self-awareness of the hero himself.

It is again the devil, but this time a ridiculous little devil of legend, who embodies the personal hell of Ivan Karamazov in Dostoyevsky's *The Brothers Karamazov* (1879–80). The conversation with the devil at the denouement of the story before Dmitri is condemned symbolizes the dialogue with the self in the form of the examination of one's conscience.

When he becomes aware of his double nature, Dostoyevsky's hero seeks the best way to become whole through accepting evil, and integrating it into himself, in keeping with the example of Christ. Ivan has tried to deny that he carries his paternal heritage within him but each brother emphasizes some aspect of these inherited demons, Dmitri representing sensual passion and Smerdyakov crime. Thus when Ivan endeavours to protect himself by resorting to fiction, his own ideal, magnified double becomes equated with the Grand Inquisitor. However, by breaking away from his family in this way and imagining that he can remain innocent, by 'leaving the serpents to devour one another', Ivan has become guilty of omission. Thus his attitude encourages Smerdyakov to go from words to deeds and actually murder their father. Indeed, in his own mind he has irrevocably condemned his father, and by destroying the idea of God and espousing the moral attitude that 'everything is allowed', he has made man divine ('parable of the Grand Inquisitor').

In contrast to Ivan, Alyosha represents someone who has identified with his positive double, the Elder Zosima, and who has passed through the processes of confrontation with evil and acceptance of it, symbolized by the odour of corruption and the wedding at Cana. Ivan accepts and reintegrates the parts of his own nature he identifies in his living double. His passion for Katerina Ivanovna represents the Dmitri elements and his saving of the poor drunkard the Alyosha element, while his aceptance of his own guilt reflects the Smerdyakov component. Ivan comes out of the confrontation with himself, 'with myself everything low, vile and despicable that there was in me', morally regenerated, even if physically he is destroyed.

The resolution of the identity crisis represented by the concert of the double starts with the acceptance of human nature as a dual entity comprising both angel and beast. Men such as the Elder or Alyosha are proof that it is possible to change. Coming face to face with one's double takes on a social resonance: we need to know who we are in order to act alongside our fellow creatures, as the story of Alyusah shows. At the same time, the double is a symptom of modern man's crisis of faith, brought about by substituting consumer goods for the concept of transcendence. It thus reflects the opposition between the atheist European world and the Russian world.

In Dostoyevsky's writing the figure of the double features in the search for the better self, a quest that is undertaken by human beings but that, at the same time, means that God is not dead (compare *The Devils*, 1871–2, 'The young man', 1975). Meanwhile the theme of confrontation with a double acting as a catalyst for the moral transformation of a hero also occurs in works by Dickens (*A Christmas Carol*, 1842, 'The Haunted Man', 1848) and by Kipling ('The dream of Duncan Parrennes', 1891).

The idea that the double represents loss of the self – its draining by a vampire attack – which has its roots in the stories of Jean-Paul, acquired real prominence in the works of Edgar Allan Poe and Maupassant. It is 'the demon of perversity' that impels the hero of 'The black cat' (1843) by Poe to confront his personal hell; yet, like William Wilson, the hero is frightened of shedding light on his innermost being, the black cat of the title, which answers to the symbolic name of Pluto. He first loves the cat then hates it, enucleating and walling it in. But the terrifying animal lies inside himself, and he is still a prisoner of his murderous impulses. The cries of the beast from behind the wall symbolized the impossibility of continuing to hide one's innermost being.

Though his awareness of inner demons fills him with a horrifying sense of imprisonment, the hero who is possessed by his double simultaneously feels a fatal attraction towards it. Thus the work of Maupassant suggests a morbid taste for the experience madness that has a hint of autobiographical detail. The horror of the double symbolizes the fear of living with oneself. To escape the agony of discovering what he really is, the hero of 'Lui' (1883) suddenly feels the need to live in a couple, though previously he had always preferred to avoid this by living a life of promiscuity instead.

A specialized use of the concept of the double reappears like a leitmotif in works in which the hero-narrator is both the protagonist and writer: 'he haunts me and I know full well that he does not exist'. The unknown character who appears beside the figure narrating the story in the first person, and who represents the split in the latter's personality, is already in evidence in Maupassant's poem 'Terreur' (1880). It became more concrete, and was given symbolic name (not a surname as in Stevenson's work) encapsulating all the horror of seeing oneself. Thus the name of the figure in 'Le Horla' (1886) can be broken down into the words: hors, meaning outside me, and là meaning there (not here), or alternatively present. The result is the name 'there and not there', which is merely a euphemistic disguise for the figure of the double, which is outside and therefore not within. It thus represents the denial of madness, as he who is outside me is not me. By this device, the hero of the 'hors-là' maintains a substantial distance between himself and the person whom he does not want to reveal his own psychic characteristics. The latter is the ultimate symbol of heterogeneity, the individual, a new individual, a mutant who has come from the alien land of Brazil and who will cause an epidemic.

Everything is a pretext for keeping what is inside the self at a distance, or for making it concrete in the form of a double ('I felt someone hunched over me') or of a vampire. Yet the sudden introduction of metaphor of the transparent body, represented by the absence of a reflection in the mirror, contradicts all these attempts to distance the innermost self and so be free of it. The absence of a reflection in the mirror shows that the double is just an illusion; an 'hors-là' or out-there with no substance, the sign of madness.

Maupassant gave the double its conventional modern significance while at the same time managing never to mention it explicitly by its conventional name. Instead, he described it in a multitude of ways that skirt round the idea but never pin it down precisely. He used the riveting image of the window, the image of the book placed on the table and the page that turns itself. The armchair seems empty to others but is all too occupied by an unseen being, '*là*, assis à ma place', making absence represent all too great a presence. This is an image of madness that ends with the words, 'so I am going to have to kill myself', a remark that shows that the other is in fact the self.

IV THE OPENING ONTO THE WORLD

The figure of the divided person, as portrayed in literature in the form of the tormenting double, attests to the deep change in the concept of self that took place during a period of turmoil caused by political and industrial revolution. The vision of the sovereignty of the ego expressed in the maxim 'cogito ergo sum' gave way to a different vision expressed by the words 'who is speaking within me?' Individuality was discovered to be flawed.

Various psychoanalytical case studies focusing on dreams (Freud, *Die Traumdeutung*, 1900) and abortive actions (Freud, *Die Psychopathologie des Alltagslebens*, 1901) reveal that heterogeneity is part of the human psychic condition. Meanwhile Lacan has shown that becauses of the unconscious, the alter ego is never where the individual thinks it is. Thus access to the symbolic ends with the splitting of the self (*Le séminaire* XI 'L'inconscient freudien et le nôtre', 1973).

1 Towards the new man

The influence of psycho-analysis on early twentieth-century literature is obvious. It not only led to the formulation of the idea of the duality of consciousness, but also encouraged its depiction as something to be overcome. Thus the double features widely in Expressionist plays of the *Wandlung* that examine the nature and functioning of the subconscious (Ich-Dramen).

Expressionist authors wrote what amounted to personal confessions, modelling them on the trilogy *Till Damaskus* (1904) by the Swedish writer Strindberg. This is a drama with set scenes in which the characters split into different personalities in order eventually to rediscover their original identity and unity, even if only in death. One consequence of the Expressionists' adoption of the new vision of Man is the use on stage of doubles who constitute projections of the central character. They variously represent his ideal self (Hansenclever *Die Koralle*, 1919 and *Der Sohn*, 1914), his guardian angel (Barlach *Der arme Vetter*) and his better self (Becker, *Das letzte Gericht*, 1919), or take monstrous forms, such as that of the man-goat in Werfel's drama *Der Spiegelmensche*

(1920). Even when the meeting with the double ends in the death of the hero (Kayser, *Zweimal Olivier*), the latter achieves moral regeneration by killing himself. Death is a second birth as it affirms the better self even at the cost of sacrificing one's life. The person who makes this sacrifice is the antithesis of the 'looking-glass man', whose self-indulgence allows monsters to come into existence.

The everyday world is peopled with ghosts created by mistakes and crimes. Thus the doubles of the victims and killers of the 1914–18 War resurface to the level of human consciousness in Frey's novella *Verzweiflung* (1920). To escape from despair heroes torn between good and evil set off in search of a new creed, whether it be purely humanist (Goll, *Methusalem oder der ewige Bürger*) or drawn from the mainstream of Christian faith (Beckmann, *Das Hotel*, 1923–4; O'Neill, *Days without end*, 1934). In the theatre this theme of internal division is portrayed by the confrontation between the hero and his double. In O'Neill's play, the split pesonality formed by John (representing good) and Loving (representing evil) is eventually reconciled with himself in the faith of his childhood, and once again becomes John Loving.

In the early twentieth century a moral preoccupation was the driving force behind works that used the double as a metaphorical element in a process of transformation designed to integrate the individual into society. In the Viennese 'Volksstück' *Der Alpenkönig und der Menschenfeind* (1928) by Raimund, the misanthropist of the title observes his double, who is conjured by the magical powers of the Alpenkönig. This enables him to see himself objectively and consequently cures him of his hatred for mankind (see also the theatrical fairy story *Der Verschwender*, 1834).

2 'Discourse with the Other'

In one way or another, it is the search for one's true identity that constitutes the theme of stories involving a double written from a Freudian perspective. In this context, exploring one's unconscious represents a 'discourse with the other' set in motion by the double. The novella *Die Reitergeschichte* (1898) by Hofmannsthal centres on a soldier who beings to experience unadmitted sensual desires, represented by a meeting with the knight who is his double and counterpart, and who will lead him to rebellion and death.

In 'Les dialogues du Petit moi et du Grand moi' (1897–1906), Pirandello confides his awarenes of his own double nature. Thus, the main subject of his plays and his stories is the drama of the individual split by fear of his unconscious. For him the self has no reality other than its own other side, or even its own opposite.

Gardair (1972) has analysed the countless stories by Pirandello that have plots involving doubles or that contain dualistic elements or characters, as well as his use of doubles in his theatrical works. To express the concept of the double Pirandello employs the image of real or symbolic twinship, which is most reliably indicated by at least partial homonymy (as, for example, in the case of 'Tanino e Tanotto', 'Nenè e Niní' and 'Rondone e Rondinella'). His story 'La Disdetta di Pitagora' tells how the narrator re-encounters a double of his friend Tito that is more genuine than the original, after an interval of three years during which Tito has got married.

The double recurs like a leitmotif in Pirandello's work, and in his plays he reverts to the themes of his short stories. In particular, the theme of imprisonment within one's personality, with the gaze of the other fixed on the self, keeps on cropping up like an obsession. Thus, in the novel *Il fu Mattia Pascal* (1904), the hero discovers that, whether he is actually alive or dead, his fictitious death does not guarantee that he can become a different person. Instead, he reverts to being what he was before, a prisoner of the other – with the added disadvantage of being deceased.

In 'Première et deuxième manières', Stefano Giogli is likewise imprisoned by the personality invented for him by his wife. Meanwhile Eve-Lyne Morli, the heroine of 'La Signora Morli, una e due' (1922) is a woman with two faces. Like a true chameleon, she adapts equally well to the company of the respectable lawyer Lelio and to that of the hedonist Ferrante. Who is she: Eve the madcap or well-behaved Lyne? The impossibility of achieving a sense of identity when one's personality varies according to circumstances and to how one is perceived by others is also illustrated by the agonies of the actress Donata Genzi in 'Trovarsi', who continues to act out her roles even in life. Finally, in *Enrico IV* (1922) the idea of duality is conveyed by means of a theatrical metaphor.

Raising the veil on the mystery of the psyche lays bare the face of the individual behind the mask, uncovering the puppet worked by others. Pirandello uses role-play to demonstrate this, revealing what his protagonists would like to be or should be; and the double plays a crucial part in this process of elucidation by acting a metaphor for the original. We are all our own puppets, and it is up to each of us to discover our mask.

Thus in Conrad's 'The secret sharer' (1925) the stowaway who emerges naked from the sea enables the capain to discover his own identity, since the latter's decision to save his criminal double, risking his own fate and the fate of his crew, makes him the true master of his vessel.

Recognizing the double in oneself has ceased to be the end of the process, and has become a new point of departure. This immediately raises questions about the allegory of the animal double in *Der Steppenwolf* (1927) by Hesse, which acts as a mirror that Harry Haller holds up to himself when going through a period of crisis and represents the metaphor of the split man. Hesse tells us that we must go beyond the myth of the oneness of the self, abandoning the alienating tendency to project the unity of the body on to the mind as well. We are made up of a multiplicity of souls, and he invites us to break the self down into its various components and recognize that its finest element may actually be the 'wolf' part. Taking his inspiration from oriental philosophy, in *Siddhartha* (1922), Hesse imagines a new man who no longer suffers from the chronic effects of a split pesonality, but remains open to all the possibilities of human existence by living fully according to mind and instinct and his dual male and female nature. The same theme of a reconciliation between opposites represented by a hostile double recurs in *Demian* (1919).

It is at this point that the theme of metamorphosis, with its links with animals, intersects the myth of the double. Man carries his animal within him (Mérimée, 'Lokis', 1869) and in twentieth-century literature he often appears as a mutant (Kafka, *Die Verwandlung*, 1911; Cortázar, *Axolotl*, 1963) who becomes imprisoned in another body, or is even transformed into part of a body (Gogol, 'The nose', 1836; Roth, 'The breast', 1972), with no impairment of the peculiarly human capacity for thought. Sometimes he dies, but generally he adapts; and here we return to the Platonic myth of human malleability.

Social preoccupations come to the fore in works where confrontation with the double represents the sudden perception of what is important for the self and of the role that the person is playing in his or her personal environment. The problem that arises is how to accept oneself and be oneself in society.

Significantly, American writing emphasizes the recognition of the principle of reality. Thus in 'The last Mohican' (1955) by Malamud, the significantly named Jew Fidelmann finally accepts the lesson taught him by his double, the Central European Jew Süsskind, who seems to persecute him but is fundamentally a redemptive figure: Fidelmann's vocation as an art critic was just an illusion. The positive consequences of coming face to face with one's own deficiencies and complexes are presented in a similar fashion in Bellow's novel *The Victim* (1947) featuring the confrontation between a Jewish petty official from New York and his parasitic counterpart, a man transparently named Albee. The hero Lewenthal is a symbol of modern man: a victim of his exploitative family and of his work in the office, who is a prey to racial prejudices. By driving his decadent image Albee out of his home, Lewenthal conquers 'the victim' in himself and is ready to embark on a new life.

Such rational optimism seemed out of place in Europe after the Second World War, particularly in Germany. Thus in Nossack's novel *Der Jüngere Bruder* (1949), the quest for the better self, symbolized by the search for the younger brother, the 'angel', is doomed to failure. In the land of Aporée (an obvious allusion to Europe), which has been devastated by a cataclysm, the better self has ceased to exist. The hero Schneider dies stupidly in an accident, after meeting Carlos, the caricatured double of the 'angel' and 'a right little bastard', in a cabaret of the type found in Hamburg. The utopian dimension associated with the figure of the double, the better self towards which Europeans wished to aspire, comes up against the notion, 'Nothing has changed . . . Still the same sham.' In a Europe scarred by the ruins left by war, Anouilh's *Le voyageur sans bagage* (1958) announces a radical break with the past, implying the rejection of one's previous personality. The story concerns the 'second birth' of an amnesiac who refuses to go back to being what he was and to resume the personality of his earlier shadow. In it, the rejection of the double gives birth to a completely new, emancipated, rootless man.

3 Literature as a double

The question that follows logically from the themes of the works just discussed is how we can erase the painful self that is burdened with the past, the family and tradition. Rimbaud had already indicated the necessary course of action in his triumphant declaration, 'Je est un autre' (Letter to Demeny, 1871), which was to become one of the guiding principles of his poetry. Finding himself 'in a soul and a body' ('Adieu', *Une saison en enfer*) and thus a prisoner of himself, Rimbaud opens up his own escape route: the 'I' undergoes a series of metamorphoses ('Botton'), shattering the principle of identity. The poet is a visionary who actually cultivates hallucinations within himself (Alchimie du verbe') and aspires to union with nature 'Bannières de mai'). He seeks to enlarge the self to the size of the world, and to effect an alchemical transformation ('Age d'or') – 'I became a fabulous opera'. Being split into two personalities is an experience of madness the deadly effects of which are ended by the confrontation with the double (a story in *Les Illuminations*). Finally, 'Le voyant' expresses the view that 'every being' is owed several lives ('Alchimie du verbe').

In its use of the double, literature turns the principle of identity upside down: what is single is also multiple, as the writer demonstrates. The desire to erase the self, to escape from the prison of self by travelling, to create an escape-self through the imagination is a constant theme in the works of Julien Green. Thus, the figure of the double recurs obsessively, even featuring prominently in his most recent collection of stories, 'Le langage et son double'/ 'The language and its shadow' (1985), which portrays the author divided between two native tongues, and two countries, the United States of America and France. Through the poetic image of the double, contemporary writers free their heroes, who are often doubles of themselves, from the prison of a particular self moulded into a particular personality. Thus, through the character of Fabien in *Si j'étais vous* (1947), Green assuages a small part of his desire 'to move through mankind like you drive through unfamiliar countries'. With each new transformation he is himself, then someone else. In this way, he experiments with the qualities in which he himself is most deficient, representing the writer in his relationship with his characters, who are simultaneously like him and different from him.

The earliest example of Green's predilection for plots involving journeys through people's characters occurs in *Le voyageur sur la terre* (1924) which involves the almost clinical study of a man with a split personality who dreams of an impossible spiritual liberation. In Julien Green's writing the imaginary inevitably takes over from disappointing reality. Thus in *Le Visionnaire* the dream of assuaging sensual desire represented by Manuel's story is accompanied by an account of everyday life formed by Marie-Thérèse's story, while Manuel has another double who is firmly anchored in disappointing everyday life, in the form of the bedridden old man who is taking forever to die in his windowless room. In his dream the latter is an alter ego who conforms with reality even to the extent of sharing the fantasies summoned up by the principle of pleasure.

In the works of Rimbaud, Hesse and Green, the proclamation of the erasure of the self through the appropriation of the double is accompanied by jubilation. However, this is always matched by a tragic sense of the loss of the self and a haunting fear of madness. The darker implications of discarding the self are also broached in Beckett's storiers *Textes pour rien* (1955). In these, the narrator carriers on a monologue that is not anchored in space or time, showing that even his link with speech, with the 'here and now' of saying 'I', is no longer enough to make him identifiable. The person who says 'I' betrays himself in a fatal way, continually overwhelmed as he is, haunted by all the voices that speak within him willy nilly. In Beckett's works, the self is emptied of its substance, emptied of existence; while all that appear on the stage are thin shreds of humanity that are taken to be the self. Here we are at the opposite pole from the Romantics' ambition to integrate the self, the myth of the infinite self corresponding to the world. The double symbolizes doubt about reality. The self, which is pure discourse, is at the intersection of a web of voices (Beckett, *Molloy*, 1951).

If the elements that demonstrated that the 'I' was anchored in reality disappear, the imaginary takes over from the real; we no longer know who is the original and who is the double. Fiction then takes on a semblance of reality, and the author may introduce himself into the story that he is telling, and become one of the participants. As a result, it seems quite natural when the narrator of L.P. Hartley's story 'W.S.' (1951) is murdered by one of the characters, a projection of the dark side of his own personality, the 'character in search of an author' who is also himself.

The negation of the first-person narrator leads to the abandonment of the idea of someone who presides in a sovereign way over the act of writing (compare Cortázar in 'Rayuela', below). The result is a dualistic element in the plot whereby the novelist also becomes a character.

4 Beyond space and time

In some works, a character may live simultaneously at two different periods, or be in two places at once, so that he is living two or more lives at the same time (compare Blackwood 'The man who has been Milligan', 1930). Indeed, in the story 'Les Sabines' (in *Le passe-muraille*, 1953) Ayme endows his heroine with ubiquity – she fills the earth with her doubles.

The myth of the double has also become a means of expressing contact beyond the self, between two lives or two cultures: the meeting of East and

West (Nerval, Rimbaud, Hesse), and of the New World and the Old World. In each instance, the journey in space is also a journey in time, representing a spatio-temporal form of duality. This denial of the irreversibility of time appeared in the nineteenth century in stories of metempsychosis. Thus in 'A Tale of the Ragged Mountains' (1844) by Poe, Bedloe relives an episode from the life of his counterpart who had died fifty years earlier. Then, as he himself finally dies he slips into the latter's identity, in accordance with the belief that the boundaries between individuals are abolished through the rebirth of the dead in the living. Julien Green's story 'Varouna' (1939–40) is also a tale of metampsychosis' in which the succession of couples whose lot is to have the heroine as their child are linked together in a chain. The future appears as a duplicate of the present in which one possible eventuality becomes fixed. Again, in Hawthorne's 'Howe's Masquerade' (1837) Sir William Howe is confronted by his double in a premonitory hallucination. The vision tells him that he will be the last English governor of Massachusetts and represents a spatial transference of the fear of defeat and death by which the governor is obsessed.

The coincidence of two periods within the same moment often goes hand in hand with the coincidence of two places, producing metaphors that give visual expression to the idea of the double as an identity that brings two lives together at the same time. Henry James has a fondness for telescoping time, place and identity in this way. In his incomplete novel *The Sense of the Past* (1917), as soon as the American Ralph Prendel crosses the threshold of an old house in London he also assumes the identity of a young American from an earlier era. This double is involved in a love affair in 1814, while the original lives in Prendel's present, 1910. In 'The Jolly Corner' (1908) the situation is completely reversed; on returning to the house of his birth in New York after living in Europe for thirty-eight years, the hero tries to flush out the ghost of the past in the form of another self who apparently did not leave, only, in the end, to avoid any confrontation with this double. Yet another story involving the avoidance of a double and the telescoping of time and identities is told in 'The Beast in the Jungle' (1903). Here, the confrontation with the beast, 'the other destiny', is constantly deferred. If it took place, it would raise a mask that has a purely social function (persona), and make it possible to experience the reality of passionate love.

The telescoping of time and place as a necessary precondition for the appearance of a double leads to the notion of a mythical instant, all-important for the future destiny of the hero. The message of Osbert Sitwell's story 'The Man Who Lost Himself' (1930), originally called 'The Man Who found Himself', is conveyed by the two different accounts of the same meeting, reflecting two different points of view. The meeting in a hotel in Granada between the writer Tristram Orlander and himself when he is fifty years older is crucial for the younger man who renounces his ideals and decides to strive for literary success. Meanwhile for the old successful writer, coming face to face with the young man that he once was, marks the moment of death.

The idea of an aperture into eternity formed by identity of fate, and the concept of the eternal return as an obsessive element in the imagination that denies the passage of time, are conjured up by Borges in 'El sur' in *Ficciones* (1956), which evokes the myth of double death. In it someone dying in a Buenos Aires hospital afer a mundane accident sees himself back in the gaucho country of his childhood where he is involved in a deadly duel, reliving the romantic death of his grandfather, who had been run through by the lances of the Indians. A death dreamt of during an actual death 'is as if two men existed at the same time'. Borges thus depicts the imaginary as triumphing over the real. The self is no longer defined by its position in the here and now; instead, the individual experiences the present as an illusion.

To be multiple and to be nobody is a part of the human condition. The collection of stories entitled *El Hacedor* (1960) contains myriad variations on the myth of the double, portraying the self and the alter ego, and Borges and the self ('things happen to the other one, to Borges. I myself walk around in Buenos Aires'), until the two characters merge in the myth of literature. There is a constant play with time in which the self becomes lost. The 'I' of narration changes into a 'he' equated with the non-person Borges the writer. The individual rejoins the human archetype, and the Romantic self is reduced to silence. In the twentieth century the self undergoes a process of dissolution and is lost in a larger grouping.

However, in a world that is experiencing an identity crisis, dreams and poetry bring us close to 'what we were before being what we don't know if we are' (Cortázar). In this world, truth and error have ceased to be the absolute criteria dividing dream and reality, because dreams are the truer of the two. In the story 'La lointaine' in *Las armas secretas* (1963) Cortázar imagines an upside-down world in which a woman from Paris called Alina Reyes meets her double, a female beggar from Budapest, on a bridge. The beggar woman is the inverted double of Alina, the queen (an anagrammtic play on her name), and represents Alina's guilty conscience. She thinks that she can easily oust Alina, but perhaps the improper act of usurpation was actually practised by the happy, well-loved, pampered queen, and the undignified clinging beggar represented reality. The duplication of the self emphasized by distorting space and time shows that Alina discovers her reality in the imaginary.

In 'The out-sider' by Onions (*Widdershins*, 1911) two characters appear superimposed upon one another, one just as real as the other and yet each one different. This represents a bringing together of opposites: the outside is the inside, and the woman drawing is the nun, or vice versa. In 'Der Nachbar' (1917) by Kafka the usurping double may only be the dream of the person who feels that he is being deprived of existence. Amidst the bustling idleness of the bureaucratic circus, which trundles purposelessly ever onwards, he seems to be being dispossessed of himself, his identity reduced to the sign on his door, 'Harras, Office'.

Dream and reality are also turned upside down in Cortázar's story 'La nuit face au ciel' (*Las armas secretas*), which is told in the third person. The realistically presented motorbike accident and journey to hospital apparently turn out to be the consoling dream of a prisoner who is about to be stabbed by the Aztecs as a sacrificial victim. Yet it is still unclear whether the accident and the stone town are the dream of the person about to die on the sacrificial pyre, or whether the accident in fact conjures up the image of the sacrifice. Thus the consciousness of the individual creates a bridge between two separate universes. Cortázar's treatment of the double in this work contrasts with his vision of it earlier in his career, when he portrayed it as just a variant form of self-absorption (compare 'Récit sur fond d'eau' and 'Une fleur jaune').

However, for Latin American writers the enclosed universe of normal human existence is extended, with characters living simultaneously in numerous different places and times. Thus, whether they present the myth of the double as something real or imaginary, dreamt of or fantasized about, they employ it as a way of approaching their relationship with history and folk memory. It serves to create a syncretic mythology that takes account of their own civilization, establishing links with the pre-Columbian divinities, and of what has come to them from Europe, highlighting their position as men torn between two cultures and two worlds: the Anglo-Saxon and the Mediterranean.

Thus the double keeps reappearing as a prominent theme in the work of the Mexican writer Fuentes. It underlines the myth of the return to the mother's womb, and regression to the foetal state that features in the 'Zona sagrada' (1967). The 'sacred zone' of the title is the focal point on which all the desires of the narrator Guillermo converge, culminating in an incestuous reunion with his mother Claudia Nervo, who wills herself to have no memory.

In Fuentes's work, the narrative element tends towards myth and allegory. This is true, for example, of the story in his play *Todos los gatos son pardos* (1970), in which the reintegration of one person and his counterpart takes the form of one oppression expelling another. Thus Cortés drives out Montezuma, who ruled as a tyrant over the Aztec people, and Cortés in turn will be driven out by the power of Catholic, imperial Spain. Montezuma is the fragile double of Cortés, while the latter is the blind double of Montezuma (scene 9); but both the conqueror and his vanquished opponent are victims of the power that they thought they could control. Nothing in the destiny of the Mexicans will change. Thus, at the end of the play, Cortés appears on stage with the features of an American general, while Montezuma is portrayed as a president of Mexico. Montezuma masquerades as a false double in order to sound out Cortés. An Aztec princess who has become Cortés's mistress will give birth to a son who supposedly represents future generations of Mexicans living in a nation that has finally acquired its freedom. But the double represents the permanent return of the original; beyond the appearances of life in Mexico there will always be the colonized, and the colonizers – who are themselves in turn colonized.

The same themes are given a more general application in *Terra nostra* (1975). Here, the figure of the double symbolizes the quest for the personality concealed by the complexities of an historical character, with successive Spanish monarchs rejoining the eternal monarch of all the Spains, and Don Juan being portrayed as the double of Don Quixote. As more than one life is required to perfect a personality, the search for the double is a quest for a personality disguised in successive incarnations of an historical experience. This experience involves the conflictive relationship beween the civilization of the New World centred on Spain, which is now in tatters, and the civilization of the Anglo-Saxon world. The question that arises is how a balance can be achieved between these two worlds that have both brought grief to the people of Latin America. Their meeting-point is again represented as being in Paris, which thus forms an intellectual and moral crossroads. The theme of the resolution of the dualistic conflict between the 'Old World' and the 'New World', determines the very structure of Fuentes's book. It is achieved through a synthesis between the opposed elements that symbolizes, and serves as an allegory for, the new man or 'the other world'.

For Fuentes, the double represents the integration of an old personality into something new, both in individual terms and in terms of societies at large. *Una familia lejana* (1980) again conveys a political message symbolized by the meeting between the young Mexican Victor Heredia and his young French friend, André Hérédia. Together, these twin characters represent a dialogue between two cultures, and emphasize that the past is still here in the present.

The difficulty of establishing a dialogue between two continents and between two inextricably connected cultures is also expressed in Cortázar's novel *Rayuela* (1963). In his wanderings across Paris, the Argentine hero Horacio Oliveira experiences how it feels to be a 'man without quality'. The exile who hops from one lodging to another is attempting to get near to his own 'centre'. In doing so, he demonstrates a readiness for adventure, and shows the sense of liberty of someone who is eager to experiment with ways of expresing his existence as a man other than those sanctioned by a self conditioned by social conventions. Indeed, to pursue his objective his is even prepared to become a tramp. In this symbolic game of hopscotch referred to by the book's title, he passes through different 'stages' on a journey of initiation, involving a concentration on the self that culminates in a meeting with his double. At the same time, he is a spectator on the sidelines, who remains available for play, and is receptive towards other worlds. (The three parts of the book are entitled: 'On the other side' (Paris), 'On this side' (Buenos Aires), and 'On all sides'.) The feeling of being in unfamiliar surroundings ends with a return to his country – to Traveler, the traveller who goes nowhere and is his double, the man who belongs, unlike Oliveira himself, who represents the man who is just passing through. Solitude becomes friendship and shared love. The ringmaster is the writer Morelli; like the author himself, he offers two books in one, two-speed reading, linear or paradigmatic. We leap from one chapter to the next as in a game of hopscotch. (Indeed, the name Morelli is a word play on the French name for the game.) Cortázar too lives between two languages and the analogy with writing explains the full significance of what happens to Oliveira, the man who does not exist but is attempting to do so.

Behind the concept of this 'man of the future', we can clearly discern the influence of a key twentieth-century novel in which the myth of the double forms a central element: Musil's *Der Mann ohne Eigenschaften* (Book I, 1930; start of book II, 1933). The fact that the book is unfinished is no dioubt related to the role played in it by the double, which involves the relationship between the brother and sister Ulrich and Agathe. In a first draft of the work, Ulrich was called Anders (Other). However, the 'other' appears as a potential manifestation of his character only when the central theme of the development of a personal moral philosophy to suit real life takes over from the satire on the Austro-Hungarian empire.

Musil does not borrow from just one of the traditional forms of the myth, but from them all, juxtaposing them to form a syncretic vision. He sets himself in the Romantic tradition of writers such as Jean-Paul by defining Ulrich's love for Agathe as love of self. However, the main myths associated with the double crop up as topics in learned discussions between the brother and the sister. The latter involve the retelling of a long story that is bound up with that of Western man. Meanwhile, the myths themselves include the Platonic myth of the half-beings in search of wholeness, the story of Pygmalion, the tale of the hermaphrodite, and the myth of Isis and Osiris. In the first version of the novel entitled 'The Twin Sister', Musil had intended to exploit the resemblance between the brother and sister as a Picaresque device in a plot involving spying. In the work as it stands, the two characters Ulrich/Anders and Agathe are simultaneously friends, man and woman, brother and sister, twins and even Siamese twins, and Musil turns their relationshlip into a story representing 'a journey to the edges of what is possible'.

This undertaking of a lifetime concentrates more and more on the story of Ulrich and Agathe, progressively setting the central fantasy in motion. Musil escapes from it by including discursive passages opposing the msaculine and feminine principles. These relate to various pairs of concepts: the perspectives of giving and taking; the convex and concave experience; and motivation based, or not based, on sexual appetite. The work takes the form of a long reverie centred on the mystery of 'the appearance of the human being in two states: man and woman' (book II, chapter 3).

A PROTEAN MYTH

The myth of the double still continues to represent a productive source of inspiration. It is easily modified, and lends itself equally well to the totalizing outlook of the Romantics, who claimed that the infinite world is reflected in the finite self, and to the more recent concept of the erasure of the self. According to some versions of the latter view, the self is prepared to adopt different manifestations, hinting at and sometimes accepting its fragmented nature, and seeing this as a means of enrichment and of dialogue with the world. However, this modern vision based on considered optimism, was tempered during the period of absurdist literature by writers who portrayed a self no longer capable even of postulating its own existence on the basis of speech (Beckett).

The Romantic image of being locked up in a painful, closed self, frightened of losing its substance, because crossing its boundaries leads to madness, was followed by an image of openness towards the world. This suggested that it is precisely the otherness at the heart of the self that will produce a dialogue and a meeting with the other, leading to a sense of solidarity. As a consequence dispossession ceased to mean inpoverishment and the annihilation of the individual, representing instead a possibility of enrichment. The *homo sapiens* who breaks away from his divine double is transformed into a *homo ludens* and a *homo communicans*.

The theme of the socially maladjusted character (Poe, Stevenson) is expanded into that of the search for a new form of sociability (Hesse, Cortázar). While the double can symbolize the alienation of the individual in a society that is becoming incrasingly massive and impersonal (Dostoyevsky), recognizing its existence can also be the means for achieving social and political liberation (Fuentes). Modern writers portray Man as a plural being, in works of fiction that operate at several levels. This provides an opening into other possible worlds, so that the double is a popular figure in science fiction.

The ambiguity, uncertainty and indefinable nature of the intellectual interplay between the self and its double cloud references to the latter, thereby expressing a constructive doubt about what is real and enabling us to imagine that it may be possible to go beyond the individual (as in the utopia vision expressed by Musil).

However, in parallel with this theme of the search for a better self there is also the theme of the special relationship between the double and the circular process of history (Borgès) which gives the myth a more ambivalent significance in the context of the present. Nonetheless, the double always rises from the ashes of its association with death, so that, rather than the circle, the spiral would be a more appropriate symbol for it, representing death and rebirth. Finally, the image of double forms a suitable vehicle for representing anything that denies the limitations of the self, and for portraying the enactment of the hallucinatory fantasies produced by desire.

Nicole Fernandez Bravo

Echo

Although the story of Echo presented in Ovid's *Metamorphoses* (III) is the best-known version of the myth and evidently formed the starting point for its development in relation to that of Narcissus, it seems to reflect the influence of oriental legends rather than reproducing the tale in its original form. Thus, other versions of a legend explaining the origin of the physical phenomenon of the echo must have existed. However, only faint traces of these have survived, passed down to us in late classical texts or by way of the works of Renaissance mythographers.

ECHO AND NARCISSUS

For Ovid, Echo is the double or reflection of Narcissus. The way in which she repeats words in shortened form is similar to the way in which Narcissus's image is reflected imperfectly by the shimmering surface of the water, because it is unreal. Ovid tells the story of Echo as a prelude to that of Narcissus, whose disdain is given as the reason for her being changed into a rock; previously she had had a body, although she had already been deprived of the power to initiate a conversation. The story of Echo thus falls into two parts. In the first place, she was punished by Juno as a result of her excessive flair for speech which she used to hold the goddess's attention and prevent her from noticing the adulterous activities of her husband Jupiter. Consequently, when she was stripped of her facility with words and her ability to start a conversation this was because she had spoken too much as well as because she had spoken in a deceptive, even deceitful, manner. Having lost her previous powers, she can only repeat the last words that she hears and is unable to express desires, anxieties or warnings, although she does retain the basic ability to choose the sounds that she sends back (*Metamorphoses* III. 359–77). In the second place, Echo is the victim of Narcissus's scorn for love. Because of this, she loses her physical substance and fades away with yearning (as Narcissus does later), until only her voice remains. Ovid stresses the symbolic relationship between Echo and Narcissus by the use of symmetry. Unaware that the voice that he hears is repeating his own words, Narcissus responds by asking the same question that he later puts to the reflection that he does not realize is his own: 'Why do you flee from me?' And as the dying Narcissus fades away, consumed by his unrequited love, Echo returns to haunt him and echo his lament as her own.

The analogy drawn by Ovid between the reflection of sound and the reflection of an image later gave rise to a whole tradition of interpretation illustrated by Isidoro de Sevilla's *Etimologías* (seventh century AD). In it the name Echo is understood in the sense of 'eikon' (image), and the phenomenon is defined in the following terms: 'in replying to the voice it presents an image of its words' (XVI. 3.4). However, Echo's status as an image or an empty mockery of sound is considered paradoxical in most literary treatments of the myth. There, she is generally dissociated from her double Narcissus. However, in the field of art the two figures remain inseparable, as for example in the works of Poussin.

ECHO AND PAN

The pastoral poem *Daphnis and Chloe*, by Longus (second century AD), gives a completely different version of the story from those mentioned above. In it, Chloe is filled with wonder at having heard heavenly music echoed by the earth, and Daphnis recounts how Echo, the mortal daughter of a nymph, was brought up by the Muses and was able to play every instrument and sing every kind of song. This wonderful gift aroused the jealousy of Pan, who had also been unable to win Echo's affections (since, in this version of the myth, Echo is the one who scorns love). Pan therefore 'drove the shepherds and goatherds mad' so that they tore Echo to pieces and 'scattered her body throughout the world while it was still singing'. The earth preserved both her limbs and her voice, which it caused to echo everywhere and which 'as before imitated all kinds of sounds: of gods, of men, of instruments and the cries of animals' (III. 23). The dismemberment of Echo is extremely reminiscent of the death of Orpheus, and may represent Longus's own version of the myth. However, it also reflects a very early association between Pan and Bacchus. (Meanwhile, there may also be an analogy between ritual dismemberment and the fragmentation of sound by its echo.) In any case, this version of the story does not appear to have been adopted by later authors, although Echo, like Orpheus, seems to have been increasingly associated with the spiritual powers of music. On the other hand, Echo's association with Pan is confirmed by several sources and appears to have inspired an important literary tradition.

Macrobius, in particular, makes Echo the symbol of Universal Harmony, loved by Pan, who represents the Divine Principle (*Saturnalia* I. 22). Meanwhile, Renaissance mythographers, such as Gyraldi (*De deis qentium* . . . 1548), associate Echo with a Pythagorean tradition and quote a strange adage: 'Pray to Echo when the winds blow'. Cartari (*Imagine degli dei*, 1556) also attributed a new significance to the story, in his chapter devoted to the representations of the god Pan, who is himself considered to be a manifestation of Jupiter in the sense that he is an archetype of divinity. Here, Echo is interpreted as an analogy of the Seven Spheres of the Universe, which produced a heavenly music. This concept coincides with a very common ancient belief that in certain hallowed places the echo was repeated up to seven times. Its implications in the context of Christianity will be seen later. Thus, in the works of these writers, Echo appears to be associated with an original myth concerning Music rather than the unreality and culpability of human speech. Nor do the mythographers appear to have retained the idea of punishment or of Echo having wronged a god. On the contrary; Echo is herself presented as a divinity: 'the daughter of the air and language'. the emphasis is placed on her invisibility and, in the work of Cartari, which is concerned with iconography, on the fact that she is 'unrepresentable'. As a consequence, later interpretations of the myth tended to associate Echo increasingly with the divine order of the Intelligible by clearly dissociating her from the order of the perceptible and the falsely representational. Cartari does not dismiss Ovid's account, but presents it as a sort of exception when compared with other works, in which Echo's unique characteristic is precisely that she is not a 'figure'. As a result, she can only be represented in association with Narcissus and a metamorphosis. On other occasions, as in an epigram by Ausonius quoted by Cartari, she is defined in terms of her relationship with the 'desert', silence and the unimaginable: 'Why do you try to represent me, oh, foolish artist? For I am such that no mortal eye has ever been able to behold me, I have neither form, nor substance, nor colour.'

The discussion of these works makes the paradoxical aspect of the myth of Echo clearer. As a shadow superfluously imitating the words of others, Echo may be regarded, in Platonic terms, merely as a representation of appearances, in contrast to the substance and truth of Being – as, indeed, she sometimes is, though always within the context of ambiguous speech. This interpretation would coincide with the Plotinian portrayal of Narcissus as a symbol of humanity deceived by appearances from which it is unable to turn away. However, it is not the one favoured by the most common literary tradition. On the contrary, according to this, Echo actually represents prophetic speech, revealing the hidden truth of the words that she hears. Indeed, this tradition tends to be dominated by a symbolism that associates the invisible with spirituality, the same spirituality that lies behind the theological function of music.

THE DIALOGUE WITH ECHO: A LITERARY GENRE

The revelational function of the echo is not apparent in the two dialogues between Echo and Narcissus in Ovid's version of the myth. However, there is a wealth of literature that imitates Ovid's technique, systematizing it to the point where, during the sixteenth and seventeenth centuries, this form of dialogue became a literary genre known as the 'echo'. Although the counterpart of Echo was no longer, or very rarely, Narcissus, the structure remained the same. It involved poems, or scenes incorporated into the pastoral (*Il Pastor Fido*), or short musical pieces (Orlando di Lasso), in which each line or group of lines was extended by an echo. Its characteristic feature was that the echo was not merely a mechanical repetition of the rhyme, but always provided the answer to a question. In this way, the dialogue assumed a didactic, consolatory or sometimes disputative quality. Significantly, a typical example of these 'echoed' lines is quoted by the mythographer Cartari (in the article 'Giove' in *Imagini degli dei*). He thus implies a continuity in symbolic terms between the myth, as he himself analysed it, and the literary genre, even though Echo no longer appears the latter – except in allusions – and her story has ceased to be told. The anonymous poem in Italian to which he refers presents a young, misunderstood lover who is sought out by Echo as he is lamenting his fate, asks her name and then begins to question her further. His questions initially concern matters of love but imperceptibly become questions of a mystical nature: 'Tell me the true way of Love, please tell me the truth? – Truth.' The dialogue ends with an enigma since the lover is unable to understand the echo's final, insistent reply, whereas all the previous ones have led to other questions. The poem contains all the characteristics of the 'jocoseria', the name given to this type of dialogue. Echo is not directly involved in the love story but remains as a confidante. Secular love and Divine Love are treated as both separate and complementary, while plays on similar sounds convey a symbolic message invariably related to enigma and prophecy.

Two main tendencies emerged from the many literary and musical versions of the dialogue with Echo. These may be linked to a slow thematic development, but, in any case, they are always closely associated. The first involves a secular approach, whereby Echo is seen as the 'Minister of Love' (Marino, 'Echo', *La Sampogna* VI, 1623) or the interpreter of the god of Love, with whom, for example, the hero of Guarini's *Il Pastor Fido* (1590) confuses her. Like Narcissus, this hero intends to resist the power of Love and, believing that he is speaking to the god himself, embarks upon a veritable *disputatio* with Echo, which ends with an ambiguous exchange: 'You are nothing but a false Prophet, forsooth! – Sooth' (act IV. scene 7). The second tendency is to see Echo as an oracle of the Divine Word. This is particularly evident in the Christian epic *La Madeleine au Désert* (1668) by Pierre de Saint-Louis in which Echo teaches Faith and Divine Love to the anchorite to whom the work is dedicated. The latter herself makes use of a play on sounds to turn the 'résonnement' (resonance) of the echo into 'raisonnement' (reasoning), making it a source of knowledge. Similarly, in an aria in the fourth cantata of Bach's *Christmas Oratorio*, God's concise replies to the questioning of the soul take the form of an echo that confirms the soul's own certainty: 'You say yes yourself'. Thus, to borrow the words used by Tesauro in *Cannocchiale Aristotelico* (1654), Echo is a 'wild Sibyl who delivers her oracles in the caves'. The sounds that she 'reflects' – 'Solitary Sybil or voice of Paradise /Who reflect so well on all that you say' (*Madeleine au Désert* II) – in fact express truths and not the deceptive unreality of Narcissus's mirror. At the same time as she reveals the closeness of the relationship between sound and meaning, she also reveals the ideal closeness of opposites, for musical harmony consists of the harmony of discord. This explains why Kircher, who based his *Musurgia Universalis* (1650) on the analogous principle uniting the cosmos and music, became fascinated by the concept of an 'echosophy'. This was based on the symbolic similarity that exists, in physical terms, between sound and light, and that the echo reveals in its guise as a sign of communication between the two phenomena. The Hermetic tradition also employs Echo as a sort of metaphor for biblical interpretation because, like Echo, the Cabbala uses homophony and 'is in harmony with the Whole of which it is a part' (Le Fèvre de la Boderie, *La Galliade*, 1578).

THE TRUTH OF THE DIVINE WORD

In her role as revealer of truths concealed by deceptive appearances, Echo appears as the very symbol of the Divine Word, which can only be revealed through enigma. She is therefore the intermediary between the human soul and the divine, and the symbolic nature of the echo lies in the fact that it 'is only a voice', condensing into a single word an entire discourse which it is unable to pronounce. Some writers even went as far as to associate Echo explicitly with the Word incarnate, 'which is the elemental note emitted by the Intellect of the Father' (Marino, 'La Musica', *Dicerie Sacre* II, 1614). At the same time they stressed the importance of the mystical belief linking the echo to the origins of music. This belief was based on the echo's association with the sacred number '7', recalling the seven words of Christ on the Cross, and constituting the original form of all music. Each of Christ's seven words is also an echo of the divine will, and a reply, which is musical as opposed to discursive, because it is pure and absolute, denoting the union of the soul with the divine (ibid.). As an intermediary between the perfect music of the Spheres, of which she is the unrepresentable image, and human speech, which she endows with its true meaning, Echo renders intelligible the very substance of Being.

Thus, with the development of mystical and specifically Christian interpretations of its nature, this disembodied and insubstantial voice came to be seen as the stimulator of awareness. It was viewed as performing an initiatory function, by eventually turning its questioner back upon him or herself, in the same way that Narcissus finally achieved self-knowledge through contemplating his own image. The dialogue with the Echo is always a dialogue with the self that the person involved has not yet been able to identify. Thus it is actually the 'otherness' of its oracular pronouncements that is illusory, rather than their message. While Ovid portrayed Narcissus's contemplation of his reflection as sterile and ultimately fatal, the literary genre of the dialogue represented Echo's reflection of speech as creating a whole new area of meaning. It surpassed human limitations and brought hope and knowledge – though that knowledge was disturbing and might be rejected by its recipient. Towards the end of the seventeenth century, Tesauro's treatise on metaphor

(*Cannocchiale* VII) provided an important synthesis of interpretations of the phenomenon of the echo. These no longer had to be based on legend to make their symbolism apparent: ‘(Echo) lives as long as you are speaking (. . .) A single life and two voices (. . .) She is your other self (. . .) If you die, she dies.’

Françoise Graziani

Eden

THE SOURCE OF THE MYTH

The account of the dramatic events in Eden in chapters 2 (7–25) and 3 of Genesis may be regarded as the most truly mythical of all the stories in the Bible. It is in fact a story of foundation, and for Westerners it represents a portrayal of the origins of mankind. Thus it explains where mankind, the couple, the hardship of labour, suffering and death have come from. It is a story with a religious function, since it teaches that all our misfortunes spring from our disobedience towards a divine command. It sets out to be accepted as the truth; though Jewish, the author addresses Everyman, which is the meaning of the name of the hero, Adam, the vaguest term by which anyone could possibly be described. And, finally, the story has been incorporated into the holy book of the West, the Bible.

To adopt Lévi-Strauss's definition, the characteristic feature of a mythical story is that it is constructed in terms of structural oppositions and oppositions of meaning. His famous presentation of the myth of Oedipus can be used as a basis for analysis:

Over-estimation of blood ties	*Under-estimation of blood ties*	*Victory over the monster*	*Name, sign of the bond with the earth*
adam & adama (the earth) 2.7 (as the son of the earth, Adam must 'serve' it/her) issh & issha (husband and wife) 2.23 (the woman is born from her husband, is his daughter)	adam & adama 3.19 (the mother turns into Death) issh & issha (husband dominates wife) 3.16 'your desire shall be for your husband, and he shall rule over you'	the human race triumphs over the race of the serpent 3.15	Adam = the Man of Earth 2.7 & 3.19 the race born of woman is bruised on the heel 3.15 the serpent will eat dust 3.14

According to Lévi-Strauss in his *Anthropologie structurale*, the myth of Oedipus expresses the conflict betwen the archaic belief in the chthonic origin of Man and the later belief that all human beings are born as a result of intercourse between a man and a woman. Similarly, Edmund Leach sees this conflict as providing the key to our understanding of the myth of Eden. Indeed, we can apparently go even further and analyse the myth in terms of the table given above. Thus the over-estimation of blood ties may be seen as representing a rejection of the desire for an incestuous relationship while their under-estimation may reflect a rejection of the desire to commit parricide. In a similar vein, the serpent – the 'monster' of the third column – would represent the phallic Father, while the 'mark' in the fourth column (a bruise denoting a bond with the earth) would be a euphemism for castration.

Useful as these considerations may be in helping us to grasp the full meaning of the biblical story, they are of little relevance to an attempt to define the originality of the literary works that it has inspired. Nonetheless, they do provide an explanation of the success of the biblical model, if we accept that the story gives orderly expression to the workings of the human unconscious. Only in *Le Paradis perdu* by Pierre Jean Jouve, according to whom the Serpent is in fact the Phallus, are they explicitly perceived.

In fact, Greimas's method of structural analysis is more useful in identifying the units that make up the biblical story and the literary myth constituted by the works that it has inspired. After analysing the story in purely narrative terms and then in terms of its underlying message, it is possible to establish the following elementary structure of meaning (or semiotic square):

LIFE without death →	vs	↙LIFE ending in DEATH
conjunction:		disjunction:
Man & animals 2.19		Man ≠ animals 3.15
husband & wife 2.23–4		husband ≠ wife 3.16
creature & Creator 2.7		creature ≠ Creator 3.23
irrigated garden & fruit-bearing trees 2.9		Man's sweat & thorns and thistles 3.3,18,19

Two opposites are involved: life, and death, with conjunction set against disjunction. Life was 'elsewhere', while death is 'here' in our everyday life. It is the rejection by the creature of an Order established by the Creator that has allowed the 'passage' from one to the other, and this occurs precisely at the place where 'temptation' occurs, by the tree in the middle of the garden round which the tempting serpent is coiled.

Though, in many respects, the story can be called mythical, it starts off as a literary work. While we do not know the name of its author, he is easy to identify as a writer through his original style and his powerful ideas. Some commentators believe this he was a scribe at the court of Solomon around 950 BC.

The sobriety of the tale and the use of poor, commonplace vocabulary suggest that it is by a local writer. The most frequently used word is 'eat' which occurs some twenty times. However, the story is cleverly composed: there are two corresponding sections hinging on a passage seven verses long that forms the central element in the drama. The narrative rhythm is maintained by the use of parataxis, by placing 'and' at the beginning of each sentence, and by word play. The latter involves chiasmus, punning and repetition ('you are dust, and to dust you shall return'), as well as popular etymology (*adam-adama* = earthy-earth, or homo-humus, *issh-issha* = husband-wife).

Indeed, it was because of its very literary nature that the original text came to be accepted as a model for later works, and most of those that it has inspired contain quite explicit quotations from it. The popular character of the original story was, in any case, modified in the Latin translation, the Vulgate; by giving it a more elevated tone, this has to some extent made it seem more solemn and holy.

VARIATIONS OF THE STRUCTURE

It is easier in a mythical story than in a story of any other type to distinguish between the logical structure, made up of opposing forces, working through a process of reversal that gives rise to antithetical situations, and the treatment of the plot, involving particular episodes and characters. In tracing the development of the biblical myth, the first step is to pick out changes made to the initial scheme, to the very drama that was played out in Eden, across a range of literary works of established quality. After this we can turn our attention to the embodiments in space and time of the forces that are balanced against each other in the myth, in other words to the mythical figures themselves.

Variations in the structure of the myth can take four possible forms, discussed in the four sections that follow.

Christianization in dramatic form

Even though it constitutes a closed unit and follows a strict logic, the story in Genesis 2 and 3 still seems to carry a label saying 'to be continued', or rather 'to be set right'. Talk of 'paradise lost' will sooner or later lead to the vision of a 'paradise regained'; destined to mortal life, Man still aspires to immortality. Even in the Old Testament there is the suggestion that the regeneration of mankind may be effected through the regeneration of Israel. Belief in a Messiah made this hope concrete, culminating the New Testament. This proclaims the salvation of the first Adam through the righteousness of Christ, his successor, who restores to man the values that have been lost: 'For as by one man's disobedience many were made sinners, so by one man's obedience many will be made righteous' (Romans 5.19). Seen in this light, the original story of Eden is just the first stage in a discussion about salvation that runs through the entire Bible. Thus it effectively constitutes a single element inserted in a whole that completes its initial plan.

The story of Eden has been read by people in the West in the light of the Epistle to the Romans, and seen as the archetype of mankind's tragedy. Consequently a large number of literary works present it in this religious, primarily Christian, light. Among them is the *Jeu d'Adam (Ordo representationis Ade)*, the first piece of drama in French literature, written partly in the vulgar tongue at the end of the twelfth century, the influence of which is still discernible in Byron's *Cain*.

This type of work was intended for an audience that had assembled specifically to hear the Word of God and then to celebrate ritually what the Word had proclaimed. *Mimesis* followed *diegesis*, actions were based on words. After coming out of their place of worship, the faithful adopted the same attitudes that they had been told about inside it, knowing that what was *re-presented* on the stage was what they should enact in their own lives. Reading the story in the present reproduces its original structure. The spectator is Adam, Man. As such, he is the object of divine benevolence, but he is tempted to refuse to submit to God's will, and is unhappy because he has broken the pact between himself and God. Furthermore, as he is Christian, he superimposes on the figure of Adam, representing Everyman, that of Christ, a new Adam, who enables him to escape from the hold that the first one has over him. Adam is the antitype of Christ, and the Christian is a repetition of both the first Adam and the second. In this instance the text is explained through observance.

Almost the same is true in the case of the theatrical works produced during the golden century of Spanish literature. Like the authors of the medieval mystery plays, and following in the same tradition, writers such as Lope de Vega (*La Creacion del mundo y primera culpa del hombre*) and Calderón (*La Vida es Sueño*: an *autosacramentale*) tell the story of mankind from its beginnings until the coming of Christ the Redeemer – from Genesis to the Apocalypse, from the tragic forfeiture of Man's original state to its restoration through the intervention of a hero. The biblical text is understood symbolically, and Genesis is relocated in a continuum dominated by the dialectic of salvation. Lope de Vega's work exhibits two significant original features: God does not appear on stage, thereby preserving His transcendence; and the serpent becomes the Devil, the fallen angel, and an implacable and powerful enemy.

Throughout the centuries, poets paraphrasing Genesis 2 and 3 have reproduced the christianized structure of the story with its three phases – happiness, misery and salvation – placing particular emphasis on the last of these. Because of their absolute faith, they have returned to the medieval tradition and revived the interpretation of the myth in terms of types of characters. To them too, it seemed impossible that the tragic story should end with the expulsion from Eden; the original state must surely be restored. But in addition, they believed that the very structure of the myth's plot foretold the conditions under which salvation would occur. The Tree of Knowledge was balanced against the tree of the Cross, the first Adam against the new Adam, in the form of Christ.

Thus in his poem *Eve* Charles Péguy stresses the division between two *climates* – the one that existed before the fall (during the time of riches) and the one that existed after the fall (during the time of alienation) – a division emphasized by the tone of disappointment that accompanies his portrayal of the former: 'You have never known [it] since'. Nothing intervenes between these two times, no tempting serpent. Rejecting the anecdotal elements, the poet adheres to the great underlying structure of the myth. Nonetheless, he does evoke the symbolic image of the tree in the Garden of Eden, which blends with the tree of Calvary: 'The tree with the double destiny, the arbiter with the double seal,/The tree of knowledge and the tree of the cross . . .'

The same structure recurs, albeit in exploded form, in various poems in *Sodome* by Pierre Emmanuel, which also emphasize the wider typological associations of the Tree of Knowledge: 'O absolute witness of man, Tree of Life/which is the tree of knowledge, but wounded/bearing a second fruit like the autumn fig-tree . . .'

Similarly, *Le Paradis perdu* by Pierre Jean Jouve gives poetic and dramatic expression to the parallels between the two Adams. Jouve's Adam prefigures the most perfect of his sons, and while his story foretells prolonged suffering, it also promises redemption.

These works use one other final, stock theme, or topos to indicate the intention that the biblical plan should be fulfilled, that of the *felix culpa*. Like the 'tree with the double destiny' and the antithetical figures of the first and second Adam, the concept of the 'fortunate offence' implies a belief in the redeeming powers of Christ.

Elaboration of the myth

Several paraphrases of the story from Genesis are preceded by a 'prologue in heaven'. This generally features Satan and Michael, the rebellious angel and the angel loyal to God, or occasionally Satan and God himself. The activities of these supernatural beings herald human action, or prefigure, trigger, deflect, interrupt or accompany it. In any event, they envelop it in a superterrestrial atmosphere that makes a powerful contribution towards turning the story into a myth. The original rule seemed too mundane and to need to be made more solemn; the device of the 'prologue in heaven' established the reality of what was to follow, giving a cosmic dimension to the story of two individuals. By linking the two dramas, one celestial and one human, not only could the writer mutiply the events and characters, he could also elevate them to heroic status. The figure of the opponent, a simple serpent in Genesis, becomes Satan, or Iblis, or Lucifer. In the work of Milton and of the seventeenth-century dramatists who preceded him, he is surrounded by a court and an army. As a consequence, in *Adam in ballingschap* (*Adam banished*) Vondel is able to extend the two short chapters in the Bible to the proportions of a classical tragedy, written in verse in five acts and including choruses.

Similarly, in the nineteenth century the Hungarian dramatist Imre Madách devoted several scenes in his huge drama, *Az ember tragediaja* (*The tragedy of man*) to a paraphrase of the story in Genesis. While his work is reminiscent of the medieval mystery plays with their vast perspectives covering the history of sinful mankind and its ultimate redemption, it lacks the vivid faith that informed them and the reverent atmosphere with which they were imbued. The Christian mythology is not reanimated from within; instead, it merely forms a dead structure, and the great symbols express philosophical concepts. The Creator's final words to Adam are 'Man, I have told you, fight and have faith', but, at the same time, the master of the system accords Lucifer his place in it as a personification of critical, negative Reason, forming a necessary yeast to stimulate Man in his quest.

Milton's epic poem *Paradise Lost* stands in a category of its own. The theme is announced in the very first lines in an initial resumé that is developed in more detail in the hundred or so lines that follow. We are often reminded of it, and it extends over a great expanse of space and time covering both heaven and earth before, during and after the fateful event in Eden. It involves a broken contract and the alienation that resulted from the act of transgression, but there is also an affirmation of the belief that the old values will be restored thanks to a redeeming hero. The scheme is identical for both the human drama and the celestial drama that heralds, prefigures and shadows it. The Divinity is conceived along the lines of an Eastern despot – God in the clouds – while angels and demons zoom through space from the heights of heaven to the depths of hell, clashing in noisy battles. The result is the sort of prodigious atmosphere found in classical epic, and is very far removed from the naive sobriety of the story of Yahweh. Nonetheless, the poem can be described as Christian, for Milton's interpretation of the story is completely in line with traditional perceptions of its meaning.

The rebellion

Starting with Byron and continuing up to the present day, there have been several writers who have faithfully preserved the structure of the original biblical account, but reversed the characteristics of the elements that it opposes to each other, so that positive becomes negative and vice versa. Thus life in Eden is seen as a misfortune, a period of alienation, while life outside Eden, though ending in death, is declared to be happy, since it enables Man to exercise freedom of choice. From *not knowing* (the knowledge of good and evil) the serpent allowed man to pass to *knowing* (even if this involved awareness of shameful nakedness, hard labour, suffering and death). The drama of Eden always contained this potential ambiguity, making it possible to see the seeming opponent (the serpent) as a helper. After all, this 'hostile' creature offered human beings *knowledge* and *power*, and actually presented itself in the role of the Benefactor. Moreover, it gave Man the opportunity to occupy that same position, and become master of the system. Viewed in this light, the deity becomes the Adversary and the serpent the Benefactor, and it is this point that the rebellion against the order established by God erupts with a vengeance. The modern writer reads Genesis back to front, or accuses it of lying, as Byron does in the first scene of *Cain*: 'The snake spoke the truth. It was the tree of knowledge;/It was the tree of life. Knowledge is good/And life is good, and how can both be evil'.

This assertion is expressed differently by different writers, but invariably in a violent fashion. The drama of Eden is seen through the eyes of the Adversary, i.e. through the eyes of Satan. However, Man too must express himself, and the poets that extol rebellion put his words into the mouth of Adam's son, rather than that of Adam himself. Nonetheless, Cain, with his regrets for Eden, is often only his father by another name. Thus the events of chapter 4 of Genesis contaminate the chapter preceding it, while the story of Cain's murder of his brother is amplified by the introduction of another element: the duplication of the sin of his parents. It is because of this assimilation of the father with his son that the myth of Eden is central to the Romantic rebellion.

The last verse of chapter 3 of Genesis is the one that is paraphrased the most faithfully chapter 4, being repeated three times and developed in a powerful fashion: 'at the east of the garden of Eden he placed the cherubim, and a flaming sword which turned every way'. Eden now offers only walls, gates and ramparts guarded by armed warriors, whose flaming swords stand out against the darkness of night. It symbolizes a cruel, repressive deity who conceals the Tree of Life behind 'forbidding walls', and provides a classic image of Byronic rancour.

Reflecting Byron's influence, similar violent images and a similar inversion of the message of the original biblical account recur in the works of William Blake (*Songs of Experience*), Alfred de Vigny (*Eloa*), Lermontov (*The Demon*), Leconte de Lisle (*Oaïn*), Laturéamont (*Les Chants de Maldoror*), Strindberg (*Inferno*), Paul Valéry (*Ebauche d'un Serpent*), André Spire (Samaël), Rainer Maria Rilke ('*Adam*' and '*Eva*') and of many others who have read Genesis 'in its diabolical or infernal sense', as William Blake put it, adding: 'thou read'st black where I read white' (*The Everlasting Gospel*).

The cult of nature

Several works inspired by the biblical story of Eden cover only its first section. They stop before the actual drama, suppressing an important element in the evolution of the plot: the prohibition that triggers its second part. Their approach, which may be described as 'naturistic', involves the belief that evil does not exist, and that human nature is good. Though the structure of the original story is preserved implicitly, it is nonetheless truncated.

Thus, Walt Whitman's collection of poems *Children of Adam*, which is full of references to Genesis, contains the striking declaration: 'I claim that evil does not in fact exist'. Life is a marvellous gift, and Paradise is a reality, extending to the very limits of the world – or at least to the limits of the continent of America. Meanwhile the human couple preserve their innocence through a love that joins man and woman 'in a single flesh'. Whitman's assertion 'I cannot see one single imperfection in the universe', sets his work at the opposite pole from that of writers such as Byron and Leconte de Lisle. Sarcasm is replaced by praise, but praise of a god who is Man himself.

By contrast, in Victor Hugo's famous poem *Le Sacre de la Femme*, it is the Creator of the biblical Genesis who appears 'in his calm grandeur' to bless the union of the human couple, who are 'modest in their nakedness', and still innocent, thereby consecrating physical love. The tone of these lines is exceptional for Hugo. They depict an ideal dream: the world as it was before the Fall, an Eden that has since disappeared, where nakedness could be unashamed.

Following on from this in *La Fable du Monde*, Jules Supervielle also concentrates on the story in Genesis 2, notably in his poem 'Dieu crée l'homme'. This portrays a generous Benefactor, an artist filled with love for his work, whose solicitude is conveyed in human gestures, just as in the version extolling Yahweh: 'My fingers encountering no opposition/Forming the flesh in readiness for such delight . . .'; '. . . Let my hand linger on your heart . . .'

Similarly, Jean Giraudoux ignored the sequel to the events in chapter 2 of Genesis, proclaiming his determination to go no further than the idyllic vision that it portrays, and thereby making himself a champion of Edenism, or, to be more precise, a 'diviner of Eden'. Through the words of his hero in *Juliette au Pays des Hommes*, he provides the most striking expression of the 'naturistic, attitude: 'I am still alive, as he [Adam] was in the interval between creation and original sin. I have been exempted from the general curse . . .'. Giraudoux's Eden is a rare oasis free from God, a brief interlude of pleasure – that 'tender word' that sees 'Jehovah vanish'; but it seems nearer to dream than reality.

All these modifications to the original biblical story seem to result from one or other of two conflicting logical demands. The aim may be to impose symmetry by rounding off or duplicating what seems to be an incomplete scheme; or conversely to create dissymmetry, by turning it upside down or truncating it. In other words, the changes are prompted by artistic intentions that are then overlain by other aims of either an ideological or an emotional nature. Those who linger in the Eden that existed before the Fall and want to know nothing of Man's expulsion from it are pining for the innocence of adolescence. As poets contemplating the world through the eyes of the first man, they briefly succeed in conjuring him up in our midst: 'how distant you are, perfumed paradises!' Writers who illustrate this 'naturistic' tendency include Hugo in *Le Sacre de la Femme*, Walt Whitman, Alfred Jarry, Charles Guérin, Karlfeldt, Van Lerberghe, Giraudoux and Supervielle.

By contrast, others see Eden as a place of boredom, where there is too much balance and passivity. There, Man dozes off in lethargic bliss and cannot really fulfil his destiny. This state of excessive order had to be disturbed: 'A little dissonance, for the devil's sake!' André Gide murmurs in his *Traité du Narcisse*. Man's transgression will be beneficial: a *felix culpa* in the secular sense of the term. By refusing to accept God's prohibition, Man gains knowledge and liberty, and in defying his master, he begins to exist. Chapter 2 of Genesis is neglected in favour of chapter 3, which ushers in the 'tomorrows that sing'. Adherents of this 'pessimist' tendency include Byron, Leconte de Lisle, Lautréamont, Zola, Verhaeren, Rilke, Salmon, Spire and Valéry.

Finally, there are the writers who are committed believers. Because they endeavour to maintain the initial balance between the forces involved in the story and stress both the bliss of its first part and the misery of its second, they are close in some respects to both the 'naturistic' writers and the 'pessimists'. Their exaltation of the original state of bliss links them to the former while their dark portrayal of the consequences of the Fall connect them to the latter. Like the 'pessimists', they too write of the *felix culpa*, but their vision is of a future in which Paradise is regained in all its splendour through the intervention of a redeeming hero. Thus they emphasize one possible outcome to the dynamic process operating in the Bibile. According to their interpretation, the Benefactor cannot totally deny his own nature, and after punishing Man he allows a glimpse of restitution. This outlook was shared by all the authors who preceded Byron, as well by as Hawthorne, Claudel, Péguy, Jouve, Carmen Conde, Pierre Emmanuel and others.

THE THREADS COLOURING THE WEAVE: THE MYTHICAL FIGURES

So far we have concentrated on the varying treatments given to a single situation: the drama played out in Genesis 2 and 3 and in works based on it. Now we must turn from the structure to its plot and characters – its various incarnations of the story in space and time. The drama is played out in different settings, but though the actors are new on each occasion, their features are restricted to a limited number of masks.

Adam

Some works portray Adam as a model of perfection, with a body combining strength and beauty. Thus, Whitman and Zola describe him as the epitome of the handsome male, the hero of nature and all that is natural. Alternatively, he can be the faun-like figure resembling the Donatello statue described in *The Marble Faun* by Nathaniel Hawthorne.

However, other writers (Lope de Vega, the seventeenth-century playwrights, Hugo, and Imre Madách) describe a completely different Adam. They see him as a 'rational animal', a 'speculative philosopher', in stark contrast to Woman, a child of nature. Milton represents him as harmonious and balanced, 'new flesh and a virgin soul'. The terms 'soul' and 'flesh', which are more Greek than Hebrew, convey the dual aspect of his nature that has been emphasized by poets on the basis of the verse in Genesis recounting how

Adam was kneaded from the dust of the ground and brought to life by the breath of the Lord God.

The fact that the first man had such a double nature excuses his weakness and even his Fall. Literary figures ranging from the Dutch writers to Milton, from Lope de Vega to Byron, from Madách to Péguy all adopted this concept of Man's double nature, and a multiplicity of terms were used to describe the material from which Adam was formed: clay, loam, mud, dust, soil, earth. Milton's hero even reproaches God: 'Did I request thee, Maker, from my clay/ To mould me Man?' (*Paradise Lost* X 743–4). Influenced by Byron, Leconte de Lisle casts the words of the Bible text back in God's face: 'My breath, oh Kneader of the ancient loam,/ Will one day raise thy victim living . . .' Meanwhile, Valéry's demon even describes God's 'breath on the loam' as a 'sigh of despair'. Even Péguy piles up pejorative terms, speaking of Man as this 'sod', this 'mire', this 'mud', this 'sticky weakness', perhaps implying some antagonism towards the Creator.

Eve

Eve is the epitome of Woman, and no verses have been paraphrased more often than those in Genesis devoted to her. The latter describes her birth, her union with Adam, her temptation by the serpent, her Fall, her condemnation, the meaning of her name and her destiny. Thus three strands are mixed together: the woman, the victim and the mother.

Eve is the second Venus, but closer to mankind and more familiar – a Venus who is a wife and mother, who would understand our tragic fate. According to Genesis, Eve was born from Adam. However, there are those who represent her as really being the daughter of Nature – a creature halfway between animal and Man, the daughter of Eden, the daughter of the Tree. Woman is the most beautiful flower in Eden – the 'most brilliant', in the words of Milton – and this theme had proved to be an enduring one, appearing, for example, in the works of Hugo, Zola, Jouve and Shapiro. At the same time, Woman is often also linked to the serpent. In *La faute de l'abbé Mouret*, Frère Archangias sees 'the tail of the serpent twisting among the locks of her hair'. Meanwhile, illustrating the perspective of a modern Eve, Carmen Conde writes, 'the beast smiled at me; I saw its smile clothing my never naked nakedness'.

Eve is born, and offers herself naked to the gaze of her husband, the poet and the reader – though the audience in the theatre has to make do with a description of her hidden charms. Indeed, Eve is a more famous symbol of naked womanhood even than Venus. The thought of her nudity inspires fervent expressions of poetic adulation, from Victor Hugo's 'Flesh of woman, ideal clay, oh wonder! . . .', to Pierre Emmanuel's 'Woman! here you are naked as in the beginning/And smooth beneath my godly hand!' Turning to an artistic context, Verhaeren gives a description in verse of Michelangelo's fresco in the Sistine Chapel featuring a buxom, healthy-looking Eve 'with beautiful high breasts'. Changes in fashion resulted in alterations to this prototype. Thus Van Lerberghe presents a Pre-Raphaelite Eve, a woman 'with pointed breasts' of the type painted by Gustave Moreau.

Depictions of Eve's nakedness range from the innocent to the perverted, from naive candour to murky eroticism. Milton provides one of the most discreet portrayals, though even he describes her as an attractive woman with 'half her swelling breast naked' (*Paradise Lost* IV. 495–6). Maurice Scève is less reserved, itemizing the main features of the female anatomy including the 'ample, fecund belly' and its 'mossy orchard'. Four centuries later, Pierre Jean Jouve employs equally daring circumlocutions: 'her belly is smooth and disappears below a shadow'. Sometimes a demon is madc to list the charms of the first woman. Thus, the one in Vondel's *Adam in Ballingschap* admires '. . . a more delicate body, sweeter flesh and charms, two ivory globes, beforc concluding 'We will pass over the rest in silence before the holy angel is tempted'. Valéry conceals an even more shameless devil in the skin of a serpent; this drooling voyeur enthuses over 'a great flank fringed with gold' and 'fair-haired lower parts mingling with shade and amber'. From Hugo's 'holy nakedness' we have moved on to a nakedness that arouses desire.

The naked Eve is not a beautiful, motionless statue, she is a living woman with what purports to be a typically feminine psychological make-up, in which naivety, emotionality and sensuality alternately have the upper hand. As an unsophisticated countrywoman who is flattered to be treated as a lady, the medieval Eve cuts a poor figure beside her later sisters. She is merely a plaything of the Deceiver, carried along in a drama that is beyond her comprehension. In contrast, the seventeenth-century Eve, whether portrayed in Spanish, Dutch or English works, invariably has a strong personality. Thus Lope de Vega's Eve is on equal terms with her husband, and is able to talk intelligently, debating with herself and listening to her own arguments. She is motivated less by greed than by curiosity and a desire for independence, though to persuade her husband, she resorts to coquetry and tears. The same thirst for independence is apparent in the figures of Eve depicted by Grotius and Vondel, who make her even fonder of reasoning. Similarly, Milton's Eve is able to reason that God 'Forbids us good . . . Such prohibitions bind not' (IX. 759, 760). In addition she always wants to have the last word – 'Eve persisted; yet submiss, though last replied' (IX. 377–8). This Eve is not the secondary figure that she became in the Classical period. Finally, Madách's Eve is just as rational, so that Satan can ironically describe her as the 'first philanderer'. Nor are reason and sensitivity treated as mutually exclusive: the earlier Eves are certainly not insensitive. Milton's Eve, in particular, is a balanced, complete, fully fledged woman. Her character is lovingly developed and is unforgettable – an ideal image, like the idyllic garden described in book IV of *Paradise Lost.*

Eve epitomizes the loving woman, and Milton, like Vondel and many later writers, enjoys depicting love. He vividly evokes the carnal desire that grips the first couple once they have eaten the forbidden fruit, describing how Adam 'on Eve/Began to cast lascivious eyes; she him/As wantonly repaid' (IX. 1013–5).

The embraces of the first lovers form an endlessly recurring theme portrayed in Milton's bower and Zola's Paradou. Verhaeren speaks of the moment 'when the spasm at last leapt from their breasts', while Shapiro talks of how 'the hard blood flows back into the human spring/the sweet door recloses under the mount of Venus'; and similar descriptions occur in the works of Jouve, Carmen Conde and others. Does this represent the final liberation of some exhibitionist desire or of an Oedipal curiosity about our (first) parents? In the works of some writers, Eve is more sensuous than her husband and invites him to enjoy the pleasures of love. This is true of Albine in Zola's novel *La Faute de l'abbé Mouret*, and of the Eves of Verhaeren and Spire. Sometimes we even encounter an Eve who is unfaithful to her husband, as she has been to her Creator, enjoying intercourse with the serpent.

Similarly, Eve is often depicted as being responsible for Man's transgression, inciting Adam to sin. The puritanical Nathaniel Hawthorne speaks of 'her damaging, vengeful role towards the man', and these sentiments are echoed by the French poet Saint-Pol-Roux, who refers to Eve as a woman who 'attracts through the honey of her large eyes' and spreads 'the poison of her disturbed blood'. Similarly, for Strindberg Eve is 'a double demon', while Claudel, the author of the *Cinq Grandes Odes*, claims that if he has been led to 'sin grievously' it is 'the woman's doing'. Pierre Jean Jouve and Pierre Emmanuel were obsessed by the idea of original sin, especially in relation to Man's sexual instincts, and wrote in a still more sombre vein. Meanwhile, misogynist sentiments – which may be present in the original text – and the fear of sex are expressed in extreme form in *L'Eve Future* by Villiers de l'Isle-Adam.

Eve epitomises Woman, but also the Mother, Hawa, the Mother-of-those-living. Hugo develops this theme, summarizing it in the last line of *Le Sacre de la Femme*: 'Eve, pale, felt movement in her side'. The same idea is present in the works of Madách and Rilke; Rilke's Eve is to some extent redeemed by motherhood, first from her coquetry, and secondly from her frivolity. Through it, she acquires a heavier burden of responsibility than Adam, while at the same time giving him back hope: 'Man has survived, for she will produce a child'. Both Péguy and Spire depict Eve growing old, the former portraying her as Man's 'bony-fingered ancestress, lonely toiler' the latter referring to her 'trembling hands flecked with grey blotches' (*Samaël*); and these graphically realistic descriptions result in an epic, mythical vision. Eve becomes the Pietà, the *Mater dolorosa*, reliving the tragic history of unhappy mankind.

These images of Eve the woman and Eve the mother have merely been superimposed on the bare outlines of her character given in the original text.

There, her crucial role in the deception scene is in the guise of the Victim. However, before that episode can be discussed, we must first examine the nature of its central figure, the serpent, the bringer of temptation.

The Serpent

In the *Jeu d'Adam*, the serpent is portrayed in two guises: as 'a cleverly contrived animal'; and as a gallant charmer dressed in ordinary clothes. The latter introduces himself to Eve and uses his mastery of flowery speech to flatter her and so obtains her acquiescence in his designs.

Madách's Lucifer comments pointedly on this scene in Eden that 'we will see it/Played out millions of times'. It answers the requirements of a stereotype, representing the process of deception. From century to century its depiction becomes more elaborate, reaching its apogee in the seventeenth century in the drama by Vondel and in Milton's epic. At a later period, Paul Valéry transcribed the account in Genesis into classical verse, making the serpent speak with an eloquence worthy of the preacher Bossuet.

Beneath the various guises that he has donned over the centuries, the deceiver has certain enduring characteristics. He talks, and he talks well, using, abusing and misusing the spoken word. He is loquacious and discursive, a rhetorician who is a master of the art of winning people over. In the works of Milton and Vondel, as well as that of Valéry, he makes use of antithesis, hyperbole and the telling phrase, attaining the status of an 'orator renowned in Athens or free Rome' (*Paradise Lost* IX. 670–1). His use of language demonstrates a certain snakelike sinuousness, so that, in Valéry's words, 'the style is the devil'. The serpent is also the first poet: according to Hugo, 'Master serpent obviously spoke in verse.' The portrait that emerges is of a courtly poet, a great illusionist – and thus a liar and a consummate actor. The element of deception is emphasized by authors who put revealing asides into the mouths of their serpents. Milton, for example, prefaces the temptation scene with a long monologue, while Madách's Lucifer speaks behind the scenes, and Valéry's serpent recounts the entire episode.

Lope de Vega metamorphoses the animal in Genesis into a huge, fearsome creature. He is a demigod, a rival even to God himself, the epitome of the Adversary. Even as early as the first staging of the *Jeu d'Adam*, audiences had recognized the serpent for who he really was: the Devil emerged from hell. Following in Lope de Vega's footsteps, Milton too gave his hero a formidable stature, and in the works of Byron and the Romantics Satan appears on an equal footing with God. Goethe, however, treats him with irony, while Madách recalls the image of Mephisto and the Spirit that-always-denies.

The gallant speech and seductive appearance assumed by the serpent have implicit, and sometimes explicit, erotic connotations. Valéry and Jouve make their serpent so full of spite that passages burning with the lava of sensuality are punctuated by ones that create embarrassment and unease. As a consequence, the Seducer comes to bear a closer resemblance to de Sade than to Don Juan, and becomes the figure on which 'vampires are based' (Valéry). As a salacious voyeur, a 'reptile who experiences the ectasies of a bird', he cannot resist the 'peril' represented by the body that is offered to him and admits experiencing 'fruitless pleasure' at the sight of such a fresh back. Speaking of Valéry's treatment of the episode in Eden, Alain maintained that 'it was impossible to provide a bolder depiction', but he was not familiar with the work of Pierre Jean Jouve, beside whose highly suggestive, indeed detailed, descriptions the timid hints of Valéry's 'Ebauche d'un serpent' pale into insignificance.

The Cherubim

The account in Genesis of the Temptation and the Fall concludes with the sombre, chilling verse describing the 'cherubim, and a flaming sword which turned every way' (3.26). The latter's tone retrospectively colours both chapter 3 itself and indeed the entire story. The cherubim were originally figures in Assyrio-Babylonian mythology conceived as being lions with men's heads or as winged bulls. However, the influence of art led eventually to their portrayal as angels with human faces, and this is how they appear in the medieval mystery plays, Spanish and Dutch dramas and Milton's *Paradise Lost.* They are fearsome 'men at arms', whose numbers can be increased at will to form a veritable militia: 'The Cherubim descended . . . High in front advanced,/ The brandished sword of God' (*Paradise Lost* XII. 628, 632–3). Byron speaks of the 'proud Cherubim' and 'their flaming swords', while Dierx, Samain, Verhaeren and many others also portray 'the blazing angels, their swords held in their hands'. In the spirit of Byron's *Cain*, and indeed outdoing Byron himself, Leconte de Lisle ascribes an important role to the cherub shining amidst the darkness. In the process, he introduces a sad dialogue between Man, who has been banished from Paradise, and the guardian of Paradise's threshold, a barbarous sentinel worthy of a tyrannical God. Jean Grosjean ('Le Kéroub accuse . . .') imagines a similar dialogue between his Angel and Adam, with the former acting as the spokesman of an angry God and upbraiding the latter. Meanwhile, Jouve conjures up monstrous creatures that seem to have come from another planet: 'the body small/the wing huge/the head hard and smiling . . . on the brow a pointed object/fearful yellow fire, an instrument of murder'.

However, whereas Leconte de Lisle champions mankind in the face of its opposition by the Cherub and condemns the injustice of the divine Master, Jouve seems to justify God, arguing that he had to take drastic action to deal with the fundamental impurity of human nature.

This is the attitude of a believer who stands in crushed submission, shoulders bowed, below the flushed face of an angry God, and it recurs in the work of Carmen Conde. The poems in her collection *Mujer sin Eden* are aflame with two fires: the fire of the flesh kindled by desire, and the fire lit by the angel's sword. The latter acts as a blazing celestial barrier, expressing an agonizing conflict within the poet between her sensuality and her Catholic faith, between irrepressible instinct and the prohibition that the current religious tradition – perhaps mistakenly – places in the mouth of the God of the Bible.

Starting from the same conception as Leconte de Lisle, Zola presented it in a completely different way. Thus his treatment of the biblical verse about the cherubim involved downgrading it rather than amplifying it, and using it to provoke disgust rather than sacred horror in the reader: '. . . Lying full length, he barred its threshold, his limbs spread out in a shameful posture . . .' There is nothing grand about this Frère Archangias who so incenses the novelist, and Zola uses his damning portrayal of him as a means of attacking the higher authority whose 'policeman' Archangias claims to be – the dreadful, jealous God of anger.

Pierre Emmanuel had the highly original idea of identifying the cherubim with his weapon, and, like Jouve, sees him as a symbol of sexual prohibition: 'Angel, you are the Sword that guards the Origin/The Sword that opens impure woman through to her back/The Sword as the mark of prohibition marking the Book.'

Finally one poet more than any other has succeeded in mixing myth and realism. He has demythologized the account in Genesis by abandoning its exotic imagery, but has not impaired the real myth itself: on the contrary, he has renewed it through associating it with everyday life. In *Eve* by Péguy the obsession with the image of the 'door' runs on from page to page, first involving the door to the garden, the great lost domain, and then the door to the dungeon. Eve's gesture in raising 'towards the first doorway/Eyes made heavy by a mournful prayer' is answered by a vision: 'And you alone saw the key in the lock/And the archangel in front of it, beloved mother.' A single angel has replaced the cherubim, but he is an archangel and therefore to be regarded with awe. There are no further details and no sword of fire, but, in their place, a single prominent figure given the seal of sanctity by means of allusion.

THE TRANSPLANTATION OF THE STRUCTURE

There are certain literary works in which the mythical structure of the story in Genesis is preserved, but in which it is displaced in time so that it occurs 'in the present' or at some other given period. These include several pieces of fiction dating from the mid-nineteenth century: *The Marble Faun* by Nathaniel Hawthorne, *La Faute de l'abbé Mouret* by Emile Zola, *La Madre Naturaleza* by Pardo Bazán and *L'Eve future* by Villiers de l'Isle-Adam.

The plot of the first two books can be summarized as follows: in the midst of a marvellous garden, a young couple experience the innocent happiness of an idyllic way of life; the man is a simple, unsophisticated creature, who is induced to commit an offence by his companion, the woman, who loves him; their happiness is lost, and the guilty pair are punished. The setting and the characters are similar in both works, but the atmosphere and intentions are very different. Hawthorne's Eden is pure, while Zola's acts as the embodiment of temptation 'whose every voice taught love', where the legendary tree is phallic: 'It was all voluptuousness; its sap was so strong that it ran from its bark . . . the very manhood of the earth.' Zola omits the presence of the Devil, and denies the existence of Evil, or at least suggests that it is a concept invented by the church, which regards carnal intercourse as the ultimate transgression, and the Fall of Adam and Eve as the Original Sin. Hawthorne, on the other hand, regards the church's dogma as encapsulating a fundamental truth. His protagonists, who bear the marks of their heredity, commit a real crime by killing a man, and are then expelled from Eden, in other words, from their state of happiness. 'Paradise has been relost and shut for ever, with swords of fire shining at its gates.' Yet Good will be born from Evil, the repentent sinner can be saved by a Redeemer: *Felix culpa*!

Pardo Bazán's novel follows Zola's very closely, but alters it by giving it a Christian emphasis. In contrast, the novel by Villiers de l'Isle-Adam is far more original. It is like a tracing of the episode in Genesis, or like its negative image on film – as the title itself indicates. We are no longer dealing with 'the Eve of the forgotten legend' but with 'the scientific Eve' who has come 'from the clay of current human Science'. In a repetition of words of the Bible, the American inventor Edison 'breathes the breath of life' into a robot in the form of a woman. In the process, he simultaneously plays two roles: that of the Benefactor who imparts life; and that of the Tempter, a 'sorcerer' who employs magic. The latter is a rival to God, whom he 'defies' and tempts by aspiring to the highest form of knowledge, 'the old forbidden Knowledge'. However, the new Eve escapes from the control of her demoniac creator and turns out to be a paragon of virtue, a woman with a soul, who affirms her faith in God. In complete contrast to Zola's novel, this work is close to that of the puritan Hawthorne in its suspicions of the temptations of the flesh, but goes still further because of its philosophical idealism.

APPROPRIATION

The drama of Eden which has been re-enacted in the works of thousands of artists and writers is sometimes played out in the heart of the individual. There are even instances when lyric poets have assumed the garb of Adam (or, less often, that of Eve). Thus Walt Whitman portrays himself going on his way 'like Adam, early in the morning'; while Paul Claudel explicitly admits to reliving the Bible story in the Seconde Ode, 'L'Esprit et l'eau'. Created from dust and the breath of God like the first man, he too has experienced temptation and he too has fallen; to become like a god is an illusory aspiration: 'Oh dear friend, I am not a god!'

When writers rework the story of Eden they often use it as a medium for confession. As this myth concerns the very roots of life and raises the question of the relationship between Man and God, almost all those authors who have chosen to evoke it have done so because they themselves were living out its drama by accepting or rejecting the notion of God as the Benefactor and accepting or rejecting its vision of their own status.

A good example is provided by Charles Van Lerberghe. His minor work *Chanson d'Eve* might appear to be merely a Symbolist version of the Hebrew story. However, it is actually the expression of a deep personal crisis, an imaginary dramatization of an internal debate. In the poem, as in life, God is confounded – a God who is defined as the enemy, 'he who imposed himself through fear', 'he who taught hatred'.

Described in similar terms, this aspect of God glowers through the lines of many writers who believe that they have found such a vision in the verses of Genesis: 'a god-that-terrorizes' with whom Jules Supervielle wants no truck; Byron's 'Proud one', 'who will not let human beings live'; Blake's 'selfish Father of the human race'; Leconte de Lisle's wicked, murderous god; Strindberg's god 'with a severe, almost angry countenance'; Zola's god of whom his lieutenant, Frère Archangias, is a repulsive copy, a cruel stupid brute; Rilke's god who 'threatens man with death'; and Spire's 'god-who-punishes, a real God'. These many descriptions of this one being all convey the same impression.

Some authors effectively admit that it is their intention to humble this wicked god, while others achieve the same result less explicitly. In doing so, they act in the name of hedonism, or human progress, and particularly in the name of individual freedom. Their attitude is based more on anti-theism than on true atheism, and their works give poetic expression to ideas current since the end of the eighteenth century, according to which God – who is first and foremost the God of Genesis – is responsible for the alienation of Man. Their paraphrases of the myth of Eden constitute an arena where they can confront their adversary. Here, their innermost beings are engaged in a struggle in which the very death of a god is at issue.

In stark contrast to this group of works, there is another in which the Lord of Lords is represented as a benefactor and celebrated as the God of Love. It includes the medieval mystery plays, the writings of the Renaissance period by Scève and du Bartas, Spanish and Dutch dramas, Milton's epic, the poems of Hugo, Claudel, Péguy, Jouve and Emmanuel, and a whole host of other works. Péguy's *Eve* represents the 'handsome, young' God placing the first human couple in Eden, while Supervielle portrays him as a 'god as good as good wine', and Emmanuel as 'a smiling God'.

However, one must be careful not to overemphasize the opposition between these two approaches. In some works, such as Jouve's *Le Paradis perdu*, the two views of God alternate, so that he is shown first as the God of Love and then as the God of Justice. Meanwhile, many writers, such as Gide and Shapiro, are less committed to one particular outlook than others. Both groups exploit the same original text either to make a god live again or to make a god die, to exalt a god or to kill him. It is not enough to call one group believers and the other unbelievers: rejecting a spiteful God may indicate nostalgia for a good, just God, as most critical studies of Leconte de Lisle's work have recognized. Similarly, the rationalism of some writers is still imbued with religious feeling, and thus is not radical; they may be seeking a god, but, unlike others, they fail to recognize him in the first pages of Genesis. Moreover, it must be remembered that the original text of Genesis has been severely distorted both by broad external influences, such as translations, and religious and philosophical traditions, and by subjective interpretations stemming from a so-called religious education and personal experiences.

Thus the images and words of the poets discussed above express all the emotions, both simple and complex, experienced by Western man: happiness and wretchedness; joy and pain; love and the passions of the couple, and nostalgia for lost innocence, and the anguish of guilt. These constitute the very essence of existence, what Péguy would call 'the common web'.

Such are the depth and scope of this myth of myths!

Robert Couffignal

Eldorado

Drawing on his knowledge of the Spanish chroniclers of the Indies, in his *Essai sur les Moeurs*, Voltaire recalls the legend of the Gilded Man (subsequently recounted in *Candide*) who lived in a valley filled with cinnamon trees by the green waters of a lake:

> from what we understand of the stories of the Indians, this great lord or prince is continually covered in gold dust as fine as the finest salt . . . and he shines with the same brilliance as a gold statue created by the hands of a great artist.

Voltaire's main source, *Comentarios reales de los Incas* (1586–1605) by Garcilaso de la Vega (1539–1615), and his other sources, *Historia del Descubrimiento y Conquista de la provincia del Perú* (1555) by Agustin de Zarate (1514–?) and *La Crónica del Perú* (1553) by Pedro de Cieza de León (1518–60), refer to gold as a mirage pursued by the Spanish conquistadors across the vast continent of America. The geography of the continent was still largely unknown and it was the conquistadors' lust for riches that indirectly brought about its exploration. Zarate, and particularly Pedro de Cieza de León, constantly refer to the fantastic nature of the territories discovered, and especially to the incalculable amount of gold and silver to be found in the region, which the Spaniards named Castilla del Oro. As well as the works of art that filled its temples and tombs, there were also gold nuggets washed down by the rivers. Cieza recalls the words of an Inca lord who claimed that in comparison with the treasures that remained, those seized by the Spaniards were like a single drop taken from a large pitcher overflowing with water. However, he added that those treasures that did remain were in places unknown even to the Indians themselves. This sort of remark was all that was needed to send the Spaniards flooding into the region to cause the Gilded Man to be transformed into a gilded land, Eldorado.

> Near a certain Lake Parima where the sand was made of gold . . . there is a city where the roofs were made of gold; the Spaniards called this city 'Eldorado' and spent a long time searching for it.
>
> (*Essai sur les Moeurs*)

In their searches for Eldorado, Gonzalo Pizarro (the brother of Francisco Pizarro, the conqueror of Peru), set out in the direction of Ecuador, while Diego de Almagro explored Chile, and Francisco de Orellana – and later Lope de Aguirre – sailed down the river Marañón. The latter was renamed the Amazon because, according to Zarate, 'it ran through a land inhabited only by women', and it is interesting to note how the frustrated conquistadors actively promoted this myth, to create another Eldorado from their failure. Orellana had betrayed his leader Pizarro by leading an expedition of his own, even using the vessel that Pizarro himself had built. The current carried him more quickly than he had dared to hope but he was deceived by the Indians, who managed to get rid of him by inventing stories. As a consequence, he sailed on, in the direction of the land 'inhabited only by women', but 'without finding either gold or silver or traces thereof in these parts'. After continuing along the river Marañón (originally called after the Spaniard who had been the first to navigate it) he finally emerged, empty handed, a long way to the north near the island of Cubagua. According to Zarate, as soon as Orellana returned to Spain, he asked the king to grant him the rights of discovery and conquest of the 'very rich [land] inhabited by those women, which was commonly known throughout the kingdom as the conquest of the Amazons'.

In a similar way, the conquest of New Granada (part of which lies in present-day Colombia) was linked to the search for a native Indian chief who immersed himself in a lake during certain festivals and then was coated all over in gold dust while priests and dignitaries threw gold objects into the water. The *muiscas* Indians had a reputation for their goldwork and the Spaniards, who were already spreading through the region at full gallop, believed that their territory must be Eldorado. Subsequent events might have formed part of an adapted version of a La Fontaine fable; there was indeed hidden silver, but the Indians wisely sent the Spaniards on a little beyond where it lay:

> Gonzalo Pizarro continued to advance with the healthier members of his expedition along the road indicated by the Indians. Sometimes in order to keep [the Spaniards] away from their land, the Indians gave them false information on what was awaiting them, deceiving them in the same way that Zumaco's men had done by telling them that further on there was a densely populated and fertile land, which information had proved to be false.

Sebastian de Belalcazar left Quito and travelled northwards, while Gonzalo Jiménez de Quesada, who had recently founded Santa Maria on the Caribbean coast in 1525, took the southerly route, following the Magdalena river upstream and reaching the Upper Orinoco, where he founded Bogotá in 1538. In fact, from the outset, the discovery and conquest of America was inextricably linked with the search for Eldorado. Christopher Columbus had suggested to Queen Isabella that he should go westwards in search of Cathay and Cipango, since the gold from these regions would finance a new crusade against the Turks, who were then threatening the West. (The recapture of mainland Spain from the Moors had just been completed.) Thus it was due to Columbus himself that the Gilded Land was seen for a short time as representing paradise on earth. This notion coincided with the belief current at the time that the Turks would be allowed to destroy the Church in the

West because God was giving Man a second opportunity for salvation in the new paradise of the Indies.

Another illusory Eldorado that attracted attention before the term itself was actually coined, was the great Aztec city of Tenochtitlan, which formed the objective of the expedition led by Hernán Cortés. From the outset, Cortés had been persuaded of the truth of Marco Polo's accounts of the existence of a kingdom of fabulous riches, and his beliefs were reinforced by the sumptuous gifts sent to him by Montezuma, who believed that he was the Aztec god Quetzalcoatl. A further version of the quest for Eldorado took place in Central America after the discovery of the Pacific by Balboa in 1513. This time it took the form of a search for the place where, again according to the Indians, the two oceans met; while Balboa's exploit inspired a beautiful poem by Pablo Neruda in the *Canto General* entitled 'Homenaje a Balboa'. In his novel *Maladrón* (1969) Miguel Angel Asturias describes 'the Epic of the Green Andes' (to quote the book's subtitle) near the place where the Atlantic and the Pacific meet. This is a metaphor for the ethnic and cultural interbreeding that has taken place in America, while his mad hero, who chooses the Bad Thief in preference to Christ and attempts to carve out a kingdom without being subject to any form of human law, is reminiscent of Lope de Aguirre. Indeed, it was with the revival of interest in the legendary figure Aguirre (1513?–61), the insane protagonist of a real-life adventure that hardly seems credible even today, that the legend of Eldorado entered the field of contemporary literature. Works such as *El Camino de El Dorado* (1947) and *Lope de Aguirre, Príncipe de la Libertad* (1979) by the Venezuelan writers Arturo Uslar Pietri (born 1906) and Miguel Otero Silva (1908–85) respectively as well as Werner Herzog's film *Aguirre, der Zorn Gottes* (*Aguirre, Wrath of God*) have popularized the figure of the Tyrant, the Traitor and the Pilgrim. However, even before this, the famous 'libertador' Simon Bolivar had persuaded Latin Americans to hail Aguirre as the figurehead of emancipation and, in 1821, had actively encouraged the circulation of the letter of rebellion sent by Lope de Aguirre to Philip II in 1561, declaring the kingdom of Marañón independent of Spain. Inspired by these events, Miguel Otero Silva wrote *Lope de Aguirre, Príncipe de la Libertad*, in which the brilliant narrative technique blends a stream-of-consciousness approach with theatrical dialogue and the author's pseudo-academic footnotes. One of the latter reveals that the author had scoured the abundant literature already available on the subject of Lope de Aguirre, reading, commenting on and annotating no fewer than 188 works by chroniclers, biographers, historians, essayists, psychiatrists, moralists, storytellers, poets and dramatists for the purposes of writing his novel. However, it goes on to say that no further reference will be made to them, since the novelist is under no obligation to reveal his sources – a jibe directed at the novel *Yo El Supremo* by the Paraguayan writer Agusto Roa Bastos. Although he follows the historical biography of Aguirre both closely and at a distance, Otero Silva makes it clear that he is not attempting to resurrect the figure of a bloodthirsty madman, emphasizing that the Eldorado sought by his 'Prince of Liberty' who declared himself to be 'the wrath of God', was Liberty in the sense of the American ideal of emancipation – freedom from the administrative and religious yoke of colonialism.

Otero Silva's treatment of Aguirre is by no means without humour, and this is amplified still further in the novel *Daimón* (1981) by the Argentinian writer Abel Posse (born 1936). Again, there is a reference to *Yo El Supremo*, in that the story's protagonist is an old man who has died (like Roa Bastos's dictator Francia), as have all the other characters, who are the ghosts of Aguirre's companions on Marañón expedition. According to Posse, the Eldorado pursued by Aguirre was actually close at hand but he was unable to see it: it was the whole of America, vast, incredibly fertile and invested with a beauty that would touch even the hardest of hearts. Aguirre, however, believed that gold was essential in order to have a 'place at Court with a well-paid, happy and arrogant regiment whose captains were dressed in velvet and wore hats trimmed with the feathers of Cuban parrots . . .'. Gold meant that you could go into a Cordoba brothel, clap your hands and order wine for everybody! The Amazon queen, who does not understand this use of gold, tells him that not far from her country is Eldorado. 'Such an unhappy land! The golden sand only serves to breed scorpions and mygales!' But Aguirre does not share this concept of unhappiness:

> If the purpose of life is to cry, then I would prefer having to cry with my backside resting on sand made of gold.

Posse's novel is brilliant and scathing, and was inevitably labelled as 'baroque' by the critics. In contrast, Otero Silva's is more ideological, while Uslar Pietri's is more historically accurate, and Asturias's work is more lyrical. However, all agree that Eldorado is undoubtedly America itself, their America, without the taint of gold – particularly in a modern context, when gold means the dollar. In short, the lesson is the same one that Candide and his manservant learned from their stay in Eldorado.

Thus Eldorado was originally an historical reality of a sort. Its historical existence was as a fiction based on stories told by the Indians and lent credence by Spanish wishful thinking: and, consequently, it provides a classic illustration of how myths develop. In a second phase, the historical fiction was transformed into literary fiction, thereby preparing the ground for a third stage, represented by visual media. Prominent among these is the cinema, which conveys the metaphorical image of Eldorado as a land of dreams and plenty. Charlie Chaplin's film *The Gold Rush* exemplifies this vision of 'happiness, somewhere else, in the future' (with gold, as always, used as a metaphor), while the reverse of this vision is represented by Fritz Lang's *Metropolis*, in the 'horror, here and now,' of daily drudgery. Fabulous America conjures up dreams and myths. Thus, in his imaginative vision of discovery *The Dream of Christopher*

Columbus, painted in 1959 for an American millionaire, even Salvador Dali interprets the New World as the land of *gold*.

Dorita Nouhaud

Eros

Eros is one of the divinities in the Greek pantheon who features most prominently in literature. Admittedly, painters have played a major part in creating our image of him, but it is primarily poets who have developed his characteristics as a mythical figure. This figure has a strange duality, since the familiar image of the young god of love was superimposed on a more ancient aspect. The latter represented the abstract force of desire implied by the noun *eros*, and explains the nature of the primeval Eros conjured up in some myths concerning the creation of the world.

THE EROS OF THE COSMOGONIC THEORIES

Hesiod's *Theogony*: Eros, a generative force

Hesiod's *Theogony* (seventh century BC) is the first Greek text in which Eros appears, since Homer makes no mention of him as a god of love. It presents him as one of the three primordial entities that existed prior to the formation of the universe: '. . . Chaos was first of all, but next appeared broad-bosomed Earth [Gaia] . . . and Love [Eros]' (116 ff). In the context of this triad from which the cosmos and the gods emerged, Eros played a special role. Though he himself did not procreate, he represented a third force, a force of attraction, that became necessary for reproduction after the birth of the very first generations, which had emanated from a single parent 'without the help of tender love'.

The first union to bear fruit was that between Gaia [Earth] and her son Uranus (the Sky). To prevent his monstrous children from seeing the light of day, Uranus buried them in the breast of their mother, thereby impeding the process of generation. This interruption can be interpreted as reflecting the excessive power of Eros, while the action of Cronos in castrating his father Uranus to keep him away from his mother may be seen as a distancing measure essential for the equilibrium of the cosmos.

This seems to imply that, when abused, the power of Eros is capable of self-destruction. In any case, its influence in Hesiod's cosmogony is sufficiently widespread to ensure both the cohesion and the perpetuity of the universe. Meanwhile, the Orphic tradition went still further, attributing creation itself to the god's power.

The demiurge of Orphism

In his play *The Birds* (414 BC), Aristophanes parodies Orphic beliefs concerning the origin of the universe:

> In the beginning there existed only Chaos, Night, Black Erebus and Dreary Tartarus; there was no Earth, no Air, no Sky. It was in the boundless womb of Erebus that the first egg was laid by black-winged Night; and from this egg, in due season, sprang Eros . . . (693 ff).

Featuring prominently in this passage is the concept of the cosmic egg from which there hatches out the *protogonos* (first born), who is variously called Eros, Phanes, Metis or Erikepaïos in the Orphic poems. According to Aristophanes, it is from Eros that the race of the immortals is descended.

Philosophers such as Empedocles and Parmenides also endowed Eros with the role of a demiurge, originally suggested by Proclus. According to their account, Zeus devours Eros and, having thus appropriated his identity, creates the gods and recreates the universe. This episode is doubly important. In the first place, it shows that the function of demiurge is sufficiently closely associated with Eros for another creator to have to be assimilated with him. In the second, it is clear that in Orphic legend Eros has ceased to represent the principle of union and has become the principle of organization: he is both the father and the master of the universe.

A universal power: Eros and nature

The breadth of Eros's power, which extends not only to the gods and men but to the elements and nature itself, is due to this original conception of him as a primordial god.

For Aristophanes, as for Hesiod, Eros's power is connected with his outstanding beauty. Aristophanes calls him 'Eros the deeply-desired, Eros the bright, the golden-winged', while Hesiod describes him as *kallistos*, 'the most beautiful of the immortals', and also remarks 'He makes men weak,/He overpowers the clever mind, and tames/The spirit in the breasts of men and gods'. The association made between beauty and power no doubt reflects the irresistible attraction of desire – 'desired' desire as Aristophanes puts it. In addition, it is worth noting that neither of these evocations of Eros's beauty endows him with any anthropomorphic traits, leaving him instead as an abstract or unreal (winged) being.

In his guise as a fundamental cosmic force, Eros is in fact a deity without distinctive physical features, and perhaps he was originally worshipped as such at Thespiae in Boeotia, where, for a long time, he continued to be represented by an unhewn stone. This form of representation associates him with the oldest chthonic gods and gods of nature, an association that is confirmed by his links with fire, wind and plant life.

The god's connection with fire is clearly revealed by the fact that during the Panathenaic festival at Athens a torch race was held in his honour, before his altar at the entrance to the Academy – as by the altars of Prometheus and Hephaistos (whom Ibycus represents as Eros's father). His links with the wind are equally clear, since Alcaeus makes Zephyr his father, and Aristophanes says he is 'like the quick eddies of the wind'. Meanwhile, as a force bringing fecundity to the universe, Eros was linked with vegetation, and particularly with its revival in springtime, the season of love. In paintings, he was represented with a wreath of foliage on his head and leaning against a tree, a reminder of the sacred woods that were dedicated to him. Indeed, pictures portraying him can sometimes be confused with those depicting Adonis, the symbol of plant revival. Moreover, like Adonis, Eros also had a funerary role, since representations of him occur on tombs.

Nonetheless, even in the context of funerary rites, Eros represents the principle of life, and the extensions of his power over the whole domain of nature mentioned above merely represent a development of his original attributes. The universal power of the primordial god is perpetuated by the omnipotence of the young god of love who is Aphrodite's companion, and this perhaps forms the most obvious link between Eros's two very different aspects.

THE GOD OF LOVE

Eros and Aphrodite

The paradoxical co-existence of the two aspects of Eros is already apparent in Hesiod's work. He is first evoked as a primordial god, but later – alone with Himerus, another figure representing desire – he is present at the birth of Aphrodite, and from then on forms part of her retinue, as a subordinate divinity.

A festival in honour of Aphrodite and Eros was celebrated at their shared temple on the Acropolis at Athens. However, it was primarily art and literature that consecrated their association. Not only were they repeatedly depicted together, but, more importantly, Eros was also portrayed as Aphrodite's son, by a father who was variously identified by different writers – Uranus according to Sappho, Ares according to Simonides, Hermes according to Cicero, and so on.

However, even before the fifth century BC, when Eros became the patron deity of ephebic love, the two divinities had separate and distinct domains. Thus Eros tended to personify abstract desire, while Aphrodite personified its realization and the accompanying physical pleasure.

Greek erotic poetry: affectation and cruelty

Love poets gradually established Eros's character by adopting two complementary approaches that often operate in unison. One relates to the god's form and involves the elaboration of his physical attributes, while the other relates to abstract issues and examines his influence on mankind.

Portrayals of the god's appearance evolve towards a prettiness that often verges on the precious. At the same time, as he is made younger, changing from a handsome young man into a small child, he is placed in settings in which his attributes and attitudes seem all the more anodyne, because the painters and poets who have taken them up have turned them into stock themes. Anacreon describes him as a young boy with wings who plays with balls and knuckle-bones, and Euripides introduces the bow and arrows with which he wounds lovers' hearts, while in works by other writers he has a torch to set hearts on fire. Alternatively, he can also be depicted bearing a crown and fillets to decorate the altar of Aphrodite. In Alexandrine poetry the image of the god became fixed, and he was turned into a simple literary device. As in vase paintings, he was no more than a decorative motif, symbolizing a loving relationship between two people.

Yet even when Eros appears to be at his most harmless he is still a fearsome god, since the game of knuckle-bones surely symbolizes the careless cruelty with which he manipulates his victims. Similarly, the conflicts between Eros and his mother evoked by Apollonius show that the little god has preserved his autonomy.

The abstract influence exerted by Eros can be summed up as involving suffering. Thus, poets such as Sappho attribute to him a cruelty that is in stark contrast with the tender-heartedness of Aphrodite. According to Sophocles, Eros engenders madness, and the theme of Eros-*nosos* (sickness) is developed by Euripides. In a more subtle approach to the subject, Euripides makes a distinction between two Eroses, according to whether the love concerned has a virtuous or a shameful outcome. This question of Eros's dual character is central to the debate in Plato's *Symposium*.

Plato's *Symposium*: the dual aspects of Eros

The six speeches in honour of Eros in the *Symposium* express diverging views as to his nature, but they can be grouped together into three series.

As far as the first two speakers are concerned, there is only one Eros; Phaedrus regards him as the most ancient god, and Agathon as the youngest. Through this contradiction Plato draws attention to an initial dual aspect of Eros, who may originally have been represented as an old man (as the rough stone at Thespiae might suggest).

The next two speakers both think of Eros as double. According to Pausanias, Eros resembles his companion Aphrodite in being able to adopt two forms.

Thus an Eros interested primarily in masculine love and spiritual matters corresponds to Uranian Aphrodite (the daughter of Uranus), while an Eros concerned with heterosexual, physical love is associated with Aphrodite Pandemus (the daughter of Zeus and Dione) – the former being clearly preferable to the latter. Meanwhile, Eryximachus extends this concept of doubleness to the whole of nature, the arts and sciences.

The last two speakers, Aristophanes and Socrates, are both thinkers. Aristophanes recounts the story of how men were originally double but were cut in two as a punishment for their effrontery in challenging the gods and have ever since been desperately seeking reunion with their missing halves. Eros represents the instinct that enables men to rediscover happiness for an instant, along with their original wholeness.

Finally, Socrates claims that his highly original theory of the nature of Eros is based on the teachings of Diotima, a priestess at Mantinea. According to him, Eros is not a god, but a demon, or a go-between linking gods and men. Poverty is his mother and Expediency his father; from the former, he derives his lack of looks and property, and from the father, he derives the means of obtaining them, through procreation by means of the body (heterosexual love) and through creation by means of the soul (homosexual love). This second form of love allows one to move on from appreciation of the beauty of a body to appreciation of the concept of beauty itself, and so to attain the realm of understanding – a process that represents the stages of a true spiritual initiation.

Plato's dialogue thus highlights two essential points: that love between men is regarded more favourably than love between men and women; and that Eros has an initiatory role. Both of these phenomena have shared antecedents in certain initiatory rites.

Eros as an initiator

Significantly, the Eleutherian festival was celebrated in honour of Eros of the gymnasia, the god of ephebic love, who was often associated with Anteros, who was seen as representing reciprocal love. This cult, which predated the homosexual idea of Plato, can be compared with the sacrifices to Eros (the archer god, and son of Ares) made in Sparta before battle, and the Theban and Cretan custom according to which a lover provided his (male) beloved with military equipment. In this context homosexuality is the consequence of a rite of passage from childhood to adolescence, linked with training in citizenship and as a soldier.

The initiatory function of Eros recurs in a different form in the *Tale of Psyche*, a story inserted into *The Golden Ass* by Apuleius (second century AD). This tells how Psyche, a mortal woman whose beauty aroused the jealousy even of Venus herself, was wedded to Amor (Eros) but was not allowed to see him. Her curiosity led her to transgress this prohibition, and she had to submit to harsh trials imposed by Venus before finally being saved by Amor, who won her immortal status.

As the plot of Apuleius's novel concerns the initiation of the book's hero into the cult of Isis, the story of Psyche may seem to be intended to prefigure it. Eros would then be a double of the goddess – like her, invisible to start with, and only attainable after the completion of a series of trials. However, the legend also has an allegorical meaning, evoking the wanderings of the human soul in search of ideal beauty. The role of Eros is thus analogous to that attributed to him by Socrates in the *Symposium*, and involves providing access to the world of the intellect, here symbolized by Olympus.

The variety of moral and philosophical concepts vested in the figure of Eros contrasts strangely with the stereotyped depictions of his outer appearance. However, this doubtless results from the literary character of the god; the more that poets vied with one another in describing the same unchanging ornamental motif, the more that thinkers sought to deepen and renew their philosophical analysis. The same vacillation between conformity and originality characterizes the evocations of Eros in Western literature since the Middle Ages.

EROS IN WESTERN LITERATURE: TRITENESS AND RENEWAL

The stereotyped Eros of Alexandrine poetry reached the West by way of Byzantine and Latin verse under the Latin names Amor or Cupid. Nonetheless, his image was adapted to suit the tastes and requirements of different periods and authors, and he was sometimes portrayed in an original fashion.

The God of Love in Guillaume de Lorris

Amor was a favourite figure in medieval allegory, but his appearance in this context in *Le Roman de la Rose* (*c.* 1230) by Guillaume de Lorris is given a richer significance than usual because he appears as the spokesman for the courtly ideal.

Here, the portrait of Amor is not based on the Eros of the Greek poems. Instead, he is an adult god, with no wings, and is described mainly in terms of his dress of flowers and his crown of roses, which bear clusters of symbols representing the orchard of paradise. Following the logic of the allegory, the double nature of the god is indicated by his double array of weapons. An ugly, battered bow is matched by five black arrows symbolizing vices, while a fine, smooth bow is accompanied by five other arrows symbolizing the female virtues. When wounded by these, the lover becomes Amor's vassal. Recalling the ancient theme of Eros the turnkey, the latter locks his heart and makes him subject to the code of courtly love.

Thus Amor is the allegorical representation of a particular emotion, with all its ambivalence and violence. The plot of the romance also involves a process of initiation similar to that described by Apuleius, but here, Amor sets the tests himself, so playing the role of Venus as well as his own.

Renaissance: From Blind Love to Divine Love

During the Middle Ages the favoured image of Amor was as a clear-sighted adult. However, the Renaissance witnessed the re-emergence of the ancient idea of the *puer alatus* (winged boy), and the development of the notion that Amor was blind. Thus, painters in general, and Piero della Francesca in particular, depict him with his eyes bandaged, symbolizing the arbitrary and unconscious nature of love.

The Renaissance poets also reverted to the idea that Mars was Amor's father, making it possible to interpret Amor as a principle representing the union of opposites (Venus and Mars). This explains the little god's association with themes involving war: 'Amor and Mars are almost two of a kind:/One fights by day, the other by night . . .' (Ronsard, *Amours de Cassandre* 1552, sonnet CLXXX).

Indeed, the very character of Amor is a combination of conflicting elements, and in the *Canzoniere*, Petrarch (*c.* 1330) emphasizes his ambivalence:

> Amor simultaneously spurs me on and holds me back
> Reassures and frightens me, burns and freezes me,
> Makes up to me and spurns me, summons me to him and drives me away,
> Keeps me now in hope, and now in distress.

Moralists and humanists gave new life to the dual concept of sacred and profane love. Thus Anteros, who in classical antiquity had personified the reciprocity of love, became Anti-Eros, a figure of purity contrasting with the sensuality of Eros himself. The Neoplatonist Marsilio Ficino defines Love as the desire to enjoy beauty, and in his *Commentary on Plato's Symposium* (1468), he opposes *Amor divinus* (the son of celestial Aphrodite), representing the aspiration towards cosmic beauty, to *Amor vulgaris* (the son of Aphrodite Pandemus), who makes the reproduction of an image of cosmic beauty possible in the physical world. However, even earthly Amor verges on the sacred. Not only is it one of the four divine passions (along with poetic frenzy, the comprehension of mysteries, and prophecy – which is inspired by the Muses, Bacchus and Apollo), it is also the most powerful. Amor is a circular current linking God and the universe, and anyone who feels love is integrated into its divine flow. This idea is illustrated by Ronsard in his *Amours de Cassandre* (LII): 'Amor made my nature perfect,/My essence became pure by his means/ He gave me life and power . . .'

Conversely, Plato's special esteem for an Eros representing homosexual love, seems to have been forgotten in the Christian West, though there is a suggestion of it in Shakespeare's sonnet CXLIV (*c.* 1590). There, the poet presents a striking contrast between his 'two loves', a fair man and a dark lady, one angelic and the other corrupting, and though he does not mention the god of love by name, he may be taking up the ideas presented in the *Symposium*. If so, he has given them even more radical expression, since he actually curses heterosexual love.

Two Allegorical Plays by Marivaux

Two short allegorical comedies by Marivaux shed new light on the Platonic view of Eros's double nature. In *Dialogue de l'Amour et de la Vérité* (1720), the true Amor is wise and circumspect and curses his impudent usurper. Meanwhile, in *La Réunion des Amours* (1731), the two rivals confront each other before the gods of Olympus. Cupid preaches the law of pleasure, and Amor's bashfulness prevents him from imposing his sentimental ideal. Jupiter's verdict reconciles the two, and this rehabilitation of carnal love seems to herald the libertinism prevalent in works of literature written later in the same century.

Conclusion

That Eros has been largely forgotten is doubtless due to over-use and to the fact that the preciousness of his image has eclipsed the inexhaustibly rich theme of love and desire that he actually embodies. In addition, psychoanalysis may have contributed to a 'depoeticizing' process by adopting the concept of *eros* as one of its central elements, representing it as the principle of action and life, as opposed to the drive of death (*thanatos*), and as being fulfilled in the libido. Though this idea conforms with the original image of Eros, it demythifies the allegory, and reduces desire to something within the individual.

Indeed, it is perhaps here that the key to understanding the transition from Eros the cosmogonic figure to Cupid the little god of love also lies. The latter may simply represent the adaptation of the former to the demands of the poets' own personal feelings. In this process of adaptation, the universal force of desire is reduced to human proportions – which explains the miniaturization of the actual figure of the deity. The eclipse of Eros shows the dangers for a god in being too human.

Ann-Déborah Lévy

Eternal Recurrence: Nietzsche's 'Great Thought'

Paradoxically, it was in the time of Hegel, during the century in which historical science developed and the ideologies of progress were born that Nietzsche rediscovered the idea of Eternal Recurrence. Indeed, the concept itself reflected a desire to strike back at the cult of the historical fact and the dreams of the determinists, which represented the last manifestations of metaphysics, while it was also a weapon against nihilism. Nonetheless, the notion of the Recurrence does not represent a philosophical strategy. On the contrary, it exceeds the grasp of Nietzsche's philosophy and work. Everything converges on this exorbitant centre where thought meets its Other, its source and breakdown point. The notion of Eternal Recurrence is so vast that Nietzsche could not formulate it himself: instead, he delegated the task to several 'voices', none of which has the last word on the subject. The 'great thought' cannot be confined to a single interpretation and, to grasp it, one should not ask the philosophical question, 'What does it mean?' but rather 'Who is explaining it?' Its meaning and status depend on who is putting it forward. For Nietzsche himself it was a revelation, in Zarathustra's words it becomes a doctrine and in relation to Dionysus it remains the god's own enigma.

THE REVELATION OF SILS-MARIA

There is apparently nothing original in the idea of Eternal Recurrence, and Nietzsche himself admitted that he owed it to the Presocratics and the Stoics 'The Birth of Tragedy' (*Ecce Homo*). Indeed, he was returning to the idea of the infinite recurrence of the same events formulated by Chrysippus, and to the active fatalism of Epictetus, for whom freedom consisted in wanting what happens. At first sight, the two passages in which he presents his conception of Recurrence (*The Gay Science* 341 and *Beyond Good and Evil* 56) confirm this. Moreover, to explain the theory, Nietzsche uses conventional images: those of 'the eternal hourglass of existence' and the circle. He also stresses the fact that there is 'nothing new' and that everything will return ('this spider and this moonlight') in an identical form.

The idea seems simple and its formulation human, all too human. Thus, in *Ecce Homo* Nietzsche almost turns it into a family story: the terror aroused in him by the thought of the eternal recurrence of his mother and sister are almost enough to cause him to abandon the idea of recurrence altogether. However, we should also note that there is a connection between the frightening domain of Mothers (from which Dionysus comes) and the notion of Eternal Recurrence, which Nietzsche presents as his 'truly "abysmal" thought'. A sort of monstrosity is thus inextricably attached to him, explaining his reference to 'the greatest weight'. Nietzsche seems undermined by his own thought. Is he able to accept even his mother's recurrence? Is he strong enough for that? The simple concept of Eternal Recurrence is in fact a criterion for identifying strength and weakness. Unbearable to the weak, it gives extra strength the strong. Faced with this thought, Nietzsche questions himself as if in a mirror. Is he worthy to be its prophet? Is he a 'decadent' or a man of the future? (See Klossowski 1969.)

Nonetheless, one certainly remains, which is more powerful than the vacillation of Nietzsche the man: the ecstatic experience that he underwent at Sils-Maria, where he had the revelation of Eternal Recurrence (August 1881). Linked to the 'great affect' and representing a spiritual experience of the greatest intensity, this event served as a sheet anchor for Nietzsche's consciousness. He continually questions his memory and himself in the blinding light of this revelation. Finally, the very circumstances under which it occurred to him prove the originality of the idea in relation to similar ancient concepts. Aware of its absolute foreignness, of his total inability to conceptualize it and even of the mistake that it would be to make it the pivot of a philosophical system, Nietzsche holds back his thought and delegates the risky task of formulating it to Zarathustra.

ZARATHUSTRA THE DOCTRINARIAN

Nietzsche refers to Zarathustra as the 'doctor' of Eternal Recurrence. It is up to Zarathustra to make this thought into a doctrine (*Thus spoke Zarathustra* X. 313), in other words to formulate it coherently and to link it to other themes in Nietzsche's philosophy. Zarathustra, the prophet of the 'superman', encourages us to see Eternal Recurrence as a superhuman idea, the idea of one strong enough to want life over and over again for all eternity. Nevertheless, the idea makes him ill and Nietzsche himself writes, 'The teaching of this doctrine must be stopped and Zarathustra killed' (X. 313). This is because the idea of recurrence seems 'at first crushing to the most noble'. Insofar as it implies an absence of goals, it confirms the nihilist sense of life's absurdity. It asserts that, in the eyes of eternity, the 'strongest' and 'weakest' are of equal worth, that they will always recur and that the 'superman' does not represent the final goal of Eternal Recurrence. However, Zarathustra teaches us how to transcend this outlook through the abandonment of individual perception. For one who understands that it is not his ego that counts but the general economy of the world and the great 'Yes' addressed to life, the concept of recurrence becomes the idea 'most overflowing with courage' (XI. 218).

However, Zarathustra's doctrine remains unsatisfactory and perhaps even misleading, for he himself is not equal to the idea that he puts forward. The latter is covered in two main passages. In the first, 'On the Vision and the Enigma', Zarathustra uses the image of two paths that converge and collide under the gateway of the 'moment', followed by the parable of a shepherd bitten by a snake. It is significant that Nietzsche chose to present his 'doctrine' in *Zarathustra*, a poetic work in which all is riddle and symbol and there is no question of formulating any real philosophical system. Yet, when they have barely even been outlined, Zarathustra's ideas are immediately exposed as flawed, first by the dwarf crouching before the gateway, who is passively contemplating the circle of recurrence instead of actively participating in his return in the 'moment', and then, in the second passage referred to above, 'The Convalescent', where the animals have already made Eternal Recurrence into an unbearable 'hurdy-gurdy song'. As a result, this idea that is beyond him and whose 'spirit of gravity' he quickly grasps, makes Zarathustra ill.

Any attempt to explain Eternal Recurrence is dangerous, if only because it then falls prey to the philosophers, who turn it into their 'hurdy-gurdy song'. However interesting the interpretations of, for example, Heidegger and Deleuze may be, they always reduce the scope of the revelation or even betray it. Thus Heidegger concludes his analysis of the concept of Eternal Recurrence by asserting that it is Nietzsche's own metaphysical idea. Similarly, though Deleuze shows a greater awareness of Nietzsche's intentions, he still tries to explain the 'great thought' through the notion of 'selective ontology', which is suspect on two counts. Despite this, Nietzsche himself subscribed to philosophical and rationalist attempts at interpretation, going so far as to hope to find scientific proof of the law of recurrence (Klossowski).

However, hope makes it possible for Zarathustra to be cured. Indeed, the passage entitled 'Of the Vision and the Riddle' already ended with an optimistic parable. In it, a young shepherd is sleeping when a snake slips into his throat – a 'heavy, black' snake representing a bad, depressing nihilist interpretation of Eternal Recurrence. Zarathustra cannot tear it out and shouts at the shepherd to bite its head off and spit it far away, whereupon the shepherd springs up, 'a transformed being . . . *laughing*'. This victory and this laugh fill Zarathustra with 'a longing that is never stilled' (1961: 180), and that perhaps represents Nietzsche's own nostalgia for the moment in Sils-Maria when he was the young shepherd suddenly struck by the meaning of Eternal Recurrence which the dogmatist Zarathustra and the philosopher Nietzsche could never formulate. However, it is in the second passage that Zarathustra's recovery is assured, not because he has managed to find the right formulation for his thought, but because, on the contrary, he has learned to keep silent. For this thought cannot merely be spoken, it must be sung, by a voice that is not his and to a tune that he does not know. To use the words addressed to him by his animals (1961: 237): 'For new lyres are needed for your new songs!' The next chapter of *Thus Spoke Zarathustra* reveals who is represented by that tune and that voice, which Nietzsche once heard in Sils-Maria and whose memory he nostalgically preserves: 'he, however, is the vintager who waits with diamond-studded vine knife,/your great redeemer, O my soul, the nameless one'. Zarathustra keeps silent and understands that he must die to permit the coming of the unknown god: Dionysus.

THE RIDDLE OF THE GOD

In *Beyond Good and Evil* (56), Nietzsche calls Eternal Recurrence a '*circulus vitiosus deus*'. It involves an element of the divine, but nothing strictly religious. The desire for Recurrence is an act of love that sanctifies life in its mystery: *Amor fati*. Through its irrational and yet irrefutable nature, it answers the world's 'unreasonable need' and makes it possible to imagine the coherence of chaos as a circular movement whose fragmented centre is Dionysus. The god is both the very image of Recurrence, through his eternal dismemberment and rebirth, and the keeper of the secret of which Nietzsche is the high priest. For Nietzsche the philosopher and for Zarathustra, Eternal Recurrence is a 'truth', a fetish as ambiguous and dangerous as a Medusa's head, not just a weapon against nihilism but also the illusory sun of Nietzsche's philosophy (see 'Medusa'). However, for Nietzsche the disciple of Dionysus it is an object of sacred 'faith' (*Twilight of the Idols* 49). Philosophical discourse must reunite with mythical discourse to render communicable a secret for which there is as yet neither word nor ear. Dionysus shows the way to a new love of life, that recalls his own love for Ariadne and is sealed by the 'wedding ring' of recurrence (see Deleuze 1983).

Eternal Recurrence is thus not really an 'idea' or a 'concept' and means nothing outside the ecstatic revelation. Its central character bears witness to Nietzsche's attempt to shatter the established structures of reason and language and to escape from metaphysics in order to inaugurate a 'tragic' philosophy that conveys a new sense of life. In annulling the opposition between life and death, being and becoming, Eternal Recurrence opens the way to a new immortality. However, in its effort to follow this path thought encounters its own limitations and must risk collapse. As Klossowski has shown, the law of Eternal Recurrence 'required the destruction of the very organ that divulged it' (1969: 320). Having rid himself of all the pretensions of reason, Nietzsche manages to relive the ecstatic moment of revelation in the 'euphoria' of Turin. Here, he at last identifies himself with Dionysus, the exorbitant centre of Recurrence around which his philosophy constantly resolved.

Eternal Recurrence is the law of the world of the 'will to power'; it assumes that the highest degree of power corresponds not to a state, to a halting of movement, but to the shattering of meaning, to Dionysian 'dismemberment' – ' "God" as the culminating moment: existence, an eternal divinization and undivinization'. The divinity of the 'god', like that of one who manages to identify himself with the pinnacle of power, consists in willing his own disappearance, because he wants recurrence and accepts the tragic and cruel law of existence.

Camille Dumoulié

Europa

The myth of Europa has been popularized both by Greek and Roman works of art, such as temple metopes, vase paintings, frescoes from Pompeii, mosaics, medallions and coins, and by the great paintings of the Renaissance, such as Veronese's *Rape of Europa* (Palazzo Ducale, Venice). It is therefore hardly surprising that it has been a source of inspiration for classical and modern poets alike.

Europa is sometimes referred to as 'the granddaughter of Neptune', in accordance with the version of the myth that portrays her as the daughter of Agenor (Ovid, *Metamorphoses* II. 858: 'Agenore nata'), since Agenor himself was the son of the nymph Libya and Poseidon. However, the commonest version of the story represents her as the daughter of one of Agenor's sons, Phoenix, and as the sister of Cadmus, founder of Thebes. This relationship is already attested in Homer's *Iliad* (XIV. 321 ff), where Zeus describes Europa as 'the famous daughter of Phoenix who bore my sons Minos and the godlike Rhadamantus'.

In fact, the story of Zeus's sudden passion for Europa is among the most ancient of legends. It recounts how the god carried off the Phoenician princess from the shores of Tyre or Sidon after assuming the form of a beautiful bull to elude the watchful eyes of his jealous wife Hera, as well as to allay any suspicions on the part of Europa herself. Zeus carried the girl off to Crete – or, in other versions, Boeotia, where the legend of Europa may have originated – and there resumed his usual form as ruler of the gods, while she became the mother of his sons Minos, Rhadamanthus and Sarpedon. An account of the main episodes of the myth occurs at an early date on papyrological fragment 1359 of Hesiod's *Catalogues*, while there are also several surviving fragments of a hymn entitled *Europeia* by the cyclical poet Eumelus, dating back to the end of the eighth century BC. The vitality of the myth was maintained throughout the history of Greek poetry by writers ranging from Stesichorus and Bacchylides to Moschus and Apollonius of Rhodes. And, finally, in the wake of Alexandrianism, the story of the love of Jupiter and Europa was frequently evoked by writers of the golden age of Roman poetry. Ovid tackled the subject with somewhat facile sensuality in his *Metamorphoses* (II. 833–75), but with more gravity in his *Fasti* (V. 604–20), while Horace ends his account of the myth in *Odes* III. 27 with the words: 'For half a world . . . shall take its name from thee'.

It is important to appreciate the antiquity of the idea that the continent of Europe was named after the princess. It appears to have been current during the Alexandrian period, as it is referred to briefly during the second century BC by Moschus, a Sicilian poet and philologist and disciple of Aristarchus. He attributes an allegorical dream to the character that he calls 'Europa' in the opening line of his poem and then, for the sake of the metre (in eight clausulae of spondaic hexameters), subsequently refers to her as 'Europeia', the form of the name that was later adopted by Leconte de Lisle:

> Europeia, the virgin daughter of Phoenix, dreamt that two continents did battle on her account, the continent of Asia and the continent which lay opposite; and they took the form of two beautiful women. One was of foreign appearance while the other looked like a woman from her own country and held on more tightly to the girl as if she were her own daughter, claiming that it was she who had borne her and brought her up. However, the other seized her with her strong hands and dragged her away while she herself offered no resistance: this woman maintained that Europeia was hers, that she was a present with which she had been honoured by Zeus, the protector.
>
> (Moschus, *Europa* 6–15).

However, it is also clear that the association between Europa and the geographical region of Europe was questioned from a very early date. Two centuries before Moschus, the legendary 'Father of History', Herodotus began his great historical work (I. 2. 6) by proposing a rationalizing Persian interpretation of the myth of the rape of Europa to explain the origin of the traditional hostility between the Greeks and the Barbarians, adopting an approach that could be described as euhemeristic, had the term been developed at that time. However, in book IV (45) he felt the need to refute the most widely accepted explanation of how the continent of Europe acquired its name:

> Nor is it clear whence it received this name, nor who gave it, unless we will say that the region received the name from the Tyrian Europa, but was before without a name, like the others: yet she evidently belonged to Asia, and never came into that country now called Europe by the Grecians; [Herodotus disagrees on this point with certain classical and Alexandrian mythographers] but only passed from Phoenicia to Crete, and from Crete to Lycia.
> Herodotus, *The Histories* (*c.* 1847), trans. Henry Cary, London: Bohn's Classical Library)

In fact, the *Homeric Hymn to Apollo* (end of the eighth century BC) makes a toponymic distinction that is not consistent with the portrayal of Europa as the eponymous heroine of the continent of Europe:

> and as many as dwell on fertile Peloponnesos, and on Europe and throughout the sea-girt isles.
> (*The Homeric Hymns*, trans. A. N. Athanassakis, (1976), Baltimore & London: The Johns Hopkins Library 250–1 and 290–1.)

This implies that it was originally continental Greece alone that was known as 'Europe', as opposed to the Greek islands and peninsulas, which included the Peloponnese. Another, more convincing piece of evidence against the traditional association between the name Europa and the continent of Europe is provided by a gloss by the lexicographer Hesychius of Alexandria. This relates the Greek adjective *europós*, which he defines as 'extensive, dark', to the name of the continent 'Europe: land of the setting sun; land of shadows'.

It can certainly be objected that there is no evidence to support Hesychius's interpretation of *europós* as meaning 'dark'. However, it is not beyond the bounds of possibility that an erudite early poet attributed such a meaning to the word in lines that have not survived (compare the adjective *euróeis* 'musty', which could be used to describe the shadowy depths of hell and which Hesychius explains as being equivalent to *skoteinos* 'dark'). In short, semantic development of the name of the continent in Greek probably parallels that of the Latin word *Occidens* or *Occasus*. In any case, we must concur with the opinion of Chantraine:

> It is possible to wonder whether the two homonyms 'Europe', the one designating the Tyrian princess and the other the continent, are not unrelated, and whether the name of the continent is not derived from the adjective 'europós'.

Let us ignore the theories developed since the beginning of the nineteenth century in an attempt to attribute a semitic root to the name of the continent. These involve an association with the words 'enter' and 'disappear' used in connection with the sun, and so recall the process of metaphorical extension lying behind the use of the term *Occidens*. Following this line of argument, there is no reason why the development of a Phoenician term should preclude the existence of an earlier substratum of which we know nothing. The maritime supremacy of Crete antedated the expansion of Tyrian commerce, and it is quite possible that the inhabitants of the Aegean Islands had already given a name to the continent of Europe beforc the Phoenicians began to trade with it!

What really matters in the present context is that, for many centuries, artists and writers were convinced that the name of the continent was derived from that of the charming Phoenician princess. Thus Ronsard not only wrote:

> Oh, Bull who on your back
> Bore off the beautiful Europa
> Across the waves
> . . .
>
> (Ode XIX, 'Avant-venue du printemps')

but made a more specific connection by saying:

> . . . and she
> That the Bull bore off upon its back,
> A Princess so young and beautiful
> That Europe bore her name.
>
> (*Discours à très-illustre et vertueuse Princesse Marie Stuart*)

Written in the eighteenth century, André Chénier's adaptation of Moschus's epyllion *Europa*, entitled 'L'enlèvement d'Europe' (*Bucoliques*), is a work of such masterly originality that it effectively recreates it ancient model. Chénier not only omitted the episode of the dream with which Moschus's poem began; in spite of its prophetic interest, he also excluded the description of the *talaros* (the vessel made of precious metal and decorated with scenes from the story of Io), which Moschus intended to perform a similar function to the prediction in the dream by setting the scene for the central episode. Thus his adaptation begins only at line seventy-one of the original work – 'Europe was as different from her companions as the goddess born of the foam of the waves was different from the Charities' – so that it was on this that he based his splendid opening Alexandrine:

> Just as Venus' beauty, the three sisters' outshone.

As a perfect Hellenist as well as a master of elegance and metre, the French poet showed equal virtuosity in transcribing hexameters by Moschus that followed: 'Indeed, not for long would she continue to enjoy the delights of the flowers, nor would her maidenhood remain unsullied'. His version is more harmonious and delicate than the original, yet exhibits a continuing concern for exactitude:

> But her destiny was not to love the flowers alone
> Nor keep her maiden's chastity forever.

Similarly, although Chénier certainly found the original description of the bull precise and picturesque, he seems also to have considered it rather laboured and difficult to read:

> Indeed, the rest of his body was of a golden colour, but a circle of brilliant white gleamed in the centre of his brow while below it his two eyes shone and glowed with passion; and his well-spaced horns of equal length, curved above his head, like the horned crescent of the moon.

As a result, he adapted it to read as follows:

> His body shines with a pure and golden sheen;
> While on his silken brow, a silver star
> Gleams; the burning flame of love glows in his eyes;
> And on his handsome head, two ivory horns
> Curve upwards; thus the shining crescent in the sky
> At night is lit by returning Phoebus.

In undertaking the delicate task of transposing the rapid rhythm of Greek metre into French verse, Chénier succeeded in making his Alexandrines more flexible by the judicious use of expressive monosyllabic or disyllabic enjambements:

She speaks and takes her seat. Just then the herd
Approaches; but rising with his beloved burden
The God flees towards the sea.

The daughters of Nereus, encircling the travellers,
Emerge. The god of the seas calms the troubled waters and
Opens the way for his brother, like a skilful guide.

On the brow of the bull the quivering beauty
Leans, and with her other hand she holds her floating dress
. . . For these waves with errant crests
Move aside; but the herds mistrust the watery depths.

But you alone
Run on the land and on the moving waves.

Mention has already been made of Leconte de Lisle's 'L'enlèvement d'Européia' which appeared in his *Dernières Poèmes*, published posthumously by José Maria de Heredia. The poem consists of fifteen quatrains, written in Alexandrine verse with alternate rhymes, and the first line alone was sufficient to guarantee its renown:

The mountains were blue and the sea of rosy hue.

Like Chénier, Leconte de Lisle departed from Moschus's version of the story by omitting the description of the dream and all mention of the episode in which Europeia and her companions gather flowers in the meadows by the seashore. (Indeed, Leconte de Lisle's account involves only three people.) In addition, he transfers the scene from Phoenicia to Greece. Thus, Europa is described as 'fleeing the sweet land of Hellas' as the bull carries her off into the sea, while when Jupiter finally reveals his identity to the young maiden he addresses her as 'Oh, beloved Flower of Hellas'. It is easy to demonstrate that Leconte de Lisle was inspired by Moschus and Chénier, both in general terms and in his use of descriptive and narrative detail. However, for all this, his adaptation was still an extremely personal one. An example is provided by his description of the fragrance of the divine bull whose breath, according to the mythographer Apollodorus of Athens (*The Library* III. 1) was scented like saffron. While Moschus described the scent of the charming bull as 'more exquisite than the perfume of the meadow' and Chénier wrote that 'the gentle creature . . . from afar gave off an ambrosian scent sweeter than that of any flower', Leconte de Lisle created his own beautiful version:

His splendid nostrils breathed in ambrosian scent
Which now and then embraced her in vermilion cloud
Just as the Cronian Spouses in a golden mist
Enveloped their gods' love and their celestial sleep.

However, while this is certainly a wonderful image that provides a highly successful example of Parnassian artistry, closer examination reveals an element of humour beneath its polished exterior. For one has only to remember that Jupiter is just about to be well and truly unfaithful to his 'Cronian Spouse' by adding the beautiful Europeia to his already substantial list of mortal female conquests!

For his 'nuptial' epilogue in Crete, André Chénier merely paraphrased Moschus's version of the story, in which the 'dénouement' of the whole affair appears somewhat hurried, indeed, while Moschus wrote 'and she, the erstwhile maiden, at once became the bride of Zeus: she bore the children of her Cronian spouse and at once became a mother' (lines 165–6); Chénier condensed the episode into a single line:

> And in his arms the maid became a bride and mother.

In contrast, Leconte de Lisle must have considered this ending to be too abrupt, while he clearly admired the short speech, full of authority and *gravitas*, that Horace had made Venus utter on the occasion.

> Know that thou are the bride of conquering Jove;
> Hush all thy sobs, learn what thy fate shall be,
> For half a world in memory of thy love
> Shall take its name from thee!
> *Odes and Epodes of Horace*, selected by S. A. Courtauld, (trans. J. L. S. Hatton, (1929), London: Bickers & Son Ltd.) (*Odes* III. 27. 69–76)

Thus, in the final two verses of his poem, Leconte de Lisle adopts an extremely eloquent lyrical style, with a solemn and prophetic tone entirely worthy of a hierogamy:

> I am the Ruler of the Gods, the son of Cronos,
> Come down from the immense Ether to kneel before you!
> You should rather rejoice, oh, beloved flower of Hellas,
> At being immortal in the arms of your immortal Spouse.
> Come! Here is the sacred Island with its prophetic caves
> Where you will celebrate your glorious marriage,
> And your Offspring will be heroes,
> Rulers of the world who will become Gods!

Jean Granarolo

Faust

The story of Faust provides a virtually complete illustration of the nature of the literary myth. It is one of those myths whose development reveals most clearly the stages in the process by which history is transformed into legend and cross-fertilization then takes place between popular legend and works of literature. The later stages of its development offer numerous, varied examples of the interaction between literature and political events or collective attitudes, and illustrate the interplay between stereotyped truisms inherited from the past and texts that perpetuate the living myth.

FROM THE HISTORICAL CHARACTER TO THE LEGEND

To judge from the few surviving documents, such as administrative entries and correspondence written during his lifetime (apparently between 1480 and 1540) Georg (or Johann) Faust was something of a bad lot. Whilst he was often esteemed as an astrologer, he was also often suspected of being a charlatan; and whilst he was sufficiently well read to act on occasion as a schoolmaster, he was also vilified and despised by all the humanists and scholars who mention him. He led a wandering existence in South Germany and the Rhineland, while his study of magic at Cracow and journeys to Paris and Rome seem to be embellishments attributable to the later growth of his legend. He evidently died in fairly horrific circumstances with his throat cut, for his death caught the popular imagination and was fairly soon ascribed to the Devil. In any case, it was from this point that a double legend grew up around his memory. On the one hand, there were popular anecdotes (sometimes already used about other 'magicians' such as Trittheim, Paracelsus or Agrippa) that recounted his magic tricks with unsophisticated admiration. On the other hand, there was a sinister tradition attributing his powers to his association with the Devil, Mephistopheles. A document dating around 1580 is the first to mention the crucial word '*pact*': Faust had made a formal *pact* with the Devil, which had given him his powers, but also resulted in his dreadful death.

FROM LEGEND TO LITERATURE

In 1587, these fragmentary anecdotes and legends were stitched together for the first time into a continuous story, which was written by an anonymous author and published at the Frankfurt fair under the title *Historia von Dr*

Johann Fausten, dem weitbeschreyten Zauberer und Schwartzkünstler etc. Often simply referred to as *Volksbuch*, this is an impressive popular tale, even if its structure is not always coherent. In the first part, the writer embarks straight away on the tragic story of Faust's imprudence, describing how his pride leads him to enter into his presumptuous pact and how, after twenty-four years devoted to magic and pleasure, he is destined to meet a terrible death. Meanwhile, in the second part, the author virtually copies out some quite scholarly chapters relating to cosmography and geography, the latter being rather ancient and outdated. In contrast, the third part of the work starts by providing a rumbustious, unsophisticated account of Faust's pranks and magic tricks. However, it then finally reverts to the moralizing style of the beginning of the book, but increases its dramatic overtones when describing the magician's last days and death. To sum up, sections intended to arouse mirth alternate with ones intended to arouse fear. It was a successful formula: twenty-two editions, gradually embellished with yet more anecdotes, were brought out within ten or so years of the first, followed by other fairly radically amended or augmented versions published on into the eighteenth century. Indeed, a much abridged version current from 1725 was no doubt read by the young Goethe. Translations of the original story were also republished frequently for two centuries; there were thirty editions of the Dutch translation, twenty-five of the English edition and twenty of the French edition, as well as versions in Danish and Czech. The English translation of the *Volksbuch* provided the inspiration for one of the finest plays by Christopher Marlowe, *The Tragical History of Dr Faustus*, which was staged in London shortly after 1590. In it, the composite structure of the original story is replicated by a strange alternation between scenes of tragedy and episodes of grotesque buffoonery. Faust has become a Renaissance man, thirsty for knowledge, experience and power, but he is quicky disappointed by his pact. He conjures up Helen of Troy, whom he regards as a symbol of antique beauty, but what actually appears to him is really a spirit. His ambitions endow him with a certain heroic grandeur, but lead him inexorably to damnation.

In the seventeenth and eighteenth century, enthusiasm for the story of Faust is attested not only by the reprints of the popular tales, but by its great success as a theme for plays at fairs, or, a little later, in the puppet theatre. The scheme of these plays was derived from that of Marlowe's work, which was brought to the continent by English actors and gradually corrupted. However, farce increasingly took over from drama, so that the most important role was often that of a burlesque servant known as Hanswurst, Kasper or Pickelhäring. The audience could laugh out loud, but moral values were preserved intact. The happy clown with his down-to-earth good sense escapes from the Devil, while Faust, the intellectual, remains entangled in this half-terrifying, half-incredible story, heading inevitably towards his doom.

Further indications of the vitality of the myth at this time are provided by H. Henning's bibliography, which lists some four hundred mentions or descriptions of Faust in works of all sorts, literary and otherwise. Even folk songs about Faust were circulated on fly-sheets. Meanwhile, in the eighteenth century, especially when books and documents about magic were in great vogue, almost a hundred such works were indiscriminately ascribed to Faust, against all probability.

The story of Faust originated in a Lutheran area, but it owes less to genuine evangelical theology than to popular religion based on fear of the Devil and of divine judgement. Stories concerning a pact with the Devil were by no means rare in the sixteenth century, and, in a Catholic context, adaptations of *Theophilus* featured prominently among the plays in Latin performed at Jesuit colleges around 1600. The hero of *Cenodoxus* by P. Bidermann (1602) listened too closely to his devils and was condemned, whereas in Spain Calderón's Cypriano (*El Magico Prodigioso*, 1636) was saved through his conversion from paganism to Christianity and his subsequent martyrdom.

THE ROMANTIC TRANSFORMATION OF FAUST

Writing between 1760 and 1780, Lessing did no more than sketch out a new scheme for the traditional story, whereby Faust was promoted to the rank of a hero of learning and was destined to escape from the Devil: 'Divine power did not give Man the most noble of instincts in order to make him eternally unhappy . . .' It was only in a sort of bourgeois drama written in Vienna by P. Weidmann (*Johann Faust, ein allegorisches Drama*, 1775) that the story of Faust concluded for the first time with his conversion and attainment of salvation.

The vision of a new type of Faust was established principally by the young poets of the following generation, who constituted the forerunners of the Romantic Movement (Maler Müller in 1776–8, Klinger in 1791, etc.). In their works, the character of Faust is based on their own image of themselves. He is a titan rebelling against this imperfect world, an individualist bold enough to defy morality, society and religion, and to enter a pact with the Devil.

STAGES IN THE DEVELOPMENT OF GOETHE'S *FAUST*

The most brilliant of these 'Angry Young Men', Johann Wolfgang Goethe, put much of himself into his portayal of Faust – his frenetic desire to experience everything, his unbridled dreams and his feelings of rebellion, his interest in magic and alchemy, and even his recollection of a love affair with a pretty girl from Alsace. His Faust is a disappointed man who no longer believes in human learning and who accepts Mephistopheles's proposals out of despair, convinced that they will not be able to satisfy him. Restored to youth, he seduces Gretchen, then abandons her, thereby causing her death. Goethe's first version of the work (known as *Urfaust*, 1771–5), which was written partly in prose and in a rather Shakespearean style, was never published. However, he subsequently rewrote it in verse, first as *Fragment von Faust* (published 1790), and then in its final form as *Faust, der Tragödie erster Teil (Faust, Part 1*, 1808). By this time, with the encouragement of Schiller, Goethe had widened the scope of the drama. The pact now takes the form of a wager over whether Mephistopheles can divert Faust's aspirations (*Streben*) towards pleasure and gratification; in other words, towards evil. A similar wager is made between the Devil and the Creator, who puts his trust in human nature. In contrast to a Mephisto with a somewhat Voltairean outlook, Faust has become the embodiment of the Romantic, with his great surges of feeling and his constant hesitation between gratifying immediate desire and satisfying the profound aspirations of his being.

Goethe did not complete *Faust, Part 2* (*Faust, der Tragödie zweiter Teil*, 1832) until a few months before his death when he was eighty-three years old. In it, Faust undergoes a variety of experiences. To begin with, he is at the court of the emperor, where, as in the traditional legend, he conjures up Helen, the symbol of classical beauty. After a long search among ancient allegories he brings her back to earth and marries her, but she soon disappears, with their prodigious child, Euphorion, the symbol of poetic genius. Later, tired of politics and war and seeking an opportunity for 'real action', Faust sets about founding an empire by colonizing a swampy coast. As in the case of his earlier ventures, this obliges him to seek the help of the Devil and to resort to crime. Symbolically rendered blind, Faust may be deluding himself when he believes that he has found perfect, selfless satisfaction in his undertaking. He dies in this belief, and his soul escapes Mephisto, who thought that he had won his wager, and is borne up to heaven by angels. The 'human tragedy' thus ends in heaven in a 'divine comedy'. Faust is admitted to paradise *mute* and contrary to the opinions of many critics, we still cannot be absolutely sure whether his salvation is due to his noble aspirations, or rather to divine grace and Gretchen's love for him.

FAUST DURING THE ROMANTIC PERIOD

The German Romantics preferred to lead their hero to damnation, thereby simultaneously punishing the grandeur and immoderation of his ambitions and actions, his nostalgia for the infinite and for love (a context in which he is associated with Don Juan), and his proud individualism. This is true of the poem by Chamisso (1804), the play by Grabbe (*Don Juan und Faust*, 1829), the ballet scenario by Heine (1856) and especially of the long, brilliant poem by Lenau (1836) in which Faust reflects the doubts, rebelliousness and despair of the poet himself. In addition, Faust also inspired musical works such as Spohr's opera (1816), Schumann's *Szenen zu Goethes Faust* (1853), Liszt's *Faust-Symphonie* (1857).

The English Romantics borrowed only small elements from the traditional legend or from Goethe's reworking of it, notably the fantastic theme of Faust's involvement with the Devil and the boundless ambition of the doomed titan. These feature most prominently in the works of Byron and Philip James Bailey (*Festus*, 1839). In France, by contrast, the influence of Madame de Staël and Nerval's translation (1828–40) ensured Faust's adoption by the young Romantics, as evidenced by Delacroix's lithographs (1828) or the *Huit scènes de Faust* (1828) by Berlioz, later transformed into *La Damnation de Faust* (1846). This Romantic vision inspired by Goethe was perpetuated in the operas of Gounod (1859) and Boito (*Mefistofele*, 1868), in Villiers de L'Isle Adam's drama *Axël* (1872–86) and elsewhere in *Peer Gynt* by Ibsen (1867).

Almost the only elements of Goethe's *Faust, Part 1* that are retained in Gounod's opera are the demoralized state of the hero and the tragic episode with Gretchen (who is called Marguerite in the opera). However, in its limited way, this facile example of Romanticism touched the hearts of the general public. As a result of the opera's successes on stages throughout the world (and the countless parodies that it inspired!) its moving story of Marguerite popularized the sketchy figures of Faust and Mephisto. The story of Faust was one of the most popular themes in the early cinema, before the First World War: in sixteen years there were no fewer than sixteen films on the subject (six by Méliès alone), most of them inspired by Gounod's opera.

FROM THE IDEALIZED FAUST TO THE 'FAUSTIAN MAN'

Goethe's play is still rarely staged. Indeed, the second part, in particular, is not much read, despite the existence of numerous translations, and is still less understood. Nonetheless Goethe's work has exerted a deep and perceptible influence on many writers, from Balzac and Mickiewicz to Melville, Hawthorne and Madách. In the wake of Goethe, an optimistic vision of Faust's grand destiny gradually became prevalent. While Faust is more hesitant than heroic in Goethe's text, after 1870 he begins to be idealized, especially in German commentaries on Goethe's work. As a result, he gradually takes on the character of a national hero and is portrayed as the typical embodiment of the German soul, even in the parody by Vischer (1861 and 1866). At the same period, scientistic thinkers interpreted him as a figure cast in the mould of Prometheus, and sometimes paired the two together (as in Hango's *Faust und Prometheus*, 1895). To them, he was an idealized representation of modern mankind aspiring towards liberty, action and progress. This idea can be recognized in a variety of forms in the anthroposophic writings of Rudolph Steiner (1902–31), the Nietzschean drama by Ficke (in Seattle, 1913), the screen-play by Lunatcharski (*Faust i gorod*, 1908–18), and elsewhere. Even parodies, such as *Franziska* by Wedekind (1912) or *Mefistófela* by Benavente (1918) demonstrate the same idealizing tendency.

In Oswald Spengler's philosophy of history *Der Untergang des Abendlandes*, published at the end of 1918, the 'Faustian man' is presented as the constant epitome of Western Man from the Middle Ages onwards. His strength and greatness are derived from his passion for infinite space and his will to power. Owing much more to Nietzsche than to Goethe, he knows nothing of pacts, or love affairs with Gretchen, and his aspirations carry him towards action, technology and conquest rather than towards knowledge. The modern German, in particular the Prussian, has remained most faithful to this 'Faustian' drive, and therefore the future belongs to him.

The historical synthesis set out in this book seems highly debatable today. Nonetheless, it provided a broad, epic vision of Western Man that would often distort Goethe's vision of Faust. There are very few critics who have claimed that Goethe's Faust is not 'Faustian', and confusion between the character created by Goethe, Faust the symbol of German nationalism and the 'Faustian man' is very widespread. The success of this ambiguous stereotype is due to the fact that in 1918 it conjured up the idealized image of a mythical hero standing erect amidst catastrophe. Thus German nationalists used it to compensate for their shattered dreams. Paradoxically, the concept of the 'Faustian man' was also welcomed in other countries (particularly Anglo-Saxon and South American ones). There, the figure was recognized as an embodiment of the will to power of modern Man – a simplified version of Nietzsche's superman.

FAUST IN THE TURMOIL OF TWO WORLD WARS

The First World War and the economic crisis during the 1920s made Faust topical once again. He had already finally achieved the status of a German national hero through the reading of Goethe's play in the trenches, while on the opposite side he was regarded as suspect and questionable.

In post-war Germany versions of the story of Faust proliferated in every literary form imaginable, from popular genres such as puppet theatre, semi-legendary historical tales, idylls, and, indeed, the famous film by Murnau (1926) to the highly ambitious poetic works echoing Goethe (in the case of the drama by Avenarius, 1919, or Busoni's opera, 1925) or Nietzsche (Pannwitz's poems, *Faustus und Helena*, 1920, and *Mantô*, 1922). As the years passed, the nationalist element became more pronounced, especially in the two works entitled *Jungfaust* by Wieprecht (1925) and Blumelhuber (1932) and in Kratzmann's historical novel, *Faust, ein Buch vom deutschen Geiste* (1932).

There were, of course, some writers who resisted this idealizing tendency, recognizing the ideological impetus behind it. These included the Expressionists (for example, Werfel in *Spiegelmensch*, 1920), as well as other writers, such as Payer von Thurn, who portrayed Faust as a librarian (*Doktor Faust, ein Gelehrtenschicksal*, 1919)? Irony was often used in the same defensive fashion in other countries, for example in plays by Silvio Pagani (1925), Ghelderode (1926) and Ribemont-Dessaignes (1931). Nonetheless, panegyrics predominated, especially on the occasion of the centenary of Goethe's death. Indeed,

Faust was even put forward as the ideal personification of religious humanism (Korff, *Der faustische Glaube*, 1938).

The establishment of the Nazi regime in Germany in 1933 seems to have dried up inspiration at its source, and after a few years there were no further versions of Faust! Theorists of the new nationalist mythology even announced 'the end of the Faustian millennium' (Kummer, 1933). After being alienated from their traditions since the Middle Ages by a foreign faith, Germans were to repudiate the Christian problems posed by Faust, and to renew their allegiance to their ancestral hero, Siegfried. Not surprisingly, elsewhere, especially in countries where the growth of German power was felt to pose a threat, Faust was subjected to psychoanalysis on more than one occasion. This approach was adopted in comedies by Soya (Copenhagen, 1932) Beskov (Stockholm, 1936) and Grande (Rome, 1934), while Faust was condemned to purgatory by Dorothy L. Sayers in her 'sacred play', *The Devil to Pay* (London, 1939).

In spite of his eclipse, Faust had embodied German nationalism for too long to avoid being dragged into Nazi propaganda entirely, and the inevitable result was that between 1945 and 1950 he was, in a strange sense, 'put on trial'. As a character, he seemed to symbolize a Germany that had made a pact with the devilish forces of Nazism, and it was felt that both he and it *had* to come to a catastrophic end! Schneider, Beutler, Jung and many others protested against this misguided triumphalist interpretation of Goethe's play, and their sentiments were echoed by many poets and writers, who emphasized the fateful pact and the resulting condemnation of Faust. Examples of the latter include Egk (*Abraxas*, 1948: a ballet), Orson Welles (*Time runs*, 1950: a play), Eisler (*Johann Faustus*, 1952: an opera), Schwarze (*Faustens Ende*, 1957: a play), Autan-Lara (*Marguerite de la Nuit*, 1955: a film), and Candoni and Nascimbene (*Faust in Manhattan*, 1963: an opera).

Admittedly, for many others Faust has remained the ideal figure of modern Man, with his 'Faustian' passion for self-fulfilment and world domination; and, for a significant number of humanists Goethean noble optimism is as topical as ever. Meanwhile, the Marxists regard Faust merely as a new Prometheus, as is apparent to varying degrees in the work of Eftimiú (*Doctor Faust Vràjitor*, Bucharest, 1957), Levada (*Faust i smert*, Kiev, 1959) and Block (*Das Prinzip Hoffnung*, Berlin, 1953), as well as in Bulgakov's subtle satire *Master i Margarita* (Moscow, 1940–66), which approaches the subject from the opposite perspective.

The Faust of Salacrou and René Clair (*La Beauté du Diable*, 1950: a film) lies halfway between the ideal hero and the man on trial. Portrayed as youthful and extremely romantic, he is eventually saved by repudiating the false splendours that his association with the Devil has brought him. Behind the irony of the dialogue, the pact is taken seriously, but, equally, so is human freedom.

TWO GREAT MODERN INTERPRETERS OF FAUST

Paul Valéry sketched out the two dramatic dialogues that make up *Mon Faust* during the political collapse of France in the summer of 1940. *Le Solitaire* is a fantastical 'fairy story', which is somewhat bitter in tone. In it, Faust debates the problem of evil with a wild hermit, a new Zarathustra, only to find that he himself is almost equally pessimistic when he is confronted by pretty fairies who would like to give him back life and youth. In *Lust ou la Demoiselle de Cristal, comédie* Faust is a wise old man hesitating between 'games of love and games of the intellect'. His lucid mind completely transcends the limited outlook of Mephisto, who would like to draw him into 'another Gretchen-style affair' with his pretty secretary, Lust. Valéry was eager to impart greater depth still to this dialogue between the Self and the Other, but the two fragments remained unfinished on his death in 1945.

It was whilst in exile during the terrible years when Germany was at war that Thomas Mann wrote *Doktor Faustus, das Leben des deutschen Tonsetzers Adrian Leverkühn*, which was finally published in 1947. In accordance with a characteristic theme, his Faust is a brilliant artist, and therefore sick and doomed. On the one hand, his life recalls that of Nietzsche, while on the other, it is based, not on Goethe's story of Faust, but on that in the original *Volksbuch*. Adrian nurtures great ambitions, and to obtain the creative power to write a new (dodecaphonic) kind of music he is drawn into a kind of devilish pact, which brings him inspiration, but also loneliness and finally madness. The path that he takes symbolizes the path travelled by German society as a whole during the first third of the twentieth century. Like him, it allowed itself to be swept giddily along, in its case into the collective vertigo of a fatal nationalism. In this double story, the reader detects an implicit allusion to the destiny of Faust and to that of Germany itself since the Reformation. These symbolic associations make the book a little heavy, but give it an original historical and philosophical breadth. Its tragic vision of Faust's destiny is in sharp contrast with Goethe's vision, which was more optimistic, at least in terms of its conclusion.

. . . AND SO THE STORY GOES ON!

Since 1960, we seem to have moved on to some extent from the concept of the great global crisis, and perhaps feel less need for symbolic figures representing Man wrestling with his demons. Nonetheless, the figure of Faust continues to give rise to new images and new forms of expression. The most important works inspired by its include: *Votre Faust, fantaisie variable*, an opera by Michel Butor and Henri Pousseur (1962); *An Irish Faustus* by Lawrence Durrell (1963); *The American as Faust* by L. Lee (1965); *La Damnation de Faust*, a ballet by Maurice Béjart (1966); 'Le Veston ensorcelé' by D. Buzzati (*Le K.*, 1966); *Faust 67*, a comedy by T. Landolfi (staged in Milan, 1967);

Die Fabel von der Freundschaft, ein sokratischer Roman by A. Paris-Gütersloh (Vienna, 1969); *Pasja i pot epienie doktora Fausta*, a drama by J. Sito (Warsaw, 1971); *Savellicus*, an opera by R. Kunad (East Berlin, 1974); *La femme Faust*, a novel by V. Voutcho (Zagreb, 1978); *Faust*, a novel by R. Nye (London, 1980); *Faubourg Antoine*, a novel by J. Mistler (1982); and *Théorèmes pour un Faust*, meditations and poems by G. Thinès (Brussels, 1983). In addition, the novel *Mephisto*, written by Klaus Mann in 1936 and aimed at his brother-in-law Gustaf Gründgens, who was with the Nazis, regained a certain topicality with the film by Szabo (1979) and the stage version by Mnouchkine (1981).

No doubt it represents something of a misuse of terminology when historians talk about the Faustian art of the twentieth century, or a jurist (J. Marchal) talks about the modern 'Faustian State', or a physicist (H. Stannard) even talks of a 'Faustian universe'. However, the very phenomenon of the term's misuse indicates that the figure of Faust is still alive, and that his is still a name to conjure with. The most recent Faust opera, *Doktor Faustus*, written by a German living in Holland, was staged at the Paris Opéra on 8 January 1985; so the story may go on . . .

THE THREE STAGES OF THE FAUST MYTH

When one looks at the development of the story of Faust, it is almost possible to talk in terms of three successive myths. The sixteenth-century Faust, a magician who has insane ambitions but is also terror-stricken at the idea of damnation, already embodies two different conflicting archetypes. On the one hand, like Paracelsus, the learned doctor who was his contemporary, Faust feels the confused impetus of the Renaissance, directed towards power, knowledge and pleasure. On the other, like the medieval Theophilus, he makes a pact with the Devil. This means that he repudiates his loyalty to God to swear loyalty to God's adversary, and in so doing, forgoes his freedom, in the belief that he is asserting it. Even Marlowe, who had a sneaking admiration for his hero, still felt it necessary to make him meet his doom. The pact with the Devil is an aberration in itself in the context of sound Christian sense and theology. Thus, when it is taken seriously, the story of Faust is the story of a sinner, dragged down by the weight of a transgression for which popular religion – dubious as it may be – sees no possible expiation.

The Romantic movement transformed the meaning of the drama. The very immediate desires of the original Faust were transfigured into an almost metaphysical desire for the infinite. This aspiration towards Knowledge and Love is the basis of Man's greatness, but it will inevitably lead him to strive to transcend the limits of humanity and therefore reduce him to ruin, failure and despair. The pact with the Devil represents a bold involvement with the forces of evil that will inevitably end by corrupting the hero, or at least by destroying him. In this context, Goethe's drama is unique: even though its precise message is hotly debated, it displays a certain trust in Man's aspiration towards the ideal, reflecting the old theological tradition of the *desiderium naturale perfectionis divinae*, while at the same time tragically measuring out the limits of human freedom. In any case, whether saved or destroyed, in the works of the Romantics Faust tended to become a model for Mankind, the sort of splendid hero that he had never been previously, even in Marlowe's play.

Subsequent generations continued the process of idealization. The pact was sometimes suppressed or treated dismissively: freed of the burden of the earlier portrayals of his character, Faust was transformed into the ideal image of modern Man effortlessly conquering knowledge, power and happiness. Representing the culmination of this process, the simplistic figure of the 'Faustian man' developed by Spengler embodied little more than the will to power and the lust for life of twentieth-century Man. Having started off as a realistic character in a dramatic *situation* that eventually destroyed him, Faust initially became a Romantic hero writ on a larger scale than the burden that weighed him down, before finally becoming the *hero* bereft of drama who features in our most chimerical dreams.

These three mythical images of Faust, which have arisen successively over four centuries, now coexist in contemporary works of literature. It is hardly surprising that the Romantic image is perpetuated in the work of René Clair and many other writers. A rarer approach involves resuscitating the totally dead and forgotten mythical image of the original Faust and investing it with new meaning. The works of Dorothy L. Sayers, Thomas Mann, Hanns Eisler and others demonstrate that the murky character from the old legend has regained genuine contemporary relevance in the twentieth century, especially since the catastrophe in Germany and the invention of the atomic bomb. The generation of writers active in the 1940s regarded these events as two clear indications that the 'Faustian' enthusiasm for knowledge and power still concealed some diabolical temptation, some fatal vertigo. In their works, Faust illustrates a growing awareness that it is not an easy task for Man to remove evil and wrong-doing from his life, and, furthermore, that his greatest aspirations and his immoderately increased powers are still fundamentally ambiguous.

Thus the pact with the Devil, which is clearly an aberrant idea in conventional theological terms, retains its symbolic value. It expresses the extent to which human liberty can become enmeshed in evil, to the point of allying itself with it, to the point of locking itself up in it and becoming totally estranged from itself. (Compare the concept of psychological determinism in relation to crime, habit and the urge to conform.) Indeed, it is actually Man's most profound desire – the desire for eternity, reflecting an impatience with restrictions and the will to assert oneself – that leads him into this fundamental temptation. In short, the figure of Faust reminds us that everyone *must* choose to commit his or her freedom to good or to evil – or to be more precise, that everyone must choose between loyalty to Someone and alienation to an Other.

In the process, it also emphasizes that by choosing satisfaction we may also choose gradual or total alienation.

If one of the two mainsprings of the drama disappears, and either Man's aspirations or (as is more likely today) the weight of evil and temptation is denied, the myth withers and dies, and Faust is reduced to a shadow (i.e. the 'Faustian' shadow) of himself. On the other hand, even if the Christian emphasis of the original story is effaced, as long as evil and the alienation that it represents continue to be taken seriously, and as long as the ambiguity of human desires and aspirations is recognized, Faust can continue to embody the double vertigo that is at the very core of the human condition. If this vertigo is removed, is Faust still Faust – is *Man* still Man? For fifty years, the world has hesitated between the realistic, tragic myth bequeathed to it by its past, and of which its present is a continuing reminder, and the ideal myth in which it pursues the image of its dreams.

André Dabezies

The Feathered Serpent

1519: year of grace, as the phrase went, for the Spanish Christians who discovered and conquered the Aztec empire.

1 Acatl: this is the name given to the year 1519 in the native calendar, a disastrous year according to daily presages in Tenochtitlan.

Hernán Cortés disembarked on the coast of the Gulf of Mexico, at the place he was to call True Cross, Veracruz. A few weeks earlier he had left Cuba (the island, whose autochthonous population died out with great speed, did not contain the resources of precious stones and metals that the Spanish had expected), and, sidestepping the authority of the governor Diego Velasquez, he decided to explore on his own account, guided by the illusion that on this new continent the fabulous kingdoms of which Marco Polo had spoken more than two centuries before were to be discovered. Cortés' lucky star took him first to the banks of the Yucatan, where he happened to find the Spaniard Jeronimo Aguilar, who had learned the language of the Indians, having escaped from a shipwreck in 1512 and been held prisoner in a Mayan village for seven years. His second stroke of luck came some time later, again in Mayan lands, in Tabasco, where Cortés and his men received a present of twenty young slaves as a pledge of feigned or opportunistic friendship. Among these slaves was an Aztec, Malintzin, whom the Spanish called Marina. She had also learned Maya during her captivity and her mother tongue was Nahua. Between Aguilar, who spoke Spanish, and Maya and Marina, who spoke Maya and Nahua, Cortés possessed the ideal means not only to converse and negotiate, but also, through the inevitable informers or through simple gossip, to discover the plots that were being hatched against him (as he did later in Cholula), and, above all, to hear the tales of a fabulous empire and its very wealthy ruler that were going around among the natives. These stories concerned the Aztecs, their city Tenochtitlan and the *tlatoani* Moctezuma. They strengthened Cortés' conviction that in the interior of the country there was an empire to pillage. He threw himself into this enterprise.

In Tenochtitlan, Moctezuma was also very interested in Cortés. For weeks his spies had been bringing him information (their practice was to produce painted images on prepared canvases) about the astounding caravels and wondrous horsemen (which the natives found hard to image consisted of a man and an animal) and were not a single entity). Moctezuma looked at houses using wings to move over the sea, huge beings with four legs and human heads, heads of such a pale hue with beards. Had Quetzalcoatl, the Feathered Serpent, returned, as he had promised so long ago? If it were so, it would mean the end of the rule of the tribal god, Huitzilopochtli the warrior, since Quetzalcoatl was opposed to human sacrifice. Moctezuma did not wish for the return of the peaceful god, but he had even less desire to risk irritating him in any way. He therefore sent ever more ambassadors and lavish presents, hoping thus to dissuade Quetzalcoatl from taking the trouble to go all the way to Tenochtitlan. This might have been a well-judged tactic to use when dealing with a god (perhaps it was also psychologically appropriate to the native mentality), but it was disastrous where the Spanish were concerned. Its inevitable result was to enflame their greed and their imaginations. Let others make do with presents alone, they would go to Tenochtitlan, whatever the cost, to see for themselves what there was to take and to take it all, whatever the cost. Everyone knows what happened next.

The march of the amazed Spanish towards the great city of Tenochtitlan formed a stage in the founding of a new myth, that of Eldorado, the land of gold or man of gold (*el dorado*, the gilded one), whom the conquerors were madly to seek for more than a century throughout the continent. As we shall see, no one has better dramatized in fiction the shock produced by the meeting of two worlds that fascinate and loathe each other than the Mexican Carlos Fuentes. But what Fuentes and many others among Latin America's finest writers have taken from the culture is the myth of the Feathered Serpent – the educating, peaceful god who promised to return; in other words to bring new access to prosperity in peace and happiness. In the socio-political context of the South American continent, we can see why and how the meaning of the myth of Quetzalcoatl has been constantly reinterpreted.

In mesoamerican archaeology the Feathered Serpent is an omnipresent motif. He is painted on frescos and codices, engraved on sarcophagi and sculpted on monoliths; he runs across the stucco at the bottom of the pyramids and on temple walls, stylized into Greek *scalares*; his iconographic importance is unmatched and allows us to grasp his cultural, in other words religious, importance. The name Feathered Serpent (*Quetzalcoatl* for the ancient Mexicans, *Kukulcan* for the Mayas, *Gucumatz* for the Quechuas) is simply the phonetic reading of the hieroglyph which, in mesoamerican cultures, refers to a historical figure, a priest-king of the Toltecs, who was later promoted to the rank of a god. As a god, he is the protagonist of myths telling of the restoration of human beings on earth, under the Fifth Sun, after the destruction of the preceding Sun (or age), as a result of the invention of maize from which human flesh is made. In short, the myth explains that the domestication of maize was demographically useful in allowing the tribes to become settled, since food was no longer a problem, and encouraged the development of the arts in an urban context. Tradition attributes to Quetzalcoatl the invention of weaving, ceramics and the zero – in other words mathematics, which was applied with celebrated skill to astronomy.

The native 'informers' of the Spanish Franciscan monk Bernadino de Sahagun told him how the black god Tezcatlipoca had used intrigue to force

Quetzalcoatl to leave his capital, Tula, leading to its ruin; how Quetzalcoatl and an escort of his faithful followers had gone to the eastern coast and how he had burned himself at a stake, turning into the morning star and promising to return to the place he started from in an anniversary year of his birth; in other words a year of 1 Acatl. Since then he had always been expected every time the calendar's cycles brought the year 1 Acatl round again. At the time when the Old World was becoming interested in the New, two dates were possible: 1467, which was too early, and 1519. However one chooses to explain it – coincidence, fulfilment of the promise or whatever – it was in 1519 that Cortés landed.

In Madrid in 1929 the Guatemalan Miguel Angel Asturias (1899–1974) published the first version of *Leyendas de Guatemala* which, in its French translation by Francis de Miomandre, was admired by Paul Valéry. Allusions to the civilizing god were to be found here and there in the text, but it was above all in the second, definitive edition published in Buenos Aires by Pleamar in 1948 and reprinted by Losada in 1958 that one of the two added texts, 'Cuculcan, the Serpent Covered in Feathers', freely applied the myth to the problems of creation, a metaphor for what became, a quarter of a century later, a text on general artistic and, more particularly, literary creation called *Tres de cuatro soles* (1971).

In 1959 Asturias started writing a cycle commonly called 'the banana trilogy', denouncing the abuses of the American company United Fruit. The first novel in the trilogy, *Strong Wind*, tells how a mysterious figure, who is at first taken for a slightly mad pedlar and is in fact none other than one of the company's chief shareholders, disappears in one of the cyclones that sweep the coasts every now and then, leaving a will which names the Indians of the plantation as his heirs. The end might appear 'unhappy', since the sympathetic couple of benefactors, Lester Mead and his wife Leland Foster, die in the tempest which ravages the banana plantations. Following the title denoting violence ('strong wind'), the first sentence foreshadows the end of the narration with a description of the final disaster. And yet, although the novel's end is also the end of the Mead couple, it is above all an account of how they are reunited: 'She tried to make her husband feel that they were together, that she was his companion in the hurricane'. So this departure for a 'foreign' place beyond the ocean, which the text allows us to identify both as North America, the Meads' homeland, and as the Setting Sun, is thus a 'happy' end: 'Leland, I knew that great darkness was awaiting us'. The couple (in conformity with the double – feminine and masculine – nature of mesoamerican gods) incarnates the civilizing hero, the god who is also commonly called Ehecatl, god of the wind.

Tres de cuatro soles plays on the similarity of the signifiers *volver* (to return) and *envolver* (to cover), a similarity which in one sense establishes the myth where the Serpent covered in feathers promises to come back.

In his 1970 play *Todos los gatos son pardos*, Fuentes particularly concentrates on Quetzalcoatl, who appears in it as a character, as do Huitzilopochtli and Tezcatlipoca, his rivals, during a scene intended to emphasize the work's meaning:

> Quetzalcoatl: One day when I was washing my penis I stroked it and played with it; my sperm spurted out and struck the stones of the earth. The dust came alive and that is how human beings were born . . . I had invented human beings, but to distinguish them from gods I gave them freedom, a face which is the mirror of time, a time which is the reflection of desire and a desire born of necessity.

But Quetzalcoatl is a character and not the protagonist: the role of the double protagonist Cortés/Moctezuma (we shall discuss below the traditional function of duality and its constancy in Fuentes' work) in the action of the play is to take on the meaning defined by the character. Since the protagonist Doña Marina more or less ends the play with a scene during which, with legs wide apart, she gives birth to the first mixed-race child, son of the white Cortés and the Indian Marina, it is easy to see that what Fuentes is dramatizing is precisely what the myth of Quetzalcoatl recounts; that is the birth/restoration of a new race of people, the Mexicans, who for better or worse are of mixed race.

In a 1967 novel, *Cambio de piel*, Fuentes sums up the text in the title. His protagonists, a German architect responsible for the installation of gas chambers in a death camp, who has fled to Mexico after the defeat of the Third Reich, and an American Jew married to a Mexican, enable him to play on both the ophidian sense of a 'change of skin' – the ritual stripping of the 'old man' and the change into new personalities (in Latin America, Nazi refugees have become masters of the art of 'changing their skin') – and the symbolism of the regenerative new beginning which comes from the myth of Quetzalcoatl: 'What did Frantz do? What does it matter . . . It doesn't matter what he did. That's old stuff. It has to die. The cycle is finished and something new has to come into being on the slough of what was old'. As is only right, the last scene takes place inside the great pyramid of Quetzalcoatl at Cholula, and at the last minute 'the yellow dog' is called, the coyote/Xolotl, who is Quetzalcoatl's double, the one who accompanied him in his subterranean journey and disappears when the god is revived as the Morning Star (Venus).

In 1975 Fuentes published *Terra nostra*, a voluminous novel which on first reading seems rather disparate, apparently caught between a depiction of the scientific future (Paris in 1999) and a historical pageant (the Spain of the Hapsburgs, the Rome of Tiberius and the pre-Columbian world), but which, once again, is a magnificent, ambitious reinterpretation of and meditation on the myth of Quetzalcoatl. I shall begin by stressing some interesting points of contact between *Terra nostra* and *Tres de cuatro soles*.

First there is the old woman who amazingly gives birth, without the intervention of human sperm, to a supernatural child, Juan Girador's skeleton.

(Asturias had earlier broached this subject in a tale called 'Juan Girador' in *El espejo de Lida Sal*, in which the Herb Woman 'carries' twins from the other side in her hump. Instead of starting from birth and moving towards death, these twins travel in the opposite direction, from their death to their meeting with their father.)

Then there are young and old women in general who are mysteriously impregnated and give birth: 'quantities of pregnant women. The Sun of fire takes the place of men. His rays penetrate dark vaginas' (*Tres de cuatro soles*); 'Into the far distance – the Alexander III Bridge on one side, the San Miguel Bridge on the other – women lay on the pavements and other women helped them . . . ladies of all ages, corpulence and situation, were giving birth' (*Terra nostra*).

Tres de cuatro soles is enriched by two complementary episodes from the myth. First the creation of the Fifth Sun at Quetzalcoatl's request and the inevitable sacrifice of one who agrees to be a god ('The sun sacrificed himself every day. It was for that reason that he was a god. Every day the wild cats and giants of walking evil cut him to pieces and his bloody remains filled the twilight with blood'). Second Quetzalcoatl's descent into the world of the dead to find the bones of the earlier humankind, so that, by grinding them with maize and his sperm, he could bring new beings to life.

But although in the 'descent' to the dark world, the Guatemalan writer's fiction, written towards the end of his life, gives prime importance to the search for the true face, the 'mask of white bones' revealed by death, in a more particular way Fuentes insists on Quetzalcoatl's generative role: 'He had invented human beings, but to distinguish them from gods he gave them freedom, a face which is the mirror of time, a time which is the reflection of desire and a desire born of necessity'. This quotation is from *Todos los gatos son pardos* and it is Tezcatlipoca speaking, the smoking mirror, Quetzalcoatl's black double. The allusion to the mirror takes us back to the mythical episode in which Tezcatlipoca goes to see Quetzalcoatl in Tula and shows him something he has never seen before: his face in a mirror. Quetzalcoatl, horrified (at seeing himself so old? at seeing only a blank according to some versions), leaves Tula but promises to return. Fuentes was always fascinated by this scene, to which he returns in brilliant variations in *Terra nostra*: Philip II in the crypt of the Escorial, seeing in a mirror he holds in his hand how at each step time passes on his face and ages him, and so on until the end, the 'mask of white bones'; the death, from the same horror at his decrepit image, of the old man who is the guardian of memory in ancient Mexico; the certainty of the 'self' for Polo Febo (Quetzalcoatl's Parisian avatar) each time he looks at himself in the mirror which never leaves him; and so on. *Tres de cuatro soles* fleetingly describes this mythical temptation of the mirror: 'Life, attracted by the whitness of ash, almost lent an ear to death and took shelter in its white seas. But it preferred shadow and sheltered in the coals'. But the truly organic reinterpretation of the myth lies in the resolution of a fantasy of Fuentes' own, the theme of the twin which appears in almost all his works: in *Terra nostra* Quetzalcoatl and Tezcatlipoca are the two sides of a single personality:

> It was him again. It was me, the same face that the mirror jealously hidden beneath my torn clothes faithfully reproduced . . . serpent of feathers in what I remember, smoking mirror in what I do not remember . . .
>
> Once again you have killed only your brother enemy. He who struggles against you. He who fights within you. The dark twin will be born again within you, and you will go on fighting him . . . what you represent will only live if it is denied . . . your good, my dear, remains alive only because your double denies it.

This dialectic was already present in the work of Asturias: 'Fire changed into smoke . . . smoke changed into cloud . . . cloud changed into feather . . . feathered serpent in the highest point of the sky.' Quetzalcoatl/Tezatlipoca (a mask of green feathers and smoke are constant signals of their presence in the narrative) leaves his world and is hurled by the sea into Europe. He leaves/comes back, as promised, to the old/new world, but only for a short time, for his sign is that of recommencement:

> You will always fail. You will always come back. You will fail again. You will not let yourself by defeated. You know the original order of human life because it was you who founded it, with human beings, who were not born to devour each other like wild beasts but to live in harmony with the teachings of the dawn: your teachings.

We can see that the figure of Quetzalcoatl, the peaceful one, vanquished at Tula by the machinations of the black god (a still current model for dictatorships, the enemies of democracy), forced to emigrate but promising (himself) to return with peace and happiness, serves as a key to such contemporary fiction as *Libro de navios y borrascas* (1984) by the Argentinian Daniel Moyano. The *Cristoforo Colombo*, a boat with a predestined name and flying, as is only right, the Italian flag, sails from Buenos Aires to Barcelona carrying several hundred 'undesirables' from various countries from the 'southern cone' – exiles and expelled persons, 'survivors of a shipwreck carefully sought out by what is called History'. Among these is the narrator, who leaves his vine untrimmed and his violin hanging on the trellis where he used to take the gentle sun in a little village in northern Argentina. The three strangers who appear and take him away in a van do not give him the time to go back to his house to change his clothes, nor even to put his violin in its case. One day he is put on to the *Cristoforo Colombo*, and thus he retraces the journey his grandfather once made, but in the opposite direction. But unlike his grandfather, who left Spain with no idea of return, Rolando wants to come back. In the Latin-American political context of recent years, the leitmotiv of return is loaded with echoes of the old myth of the feathered serpent:

> Hard to arrive, isn't it? Of course, since we are in the process of returning

> without knowing we are returning. In more than a hundred years of migratory absence, everyone ends up forgetting that they left one day.
>
> [...]
>
> Do you think we'll return soon?
> Just in time to trim my vine.

Without claiming to reduce the meaning of the fiction to a myth which does not, strictly speaking, belong to the same cultural space, I should like to emphasize the inevitable literary diffusion of the American cultural inheritance throughout the continent, which legitimates, with the usual provisos, the reading of the return as an indefinitely renewed avatar of Quetzalcoatl's promise:

> A democratic god, a decent sort, with no sword and no rewards, the god in whom we have believed until now is the god of war and rape, he is no good to us... Now we need a god who fits our needs better, let's say a god who is reformist if he's not going to be revolutionary, even if he is provisional, transitional, half sacred and half profane at the same time.

In a continent which was once the cradle of prestigious civilizations and which is characterized today by economic underdevelopment and a high rate of illiteracy, the figure of an educating god who returns to teach physical and mental health inevitably underlies fictions informed in the first degree by a different ideology. This is the case of *Doña Bárbara* (1929) by the Venezuelan Romulo Gallegos (1884–1969), a novel in which Santos Luzardo (much has been made of the signified 'light' in his patronym, but here we should like to stress its possible relationship to the solar myth of the educating god), a young man who grew up in the city and studied at the unversity, returns to the *llanos* to introduce 'civilization', in the form of respect for property rights, the education of women and the use of fresh water in physical cleanliness. This ideology, reminiscent of the teachings of the schoolmasters of yesteryear, is certainly informed more by a European decimononic positivism than an indigenous mythical tradition, although the latter cannot be excluded, if only as a 'coincidence'. I should also like to quote the novel by the Uruguayan Enrique Amorim (1900–60), *Corral abierto* (1956), because the protagonist, Horacio Costa (Costita), returns to the poverty of his village, 'Corral abierto', and there naturally adopts a charismatic role which is easily assimilatable to that of Christ, a figure whose significance is far from being incompatible with that of Quetzalcoatl. Both answer the epigraph chosen by Amorim for his fine novel: 'the priest of the god of things as they are was losing ground in relation to the priest who serves the god of things as they should be' (Rudyard Kipling, *The Judgement of Dungara*).

On the question of the possible assimilation of Christ to Quetzalcoatl, let us consider, with all the usual provisos and reservations, how early in the twentieth century in Mexico, Quetzalcoatl's traditional cultural space, an extremist movement development in the countryside, with Christ the King as its spiritual head and whose partisans, the *cristeros*, became the protagonists of an abundant literature, which was itself called *cristera.*

The quality, quantity and variety of Latin-American fiction in which the old myth emerges – deliberately or unconsciously – render pale and above all artificial such novels as D. H. Lawrence's *The Plumed Serpent* or *Le Jade et l'obsidienne* by Alain Gerber, whose declared references to pre-Columbian culture are no more than a romantic but meaningless folklore, despite their other qualities. On the other hand, the death of the gods, of the fallen god, bound hand and foot in stone in the middle of the jungle, incapable of defending his territory against the usurpers who are coming (whereas he has been unable to return), overturns the order of a world which will henceforward be 'new' for all. This death is the theme of a magnificent poem in Pablo Neruda's *Canto General*, 'A Soldier Sleeps' ('Duerme un soldado'), describing a Spaniard, barbarous and almost childlike in sleep, who for a moment and a moment only is as inoffensive as the monolith of the Feathered Serpent at whose foot weariness has laid him.

Dorita Nouhaud

The Flood

IN THE BEGINNING . . .

Anthropologists have come across nearly one hundred mythical stories concerning a flood, yet in the West only one is widely known: the biblical account of Genesis 6–9. Nonetheless, this has given rise to a great many picturesque images. Wild and domestic animals move along two by two. 'The sky and the sea are black as ink' (Baudelaire), but the 'ship of salvation' (Rimbaud) shows up brightly. This is 'the ark in the storm' and, miraculously, *fluctuat nec mergitur* (it floats and is not submerged). Around it is the beating of wings: the black wing of the raven and the white wing of the dove who brings the olive twig in her beak. Finally, above the verdant ground from which the smoke of the sacrifice rises, there shines the multicoloured bow, 'that rainbow that promises that the thunder has passed' (Louis Aragon).

Poets and painters have produced such evocative images from a text that in itself is not at all picturesque, a text that includes no actual description and is quite literally a tale. This is really a compilation of sequences, which at least at first glance, appear confused, complex and heterogeneous, for its final writer has been none too successful in welding together two versions of the story: the Yahwist (J) version, which is the older, and the so-called priestly version (Priester codex = P), which complemented it. This has resulted in a great deal of repetition and even in some contradictions.

Nonetheless, even if the story of the Flood is less elegant than the story of the Garden of Eden, it has the same logical rigour: reparation for an initial *misdeed* ('the wickedness of man', Genesis 6.5) takes the form of the extermination of 'every living thing' (7.23). This motif is readily recognizable as an example of the *main test* found in tales and myths. Meanwhile, other conventional mythical elements are also clearly in evidence. First, a Donor grants to a human being (Noah) what may be considered a *magic attribute*, the ark (6.13–14), in which is evidently a *qualifying test*. And, finally, the hero fulfils an *arduous task* ('Noah built an altar . . .' 8.10), which brings him a *reward*. This reward is indicated by a word play on Noah's name, since the original wording of 'when the Lord smelled the pleasing odour' (8.21) made punning use of the letters, N, O, AH. The story is thus a perfect example of a traditional tale, with the peculiarity that it assigns the *decisive test* to the deity, while in the two other tests the chief protagonist is a man. The action of the Almighty has two aspects. On the one hand, he punishes the breaking of a contract drawn up between himself and mankind. On the other, he rewards the faithfulness of his servant – saving him by telling him to build the ark as a refuge, and, in the priestly version, making a new covenant with him, sealed by the sign of the rainbow. Two story lines are in evidence: the deity *proceeds against* mankind as a whole, but one man with his family and the seeds of all life is *succoured*, and we have the impression that this rescue represents the crux of the story. While the anonymous masses are *liquidated* (literally!) in a few words, the hero has a name that is meaningful and that recurs in the story more often even than that of Yahweh Elohim (the Lord of Lords). In the final analysis, the flood is important only because it resulted in the exaltation of a human hero, and the story might properly be called 'Noah rescued from the waters', rather than 'The Flood'.

This becomes clear when we consider the opposition between the two main concepts in the text: Life and Death. In relation to the former, there is the life of mankind before the Flood which the Gospels describe thus: 'They ate, they drank, they married, they were given in marriage, until the day when Noah entered the ark, and the Flood came and destroyed them all' (Luke 17.27). That life was attacked by the Flood, the means used by Yahweh Elohim to put mankind to death; and this can be seen as the *decisive test.* However, Noah was saved from Death by means of the ark and so regained Life, regained a life that was better than before, a life bound up with God. There has been destruction, but it ends in regeneration. We should note that the opposition between the two great universal concepts Life and Death is echoed by the opposition between two concrete objects: the *Flood* and the *ark*, water that brings death and the 'ship of salvation', two tools used by God to achieve his ends, the final one being a work of salvation. On the one hand, we have the universal tragic conflict, 'Mors et vita duello / Conflixere mirando . . .' (part of the Easter Day order of service), on the other, the contrasting image of the 'ark in the storm'. A supernatural power that presides over life and death has shown its terrible countenance to sinful mankind, but the same power now turns a benevolent face towards the man who will establish a new creation.

If we return to the schema of the tale outlines earlier, the stages involved in it and the movements linking them show that it reflects a process of initiation. Leaving the land familiar to them, Noah and his children go aboard the ark, which takes them on a voyage on '*the great deep*' (Genesis 7.11) – the dreadful sea, representing death. The numbers used in the account indicate the sacred significance of things and events: there is an interval of *seven* days before the catastrophic downpour, and Noah waits for the same period before sending the dove out of the ark a second time; while the rain falls for '*forty* days and *forty* nights', another magic figure. Finally, after a period spent in *another place*, the kingdom of death, Noah emerges from the ark, *returning* to life. The concepts of both space and time are sacred. What is involved is the supreme initiation ending in union with the deity. In the Yahwist version, this is expressed through the image of the offering made by the hero, which is approved by the Lord, who smells the pleasing 'Noah' odour (to recall the original word play). Meanwhile, in the priestly version, the rainbow in the storm clouds provides the *light* that features in most accounts of initiations.

THE STORY'S IMPACT ON LATER LITERATURE

As portrayed in art and literature the biblical story of 'Noah rescued from the waters' illustrates the multiple facets of a myth, in all the accepted senses of the term, ranging from the most profound religious ones to the most banal involving its use as a cliché. It is a myth dealing with the relationship between God and Man. As such it is a living myth in Judaism, Christianity and Islam as is demonstrated by the writings of the Jewish rabbis starting with the *Siracide* (44.17–18), of the apostle Peter (I Peter 3.20–21, II Peter 2.5 and 3.6) of the Fathers of the Church, and in the Koran (Sura XI.40–48).

In Western secular literature the traditional interpretation of the story has prevailed. An example is provided by the medieval mystery plays (*Chester Plays* etc.) in which it is assumed that the spectators will share the faith of the authors: God is just, he sends the Flood to punish sin, and saves one human family through an act of pure grace. As well as adopting the familiar tone of the Yahwist version, most writers also follow its anthropomorphic approach – a tendency illustrated by thirteenth-century miniatures, in which God is depicted directing the animals towards the entrance of the ark. This God seen as a 'good father' goes on scolding, then smiling, right up into the twentieth century: in Marc Connelly's play *The Green Pastures*, in some negro spirituals, and in André Obey's *Noé.* These writers add an element of family psychology to the tale told in Genesis, stressing the relationships between Noah and his sons to such an extent that the tragic story often verges on the comic. However, certain epic and lyrical works – by Du Bartas, Milton (*Paradise Lost*) and Pierre-Jean Jouve (*Les Noces*) – retain the gravity befitting paraphrases of the Bible.

This orthodox interpretation of the story of the Flood, based closely on Genesis, was challenged by the Rebels. The instigator of the attack was Byron in his mystery drama *Heaven and Earth*, and he was followed by Alfred de Vigny ('Le Déluge'), Victor Hugo ('Les Sept cordes') and Leconte de Lisle ('Qaïn'). These poets were not so much atheist as anti-theist, and sought to highlight the scandalous nature of a Creator who destroys what he himself has created. 'If he hath made the Earth, let it be his shame,/ To make a world for torture!' intones the Byronic chorus. And this sentiment is echoed by Vigny's hero: 'The death of innocence is a mystery to man./ God makes no pact with the human race:/ He who created without love will destroy without hatred.' Meanwhile, Hugo writes in the same vein: 'What! I said, Are we created so as to be annihilated?/ Oh earth, is the fault yours? Oh Heaven, is the crime yours?'

The only part of the story that is retained is the cataclysm, and its horror is heightened. We hear of nothing but 'awful rain', 'ghastly waves', a 'howling' sea, a 'dead universe' (Leconte de Lisle's), and 'limbs snatched from the corpse of the World' (Vigny). The Romantic vision, illustrated by Gustave Doré, is of a magma of naked human beings attacked by ravening animals and swallowed by the waves while, above them, sails a monstrous ark.

The Romantics delighted in developing one theme in particular, that of the love between the sons of God – the angels – and the daughters of men (Genesis 6.1–4), as a means of heightening the tragic aspect of the story. In this, they were following Milton, who had in turn been inspired by *The Book of Enoch*, but, unlike him, the Romantics sided with the rebellious angels. Thus the human drama was matched, explained and magnified by the celestial drama. The relevant verses from Genesis were used in the same way by Pierre-Jean Jouve and by Jean Grosjean ('Sémiazas accuse').

Rimbaud's work 'Aprés le déluge' shares its title with several later poems, for instance by Pierre-Jean Jouve and Pierre Emmanuel, and in these it is the mythical symbolism of the episode of the Flood that is exploited rather than its religious content. The Flood is seen as an enormous 'washing-day' that was required to 'cleanse' the old, sullied world and recreate another, 'clean and smooth as it if had just stepped out of the bath' (Pierre Emmanuel, *Babel*, 1951). Writers portray concepts established by anthropologists: 'the Flood, [representing] a return to chaos from which the regenerated being is to emerge' . . . 'annihilates the old human species and prepares the way for the emergence of the new human species'. In André Obey's play the characters exclaim, 'Now we are nice and clean!' Meanwhile, Julien Gracq writes of one of his heroes that after a storm, 'the earth appears beautiful and pure to him as it did after the Flood', and makes the same character express '. . . the wish that a cataclysm would mark an end, an end to impurity, followed by a new beginning'. It is in this context that touches of colour are introduced: Rimbaud's 'precious stones', Pierre Emmanuel's 'earth varnished in green', and above all the rainbow, 'God's seal' (Rimbaud) that appears at the end of both a poem by Vernon Watkins ('. . . the rainbow's covenant is fulfilled') and the play by André Obey, and that extends like a blessing above a painting by Marc Chagall.

For some this 'return to chaos provides an opportunity to re-experience the primordial, preformal state', in short to indulge in *orgies*. It was this idea that Tennessee Williams and Günter Grass developed in their plays *Kingdom of Earth* (1968) and *Hochwasser* (1955), respectively, in their plays which were inspired by Genesis 6–9. In these works transposing the story of Noah into modern times, the heroes take advantage of the disaster to give vent to their instincts – primarily their sexual instincts.

Another popular theme that has lost all religious significance and has perhaps come more to represent a psychological state that could be described as the 'Noah complex' is that of the ark as a refuge. The ark is incontrovertibly a symbol of the mother's arms, where the child huddles to escape the wrath of the father. It provides the illusion of being a passive foetus again, of sleeping in the belly of the waves 'as you sleep at your mother's breast', as Hugo says in 'Moïse sur le Nil'. It represents the return to the womb, an essential phase in any story of initiation. Thus it is hardly surprising that Marcel Proust identified himself with the biblical patriarch, who '. . . could never see the world better than from the ark, for all that it was enclosed and the earth was in darkness . . .' (Dedication in *Les Plaisirs et les jours*). The main character in Julien Gracq's novel *Un balcon en forêt* shares the same complex; as a soldier huddled in his blockhouse in 1940, he muses jocularly on the dove and the raven. It is in this sort of context that the myth can become worn-out, and degenerate into cliché. If heavy rain lasts, mention of the biblical Flood is made almost automatically as in a recent novel by Anne Hébert – 'I live in Noah's ark . . . At the centre of the flood, but well protected in a transparent bubble' (*Les Fous de Bassan*) – or in Georges Brassens' famous song with its predictable French rhyming pattern: 'I would have liked the rain to fall without stopping as in the Flood, so that I could keep her in my refuge for forty days and forty nights . . .'

Nonetheless, even if myths that were originally sacred do become secular over the course of centuries, they can still be reinvested with their original power through creative genius, like that shown by Jouve in his poem *Diadème*. In it he assimilates himself with Noah, the prototype of the man who hopes: 'A deep, distant hope/ Sometimes surmounts this flood of darkness/ Over which I steer, an omen of the rising sun . . . The dove of a day in the world/ The naked herald and as a gift/ A continent of earth of light . . .'

As Ernst Jünger commented so appositely, 'The antiquity of Genesis is manifest in the great dream-inspiring figures contained within it.' Noah is indeed one of our great ancestors.

Robert Couffignal

Germanic Myths

This article covers only those myths that in the author's opinion relate to the continental Germans, and thus omits ones relating to the northern and western branches of this important group within the great Indo-European family (involving the Scandinavians, the Anglo-Saxons and the Dutch). Even so, the differences in traditions between German-speaking Switzerland and Austria, or between Prussia and Bavaria are still considerable, and an overall survey by definition runs the risk of hasty and therefore incorrect generalization.

For it is quite wrong to lump together under one name ethnic groups that are more striking in their differences than in their shared traits. The Germans, more than any other people, represent a conglomerate unified only by its language and whose existence in historical, political and even geographical terms is extremely recent. From the very beginning, the Germans have never used the word 'German' to describe themselves and it was thus the non-Germans who effectively 'created' the Germans. (Incidentally, the name must be Celtic in origin and is associated with the word 'shout' – probably because of the way in which they behave at public meetings – and definitely not with the ideas of 'army' or 'war'.)

The first person to conceive of these heterogeneous peoples as Germanic was probably Tacitus (*Germania*, 98 AD), who was clearly writing from a partisan, moralistic standpoint. He contrasted the soft, decadent Latin races with the energetic, pure, hard Germans – by whom he obviously meant 'barbarians' in the Greek sense of the term. At a later date, this theme was taken up again and orchestrated by Montesquieu, and it has lost none of its force today. Yet, even allowing for the literally formative power that a language can have on those using it, the first thing that must be observed is the extreme diversity of the peoples grouped together under the epithet 'Germanic'. Their characteristics are manifold, ranging from the love of life and fanciful transports of the Bavarian, evidenced by the famous castles of Ludwig II, and the smiling imaginativeness of the Tyrolean to the dry efficiency of the Prussian, from the rustic good sense of the Silesian to the dreamy mysticism of the Rhinelander . . . so what common denominator can possibly bring together these disparate men and women? Perhaps Albert the Great and Goethe, Marx and Wagner, Thomas à Kempis and Luther, *Narrenschiff* and *Simplicissimus*, or *Hoffmann* and Musil!

Given the diversity of the German people, it is not surprising that Germanic myths are also multiple and often contradictory. They have been included in the present work mainly because they attest to the fantasies and preconceived ideas of the non-German observers rather than because they correspond to any great degree to a reality too fleeting to be monolithic. For the purposes of this article, three aspects of the myths are of particular relevance.

The one that springs to mind first, because it has been reinforced by the tragic events of recent history, is the concept of the 'Teuton' a cruel, brutal warrior. This motif, which has kept recurring since the time of Jordanes, centres on the image of barbarian hordes streaming westwards in compact, endless cohorts to overthrow the civilized world, enslave it and subject it to martial law. Meanwhile, the impression of harsh barbarity has been consolidated by the reputedly guttural accents of a language that is actually capable of the most subtle melodic variations. As a consequence, the Cimbrians, Vandals and Ostrogoths (to choose the names that have acquired the most sinister connotations) are seen as remote prototypes of the Prussians who manned the armoured columns of the Third Reich and showed a fanaticism relating to 'Blut und Boden' that amounted to collective, systematic dementia. The scenes of apotheosis in Nuremburg were nurtured by an unquestioning, wrongheaded Romanticism, which had lost none of its childish magnetism, associated with the prefix *Ur–* ('original', as in *Urvolk, Urheimat, Ursprache*). This constant harking back to the purity and authenticity of the beginnings of the German race was intended to convey a simple implicit message. It told Germans that this was the state to which they must return in order to achieve redemption, for it was here that a cursory, unintelligent reading of Nietzsche located the Übermensch. History records in all too gory detail the criminal excesses that were inspired by the murky magic of the image of the tall fair-haired blue-eyed Aryan, despite its obvious falseness.

Yet even non-Germans do not want to admit that this image is false: the figure of the Teuton crystallizes the disguised hatred instinctively felt towards a hereditary enemy, and we cannot do without it, for it fulfils the terrors that we secretly cherish and makes good our deficiencies. We want to see the Teuton as the epitome of blind order and iron discipline. His image evokes dark depths associated partly with the sun, partly with sex. He is resolutely male-oriented and proudly contemptuous of the obvious blemishes in our collective unconscious, of which we are to varying degrees aware, and which we sense behind the symbol of the swastika. In our eyes, the Teuton expresses himself in the titanic, the monumental, the Kolossal (with a K). Through his superhuman efforts, the Bavarian castles sink into oblivion in comparison with the huge projects achieved in Berlin. He evokes inspiring militaristic slogans: 'Wer will, der kann'; 'Ich bin ein Mann, das ist ein Kämpfer zu sein.' He evokes the helmet and the boots; fire and blood; Wotan and the *Twilight of the Gods* (a singularly inappropriate name).

The second generally accepted manifestation of the Germanic myth is to some extent indirectly linked to the first, through its emphasis on efficiency and method. Germanic is synonymous with technical precision, unparalleled practical achievements and the triumph of the systematic approach. Those who espouse this view show a marked and undeniable tendency to push the theories that they base on it, and the application of these theories to their ultimate logical conclusion. They conjure up the images of beetle-browed scholars who have written vast theses on infinitesimal points of detail. They point out the achievements of German industry, particularly in the fields of mechanical engineering and physics, which seem especially impressive in the present technocratic era. And they posit the existence throughout German society of a flawlessly honed system, the success of which is due in equal parts to the ingenuity of those who have the ideas and the conscientiousness of those who put them into effect. After all, despite the protests of writers such as Rilke or Musil and the gentle but corrosive irony of ones such as Heine, in almost every field the great systems of thought that have made an impact on the West over thc centuries are Germanic in origin, while, conversely, the German world very rarely provides an image of a dilettante or a worthy man with nothing special on which to pride himself. Faust is continually set to penetrate the Great Secret, and in that he remains faithful to an entire Germanic tradition. Even in the contexts of German art and poetry, we invariably have the impression that a great overall theory has guided the creation of the works concerned, which are generally on a gigantic scale. As a result, we are reluctant to recognize that such works have often undergone considerable modification during the course of their development. Yet Wagner himself can be cited as an example of this process: under the influence of Schopenhauer and of Buddhism, he ended by turning his (originally) ardent, radiant tetralogy into the mournful *Twilight of the Gods*.

However, despite all this, it is still true that from the time of Meister Eckhart to that of Heidegger the systematic approach, however subtle a form, seems to preside over all expressions of the Germanic genius. Moreover, this is despite the fact that, because of a desire to be exhaustive or flawlessly precise, many German theories end up developing a dialectic that is so ferociously abstract that it often becomes virtually incomprehensible. In addition, because of its remarkable capacity to enrich itself through the use of compound works or derivatives, the German language has the peculiar property of being able to push back the boundaries of the dictionary indefinitely and so subdivide the possibilities of conceptualization. Not enough attention is paid to this point: whether one maintains that the German language merely transmits thought or actually generates it, its natural tendency is to organize it.

As a consequence, it is not surprising, for example, that the two great currents of thought that have dominated the entire twentieth century are both of Germanic origin: psychoanalysis, pioneered by Freud, Adler and Jung); and the form of socialism promulgated by Marx, Engels and Lassalle. This returns us to our point of departure: opposing the Mediterranean ideal of balance and the oriental ideal of escape, there is this radical and seemingly uncompromising approach, involving a search for what is fundamental and universal that is indissolubly linked to the will to put it to a practical application. The Lutheran reformation provides a good early example of this tendency: after starting off as a practical measure to combat the abuses in the Church, it was quickly structured into a system of imperatives. There is no need to delve into its subtleties or limitations: the concept of a system is sufficient, enabling us to crystallize this aspect of the Germanic myth.

However, there is nothing exclusively mathematical about the German systematic approach. In this context, one should remember the Hanseatic League. This superb commercial and political organization eventually imposed its control over a large area of Europe from the end of the Middle Ages onwards, but people do not realize that it was based on mystical, or even spiritual, beliefs that were very far removed from dull economic realities.

This brings us to the third aspect of the Germanic myth, which actually clashes with the other two – for Germanic also means mystical. The famous northern mists are seen as also descending over the landscape of Pomerania and Mecklenburg, and, however paradoxical this may seem, the Romantic soul and the dream (to borrow the title of Albert Béguin's famous book, *L'Ame romantique et le rêve*) come with them. To revert one last time to the subject of language, it is perhaps because of the very organization of a German sentence, which permits every kind of digression before one finally reaches the verb at the end, that German writing has a certain mystique. Be this as it may, we seem to be able to detect a whiff of mysticism behind every Germanic work and every Germanic thought. After all, from the cloistered nuns of the Rhineland in the high Middle Ages (Hildegard von Bingen) to Schelling and his philosophy of nature, there are so many German thinkers who expose the limitations of shallow Cartesianism. Conversely, what a multitude of incoherent meditations there are on the outpourings of Novalis, Hölderlin and Hofmannsthal! And, earlier still, Dürer and his *Melancholia* gave rise to countless learned essays. Expressionism is really as much Scandinavian as German, given the contributions of Edward Munch and Strindberg, but the Scandinavians themselves are also Germanic. Thus the Expressionist movement from Wedekind to Brecht proves that the endeavour to convey emotional turmoil as directly as possibly through written or pictorial means by striving to abolish the screens interposed by convention or nature is also a reflection of the Germanic mentality.

Moreover, Germany is surely the earthly paradise of music, especially Romantic and modern music, though the huge shadow cast by Johann Sebastian Bach and the airy grace of Mozart can vie with either Schubert's lieder or the rolling expanses of Wagner and Mahler. For all that Stockhausen is German, nothing will ever dislodge the 'Ode to Joy' of Beethoven's *Ninth Symphony* from its pre-eminent place in our affections. Indeed, Beethoven undoubtedly epitomizes a notable part of the Germanic myth.

That is, unless the myth resides in the person of the woman from beyond the Rhine. She sometimes takes the form of the Lorelei, who has dealings with the supernatural spirits that guard the Rheingold and who captivated

Nerval. She is sometimes a Valkyrie in at least two of the accepted senses of the word: the swan-woman, simple and just a little animal-like or natural, who is stripped by Siegfried and, in return, teaches him the secret of the magic runes; or the female warrior, the virgin with a shield, who decides the consummation of every heroic destiny. She can embody virtually every aspect of the myth, not merely the trite image of 'Sturm und Drang' – she *is* Germania.

Régis Boyer

The Golden Age

If a myth is a story, whether oral or written, that can awaken in the mind of the hearer or reader ancient collective images related to contemporary aspirations and events, then the Golden Age is the most representative of humanity's great myths. It is attested in many cultures, from the distant past to our own times, and provides an enduring image of a state of human happiness presided over by the gods or of God, as the fulfilment of a universal destiny. Whilst, initially, its religious dimension was uppermost, over time, the myth of the Golden Age has adopted forms that have turned it into a commonplace in the oral tradition and led it to undergo complex mutations in the literary tradition. Far from being simply an aesthetic motif landing itself to mechanical imitation, in Western culture it has a philosophical aspect and a political relevance that have encouraged its survival. The myth of the Golden Age has an admirable plasticity: its themes are constantly taken up and reshaped to fit the requirements of a given philosophical argument or the political aspirations of a particular people. By being transformed in this way, they provide the imagination with an updated image of complete human happiness.

To identify the living myth of the Golden Age beneath its various disguises, we need to bear in mind the archetype underlying the structure of all the relevant stories, developed over four millennia in the east and west and of the region surrounding the Mediterranean. The myth of the Golden Age is evoked every time that the gods bring about peace, abundance and justice for human beings in the context of an order that is both natural and divine, and this is done by means of images whose everyday simplicity encapsulates both a link with the collective unconscious and the persistence of certain specific mental outlooks.

Various names have been given to the myth of the Golden Age in each culture and, despite its long history, its unity and importance are only now coming to be recognized. The conventional term 'Golden Age' first appeared in Rome, in the first century BC in the form of references to a *tempus aureum* in Horace's *Epodes* (XVI. 64) and an *aurea aetas* in Ovid's *Metamorphoses* (I. 89). The myth itself had doubtless come into existence two thousand years earlier in Sumer, but had previously been represented as a creation myth involving the act of a great god. In this context, it must be emphasized that it is modern readers of the old cogmogonic epics who have arbitrarily given the world's oldest myths of the Golden Age their names, basing them either on the names of the deities involved or on those of the places where the gods manifested their benevolence. Notable examples are as follows. In Sumer the myth is the 'myth of Dilmun' in Egypt, the 'myth of Re and Isis', and in Israel, the 'myth of Eden'. Meanwhile, in Greece there is the 'myth of Cronos' – although there are also Greek 'paradises' represented by the Isles of the Blest or Homer's Scherie – and, in Rome, the 'myth of Saturn' competes with the concept of the *tempus aureum*. The Roman period was of primary importance in this connection, since thereafter the name Golden Age was definitively established in the European literary tradition. By contrast, despite the success of Virgil's fourth *Eclogue* throughout the whole of the Middle Ages, due to its interpretation as a messianic poem announcing the Christian 'Golden Age', the *Saturnia regna* did not leave their mark on European literature. However, the political influences of the 'myth of Cronos' and the 'myth of Saturn' have increased continually ever since the Renaissance. The Greco-Roman myth of the Golden Age nourished the sixteenth-century utopian concept of the ideal city, the social criticism of the eighteenth century (Voltaire's tales) and the revolutionary thinking of the nineteenth and twentieth centuries. In fact, by linking the myth of the Golden Age to their own history, the Romans politicized a myth that had previously been essentially religious and, in so doing, explored the conditions required for imposing an ideology.

When, in his fourth *Eclogue*, Virgil announces the imminent return of the *Saturnia regna* under the aegis of the *princeps* (Augustus), he is offering people the hope of the restoration of peace, abundance and justice in quite exceptional circumstances.

At the end of the twentieth century, many peoples still cherish similar hopes, and this explains the resurgence of the myth of the Golden Age in contemporary thought. Certain images representing the 'triad' of peace, abundance and justice that lies at the very core of the myth persisted through its oriental and Greco-Roman variants. These images often retained the colour of the archetypal story at the source of the later literary versions of the myth even when they changed their cultural context.

The first element of the triad is illustrated by the portrayal of gods and human beings as living together in a state of original peace. This conception, which is related to the myth of primordial unity, can be traced back as far as Sumer. There, it is represented by 'the Golden Age of Dilmun', which is situated before the first stirrings of history, since history recounts human divisions and struggles. This myth is the opposite of that of Babel, since it asserts that, in the time of Enlil, all humankind praised the great god in a single language. Mesopotamian unease probably explains the emphasis on global peace, which the Sumerian text portrays as reigning on an island at the dawn of time.

Turning to the other great power of the oriental world, from the fourth millenium BC onwards Egyptian mythology associated peace between the living with the perfect standard of 'the first time. During the reign of Ra in heaven and on earth which ended with a rupture between the divine creator and his creature, the unity of cosmic order, both divine and human was expressed in the figure Maat. In the same way, in the Bible, Eden illustrates the intimate relationship enjoyed by Yahweh and the first human couple in the peace of a garden.

Greek mythology also retains the memory of a time of peace between gods and human beings before the rift immortalized in the 'myth of Prometheus' and the evils brought by Pandora. Indeed, these two myths lie at the root of a disputed line in Hesiod's *Works and Days* (108), 'For gods and mortals have the same origin'. Meanwhile, in accordance with their Orphico-Pythagorean convictions, Empedocles and Pindar also echo this great dream of primal unity, the basis of peace.

The second element in the triad, abundance, is illustrated by the image of the garden, island or oasis, which represents the earth's fertility in the form of fruit, flowers, trees and plants, growing near running water. Israel offers the most powerful archetypal image in the form of 'Yahweh's garden'. The abundance of Eden was restored when the new covenant was established between the people and their god (Ezekiel 36. 28–30), as well as by the miracle of the oasis (Isaiah 55. 1). The miraculous abundance manifests the presence of god in the world.

In Mesopotamia and Egypt this religious concept was introduced into royal ideology, so that sovereigns became guarantors of abundance for their people.

The Greeks describe their islands as paradises and, starting with the *Works and Days* of Hesiod, the earth's spontaneous abundance became the characteristic feature of the Golden Age. Thus, when Virgil made Italy the land of abundance, he was simply Romanizing earlier versions of paradise.

The third element of the triad, justice, was the slowest to take shape. In this context, stress is laid on the idea that human beings should model themselves on their god. In Mesopotamia the integration of the myth into royal ideology created an 'ideal' relationship between ruler and subjects. In Egypt, justice was assimilated to Maat, who symbolized the unity of the structures of the cosmos, nature and society, while, through his identification with justice, the Pharaoh embodied divine perfection in Man. Thus, these two great civilizations gave rise to the persistent image of a God-king who guarantees his people's happiness.

Israel made justice, in its religious, social and human dimensions, the leaven of history, and, by directing the people of God towards a new Golden Age set at the end of time, the Hebrew prophets liberated humankind from cyclical time and placed it on the path of regeneration.

In Greece, following Hesiod's affirmation of the religious root of social justice, thinkers began to meditate on the sort of ideal constitutions that might ensure the stability of cities. Thus, Plato returns to the 'myth of Cronos' to give a definition of good government. The conclusion drawn from these ponderings is clear: the origins of justice are divine. Consequently, the man who is *divinely royal* and perfectly just is the symbol of regenerated humanity.

Virgil was a faithful heir to the Greek tradition and placed justice at the heart of his *Saturnia regna*, making it the prerogative of the old god Saturn and of the Latin people. As a result, the Roman Golden Age, *Saturno regnante*, became the prototype for the rule of the Latin kings, which in turn provided a model for the Augustan 'restoration'. Thus the political significance of the Golden Age came to be emphasized in Rome, as it had earlier been in the Orient and in Greece.

The history of the myth in the five cultures briefly discussed here reveals an important recurrent feature: it is in times of crisis, when everything seems ready to collapse, that the myth is revived, and this revival occurs in a prophetic context closely linked to that of the apocalypses. In Alexandria, for example, during the last three centuries BC, the clash of cultures following the collapse of Alexander's empire created an environment that encouraged pronouncements on the fragility of kingdoms (Book of Daniel) and predictions of the coming of a *regnum* without end. As a consequence, apocalyptic literature appeared offering visions both of the 'end of the world' and of the definitive 'Golden Age' (*Oracula Sibyllina*). Similarly, at Rome in the first century BC, there were fears of an impending 'end of Rome' and hopes for the return of *Saturnia regna*. This crisis, in which despair and hope go hand in hand, is reflected in Horace, *Epodes* XVI, and Virgil *Eclogues* IV. The tone of these works is identical to that of the Hebrew prophets setting their 'curses' and 'blessings' before the people. At such times, daring syntheses appear. Alexandrine influence revived the Greek and Italic legacies. People remembered Pythagoras's prediction linking the happiness of Hesiod's golden race to the eternal return of things, and Neopythagoreanism, in particular, spread the idea of the return of the *Saturnia regna*. The disarray of the Romans after a century of civil wars created the urgent need for reassurance, and it was through the myth of the Golden Age that their greatest poets provided the necessary message of hope. Following them, thinkers and politicians then attempted to bring those hopes to fruition.

At the end of the twentieth century, hope is still what the living myth of the Golden Age has to offer: is it a promise of happiness for the world, or merely a mirage?

Marie-Josette Bénéjam-Bontems

The Golden Fleece

The origins of the myth date back to the beginning of Greek history. In fact, Aristarchus confirms that Homer was already familiar with the story of the Argonauts, and the very earliest texts refer to it. The basic scenario is as follows. The oracle had told King Pelias that he would be deposed by a man wearing only one shoe. When Pelias saw Jason (who had just lost one of his sandals) approaching, to avoid the danger he sent him in search of the Golden Fleece, knowing full well that Jason was extremely likely to lose his life during the expedition. The Golden Fleece came from the divine ram which had carried Phrixus, the son of a Boetian king, through the air. The ram had been offered to Zeus as a sacrifice and its golden fleece had been hung from the top of a tree which was guarded by a fearsome dragon. Jason gathered together the best Greek warriors, including Heracles and Orpheus. The building of his ship, the *Argo*, was supervised by Athena, who wove the sails and gave Jason an oak from the forest of Dodona for a mast. The Argonauts sailed towards the east, experiencing many dangers and encountering many obstacles. They made their first stop on the island of Lemnos which was inhabited solely by women. They stayed there for two years and Jason fell in love with their queen. Their second stop was on the island of Cyzicus where they had to fight giants who tried to capture their ship. On the Thracian coast, they rescued the unfortunate soothsayer, Phineus, whose food was snatched away by the Harpies. Phineus told them how to reach the Golden Fleece and how to gain possession of it. The adventurers has to pass through a narrow channel bordered by two immense cliffs which crushed the ships daring to pass between them. They negotiated the channel in the midst of storms, and came to Colchis. In his palace at the foot of the Caucasian Mountains, King Aeëtes refused to agree to their request to be allowed to carry off the Golden Fleece and decided instead to subject Jason to a series of tests. In one day, the hero had to harness two fire-breathing bulls, plough four acres of uncultivated land, sow giants' teeth and kill the giants born from them. Using a salve provided by Aeëtes' daughter, Medea, Jason succeeded in accomplishing all these tasks. He killed the monster guarding the Golden Fleece which he then carried off. On the return journey, the Argonauts escaped the evil spells of the Sirens who were reduced to silence by Orpheus' song. When they reached port, Jason consecrated his ship which was carried up to heaven and became a constellation.

The myth therefore has a double significance. The Golden Fleece represents first and foremost what is usually inaccessible to men. It symbolizes all that is sacred, which is both fascinating and awesome. Jason wants to gain possession of the Fleece, but those who are bold enough to try run the risk of dying in the attempt. It is therefore possible to see the Fleece as the symbolic representation of Transcendancy, absolute love and perfect beauty, which seem to be denied to men during their life on earth. But the myth also demonstrates that love manages to achieve what was apparently impossible. Through a series of tests, of an initiatory nature, Man manages to enter the forbidden kingdom.

In the *Iliad* and particularly in the *Odyssey*, Homer makes brief references to the legend and seems to be referring to an earlier epic. The same applies to Hesiod, whose various works provide evidence of the existence of a complete and entirely coherent myth. In 462 BC, Pindar devoted an entire ode, the IVth *Pythian Ode*, to Jason's adventure in the kingdom of Aeëtes. Retaining only the essential elements, i.e. the trials of the hero, the seduction of Medea, the capture of the Golden Fleece and the departure of Jason and Medea, he condensed the legend to present, in strikingly dense verse, the main lesson, i.e. the triumph of love.

Apollonius of Rhodes (third century BC) composed the *Argonautica*, a vast epic in four books, the earliest surviving work which recounts Jason's entire expedition. In book I, King Pelias orders Jason to leave and the *Argo* is built. Book II traces the events of the expedition up to Jason's arrival in Colchis. The trials imposed on Jason are the subject of book III while, in book IV, Jason captures the Golden Fleece and makes the return journey. In learned and sophisticated language, Apollonius demonstrates his very keen interest in mythological scholarship. In spite of the cyclical nature of the epic, Apollonius follows the aesthetic format advocated by his master, Callimachus. He skilfully juxtaposes elements drawn from different sources and combines the colloquial and picturesque with the epic. This can be seen in his presentation of the Golden Fleece:

> 'It was the Fleece, as big as a young ox's hide,
> Or of the deer that hunters call the Achaean hind,
> And the golden wool hung down to the hero's feet.
> Covered in flocks of gold which weighed it down.'

In Idylls XIII (Hylas) and XXII (the Dioscuri), Theocritus wastes no time in recalling the bravery of the Argonauts. Valerius Flaccus (*c.* 70 AD) also gives an account of the expedition in the eight Books of his *Argonautica*, which he never finished and in which he freely imitates the work of Apollonius of Rhodes.

During the Middle Ages, the Golden Fleece gave its name to the most renowned chivalric order. On 10 January 1430 the Duke of Burgundy created the Ordre de la Toison d'Or (the Order of the Golden Fleece). Philip the Good hoped that the image would serve as a reminder of the Crusades. The Fleece represented Jerusalem which had to be saved from the Infidels, who were represented by the dragon. But the acquisition of this prestigious decoration soon became the object of ambition and the cause of intrigue. In his *Lettres Satyriques* (Letter XX: 'D'un songe', 1654), Cyrano de Bergerac treats the myth in an amusing manner. Descending into Hell in a dream, he describes Jason who is amazed to find himself in a throng of Spanish courtiers whose activities are entirely centred around obtaining the Golden Fleece.

Corneille wrote a tragedy, *La Conquête de la Toison d'Or* (1660), in which he modified the ending of the legend. Aeëtes is afraid that his many enemies will steal the Golden Fleece from him:

> 'This treasure to which the Gods have linked our destiny
> And which many jealous neighbours are trying to usurp.' (I, 2.)

The arrival of Jason, who fights alongside him, enables him to conquer and preserve this talisman on which is royal destiny depends. The gods have made his power dependent on his possession of the Fleece. To reward Jason, he promises to grant the hero's every wish, but Jason wants to gain possession of the Fleece. Aeëtes refuses to grant the wish, but his oath obliges him to allow Jason to try to obtain it. Medea reveals the dangers that await whoever dares to lay hands on the Fleece and Juno advises Jason to win Medea's love as she will be able to counter the magic spells protecting the Fleece. But Jason has promised to marry Queen Hypsipyle and still loves her. He hesitates between her and Medea who retains her sense of duty:

> 'I will not betray my country and my father;
> The destiny of the State depends upon the Fleece.' (II. 2.)

Jason emerges victorious from the trials. But Medea, who is passionately in love with him, is vexed by the fact that he does not prefer her to Hypsipile and seizes the Fleece in order to provoke Jason into choosing between love and glory! He must either give up the Fleece out of love for Medea or kill her to gain possession of it. Jason submits and withdraws to his ship. He has renounced glory for love. Then Medea (Corneille borrows this detail from Denys le Milésien) brings him the Fleece. The hero has renounced his heroic ideal for love, but for Medea, love and glory are synonymous.

More recently, the Austrian writer, Franz Grillparzer, has produced a very free adaptation of the myth in his trilogy *Das Goldene Vliess* (1818–21). He based his three plays on the idea that the Golden Fleece will continue to bring ill fortune to whoever possesses it as long as it is not returned to the Temple of Delphi from whence it was stolen. *Der Gastfreund* tells the story of Phrixus who takes refuge in the Temple of Delphi and is told in a dream to seize the Fleece and carry it off to Colchis. While staying as the guest of King Aeëtes, he is killed by his host, who takes possession of the Fleece. The king's daughter Medea predicts the disastrous consequences of the crime. *Die Argonauten* tells the story of Jason's expedition to bring the Golden Fleece back to Greece. Aeëtes is unable to rely on his daughter because she has fallen in love with Jason and saves his life. With her help, Jason gains possession of the Fleece and leaves for Greece, taking Medea with him. *Medea* is set several years later. Having borne him two children, Medea realizes that Jason is about to reject her. She manages to destroy her rival, Creusa, and the palace. She then kills her own children to prevent them being taken into slavery. Jason is exiled and, as he leaves, Medea shows him the Golden Fleece which she is going to return to the Temple of Delphi. The Fleece is an evil talisman which has always brought misfortune. The transgression of an interdiction does not go unpunished. The sacred should remain beyond the reach of men.

Yves-Alain Favre

The Golem

The myth of the Golem grips our attention for various reasons. First, it belongs to the category of 'biblical' myths, and, as such, embodies the nostalgia for our origins and the feeling of proximity to the sacred that, according to Mircea Eliade, lie at the basis of myth in general. Then again, it is derived from the Old Testament, and therefore linked with Jewish mysticism and, in a broader context, with Hebrew culture. The myth arose in the countries of eastern and central Europe (such as Poland, Czechoslovakia and Russia) where the Jews settled after the Diaspora, but it was in Germany that it really took root. Thus it occurs frequently in German literature, and can also be found in works written in Hebrew or Yiddish. By contrast, it is relatively little known in Great Britain. The whole story is replete with wisdom: the paradoxical lesson of the Golem is that it may sometimes be a greater sin to create than to destroy. Whether creating an artificial being is a Promethean act or a sacrilegious transgression, it is fraught with danger. Finally, the story of the Golem provides us with the opportunity of following the development of a literary myth in specific detail. Religious exegesis and popular legends form indispensable stepping stones leading to the evolution of purely poetic forms of expression.

SOURCES IN THE BIBLE AND THE CABBALA

Unlike the story of the Wandering Jew, the myth of the Golem has relatively little basis in the Bible. The legend comes not from a story, but from a single word, and the way in which it has been interpreted by the Jewish mystical tradition.

Psalm 139

The word *golem* appears for the first time in Psalm 139 (16). The psalm itself is generally taken to represent the words of a man thanking God for making him, and recalling the different stages of his creation: 'Thy eyes beheld my *unformed substance [golem]*'. The word *golem* is used here in its normal Hebrew sense meaning 'embryo'. However, from a very early time, some commentators have maintained that the speaker is Adam himself and that he is reliving the relevant episodes of Genesis. In that event, the term *golem* would take on further connotations. It would denote a formless lump of earth, the inert matter from which Adam's body was moulded before the divine *pneuma* was breathed into it, a piece of earth not yet inhabited by the spirit, waiting to be turned into a living being by the breath of life.

Talmudic Literature (Second to Fifth Century)

These concepts were developed during the Talmudic period. The word *golem* was applied to anything that was in its primitive, unrefined state, and to anything that was in the process of turning into something. There were those who regarded the clay from which Adam was kneaded as full of potential, already containing his hidden light. However, most of the Talmudic commentaries (Midrashim) continued to associate the idea of *golem* with the story of Genesis, while at the same time portraying a special image of Adam. This Adam (the first Adam, the Adam who predated the Fall) is described as androgynous and huge in size. He is the primordial man of the cabbala (Adam Kadmon), the hero of the episode relating to the cosmogony, a cosmic being capable of expanding to the size of the universe, a sort of macrocosm condensing within himself the whole of creation (macranthropos). Predating the world of the spirit, the concept of *golem* is part of the corporeal principle. Before he was animated by the breath of life, Adam was closely associated with the dark, mysterious power of the earth (*adamah*). In the Haggadah the telluric weight of the first man is contrasted with the lightness of the divine breath, and it is even maintained that it took all the earth in the universe to make him! By extension, the Golem came to be seen as prefiguring the succession of human races that followed.

The Dark Ages (From the Fourth Century) and the Middle Ages (Twelfth-Thirteenth Centuries)

This was the period when the cabbala exerted its greatest influence, through the *Book of Creation (Sepher Yezirah)*. A multiplicity of combinations of numbers and letters was used to develop a 'recipe' for creation, the underlying principle being that as emanations of divine power letters also constitute the 'signature' of things, and that combinations of letters hark back to the structure of the cosmos. Various accounts and commentaries on this book relate how, after taking part in magic rituals, rabbis succeeded in creating a Golem. However, the Golem is never actually described – it remains an abstract entity. It is real only insofar as it is the object of a mystical experience that can even amount to ecstasy and the product of a successful initiation that leads the Talmudist to an understanding of the secrets of the universe. The motif of the magic letter was already present at this point, but the Golem was also destroyed as soon as the creative power of the rabbi had been demonstrated:

> Jeremiah and his son Ben Sira, with the help of the *Book of Creation*, created a Golem, and on his forehead was written: (*aleph*) [*a*]*emeth*, truth, like the name

which God pronounced over his creature to show that his creation was finished. But the Golem rubbed out the first letter to show that God alone is truth, then died.

Hasidic Judaism in the Rhineland placed a special emphasis on demiurgic practices, and Eleazar of Worms has left a famous description of such a ceremony, recounting how a group of three or four rabbis go about creating a Golem. The process involves going round the figure a certain number of times reciting certain formulas, while to make the body, they bake water and clay, and breathe on to it ritually . . . However, the dangers of such an act of creation, which would put Man on an equal footing with God, were already stressed. The fact that the Golem could not speak indicates that it belonged to a lower, imperfect form of creation, resulting from an act involving lack of moderation, and transgression. The threats that hovered over the cabbalist came from the very core of his work. There was the danger that the Golem might take up arms against its creator, the danger that the demon (Samael or Lilith) might slip into this empty husk, imbuing it with the power of evil, and the danger that the Golem might degenerate into an idol . . . During the Renaissance, Paracelsus was probably inspired by these Hasidic writings when he developed his concept of the *homunculus* (formed in a test tube from a mixture of earth and water).

Progressing several centuries, it is in this light that we should view the passage concerning the Golem in Thomas Mann's *Joseph und seine Brüder* (Part II, *Der junge Joseph*, 1934). In it, Jacob is inconsolable at the disappearance of his son Joseph, whom he believes to be dead, and ponders on ways of bringing him back to life 'using mystical practices'. He then has the idea of making a creature from earth and water to replace him, and, the ritual that he follows faithfully reflects that in the Judaic tradition. As in alchemy, the elements are regarded as very important. By virtue of the breath of the father, which is assimilated to fire, a real transmutation takes place, and the description finishes with the vision of the child opening his eyes. However, the experiment is regarded from the outset as belonging to the domain of dreams and sacrilegious practices and is condemned forthwith, as was the descent into hell that preceded it.

THE POPULAR LEGENDS

The legend of the Golem that has inspired writers is known to us in two forms, which differ considerably from one another and are already highly dramatized.

The Polish Version

This is the earlier of the two forms of the story, and is associated with Rabbi Elias Baalkschem, who died at Chelm in Poland in 1583. It spread further afield in the sixteenth and seventeenth centuries, and the earliest formal written version that survives dates from 1674. This form, which is the closest to the original scheme of the myth, was the one used by the German Romantics during their efforts to revive mythological tales. Achim von Arnim (*Isabella von Ägypten*) and Jacob Grimm (*Die Golemsage*, 1808, quoted below) give the following account:

> After reciting certain prayers and fasting for a prescribed time, the Polish Jews shape a man from clay and bird lime and if they say the miraculous *Schemhamphoras* (the name of God) over it, it should come to life. Admittedly it cannot speak, but it understands perfectly well what is being said and what it is ordered to do; they call it 'Golem' and employ it as a servant to perform all kinds of household tasks. On its forehead is written the word *aemaeth* (*Emeth*, truth), and it grows ever larger – while to start with it is small it rapidly becomes bigger and stronger than everyone else living under the same roof. It is for this reason, because they are afraid of it, that they rub out the first letter so that only *maeth* (*Meth*, meaning he is dead) is left – whereupon the Golem collapses and reverts to clay.
>
> One man was careless enough to let his Golem go on growing, and it became so big that they could not even reach its forehead. Through fear, the man then ordered his servant to take off his boots, thinking that when it crouched down he would be able to reach the forehead. The stratagem was successful, and the first letter was rubbed out without difficulty; but the whole weight of the clay fell on top of the Jew and crushed him.

It is clear that the myth has undergone a profound change. The emphasis is no longer on its mystical aspect and on the process of creation, whilst, conversely, the motif of the *schem*, the magic word, has become increasingly important, and the Golem, which is still dumb, has become a servant or famulus. Its inexplicable growth, which is seemingly so hard to control, contains a latent danger and reflects a hidden power, while the rabbi in the end becomes the victim of the creature that he has created and is punished for his illicit deed. In the context of a critical interpretation of the myth (*Erklärung der sogenannten Golem in der Rabbinischen Kabbala*, 1814) Clemens Brentano presents a poeticized version of it, in which the servant threatens to become a 'tyrant' controlling its master. In addition, the author uses the short commentary that follows to expound the Romantic view of the myth, which is characterized by its emphasis on symbolism and on the story's moral significance:

> This fable is a myth that does not lack depth. All false, external art in the end brings down the master who created it . . . Only true art which is creation itself is eternal; only a great artist is always superior to his work and capable of

achieving the *emeth* that is inscribed on the forehead of the creature Man has made in the human image.

The Prague Version

This version of the myth, which is by far the better known only became current much later at the beginning of the nineteenth century. It introduces the figure of the famous cabbalist Rabbi Löw (1512–1609), placing him in the unusual setting of the Prague Ghetto. In his novel *Spinoza* (1837), Berthold Auerbach gives a comprehensive account of the new form of the legend, in which the various themes are differentiated out to a notably greater extent and a number of supplementary motifs have also appeared. Rabbi Löw creates a Golem to help him in his household tasks. He brings it to life, no longer by combining the four elements, but through the magic power of a parchment, which he slips into the back of its head after making an opening in its skull. Every Friday evening the rabbi removes the parchment, and the Golem reverts to being lifeless clay. However, one Friday the cabbalist forgets to do this and while everyone is at the synagogue, the servant goes berserk and starts to destroy everything around it. The rabbi is alerted, and manages to snatch the parchment from the Golem's head, whereupon the Golem collapses lifeless at his feet. Around 1850, several authors took up this scenario, and though they were careful to remain faithful to popular sources, they nonetheless introduced some variations. In a poem written in 1842, (*Der Golem des Hoch-Rabbi Löb*) A. Tendlau describes the Golem as an 'idiot' endowed with exceptional strength. After destroying it, the rabbi buries the remains in the synagogue granary. By contrast, the servant in G. Philippson's poem (*Der Golem*, 1841) is a spectral creature, and his frenzied delirium summons up the spirits of the dead. Meanwhile, in other accounts, the magical parchment is slipped between the Golem's teeth or below its forehead rather than into the back of its skull. Nonetheless, whatever alterations are made, we can still discern the continued existence of a highly structured dramatic nucleus at the heart of all these versions of the story. The anecdote is related to the Jewish liturgy and the recurrence of the Sabbath. Here, it is the rabbi who overcomes the golem, while his own lack of moderation is no longer punished by death. The motif of the Golem running amok is developed considerably, and in the work of some writers its rebellion even endangers the entire world.

'The Book of Wonders'

Starting from this model, the Jewish tradition went on to invent a great number of varied stories. A new version of the Prague story, which was to become familiar to writers at the turn of the twentieth century, appeared in 1846 in a collection of Hebrew legends (*Die Galerie des Sippurim*) by

K. Weisel. Meanwhile, the events in the story of the Golem's life were multiplied in the works of Yudi Rosenberg (*Le Livre des miracles du Mah'Aral de Prague*, 1909), C. Bloch (*Israël, der Gotteskämpfer*, 1922), O. Wiener (*Böhmische Sagen*, 1919), J. M. Bin Gorion (*Golem-Geschichten um Rabbi Löw*, 1921), as well as in the books of Martin Buber. The role of the Golem is reversed, and related very closely to the Jewish problem. According to the new tradition, the Mah'Aral created the Golem during the anti-Jewish pogroms to defend Jews against accusations of ritual murder that were being brought against them. The Golem plays the role of hero and protector of the ghetto, of saviour and Messiah even, and, as such, it can perform miracles. Thus it exposes the deceit of those who bring out dead children and pretend that the Jews have killed them, prevents a young woman from being converted to Christianity, and brings to light an act of adultery. It can make itself invisible, enter into contact with spirits, drive away demons and cure illness, while it is also invulnerable. With the completion of this phase of the myth's development, it is evident that much of its original density, pattern and religious significance has been discarded to make way for affected, melodramatic adventures of a fantastic or miraculous nature. Thus, in a children's story (*Wohin der Golem die kranken Männer bringen liess*, 1918) combining fairy-tale elements with Zionist nostalgia, I. Singer was able to give his imagination free rein. Here, the Golem is a benevolent miracle-worker, and effects the cure of four sick people by taking them to Israel, the land of Eden.

THE LITERARY MYTH

The myth began its literary history at a relatively late date – the beginning of the nineteenth century – while it came to prominence in relatively important works particularly during the Romantic period and around 1900 (with the *fin de siècle*, new Romanticism and Expressionism). Its rise thus coincided with periods during which the imagination was set free and during which there was much metaphysical soul-searching or questioning of what was held sacred. Nonetheless, it also features quite frequently in literature of the second half of the nineteenth century, albeit in minor works.

The Romantic Period

The Romantics used the Polish version of the myth, but treated it so freely that their account of the Golem ceased to bear much relationship to the original story. They retained the character of the Golem, but largely abandoned its dramatic context, integrating it instead into an entirely different narrative scheme. It occurs in a novella by Achim von Arnim (*Isabella von Ägypten, Kaiser Karls des Fünften erste Jugendliebe*, 1812) and in two tales by E. T. A. Hoffmann, *Die Geheimnisse* (1820) and *Meister Floh* (1822). Hoffmann actually used the term 'Teraphim' rather than Golem, but the definition that he gives of the figure implies an element of confusion. (Teraphim were clay figurines used by the Hebrews for oracular purposes. They were imported from Egypt and were often believed to have evil powers.)

The Golems in these works have nothing to do with mystical speculation, and belong instead to a fantasy world or wonderland, in the same way as a mandrake, someone who rises from the dead or an old witch. This universe has to do with doubles, or rather with replicas: in the works of both Arnim and Hoffmann, the Golem is a supernatural character who imitates a real person or is substituted for him or her in some amorous adventure. In *Die Geheimnisse*, the Golem is a handsome young man, Theodor von S., and a cabbalist has substituted him for a vain, elegant young nobleman who is in love with a Greek princess. The intention is to prevent the princess from reciprocating his love, and so escaping from the cabbalist. In Arnim's novella and in *Meister Floh* the Golem is a woman. Arnim's story recounts how the Emperor Charles V falls in love with Isabella, a young and beautiful gypsy, but she is fiercely guarded by the mandrake von Cornelius, which she herself has created. So that he can be free to meet her, the emperor commissions an old Jew to make a Golem (Bella) that looks like Isabella, and can take her place alongside the jealous freak. However, Charles V falls into his own trap and mistakes the false Isabella for the real one, who is sent packing. In *Meister Floh*, Peregrinus loves a beautiful Dutch girl, Dörtje, who behaves capriciously, and at the end of story, it is revealed that a Golem has sometimes taken her place. This motif of replication also featured much later in a novella by W. Rathenau (*Rabbi Eliesers Weib*, 1902). Here, a rabbi who is dissatisfied with his wife because she has borne him no children creates an artificial creature to take her place.

The Romantic Golem is a simulacrum, a disembodied figure with no tangible reality. Theodor von S. has none of the solidity of clay, but instead is sculpted from cork, and he walks hesitantly, with jerky movements. There is something in Dörtje's eyes in *Meister Floh* that is strangely lifeless and empty; Peregrinus is fascinated by her silver clothing, and experiences 'an icy shiver' caused by her 'electric heat'. Thus the Golem is always a base, incomplete or inferior creation. Like Theodor, Bella is 'remote-controlled', set in motion by a will outside herself and with no real autonomy; her head contains only what was in the mind of the Jew when he brought her to life. She has a memory but no 'spiritual aspirations'. As an illusory being, the Golem is ultimately very vulnerable, and all Golems are eventually exposed and destroyed. In *Die Geheimnisse* the princess's talisman is enough to make the false Theodor collapse into dust; while in Arnim's story, Isabella easily rubs out the word *aemaeth* on Bella's forehead, whereupon the replica immediately crumples, devoid of life. In this sense, the Golem embodies Man's original Fall. In the beginning, Man, being in the image of God, was theoretically capable of imitating divine creation; he only needed to know the right words. But when Man was driven out of Paradise and had only mediocre clay at his disposal, the Golem too became defective: it lacked the breath of *neschamah*, divine inspiration. Such is the theory propounded by the old Jew. Finally, in *Meister Floh*, Dörtje is depicted as breaking into grating laughter and starting to leap around in an unco-ordinated way. This behaviour, suggesting a mechanism that has started to malfunction, leads on to the themes of the automaton and the puppet, which became popular with the Romantics following Vaucanson's discoveries.

These Romantic Golems continued the process of loss of religious significance noted above, with magic taking over from mysticism. The demiurges here are strange, disturbing figures: the honorary clerk of the court, or the old Jew who is more or less a charlatan. In contrast to true mysticism, magic is the art of illusion, or even of mystification, and these Golems are actually the products of mysterious optical techniques. The mirror is the instrument that gives rise to life. To ensure that Bella will resemble her, Isabella has to look into a magic mirror located in a room devoted to optics; while the sorcerer in *Meister Floh* conjures the image of Dörtje out from a luminous mirror. At the same time, however, the mirror effects the passage from the real to the artificial. In it, the character can contemplate another self, more or less remote and distorted, which inevitably lays his or her own existence open to question. Thus, by placing a person opposite his or her reflection, and so opposing being and seeming, the Golem is also among the figures used to convey Romantic irony.

However, even at this point, the Golem did not completely lose its cosmic character. Magic is not just a pseudo-science: it is esoteric knowledge related to magnetism and astrology, and based on an intuitive insight into the relationships between things and the affinities that form the hidden web of the universe. In *Die Geheimnisse*, Theodor's counterpart is said to derive his apparent life from his capacity to arouse and tap into the secret forces of the universe. The sorcerer uses the Golem to deflect from himself the misfortunes that have been prophesied for him. According to his theory, the world is ruled by a dynamic based on opposites. Being a third force, the Golem acts as a principle of dissociation, and should be able to disrupt the maleficent system, making it possible to 'conquer the power of the stars'.

The replica is not just a double, it is a wicked, hostile double. The woman created by Rathenau's rabbi has absolutely no feelings or moral sense; she can neither laugh nor cry. Meanwhile, the Bella Golem in Arnim's story is invested with the passions of the old Jew: pride, sensuality and avarice. Unlike the mythical figure, which traditionally was formless and sexless, the counterfeit literary Golem has a definite sex and is invariably beautiful. It features mainly in seduction scenes with barely disguised baleful overtones. Substituted for a real person without his or her knowledge, it serves to deflect love felt for that person towards itself, stealing part of the person's individuality. In addition, the Golem embodies carnal temptation and eroticism. When confronted by Dörtje, Peregrinus experiences a feeling of guilt: he senses that she is distracting him from higher concerns and that the love that she has for him is not true love. The Golem can thus be regarded as an unconscious projection of the self torn away from the true individual. Isabella's repressed instincts and narcissistic impulses find expression in the Golem figure of Bella.

Nonetheless, the figure of the Golem was still imbued with a more metaphysical form of symbolism. In *Meister Floh*, the beautiful Dutch girl who exploits all her charms to the full is described as the 'serpent of Paradise', and the equation of Woman with the serpent refers us back, not this time to the creation of the world, but to the other aspect of Genesis, to the Fall. The sorcerer is a devilish being, who implements the cunning schemes of the Evil One. In the world of the Romantics, which was highly structured in terms of antagonistic powers, the Golem incarnated the 'power of darkness', the 'principle of error', the 'demoniac illusion'. When Dörtje combats Meister Floh, Peregrinus's diminutive adviser, the weight of the body is opposed to the transfiguring strength of nature and the spirit. Thus Peregrinus himself (who is also King Sekakis) is addressed in the following words: 'Wretched King Sekakis, because you have neglected to understand nature, dazzled by evil charm and the cunning devices of the devil, you have contemplated the deceitful appearance of the Teraphim instead of contemplating the true spirit.' Echoing the earthly plot, there is also a 'story in the heavens', the realm of spirits, of the imaginary and of pure poetry. There, Dörtje has her counterparts in the hostile power of Famagusta, in Prince Egel, the terrifying vampire, and in the coarse genie Thetel. Meanwhile, she is the opposite of Rose, the ideal woman, the 'angel of light', who represents beauty and pureness of passion.

The symbolism of these stories is kept discreet, or at least is completely integrated into the logic of the world of marvels that they conjure up, but the same cannot be said for the Romantically inspired works that followed. In these, the motifs of the Golem's rigidity and lack of real life are retained primarily as devices to satirize society, while the allegorical element and often heavy-handed irony threaten completely to obscure the fable itself. The Golem represents Man with all his imperfections. In his novella, *Die Vogelscheuche* (1835), Ludwig Tieck turns it into a grotesque puppet, a leather scarecrow with crazy ideas who founds a secret society to defend bourgeois values. Subsequently Theodor Storm also used the image of the 'leather man' in his poem *Der Golem* (1851), as a device for criticizing bureaucratic immobility and conformism. Much later, this negative view of the Golem received even more pronounced emphasis. Thus, in his poem *Der Golem* (1882), L. Kompert stresses the instinctive brutality and thirst for destruction of Golems, whom he uses more or less overtly to represent anti-Semites. Finally, Annette von Droste-Hülshoff is the only writer to portray the Golem in a more poetic and original way, in her poem *Die Golems* (1844). Here, Golems are the spectres of ravenous time, dragging in their train the weight of destruction and death.

They impede the memory and thwart all efforts to recapture the world of childhood with its angelic innocence and enthusiasm.

Realism and Naturalism

During the second half of the nineteenth century the rationalizing process started by the Romantics was developed still further. A return to historical sources and an approach based on scientistic positivism were characteristic of the period, and writers tended to emphasize scientific or pseudo-scientific explanations of the myth at the expense of its mystical and irrational aspects.

The Prague version of the legend generally formed the basis for stories written at this time. Mention is made of the legendary visit paid by Rabbi Löw to Rudolph II, an emperor with a penchant for the esoteric and astrology. Meanwhile, there is a perceptible concern for historical reconstruction. Thus the persecutions of the Jews by the Christians, and the difficult relationship between the two communities, form the background to U. D. Horn's novella *Der Rabbi von Prag* (1842) and to Friedrich Hebbel's libretto for Anton Rubinstein's musical drama, *Ein Steinwurf* (1858). Here, the Golem once again became the rabbi's servant. Treated realistically, it is a dumb and often deaf colossus, which is compared to Goliath. The coarse creature is totally dependent on its master and passively obedient to him, and when it is not working, it crouches in a corner. Its material aspect is particularly emphasized – it is primarily a body without a soul, and is reduced to a subsidiary role, or even to the level of a fictional being. This may explain why it ultimately features so little in post-Romantic works.

Rabbi Löw takes on various guises, becoming a scholar, a physicist, a chemist, a doctor, or even an engineer or a clock-maker. He turns his back on the idea of transcendence, contenting himself with 'reading in the book of nature'. The Golem is the product of his faith in Progress, and its figure really forms part of a critique of the technological culture. Horn represents the servant as a kind of 'man-machine', a wooden figure with a clockwork mechanism in its head. The rabbi winds it up every Sunday and the Golem comes back to life, while on Fridays he presses a spring to stop it. But one day the worn spring breaks and the famulus goes berserk in the house, though its master does manage to regain control of it. Thus the Golem is an automaton, or, to be more precise, an android. In Horn's work it offers the illusion of real life for quite some time before being finally exposed (compare *L'Eve future* by Villiers de l'Isle-Adam written at about the same period) but technology frightens people when they do not understand it, and sometimes those living in the ghetto take the Golem for the devil.

Deprived of its dramatic presence, the figure of the Golem became an integral element in a type of plot stressing social problems and religious questions within the Jewish community. Horn describes the rabbi as a moderate person, full of humanity and wisdom; he is fighting for the emancipation of the Jews, for tolerance, for social equality and for freedom of expression. The central theme of the novella is a young nobleman's love for a Jewish girl; this love develops when the Emperor Rudolph visits the cabbalist, an encounter that allows the Golem to be introduced into the story. The love affair has a tragic ending, with the father, an orthodox Jew, killing his daughter to prevent her from marrying a Christian. In Hebbel's work the Golem appears for the first time as the saviour of the Jews and a kind of national hero. However, it is a completely imaginary saviour, invented by the rabbi to ward off the looters who are threatening his house and to protect his fellow Jews. In a different vein, the romances by L. Kalisch (*Die Geschichte von dem Golem*, 1872) use the motif of the unleashing of the Golem to condemn the pride of the cabbalist. At the start of the story, the writer conjures up a highly poetic image of the process of creation. However, faced with the brute force of his servant, its master realizes that he has been surpassed by his creation and recognizes that his work is sacrilegious. He then repents, does penance and is finally delivered by an angel disguised as an old man.

Some of these elements recur in the late nineteenth and early twentieth century in the work of authors who are more concerned with rational explanations of the myth than with literary forms of expression. At the start of G. Münzer's novel *Der Märchenkantor* (1908), the Golem is a marvellous creature, portrayed in a romantic, fairy-tale atmosphere, but, in the end, it is exposed as a marionette, controlled by very fine strings and guided on rails. Very much in keeping with the contemporary taste for decadence, C. Torresani's novella *Der Kiener* (1904), combines an interest in anatomical aberrations with fantastical effects. The Golem is an automaton, and its inside is described in detail. This consists of a completely empty clay cone, at one end of which there floats a piece of paper – a debased manifestation of the *schem*. There is little hint here of any technological nostalgia, and the picture of science that emerges, is somewhat ambivalent. In a different vein, M. Bermann's attempts to explain the Golem's violent behaviour in the novella *Die Legende vom Golem* (1883), amount to giving it a semblance of psychology. When creating it, the rabbi forgot to recite a magic formula and, as a result, the colossus is subject to fits of rage. Meanwhile, in his poem *Der Golem* (1898), Detlev von Liliencron gives a humorous description of the struggle between the master and his unleashed creation, and criticizes the rabbi's imprudence.

Though, in chronological terms, it belongs to the Expressionist period, the drama by J. Hess *Der Rabbiner von Prag* (1914) continues the tradition of the works just mentioned, picking up some of their motifs. The subject is tackled in a realistic fashion, with a mixture of amorous intrigue and action involving religious upheaval, while the historical setting is preserved. As in Hebbel's work, the story takes place during the persecutions of the Middle ages and the rabbi spreads rumours that he has a servant made of clay, who does not actually exist, in order to protect himself. The rabbi is eager to lend substance to his fiction and one day chances upon a Christian suffering from madness.

He 'awakens' the man to a new life and confers supernatural powers on him by placing the *schem* under his tongue. This new-style Golem then protects the Jews, and especially one particular girl, though in the end she succumbs to the blows of their persecutors. Finally, the servant relapses into madness, falls into his bad old ways and starts ravaging the ghetto.

FIN DE SIÈCLE AND THE START OF EXPRESSIONISM

During the Neo-Romantic period and the beginning of the Expressionist period the myth acquired considerable importance. It featured particularly prominently in novellas and drama, and was also adopted by the early cinema. The works in which it occurs are marked by the great literary trends of the turn of the nineteenth century: an emphasis on the need for transcendence and spirituality; a return to myth and symbol; stringent aesthetic demands; a penchant for the supernatural and for melodrama; an association between mysticism and eroticism; and an interest in psychic phenomena and the exploration of the depths of the soul. Writers of the Belle Epoque always used the Prague version of the story, featuring Rabbi Löw, though they sometimes also drew inspiration from supplementary episodes taken from the *Livre des Merveilles* and collections of popular legends. The Golem ceased to be an inferior double or a creature totally subservient to its master, acquiring an individuality and becoming human. It now took an active part in plots that were often dramatic and highly coloured. Amorous relations played an essential role in these and this time they were real.

One significant development was that the outer appearance of the Golem changed. The creature was still the rabbi's servant, but it was formed from a substance that was neither corporeal nor spiritual, and it cut a figure that was both primitive and exotic. In A. Holitscher's play *Der Golem* (1908), it combined huge stature with a livid complexion, steel hands and a fixed, empty stare. When it had nothing to do, it remained crouching in a corner like someone asleep; then, when given an order, it got up stiffly and moved in jerks. P. Wegener was inspired by several aspects of Holitscher's play, and made at least two films with the title *Der Golem*. Only the second, dating from 1920, has been preserved – along with a sort of commentary by the film-maker (*Der Golem, wie er in die Welt kam*, 1921). Wegener himself played the role of the clay colossus, which had a flat nose, slanting eyes and prominent cheekbones, and was dressed in the tunic of primordial man. Its appearance was based on the famous 'Mongolian type', which no doubt inspired Meyrink, while the heavy, rhythmic gait and the impassive face also reappear in A. Hauschner's novella *Der Tod des Löwen* (1916).

The setting for the myth ceases to be a simple backdrop and becomes an essential element of the story. Prague provides an especially evocative milieu, which lends itself to fantastic or strange effects and Hauschner tries to bring back to life the confused baroque atmosphere of the city on the eve of the

Thirty Years' War. The central character is surrounded by a constellation of mystical images. Gloomy neighbourhoods, a maze of narrow streets, unending stairways and huge mysterious buildings are conjured up in a three-dimensional way, as in Wegener's film, along with the teeming, phantomlike crowds. Because of the very origins of this town set at the meeting-point of two civilizations, Jewish life in Prague is influenced by the East. Münzer places the action of his story in a strange setting, portraying the rabbi as an old clock-maker dressed in Turkish garments who repairs 'living' clocks. In F. Lion's version of the myth (in the libretto of the musical drama *Der Golem* by Eugène d'Albert, 1926) the Golem is a kind of guardian angel that, according to legend, accompanies Jews on their travels. It thus becomes confused with the messianic figure of Ahasuerus, the Wandering Jew, popularized by the Romantic Movement.

Generally, however, the character of Rabbi Löw tends once again to be portrayed more or less in conformity with the mystical tradition. In his play *Der Golem* (1920) the Russian Yiddish writer Leivik depicts him beside the Moldau (River Vltava) kneading mud and water from which to form the Golem. In keeping with the Decadent taste for the supernatural and the occult sciences, the Mah'Aral is often portrayed as an alchemist or a magician. Thus Hauschner describes the 'alchemist's kitchen' in which Rudolph II receives the rabbi and in which spirits are conjured up. In a similar scene in Wegener's film, the rabbi invokes the demon Astaroth to give life to the clay, using the word meaning 'dispenser of existence', and Astaroth does in fact appear, amidst flashes of lightning and sulphurous fumes, in the form of a gelatinous, phosphorescent head. In addition, the idea of Golem's relationship with the cosmos at large is also retained, so that the creature can be created or destroyed only during certain conjunctions of the stars. However, the cabbalist appears in many different guises: while some authors portray him as an astrologer, others depict him as a noble, idealistic being, in pursuit of true knowledge. Well-versed in the *Zohar* and its theory of skins, the rabbi in Lothar's novella *Der Golem* (1900) tries to recapture the innocence of Adam. His idea is to create an artificial being and to project into it a soul that retains all its original purity, but this soul cannot come from nothing. In a clear reflection of the influence of oriental religions, Rabbi Löw believes in transmigration and breathes into a carefully prepared body of clay the soul of a living man who is in a deep cataleptic sleep. The almost perfect result produced by this procedure inevitably represents a challenge to the Creator. The rabbi, in his pride, is rivalling God: he is a modern Prometheus or an incarnation of the Nietzschean superman. At the same time the rabbi's creation of the Golem is an expression of his revolt against the human condition, and Holitscher is thus able to turn him into the mythical hero of the combat with the Angel of Death. However, 'stealing the sacred fire' is fraught with danger: right from the start of both Leivik's and Holitscher's works the wretched rabbi is portrayed as being assailed by doubt and tortured by metaphysical worries, while his desperate enterprise is depicted as being doomed to failure.

Since the body is the reflection of the soul, the Golem ceases to be portrayed as ugly and monstrous, and in a significant reversal of the myth, Lothar's Golem is a handsome, attractive young man. The same idealization (or transfiguration) of the character occurs in a ballad by H. Salus, *Vom hohen Rabbi Löw* (1903). Admittedly here, the man created from the clay still has a fixed impassive stare and never smiles. However, his youthful freshness and Herculean strength, combined with his propensity for hard work and his loyalty, are enough to make him attract the attention of the rabbi's daughter. The idea was not new – there was already an old tradition that alluded to the latter's love for the Golem, or to his love for her – and at the turn of the twentieth century most writers took up this theme of passion, making it the dramatic heart of the story. The exception is Wegener, whose film contains virtually no mention of love. In the work by Hess mentioned above, the Golem falls in love with his ward, a beautiful Jewish girl who eventually falls victim to anti-Jewish persecution. However, the affair can go no further: right from the beginning, as an automaton and a former Christian, the Golem must renounce all hope. Salus portrays the opposite scenario, in which it is the girl who quite spontaneously becomes enamoured of the handsome young man. The symbolism of the body without a soul is barely disguised, and harks back to the works of the Romantics: the Golem represents Eros and carnal temptation. Thus, to teach his daughter a lesson, her father orders the colossus to kiss her; in its roughness it almost breaks her bones and she is brusquely cured of her insane passion.

Other works introduce a supplementary character in the form of the fiancé. In Lothar's novella, the Golem once again fulfils the function of a substitute or double, but the theme of love is still related primarily to a mystical notion: the spirit gets the better of matter, and sensuality must give way to a more spiritualized concept of passion. Esther is engaged to a young man who is very worthy but very ugly and, to get his daughter to agree to marry him, her father has the idea of 'projecting' the soul of his future son-in-law into his servant. Drawn initially by the Golem's good looks, Esther later discovers his spiritual attractions, and when the soul of Elasar returns to his sleeping body (compare above) after the Golem has been destroyed, she continues to love the young Jew. By contrast, Holitscher's play adopts an entirely different approach: there, the daughter's fiancé returns home, and the Golem to some extent becomes his rival. While the young man talks to the girl, she and the Golem, who is seated in a corner, begin to feel love for one another. At this point a new myth theme appears. Abigail's love has a transfiguring quality and the power to bring about metamorphosis. As a result of this ardent, sensual passion, Amina progressively emerges from his vegetative state, learning to speak and acquiring a semblance of sensitivity and consciousness. Lion picks up this theme and enlarges on it, contrasting Léa, the primordial woman, the spiritual principle, with the Golem, the primordial man, the material principle. Through the power of love, and stirred by the girl's caresses, the Golem, which started off as an idiot, is transformed into a being capable of thinking and of experiencing emotions. The process whereby the opposing principles are brought together occurs in three stages. The first involves anger towards the Master; the second, the discovery of sexuality; and the third the discovery of human suffering.

The development of a complex personality is not always the result of passion, however. Especially in Wegener's work, but also in Holitscher's, the Golem is half-conscious of its own condition right from the beginning – it is 'the upsetting silhouette of an incomplete being *Halbwesen*, that is struggling to gain access to the world of feelings and become a human being'. This obscure realization of its condition makes it deeply aware of the tragic aspect of its existence. The images produced by Wegener convey its unsuccessful efforts to reach a higher level of perception and intelligence – for example, when it breathes in the scent of a rose, when it looks at a small fair-haired child, when it blindly touches the body of the rabbi's daughter. But its tragic inadequacy relates primarily to emotional and metaphysical matters. It is love, or its inability to experience love, that makes the Golem sense that it is different from other people. 'To be a man! To feel joy! To suffer!' Amina exclaims in Holitscher's play. The Golem is excluded from the world of pure thought and from the world of tenderness and love, and, as in Hess's play, it is prohibited from having any human contact. It thus becomes a marginal, solitary figure, a 'stranger to fate'. Indeed, it may even be a condemned creature eager for deliverance (Wegener) or a victim of science pleading for annihilation (Torresani).

As a consequence the Golem quite naturally became a rebel and Expressionist writers placed special emphasis on the tormented links binding the creature to his creator. In Leivik's play, while the Golem is still just a shadow, it asks the Mah'Aral not to create it, and subsequently it goes so far as to raise the axe that it is carrying against its creator. Thereafter, it drifts into the life of a wanderer and, as a new Messiah, it travels the world defending the poor against the oppression of the ruling classes. In Holitscher's play it curses the master who has made it in the form of an inferior creature, and refuses to open the door for him. Meanwhile, in Salus's ballad the Golem's rebellion is the expression of a pure, noble soul that cannot accept the finiteness of earthly existence. The outbreak of violence, resulting from pain or despair, often takes on apocalyptic dimensions. Thus Wegener's Golem reverts to primitive, almost monstrous animal behaviour. A long passage in the film depicts the havoc that it wreaks in the ghetto, throwing the rabbi's daughter's fiancé down from the top of the observatory, dragging Mirjam through the streets by her hair, hitting out at passers-by and setting the ghetto alight . . . In Torresani's work the episode takes on a fantastical character. From the start, the Golem is presented as a ghost. It then becomes a blind, uncontrolled force and turns into a devil spitting flames, tearing the rabbi to pieces and setting fire to his house.

The death of the rabbi does not always form part of the plot. However, in general, even if he is not confronted by the hostility of his servants he is at least confronted by the failure of his attempt at creation. Conversely, death is inherent in the Golem's very existence. But its destruction is no longer portrayed as something purely mechanical. Instead, it is made to seem more like a final test perhaps enabling the Golem to achieve complete humanity, or is depicted as the inevitable conclusion to a life of suffering or an impossible love. The Expressionists gave great dramatic intensity and a new mystical dimension to this theme, which forms the climax of the story. Holitscher's play is laden with passion to the very end. Pursued by her fiancé and realizing that her father is incapable of making the Golem into a complete human being, the rabbi's daughter throws herself out of the window. Then, with a demoniacal grimace the desperate servant also renounces existence by snatching the red amulet out of his own chest. The conclusion of Wegener's film is even more clear-cut. The Golem's life is conceived as a cursed existence in a world of mystery and suffering, subject to the arbitrariness of fearsome and uncontrollable forces, so that the death of the colossus is portrayed as bringing deliverance and salvation. This message is conveyed by the symbolism of the film's final images. After his fit of rage, the Golem reaches a meadow filled with light and covered with flowers where children are playing. One of the children removes the pendant containing the *schem*, whereupon the Golem becomes an inert mass and returns to nothingness. Is there a hereafter for the creature of clay? This is the question clearly raised at the end of the novella by Lothar, who is always more overtly mystical then the other writers. In accordance with the rabbi's theories concerning the exile of the soul, the Golem is invited to return to heaven by the angelic powers. However, the creature is torn between the spiritual principle and the material principle. Consequently, when it takes flight to return to the divine land of its birth, a force draws it downwards and it falls to the ground and shatters.

MEYRINK'S GOLEM

Written at the cross-roads between neo-Romanticism and Expressionism *Der Golem* (1915) by Gustav Meyrink deserves special attention. The novel is set in the Prague ghetto at the beginning of the twentieth century and the main part of the story is presented as the narrator's dream. Not unnaturally, Meyrink mentions the Prague version of the myth, and reproduces it extremely faithfully, but it is actually a different form of the legend that serves as the basis for the novel. According to this account, which no doubt belongs to a later tradition, if it is not the author's own invention, the Golem is a kind of ghost, the spirit of the ghetto, an exotic apparition, 'a totally foreign being'; it is hesitant of gait, with a yellow skin, slit eyes and no beard, and is enveloped in tattered clothing. A person may come upon it unexpectedly round a bend in the road, but as soon as it is recognized, it mysteriously vanishes or shrinks. It is linked to the fantastic topography of the ghetto. People say that it lives in the area around the Old-New Synagogue, in an inaccessible room with only a single window opening to the outside. One day a man tries to look into the room by dangling from a rope, but the rope breaks and he is shattered on the ground. A friend of the hero of the dream story recounts several appearances by the Golem in different forms. These appearances are believed to occur every thirty-three years, recalling the myth of the Wandering Jew. Anyone who witnesses such an appearance loses consciousness or suffers an epileptic fit. The hero of the story within a story, the goldsmith Pernath who, we learn, has been mad but is now cured, will also come face to face with the Golem on several occasions. The Golem appears in different forms that are often disturbing and misleading, and sometimes there is even a residual ambiguity. However certain characteristics usualy make it possible to identify the mythical being and trace his successive transformations. For example, he appears as a stranger with slit eyes and an odd gait who brings a mysterious book to be repaired, and as a puppet that is being carved. Then he is associated with a playing card – the Fool in the tarot pack – and later with the completely fanciful and enigmatic figure in the 'dream about the corn' , a wide-shouldered creature with his head lost in a mist and a white stick in his hand. The 'Mongol type' of Golem is most clearly represented by the murderer of a girl, with whom Pernarth finds himself in prison. Finally, the Golem is no doubt also represented by the old servant in court dress in the main story, who opens the door to the enchanted world for the narrator. In addition to the theme of the successive appearances of the Golem, there is also a love story, since Pernath falls for the beautiful Mirjam, the rabbi's daughter. This raises the question of whether Pernath himself is the Golem, or, alternatively, the Golem's rival.

Because of the wealth of suggested meanings and the importance of symbolism the book can be read at three levels: the fantastical, the psycho-critical and the esoteric. Traditionally *Der Golem* is classified as a fantasy. Pernath relives the mythical adventure of the unwise busybody whose rope broke when he was opposite the mysterious window. But is this a simple dream dreamt by the narrator, or does the dream have some element of reality? We do not know, any more than we know if Pernath is really mad, or if the Golem might not actually be a ghost, a supernatural being of course, but one with the unquestionable ability to manifest itself in an objective manner. There is an abundance of strange and disturbing elements in the story. To begin with, the Golem itself undoubtedly creates a threatening atmosphere that hovers over the Jewish district – it frightens people. Likewise, certain beings, such as the antiquarian, Wassertrum, seem to be endowed with demoniac powers. Meanwhile, the ghetto is a labyrinth, which, like the Golem itself, can be transformed in a diabolical way. The room with no entrance in which Pernath finds himself a prisoner after a long journey underground and where the combat with the Fool takes place is an example of the sort of trap that it can form, while we are explicitly told that the Golem is a kind of vampire that feeds off the spiritual substance of the inhabitants of the Jewish quarter. In addition, all the misfortunes that befall Pernath may also be due to the Golem's baleful influence. The novel ends in an apocalyptic scene in which the goldsmith's house mysteriously catches fire, and the suspicion springs to mind that the Golem may have caused the blaze by magic means.

On the other hand, the constant allusions to dreams, madness, hallucination and visions, and the dreamlike quality of the images are clear indicators of a disturbed psyche – and Meyrink was familiar with the works of Freud and Jung. Here again the Golem is a projection of the unconscious, a figure representing the Double; but, unlike in the works of the Romantics, it is a Double whose ambivalence is emphasized. Sometimes it is the schizophrenic, terrifying Other, the Adversary; sometimes a kindly, helpful being, assisting people in distress. In addition, it becomes apparent that the fantastic metamorphoses of the Golem accompany or set in train an oscillating process involving the destruction and restructuring of consciousness. Thus, when the puppet carved by Pernath's friend turns towards Pernath, it reveals his own grimacing, worried face, and the goldsmith feels as if he is being transported inside this object that is drawing life from his own being. The same phenomenon recurs in the episode involving the tarot card, when it is evident that 'the point shining like an eye' that is fixed on Pernath during the staring duel and that starts to grow, is a metaphor for a tormenting conscience and for the instinctive appeal of Death. In contrast, the need for life and hope is expressed through the mouths of Rabbi Hillel and the ancestor in the dream about the corn – and indeed, through that of the murderer, though here there is much greater ambiguity. The evil self is contrasted with these idealized characters, who are nostalgic incarnations of a sublimated self. In a parallel development, the angelic figure of Mirjam is opposed to that of the femme fatale, the temptress or the woman of the world. On this second level, Meyrink's novel may be seen as an account of a process of individualization, a mental transformation whereby the hero integrates opposed images and so rediscovers his Self (the hermaphrodite on the mother-of-pearl throne).

Finally, a very obvious form of esoteric symbolism is grafted on to the phantasmic world of dreams. Thus, the silhouette in the dream about the corn represents Thoth/Hermes, while throughout the novel, the Golem plays the role of a spiritual guide. Similarly, Pernath's different visions or hallucinations amount to a series of trials or revelations defining the stages of a initiatory process. The underground wandering that precedes the battle with the Fool is in fact a necessary journey, a form of test, marked out with geometric signs evocative of Free Masonry. The tarot cards – the Fool and the Hanged Man – are material representations of the stages in a process of spiritual alchemy that opens up the way of rebirth through successive deaths.

Much attention is devoted to Hebrew tradition with its rituals and its emphasis on the symbolism significance of letters. The ceremony when the lights are inverted constitutes an important landmark in the process of illumination. Thus the Golem can appear simultaneously as the messenger of the unconscious and as the mystical double (in Nerval's sense of the word) in any case, as a messianic creature whose coming is announced. The Golem is:

> the true double, the one that is called 'Habal Garmin', the 'breath of the bones' [and of whom it is said] Thus he descended into the tomb, and thus he will arise on the day of Judgement . . . He lives very high above the earth in a room with no door . . . The person who succeeds in charming . . . and taming him will be reconciled with himself.

The novel is thus able to conclude on a happy note, with the vision of the mystical union of Mirjam and Pernath.

Meyrink's work had a great impact. In his novella 'Spuk' *Phantasien zur Nacht*, 1922) H. Nottebohm created a scenario in which the horrific vied with the fantastic. Rabbi Löw, a new Wandering Jew, must drink the blood of a Christian every hundred years to restore his youth. On each occasion he creates a Golem, which he uses to commit a murder in his place and which he destroys immediately afterwards. Meyrink's influence is also perceptible in the film *Le Golem* by J. Duvivier (1936) starring R. Karl, in the role of the Golem, and H. Baur. In addition, there are frequent references to the German writer's novel in twentieth-century literature. Thus E. Triolet (*L'Age de Nylon, II L'Ame*, 1963) gives an abbreviated account of the second state of the legend and the story of the room with no entrance in the surrealist framework of a story about animated objects and childhood, and of reflections on the relationship between technology and poetry.

Since the Second World War, the Golem has appeared increasingly rarely, though the theme has been revived to a significant extent quite recently in works that have appeared as a legacy of the Diaspora and that tend to go back to the popular sources of the myth. Thus the Golem resumes its role as a saviour of the Jews in D. Meltzer's poem *The Golden Wheel* (1967), A. Rothberg's novel *The Sword of the Golem* (1970) and F. Zwillinger's play *Maharal* (1973). Meanwhile, in the poem *Einem, der vor der Tür stand* (1964) the story of the servant prompts P. Celan to meditate on the difficulties of creation and the power of words. By contrast, E.-E. Kisch 'buries' the Golem as early as 1925, in the novella *Dem Golem auf der Spur*. Setting out from Russia on the advice of an old Jew, the journalist looks in vain for its legendary remains, first in the synagogue granary, then in the poor districts of Prague. Finally, in the poem *El Golem* (1958), J. L. Borges casts a sceptical, distant eye over the rabbi's work, enquiring whether the Golem is not just another aberration in the skein of human sufferings, a cumbersome and useless toy that we contemplate with a mixture of tenderness and horror. Be that as it may, the real question that wells up from between the lines is this: is a fantasy about the naive adventures of a slightly crazy rabbi and his clumsy servant made of clay still relevant in an age of robots and mutants? The near future will no doubt decide whether the story will continue to inspire writers, or whether, with the transition from the 'mystical imagination' to the 'technological imagination' we are in the process of witnessing a change of myth.

Catherine Mathière

The Grail

The literary history of the Grail began around 1200 with a period of creative activity that produced numerous surviving texts. These included several indisputable masterpieces, such as the romances by Chrétien de Troyes and Wolfram von Eschenbach and the anonymous *Queste del Saint Graal*, and the tradition thus established persisted up to the end of the Middle Ages. Certain major texts were printed at the beginning of the Renaissance, and though some were reworked, they were not distorted. However, their faithful preservation was also, paradoxically, the cause of their progressive neglect, with the result that during the Classical period, the story of the Grail was virtually unknown.

Although it was revived during the Romantic period, this was a very gradual process. It was absolutely indispensable that the early texts should be edited and this was a huge undertaking that could not be accomplished in the space of a few years. As a consequence, the poetical works inspired by the Grail at this time belong to the second half of the nineteenth century. Two stand out in particular – Tennyson's *Idylls of the King* and Wagner's *Parsifal* – and twentieth-century literature is still greatly indebted to both.

THE TEXTS AND THEIR HISTORY

Since any earlier tradition, whether written or oral, is now inaccessible to contemporary readers, the poem by Chrétien de Troyes entitled *Perceval* or the *Conte du Graal* (*c.* 1185) marks the absolute beginning of the tradition. Nothing is known about the 'book' on which the poet claims to have based his work and it is even questionable whether it ever existed, in the same way that unanswerable questions have been raised about the poem by Kyot le Provençal that Wolfram von Eschenbach maintained had inspired him to write his *Parzival* (c. 1210). It is even possible that Kyot himself never existed: we shall probably never know.

Nor shall we ever know how Chrétien intended to complete his poem, which he left unfinished in the middle of an episode. Four continuations have been handed down to us, together amounting to nearly 60,000 lines. Some of the narrative material used in these can be found in other texts on the Grail which will be considered in due course – those attributed, rightly or wrongly, to Robert de Boron and Walter Map. The questions raised by these continuations are: where did their material come from, did Chrétien know about it, and did he intend to use it?

Many questions have also been asked about the short Welsh romance entitled *Peredur ab Evrawc*. The text, which is difficult to date, echoes themes that were also used by Chrétien and seems to have been inspired by *Perceval*, before being modified by the introduction of completely original episodes.

It is quite evident that Wolfram too relied heavily on the work of the poet from Champagne, even though he accused him of being ill-informed. This type of denigration was common at the time. He managed to bring his own work to a successful conclusion, but not without incorporating a great deal of oriental material, which raises the question of whether this new subject matter was the product of his imagination and of his reading, or whether it derived from actual contacts with the East as a result of the Crusades.

Whatever the answer, all these texts have one thing in common: the story is told from the standpoint of the hero. In fact, they could all be called 'Perceval romances'. This perspective means that the narrative is structured in the form of an enigma in which the innocent man sees a wonderful spectacle almost by chance. Having refrained from showing his amazement and from asking a single question, he then goes in search of the Grail to discover exactly what it is, and has the most varied adventures on the way.

Seen in this light, the subject matter seems to justify the retrospective technique that the authors employed in their poems with a greater or lesser degree of skill. The sub-plots proliferate, especially those in which Gawain is the protagonist, while the list of episodic figures grows in an alarming manner. Similarly, the hero himself delivers countless thrusts of the sword, saves many victims and fights a plethora of evil characters before finally becoming king of the Grail.

The second feature uniting these works is that the story being told is relatively independent of the world of Arthurian legend. Arthur and his court are certainly always present, but the former as a witness, even a spectator, and the latter as a place where people constantly come and go, or stay only briefly, a distant point of reference. The Perceval romances are romances about a single individual.

The poem by Robert de Boron, *L'Estoire du Graal* (*c.* 1200), and the prose trilogy derived from it, seem to be quite different in character. The poet starts his story from the very beginning. The Grail is the chalice which was used at the Last Supper and in which Christ's blood was collected, while the Spear is the one that pierced Christ's side on the cross. Preserved by Joseph of Arimathea, the secret disciple, the Grail is taken to Brittany. Merlin the prophet knows its history and has the Round Table made as a replica of the table on which the Last Supper was celebrated and of the one used by Joseph for the Grail service. Perceval's adventure is the continuation and conclusion of this long story, and the novelistic prose trilogy is actually structured in three parts: *Joseph*, *Merlin* and *Perceval*.

Thus the narrative scheme no longer takes the form of a progressive revelation. There is no longer an enigma, and, rather than discovering the world, the individual seems to be performing a role that has long been predetermined. Meanwhile, the work itself is presented as the fulfilment of a prophecy. This may explain why it is less elaborate than either the body of material formed by Chrétien's romance and its continuations, or even the poem by Wolfram. It is apparently the first work to give the legend a Christian interpretation – though this still remains to be proved – and thus tends to attach greater importance to the story's meaning than to creating a profusion of adventures.

Robert de Boron's work is also distinguished from the Perceval romances by the way in which it deals with the Arthurian subject matter. Instead of taking the Grail adventure as one episode among thousands chosen from the countless legends involving Arthur's companions, it incorporates historical information about the king, derived from the chronicles. However fanciful Geoffrey of Monmouth's *Historia Regum Britanniae* or Wace's *Brut*, which was inspired by it, may now appear to be, these works paint an historical portrait of Athur. They depict a statesman and a warlord imposing his power on rebellious vassals, strengthening his royal prestige, waging war on and conquering distant lands (including Rome), and finally being defeated and killed while fighting against his treacherous nephew Mordred, to whom he had entrusted his kingdom during his absence.

Robert de Boron subordinated these events punctuating the history of Arthur's reign to his own fiction. The story unfolds as if the Round Table had no other function than to commemorate other more renowned tables, and as if, once the quest for the Grail was accomplished, Arthur had nothing better to do to preserve his worthless prestige than to involve himself in campaigns that were dazzling but ultimately disastrous. The Grail adventure was the culmination of the story of the Arthurian empire.

A similar idea is found in the vast body of prose implausibly attributed to Walter Map and still referred to under his name for pure convenience, except by those who prefer the somewhat unsatisfactory practice of referring to it as the *Lancelot-Graal*. This comprises three romances, which, despite being self-contained, are closely related: an extremely voluminous *Lancelot*; *La Queste del Saint Graal*; and *La Mort le Roi Artu*. The last describes the magnificent death throes of the world of Arthurian legend, following the successful conclusion of the most noble of all conceivable quests, the quest for the Grail.

Despite the fact that the three romances are clearly by different authors, who must have written them between 1210 and 1220, the unity of the project is outstanding. Its aim was to establish a link between the noblest knight in the world, Lancelot, and the knight who would accomplish the quest for the Grail. To this end, Perceval was relegated to a secondary role, in favour of a newly invented character, Galahad, the son of Lancelot, and the young woman who looks after the Grail. The most perfect knight on earth is tainted by his love for Queen Guinevere and superseded by his son, who is the epitome of purity.

Thus, throughout the work, the reader witnesses substantial changes in the treatment of the narrative. Initially, the story concentrates on Lancelot, describing his childhood, his first exploits and his love for the Queen against the background of Arthur's early campaigns. However, these wars are not the real subject of the story, and Arthur himself is more interesting as an individual than as the ruler of a kingdom. The profusion of individual adventures leads to a certain shift in perspective, so that we follow the progress of first one knight and then another, but a degree of unity emerges when the Castle of Corbenic, where the Grail is kept, is visited successively by Gawain, Lancelot and Bors. The theme of the Grail also has a unifying effect and, at the beginning of *La Queste*, all Arthur's companions depart together, leaving the king virtually alone. True, they soon go their separate ways and only three of them achieve their goal, but the precision with which this goal is defined creates a form of narrative that is very different from the one that predominates in the *Lancelot*, which occasionally resembles a mosaic of episodes.

The writer of *La Queste* further develops a device already used in the last pages of the *Lancelot*, whereby a sign is revealed through the deciphering of an allegory. To a certain extent, this recalls the device of the enigma employed by Chrétien, but its use has been extended, and it would be highly inappropriate to apply the term 'enigma' to these images, which subsequently reveal magnificent truths. The word 'senefiance' (significance) is not a synonym for 'solution'.

The writer responsible for organizing the work as a whole, who, one would like to believe, was also the author of *La Queste*, skilfully manipulates this system of premonitions and obscure revelations. This has the effect of focusing all the 'senefiances' on the Grail and its distant kingdom, from which neither Galahad nor Perveval return. Thus the quest is the ultimate adventure, after which Arthur's kingdom can only disintegrate. Individual exploits give way to the tragic epic of great battles in which the fate of empires is at stake. This terrible and necessary dénouement tends to be forgotten when the term *Lancelot-Graal* is used.

Like Robert de Boron and his successors, the pseudo Walter Map produced a general survey containing the basic elements of the Arthurian legend, dominated by the story of the Grail. Probably a little after its completion, this survey was extended – as if by a narthex – by the inclusion of two books, which were placed before it in the finished manuscripts: an *Estoire del Saint-Graal* and an *Estoire de Merlin*. In this way the fusion of the works of Robert de Boron and the pseudo Walter Map was accomplished up to a point, while the cycle provides a contrast with the Perceval romances described above.

These, then, are the texts that, for nearly three centuries, were recopied, enriched and abridged. Modifications to their details did not destroy the overall economy of their structures, and it is possible to recognize the work of Chrétien de Troyes and of some of the writers of the continuations in the *Perceval* published in 1530. The monumental compilation that its author, Sir

Thomas Malory, entitled *Le Morte Darthur*, draws on all kinds of source material, some of which no longer exists. However, the entire section dealing with the Grail remains very close to the *Lancelot* and *La Queste*, and sometimes appears to be a word-for-word translation. The early printed text of 1485, reprinted until 1634, gave English readers a magnificent and highly authentic account of the legend. Meanwhile, another author to benefit from the development of printing was Wolfram von Eschenbach, whose poem reappeared in Strasbourg in 1477.

At this point, everything seemed to favour the continuation of tradition. Yet, when Ronsard referred to King Arthur and Merlin, it was in a poem dedicated to the Queen of England, as if the world of Arthurian legend was no longer of interest to anyone in Europe. Similarly, although Arthur features in Spenser's *Fairie Queene* (1590–6), the author only attributes previously unrecorded adventures to him and gives him hitherto unknown companions, completely ignoring the Grail. The same approach was adopted by Dryden when he wrote his *King Arthur* (1584), which was set to music by Henry Purcell. People obviously knew who Merlin was, but did they still know of Lancelot?

French dictionaries occasionally included a short entry on the Grail. Following Furetière, the entries in the *Dictionnaire de Trévoux* and the *Encyclopédie* first referred to a relic preserved in Genoa and then mentioned that it appeared in 'the old romances'. It was written, not as 'Saint Graal', but as 'Sangréal' – the 'Sankgreal' of Malory – and was described as being sought by 'paladins', as knight-errants were called from 1550 onwards.

It was but a short step from the paladins to the tradition of the troubadour, a step that was taken by the Comte de Tressan, without much benefit to the Grail itself. In eighteenth-century Europe, mention of the ancient paladins evoked the images of Amadis (de Gaule) or Ariosto's Orlando rather than Gawain or Perceval.

By a strange coincidence, in 1784, barely a year after the death of the Comte de Tressan, Bodmer published part of Wolfram's *Parzival*. This edition, which was the first to have appeared for several centuries, was of poor quality, and it was not until 1833 that an accurate text, the Larchmann edition, became available to the public. In England a similar interval separated the first 'scientific' edition of Malory, published in 1856, from two earlier editions that had appeared in 1816 and another that had appeared in 1817. Finally, Robert de Boron's *Le Roman du Saint-Graal* was published in Bordeaux in 1841 by Francisque Michel, while *Perceval* and its continuations were published by Potvin in Mons in 1866–71. It is interesting that during the second half of the nineteenth century many French texts were published by British scholars: French readers seem to have been more interested in Charlemagne, following Fr. Michel's publication of the *Chanson de Roland* in 1837. Nationalism played an important part in the disinterested pursuit of rediscovering of early texts.

It is not without significance that Tennyson dedicated his vision of the perfect prince, the *Idylls of the King*, to Queen Victoria. The work, written between 1857 and 1885, consists of twelve poems, in other words, twelve juxtaposed episodes, and uses a technique reminiscent of both *La Légende des Siècles* and Malory's mosaic effect. Indeed, the episode entitled *The Holy Grail* published in 1869 drew freely on Malory's work, and therefore, through it, on the *Queste del Saint Graal.* The innovative modern feature that transforms the nature of the account, involves entrusting the task of narration to one character, Perceval, who often retells stories that he himself has heard. In this highly erudite work, the text puts the story into perspective and tends to present it in terms of something unattainable and infinite. Thus, in the absence of any definitive authority, the reader may wonder whether what the characters saw were really illusions. Perhaps the quest for the Grail represents a subjective and individualistic form of temptation calculated to disrupt the harmonious order established by the best of kings. Arthur does not participate in the quest and seems to wish that it had not taken place.

In *Merlin* (1832), Karl Immermann adopted the same idea, but went so far as to portray the quest as an organized expedition, led by Merlin, and also involving Arthur and Guinevere. When the prophet is seduced and imprisoned by Niniane, Arthur's troop loses its way in the desert, perhaps not far from the castle of the Grail, where Titurel, Perceval and Lohengrin reign.

These three names remind us that the daydream images of the German Romantics were inspired by comparatively late works such as *Lohengrin* and *Le Jeune Titurel*, which were reprinted even before *Parzival.* Indeed, it was *Titurel* that provided Görres with the description of the castle of the Grail that he reproduced and commented on in his *Christliche Mystik* (1836).

In *Lohengrin* (1848), Wagner represents the castle of the Grail as the domain of eternal happiness and portrays it as being in another, inaccessible, world. In *Parsifal* (1882), he adheres more closely to the original sources, building his drama around the illness suffered by Amfortas, king of the Grail, and around Parsifal's role as saviour. In this barren 'waste land', it is, in a sense, the Grail itself that must be saved.

Julien Gracq's play, *Le Roi Pêcheur* (1946), is deliberately based on the Wagnerian concept, which it is intended to call into question. Perceval's coronation would represent the end of all adventure, a fatal form of immobility. Thus it seems that the quest should never reach its conclusion.

T. S. Eliot may also have been thinking of the Wagnerian vision when he wrote *The Waste Land* (1921–2). In his 'arid plain', a desolate contemporary landscape, there is no Grail to be seen, but the poet himself deliberately stresses the allusion to the ancient story. Conversely, it should be noted that the image evoked is completely alien to the world of Arthurian legend.

In contrast, it was the Arthurian theme that tended to inspire other authors writing in English for an extremely diverse readership. Thus the Grail appears only as a subsidiary element in Marion Bradley's *The Mists of Avalon* (1982), where it fulfils a purely Tennysonian function, appearing in connection with the last offensive of the druid world against Arthur's Christianized kingdom. Meanwhile, in his film *Excalibur* (1981), John Boorman makes it a symbol of the king, perpetuating the old and possibly unintentional pun on the word 'San[k]greal' (which can be taken to mean 'royal blood').

Fittingly, this venerable theme, which attracted the most respectable of Victorian poets, has also been treated with humour. Examples of this approach are Jack Spicer's poem, *The Holy Grail*, published posthumously in 1975, and Tankred Dorst's strange drama, *Merlin* (1981). Following a German tradition dating back to the Romantic works of Tieck, the latter combines tragedy and farce, and constantly challenges the illusion of theatre. In addition, like Bradley's novel and the *Graal-Théâtre* (1977) of Florence Delay and Jacques Roubaud, it is based on a thorough knowlege of the early texts, which now seem to be as much a part of general Western culture as the poems of Homer.

THE MYTHICAL STRUCTURE AND ITS INTERPRETATIONS

Whatever flights of fancy revisers may have indulged in, either through innocence or malice, from the time of Wolfram onwards, it it true to say that Chrétien provided virtually all the fixed elements in the mythical tradition. Indeed, he may have been the first person to combine the story of an inaccessible talisman with that of an innocent individual who slowly gains worldly experience. What is certain, is that since he wrote his poem, these two elements seem to have been inextricably linked.

The word 'innocent' must, of course, be interpreted in its widest sense. Chrétien's Perceval is a sort of naive countryman, while Galahad is in every respect the perfect knight and might better be described as 'pure'. However, in both cases, the character does not belong to organized society. Perceval does not stay long in the places where he receives his – remarkably rapid – education, while Galahad is more solitary and even more unsociable than his father, Lancelot, because he pays no heed to courtesy and its 'fine flower', love. The knight of the Grail has always come from 'elsewhere'.

The Grail, is also 'elsewhere', in a castle that may be invisible, or in an inaccessible kingdom. The idea of hiding it in India, with the legendary priest John, is in keeping with the basic tenor of the myth, as is the oriental exoticism used extensively by Wolfram and adopted in a modified form by Wagner.

The magnificent ceremonies that these two authors describe in such detail, are also an extension of the simple procession described in Chrétien's work. The Grail is, first and foremost, an object used in a ritual, and this is perhaps the most important of all the constant elements in the myth. When a question is posed, it is not about the Grail itself, but about the purpose for which it is used. One should not ask what the Grail is, but rather who is served with it, which is equivalent to asking what is the destination of the procession.

The ritual nature of the story is also apparent in the idea of predestination, which is constantly in evidence. The hero cannot fail to accomplish the deeds that are expected of him, because he is the chosen one, for all eternity. His heredity does not account for everything. The story of the Grail is a family affair, even in the aberrant version given in *Peredur*, where the object carried by the procession is a dish containing the head of a man whose death must be avenged. But the Promise is not related to ties of blood. The hero's alternatives are limited: either, like Perceval, he is unaware of his calling and discovers it after making several mistakes; or, like Galahad, he is taught about it, and moulds himself to suit a predetermined plan. The theme of a mission remains constant through all the variant accounts. Only Julien Gracq suggests that the wandering life itself is the noblest form of mission, and that the redeeming venture is merely a delusion. In this respect, he can be compared with Chrétien, who endeavoured to leave his poem unfinished.

The legend of thc Grail presents a double form of ritual: a ritual that takes place somewhere else and a ritual that leads somewhere else. As Wagner realized, this is basically a theatrical device. The first and third acts of his opera portray characters walking through a place that cannot be found, followed by the vision of the Grail.

This device has been interpreted in various ways. Thus there have been attempts to identify the Grail by discovering its origins. Some scholars have taken Robert de Boron literally and are convinced that the legend is primarily Christian. Others, with good reason, have suggested that it might be based on a Celtic theme, which was later given a Christian interpretation. While these two hypotheses are useful in their own restricted context, they are of correspondingly little assistance in the literary analysis of the surviving texts. The Christian hypothesis encounters more than one obstacle, especially as regards the esoteric aspect of the adventure – for example, there are some Grail secrets that cannot be revealed to ordinary Christians. By placing a guard of Templar Knights around the Grail, Wolfram gives the impression that his own vision of the secret was not entirely orthodox. Even if the texts that do lend themselves to a theological interpretation are considered in a theological light, we still have the impression that the body of thought surrounding the Grail belongs elsewhere, somewhat on the fringe of accepted doctrines.

The Celtic hypothesis, which is probably the more convincing, is only of quite tenuous relevance in accounting for the various talismans that guarantee perpetual nourishment, cures, and even resurrection. Meanwhile, the absence of undisputed texts devoid of any trace of Christianization effectively prevents further progress.

Allegorical interpretations of the legend, which abound in commentaries on Wagner, tend to focus to a greater or lesser extent on the word 'ideal'. In spite of Baudelaire's arguments to the contrary, this may well seem less colourful than the rituals evoked by Chrétien and Wolfram. However, it was Baudelaire himself who produced one of the most extraordinary pieces ever written indirectly about the Grail, in the context of the prelude to *Lohengrin*.

Wagner describes this music as being a representation of the descent of the Grail, but Baudelaire contemplates it in a 'more vague and more abstract' manner. Nonetheless, this emphasis on abstraction does not prevent him from describing 'a sensation of spiritual and physical bliss' and 'the sensation of space extending to the farthest conceivable limits' (*Richard Wagner et Tannhäuser à Paris*). It is hardly surprising that this feeling of fascination, which is simultaneously physical and spiritual, leads to a quest. The poet is 'powerless to define' the new feeling that he has experienced and he writes: 'this impotence gave rise to feelings of anger and curiosity mingled with a strange delight'. This passage, which is appositely commentated on by Bachelard in *La Poétique de l'Espace* (177 ff), could be taken as the starting point for any literary analysis of the Grail texts. It enables us to understand why *La Queste du Saint Graal* does not end in colourless allegories, in spite of the obvious intentions of its author, why the description unceasingly draws on the imaginary, and why the book is not a treatise on mystical theology disguised as a romance. It is through Baudelaire that we can perhaps understand why the acknowledged ambiguity in Tennyson's poem was inevitable. This helps to explain the enigmatic nature of its final lines. 'Ye have seen what ye have seen. So spake the King: I knew not all he meant.'

The legend of the Grail is dominated by the vision. But this theme remains inseparable from another – the theme of ill health – which is expressed in a variety of different ways. The Grail king is ill and his kingdom suffers with him. The chosen one is also the healer. However, it is difficult to follow up this point in further detail if we look for constants within the mythical structure, since the theme tends, in fact, to occur in a somewhat random manner within the narrative sequence. In the work of Chrétien de Troyes, we are told about the king's illness at the start of the story, but the barrenness of the land seems to result from Perceval's first failure. It is because he did not dare to ask the long awaited question that the land must suffer. In *La Queste*, there is only an allusion to the illness of King Mordrain – who is not the Grail king. His suffering is relieved by Galahad, but this deliverance is more than a cure. When he was struck down with the illness, King Mordain asked God to keep him alive until his descendant the Good Knight should appear. Once he has recovered his sight and his wounds have been healed, Mordrain dies in Galahad's arms.

It is possible that for Tennyson, the quest itself represented an illness, a type of madness that attacked Arthur's knights and compromised the well-being of the kingdom. Galahad is a source of disease because he spreads a sort of contagion. This disease is undoubtedly essential, for it is important to provide Man with a form of desire that is not purely temporal. Most men, however, are not strong enough to bear this new desire and are broken by the quest. Tennyson retrospectively casts light on Malory and the *Queste del Saint Graal*, showing that, because the goal of the quest is the supreme goal, once it is attained there is nothing left for the spiritual knight to do, except wait for death, which is also a transfiguration. Galahad, like King Mordrain, wants to die.

When Wagner's Amfortas wishes for death, it is in a completely different context. He is merely waiting for the obliteration of his being to put an end to his suffering. For the Grail king, who is suffering from an incurable wound, death is a despairing solution that is directly opposed to the concept of salvation. In this instance, it represents the wages of sin, until grace is granted. Taking up a hint in Wolfram's poem, Wagner went further than any other author in interpreting the king's illness as a punishment. This interpretation had already been suggested in *La Queste*, where Mordrain was struck down for having come too close to the Grail when he was not a priest. At the end of the romance, Lancelot commits the same sin through an excess of love and is punished with the same suffering, although this time it is of shorter duration. However, Lancelot has already realized that he will never reach the ultimate goal of his quest, because his guilty love for Guinevere has made him unworthy. Wolfram and Wagner combine the two themes. The sin committed by Amfortas is a sin against purity. He is wounded for having had a love affair. Thus they echo and give a moral connotation to what is probably a very ancient theme; the idea that the wound has affected the king's virility.

Although this theme can be found in the work of Chrétien de Troyes, he does not appear to link it to any sinful act. Meanwhile, in Malory's version of the story, the 'dolorous blow' was struck in ignorance and could not be considered as a punishment. However, more than one commentator has questioned this appearance of innocence and, for several years, psychoanalysis has been used in an attempt to clarify two sinister episodes. The questions to be answered are why the king is wounded directly between the thighs and why Chrétien's account represents Perceval's first failure as a punishment for the hero. In the latter context, it has been suggested that by leaving his mother, the 'widowed lady', the young man had unwittingly caused her death.

In addition to the moral interpretation of the king's illness, naively adopted by Wagner, and the varied, but all equally impressive, psychoanalytical interpretations, there is also an ethnological interpretation based on the connection found in some authors between the impotence of the king and the barrenness of his kingdom. Disciples of Frazer have seen the story of the Grail as a confirmation of their master's hypotheses. Thus, Perceval is portrayed as the young man who replaces the ageing king whose weakness is jeopardizing the prosperity of the kingdom. This interpretation is probably more relevant to the stories in the oral tradition that form the basis for Chrétien's work. The idea of a magical link between the king's illness and that of his kingdom is no longer apparent and the old king is not put to death. Searching for the origins of the Grail legend, and many other literary myths, often seems like trying to pursue ghosts. However, there is one fact that historians cannot ignore: the highly controversial book by Jessie Weston, *From Ritual to Romance*, which has recently been much neglected by specialists and which develops a theory similar to that of Frazer, was the acknowledged source of inspiration for T. S. Eliot's *Waste Land*. As has already been pointed out, scholarly works exerted a considerable influence on modern literary versions of the ancient legend.

It seems that an aesthetic reading of the early texts leads us to make a certain shift in emphasis. It becomes less important, from the poetical standpoint, to identify the Grail and the objects that accompanied it and to discover its history, than to understand the role that it plays in a ritual that implies a process of initiation. In the same way, it is less important to identify the illness suffered by certain characters in the story, to ascertain its cause, and to apportion responsibility, than to understand how it affects its victims. Two elements should be taken into account.

The first is the existence of a contagion that, in the story, is spread through a process of 'identification' – a term that should, of course, be understood in its psychoanalytical as well as its theatrical sense. In the work of Tennyson, all Arthur's knights imitate Galahad to the point of identifying with him psychologically. Meanwhile, the compassion that Wagner's Parsifal feels for Amfortas, should not be taken purely as a feeling of pity. It is 'Mitleid' – sympathy, empathy, suffering because of another's suffering; while Parsifal also follows the same route that the king had formerly taken, to the castle of the evil magician, and even into the arms of Kundry, the sorceress. In a completely different vein, as has already been shown, in *La Queste*, Galahad wishes for death in the same way in which King Mordrain wished for it: the aura of the 'Nunc dimittis' surrounds both characters. The same phenomenon of assimilation also appears in the work of Chrétien: in spite of Frazer's theory, it is Perceval's failure that seems to bring about the decline of the kingdom, as if this failure were the equivalent of the 'dolorous blow' that reduced the king to impotence. However, it is also his failure that leads Perceval to dereliction and to desert, where for five years he forgets God. After sinking to the depths of the abyss, he is then transformed by his meeting with the hermit, whereupon he emerges from oblivion and begins the long wait.

This word 'wait' is extremely significant, as it is perhaps the one that best conveys the way in which the theme of illness is portrayed in the texts. This illness assumes various aspects. While for Wagner it is a terrible agony, in Chrétien's work it appears to be a quite tolerable discomfort that prevents the king from mounting his horse to go hunting and causes him to take up fishing. It is the wait for the cure, which is identified with the very meaning of the quest itself, that is the common element in all versions of the story. This is because the illness cannot be cured by the usual methods – a point stressed by Wagner. No balm is effective. Indeed, no doctor can even find a treatment. There is no alternative but to wait for the granting of grace. Similarly, it is impossible for the quest to be planned according to any particular strategy. It can only be carried out in a random manner and can only be experienced as a period of waiting and constant surprise, even when the hero knows that everything has been predetermined. Its unpredictability is emphasized by the words: 'Therefore, be on your guard; you know neither the day nor the hour.'

It is the theme of waiting that Gracq emphasizes most clearly in his *Roi pêcheur*, as in most of his works. In so doing, he seems to explain retrospectively why the story of the Grail is incompatible with the narrative continuity so dear to writers of the Classical period, why Wagner includes long pauses between his scenes, why Tennyson revives the medieval technique of interlocking tales, and perhaps why – whether as a deception or a necessary diversion – Chrétien abandoned Perceval to recount the adventures of a Gawain who was destined for failure before finally leaving his poem unfinished.

The last word on the Grail is impossible, or perhaps unpronounceable.

Jean-Louis Backes

The Great Serpent

Let us start with an observation: there is almost no mythology that does not have its own Great Serpent, almost always a marine creature and always ambiguous in character. This is true of the Indo-European domain, but pre-Columbian America has its plumed snake, Quelzalcoatl, the Toltec deity appropriated by the Maya.

We shall not consider here the countless snake-like creatures of all sizes, the amphisbaenae, basilisks, hydras, chimeras and dragons to be met in well-known tales in the folklore of all countries, associated both with a beautiful girl they are guarding and with a hero, whom they reveal to himself, like Fáfnir and Sigurdr. Our concern is the supreme Great Serpent, the cosmogonic, ethical and eschatalogical Trismegistus. This serpent has constantly haunted our imaginations, from Ras Shamra to the Loch Ness monster, it is one of the rare symbolic figures that can claim to solve the mystery of the world. In it our immemorial terrors, our hopes and tenacious desire for lasting existence are combined and crystallize. When it bites its tail – the position it adopts in some representations – it is a circle, the emblem of all perfection. When it rises up erect, it is a pillar of the world, a universal column. And when it weaves along, its phosphorescent track follows the detours of our dialectics. Like the sun, whose declared adversary it is, it cannot be looked at directly, for it never blinks.

In brief, we cannot avoid this image with its inexhaustible richness, for it carries every spell of attraction and repulsion which, all things considered, determine the great unexplainable drives which govern us and are, like the serpent, irresistible.

This is because, once again apart from the sun and fire, the serpent incarnates the great elements from which life draws its sustenance: the earth, which is also the resting place of the dead, enriched by their substance through the equivalence of *homo* and *humus* so dear to Mircea Eliade; and the ocean water which, as Pliny said long ago (*Natural History*, II.10) is the mother of all monsters. The serpent is assimilated to earth through its body, which is perpetually in contact with that element; and it remains linked to water through the scales, which liken it to a fish, through its movements that evoke the undulating waves, and through a whole spectrum of complicity which makes it as familiar with water as with the ground. It is the creature that plays with our spatial categories; it is hardly surprising that some mythologies have endowed it with wings.

The very notion of distance in which so many of our anxieties and dreams are grounded does not exist for the serpent, since it is the living image of the end and the beginning combined. The *Mahâbhârata* clearly shows this, assimilating the serpent, to which it gives the name Pinâka, to Siva's bow, which, it tells us, 'is really the great serpent' that is 'rolled up with the string used to draw back the bow . . . whose colours are like those of the rainbow' – a pertinent comparison that blurs the contours of this heavenly – aquatic representation. The rainbow has always been felt as a 'bridge' between our world and 'heaven', an impalpable but charming intermediary with elements of both created nature and the ethereal sphere where all our hopes reside. Like the rainbow, the Great Serpent connects kingdoms whose antagonism grieves our understanding.

For there is something disturbing about this creature – which is moreover dangerous because of its venom, and able to compete successfully in all habitats of the animal world – to us biped mammals. We can indeed fly, but only through artifice (Icarus, Völundr), and swim, but only after learning how. It is thus not surprising that we have instinctively enlarged it out of all proportion to make it the symbol of our deepest desire, that for totality.

Let us return to the sea; to the Great Sea, where the serpent prefers to remain, or where we have sent it because it was awkward for us. The serpent incarnates all the sea's fearsome prestige: the unfathomable danger in the mastery of which lies the fame of Odysseus, Brendan, the Conquistadors, the Argonauts and the Vikings; the magnetism which Bachelard analysed so well, which is troubled because it is fleeting, unreal and at the same time clearly present and eternal like our dreams; the sparkling darkness of Rimbaud's wild imaginings – in short, all that is concealed and dangerous, the deliciously desired and secretly feared deadliness of the unmanifest. Faced with the blinding clarity of the sun, which reveals the world to us but whose over-bright effects leave our unformulated longings unsatisfied, the Great Serpent and the sea are the ones we would need to know in order to be gods like them. Although the serpent does not speak, it hisses, or is said to hiss, and no one has ever been able to elucidate that language. In extreme cases it breathes fire, which is to say that it has also assimilated the phlogistic element. For, as we have said, the serpent always lies beyond all our categories.

Or indeed, it is, quite simply, *beyond*. What is unmanifest may be something that is yet to come; it may also refer to a great secret that is silent because it is uncommunicable. It is to this extent that the serpent is of the earth: it incarnates the spirits of the dead who haunt and form the earth, and this gives it an eternal dimension. Just as the contrast with the sun is too obvious, the serpent now becomes lunar and thus eschatalogical. There is such a degree of complicity between the serpent and the spirits of the dead that it knows all their secrets. This makes it a source of all wisdom, gnomically unveiling a disturbing but vital knowledge to the confounded hero (Sigurdr again, or Marduk). It is also able to predict the future, having assimilated space-time, particularly if that space-time is seen as an eternal recurrence, as expressed by the serpent's coiled body, or as an upward spiral enchanted by the cunning fingers of the flute-player, or again as an eternal and immobile instant which can be assimilated to the great orb of its resting body.

Further, the serpent is an animal that changes, that regenerates itself. When the time comes it changes its skin, fulfilling what is certainly the most ancient of our wild aspirations. It is now rejuvenated, reborn. In this way, too, death, with whom it exists in such intimate collusion, gives up its rights. The serpent instinctively knows the great secret of the alchemists: is not the philospher's stone said to lodge in its great oblong head?

We were speaking of death: in fact the serpent is the sign of undying life, going beyond all boundaries, sometimes certainly by insane transgressions, but also in a literally perennial affirmation. If the serpent personifies the moon almost everywhere, it is because of the feminine connotations of the nocturnal orb. Both are the foundation of all fertility and regeneration, their cyclical nature obeys this primordial law. And yet we know that in many religions, particularly the oriental or germanic ones, the moon is masculine. What does it matter? This does not contradict our former assertion: all we need do, from our vitalist standpoint, is to shift the lighting, and here is the Great Serpent phallic and erect. The dead are also always considered to be guarantors of fertility, not only through their physical substance but also through the contagion of their creative or regenerative knowledge.

Let us for a moment consider the series Moon-Rain-Fertility-Woman and Moon-Death-Sea-Regeneration-Knowledge: the Great Serpent fits naturally within them, present in each link of the chain.

Its strangely icy body has the paradoxical prestige of the moon, of a life which can do without warmth and thus undermines our too familiar dichotomies. It has the cold blood (the coldbloodedness) of fish and, as we have said, it can also have wings. It cannot be placed in any Linnean classification, like the bat of the fable.

It has retained the glaucus colour, the fearsome caprice and unimaginable powers of fertility of the rain, the sea – of the regenerative water, whence all life undoubtedly came. This is why it often connives with Woman, whose hair recalls its coils, whose bodily forms resemble its aversion to all that is crude and hard, and whose real or supposed psyche reflects its inconsistencies. Whether it be in the Garden of Eden or beneath the Virgin Mary's feet, the serpent is chosen interlocutor of the great feminine mystery, with which it harmonizes with spontaneous grace. It matters little whether this is because it knows the language of temptation or whether it suffers punishment for its treachery. A harmony is instinctively established between the ambiguous appeal of its meanderings and the fleeting contours of the anima that our animus is desperately seeking. And then woman is, by definition, a vector of regeneration, source of fascinating metamorphoses and proof of redeeming losses, like the serpent. For all that, who has never been disturbed by her genitals? They superbly synthesize all our polarities, for they may be both beginning and end and are indeed the negation of all categories.

In all, we can only marvel at the unparalleled profusion of images to which the serpent gives rise within us. Human beings have found few creatures as betwitching. From the most sublime religious or mythological texts to the 'sea serpents' of our daily papers in search of the sensational, the serpent has always known how to plunge the depths of the unknown – the sea, woman, night, death – to bring back something new.

But there is more. For it has a story. Or rather, it is always associated with a story, which is itself also fundamental and provides a resolution of our essential or existential anxieties.

This story can be summarized in simple terms: everywherc the serpent is struggling against a god, the God. The reason for this is very clear. As we have said, the serpent represents too much that is unknown or irritating, it is too compromised with the great mysteries of our being. Lastly, this great ungraspable, perverse transgressor is so highly charged with exasperation that in the end there has to be an explosion. And we have confronted it with our last hope, the representative of our irrepressible need for light, our god of clarity, order and reason.

The Hebrews seem to have best expressed this. They have the myth of a primordial ocean encircling dry land. In it was coiled a sea monster, personifying this hostile element, the sea dragon Rahab (Job 16:12) or serpent Leviathan (Isaiah 27:1). And it was against this monster that Yahweh – who corresponds to his definition, he is the one who is, he is that he is, *par excellence* – begins a battle (Exodus 34:22), thus inaugurating the origin of time, the start of history, the necessary categories of the beginning and the end. There is no shortage of proof of Leviathan's ancient nature: the Phoenician mythological poems of Ras-Shamra (1300 BC) mention him. Let us be aware, in the first analysis, that this confrontation is rich in deep meaning: this is not so much a struggle between heavenly light and the shadows of the abyss, as a desperate desire to create meaning in the face of so much that is unexpressed and inexpressible. Ethical connotations will interpose later, and we shall state them. For the moment we are far ahead of these, at the very heart of metaphysics. The desire for knowledge is straight and direct: it is instinctively repelled by all that is sinuous, what Ibsen would one day call the Great Curve.

And if the supreme god is not involved, then it is one of his avatars who is best placed from the point of view we have adopted here: the god of storms – sudden force, sovereign violence, terrifying effects – and thus of patent, obvious and expected fertility. Indra against Vritra, Zeus against Typhon, Marduk and Tiamat, Thórr fishing Midgardsormr (but terrified and even momentarily paralysed by the latter's eye). Or else, if we are thinking not of great gods confronting the beast, but of demi-gods or human beings with divine status, Thraetona and Azi Dahaka in Iran, Apollo and Python, or Heracles and the Hydra of Lerna.

In fact each of these categories should be considered separately. In the first case – the thundering gods against the reptilian monster – we are rightly surprised. There seems to be an inconsistency in this confrontation, since both govern fertility. Precisely: the former are light, and their actions are orthodox, bringing neither surprise nor enigma. In all domains violence is always necessary to bring about fertility: violence, rape, sacred terrors which cause the act of giving birth to be sensed as deliverance and liberation. This is how the *Rig Veda* (1.32) sees it, in this case in relation to the anatagonism between Indra and Vritra. It tells us that he killed the dragon, pierced the waters, broke the mountain-sides. In a male act, he loved the *soma* and he killed the first-born of dragons. But what of the Great Serpent? As we have said, it too is a symbol of fertility, but in some way obscurely so; through an almost inadmissible complicity, indeed through perfidiousness. There is too much duplicity, evasion and sinuosity in the indefinable nature of this creature, which is more *lively* than *alive.* This is clearly shown in Isaiah (27:1): 'In that day the Lord with his sore and great and strong sword shall punish leviathan the piercing serpent, even leviathan that crooked serpent; and he shall slay the dragon that is in the sea'.

Let us repeat it: the primordial and inevitable Great Serpent bothers us; there is no way that we can deny its necessary existence and exemplary vitality. But, while we must integrate it into our universe, whose unfathomable powers it combines, we do so against our will. We have tried to exorcise it by calling up against it a true god, born of the deficiencies and aspirations of our clear awareness. This serpent moves in an extreme territory: it is not really part of us, that is why we have cast it out into the Great Sea or – like the Arabs, who give the name 'Dragon' (*tannîn*) to both a giant serpent and a constellation – we have exiled it in heaven, the symmetrical pendant of the bottomless ocean in our symbolic imagery.

We may, however, choose the other kind of hostile confrontation, which brings together either heroes and the serpent, or animals that are always winged – preferably an eagle, or some other bird – and the monster. Here, reinforced by Gnostic or Manichaean tradition, the opposition is more immediately within our grasp. Supported by the observations we have just made, it is easier for us to understand that such conflicts have an ethical meaning. The serpent may indeed carry the inexpressible, if real, element that we bear within us. However, there is too much mystery, too much that is unsaid in its being. It is beyond our reach in every configuration that we seek to give it. Its exasperating obviousness humiliates us.

So let us make the serpent the figure of evil, of trickery, disorder and chaos. But this reflex is in itself illogical, since we well know that it belongs to our shadows, and that these cannot do without it. Moreover, it is also natural; it is neither compensation nor sublimation but an attempt to create order or an equation. Therefore let the conquering or avenging heroes appear when the time is right. Their deeds will be an act of justice that we perform for ourselves. The serpent bears the weight of our sins. Does the Bible not expressly tell us that it is responsible for their fatal appearance in Eden? With the serpent began time and history, sources of all our woes. On this point, human imagination has produced many right-thinking justifications. Let us punish the serpent, for it has devoured sun and moon and is thus responsible for the eclipses which were so long the bearers of our blindest terrors. At once the serpent takes on an obvious cosmogonic character: a circular being, it is the one that prevents things turning as they should. Why should we be surprised to see it assume the face of Satan, the one we do not need to seek to know where he is?

We are dealing here with the powerful images that simple maieutics draw up from our inner depths; a fascinating story, whose internalization we all experience within ourselves as the true sign of our unique and supreme good – this life that we treasure above all else, knowing from thousands of years' experience that it will always kill us in the end.

All our mythologies and religions have placed this truly fantastical fantasy of the Great Serpent at the occult centre of our vision of things. It would be easy to draw up a comparative catalogue of expressions that human beings have tried to give it. We shall however take a well-placed example which seems to exhaust the multiple aspects of the subject, that of the Scandinavian Midgardsormr. Through the various myths in which he appears, he seems to combine in concentrated form all the ideas and representations whose details we have just outlined.

The texts present him to us in five different forms. He lives, of course, in the primordial Great Sea which surrounds the 'Middle World' (Midgardr, hence his name); in other words, the land of men in the centre of which is the domain of the gods, Ásgardr. Beyond the sea, in this concentric conception of the world, there is the outside world, Útgardr, home of the evil powers, the giants and forces of chaos. The role of the serpent is essential: as he is coiled around Midgardr so that he is biting his tail, he literally girds our human and divine world, ensuring its cohesion. He is both a rampart and the guarantor of its solidity.

The second image is more subtle, although it reflects the same logic. Instead of the horizontal image we have just described, we have a 'vertical' image. The world is then imagined as a kind of gigantic spindle whose axis is the great tree Yggdrasill, which is perhaps quite simply the Great Serpent with another name. Indeed Yggdrasill is sometimes called Jörmungandr (magic/giant/wand), and in some texts this name also applies to Midgardsormr. Its function is the same as that of the serpent: it is to ensure the coherence of the universe, and the image of the Great Serpent erect is far from unthinkable. Moreover, collusion between the two symbols is to be found elsewhere, where the serpent is shown coiled around the base of Yggdrasill's trunk. This superimposition, so familiar to our ways of thinking, thus brings about the synthesis.

However, if Midgardsormr should let go – in the horizontal view of this cosmogony – or, in the vertical representation, the tree should come down, the result is catastrophe, universal cataclysm, Ragnarök. This threat, ultimately the same as the Celts' terror of the sky falling on their heads, was so deeply felt that, as we know, here as elsewhere the mythology produced a supreme god of force, Thórr, to fight the potential enemy. A very elaborate myth relates how the god of thunder tries to catch the Great Serpent without succeeding, because, at the last moment, the giant who is witness to this combat (in other words a representative of the truly telluric zones of our world) intervenes and frees the monster. But this does not settle the duel: Midgardsormr and Thórr kill each other at the Ragnarök, in an apocalyptic setting.

This is why the serpent was finally assimilated to the most malevolent creatures. It was made the son of Loki, the god of evil, or, more precisely, in the germano-nordic mentality, of supreme disorder, of chaos. It is not irrelevant, then, that in this context Midgardsormr is the brother of the wolf Fenrir, another sinner straight from the Ragnarök, and of Hel, mistress of the Empire of the Dead. Once again, the Great Serpent remains outside our limited categories and, particularly, our too-clear-cut dichotomies. The striking thing in the complex of ideas and images that ancient Scandinavian mythology offers us, seemingly more clearly than elsewhere, is the ambiguity, the bivalency – that is to say, ultimately, the transcendental quality of the Great Serpent. He is bound up with death while symbolizing the most tenacious life; he defies our limited reason because he is knowledge; he attracts our sensibilities above all with his instinctive power of repulsion; he offers our imaginations a figure that goes considerably further than our most violent fevers because of the margin of indefinability that he carries and that we can never fill.

He is both the guarantor of the world's order and the expected cause of chaos, both the reassuring proof of our diurnal being and the delicious terror of our nocturnal dreams.

Régis Boyer

Gyges

The exploits of Gyges the Lydian are known to us in four different versions from classical Antiquity; these amount to four coherent, autonomous stories with diverging, even contradictory episodes indicating the different levels at which the hero may be apprehended – mythical, legendary or historical. The thematic tradition associated with Gyges suffers from this diversity of origins; it was slow to become established, as if suspended between opposing interpretations, and really only crystallized into a literary myth in the nineteenth century, when it flowered only briefly. Thus its line of descent, with many unexpected revivals, produces a rather charming pointillist effect.

THE SOURCES OF THE TRADITION

Plato's version (*Republic* II. 359b–360b), though later than Herodotus', is the richest in fabulous detail and the principal one involving the recurrent and influential motif of the invisible man. The question posed is whether good men are good only because their deeds can be observed by others; if they enjoyed invisibility and hence impunity would they not be tempted to do wrong, as Gyges did? Gyges, a simple shepherd employed by the King of Lydia (who is not named) sees his flock being swallowed up by the ground during an earthquake. Setting out in search of it, he explores a chasm in the earth where he discovers a hollow bronze horse containing the corpse of a giant; he appropriates the giant's ring, which allows him to become invisible. Secure in his power, 'arriving at the palace, he seduced the Queen, plotted with her against the King, killed him, and so obtained the crown'. Setting aside its moral implications this is unquestionably a terrifying fable, and it may even be part of an initiatory scenario involving a descent into the underworld and a rite of passage, which would conform with the symbolism of the ring.

Plato relates a myth while Herodotus (I.8–13) writes a short story, replacing the muthos with the logos. His story is part of a summary of past history intended to inform the reader about the ancestors of Croesus, including Gyges, the founder of his dynasty. The Lydian King Candaules, the last of the Heraclids, is so in love with his wife that he thinks she is the most beautiful woman in the world; he takes Gyges, his favourite bodyguard, into his confidence and persuades him despite his reluctance to hide in the royal couple's bedroom and look at the Queen naked. But the Queen catches sight of him as he is slipping out; she greatly resents the slight she has been subjected to, for 'with the Lydians, as with most barbarian races, it is thought highly indecent even for a man to be seen naked'. The very next day she sends for Gyges and presents him with the alternative of dying himself or killing Candaules, succeeding him and marrying his widow. Once again Gyges demurs, but to no avail. The Queen in her turn conceals him in the bedroom, he kills the King in his sleep, then inherits his wife and his kingdom. The Pythia in Delphi legitimates the usurper, but prophesies that the Heraclids will be avenged on the fourth generation descended from Gyges, that is on Croesus, the last of the Mermnades.

It would be superfluous to underline the differences between this and the previous version: here everything is logical and lifelike, everything is explained psychologically or ethnologically, everything hangs together firmly within the context of inevitable fate, 'for destiny intended that Candaules should end badly'. The events unfold within the narrow confines of Greek tragedy – in a single place, within twenty-four hours – so much so that Herodotus' text has been thought to be the summary of a dramatic work of which only a fragment has survived (published by Lobel, *Proceedings of the British Academy* 35). In it the Queen tells how having recognized Gyges in the bedroom she decided on vengence, got rid of the King and sent for his favourite. The theory of a summary is tempting, but it is not at all certain that the tragedy is as early as the fifth century BC. To return to the theme of the story, several points should be noted. The disappearance of the ring which neutralizes the mythical potential of the episode is compensated for both by the importance assigned to the taboo of modesty and the space given to the personal motivation of the protagonists. The geometric pattern of the story which was previously centred only on Gyges is now focused on the very crux of the situation; once set in motion it is as if a chain reaction carries the story to its final resolution. This scenario welds the three constants of the theme together into an indissoluble trio – the King and his folly, the Queen and her modesty and, moving obliquely between them, the 'knight' Gyges, manipulated by first one and then the other – in such a way as to place the pieces in the arrangement in perfectly symmetrical positions; a fine subject, perhaps too fine, for it does not leave much room for 'play'. Anyone wanting to reinsert the motif of the ring, superfluous in this version, will have to open up the schema to some extent and distort its dynamics.

Another Gyges, a historical-cum-legendary figure this time, turns up in Nicolaus of Damascus (in *Fragmenta Historicorum Graecorum*, Müller, III); he drew on the *Lydiaca*, a lost work by Xanthus, a contemporary of Herodotus. Gyges, a handsome, brave young man belonging to the noble Mermnades family, attracts the attention of King Sadyattes (= Candaules) who summons him and entrusts him with dangerous missions, possibly in order to get rid of him. Gyges succeeds in these undertakings and the King is won over, awarding extensive lands to him. But love crosses the path of politics: Sadyattes entrusts Gyges with the task of escorting his wife-to-be to him; Gyges tried to seduce her and she denounces him to the King, but a servant who is in love with Gyges overhears their conversation and alerts him. With the servant's help Gyges gets into the royal bedchamber and kills Sadyattes in his sleep; he then marries Sadyattes' widow, bearing her no malice. As we can see, this version favours adventure and romance, but it could not supplant Herodotus' account of events. With its twists of fate, however, it can often dilute it.

Finally Plutarch in a brief passage (*Questiones convivalium* I.5) alludes to yet another tradition according to which Candaules, because he had given away the axe he had inherited from Hercules to one of his henchmen, drove Gyges to rebel and was killed not by Gyges himself but by one of his allies.

Of course there have been plenty of attempts to reconstruct a kind of all-embracing Ur-form of the 'exploits of Gyges' incorporating all the known elements, from which the four basic versions given above could have been derived in a corrupted form; such attempts are laborious and merely plaster over the cracks. We must resign ourselves to accepting only one single common source for these various tales: the real accession to power of the man who was the first tyrant, what Georges Radet (*La Lydie et le Monde grec au Temps des Mermnades*, 1893) called the 'Lydian revolution of 687 BC' at Sardis. From the literary point of view these roots in time and place can only serve as an opportunity to enrich the story with colourful detail, derived from the plethora of symbols of ceremonial and opulance that has always surrounded the country of the Pactolus.

From this complex tradition we should take special note of the malleability of the character of Gyges – first a shepherd then a lord, submissive or rebellious, the holder or otherwise of a magic object – which offers great scope to retellings of the myth. And finally Gyges comes into the picture only in relation to his opposition to Candaules: from the moment Gyges becomes involved in Candaules' misguided scheme, the power to make himself invisible, vital to the original myth, can survive only as evidence of an archaic religious context or as a floating symbol in search of a meaning. We are faced with the paradox of a myth that is out of phase, its nucleus shifting from its central position on contact with another adventure – a strange, unsuitable adventure, foreign to its essence – and which will much later find a source of renewal in this thematic lopsidedness.

RECORDS OF SURVIVAL

For centuries the interconnected exploits of Gyges and Candaules survived in a modest way thanks to the rhetorical tradition which included them in its repertory of *exempla* or *topoi*, beloved of textbooks and moral treatises. Allusions, glosses or simple summaries – in Cicero, Justin, Dionysius of Halicarnassus and Plutarch, but also in obscure commentators such as Ptolemy Chennos alias Hepaestion (who did not escape Gautier's painstaking research), Aelius Aristides or Nicholas the Sophist – ensured that the subject was kept alive until the *Chiliades* by the prolific, confused and wordy twelfth-century Byzantine writer Johannes Tzetzes.

The story-tellers then took over, alive to the moral connotations of the episode: Boccaccio (*De casibus illustrium virorum*, II; between 1355 and 1360) accused Gyges of licentiousness, William Painter (*The Palace of Pleasure*, story 6; 1566–7) condemned the King's vanity and ostentation and Henri Estienne (*Apologie pour Hérodote*, 1566) his 'infamy', while Hans Sachs ('Die nackat königin aus Lidia', 61 lines; 1538) who reproached the wicked (*arg*) Queen can still be savoured for his uncouth, naïve awkwardness. It is when we come to Branthôme (*Les Dames galantes*) that the story of the three, freed from Puritan commentaries, takes on a Gallic flavour; Candaules deserved to be 'well and truly cuckolded'. The patron saint of betrayed husbands inspired one of La Fontaine's *Contes* (1674), which is by and large based on Herodotus' account, but overlaid with sly allusions and misogynous raillery. Fontenelle (1683) created a dialogue in the underworld between the murderer and his victim, who agree that honour does not enter into affairs of the heart. Thus the motif of love which was dominant in Plato's version recovered its full influence (which it was to keep), and thus the Queen of Lydia was able to take her place in the gallery of *Femmes galantes de l'Antiquité* by Dubois (6 vols, 1726–32; vol. III). The sole exception is La Mothe-Fénelon, in a tale freely inspired from the Platonic account alone ('L'Anneau de Gygès', 1690), though it is still a very watered-down version 'for the use of the Dauphin'.

On the stage the story was used in an opera libretto by Adriano Morselli (*Candaule*, in three acts, Venice, 1679), a sort of musical comedy chase ahead of its time, where it in fact served only to introduce another plot, full of misunderstandings, disguises and tit-for-tat, against a background of ballet and spectacular stage effects. The same kind of machinery is also brought into play by Jose de Cañizares in his interminable 'comedia famosa' in three parts, each consisting of three acts (*El Anillo de Giges, y maxico Rey de Lidia*, 1764). This uses Plato's version as its point of departure and as a pretext, the existence of the ring justifying both a spectaular stage set and some innocent tomfoolery. Declarations of war follow hot on the heels of declarations of love, each resembling the other and the whole at an exaggerated pitch of gallantry and heroism, while Gyges who is here in love with Claridiana, Candaules' daughter, spends his time losing and recovering his ring, which takes the place of any dramatic progression; in the third part, now a widower after Claridiana's death, he even embarks on a second marriage.

This is how the story provided by Herodotus and Plato was neglected or mistreated: renewed appreciation of the theme resulted from a return to the sources, and from a deepening and readaptation of its meaning after so many clichés and stereotypes.

REBIRTH

With his novella *Roi Candaule* (serialized in *La Presse*, 1844) Théophile Gautier wrote the first substantial work devoted to the subject. He was well versed in the earlier ramifications of the theme, using them as his inspiration while embroidering happily on the canvas sketched out by Herodotus, highlighted with picturesque touches and historical and local colour. In his reconstruction of Antiquity he seizes every opportunity for description – processions, ceremonies, monuments, etc. – exploiting it as a virtuoso of the written word. He powerfully contrasts the 'Greek-Lydian' Candaules with Queen Nyssia from the remote, archaic land of Bactria, and the King's aestheticism (a motif borrowed from La Fontaine) with the fierce modesty of his veiled wife. He sees Candaules as a failed artist; marriage has put him in possession of a living masterpiece and he suffers from having to enjoy it alone. He wants to keep alive the memory of this perfect, but moral and fragile body, which he cannot record permanently in marble, by at least allowing Gyges too to gaze upon it, which is why he invites him to spy on the Queen as she undresses. Gyges is a connoisseur of women (and very much responsible for the 'Parisian' tone of the novella); moreover his appetite has already been whetted because he had caught a glimpse of Nyssia's face when a gust of wind lifted her veil as he was escorting her from Bactria (reminiscent of Nicolaus of Damascus). However, he is very soon reduced to the role of a mesmerized lover. As for the Queen, she is a complex creature, a kind of *femme fatale* with the gaze of a Medusa, transformed from an angel into a devil by the 'visual adultery' to which she has been subjected. But for all his endeavours to find a divine equivalent in Isis for the unveiling of the Queen, and to compare Candaules' torments with those of Pygmalion – following his path in a diametrically opposite direction, since he wants to turn Nyssia into a living statue (Pradier did make a statue of her in marble) – despite all these comparisons Gautier did not raise the subject to the level of a literary myth.

Nonetheless the subject had been given a new lease of life; parodies and works influenced by Gautier as well as a small but fruitful clutch of original works are evidence of its new vitality.

PARODISTS

As might be expected, parodists exploited the ribald aspect of the story. This produced *Monsieur Candaule ou le Roi des Maris* by Fournier and Meyer (1858), an unpretentious sketch in one act that transposes the adventure to sea-bathing at Trouville; or *Roi Candaule* (1865), an opera in two acts with a libretto by Michel Carré. Gautier had written that Gyges looked at the Queen 'with the impassioned eye of a southern commercial traveller', that Candaules 'wears his purple like a jacket from the Belle-Jardinière', etc. Meilhac and Halévy produced a farce (also called *Roi Candaule*, 1873) which speaks for itself: 'the fat man with a crown' tells the 'little man with the eye-glass' 'I've got a smashing wife!' Maurice Donnay used the same title yet again (1920); he was perfectly familiar with Radet's theory, but remained bound by the narrow conventions of operetta and the boulevard to make things funny at all costs, by laboured puns in particular. There was just one innovation: Candaules' ghost returned to the palace each night to be tortured by the sight of his successor disporting himself.

FOLLOWERS

Like Gautier these writers were ardent in the cult of Beauty, to the point of being funny (they themselves lacked a sense of humour) and without their precursor's genius for erudite eroticism. In 'Gyges and Candaules' (268 lines; 1868) Robert Lytton was inspired by Gautier but also Keats' 'The Eve of St Agnes'; he exaggerates the fascination the Queen exerted on both Gyges and Candaules, portraying the latter as a lover besotted to the point of silliness; 'fine writing' and 'word painting' nonetheless ensure that the royal striptease is portrayed with a calculated slowness likely to increase its eroticism. An anonymous English scholar in 'The Folly of King Candaules: A Lay of the Ancient World' (207 lines; 1880), celebrating in well-worn clichés the golden age of the Lydian El Dorado and the dream of an Eden where it was still possible to live '*in statu naturae*', makes us long for the impassiveness of the 'son of Halicarnassus' whon he cites as his inspiration. In *Gyges' Ring: A Dramatic Monologue* (989 lines; 1901) Rupert Hughes, an American writer, juxtaposes the two main versions; even more than the previous writers he piles up gold, silver, precious stones and transliterated Greek words to describe the 'dear disrobing'. Gyges, a poor but worthy man, is a plaything in the hands of the experienced Nyssa, while Candaules is depicted as a doddering, lubricious dotard. If the episode of the Queen's body is very coy, the murder scene is bathed in an unending deluge of blood, and the fundamental antagonisms – between town and country, youth and age, wealth and poverty, etc. – relentlessly dominate the whole story. Every literary and historical source is poured into *Candaule* (1921), a play in four acts by G. Radet which is a complex hotchpotch of pedantic scholarship and doggerel verse, with Homer playing his part alongside a Candaules who is 'crazy about beauty' and based on the figure of Renan!

Thus the followers of Gautier degenerated into farce, exaggeration or ludicrousness.

REBIRTH OF THE MYTH

The person who really restored the myth was Friedrich Hebbel in *Gyges und sein Ring* (a play in five acts in verse, 1854); despite many points of resemblance between him and Gautier, the climate in this 'Romantic' tragedy, ennobled by the joint influence of Racine and Goethe's *Iphigenia* is completely different. The mystical dimension is immediately restored by the insertion of the motif of the ring into Herodotus' fable, and a renewed appreciation of the subject, reinterpreted in terms of the philosophy of history as a conflict between tradition and modernity, takes root on this 'prehistoric' ground. The protagonists are clearly characterized: Candaules is a social reformer, a man with a powerful intellect, but his people find him hard to understand and enemies are threatening Lydia from without; set against him is his Indian wife Rhodope who lives shut away in her woman's quarters, claiming the inviolability of what might have been called her *Schleierrecht*. The King has befriended Gyges, a young Greek temporarily staying at his court in Sardis, who represents Hellenism. Gyges is frightened of the ring which he has discovered in circumstances similar to those described by Plato, and offers it as a tribute to Candaules who uses it jokingly and to create mystification despite the solemn warnings of Rhodope; he offers to give it to her if she in return will abandon the veil. Thus the main motifs are rapidly brought together without disturbing the basic triple arrangement, and this is achieved by making the talisman something that is passed from one person to another. It returns to Gyges' possession for the bedroom scene before being given back to Candaules who does not use it again: the magic object therefore represents the pledge of friendship, the accessory to permissiveness and the invisible, dread base of things that Candaules cannot disturb with impunity. Rhodope senses that she is being visually violated and two acts are devoted to the close inquiry she undertakes to learn the truth, questioning first the King and then Gyges – an inquisition which is reminiscent of the one in *Oedipus Tyrannus*; underlying it is an intense dialectic relating to the veil and the ring, the prohibition and the transgression of it. Hebbel is the first writer to give Gyges a substantive role in which are combined horror of the crime (the young man had hitherto known women only as mother figures), awakening sensuality, and loyalty towards Candaules, his spiritual father. Rhodope, who is the strict embodiment of moral law, an innocent victim of the battle between the sexes, sullied in her womanhood, betrayed in her religious faith, cannot persuade Gyges to kill Candaules. The two meet in a duel, but the Queen commits suicide immediately after her marriage to Gyges.

The end is not as pessimistic and nihilistic as it sounds. Lydia has found its saviour in Gyges who fulfils his historic destiny by means of one of those stratagems which Reason, according to Hegel, is fond of using. If Candaules failed in his attempt to waken the world from its sleep, it was because he had come before his time. Thus the fate of the protagonists conveys in three different ways the tragedy inherent in any process of individualization. Hebbel's treatment of the theme, while preserving much of the arbitrary incongruity of Candaules' deed, at the same time turns it into the trigger, powerful because it is erotic in nature, of the crisis that will overturn the established order by liberating individual forces. But none of the protagonists is a wholly positive character and none is wholly sanctioned: the ideas defended or embodied are shown as merely relative. Even Rhodope, whose moral law is represented as the simple product of a civilization that is limited in time and space, does not justify that law by sacrificing herself, for the idea is conceived in a very modern way by Hebbel, as containing within it two contradictory parts, one positive and the other negative, confrontation between which, here brought about by setting ethics against the erotic, results in human tragedy.

In his *Roi Candaule* (play in three acts, 1899) André Gide is interested in the other side of the subject, that leading up to the bedroom scene. He introduces a large number of original features to the treatment of the theme, both in relation to Gautier whom he rejects utterly, accusing him of being the 'father of journalism', and to Hebbel whose work he did yet know. Candaules, totally Hellenized, is surrounded in his palace by courtiers whom he entertains and with whom he converses in a very 'Platonic' atmosphere. Gyges is still further removed from the known models: he appears in the role of a poor, brutish fisherman (he kills his adulterous wife without ado), who in his childhood had been a playmate of the King, but now is forgotten by him. He represents the poor man *par excellance*, perhaps the only one in the kingdom, the very person required by the prodigal Candaules, who has a 'giving nature', is 'generous to a fault' and feels guilty because of his immeasurable wealth. As for the introduction of the motif of the ring, this is radically altered through being contaminated by the fable of Polycrates: for the King finds the ring in the belly of a fish caught by Gyges, and the talisman bears the ambiguous message: 'I conceal happiness'. Candaules, alienated by his possessions, cannot wait to share them with Gyges, overwhelming him with gifts in a one-sided relationship which inevitably irritates the recipient. Step by step, constantly exhorting himself to go further, he gets to the point of 'risking' the possession he holds dearest: Nyssia. 'Taking risks! It is the other form of happiness, that of the wealthy . . . It is mine.' This leads to the experiment which consists of offering Gyges – through the power of the ring – a night with the Queen. The climax of the action is the scene where the lover is substituted for the husband, a masterpiece of 'self-conscious theatre', and very daring for the period, so much so that it brought a volley of invective down on Gide's head when the play was staged in Germany.

The play moves very rapidly to its conclusion: Gyges reveals the truth to Nyssia who immediately becomes emancipated, throwing off her veil and giving orders; but after the King has been murdered Gyges will have none of it – the Queen has to pin her veil back on! In this parable of the good rich man and the nasty poor man (unless things are the other way round) Gide allocates a very minor place to the woman: the erotic element is overvalued, and prohibitions are undermined, so that wearing the veil here amounts to little more than a piece of coquetry on Nyssia's part. If Gide puts a lot of himself into the character of the King whose 'idiosyncrasy' powerfully colours the whole drama, Nietzsche also has an influence, as the King stakes his whole *amor fati* in provoking destiny; but does not the uncouth figure of Gyges, whom the King never succeeds in corrupting, also have Nietzschean overtones? If in fact we are to 'generalize' the figure of Candaules as Gide invites us to do, the lesson to be drawn from him is no doubt that it is impossible to come to terms with oneself as a man or as an artist without being prodigal with oneself, giving oneself, going beyond what one has already done.

König Kandaules: Ein Trauerspiel (1903) by Hugo von Hofmannsthal did not get beyond the stage of a barely coherent outline. As several crucial scenes are missing, to follow the action we have to turn to Hebbel, who echoes the general outline of his work, particularly in the eventual suicide of Rhodope. However, the bedroom scene passed over in the interval by Hebbel would have been very detailed here, as in Gautier's version. The main quality of the play lies in the atmosphere of barbarity, even savagery, in which thc plot with its many vicissitudes of fortune unfolds: Hofmannsthal depicts the despotic King and the Queen – a living idol and well versed in the *Kama Sutra* – as Orientals. The sound and the fury are unleashed after the murder of Gyges' mistress (he is the head of the Greek mercenaries), who is killed by her husband, then mutiliated and cut to pieces. The King is threatened by a conspiracy, the members of which confer with Gyges who owns the ring. In contrast to Hebbel's or Gide's account, relations between the King and Gyges are very hierarchical: the young man obeys orders as a matter of course, even when he hides in the bedroom where he suffers from contemplating what is going on 'as a decoy'. The story of the conspiracy unfolds: the Old Lydians persecute the Greek mercenaries who rebel. After killing the King, Gyges is himself murdered by the wives in the harem while the mercenaries are carousing. A surprising overlap of the Gyges-Candaules theme with that of *Salammbô* is apparent here, and there are many other traces of it: a severed aqueduct, a veil scattered with hieratic signs, the cult of Baal, of Melkarth, of Tanit and so on. Both the drama and the characters, however, race out of control into a nightmare of gratuitous violence and death, into 'the long, heavy, confused dream of humankind' to which Schopenhauer reduces the discourse of history. Thus the way opened up by the works of Hebbel and Gide, who restored the myth within the context of historical and moral development, ends up in a blind alley with the uncompleted work by Hofmannsthal. The revitalization of the mythical substratum brought about by the giving and handing on of the ring was not enough to provide a lasting impulse to literary creativity.

After an almost endless period of maturation, then a short, sudden explosion, it seems as if the theme exhausted its pent-up potential all in one go, perhaps because the values it expresses have been transferred to other fables; but it has passed through so many arid periods that we may hope that the unsettling silence now shrouding it will prove temporary.

N.B. An important though not exhaustive list of thematic references to

Gyges can be found in three articles by Kirby F. Smith in the *American Journal of Philology* 23 (1902) and 41 (1920).

Michel Potet

Hamlet

'... but the lord unrealized and unable to fulfil himself advances, the youthful shadow of us all, inherited from the myth'

(Mallarmé)

Ever since the second half of the eighteenth century, Shakespeare's tragedy (written circa 1600–1) has continued to exert a strange fascination over audiences, critics and authors alike. The figure of Hamlet, like those of Ulysses, Faust and Don Quixote, belongs to the group of fictitious heroes who, according to Döblin, are an excellent illustration of the essential aspects and 'basic situations' of human experience. This decisive influence is probably explained by the universal nature of the sources from which Shakespeare drew his inspiration. The early legend recorded by Saxo Grammaticus in the twelfth century (a version which was later adapted by Belleforest to suit the contemporary taste of the 1570s) combines elements which belong to the imaginary world of saga (as collected by Snorri Sturlson in the *Prose Edda*) as well as to the mythology of the Mediterranean. The figure of the son called upon to avenge his father – murdered by his uncle – is reminiscent of Amlodi, the apparent simpleton, who contemplates the sea whose depths contain the 'Windmill of the Universe', which crushes rocks and reduces both the quick and the dead to sand. These characteristics of Nordic origin are combined with those of Orestes and Electra, and of the semi-legendary Lucius Junius Brutus, all of whom are motivated by the hatred they feel towards their mothers and the usurpers who persecute them. As the young man bearing the letter containing his own death warrant, but who nevertheless manages to save his own life, Hamlet is also the brother of Uriel and Bellerophon.

Shakespeare's tragedy recalls a legend (which he either knew directly or via the intermediary of the famous 'Ur-Hamlet') that is full of mythological references. At the same time, the playwright also revives the conventions of the revenge tragedy and, within the context of a play characterized by teasing ambiguity, presents themes concordant with a magical understanding of the universe and the religious and philosophical preoccupations of the turn of his century. His hero – who by feigning a 'strange attitude' is preserved from the murderous rage of the traditional avenger – is visited by his father's ghost, which 'usurps this hour of the night'. Whether the ghost inhabits hell, purgatory or heaven, he breaks down the boundaries which separate this world from the next; whether he is a corporeal ghost or purely a spirit, he actually exists in theatrical terms at the beginning of the play, whereas he subsequently appears to be nothing more than a figment of his son's imagination. The new king, who is younger, stronger and more virile than his predecessor – who was betrayed by his declining strength and abandoned by his queen – could have introduced an age of renewal. But as a base murderer, he is merely a source of corruption. Hamlet, as the hero of a cosmic, philosophical and family drama, has to find his way through a labyrinth of doubt and uncertainty. This melancholy figure, deeply wounded by his mother's remarriage and obsessed by the impossible task of avenging his father, successfully thwarts his uncle's intrigues. By the end of the tragedy he has achieved the strange serenity – which is either fatalistic or indicative of his confidence in the designs of Providence – of the adolescent subjected to paternal authority and constantly brooding over a vengeance which he is unable to accomplish. He becomes a prince in his own right and puts to death the usurper whose guilt has become apparent. (See introduction to the bilingual edition, Aubier, 1988.)

Hamlet is a drama of individual as well as collective awareness. It is a play which glorifies the dramatic art, and is an unrivalled example of that art, full of myth and mystery, a source of inspiration for many writers. For them it is a question of plumbing the depths of a character, exploring the hidden dimension of a text and rewriting it to suit the tastes and particular sensibilities of their age, in an attempt to achieve a better understanding of the masterpiece. It is possible that the 'commemorative' interpretation, to use Genette's expression, is inspired by a feeling of rebellion against the text which has become a cult object.

The novelistic literature inspired by *Hamlet* is characterized by two major works: *Wilhelm Meisters Lehrjahre* (1795–6) and *Ulysses* (1922). In Goethe's novel, the development of a fine personality has close links both dramatically and theoretically with *Hamlet*. Nevertheless, it becomes clear that the identification with Hamlet is merely a stage in the apprenticeship of life of Wilhelm, who must realize that the way to love and true society lies through his renunciation of his passion for the theatre. Goethe creates numerous links between the action of the novel and the plot of Shakespeare's tragedy. Twentieth-century authors of the 'Bildungsroman', such as Hauptmann and Döblin, imitated this technique of association. In Joyce's *Ulysses*, the myth of Hamlet is superimposed upon the Odyssean myth. A young writer, Stephen Dedalus, believes in the creative autonomy of Shakespeare, rejects the idea of paternity of the flesh and is violently opposed to the dogma of the 'consubstantiation' of father and son. On this sixteenth day of June 1904, Hamlet-Telemachus is searching for a spiritual father. However, it is possible for Vurág-Bloom, living in exile in Dublin and dreaming of Central Europe – a Ulysses deprived of all Homeric glory – and pursuing the ghost of his dead son Rudy-Telemachus, to offer Stephen this spiritual paternity when he himself is hoping that he will prove to be a suitable new lover for his wife? Like Hamlet, Stephen has to rid himself of destructive parental images and free himself from all friendly, family, patriotic and cultural attachments in order to win his freedom as a creator.

Between the two summits of achievement represented by *Wilhelm Meister* and *Ulysses*, there are other works which are worthy of interest and representative of the influence and 'purpose' of the myth. In Melville's *Pierre: Or the Ambiguities* (1852), the creative impetus of a young writer who wants to produce a mature work while he is still emotionally immature is destroyed by a Hamletesque heredity, namely an adulterous father and a half-sister whom he marries against the will of an authoritarian mother. Pierre suspects that he has guilty ancestry and his doubts degenerate into madness. The family group – like the one in *Hamlet* – destroys Pierre as surely as the 'Ghost' of *Moby Dick*, the white whale, destroys the rebellious and fanatical Ahab. In France, during the second half of the nineteenth century (circa 1886–7), Paul Bourget (*André Cornélis*) and Jules Laforgue (*Hamlet ou les Suites de la Piété filiale*) tried to 'rewrite' Shakespeare's tragedy. While Bourget's psychological detective novel was a partial failure, Laforgue's 'legendary morality' was quite successful. Laforgue's Hamlet, the son of the assassinated old king and a young gypsy, and the half-brother of Yorick, is a dandy of the Decadent period. He is an irritating individual, cynical, full of surprises, offhand, an impassive aesthete, a perceptive actor, a nihilist philosopher and a skilful juggler with the Shakespearean text: 'But to be no more, to be no longer here, to be no longer part of things' causes him to experience a sort of 'secular sadness'. More recently, Iris Murdoch (*The Black Prince*, 1973) skilfully presents an inhibited writer who can only love Ophelia when disguised as Hamlet and reminding her of Octavian, the count of the *Chevalier à la Rose*.

On stage the myth of Hamlet appears to have a curiously destructive effect. Ivanov, Chekhov's 'superfluous' man, and Treplieff, the hero of *The Seagull* (1896) who is the victim of Trigorin-Claudius and Arkadina-Gertrude, both die because they enjoy the role of Hamlet. Chekhov was familiar with Goethe's interpretation of *Hamlet* and also with Turgenev's essay. Over the last quarter century we have witnessed a revolt against the Shakespearean masterpiece. In *Rozencrantz and Guildenstern are Dead* (1967), Tom Stoppard, inspired by Beckett, rehabilitates these minor characters who, as the heroes of a tragedy of the Absurd, diminish and discredit the figure of the 'sweet prince'. Marowitz' adaptation of *Hamlet* (1965) is in fact a 'dismemberment' of the masterpiece in which Hamlet's monologues are transformed into dialogues and the reproaches that Hamlet makes to himself become vehement accusations in the mouths of his friends and enemies. From this point on Hamlet's theatrical destiny was in the hands of the producers. During the Théâtre de Chaillot's 1982–3 season, Vitez presented Hamlet's father as a weak, wretched individual, a 'poor tramp' who was fatally wounded in both body and spirit. At the 1988 Avignon Festival, by presenting the action on a dark, moving stage, which was full of holes and divided into sections like a board game. Chéreau and his set designer, Peduzzi, attempted to express hidden anxieties which – according to Michel Cournot – lead straight to the grave.

Paradoxically it was the great poets who, like the philosophers who reflected on Hamlet (such as a Kierkegaard and Nietzsche), were best able to understand the important lessons of the myth through their own subjective appreciation. According to Baudelaire, in the eyes of the general public the poet played the role of the Prince of Denmark. He chose Hamlet as the symbolic figure of the 'poète maudit', threatened by the Ghost of Silence. Just as Hamlet wonders as to the origin of his father's ghost – 'Be thou a spirit of health or goblin damn'd,/Bring with thee airs from heaven or blasts from hell' – Baudelaire asks, as he contemplates Beauty: 'Do you come from on high or out of the abyss?' ('Hymne à la Beauté', 1860). In the opinion of the author of *Igitur* (1869), Hamlet 'externalizes, on the stage, this unique figure of an intimate and occult tragedy whose very name exerts upon me, and upon you, the reader, a fascination which is akin to anguish' (1896). The fear that the ghost may be merely the revelation of the void led poets to question the very nature of language, and the arbitrary nature of symbolism. The fascination of the word with no referent offered the poet the vision of a 'pure work of art'. Surely Hamlet, Mallarmé's 'lord unrealized and unable to fulfil himself', pays tribute to a heroic past of which he is not part? Surely poets should free themselves from the 'confines of the history of their race which weighs upon them as the experience of the finite', in order to attain the Absolute, which involves forgetting 'the human word within the illegible scrawl'. Poets, who sometimes doubt the validity of their undertaking of negation and self-sacrifice – the very basis of their poetry – are obviously haunted by Hamlet's dying words which express the essence of tragedy itself: '. . . the rest is silence'.

In our modern age of transition and change the myth of Hamlet, like all great literary myths, has inevitably become impoverished. Are the minor works disappearing to make way for The Work which enjoys a disproportionate amount of success? Surely the time has come for Hamlet to be understood via poetic creation and 'the palimpsest of the memory'. Or perhaps, like Oedipus, Electra, Amphitryon and Ulysses, Hamlet will have a new incarnation.

André Lorant

Helen of Troy

Did the Trojan War take place? We have little reason to doubt it, but we have little more to believe that it was the greatest conflict ever to have occurred. The Greeks however, thought that it was: before telling the story of the Peloponnesian War the historian Thucydides felt the need to establish a parallel between it and the Trojan War to emphasize the importance of his subject. With the passage of time these heroic exploits had entered the realm of legend, people were convinced that the gods had taken part, and history became myth. The Trojan War glows with a dark fire at the dawn of time as the unsurpassable model for all the wars that were to come.

An extraordinary phenomenon must have an extraordinary cause. Did Homer think so? It is impossible to tell: his *Iliad* recounts only one episode in the conflict, the death of Hector, otherwise contenting itself with allusions or prophetic pronoucements. One thing is clear: each time the contenders started negotiations, it was said that the Trojans would have to hand back 'Helen and the treasures'. The affair started with a woman being raped and a raid – an act of brigandry. Paris went off with plundered treasure, and a queen to boot. With Aphrodite's blessing, he made the queen his wife.

But other bards, whose work has been lost, were not satisfied with such a humble explanation. They built up a cycle of epics telling the whole story of the war from the beginning. They described the origin of the affair *ab ovo*. They accepted that Zeus wanted to decimate the human race which had become too numerous, and posited a whole series of events: rivalry among three goddesses over an apple given 'to the most beautiful' by Eris (Discord); a verdict favouring Aphrodite pronounced by Paris, a Trojan prince brought up among shepherds; Paris being rewarded with the most beautiful woman ever seen. This woman, Helen, was the daughter of Zeus and Leda; as Zeus had disguised himself as a swan to seduce his beloved, Helen and her brothers the Dioscuri were born *ab ovo* – from an egg.

This explication of the whole episode entails several difficulties. The main question is the extent to which Helen accepted the fate assigned to her. Did she act of her own free will? It was not long before people wondered if she had followed Paris voluntarily. It is an important distinction. In the first instance it could be said that she was the occasion of the war, which makes her no less odious; in the second she was responsible for the war, and could thus be hated as a scourge, and also condemned on moral grounds.

Such condemnation became increasingly necessary in the eyes of the Greeks, who were developing a personal morality, but was ever less acceptable to those among them who saw Helen as a goddess. The immorality of religious myths shocked more than one right-thinking person in the fifth century BC. In some towns, Sparta in particular, there were temples to Helen, feasts of Helen and a cult of Helen, who figured as the protectress of adolescent girls and young married women. It would be shocking if elsewhere she had set an example of adultery. And the closer we go towards presenting the story in human terms, the closer we come to the unacceptable. Aeschylus turned Helen into a being who was both abstract and divine, a sort of curse closely allied to the goddess Nemesis, – who according to some traditions was her mother, and not Leda. But Euripides saw his heroine purely as a woman; he did not even accept the possible intervention of Aphrodite to inspire Helen with an irresistible passion. Hecabe says so very forcefully in the *Troades*: 'Paris was an extremely handsome man – one look,/And your appetite became your Aphrodite. Why,/Men's lawless lusts are all called love' (v. 987, trans. Vellacott).

How far is this psychological speech, which uses allegory, also an impious speech casting doubt on the existence of the gods? It is not easy to say. In any case it is almost at the opposite pole from the chorus in *Agamemnon* where Aeschylus says of Helen that she is the Erinyes, the 'wife of tears' and 'the priest of Ate'; we are also a long way from the suggestion that Helen a has a sort of divine mission, making her the instrument of fate: as it is expressed in Vellacott's translation, 'Was born that fit and fatal name,/To glut the sea with spoil of ships' (*Agamemnon* 689).

The virtual disappearance of the religious aspect of Helen that surrounded her with an aura of sacred terror laid her open to the most scathing insults. People expressed amazement that the Trojan War should have been fought over such an unimportant creature – a woman – adding that the woman in question had absolutely no value because she herself had no sense of her own dignity. A fine assortment of insults could easily be garnered from Euripides. This tradition did not stop with him; at the height of the neoclassical period in Europe the name of Helen became a simple figure of speech, a metonym that could be used to designate any woman who was dangerous because she was flighty; in Schiller's *Maria Stuart* one of the queen's most persistent opponents can find no worse epithet for her than this: she is a Helen.

Euripides was alive at the time when sophistry was born. No doubt he was as amused as anyone else by the idea of pleading lost causes. Gorgias and Isocrates each produced a eulogy of Helen. The tragic poet had shown them the way by putting a plea in the heroine's own mouth (*Troades* 903ff.). There is censure of the power of the gods, the origin of desire and the power of seduction: a suitable subject for rhetors whose prime concern it was to attract an audience. Or there is praise of beauty.

From whatever angle it was approached it was not a comfortable morality: was it possible for a woman who was perfectly beautiful to be corrupt and vile? A philosophical dimension loomed. Homer was happy to concede that the Trojan populace felt ill-will towards Helen, but the finest Trojans, Priam, his advisers and Hector, found it impossible not to respect her. At one point in the *Iliad* (VI.358) a strange complicity is established between Helen and Hector, both of them unhappy, but sure that they will for ever be celebrated by poets.

Homer's successors never tired of pondering a parallel between Helen and Achilles. One of the poets of the epic cycle had proposed a meeting between the most beautiful daughter of Zeus and the most valiant of heroes. Much later it was imagined that these two marvellous beings were united beyond death on the fabled Isles of the Blessed. But Euripides had already pointed out (*Helen* 99) that Achilles had been prominent among Helen's suitors, and that the Trojan War had been envisaged also with a view to allowing Achilles to distinguish himself (op. cit., l. 41); moreover the apple of Discord, the origin of the whole affair, had been produced on the occasion of the wedding of Thetis and Peleus, Achilles' parents-to-be.

Paradoxically the concern to elevate Helen from the realm of sordid anecdote and restore her to an epic role, was to have the effect of casting doubt on the epic itself. Since it was vital that beautiful Helen should be virtuous, it was claimed that she had never been in Troy, that Zeus had put a phantom in her place or that a king of Egypt had snatched her from Paris to protect her. The second version, which was known to Herodotus, has had a long life: it can be found in the novel *Kassandra* (1983) by Christa Wolf. Wolf imagines that the Trojans pretended Helen was within their walls so as not to lose face. The first version also effectively makes Helen an object of derision, and again presents in an exaggerated form the bitter judgement so often repeated – a woman was not a worthwhile cause for people to kill one another.

Yet this was not the point of view expressed by Euripides, the poet supposed to hate women, in his tragedy *Helen*. Not only does he depict her character in the same touching, majestic light as his Alcestis or his Polyxena (in *Hecabe*), he even extends the study of the sufferings of misrepresented innocence to a tragic interrogation of the identity of the person: Helen is a woman who has been robbed of her very name and face. Saved because the gods finally proclaim the truth, she can rejoin or at least expect to rejoin the pleasant atmosphere of the feasts in Sparta (l. 1451ff.), the young girls dancing and the husband towards whom she was led with songs.

Writing his 'Epithalamion of Helen' (*Idylls* 18) more than two centuries after Euripides, Theocritus did not even mention the Trojan War. No doubt he bore in mind that according to a tradition relayed by Plato (*Phaedrus* 243a) the poet Stesichorus had been blinded by the gods for speaking ill of Helen, recovering his sight only after reciting the *Palinode* (a recantation).

It is impossible to know which of the two traditions Euripides was more committed to, that which he followed in his *Helen* or the other which is evident in the rest of his plays, where he attacks her as fickle, flirtatious and brazen. We can only note that other heroic characters were also depicted by Euripides in a none too favourable light: wily Odysseus, for example, whose wisdom and ability to confront the most disconcerting situations unperturbed were described by Homer with admiration, tends to become an unscrupulous sophist who loves traps and machinations. If Hecabe reproaches Helen, she does not spare Odysseus. Reading the great tragedies that conjure up the fall of Troy (*Traodes, Hecabe* and to some extent *Andromache* as well) we get the impression that the judicious balance that Homer's epic poems preserved between the two opposing sides has been upset, and certainly not in favour of the victors.

The legend also became degraded. Once seen as a divine scourge, Helen was now regarded as a hateful woman. She was the butt of obscene jokes even in Euripides' day (the *Cyclops*), a tradition that was continued in Horace, Jean de Meung, Hofmannswaldau, and Meilhac and Halévy. Others merely adopted a light, frivolous, scornful tone when writing about her.

The whole legend suffered in the process, as will be realized by anyone brave enough to tackle the depressing task of reading the short summaries made in Late Antiquity – the whole Trojan War in forty pages – that have come down to us under the fine-sounding names of Dictys Cretensis and Dares Phrygius. These works would be devoid of interest but for the fact that they, rather than the *Iliad*, were read right through the Middle Ages and well beyond; they were published in Amsterdam as late as 1702 in a superb edition with scholarly notes 'for the use of the Dauphin'. In them we learn more than one surprising fact. The fearful duel recounted in Book XXII of the *Iliad*, for example, never took place: Achilles killed Hector in an ambush at no risk to himself. This detail is repeated in Shakespeare (*Troilus and Cressida*), Montchrestien (*Hector*) and in *La Pomme de Discorde* by Guillén de Castro, a writer best known for having blazed the trail for Corneille in his *Las Mocedades del Cid*.

Although Dares does not fall into that particular trap, he does claim that the Trojan horse never existed. He did not gain much credence. He also claims that the judgement of Paris took place in a dream, and to explain the Trojan War he relates a complete earlier history of conflicts between the Trojans and members of the Argonauts' expedition, punitive expeditions in every direction, raids and abducted princesses. The episode involving Helen is downgraded in the process.

We also find new heroes being put forward. Troilus plays a major role alongside Hector. Polyxena rivals Helen in her beauty. From the time of Euripides it was known that Polyxena was sacrificed on Achilles' tomb after the fall of Troy, and some time later it was deduced from this that Achilles had demanded that his beloved should join him in death. The legend of Achilles' love for Polyxena is not expressly mentioned before Late Antiquity; it plays an important role in the work of Dares, Dictys and those that followed them, since it was on the occasion of the secret marriage of the two lovers that Paris treacherously killed the Greek hero.

At the end of Antiquity Greek poets recounted in verse all that Homer had omitted (Quintus Smyrnaeus, *The Fall of Troy*; Colluthus, *The Rape of Helen*; Tryphiodorus, *The Capture of Troy*). Their version of events was in general closer to tradition, but it was Dares and Dictys that were studied and followed in the Middle Ages, no doubt because they were available in Latin.

In the mid-twelfth century a clerk from Touraine serving the Dukes of Normandy, Benoît de Sainte-Maure, wrote a 'romance', that is a version in the Romance, French or vulgar tongue of a Latin original. His *Roman de Troie*, a vast poem 30,000 octosyllabic lines long, is fortunately not a translation, though neither was it really an elaboration on the original story. This book brought Helen as well as Hector, Troilus and Polyxena immediate glory, rather different from the glory that the scholarly tradition might have afforded them. In the courtly atmosphere which was then becoming prevalent Helen and Paris became a pair of perfect lovers, comparable with, say, Tristan and Isolde or Lancelot and Guinevere. The Middle Ages also honoured Achilles and Polyxena as a couple, as well as Troilus and Cressida (perhaps arising from a confusion between Chryseis and Briseis), though they did not enjoy favour for long.

It may be because Dares provided an acceptable explanation for the start of the war that in mediaeval literature Helen escaped the reproaches levelled against her in Classical Greece. Only a few scribes brought up on Latin studies still thought of casting insults on her: 'Causa rei talis meretrix fuit exitialis,/Femina fatalis femina fet malis' (*Carmina Burana* 101.45). But another poet in the same collection wrote ecstatically of his beautiful heroine: 'Deus, Deus meus! estne illa Helena vel est dea Venus?' (*ibid*, 77.14). And his colleagues writing in the vulgar tongue, from Arnaud Daniel to Villon, followed his example. Helen is one of those radiant beauties comparable to a stained-glass window or a polished ivory, the sight of which turns men into knights and poets.

We may wonder at the readiness with which the female characters who appear in the legends of the Grail are given her name. Of course there was a St Helena, the mother of Constantine, who discovered the relics of the True Cross. Nonetheless if the name Helen had still been as disreputable as it was in Euripides' plays it would be hard to conceive of it being used for the maiden who carried the Grail and who would become the mother of Galahad (Malory, *Le Morte d'Arthur*, XI.2).

There is undoubtedly a reminiscence of that chivalric vision in the famous sonnet by Ronsard adapted from Homer: 'We must not stand gaping, said these good old men . . .' (*Sonnets pour Hélène* II.67). The old men did in fact admire Helen; in their eyes she had a superhuman beauty which justified the fighting. Yet in Homer they have second thoughts, and say they would prefer her to be sent back to Greece so that Troy might continue to prosper. Ronsard does not find this admissible: 'all of you together should have risked body, possessions and city for her'. This mediaeval fury will come as no surprise to those readers who have noticed how often Ronsard used the word 'chevalier' even when talking of antique heroes.

The rediscovery in the sixteenth century of the Greek authors, however, especially of the minor writers from the period of the late empire mentioned above, but also of Euripides, tended to revive the image of Helen as a hateful woman, a criminal aware of what she was doing and the prime cause of an unrelenting war. The fireworks with which Ronsard celebrated the name of Helen perhaps marked the end of an epoch. When the poet in his *Hymne de Charles, Cardinal de Lorraine* compared to the niece of the Cardinal to whom the poem was dedicated to Helen he does not appear to have committed a solecism. This could probably not have been done at a later date.

Perhaps a ruse was called for. Guillén de Castro described the rape of Helen in a very odd way: like Dares or Benoît de Sainte-Maure, he assumes that through the agency of Eros Helen and Paris were drawn to one another irresistibly. But could the Queen follow her lover without at least token resistance? What would become of her good name? They agree to pretend. And right in the middle of a violent scene they murmur to one another: ' – Oh, Helen, how well you are acting! – Oh, Paris, how well you are ravishing me!' Guillén de Castro's poem is not outstanding. In Racine's *Iphigénie*, which is rather more distinguished, Menelaus' indulgence for 'His guilty better half of whom he is too fond' is constantly stigmatized. In that play, as earlier in *La Troade* by Robert Garnier, it is accepted that Helen was responsible for the war. Racine will have nothing to do with the ancient tradition, liberally used by Isocrates in his *Eulogy of Helen*, according to which Theseus abducted Helen when she was still a child; the poet seems to infer from this that she had always been depraved.

The imagination of a clerical schoolmaster, however, prepared the way for a turnaround. According to the *Volksbuch* Faust rounded off his career as a magician by bringing Helen back from the underworld; he must have learnt in his textbook of rhetoric that the Queen of Sparta was the paragon of beauty. Marlowe took up the story and at the end of the sixteenth century composed an amazing silent scene for his play about the damned scholar. Helen appears, but she does not speak.

It is worth asking why there was this link in the so-called Baroque period between Helen and the theatre, the opera in particular. Helen could appear, she could be made to sing, she could be seen acting. But apparently she could not be talked about, and her fiercest detractors were in fact those who did not put her on the stage. First Cavalli, then Gluck wrote tunes for Helen.

It was again for the theatre, though almost a theatre of dreams, that Goethe wrote his *Helena* which was to form the third act of *Faust II*. At the same time as taking the motif from the *Volksbuch*, the old poet was quite happy to write a classical tragedy in a metre adapted from Antiquity. He takes up the story at the time of the fall of Troy, which allows him to summarize in a few lines what was henceforth to be the standard popular version, the version that permeates the work of Euripides, for example. Nothing is left out, neither the doubts about whether Helen had consented to her abduction, nor the rumours about her stay in Egypt and the ghost that took her place in Troy, nor the mention of Achilles' passion. The whole scenario is summed up in the contradiction contained in the first line uttered by the heroine: 'So much admired, burdened with so many outrages, Helen . . .'. Helen is going to be put to death, in keeping with the wishes expressed by Menelaus in the *Troades*. A mysterious mist saves her, and the intervention of a frightening old woman who once her mask has been removed turns out to be Mephistopheles: Helen is in Faust's power. What follows is no longer part of the legend of Troy, but it does go back to a very old tradition from the end of the heroic period that describes the apotheosis of Helen. For a while Faust plays the role of an attendant to a supreme divinity who, by him and for him, gives birth to the too beautiful Euphorion; the interlude ends in despair after the child's disappearance. But for a while Helen and Hellas reigned, and some magicians know how to conjure them up again.

What is important is not Helen's eternal residence in a rather vague Empyrean but her enthronement, the act by which a superior power restores her to her rightful place. Though the Queen hardly plays a distinguished part in it, Euripides' *Orestes* in fact ends with these words from Apollo:

> Now, soaring aloft to the star-bright sphere
> Helen I will conduct to the mansion of Zeus
> There men shall adore her, a goddess enthroned
> Beside Hera and Hebe and great Heracles.
> There she, with her brothers, Tyndareos's sons,
> Shall be worshipped for ever with wine outpoured
> As the seamen's Queen of the Ocean. (v. 1633)

This development was probably conveyed on the stage, with Helen appearing high up beside the *deus ex machina*.

Helen's salvation is again the issue in *La Tentation de saint Antoine*, in which Flaubert refers to the Gnostic tradition according to which Simon Magus met Helen of Troy in an area of ill-repute in Tyre, and restored her to her true condition of primordial Goodness.

The rehabilitation or apotheosis of Helen is not well suited to speeches, pleas, eulogies or apologies. Thus in lyrical poetry this process coincided with a movement to abandon the rhetorical tradition. Perhaps as poems became shorter, renouncing argumentation and often confining themselves to a mere image, gesture or snapshot scene, an almost ritual return to the original scenario as described by Homer was made possible: Helen walks along the rampart, approaching the Scaean gate. The Symbolist movement justified its name – given to it retrospectively by literary historians (through a misguided broadening of the concept) – when the poets involved in it succeeded in avoiding allegory, the transformation of Helen into a vignette suitable for illustrating the abstract idea of beauty, and instead were simply fascinated by the trembling silence that greeted a woman's walk. Valéry, Yeats, Samain, D'Annunzio, Apollinaire, Mandelstamm and Elytis come to mind. The list could easily be extended with the names of those who expanded – but did not develop – the one- or two-line glancing allusions of their precursors, including Ronsard, into a sonnet or a poem barely any longer.

The return of Helen that Goethe brought about also gave rise for the first time for many centuries to works in which the Queen is the central character: very classical, rather scholarly poems such as *Hélène* by Leconte de Lisle or *Helen of Troy* by Andrew Lang; low-brow farces such as *La Belle Hélène* by Meilhac, Halévy and Offenbach; pretentious light comedy such as *Hélène ou la Joie de vivre* by André Roussin, a brave attempt to vie with the ambiguous play by Giraudoux called *La Guerre de Troie n'aura pas lieu*; lyrical tragedy short on plot such as *Hélène de Sparte* by Verhaeren; enigmatic fantasy such as *Protée* by Claudel; pure tragedy such as *Die ägyptische Helena* written by Hofmannsthal as a vehicle for Richard Strauss' music. Different as they are, all these texts but one were written for the theatre.

What is striking in the best of these works is the refusal to condemn Helen, or to excuse her for the sake of her resigned goodness. Claudel turns his Helen into a complete fool, as part of his transformation of the Egyptian version of the legend into a farce. Nevertheless there are moments when he achieves an unexpected lyrical power, as if the beauty of Helen's speeches had a life of its own, independent of the will of the person uttering them. Giraudoux makes Ulysses say of Helen that she is 'thick-headed' and 'of limited intellect', but he endows her with a fearful clairvoyance which fills her with vivid imaginings and enables the playwright to know, when all those arguing in favour of peace are going about their business, that the Trojan War will nevertheless take place, that Paris will die in it and that little Astyanax will be killed.

Hofmannsthal's distortion of the pious legend of Stesichorus is still more dreadful: an Egyptian sorceress is ready to convince Menelaus with the help of philtres that Helen of Troy is a ghost and that the real Helen was in Egypt throughout the course of the war. The illusion will be broken at the behest of Helen herself who needs to be accepted such as she is, formed by her complex and contradictory legend. Have we gone beyond the concepts of Good and Evil?

Or have we in fact discovered tragedy when the certainties of connected speech, the assurances of reason and judgements based on immutable principles start to unravel? Homer realized this from the start: Helen has had an intolerable role thrust upon her. 'Ah how I wish that on the very day when my mother bore me the Storm-fiend had swept me off into the mountains or the roaring sea' (*Iliad* VI.345). Although Benoît de Sainte-Maure had not read Homer, he also divines that his heroine must curse the day of her birth (*Roman de Troie* 22,920ff.). Montchrestien chops and changes the *Iliad* as he sees fit, but he too makes Helen say: 'Eyes too awake to my doom cover yourselves in darkness;/Cease to see the days that you darken;/Alas, cease to look on these lovely green fields/Which are covered with murder and blood for you' (*Hector* 1349ff.). And in his 'A Dream of Fair Women', a poem from his youth freely inspired by Chaucer, Tennyson tells how he heard Helen say:

> Many drew swords and died. Where'er I came
> I brought calamity . . .
> I would the white, cold heavy-plunging foam,
> Whirled by the wind, had rolled me deep below,
> Then when I left my home.

The forms in which this myth is expressed are so diverse that it is hard to determine its invariables. How could we justify censuring those poets for whom Helen is perfectly and impudently at ease with her conscience, always supposing she has one? All the same, Helen is cast with remarkable frequency as a burdened soul who finds it hard to recognize her own identity, in the work of both those who stick to the Trojan version and those who adopt the Egyptian variant. One of the first times he mentions Helen Homer speaks of her 'sobs'. And the distress of the innocent Helen in Euripides' play is immense.

Beside this motif there is another: Helen is *par excellence* the woman carried off by a stranger. Abducted by Theseus, then by Paris, recaptured by her brothers, then by her husband, snatched from Paris by an Egyptian king, then from the son of that king by Menelaus, taken off by Simon Magus, then by Faust, sent to the heavens or to the Isles of the Blessed: is Helen the mistress of her fate?

It will be remembered that in *Troades* Helen is 'held prisoner with all the women taken in Troy' (1. 872). She is imprisoned like Hecabe, Andromache and Cassandra. For the film he produced in 1971 Cacoyannis had a cage built in which Helen was discovered, and suddenly booed. And in the plea she makes, however sophistical it may be, the reviled princess claims that her time spent in Troy has always been to her a period of captivity.

Morality and psychology would lead one to expect many subtle differences in the relationships between the characters. Euripides, for example, organized his tragedy round a conflict between Helen and Hecabe, and Tennyson made his poem a complaint levelled at Helen by Iphigenia. Beyond these incontrovertible specific aspects, however, one feature remains: of all the heroic chronicles that have attained the status of myth, the saga of Troy is perhaps the one in which the roles played by women were most developed. From the mourning lament in Book XXIV of the *Iliad* to Christa Wolf's *Kassandra*, taking in the highly original adaptation by Jean-Paul Sartre of *Troades*, a veiled figure stands over the corpses, a pitiful victim left to her fate. When the warriors have perished, the women will be dragged far away from their land to the houses of new masters. The epic of Troy tells us that a city can die.

Homer finishes the *Iliad* with a lament. Standing beside Hector's body Helen speaks to him, thanking him for never having insulted her. She is not afraid to compare their misfortunes; there are sensitive feelings that the old myth, facing darkness, may neglect: '. . . these tears of sorrow that I shed are both for you and for my miserable self. No one else is left . . .'.

Jean-Louis Backès

Hermes

According to the author of the Homeric hymn, just as the light of dawn creeps into all nooks and crannies, Hermes slipped silently out of the cave in which he was born. Hermes was by nature flexible, changeable and ambiguous, a nature shared by his assistants, Hermione and Harmonia, and especially by his predecessor, the light-footed, golden-winged Iris. In Greek mythology he is an engaging and complex figure who appears in both changing and constant forms. Therefore, in order to follow him on his long journey through the western imagination, in mediaeval and modern times, it is first of all important to understand him in terms of Greek mythology. As an essential point of reference and a permanent background it is so well known or at least easily accessible, that there is no need to summarize the story in which the Greek god Hermes, or the Roman god Mercury, appear as either the main character, the hero or in a minor role. A few reminders should suffice, which focus on his unchanging characteristics, often repeated from Antiquity to modern times. Two of these in particular stand out from the general mass of details. The first is his role as the guide of souls, which is linked to his extreme mobility, and the second is his mastery of discourse and interpretation which is the guarantee of a particular type of knowledge.

Aware of his mercurial qualities, Virgil describes how the agile messenger of the gods controls the wind and clouds with his magic wand as he flies through them like a bird. But this messenger tends to follow clearly defined routes from which he does not deviate. As Karl Kerenyi suggested, he is more of a 'journeyer' than a 'traveller', and likes to move about and communicate for the pure pleasure of doing so, in much the same way that the geographical destination of a honeymoon is of relatively little importance. That being the case, the route is not seen primarily as the link between two points, but rather as a world in its own right, made up of winding pathways along which anything could happen in a chance encounter with the unexpected. 'Hermaion' means a 'windfall' or a 'stroke of luck', and taking advantage of windfalls does not preclude the possibility of giving destiny a helping hand in the form of the occasional ruse. Hermes is therefore sometimes represented as discovering hidden treasures, and it is only one step from there to stealing them. 'Hermes' [Ermaïon's] share!' was an expression used by the Greeks when they had a lucky find, just as the French use an expression 'Part à deux', which means 'extra share'. It is possible to justify both the eclecticism and the plagiarism, but it should be remembered that 'steal' is a poor translation of 'klepteïn', which rather suggests the idea of cunning in the sense of 'secret action' (cf.

the German 'Täuschung' and the wonderful verb 'verschalken'). And after all, isn't discovering hidden treasures the prerogative of hermeneutics? Therefore Hermes, unlike Prometheus, only steals to put these treasures back into circulation. It is even possible to talk of a 'circulation' of souls since Hermes fulfils his role as the guide of dead souls in two respects. He not only leads them down into Hades, but also brings them back to the land of the living (see *Aeneid* IV.242, as well as many examples in mediaeval and modern literature). Through a wide variety of representations in folklore, painting and literature, the western imagination has stressed this intermediary aspect, which is the common denominator for Hermes' attributes ranging from the guiding of souls to theft via trade, magic, poetry and learning.

Thus Hermes, like Athena, claims the glory of having discovered the sciences and arts, and it is well known that the Homeric *Hymn to Hermes* (1. 25ff.) considers him to be the inventor of the seven-stringed lyre. He is the keeper of a particular type of knowledge, or rather of a way of achieving knowledge – divine, gnostic, eclectic, 'transdisciplinary', or all of these at once. In this respect it is possible that he is greatly indebted to Plato. Shortly after Aristophanes' *Plutos*, in which Hermes appears in a comic role, Plato's *Cratylus* (407ff.) considers the name 'Hermes' to be derived from the Greek word for 'interpreter': 'Let us consider what the name Hermes means . . . Well, . . . the name Hermes appears to be related to discourse ('logos'); the characteristics of the interpreter ('hermeneus'), the messenger, the accomplished thief, the deceiver with words and the clever merchant, all such activities are related to the skilful use of speech.' This is the only aspect retained by the New Testament where, according to Acts XIV.12, the people of Lystra mistook Paul for Hermes when they discovered that he was extremely eloquent. It was in this role that Hermes was revered by poets and philosophers. Horace, Virgil's contemporary, placed himself under the specific protection of Mercury, while Lucian in his *Fugitivi* (XXII) describes him accompanying Heracles and Philosophy in their pursuit of the Cynics because, according to Apollo, he was best able to distinguish between the true and false philosophers. His role was more that of a wise man – albeit a facetious and mischievous one – than of a hero, an aspect which is taken one step further in the *Iliad*, whose world is so far removed from that of Hermes that he isn't even given the opportunity to guide a dead soul and remains at a distance from any form of heroic action. Although he does oppose Leto, he then evades the issue in order to avoid a confrontation. When Zeus sends him to help Priam, who is about to retrieve his son's body from Achilles, he is not so much a messenger as a guide, and it is he who prepares their escape by ensuring that the guards fall asleep. Wotan, whom the Romans were already correctly comparing to Mercury (Tacitus, *Germania* IX), possessed similar characteristics. Furthermore, when the Germanic deity was invested with certain comic connotations, he was soon followed by Harlequin with his wooden stick or sword, a derisory imitation of the caduceus.

HERMES TRISMEGISTOS

With the appearance of Hermes Trismegistos during the first century AD, the characteristic flexibility of Hermes–Mercury was represented in a very specific form embodying the most serious and least mischievous aspect of the character, which has survived up to the present day. It seems to be associated with two main factors. On the one hand, the allegorical interpretation of mythology, which began with Homeric criticism in the fourth century BC, and moved increasingly towards euhemerism, which resulted in a tendency to see Hermes as a historical personage who had been deified. (Euhemerus, a Greek philosopher of the third century BC, had propounded the theory that the gods were in fact real men who had been deified posthumously.) This tendency was reinforced by Christian thought, which from the second century AD was firmly orientated towards euhemerism. The second factor was the interest shown by Greek and Roman paganism in ancient Egypt, in accordance with the need felt by the Greeks to extol the philosophy of the barbarians to the detriment of their own. This interest was greatly fostered by the existence of an Alexandrian Greek culture, firmly established on Egyptian soil, which involved pyramids and hieroglyphics. The Greeks of the first century AD rightly saw in Thoth the first image of Hermes, or even Hermes himself under a different name. In accordance with euhemeristic theory, a large number of existing books were attributed to Thoth–Mercury under the general title of the *Hermetica*. They were nearly all written in Greek, in the Delta region, during a period which dated from the end of the first century BC to the third century AD, and were devoted to astrology, alchemy and theosophy. The most famous of these (from the second and third centuries AD) are grouped under the general title of the *Corpus Hermeticum*, into which have been incorporated the *Asclepius* and the *Fragments* attributed to Stobaeus. But a legendary tradition attributes thousands more books to Hermes Trismegistos.

Fragment 23 by Stobaeus described the court of the Lord, creator of the universe, as it was before mortals existed. Hermes is featured as a 'soul' ('psyche') who is able to understand the mysteries of heaven and has been sent by God into the lower world of mortals to teach true knowledge. The Lord asks Hermes to participate in a supervisory and administrative capacity in the creation of mankind, with the result that it is possible to see him as the main protagonist, after the supreme god, in the anthropogenic drama. He is a soul who has come down to earth as the first divine manifestation, before the second manifestation represented by Isis and Osiris, who are also sent into the lower world to bring knowledge to humanity. Although he is not in this instance referred to as 'Trismegistos', thrice great, the other texts of the *Corpus Hermeticum* provide more than a suggestion that this is in fact he. This is one of the many examples of the transition from the figure of the wise man of that name, who is mortal, to the Olympian god. This means that, during this period, we are not only dealing with euhemerism but also with the reverse process. Hermes Trismegistos is a projection of Mercury into the history of humanity as well as the redirection of history towards Mount Olympus. This fluctuation, or rather this two-way process, is favoured by an erratic genealogy and by the presence of several Hermes.

During the Hellenistic period, the most usual genealogy, developed during the third and second centuries BC, considered that the series of representations of Hermes began with Thoth, who engraved his knowledge on steles before hiding them. He was the father of Agathodaimon, whose son was the second Hermes, known as Trismegistos, who was the father of Tat. In his *Argonautica* (I.640ff.), Apollonius Rhodius informs us that Hermes, through his son Aithalides, is the ancestor of Pythagoras. But there is nothing more uncertain than divine genealogies. According to the traditions reported by Plutarch, Isis was supposed to be the daughter of Hermes, while in *De Natura Deorum* (I.3–22) Cicero lists no less than five Mercuries: the son of the sky and light, the son of Valeus and the nymph Phoronis, Thoth, the son of Jupiter and Maia, and finally the one who, according to Cicero, was called Trismegistos and was supposed to have 'taught the Egyptians the laws of writing'. In *The City of God*, St Augustine makes Trismegistos the great-grandson of a contemporary of Moses and indulges in euhemerism by seeing the origin of this and other Greek gods in remarkable human actions. Isidorus of Seville (sixth to seventh century AD) also subscribed to the euhemerist theory and devoted a number of passages in his *Etymologiarum sive libri XX* (cf. VIII, XI.1ff. and XI.45–9) to Hermes, where he considers him to be a pagan invention based on the historical figure of the inventor of the lyre, the flute, conjuring and illusions ('Praestigium vero Mercurius primus dicitur invenisse').

Although based on Isidorus' *Etymologiarum*, Adon de Vienne's *Chronique des six Ages de Monde* illustrates, as do many other works, the significance of the ambiguity of Hermes (Mercury and/or Trismegistos). According to Adon: 'It was at that time that Prometheus was said to live, who is supposed to have created Man out of mud; at the same time, his brother Atlas was considered to be a great astrologer; Atlas' grandson, Mercury, was extremely skilled in several arts and for this reason, after his death, an aberration on the part of his contemporaries placed him among the gods' (*P.L.* CXXIII, col. 35). Similarly, *Li Livres dou Trésor* by Brunetto Latini considers Mercury, like Moses, Solon, Lycurgus, Numa Pompilius and the Greek king, Phoroneus, to be among some of the first legislators to whom humanity is greatly indebted. Thus Hermes–Mercury, in a double form, takes his place among the divine forerunners of civilization. According to Strabo, he made laws for the Egyptians and taught philosophy and astronomy to the priests of Thebes, and Marcus Manilius even makes him the founder of religion in Egypt. For Jacques de Bergame, Minerva was the first woman to master the art of spinning wool, and Cheiron was the inventor of medicine, Hermes Trismegistos was the first astronomer, Mercury the first musician and Atlas taught astrology to the

Greeks. Similar attributes are found in the works of Polydore Virgile, who thought that Hermes taught the concept of the division of time and Mercury taught the Egyptians the alphabet and astronomy.

THE ARABIC GOD, IDRIS, AND MERCURY, GOD OF ALCHEMY

From this point onwards the name of Hermes, whether qualified by Trismegistos or not, served as guarantee and signature for a number of estoteric works on magic, astrology and medicine throughout the Middle Ages, although this was a period unfamiliar with the *Corpus Hermeticum*, with the exception of the *Asclepius*. At the same time, mediaeval Latin and Arabic literature produced a succession of visionary accounts with inspired imagery, grouped around this central figure. The ancient belief that Hermes was supposed to have founded a city is echoed many times, particularly in *Picatrix*, probably written in Arabic during the tenth century and then translated into Latin. In it we are told that he was the first to construct statues which he used to control the course of the Nile in relation to the moon, as well as a city of which the richly symbolic description has not yet revealed all its secrets. This literature, and particularly the works in Arabic, produced numerous scenarios of a character discovering theosophical, astrological and alchemical secrets beneath a stele in Hermes' tomb. Most of them use the same 'topos': the first Hermes, the one that lived before the great flood, had anticipated the disaster and constructed the pyramids so that he could conceal the secrets of knowledge in them before the world was destroyed. This is the scenario presented in the *Book of Krates*, an Arabic text dating from as early as the sixth century. The texts, which are often very beautiful, also illustrate the pervasive influence of local Egyptian colour and Greek culture on the Arabic imagination after the introduction of Islam into Egypt, that is from 64 AD. The short but famous text of the *Emerald Tablet*, attributed to Hermes Trismegistos, forms part of this literature. It is attached to a group of writings to which Apollonius of Tyana and Hermes had both made significant contributions. For example, their names are both associated with the extraordinary *Book of the Secret of Creation*, composed sometime between the sixth century and 750 AD. In the Latin countries this could evoke the story of Perceval in which the hermit Trevizrent (triple knowledge) reveals the history of the Grail, all the more so since modern research has suggested a possible origin of the world 'Grail' in the Greek word 'krater' ('bowl'), with reference to Hermes' bowl described in the *Corpus Hermeticum*. There is also a Saracen god, Tervagant, who has been identified with 'Hermes ter maximus' and who also appears notably in the sixth-century mystery play *Barlaam et Josaphat*.

Hermes in fact occupies an important place in the Islamic tradition. Although his name does not, of course, appear in the Koran, hagiographers and historians of the first centuries of the Hegira soon identified him with Idris, the 'nabi' mentioned twice in the sacred text (Koran XIX.57 and

XXI.85). This is the Idris that God 'raised to an exalted position' and in whom the Arabs also recognize Enoch (cf. Genesis V.18–24). Idris/Hermes is known as the 'Triple Sage' as he was represented in three different forms. The first, who could be compared with Thoth, was a 'civilizing hero', an initiator into the mysteries of the divine knowledge and wisdom which inspire the world. He engraved the principles of this sacred knowledge in hieroglyphs (the Arabic word for 'pyramid', 'haram', is even linked with the name of Hermes, 'Hirmis'). The second, who lived in Babylon after the great flood, was the teacher of Pythagoras, while the third was the first teacher of alchemy. In this way, the figure of Hermes links the pagan past with the Muslim consciousness, but is as elusive as the western figure of Trismegistos. To quote the Islamic scholar, Pierre Lory, from whom the elements of this account have been borrowed, he is a 'prophet without a face', with no substantial or particularly outstanding features. The indefinable nature of his character distinguishes him from most of the major figures in the Bible and the Koran. The same applies in the *Corpus Hermeticum*, which sometimes presents Hermes as a god, sometimes as a sage and at others as a disciple of Nous. According to Arabic tradition, he exists on both a physical and timeless plane, as does Elijah, and his very body is proof of his eternal existence. Pierre Lory recalls that Idris/Hermes is also supposed to have written poetry, particularly odes, in Arabic, Hebrew and Syriac. He therefore rises 'above denominational divisions and transcends religious mysteries and historical chronology'. He speaks 'the languages of heaven and earth and the language of Man in a state of fulfilment, i.e. Arabic'. We noted above that the *Emerald Tablet* was handed down to us in this language.) Finally, there is a very appealing story associated with the character of Hermes/Idris which provides a wonderful example of the myth of the 'Saviour saved'. An angel who had incurred the wrath of God is said to have had one of his wings cut off and been exiled to a lonely island. Having asked Hermes/Idris to intervene on his behalf, and the intervention having proved successful, the angel offered him the opportunity of ascending to the Seventh Heaven while he was still alive.

It comes as no surprise that Hermes, whether qualified by Trismegistos or not, should be considered from very early on, that is from the Alexandrian period, as the founder of alchemy. Greek – or Alexandrian – alchemy, disappeared around the sixth century, only to reappear in the Arab countries in the seventh and eighth centuries. The Arabic translations of the Greek Hermetic texts were to prove a major source of inspiration for authors writing in Latin from the twelfth century onwards, a period which corresponded to the development of alchemy in Europe. A great many authors writing in both Arabic and Latin up to the twentieth century referred to Hermes and Mercury when writing about the Great Work. The references were to him not only as a figure but also, and this was particularly true in the case of Mercury, in such expressions as 'spiritus mercurius', when describing a specific substance or property. According to them, Mercurius was the 'prima materia', the 'ultima materia' as well as the alchemical process itself! As an entity, he was the 'mediator' and 'salvator' – the Mercury of the unconscious described by Jung. As a substance of the Arcanum, he was mercury, water, fire and the divine light of revelation. He was the soul, the principle of life, air, hermaphrodite, both 'puer' and 'senex' and 'tertium datum'. The Mercury of alchemical literature was part of a continuous tradition which attributed a certain metaphysical significance to the gods of Parnassus. Thus towards the end of the pagan era, the Greek Phornutus, in his *Commentary on the Nature of the Gods*, described the virile attributes of Mercury Quadratus as symbolizing the richness and fertility of reason. The Neoplatonists went even further and applied this method to all religious traditions, including those from other countries. They considered the entire universe to be one great myth, the spiritual meaning of which had to be deciphered by our intelligence. This was what Sallustius, the friend of the Emperor Julian, tried to achieve in *De deis et mundo*.

THE FORMS ASSUMED BY HERMES DURING THE EARLY MIDDLE AGES

For this reason, the wealth of archetypes which embellish the figure of Hermes prevent the latter being limited solely to the form of Trismegistos. The Mercury of Parnassus occupied a prominent position in the Christian imagination, but not without undergoing strange transformations, to which his volatility predisposed him. On the one hand he was condemned, ridiculed and represented as a devil, while on the other, he was recognized as a benefactor, a champion of humane values and Christian virtues, the image of Christ, as well as being the keeper of an esoteric philosophy.

Leaving aside this last aspect, it is possible to identify several prominent and constant characteristics in the mediaeval imagery. First of all, there is the allegorical significance of Mercury as 'sermo' and 'ratio', which was frequently evoked by compilers and authors of glossaries until the Renaissance. It was via this route that Mercury was incorporated into Christianity as the god of eloquence. There is nothing surprising about this if it is remembered that in its early stages, and even in the Middle Ages, Christianity saw Greek mythology as a form of preparatory teaching for the true revealed religion, and examined the ancient legends in the hope of discovering prophetic announcements of the Scriptures. From very early times Hermes-logos was compared with Christ-logos (cf. for example Justin, *Apology* 1.22), and several passages by Clement of Alexandria), possibly influenced by Origen (*Contra Celsum* IV). He was seen as the god of flocks, the good shepherd, as shown in early Christian representations where he appears in the form of Hermes 'kriophorus', that is carrying a ram or ewe, an aspect which is indissociable from his role of 'psychopompos' or guide of souls, and is an obvious attribute of Christ. This gave rise to the relatively widespread tendency to imagine this Mercurial guide as an 'angelus bonus' of which one of his incarnations, particularly in the Christian folklore of the East, was none other than the Archangel Michael – or Gabriel. Mercury as an archangel is sometimes represented in iconography with a dog's head, in accordance with a tradition which dates back as far as the Egyptian god Anubis (Hermanubis!) and of which echoes can be found in the Latin world, particularly in the writings of Isidorus of Seville. Three centuries later, in the ninth century, Raban Maur's *De rerum naturis* depicts Mercury with a dog's head among ten or so other divinities. He is holding a stick and there seems to be a bird trapped between his legs, an inaccurate interpretation as the artist was not aware that these were heelpieces. A serpent, a distortion of the caduceus, lies at his feet. In the copy of an Arabic work by Kazwini, the heelpieces are attached to his belt and the wings of his hat have been transformed into a cock's comb. In another illustration reminiscent of Albricus, the wings have been extended to the point of covering his legs and head, forming a sort of crest. Elsewhere, in one of the drawings published by Jean Seznec, the caduceus has been replaced by a two-branched candelabrum.

These unusual representations resulted from errors or inaccurate interpretations and were perhaps responsible for encouraging and indeed aiding the Church to demonize Hermes–Mercury, whom it has often depicted as an evil character. He is therefore sometimes the reflection of Christ-logos, and sometimes a soldier of the infernal legions! In the fourth century AD Sulpicius Severus reported that two demons had appeared to St Martin: 'ille se Jovem, iste Mercurium ferebantur'. The second was the more dangerous: 'Mercurium maxime patiebatur infestum'. And the author added that Satan himself readily assumed the form of Mercury (*Dialogus* I–III, IV.4; XIII.6; IX.1). During the sixth century Martin de Bracare was inspired by the same source. But we have only to recall the passages on the immorality of the gods in the *Republic* to realize that Plato had already set the example. This interpretation was continued by Lactantius and echoed in various other works, for example in *Barlaam et Josaphat* (sixth century, cited above) where Hermes is described as a thief, a liar and a libertine, and in Iacopo da Varazze's *Legenda aurea* (thirteenth century), which repeats the accusations made by Sulpicius Severus. However, one of the most famous works of the early Middle Ages, Martianus Capella's *De nuptiis Philologiae et Mercurii* (fifth century), which was destined to be widely read at least up to and including the seventeenth century, in no way subscribed to this view. Rather, it contributed to the near-definitive establishment of most of the allegorical interpretations of Mercury in the European tradition. In the marriage of Philology and Mercury, the latter represents eloquence while Philology represents love, wisdom and reason, and the seven arts are the bridesmaids. When they are divorced, they are both condemned to sterility, since Mercury has nothing more to say and Philology can no longer express herself. Jupiter, who presided over the divine assembly during the marriage ceremony, said of Mercury:

nam nostra ille fides, sermo, benignitas
ac verus genius, fida recursio
interpretesque menae mentis, o nous socer.

The couple, Mercury and Philology, were to have a long literary future ahead of them. They appeared in the poetry of the Goliards which, although a lesser-known form, had a widespread and persistent influence, while Renaissance writers obviously enjoyed playing with the allegories of the *De nuptiis*.

In direct opposition to the diabolical representations, but also beyond the limits of the tradition defined by Capella, Mercury has also been known to be represented as a bishop. He can be seen in this role in the illustrations for the astronomical and astrological treatise composed by Michael Scot between 1243 and 1250 at the Sicilian court of the Emperor Frederick II. In these illustrations his attribute is a book rather than the caduceus, which according to Fritz Saxl demonstrates Babylonian influence through Islam. Michael Scot's pious and wise Mercury corresponds to Nebo, the author-god. Holding a book, and sometimes even depicted with a halo, the 'Mercury' of the Babylonian images is a scholar or a dervish for whom, having reached the west, it is almost natural to become a bishop. In the same way, the forerunner of Jupiter, who is represented as a judge, is Marduk, the god who controls destiny. These attributes basically illustrate the relatively common tendency during the Middle Ages of presenting the pagan gods in contemporary dress as well as vice versa. This explains why, as Jean Seznec has pointed out, the Virgin of Reims looks like one of the Vestal Virgins. In the chancel of the Erimitani Church in Padua and on the capital of the Doges' Palace in Venice, Mercury assumes the characteristics of a professor, while for Alexander Neckham (d. 1217), the planetary gods correspond to the seven gifts of the Holy Spirit and Mercury is given the title of the dispenser of the 'donum pietatis'. This must surely be one explanation, among many others, for his transformation into a bishop. It is possible that Neckham was the author of the famous *Liber imaginum deorum*, although it was circulated under the name of Albricus at the same time as the *De deorum imaginibus libellus*, which was illustrated with ink drawings. The *Liber* and the *Libellus*, which were widely read and often recopied until the seventeenth century, are an example of a very old tradition dating back at least to the fifth-century Greek poem *Aratos*, as well as to Cicero (*De natura deorum* II.15), that identified the gods with the planets. It was a tradition that inspired many illustrated mediaeval manuscripts from the Carolingian period onwards. Known as 'Aratea', they have contributed to the association of the gods with the planets, and therefore of Hermes with the planet Mercury. But it was mainly as a result of the two works attributed to Albricus, the *Liber* and the *Libellus*, that the Olympian gods were able to re-establish their sovereignty.

AT THE DAWN OF THE RENAISSANCE

As Dante's guide through hell, purgatory and heaven, was Virgil not fulfilling a Mercurial role? We will return to the problem posed by this type of parallel, the question of whether a myth can only be identified by a name. For the moment, let us continue to follow the trail of Hermes–Mercury. Even in the works of Dante, the planets are compared with the seven liberal arts: Dialectics corresponds to Mercury, the sphere of Grammar to that of the Moon, etc. But although the fourteenth century began with the *Divine Comedy*, it also witnessed the development of the works of Boccaccio and Petrarch, with the result that Italy remained the chosen country of the god up until and during the Renaissance, which glorified him as a figure of great importance. Boccaccio saw him as the intepreter of secrets who dissipated the clouds of the mind ('ventos agere Mercurii est') and his *De genealogia deorum*, which subsequently became an indispensable reference source, was perhaps the work which most effectively bridged the gap between the mythology of the Middle Ages and the Renaissance. Loyal to the spirit of his century, he defended the idea that poems and stories always have a hidden meaning 'sub cortice' (a tendency already present in the works of Raban Maur), and demonstrated a marked interest in the idea of identifying each planet with a god. Boccaccio explained that the planet Mercury was characterized by its flexible nature and described all its attributes at great length. These were, of course, also the attributes of the god. Petrarch tended to favour the idea of removing Hermes from an allegorical and interpretative context, but he also made extensive use of Albricus when writing his *Africa* in Latin verse. This was written not long after Pierre Bersuire's *Ovide moralisé* (*c.* 1328 or 1340), a work which was accompanied by commentaries by several different authors and in which Mercury appears as the patron of eloquence and those skilled in the art of discourse, as well as the patron of 'false indoctrinators'.

The works of Dante, Boccaccio and Petrarch fall within the province of learned literature. But popular representations of the gods were also increasingly successful during the fourteenth century. Until the twelfth century virtually the only works on astrology available to western scholars were the texts of Macrobius on the *Dream of Scipio*, the works of Firmicus Maternus and the Latin commentaries on the *Timaeus*. Then suddenly astrology began to enjoy an unprecedented popularity, as many Arabic texts began to be translated into Latin. These translations were carried out mainly by Jews and gave rise to a growing interest in the subject, the extent of which can be measured by the increase in the number of calendars, almanachs and *Pronostica*, a flourishing astrological imagery in which Mercury obviously occupied a prominent position. There was a unique development of two types of images. On the one hand were images representing the association between astrological signs (which, of course, tended to be the signs of the zodiac) and parts of the human body, while on the other were planetary images representing the gods associated with each of the seven planets, which explains the many representations of Mercury. In the latter, the god usually appears in a chariot, above a group of figures known as the 'children' of Mercury, which gave rise to the term 'children of the planets'. This type of iconography occurs in a great many documents that have reached us intact. In these drawings the 'children of Mercury', figures which are supposed to represent the human characteristics of the god, are distributed in series or in groups which are always presided over by Mercury, enthroned in his chariot at the top of the picture. Below him, the 'children' bear the attributes of musicians, conjurers, scribes, merchants, etc., in other words of all those professions traditionally placed under the sign of Mercury. The 'children of the planets' are found not only in illustrated manuscripts, but also on both secular and religious buildings in Italy, and particularly on frescos.

During the fifteenth century, the children of the planets increased in number and the famous Tarot de Mantegna appeared *c.* 1460. This collection of 'tarocchi' is a veritable initiatory work, structured like a scale or 'ladder' of mediations, which summarizes the spiritual speculations of Klimakos, Dante and St Thomas. Mercury (card XXII) has remained famous, with his tricorn hat, soft boots, flute and caduceus, on which the two serpents have been replaced by two dragon-like, winged creatures. Beneath his foot lies the severed head of Argus. This image of Mercury is a combination of the Hermes of Antiquity and the mediaeval version handed down by Albricus. But the overall image was inspired, as Fritz Saxl has shown, by a Greek bas-relief discovered several years earlier by Cyriacus of Ancona, who had made Hermes his own personal god. Numerous reproductions of this relief had passed from hand to hand and various adaptations had appeared in Italian art before it was adopted by the 'tarocchi'. These were still being used in 1471 to illustrate the manscript of a poem by Ludovico Lazarelli, *De gentilium deorum imaginibus*. Jean Seznec has identified the Mercury of the Mantegna Tarot 'in the works of the Cassoni, in the Virgil of the Riccardi Palace, in a medallion by Niccolo Fiorentino for Lorenzo Toruabuoni, and in a wood engraving illustrating the *Metamorphoses*', while in an interesting representation in the Arsenal in Paris, he appears between a sleeping Argus and an ox from whose open side Io looks out as if from a window. He also joins Apollo, Pallas and Peace as one of four beautiful statues by Jacopo Sansovino in Venice where, in his tunic, tricorn hat and soft boots, and with the severed head of Argus beneath his right foot, he is recognizable as the Mercury of the 'tarocchi'.

None of the insignia of the Mantegna Mercury and others distort the traditional representations, and during the second half of the fifteenth century the gods just as easily reassumed their early form which, as we have seen, had so often been subject to fanciful modifications. The Renaissance was more a period of synthesis than revival and the German contribution enriched the representations. Aby Warburg has shown how Cyriacus of Ancona's Hermes was the subject of adaptations by Albrecht Dürer and Hans

Burgkmair, was popularized by a calendar in Lübeck and finally became a decorative motif on the façades of German and Austrian houses. In this way the countries of northern Europe incorporated the traditional forms of the gods and their attributes, while frescos such as those of the Schifanoia Palace in Ferrara, by Francesco Cossa (*c.* 1470), continue to extend a joyous welcome to the planetary gods and their 'children'.

Botticelli's *Primavera* (*c.* 1480) evokes Hermes in his traditional role as guide of the Graces, but is equally reminiscent of Virgil's description of the lively messenger of the gods who controls the winds and clouds with his magic wand as he flies through them like a bird. He is also a reflective divinity with an element of 'melancholy' in the Ficinian sense of the word. As well as being the god of eloquence, he is also the god of silence and meditation. The humanists saw him as the ingenious patron of inquiring intelligence, the intelligence of the grammarians and metaphysicians who, according to Marsilio Ficino, recalls the mind to celestial matters through the powers of reason (*Opera* 1559). As Boccaccio had done earlier ('ventos agere Mercurii est'), Botticelli represents him dissipating the clouds of the mind, controlling them (cf. *Aeneid* IV.223) like a Platonic hierophant who shakes the thin veils so that divine truth filters through and reaches us without blinding us. If he looks thoughtfully towards the heavens, we sense that it is not with the intention of disappearing into them forever, but rather with the Ficinian intention of returning from them, of returning to the world with the impetuousness of Zephyr. For Mercury and Zephyr (who is depicted on the right of the picture) are in fact, as Edgar Wind realized, two stages of the same process: what descends to earth like a wind of passion, later returns to heaven in a spirit of contemplation. The picture can therefore be seen as an expression of the three stages of the hermetic process: 'emanatio, conversio, remeatio', that is emanation in Zephyr's descent to Flora, conversion in the dance of grace and re-ascension in the form of the world.

Mercury is referred to particularly in mystery plays such as the *Conversion de saint Denys* or the *Mystère de la Passion* by Greban. He plays a remarkable and unceremonial role in the *Geu des trois Mages*, in which King Herod's councillor bears his name, possibly reminiscent of that other function that, according to St Augustine, he performed for Osiris, but more probably a survival of the mediaeval legacy which gave his name to the devil. In the famous legend attributed to the Emperor Julian, he is well and truly an agent of the devil: according to the story, Julian's mother-in-law finds a statue of Mercury in the Tiber. Julian sells his soul to the statue and becomes an apostate and then emperor thanks to his diabolical servant. In addition and by way of contrast, the second part of the story presents a St Mercury who is none other than the counterpart of St Sergius of the Armenian Church as well as an avatar of Hermes, the guide of souls.

HERMES AND THE NEW SPIRIT OF HUMANISM

During the sixteenth century the image of Hermes began to appear in encyclopedias, particularly Italian ones, which immediately became an indispensable and standard source of reference. They were mainly inspired by Boccaccio's *De genealogia deorum*, and particularly by the dictionaries of classical mythology by the German, Georg Pictor (*Theologia mythologica*, 1532), Natale Conti (*Mythologiae sive explicationum fabularum libri decem*, Venice, 1551), Lilio Gyraldi (*De deis gentium varia et multiplex historia*, Basel, 1548) and Vicenzo Cartari (*Le imagini colla posizione degli Dei degli antichi*, Venice, 1556). The illustrations for Cartari's book, which were surrealist long before the term existed, recapture the fantastical and syncretic style which had virtually disappeared during the previous century. The illustrations of Hermes are quite extraordinary and varied. The emblems of Achille Bocchi (*Questiones symbolicae*, Bologna, 1555) are in a more classic style and include one of Hermes holding a seven-branched candelabrum in one hand placing the index finger of the other on his lips, a gesture associated with Harpocrates. What a wonderful oxymoron to apply to the god of eloquence! In Alciato's *Emblematum liber* (1531) Hermes personifies wisdom, while the famous illustrator, Junius, portrays all his attributes in *Insignia Mercurii quid?*. There are also some very fine illustrations of Mercury in the *Inscriptiones sacrosanctae vetustatis* (1534) by Petrus Apianus. Most of the mythographers of this period were questioning the more recent representatives of paganism, namely Egypt and the Orient, while at the same time more archaeological documents were being discovered than ever before, and from a wide range of different sources.

And what discoveries were made! A year after the first Latin translation of the Homeric *Hymn to Hermes*, the *De rerum inventoribus* by Polydore Virgile was published, which presented a large number of classical traditions relating to the god. In 1499 the *Noces de Mercure et de Philologie* was published for the first time (there were eight editions between then and 1599), as well as the translation of the *Corpus Hermeticum* by Marsilio Ficino. Hermes–Mercury had probably never been so widely discussed as during the sixteenth century. In his *Adagia* Erasmus echoes what was being said about him. He comments on the expression 'Mercurius venit' – the equivalent of 'an angel passes' – but in order to refer to reflective silence, thus contributing to his identification with the archangel, St Michael. In *Encomium morias* (1509) he considers him to be the creator of illusions and inventor of conjuring ('Quos nos ludos exhibet furtis ac praestigiis Hermes?'), as does Isidore of Seville. But it is in his capacity as 'ratio' and 'sermo' that he appears in numerous anthologies and dictionaries, qualified by the appealing formula 'quasi medius currens'. He appears in this role in *Catholicon* (1490) by Johannes Balbus, *Dictionarium* (1510) by Ambrosius Calepinus, *Lectionum antiquarum libri XII* (1517) by Caelius Rhodoginus and the works by Guillaume Budé, Pictor and Gyraldi referred to above.

In *Baldus* (1517), a Latin epic poem by Teofilo Folengo, Baldus, who represents Mars, is imprisoned in Mantua for five cantos, and is liberated, as in the *Iliad*, by the cunning of Cingar, who represents Hermes. Then Cingar intones a long and beautiful anaphoric hymn to Hermes in which nearly all the god's attributes appear:

> Te patrone meus, pochinas cerno fiatas.
> Mercure, qui doctor primarus in arte robandi es;
> Namque times ne dum per coeli rura caminas,
> Te rapidis jungat furibundus Apollo cavallis,
> Et sburlans faciat tibi forsan rumpere collum.
> Tu sopra lunarem arcem tua regna locasti,
> Per quae tercentum pegorae faciendo bebeum
> Pascuntur, grassique boves, asinique ragiantes,
> Atque casalenghi porci, gibbique camelli;
> Nam tu per mundum vadis faciendo botinos,
> Quos introducis coeli sub tecta secundi.
> Alatum portat semper tua testa capellum;
> Alatum portat semper tua gamba stivallum;
> Fatidicam portat semper tua dextra bachettam;
> Ac imbassatas patris Jovis undique portas.
> Tu mercantiam faciens vadisque redisque.
> Tu ventura canis, tibi multum musica gradat,
> Tu pacem, si vis, furibunda in gente reponis,
> Tu litem, si vis, compana in gente ministras;
> Tam bene dulcisonis tua cantat phistula metris,
> Quod male delectans ad somnum provocat artus:
> Argos centoculus fuit olim mortuus hac re.
> Sic, patrone meus, tibi me recomando ladrettum,
> Ne triplicem supra forcam me lazzus acojet.

In *Lozana Andalusa* (1528) by the Spanish writer Francisco Delicado, Hermes appears to the heroine in a dream in order to save her from Pluto and Mars. Also in Spanish, the *Dialogo de Mercurio y Caron* (1529) by Alfonso de Valdès describes him as the god with clear gaze, the critical observer *par excellence*. Bonaventure des Périers describes him very differently in *Cymbalum mundi* (1538) where in the first three dialogues he is the object of satire, a negative Christ figure. This may be the result of Rabelaisian influence because he shares Panurge's liking for drink and claims that he, too possesses the philosopher's stone. He makes a further discreet appearance in two triplets in a sonnet by Du Bellay dedicated to Ronsard, but it is in the works of the latter that we find the most beautiful and detailed sixteenth-century evocation of the god with the caduceus. In 'De Mercure', the tenth *Hymne* of Book 2, inspired by the Homeric hymn and dedicated to Claude Binet, Ronsard describes Mercury's various roles and recalls in some fine lines the main points of the story of Mercury according to the Greeks. He also includes the psychological characteristics and activities of the 'children' of the planet, as well as the alchemical aspect. Such a wide range of attributes does not, however, make Ronsard forget the true nature of his character:

> It is you, Prince, who makes our minds more skilled
> In finding a solution to difficult problems,
> Ambassador, agent, who does not fear the dangers
> Of land or sea, or of foreign Rulers,
> Always active, with rest or repose,
> So that the work you have undertaken is completed.

He reappears in the form of a messenger in *Maistre Pierre Faifeu* (1532) by Charles Boudigné, which opens with an 'Epistle sent by Maître Pierre Faifeu to "Messieurs les Angevins", by Mercury, Herald and Messenger of the Gods'. Perhaps Boudigné was inspired by another book written in French, the *Illustrations de Gaule* (1512) by Jean Lemaire de Belges, in which each of the three parts opens with a prologue spoken by Hermes. He introduces himself in the book as the 'formerly renowned god of eloquence, ingenuity and inventiveness, herald and messenger of the gods' and his role is in line with that of the traditional allegory: 'Mercury means the word, by which all teaching is expressed and admitted into our understanding'. 'Understanding' means 'clarity of mind', since Hermes' subjects are 'all noble and clear-thinking people of both sexes, who form the band of Mercury, and like reading good things'. One cannot help thinking of the pleasure experienced shortly afterwards by Rabelais when confronted with the re-establishement of 'good literature'. Jean Lemaire reinterpreted the traditional allegory of Mercury in the sixteenth century by giving it a new meaning, taken from Lucian's *Charon* in which Hermes opens the eyes of his companion, Charon, and enables him to take a broader look at the theatre of the world. In the works of Boccaccio, 'claritas' was already featured among his attributes, as was his flexibility. In this respect, too, Jean Lemaire echoes Boccaccio when he refers to the 'noble god Mercury whose planet is neutral and impartial, looking kindly upon the benevolent and unfavourably upon the malevolent, master of imaginative, fantastical and constantly active virtue'! Most of this reappears in Giacomo Zucchi's *Discorso sopra li dei de Gentili* (1602).

GEOFFROY TORY AND FRANÇOIS RABELAIS

Also inspired by Boccaccio, Geoffroy Tory gave Mercury a prominent position in *Champfleury* (1529), an unusual work that comprises a sort of cabbala of the Latin alphabet. After reminding his readers of the story of Io, changed into a cow by Juno, mistreated by the herdsman Argus and finally saved by Mercury who lulled Argus to sleep and then killed him, Tory puts forward an interpretation of the story:

> Mercury playing his pipes and cutting off the head of the said Argus, is here the interpreter and prince for men desirous to pursue the purity of all good

> writings and ancient Knowledge by devoting themselves to the task of teaching others, as much by their words as by their writings, and by casting aside and destroying the deep-rooted barbarism of the unenlightened, just as we see three noble figures doing so today, the Dutchman Erasmus, the Sieur d'Etaples in Picardy and Budé, the jewel of the Parisian nobles and scholars, who night and day watch over and write for the general good, and extol perfect Knowledge.

In the work Mercury, (Jupiter's) messenger of enlightenment comes to free Io (literature and the arts) from Argus (intellectual obscurity), the servant of Juno (wealth). He is responsible for breaking down barriers, re-opening routes that had previously been blocked off and bringing back into circulation the knowledge imprisoned by the guardians of the established intellectual order (Argus). In short, he represents the new spirit of humanism as perceived by Tory.

Rabelais was certainly familiar with the figure of Hermes. In his poem dedicated to Jean Bouchet, he refers to him as the patron saint of Bouchet because the latter liked to describe himself as 'treading perilous paths'. Rabelais knew that Pan was the son of Hermes and Penelope, had heard of the oracle of Hermes at Pharai, and mentions the fountain of Mercury in Rome and the Mercurial plant described by Pliny. He also refers to the Gallic Mercury, to a statue of the god in solid quicksilver, and makes several references to the planet of that name. We are indebted to Ludwig Schrader for a fine study on the subject in which he focused particularly on Panurge and demonstrated to what extent the latter was inspired by Folenzo's Cingar, as well as by other sources so numerous that it is impossible to locate them all. However, it is possible to identify basic similarities between Panurge and Hermes. Describing how he escaped from Turkey, Panurge says: 'by divine will the thief fell asleep, or thanks to the good offices of some kind Mercury who lulled the hundred-eyed Argus to sleep'. Before questioning Raminagrobis he offers him a cockerel, and gives Triboullet a bag made out of a tortoise shell. His good relations with dogs are reminiscent of Hermes as the shepherd, and this is reinforced by the fact that Panurge also carries Dindenault's ram.

Before visiting the sibyl of Panzoust, Epistémon realizes with horror that they have forgotten to provide themselves with a golden branch. Panurge replies that he has seen to it and has it in his leather bag 'in the form of a golden rod with beautiful and joyful copper coins . . .' Like Hermes 'empolaïos' he carries a purse, and like Ronsard's Hermes, sells theriaca. He can open any door or box as easily as Ovid's Mercury ('caelestique res virga patefacit', *Metamorphoses* 2.819). He appears to be as proficient in languages as his paradigm and, like him, does not seek glory. He has the same gift of prediction as his patron saint and practises it by 'praestigium', in dreams or in verse. The curing of Epistémon by Panurge is more than a skilful surgical operation, it is also the parody of a conjuration, which demonstrates his ability to bring back souls from Hades into the land of the living (here by means of an ointment with the power of resurrection). But he also has the power to direct them towards the other world, and the staff with which he prevents Dindenault and his servants from fleeing is recognizable as the staff with which Hermes drives dead souls before him (see Lucian's *Cataplus*); along with Carpalim and Eusthenes, he joyfully administers the *coup de grâce* to the enemy lying on the battlefield.

The points of comparison continue. Tertullian and Eratosthenes, among others, attributed to Hermes a very distinctive taste in clothes which is shared by Panurge, especially during his Parisian adventures. Like the Hermes of the Homeric hymn, he is fond of food and drink. In *Cataplus* Lucian had revealed that Hermes was not a willing resident in the world of mortals because there was not enough to eat (see also *Pax* and *Plutus* by Aristophanes). As well as being an out-and-out drinker, Panurge's bawdiness is also centred around sex. We know that Herodotus and Pausanias represented Hermes in an ithyphallic manner and, according to Hyginus, he is even the father of Priapus. Panurge has secret affairs (it will be remembered that Hermes was born of the secret union of Maia and Zeus) and like Harpo Marx, that other little Hermes, he eagerly pursues nymphets: impotence is certainly not a problem. Indeed, according to Petronius, this affliction is in fact cured by Hermes, who is also the god of cuckoldry (see Lucian's *Fugitivi*) a subject dear to Panurge's own heart. The latter identifies himself readily with his codpiece which he qualifies as 'thrice great', and it is in fact his codpiece which helps to cure Epistémon: Panurge 'took his head and held it against the warmth of his codpiece to prevent it catching cold'. But he also uses the adjective 'thrice great' to describe his bottle. 'May you also receive the word/ Of the thrice great Bottle.' It should be added that Panurge has trouble getting married, as did Martianus Capella's Mercury, while Pantagruel here assumes the role of Apollo and Raminagrobis that of Zeus.

Finally, his medical knowledge does not mean he is associated solely with the hermetic tradition. There is also an element of Hermes the humanist, the contemporary scholar, although this does not prevent him being a sort of alchemist at the same time, for he claims to possess the philosopher's stone: 'I have a philosopher's stone, which attracts money from purses as surely as a magnet attracts metal.' And in his praise of debtors, he refers to the 'joy of alchemists when, after a great deal of work, effort and expense, they see the metals transmuted in their ovens'. The aim of the hermetic art, transmutation, is joyfully parodied in Rabelais' *Quart Livre*: 'Haven't I given enough explanation of the transmutation of the elements and the simple symbol which lies somewhere between roast and boiled, and between boiled and roast?'

THE REAPPEARANCE OF TRISMEGISTOS DURING THE RENAISSANCE

The interest shown in Hermes–Mercury during the sixteenth century is accompanied by the rediscovery of Hermes Trismegistos, who became even more popular in Europe during that period than during the Middle Ages. He suddenly occupied a position at the forefront of the philosophical scene at a time when, partly because of him, a doctrine was beginning to develop which would later be known as esotericism. The discovery of the Jewish Cabbala, especially after the diaspora of 1492, is one of the two major events which gave rise to a specific kind of esotericism. The other event was the rediscovery of the *Corpus Hermeticum*, which had been neglected during the Middle Ages when only the *Asclepius* was known. The *Corpus* was introduced into Florence circa 1460 by a monk from Macedonia, and was translated into Latin by Marsilio Ficino in 1471. There were numerous editions during the sixteenth and seventeenth centuries, as well as many learned and enthusiastic commentaries by such authors as Lefèvre d'Etaples, Ludovico Lazarelli, Symphorien Champier, Cornelius Agrippa, Gabriel du Préau. François Foix de Candale, Hannibal Rossel and Francesco Patrizi, to name only a few. At the same time there was a tendency to 'Apollinize' Hermes Trismegistos, as if to relegate and obliterate the magical and theurgical aspect of the Alexandrian writings. The success of Trismegistos during the Renaissance was undoubtedly due to its general fascination with Mercury, with the result that the sixteenth century saw Hermes, in both forms, take such a hold over the cultural imagination that he was used as a receptacle for all kinds of ideas. Finally, one of the most remarkable aspects of the presence of Trismegistos, that is of hermetism in the strict sense of the word (the editions, studies and commentaries of the *Corpus Hermeticum*), was its irenic quality. The milieux in which Hermes moved were characterized by religious tolerance.

Because of the variety and richness of his attributes, as well as his intermediary position between religious and literary myth, Trismegistos fulfilled all the conditions for becoming the central character of a philosophical history of humankind. We have seen that classical authors such as Strabo and Marcus Manilius had already presented him in this way. Roger Bacon gave him an important, although negative, place in this history. During the Renaissance there was an even greater need than during the Middle Ages to conceptualize the notion of 'Tradition' (in the esoteric sense as understood since the nineteenth century). At the time it was known as 'philosophia perennis', a term defined by Agostino Steuco in 1540 in his book *De perenni Philosophia*. The name of Trismegistos is indissolubly linked to this philosophy. Pico della Mirandola and Marsilio Ficino paved the way for Steuco by referring to Hermes as 'the first theologian', and by seeing the 'prisca theologia', which they considered to have begun with Mercury, as reaching its peak with Plato. The typical list, the 'philosophical' genealogy compiled during this period, was as follows: Enoch, Abraham, Noah, Zoroaster, Moses, Hermes Trismegistos, the Brahmans, the Druids, David, Orpheus, Pythagoras, Plato and the Sibyls. And it is not the least curious aspect of the western 'tradition' that mythology and history are continually confused. The great importance attached to the idea of 'prisca philosophia' presented a certain danger from the outset, insofar as the degree of authority of a text or doctrine depended on a guarantee of its ancientness. The inevitable occurred in 1641 when Isaac Casaubon discovered that the texts of Trismegistos dated from no earlier than the second and third centuries AD.

Nonetheless, Trismegistos has continued to enjoy a long, albeit more discreet, career until the present day. But from that point onwards there was a tendency to refer to sources other than the hermetic writings for the mythical reference which would provide the 'guarantee' of authenticity, even if it meant producing a complete fabrication of stories and rituals, which possibly accounts for the appearance of the Rosicrucians at the beginning of the seventeenth century and speculative Freemasonry a hundred years later. As for Paracelsism and the great Germanic Christian theosophy which developed with Jakob Boehme, they derive little from neo-Alexandrian hermetic philosophy and allocate only a relatively minor place in their teaching to Trismegistos.

In 1488, only seventeen years after the publication of Ficino's Latin translation of the *Corpus Hermeticum*, and about ten years after Botticelli's *Primavera*, an artist inlaid the courtyard of Siena Cathedral with a beautiful representation of Hermes Trismegistos, still visible today. He is a tall, bearded old man dressed in a long gown and cloak, wearing a rimmed mitre and surrounded by various figures. The inscription reads: 'Hermes Mercurius Trismegistus Contemporaneus Moysii'. Not long afterwards Pope Alexander VI, the patron of Pico della Mirandola, commissioned a painting by Pinturicchio for the Borgia's apartments in the Vatican. The huge fresco is rich in hermetic symbols and signs of the zodiac, and depicts a young and beardless Hermes Trismegistos accompanied by Isis and Moses.

HERMES DURING THE SEVENTEENTH AND EIGHTEENTH CENTURIES

However, the iconographic representations of Hermes – usually bearded and venerable men – are relatively rare; the author of the present article has not been able to locate more than thirty. Of these, we will mention only Manor Finiguerra's Trismegistos (*c.* 1460) in the 'Florentine Picture Chronicle' (British Museum, London). Hermes–Mercury, on the other hand, is featured in numerous paintings, drawings and sculptures, wherever one sees artists drawing their inspiration from classical subjects. The list of outstanding and significant works of art is endless. Statues include the fragile and sylphlike Mercury of Giovanni da Bologna in the Florence Gallery and the beautiful version by Adriaen de Vries in the National Gallery of Art in Washington, while the painting by Dirck van Barburen (*c.* 1595, Rijksmuseum, Amsterdam) a red-faced Hermes witnesses the chaining of Prometheus by Vulcan from his vantage point between the two figures (where else?). Other paintings are of the helmeted and bearded Mercury of Baldung Grien, and the Mercury of Johann Rottenmayr (*c.* 1690, Chicago Museum of Art), one of the many variations on the theme of Mercury killing Argus to free Io. He was also constantly revived for mythologically inspired emblems.

But he is not only to be found in paintings and emblems. He was also present in the political and literary imagination, which, through narrating historical and local events, recreated the mythological and mythical role of the sovereign. This was the case in England with the theme of the magician king. Thus from Spenser and Queen Elizabeth to Pope and Queen Anne, the planetary god Mercury, who was identified with the monarch, was often used to represent the magical powers of kings and queens. In Spenser's *Faerie Queene* (1590), Gloriana, that is Queen Elizabeth, revives, from within the heart of Protestantism, the mediaeval notion of a world ruler who will restore the Golden Age by repairing the devastation caused by the fall of Adam. The real Elizabeth had no hesitation in seeking advice from the magus John Dee (whose *Monas Hieroglyphica* dates from 1564), just as Arthur was counselled by Merlin. A recent study by Douglas Brooks-Davies examines the consequences of the identification of the English monarchy and magic using the images of Mercury and Trismegistos. This identification explains the desire to achieve an ideal kingdom or empire, similar to the Arthurian ideal. Here again various 'traditions' combined in an interesting manner. On the one hand, like so many of his fellow countrymen, Spenser saw England as another Egypt, while on the other, the anti-Roman hermetism of Giordano Bruno was a striking success there, particularly his book *Lo Spaccio de la Bestia trionfante.* Finally England kept alive the tradition of the Druids who were thought to be descendants of Noah through his son Ham, and therefore holders of power associated with the priestly and magical role of the monarch. The Druids were also frequently included in the tradition of 'prisci theologi', in spite of, or perhaps because of, the absence of texts produced by them. For this reason the English monarch, an amalgam of all these various elements, tended like Mercury being, to represent a tension between heaven and earth, the sceptre being the caduceus (and vice versa). The wisdom of Trismegistos was therefore also attributed to the monarch. During the seventeenth century, after the publication of Spenser's poem, many other works presented this image, including Ben Jonson's *Mercury Vindicated* (1616), which was performed at court and was a panegyric of the monarch endowed with mercurial and magical qualities, and Milton's *Il Penseroso*, which presented the idea of a reformed monarchy on earth, described by a poet who acted as a visionary intermediary, much as Merlin did for King Arthur.

These representations of Hermes, that were peculiarly British in their political and literary concerns, tended to combine the two forms of the god. In the art of the same period, Mercury is often lost in academicism, appearing as one figure among many others in a classical setting; this is increasingly the case as we leave the Renaissance behind. Renaissance artists were adept at reviving the attributes of the gods in creative, even exuberant, manner, but later and more conventional artists lost track of the particular significance of the myth of Mercury. This significance did, however, continue to exist in an esoteric form amongst alchemists, the Cambridge Neoplatonists (Henry More, Ralph Cudworth), the cosmosophy of Robert Fludd and the hermetic Egyptomania popularized by the Jesuit scholar Athanasius Kircher in *Oedipus Aegyptiacus* (1652). Kircher had no hesitation in associating the Cabbala with hermetic philosophy. As Ficino had done before him, he saw Hermes as the inventor of hieroglyphics and the truths engraved on the stone of obelisks. But however widespread Egyptomania may have been in the literary, artistic and philosophical imagination of the seventeenth and nineteenth centuries, Hermes only played a token part, although he made a significant appearance in the translations and new editions of the *Corpus Hermeticum*, particularly in the German speaking countries.

In fact, he continued to appear in these countries from the second half of the seventeenth century onwards, whether in connection with hermetism in the true sense of the word, which in these countries was linked with the late appearance of humanism, or with alchemy. In *Conjectaneorum de germanicae gentis originae* (Tübingen, 1648), an unusual work which testifies to the revival of Hermes in Germany, Kriegsmann uses a number of philological arguments (in which he associates the Egyptian god Thoth with 'Theut' and 'teutonic') in support of his attempt to demonstrate that Hermes was the founder of the Germanic races. This is a revised form of euhemerism, whereby a mythological figure appears not so much as a benefactor of humanity but rather as the patron of a race. Not long afterwards the Jesuit sinologist, mathematician and musician, Joachim Bouvet, demonstrated the continued survival of Hermes by writing to Leibniz in 1700 that the *I Ching* was a 'universal symbol devised by an amazing genius of Antiquity, such as Hermes Trismegistos, to provide a visual representation of the most abstract principles of all forms of knowledge'. Hermes appears again in Michel de Ramsay's *Les Voyages de Cyrus* (1727), where his meeting with Cyrus is one of a series of events designed to demonstrate that Egyptian and Persian mythology are based on the same principles: 'it was simply a matter of using different names to express the same ideas'. Scholarship and learning, which were even more systematic than during the Renaissance, contributed to the fascination with the god and hermetism and produced such works as the monumental *Bibliotheca Graeca* (1705–28) by Johann Albrecht Fabricius, and Jacob Brucker's *Historia Philosophiae* (IV, 1743).

In fact the seventeenth century witnessed the largest number of alchemical works published in Germany, all illustrated with drawings and figures. Mercury is the best represented of all the gods in this exuberant baroque iconography, and the traditional images of Hermes occur often and naturally, without a hint of academicism. He is fully at home, with all his attributes intact. He reigns as a master skilled in the art of resolving contradictions, reconciling conflicting tendencies and channelling our active imagination. The many examples include Michael Maier's *Atalanta Fugitiva* (1617) and Adolph Beute's

Philosophische Schaubühne (1706). The Germans continued to represent Hermes in books on alchemy until the middle of the eighteenth century, when he began to assume rococco forms and was incorporated into settings in the same style. For examples of this, see the drawings in the *Deutsches Theatrum Chimicum* by Friedrich Roth-Scholtz, the *Neue Alchymistische Bibliothek* by Schröder, *Lumen novum phosphorus accensum* (1717) by Cohaussen, *Famae alchemicae* (1717) by Boethius, and *Besondere Versuche vom Mineral-Geist* (1772) by von Respur.

Although alchemical iconography did not develop in the same way in France, interpretations of Mercury were inspired directly by the 'hermetic art'. The Benedictine scholar Antoine-Joseph Pernéty is the best-known French representative of the alchemical interpretation of the classical fables. His *Fables égyptiennes et grecques dévoilées* (1758 and 1786) still enjoy a certain degree of success today, a fact borne out by several recent editions. He made use of some of Michael Maier's commentaries, but extended them and presented them more systematically according to a tradition first introduced by Olympiodorus and still in use, namely the interpretation of mythology as if it were a coded language which contained all the principles of the Great Work. For Dom Pernéty, Cybele (or Maia), the mother of Mercury, is the 'nurse' referred to in the *Emerald Tablet*. (The text in fact reads 'nutrix eius terra', which is the translation of the Greek name, Cybele.) The messages that Mercury 'carried day and night' for the gods represent 'his stirring of the contents of the vessel throughout the entire work'. Similarly, 'the harmony of the instruments that Mercury invented indicates the proportions, weights and measures' of the materials of the magistery and of the temperatures of the fire. The role of guide of souls attributed to Mercury 'is nothing other than the dissolving and congealing, fixation and volatilization of the materials of the work'. After decomposing, the philosophers' materials assume all sorts of colours which disappear at the moment when the materials congeal and set: 'This is Mercury killing Argus with a stone'!

In addition to the hothouses of alchemical works, the first volume of *L'Antiquité expliquée, et représentée en figures*, by Dom Bernard de Montfaucon, appeared in Paris in 1719. Each chapter of this collection of large folios is devoted to a god, with a wealth of drawings that reproduce classical works belonging to museums and private collections. The first volume, in which Hermes occupies a very prominent position, was enriched by the first part of the 'Supplément' in 1724, in which he appears in many other classical forms. So many images of Mercury are unlikely to have been presented in one collection before. Looking through these plates, it is possible to see how easily he is assimilated with other characters to form a single figure: Hermathena (Hermes with the head of Minerva), Hermeros, Hermanubis, etc. Montfaucon's compilation continues to be used today as a work of reference, but there still does not seem to be a collection of images of Hermes as seen in modern times. Court de Gébelin) devoted a long chapter to him in his *Monde primitif*.

On the frontispiece, beneath a starry sky, Hermes the geometer and Minerva consult a collection of mathematical symbols. Court de Gébelin's is one of the most careful and engaging studies to appear during the French Enlightenment.

However, if eighteenth-century French illuminism, European Romanticism and finally nineteenth- and twentieth-century esotericism present Hermes in an equally diverse number of ways, it is rather the result of a particular direction of thought and type of awareness than a conscious act of evocation or invocation. This does occur occasionally, however, when Mercury's traditional attributes are revived, or when specific references are made to Trismegistos, from *Séthos* by the Abbé Terrasson (1731) to the *Essai de palingénésie sociale* by Ballanche, via the works of André Chénier. But it is the myth of Orpheus that is referred to explicitly in this respect. Orpheus, as has been demonstrated by Brian Juden, was the favourite god of the Romantics and haunted the Romantic imagination. Later, during the age of Symbolism, the syncretist Edouard Schuré dedicated an emotive homage to Hermes, but the god was rarely described in such a wealth of colourful clichés as by the author of the *Grands Initiés*. It was Carl Gustav Jung who considered Hermes in a way that appealed to anthropologists rather than historians. One Jungian work worth mentioning is a very fine book by Rafael Lopez-Pedraza (translated into French in 1980 as *Hermès et ses enfants dans la psychothérapie*), but other works of the same type are usefully devoted to the presence of gods and goddesses within us.

ASPECTS OF HERMES

The extremely varied nature of the representations of Hermes from the Enlightenment to the 'decadent' period, and the almost obsessional presence of Orpheus – who, on occasions, resembles Hermes like a brother – during the long career of Romanticism, presents a problem which is posed by any serious reflection on mythology: is it enough, in order to locate the occurrences of a myth, to trace it using the name by which it is identified? In other words, is the name alone enough to identify the myth? On two occasions at least, we have encountered Hermes under an assumed name, that is Dante's Virgil and Rabelais's Panurge. He occurs in disguise in other important literary works too, such as *Der Zauberberg* by Thomas Mann. In a recent work (1985) both valuable and precise, Gilbert Durand answers this question in the negative by referring to the 'permanent and derivative aspects of the Mercurial myths' (see bibliography). He propounds the theory that the caduceus does not make Mercury, and identifies the myth in question in terms of the following elements: a) the power of the minuscule (it is true that Mercury is sometimes tiny as shown by several of Montfaucon's drawings and many alchemical illustrations; when his phallus is large, he symbolizes spiritual fertility) b) the role of intermediary c) the role of guide of souls.

In this way Durand identifies several points in history at which the myth of Mercury 'explodes', or intensifies. The first of these occurred in Egypt with Thoth, and continued for five to eight hundred years. Then came the Greek and Roman periods, although in Rome he was not considered a truly Roman god. Rather, for Caesar he was a Gallic, Celtic god and many Celtic churches and locations bear his name. He is basically a god of semitic origin: Phoenician, Carthaginian, Hebrew and Arabic, that is, associated with trading and travelling races. The next four periods identified by Durand are more indicative of an 'explosive' process: A) the 'Gothic Renaissance' of the thirteenth and early fourteenth century when alchemy flourished, and which produced such figures as Arnauld or Albert le Grand. During this period Mercury appeared as the agent of transmutation, the 'intermediary' of the Great Work, often associated with the moon, silver being representative of the state of the moon and quicksilver of the planet's rapid movement. This was the age of San Bonaventura and of Joachimism (when the reign of the Holy Spirit was coming into its own), but all this collapsed into economic chaos, the black death and the great schism of the fourteenth century. B) The next period was the age of humanism, during which Mercury appeared as an intellectual figure, presiding over printing and the dissemination of information. He is the sun of the Word which destroys the star-studded sky, that is, studded with the thousand eyes of Argus. International trade developed under his new 'reign'. Here Mercury is 'mercurial' in the extended rather than the original sense of the word. But this world collapsed, at the same time as hermetism, in favour of the Enlightenment. C) Towards the end of the eighteenth and the early nineteenth century, Mercury was an ambiguous figure. He represented obscurity as much as he did enlightenment, as testified by the fascination of the age with hieroglyphics and secret societies. The style of the whole period was characterized by Mercury's ambiguity: the language of the Enlightenment was used by the enlightened to talk about obscure subjects. At the end of the nineteenth century, however, scholars such as Marcelin-Berthelot cast Hermes–Mercury in a Promethean role, and the positivist and scientistic age that followed placed itself under the sign of Prometheus. D) As a reaction to this, the epistemological revolution of our own time, especially the second half of the twentieth century, has called upon intermediaries, extending the 'relational' concept into all scientific and intellectual spheres (relativity, pluralism, polarities, polysemy, exchange of information, etc.), and has probably considered in greater depth than ever before the various ways of pursuing the internal quest. Such a revival of Hermes favours a form of 'angelism' (in the sense of 'angelos', used to describe Hermes the messenger), of (creative) controversy specific to periods when institutions are disintegrating, and when the west is confronted with the breakdown of civilization.

It is easy to see how intellectually stimulating such a subtle and discreet division of history can be. There is no doubt that it is Hermes who presides over the periods so accuratcly placcd under his sign by Gilbert Durand, although at the same time the ambiguity of the very concept of 'myth' when applied to mythological and literary figures such as Prometheus, Hermes, Faust and Don Juan should be appreciated. In fact, tracing Hermes through history in an attempt to identify the cultural characteristics that he has inspired anonymously (indicative characteristics which make it possible to identify constants within the imagination), means examining what amounts to the history (whose relevance is not here under consideration) of esotericism within a broad perspective which includes the philosophy of nature, in the romantic sense, the eclectic synthesis of a Pico or Ficino, as well as traditional alchemy and theosophy. The undertaking is undoubtedly legitimate insofar as the esotericism thus defined relates entirely to Hermes, and insofar as the quicksilver god exceeds the boundaries of that same esotericism (Durand also discusses maritime and commercial trade during the sixteenth century). Such a process inevitably runs the risk of a certain number of (often interesting) images escaping analysis because they do not correspond to the three indicative characteristics suggested. For example, it is not specific to Hermes to disguise himself as a bishop, to be considered as the founder of Germany, or to double as a god (Mercury) and a mortal (the Trismegistos of the euhemerists). But the two paths are not mutually exclusive. Although methodologically distinct, they complement and enrich each other. It requires both determination and ability to locate the name of Hermes–Mercury through the ages, and to try to identify his active presence in areas where he disguises his name and explicit attributes.

On the basis of Celtic etymology, Court de Gébelin suggested that 'Mercury' was composed of the words 'sign' ('merc') and 'man' ('cur'). This would mean he was a figure associated with signs, who erected signposts and beacons, that is who helped us to interpret history, and our own lives, by providing us with significant points of reference. These signs are neither abstract nor fixed, and their mediatory function reflects the nature of the 'medicurrius' and 'medire currens' of St Augustine and Servius, that is of 'he who runs between two' or 'in the middle'. These routes and journeys, which are totally distinct from those of wanderings and ideologies, provide a connection for the unconnected and link conflicting terms in configurations which are constantly renewed. And if, en route, Hermes sometimes steals the substance of what he touches with his wand, it is in order to regenerate it by putting it back into circulation. It is thanks to him that the paradoxical chariot, card VI in the Greater Arcana of the Tarot, can start out. But what is its destination and what is the purpose of its journey? The difference between Hermes–Mercury and Hermes–Trismegistos therefore appears all the more significant as it focuses on a double form of mediation. Mercury ensures the balance between Apollo and Dionysus (the gods must not be left to their own devices) and is a 'guide' rather than a messenger, whereas Trismegistos, who unites reason and inspiration, 'logos' and the sibyls, history and myth, is given the title of 'regenerator'.

Antoine Faivre

Heroism

The Indo-Europeans have specialized in the epic, to the extent that having devoted six chapters of his *Heroic Song and Heroic Legend* (1963) to the Greeks, France, Germany, Ireland and Iceland, India and so on, Jan de Vries discusses 'the epic poetry of non-Indo-European nations' in a single chapter. However, this predominance in no way denies the fact that dreams of heroism are widely shared throughout the world, as is clear as soon as we turn to the Babylonian epic *Gilgamesh*, the Finnish *Kalevala* and many other works.

In the early twentieth century a strange phenomenon began to emerge: as well as speaking of cultures influencing each other, as people had long done, it became clear that narratives with striking similarities had appeared at different times almost everywhere on the planet. These were the 'lives of heroes', of supermen, people halfway between the status of gods and ordinary human life. Two new sciences, psychoanalysis and mythology, established the previous century, combined and intersected to explain these constants. The definitive study was the work of Otto Rank, a disciple of Freud's, who in 1909 published his *Mythus von der Geburt des Helden (The Myth of the Birth of the Hero)* which was soon followed by an analysis of the story of Lohengrin (1911). After this many works appeared, the most famous being those of Campbell (1949), Baudouin (1952), Jung (1953), Durand (1961) and Jan de Vries (1963).

A particular strand of fantasy – the dream of excelling, the secret desire to be a god – which is at work in epics, fragments of epics and narratives concerning politics and war (such as those of Alexander, Caesar, Louis XIV of France or Napoleon), also became apparent in quite recent literary undertakings, such as the novels of Romain Rollan (*Jean-Christophe*, 1903–12) and Malraux, or the poetry of Saint-John Perse. Nor could its presence be missed as the underlying factor in many of the productions of 'mass culture': westerns, crime novels and films, sporting narratives, posters, cartoons and so on. Of course the very frequency of these 'heroic' narratives explains why every now and then the scenario seems to have been flogged to death, hence the importance of parody from Cervantes' *Don Quixote* (1605) or Scarron's *Virgile travesti* (1649–59) to *Lucky Luke*, the famous cartoon by Morris and Goscinny.

THE SEQUENCES OF THE 'HEROIC MODEL'

Analysis of epics or epic fragments leads to the discovery of a basic theme beneath the variations: the hero's increasingly brilliant manifestations through successive births until the ultimate birth as an immortal. The narrative takes its rhythm from alternating birth, death and rebirth.

The hero is generally born to illustrious parents: his father or mother is divine (Herakles, Achilles) or, at the least, his parents are the earthly reflections of divinity, being kings or princes, those people most similar to gods. In many cases the parents have had problems, either in the political domain or in that of the family (for example, a long period of sterility on the mother's part in the case of Samson). The child's birth is preceded by oracles or dreams accompanied by miracles (the 'presages'). Often these omens prove threatening to the father: the new-born baby is then rejected by his family, abandoned, 'exposed' and condemned to die (Oedipus, Cyrus). The most widespread form of this abandonment is exposure on water: this represents the uncovering of a 'piece of silent literature' (Robert 1980) which is usually buried deep within us, the fear of making that journey which brought us into life from the belly and waters of our mothers in the opposite direction; through an inversion, which is common in fantasy life, instead of the waters in the casket (the amniotic fluid in the mother's womb), the narratives depict the casket on the water. The biblical flood and the early life of Moses fit here, as does the exposure of Perseus in the casket on the water, accompanied by his mother Danaë and protected by his father, who was none other than Zeus himself, lord of the gods.

Surrounded by death, threatened from his glorious birth by a hostile universe, given up to the caprices of the waters (as were the Assyrian king Sargon and the founders of Rome, Romulus and Remus), the child is saved by fishermen (Perseus), shepherds (Oedipus), a herdsman (Cyrus) or indeed looked after by kind animals (Romulus and Remus). He then lives an obscure life, very different from the one for which his birth should have destined him. This is the period of hidden life, of apparent death.

Various events bring this 'occultation' of the hero to an end. Sometimes he has retained a 'sign' of his origins and is 'recognized' (Theseus, Cyrus), or else one day he meets his real parents, attacks his father and is then recognized (Oedipus). Most frequently he reveals himself to the world by mighty 'works'. This is the heroic 'epiphany'.

The most famous examples of these exploits are those of Gilgamesh and Hercules. The most typical of them is combat with a monster. The fact that the monster is jealousy guarding a girl in many tales (Andromeda) suggests that for the male hero the enemy to be brought down is none other than the guardian of the desired mother, a paternal imago. Sometimes the dragon is replaced by a horrible giant (Goliath in the Bible, the Morholt in *Tristan et Yseut*), or by a host of enemies whose great number appears monstrous in itself (Samson against the Philistines, Roland against the Saracens). Indeed, there is a fairly constant relationship between monstrosity and multiplicity: the monsters of fables are usually composite creatures, having a number of heads (Cerberus) or being a mixture of species (the Sphinx). Victor Hugo 'sees' 'two prodigious snakes of steel' in the two columns charging at Waterloo (*Les Misérables*, II, 1) or, in the open sea with its myriad reflections, 'the ocean hydra twisting its star-scaled body'.

Having emerged victorious from his fearsome 'ordeal', the hero appears as the 'saviour' of an entire people. His greatness is such that it obliges him to become a political leader. This is why either the hero is originally a king, who reclaims the throne that is rightfully his (Oedipus, Theseus, Cyrus) or his coexistence with the political authorities proves difficult and full of risks: in the *Iliad* it matters little that Agamemnon is the king of kings, he pales in comparison to Achilles and tempers his treatment of the latter as a subordinate. In *Le Cid* Corneille, carried away by his vision of heroism, has some difficulty placing Rodrigue in his proper political context. In *Suréna* King Orode understands perfectly that life with heroes is dangerous for monarchs, thus he has Suréna murdered. In some cases creators of epic narratives give themselves over entirely to the logic of the 'model': then the hero kills the king, whose weakness is ridiculous in comparison to the power of his position. This is what happens in Claudel's *Tête d'or* (1889). The conflict between the hero and the political leader is a reproduction in the realm of war of that which, in the religious domain, opposes prophet and priest, the person inspired by God and the functionary, the incandescent soul and the trickster. Like prophets, heroes tend to be antisocial and outside the law, in the *Iliad* as in westerns.

This sovereignty of the hero and his overwelming pride – the psychoanalyst would call it a fixation at the phallic phase and a persistence of the ideal ego's megalomaniacal desires – eventually lead to excess. Intoxicated by greatness, the hero defies the gods themselves. Failure and punishment are not long in coming, for example in the form of the killing of the hero's companion or 'double' (Enkidu for Gilgamesh, Pirithoüs in the life of Theseus).

The well-known episode of the descent into hell is a quite different matter. Here the hero does not take on the gods; he sets off on one of those extraordinary undertakings which, like the fight with the monster, demonstrates his epiphanic nature. He enters and returns from a kingdom from which no ordinary mortal has ever returned (Odysseus, Aeneas). In westerns the hell of the ancients is replaced by the 'devil's gates' or 'death valleys' which no one has ever crossed alive, but from which the hero re-emerges into the land of the living.

Because he is partly human, the day comes when the hero has to face inevitable physical death. Because he is in essence invulnerable in his conflicts with ordinary, mediocre human beings, he cannot be defeated in a fight. To bring about his death, the imagination has turned to two solutions in particular, the first being that of the traitor. The invincible one is struck in the back, as in the stories of the two magnificent deaths of Achilles and Siegfried, both of whom were rendered invulnerable at birth by being dipped in magic water, except for Achilles' heel (since his mother was holding him behind his foot) and a few centimetres of Siegfried's back (a leaf fell when he was being bathed and prevented the water from touching the skin). Both are struck in the back by cowards (Paris and Hagen). Hercules is betrayed by his own wife, Deïaneira, who makes him put on a poisoned tunic. The second possibility is that, through weariness with life's shortcomins or for some other reason, the hero freely decides to die; thus in Corneille's *Le Cid*, the despairing Rodrigue chooses to let himself be killed in the duel he fights with Don Sanche, and only Chimène can make him change his mind. There is at least one case where both solutions – betrayal and freedom – coexist: the death of Christ. Such superimposition is not surprising in the context of a personality who appears as a kind of sun of human symbolism: here is both the rite of passage and the scapegoat device (as the anthropologist René Girard has demonstrated). What should be stressed here is that the life of Jesus reproduces the 'heroic model' in an original way. The same is true of the heroine whom Michelet regarded as the most perfect imitation of Christ: Joan of Arc.

But a hero cannot be prey to the horror of death; his apparent death is seen as a victory. The betrayed Hercules erects his own stake, but the flames are hardly alight when he is carried off to Olympus. In the same way Claudel imagines the dying Joan of Arc already hearing the heavenly voices welcoming her (*Jeanne d'Arc au bûcher*, 1937). Lastly, Jesus Christ goes through physical death to reveal himself in a supreme epiphany, the Resurrection and Ascension. In Mythology, this last victory bears the name of heroic 'apotheosis'.

FRAGMENTATION OF THE 'MODEL'

Heroic narratives do not necessarily display all the sequences described above. If we consider each sequence as a frightening oscillation between life and death dominated by the law of contrast, we will discover that many works can be constructed around just one of the oppositions that have been brought to light here. An obscure child becomes hero and king: David. Or the hero, unknown to all, is recognized by a sign: Odysseus by his dog, his nurse and then by the suitors at the end of the *Odyssey*. As we see in this example, the simple opposition between 'unknown' and 'recognized' can produce many variations, for the greater pleasure of reader or spectator. This explains not only the three recognitions of Odysseus, but also the twelve tasks of Hercules, the countless single combats of the *Iliad* and contemporary epic forms (westerns, crime stories and so on). These excess elements, these 'duplications', are extremely numerous in heroic narratives and help to explain the latter's structure as 'strings' of events, where all kinds of independent feats follow one on the other. In previous centuries this independence of the different episodes allowed Louis XIV of France to preserve the 'metallic history' of his reign in a succession of medals; in the same way the traditional scenes featured in the popular coloured prints of the period did much to assist the diffusion of the Napoleonic myth. Today the ease of reproduction encourages the creation of 'series' of adventures, both in cartoons and on television.

THE HERO AND THE FEMININE WORLD

A glorious character who is always imagined with solar features (shining eyes, radiant face, magical hair), the hero rises like the sun in the sky, alone. This essential solitude is preserved even when he has an inseparable friend, a 'double' (Achilles and Patroclus, Tête d'Or and Cébès), who is moreover soon carried off by death. But what happens when the superman meets young and beautiful women on his path?

In most cases the feminine world is presented as a threat to the brilliant fulfilment of the heroic task: the softness of the nest, spellbinding curves and opulence, warmth and seduction into inactivity. And yet woman attracts and seems to bewitch the hero, thus she often appears as a witch (Circe in the *Odyssey*, Armida in Tasso's *Jerusalem Delivered*). The list of the ephemeral loves from which the hero finally escapes with a sudden burst of will is a long one: Odysseus leaves Circe and then Calypso; Aeneas tears himself from Dido's arms to go and found Rome; the secret agent escapes the charms of the fascinating woman spy and successfully carries out his mission.

Very often the woman is thus merely there for the warrior's recreation. Having enjoyed the delights of her company for a brief or longer period, he abandons her. Some of these 'abandonments' are famous, such as those of Medea or Ariadne:

> Love left thee dying, sweet sister Ariadne
> Lying forsaken by the alien waters
>
> Racine, *Phaedra*

Although this imaginary solution to the encounter between hero and woman seems by far the most frequent, there are others. The most striking is that which enchanted the authors of the 'courtly' literature of the twelfth to the seventeenth centuries, particularly in France. Having become her knight's suzeraine, it is the 'lady' herself, appreciative of warlike exploits, who sends her lover far away to prove his valour. His great deeds make him deserving of his beloved's favours and he receives her as the 'prize' for his courage. Love and desire thus stir up heroism rather than threatening it.

There is a possible third outcome, which highlights a valuable aspect of femininity. The hero lives in a world of brutality and crisis: is this excessive virility really so all-satisfying? Women may then appear as 'wisdom' or, in a Christian world, as 'grace', bringing gentleness, the reconciliation of the driven man with himself, serenity and a different kind of joy from that of the warrior's triumphs. This is true of the princess of *Tête d'Or* and Jean-Christophe's last woman friend, who, significantly, is called Grazia.

With the very recent liberation of women from the fate of unwanted mother-

The 'heroic model'

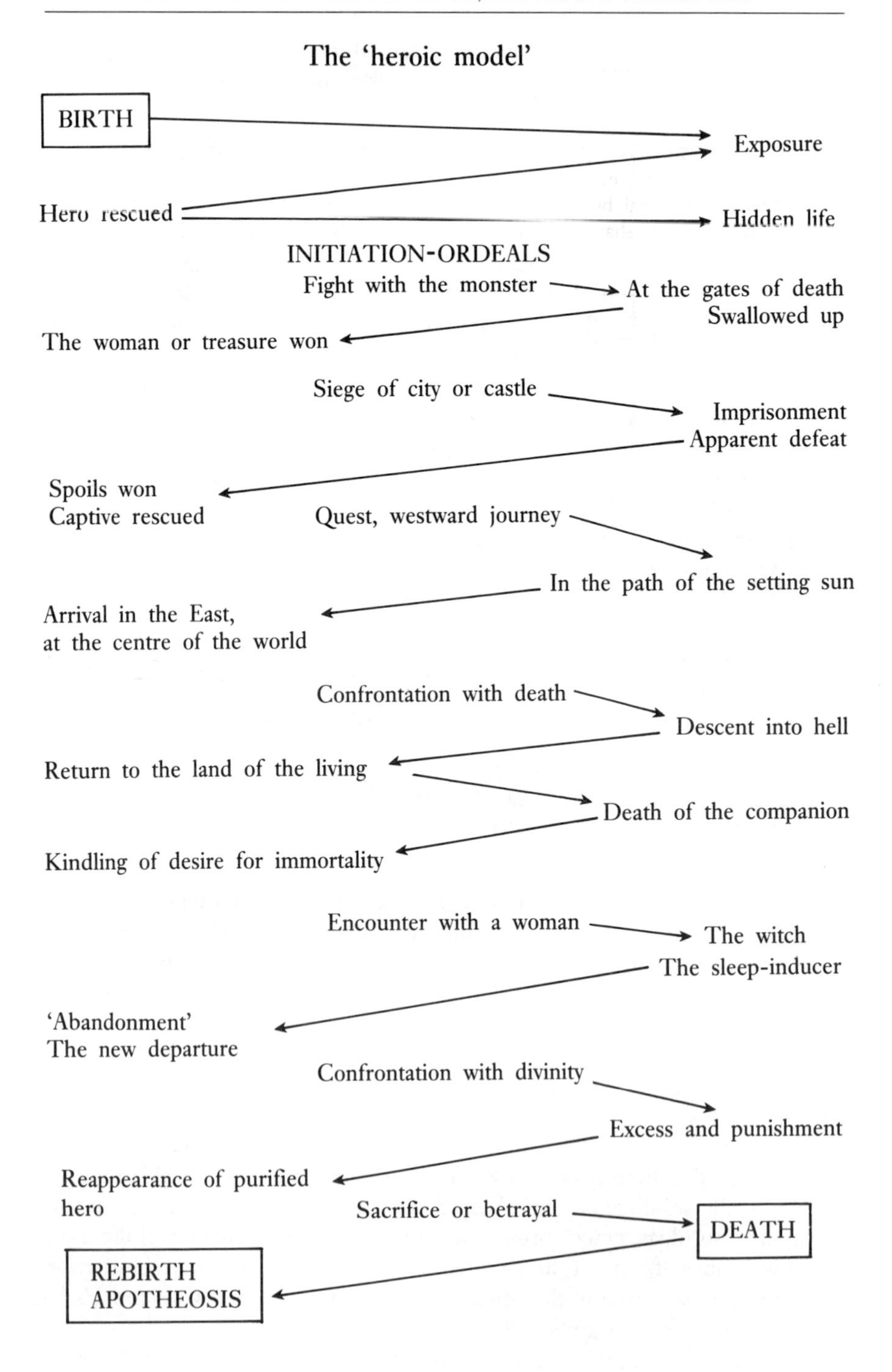

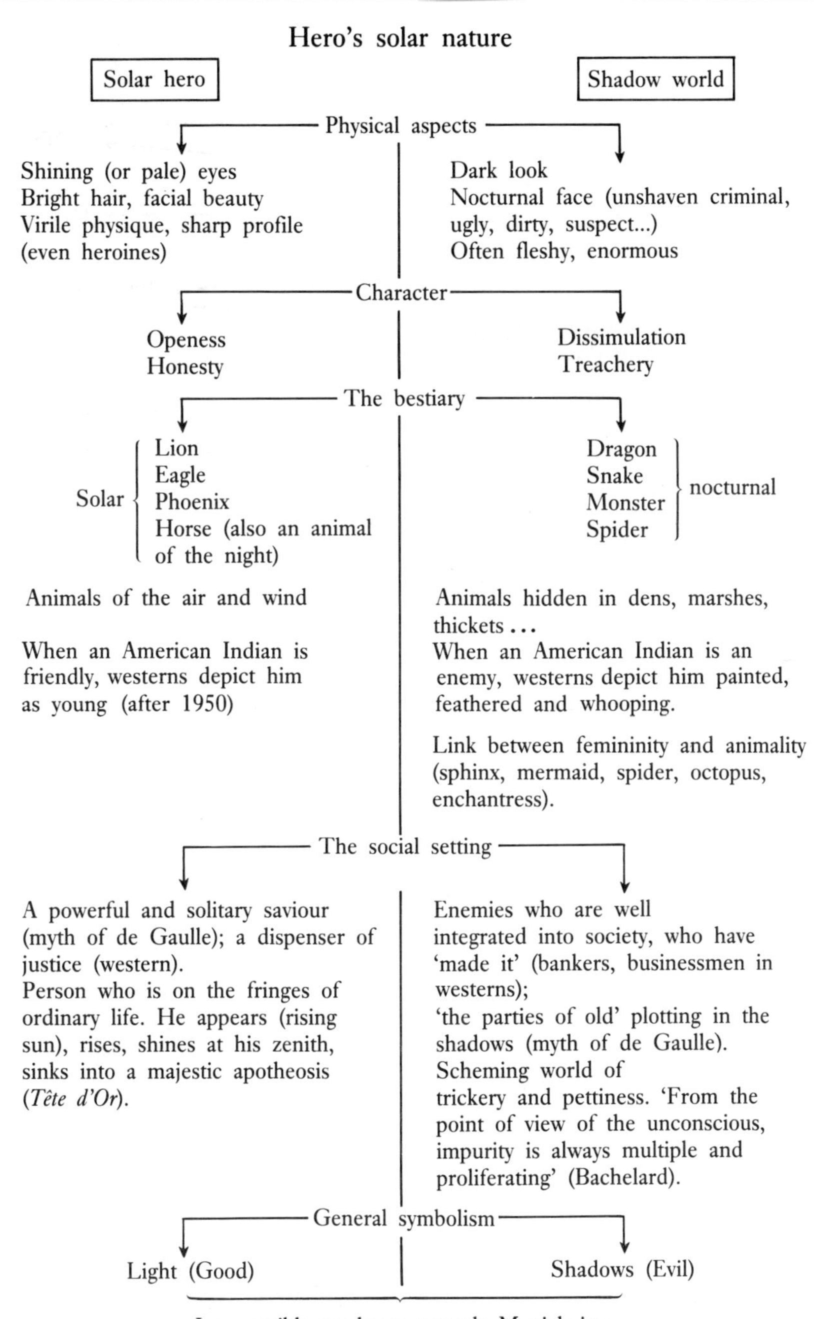

Table taken from Sellier (1985) *Le Mythe du Héros*, Paris: Bordas.

hood and with their new freedom of appearance, a fourth possibility should emerge, one already present in the mediaeval romance *Erec et Enide*: that of the heroic couple.

FEMININE HEROISM

The heroic fantasy almost always creates masculine figures: this phenomenon can be explained by the physical superiority of men, the social position of women until recent times, and by motherhood. At a deeper level, we should consider the hypothesis that the heroic is a masculine fantasy: there are many women creators in the history of literatures, but none have been tempted by the epic world.

Nevertheless there are 'heroines'. However, they are usually portrayed as slim, hard, unattainable virgins, quite the opposite of the feminine opulence which bewitches the heroes. The companions that Saint-John Perse gives to his conquerors are slender warrior women who know how to 'harden themselves beneath their helmets' (*Vents*).

Greek mythology provides the example of the fleet-footed Atalanta, who was exposed at birth on Mount Parthenius, suckled by a bear and so on. But her heroism comes to an end when she marries Melanion. Girls lose their heroism with their virginity. The Amazons themselves had difficulty reconciling their desire to be effective warriors with their desire for the fine young men they fought: according to Herodotus their Scythian adversaries were very good at finishing their battles without a single death. They had an additional handicap: their breasts got in the way of their bows. They therefore had to mutilate their daughters so that they could fight.

There is, however, one case where reality is more impressive than fiction and that is the story of Joan of Arc. With disturbing precision, the facts made real that which imagination had found so hard to conceive of for a girl. Joan, born to an obscure family and a keeper of animals (like David) was chosen by God. After her hidden life her epiphany began: she was 'recognized' by a king by a 'sign' which remained secret. Victory then followed victory. She was a virgin; her personal magnetism was so great that the soldiers respected her. One day she was betrayed; she was subjected, like Christ, to an iniquitous trial, but her stake was merely the place of her apotheosis. It is not surprising that so many artists have been fascinated by this story, a true myth.

HEROISM FOREVER . . .

Heroic fantasies have always been subject to virulent attacks. Perhaps the most violent date from the second half of the seventeenth century: after the exaltation of the period of Louis XIII of France (Corneille's plays) came a period in which 'heroic' pomposity was viewed with irony, and in which a veritable 'demolition of the hero' took place, to use Paul Bénichou's apt words in *Morales du grand siècle* (1948). In the following century, heroism fared no better: in *Candide* (1759) Voltaire was no kinder than Pascal and La Rochefoucauld had been. But with the Revolution and above all the Napoleonic empire, a powerful epic literature was reborn. Today feminist theorists have roundly attacked that male madness, 'heroism against a backcloth of death', seeing heroes as those who have failed in their lives, as being obsessed with control (Leclerc, 1975).

But such attacks are doomed to fail, having no purchase on an almost primal fantasy, which is probably more tenacious than any other, judging from the enormous role it plays in cultural productions, from high literature to popular fiction.

Philippe Sellier

Hindu Myths in World Literature

Mircea Eliade marvelled at the 'grandiose, exuberant mythology of ancient and mediaeval India' (*La Nostalgie des Origines* (1978)), as have all those, such as Jung or André Malraux, who have preserved their sense of the sacred and of symbolism. It should not be forgotten that India is the oldest great non-Semitic civilization, and the only great civilization from the intertropical area that is still alive today. In every language in use in the subcontinent there are countless poems and dramas tirelessly harking back to stories about the gods. These stories form the common background of the Hindu imagination; mothers hand them down to their children and like young Apu, the hero of B. B. Banerji's *Pather Panchali* (on which Satyajit Ray based his famous film), the children live in constant familiarity with the heroes of the *Mahabharata* and the *Ramayana*.

Of the great myths which became established in ancient times the ones that have a real literary history and that have been enriched or even transformed in the course of time are in fact those that relate to divinities who are especially venerated and loved (*ishta devata*, 'chosen gods'), with stories that serve as much as an example and model as an explanation or justification, if not more so. These are mainly the great gods Siva and Vishnu, and two of the *avatara* ('descents' to earth) of Vishnu, Rama and Krishna, and the Great Goddess in her awe-inspiring and fascinating aspects. The *patua* of Bengal, a community of semi-nomadic minstrels, sing about the exploits of the goddess Durgha on village squares, displaying painted scrolls that are basically strip cartoons depicting mythological stories. Cinema, which is the most popular art form in modern India, also draws widely on myths, whether in their traditional version, as was generally the case until the 1960s, or transposing them into the realities of modern life; it could be said that such films, with their singing, dancing, archetypal situations and simplistic psychology, have carried on where the traditional popular spectacles left off. The power of myth is so great that the actors who play 'nice' gods are imbued in the eyes of the public with the qualities of these gods; some stars of the Indian cinema in fact owe their brilliant careers in politics to a very clever exploitation of their screen image.

Mythical stories also provide material for innumerable publications, especially a huge quantity of children's literature – collections of tales and legends derived from the *Mahabharata*, the *Ramayana* or the *Purana* – most recently in the form of strip cartoons. The 'Amar Chitra' collection published in Bombay brings the main mythical and legendary stories within the range of children: 200 albums have already been published.

There is no doubt that the gods of India are almost as 'alive' now as in former times. Ramakrishna, the Bengali guru whose life was made familiar to French readers by Romain Rolland (*La Vie de Ramakrishna*, 1929), told how the goddess Kali used to appear to him at night on the balcony of his temple. It was after he had had a vision, while in prison for political reasons, of union with Krishna that the thinkers Aurobindo decided to give up his activities and found an ashram. Gandhi spent one or two hours daily listening to the feats of Rama being read aloud, and died with that god's name on his lips. For Hindus stories about divinities and heroes still retain all the power that they have in a traditional society, linking modern man to the remotest past, the time before time began.

Myth effectively associates historical man to what Mircea Eliade called the 'Great Time'. The 'descents' (*avatara*) of Vishnu to earth, intended to re-establish good order in the universe (*dharma*) whenever it is under threat, are irruptions of eternity into history, or ordinary time. In the words of a famous verse from the *Bhagavad Gita*, 'For whenever the law of righteousness (*dharma*) / Withers away, and lawlessness (*adharma*) / Raises its head / Then do I generate Myself (on earth)' (IV. 7, trans. in *Hindu Scriptures*). Epics are the chronicles of a time when men communicated with the divine in a 'natural' way. Festivals celebrating the gods or the recital of sacred texts do not 'commemorate' or 'recall' these primordial events, rather they give them contemporary relevance, relive them, and in these special moments there is a virtual suspension of ordinary time. The traditional spectacles allow people to meet the gods in flesh and blood, rather as our mediaeval mystery plays did. The devotees of Krishna, who at certain times perform the round-dance of the girls tending the cows (*gopi*) and their Beloved, singing ardent poems, feel that they are being transported not just to the period when Krishna was alive but to the eternal *Vrindavan* (the name of the village where the god spent his childhood), the Paradise where the object of their love welcomes his devotees for an endless *lila* ('game' or 'dance'). Thus if Rama or Krishna are more 'real' to a Hindu than Emperor Ashoka who lived in the third century BC it is because they do not care about Ashoka's life – it belongs to a past that it truly dead, in the world of the historically ephemeral, fortuitous or contingent, whereas mythical heroes will never cease to be present, or 'alive'. It is this lesson relating to eternity that explains why André Malraux, who was so haunted by the futility of 'what passes', was so receptive to the teachings of Indian myths; in his book *Antimémoires* he recounts several stories all highlighting the opposition between the *maya*, the universe in which we move and the power animating it, and the absolute, the single Reality. There is also a story demonstrating the power of the *maya* in the 'Indian biography' at the end of *The Glass Bead Game* by Hermann Hesse; the character in question thinks he has lived a whole life whereas only a few seconds have elapsed – 'it had been the *maya*!'

By imitating the exemplary deeds of heroes, not only does man become detached from historical time, but like the divine avatars themselves he contributes towards maintaining the cohesion of the universe. We know that the fundamental concept of Hinduism is that of *dharma*, which can be translated as the good order or harmony of the universe and all the rules that each man should observe in order to preserve it. Krishna says, 'Better one's own duty (*dharma*) [to perform], though void of merit, / Than to do another's well' (*Bhagavad Gita* III. 35, op. cit.). According to a very ancient belief, all levels of reality are interconnected, and only the recital of sacred texts enables the universe to 'hold together'.

In addition to the characteristic whereby myths link us with the 'Whole' and enable us to preserve its cohesion, they have an instructive aspect, or an exemplary value: the story itself permeates us and can transform us. Peter Brook, who directed a stage adaptation of the *Mahabharata*, was completely faithful to the Indian tradition when he said with regard to his play:

> In the great poem that is the *Mahabharata* we are continually being told something that is rather strange to us: if you listen to a story, at the end of it you will be a different person; the very fact of listening to the story will give you virtue. . . . In the sense that a real story has an action.
>
> (G. Banu 1985: 5).

In India, for the mythical story to be really *effective*, it should be *uttered* for Sanskrit is a language that is regarded as sacred and its rhythm is attuned to the cosmic order; it can also be sung, mimed or danced. More precisely still, it is possible to talk of myths having a 'psychagogic' function; the story of the life of a god or hero is intended to help us overcome the obstacles that will inevitably arise in our own spiritual journey. The 'childhoods' of Krishna as described in the *Bhagavata Purana* (fifth to tenth century) and the huge literature that followed depict a succession of fights against demons, with the god always emerging victorious; these demons obviously symbolize tendencies within us which may hinder our progression towards the deliverance and ecstasy afforded by divine love. Thus superimposed on 'cosmological', 'cosmogonic', 'astronomical' or even 'meteorological' interpretations of the myths there is a 'psychagogic' interpretation, which in no way contradicts the others; it could even be called 'yogic' since ultimately the word *yoga* is used in India to describe all forms of spiritual discipline.

In the earliest texts known to us, the Vedic hymns and the *Brahamana* which carry on directly from them, the main function of the stories that we call 'myths' seems to be to justify some element or another of sacrifice – sacrifice being at the heart of ritual activity, as it makes it possible for the forces of the universe to be reconciled. Indra, the head of the family of the gods, is the hero in numerous stories. His most celebrated exploit is the killing of the demon Vritra, who was holding the waters imprisoned within the mountains. Among the other divinities of the Vedic pantheon we may also mention Varuna, the sky, guardian of the order of the world, looking down on mankind with as many eyes as there are stars. Julien Green uses his name as the title of one of his novels, *Varouna* (1940), which tells the stories of three characters who live at different periods, but who are united in time by a chain symbolizing the ego of each of them (here of course we recognize the Indian concept of metempsychosis). In the course of each of these three lives, crimes are committed and then pardoned: 'Varuna is the Vedic god, the night sky watching for the guilty', Julien Green explains (*Journal*, p. 180).

The composition of the two monumental poems that really lie at the heart of Hindu tradition, the *Mahabharata*, the 'great story [of the war] of the Bharata' and the *Ramayana*, the 'feats of Rama', in the form that we know them must have got under way in the second century BC. In its final form the former consists of no less than 90,000 couplets, i.e. eight and a half times the combined length of the *Iliad* and the *Odyssey*, or three and a half times the length of the entire Bible, while the latter runs to 'only' 24,000 couplets. Originally the main heroes of these epic poems, which were probably based on poems sung by bards in castles, would surely not have been incarnations of gods. It was the evolution of religious life that later gave them that dimension, to the point of turning them into manifestations of the supreme Spirit.

The *Mahabharata* tells of the conflict between two rival lines of the same family, the hundred Kauravas and the five Pandavas. After a game of dice which had been fixed the Pandavas had to abandon their kingdom to their cousins and go into exile in the forest along with the wife they all share, Draupadi. When they go home after the elapse of a set period of time they have to fight to recover their throne. They wage a great battle in the course of which prince Krishna, who is the Pandavas' ally, teaches Arjuna, one of the five brothers, the paths of supreme knowledge, and reveals himself as the absolute Spirit; this teaching constitutes the *Bhagavad Gita*, unquestionably the most popular religious work in India. The Pandavas emerge victorious from this test in which so many heroes have died, and the story finishes, at a much later stage, with the ascent of the five brothers into the sky.

While the event that may have prompted this tale was certainly not particularly memorable, its literary importance can be compared with that of the Trojan war to Greek culture. In many Hindu calendars, year nought is that of the battle of the *Mahabharata*. While in the words of Sylvain Lévi (*L'Inde et le Monde*) the *Mahabharata* is a 'veritable encyclopaedia of the perfect knight', it is of course far more than that. The *Kurukshetra*, the battlefield where the two armies confront one another, is described at the very beginning of the *Bhagavad Gita* as the 'field of justice' (*dharma-kshetra*): 'On the field of justice, the Kuru-field, / My men and the sons of Pandu too / Stand massed together, intent on war . . .' (I. 1, op. cit.) The heroes are supernatural beings, incarnations of gods, or *asura* (anti-gods). The situations described are situations that exemplify all Indian societies. Thus the story is played out at a number of different levels, with the protagonists representing particular values or particular psychic abilities. For example Arjuna, who is the son of Indra, represents the highest level of consciousness that man can attain through his own efforts, but he gladly bows his head to Krishna (Vishnu), the power of spiritual illumination. Each person can find the sustenance that suits him in this saga. Lamartine, who wrote at length about early India in his *Cours familier de Littérature* (1856), said of this epic poem: 'when you close the book you have not only been entertained, you are a better person' (IV: 139). And for Peter Brook, 'in the *Mahabharata* a positive attitude is continually being called for . . . , a way of surviving in a world in a state of catastrophe without losing contact with whatever it is that enables man to live and fight in a positive way' (Banu (1985): 9).

The *Mahaharata* has exerted an enormous influence on literature. Sanskrit theatre has taken many of its subjects from it: *Sákuntala*, the most famous play by Kálidása (fifth century), develops one of the countless legends adorning it. Numerous translations and adaptations in Tamil (from the seventh century), Telugu, Bengali, Orya, Hindi etc. disseminated it throughout the country, and these versions are often the source of local literatures. It provided the inspiration for the *kathakali* theatre in Kerala, and for popular spectacles more or less everywhere. The spread of the cult of Krishna confirmed the major place it occupied.

However, from the literary point of view, India's other great epic, the *Ramayana* by Valmiki, is in every way its equal. Less overloaded with heterogeneous accretions, in general outline the story is fairly simple. Normally Rama should have succeeded his father to the throne of Ayodha. However, in order to benefit her own son, one of the king's wives contrives that Rama should be exiled to the forest for fourteen years while her son takes his place. So Rama has to leave the city accompanied by his loyal brother Lakshamana and his beloved wife Sita. During their sojourn in the forest Sita is kidnapped by the demon Ravana, the ruler of Lanka (Ceylon). With the help of an army of monkeys commanded by Hanuman, Rama lays siege to Lanka and frees his wife after a fierce battle in which Ravana is killed. Rama is then able to return to Ayodha where he is crowned. His reign is a period of peace and prosperity.

There is greater unity in the action than in the *Mahabharata*, and there are not the same skilful networks of kinship; at whatever level it is taken, the interpretation also seems simpler. No doubt it is possible to see this adventure as a mythical transposition of the conquest of southern India by Brahmanical society, as some historians have done (according to this interpretation the army of monkeys represents aboriginal peoples). However, the fact that the myth has remained so alive in Hindu consciousness must obviously be due to other reasons. More than those in the *Mahabharata* and always in a more obvious, explicit way, the characters here are models of good conduct: Rama epitomizes the just king, the virtuous *kshatrya*, Sita the perfect wife, and Hanuman the ideal servant, devoted to the end. The exile in the forest and the journey through Ceylon are tests on the difficult path leading to the ultimate coronation. And Rama is presented as an avatar of Vishnu.

The simplicity of the narrative plot and personalities of the protagonists and the ease with which a moral can be drawn from it have resulted in the myth being very widely known indeed. Rather than attempt to list the principal works derived from the *Ramayana*, we will mention just the main landmarks, the most distinguished from the literary point of view: in Sanskrit an epic poem by Kálidása, the *Raghuvamsha* (the family tree of Raghu, a solar dynasty to which Rama belonged); the *Uttaramacarita* (the 'end of the story of Rama') by the playwright Bhavabhuti (seventh century) recounting the second half of the hero's life; and by far the most important text and one that was to exert considerable influence on Indian life, the *Ramacaritmanas* ('treasure of the life of Rama'), an epic poem by Tulsīdās (1532–1623), more commonly known as the *Ramayana.* Though written in a very literary Sanskrit-influenced form of Hindi, it nonetheless has relevance for all social strata. Despite the fact that it presents an extremely conservative vision of society, it appeals to the poor because Rama, who ultimately attains the rank of supreme God, extends his pity to the humblest. Intended to be read aloud or chanted, the poem is still regularly recited at public gatherings. It is the basis of the theatrical performances that take place every year in autumn on the plain of the Ganges, at Benares in particular, known as *Ramila* (the play or deeds of Rama), with huge crowds participating. There are versions of the *Ramayana* throughout South-East Asia, which is permeated with Hindu culture, versions that are sometimes very far removed from the original story. Thus in Malaysia Sita is presented as Rama's half-sister; Rama and Sita are metamorphosed into monkeys, and Hanuman is their son . . .

Besides these two epic poems, the other great source of legendary stories is a collection of books that are held sacred, the *Purana*, '[stories of] ancient times'. In theory each book is devoted to one of the great divinities in the pantheon, and a few gods are even central to several collections, the most popular by far being Vishnu.

Siva, who occupies an important place in all Hindu mythology and worship, being regarded as the 'patron' of dancing and the theatre (the two are indissolubly linked in Indian spectacles), with his exploits being widely reproduced on the walls of temples and in paintings, is the central figure in a great many stories, either on his own or along with his 'wife' Parvati. The origin and symbolism of the *lingam* (the representation of Siva in the form of an upright stone), the god's various dances, graceful or frightening (he is the *Nataraja*, the king of the dance) and his fights with demons are amply developed in the *Purana* and the popular stories inspired by it. The *Kumarasambhava* ('the birth of Kumara', Siva's son) tells of the wedding of Siva and Parvati, and describes their love-making in extremely crude terms. Tulsīdās composed some nuptial songs inspired by this love between the gods, a theme that was also developed by Tamil mystics and the Sivaites of Kashmir. However, Siva's failure to inspire poets and playwrights further must surely be due to the fact that his compassionate traits, while not negligible, are often obscured by his more awful aspects that can verge on the frankly terrifying; it is hard to celebrate the fierce ascetic who haunts funeral pyres at night in the same terms as likable Rama or attractive Krishna. Pierre Loti described his visit to the sanctuary of Ellora, which is devoted to Siva, as a nightmare: 'Siva, always Siva . . . Siva who makes fertile and Siva who kills. . . . Siva who howls in triumph over twitching remains' (*L'Inde sans les Anglais*, Calmann-Lévy, p. 260). But it was in the same shrine that Malraux discovered 'the immemorial domain of the archetypes and the great symbols', adding 'I was in the nocturnal garden of the great dreams of India' (*Antimémoires*).

Devi, the 'Great Goddess', often identified with the wife of Siva, seems to have been a great inspiration to poets, especially in north-eastern India where the tantric influence was stronger. In the eyes of the *tantrika* the goddess represents the power that enables desire to be fulfilled, both for human beings and for the supreme Being. In a general way she symbolizes the life-force, in the theological terminology '*nature naturante*'. It is that vision of her that Claudel developed in 'La légende de Prakriti' (*Figures et Paraboles*). However, for those who worship her and the poets who celebrate their faith, the goddess is a divinity who is very much alive, with features that are completely individual, not just a representation of energy or of a principle. Sometimes she appears in her lovable, kindly, even seductive aspect, sometimes she is the opposite, showing herself as terrible and implacable. The origin of the goddess and the story of her exploits (particularly her victory over the demon-buffalo) are described in a long passage in the *Markandeya Purana*, the 'Devi mahatmya' ('Celebration of the Great goddess'), which was the source of many Bengali poems and of popular spectacles (the *yatra*, a kind of musical drama or mystery play in Bengali). The ambivalence of the feelings she inspires was experienced in full by the mystic, Ramakrishna: 'Constantly you dance in battle, oh Mother. Never was there beauty equal to yours' (*L'enseignement de Ramakrishna*, Albin Michel). This ambivalence is highlighted by Marguerite Yourcenar in 'Kali décapitée'. The story explains how the head of the goddess had been placed on the body of a woman who was an untouchable; the lesson is that the two principles, *dharma* and *adharma*, what is within the divine order and what is not, must live together, and that knowledge of vice enables us to become aware of perfection (*Nouvelles orientales* 1963). That is why, so it is said, some devotees of Siva walk at night through incineration sites in order to learn to control the feeling of fear that death inspires, and gain better understanding of the call of the divine.

But of all the gods whose story is told in the *Purana* the most popular is Krishna; he has inspired the most ardent feelings in his devotees and most excited the imagination of poets. The dark-complexioned god who was depicted in the *Mahabharata* in the guise of a prince and warrior is described in the *Prana* ('stories of olden times') as a child and a young man. These huge collections in verse of myths and legends relate the thousand tricks he played and his 'labours' (in the sense of the 'labours of Hercules'). Threatened with death through the anger of an uncle, a cruel tyrant who has been told that Krishna will come to earth to kill him, his father hands him over to the head of a village of herdsmen, amongst whom he spends his entire youth. The uncle sends several demons to attack him with orders to exterminate him, but on each occasion they are overwhelmed by the young god. His strength and charm make him the village favourite. It is this irresistible boy, beloved by his male and even more by his female companions, the *gopi* (cow girls), who has aroused feelings of love in the hearts of millions upon millions of men and women – feelings that are maternal as well as sensual and erotic. The image of this herdsman god seems to have become established in the first centuries AD. The story of his adventures is told in the *Harivamsha*, a supplement to the *Mahabharata* dating from the fourth century; mention is made of them in some early plays. The story becomes clearer in the *Vishnu Purana* (sixth century) and more especially in the *Bhagavata Purana* (tenth century), in which the erotic component is very pronounced. However, Radha, the god's favourite *gopi*, does not appear as a character until much later in the Sanskrit poem the *Gita Govinda* ('Song of the herdsman') by Jayadeva, written in the twelfth century; from then on, whether in the innumerable mystical poems celebrating their love, in dance, or in painting, the figures of the two lovers are inseparable. Theirs is a total love, irrational, unlimited, outside the social norms (Radha is not usually Krishna's wife, though according to some traditions she is described as such), in which sensuality and desire have full play (though in some areas such as Maharashtra it is Krishna's 'legitimate' wife, Rukmini, who is given pride of place, while Radha is virtually unknown). In contrast to Rama and Sita as a couple representing the triumph of normality, of *dharma*, Radha and Krishna are the prototype of insane love and irresistible passion. Desire and physical pleasure are present in a very open, explicit way (a number of commentators have been prudish enough to interpret this as being purely allegorical!).

The *Gita Govinda* is a pastoral intended to be sung at festivals (especially in the great temple at Puri) while the dancers mime the episodes; it is a series of cantilenas and refrains featuring three characters, Krishna, Radha and a female confidante of Radha's who acts as a messenger between the two lovers. Krishna and Radha are both closely associated with the development of the arts. A huge wave of devotional fervour swept across the north of the country from the fifteenth century on, especially in the Delhi region of Bengal (Krishna is supposed to have spent his early years near Mathura, a hundred kilometres south of Delhi) and in the west (Maharashtra and Rajasthan), inspiring not only tens of thousands of poems intended to be sung, but also temple and village dances, spectacles, paintings and sculptures. An extraordinary proliferation of paintings, in the Rajasthan and Punjab between the sixteenth and nineteenth century in particular – miniatures illustrating manuscripts or kept as treasures in portfolios – are devoted to the god's adventures. The *ragamala* – 'garlands of raga' – collections of paintings are thought to offer a visual transposition of the feelings contained in musical modes (*raga*) and the poems that accompany them; Krishna is often represented in them, with or without his beloved *gopi*. Generally speaking the paintings 'illustrate', sometimes in a very explicit way, a passage from the *Purana*, the *Gita Govinda* or some poem that is familiar to everyone.

In Indian art the same fundamental principles apply to drama and dance, or sculpture and music, for all art is directed towards the same objective: engendering in the spectator a certain aesthetic response (*rasa*) which is often considered analogous to a mystical experience. It is the artist's role to communicate what is permanent and transcendent about this emotion, in other words its divine aspect. This leads on the one hand to a refusal to resort to anecdote, sentimentality, individualized emotion and any personal feeling, and on the other to a codification which, while it certainly does not prevent talent from being expressed, is nonetheless extremely rigid and restrictive. The room for manoeuvre within the limits of each style seems fairly narrow, and in the struggle between constraint and freedom constraint seems to win the day.

In the Krishnaite tradition, however, the situation seems to be reversed; the artist has a freer hand, and imagination can be freely shown. No doubt this is partly related to the period. The veneration of Krishna spread mainly from the tenth century on (when the *Bhagavata Purana* was written), with the figure of Krishna being virtually absent from great shrines built before that date. Painting on paper did not come into being until quite late, and non-Hindu painters, first at the court of the Moghuls and then working for princely regional courts, were asked to depict the life of Krishna. It must be added that lyrical poetry, like painting, is a more personal, less 'collective' art than statuary sculpture or dancing, and it is in these two forms of art that the absence of constraints and the possibility of improvisation are most evident.

The poetess Mirabai (1567–1614) personally experienced the myth of Krishna, and it took possession of her. As a member of a princely family in Rajasthan she was subject throughout her life to persecution from her relations, who found it hard to accept that she preferred her divine lover to them.

In country areas in Bengal the figure of the 'Adorable' is still celebrated today by the *baouls*, nomadic musicians most of whom belong to the *vaishnava* (devotees of Vishnu) sect. Their life is described by T. Banerji (1898–1971) in his novel *Radha au Lotus*. This story deserves special mention in any case as a good example of the modern treatment of a 'myth'. The heroine, who is a worshipper of Vishnu, tries to bring the passionate love of the divine lovers into her own life; she venerates Krishna but in her dreams he always has the features of the man she loves. However she comes up against the mediocrity of her male companion, a Vishnuite like her but totally devoid of nobility of feeling. For him therefore myth is a poetic reference or a social affair, but it has ceased to be a model of behaviour.

Rabindranath Tagore (1861–1941) alawys acknowledged the debt he owed to the humble *baoul* minstrels he had heard as a child in the villages in Birbhum (a district north of Calcutta where he founded his university of Santiniketan), sharing their love of life and their 'pantheist' feeling for nature; he also praised Candidas, other poets of the *bhakti* school and the great seventeenth-century mystic Caitanya. Like many Hindus he also knew the *Bhagavad Gita* through and through. Many pieces in *Gitanjali* (Song Offering) and *The Gardener* in turn develop the themes of separation from the Beloved and the wait for him:

> I burn to play games of love with you, my love
> But you too feel this burning desire
> For your lips cannot smile nor your flute sing
> Except when my love is fulfilling you . . .

For him Krishna is perfect beauty and infinite joy.

Just as each poet relies the myth in his own way, identifying with Krishna's companions and sometimes with Radha herself as Mirabai did, enriching the myth with their own sensibility, and dwelling on the elements to which they respond most vibrantly, so in their turn painters, whether the miniaturists of earlier times or the image-makers of today, allow their imagination to speak and echo the dreams of their day. Often miniaturists gave the characters they were painting, Krishna or Radha, the features of the prince for whom they were working or of his favourite wife. In Rajput or Punjabi paintings we can also recognize the setting in which princes of the Moghul period lived, and the natural landscapes which are very realistically conveyed. Another example of the freedom associated with Krishna can be found in the 'garlands of *raga*' mentioned above. While the poems inspired by a particular musical mode do not precisely conjure up Krishna, painters associate him with the representation of spring or autumn – we see him swinging gaily at the 'feast of the swing' or romping in the woods with the young girls tending the cows. What is it that promotes such imaginative freedom?

It seems to us that the freedom accorded to flights of fancy are integral to the meaning of the myth and can legitimately claim to be part of it. *Pace* the many commentators in India and the west who have wanted to consider only the 'spiritual' significance of Krishna's amorous exploits, it is an undeniable fact that devotion to Krishna contains within it an immense love of life and a rejection of shackles and constraints; this distinguishes it from a quite different tradition of Indian thought, which we sometimes mistakenly identify with Hindu thought in its entirety. It is certainly no accident that a person such as André Malraux, who was fascinated by the austere path of *vedanta* which advocates contempt for appearances, drew only on the most hieratic trend in Hindu art; Elie Faure, on the other hand, who had been affected by the theory of evolution and was receptive to vital dynamism, saw only the burgeoning of forms and naturalistic luxuriance in India.

Krishnaism is a far cry from denying all dignity to existence: on the contrary it glorifies it. Krishna is a god incarnate, and it is in the splendour of his body that the *gopi* and all those who have come after them adore him. It is a glorification of the life of the body and the senses; miniaturists and poets alike portray the young god amidst resplendent nature, with nature participating in the gaiety and frenzy of love that surround the divine herdsman. Far from despising the world, people progress imperceptibly, rather as with Plato, through personal love to contemplating nature in its entirety, and thence to the love of the divine.

The tenderness of Krishna is not a grudging, mean tenderness. *Vrindavan*, the name of the country where Krishna spent his adolescence, contains the Sanskrit word *vrinda* meaning multitude. The milk that the little boy shamelessly spills is the very milk from which the universe sprang in the beginning of time; it is abundance itself, rich with every possibility.

Prodigality knows no bounds. Though some people have tried to interpret the exaltation of the *gopi* as just the fervour of souls in search of their Lord and in some areas in the west of India – which have perhaps been more affected by Islamic puritanism – Radha has sometimes been represented as Krishna's legal wife and sometimes just been simply ignored (the iconographic portrayals of Krishna are much more static in these areas), nonetheless in the dominant tradition the *gopi* are indeed passionate young women who abandon everything, home, children and husband, the moment they hear the call of the flute, and Radha, far from representing the ideal wife, is the female prototype of the passionate lover. The poetess Mirabai was persecuted by her family because she discounted all human respect for the love of her Beloved. Likewise Candidas (1417–77), whose lyrics are still just as popular in Bengal, brought down the wrath of the other Brahmans on his head and was excluded from his caste because he took a fancy to a young laundress (i.e. someone of very low caste) and celebrated their love in terms of the love between Radha and Krishna.

Readers will see what we are suggesting. Siva, like Krishna, is a dancing god. But whereas Siva dances the great cosmic dance which unmakes and remakes worlds and encourages us to go beyond them, Krishna draws us into a joyful whirl which *transfigures* existence. Unlike Siva, Krishna does not attempt to purify Kama, the god of desire and love, by fire. Painters and poets are fully justified in giving their imagination free rein; they are not going against the spirit of the myth. The profane, the world of multiplicity and of the mirroring of appearances, does not have to be destroyed, nor does time have to be denied.

The legend of Krishna was one of the earliest to be known in the west. Since Wilkins first translated it in 1784 there have been many translations of the *Bhagavad Gita*. Burnouf translated the *Bhagavata Purana* into French in 1840. However, because of the cultural gulf the story of the flute-player and his *gopi* has had very little literary impact in France. André Malraux, perhaps the French writer most naturally attracted to Indian myths, was more responsive to the aloof ascetic figure of Siva or to Vishnu as master of the *maya* than to the sensual charm of Krishna, which he no doubt saw as rather too lax. Of French writers, only Marguerite Yourcenar seems to have been attracted by this combination of sensuality and happiness ('Sur quelques thèmes érotiques et mystiques du *Gîta Govinda*).

With a few exceptions, the west has not been conversant with the huge mythical heritage of India. In India itself, on the other hand, the great 'myths' occupy a major place, but they are not perceived as myths in the current sense of the word, for they are *lived*. Unflaggingly returned to, translated, adapted to suit the taste of the day, they are the fundamental source from which literary and other artistic inspiration is drawn. They are not fixed, versions vary in the different regions, and, as *living* myths, they play a crucial role in the formation of the world of the creative imagination.

Yves Beigbeder

Historical Figures and Mythical Figures

Following in the wake of Athens and Jerusalem, the modern West has produced narrative scenarios such as those of Tristan and Isolde, Faust or Don Juan that correspond to the definition of myth given by Denis de Rougement in *L'Amour et l'Occident*:

> A myth is a story, a simple yet striking symbolic fable that encapsulates an infinite number of more or less analogous situations. The myth enables us to comprehend at a glance certain types of constant relationships, and disengage them from the muddle of everyday appearances.

However, everyday life and history itself can also directly provide the material for great literary myths – what we will describe as politico-heroic myths and what Philippe Sellier refers to in the following terms:

> Sometimes we are dealing with glorious figures, Alexander, Caesar, Louis XIV, Napoleon, sometimes with events . . . the French Revolution in 1789, the Spanish Civil War . . . With these great political myths the heroic 'model' that exists in the imagination always tends to come into play: dreams about a superman or supermen who are confronted with all sorts of tests (monsters, countless enemies) and who are destined – in spite of death – for apotheosis.

No myth of a politico-heroic nature is derived 'solely from the feats and deeds of a hero', as Pierre Barbéris pointed out in 1970. In other words, it does not result from his behaviour at any given time, which can easily be dated, understood and explained. Moreover, the myth very often springs up after the event, as in the case of the myth of Talleyrand, which was created by Balzac. Neither history nor reality are mythical in themselves, but they may become mythical if, for example, they are imbued with an unfathomable mystery or cease to be comprehensible and to develop logically. When an historical event or the behaviour of a great man or woman seems to interrupt the passage of time or the normal pattern of human behaviour, when an area of shadow and incomprehensibility suddenly floods over them, concealing them from science and the intellect, groups of people and entire nations defy the laws of everyday life, and use their imaginations in a quite natural way to metamorphose, distort and elaborate these phenomena and to invest them with their own colours.

In this context, death often provides favourable conditions for the emergence of a myth or supplies an existing myth with new impetus. At this point, when every life turns into destiny, and the hurly-burly of reality recedes to a distance, the collective imagination can transform history and transfer it into the realm of myth – a world that is grandiose yet simplified, meaningful yet sacred. Because any gesture, or cry, or other form of behaviour perceived at this time is final, it cannot only readily take on a paradigmatic value, but can also appear so incomprehensible that no explanation can succeed in plumbing the depths of its significance. Questions are posed with great force, and numerous interpretations are conjured up, with the result that history, which is too easily codified, gives way to myth. Thus, because it did not seem to have any logical basis and could not be analysed 'scientifically', the saintly conduct of the martyred Archbishop Thomas à Becket when he came to his end suddenly transformed the historical hero into a different character, thereby 'sparking off in the imagination of the peoples of Europe a fascinating and prodigious existence' – a phenomenon studied by Jean-Marie Grassin. Because death is imbued with mystery and associated with sacred matters that cannot be explained or put into words it creates a context in which myth can develop naturally. Other myths associated with an individual's death, besides that of Becket, include the myth of Henri IV of France, which was orchestrated by funeral orations and thus belongs to the epideictic category analysed by Jacques Hennequin.

However, not all myths relating to particular individuals only emerge when they die – some start to develop as soon as they appear on the scene. In this case, the myth has already to be seen as necessary even while the event to which it relates is actually happening. Thus, the myth of Clovis came into existence immediately, for in one fell swoop he acquired the status of founder of the French Christian monarchy, and simultaneously created the tradition of royal miracle-working. There is no perceptible interval between the appearance of Clovis on the historical stage and the appearance of the definitive model of French monarchy, that came into being through him and with him.

The need for a myth may also arise from an accumulation of events. This is true in the case of Louis XIV. Here, the birth of the royal baby was so long awaited that it seemed to verge on the miraculous, while the king's recovery from illness in 1658 appeared to be due to the will of Providence alone, and, finally, the death in 1660 of Gaston d'Orléans, who might have seized power had he lived, was also ascribed to divine intervention.

It is extremely hard to pinpoint the date at which a myth comes into being, because its emergence has to take place in a particular context separate from the one or several events that inspired the myth itself. Georges Dumézil alerts us to this in his book *Mythe et Epopée*:

> Myths . . . are not gratuitous dramatic or lyric inventions, with no relation to social or political organization, structure, law or custom; on the contrary, their role is to justify all of those, to express in large images the large ideas which organize and sustain them all.

The politico-heroic myth is, in fact, the expression of a drive that comes from the depths of the collective psyche; before the mythical character even reaches the forefront of history, his arrival is already anticipated in a strange kind of way. In people's minds, or in the collective psyche, there is a group of old dreams, old hopes and hatreds that are just waiting for an opportunity to attach themselves to a real figure. Thus, when someone emerges who is invested with a certain power or a certain function, that person immediately crystallizes these hopes, hatreds and dreams. For example, when the future Louis XIV was born, in 1638, all Catholics vested the hopes that they had nurtured for many years in that particular child. He would defeat the Turks; he would be the sovereign who would at last re-embark on the Crusades and achieve the triumph of a worldwide monarchy. The myth of Louis XIV immediately acquired imperial aspect. Similarly, in 1660, when the French were longing passionately for peace, Louis XIV's ending of the war with Spain through his marriage to the Infanta Marie-Thérèse endowed him with the almost divine prestige of a saviour. Thus collective fantasies play a major role in creating a context conducive to the emergence of the myth, for a politico-heroic myth is, in fact, the product of the collective unconscious.

This collective psyche is often guided in a certain direction, in other words manipulated. This is why it is important to give special attention to propaganda as one of the catalysts stimulating the myth's emergence. How frequently the hero can be seen elaborating his own myth! Caesar, Louis XIV and Napoleon are cases in point. Propaganda sets in motion big ideas that are clear and simple to understand, and that are constantly repeated in exactly the same form so that they are all the more readily impressed on people's minds. Indeed, a myth must be simple – the mythical image of an historical character is a simplified, amplified image. It is partly through this that a myth can be distinguished from a symbol; the symbol respects historical identity, whereas the myth starts from the point at which the imagination takes over and constitutes a form of deification. The examples of Louis XIV and Napoleon provide sufficient proof of this.

The elements discussed above are not mutually exclusive, and sometimes come into play simultaneously during the formation of a myth. Conversely, it is not essential that every single one should always be present: some elements may be missing. For example, there is no aura of mystery surrounding Napoleon, whose myth is specifically political in nature, as Jean Tulard demonstrates.

Once the myth emerges, its development is conditional on several virtually indispensable factors. Propaganda, which is often crucial in providing the initial stimulus, may again be employed to sustain and nurture the myth. Indeed, it is frequently used to inject new sources of impetus at appropriate intervals. Propaganda may be dependent both on scholarly artistic media and on popular media. Thus the myth of Louis XIV was promoted not only in official literature but also in almanacs; similarly, the myth of Napoleon was established in great works by the Romantics and then perpetuated in songs and pictures.

What is more, politico-heroic myths continue to be very closely associated with specific events, even if they are able to transcend them or even distort them. Myths may also be transformed as a result of altered circumstances, and it is possible for a 'golden' myth to turn into a 'dark' myth or a myth of some other kind. For example, a change of fortune may bring a new 'deity' crashing down from the exalted heights that he once occupied. In the process, the original dreams vanish and make way for ones that match the new needs and new ideas. Likewise, the particular element in the collective unconscious or the particular expectation that bore the myth along may change into something different, if they are shattered by reality. The chronology of political events often imposes its rhythm on the myth's development. Obviously, too, the life of the hero who has been mythicized is a human life, and so naturally forms a contrasting patchwork of shadows and brightness. A failure, an illness or death suddenly show that the god is a man. However, the myth will accommodate the paradox of a god who is murdered: the myths of Caesar and Louis XIV are evidence of this. The myth is changed, restored and transformed by contemporary demands and the contemporary imagination.

One should also remember, as already indicated, that the myth may evolve at the time of its hero's death, after which a distancing process takes place, which is even more conducive to mystery and simplification. Moreover, it is often after death that the hero acquires an image that transcends his historical identity and satisfies the expectations felt by the nation at that particular period. All literary myths tend to vary according to the political, social, economic and, indeed, spiritual circumstances of a community, which are not necessarily identical at different stages of its history. Thus, in his analysis of the transformations undergone by the myth of Napoleon, Tulard points out that in the early days of the Restoration difficult economic conditions, which made life hard for wage-earners and thus created ill-feeling towards the Bourbons, had the corresponding effect of fuelling the cult of the Emperor and the myth of the Napoleonic Golden Age. In 1840, it was the Romantic generation that identified itself with him: 'Napoleon became the god of the generation that was bored.' The myth of the great man took on the character of a protest against modern society.

One feature of the politico-heroic myth is that during the course of time, it may be readopted or resurface, either in the same form or in a different one, but, in any case, in one that is specifically dictated by the needs of politics and devoted to them. In some cases, new images are developed that are totally at variance with history. Indeed, due to the distorting effect of variations on the myth, historical characters who were good often become wicked, while the wicked often become good. Thus Frederick II of Germany, a thirteenth-century ruler who lived in Sicily with his monkeys (apes?) and chose to come to an understanding with the infidel rather than to hack him to pieces, has gone down in mythology as the Antichrist. Conversely, St Louis and Henri IV of France have acquired undeservedly good reputations through the metamorphoses of myth. The concerns of Christian propaganda have often been a crucial factor behind the use of myth to distort or even contradict history: Cesare Borgia and Nero afford convincing evidence of this. Similarly, the French parliament succeeded in making a prejudiced and distorted image of Louis XV prevail, working on the collective imagination in such a way that the king was soon perceived as corrupt and debauched. Amongst other allegations, pamphlets written in the reign of Louis XVI branded him as the monarch who had sold off the colonies. However, contemporary historians, who are in a sense climbing back up 'the natural slope of intelligence', to use a phrase by Bergson, and are eager to study the institutions and economic and financial conditions of the period of Louis XV in a scientific fashion are in the process of rehabilitating the French king. They find someone very different from the character who has entered the world of myth, borne along by the political requirements of earlier periods. Thus a myth is never innocent; the character around which it develops is immediately categorized, and can only really be rediscovered by looking at the history of mental attitudes.

Even if we do succeed in getting back to reality, it is never possible to clear away all traces of the image created by myth, as the example of Louis XV proves. The hero derived from myth-making and the historical hero exist side by side, like two distinct realities that are almost foreign to each other. They never destroy, exclude or impinge upon one another, for they belong to two different universes, those of art and history. Art leaves an indelible mark on the myth. The latter assumes the form of a literary work, a story, a painting, a sculpture or a musical score and these establish a certain image for perpetuity. Eminent individuals who wanted to use myth to foster their aggrandizement while they were still alive were not unaware of this crucial element. Indeed, many personally supervised their own propaganda in order to orchestrate the various artistic media so that they produced a consistent image, and in order to nurture and even stimulate the talent of selected writers, painters, sculptors, print-makers and musicians. Just at Augustus had needed a Virgil, Louis XIV needed a Petite Académie – as well as exceptional material. He used the latter to strike medals, which withstand the test of time much better than poems or plays, and constitute an independent form of account. Similarly, the popular aspects of a myth never fail to be striking and unforgettable, whatever form they take and whether they are in harmony or at variance with its scholarly aspects. Here, again, the myth is extended until it incorporates certain 'autonomous' forms, such as the scrapbook pictures – 'images d' Epinal' – that bring the figure of Napoleon so vividly to life.

So great is the genius of art that it can sometimes confuse the trail of reality to such an extent that it is impossible ever to rediscover it with complete certainty, as in the case of Alexander the Great. The magic of the word recreates, reinvents and reincarnates characters and their actions so effectively in the colourful world of the imagination that their historical anchorage loses all significance. History tends to put a brake on the imaginary, and even when historical factors give a myth its impetus and dictate its transformations, the imaginary element can still be recognized by its remoteness from the actual events and by the distortion that it imposes on them through the glamour and creative properties of a dramatic structure, of a great work of fiction or of poetry. Because he is never accorded such treatment and never acquires an independent life through literature, a character such as Maecenas never achieves mythical dimensions. As Bernard Beugnot remarks: 'He has many roles, but they are fixed . . . ; it would be more appropriate to talk of idealization based on rhetorical amplification than of reincarnation or metamorphosis.' Beugnot demonstrates that, in contrast to the Emperor Julian, Maecenas gave rise to a legend and not to a myth: 'once he had left the historical stage, Maecenas was immediately robbed of his own name only to be reborn in the crucible of texts praising him as a symbolic figure'.

The literary myth has a demiurgic quality and corresponds to Paul Ricoeur's general definition of a 'founding story', as well as conforming with Mircea Eliade's declaration that this type of story 'is the real foundation of the world'. Similarly, it 'is distinct from the saga, in which there is an historical anchorage', as Sellier puts it.

This autonomy from history that is characteristic of myth supplements and inevitably implies the independence that separates myth just as radically from everyday life. As a result it is not possible to confuse a myth with a folk or fairy tale. In spite of a few concessions to the fabulous, such tales inevitably refer back to everyday life, and draw their very substance from it. In addition, characters in tales are endowed with a psychology that is fairly similar to that of ordinary people. Mythical heroes, on the other hand, are totally devoid of such a psychology and obey the laws of the imagination. Consequently, they 'symbolize fundamental forces and realities', as Sellier puts it. Thus, in *Horace et les Curiaces* (1942), Georges Dumézil writes:

> The simultaneously terrifying and fascinating mysterious manifestation of 'furor', a state of fury or frenzy made up of pride and untamed impetuosity, has very little in common with our petty 'tempers'. What we are talking about is the trance-like state of a warrior, which may fortunately first of all ensure the salvation of Rome, but which by its very nature constitutes a threat to all human order.

To become established, a myth must focus on a virtue, or a vice, a strong tendency, or a powerful idea. It is then up to the artist to highlight this inevitably bald and seemingly schematic element, using his style to impart colouring and shading. The myth is nurtured by powerful representation, and generally draws life from the shock of contrasts. As Tulard points out: 'The fantastic rise of the soldier of fortune and his no less vertiginous fall are the two – complementary – aspects of the Napoleonic myth.' In the same way, the myth of Louis XIV brings together, in succession and in a complementary fashion, the image of the glorious victor, who might easily believe himself immortal and that of the old king weighed down by bereavements and reverses. Extraordinary destinies, generally with a tragic dimension, representing some Prometheus struck down by a thunderbolt, are what suit the universe of myth: they serve as models, which seem to be offered to the human race by Providence itself. Moreover, the historical characters that art succeeds in raising to this grandiose realm give the impression of being guided by a divine or diabolical light. They seem, in some way, to be in league with the supernatural. Their gaze is not directed at this world, but seems more often to be contemplating the world beyond it. And in any case, surely literary myths, like myths in general, describe what Eliade rightly calls 'the various, sometimes dramatic irruptions of the sacred into the world'?

The artistic orchestration of these great imaginary images often takes the form of repetition. However, if a literary myth is really to exist, such repetitions must ring the changes from one work to another, like variations on a musical theme. This means that the works concerned are not creations of fantasy, mere ornaments that actually dismantle the myth. Instead, they involve the presentation in various guises of the myth's innermost meaning. They may take the form of poetic narratives, novels or plays. They may be epideictic in character or return to the epic approach. In any case, it is not the number, or, indeed, proliferation, of works that counts, but their quality – to be more precise, their richness of meaning and their unity. Sellier has defined the limits outside which it is incorrect to talk of a literary myth. At one extreme, he places the category of the emblem with its too 'relative simplicity': 'A great many over-simple episodes in the Greek myths or the Bible immediately achieved the status of emblem: Sisyphus pushing his stone, the Flood, the Tower of Babel, the rain of brimstone and fire on Sodom.' At the other extreme, he cites rhapsodies, such as those evoked by *The Odyssey*, constructed from overloaded situations, the 'structure [of which] is debased into pure sequence'. Myth lies between these two. It does not just imply the recurrence of a theme in several works over the course of time, but requires the elaboration round the hero of a whole structure fed by the most profound reactions of the imagination. As already indicated, a myth takes shape only if it corresponds to some necessity that gives it a concentrated form and a particularly solid structure, along with its meaning. Not only are these factors more crucial than the simple phenomenon of being repeated from one story to another, they must in some way initiate and propel the myth. It is their power and their deep-rooted hold on the minds of men that continually resurrect the myth over the centuries by means of works of literature. Employing this perspective, Sellier demonstrates that, while Oedipus's adventures are redolent of saga, *Oedipus Rex* demands acceptance as a literary myth. Similarly, the continued appeal of the myth of Caesar is due to three factors (amongst others): that he is embedded in the memory of the West as a literary character, that he occupies a fundamental place in our cultural heritage and that he represents a cultural phenomenon.

Are politico-heroic myths destined to disappear with time? If this were so, they would really belong in the domain of hagiography; but, on the contrary, they have a Protean quality that enables them to change into something different without ever completely disappearing. The myth of Louis XIV has unquestionably now become the myth of Versailles, but the name of the great king still conjures up the image of a complete world that is varied and passionate.

Myths can also be eclipsed or lose their power, but, even so, they are anchored in human dreams in such a way that they always arouse a reaction very different from one based on simple reason and cold logic. The names of Caesar and Alexander retain an aura and a resonance; it is as if they have preserved a tinge of magic. And perhaps it is through appreciating this that we can learn to listen to the message of the great literary myths of our own political history.

Nicole Ferrier-Caverivière

Image and Myth

At the beginning of the second century, Theo of Alexandria gave the following definition of the myth: 'the myth is a deceitful discourse which expresses the truth in images' ('logos pseudès eikonizôn alêtheian', *Progymnasmata* III). This definition marks a decisive stage in Antiquity's conception of the function of the myth. We know that Plato contrasted the 'muthos', as a lie, with the 'logos', which expresses what is true; in the same way he regarded the image ('eidolon'), the appearance which is alone accessible to the human mind through the senses, as inferior to its model, the intelligible idea. For Plato any simulation, of which the myth was one, was an illusion to be distrusted and it was important not to identify the copy, which was by nature misleading, with its model. We can translate this in art historical terms as meaning that any representation in the form of an image is a fake. This negative conception, which amounts to a condemnation of representation leading to a total condemnation of poetry, was radically modified by the Neoplatonists who, justifying myths as allegories, saw them as a means to gain access to the 'true', just as the perceptible image is a way of attaining ideas. For Plotinus, the justification of the image and that of the myth were indissolubly linked by their identical status: both belong to the order of things perceptible by the senses, but refer back to the intelligible, from which they spring. The myth is a figurative discourse and hence a mode of indirect knowledge.

This conception of myths as allegories determines the value given to Art, which was defined as a 'theology' by identification with poetry in the Renaissance, as well as the particular treatment of mythical subjects in the painting of that time. In the history of art the Renaissance was an exemplary time for the foundation of the concept of art and it was renaissance Italy, a good location for contemplating the relationship between painting and poetry, that provided the principle elements in an analysis of the complex exchanges between myths and images, images and texts and myths and metaphors. The question of the status of myths in painting extends far beyond the area covered in this volume; we shall therefore approach it here only in terms of its relationship to literary form, and more particularly to poetry or to the poetic in the wider sense.

Over the centuries the different artistic schools have clearly regarded the treatment of mythical subjects differently. If we are agreed that, overall, Antiquity saw mythical images as idols, it is possible very schematically to retrace the principle stages in the evolution of the mythical subject in art by reference to a definition of the myth as an allegory: we move first from idol to allegory, which was dominant until Poussin, and then to the representation of 'fables', in which the myth is no longer either reality or allegory, but perhaps already a pure 'image'. Starting with the eighteenth century, when mythical subjects were no longer predominant in painting, or in poetry, they seem to be portrayed more and more literally, becoming simple representations with reference to a 'story'; however, the allegorical form persisted until Watteau, and reappeared, modified and adapted by the Symbolists at the end of the nineteenth century. The few appearances of myths in modern painting are particular and while one can still see allegorical ('metaphysical') treatments in Chirico's work, Picasso's mythological drawings have no such elements, on the contrary manifesting a return to the primitive function of myths, a function far more anthropological than philosophical, and an analysis of the image itself (of the 'figure' as a subject) as a mythical expression, fundamentally bound to the order of the senses alone (the *Minotauromachy* series).

We shall not study each of these stages here; we shall simply consider the general problems which set this evolution in motion.

IMAGES OF THE GODS

In Antiquity, the representation of a god was called an idol or a simulacrum: it was later to be called an icon, losing its status as a representation to take on that of a disputed symbol in the Byzantine Christian tradition. It is significant that, in the Christian tradition, the status of the religious image was a subject that gave rise to violent attacks, to the point of iconoclasm, the divinity being fundamentally unrepresentable as such, while at the same time, sacred art was developing on the same level and often using the same forms as profane art, from which it became separate much later.

The commentators agree that the invention of myths was linked to the anthropomorphic representation of the gods – who were not differentiated in archaic rites, being merely symbolized by trees or standing stones – whereas the Hebrew religion distinguished itself from the others by an absence of images. The origins of painting (the term is used generically to refer to all the plastic arts) are likewise linked to the representation of bodies and to portraits or images of the gods: they are attributed either to Apollo, or to a craftsman hero such as Prometheus, Dedalus or Ninus. Once the divinity was represented, people wondered what the reality of the idol might be in relation to the divine power it represented. Until the fourth century BC the dominant opinion was that the statue contained the power of the god and was itself endowed with a soul, indeed that it was a real incarnation of the god, his physical 'body', which was necessary to allow human beings to worship him directly, the tangible form being necessary as a mediation so that human beings could communicate with the god. It was this allegorical interpretation that St Augustine attacked in *The City of God* and the *Enarrationes*. He also rejected a similar tradition, that of the *Asclepius* (*Corpus Hermeticum* II), which distinguished two different sorts of god, corresponding to two levels in the perceptible world: the 'heavenly' or mythical gods (stars), who were created by the supreme God in his own image, and the 'temple gods' (images), who were created by human beings in their own image, but were equivalent to the former. For Augustine, everything that human beings made was an illusion and he defined idolatry in the same terms as the sins of the flesh, for it was concerned with appearances (bodies) in themselves, honouring 'the creature rather than the Creator' in the words of St Paul (*Letter to the Romans*, I, 25).

The motive of making a likeness which unites the image with the model is fundamental. Indeed it is this that determines all creation, both by God and human beings, and it is here that the danger lies in Augustine's eyes. In the archetypal schema of the cosmogonies, including *Genesis*, the human being is seen as an intermediary between the divinity, whose image the human is, and the world, which is made up of images, some of which may be of human production. This is why, for the Neoplatonists, the different 'worlds' correspond to each other, for they are images of each other: on the one hand the three worlds of the macrocosm (intelligible, heavenly and elemental) and on the other the human being, the 'fourth world' or microcosm, also called the 'miniature of the world'. The 'four worlds' can 'exchange their natures and even their names' and if 'the Ancient fathers could properly represent one reality by the image of the other', this was because they knew 'the occult friendships and affinities of all of Nature' (Pico della Mirandola, *Heptaplus*).

The image, which Plotinus defines as 'a mirror capable of grasping the appearance of its model' (*Enneades* IV. 3, 11), is an imitation, a 'figure' or 'sign' of the model. In the linguistic series used to refer to the image in Latin, we find the fundamental problem of *mimesis*, which is expressed in a contradictory way according to the types of exegesis used, depending on whether one understands it in a Platonic or an Aristotelian sense: *similitudo – simulare – simulacrum*; we can give this series strictly physical connotations, around the idea of the likeness of an image to its model, or on the other hand we can give it a negative moral value, following Plato and Augustine. Significantly Augustine also associated the metaphor, 'which explains one thing on the basis of another', to myths, images fables, fiction, figures and likenesses – *similtudo* (Pépin, 1976: 91). The literary work is likewise defined, negatively by Plato and positively by Aristotle, as essentially mimetic: its function is to imitate nature and the poet is a 'maker of images' like the sculptor or the idol painter. Poetry is thus a double of the perceptible image, and has the same status as the latter, as does the myth, by means of which it first expressed itself. Like twin sisters but more so, painting and poetry are reflections of each other and are ultimately identical: their similarity, defined by Horace in *Ars Poetica*, was taken up in the Renaissance as a basis for justifying mimetic arts in their relationship to the divine.

PAINTING AND POETRY

From a very early period and for a long time, painters used descriptions by poets for models. These were associated with 'pictures' and, like didactic practice, the practice of painting was based on ancient texts, whose principal subjects were mythological tales. According to De Prezel's *Dictionnaire iconologique* (1779), 'Rubens, that fertile genius, was so convinced of the succour that the richest imitation could draw from Poetry, that he had had a collection made of the finest extracts from the poets, which were like so many Pictures . . . These descriptions from the Poets are in fact the best Poetics that could be offered to artists'. Similarly Titian called his mythological pictures 'poems'.

Literary utterance being generally considered as the origin of myths, the image was supposed to reproduce in the order of the visible the 'idea' expressed by the poets both in the founding narratives of Homer, Hesiod and later Virgil and in the successive commentaries of later Antiquity and the Middle Ages. This was the position of the mythographers and theorists of art in the Renaissance, when the similarity between painting and poetry implied an allegorical type of relationship between them and a transposition which was usually reversible. In the eighteenth century, when this relationship was no longer accepted, Lessing, in *Laokoön* (1766), established a fundamental distinction between the two arts, in order to define their respective fields. From a methodological and no longer symbolic point of view, this distinction revealed another transposition based on the difference between the nature of literary description and that of visual images: the two arts are different in their relationship to time. Poetry is primarily narrative, in other words it is based on action and movement, and when Homer describes Juno's chariot, his description is not 'pictorial' or informative, but 'narrative', for it describes not so much the thing itself in visual terms as its effects spread out over a period of time. Painting, on the other hand, is static and can only suggest a continuous and permanent action: its place is in the instant, even though that instant may be equivalent to an eternity. Likewise for Winckelmann, whose ideas were similar to those of Lessing, the fable's relationship to its representation can be summed up in a paradox: Hercules' immobile body (in the Belvedere gallery in the Vatican) 'seems given up to the contemplation of all his works', in some way it represents the 'idea' of Hercules at the same time as a summary of the myth (Winckelmann, 1764; Heinrich, 1970: 31). Thus the fact of reducing the narrative of a myth to a figure is analysed as a complex act of fixing, involving the realization of the combination of temporality and eternity, movement and stasis, within a code of representation. It is thus an act of condensation and transposition analogous to the process of metaphor (*trans-latio*).

Renaissance theorists of iconology constantly emphasized the similarity of structure and function that unites the poetic image and the visual image, which is 'made to signify a different thing from what the eye sees' (Ripa, 1593), because they wanted to point out the superimposition of two 'images' in the process of transposition. In this context, mythological painting was regarded as necessarily containing a symbolism based on the codification of divine figures and attributes. This codification was equivalent to the structuring of a language, in which the relationship between the narrative 'fable' and the visual 'figure' could be read as an analogy of the relationship between the soul and the body in a general theory of representation: the body, 'dress of the soul', is the figure beneath which the sense of the fable is hidden (Ripa). Here we see once again the allegorical conception of the Neoplatonists. But for the theorists of art, this conception of the image as body was always tied to a symbolism of the surface, of the perceptible appearance which was the preserve of the visual arts, whereas poetry dealt with the 'internal'.

It was the mythographers' task to codify the figures. Their teaching was primarily intended for painters and was based on the recognized didactic and allegorical role of myths themselves. In the process of simplification, the mythographers' encyclopaedic project soon turned into iconology. The role of Renaissance mythographers was essential to the transmission of myths insofar as they discussed not only the fixed state of images based on texts, but also all the variations introduced by later interpretations and distortions: in their work we find a synthesis of the ancient state of the myths, their variations and correspondences with the Egyptian and Asiatic traditions, and allegorical and Christian interpretations (those of the Fathers of the Church and the mediaeval authors). So their codification was fundamentally syncretic, and myths were passed on in series of stratifications like those revealed by archaeology.

The syncretism of images was not always accepted, particularly when painters or poets juxtaposed mythological figures with Christian or biblical ones, which they treated allegorically. Mediaeval symbolism often linked the two codes (one can see a Jupiter dressed as a monk on Santa Maria dei Fiori's Campanile in Florence) and in the Renaissance Christ was still often represented with the features of Apollo; this tradition remained in evidence in paintings until the seventeenth century.

Such obvious syncretism then had to be justified and this was done in terms of the metaphorical function of the image, regarded as a 'poetry of style', and invoking the authority of Christ himself, who 'hid a great part of his divine secrets beneath the obscurity of his parables' (Ripa). This is how, as late as 1779, De Prezel's dictionary justified Poussin: 'it was doubtless with too great severity that Poussin was accused of having mixed Fable with Truth because in his picture of Moses Saved he introduced the Nile in the form of a human face, instead of simply representing a river. The artist never represented this River as a God of Antiquity: if he gave it a body, he did so purely to conform to the figurative style of the Scriptures'.

THE PHILOSOPHY OF IMAGES

Painting as a figurative language and the universal language of the sacred was soon compared to Egyptian hieroglyphs, and then to Pre-columbian pictograms: 'the Pictures that it makes can be called so many Mystic Letters, which are generally known to all the peoples of the world. It is not therefore surprising that such Figures used to serve as Characters for the Egyptians and are still used as such today in most nations of the New World' said Baudoin in the preface to his *Recueil d'emblèmes* (1646).

According to Conti's *Mythologia* (1627), any representation is an enigma, the image being a 'skin' or 'veil' concealing 'the mysterious secrets of Physics and morality'. Myths themselves were defined as allegories in exactly the same way. The aim of emblematic science, which was based on this postulate, was to make a figure, usually one borrowed from the codification of the mythographers (who were regarded as an authority until the eighteenth century), coincide with a moral meaning condensed and signified by the image itself. This science came into being during the sixteenth century, on the basis of three dictionaries of figures: Horapollo's *Hieroglyphics* (1505), Alciati's *Emblemata* (1531) and Ripa's *Iconologia* (1593). An entire literature of commentaries and exegeses of these three works later contributed to the basing of a 'divine science' on the interpretation of images. In pictographic language, mythical and allegorical figures (virtues, vices, passions) were placed on the same level and often combined. Thus Piero Valeriano, in his commentary on Horapollo (1556), interprets images of the gods as elements in a hieroglyphic vocabulary, next to non-mythical symbols (geometrical figures, trees and plants, stones, animals): Vulcan 'signifies' fire, Silene the movement of the mind, Argus 'the Mass or Machine of the World', for 'his head represents the heavens, his eyes the stars', Juno the four elements, Danaë 'the affluence of heavenly wealth', Europa 'the state of the soul in the human body', and so on.

This perception of the myth through the image is literally reductive: it is the result of a substitution by which the narrative fable's individualized and dramatized representation is condensed in order to codify it as a 'moral' representation, which is more abstract and general (more 'eternal', in Lessing's words) and is based on the analysis of myths, whose narrative aspect then becomes merely a reference point. The allegories which took the place of the gods in the mediaeval moralizations were largely iconographic schemes of the gods' attributes, while also being their exegesis.

In the Renaissance, the exegesis of mythical images was regarded as a mode of knowledge, linked to the hermetic tradition, in which symbols and allegories superimposed on the myth's original narrative structure (which remains in the memory) reconstruct a 'Philosophy of Nature' in a new cryptography. Thus in his *Philosophie des images énigmatiques* (1682) Menestrier analysed the symbolism of emblems and figures in general intended to penetrate the 'obscurity of the Mysteries' to which the mind cannot gain access without the mediation of images. Use of images also made it possible to condense encyclopaedic speculations and, ideally, all human knowledge into a small space. Such was the project of Giulio Camillo Delminio's 'theatre of memory' at the end of the sixteenth century; this was a pool of images linked to the senses, to science and to technical skills, making it possible to offer the image of the structure of the mind itself through the symbolic combination of mythical figures – Prometheus, Mercury, Pasiphaë, Apollo – and abstract categories (Yeates, 1969).

PAINTING AS MYTH

Since the image was regarded as a mirror of truth, the art of making images, whether called painting or poetry, was given particular value in the Renaissance and afterwards. First art was assimilated to the Creation, giving a basis to what Curtius calls the 'theocentric conception of art', which gave painters themselves divine status to the extent that they interpret and represent the Deus Pictor. When nature as a whole is seen as an illuminated book, written in hieroglyphic letters, the mimetic function of art simply celebrates the act of creation by reproducing it.

At the same time a basis for the nobility of the mimetic arts was sought in their mythical origins. The first theorist to argue for the mythical status of painting was Alberti in *De Pictura* (1436). Alberti, for whom painting was the very expression of the divine, saw Narcissus as its inventor: 'Would you say that painting is anything other than embracing, with art, that image on the surface of the water?' This interpretation of Plotinus who, for his part, saw Narcissus as the symbol of imperfect humanity who 'prefers the vision of the eyes to that of the inner eye' (*Enneades* I. 6, 8), rests on the positive value given to what can be perceived by the senses, to the surface, which we have seen was the preserve of painting. It is interesting to compare Alberti's interpretation with Isidorus of Seville's etymology (*Etimologiae* XVI. 3, 4) of the name Echo – Narcissus' double in sound, the private voice of the body, just as in his reflection Narcissus only reaches a bodyless image – which he associates with the image, 'eikôn', to point to the latter's negatively mimetic and meaningless function. For Alberti, on the other hand, painting has value precisely because it is the reflection of the 'invisible Beauties of God painted in the visible Beauties of his paradise' (Fontaine, *Dictionnaire chrétien*, 1691). Here again we find the tripartite structure of the Neoplatonists, with the analogy between the three levels: supreme intelligence, images created by God and images created by the human intellect containing a divine 'soul'.

From this point of view, the simulacrum created by human beings cannot be stained with negative connotations or with sin. For if God created human beings in his image, it was so that they would contemplate his work in order that they themselves might make its reflection. Imitation is thus part of human nature. This conception, taken to the extremes of its implications, led the baroque poet Marino to a hyperbolic analysis in which he presents the imitation of Jesus Christ in the same terms as the Incarnation, by virtue of the principle of universal imitation according to which human beings, like the sun, angels or the Word are 'portraits of God' (*Dicerie Sacre*, 'La Pittura', 1614). In the same way the painter and theorist Zuccaro used etymology as the mythological commentators had done to justify his view of painting as divine through an analysis of the words *Dio* (God) and *disegno* (drawing). On the one hand, disegno is translated as 'sign of God', the words thus guaranteeing the sacred value of art. On the other, the word *Dio* is interpreted as a hieroglyph and as the very image of the Trinity: D, first letter of *Dono* (gift of God), represents the Holy Spirit, the 'union of the Father and the Son' in the very way it is written, for the letter D is formed of a circle, first letter of 'Omnipotence' and symbol of the Father, and a straight line, the first letter of 'Image' and hieroglyph of the Son (*Idea* 1607: II, 16). Thus the central position of the straight line in the name of the Creator emphasizes the symbol of the Incarnation, which Zuccaro automatically associates with the creation of human beings who were made 'in the image of God'. If the incarnation is the giving of an image to the divinity, a way of giving him a body, how can the image be misleading, since it definitively springs from God himself and not from the human mind, which is only his mirror? We can see the radical change of perspective in relation to the allegorical interpretation of the pagan idols: here the image, the body of God, is no longer a simulacrum of human manufacture, for the relationship of God to human beings has been reversed. It is the act of imitation itself, and no longer the idol, which is valued as a celebration. Here the painter is not an artisan, but an *artifex*, not an idolator but a theologian, as 'inspired' as the poet. Painting is thus superior to the other arts because its subject is the image, the figuration of the divine plan.

MYTH AND METAPHOR: THE MYTHICAL IMAGE IN LITERATURE

The image as a figurative language cannot be dissociated from the rhetorical figure and notably from metaphor. We have seen that its fundamentally ambiguous status is based on the fact that painting and poetry have identical functions, despite their differing natures. Once the status of the myth as an image and that of the image as a myth have been defined, it is important to examine the transformatory function of the mythical image in the field of literature, when the text reworks mythical material by combining description with interpretation, at the level of both the fable (founding narrative) and the representation (codified image). To do this we shall consider a few examples.

The mythical image, subject to the transformations and contaminations which define its stratified nature, in turn produces 'fables' which are either its description or its amplification in the form of new narratives, which thus themselves appear as metaphors. These products of the image, whose structure and literary status are particularly complex, can be defined as the second degree of perception of myths in terms of a system of representations to which they have given rise: as the image of an image.

The most immediate presence of the image in literature manifests itself in description or 'ecphrasis', where the text is offered as a copy of an image to show what the narrative only suggests through the succession of events or actions. But, as Lessing's analysis shows, in its very principle description always contains the narrative characteristics of the story: the image described can never be superimposed on the iconic image, it is always hyperbolic and analytic. The paradigmatic description of works of art in literature is that of Achilles' shield forged by Vulcan in Book 18 of the *Iliad*, which Vico (*Scienza nuova*. II, 6) analyses as the condensed image of 'the history of the world', from the creation of the universe (representation of the stars, the heavens, the earth and the seas) to the various stages of human civilization (laws, wars, agriculture and husbandry, architecture, dance symbolizing the accomplishments). Each stage is represented on the shield by an animated scene, which Homer's text describes, simultaneously stressing the iconographic, material element of the engraved object and the illusion of life and movement reproduced by a dramatic narrative. Far from being the redundant copy of an image, this description points to the fundamental gap between the visual object and its poetic transformation, which prevents the reverse operation, which would be to represent the object which is described iconically.

A second level of literary production of images comes into being in the Hellenistic period with the emerging genre of the novel: Longus' pastoral work, *Daphnis and Chloë*, is presented as the narrative development of a painted subject that the narrator is contemplating. Achilles Tatius' novel *Leucippe and Clitophon* opens with a thanksgiving representing the rape of Europa, and analysis of the image provides the allegorical structure of the story which Clitophon recounts to the person looking at the picture, who represents both author and reader; the subject of the image and that of the novel are different here, but they are metaphorically connected to each other in that they are both stamped with the power of Eros. Lastly, in Helidorus' *Aethiopica*, the heroine Chariclea is the incarnation of an image representing Andromeda, founder of her lineage, which her mother was contemplating when she conceived Chariclea; the myth of Andromeda here determines the heroine's wanderings and the narrative is presented as an analytical and hyperbolic discussion produced, in the image of its heroine herself, by a painting.

At the same time the rhetorician Philostratus wrote a singular work which was very popular right up to the seventeenth century, *Imagines*, the description of an imaginary gallery of paintings representing mythological subjects, which gives a didactic pretext for a series of rhetorical variations on interpretation, illusion and the status of the image. Based on an iconography which was absent (but present in all memories by reference to the myths), Philostratus gave the images a philosophical and symbolic commentary, which was to be magnified by his translators (notably Blaise de Vigenère in 1578), and was more important than the actual description. The myth of Narcissus, for example, is analysed in a conceptual way as a reciprocal attraction between the body and its reflection: the water is 'attentive to him, as though it had been dried out and was thirsty for his beauty'.

Following on to some extent from Philostratus' undertaking, in 1620 the Italian poet Marino wrote a collection of short poems called *La Galeria*, which is an ideal catalogue of mythological subjects, some attributed to modern (and actually identifiable) artists, others probably imaginary. The poems, each of which is devoted to an image, are grouped into 'stories' (either mythical or biblical), 'portraits' and 'sculptures', and here again, the description is not literal, but analytic. Whereas Philostratus sought to read images like metaphors, to give their meaning and iconological function, Marino gives a metaphorical interpretation of the structural and analogical implications of the myth, which he reads in the symbolic expressivity of the figures shown in the images. The short, non-narrative (as in Homer's work) form of the poems, which are mostly sonnets or madrigals, facilitates as full a grasp as possible of the image's condensation of the myth. At the same time the poems take up and analyse the problems of how far the image matches its model and of the illusion and fundamental reflexiveness of representation. Here again Narcissus, 'idol and idolator of himself', appears as the very image of painting. Beyond the individual meanings of the images, *La Galeria* establishes a mode of interpretation which is no longer based on allegory, but on metaphor, ambivalence and the reversibility of the myth and the image. In other words, description is here replaced by a mytho-poetics of the image.

MYTH AND ABSTRACTION

In the few examples we have just examined, it would seem that, in the context of global thinking on the function of art, the rhetorical status of the mythical image can be defined in terms of the combination of two transformational functions: firstly, the image has a pre-text, in other words it refers to a narrative fable of which it is the 'figurative' representation and condensation; then, as a result of the self-reflexivity of the image, or its reflexivity in relation to what it has condensed, it produces a new, hyperbolic text through an analysis of its attributes or the intermediary of allegorical exegesis, which incorporates both its iconographic status and its polysemous mythical function at the same time.

An extreme form of the permanence of this reflexivity of image and text in art can still be seen today in the work of the American painter Cy Twombly, who reverses the relationship in an exemplary way: an enormous series of paintings (1960–80) formed of abstract lines, graffiti and unusual colours, with titles that refer to mythological culture (*Narcissus, Bacchus, Bacchanalia,*

Birth of Venus, Orpheus, Mars and the Artist, Virgil and so on) show, in the place of the figures, their names written on the paper or canvas. Here, the image is literally abstract, and it is the name alone which condenses the fable, with the same role of graphic symbol, of pictogram, that the figure had in figurative art. Written on the painting, the name of a god, a poet or a painter takes on the status of an image and refers us back to the mythical structure of the fable by allusion and by joint reference to the dual literary and artistic tradition (Barthes, 1982: 168–74).

Françoise Graziani

Iphigenia

The tragedy of Iphigenia, initially a victim and then a priestess, unfolds at Aulis and in Tauris, not far from the sacrificial altar and in an atmosphere of impending sacrifice. It also takes place near the shore, but this offers no opportunity for escape. The gods are not involved. They have made the rules and leave the drama to take its course. It is the drama of *raison d'etat* and private affections, of the dangerous relationship between ritual and massacre. Heaven will eventually resume control, or not, as the case may be, and it is possible to see how far mortals have gone in the meantime.

ASPECTS OF THE MYTH

A myth of war

As part of an overview of the Trojan epic, the Aulis episode – Artemis demanding the sacrifice of Agamemnon's daughter so that the Greek fleet could set sail – resembles a propitiatory liturgy. According to Cicero, Iphigenia's blood was destined to summon the blood of enemies by incantation and Agesilaus, when embarking his army for Gerestes, went as far as Aulis to sacrifice a hind in memory of Agamemnon's sacrifice.

Whatever its magical influence, the sacrifice guaranteed the political unity of the Greek camp which was threatened by the recantations of its leader. In Tauris, Thoas and his subjects seemed as insistent on performing the ritual as the Greeks of Aulis, as if the survival of the group depended on it.

It is therefore a political myth as much as a myth of war. It is also a national myth. Euripides' Iphigenia, sacrificed to the threat from the barbarians, takes her place – before Joan of Arc – among the maidens who saved cities, while the image of Tauris, a place of exile and cruelty, is a hymn to the land of Greece.

A religious myth

In Greek tradition, it is rare that a liturgical issue occupies a central place in a myth. There is a dangerous confusion of rituals. The victim, brought to Aulis on the pretext of marriage, is in fact destined to be sacrificed. In some versions, Agamemnon is forced to sacrifice his daughter for having boasted of his prowess as a hunter. In others, the girl is replaced on the altar by a deer. The victim, sometimes sacrificed and sometimes replaced on the altar by an animal, is also sometimes carried up to heaven and immortalized. According to Euripides, the victim of Aulis becomes the priestess of Tauris, which is no longer simply a confusion in terms of rituals, but of the entire spectrum of the religious hierarchy, i.e. the association of the animal with the human and the mortal with the immortal.

Furthermore, there is a variation in the religious ethic, depending on whether or not Agamemnon has committed a misdemeanour, which explains the demand made by the gods, and according to whether or not a divinity, 'ex machina', mitigates the crulety of the sacrifice. But without exception, the sacrifice at Aulis was successful while the one in Tauris did not take place. Does this mean that the first was legitimate because it was successful and illegitimate because it was cruel? Was the second prevented because it was intended to be introduced into Greece and civilized because it was reduced to a symbolic gesture? The myth of Iphigenia clearly raises the issue of the legitimacy of sacrifice.

A family myth

The sacrifice at Aulis took its place among the series of murders which characterized the family of the Atrides and of which the death of Agamemnon, followed by the deaths of Clythemnestra and Aegisthus, were more or less the direct consequences. The Tauris episode, involving an imminent involuntary fratricide, would have provided the sequel had it not been decided that Iphigenia would help to purify Orestes.

But the family also provides the privileged context in which the sacrifice is questioned. Thus in contrast to the demands of the gods are the conflicting and convergent rights and feelings of the daughter, father, mother, fiancé, brother and childhood friend. These give rise to the confrontations which invest the myth with its intensity and pathos.

GREEK AND LATIN LITERATURE

A heroic myth

Although Iphigenia appears in the Trojan epic, for reasons which are much debated she is not evoked by Homer. The Aulis episode is certainly featured in another poem in the Greek epic cycle, *Cyprian Hymns*, but this only became known to us through a later summary, according to which Agamemnon is punished for boasting of his prowess as a hunter and Iphigenia, who is replaced on the altar by a deer, is taken to the land of the Taurians where she is immortalized. There are traces of the various genealogies of the heroine (according to which she is said to be the daughter of Theseus and Helen or of Chryseïs and Agamemnon) and, as we have seen, many versions of how her story ended. These variants provide proof of the vitality of the heroic myth which, however, only achieves its full potential and durability within the tragic dimension.

A tragic myth

Although only the two versions of *Iphigenia* by Euripides (*Iphigenia in Tauris*, ?411 and *Iphigenia in Aulis*, 405) have survived, both Aeschylus and Sophocles also wrote tragedies with the same title. Another tragedy by Sophocles (*Aletes*), which is also lost, provided the sequel, set in Delphi, to the Tauris episode. In the play, Electra came to Delphi to seek revenge against Aletes, the son of Aegisthus who had seized the Mycenaean throne. Iphigenia and Orestes also arrived in Delphi, on their way back from Tauris. Electra was about to kill her sister, whom she believed had killed their brother, when Orestes revealed who he was.

At Aulis, in Tauris and at Delphi, the tragic unit is characterized by the imminent killing of a child or brother and by the exertion of the various wills, whether or not they are working in conjunction, which try to prevent this happening. This gives rise to the alternation of hope and despair in a series of scenes whose many metaphorical representations provide evidence of their impact, as well as contributing to the myth's survival, for example, the reunion of the happy daughter and the tormented father; the revelation to the mother; the supreme self-sacrifice of Iphigenia and, in Tauris, of Pylades; the recognition of brother and sister.

A cultural commonplace

For the moralists, the myth was often no more than an 'exemplum' fixed by tradition and used in an illustrative capacity. When Lucretius (*De Rerum Natura*, I. 101), Cicero (*De Officiis* – On (Morall) Duties – III. 25) and Horace (*Satires*, II. 3) evoke Aulis, it is, respectively, to condemn a religion which has generated such cruelty, denounce the folly of Agamemnon and blame the king for having made – and kept – an irresponsible promise to Diana.

The myth also provoked reflection on literature, for example, Aristotle's *Poetics* and painting, particularly a work by Timanthus which depicted the sacrifice, with Agamemnon veiled to conceal his grief. Finally, the schools seized on the myth and made it the subject of exercises in rhetoric. This had the effect of gradually destroying its realism and vitality and reducing it to the level of a 'bookish' reference.

MODERN LITERATURE

Scholarly humanism and the temptations of annotation

The *Roman de Troie* of the Middle Ages and the great treatises on mythology written during the Renaissance tended to transmit the classical tradition without developing it in any other way than by improving the quality of its scholasticism. The first (humanist) translations of Euripides were characterized by their faithfulness to the original. The first of these was the Latin version of Erasmus' *Iphigenia in Aulis* (1509).

However, other scholars subjected the tradition to systematic misrepresentation. From the end of the Middle Ages, 'moralisers' of the works of Ovid and then, until the end of the seventeenth century, the authors of the many manuals on mythology, tried to demonstrate that the sacrifice of Agamemnon was a prefiguration or even an imitation of the sacrifice of Abraham or Jephthah, or even of Christ himself.

This attempt at apology was succeeded during the eighteenth century by a euhemeristic reaction which, by placing mythology – explicitly or implicity – on an equal footing with Christianity, had the effect of discrediting rather than reinforcing it. In his *Dictionnaire*, Bayle ironised the relationship between Achilles and Iphigenia while in *Gil Blas*, Le Sage made the paradoxical statement that the basic element of the myth was air. Such irony opened the way for the attacks launched by Voltaire against human sacrifice, the fruit of fanaticism, and as cruel in the case of Jephthah as of Agamemnon.

Attic simplicity and the temptations of complexity

In the same way that scholars, until the eighteenth century, had to choose between the rigorous approach of humanism and the use of the myth for the purpose of propaganda, dramatists had to choose between remaining faithful to Euripides, who was acclaimed by all as a model of purity and simplicity, and the need to conform to the tastes of the age.

In *Iphigénie* (1640), Rotrou did not complicate the plot of Euripides' tragedy, although he did introduce a motif which was to seem indispensable for almost a century, that of love. Achilles was no longer simply Iphigenia's fiancé, ridiculed by Agamemnon's decision. He was the lover whose loved one was being snatched away from him. By introducing the character of Eriphyle (simply a name in the classical tradition), Racine (*Iphigénie en Aulide*, 1674) gave Iphigenia a determined rival and, in so doing, seriously complicated Euripides' plot. Eriphyle's destiny, the secret of her birth and the evocation of her captivity, also introduced a relatively new element of fantasy to the tragedy. The same element is found in the plan for the first act of an *Iphigénie en Tauride* in which Racine made one of Thoas' sons – unknown to Euripides – Iphigenia's lover as well as inventing the fact that the victim was snatched from the altar at Aulis by pirates.

The following decades were characterized by a Racinian cult. For would-be imitators, such a cult meant that they were forbidden to write new versions of *Iphigénie en Aulide*. On the other hand, it led them to take the complications of the plot and its elements of fantasy to extremes. As a result, during the first half of the eighteenth century, there was a whole series of *Iphigénie en*

Tauride, full of political and romantic episodes, from France (La Grange-Chancel's *Oreste et Pylade*, 1699), Italy (Martello's *Ifigenia in Tauri*, 1709 and Carli's *Ifigenia in Tauri*, 1744) and England (Dennis's *Iphigenia*, 1699 and Theobald's *Orestes*, 1731).

The trend persisted in the librettos for 'opera seria' devoted to Iphigenia which abounded until the end of the century. But, circa 1750, theatrical productions were strongly marked by a new image of Greece. Père Brumoy's translations of Euripides (1730) undoubtedly contributed to this new image, as did certain views expressed by Diderot to the effect that the modern theatre, as Euripides' *Iphigenia in Tauris* had done in the past, should 'disturb and terrify' the soul. During the same period, Winckelmann glorified the 'noble simplicity' and the 'calm grandeur' of classical Greece, and a little later, Schiller translated Euripides' *Iphigenia in Aulis* from the Greek as a tribute to its harmony.

According to *La Correspondance littéraire*. Guimond de La Touche (*Iphigénie en Tauride*, 1757) had shown 'a certain amount of courage in eliminating a secondary love interest with which Racine, as was his wont, had distorted his plot'. Gluck's librettist (*Iphigénie en Tauride*, 1779) merely adapted his tragedy. The libretto for *Iphigénie en Aulide* by the same composer (1774), although inspired by Racine, suppressed both the amorous intrigue and the character of Eriphyle.

It is undoubtedly because Iphigenia refuses to marry Thoas that the latter orders her to be sacrificed at the beginning of Goethe's tragedy, but from that point on, the source of the drama lies in crises of conscience rather than specific events.

What is internalization in the works of Goethe is often, in the works of other authors, nothing more than a more or less fortunate compromise between hieratic rigidity and ostentatious pathos. This accounts for the success of the parodies by Favart, Guimond and Gluck.

Mystery and passion

These aesthetic variations alter the impact of the issues raised by the tragedy. For Euripides, consent on the part of Iphigenia was patriotic self-denial rather than an acceptance of divine will, while for Rotrou, her stoic resignation is converted into religious vocation. In Racine's version, where the decrees of heaven are more likely to inspire anger than piety, the sacrifice becomes the fulfilment of a religion of the heart while, conversely, the theatre invests the emotions with the colours of sacrificial cruelty. Bloody images are confused with images of love, and the death of Eriphyle – against a backcloth of monstrous heredity – also satisfies the logic of sacrifice and hopeless passion.

Later, when playwrights were looking for 'classical' emotion, the cult of virtuous humanity, the rejection of fantastical dénouements, only served to illustrate the difficulty of reconciling the argument of the legend, the essence of tragedy and the themes of political propaganda.

Goethe, however, invested the myth with new poetry and depth. He saw the origin of tragedy as Tantalus' crime against the gods of Olympus. But Iphigenia, choosing to be frank in respect of Thoas, implores the gods to redeem their image within his breast and put an end to the spiral of violence. Similarly, the voice of Iphigenia, the 'innocent sister', saves Orestes by purifying him of the blood of Clytemnestra.

Cruelty and disgust

The eighteenth century was a century of would-be imitators who tried to rewrite the Aulis episode in the style of Goethe.

However, Burckhardt and Nietzsche opposed a new, Dionysian image of Greece to Goethe's Apollonian interpretation. It is echoed, during the twentieth century, in the *Dionysische Tragödien* by Pannwitz (*Iphigenie mit dem Gotte*, 1913). But more significant is Hauptmann's *Atriden-Tetralogie.* In the two 'Iphigenias' included in this collection (*Iphigenie in Aulis*, 1944 and *Iphigenie in Delphi*, 1941), human sacrifice is seen as 'the bloody origin of tragedy'. It is no longer the gods who reign, nor Goethe's pure humanity, but the furious cries of Ares. The myth has become (or reverted to) a myth of war, cruelty and chaos in which the main issue is to court death.

The myth is far from having such strong echoes outside Germany. Jean Moréas's *Iphigénie à Aulis* (1903) is merely a re-write of Euripides in the style of the Romance School. In *Une Fille pour du vent* (1953), André Obey uses the death of Iphigenia to denounce 'the greed and cowardice' which make it possible to survive 'in a world of folly and crass stupidity'. The figures of the myth are absent from Michel Vinaver's *Iphigénie Hôtel* (1963) except in the – problematic – attraction of tourists for the remains of an ancient past which can also 'turn your stomach'.

PAROXYSM AND LITOTES

Paroxysm is central to the myth of Iphigenia which, in a combination of horror and the sublime, presents a series of decisive crises in terms of power and the emotions. The ancientness of its convention provides the litotes for truths which are restated by every age.

Also central to the myth is the attraction of an elusive vision. The search for simplicity and the complications of the intrigue, the surges of virtuous humanity and the 'ex machina' dénouements soften, as well as intensity, the cruel and disturbing image of sacrificed virginity.

J.-M. Gliksohn

Ishtar

The nature of the Babylonian goddess is the result of a fusion between two earlier deities, Inanna, the Sumerian earth goddess and Mother Goddess, and Ishtar, whose name she took, a Semitic goddess of battle and the morning star.

Ishtar has an ambiguity of character which comes from her composite origin, and this is borne out in her genealogy since she is sometimes described as the daughter of Anu, the god of the sky, and sometimes as the daughter of Sin, the god of the moon. The conflicting attributions of the two earlier goddesses, particularly love and war, brought together in Ishtar, contribute even more to her ambivalent character: kindness and cruelty, life and death meet within her. Among her emblems the dove (sky), the lion (war) and the serpent (earth) are found side by side, symbolizing the contradictions in the myth. However, in the cult of Ishtar in the ancient Near East, priority was given to the fertile, fecund goddess of love.

THE EARTH MOTHER

Goddesss of fertility: Ishtar mourning Tammuz

The mainly peasant population of Mesopotamia saw Ishtar as a local goddess (texts speak of an Ishtar of Nineveh, an Ishtar of Arbela . . .) called Ninhoursaga (the 'lady of the mountain'), the mistress of the earth and of vegetation.

One of the main rituals in the Babylonian cult consisted of staging and ceremonially re-enacting Ishtar's lamentations over the death of the young shepherd-god Tammuz (or Dummuzi), who was sometimes her son, and sometimes her brother and husband. After long liturgies, demonstrations of joy greeted the resurrection of the god, brought back to life by Ishtar; he appeared huddled in her arms. Tammuz personified plant life, an identification better illustrated by the legend according to which he was crushed to death in a mill, rather than by the commoner version in which he is killed by a wild boar. Thus his temporary death symbolizes the withering of plant life, not in winter as in western myths, but in the July drought (July being the month of Tammuz). These rites, which are mentioned in the Bible (Ezekiel 8:14), were celebrated up until the Middle Ages.

Ishtar and Tammuz were again associated in the ceremonies for the New Year when their sacred marriage was simulated by a priestess and the ruler of the city. Only the bond of marriage had the double power of confirming royal authority and ensuring that Tammuz would return to the city, i.e. that the cycle of seasons would be stable and provide a fertile year.

Ishtar's descent into the underworld

Another version of the myth makes Ishtar herself the divinity of plant life who dies and is reborn, like nature; the goddess goes down into the underworld, the realm of drought. At each of the seven doors of the kingdom of the dead she must divest herself of a garment or an ornament, just as in purgatory Dante lost one of the seven Ps (representing the seven deadly sins – *peccato*, sin) engraved on his forehead at each gate (*Purgatorio*, IX: 112). The goddess arrives naked before Ereshkigal, the queen of the underworld, who inflicts sixty tortures upon her. Ea, the god of the deep, the wisest of the gods, then intervenes on Ishtar's behalf; sprinkled with life-giving water Ishtar returns to the world of the living, finding one of her seven discarded garments at each of the doors.

But Ea's intervention is due less to the sufferings of the goddess than to the sufferings of mankind without her. Strangely enough, though Ishtar's descent into the underworld does in fact symbolize the death of plant life in summer, it also brings about a halt in animal and human procreation, as the Akkadian version of the legend demonstrates: 'Since the goddess Ishtar had gone down to the country from which there is no return, the bull had stopped mounting the cow, the ass had not mounted its mate, and boys in the street had shunned girls . . .'. Thus it is impossible to dissociate Ishtar the fertile from Ishtar the fecund, the Mother Goddess, goddess of love.

The 'lady of love'

The figure of Ishtar, the Mother Goddess, is surprisingly ambiguous since she is sometimes portrayed as a virgin and sometimes as a courtesan of the gods. These two extremes are in fact reconciled in the goddess's maternal role: called Nin-lou amakalamma ('the lady who gives birth, the mother of the country') and regarded as the mother of kings (we have seen that she was also their wife) she presides over birth. Statuettes showing Ishtar naked, stretched out on a bed with her legs drawn up to her body and her hands cupping her breasts must be intended to illustrate this function. Nakedness is often associated with the figure of Ishtar, as has already been noted in the case of her descent into the underworld.

Be that as it may, it would seem that procreative power as one of the goddess's attributes only results from the first aspect of love, sensuality. In her temples sacred prostitution was practised using young girls and boys who simulated the sacred marriage of the goddess, possibly on the altar. In Carthage the cult of Astarte, the Phoenician version of Ishtar, was celebrated by orgiastic rites.

Being in charge of births, Ishtar continued to protect life, and so had a role as a healer; in this she was again associated with Tammuz, the god of the sick. It has even been suggested that the story of Ishtar's descent into the underworld was recited as an incantation to cure the sick, the ordeal and rebirth of the goddess in fact reflecting the sufferings and convalescence of the ill.

But if Ishtar could give life she could also take it away. And oddly enough the two poles of her action, life and death, are closely linked since her cruelty cannot be dissociated from her erotic aspect.

BALEFUL ISHTAR: VOLUPTUOUS AND CRUEL

The epic of Gilgamesh: Ishtar, the pitiless lover

On seeing the hero Gilgamesh, King of Uruk, dressing Ishtar is attracted to him and asks him to become her lover, offering him gifts and honours in return. But Gilgamesh has the audacity to refuse, and worse still to insult the goddess by enumerating the base events in her amorous career, governed by infidelity and cruelty:

> . . . you are just a trap concealing treachery . . . Which of your lovers did you ever love for ever? Who of those you have belonged to has ever come to any good? . . . . You loved the little wagtail with his pied feathers: you struck him and broke his wing . . . You loved the shepherd . . . you struck him and transformed him into a jackal; . . . You loved Ishallanu, your father's gardener, . . . you transformed him into a *tallalu* [spider] . . . (Tablet VI)

Ishtar is outraged; the Babylonian Circe goes to the sky in search of her mother Antu and her father Anu, asking the latter to send a raging bull to attack Gilgamesh; in return she promises that there will be seven fertile years of plant growth.

But the cult of Ishtar credited her with even crueller acts than metamorphosing her lovers into animals; like the queen of the Tour de Nesle she demanded their death. Some ceremonies celebrating the sacred marriage finished with the husband being sacrificed, a new victim taking his place each year.

A destructive power

Thus the reverse face of Ishtar's procreative power shows her destructive force, which is its counterpart. The goddess in fact threatens to wreak vengeance on all humankind if the raging bull is not granted to her: '. . . I will fill the world with carnage,/and the dead will outnumber the living!' Yet immediately afterwards Ishtar promises 'to make the grass grow profusely for seven years'. The threat of destruction is thus immediately set against this promise of fertility.

The myth of Ugarit again emphasizes the bond that links creation and destruction, life and death in the personality of Ishtar. The hero Aleyan-Baal is assassinated by Mot, the master of the underground world. His wife Anat (one of Ishtar's names) seizes the guilty party, cuts him to pieces with a sacred sickle, winnows him, burns him, crushes him under a mill and scatters his remains in the fields. Mot will then come back to life, having thus undergone the same fate as corn. The figure of the plant god seems here to have split into two in the person of Aleyan who dies and Mot who suffers and is reborn. Together they make up the figure of Tammuz, or of the Egyptian god Osiris. But it should be noted that the very manner in which Ishtar kills Mot brings about his resurrection. This shows how closely the power of death and the power of life are mingled in the character of this goddess.

The 'lady of hand-to-hand fighting'

In Assyria in particular, a land of warriors, Ishtar was worshipped as the goddess of battle, a kind of Bellone, as representations of her bearing weapons prove. A certain virile quality in the goddess, whose very name has a masculine ring to it, has been associated with this role. She seems to have the same origin and the same attributes as Athtar in southern Arabia, who is a god.

Nonetheless, the link between the goddess of love and the goddess of battle seems problematic. Theologians have explained Ishtar's duplicity by reference to her star, the planet Venus, which is sometimes a morning star (corresponding with Sin's warrior daughter) and sometimes an evening star (Anu's daughter, the goddess of love). This explanation emphasizes the goddess's ambivalence but does not justify it. It may be that her warrior role should be associated with her protective power as a local goddess; on the other hand, battle can be seen as a means whereby a goddess who is 'to be dreaded by her enemies' can give want to her destructive violence.

THE GREAT GODDESS

In the course of the centuries Ishtar became increasingly important in the Babylonian pantheon, eventually becoming one of its main figures. It has already been noted that in her amorous relationships the goddess always took the initiative, whether her lovers were gods or men. But her authority gradually extended beyond the domain of love, establishing her as a sovereign over all gods and human beings. A hymn to Ishtar bears witness to her supremacy:

> Celebrate the most august of goddesses . . .
> Ishtar, she who occupies a place apart among the gods,
> Whose orders carry authority . . .
> She is their Queen: they accept her commands,
> They all bend the knee before her.

At the same time as acquiring this supremacy, Ishtar absorbed into herself other female divinities in a concentration of power that was no doubt encouraged by her ambivalent characteristics: Antu (Earth), Ningal (the 'great lady'), Aya (a subordinate divinity of the god of the sun) and then all goddesses became no more than different forms of Ishtar, who had become universal. This offers the most striking example of Babylonian syncretism, along with that of Marduk, Ishtar's equivalent among the gods, and it is reminiscent of the importance accorded to Isis in Rome in its declining days. The famous gate of Ishtar, one of the grandest monuments in Babylon, bears witness to her pre-eminence. But it is literature rather than architecture, from the Bible to the twentieth century, which has kept the memory of Ishtar alive, ensuring that the myth has endured albeit with some transformations. Evoked under other names and in other forms, the goddess has remained recognizable through the great constants in the myth surrounding her.

ISHTAR'S LITERARY POSTERITY

Esther in the Bible and in Racine

Though the Bible makes her a queen and not a goddess, Esther may be seen in many respects as a sort of survival in Hebrew mythology of the figure of Ishtar. To start with their names are allied. Moreover, Esther's birth sets her apart from her husband Ahasuerus, King of Persia; because she is Jewish she is closer to the Lord, for all that she is human. Thus the relationship between Esther and Ahasuerus is analogous to that between the goddess Ishtar and her human husband, who was also royal, in the rite of the sacred marriage. Racine's Ahasuerus (*Esther*, 1689) recognizes that his wife affords him some sort of divine protection: '. . . sitting beside you on the throne/I am less afraid of the wrath of the hostile stars,/And believe that your forehead endows my diadem/With a brilliance that makes the very Gods respect it' (Act II. Scene 7).

Finally, Esther's mission is accomplished at the end of the dinner to which she has invited the king and Haman, with Haman being condemned to death just as the husband of Ishtar might be after the New Year ceremonies. While Haman is not Esther's husband, it is significant that he tries, or seems to try to violate her: 'What? The traitor laid his bold hands on you? . . . Let the soul of this monster be snatched from him instantly . . .' (Act III. Scene 6). It is after this incident, which symbolically unites him with Esther, that Haman is finally condemned to death.

Astarte

Astarte and Ishtar resemble one another much more closely: Astarte is Ishtar's Phoenician counterpart, with almost identical attributes. In Carthage Astarte was of prime importance, as the Great Goddess, the protectress of the city. In *Salammbô* (1862) Flaubert refers to this role of the goddess whom he calls by her Greek name of Astarte (the Phoenician form being Ashtart), or more often by one of her other names, Tanit. The heroine's prayer is addressed to her: 'Oh Rabbetna! . . . Baalet! . . . Tanit! . . . Anaïtis! Astarte! . . . by the furrows of the earth – by the eternal silence and everlasting fecundity – commander of the dark sea and the azure beaches, oh Queen of all things moist, hail!'

In this invocation we recognize fertility and fecundity, associated as they are in Ishtar, but a new characteristic has appeared with the linkage of fertile humidity and the marine element. This association may have originated in the influence of the Greek goddess Aphrodite on the figure of Astarte, as Flaubert conceives of her.

The Parnassian Astarte

For nineteenth-century poets Astarte was first and foremost one of the forms of Venus. Perhaps the poets' fondness for her relates less to her specific qualities than to the harmonious sonority of her Greek name, which in French provides a rhyme for 'clarté' – which is hard to find! This is no doubt partly why the Parnassians, preoccupied as they were with musicality, gave Astarte a place in their wide-ranging mythology, as in these lines from Banville's 'Prosopopée pour une Vénus':

Hélas, qui me rendra ces jours pleins de clarté
Où l'on ne m'appelait que Vénus Astarté . . .
[Alas who will give me back those clear days
When I was called nothing but Venus Astarte . . .]

Rimbaud in his Parnassian period also conjured up Astarte. Though she is here named alone, the goddess is still close to Venus:

Oh, if man still suckled at your breast,
Cybele, great mother of the gods and of men;
If he had not abandoned immortal Astarte
Who in bygone days emerging into the immense brightness
Of the blue sea, flowers of flesh perfumed by the wave,
Showed her pink navel where the spume broke like snow . . .'
('Soleil et chair', 1870)

Apart from the Parnassian images mainly evoking the birth of Venus, these few lines connect Astarte with the original figure of the mother-goddess since her name is beside that of Cybele, the Great Mother of Anatolian mythology, who like Ishtar represents the generative power of nature.

The Decadents: a disturbing Ishtar

At the turn of the century, Ishtar appears as one of the recurrent figures in Decadent literature. The duc de Fréneuse, the hero of Jean Lorrain's novel *M. de Phocas* (1901), feels he is possessed and spellbound by a gaze that torments him:

> the gaze I am seeking, the gaze of Daghut, daughter of the king of Ys, the gaze of Salome too, but above all the limpid, green clarity of the gaze of Astarte. Astarte who is the demon of lechery as well as the demon of the sea.

The marine aspect of Astarte still ties in with Parnassian themes, but here we recognize the malignant aspect of the goddess (the demon of lechery), as she was portrayed in the Gilgamesh epic.

A disturbing version of Ishtar can also be found in the work of Péladan, in his novel *Curieuse:* the heroine, Princess Riazin, identifies with 'great Ishtar, the Aphrodite of Chaldea'.

The interest the Decadents took in the goddess seems to have had a double origin, resulting on the one hand from their fascination with figures representing the *femme fatale*, and on the other from their predilection for unusual divinities who satisfied the aesthetes' love of the strange.

Saint-John Perse's interpretation

Unlike the poets of the Parnassian school Saint-John Perse reverted to using the goddess's original name, Ishtar, reinstating her among other Babylonian gods who are featured in his work. In *Amers* (1957) Ishtar, though she is still linked with the sea in an association that is by now familiar, recovers her original personality (better known in the twentieth century due to the discovery and deciphering of cuneiform texts) and her original contradictions:

> Let Love and the sea be heard! Birth and death in the same garb! . . .
> Thus she who is named strikes the dazzling heart of the waters at midday: Ishtar, splendid and naked, with flashes of lightning and green eagles as her spurs, in the great green gauzes of her flotsam fire . . .
>
> (Strophe, IV)

In these verses we recognize the original duality of Ishtar, 'birth and death'; likewise we recall that nakedness was associated with the fecund Ishtar. Her appearance at midday, which seems to relate her to the sun ('dazzling', 'flashes', 'fire'), is more surprising. Perhaps this should be seen as a reminder that Shamash, the god of the sun, was Ishtar's brother. However, Saint-John Perse is aware of Ishtar's astral symbolism since a little later in the poem he evokes the 'green star of the morning'. As for the dominance of the colour green, in a poem devoted to the sea it seems that this has to be explained not as a reference to the goddess's fertile role but by a marine vision of Ishtar, yet again related to Venus Anadyomene.

Conclusion

Ishtar's abundance cannot be dissociated from her contradictions: now kind, now cruel, she may simply reflect the Mesopotamian natural world that she represents, changeable and capricious.

It may seem surprising that such a rich, powerful figure is not better known to us. And yet the most striking episodes in the Ishtar myth strike us as familiar. This is because we know them, but in association with different names: Orpheus for the descent into the underworld, Isis and Osiris for the dead body cut to pieces and scattered, Venus and Adonis for the lamentations over the death of the young god . . . All these legends originate from the Near East or the Middle East, some being derived from Babylonian mythology. Has Ishtar perhaps been eclipsed by her own heirs?

Ann-Déborah Lévy

Isis

Depicted simply as a woman with a high-backed throne – the hieroglyphic symbol of her Egyptian name, Aset – as her head-dress, in ancient Egypt Isis was the daughter of the sky and the earth, begotten by the sun god Re. As he was growing old Re appointed Osiris, the brother and husband of Isis, to succeed him, and as a beneficent couple symbolizing the fertility of the Nile Valley they brought agriculture, civilization and laws to mankind.

THE EGYPTIAN GODDESS

The legend of Isis and Osiris

Osiris's brother Seth was jealous of him and murdered him, cutting his body up and scattering the pieces. Isis then went in search of his remains, managing to reassemble the pieces and breathe new life into the corpse. Finally the goddess used clay and saliva to refashion Osiris's penis, which could not be found, then conceived Horus, whom she had to bring up in secret because of Seth's hostility.

The general outline of the Isis myth at the time of the Pharaohs was based on this story, so far as it can be reconstructed from fragments, or as it is recounted by Plutarch in *De Iside et Osiride* (first century AD).

Isis's attributes: magic, fertility, motherhood

Because she was able to bring her dead husband back to life, Isis was first and foremost a healer, a magician whose incantations ensured that effectiveness of remedies (she was able to save Horus when he was stung by a scorpion just by the words she spoke). As the goddess of medicine Isis was primarily a magician to the people, and her symbols, the 'knot of Isis' in particular, were worn as amulets.

Osiris's resurrection symbolized renewed plant growth, and Isis was also the agrarian goddess of fertility, which is why the water of the Nile (still to be found in hydrias at ceremonies in Rome to represent the goddess) was so important in her cult. As bearer of fecundity, since she gave Osiris back his sexual power, she became a subordinate divinity of Min, the god of procreation; this attribute is closely linked to her maternal role.

As the protectress of love and childhood, Isis the wife and mother was depicted suckling her child; her original head-dress was then often replaced by the horns of a cow enclosing the disk of the sun. This feature marks the assimilation of the social aspect of love and childbearing (Isis) with their physiological aspect as represented by Hathor, the nursing cow-goddess. Isis-Hathor, whom the Greeks identified with Aphrodite, was invoked for her love charms and philtres.

These two areas of Isis' power – agriculture and motherhood – came together in the Late Empire period in the figure of the universal mother, successor to the original myth of the Earth Mother.

The power of Isis

No longer a secondary figure beside Osiris, through her power as a magician Isis joined the front rank of the Egyptian pantheon, overtaking Re himself; she fashioned a serpent from clay which bit the god, and agreed to cure him only if he would reveal his secret name to her. She then became 'Isis, mistress of the gods, who knows Re by his very name' (Turin papyrus). Her supremacy, along with the increasing breadth of her attributions (she was henceforth given sole credit for bringing civilization), tended to turn Isis into a universal goddess, and this tendency was confirmed through contact with Hellenistic culture.

ISIS AND THE GRECO-ROMAN WORLD

During the period of Greek hegemony the Isis myth underwent a double modification: she was Hellenized, while at the same time her cult, with assimilations, moved towards virtual monotheism, which triumphed in imperial Rome.

Isis and Demeter

Similarities between the two goddesses opened the way to an ever more pronounced syncretism; according to Diodorus Siculus and Apuleius the only difference between them was in their name. Like Isis Demeter was faced with the loss of someone dear to her, her daughter Core, abducted by Hades; she too set off in search of her lost love, gaining the concession that each spring Core would re-emerge from the underworld where she was detained in the winter. Thus the two legends are similar explanations of the renewal of plant life.

In *De Iside et Osiride* Plutarch heightens their resemblance by inserting into the story of Isis's search an episode that is Greek in inspiration; while looking for Osiris's body in Byblos the goddess is taken on as a nurse to the king's son. The child's mother one day surprises her exposing her son's body to the burning heat so as to confer immortality upon him, and this interruption brings Isis's benefactions to an end. Such an episode seems to have been borrowed from the legend of Demeter; when she was unable to immortalize her nurseling Triptolemus she turned him into the founder of agriculture.

This explains why Isis was introduced into the Eleusinian pantheon, becoming the object of a mystery cult like Demeter, while at the same time her image was modified.

Isis Hellenized

Isis adopted the long tunic of the Greek goddesses, but could still be recognized by her head-dress (long curls falling over her shoulders and a garland as a reminder of her role in plant life) and more particularly by her fringed shawl, tied in a knot between her breasts in an adaptation of her original knot.

Under Greek influence the cult of Isis experienced a renewal in Egypt: the Ptolemaic queens identified with the goddess, and Cleopatra used the name Nea Isis. She was then regarded as a divinity symbolizing the whole of Egypt, not just the Nile valley; this must be the meaning of an inscription on the shrine of Isis at Denderah, where Isis is said to be born 'in the form of a black and red woman' – black being the colour of the earth, while the desert was designated as red.

Paeans of self-praise (aretalogies)

These hymns sung or recited at the feasts of Isis are often written in the first person: the goddess herself is speaking, and after introducing herself ('I am Isis'), she lists the domains of her now universal power. As well as civilization and law-making the Kymé aretalogy (first century BC) credits her along with Hermes (Thot) with the invention of writing and languages, and depicts her as the creator of the universe, the sovereign of the three worlds, earthly, celestial and subterranean, a cosmic power reigning over the elements and the stars. The first hymn by Isidoros dating from the same period lists the names of the goddess (Astarte, Artemis, Hera, Aphrodite, Hestia, Rhea, Demeter, etc.); she is *myrionyma*, and while her cult verges on monotheism, it also seems very close to pantheism. There is a return to this form of hymn in Apuleius's novel (second century AD).

The Golden Ass of Apuleius

In this myth the hero Lucius finds himself transformed into an ass as a punishment for having tried to learn a sorceress's secrets. Tired of the hellish life that his metamorphosis has condemned him to, he invokes Isis in the form of the moon (XI. 2); the goddess appears to him with snakes coiled round her head encircling the disk of the moon, wearing a tunic of shimmering material and a black shawl brocaded with stars and tied in a knot. She agrees to give him back his human form if he will consume the roses that the priest will be carrying at a feast of Isis soon to take place. In return Lucius will have to devote himself to her cult, which will ensure him a long life, happiness, and a place in Elysium. When he is a man again, he undergoes the initiation of Isis (XI. 23–4); Apuleius writes that 'The very act of initiation includes a voluntary death and salvation obtained through grace' (XI. 21).

Isis in Rome

From the time of Sulla, but especially during the empire, Isis and her initiation ceremonies were immensely popular in Italy, where she was associated with Io, no doubt because as a woman transformed into a heifer Io was reminiscent of Hathor. Assimilated with Venus (Venus-Isis of the Esquiline Hill), she was depicted naked, recognizable by her fringed shawl placed nearby on a hydria, and surrounded with roses (one of her symbols). Under the name of Isis-Pharis she was the protectress of sailors, and as Isis-Pelagia was worshipped as the goddess of the waves, bearing a wind-filled sail. But her main role as a protector was as Isis-Fortuna, *victrix et invicta:* all-powerful providence, supplanting the forces of destiny and removing her initiates from the power of blind *fatum*.

The cult of Isis was one of the most active in the declining years of paganism, only yielding to Christianity. It seems, in fact, that the myth of Isis may have prepared the way for this new monotheistic religion; in Christianity too a providence promises life after death if certain purifications are carried out, and like Isis the Virgin is portrayed carrying a child, with both mothers raising their son in secret to escape a murderer. Nerval, moreover, stressed the kinship between the *mater dolorosa* and the grief-stricken wife of Osiris: 'A divinity, mother, wife or lover, bathes the bleeding, maimed body with her tears, the victim of a hostile principle' (*Isis*). And finally the resurrection of the god in spring is still the symbol of the renewal of plant life.

However, the myth of Isis lived on after her cult has ceased, and European literature bears witness to rediscoveries and adaptations of it.

REDISCOVERIES IN MODERN LITERATURE

Isis continued to be studied throughout the Middle Ages, and the mystery cults, epitomized by that of Isis, are echoed in the initiatory structure of many mediaeval romances.

The quest in mediaeval romances

The grail in the stories of the Round Table could be seen as one of the avatars of Isis's hydria, the contents of which symbolized the divine presence. As the rose is one of her symbols it is tempting to interpret the *Roman de la Rose*, which proclaims itself as a story with a veiled meaning (the unveiling of the statue of Isis was the supreme reward for initiates in ancient times), as the search for a divinity who is also the goddess of love. Even if we do not go that far, it is clear that the grail, like the rose, is a feminine object which is essentially inaccessible and can only be approached through a series of tests or ordeals. But the legend of Isis itself did not reappear until the end of the Middle Ages.

The Renaissance: attempts at interpretation

In *De Genealogia Deorum* and *De Claris Mulieribus* (*c.* 1360) Boccaccio gave a dual interpretation of the myth; on one hand he integrates Isis into a religion of nature in which she represents the earth, and on the other hand, in a historical explanation, he makes her the daughter of Prometheus, a significant association since it ties in with the image of Isis bringing knowledge of a divine nature to men in the form of writing.

At the beginning of the fifteenth century Christine de Pisan in the *Epître d'Othéa* drew an allegorical and theological interpretation from the myth; as the goddess of vegetation Isis invites us to nurture within ourselves the seeds of the mind: 'All virtues grafted and planted/In you, as Isis makes the plants/ And all the seeds bear fruit:/Thus you should edify them in yourself'. Moreover as a divinity of fertility Isis heralds the conception of Christ: an illustration in the manuscript shows her grafting a young branch onto a dead tree, an act symbolic of child-bearing.

These interpretations signal nascent humanism through their concern for erudition and investigation on the one hand, but also because they steer the myth of Isis in the direction of a defence of knowledge and intellectual development.

Egyptomania: The Magic Flute, a Masonic opera

Freemasonry, as heir to the mediaeval and ancient guilds, adopted its oriental rites during the craze for things Egyptian which resulted from the work of the Egyptologist Kircher (1601–80), and more especially from the novel *Sethos* (1731) by Abbé Terrasson. This book lay behind a series of operas of Egyptian inspiration: *La Naissance d'Osiris* by Rameau (1751), *Osiris* by Neumann (1781) and – the most typically Masonic of them all – *The Magic Flute* by Mozart, with the libretto by Schikaneder. It follows the initiation to the cult of Isis of Tamino and Pamina, a prince and princess. Threatened by the powers of darkness the aspirants enter the night of the tombs where they have to face ordeals involving the elements; at each of these the sound of the hero's flute calms the wind elements, and the couple eventually reach the temple. The choir of priests then proclaims the end of the initiation: 'Hail, initiates! You have penetrated the dark mysteries of the Night, Isis and Osiris, accept the tribute of our gratitude. Virtue has triumphed. Vice is routed'.

In 1798 Goethe, who was a Freemason, wrote a sequel to Mozart's opera,

Der Zauberflöte zweiter Teil, and Novalis also sketched a sequel in *Die Lehrlinge zu Saïs* (1798). But the link between the myth of Isis and Romanticism extends beyond Masonic ritual; it was above all the theme of initiation itself that captured the poets' imagination.

Isis in the Romantic period

For the Romantics Isis had two main aspects: she was Nature, the universal mother, and she was the goddess hidden from the uninitiated by a veil.

In the figure of maternal Nature Novalis emphasizes the nocturnal part of her being: 'Would you too [as a mother], dark Night, show us kindness? What is it that you wear under your mantle?' (*Hymnen an die Nacht*, I, 1800). The image of the mantle of night, commonplace in itself, may here suggest Isis's black shawl, which Apuleius had described as resplendent with stars.

The development of a nocturnal interpretation of the myth was due to the fact that in the Romantic period Isis was first and foremost a veiled goddess. Her invisible face became the crystallization of all mysteries and all taboos. In 'Das verschleierte Bild aus Sais' Schiller faces his hero with the hierophant's warning:

> '. . . No mortal,' she says,
> 'Sets this veil aside until I myself raise it.
> And anyone who with an impure, guilty hand
> Raises the holy, forbidden veil sooner,
> Will . . .' said the goddess . . .
> 'Yes?'
> 'He will see the
> truth.'

After breaking this prohibition the hero receives a punishment worse than that meted out to Lucius in Apuleius; he soon carries his secret with him to the grave, and the reader never learns what it was.

At the end of *Die Lehrlinge zu Saïs* Novalis outlines two dénouements following the raising of the veil: 'Someone succeeded in doing it – he raised the veil of the goddess at Saïs – But what did he see? Wonder of wonders – he saw himself.' In the second version the initiate finds himself gazing at his fiancée. It is doubtless significant that these two outlines for a scenario were never implemented: a finished story involving the unveiling would be a transgression in itself. For Novalis and Schiller alike the secret had to remain inviolate.

Nerval, as heir to the German Romantics, made the myth of Isis one of the central themes of his whole work. A chapter in *Voyage en Orient* (1851, Part 2, IV) gives a detailed description of the Isiac initiation: after the elemental ordeals and a series of purifying fasts the initiate discovers his beloved, or ideal, woman beneath the veil. But in Nerval's other works essentially the unveiling is never completed. Thus in *Octavie* (1854) the recurrent image of Isis appears in an episode in which the goddess is not in fact named; it is the nocturnal scene in which the narrator is in the house a mysterious Neapolitan woman, a scene which brings together the symbols of the Isiac initiation. In a disturbing atmosphere 'a black Madonna covered with tawdry finery' (the veiled statue), roses, mythological pictures of the four elements (corresponding to the elemental ordeals) and a treaty on divination can be seen; the hostess, a magician, finally appears carrying a child.

But this metaphor of initiation is not completed, any more than is the quest in *Aurélia* (1865), in which madness itself is understood as 'a series of ordeals' undergone for love of the goddess:

> I am the same woman as Mary, the same woman as your mother, the same woman that you have always loved in all her forms. At each of your ordeals I have discarded one of the masks with which I conceal my features, and soon you will see me as I am. (II: 5)

What is revealed in the final unveiling can only give rise to conjecture: will it be the mother, or 'the image of Death' (*Isis*)? In the final analysis it is the actual pursuit of the unveiling which takes over from its fulfilment in a work where everything is subordinated to the quest.

Another Romantic concept of the impossible quest can be found in *Isis* by Villier de l'Isle-Adam (1862), but here the mystery is evoked as a model beyond which the heroine aims to go in her philosophical search. The mention made of it, though it is at the heart of the work in a chapter entitled 'Isis', hardly seems to justify making the goddess the subject of the novel; she serves mainly as a point of reference.

Rimbaud and Flaubert: two original adaptations

After the Romantic period the theme of the unveiling of the goddess recurs in *Les Illuminations* by Rimbaud (1872–3, published 1886). The myth of Isis (she is not named) is interpreted in a strange way since the goddess is simultaneously the incarnation of nature and the veiled woman: the poem 'Aube' describes the slow unveiling of the 'summer dawn' by a child, who may represent a novice. The pursuit ends with a simulacrum of death: 'I swathed her in her heaped-up veils and had some awareness of her huge body. The dawn and the child fell at the bottom of the wood'. And this fall is followed by a re-birth, a reawakening. We see that Rimbaud has returned Isis to her original line of descent from Re by integrating her with the myth of the sun (the dawn is a veiled sun which is stripped bare at midday).

If 'Aube' reduces the myth to its bare essence, Flaubert's very detailed text in *La Tentation de saint Antoine* (1849–74) can be set against it, bringing the various legends of Isis together in a few lines: her shawl and her veil come together as 'a long black veil that hides her face', and she is suckling her child while at the same time lamenting the death of Osiris. Thus Flaubert reactivates the theme of the search for the body of Osiris, which had been neglected by the Romantic interpreters of the myth: 'Hideous red-headed Typhon [Seth] had killed him, chopped him to pieces! We have found all his limbs, but not the member that made me fecund!' Antoine wants to stone this shameless woman, but Hilarion stays his hand: 'It was the religion of your ancestors'.

As the text continues it is reminiscent of the first-person paeans of self-praise: 'I am still the great Isis! No-one has yet raised my veil! My fruit is the sun!' Eventually the funereal lamentation takes over again, but this time it is directed towards Egyptian religion: 'Egypt! Egypt! Your great motionless gods have shoulders white with bird droppings, and the wind blowing over the desert scatters the ashes of your dead!'

Conclusion

It would, in fact, be possible to trace an adaptation of the mysteries and ordeals of the Isis myth in all works constructed according to an initiatory schema, from the folk tale to the *Bildungsroman*, but to see them as the heirs of the myth of Isis we would certainly have to forget that Isis herself is only one of the archetypal figures of quest.

Nonetheless the myth of Isis always confers an essentially dynamic structure on its literary interpretations; the movement of the quest is at the very basis of the myth, whether Isis herself is searching, gathering together Osiris's remains, or whether she is the object of the quest in the initiation rituals. In both cases the quest of or for Isis, whether it is a frantic or a methodical search, is a path that has to be followed, an apprenticeship.

Ann-Déborah Lévy

Jacob

Like the *Oresteia* or the *Oedipus* cycle, the colourful life of the patriarch Jacob which begins in Genesis 25 seems to consist mainly of 'family matters': an extraordinary birth, a marriage involving trickery, a duped father, a deceitful father-in-law, a possessive mother, brothers who are enemies, sisters who are rivals . . . But alongside these family scenes there are two which – at least on the surface – are not connected with kinship and which cut across the others because of their miraculous nature: 'Jacob's dream' and the 'struggle at the Jabbok', episodes that have already been linked by the prophet Hosea: 'In the womb he took his brother by the heel, and in his manhood he strove with God . . .' (Hosea, 12:3). There are obvious similarities between the two scenes: both are nocturnal, after 'the sun had set' (Genesis, 28:11) and before 'the breaking of the day' (Genesis, 32:34); both are filled with anguish – 'How awesome is this place!' Jacob exclaims at Bethel, and he could have said the same at the Jabbok. Likewise when he says beside the River Jabbok 'and yet my life is preserved', the same remark would be equally valid in both situations. And lastly, in these places that are consecrated by a name alluding to God (Beth-El, Penu-El), beings from another world manifest themselves.

Thus here we have two obscure texts which commentators have traditionally explained in terms of their ultimate intention, which is confessional or predicatory, neglecting the mythical background and being very hesitant about following the path opened up by Gunkel. They have been anxious to list sources, without attempting to decipher symbols; this is essential, however, especially in the case of dreams – we know that the secret component of these is just as meaningful.

THE SOURCE OF THE MYTH

There are two models that seem to shed light on the meaning of the cycle of episodes involving Jacob; first is the matrix of the wondrous tale or mythical story, as established by Vladimir Propp, regarding the sequence of events. If we place the schema suggested in the *Morphology of the Folktale* alongside the verses from the Bible we can see that the latter correspond with the elements that constitute the former. First there is a preparatory part including a 'process of deception' (Genesis, 25–27: 1–24); this 'snaring process' sets the action in motion, the theft of his father's blessing constituting the mainspring for the whole cycle; it is a misdeed which sets the plot in motion. A mediator comes on the scene (in the person of Rebekah), sending the hero-victim away; his departure from the family takes the form of a flight (Genesis, 27:18–29; 27:41–46; 28:10).

The episode involving the 'dream' may be described as 'the qualifying ordeal' or 'the first function of a donor', for the Lord makes the patriarch the gift of a dream in which he is shown a magic object, described as a ladder reaching from earth to heaven, or as 'the house of God', or at least the doorway into it, 'the gate of heaven'; this vision is understood by Jacob as a benefaction from the Lord.

The Jabbok episode is the 'main ordeal': the hero, arriving within reach of the object of his quest, in a strange place, fights a mysterious assailant and gets the better of him, but not without being physically wounded in the thigh, – his limp (Genesis, 32:23–33) – and also being marked spiritually: his new name of Israel acknowledges the true nature of the hero, and is likewise a name that refers to God.

Beneath the web of the Jacob cycle we can thus identify the structure of an initiatory narrative, and the Bible story can therefore be regarded as the dramatic transposition of a universal archetype, a fantasy, and so belongs among myths.

Now we must turn to a second model, established by Freud, that of Oedipus. Jacob is indeed the Bible version of Oedipus, and each sentence of the following analysis by Ferenczi, a disciple of Freud, can be illustrated by an episode in the Jacob cycle:

> Every meaningful but unconscious psychic prompting (aggressive fantasies towards one's father, sexual desire for one's mother, fear of castration by one's father as a punishment for guilty thoughts) has produced an indirect symbolic representative in the consciousness of all men.

Thus Jacob's fault – similar to that of Oedipus – was originally aggression towards his father (Genesis, 27), then at Bethel (Genesis, 28) the symbolic consummation of incest (the raised stone and the pouring of oil over it . . .), and finally at the Jabbok, because of what has gone before, the hero is hit in the hip, representing castration inflicted by the unknown adversary, who can be seen as the father figure.

However, and this constitutes the originality of biblical myths compared with Greek ones, the man in the Bible, breaking free of the network of fatalities we find in the Oedipus story, is invited by his God to overcome his secret desires and achieve full possession of himself in recognizing his heavenly father. The legend of Joseph, which emerged from the most archaic layers of the human psyche and was subject to the constraints of the unconscious, proclaims the responsibility of the individual and at the same time the unfailing benevolence of the divinity; like all Bible texts, the story of Jacob is essentially *religious*, uniting earth and heaven, human and divine.

THE MYTH OF WRESTLING WITH THE ANGEL

Of the various episodes in the legend of the patriarch, the account in Genesis 32 of Jacob wrestling with a mysterious stranger is in fact the one most laden with symbols, and has given rise to one of the most famous of western myths, wrestling with the angel, a stereotype that can be traced back to the prophet Hosea: 'He strove with the angel and prevailed' (Hosea, 12:4).

Three characteristics are always present in the countless texts devoted to this episode involving a fight between a man and a superhuman being of a religious nature; its basis lies in the initiatory scenario.

Description of a struggle

Anxious to avoid the blasphemy implied by physical contact between a divinity and a human being, the first Jewish commentators on Genesis interpreted the title of 'angel of the Lord' literally, and the fathers of the church fell into line, insisting that the image of a winged white-clad figure should be used in iconography. The mediaeval mystery plays still identified God beneath the angelic trappings, but thereafter the angel was seen as separate from God, and the pictorial image came to be accepted. Saint-Amant describes 'the gliding wing with golden feathers'; Lautréamont's Maldoror singed the same wing with his foul breath; Pierre Emmanuel mentions its 'talons' and 'nails'; according to Cocteau the wing turns the angel into a 'hunchback'; Gide does not venture to describe the winged figure, but remarks that it glides rather than walks.

The superhuman side of the figure is emphasized almost to the point of turning it into a monster, or an animal, which leads us back to the origin of the mythical figure, the Assyrian-Babylonian cherub, a winged bull mentioned by the Prophets (Ezekiel, 1:6 *ff*). Cocteau drew attention to its 'squashed muzzle', Thomas Mann to its 'bovine eyes' and stiff body, Pierre Emmanuel to the 'squinting eye' and 'lowered horns' of this 'wild creature', this 'yellow dog', and Georges Bernanos commented on its 'whinnying'. For Bernanos his hero's adversary was Satan, and others before him had made this association between the attacker at the Jabbok and a demon, for example, the shining angel in Lautréamont who metamorphosed into a devil with blackish wings, Fleg's black angel, and Beer-Hofmann's Samaël. Here another episode from the Bible is superimposed on the events of Genesis 32, that in Revelations where Michael overcomes the Dragon, 'that ancient serpent, who is called the Devil and Satan' (Revelations, 12:7–9). Bernanos interposes a further scene from the Gospels in his work, Satan's temptation of Jesus in the desert for forty days and forty nights (Matthew, 4:1–13). The substitution of the angel for Elohim, therefore, led to a strengthening of the fantastic aspect of the story, so that alongside the old archetype of a hero's struggle against the dragon there is a trend towards the marvellous.

The initiatory scenario

The mythical elements of the initiatory scenario can be seen in the works inspired by the story of Jacob as clearly as they can in the original. Thus the Hebrew patriarch's assailant corresponds to the infernal monster that aspiring initiates have to confront; the author in the Bible boldly assigned the role of opponent to his god, the Jewish Elohim, whereas several writers subsequently modified that figure in accordance with a thousand-year-old tradition, making him a demon, Satan, the consummate adversary ('*Adversarius vester*' – 'your adversary the devil', as the writer put it in 1 Peter, 5:8). Jean Grosjean and Pierre Emmanuel are closer to the mythical origin in making the adversary a sort of river spirit, the Jabbok itself, but they do not forget the Bible version of the story and build their character from a combination of the opposing characteristics of the demon and the divinity. The novice who experiences the torment of the ordeal, then illumination and a final rebirth is Jacob under a variety of names, such as the vicar in Bernanos, or Bernard Profitendieu in Gide; for Pierre Emmanuel he is each of us, for 'every man is Jacob', 'Jacob Anybody', called upon to endure suffering before being reborn to truth. Thus we see that the source of the legend, the *need* for it, is essentially psychological, but whereas for Gide the tale serves just as a convenient illustration for a current situation, for Laurence Housman it conveys the agonizing conflict between the two selves: the instinctive ego and the moralistic super-ego. Even so, the English playwright does not reduce wrestling with the angel to a commonplace struggle, stripped of its religious elements: for him the voice of the moral conscience is in fact the voice of God – as Rousseau expressed it, 'Conscience, immortal, heavenly voice! . . .'. Jacob is generally seen as symbolizing man struggling with something beyond him, Nature or the Ideal. It is in this sense that Gide reduces the myth to human dimensions, in accordance with the Romantic tradition that can already be seen at work in a poem by Lamartine, 'L'Esprit de Dieu'. For Lamartine the 'divine spirit' is poetic inspiration seen as a divinity, with prayer being confused with poetry. In Gide's *Les Faux-Monnayeurs* the biblical model has lost its religious value, and the young hero, Bernard, a new Jacob, tells his story in rational terms: 'I struggled over it all night,' he confides, forgetting any reference to the angel and attributing the ordeal imposed on him by the angel to a demon, in the vaguest sense of the term: '. . . driven by I don't know what demon'.

The meeting with God

While some writers have omitted the religious context of 'wrestling with the angel' – we have already cited Gide who used it as a personal allegory, as did Cocteau, but Thomas Mann, who treats the divinity objectively or scientifically in the manner of an ethnologist, should also be mentioned – most have highlighted the sacred character of the episode, whether in order to exalt or destroy it.

Thus Lautréamont and Jacques Prévert, not content with being coldly sceptical, launch virulent attacks on the God exalted in the original work. For them the banks of the Jabbok are the scene of confrontation, the lists in which the struggle with the Creator is played out, a struggle that should end with the Creator's death; through blasphemy and sacrilege, their works are still *bound* to the power but for which the story of Jacob would not exist.

In most works that draw their inspiration from Genesis 32, the relationship with the biblical Lord of Lords is central, constituting the actual message, delivered with greater or lesser conviction; it was always taken absolutely for granted both in the centuries influenced by classicism and in the Middle Ages. In the traditional paraphrase, the episode from Genesis is *re-presented*, in the literal sense of the word, on a stage, with living actors; these are faithful repeats of a model. As well as the mediaeval mystery plays, the passage devoted to Jacob's struggle in *Moyse sauvé* by Saint-Amant belongs in this category. He is content to tell and describe, but other seventeenth-century writers – an anonymous Spaniard and Laurent Drelincourt – extol the Divine Being, and deliver a message. These are just examples of a huge literary output that must be described as 'spiritual', in which the literal text is cloaked with ideology, and repetition of the original text serves as no more than a pretext for commentary, and itself becomes commentary. This applies to pages devoted to the struggle with the angel in the work of Gregory of Nyssa or St Jerome, Augustine or Tertullian, Ambrose, St Bernard and countless others, as well as to Reformation writers including Luther himself, who recognized the figure of Christ, God incarnate, in the stranger at the Jabbok. Since then, those who have reflected on the biblical text have adopted the feelings of the patriarch, seeing in the stranger at the Jabbok a God made man so as to save man. This is true of a poem by Wesley and of a negro spiritual, original adaptations of the episode that are direct in tone: 'Oh wrestling Jacob, here comes the dawn! I've still got you . . .' The speaker plays the role of the initiating angel; he is 'the professional converter who struggles . . . to regain the sinner's soul . . . he is evoked in the form of the night-time fight in the country of Galahad'.

Jewish poets – Edmond Fleg and Claude Vigée for example – project themselves into ancestors who for them are 'corporate personalities'. According to Vigée:

> The story of Jacob is not a myth or a dream, like the dream of Icarus. It is an exemplary experience, that of the Jewish people . . . Jacob struggles with an infinite being that is unavoidable but bad, until such time as we subdue him. Moreover Jacob does not vanquish the angel, all he does is withstand the attack until morning . . .

Pierre Emmanuel, as a Christian poet, adopts the attitude of a spiritual commentator, giving a symbolic or even allegorical reading, like the Jewish rabbis or the Fathers of the Church. He breathes new meaning into the ancient story, mythical meaning first of all, and as he is a modern writer this is myth interpreted through theories of the unconscious; in his work, as in that of many others, the struggle is transformed into a lovers' embrace. As in the famous fresco by Delacroix, the angel is feminized and faces a Jacob who is the epitome of masculinity, pleading with his adversary in language charged with eroticism ('When will I feel your nakedness against me?'). Another characteristic of the poems devoted to this episode by Pierre Emmanuel is that they place this struggle in the present: the fight at the Jabbok takes place 'a thousand years ago today' and may equally well be located at Sodom or Auschwitz. Similarly, Jacob as modern man is still under attack, threatened by death from outside while at the same time experiencing within himself an equally testing confrontation between the instinct for death and the aspiration towards life, between the spirit of mendacity and the spirit of truth. To make the spirit whole, it is necessary to undergo the ordeals of an initiation at the end of which man will be able to 'stand up straight' and will receive a new name, like Jacob who was reborn as 'Israel'.

The biblical source is so prestigious and the name by which it is known, wrestling with the angel, so suggestive that it has served and still serves as a springboard for dreams; Jacob, just as much as Adam or Cain, has been seen as the image of eternal man, struggling against a transcendent power, whether it is vague or precise, secular or religious.

Robert Couffignal

Japanese Mythology

Orientalists can no longer simply dismiss Japanese mythology as a 'collection of folk tales'. However, although western perception has become more acute, and the restrictions which existed in Japan concerning the study of Shinto texts have now been lifted, many difficulties of interpretation still remain. Today opinion is united in rejecting the theories of both the nationalists, who tried to find evidence in the Annals of the elusive *Volksseele* (or national spirit, a virgin figure of purely western origin) and the positivist historians, who claimed that these same texts had been compiled much later by the official Court writers. But the recent popularity of mythological studies and the many different approaches taken have given rise to new problems. Too many writers adopt a cryptic style and lose touch with the myths in an attempt to 'read between the lines' and discover fragments of different areas of knowledge, e.g. traces of historical events, ethnographical information, references to rituals, etc. This reductionist approach has two main results. Either the unity of Japanese mythology is ignored and its stories are rendered into a mosaic of motifs to which a wide range of different origins are attributed or, if it is considered to have a systematic organization, this is believed to originate outside the mythological field, and the texts are interpreted in political or ritualistic terms. Thus modern writers' very laudable desire to separate themselves from the chauvinism of the 1930s has often forced them to reject Motoori Norinaga's 'tautegorical' approach.

THE TEXTS

In 682, the Emperor Temmu, anxious to preserve Japanese traditions, commissioned a work of compilation which appears to have been based on two main sources (or two types of sources): the *Sumera mikoto no pi-tugi*, a chronicle of emperors containing basic genealogical information, and a collection of legends and anecdotes entitled *Saki-no-yo no puru-goto*. Piyeda no Are was entrusted with the task of learning (and unifying?) the texts, but Temmu's death in 686 interrupted the work which was not resumed until the reign of the Empress Gemmei in 711, a year after the capital was installed at Nara. The chronicle of ancient Japan, the *Kojiki*, appeared in 712. It was a mythological and literary text, and the first work written in Japanese (Shotoku Taishi's *Hokkekyo Gisho*, written a century earlier, had been in Chinese). By using a dual system of notation in which the characters function either phonetically or semantically, the compiler, Opo no Yasumaro, had obviously made every effort to try to preserve the sometimes incantatory rhythm and character of the narrative. The three books of the *Kojiki* cover the history of Japan from its origins to the death of the Empress Suiko (628), and combine a number of elements, i.e. the traditions of the Imperial Court and of the great Japanese families, the repertoire of the Court musicians, the oral traditions of the *katari-be* reciters), and the folk tales stemming from different cultural centres. It is possible to identify three types of documents within the text.

The genealogies

Their function was to ensure the dynastic continuity of the country by linking the great families to the divine ancestors of Japan. They mention only the residence, duration of reign, wives, descendants and place of burial of the emperors. Entire chapters of the *Kojiki* (from Suisei to Kaika and from Ninken to Suiko) are nothing more than a summary of these genealogical details.

The narratives

The distinction between the age of the gods (Book I) and the semi-legendary episodes of Books II and III has been established by usage. A more detailed study also makes it possible to interpret the 'historical' drama of the conquest of the kingdom in terms of the repetition, on a lesser scale, of the mythological structure of the first book. It is a vast undertaking which is a variation on the theme of genesis.

The poems

The literary value of the narrative is enhanced by 113 poems. They are virtually all written phonetically and often attest to a highly sophisticated poetic talent covering an extremely wide range: rural poems telling of daily work, and songs of love, departure, victory and gastronomy. They are linked, retrospectively, to the body of the myth by a simple place-name relationship, but they are also sometimes minor dramas invested with a narrative and choreographic structure which is so precise that they could be performed in the extremely complex ritual of the Court, e.g. the *Kume-uta* and the *Kamugatari*.

Eight years later, in 720, Prince Toneri and Opo no Yasumaro completed a second, more extensive Annal, the *Nihon shoki*, which included the abdication of the Empress Jito in 697. Written entirely in Chinese (with the exception of the poems and names of places and people), the *Nihon shoki* was based on the system used in the Chinese chronicles, whereas the *Kojiki* had no system for recording dates. It was a scholarly work, punctuated with numerous Chinese references, which served as official historical reference during the Heian period and was embellished with a continuation (*Shoku Nihongi*) and later commentaries (*Shaku Nihongi*). Although, like the *Kojiki*, it contains mythological details and 128 poems, the *Nihon shoki* demonstrates, by the very exhaustive nature of its approach, a conscious effort to present tradition objectively. For example, it goes as far as quoting six or seven versions of one episode. These – certainly valuable – versions of secularized mythology were no longer the subject of contradictory repetitions, but were examined selectively to produce a body of knowledge which could subsequently be extended.

The *Fudoki* were the result of an initiative of the Empress Gemmei in 713. A series of 'notes on customs and regions' compiled over a period of more than a century, these descriptions of the provinces provided a mine of ethnographical information, supplied an inventory of local resources and recorded provincial folk tales which could be situated on etymological grounds.

The proliferation of texts at the beginning of the eighth century occurred at a time when Japan was already so deeply swayed by Chinese culture that it is often impossible to distinguish between external influences and indigenous traditions. Although the Annals attempt to give the young nation an awareness of its own identity (*Kojiki*) as well as to develop a diplomatic identity (*Nihon shoki*), they also contain concepts introduced from outside. The influx of Korean immigrants during the third century resulting from the pressures of the Wei dynasty on the peninsula, the landing of 369, the founding of the colony of Mimana, the introduction of Confucianism and Buddhism, the role played by Chinese scholars (after the conquest of the kingdom of Paekche) in founding libraries and introducitng archive systems all counter the legend of Japan's cultural insularity.

CONTEXT

The search for a truly mythological dimension should not lead us to ignore the political aim of the Annals. The stages of the compilation of a national history correspond to the different stages of unification of the country. Initiated during the sixth century under Keitai and Kimmei, the compilation project was extended with the *Tenno-ki*, *Kokki* and *Hongi* put together in 620 under the patronage of Shotoku Taishi. Centralizing and Sinophile tendencies were strengthened by the reforms introduced by Taika (645), which had the effect of strengthening the resistance of the great families and in order to ensure its authority, the imperial family was occasionally obliged to negotiate with the more peripheral groups. They were faced with the task of justifying the supremacy of the ruling family, introducing administrative reforms, ensuring that the new hierarchies were respected, and promoting the nationalization of land while at the same time offering compensatory economic and political advantages to the non-exempt aristocracy. This ambiguity already constituted an initial betrayal of the Chinese model. It is easy to understand how the control system of the past, guaranteed by the Annals, was able to play a major ideological role in the allocation of these privileges. The most famous instigator of the compilations, the Emperor Temmu, worked directly for political unification. One of the first decisions made by this sovereign, who acceded to the throne after the rebellion of Jinshin, was to promulgate a new system of titles (*yakusa no kabane*) to provide a clear explanation of his power. When he speaks of correcting the errors which had crept into tradition, this should be understood in terms of wanting to replace the multiple history of the great families with the official monologue of the Court. It is impossible to ignore the fact that the writing of the Taiho Code and the establishment of the first fixed capital at Nara occurred only a short time before the *Kojiki* was compiled. Although the Court used the *Kojiki* and the *Nihon shoki* to consolidate the new hierarchies by ensuring its control over time, it was also anxious to strengthen its hold in spatial terms. The *Fudoki*, which are read today as collections of legends and appreciated for their ethnographical value, were in fact a test of the loyalty of the provinces, confirmed their division into *kuni/gun/ri* and provided a list of the kingdom's wealth and resources of crucial significance for estimating taxes.

Should one agree with Tsuda Sokichi in reducing Japanese mythology to the level of pathetic political manipulation? Texts such as the *Kogoshui* (807) demonstrate that the struggles for supremacy between the great families only affected the genealogical dimension of the myths, leaving their narrative structure virtually intact. The significance of the Annals is not purely political. Many cultures have been able to legitimize their power without having recourse to mythology. It is in fact the mythological significance of its origins which distinguishes Japan from its immediate neighbours. Compared with China (which rejects any form of cosmological explanation and clearly establishes the rule of history, restricting its legends to collections of strange tales) and with the official history of the Korean Samguk Sagi and the anecdotes of the Samguk Yusa, the *Kojiki* illustrates the great importance of the myth in Japanese culture.

THE MYTHS

A linear interpretation of the *Kojiki* reveals a series of seven sequences: Cosmogony sequence; Izagani-Izanami sequence (or Theogony, i.e. the engendering of the islands and the elemental gods by the primeval couple); Takama-no-para sequence; Idumo sequence; Land-ceding sequence; Heavenly Descent sequence (the descent of Ninigi); and finally the southern sequence based on the adventures of Po-wori.

The genesis account traces the progressive formation of the universe which was concomitant with the emergence of the first divinities. Three invisible monads, the god of the centre of Heaven and the two *kami* of generation came into existence on the Plain of High Heaven (Takama-no-para). Reed-shoots sprouted forth from a liquid *materia prima*, which the text compares to a jellyfish, and from these shoots two new *dei otiosi* came into existence. The ensuing genealogy consists of pairs of deities whose bodies appear to materialize and differentiate with the development of the world. The birth of Izanagi and his sister Izanami marks the end of the Cosmogony sequence. The celestial divinities gave them the task of solidifying the Earth which was still drifting. They were carried down to Earth by the Heavenly Floating Bridge (Ame no uki-pasi) and created an island by plunging a magic weapon, the Heavenly Jewelled Spear (Ame no nu-boko), given to them by the gods, into the primordial ocean. Standing on the island, which they called Onogoro, they erected a pillar (Ame no mi-pasira) and a palace (Ya-piro-dono). Discovering the difference between their bodies, the gods decided to 'have conjugal intercourse' after walking in a circle around the *axis mundi*. The brother and sister became man and wife: the pair became a couple, a complementary identity. The two offspring born to them (Piru-go the leech-child and the island of Apa) were failures. They returned to Heaven to report their lack of success and were told that it was the result of a fault committed by the woman as they circled around the pillar. She had made the mistake of taking the initiative when pronouncing the ritual formula of marriage. The two gods returned to Earth to repeat the process and the islands of Japan were born of this second union. Although there is an undeniably cosmogonic dimension to the 'labour' accomplished by the two demiurges, this is not the only level of interpretation. They did not create an abstract universe but a cultural space centred around the Inland Sea whose importance as a means of communication during the protohistoric period is well known. The itinerary traced by the gods reveals a political geography already illustrated by the administrative division into *kuni*.

A second genealogical series records the appearance of the divinities of nature, the *kami* of the sea, rivers and mountains. The sequence ends with the birth of the god Pi-no-Kagu-titi. The goddess Izanami, whose genitals were burned as she gave birth to this last child, died after spewing forth from all her bodily orifices the gods associated with the arts of fire, i.e. pottery and metal work. Izanagi mourned over the body of his sister-wife and then took his revenge by killing the guilty son from whose body new divinities came into existence by schizogenesis. He then went in search of his dead wife and reached Yomi, the land of the dead. He was allowed to enter, but could not bear to wait in the antechamber of Hades and so he lit the shadows with an improvised torch, ignoring Izanami's instruction not to look upon her. He made the horrifying discovery that Izanami's body had given birth to eight monsters, the Ikaduti-gami (thunder-deities). The over-curious husband fled, pursued by the hags of Yomi and finally by Izanami, who had been transformed into a chthonic deity and the goddess of death. Having delayed his pursuers, the fugitive managed to block the entrance to the land of Yomi with a huge boulder, on either side of which the spouses 'broke their troth'. This formula introduced death into the world and established the separation between the lands of the living and the dead.

'O my beloved husband, if you do thus, I will each day strangle to death one thousand of the populace of your country!' – 'O my beloved spouse, if you do thus, I will each day build one thousand five hundred birth huts!' Having returned to the land of the living, Izanagi went to purify himself on the shores of the Tati-bana. When he had completed his ablutions (*misogi*), three children, Ama-terasu, Tuku-yomi and Susa-no-wo, came into existence from his eyes and nose to ensure the continuation of the line. As one of his last recorded actions, Izanagi carried out a ceding of power which was accompanied by a spatial division. Ama-terasu, the sun deity, would rule Takama-no-para, Tuku-yomi, the moon deity, would rule the realms of the night and Susa-no-wo would rule the ocean.

This is the end of the first sequence of the myth but the second, based on the conflict between Ama-terasu and Susa-no-wo, can be interpreted as a transposition of the first, since the exclusion of the third deity (Tuku-yomi) reintroduces the initial polarization. The two myths follow the same formal structure as they open with an act of incest and end with an expulsion. Rebelling against his father, and refusing to rule the kingdom which had been entrusted to him, Susa-no-wo wept constantly, howling for his mother, and caused calamities throughout the world. The enraged Izanagi took the trouble-maker at his word and exiled him to the land of his mother. Susa-no-wo decided to take his leave of his sister Ama-terasy but, because she suspected him of having come to usurp her kingdom, he proposed a ritual test (*ukepi*) to prove the purity of his intentions. He was in fact proposing an indirect marriage, as both gods had to chew and then spit out certain attributes (i.e. sword and beads), to engender children whose sex would determine the winner. Susa-no-wo emerged from the test with his name cleared but, 'raging with victory', he committed further acts of violence, even going as far as to ravage the rice paddies and to disrupt the ceremony of the first fruits presided over by his sister. This was too much for Ama-terasu, who shut herself inside the heavenly rock-cave and plunged the land into darkness and chaos. The ceremony that the divine assembly decided to organize to recall the sun goddess has been compared by scholars with the ceremonies of southern Asia and certain revitalizing Shamanist techniques such as the *tama-furi*. The crowing of cockerels, the reading of the *norito*, the erotic dance of the goddess Ame no Uzume and the laughter of the 800 myriad deities encouraged the goddess to leave her retreat. The cosmic order had been restored. Expelled from Heaven, Susa-no-wo descended into the kingdom of Idumo where he became a dragon-slaying hero, before marrying the young Kusi-nada-pime whom he saved. After a period of time (not recorded in the *Nihon shoki*), devoted to the trials and resurrections of Opo-kuni-nusi, several celestial divinities were dispatched to Earth to subdue the nature deities. The first two emissaries were corrupted by Opo-kuni-nusi to such an extent that it required a third ambassador to complete the process of pacification. After the defeat of his sons, Opo-kuni-nusi agreed to cede the control of the visible world (i.e. the Central Land of the Reed Plains) to the descendants of Ama-terasu, and from then on restricted himself to administering the hidden aspects of the world. The kingdom of Idumo would no longer be an enemy to be defeated but a magical power to be propitiated whenever mysterious calamities recalled the former dispute.

The stage is set for the final act, i.e. the Heavenly Descent of the ancestor of the emperors. His father's eclipse enabled the young god of Rice-ears Piko-po-no-ninigi-no-mikoto to play the leading role. Having received the three insignia of royalty, i.e. the beads, mirror and sword, from Ama-terasu, he left Takama-no-para and descended, not into the kingdom of Idumo as expected, but onto Mount Taka-ti-po, in the south of Kyushu. His arrival was celebrated with a complex ceremony which appears to combine an agrarian ritual with an enthronement ceremony originating in the Altai mountains. The mountain god offered to the divine prince his two daughters, the ugly Ipa-naga-pime (the Rock-Long Princess) and the lovely Ko-no-pana-no-saku-ya-bime (Blossoms-of-the-Trees Blooming-Princess), but Ninigi only accepted the more beautiful of the two. This ill-fated choice provoked the anger of his father-in-law and condemned his descendants to a life which lasted 'for the interval of the blossoming of the trees', whereas they would have acquired longevity had he not disdained the more enduring qualities of the Rock-Long Princess. Saku-ya-bime conceived so quickly that she raised suspicions in the mind of her divine husband. She therefore gave birth in fire to prove the legitimacy of her children. The final part of Book I of the *Kojiki* is taken up with the fortunes and misfortunes of their three offspring. The exclusion of one of the three once again produces a polarization of the action, and the rivalry between the two brothers provides a framework for the myth of the journey into the kingdom of the sea. Mistreated by his elder brother who demanded the return of the fishhook he had lent him, the hero Po-wori went to the sea-deity's palace. In addition to the lost hook, he was also offered a magic potion and obtained the hand of the princess Toyo-tama-bime. On his return to Earth, he took his revenge on his brother, and reversed the hierarchical order since the descendants of the elder brother would be subservient to those of the younger. As the time of her delivery approached, Toyo-tama had a parturition hut built by the edge of the beach and entered it, forbidding her husband to be present at the birth. This aroused the curiosity of Po-wori, who watched in secret and discovered that his wife had assumed the form of a sea monster (*wani*). Ashamed, Toyo-tama left the newly born child with her husband and, as she departed, closed the 'sea-border'. The child later married his maternal aunt, who gave birth to the first 'historical' emperor of Japan, Kamu-yamato-ipare-biko-no-mikoto, who would later become the Emperor Jimmu.

LEITMOTIFS

The reader who simply follows the sequence of the episodes risks making the mistake of adopting the atomistic approach and reading the Annals as if they were only a collection of assorted myths. The striking thing about Japanese mythology is in fact its cohesion, its underlying harmony and unity, which finds its most beautiful form of expression in the *Kojiki*. The book of divine genealogy merely develops the permutations of a very limited combination of basic situations. It even appears possible to reinterpret the historical books of the *Kojiki* on the basis of the mythological structures of the first book.

Implicit origins

It is believed that the *Kojiki* has retained certain oral characteristics. The Japanese myth therefore reflects its origins without, however, being organized according to a linear structure from an absolute starting point. It would be pointless to try and identify an original state, motive or subject. Its genesis immediately defies any attempt at an allegorical interpretation of first causes, even metaphorical. With the exception of the Chinese quotations of the *Nihon shoki*, it does not resort to such classical figures as those represented by the original egg or the cosmic giant. The origins, which are elusive because they are disseminated throughout the text, are repeated in the form of a descent, from the mission of the couple Izanagi and Izanami to the provincial expedition of Yamato-takeru. The genesis may lose its cosmic dimensions, but survives by being transposed onto a lesser scale. The chaos that it was the task of the divine protagonists to reduce becomes the vast quarrel of the harmful *kami* during the rebellion of Susa-no-wo, before degenerating into a revolt of unruly, uncivilized barbarians. The solemn descent of the grandson of Amaterasu is nothing more than a departure from the capital, but the Japanese expression *ama-kudari* (Heavenly Descent) can be applied to both situations. The creation of the country by the primeval couple, the descent of Susa-no-wo presented as a tree-planting god, the work of Opo-kuni-nusi in the province of Idumo, the unsuccessful descents of the first celestial envoys, the mission of Take-mika-duti, and the descent of Ninigi are united by an interplay of reciprocal references. By setting foot on the Ame no uki-pasi, Ninigi repeats the action of Izanagi/Izanami, and the clouds that he pushes aside are reminiscent of primeval matter. Even the ritual of enthronement (Daijosai) – whose connection with the episode of *tenson korin* (divine descent on Earth) is well known – ensures the return of the original emperor.

The 'Baitogogo' complex

Perceptive even in his digressions, Lévi-Strauss suggested placing Susa-no-wo in the category of the 'whining babies', i.e. those incestuous heroes who refuse to grow up and remain subject to female control. This extremely fruitful hypothesis provides a unifying principle which solves the problem of the generally heterogeneous nature of the list of the god's attributes. The capriciousness of the trickster, the functions of the cultural hero and the wanderings of the criminal cease to be contradictory. Born from his father's nose as the latter completed his ablutions (*misogi*), Susa-no-wo was from the very beginning destined for the role of 'sniveller'. He cried until he had reached the age when 'his beard of eight hands long extended down over his chest', he wanted to find his mother and committed acts of violence which affected the order of the world. This incestuous desire undergoes its first metamorphosis at the point of the *ukepi*, when his sister replaces his mother. Not only is the ritual exchange of attributes on the shores of the heavenly river interpreted as a symbolic marriage (using interposed symbols), but it would in no way be a distortion of the text to see the wound of the servant (or of Opo-pirume herself) as indirect rape. Surprised by Susa-no-wo who 'opened a hole in the roof of the sacred weaving hall and dropped down into it the heavenly dappled pony which he had skinned with a backward skinning', the 'heavenly weaving maiden' pierced her genitals with a shuttle. The crimes committed by Susa-no-wo are violent acts against agriculture (Ama tu tumi) or femininity, when the myth does not associate the two (Opo-ge-tu-pime). After he has been exiled and slain the dragon, Susa-no-wo, installed in his new role as a chthonic divinity, illustrates the ultimate degree of attachment to femininity by refusing to give his daughter to the young stranger who has come to woo her. The trials imposed upon the future Opo-kuni-nusi betray Susa-no-wo's jealous determination to eliminate a rival. If all the stages of the complex are combined in the person of Susa-no-wo, who is by turns a whining baby, an incestuous adolescent and a possessive father, he is by no means an exception. The 'Baitogogo' theme underlies the whole of Japanese mythology. The convulsive despair of Izanagai crying over his dead sister (which has nothing of the formalized mourning of later funerals), the murder of the son responsible for her death, and the overwhelming desire to see her body, mark, through their very hubris, the first appearance of the pattern of dependence. Later in the text, Ame-no-osi-po-mimi-no-mikoto's attachment to his mother Ama-terasu, and his refusal to descend to Earth when he should have been the protagonist in the *tenson korin* episode, confirm the strength of the attraction of the 'Baitogogo' complex, the metaphors of which can be traced to the adventures of Yamato-takeru.

Monstrosity

While the complex of the 'sniveller' illustrates attraction for those who are too close, the theme of Melusina, which occurs with an equally significant degree of frequency in the *Kojiki*, illustrates the marriage (and subsequent split) with those who are too distant. Endogamic excess (incest) is succeeded by exogamic excess (bestiality). The cultural heroes, who have descended from the Plain of High Heaven to unite with the daughters of nature, are all prey to the same profane curiosity. Violating a taboo, they all one day look upon their wife in secret and discover her true – i.e. monstrous – nature. It is always when she is indulging in an archetypal female activity that the wife reassumes her animal form, e.g. giving birth or cooking (*Kojiki, Nihon shoki*), breast-feeding or weaving (folk tales). Children, milk, excrement, 'natural' cooking and hair, all materials that men must have experienced without knowing their origin, are also products that women draw from themselves at their expense, for in folk tales and myths they often die as a result of having given too much of themselves. Thus the myth always tends to envisage generation in terms of parthenogenesis and schizogenesis. The universality of this structure is reorientated in Japanese mythology to produce a particular meaning. The violation of the interdiction and the ensuing separation fulfil a function which is both cosmological and ontological. They are responsible for introducing death into the world, and establishing frontiers between natural and cultural space. Izanagi fleeing after discovering the snake-like nature of Izanami (the thunder-*kami* are serpents), and Ninigi rejecting the ugly one of the two wives offered to him, are responsible for introducing two forms of negativity, i.e. death and a brief lifespan. In a final version, the Emperor Suinin sends for the fruits of immortality, but he dies before Tadima-mori returns, for having rejected the ugliest of Mitiusinomiko's daughters.

It is of little importance whether the frequency of the Melusinian theme in a text as short as the *Kojiki* is the result of an analogical law inherent in the mythical narrative, or due to the intention of the compilers. It is enough to have identified a system of continuity in this diffuse material which is still all too often attributed to pure chance.

LITERARY AVATARS

The combination of narrative and poetry which had already been responsible for the appeal of the *Kojiki* witnessed the creation of one of the most important literary forms of the Heian period, i.e. the *monogatari*. The preamble in prose introducing the poems of the *Kokin wakashu*, originally merely an interpretive development, became increasingly more independent until it was transformed into a narrative which eclipsed the poems (*waka*) themselves. The literary myths contained in the *monogatari* are presented in two forms corresponding to the two ways of interpreting the concept of the myth. They appear either as obsessive themes characterized more by their 'atmosphere' than by their structure (for example, the obsession of the wandering hero), or they occur as predetermined formal structures, as in the case of the folk tales incorporated into the network of the *Taketori monogatari*.

Kishuryuritan

In 1918, Orikuchi Shinobu, the ethnographer, philologist and poet who was a great disciple of Yanagita Kunio, introduced an expression to designate a recurrent narrative structure in Japanese classical literature and mythology, i.e. *kishuryuritan*, the motif (*tan*) of the wanderings (*ryrui*) of a hero of noble rank (*kishu*). At the same time when the theme was assuming a definite form of expression in the literature of the Heian period, this journeying drama consisted of three basic elements: the crime, banishment and return (apotheosis) of the hero. The crime, considered by certain specialists as a secondary development providing an explanation of the hero's misfortunes, in fact appears to be indispensable to an understanding of the theme. Even in a borderline case, such as the episode of the divine woman of the *Tango fudoki*, the crime is referred to *in absentia* by the subsequent expiation. In the *Ise monogatari* and *The Tale of Genji*, the crime involves the violation of a sexual interdiction. Arihara no Narihira has illicit sexual relations with Fujiwara no Takaiko, when she has been promised to the Emperor Seiwa, and in this way offers an example of misconduct to Hikaru Genji who is also interested in encroaching upon the emperor's preserve. If we follow Origuchi's line of thought, these illicit relations constitute a sophisticated version of Susa-no-wo's acts of violence. The punishment is as ambiguous as the crime for which it is inflicted and covers a wide range of possibilities, from the exorcism which accompanies the banishment of the culprit to the diplomatic exile experienced by those aristrocrats who feel they are no longer in favour at court. But, in all cases, the fallen hero-traveller, whether he is Ama-kudari, Azuma-kudari or Suma-kudari, 'descends' in spatial terms and within the hierarchy of beings. Although the *kishuryuritan* occupies a prominent position in Japanese literature as a result of the frequent occurrence and the richness of the theme, the mythological roots attributed to it are often somewhat doubtful. The crime and the 'descent' provide an extremely tenuous link with the comparisons made between the *Kojiki* and the *monogatari* of the Middle Ages. As demonstrated by Pigeot's study on the Michi-yuki-bun, the *kishuryuri* is defined much more by its tone than by its formal framework. The personal drama of the banishment from the capital and the evocation of the sufferings of the exile are much more important than the narrative function. Only Yamato-takeru, whose story is steeped in a tragic atmosphere, can be considered a direct ancestor of the heroes of the *monogatari*. The extremely complex ritual background to the myth of Susa-no-wo should encourage us to temper our enthusiasm for comparison, a caution which is valid for the interpretation of the 'journeys' of Sukuna-biko-na and Piru-go.

The theme of 'otherness'

The theme of wandering reaches a more easily recognizable mythical dimension if incorporated into the vast configuration of narrative structures whose common property is a relationship with 'otherness'. It was in fact in this same style (Ikyo, Iruinyobo, Iruimuko) that the authors of the Heian period sought to construct the framework for their narratives. The Hagoromo story which serves as a context for the *Taketori monogatari* on the one hand, the narratives based on the Urashima model on the other, and finally the male and female versions of the supernatural marriage are all linked by the theme of transformation. The contact and separation between the worlds lends itself to three types of treatment. According to the first, a supernatural being is exiled onto the Earth (e.g. the divine woman of the *Tango fudoki*) and has one of his/her attributes stolen which precludes any hope of return. The reascension to Heaven can only take place after many ordeals. In the second type, a human being (a young sinner) enters the other world, is overwhelmed with kindness and subsequently returns to Earth of his own accord. Having been promised immortality, he violates an interdiction which severs the means of access between the maritime other world and the Earth and renders him mortal. In the third type of example, a marriage between a human being and an animal is blessed with wealth and happiness as long as the latter is able to conceal its true identity. An indiscretion provokes a split and happiness is dissolved. The human is restored to mortality while the animal returns to nature, sometimes leaving behind offspring who are assured of an exceptional destiny.

Although it would be dangerous to see Susa-no-wo as the first manifestation of a 'basic romanticism' which has always pervaded the Japanese spirit, and derisory to reduce masterpieces of subtlety such as *The Tale of Genji* to the impoverished level of a series of narrative frameworks, it is however legitimate to consider the misfortunes of the incestuous hero, and the drama of the split with 'otherness', as two basic mythical structures which continue to recur throughout Japanese literature.

Alain Rocher

Jesus Christ in Literature

As far as myth can express mankind's profoundest experiences, speaking of myth in connection with Christ in no way implies reducing or denying his importance (the connotation of the word myth in the nineteenth century) and does not prejudge our religious attitude. Jesus Christ is considered here as a crucial figure in the cultural history of the West, as his person has been understood, experienced and formulated in religious conscience and in the literary expressions or representations, conformist or otherwise, it has provoked.

His case is unique among the great symbolic figures of humanity: the earliest traditions (first broadcast in the Epistles of Paul, and then in the Gospels), taking his death and resurrection as their starting point, immediately emphasize the fact that Jesus was really and truly both a man and also far more than a man: a divine being, the Son of God. As Christian tradition soon put it, divine nature and human nature coexist in his person, which gives him a paradoxical and mysterious status, very different from that of any other holy person, prophet or miracle-worker.

But the Gospel stories are not a 'life of Jesus' and their concern for documentary truth is only incidental. The anecdotes they cite have primarily a symbolic value – an exemplary value for Christian life or a revelatory value for the identity of Jesus, especially confirming that he corresponds with the 'figures' foretold by the prophets and fulfils the promises of the Old Testament. The Gospel stories as a whole place Jesus firmly in history, but documentary detail is always a secondary concern – this gave rise to considerable problems from the literary point of view when, from the nineteenth century on, writers felt freer to embroider on the sober stories recounted by the Evangelists; there was then a danger of drifting into anecdotal story-telling, diminishing the symbolic weight of the actual figure of Jesus. Mystery and paradox are an integral part of that figure – otherwise he is reduced to being just an ordinary man with no further dimension, whereas his originality lies in being a mediating figure: a unique, enigmatic intermediary, the face of God behind the features of a man caught up in history.

LITERARY WORKS IN THE LITURGY

Right from the beginning prayer and reflection based on Jesus were expressed in religious texts in at least three different modes.

1 The 'hymn' quoted to the Philippians (Philippians 2:6–11) is the first of a

prolific tradition of liturgical poems in every language (required for and multiplied especially by the liturgical cycle reintroducing Advent, Christmas, the Passion, Easter etc. year after year). Greek and Latin hymns flourished in the Middle Ages: we will cite just one of the best known, St Bernard's 'Jesu dulcis memoria'. Taking over from them came a blossoming of songs in modern languages, Lutheran chorales and canticles of every description, sometimes written by great poets, ranging from Paul Gerhardt or Claudius to La Tour du Pin. Cantatas, Passions and oratorios further multiplied both dramatic and musical images of Christ; here we will only mention the four Passions by Heinrich Schütz (between 1653 and 1666), the two Passions by Johann Sebastian Bach (1724 and 1729), Liszt's oratorio *Christus* (1866) and the *Passion selon saint Luc* by Panderecki (1980).
2 Reflection (and controversy) concerning faith in Christ gave rise to a huge body of literature, from the passionate sermons of St Augustine to those of John Donne, from Abraham to St Clare, or from the *Traité de l'Amour de Dieu* by François de Sales and Pascal's *Pensées* to the wide-ranging meditations of Newman or Teilhard de Chardin.
3 From the time of the first generations of Christians the need to 'recount' the deeds of Jesus and thus make it easier to imagine him by emphasizing concrete details also gave rise to a great many stories that are called 'apocryphal'; in these, anecdote takes over to delight the imagination. This then gave rise to all sorts of paraphrases, from the epic visions of the German *Heliand* or Cynewulf's Anglo-Saxon *Christ* in the ninth century to the symbolic representations of the Holy Grail, or his evocation by such people as St Bonaventure or St Margaret Mary, to mention only writers of merit.

THE CHRISTIAN CENTURIES AND THE HUMANITY OF JESUS

'Truly God and truly man': this definition was finally consecrated at the Council of Chalcedon in 453. The first centuries of Christianity were in fact much more impressed by the divinity visible through the humanity of Jesus Christ. Very often his humanity was regarded as no more than a visible 'sign' referring back to the transcendent and invisible. That perspective was endlessly seized on by sermon-writers and mystics.

However, as western man became increasingly self-aware he also became more and more interested in the example of perfect humanity afforded by Jesus, and sought a more direct and personal link with him. A complete spiritual tradition developed starting with St Bernard, St Francis of Assisi and the fourteenth-century mystics; in the fifteenth century the 'devotio moderna' and its masterpiece, *L'imitatio Christi*, and the influence of St Ignatius Loyola's *Exercitia* in the sixteenth and seventeenth centuries were also moving in the same direction. A very human symbol of Jesus Christ as a person, that of the Sacred Heart, gradually impressed itself on Catholic piety, though it also crops up sporadically in Lutheranism or the Anglican faith (T. Goodwin, *The Heart of Christ* 1652).

This spiritual tradition gave rise to a profusion of writing. Already in the Middle Ages the figure of Jesus was integrated quite naturally with his life and writings about him. With instinctive imagination and realism, he was seen as near at hand, involved in the life, sufferings and joys of men, at times as a sovereign and judge, but more often with a kindly, forgiving face. That is how he was depicted in the Crusade cycle (eleventh-thirteenth century), by Joinville (d. 1317), and in the *Osterspiele, Weltgerichtsspiele* and *Mystères de la Passion*, the most famous of which were written by Arnoul Gréban (1462) and Jean Michel (1483), though the tradition has survived down to the present day in Bavaria (Oberammergau) and Austria (Thiersee).

The Renaissance and Classical periods gradually restored literature to the principles of ancient rhetoric which advocates idealization and rejects the mixed genres and realism of the Middle Ages (see Auerbach, *Mimesis*), especially in connection with religious literature. Nonetheless epic poems written in imitation of the *Aeneid*, such as the *Christias* in Latin by M.-G. Vida (1535) or the *Christiada* in Spanish by D. de Ojeda, may be mentioned. But the poets of the Baroque period, who enjoyed making play with polarities and contrasts, devoted a lot of time to meditating on the figure of Christ as the perfect example of 'Tout-Rien' (All-Nothing), the formula of a sonnet by N.-B. de Javezac, with the infiniteness of God and the fragility of man united within him. The same poets on occasion revert to images from antiquity to describe him: Orpheus, the phoenix, Deucalion, Psyche, Hercules etc. Alongside *Los nombres de Christo* (1583–5) by Luis de Leon or the 500 sonnets on the Passion and the Resurrection (1613–22) by La Ceppède, a host of other names, including Marguerite de Navarre, Corneille, Racine, Silesius, von Spee (*Trutz Nachtigall* 1649) etc., should be cited. From *Paradise Lost* (1665) Milton moved on quite naturally to the Redeemer triumphing over the temptations of the devil (*Paradise Regained* 1671). And finally the seventeenth century was the great period of religious eloquence which was often centred on the person of Christ and the Passion, for example in the work of François de Sales, Surin and Bossuet, to mention just a few French names.

CHRIST IN THE ROMANTIC PERIOD

In the eighteenth century, in French literature at least, 'classical' taboos finally won the day. Rationalism, based on the first elements of biblical criticism, tended to discredit the union of man and God, i.e. the incarnation, as improbable. Religion drifted partly towards deism, separating a rational, remote, indifferent God from Jesus, who was brought back down to the dimensions of this earth and seen as a model of human goodness, and no more. This resulted in a relative silence about him in French literature, whereas elsewhere, in Germany for example, the Passion was evoked through a new sensibility (Klopstock, *Der Messias* 1748–81).

To those living in the Romantic period Jesus often appeared as the epitome of man unjustly overwhelmed by fate and crushed by Evil, therefore as the perfect example of a tragic existence, especially in the episodes relating to Gethsemane and his death on the Cross, and in the seeming despair of 'Why hast thou forsaken me?' So in the famous 'dream of Jean-Paul' (in *Siebenkäs* 1798) 'the dead Christ proclaims to the dead that there is no God', a cliché which was to be immensely influential, especially through Mme de Staël's translation (in *De l'Allemagne* 1810). The Romantic fondness for Gethsemane and the Cross, already signalled in *Le Génie du Christianisme* by Chateabriand, resurfaced in the poems of Lamartine, Vigny and Nerval as well as in the vehement Passion evoked by Hugo (*c.* 1860–70 in *La Fin de Satan*) or *The Divine Tragedy* by Longfellow (1871), and even as late as Péguy (*Clio II* 1914) or Pierre Emmanuel.

However, in the Romantic period in France the influence of Lamennais, Lacordaire and the so-called 'Utopian' socialists (Saint-Simon, Cabet, Leroux, Proudhon) caused Jesus Christ to be seen in the reign of Louis-Philippe as a defender of the 'people', or even as the 'prince of Communists' (Cabet's words). During the 1848 Revolution this socialist Jesus enjoyed a popularity that had no future, as the various socialist factions then turned away from him, and it took some time before an isolated writer here and there again emphasized the social aspect of his message – people like Hugo, A. Hold (*Buch der Zeit* 1885), Péguy, Dorothy L. Sayers or Henri Barbusse, with Barbusse making him out to be an atheist Communist (*Jésus* 1927).

Meanwhile biblical criticism had entered a more aggressively negative phase, signalled by David Friedrich Strauss's *Leben Jesu* (1835), the results of which were offered to a wider public in a vulgarized form by Ernest Renan in his own *Vie de Jésus* (1863). Under its scientific dressing it is a sort of biography in novel form, i.e. a reconstruction of the character of Jesus (in his purely human dimension) using the devices of the novel: psychology, description and narrative. In a way it provided advance justification for any conceivable reconstruction or flight of imagination, authorizing people to project any and every dream, obsession, value and experience onto the character of Jesus, freed of the limits imposed by faith (or by history, henceforth regarded as largely conjectural).

As with other literary genres in the modern period, literature devoted to Jesus Christ could either move towards reconstruction, evoking the Jesus of former times, a probable figure in his historical setting, or take the opposite path and aim at the imaginary transposition of him into times nearer our own.

'RECONSTITUTING' THE STORY OF JESUS

Many a novelist or dramatist, with historical accuracy as his prime concern, has set out mainly to relocate Jesus and his preaching in his own period, confronting his own enemies, and confronting final failure. Jesus appears as a misunderstood model of wisdom, or perhaps as a virtually predestined victim, and sometimes more recently as a man who has been outwitted and deceived, even himself doubting his own mission, at Gethsemane at least. If seen in this light, an explanation must be found for his life, justifying its tragic end, and showing how belief in the resurrection is probable or at least conceivable. With regard to the final point, there has been no shortage of simple explanations: either the death of Jesus was only apparent (for example, Joseph of Arimathea might have administered a powerful philtre to him on the Cross, as in the plays of F.A. Dulk (*Jesus, der Christ* 1865) or G. Trarieux (*Joseph d'Arimathie* 1898) or George Moore's novel, *The Brook Kerith* 1916); or else the resurrection is reduced to a collective illusion on the part of the disciples which was transfigured into a legend, as had already been suggested by Renan. The story has to be purged of mystery and symbol to make it more probable.

There are other possible approaches: the scholarly variant which conceals the mystery behind a cloud of historical or philological erudition, as did M. Pomilio (*Il quinto Evangelio* 1975), or the legendary or poetic variant, as found in the work of Selma Lagerlöf (*Kristuslegender* 1904) and a fair number of other poets. Péguy achieved a rare balance through a meditation on the incarnation that is simultaneously historical and religious (*Eve* and *Clio II* 1914). A masterly imagination mixes realism and symbolism in *Master i Margarita* (1940–66) by M. Bulgakov, in which he confronts Pontius Pilate and Jesus.

A recent variant of this historical reconstitution is associated with the fact that we are better able to place Jesus in the Jewish tradition from which his way of talking and his gestures emanate, now that ancient Judaism has become better known: this is illustrated in S. Asch's *The Nazarene* (1950), Robert Graves's *King Jesus* (1946), M. Brod's *Der Meister* (1952), G. Menzel's *Kehr wieder, Morgenröte!* (1952) etc.

Others are less concerned with explaining the historical context than with reconstituting the personality of Jesus, his emotions and his psychology; this is true of F. Avenarius in his drama *Jesus* (1921) and W. von Molo (*Legende des Herrn* 1927). Other writers imagine his experience of humanity, from which human love must not be excluded; these include D. H. Lawrence (*The Man who Died* 1931), A. Burgess (*J.-C. and the Love Games* 1976) and J.-C. Barreau (*Mémoires de Jésus* 1977). Others still place their emphasis on his preaching, in the manner of Buddhism (E. Arnou, *The Light of Asia* 1879) or of Christian Science (Lloyd C. Douglas, *The Big Fisherman* 1952).

A literary procedure that is convenient and fruitful because it allows objective detail and subjective memories to play their respective parts consists of showing events through the eyes of a witness, noting only what he sees, and how he sees it. As far back as the Gospels, the stories relating to the appearance of Jesus risen from the dead were presented in this way; as sermon-writers and men of religion had already done, writers and poets too conjured up Jesus through the eyes of the Apostles or Mary Magdalen, Joseph of Arimathea or Pontius Pilate, Judas, Barabbas or even Ahasuerus, the Wandering Jew, and other characters. Literature published in recent years, say from 1975 or 1980, shows a tendency to go back to the historical novel, with evocations of the first generations of Christians handing down their memories of Jesus (following the memorable example of *Quo Vadis?* by H. Sienckiewicz, 1896). Using a witness in this way can be a means of retaining the immediacy of the narrative, while at the same time suggesting mystery, as did Marcel Pagnol in *Judas* (1955) or M. Waltari in *Chmiskunnan viholliset* (1979), for example; or on the the other hand it can be a way of casting doubt on memories, as happens for example in *Lazare le Ressuscité* by A. Absire (1985) or *La Colère de l'Agneau* by G. Hocquenghem (1985).

Though it has become difficult to present Jesus on stage in a more or less realistic setting, there has been no shortage of dramatists in the past century prepared to make the attempt; among those who have done so most convincingly we may mention, besides Pagnol's *Judas*, R. Hossein's *Un Homme nommé Jésus* (1982). Film-makers, on the other hand, with the means of suggesting both realistic detail and the lighting to convey the miraculous at their disposal, have frequently been attracted by the subject; again we will cite only some 'classic' examples: Griffith (*Intolerance* 1916), J. Duvivier (*Golgotha* 1935), Zeffirelli-Burgess (1977), Rossellini (1975) and Pasolini's impressive *The Gospel according to St Matthew* (1965).

THE RANGE OF SYMBOLIC TRANSPOSITIONS

Writers, poets especially, often prefer to transpose the character into a different real setting rather than reconstitute it in a historical, probable way, accepting 'improbability' from the word go. This device can claim to be derived from the original faith in Christ's 'return': Christ Resurrected is outside time, and the first Christians waited for him to reappear amongst them; each time his presence was like a judgement, revealing to people what was in each other's heart.

Thus the writer can transpose the figure of Jesus into his own day, or at least into the fairly recent historical past, where he is shown contesting (or revealing) the vices of a modern society. This happens in the form of a kind of historical parable in the writing of Balzac (*Jésus-Christ en Flandres* 1831), Dostoyevsky ('The legend of the Grand Inquisitor' in *The Brothers Karamazov* 1881), F. Timmerman (*L'Enfant Jésus en Flandres* 1917), R. Huch (*Der Wiederkehrende Christus* 1926) and others, or in the highly amusing comedy by Jerome K. Jerome, *The Passing of the Third Floor Back*, 1908. This type of poetic device works better in short stories; attempts to elaborate it in longer works involve a great risk of using rather facile effects to show Jesus arriving from the past and having to come to terms with the modern world. He is portrayed for example in Paris among journalists (Saint Georges de Bouhêlier, *La Tragédie du Nouveau Christ* 1901), among the working classes in Berlin in M. Kretzer's novel *Das Gesicht Christi* (1897), or recently again in novels by O. Herbüger (*Jesus in Osaka* 1970, in German) or B. Raquin (*Jésus de Manhattan* 1979, in French), and even in science fiction in M. Moorcock's *Behold the Man* (1968).

The figure of Jesus can be transposed into the existence of a man who is trying to live as Jesus would live today – illustrating Paul's words, 'It is no longer I who live, but Christ who lives through me'. Thus Jesus can appear either as an ideal figure giving meaning to a life renounced for his sake, for example in 'La Légende de saint Julien l'Hospitalier' in Flaubert's *Trois Contes* (1877) or *Hanneles Himmelfahrt* by Gerhart Hauptmann (1893), or in a slightly different way in *Le Désespéré* by Léon Bloy (1886). Elsewhere a Christ figure is depicted living an evangelical existence and coming up against contradictions and persecutions, as in the path followed by Jean Valjean in Hugo's *Les Misérables* (1862) or in Pérez Galdós's *Nazarin* (1895), A. Fogazzaro's *Il Santo* (1906), Gerhard Hauptmann's *Der Narr in Christo Emmanuel Quint* (1910), M. Mell's *Das Nachfolge Christi-Spiel* (1927), Ernst Wiechert's *Missa sine nomine* (1950), or – stressing the paradox – Graham Greene's *The Power and the Glory* (1940) or William Faulkner's *A Fable* (1954). The opposition to Jesus can become the centre of perspective as in the plays *The Man born to be King* by Dorothy L. Sayers (1949) and *Processo a Gesu* by D. Fabbri (1955), or the novels *Barabbas* by Pär Lagerkvist (1950) or *Christ Recrucified* by Nikos Kazantsakis (1948).

There is yet another transposition which can claim to be based on the Scriptures: in this Jesus is identified with the whole of a community, the 'people' for example, i.e. the poor and oppressed in France between 1840 and 1850, but such language was already used by St John Chrysostom and Bossuet. After two World Wars, any persecuted, starving or tortured minority could be identified with Christ, suffering the injustice of the world today. This symbolism was willingly seized upon not only in France in particular by a whole line of Christian writers ranging from Bloy, Péguy, Bernanos, Emmanuel etc., but in Germany too, for example among the Expressionists writing between 1920 and 1930, or in the generation writing around 1950 (including Heinrich Böll, *Und sagte kein einziges Wort* 1953).

In the field of the media and showbusiness, writing about Jesus has at times become something of a 'fashion', in Paris *c.* 1900 for example, or more recently in 1970–2 (the years when *Jesus Christ Superstar* and *Godspell* were produced). These 'fashions' have very slight repercussions on literature. What must be seen as more important is the patient movement which has led, since the beginning of the twentieth century, following in the footsteps of Péguy in particular, to two or three generations of writers rediscovering a deeper symbolic understanding of the incarnation, and hence giving a new poetic presence to Jesus. In the absence of an understanding of theological language, which has become inaccessible to non-specialists, a wide sector of the public has thus found in literature a kind of 'poetic Christology' which is alive and close to them. In this, literature has regained the function of religious expression (and teaching) that it had to some extent lost since the Middle Ages or the seventeenth century.

JESUS, A SYMBOLIC FIGURE

It is hardly possible to rediscover the psychological make-up of Jesus – the Evangelists were not much concerned with it, nor were early Christian traditions. While it is tempting to attribute a rather modern psychology to him, this is always fraught with danger – as is true in dealing with any mythical figure from the past. The figure of Jesus is a religious figure weighted towards symbolism.

The Bible, and literature devoted to Jesus after it, inevitably seized on various primitive forms of symbol, even if this entailed transposing their meaning. It is not at all surprising to pick out a fair number of symbolic references to the sun, from the Gospels talking about his childhood up to the contemplations of the Sacred Heart. Moreover Jesus was more often identified with the original lunar hero, the son of the Virgin, dying and being reborn to life. In fact correspondences with the Old Testament are much more direct and significant; Jesus fulfils the 'figures', the prophecies and the promises: king, Servant, lamb etc.

The symbolism of the person is of course expressed in the evangelical doctrine that he preaches and that he himself lives: this symbolism suggests not just a simple moral code (which sermon-writing and too many moralistic poems have over-emphasized in the last two or three centuries), but a complete vision of existence and an art of 'living-with', i.e. with men and with God. But the most fundamental symbolic value of any mythical figure is primarily linked to the drama in which that figure is involved. Here this drama can be resumed in three well-known words: incarnation, death, resurrection. Incarnation: God has identified himself with a man so that men can lead the life of the son of the Father, the life for which Jesus set the example. Death: he lived the contradiction within humanity to the end, i.e. the problem of Evil. Resurrection: his seeming failure in fact reveals that life and love are stronger than death, and that every failure, every suffering can and must have meaning and engender life.

Thus every human face can be compared with that of Jesus as with a symbolic model; more particularly, all suffering and all death pangs can be set against his – and illumined with meaning and hope by his resurrection: the countenance of a Servant and a countenance of compassion, a countenance that conveys the call of the Other (and of other men), that is the true face of the God-Man, so that 'if God gave himself a face for us, then man can know his own face' (Berdiaev).

The definition 'man and God' hovers over any evocation of Jesus Christ; it is always possible to reduce such an evocation to the purely human figure of an anticonformist sage, in the style of the Just Man persecuted, since vocabulary of this kind has been employed since time immemorial to present Jesus as an example of perfect humanity. But as soon as Jesus is represented in this way as only human, in psychological terms with the 'figure' functioning as an ideal image that one is suggesting to oneself, as a projection of the desires of the writer (or of the public, or of a whole generation) – man is in dialogue with his own image. Whereas, presented as a religious symbol (in one way or another), that is as signifying a reality other than human (transcendent, in whatever way), the figure functions psychologically as a question asked by an external reality; the reader is prompted to enter a dialogue with something other than himself, to take into account the presence or at least the existence of the other. In the first case, Jesus symbolizes the dreams of mankind, or my dreams; in the second, Jesus signifies a voice other than mine, the 'voice off' which enunciates the call (or provocation) of the other. And these are two completely different symbolic functions.

Nevertheless the fact remains that literature is hardly able to evoke what it conceives of as divine except in anthropomorphic terms. Such references have here become the 'signs' and the human face, so to speak, of the Unimaginable – relating to the incarnation. Is it not the role of the very person of Jesus to signify in humanity that which goes beyond man, another dimension if not another Presence? The incarnation can suggest to us that it is no longer a question of seeing God and man in opposition. 'Man has died, after God', the young Malraux noted down in 1926; it has still to be verified whether in poetry, as G. Haldas writes, 'there is only Christ who can save Orpheus . . .'

André Dabezies

Joan of Arc

The myth of Joan of Arc existed before the historical figure. At the beginning of the fifteenth century, when France was going through one of the darkest periods in its history, the hope of a miraculous Saviour was nurtured in the most deprived regions. An ancient prophecy predicted that a female would cause the downfall of France, and its salvation would be at the hands of a young woman from the Marches of Lorraine. When Joan was seen marching on Orléans, the prediction was remembered and attributed to Merlin the Sorcerer. The general populace welcomed her enthusiastically and the only sceptics were among men of rank.

The myth is no less historical because it was predicted in this way. This unquestionably extraordinary story – in which the heroine embarks upon a glorious career which ultimately leads her to the stake – is reminiscent of the epic narrative. But in this instance the stake actually existed and was not an invention of the poetic imagination. According to Michelet, although Joan was a living legend, her story should not be regarded as legendary, since all the facts can be historically verified. An unprecedented amount of evidence has been collected about this historical figure whose public life lasted only two years, including the twelve months spent in prison. In spite of the efforts of poets and playwrights to embellish her adventure with fictitious anecdotes, its central core remains intact. Ironically, history decreed that the executioners themselves should be responsible for ensuring Joan's eternal glory. Her trial, which was biased and prejudiced, but whose minutes were drawn up by notaries, guaranteed immortality.

It took four centuries for the proceedings of the trial to be collected, collated and, where necessary, translated. Today, Joan's story forms a sizeable body of work which, in spite of some remaining obscurities, has made it possible to reconstruct the facts with an accuracy that would do justice to a meticulous biographer.

THE HISTORICAL FACTS

The adventure was exceptional in itself. Joan of Arc was a seventeen-year-old peasant girl, born in 1412 at Domrémy, on the borders of Lorraine and Barrois. She was the daughter of a 'husbandman' (i.e. from a reasonably well-off peasant family), illiterate, able to sew and spin (though a shepherdess only on occasions) and considered 'completely ordinary' by those around her. She became inspired to rally a divided France and to restore King Charles VII's legitimate inheritance, which was being challenged by the English who controlled part of the country. Her mission was successful. At Bourges, the king authorized her to participate in military operations and she was given a full coat of armour, a sword (which she hardly ever used), and a banner which she had inscribed with the phrase 'Jhesus Maria'. She played a major role in the raising of the siege of Orléans, triumphantly entering the city on 8 May 1429. Jargeau, Meung and Beaugency were subsequently recaptured and the French were victorious at Patay on 12–18 June. She then persuaded the king to go to Rheims, where he was crowned on 17 July in the traditional manner, by anointment with holy oils. Then her good fortune appeared to decline. The army commanded by the Duc d'Alençon was defeated outside Paris. She was wounded on 8 September and the winter was spent carrying out limited military operations. On 24 May 1430, while she was in command of a small troop attempting to raise the siege of Compiègne, she was taken prisoner by the Duke of Luxembourg. She tried unsuccessfully to escape and was handed over to the English, who did not want her put to death immediately, but instead wished to see her condemned as a witch, which was, in their opinion, the only way to discredit Charles VII and invalidate the coronation at Rheims. After a lengthy trial held in Rouen (then occupied by the English), and conducted jointly by the University, represented by the Bishop of Beauvais, Pierre Cauchon, and by the Inquisition, she was initially sentenced as a heretic. Then, after the recantation which was wrested from her at the cemetery of Saint-Ouen on 24 May, she was sentenced as a relapsed heretic because she had reverted to wearing men's clothes. (Strange times indeed when you could be burnt at the stake for changing the way you dressed!) She was handed over to the 'secular arm', i.e. the English, and not to the civil authorities as laid down by the law. She was burned at the stake on 30 May 1431, in the Place du Vieux-Marché in Rouen. These are all credible historical events, and the life of Joan of Arc could in fact be described in realistic terms, without any reference to miracles.

The rehabilitation proceedings – or rather the quashing of the sentence – that Charles VII wanted to instigate as soon as he had recaptured Rouen in 1450, did not come to court until 1456. The proceedings in fact concentrated more on condemning the illegality of the judges at the trial in 1431, than on clearing Joan's name. But the 115 testimonies called upon confirmed the impression that had already emerged from the trial, in spite of the prevarication and deviousness of the judges. Joan was honest, brave, tenacious, and favoured with good sense and a ready tongue.

However, one mystery remained, i.e. the visions of Saint Michael, Saint Margaret and Saint Catherine, who had advised and encouraged Joan from the age of thirteen to 29 May 1431. They were central to the sentencing proceedings during which Joan tirelessly repeated: 'No, my voices have not deceived me.' Her own certainty allows for the possibility of miracles, which contemporary rationalists have attempted to interpret realistically in terms of imagination, hysteria and hallucinations. The fact remains that Joan believed in them and historians, regardless of their own opinion on the matter, should at least take account of her firm conviction that the voices existed. The supernatural cannot be historically proven, but the mentality of that period is an historical fact. It should moreover be noted that the conflict was not between reason and faith. The judges were not rationalists and they too believed in the supernatural, especially when they saw it as the devil's work. They wanted the accused to acknowledge her contact with the devil, so that they had the right to burn her. But Joan refused to make the confession they required of her. In the twentieth century, it is impossible not to compare the story of Joan with another true story. In Arthur London's *L'Aveu*, another tribunal, with all the characteristics of the Inquisition, endeavoured to obtain by all possible means (except physical torture – Joan was not tortured either) the confession of an imaginary crime which would support a political cause.

THE MYTH OF JOAN – OVER FIVE CENTURIES

The interpretations of Joan's rule have necessarily varied through the ages. Changes in attitudes, discoveries made by historians, and inventions by men of letters have all produced dozens of 'Joans' who belong to the history of ideas rather than an authentic biography of the Maid of Orléans.

Several unlikely versions should first of all be discounted. According to these, Joan did not die but escaped, with the help of Cauchon, through an underground passage (of which no trace remains), while she was replaced at the stake by a dummy, or some poverty-stricken girl. Alternatively, she was resurrected from the flames. In 1436, a young woman named Jeanne des Armoises appeared and claimed to be Joan of Arc. She gained a certain amount of recognition, and was even acknowledged by Joan's brothers, but confessed to her deceit before the Paris Parliament in 1440. Another 'claimant', who called herself Jehanne de Sermaize, was unmasked in 1457. At one point, there were as many as three adventuresses of this type in the Anjou region alone.

There was another, later fabrication in 1802 when the sub-prefect of Bergerac, Pierre Caze, publicly advanced the hypothesis of Joan's illegitimacy. According to his theory, she was the child of an adulterous affair between Isabella of Bavaria and Louis of Orléans, and was therefore Charles VII's half-sister. He claimed that she had been brought up and manipulated from birth with a view to fulfilling a major role later in life. This was a crude fabrication which conflicted with the facts (the stillborn child to which Isabella gave birth in 1407 was a boy, Philippe) as well as being extremely unlikely, for how could Charles VII have let his own sister die at the stake? The version has, however, attracted some support in the twentieth century to which Régine Pernoud wrote an apt reply in *Jeanne contre les Cauchon* (1970).

The Amazon maid

It is more useful to make a chronological study of the testimonies provided by the cult which has evolved around the 'historical' Joan. It has had its imposters, its decline and its apogee. Over the centuries, it is possible to identify various general trends. The initial development of Joan's legend was completely divorced from any literary knowledge. Her exploits were remembered and people marvelled that a woman could have achieved them. They extolled the warrior or, more accurately, the Amazon. Thus, it was the 'epic' nature of her campaign that fired the popular imagination.

Initially, Joan was the object of local cults. The cities of Bourges and Orléans celebrated a mass on the anniversary of her death. In Orléans, this tradition has survived to the present day. In Domrémy, where her brother, Jacquemin, had continued to live, her memory was religiously observed.

The Church remained strangely silent in this respect. As early as 1429, Chancellor Gerson, who had been summoned in an advisory capacity, had supported Joan. But he died several months later and his opinion was never heard.

For the poets, she remained an extremely vivid figure. Even before Joan's death, Christine de Pisan, who died in 1431, devoted her last lines to the woman who in her opinion epitomized the noblest female qualities: 'A maid of sixteen years,/For whom weapons are not weighty/Isn't that only natural?/And her enemies flee/Before her [. . .]' (*Le Dittié de Jeanne d'Arc*, July 1429).

Even more significant was the composition of the *Mistère du Siège d'Orléans*, drafted in 1435 and written between 1453 and 1456, during the rehabilitation proceedings, and performed in Orléans on several occasions. It comprised 20,530 lines and required approximately one hundred actors. It ensured Joan's fame for several centuries.

One hundred years later, people still remembered Joan vividly. François Villon featured her in one of the most moving verses of his *Ballade des Dames du Temps jadis* (1461): 'Bertha Broadfoot, Beatrice, Alice,/[And Ermengarde the lady of Maine,]/And that good Joan whom Englishmen/At Rouen doomed and burnt her there,/Mother of God, where are they then?/But where are the snows of yester-year?'

The chroniclers also paid homage to her. In the Lorraine region, her adventure was incorporated into the *Chronique de Lorraine*, a sort of *chanson de geste*, composed circa 1480 by the Dukes of Burgundy, who attributed all victories before and after 1431 to Joan without making any mention of the voices or the trial.

From the sixteenth century onwards, Joan was no longer a memory. She had already become a remote mythical figure, whose mission was misrepresented according to the current literary fashions or political trends. Several works number her among the virtuous women who honour the female sex, for example, Alain Bouchard's *Mirouer des Femmes vertueuses* (1546), which

Mlle de Scudéry used in her *Conversations morales*. On the other hand, malicious interpretations also appeared which supported a certain secularization of the myth. With the exception of the Latin epic by Valeran de la Varanne – *De gestis Johannae virginis Franciae, egregiae bellatricis libri 14; Des exploits de la glorieuse combattante, Jeanne la Pucelle de France* (1516) – which used elaborate rhetoric to glorify Joan's epic story, there were growing doubts about her divine mission, and even about her chastity. In *De l'Estat et mercy des affaires de France* (1570), a book which can be regarded as the first French national history, Girard de Haillan stated his belief that Joan was mistress of Robert de Baudricourt, or of Dunois, the bastard of Orléans. In his opinion, she was merely an instrument in the hands of the politicians.

Furthermore, there were also the reactions of the Protestants. In 1567, they destroyed the monument that had been built in Orléans, on the pretext that Joan was becoming the patroness of the Catholics and members of the pro-Catholic 'Sainte Ligue'. Nor could much sympathy be expected from the English. The first play attributed to Shakespeare, *Henry VI* (although its authorship was disputed by Robert Greene), describes Joan as a witch, whose success was due only to demons, and a 'strumpet' who was carrying the child of Charles VII, or some other prince (1590).

However, serious historians have examined the history of the Maid in more depth. The magistrate Etienne Pasquier pays tribute to the woman 'to whom France owes so much', and sadly remarks that: 'France had never before received such timely assistance, and no woman's memory had ever been more distorted than hers' (*Recherches de la France* 1580). In the same year, Montaigne visited Joan's house in Domrémy.

During the seventeenth and eighteenth centuries, the attitude of the general populace towards Joan remained unchanged. The scholars continued their research and collected documents from the trial. Edmond Richer stressed the importance of these documents and was concerned with their preservation. He wrote four extensive books on the *Histoire de la Pucelle* (1625–30) which he did not publish, but which were used by Lenglet-Dufresnoy for his *Histoire de Jeanne d'Arc, vierge, héroine et martyre* (1753–4). A meticulous historian, Clément de l'Averdy, compiled a copious collection of documents entitled *Notices et Extraits de la Bibliothèque du Roi*, III (1790). All these works glorified Joan's memory.

Paradoxically, but perhaps not surprisingly, the clearer Joan's story became, the more uncomfortable the poets felt with the subject. For example, although Chapelain's intentions for *La Pucelle ou la France délivrée* (1656) were admirable, i.e. to write an epic based on a modern subject, to extol the heroism of women and to decisively establish Joan's immortal glory, the finished result dismayed his contemporaries who quickly tried to ignore this insipid poem, which was weighted down with classical and mythological imagery. It may have been by way of a reaction that Voltaire wrote his *Pucelle d'Orléans* (drafted in 1738 and published in 1762), a counter-epic in which he distorted Joan's character, to the great satisfaction of the libertines and anticlericals. He had, however, already acknowledged Joan's merits in the *Essai sur les Moeurs* (1753), stating that, for having saved her king, she would have been 'worshipped in heroic times'. But he used any means to attack the Church. His *Pucelle*, a mock-heroic and suggestive poem, which is no longer read, is difficult to assess because it has been distorted to such an extent by 'unofficial' versions (see the critical edition of *Le Pucelle d'Orléans*, by Jean Vercruysse, 1970). In the only version that he claimed as his own, Joan is a serving girl at an inn (the mistake was already present in Bossuet's work) and the daughter of a bawdy friar. Her brilliant feats consist mainly in defending herself against the attempts made on her virginity, and in particularly against the donkey, which serves as her steed and which, being able to fly, helps her liberate Orléans. Once the city has been recaptured, she is released from her vow of virginity and can give herself to Dunois.

This buffoonery, in which Agnes Sorel occupied the same amount of space as Joan, proved extremely successful at a time when Joan's renown was at its lowest ebb. Beaumarchais refused to attribute any form of heroism to her at all, the *Encyclopédie* treated her as an unfortunate fool manipulated by rogues, while Montesquieu reduced her story to nothing more than a piece of deceit. Only Rousseau, who was probably closer to the feelings of the general public, produced an account of the *Procès* for the Republic of Geneva.

It was another reaction to Voltaire which stimulated a revival of sympathy for Joan. Due to the emergence of the Romantic movement, the English and the Germans, scandalized by Voltaire's irreverence, once more portrayed her in a favourable light.

The 'romantic' Joan

Fired by revolutionary ideas, Robert Southey was intensely interested in the Maid, whom he saw as the epitome of the people's struggle against those in power (*Joan of Arc* 1795). He refused to read Voltaire and wanted to atone for his country's burning of Joan and for their approval of what Shakespeare had written about her. His epic glorified a republican and patriotic Joan, the personification of civic virtues, who heralded the declaration of human rights at the coronation of Rheims.

In Germany, Schiller wrote one of the most outstanding plays ever inspired by the myth. *Die Jungfrau von Orléans* (*The Maid of Orléans* 1800), which he called a 'romantic tragedy' to excuse himself from not adhering to historical fact, was his own particular response to Shakespeare's accusations. Condemned as a witch and forced to flee from censure, Joan miraculously breaks free from her chains and dies on the battlefield in a sort of apotheosis. The work was extremely successful and served as a model for many European playwrights. The only unfortunate aspect is Schiller's falsification of the heroine's character by introducing a romantic element into the legend of Joan who, in spite of herself, falls in love with the Englishman Lionel. While it is perfectly acceptable to use fiction to embellish history, it should not distort the very basis of it. Joan's chastity was one of the characteristics most consistently attested by all witnesses. It was even more important to respect this fact because the English had done everything within their power to cast doubts upon this aspect of her character, and also precisely because the success of their trial depended on being able to prove that she was no longer a virgin.

In France, at the beginning of the Revolution, there was some uncertainty with respect to Joan: surely by saving a king, the Maid had contributed to the defence of the monarchy. In Domrémy, in 1793, vandals very nearly defaced her statue, but the inhabitants intervened. Gradually, the image of Joan the patriot prevailed and in 1803 the people of Orléans again began to commemorate their liberator. Bonaparte spoke highly of her, and Louis XVIII had the house at Domrémy, which had become a public property, restored. He erected a monument which was inaugurated in 1820 and two contemporary works of literature were sealed into its base, i.e. the tragedy by Loeuillard d'Avrigny, *Jeanne d'Arc à Rouen* and the elegies by Casimir Delavigne, *Les Messéniennes* (1818). In 1843, the French king Louis-Philippe presented Joan of Arc's house with a statue of the heroine, sculpted by his daughter, Princess Marie.

In spite of the prolific literary output that she inspired, there were no outstanding works dedicated to Joan by the great French Romantic poets, unless the admirable fifth volume of Michelet's *Histoire de France* (1841, reprinted as a separate volume under the title of *Jeanne d'Arc* in 1853) which glorifies the liberator of Orléans, is regarded as a poem. The work is a true masterpiece. Although he had only read l'Averdy's incomplete version of the trials, this was however enough to move him deeply, and to enable him to understand Joan's personality, 'her good sense', 'her kind heart', her intelligence and her purity. The Maid was of peasant stock and she was a woman. Everything combined to inspire Michelet's admiration. He focused on three aspects of her mission. She was first of all a patriot. Was she not the first person to have felt the 'Pity inspired by the kingdom of France'? Secondly, she embodied freedom of thought, justifying on the scaffold 'the right of conscience, the authority of the inner voice'. She allowed the 'God within her' to speak, a striking phrase from the pen of Michelet, the unbeliever. Finally, she represented the Passion: 'the imitation of Jesus Christ, his Passion reproduced in the Maid'. 'She had redeemed France.' Thus, the historian who did not believe in the voices prepared his readers to accept Joan's saintliness. This was a very romantic attitude in a century which rejected dogma, but retained a strong need for religion.

At the same time that Michelet was writing his poem about Joan, the scholar Jules Quicherat was establishing her story as accurately as possible. The five volumes of the *Procès* (1841–9), which dealt with the sentencing and rehabilitation of Joan of Arc, published not only the minutes of the trials which were already common knowledge, but also numerous documents in Latin and

French, which had been found in hitherto unexplored archives. The *Procès* were a mine of information for all researchers, and modified the reader's point of view by placing more emphasis on the tragedy of judicial error. The tragedy – and no longer the epic – is played out in a courtroom between Joan and her judges. There is nothing like a trial, especially when its methods are suspect, to fascinate a spectator who has been admitted to the intimacy that exists *in camera*. Quicherat's work introduced a new figure, the accused, who was completely different from the plumed Amazon depicted in so many paintings.

Michelet and Quicherat, both atheists, and both passionate admirers of the Maid, paved the way for a new stage in Joan's posthumous career, i.e. as a national saint.

The national saint

From 1850 onwards, Joan's following increased considerably. On his release from prison, the insurgent Armand Barbès said: 'The greatest glory of our nation is that it produced Joan of Arc' (*La Solidarité*, 1 June 1867). In 1869, Monseigneur Dupanloup, the bishop of Orléans, asked Rome to initiate canonization proceedings. After the Prussian victory over the French in 1870, she became 'the Angel of revenge'. Poets and painters rivalled each other in enthusiasm and her portrait became a favourite theme of the 'art pompier'. She was part of the academic Pantheon of the Third Republic. In 1884, the republican Joseph Fabre defended his idea of a purely civic national holiday dedicated to Joan, but it was several decades before either the civic or the religious festival was introduced.

In the intervening period, Joan was used by all the political parties. Between 1870 and 1914, they all believed in the patriot but had differing opinions about Joan the saint. A revealing example can be found in the newspaper *Le Parti ouvrier* in which, on 14 May 1890, Lucien Herr claimed that Joan was a socialist: 'She represents the people who for the first time in history saved France. The Church should leave her to us [. . .]. You can keep your bishop. We will keep the daughter of the people.' In *La Foire sur la Place* (1908), Romain Rolland described a Jean-Christophe who was overwhelmed after reading Michelet, 'Joan's evangelist'. In 1910, Jean Jaurès emphatically paid homage to Joan's universal mission in *L'Armée nouvelle*. In 1913, the philosopher Alain praised Joan for her 'miraculous strength of character which owes everything to mankind and nothing to heaven' (*Propos*, 6 May).

In this atmosphere of generally shared enthusiasm, it came as no surprise that in 1897 a young socialist poet from Orléans, Charles Péguy, also wrote a version of *Jeanne d'Arc*, an extensive trilogy dedicated 'to all those men and women who will suffer a mortal death in order to establish the universal socialist Republic'. The first play in the trilogy, *A Domrémy*, presents a passionate child, obsessed with the suffering of her country, with Christ's Passion and prey to an obsessive fear of damnation. In the second, entitled *Les Batailles*,

Joan embodies the people, a people which joins forces with the combatants, launches attacks and joyfully wins victories. The third, *Rouen*, includes a lengthy evocation of the punishments of hell which Péguy attributes to Maître Evrard in the scene in the cemetery of Saint-Ouen, and which shakes Joan to the point of making her doubt her own salvation. There are many fine epic and tragic passages, but also some weaknesses. Péguy was unable to sustain the tone throughout the work, and shrank from staging the scene at the stake. The trilogy, which provoked virtually no reaction, is however the most poignant of the dramatic works devoted to Joan. Miracles play no part in it, and the sign that makes Joan decide to leave home is an historic event, i.e. the lifting of the siege of the Mont-Saint-Michel. But the young socialist who claimed to be an unbeliever had already made Joan 'the major guiding principle' of his life and his work. In 1910, after re-embracing Christianity, he revised the first of these plays and converted it into *Le Mystère de la Charité de Jeanne d'Arc*. In this lengthy deliberation by Joan – which is virtually uninterrupted by the brief replies – he had no difficulty in developing the same themes of salvation and damnation, or even in incorporating an account of Christ's Passion, which stresses the parallels, already identified by Michelet, between Christ's martyrdom and that of Joan. He intended to follow this first 'Mystery', which was warmly received by the critics, with fifteen or so others on the vocation, the saintliness and the martyrdom 'of the greatest saint that has ever existed'. Although he lacked the time required to fulfil his ambition of becoming the 'notary' and 'faithful servant' of his heroine, the twentieth century still regards him as the most famous of Joan's eulogists.

Léon Bloy, Péguy's contemporary – but not his friend – also chose Joan as his heroine. In 1915, 'on the threshold of the Apocalypse', he finished a book on which he had been working for a long time, i.e. *Jeanne d'Arc et l'Allemagne*. His vision of the world is quite straightforward. His homeland is a chosen nation: 'God's only nation is France.' Joan had secured Jesus' 'lieutenancy' on earth for the king of France. Her martyrdom made her the miraculous passion flower which bloomed before the demise of the Middle Ages. For Bloy, as for Péguy, Joan was a personal myth.

Maurice Barrès made the most significant contribution to giving concrete expression to the memory of Villon's 'bonne Lorraine', although he never managed to write the book he had dreamt of completing about her. He was an agnostic, a 'fellow traveller' of the nationalists, and was torn between the idea of a Celtic Joan, the daughter of a pagan land, and the Joan inspired by God and invoked by his political colleagues. He went as far as to refer to 'that fairy whom we made a saint' (*Le Gaulois*, 28 January 1908). However, it was due to his sustained efforts that, in 1920, he succeeded in achieving Joseph Fabre's ambition by persuading Parliament to vote in favour of a national holiday dedicated to Joan.

This vote had taken such a long time to obtain because the left-wing parties looked unfavourably on the Church's appropriation of Joan. The Papacy had declared the Maid Venerable in 1894 and Blessed in 1909. The anticlericals were becoming concerned. In 1904, a minor, although significant, event occurred which was known as the 'Thalamas' affair. Thalamas was a fifth-form master at the Lycée Condorcet who had denied the existence of Joan's voices in front of his pupils. Under pressure from the Ligue des Patriotes, he was reprimanded and transferred. In 1908, he was authorized to teach a class for non-registered students at the Sorbonne. There was a further scandal, which coincided with the publication of the *Vie de Jeanne d'Arc* by Anatole France, who had been interested in the psychology of the Maid since 1876. In an attempt to provide a rational explanation of the voices, France had consulted psychiatrists, including Dr Georges Dumas, and had come to the conclusion that Joan of Arc's voices were merely 'the voices of her soul', that she was a visionary, a sleepwalker who suffered from hallucinations. But at the same time, his anticlericalism led him to suspect that she had been manipulated by the priests who had devised a 'pious fraud' to ensure that she fell into their trap. This gave rise to a dual interpretation which detracted from the unity of the work. France's book was meticulously refuted by the English historian Andrew Lang in *La Jeanne d'Arc de M. Anatole France* (1909). However, it also provided arguments for the radicals and the freemasons, who resented the fact that, every year on 8 May, their saint was honoured by members of Action Française in front of the statue by Frémiet, in the Place des Pyramides.

These disputes came to an end with the Great War, when Joan once again became the symbol of a threatened nation. The Church was the first to take action. On 16 May 1920, Joan was proclaimed a saint and the patroness of France by Pope Benedict XV, who was anxious to draw a veil over the neutralist stance adopted by the Vatican during the war. The French government soon followed suit. On 24 June, Saint Joan's day became 'the festival of patriotism'. This dual patronage sealed a temporary reconciliation.

The 'modern' Joan

There was a possibility that these ultimate honours would detract from the figure of Joan, and embalm her forever in a chilly shroud. Although the pacifists had occasionally mocked the chauvinistic forms assumed by her following during the 1920s, and although the unbelievers had found her rehabilitation by the Church intolerable, her unique personality has continued to be a source of interest for writers and film-makers alike.

Quicherat's works had caused a shift in the emphasis of the myth which was reinforced after 1920. More stress was placed on the trial of 1431 than on the years of the Maid's calling and military campaigns. The secularization of society also meant that there was a certain lack of interest in the voices. Only Claudel included them in his Oratorio, *Jeanne d'Arc au Bûcher* (1938), for which the music was composed by Honegger. But the work was intended to be performed on stage and as such did not have to be entirely credible. For a number of his contemporaries, the confrontation between Joan and her judges was of prime importance. Joan was the child in the presence of the Church Doctors. This was how Bernanos, Péguy's successor, saw her in his brilliant essay, *Jeanne relapse et sainte* (1934). 'The miracle is that once, and possibly only once in the history of the world, childhood was brought before an official court in this way.' During the Second World War, Joan was finally identified with the underground freedom fighters. Writing in occupied France, Claude Vermoral saw her as the epitome of the women of the Resistance movement in *Jeanne avec nous* (1942). For Anouilh, she was the little girl 'who says no', rejecting the mediocre happiness offered by an almost paternal Cauchon (*L'Alouette*, 1953). The title that Thierry Maulnier gave to his play in 1949, *Jeanne et les Juges*, sums up this general trend which was illustrated by the Moscow trials. This was now the era of the Cold War.

But in order to understand how Joan could be adopted by both individualists and conservatives, it is necessary to go back to Bernard Shaw's *Saint Joan* (1923). Even in the preface to his play, he makes two statements to the effect that Joan was one of the earliest Protestant martyrs, and that she was one of the first advocates of nationalism. These two propositions are illustrated in a lengthy discussion between Cauchon and the Englishman Warwick. Cauchon predicts the coming of Luther, the victory of individual reason over the absolute authority of the Catholic Church, and is not afraid to call heresy by its name, i.e. Protestantism. Warwick, for his part, fears the advent of the concept of nationalism which would give the king (or the State) complete power over the feudal system. He is afraid of people like Richelieu. This very shrewd analysis explains how Joan could be acclaimed by people who are apparently very different, i.e. the nationalists and the critics of the establishment.

Joan of Arc is the embodiment of occasionally contradictory ideologies. She can be Joan the devout Christian or Joan in conflict with the Church, the unifier of France or the rebel struggling against the establishment, and has often been created by writers such as Péguy, Anatole France and Bernanos, in their own image. Which of Joan's roles has most appeal for the modern imagination? It is in fact the cinema that has generated the twentieth century's favourite view of her. Among the twenty or so films inspired by her, *La Passion de Jeanne d'Arc* (1928), a masterpiece of the silent screen by the Danish director, Carl Dreyer, and the *Procès de Jeanne d'Arc* (1962) by Robert Bresson, are particularly worthy of note. Both films focus the action on the last days, or even the last hours, of Joan's suffering. They have either eliminated or stylized the setting. Only the faces of friends or foes are real, reflecting their emotional states, hatred, anxiety, compassion and anguish. The silent film and the talking film thus initiate a dialogue which is concise, slow and insistent in the case of the *Passion*, and more rapid and incisive in the *Procès*, and which leads inevitably to a tragic end. A powerful inner existence rises to the surface, which some might call a mystical presence. This is probably the only modern form of expression which can create a living image of Joan, with all her strengths and weaknesses, intensely alive even to the point of death.

Simone Fraisse

Job, a Myth about Poverty? As Poor as Job

Following a wager between God and Satan, Job, who is a very wealthy semi-nomad, suddenly finds himself stripped of all that belongs to him – his flocks and his children. All he is left with is his wife. Then even his flesh is afflicted with an incurable and contagious disease, and he is left alone on a rubbish dump (the 'midden'). Three friends come to comfort him, but in fact make it clear that they feel he must be to blame; Job protests his innocence, and in the end becomes resentful of God because of his silence. After a long and painful debate, God finally reveals himself in a whirlwind, and vindicates Job who has submitted to him amidst the ashes. Job regains his wealth, and has more children.

Is it possible to describe the story of Job as a myth? Myths have no author, whereas the Book of Job is historical; it is a story that has a place and a date (*c.* 575 BC). It forms part of the Jewish literature that dates from after the exile, and is one of the Books of Wisdom. But where can we discover who the author of the book was? We do not know for certain: Moses? an Edomite Jew? a heathen thoroughly versed in Egyptian thought? Job himself? Moreover, the structure of Job is composite (a lamentation in verse between two sections in prose), giving the impression that there must have been a set pattern relating to the theme of the Righteous Man who suffers (Ezekiel in chapter 14 of his Book conjures up Job as a remote figure alongside Noah and Daniel). The story of the king who has been unfairly stripped of his power as a result of a wager between God and Satan may thus have been spread by Bedouins. In it they may have seen the theme of the renewal of nature in autumn after the torpor of summer; or that of a quest for immortality, as in the myth of Gilgamesh, with the expiatory consequences of immoderation that follow on from it; or again that of the search for the absent Father.

If a myth is a story in which our rages, terrors, desires and cries are expressed, and 'a symbolic fable resuming an infinite number of more or less analogous situations', then the Book of Job is indeed a story with mythical power, and its wretched hero is a mythical hero: poor as Job on his midden.

The book of Job lies at the point where sceptical Mesopotamian thought (*Poem of the Just Man who Suffers* and *Dialogue on Human Poverty*, *c.* 2000 BC) and Egyptian pessimism (*Conversation between the Desperate Man and his Soul* and *Complaint of the Poor Peasant*, *c.* 1800 BC) converge, and touches on the same subject matter as the Greek tragedies, on the one hand in its theatrical texture, and on the other in the terrible indictment of the jealous sadism of the gods or of God. But Job is not Prometheus; Prometheus's hubris leads him to defy and curse the gods, while Job's is resolved in worshipful silence before his god. A certain number of invariables also endow the story with a special mythical autonomy: quite obviously, whatever oriental influences may have had a bearing on its evolution, it is first and foremost a western biblical myth associated with Hebrew monotheism. It foreshadows the suffering Servant of Isaiah, and Christ in his hour of death. But the case of Job more explicitly involves 'setting up' human misery which is then met with the silence of God; Job suffers, therefore he must be guilty since God is just; but Job knows he is innocent, which would mean that God was unjust; the paradox can only be resolved through an appeal to Mystery, and in the silence of Illumination; Job suffers, he is innocent, yet mysteriously God is just.

Thus Job in his time of trial is alternately rebellious and submissive, someone who is being tested and is waiting for restitution, rejecting the image of a cruel God meting out justice as he pleases to herald in the image of a good, fair God. In this Job figures as the epitome of human misery, alternating between rebellion and passive acceptance.

In its tragic simplicity the theme has tempted, inspired, even obsessed a fair number of writers. In some periods it has tended to be seen more as an example of patience, while at others it has been seen as an example of rebellion.

Beyond the pilgrimages to St Job and the paraphrases and commentaries that crop up throughout the Middle Ages, it is primarily on the stage, in the Mystery plays, that the character of Job makes its most 'spectacular' impact on the literary imagination. The start of this phenomenon must lie in the twelfth-century Walloon adaptation of Gregory the Great's *Moralia in Job*, but the most successful adaptation is the fifteenth-century *Mystère de la Pacience de Job*, which provided the faithful with an example of resignation embodied in the leading character. Poets too, though for different reasons, relating to the fact they were frequently on the margins of society, were quick to compare themselves with Job in his fallen state. As early as the thirteenth century Rutebeuf drew an analogy between his poverty and that of Job: 'God has made me a companion of Job,/At one fell blow he has taken/What I had . . .' (*La Complainte Rutebeuf*).

During the same period the torment of Job was being written in stone on the doorways of Chartres and Rheims. Then in the fifteenth century Villon refers to it when alluding to the tragedy of human temporality: 'My days have wandered away/As Job says, they are swifter/Than a weaver's shuttle . . .' (*Testament*, V. 217–19).

The theme was then seized upon in the moral essay, to exalt the stoical courage of the hero who remains steadfast in face of events over which he has not control; Chassignet published *Job ou de la Fermeté* in 1592. Roland de Lassus composed his *Sacrae lectiones novem ex propheta Job* at the same time. Thus Job became an example of steadfastness in the face of misfortune. Transposed into a more worldly setting he would soon be used as a mannered reference in the famous dispute between the supporters of Uranie and of Job, regarding the merits of the two love sonnets by Voiture and Benserade: 'Job inflicted by a thousand torments,/Will let you know of his suffering (. . .)/If he suffered from incredible ills,/He complained of it, he talked about it;/I know some who are worse off' (Benserade).

In entering the literary salons Job, 'full' of woe, risked being relegated to a mere figure of speech, but the mythical potential of the character is so great that he very quickly regained his tragic aspect in hellfire theology, in particular in the work of Father Surin (*Lettres*) and the direct allusions made to him by Pascal (*Pensées* 174, Brunschvicg edition) and Bossuet (*Oraison funèbre d'Henriette d'Angleterre*). Georges de la Tour's famous painting, 'Job raillé par sa femme', also dates from this period.

In the eighteenth century the tragedy of Job was the inspiration behind Voltaire's *Candide*, but the reflections that arose from the model were now philosophical in nature rather than religious, relating to the meaning of life. Like Job, Candide discovers a more courageous way of living through his experience of the harshness of life and being galled by it. On reading the story Frederick II commented: 'It is Job in modern dress' (Letter 7554, ed. Besterman).

In the Romantic period there are a proliferation of allusions to Job as a sad witness of the longing for the infinite. Chateaubriand, Lamartine and Victor Hugo in particular made many references to him as a key figure for mankind, resuming within himself all suffering, both physical and mental: 'While crushing the vermin on his ulcers, he calls upon the stars' (Hugo, *William Shakespeare*). He is the titan of the midden. William Blake's pictures attest to the permanence of man's obsession with Job in the field of art. In the second half of the century which was given over to scientism, while not ceasing to serve as an example, Job became a hero of 'scepticism' in Renan's account (translation and commentary) or a Messiah or regenerated humanity in Pierre Leroux's five-act drama.

The modern idea of Job as a suffering Exister, a creature who has been abandoned but is still waiting for an absent God, became current after the publication of Kierkegaard's thoughts (*Edifying Discourses*), Unamuno's *Del sentimiento trágico de la vida*, and later Chestov's *Kierkegaard et la Philosophie de l'Existence*. Many of those writing at the end of the nineteenth century searching for lost values reiterated the lament of Job, without necessarily identifying it as such. Thus the rage of Rimbaud and Lautréamont could be described as Job-like, to such an extent that it is no longer necessary to use the name Job as a basis in order for work to be 'recognized' as part of the myth of Job.

In the twentieth century the two World Wars were to shed a new and terrible light on the figure of Job, as personified not only in the flayed figures of Kokoschka (*Hiob* 1917) or the tortured faces in Picasso's *Guernica*, but also in those deported to the concentration camps or the victims of the bomb at

Hiroshima, not to mention all the starving waifs from Third World countries. Gide ('Reading Job made the most vivid impression on me', *Si le Grain ne meurt* 1926), Claudel ('Of all the books in the old Testament, Job is the most sublime', *Le Livre de Job* 1946), Bernanos ('Our poor world is like poor old Job on his dunghill', *Journal*) and Julien Green ('When I felt tired as I wandered through Paris I used to sit down on a bench and read Job', *Mille Chemins ouverts*) still saw it as the drama of a single being grappling with his God. The picture by the Expressionist painter Francis Gruber (*Job sur Fond de Palissade* 1944) conjures up this type of relationship. That was also Jung's perception when he published *Antwort auf Hiob* in 1940. But increasingly Job has taken on a collective significance with the mental cataclysms that have marked our period: the work of Ernst Bloch in particular (*Atheismus in Christentum* 1968) portrays Job as the hero standing alongside a whole people in their oppression, no longer as a solitary figure, saying goodbye for ever to the theocratic God of Tradition, but going forward to find him as a 'Utopian passion'. As early as 1946 Margarete Susman wrote a book with the eloquent title, *Job ou la Destinée du Peuple juif*; no doubt even at the time when the Bible was written Job also stood for the whole Hebrew people in exile, but in spite of this collective significance he was essentially perceived through the image of an exemplary individual. After Auschwitz the figure of Job came to represent all the victims of the concentration camps; it was the start of an 'eclipse of God' from which we have not recovered, but the desire for the missing Presence is so great that even if the question of Job has gone up in smoke in the furnaces of the crematoria we make every effort to give a hopeful meaning to the Absurd: 'Our time has become ripe for Job' (Hans Ehrenberg, *Hiob der Existentialist* 1952). During these last decades that have been marked by the 'death of God' (already predicted by Nietzsche in the last century), the 'recognition' of Job has spread all across Europe; just after the Second World War it was possible to meet up with Job 'on every road in Europe' (Elie Wiesel, *Célébration biblique* 1975).

In fact more or less everywhere in Europe with the 'return of the tragic' we have witnessed a powerful resurgence of the figure of Job, not so much any more as a distinct person, but as suffering motivated by causes that are comparable to those underlying the story of the Righteous Man in the Bible. The Germans have exploited the theme more than most; it was already present in the twelfth and thirteenth century in the very similar figure of *Der Arme Heinrich* (Hartmann von Aue 1195), the knight suffering from leprosy whom God puts to the test as he had once tested Job. The theme of the innocent man unjustly persecuted was taken up again by Heine in *Romanzero* (1851), especially through the lamentations in the poem 'Lazarus'; Heine when ill at the end of his life echoed the voice of Job: 'Why does the Righteous Man crawl along, haggard and miserable,/Weighed down by the Cross,/While the Wicked Man like a cheerful conqueror/Gallops along on horseback?'

But it has been in the twentieth century and in the work of Kafka in particular that the question of Job has once again been raised, with the eternal dispute with God, a hidden, silent God. Max Brod sees innumerable analogies between the work of his friend Kafka and the Book of Job: 'It is the eternal problem of Job'. Like Job, Joseph K. and K. are reaching towards a redeeming Interlocutor who for ever eludes them; the *Brief an den Vater* is a supplication at the same time as a challenge, searching for the true Father. In his stage adaptation of *Der Prozess* Gide rightly perceived this dimension in Kafka's work when he put a Job-like line not present in the novel in the mouth of the cathedral almoner: 'Do you condemn me in order to justify yourself?'

In the years close to the Second World War the references to Job became more direct and especially frequent in countries where German was spoken: *Hiob* by Joseph Roth (1930), a transposition of the biblical myth to the period of Tsarist Russia; the short verse tetralogy by Karl Wolfskehl, *Hiob oder die vier Spiegel* (1950), in which the author starts by evoking Job/Israel in exile and ends with Job/Messiah calling upon God and forcing him to come to him; Wolfgang Borchert's drama *Draussen vor der Tür* (1946) which ends with the essentially Job-like questions: 'Warum schweigt ihr denn? Warum? Gibt denn keiner eine Antwort?' [Why are you silent? Why? Will no-one give an answer]; and finally quite recently in German-speaking Switzerland the novel by Fritz Zorn, *Mars* (1977), the tormented story of a rich young man being eaten up by cancer who in his 'anger' (*Zorn* = anger) prefers to follow Job's wife in cursing God rather than Job himself, repentant amidst the ashes: 'We have no right to allow ourselves to be comforted if the consolation on offer is only a lousy consolation'. One of the characteristics of Job as a contemporary figure is that the violence of his rebellion is as often as not stronger than the stoicism of his acceptance.

The 'modernness' of the story is vouched for more or less everywhere in Europe by works using the actual name of Job in the title: in France *Le Rêve de Job* by Jean Demélier (1971), a transposition of the Bible story into a novel set in Paris; in Poland a play called *Job* by Pope John Paul II (written in 1940 under the name Karol Wojtyla and recently staged in Italy) and *L'Homme parfait* by Jerzy Zawieyski (1945); in French-speaking Switzerland *Job le Vigneron* by R. Morax (1940) and *L'Ogre* (1973) by Jacques Chessex – containing many references to Job; in the English-speaking world *The Undying Fire* by H.G. Wells (1920: 'The whole earth is now – Job') and *J.B.* by Archibald MacLeish (1958); in Portugal the poetic lamentation by Miguel Torga (*O outro Livro de Job*, 1936: 'Injustamente, Senhor, injustamente . . .'); in Spain, where the myth was already present in Fray Luis de Léon's commentaries in the sixteenth century and in an *auto-sacramental* by Calderón in the seventeenth century, it has been taken up again in the present in a novel-form essay by Fernando Savater, *Diario de Job* (1983), and a Basque drama by Luis Haranburu Altuna, *Job* (1972), in which there is a second Job who is the antithesis of the first, a sort of Hitler who dominates the world. In Hungary a recent film by Imre Gyongvossy (*La Révolte de Job* 1983) offered a somewhat similar transposition with a man grappling with a tyrannical power.

While it is impossible to provide an exhaustive list, it must be stressed that of all the literary genres used the theatrical form is unquestionably the best suited to 'resurrecting' the myth. Moreoever, it is probable that the text of the Bible was written with the intention that it should be read aloud on stage, in a style resembling the stationary monologues of ancient tragedy, but also appropriate to the 'infra-tragedy' of modern plays. The drama of Job is an internal affair which nonetheless entails pain and violence for the 'sufferer' who is struggling with himself. A drama such as *Le Personnage combattant* by Vauthier (1955) is very close to it; the plays of both Ionesco and Beckett in their different registers often repeat the same tense expectancy found in Job, which finally dissolves into despairing relinquishment. This is the same 'pacience' that we find in the mediaeval mystery plays: 'The air is full of our cries' (*Waiting for Godot*). Ionesco sees Job as a contemporary of Beckett's (*Notes et Contre-Notes*) and his own 'foreman'; praising Philippe Nemo's essay *Job et l'Excès du Mal* (1978) he adds, 'I feel I am Job, and I am struck with the fundamental question of "What do they want of me?" ' (*Un Homme en question* 1979).

In fact all Theatre of Cruelty, giving expression to the body racked by pain and the mind tormented by anguish, has Artaud to thank for the unremitting violence of flesh that is dying and howling self-awareness; Artaud himself had the character of Job in mind when he was considering writing a play based on a great tortured figure from antiquity: 'See the Book of Job' (*Oeuvres complètes*, vol. II, 'Dans un but de décentralisation'). At the same period Ghelderode in Belgium was torn by identical torments, 'the extenuating anguish' which made him fit to perceive the deity (a letter, 1933); direct references to Job figure in some of his works (*Mademoiselle Jaïre, Marie la Misérable*).

Other more recent dramatists, all in differing proportions heirs to this tradition of 'cruelty' – such as Arrabal (*Le Bréviaire d'Amour d'un Haltérophile* the main character in which is called Job) or Billetdoux (*Comment va le monde, môssieu? Il tourne, môssieu!* in which one of the main characters is again nicknamed Job) – find an image of our condition in the biblical figure of the reprobate. So it comes about that 'the mystery of wickedness has one of the greatest clowns of all time as its main interpreter – by the name of Job' (Alfred Simon, *Beckett* 1983).

Job is perceived by us as an exemplary 'being' in whom we can identify ourselves. He is the Job within each one of us, when we are feeling put-upon, the victims of an unjust God. So it is not surprising to witness the 'resurgence' of a figure who is so painfully expressive of the 'poverty' of our existence. God is ignoring us, letting us 'fall' like the overwhelmed creatures in Beckett's play, *All that fall*. Like Job we are tempted to curse our birth and speak ill of a creator who is so careless of our happiness. Like Lazare in Grotowski's *Apocalypsis cum figuris* (1973) we utter Job's words of indignation.

Is it still possible as it was in biblical times for this 'kenosis' (renunciation of divine nature) to which we are all condemned to be a metamorphosis at the end of which the hero becomes himself again, restored, glorified and resuscitated? The richness of the myth of Job lies in the very fact that it is open to a variety of interpretations and can be used by the most different philosophies: philosophies based on hope such as found in Julien Green (*Ce qui reste de jour*: 'Have read Job a great deal') or Simone Weil (*Attente de Dieu*) – or the despairing philosophies of people like Malraux ('The most disgraceful dialogue a man ever had with his God', *Malraux, celui qui vient* by Guy Suarès) or Cioran ('Unlike Job I have not cursed the day of my birth; on the other hand I have anathematized every other day', *De l'inconvénient d'être né* 1973).

Marc Bochet

Judith

THE BASIS OF THE MYTH

Judith is the heroine of a Bible story which scholars place in the fourth century BC at the time of the persecution of the Jews by Antiochus Epiphanes. The narrator tells how, when the town of Bethulia is besieged by the Assyrians, a young widow renowned for her piety, wealth and beauty decides to go to the camp of the enemy general Holofernes, motivated by pity for her people and indignation at the cowardice of her fellow citizens who want to surrender the town to the enemy. After spending a night in his tent without losing her honour she beheads him. The sight of his head displayed on the town ramparts is enough to cause the Assyrian army to break up and take to their heels, leaving rich booty behind them. The story ends with a hymn of thanksgiving intoned by Judith amidst the women of Bethulia.

The original story was no doubt written in Hebrew, though only the Greek text of the Septuagint is known to us, repeated in Latin in the Vulgate with a few variations probably derived from an Aramaic text known to St Jerome. It forms part of the Deuterocanonical books, added to the Hebrew Bible in the Canon of the Christians, and regarded as apocryphal by Jews and the Protestant church.

There would be no point in trying to fit Judith's deed into any episode of Jewish history, as the historical and geographical details which feature plentifully in the text do not add up. We do not know where the town of Bethulia is (its name means 'door of God' in Hebrew); Holofernes' campaign from Nineveh to Damascus runs counter to geography. It has also been noted, for example by Dhorme in his introduction to the French La Pléiade edition of *Judith*, that the name of the heroine does not refer to one particular person. It is symbolic: Judith or Yehoudith is the incarnation of Jewish women in general.

As a fictional story the purpose of the Book of Judith is obvious: to reinspire the Jews with courage at one of the most tragic moments of their history. Its structure is similar to that of a fairy tale. After a 'lack' – the thirst which is wreaking havoc among those besieged – has been recognized, a heroine appears, gifted with above-average beauty and intelligence, magic tools of a very high order. She easily convinces her enemy that she has come to see him to enhance her own standing, captivates him and then, when he has collapsed on the bed, 'overflown with wine', mows him down with his own scimitar. She makes her way back to Bethulia without encountering any obstacles, and there her feat is celebrated as a triumph by one and all. The moral is the same as in a great many tales, the story of Tom Thumb for example in popular literature, or in other Bible stories too, such as David and Goliath: if the weak know how to use their assets, cunning and intelligence, they will always succeed in getting the better of those who are stronger.

The whole text is in fact built on the antithesis between strength and weakness; the first three chapters which evoke the power of the Assyrian army are contrasted with the four succeeding ones which describe the weakness of the Jewish people confined within Bethulia. The strength of Holofernes is contrasted with the weakness of Judith, which she emphasizes in her prayer (chapter 9). Then comes the reversal which lies at the very heart of the story: weakness turns into strength and strength into weakness. Facing the enemy who lets himself be captivated, misled and then made drunk stands the Jewess who is strong in her beauty and her intelligence; the arrogance of the pagan is countered by the contempt of the servant woman who throws the head into a bag of victuals; the devastation of the surrounding countryside by the Assyrians is set against the Assyrians' rout and the sacking of their camp by the inhabitants of Bethulia; the original picture of desolation within the besieged town is contrasted with the final picture of gaiety in the town that has been saved.

If weakness turns into strength, it is because Judith places her trust in God: this is the major theme of the story, reaffirmed by all the protagonists, even those who are not Jewish. In his speech to Holofernes Achior the Ammonite tries vainly to point out that the Assyrians have won so far because they have such a huge army, but that it is not inconceivable that the Jews will have the final victory: everything depends on whether they keep faith with their God. And at the time of deepest desolation it is Judith who shows her fellow citizens how she will save them, with the help of God; the Jewish people have committed no sin, therefore there is no reason why God should not come to their aid. It is not a matter of threatening him or 'bringing him to reckoning like a son of man', people must confide in his Will (8: 27). Where the Elders she admonishes have gone wrong is in losing trust. As for her, she uses the weapons God has given to her as a woman to captivate Holofernes and then kill him, without being troubled by the slightest doubt (any more than those around her) as to the legitimacy of the means used. To demonstrate that he is helping her, God gives her an appearance that beguiles everyone – the town Elders, Holofernes's guards and Holofernes himself; the narrator devotes several verses (10: 1–5) to describing her toilet preparations, her clothes and the jewels with which she decks herself. God puts into her mouth the words that Holofernes wants to hear, ambiguities which Judith can utter without compromising her faith: 'God shall bring the thing to pass perfectly with thee' (11: 6). The support of her God never fails her. He prevents her from being in any way sullied by making the heathen collapse in a drunken stupor and gives the woman the physical strength required to cut through the barbarian's neck. She is the instrument of God, blind obedience, and subsequently boasts of having carried out the murder. There can be no lingering doubts after the final hymn: 'The Almighty Lord brought them [the Assyrians] to nought by the hand of a woman' – 'Her scandal ravished his [Holofernes'] eye,/And her beauty took his soul prisoner;/The scimitar passed through his neck' (16: 5, 9).

TRADITION

With very few exceptions the narrative and dramatic works that took up the story of Judith did not alter its meaning, at least until the nineteenth century. The biblical book was quite obviously used for edifying purposes. The epic poem by Guillaume Salluste Du Bartas might seem like just another traditional version, following in the line of poems written in English and German in the tenth, eleventh, thirteenth and fifteenth centuries, but for its author's beliefs and the circumstances in which it was written. Du Bartas had been won over by the ideas of the Reformation; he was comissioned to write *Judith* in 1564 by Jeanne d'Albret, the widow of the king of Navarre, who is known to have had Protestant sympathies. In the eyes of her fellow countrymen, the political and religious situation of the kingdom of Navarre seemed to have similiarities with that of Bethulia besieged by a much more powerful enemy; Jeanne, a 'widow with the heart of a man', had more than one feature in common with the Bible heroine, reticent, weak and isolated to start with, but with an equal trust in God; as for the sworn enemy of the Protestants, Duke François of Guise, who died of a mortal wound at the siege of Orleans, fitted the role of Holofernes perfectly. In the light of the events of the day, the feat of the Jewess takes on a very special meaning: by exalting her exploit, the Gascon poet is quite specifically praising tyrannicide. The story of the widow from Bethulia was thus being used by him as a weapon, just as it was subsequently to be used as a propaganda device by dramatists who shared his faith.

Considered from an entirely different standpoint, the story attracted the Jesuits as a teaching tool. They made wide use of it in plays written in Latin for the use of their pupils, which were enacted in class at prize-givings; some of the plays reveal great mastery over dramatic construction. The staging ended with a procession inside the school and outside in the streets of the town. This led to the writing of plays for the popular theatre mixing tragic scenes with comic interludes, in the tradition of the Mystery plays. The story of Judith was even presented in a puppet theatre in Hamburg in 1785, and in London in 1663, as well as being presented several times in the seventeenth and eighteenth centuries at Bartholomew Fairs.

In the same period there were a great many operas and oratorios that used the subject without changing its meaning, by Marc-Antoine Charpentier, Opitz, Scarlatti, Vivaldi, Mozart and Salieri, for example; the last two were based on a libretto by Metastasio. Only Vivaldi's libretto stands out from the others because of the final *carmen allegoricum* in which it is clearly stated that Bethulia represents the Church under attack from the heathen, in this instance the Turks.

The dramatic and didactic qualities of the story likewise explain the many pictorial works devoted to it in the sixteenth and seventeenth centuries; one of the consequences of the Counter-Reformation was to encourage painters to depict a character that lent herself so well to allegory. In the beheading scene followers of Caravaggio among others found material for aesthetic exploration.

THE INTRODUCTION OF EROTICISM

In the prolific sequence of literary works derived from the biblical book, the play by Hebbel in the nineteenth century marks a turning-point. The German playwright did not change the events in the story; he added just one character, Ephraim, Judith's suitor. The originality of his work relates to the complex personality he ascribes to the heroine, and the new meaning he consequently attributes to her feat; at the same time he thereby gives greater importance to her adversary, Holofernes. Hebbel was horrified at the idea that a woman could kill her lover solely to fulfil a divine mission, without being herself personally involved. This led to the idea of making Judith a widow whose marriage had not been consummated, transforming the murder into an act of vengeance after she has been violated.

She depicts herself as a woman who is frustrated because she is a virgin without children, whose beauty, like belladonna, brings death. She is searching for her identity, and Ephraim, a pallid figure who cannot take up her challenge, is not able to reveal her to herself. Holofernes is the only man who equals or even outstrips her; he is the man she is unconsciously waiting for. Within her, sensual motivation is at odds with religious and patriotic motivation, and it alone justifies her deed. This erotic current is also obvious in the most powerful moments of Acts II and III, which are entirely devoted to it: the Dream and the Prayer in which she interprets her own desires as the will of God. But before embarking on her act she starts doubting its validity, already tormented by the fault that nothing can efface, even if 'through You the impure becomes pure'.

Against Judith Hebbel sets a Holofernes whose character matches hers; no doubt modelled on Napoleon, 'an individual of genius who loses himself in excess', endowed with a cosmic dimension, comparing himself with wild beasts, unleashing himself like the Titanic elements, he is an Antichrist or Superman figure before its time; on several occasions his powerful delineation verges on the grotesque. In the relations between them it is no longer a question of an opposition between Judaism and paganism, but of a triple conflict: between two individuals, within one individual and between the individual and universal law, and this endows the story with a tragic dimension not present in the original story. For Judith feels doubly guilty: guilty because she has acted for personal reasons when she thought she was simply fulfilling her mission, and guilty because she has killed the only man worthy of her. By killing Holofernes she has acted against the law of nature: God has used her as an instrument, but he cannot save her from remorse. At the end of the play she appears as the accused in the eyes of her maidservant, who embodies the judgement of the world. Consequently Judith wants to credit her with the glory of her crime, finally agreeing to assume responsibility for it and undergo the consequent suffering only on condition that they will kill her if she asks them to – if she is carrying Holofernes' child, this would be nothing short of matricide.

The character of Holofernes lent itself so easily to parody, as Hebbel himself was aware, that immediately after Hebbel's drama had been staged in Vienna in 1849 a famous Viennese writer-actor, Nestroy, returned to the subject in the form of a 'travesty'. He exaggerated the general's swaggering and substituted for Judith her brother Joad who does not care in the least about his glory and snatches up the wrong head which has been made specially from cardboard to trick him. The current situation – Vienna had only just emerged from a long siege – inspired jibes aimed at the townspeople of Bethulia in whom the Viennese were easily able to recognize themselves.

THE DESACRALIZATION OF THE MYTH

While respecting the plot, Giraudoux introduced an innovation to the Bible story, making his Judith as tragic a figure as Hebbel's. But her motivation is completely different. Whereas Hebbel's Judith owes her tragic character to her awareness immediately after her murderous deed that she has betrayed her mission and her people, Giraudoux's Judith prides herself on acting purely for personal reasons and considering neither her people nor her God. In Giraudoux's version she is not a widow, but an upper-class young woman who in spite of her worldly life and her flirtations is still a virgin. She shows no leanings towards heroism, quite the reverse, refusing to take any interest in the prophecy according to which the town will be saved by 'the purest and most beautiful of the daughters of Israel'. Thus it is with no idea of fulfilling the prophecy that she decides to go and find Holofernes in his camp, but in order to prove to her fiancé, who symbolizes Jewish cowardice, and to herself that the gift of her person to Holofernes represents an act that is so degrading that it is appropriate only for an exceptional person such as herself. She therefore refuses the help of Suzanne, a prostitute, whom Giraudoux depicts as a counterpart of the heroine in the register of human tenderness, just as he creates Egon as Holofernes' double, in the register of the grotesque – and Judith mistakes Egon for the general. The Holofernes who comes to her rescue has nothing in common with Hebbel's braggart or the monster in the Bible; he is an experienced, urbane Don Juan who expresses himself as a poet. He offers Judith a world without God in which the only rule is to satisfy one's own inclinations, in this instance to succumb to the desire which is drawing them into one another's arms: in short a world from which sin has been banished. Giraudoux's aim of desacralizing the biblical story then finds its clearest manifestation and its climax: Judith is won over, and with no ulterior motive agrees to spend some hours of happiness with Holofernes. She then kills him in order to preserve their love from any degradation and give it eternal value. She clearly assumes responsibility for the act she has carried out for love. But nobody will listen to her – therein lies her drama: not her fiancé, not Suzanne, and not the priests for whom the only truth is religious and official. What does it matter in the end whether Judith loved Holofernes and still loves him, provided the people believe she sacrificed herself in order to save her town? The revelation of a drunken guard, a guardian angel who declares that everything took place in accordance with the will of God without her suspecting it, makes it quite impossible for Judith to rebel. Thus she accepts being brought back, and agrees to keep quiet and shut herself away. The truth of the individual is stifled so as to preserve the myth, i.e. for the advantage of the powerful who will use it for their own personal ends.

Claudel's poem represents a riposte to Giraudoux's play. The poet wants to avenge 'the simple, sublime figure' of Judith mishandled by a 'lascivious, Voltairian scribbler'. He sees in her 'the flower of the wisdom of God, Shekinah, or Sophia' who is struggling against 'the huge materialistic spree in the midst of which we are floundering', incarnated by Holofernes or Nebuchadnezzar.

THE MYTH IN MODERN TIMES

The treatment accorded to the story of Judith by Georg Kaiser at the beginning of the twentieth century, turning it into a comedy, is in line with contemporary concerns, since it was an opportunity for him to illustrate a Freudian point of view. The 'Jewish widow' who was married off very young against her will to Manasses and who has no children is seeking to fill the emptiness of her life; she is disappointed in the two young men sent to her by the Elders. She then decides to go to the Assyrians' camp; Achior finds her and takes her to Holofernes. She is not interested in the old soldier, however, but is fascinated by the effeminate king, Nebuchadnezzar, and thinks she will captivate him by beheading Holofernes; the king is appalled, and takes to his heels! Judith would once again be left to her own resources but for the high priest who takes charge of her.

Henry Bernstein also adopted a modern standpoint by denouncing Judith as frigid; her forced marriage means she cannot respond to the overtures of Holofernes who is completely overwhelmed by her beauty, and she kills him to preserve her independence and guard against the humiliation of love. But the register chosen by Bernstein is at the opposite end of the spectrum from Kaiser's, as it was his intention to alert his public after the First World War to the tragic situation of the Jews.

Another dramatist, Kjeld Abell, effected a transposition of the myth into the contemporary world by setting the biblical episode in a modern plot taking place in Denmark before the Second World War; like Giraudoux's, his Judith is a member of the upper classes with neither the will nor the ability to suppress the enemy, i.e. triumphant Nazism. Holofernes is killed, but by a representative of the people, the brothel madam Mrs Branza.

When we consider the long series of literary works based on the story of Judith from the tenth to the twentieth century, we are struck by her fate as a mythical figure and the diversity of meanings that have been ascribed to her. The story is told sometimes in epic tones, sometimes in a lyrical mode, in tragic terms, but also in a comic guise.

First and foremost Judith represents the Jewess who sacrifices herself to save her people. This was true for the original text and has continued to be true until the present, in minor contemporary works: a fine example of patriotism. In the mediaeval poems, in the tragedies written for schools, and in our own day in the work of Claudel, she is depicted as the beneficient figure of a pious woman who has been turned into a saint. Her name has constantly been linked with current affairs, and her story associated with the struggle for liberty: in France during the Wars of Religion she was the symbol of the oppressed minority; in the seventeenth and eighteenth centuries she incarnated Christianity fighting against Islam; in the twentieth she has stood for democracy about to succumb to the onslaughts of Nazism.

But the story of Judith is not just the story of a people or a group caught up in a dramatic situation, it is also the account of a woman who has to confront a man and kill him after attracting him to her. How can Judith be brought to carry out the act ascribed to her in the Bible? Can she refuse the mission that has been assigned to her? Can she be held responsible? These are the questions that dramatists have set themselves from the nineteenth century on, and in answering them they have turned the heroine into a disturbingly ambiguous figure.

Marcelle Enderlé

Julian (Emperor)

Emperor Julian was born in Constantinople in May 332 AD and died in Persia in June 363 AD. Despite his short life, and a reign of only twenty months, his career encompassed several spectacular events. During his childhood he had a near-miraculous escape when his family were massacred and later, when he was sent in disgrace to Gaul by his uncle Constantius, he acquired great honour there through his victories over the Alemanni. Doubts about the exact circumstances of Julian's death during the campaign in Persia contribute to the enigmatic nature of his persona.

The character of Flavius Claudius Julianus, his actions and his historical role are complex matters that occasionally prove contradictory. Issues that remain unresolved include the real motives for his chastity, Julian's prolonged dissimulation of his move away from Christianity, and his ambiguous attitude towards Christians. He has been alternately denounced as a devious politician, or heralded as the model of the good prince and perfect lawmaker – a pattern of wisdom and tolerance. For a considerable time he suffered the punitive fate of being known as Julian the Apostate. It is difficult to reconcile the hero of the Battle of Strasbourg with the mystical pagan who wrote the *Hymn to King Helios* or *Hymn to the Mother of the Gods*. Julian's controversial personality has inspired a profusion of literary works over the sixteen centuries since his death, ranging from short poems to epics in verse, a great many historical novels and a number of plays.

During his thirty-one years Julian was a philosopher, a mystagogue – Prudentius in his *Apotheosis* (453) accused him of worshipping 'three hundred thousand gods' – a religious reformer, a military leader, Caesar then Emperor. Any examination of the man – be it from a psychological viewpoint or within the context of the history of religion, or in relation to his political roles, could lead to conflicting conclusions. Parisians, for example, have always retained a certain fondness for Julian, who liked living beside the Seine (de Jouy: *Julien dans les Gaules* 1827); while Chateaubriand made the point that the people would not 'see another emperor crowned in Paris' until Napoleon's day. To German scholars, Julian epitomizes the difference between two types of civilization – the Graeco-Roman and the Teutonic.

BIRTH OF THE LEGEND: JULIAN THE APOSTATE AND MAGICIAN

Manuscript *Add 14641* (*c.* 502–33 AD) in the British Library contains the story of Eusebius, a bishop of Rome; it describes the sufferings he allegedly received at Julian's hands. Following this is the story of 'Jovinian' (Jovian), supposedly recounted by Bishop Eusebius himself. The latter part of the tale tells of Aploris (Apollinaris)?, a close adviser to Jovian, who restored Christianity. This part of the story describes Julian's activities from the beginning of his expedition to Persia until his death. The writing conveys an atmosphere of wonders and prodigies, with constant divine interventions, visions, signs and premonitory dreams. The part relating to Eusebius in Rome, which cannot be integrated into the story of Julian – as the emperor never went to Rome, has had very little literary impact. Only the Roman writer Pietro Cossa found inspiration in it for a historical play (1876). The second part, moreover, introduced the theme of St Mercury (one of the Forty Martyrs of Sebastea who were killed by being left to die on a frozen pond), being brought back to life by the Holy Virgin specifically so that he could go and kill the Apostate. This theme became an essential element of the legend, and is present in many of the literary works that feature Julian.

A second manuscript (*Add 7192*; British Library) dating from the seventh century contains fragments relating to Julien's apostasy and his use of magic. Cupidity is cited as one of the motives for his behaviour, and the text also supplies an interesting example of a pact with the devil. Its character of Magnus the magician is based on the historical figure Maximus of Ephesus, a theurgist. The manuscript cites the dreadful practice of removing a live foetus from its mother's womb, in order to invoke the spirits of the dead. This ritual was described in the work of Ammianus Marcellinus (XXIX, 2, 17), where it was attributed to one Numerius, a member of Valens' entourage. The final fragment describes Julian's period in Athens in the company of St Basil and St Gregory of Nazianzus, and shows him conversing with demons.

It is interesting to note that the character of Faust may originate from the fusion into a single entity of Julian and Magnus; and Julian as a magician was on a par with Faust.

JULIAN, THE PERSECUTOR OF THE CHRISTIANS: THE ADVERSARY, THE IMAGE OF THE ANTICHRIST

In their writings, both St Gregory of Nazianzus and St Cyril of Alexandria are scathing about Julian, and accuse him of persecutions that never took place. The image of Julian that predominated until the sixteenth century was that of an apostate emperor who persecuted Christians.

The death of Julian was a popular subject in Byzantine art. In the iconographic programme of the churches, *St Mercury Smiting Julian* features alongside the other 'warrior saints' – Demetrius, George, Nestor and sometimes

St Michael. In such pictures, Julian is shown lying on the ground, being trampled by the horse's hooves. There are also a great many portraits of St Mercury alone, armed with his lance.

The second part of *Gallicanus* by Hrotsvitha, the Abbess of Gandersheim (after 950 AD), celebrates the heroism of the martyrs Gallicanus, John and Paul, who were persecuted by Julian. In the eighth book of his *Exceptions allégoriques* (*c.* 1150) Hugues de St Victor lists all the Emperor's supposed crimes, deliberately rendering him an odious figure; the *Kaieserchronik* written at Regensburg around the same time also describes Julian as a pitiless champion of pagan religion. The *Miracle de Saint Basile* by Gautier de Coinci (circa ?1223) and *La Légende dorée* by Jacques de Voragine (circa ?1260) bring together the story of St Basil and the killing of Julian by St Mercury. In the three poems (*Meistersänge* 1553) in which he refers to Julian, Hans Sachs perpetuates this traditional, highly negative image.

Julian occupies a prominent place in Jesuit drama in Germany. The most remarkable play in this category is *Julian der Apostat* (1608) by Jeremias Drexel, who presents a series of actions that are psychologically motivated.

In Spain (*Cardinal de Bethléem* 1610) Lope de Vega introduces Julian as a minor character who practises necromancy and who is put to death by St Mercury. Luis Vélez de Guevara in his play *Juliano Apostata* (between 1610 and 1644) integrates St Mercury into the dramatic action, setting him against the demoniac Julian. In *Die Verkehrte Welt* (1672) by the German writer Grimmelshausen, the portrait of the Apostate attains frightening dimensions: the abyss of despair at the prospect of irrevocable damnation is described through the medium of a sincere confession.

The traditional image is perpetuated by the writer Friedrich de la Motte Fouqué, who devoted two works to Julian. The first is a poem entitled *La Légende de l'Empereur Julianus l'Apostat* – a youthful work probably dating from about 1800, and published in 1816, in which the author closely follows *La Légende dorée.* The second is a long novella, *Les Histoires de l'Empereur Julianus et de ses Chevaliers* (1818), a relatively complex work set in a romantic mediaeval period and into which the author introduces the rather incongruous themes of a sworn oath, redemption and love. In 1817 in an account published in the *Journal des Débats,* Charles Nodier compared Julian to Bonaparte, who was himself the image of the Antichrist. Twenty years later in the *Dictionnaire de la Conversation* he described him as a kind of Voltaire: 'There was some connection in the direction followed by these two men, the two most violent enemies that hell ever stirred up against Christ.'

THE REVERSAL: FROM THE 'HISTORICAL' JULIAN TO THE PHILOSOPHER

The reinstatement of Julian's good name in the face of historical prejudice is based on two main factors. One is that he was a prolific writer; although his war memoirs have been lost, much informative autobiographical material remains, notably the *Hymn to King Helios* and *Misopōgōn*. Second, in anticipation that he would be misrepresented, the historian Ammianus Marcellinus, who went with him to Persia, and his friend Libanius, a rhetor, carefully established files of information rehabilitating him; these have always been accessible to anyone wishing to consult them.

Jean Larmat's researches have ascertained that *Le Mystère de Saint Martin* (1496) by André de la Vigne, which contains a very subtle portrait of the Emperor, was the start of a reappraisal of the man. (It is interesting to note that St Martin of Tours fought as a soldier in Julian's army.) In his *Traité sur la technique oratoire* (1535) Erasmus attempted to ascertain the historical truth about Julian, while Jean Bodin's *Méthode pour faciliter la connaissance de l'histoire* (circa 1560) contains a fair and reasonable portrait of him. In the famous chapter entitled 'De la liberté de conscience' in Book II of his *Essais* (1580), Montaigne completed the reversal, going from partial rehabilitation to outright praise.

> He was indeed a very great and rare man, someone whose spirit was vividly imbued with the philosophical discourses according to which he set out to regulate all his actions; and truly there is no sort of virtue of which he has not left very notable examples.

Dating that period, two very different images of the Emperor continued to co-exist. In the seventeenth century Montaigne's theme was powerfully developed by La Mothe le Vayer, who turned Julian into a sort of moral hero, devoting forty pages to him in his treatise *De la Vertu des Payens* (1642). Bossuet on the other hand saw Julian's reign as a decisive test for Christianity, part of the providential plan (*Discours sur l'histoire universelle* 1681).

JULIAN IN THE EIGHTEENTH CENTURY: THE PHILOSOPHER BECOMES A MODEL OF TOLERANCE

In the second edition of his *Characteristicks of Men, Manners, Opinions, Times* (1714) Shaftesbury dwells on Julian's spirit of tolerance, giving as example a long quotation from his *Epistles to the Bostrenians* (wrongly and tendentiously interpreted) which Shaftesbury believed was arguing along the same lines.

The *Epistles* and Julian's other texts cited above became decisive points of reference, Diderot was directly inspired by them in his *Pensées philosophiques* (1746), even arguing against the tag 'apostate' which until then had been attached to Julian's name. In his article for the *Encyclopédie* on Eclecticism, Diderot describes Julian as 'the honour of eclecticism'.

This development continued both among the Platonists in Cambridge and in the work of Voltaire and Diderot. The trail had been blazed moreover by Abbé La Bletterie; in his *Histoire de Jovien* (1746) he sought to assess Julian fairly as a 'singular man'. Now seen as a model of tolerance and respect for others, Julian almost became the prototype for the Good Prince! In his *Examen important de Milord Bolingbroke* Voltaire also turned him into a militant deist, like himself:

> I think if this great man had lived, with time he would have freed religion of the most vulgar superstitions and accustomed the Romans to recognizing a God who had formed gods and men, and to addressing all their homage to him.

In 1877 the Greek writer Kleon Rhangabe, an heir to the French philosophers, produced *Julien l'Apostat* – a huge tragedy of 10,000 lines in which a pastiche of the European Romantics is found alongside violent attacks on the Orthodox Church. His play is preceded by a crushing, explanatory Preface written in scholarly language.

CONFLICTING IMAGES OF JULIAN: THE THEURGIST AND THE ABERRANT MYSTIC

In the eighteenth century in Germany the pendulum swung halfway back, particularly with Johan Georg Hamann (*Wolken* 1761; *Des Ritters von Rosencreuz letzte Willensmeynung* 1772). He stressed Julian's leaning towards the irrational. Herder condemned him for having tried to 'paint the face of the corpse of paganism' and because of his absolutism (*Feuilles éparses* 1786).

Edward Gibbon, the author of *The Decline and Fall of the Roman Empire* (1776–88), made Julian the object of a detailed psychological analysis, finally presenting him in all his complexity with the contradictions inherent within him.

> When he was in a state to reflect coldly Julian preferred the useful, beneficent virtues of the Antonines; but his ambitious spirit was inflamed by the glory of Alexander and he longed with equal ardour for the good opinion of the wise and the applause of the crowd.

It was precisely because of the complexity of his character and the virtual impossibility of presenting it fairly that Schiller abandoned his project of writing a play about Julian.

Chateaubriand wrote about Julian on several occasions, particularly in a late work entitled *Etudes historiques*, vol. 1 (1834), in which two 'discourses' are devoted to him. Although the author makes visible efforts to be impartial and understanding when describing the redoubtable enemy of the 'Galileans', this does not prevent him from quite uncritically repeating completely fabricated anecdotes reported by such people as Theodoret, a systematic detractor of Julian's.

In 1822 Aubrey de Vere Hunt wrote a dramatic poem centred on Maximus of Ephesus, presenting him as the Emperor's 'evil genius'. Julian is given no personality of his own, and is just a plaything in the other's hands; the only act Julian carries out independently is the killing of Maximus, who has transferred his allegiance to the Persians! The best parts of the work are the lyrical passages in which the Spirit of the Empire appears to Julian.

Alfred de Vigny devoted a youthful tragedy to Julian (1816) which he subsequently destroyed. In 1832 he started to think of writing a *Deuxième Consultation du Dr Noir* – like the first, it would have contained three tales devoted to Julian, Melanchthon and Rousseau respectively, each ending in a 'suicide'. Its theme was to have been the influence of religion on morality. The part of the work that was actually written is called *Daphne* after the place where the temple to Apollo near Antioch is located; it dates mainly from 1837. Vigny did feature Julian in it, but the main character is Libanius, the Old Sage of Antioch. Julian comes to seek his advice and strangely enough the philosopher disapproves of his attempts to restore paganism: history cannot go back on its tracks. Julian's longest speech is a summary of his *Hymn to King Helios*. After realizing the futility of his efforts Julian in despair sets out on his Persian campaign, and his death is portrated as a disguised suicide (which it may well have been).

Vigny spent years reflecting on the character of Julian and there is a great deal of material for the uncompleted work in the notes and notebooks published under the title *Journal*. In 1833 he even admitted to identifying with him: 'If metempsychosis exists, I have been this man. His role, life and character would have suited me better than those of any other man in history.'

It should be stressed that Ballanche, Gobineau and Nicolas Martin (who made a verse translation of some passages in Julian's work so as to form a 'Gazette en vers', 1862 and 1875) come to the same conclusion as Vigny. Martin, speaking in the character of 'Impartial History' declares: 'You travelled counter to progress.'

To date, it is Henrik Ibsen who has produced the most striking example of the unresolved contradictions pertaining to Julian. He had originally planned a trilogy based on the Emperor, but subsequently replaced the entire section about the Battle of Strasbourg with a story; his work, published in 1873, consists of just two parts. The overall title is *Kejser og Galilaer* (Emperor and Galilean: A World Historic Drama); each part is in five acts, the first play being called *The Apostasy of Caesar*, and the second *Julian Emperor*. Very little is known about Julian's wife Helene. Ibsen portrays her as a cruel, sensual woman who, as she is dying from poison, tells Julian that she has been his brother Gallus' mistress. The dramatist does not seem to know that Julian was brought up in an Aryan culture, nor – although it is mentioned by all his sources – does he take account of the fact that Julian had reverted to paganism at a very early age and concealed this for ten years, proclaiming it publicly only when he became Emperor. The grandiose evocation scene in Act III, in which Maximus of Ephesus conjures up Cain and Judas, implying that Julian is the reincarnation of the same principle, is probably based on a passage by Neander on the Cainites.

Maximus is presented as the apostle of the 'Third Reign'; he respects

Christ because Christ is a prophet, but he foretells the coming of a religion finer than Christianity. The Third Reign would bring about the reconciliation of the spirit and the flesh, of paganism and Christianity. At the same time Ibsen, who had been deeply affected by witnessing scenes from the Franco-Prussian War and the Paris Commune, followed the idea according to which events and human beings are directed by a 'will' – the agent of rigorous determinism.

The first part of Ibsen's work covers a period of ten years; the second, which was probably written too quickly, relates to the twenty months of Julian's reign. The main protagonist is something of a caricature, with only his negative side in evidence. As a personal enemy of the Galilean he pursues Jesus' disciples with hatred, persecuting them cruelly whilst proving unable to detach himself completely from Christianity. He is all resentment, hypocrisy and vanity, to such an extent that we wonder if this can really be the same character as in *The Apostasy of Caesar*. Ibsen even goes so far as to rearrange the historical sequence of events so that Julian's order to set fire to his fleet on the Tigris seems the act of a madman. The play ends with the emphasis on predestination, and the comment that some people may be 'damned through obedience'.

In the first play Ibsen incorporated whole pages from the work of the historians he had consulted, firstly German writers like Neander, J.E. Auer and David Strauss, then the French writer Albert de Broglie who wrote *L'Eglise et l'Empire romain au IVe siècle* (1856). In *Julian Emperor*, perhaps through a lack of sufficient preparatory research, he went completely astray, and it is hard to understand how he could have thought that these two plays constituted his masterpiece.

JULIAN IN GERMANY IN THE NINETEENTH CENTURY

Julian continued to arouse the interest of German historians and writers throughout the nineteenth century, mainly because the Battle of Strasbourg was perceived as a confrontation between the Gallo-Romans and the Germans (Alemanni). In the long historical novel by Felix Dahn, *Julian der Apostat*, completed in 1893 and more than 700 pages, the character of Merowech is especially important. As the author's spokesman he advocates a Nietzschean 'Beyond Morality' and a religion of the people.

Between 1866 and 1902 many German dramatists featured Julian in their plays, sometimes seeing him through the eyes of the eighteenth century (K. Boruttau, Andreas May in *Zénobie la Dernière Païenne* 1867, Hermann Riotte, P. Seeberg, J. Wieser von Mährenheim), sometimes portraying him as the enemy of Christianity (W. Molitor, A. Trabert, J. Mayrhofer). The latter group condemn Julian with as little subtlety as the writers for the Jesuit theatre.

The most important work in this category is Eichendorff's verse epic *Julian*

(1853), which has great lyrical beauty. In it the mysterious Fausta embodies the evil seductiveness of paganism.

JULIAN, RESTORER OF PAGANISM AND DEFENDER OF HELLENISM

During the past two hundred years, the writers who have viewed Julian in a favourable light are generally those who emphasize his Hellenism and have an idealized conception of paganism in Antiquity. In *Du Polythéisme romain*, an uncompleted work by Benjamin Constant published posthumously by Jacques Matter in 1833, there is a collection of material intended to be used in writing Chapter VIII of Book XVII. Consisting of extracts from Julian's own writings, or from Libanius' *Panegyric*, it is a useful account both of Julian's fundamentally mystic nature, and of the fact that when he set out to reform paganism his sole source of inspiration was the Christian practices in which he had been brought up.

In his book *Thréicie* (1798–9) Quintus Aucler advocated a return to paganism, mentioning Julian in this connection. Subsequently, in his study of Quintus Aucler, written in 1851, Nerval made a long summary of this work with many quotations from it, and he in turn referred to Julian who had attempted to restore the cult of the ancient gods ('They will return, those gods . . .'). In his posthumously published poem 'La colombe' (*Dernières Chansons* 1872) Louis Bouilhet depicted Julian lamenting the death of paganism; he himself announced the approaching end of Christianity. *Les Rêveries d'un païen mystique* by Louis Ménard includes a poem entitled 'La Dernière Nuit de Julien' in which the Spirit of the Empire urges the Emperor to resign himself to the inevitable.

In two articles in *Le Temps* on Gaston Bossier's book *La Fin du Paganisme* (1891, reissued in 1892 in vol. 4 of *La Vie littéraire*) Anatole France speaks sympathetically about Julian. In the second volume of *L'Enquête aux pays du Levant* (1923) Maurice Barrès expatiates on the story of his visit to Daphne in June 1914, and to conjure up the memory of Julian quotes at length from Emile Lamé, a disciple of Ménard's.

The English writer Swinburne refers to Julian in two poems, 'Hymn to Proserpine' (1866) and 'The Last Oracle' (1876), expressing his own allegiance to paganism, while the Greek poet Constantine Kavafis has also used Julian as his mouthpiece, in some beautiful poems. The mystical pagan, the champion of Hellenism, is well portrayed in D. Merejkowski's novel (1908) or in the poem 'Julianus Imperator' by C. L'Andelyn (E. Pittard), 1922. André Fraigneau's sensitive story *Le Songe de l'Empereur* (1952) belongs in a category of its own.

The Hungarian writer Joseph Revay in *Hélios, tu m'as abandonné* (1961) demonstrates the untenable aspects of the Emperor's religious attitude. In an essay (1953) G. Henein sees him first and foremost as the champion of an antiChristian feeling that matches his own. *Golgatha* (1901) and *Le Poison de la Judée* (1905–6) by the Czech writer J.S. Marchar also stress this aspect. Machar's presentation of Julian, directly inspired from the Emperor's own writings, is very reminiscent of Nicolas Martin's.

OBJECTIVITY AND SUBJECTIVITY

Among recent objective treatments of Julian, *Julien l'Illuminé* by Wolfgang Cordan (1950) and *Julian* by Gore Vidal (1962) should be mentioned. Vidal's book is one of the most ambitious to have featured the Emperor as its central character, successfully on the whole, apart from the odd idea of giving Julian a natural son. In his book *Apostat* (1968) Luc Estang chose to give a parallel account of Julian's career and his own renunciation of the Christian religion – resulting in some confusion, even though the book is full of subtle insights.

The most varied and contradictory ideologies have been projected on to Julian, but this also raises the question of whether several different Julians existed at the same time – a Pirandellian concept before its time! There can be no possibility of ever arriving at a simple explanation of his character. However, his most distinctive aspect remains his attempt to restore paganism – the unique expression of a religious and metaphysical disquiet that nothing could assuage and, which, to a large extent explains the interest that he has aroused ever since.

Jean Richer

Koumen: an Initiation Myth of Peul Herdsmen

Koumen is an initiation story that was collected and recorded by Amadou Hampate Ba in a Peul encampment in the Linguère circle in Moguer, between Senegal and The Gambia. His source was master Ardo Dembo, who would recite it to his students as a test. The story, which is traditionally narrated throughout the Niger loop and the Senegal valley, takes its name from the Peul herdsmen's first master of initiation, Koumen. As the assistant of the spirit Tyanaba who, in the Peul pantheon, is the delegate on earth of the divine creator Gueno and mythical owner of the first herd, Koumen most frequently appears to human beings in the form of a child with a greying beard – the symbol of wisdom and experience. He holds the secrets of initiation as a herdsman.

The tale recounts the different stages of the initiation of Soule Sadio, the first *silatgi* (priest of the Peul community). It is structured into twelve sequences, organized around the theme of the symbolic journey undertaken by the postulant accompanied by his initiator Koumen, whom he meets under a large tamarind tree. This symbolic journey is represented by his actual physical passage through twelve successive clearings; these correspond with thc twelve months of the lunar year and form the stages of his progress towards the light of absolute knowledge.

The aim of Soule Sadio's quest is to acquire the secrets about livestock, symbolised by a sacred bovine figure, the name of which he must try to obtain from Forofforondou, Koumen's wife. The 'goddess of milk and butter', Foroforondou holds the secrets of animal health and fertility. Soule Sadio is presented to her in the tenth clearing, and she subsequently takes over from Koumen to complete his initiation.

A Peul herdsman's initiation consists of thirty-three levels corresponding to the thirty-three phonemes of the Peul language. To these are added three higher and 'invisible' levels, which are automatically acquired after the thirty-third. In a mystical comparison with the three envelopes surrounding a foetus, they are called 'the three darknesses of the womb' and signify that on a spiritual level, man returns to the foetal state to be then 'born' into a new life in which he will be able to bear the title 'son'.

During the course of his 'journey', Soule Sadio has to undergo many ordeals. These represent the fight he must have with himself in order to progress. Thus he overcomes the fear caused in him by the appearance of the herdsman of a black herd (symbol of the occult aspect of knowledge) and resists the temptations of the frog, guardian of the sanctuaries of initiation (pond, pool), and finally does not flee but confronts frightening animals, symbols of the wild forces that man must master, recalling the requirement for a herdsman to be vigilant. The supreme test, presented by Foroforondou in the twelfth clearing, comes in the form of an enigma which he must solve. It consists of untying a rope with twenty-eight knots while naming the guardian spirits of the herds to which they correspond, one by one. The group of knots represents the genesis of the world and the twenty-eight 'homes' of the moon. For each correct answer the postulant receives a reward: the right to suck the tongues of his two initiators and to suckle at Foroforondou's left breast. He also receives tools useful to a herdsman: a milk whisk, a calabash for milking, a rope to tie up the calf, the herdman's special belt, a herdsman's staff, the goddess' ring, a supply of calabash seeds and the absolute ownership of the *Ndett*, which frees him of all forms of dependency on others. He is then ordained as a 'seer', for he is the man who has met the goddess and received all the secrets from her.

Having thus reached the summit of knowledge, Soule Sadio can now return to the world of people. However, on the way back he still has to test his strength against a lion. In combat he strikes the lion on the nose with his initiate's staff and keeps the tuft of hair from between its eyebrows as a talisman. This talisman is then placed under his head while he sleeps, bringing him the dream in which is revealed the name of the sacred bovine, the hermaphrodite with a multicoloured coat, symbol of supreme knowledge of things relating to the life of the herdsman.

Each important revelation is preceded by a purification ritual and a sign of the master's approval. Thus, once the pact with Koumen has been sealed, the latter opens to Soule Sadio a thicket of creepers which forms a curtain and represents the patience and flexibility that the future initiate will need. Soule Sadio must also look at his reflection in the clear waters of the pool and wash himself in the pond he finds behind the door of creepers; the ritual bath strengthens his eyesight and enables him to see into the future (theme of transparency). Characterized by his humble attitude of strict obedience, the future initiate vows to defend 'cows, women and orphans'; he is also subject to a prohibition: he must not look at the master's navel, that sacred central point, symbolizing the profound knowledge which can only be acquired by degrees.

The first revelations relate to the cosmogony of which the postulant must have a perfect understanding before he can have access to the secrets of the herdsman's life. He is placed in contact with the four elements of creation, which come in the form of a pot (earth) filled with water, in front of which a snake blows on the fire while playing a flute (air) with seven holes. This snake with ninety-six scales represents Tyanaba, God's delegate on earth and mythical owner of the cattle; his presence signals to Soule Sadio that, like Tyanaba, he must shed his skin and change at both the physical and spiritual levels.

Soule Sadio is then instructed in the correspondences established between the four elements, the four points of the compass, and the four Peul tribes with the colours attributed to them:

Dyal (herdsmen): yellow-fire-east
Ba (warriors): red-air-west
So (knowledge of the bush): black-water-south
Bari (marabouts): white-earth-north

On his exit from the fifth clearing, Soule Sadio becomes a complete person. He has emerged from the primordial darkness of the time before Creation and can contemplate the light of the seven suns in their colours of the rainbow. Each sun dominates a different sky; its twelve rays, corresponding to the twelve lunar months, constituting the 'path of God'. The initiate then meets the 'one-eyed spirit' – the blacksmith. With his one eye 'of outer and inner knowledge' he is the spirit of war who possesses the secret of invulnerability and also serves as a reminder of an alliance between the Peul and blacksmiths.

It is only in the second stage of the initiation, once the pact with Foroforondou has been sealed in the tenth clearing, that Soule Sadio may ask questions. The goddess appears, beating cream in a calabash churn and making a terrible noise. She promises to take him to the furthest point of human knowledge and as a sign of her approval gives him a handful of jujubes (symbol of the summit of initiation) in a calabash, which is the image of the world's womb. To purify himself, Soule Sadio takes the bitter rind of the citron and the bitter juice of the dwarf baobab (symbol of longevity), which protect 'the eyes that see and the mouth that speaks'.

In the twelfth clearing a new ritual is set up, in the guise of a preparation for the supreme test: Soule Sadio washes twice in the pond, from head to foot and from foot to head, thus signifying that he dies in his old state to be spiritually reborn. This rebirth will be completed once the hermaphrodite bovine allows him to ride it at the end of the ritual and a calf comes out of the pool, in an allegory of the new birth of the initiate. For her part the goddess goes through a specific ritual that is also practised to cure the sick: she takes clods of earth from two anthills and two termite hills, one of which is inhabited and the other not, moulds them together using water from the pool and gives the clay ball to Soule Sadio to place at the foot of the tree. By these gestures she unites the full with the empty, and communicates to him 'the power which tames and the knowledge which is acquired', the power of healing. The vast area of ground in which this ritual takes place represents the universe and the first grazing land.

Analysis of this myth brings to light the themes of the meeting and pact with the initiator, of the journey and qualifying tests and of symbolic death which is the prelude to the spiritual rebirth of the initiate in water, all characteristic themes of the initiation story. The originality of *Koumen* lies in the presence of a woman master (the goddess Foroforondou) at Koumen's side, who expresses the major concern of the Peul herdsmen: the fertility and health of their animals, man being regarded as the double or twin of the mythical hermaphrodite bovine. Astral symbolism is also significant with each element of the organization of the herdsman's life having a constant relation to the cosmogony.

Nicole Goisbeault

The Labyrinth

The labyrinth in modern literature is an image of multiple significance, but it was not always so. Indeed, the twentieth century can justifiably be called the 'age of the labyrinth' in that it tends to see labyrinths where there are none. Drawings of labyrinths have existed since the prehistoric age, and the image is present in a wide range of cultures; the labyrinth is also sometimes linked to a myth or a ritual, although known cases of this are rare. Its remote and varied origins, its link with the sacred, and the multiple symbolism inherent in its image, give it a mythical structure and make it a subject of fascination for writers and artists alike.

In the field of western literature (to which the present study will confine itself), the image was not dissociated from the Greek myth of Theseus until relatively late. The theme, insofar as it is associated with wandering, and the actual term 'labyrinth', were only slowly incorporated into modern European languages. There are two types of labyrinth: those with a single passage (which were the only ones to be represented pictorially until the middle of the sixteenth century), and those with several passages containing intersections and offering possibilities for choice, error, etc. Although the labyrinth appears to be concerned with the concept of space and the problems arising in relation to it, it can also be used to illustrate the concept of time – of which the eternal return to the beginning presents a finite image. In a literary text, the labyrinth may appear as an explicit theme, but it can also serve as a latent structure. It may, or may not, evoke a reference to the Greek myth. On a basic level, its negative properties are usually in evidence, whereas in more elevated works its sacred origins are recalled and the image assumes a positive meaning.

A vast body of literature has been produced on the subject of the labyrinth although, paradoxically, the phenomenon as such *does not exist.* Classical authors writing about the famous labyrinth of Crete each imagined it in a different way, while archaeologists do not know whether it ever existed or, if it did, in what form. In the modern world, there are various updated versions of the structure – halls of mirrors at fairgrounds, mazes, labyrinth board games, etc. – although, of course, these are only weak manifestations of the concept. The labyrinth is above all a mental image, a symbol unrelated to any architectural prototype. Beyond the basic image of a winding structure in which the protagonist loses his or her sense of direction, the appearance of the labyrinth is open to imagination, and its implications are open to interpretation. By closely observing the points at which it becomes associated with related images ('natural' labyrinths such as a forest or a dream; 'artificial' labyrinths such as a city or a book), and especially by trying to understand the message conveyed by the image on each occasion, it is possible to identify five main stages in the development of the myth. Each stage seems to create a particular image of the labyrinth and to use it as a metaphor to represent a particular situation or dilemma fundamental to the human condition. For the age of Classical Antiquity it represented the single and the multiple, for the Middle Ages the horizontal and the vertical, for the Renaissance (fourteenth to sixteenth centuries) the exterior and the interior, for the Classic period (seventeenth to eighteenth centuries) reality and appearance, and for the modern age the finite and the infinite. However, each stage may continue to ask the question(s) which had been asked previously, while containing the seeds of future questions. Each period bears witness to a particular philosophical preoccupation, without precluding the others by whose presence it may in fact be modified.

The term 'labyrinth' – used by historians and geographers to describe complicated constructions whose use was not immediately apparent – rarely occurs in Greek and Latin literature other than in relation to the myths of Theseus, Ariadne, Daedalus and the Minotaur. The events for which it provides a setting are therefore associated with the myth of the labyrinth – and possibly even with the ritual which preceded or accompanied it. When the labyrinth is evoked in literature, the most obvious of these events is probably the task imposed upon Theseus of choosing between the various ways of reaching the Minotaur, and then of finding his way out of the labyrinth. A multiplicity of passageways suddenly opens up before the Greek hero, who confronts the vertiginous experience of the plurality of possibility. The first tension to be represented by the labyrinth is therefore that between the one and the many. Ariadne's magic thread shows him the only way of both entering and leaving the labyrinth. In other words, the myth presents the problem of choice, but at the same time provides the means of solving it. It offers plurality, but immediately reduces it to the singular. Conversely, in the philosophical works of Plato, the image of the labyrinth is linked to the loss of direction – an idea which may signal the first break with mythical thought.

The earliest trace of the word 'labyrinth' is probably that found in the form 'da – pu – ri – to', written in Linear B on two Minoan tablets from circa 1400 BC. One refers to a jar of honey for the 'lady of the labyrinth' (Ariadne?). Herodotus was the first to use the term in the Greek script to describe the Egyptian building with 3,000 rooms that the Pharaoh Amenemhet III had erected to the south of his pyramid at Hawara near Lake Moeris. Although this building, half of which was constructed underground, was not a labyrinth but a vast geometric combination of rooms, Diodorus, Strabo and – in Latin – Pliny the Elder, continued to use the word to refer to it. The latter two authors even claimed that it had provided Daedalus with the inspiration for the construction of the Cretan labyrinth. All three also mention other 'labyrinths' known to Antiquity (at Lemnos, Samos and Clusium) without the word appearing to be any more appropriate than in the case of the monument constructed by Amenemhet III. Although the intention of those responsible for these constructions remains unclear, the labyrinth is presented as an artificial and complex structure.

The term may have been used in the *Theseid* (sixth century), but the work has not survived; the first references to the labyrinth appear in fragments by Pherecydes (circa 450 BC) and Cleidemus (circa 375). It is worthy of note that in Euripides' *Heracles furens* (circa 421 BC), Theseus recalls that he killed the 'bull of Cnossus' (1. 1326) but makes no mention of the labyrinth. Isocrates, recounting the story of Theseus in his *Encomium of Helen*, also refers to the 'monster which was half man, half bull' (X, 28) but does not mention its legendary dwelling. In the Greek language, it was not until Callimachus' *Hymn to Delos* (third century BC) that Theseus and his companions were described as having 'emerged from the tortuous detours of the labyrinth' (311). It was only then that the image was developed in the Latin works of Virgin and Ovid where Daedalus was described as having 'unlocked the building's treacherous, winding ways' (*Aeneid* VI, 29) and 'planned the work, and traced the baffling paths, with windings intricate' (*Metamorphoses* III, 166–7). Finally, at the end of the first or beginning of the second century AD, the Greek philosopher and biographer, Plutarch, examined the nature of the structure more systematically in order to determine whether it was a place from which one could not find the way out, or simply a prison (*Life of Theseus*, 15 and 16). In all the above instances, whether the story is based on Daedalus or Theseus, the labyrinth remains associated with the myth. It does not appear independently of the group of myths of which it forms the centre, outside the context of the story of the four protagonists of Greek legend, nor without a reference to the guiding thread which winds through it and basically invalidates it. This thread may also lead us beyond the myth to the ritual itself.

It is possible that Homer was referring, indirectly but significantly, to the labyrinth when, in Book XVIII of the *Iliad*, he compared the 'khoros' sculpted by Hephaestus of Achilles' shield to the one 'that once in the wide space of Cnossus, Daedalus built for Ariadne of the lovely tresses' (1. 520–2), and from this evokes the dance that took place there. The problem arises as to how to interpret the word 'khoros', i.e. as a 'dancing floor' (the choice of most modern translators), as a low relief depicting a dance or, as one theory suggests, as a dance floor with a choreographic and labyrinthine layout. And did Ariadne herself lead the dancing? The important thing, in any event, is the connection between the stories of Daedalus and Ariadne and ritual dance, for this demonstrates that a religious ceremony was involved and that the myth was originally associated with a ritual. In the surviving narratives of the adventures of Theseus, dance is constantly used to echo the experience of the labyrinth. For example, in his *Hymn to Delos*, Callimachus describes the statue dedicated to Aphrodite by Theseus when, on their return from Crete, the hero and his companions 'danced in a circle around your altar to the sound of the cithara and Theseus led the dance' (311–3). Plutarch later recorded that this dance imitated the twists and turns of the labyrinth and noted that it was still practised at the time by the inhabitants of Delos who called it 'grenaros', i.e. 'the dance of the crane' (*Life of Theseus*, XXI). Not only do dance theoreticians frequently refer to the labyrinth, but the two concepts have also remained linked throughout the course of history and literature.

In the same vein, the labyrinth is also associated with a somewhat mysterious religious procession, the 'Trojae lusus', a sort of equestrian parade reinstated in Rome by Augustus. In Book V of the *Aeneid*, Virgil evokes it by making it the last of the games celebrated at the funeral of Anchises (l. 545–604). To convey some idea of the complexity of the training of the young horsemen, the poet compares it with the task of finding one's way through the Cretan labyrinth. The comparison is significant in that the Trojan game may have been part of the same magical and ritual representation as the labyrinth. The complexity of the latter is emphasized to suggest the highly elaborate performance of the ritual. Here too, it is possible that, to make the exercise possible for the young boys aged between seven and seventeen who took part, the idea of a layout was introduced which marked out the course on the ground and formed the pattern of a labyrinth. (On the Etruscan oenochoe of Tragliatella, beside the two horsemen taking part in the game, is depicted a labyrinth on which the word 'Truia' is inscribed, and it is a well-known fact that the names of the many stone labyrinths in northern Europe are all based on that of Troy, e.g. 'Trojaburg'.) In the parade described by Virgil, the labyrinth actually moves. Its function was possibly to prepare the soul of the dead person so that it did not take the wrong turning in its descent into the Underworld. It should be remembered that, in Book VI, it is *before* he descends into the Underworld that Aeneas contemplates the door of the temple constructed by Daedalus, on which the entire myth and the labyrinth itself are depicted.

In contrast to these traditional and pre-Classical uses, Plato employs the term in a sense that to a large extent anticipates its later meaning. In *Euthydemus* (291 b), Socrates chooses the image to describe a particular line of reasoning which, while under the impression that it is reaching a conclusion, in fact returns to its starting point. Apart from Herodotus, this is the first use of the word which does not make an explicit reference to the myth as well as being the first metaphorical use. At this point, the labyrinth embarks upon its autonomous and secular career as a symbolic structure. It becomes the opposite of the protected passageway of the myth and the ritual, and instead represents – for the mind which is daring enough to venture into it – the risk of returning to its 'point de départ', and the place of wandering. The possibility of being able to choose freely the path only partially opened up by the myth, is retained by philosophical thought as it makes the transition from 'mythos' to 'logos'. Indeed, this view of the labyrinth has made it the basis of modern reasoning: thinking means entering the labyrinth and running the risk of losing your way. The labyrinth is also a metaphor for aporia and for this reason forms the basis of western thought.

During the Middle Ages, the clerics who wrote glossaries for classical texts had a very precise idea of the labyrinth constructed by Daedalus. Notes probably written by Remigius of Auxerre (circa 900) explain that, in the works of Virgil, Prudentius and Sedulius, the labyrinth is cited as an underground structure with one hundred entrances, built by Daedalus as a prison for the Minotaur, and from which it was impossible to find an exit. Copyists also had their own idea of the meaning of the word. They vied with one another in repeating: 'dicitur labyrinthus quasi labor intus', i.e. it is called the labyrinth because of the hardship experienced within it (labor intus) – an interpretation which makes of the labyrinth a sort of immense snare opening up before the unwary and then, once it has engulfed them, imprisoning them forever. While this image is strongly associated with the idea of sin and hell, it also offers salvation – in the sense that whoever reaches the end of the tortuous pathway will enter the kingdom of God. The tension that thc labyrinth represents during the Middle Ages is therefore mainly that of 'above' and 'below'. It stresses the importance of the third – vertical – dimension. But this Christian interpretation and development of the classical image are strictly limited to religious literature written in Latin. In fact, until the thirteenth century, the term and the theme which characterized it were absent from literature in the vernacular languages, even in those areas where the modern awareness would expect to see them appear. There were various reasons for this.

Generally speaking, the labyrinth represented the world of evil, and the most developed form of this world was hell. The author (possibly Remigius) of a lampoon entitled *Visio Caroli Tertii* describes a vision supposedly experienced by the Emperor Charles III during which his soul leaves his body, is given a ball of thread which shines like a star and leads him 'in laberintheas infernorum poenas'. Here he meets his uncle who tells him to transfer the imperial office, via the thread, to his great nephew Louis de Provence (favoured by the Church of Reims and probably by Remigius of Auxerre). Charles obeys and gives the child 'omnem monarchiam imperii per ipsum filium'. In Louis' hand the thread rewinds itself into a shining ball and the soul of the Emperor is able to regain his body. Thus, throughout his descent into the labyrinthine torments of hell, the shining thread has guided the Emperor's steps, driven away demons and enabled the imperial throne to be legitimately transferred, finally reassuming its spherical shape, the symbol of imperial power. In this evil world, it symbolizes the divine grace which should show Charles the way. When, following in the footsteps of several other writers, Petrus Berchorius (Pierre Bersuire) produced a Christian interpretation of Ovid's mythology, he stressed the idea that the Minotaur represented the devil, and that God had driven him from heaven and imprisoned him in the labyrinth of hell, or even of the world: 'et in laberinto inferni seu etiam huius mundi eum inclusit'. But fortunately, Theseus-Christ saved us. We know that, at the time, labyrinths were often depicted in manuscripts, sometimes (but not always) as an illustration of the legends of Theseus and Daedalus. We also know that the image appears on the tiling of twenty or so churches in Italy and France. All these labyrinths, without exception, have a single passage, clearly demonstrating the other medieaval concept of the labyrinth, i.e. the way is long and tortuous, but there is only one way. The true way lies in God and it would be ungodly to claim or to represent the contrary. The labyrinth therefore came to represent the way to salvation, as it was its own 'thread'. It was symbolically enough to follow the 'league of Jerusalem' depicted on the floor of the church in order to reach the centre, i.e. the kingdom of heaven.

But the risk of failure was high, one of the reasons for which was heresy. While for Plato the labyrinth was the spatial representation of aporia, for clerics it soon came to represent ungodly speech, fallacious and reprehensible reasoning. During the third century, the Church doctor Hippolytus of Rome referred in Greek to a 'labyrinth of heresies'. In Latin, Boethius used the image to stress the confused nature of an argument (*Consolatio philosophiae* III, 12, 96). In the glossary to a work by the Christian poet Sedulius, Remigius more or less said, 'that the poet uses the metaphor of the labyrinth to refer to the errors of the Athenians who are more attracted by worthless songs than by the truth of the lesson of the Scriptures'. This is echoed by a twelfth-century commentary which summarizes: 'The labyrinth (domus dedali) represents heresy (. . .) from which one only extricates oneself with difficulty, if ever'. It therefore comes as no surprise that Gauthier de Saint-Victor, when attacking four of his contemporaries and accusing them of heresy, entitled his pamphlet *Contra quatuor labyrinthos Franciae* (1177) and compared them with minotaurs lurking in the depths of their labyrinth. It was this polemic meaning as much as that of the 'vade mecum' which was still present four centuries later in the title of Paracelsus' medical work *Labyrinthus medicorum errantium*, 1538.

But one can go on forever playing with words and trying to create order out of the chaos of the world, especially when philology appears to authorize the process. There is only one letter's difference between 'labirintus' and *Laborintus*, a symbolic and appropriate difference for a poetic work. Indeed this is the title of a twelfth-century work by Evrard l'Allemand (Evrard the German). But the literary art is difficult and Evrard wrote about both the problems of teaching (parents who do not pay, difficult children . . .) and the mysteries of poetic creation (ways of beginning poems, of embellishing them . . . and especially different types of verse). Some of the examples he gives, such as the 'oratorio ad virginem' – a prayer which asks for the intercession of the Rose-queen of the world and in which the metre varies with each stanza, could be considered as rhythmic labyrinths composed for his salvation. The use of the word 'labyrinth' is of particular interest because the word is associated here with the literary form itself. Although this association is certainly not very common, it is possible to observe it running between the lines in literature from Lycophron's *Anthology* (9, 191) which refers to the labyrinths of tortuous poetry, through Ausonius' 'logodaedalia' (*Idylls*, 12), before reaching the Baroque poets and our modern 'architects' of textual labyrinths.

Because the use of the word was restricted to scholastic Latin, it does not appear in vernacular literature. Nor does it appear in the epics or in the courtly romances which do, however, refer to Theseus and in which the various forms of the quest have been stressed 'ad infinitum'. Certainly, the hero's progress is often scattered with 'treacherous pathways' which lead 'where the way is most narrow' (*Chevalier de la Charrette*, 654 and 1508), and the reader frequently encounters a character daring to enter the forest 'where he is likely to lose his way', or following a 'shadowy, overgrown pathway' in order to reach the magical fountain (*Chevalier au Lion*, 378 and 769). However, the term 'labyrinth', which belongs to another cultural and intellectual register, is not used. Nor is it found in the stories of journeys, whether ordinary or extraordinary, or voyages, whether or not enchanted. The tradition of the dream or the vision, used continuously since ancient times, does not evoke the image either. In other words, the term and its theme makes no more of an appearance in the initial dream of the *Roman de la Rose* and its subsequent development into frustrated wanderings (during the course of which there is a fleeting reference to Theseus), than in the various *Songes d'Enfer* and *Voies du Paradis* by Raoul de Houdenc, Baudoin de Condé and Rutebeuf, or even the incredible spiralling descent into Dante's *Inferno* (in which the author and Virgil do, however, meet the Minotaur). With the exception of a poem by Richart de Fournival, 'Talent avoie d'aimer' (1260), in which being in love is compared with being imprisoned in the 'maison Dedalu' (the house of Daedalus) in an attractively developed metaphor, the labyrinth 'strictu sensu' does not appear in European literature until the fourteenth century. The exception referred to should be linked to the construction of 'houses of Daedalus' in certain gardens, of which there is evidence in France from the twelfth century onwards and which were probably arbours rather than simple hedge mazes.

During the Renaissance, the tension represented by the labyrinth tends to be that of 'exterior' and 'interior'. Whereas the mediaeval labyrinth was threatening, but remained external and 'other', during the Italian pre-Renaissance period (fourteenth century), it became part of the human experience. Through a process of psychological revolution which proved extremely significant, poets began to believe that the labyrinth was perhaps as much within us as we were within it, or even that it was an external projection on the part of the individual. From being objective it became subjective or vice versa, there being a relationship between internal and external space, as between microcosm and macrocosm. Is it in fact possible to escape from the external manifestation of the inner self? The individual is in any event implicated and the image of the labyrinth appears as an attractive illusion, or a fate, which it is extremely difficult to avoid.

It was in Italy that the word appeared for the first time in the vernacular in Cino da Pistoia's *Canzionere*, and then in the works of Boccaccio and Petrarch who employed it in a sense which was very different from that of the exegetes of the Latin language, since they used it to describe an amorous situation. In a section of *Il Corbaccio* (1354) entitled *Laberinto d'amore*, Boccaccio puts forward – in addition to the numerous references to the myth of Theseus in his works in both Latin and Italian – a completely new use of the image. In love with an attractive widow who has mocked him, the narrator has a vision in which, after passing through enchanted places (the delights of love), he discovers what he refers to as 'the labyrinth of love' or 'Venus' pigsty'. Here, those who, like himself, have become ensnared by the illusions of love, are reduced to the level of animals. But fortunately for the writer, he meets a shade sent from heaven, the husband of the widow, to whom he tells his story and who, in return, describes the faults of his former wife. As a result of this providential meeting, the narrator is able to avoid his punishment but because he has done so, has to tell all he has seen. Viewed in terms of a pitfall that men create for themselves, the labyrinth is in this instance entirely dissociated from the Greek myth. The metamorphosis into an animal, which reveals man to himself, gives it an original symbolic function. However, Petrarch, as well as Boccaccio, established another, starker image of the labyrinth of love in a single line of his *Canzionere* (1366). Describing the way in which Laura has captivated him, he states in the final triplet of Sonnet 211: 'One thousand three hundred and twenty-seven, exactly at the first hour of the sixth day of April, I entered the labyrinth, nor do I see where I may get out of it'. This image of entering the labyrinth is of the highest order. Combined with the first person singular, it marks the involvement of the individual in history. It is no exemplary hero but Petrarch himself who is experiencing the labyrinth, which is no longer the domain of a mythical monster but of a mortal being, a young woman called Laura. The obsessive exactitude of the day and the hour is not simply a lover's superstition. It provides all the solemnity appropriate to a moment which is also that of Man's entrance – of his fall according to some – into historical time. We are in the process of passing from the sacred to the profane. For Petrarch, this sixth of April signifies western man's entry into the labyrinth from which, since then, he has been trying to find a way out.

Liberated by Boccaccio and Petrarch, the image of the labyrinth was maintained in Italy, although it was not so easily introduced into the literature of other European countries. It is possible to consider three texts in particular as paving the way towards the Renaissance. In addition to scattered allusions to the Greek myth, all three offer the image of the labyrinth as a wonderful building which is not only allegorical but also specific. In Chaucer's *The House of Fame* (1379–80), the poet finds himself transported by a golden eagle to the House of Fame, where good and bad reputations are attributed. He is then taken to the House of Rumours from whence issues the terrible din of false reports. It is the latter which is compared to a labyrinth ('Laborintus', III, 1921) in the first inclusion of the term into the English language. This very strange, revolving building, made of interwoven branches, is inhabited by an entire band of manufacturers of lies. In his *The Legend of Good Women* (circa 1386), the Cretan labyrinth is evoked in the same very specific manner – 'For it is shapen as the mase is wroght' – which is surely due to the influence of the Irish and English tradition of the maze.

In Juan de Mena's *El Laberinto de Fortuna* (1444), the author, lost in a wood and in danger of being attacked by wild animals, is helped by Providence in the form of a very beautiful woman. She takes him to a 'great house' from which it is difficult to find a way out. This is the labyrinth of Fortune, the first and very early use of the term in Spanish, as well as the first explicit use of the labyrinth as an image of the world. Inside, the poet can in fact see the whole of the earth's surface and three huge wheels representing the present, the past and the future. Thus de Mena made use of the labyrinth which Dante had chosen not to mention. The image is not one of chaos but, on the contrary, of a wonderful world order about which Providence generously teaches the poet.

In *Hypnerotomachia Poliphili* (1499), an interesting novel by Francesco Colonna, Poliphilus enters a magnificent palace which is compared to the Egyptian labyrinth and under whose vault is depicted the Greek legend. But the story takes a new turn when, frightened by the dragon, Poliphilus plunges into the darkness of the palace, loses his way completely and wanders for such a long time that he asks himself whether he is in 'the Labyrinth of the ingenious Daedalus'. Fortunately, this is but a short episode in the story of Poliphilus' progress and, shortly afterwards, he discovers the 'labyrinth', a strange water garden in which the waterway forms a spiral of seven spheres bordered by trees, fountains and towers. The spiral closes around the seventh and last tower, the home of a fearful and invisible dragon which can intercept travellers in their boats at any point during their journey. It is impossible to retrace one's steps, and travellers who avoid the monster 'en route' are inevitably swallowed up when the current carries them to the seventh tower. They are then judged and given a fate, for better or for worse. As a general image of the human condition, this 'labyrinth' adopts the most traditional form of the single path. But having avoided the dragon, Poliphilus meets the queen of the domain, the goddess of freedom, and then Polia, the purest of nymphs.

For all three authors then, the labyrinth is a magical place in which it is possible to discover a particular truth, and its function largely remains allegorical. However the texts also contain the beginnings of a veritable tradition of imagery based on the labyrinth. Following their revolutionary visions,

Boccaccio and Petrarch conveyed the image to the very heart of the Renaissance and even further, to the Baroque period.

The last of these texts led to Ariosto's *Orlando Furioso* (1516–32). In Italy, the image of the labyrinth as a prison of love persisted in the fifteenth and sixteenth-century Petrarchan poetry of Antonio da Ferrara, Giusto da Conti, Luigi Pulci, Vittoria Colonna, etc., but Ariosto's epic revitalized the use of the image, and one of the main areas in which it did so was in relation to the theme of the forest. The forest, which provided a refuge for exiles and was the scene of many wanderings, was constantly represented in mediaeval literature. For Chaucer, de Mena and Colonna, as indeed for Dante and many others, it was the usual setting for dreams, yet although it was often the scene of 'labyrinthine' experiences, these were not actually classified in terms of the theme of the labyrinth until much later. The story of *Orlando Furioso* was possibly the first to make this connection. It also provided a strong link between the theme of enchantment and that of the labyrinth. In Canto XXII, most of the knights in fact appear in the palace of the sorcerer Atlante in the course of their quest for the object of their desire, i.e. their beloved, an enemy to fight, a lost object, etc. The palace continually offers them the illusion of what they are seeking and then snatches it away before their very eyes: 'And so they all wander in confusion within the palace, a veritable labyrinth from which they cannot find a way out'. In a poem in which the characters spend their lives wandering, the palace represents a labyrinth within a labyrinth, a whirlpool in which desire is engulfed in the pursuit of its own shadow, a doubly vertiginous experience. This is one of the high points of re-emergent subjectivity.

In French literature it was the image of the labyrinth as a prison of love which was being evolved, but even this was a slow process. In his *Rondeaux* (1440), Charles d'Orléans does not use the Greek word – which is too pedantic and infrequently used – to evoke his sufferings in love and the spiral in which he is imprisoned, but refers instead to 'Daedalus' prison'. Villon does not use the image at all. Translations of Italian works contributed greatly to the word becoming familiar, as did the adaptation of the *Huit premiers Livres d'Amadis de Gaule* (1541–8) by Herberay des Essarts. Not satisfied with the evocation in Book II of a 'labyrinth of bitterness' of which there was no trace in the Spanish original, this inventive translator introduced into Book IV, on one of the islands: 'a maze ('daedalus') comprising (. . .) four square acres' which Oriane enters and which bears out the continuity in France of the theme of the 'house of Daedalus'. Soon the poets of the Pléiade introduced other aspects of this image. In Ronsard's *Amours de Cassandre* (1552), the labyrinth is an area of contradiction which can only be transformed and liberated by poetry (XVII). For de Magny, it is associated above all with the oxymoron: 'labyrinth of joyful sadness' and of 'useful misfortune' (*Les Amours*, 31 and 85, 1553). Amadis Jamyn finds himself imprisoned 'In the Maze (Dédale) and labyrinth of love' (1574), while de Boyssières, Pasquier and

Desportes describe themselves as imprisoned in the same way. In France, the labyrinth of love, a prison with no door, a voluntary gaol, had replaced the 'house of Daedalus'. The labyrinth had established itself in the poetic imagination.

In Spain the process took a little longer. There is no mention of it in Fernandez de San Pedro's *La Carcel de amor* (1492), one of the most famous works in the romantic literature of the period. Nor does it appear in the tales of chivalry or in pastorals such as *Los siete libros de la Diana* (1559) by Montemayor, in spite of the presence of ordeals, imprisonment and metamorphoses. The only person to break new ground before Cervantes and the Baroque period, was the translator of Boccaccio's *Filocopo* who replaced the Italian title by *Laberinto d'Amore* (1546). The word was primarily introduced into the German language through 'Der Labyrinth' (1510), an allegorical poem about the state of Switzerland written by Zwingli in his youth. The term 'Irrgarten', which originated in the field of garden design, was quickly adopted by comic playwrights such as Sachs and Ayrer, but here, too, it was not until the Baroque period that the image achieved any true literary significance. Curiously enough, the same was true in England where, after Chaucer, the theme of the labyrinth fell into disuse. Apart from the first poems inspired at the end of the century by the legend of the Beautiful Rosamond (imprisoned by Henry II in a labyrinth of vegetation), it was Shakespeare who revived it.

The Italians continued to provide the models. The episode in *Gerusalemme liberata* (1580) in which the enchanted forest gives form and voice to the secret fears of the knights (XIII), is reminiscent of the forest and the enchanted palace of *Orlando Furioso*, but in Tasso's epic it is the theme of the garden which tends to be encompassed by the image of the labyrinth. The dream of a garden of love had been extremely popular during the thirteenth and fourteenth centuries, but although the structure of these dreams was ideally suited to the image of the labyrinth, and in spite of the existence of the 'houses of Daedalus', the connection between the two images was not made. With the exception of the allegorical water garden in the *Hypnerotomachia Poliphili*, it was only in *Gerusalemme liberata* that the attributes of the labyrinth were added to those of the 'hortus conclusus' and the 'locus amoenus'. Its winding detours protect the magical garden which the sorceress, Armida, has created for her love, Rinaldo, in the heart of her palace on a distant island. When he deserts her, in her grief and pain, she causes it all to disappear (XVI).

Shakespeare had read the Italian writers, but also captures his own national traditions. In *A Midsummer Night's Dream* (1595), the reader or audience enters, with the lovers, a wood near Athens. On this St John's Eve, it seems as if everyone else has arranged to meet here too, and so the lovers encounter magicians, players and other evil spirits. The forest is theoretically the kingdom of the King and Queen of the Fairies, Oberon and Titania, but because they have had a disagreement, the king, with the help of the sprite Puck, casts numerous spells which cause various misunderstandings and complications, with the result that we find ourselves in a truly 'haunted grove'. Furthermore, because Oberon has disrupted the dances that the Queen of the Fairies traditionally leads on the green, the order of the seasons has also been interrupted, the world is upside down, and marriages cannot take place . . . Dancing and the treading of the labyrinths have been forgotten: 'And the quaint mazes in the wanton green/For lack of tread are undistinguishable' (II, 1, 99–100); in other words, because they have not been trodden, the remarkable lawn mazes (which were extremely common in England at the time) cannot be distinguished from the overgrown grass. Dancing and the ritual treading of the labyrinth must occur for Time to resume its course and the forest be freed from its spells. As can be seen, the expression 'to tread a maze' is used here in its original sense which is linked to dance and the religious function of the labyrinth. Once Oberon has decided to become reconciled with Titania, the dance of the Queen of the Fairies, and then the dance of mortals, can be resumed. They dance on the very ground on which the sleepers slept (IV, 1, 86–8) and the spells are lifted. Finally, *Pyramus and Thisbe* can be performed at the palace and, although both the play and the players are poor, in this newly reconciled world, the carnivalesque performance is pregnant with the new life to come.

During the Classic period (seventeenth and eighteenth centuries), although the image of the labyrinth was not quite as central to Baroque aesthetics as is commonly suggested, it was significantly represented. The labyrinth was no longer the effect of a short-lived spell, but tended to represent the deceptive permanence of the world itself. Neither did it imply the tension between interior and exterior, but rather the associated problem of reality and appearance. Sorcerers began to disappear, to be replaced by the experience of illusion and reality. In the theatre this occurred in the form of disguise, in the novel in the form of didactic discourse followed by the initiatory experience, and in poetry via attempts to produce a formal representation of the enigma. *Don Quixote* (1605–15) is a good introduction to all this.

In Part One, Chapter 48, Sancho recognizes the masked men who have imprisoned Don Quixote in a cage, as the village priest and the barber. When he tells his master of his suspicions as to the true identity of these 'sorcerers', Don Quixote replies that although it is quite possible that they may resemble their former acquaintances, it does not necessarily follow that they are one and the same. One characteristic of sorcerers is to assume the guise they find most convenient 'and they have taken the form of our friends in order to make you think exactly what you are thinking, and to throw you into a labyrinth of uncertainty ('en un laberinto de imaginaciones') from which Theseus' thread would never help you find a way out'. The knight's argument provides food for thought: if Sancho allows himself to entertain doubts on the subject, he will enter a labyrinth of awkward questioning. As soon as we cease to believe, the nature of reality begins to pose problems. The entire novel brings us to the edge of this dizzying uncertainty. If we move outside the circle of belief, we embark upon an infinite series of questions. Don Quixote had decided long before to believe in sorcerers and to stay within the circle. Similarly – but this time within the context of disguise and the theatre – after the performance given at the duke's castle, Sancho believes he recognizes the steward's face as that of la Dolorida. When he informs Don Quixote, the latter explains that one should beware of jumping to the conclusion that, because two faces look alike, they necessarily belong to the same person and, as in the case of Dulcinea, he warns Sancho against enquiring too closely into the identity of people for fear of entering 'an intricate confusion of labyrinths' (II, 44). The knight does admit that all this is open to question, but he prefers not to venture into the realm of enquiry. He does not deny that there is a labyrinth within the world but, as far as possible, takes care not to enter it. In spite of the irony, Baroque literature followed his example and, having complacently evoked the labyrinth, immediately hastened to evade it.

The importance of the 'theatrum mundi' in the theatre of the Spanish golden age is well known. The world is shown to be nothing but a theatre of appearances which is ruled by God, who is the only reality. It is also because the theatre itself is merely an image of the world, an illusion, that it is an ideal medium through which to demonstrate the imaginary and transitory nature of our world. However, although this theme leads to the labyrinth, it does so indirectly and for the most part via the motif of disguise. This is illustrated first of all in the work of Cervantes and, for example, in *El laberinto de amor*, one of the comedies published in 1615 in the collection *Ocho Comedias y ocho entremeses nuovos*. 'The blind labyrinth' into which we, and the characters, are plunged, is the labyrinth of love and the amazing misrepresentations of identity in which it involves us – e.g. dukes disguised as peasants and princesses as shepherds, etc. – before everyone discovers their ultimate truth and the world has been restored to its former wisdom. In Tirso de Molina's *El Vergonzoso en Palacio* (1624), as the various permutations of costume which will make the many developments of the intrigue possible, get underway, the shepherd Tarso complains of the difficulty he is having pulling on the pleated breeches that he has been given and asks someone to show him how to find the 'entradas y salidas de esa Troya' (i.e. the entrances and exits to this labyrinth, 520). From the moment the characters enter the theatrical imbroglio, the repartee is extremely significant. Furthermore, these breeches will remain, throughout the play, the bizarre and persistent symbol of the many intrigues of identity. Nor are the connotations of the ancient name of Troy without significance. As well as the Roman 'Trojae lusus', and potentially defensive labyrinths, the word also suggests the city (and the court) that must be overcome. It is also said (but cannot be proved, and it is in distant, northern Europe) that a woman is possibly the prize for whoever finds their way to the centre of the stone labyrinth of Trojaburg.

Calderón's *La vida es sueño* (1631–5) is the best example of this process of penetrating apparent reality which should make us realize that the world is nothing but a 'shadow theatre'. The interaction between the images of reality and illusion in which we are imprisoned with Sigismond, has often been compared with a labyrinth. But once again, the general structure of the work is not specifically classified in terms of the theme of the labyrinth, which only exists in a secondary capacity as a background to the metamorphoses of Sigismond and Rosaura. In this way, the latter, initially lost in a 'confused labyrinth' of rocks, discovers her true self, from the tower in the mountains to the Polish Court and through the medium of various disguises. When she explains to Clothalde that her clothes are an 'enigma', that they do not belong to whom they appear to belong, and that she is not what she appears, etc., Clothalde wonders: 'What is this confused labyrinth, in which reason cannot find the thread?' (975–8). Half man and half woman, Rosaura, like Sigismond, must rid herself of her masks and find her own truth. If we consider several other fine examples of 'theatre within the theatre' – e.g. Gian Battista Andreini's *Le due commedie in commedia*, Corneille's *Illusion comique* and Rotrou's *Le Véritable Saint Genest* – we see that the image of the labyrinth does not appear. This is because their structural framework is not suited to it. In Baroque theatre, it made a more modest appearance, and was finally linked to the dramatic confusion provoked by the use of disguise, thereby addressing the question of reality via the more theatrical question of identity.

Curiously enough, the seventeenth-century novel sometimes revived the mediaeval taste for religious and moral allegory. Following the famous devotional work by the Jesuit Hermann Hugo, *Pia Desideria* (of which the 1624 Latin edition was followed by numerous translations), several lengthy prose texts used the labyrinth as the central symbol of the way to enlightenment. In *Labyrint Svèta a ráj srdce* (1631), the great Czech humanist Jan Amos Komensky describes, in the first person, a pilgrim's journey around the world. The latter discovers that the world is a vast city whose six main routes converge on a central square where the Palace of Wisdom and the Castle of Fortune are located. After visiting the two buildings, the pilgrim realizes that the entire government of the world is based on lies and illusion and he decides to pursue his investigations no further. He then attends upon the dying and discovers God, who tells him that he should have sought Him, not on the highways of the world, but within himself, within his human heart. Here the image of the labyrinth is, for the most part, negative. It corresponds to the constantly changing and misleading outward appearance of events and behaviour and is directly opposed to the seat of deep values, the true meaning of things and repose in God, i.e. the 'paradise of the heart'.

In *El Criticón* (1651–7), Gracian y Moralès does not make use of the labyrinth to present a general image of the long journey of Andrenius and Critile and their discovery of the temptations of the world, but the theme is present at several decisive points during their exploration of reality and their discovery of truth. Thus, the great city of Spain where they arrive in Part One is a 'perfect labyrinth', an accumulation of the defects of all legendary and historical cities. This dark and chaotic labyrinth contains a second labyrinth, the court, which is the focal point of pretence and deceit. No book will provide them with 'Ariadne's golden thread' to enable them to find their way. They must continue to travel and learn to exercise their powers of practical reasoning in terms of their faith in God in order to avoid the snares of this world. In a somewhat similar vein, in the unfinished novelistic account by Casper von Lohenstein (*Arminius*, 1689), Zeno, an ancient Armenian prince and philosopher, visits the Egyptian labyrinth where he discovers, on the amazing pediment of the building, a hieroglyphic poem entitled: 'Inscription on a labyrinth'. As he deciphers it, it becomes clear that, here, too, salvation cannot be separated from the exercise of reason. In Bunyan's *Pilgrim's Progress* (1678), Christian must keep to the right path and avoid many a pitfall before he reaches the Heavenly City, but the symbol of the labyrinth, which is probably too alien to the biblical register of the book, does not appear. It is also absent from Fénelon's *Adventures de Télémaque* (1699), the last great educational voyage of the century, although when they visit Crete, Mentor and his pupil do examine with great interest the labyrinth of Daedalus which is a replica of the one they saw in Egypt (V).

The difference between virtuous enlightenment and the initiation into immorality lies in the nature of the teaching and not in the symbolic form of the path followed. As well as serving as the image of the deceptions of the world which one has to learn to avoid, the labyrinth can also be the symbolic route to many other types of knowledge. The structure of the 'précieux' novels, with their sudden developments, interlocking intrigues and countless repercussions, certainly constituted a labyrinth, but since their authors were not primarily concerned with the adventure of writing, the image was not used to illustrate it. However, in *Artamène ou le Grand Cyrus* (1649–53) by Mlle de Scudéry, there is an interesting use of a labyrinth of greenery in the story of Parthénie (VI, 1). The beautiful princess is in danger of becoming the victim of an oracle which has predicted that she will only be happy with someone who will marry her without having seen her. While out hunting, the handsome Timante loses his way in the maze of a park that Parthénie happens to be visiting at the time. Fortunately, he hears her singing and she, without revealing herself, agrees to act as his guide. She promises to lead him to the centre of the labyrinth where he will find a fountain and a 'pleasant rondeau' and from whence, after an hour, the keeper of the park will release him. Invisible and inaccessible, it is the woman who controls the romantic proceedings. Although she is very much present through her voice, Parthénie is also completely hidden. The maze which conceals her also makes Timante her prisoner while making it appear that she is freeing him. The more he complies, the more chance he has of reaching the centre and of one day possibly becoming the master of the park. But for the moment, he must wait in the centre and read and contemplate a rondeau, a little labyrinth of words. We are in a story within the story, but rather than providing the thematic echo of a complicated structure, the labyrinth here forms part of the symbolism of the 'Tendre' (the kingdom of the emotions). It is a metaphor for romantic fulfilment, between the visible and the invisible, between desire and its object. Put more simply, it required nothing less than a labyrinth to frustrate an oracle!

In the picaresque novel, the image of the labyrinth is not usually employed in terms of the general destiny of the picaroon, but in an inspired novel in the genre, such as *Der Abenteuerliche Simplex Simplicissimus* (1669) by Grimmelshausen, it appears in a significant, albeit unexpected, context. Rather than being used to illustrate Simplex' thorough initiation in love by the Parisiennes, it appears instead in an episode from his life as a soldier and with the term 'Irrgarten' linked to the comic tradition. In order to deceive the enemy so that he can obtain plunder, Simplex 'invents' a sort of shoe that is worn 'back to front' and leaves inverted footprints 'more confused than the passages of a labyrinth' (III, 1). Thus, by pointing in the opposite direction to the one expected, the footprints left by Simplex as he passes through the world show an inverted image of it. But this reverse image of the world also has something to say and we should not be afraid to let it speak for itself. If we want to understand the whole story, the obscure pathways and the voices from the reverse side of the image must also be invoked. We must pay careful attention to Simplex' footprints, even if they do resemble the confused pathways of a facetious gardener.

During the eighteenth century, Illuminism and the taste for things oriental were responsible for the development of the initiatory theme. For example, the Abbé Terrasson's *Séthos* (1731) is one of the sources of inspiration for the librettist of *The Magic Flute*. However, the connection between the esoteric dimension of knowledge and the image of the labyrinth was not automatic. One of the only texts in which it is explicitly made is probably Vivant Denon's elegant and libertine narrative, 'Point de lendemain' (1777). The story told by the young narrator is both an initiation into love and an introduction to the mysterious world of the senses. Was his experience real or was it in fact illusory? Had he been surrounded by illusions or been really happy? The 'dédale' (maze) that he explored was indeed extremely strange and ambiguous. The way to love has the appearance of a mysterious ritual – 'It all seemed like an initiation' – and leads him, and us, to question, in more general terms, the nature of the information and revelations acquired via the senses.

In the style of the Pléiade, early seventeenth-century poets reverted to the image of the labyrinth to evoke the vicissitudes of secular love (La Roque, Chiabrera) and even frolicsome love (Le Villain's *Labyrinthe de Récréation*, 1602, and Fornier's *Le Labyrinthe d'Amour*, 1610). Others, such as Adam de Otradovic, presented it as the way to sacred love. In his 'Labyrinth of Sacred Love', the poet, lost in 'the darkest labyrinth', wants love to be like Ariadne's thread and lead him to Christ (*Ceskà marianska muzika*, 1647). There are some extremely interesting attempts within this religious and even mystical context to incorporate the image of the labyrinth into poetic writing itself. They fall into two main categories which can be qualified as calligrammatic and cryptogrammatic. Calligrams – which have existed since Ancient times – were extremely popular, particularly in Germany during the Baroque period, where the most elaborate 'Geistliche Irrgarten' (spiritual labyrinths) were written. In 1539, Johann Neudörffer produced a very fine example, in the style of the mediaeval text of the Freising manuscript, which was harmoniously composed and beautifully written. While some texts were merely written between the single lines depicting the passages of the labyrinth (Quad, 1609 and Kieser, 1611), others reproduced the shape of the labyrinth as part of their development (Lipp, 1645). The fashion continued during the eighteenth century with the composition, sometimes with texts in several languages, of labyrinth-poems which led to several centres, i.e. the four possible sources of grace (Koch, 1742 and Wagner, 1758). The spiritual labyrinth, which made it possible to achieve an overall appreciation of the image as well as a progressive understanding of the text, provided a symbolic written presentation of a dual approach to the enigma.

Cryptographs, which have also existed since Ancient times, were mainly found in Spain and Portugal, so much so that, in these two countries during the eighteenth century, poetic compositions which could be read in several different ways were called 'laberintos'. By adopting the 'retrograde' approach, for example, it is possible to read a sonnet by starting with the final triplet. By adopting the 'vertical' approach, it is possible to read a sonnet by Góngora (the inventor of the superlative 'dedalisimo') by following two distinct columns of words. In both cases, the poem is presented 'normally' and the second way of reading it is concealed by the first. But there were also more systematic elaborations. According to the calculations of Luis Nunes Tinoco, there are almost fifteen million possible ways of reading his text, the words of which are laid out in the form of a draughtboard with 169 squares. From combinations of words it is possible to move on to combinations of letters. In the style of the 'sancta ecclesia' inscription contained at the centre of the labyrinth of the Basilica of Orléansville (later el-Asnam), which can be read in all directions, a Portuguese poet composed an alphabetical labyrinth in the form of a rectangle in which a single phrase, repeated on each line and offset by one letter each time, can be read in an infinite number of ways. Another poet, Manuel Ferreira Leonardo, went even further by presenting this sort of reduced letter-poem in the form of a cross and thus linking it to the 'German-style' calligram. One text can conceal another text, or it can conceal an infinite number of other texts. The secret of the Word contained within it eludes us.

During the Romantic period, the image of the labyrinth occurred so frequently that it would be impossible to continue to describe it on an enumerative basis. But the occurrences can be grouped fairly easily around a certain number of themes, or topoï, of which 'labyrinthism' constitutes the common approach. The sudden revelation and emphasis of the labyrinthine dimension of images that had long been familiar in literature corresponded to new developments in the way in which the world was perceived. From this point onwards, the tension prioritized by the labyrinth during the nineteenth and twentieth centuries was the opposition of finite and infinite. There are three successive periods to this preoccupation. The first dates from the beginning of the nineteenth century, when the new themes which appeared focused primarily on the Romantic experience of limitation. Infinity, it was discovered, could be a terrible form of imprisonment. Subsequently, the question of the meaning of the world began to be asked – more frequently than the question of the exceeding of limits – in terms of the finite and the infinite. This meaning, which until the eighteenth century had been symbolized by the centre of the labyrinth (which was theoretically attainable), became extremely problematic towards the end of the nineteenth and even more so during the twentieth century. Finally, in order to define the philosophical problem of end and meaning more fairly, literature began to question itself as to its means and ability of achieving this.

The first of the 'labyrinthine' themes of the Romantic period was certainly the castle. It is omnipresent in the 'gothic' novel which developed in England at the end of the eighteenth and the beginning of the nineteenth centuries, based on the *Castle of Otranto* (1764) by Horace Walpole. Perched on top of a mountain or lost in the depths of a forest, the castle, or more usually the gothic building, proves to be an insidious trap. Having entered of her own free will, the heroine finds that she is in fact a prisoner. Essential doors are blocked while other, secret doors open. Only the tyrant controls the 'disconcerting space' of the castle: it becomes the instrument of his power, and of his abuse of their power. In Ann Radcliffe's *The Mysteries of Udolpho* (1794), there are no less than four castles. Hundreds of novels, not only in England but also in France, Germany and Russia, exploited the theme, but like all those encompassed by the labyrinth, the castle here may have a dual significance: a black castle, for example, may conceal the initiatory white castle. In *Wilhelm Meisters Lehrjahre* (1795–6), an old tower in Lothario's castle very curiously remains inaccessible to Wilhelm. At the very end of his apprenticeship, he is allowed to enter it and discovers the rolls of paper on which are recorded, among others, his 'years of apprenticeship'. These are the mysteries to which he is finally initiated and which mark the mastery of his art. In *Isis* (1862) by Villiers de l'Isle-Adam, the palace is described as 'a magnificent labyrinth whose winding passages concealed a skilful order'. At its centre, in the circular room furnished with a bed in the form of a sphinx, is the mysterious marchioness Fabriana. Through her, the young Wilhelm d'Anthas will glimpse living knowledge. In addition to the gothic castle, the palace of Corleone – the lodge in Hugo's *L'Homme qui rit* (1869) – is a magical labyrinth which is also deceptive, for, except for the transgression considered only fleetingly, Josiane will pay no further attention to Gwynplaine. We must pass through darkness in order to reach the light. 'On the edge of an abyss, built of the philosopher's stone, the shining castle opens its doors,' wrote Breton in *L'Amour fou* (1937).

But more than the castle, it is possibly the dark underground passage which runs beneath it, that best represents the labyrinth. According to Bachelard, 'Below the ground, all paths are tortuous'. The underground passage of the gothic novel expresses all that is concealed and suppressed inside the castle or the abbey. It is the metaphor for the devious nature and sombre machinations of the Evil One and is more closely associated with the theme of the labyrinth than with the grotto or the cave because the underground passage is an artificial and often perfidious structure. It traverses and explores impenetrable and forbidden regions. Thus, with this 'endless labyrinth of shadows' winding beneath the castle of Otranto, Walpole attests to the existence of Shadow in the midst of the Age of Enlightenment, asserting that beneath the familiar outward appearance of things, there is an entire world which lies dormant. In Radcliffe's *The Italian* (1797), the underground passage is the symbolic projection of the evil soul of Schedoni, the Machiavellian monk who haunts it. When in Lewis' *The Monk* (1796), Ambrosio carries off an unconscious young woman – in fact his own sister whom he has just wrested from her mother – through the underground galleries of the abbey and rapes her among the skeletons, he is certainly exploring the realm of the illicit. Julien Gracq reminds us of this when, in *Au Château d'Argol* (1938), Albert is led to the threshold of the room 'by the wavering and flickering flame of the torch'. But the journey through the underground passage can also lead into light. The fashion for gothic literature was scarcely underway when, in *Heinrich von Ofterdingen* (1802), Novalis made Heinrich's meeting with the miner and the descent into the 'labyrinth of galleries' one of the important events of his story. The search for metal within the depths of mother-earth is somewhat reminiscent of the search for alchemist's gold. In *Die Bergwerke zu Falun* (1819), Hoffmann also uses a similar type of symbolism. Eventually the underground labyrinth was to assume, and continues to do so today, many different forms, both artificial (sewers, catacombs, tunnels, urban 'rabbit warrens', etc.), and natural (grottoes, caves, conchs, intestines, etc.). Hugo provided two extremely powerful examples with the Parisian sewers in *Les Misérables* (1862) and the underwater grotto in *Travailleurs de la Mer* (1866).

Until the nineteenth century, the dream was primarily a device for rhetorical expression. It was a way of entering another dimension and thus escaping the principles governing reality. The vision was the pretext for all types of symbolic images and conjectural speeches, rather than the evocation of the impressions of a dreamer. When characters began to dream in literature and to want (which was not necessarily the case) to evoke the oneiric dimension, the image or at least the experience of the labyrinth soon occurred. In this area, too, gothic literature and the literature of the supernatural provide some early examples. In Ann Radcliffe's *The Romance of the Forest* (1791), the heroine has a premonitory nightmare in which she loses her way and wanders through the winding passages of an abbey, unable to find the exit. In more general terms, in Potoki's *Le Manuscript trouvé à Saragosse* (1804–15), Alphonse, in spite of all his efforts, keeps finding himself in the same place, beneath the gibbet of the Zoto brothers or in the Venta Quemada inn. The fear experienced in this novel does not arise from a brutal manifestation of the supernatural but from the confusion of reality and dream, i.e. walking on the spot and the obsessive recurrence of the same theme. Not content with dreaming naturally, the Romantics and post-Romantics created dreams. In de Quincey's *Confessions of an English Opium Eater* (1822), the completely colourless images of the labyrinth-city pass by in a slow, even movement in an atmosphere of unreality in which all sound seems muffled. Each gesture seems condemned to be repeated and Ann's search becomes confused with the endless approach of inaccessibility and death. In a dream, Baudelaire sees himself in a vast, crumbling 'labyrinth-tower', a veritable Tower of Babel consumed by some secret leprosy, from which he is unable to find his way out (Pléiade, p. 317). In his *Paradis artificiels* (1860), a woman tells how, under the effect of hashish, she imagined herself to be imprisoned behind the bars of a 'magnificent cage', which opened on all sides on to space (Pléiade, p. 368). From Musset to Tom Wolfe, via the works of Daumal and Michaux, the experience of drugs regularly leads to the experience of the labyrinth. The desire and the difficulties of achieving another level of awareness are inherent in both experiences, but the simple Romantic dream had already often produced initiatory journeys with labyrinthine characteristics. The first chapter of *Heinrich von Ofterdingen* tells of a dream in which Heinrich crosses seas, goes through a forest and enters a mountain through a gallery, eventually reaching a grotto where he rediscovers the blue flower. (There follows a speech in defence of dreams which persuades Heinrich's father to tell, in his turn, the story of a very similar dream.) In the same way, the dreams in *Die Jünger von Saïs* (1797–8) and *Aurélia* (1865) by Nerval above all retain the magical disorientation of the labyrinth.

The use of the image of the labyrinth in descriptions of cities is a very common cliché in modern texts. It could be considered that, with the industrial revolution, the city became the setting which most commonly inspired the experience of the labyrinth and that, from then onwards, it fulfilled the role which had for a long time been played by the forest. In literature, it was circa 1820 that the large European cities began to replace gothic buildings and underground passages as the setting and medium for adventure. As in the other instances where the labyrinth was superimposed upon another image, it was characterized by ambivalence. It certainly stressed the problems of finding one's way around cities and we see the opium eater suddenly enter 'a labyrinth of narrow streets and a maze of dead ends' which echoes all the twists and turns of the labyrinth: 'On my return, I lost my way in this vast labyrinth of a city of 1,500 souls', noted Michelet in his *Journal* (1834). However, it was also used to illustrate the journey which leads, through the town, from ignorance to self-knowledge, from anonymity to identity. The stranger who, in the opening lines of *Mystères de Paris* (1842–4), plunges into the 'labyrinth of dark, narrow, winding streets', has, by the end of the narrative, regained his name and titles. Oliver Twist, born of an unknown father to an anonymous mother, in an unnamed town, leaves for London on his ninth birthday. In so doing, he enters a world which is both extremely realistic and symbolic and where, after several deaths-rebirths, he finds his family and his identity (Dickens, 1837–8). In Oscar Wilde's *The Picture of Dorian Gray* (1890), Dorian submerges himself in the labyrinth of the dregs of London society, which is a way of discovering his true nature and affirming that beauty lies beyond good and evil and, if necessary, in the truth of death. Similarly, in all cities, whether large or small, there is likely to be a metaphorical labyrinth which lies behind the stone façades. However, from Beckford to Byron and from Ruskin to Morand, the story of one particular city is more often associated with the labyrinth than any other. That city is Venice – a place of paradox, of reflected architecture, a cosmos built on chaos, immovable in the midst of movement, a city of masks and metamorphoses, of light and death, whose labyrinth, when glimpsed, takes one beyond the mirrored façade of its waters.

All journeys may involve glimpses of the labyrinth – in disconcerting architecture, an unknown city, or a confusing natural site – or, taken as a whole, the journey itself may be compared or likened to a labyrinth. During the Romantic period, there was an increasing number of accounts of journeys during which certain important moments were experienced in terms of the labyrinth surrounding the mystery of the world. In Lamartine's *Voyage en Orient* (1835), Baalbek, Damascus and Constantinople suggest, each for a different reason, the metaphor of the labyrinth. In Nerval's account (1848–51), the visit to Cairo (II, 131) is a systematic entry into the labyrinth and the crowd, as if in an attempt to become absorbed by the chaos and decay of the city. Considered as a whole, the Romantic journey to the Orient also represented a search for another culture as well as an attempt to discover the origin of mystery. Underlying the poetics of the sea journey and the illicit journey in the labyrinthine hold of the ship in *The Narrative of Arthur Gordon Pym* (1837) by Edgar Allan Poe, is the magnetism of the South Pole where the narrator and his companion disappear (and the story comes to an end) after seeing a huge figure, white as the driven snow, which looms across their path. Only shortly beforehand, they had explored winding chasms of which the hieroglyphic design constituted a message in Ethiopian script and was completed by words in Arabic and Egyptian carved into the rock. Through these black granite chasms, which Baudelaire referred to as 'alphabetic chasms', they were possibly drawing close to the 'white' source of the symbols. Jules Verne in *Le Sphinx des Glaces* (1897) and Lovecraft in 'At the Mountains of Madness' (1931) both echo the theme of Poe's novel. Jules Verne's extraordinary voyages are more likely than most to present his readers with the many forms of the labyrinth. The *Voyage au Centre de la Terre* (1864) consists entirely of an underground labyrinth, with a difficult but successful descent, a euphoric entry into the elemental body of the earth. In *Le Château des Carpathes* (1892), the hero reaches the castle after crossing the chaos of the rocks, only to find that its 'geometrical layout constituted a system as complicated as those of the labyrinths of Porsena, Lemnos and Crete' and the entire story teaches him to be wary of illusion. Even were we to consider only adventure stories, there would be no difficulty in extending the analysis. The story may be set in darkest Africa, as in the forests of *She* (Haggard, 1887) and *Heart of Darkness* (Conrad, 1902), or in the underground galleries of *King Solomon's Mines* (Haggard, 1885) and *L'Atlantide* (Benoist, 1918), or adventure may even occur, crazily and unexpectedly, at one of the turns of the Hampton Court Maze, as in *Three Men in a Boat* (Jerome, 1889).

With the 'invention' of the detective novel by Poe in 1842, it is possible to observe a shift in the image of the labyrinth, i.e. from the experience of limitation in terms of existence to the more intellectual experience of the limitation of knowledge. The enigma in which the criminal envelopes the characters and the detective in the novel is in fact an exasperating aporia, a labyrinth of logic: 'He had the impression of being in a labyrinth in which he encountered the same obstacles at every turn' (Steeman, *L'assassin habite au 21*, 1939). The preferred settings of the classic detective novel – the town and its narrow streets, the manor house and its outbuildings, all enclosed and irregularly shaped places – are a form of labyrinth and thus the spatial metaphor for the enigma. But there is always someone cleverer than you. The detective responds to the criminal's labyrinth by systematically developing the labyrinth of the enquiry. This is summarized by Ellery Queen in *Ten Days' Wonder* (1948): 'And that's what you have given me to work out (. . .) A difficult trail in the form of a labyrinth'. To completely reconstruct the labyrinth, he would have to follow that trail to the end or, alternatively, to recognize it, he would have to catch hold of a thread and not let go, as was the case for Arsène Lupin in *Les Huit coups de l'horloge* (1923): 'I had the Ariadne's thread which would guide me into the labyrinth'. Whether reconstructed or recognized, the labyrinth is destroyed and the enigma solved. By producing a counter-labyrinth, the detective in fact invalidates the original structure. He identifies the criminal, achieves knowledge and assumes control. In its own way, the mystery detective novel forms part of all twentieth-century literature, insofar as it represents the triumph of meaning over the obscurity and absurdity of the world, symbolic of our age of search and enquiry. However, novels of enquiry and poetry are not always as optimistic as the extremely positive detective novel. While for some the experience of the labyrinth – the symbol of knowledge – means enquiry, and for others it means wandering, it is more often an inextricable combination of the two.

During the Symbolist movement, d'Annunzio's *Il Fuoco* (1900) provided a very fine example of this double postulation. Completely absorbed in his quest for fire (an ideal of superior humanity inspired by Nietzsche and Wagner), the poet Stelio is torn between a young singer whom he has just heard and the – older – great actress who, until then, had been his perfect Egeria. Following a performance of Benedetto Marcello's *Ariane* which stressed the Dionysian and liberating aspects of the story, the singer nicknames Stelio Ariadne. Later, during a walk at Stra, he allows the actress to lose her way in the famous hedge maze at the Villa Pisani. But things go badly wrong and Stelio cannot prevent the joke turning into torture. In this unusually violent scene, we in fact witness an abandonment to wandering, an exposure to torment, a veritable sacrifice within the labyrinth: 'And she was unable to make the distinction, within her own mind, between the reality of the place and the image of her inner suffering'. In Alain-Fournier's *Le Grand Meaulnes* (1913), it is after losing his way in the forest that Augustin discovers the magical domain, takes part in the fête and catches sight of Yvonne de Galais. In his ceaseless attempt to recapture this chance vision, he even goes as far as to carefully reconstruct a map of the mysterious region. Strangely, thc path of his romantic and mystical search crosses that of the unfortunate fiancé of the fête. Each has the potential to enable the other to find the key to the enchanted kingdom, but the search never precludes the element of chance. A dazzling memory is all that remains of the unattainable château of the soul.

The works of Henri de Régnier are entirely dominated by the idea of the labyrinth. In the stories in *La Canne de Jaspe* (1897), it very often takes the form of the castle which conceals a secret, in *Romaine Mirmault* (1914), it takes the form of the garden and in *Escapade* (1926), that of the forest. On other occasions, it is a town: Bruges in *Le Bosquet de Psyché* (1894) and Venice in the *Illusion héroïque de Tito Bassi* (1916) and *Le Voyage d'Amour ou l'Initiation vénitienne* (1930). Although these associations are not new, there is possibly something new in the way they are constructed and the author's perception of them. For example, in the foreword to *La Canne de Jaspe* he writes: 'Find your way through the labyrinth, enter the copse and read my book, page by page.' Although the term itself scarcely appears, the Venetian tales of Hugo von Hofmannsthal are certainly labyrinthine while Thomas Mann's *Der Tod in Venedig* (Death in Venice, 1912) is, of course, as dazzling as a petrified labyrinth. For certain poets, the search is also linked to the experience of the labyrinth. For example, it is used lightheartedly in connection with the romantic intrigue in Bierbaum's *Irrgarten der Liebe* (1901), is referred to 'en passant' in Cocteau's *Plain-Chant* (1923) – 'Our lovers' embrace is like entwined letters/carved on a tree' – and is used more seriously in connection with the theme of solitude in collections by Jimenez such as *Laberinto* (1911).

Just as all nineteenth-century 'Bildungsromane' can be analyzed in terms of the labyrinth, the great novelistic sagas of the beginning of the twentieth century (e.g. those of Rolland and Galsworthy) could also be considered within this perspective. Two extremely popular and often-quoted works which are both 'Künstlerromane' (stories of the artist) and also great novelistic sages, are James Joyce's *The Portrait of the Artist as a Young Man* (1916) and *Ulysses*

(1921). They do not tell the story of Daedalus or Ulysses but, through the characters Stephen Dedalus and Leopold Bloom, continuously pose the question of artistic creation while at the same time develop a vision and history of Ireland. Taken as a whole, the story of the *Portrait* forms a spiral. Each of the five chapters repeats and extends the experience of the previous one until the final liberation. It is possible to consider the major difficulty confronted by Stephen within each of these experiences as a sort of ordeal of the labyrinth. But most importantly, Stephen, in danger of being imprisoned by the universe which surrounds him, constructs a labyrinth of words with which he hopes to control the labyrinth of the world. His story is a microcosm of the whole of reality and as such puts the powers of writing to the test. The text, first and foremost a symbolic equivalent and subsequently a magic formula, is engraved upon the heart of the world like an 'open sesame'. It gives the young artist his freedom, which he uses to construct another labyrinth – *Ulysses* – for there is always more to discover about the world and freedom can always be explored in more depth.

It has often been said (to repeat Gilbert) that Chapter X of *Ulysses* constitutes a perilous passage through the 'wandering rocks', that the characters risk losing their way and the reader is in constant danger of taking a wrong turning; and that Joyce specifically uses the technique of the 'labyrinth' (which involves incorporating an element from another sequence into a narrative sequence and thus introducing the interplay of harmony and conflict). In fact, the metaphor could be used to illustrate many other processes within the text where the reader continually runs the risk of losing his or her way among the interwoven stories, ambiguous words, intricate symbols and other such devices. The risk is even greater in *Finnegan's Wake* (1939) in which each word has a host of different meanings and the dream of the book as a whole is even more vivid than in the previous works. However, with the exception of the *Portrait of the Artist as a Young Man*, the theme of the labyrinth does not appear. In terms of structure, it is not more relevant than in any other odyssey or wake and, as a specific technique, is only used as an arbitrary metaphor. However, the labyrinth is certainly, from the reading point of view, one of the most suggestive images in Joyce's work.

There are several places in Proust's *A la recherche du temps perdu* (1913–27) which are reminiscent of the concept of the labyrinth: not only Venice, where a magnificent 'campo' discovered during a nocturnal stroll proves impossible to find the next day, but also the Grand Hotel in Baalbek (where the term itself is used), the Bois de Boulogne, the Opera House, etc. It is possible that some of these places are part of a system and constitute the specific labyrinth of Proust's own experience. Thus Butor sees in the combination of the various rooms occupied by the narrator, of the gardens placed at his disposal and of the 'salons' where he is received, the 'labyrinth of the world' that it has fallen to him to explore. The *Recherche* ostensibly undertakes to understand reality, to penetrate its opacity. It is only through studious asceticism and extreme patience that the narrator is eventually in a position to impose meaning. It is indeed a search, a successful search, at the end of which the tireless identification of signs and minutely-detailed writing make it possible to establish that time is reversible in psychological terms, and to discover the value of time. But the novel is also, like Joyce's *Portrait*, a 'Künstlerroman' which recounts the difficulties experienced by the emergent artist. At the end of the *Recherche*, the narrator finally becomes the writer that he dreamt of being. His first work could be an account of his apprenticeship and would be, neither exactly the same, nor an entirely different *Recherche*. Thus, as in the case of Joyce's *Portrait*, the dynamic structure of the *Recherche* appears to bear more relation to the spiral than to the labyrinth. It is a spiral which develops according to a pressing inner need until the final full stop which, when written, interrupts the movement of the spiral just as it has finally been fixed within itself by the writing.

Reaching the centre of the labyrinth is not always a euphoric experience, nor is the search always successful. Bely's *Petersburg* (1913) is an outspoken challenge of the validity and implications of this centre. Installed at the top of the administrative hierarchy of the artificial, geometric town, the senator Apollo Apollonovitch is the 'unique centre of both the real and imaginary universe'. In the heart of his fortress, the old man is constantly legislating and developing the increasingly complicated network of regulations, like a defensive labyrinth which will protect him from the world around him. But the regulations are ineffectual and his directives are ignored. The centre of the empire no longer controls anything. The building is cracked and the senator himself is prey to uncontrollable intrusions of the unconscious. He is constantly obsessed by the 'breach' through which the great Threat will appear. The target of a bomb prepared by his son and the victim of schizophrenia, the wizened old man sees his reflection in the mirrors of the 'salon Tsoukatov' as a multiplicity of scattered images. The naked king explodes into a myriad of reflections and the centralized oppressive power is shattered. But on what do the doors of the mirrors open?

In the narratives of Kafka, the nature of the centre is a matter for conjecture, and access to it generally proves impossible. As we know, Kafka's characters push open doors, pass along corridors, seek help from intermediaries, but never reach their goal. They repeat the same process to no avail, for they are always brought back to the point from which they started and never manage to cross the threshold. They only know what lies beyond the threshold by hearsay and they will only ever have an extremely indirect contact with this reality or truth. They will never know the law itself, only the story of the guardian of the law. The fate of the character anticipates the fate of the reader. Just as there is no truth other than the relative and hypothetical truth contained in the story of the guardian, so the meaning of the narrative is contained within the text of the narrative, even though this is precisely where it continues to elude us. The wanderings of the character lead us to and present us with the indefinable nature of this meaning. This is the basic experience of the labyrinth in Kafka's works. However, if we consider his very persistent use of the term in a – probably later – text such as *Der Bau*, we observe a noticeably different use of the image. The animal-narrator can in fact be compared with Apollo Apollonovitch. To protect itself, it is continually perfecting a burrow with a network of defences. Virtually at the centre of its 'fortified castle', it has stored up abundant supplies, some of these having been placed in various secondary galleries as a precautionary measure. In the heart of its structure, the animal is therefore in the 'castle', but it is soon overcome by a nagging fear because, wherever it is in the burrow, it hears, or thinks it can hear, a 'faint whistling'. Its attempts to burrow deeper are pointless as it only succeeds in burying the noise more irremediably with it. Wherever it goes, it is accompanied by the noise, which becomes increasingly disquieting. Is there no way to escape it? The narrative leaves little room for hope . . . To return to the little-used entrance to the burrow: the system of passageways leading to it, and which is of an earlier construction, is in fact called the 'labyrinth'. Although now dissatisfied with it, the animal will probably leave it intact for, as it explains, it 'has a soft spot for this early piece of work'. Literary critics see the labyrinth as a symbol of Kafka's early works. They point out that, despite the fact that this labyrinth-burrow is curiously called the 'way out', it does not for all that provide a means of escape from the curse: '(this) way out (. . .) is undoubtedly unlikely to save me under any circumstances; it would be more likely to bring about my downfall, but it offers hope and I cannot live without it'. Thus the labyrinth could be said to be not so much a space to be explored, as something that is burrowed out with the brain, or 'forehead' as in the case of the animal. The work may be inadequate, and even when perfecting it 'ad infinitum', the ominous whistling sound remains trapped inside. However, it still helps us to live. Thus literature is presented as a labyrinth – a pointless and extravagant structure – but one which may be vital for survival.

Even before Bely and Kafka, it would have been possible to say that the fantastical narratives of the nineteenth century were constructed like labyrinths whose unreliable, or frankly alarming, centre challenged the 'usual' image and meaning of the world. From the gothic to the 'Angst' novels, there are numerous examples of supernatural dimensions which are divorced from the rest of the world and strongly focused on abnormal manifestations. Some works developed the theme of the labyrinth very explicitly on this basis. For example, in the short story by Henry James entitled 'Mr Humphreys and his Inheritance' (1911), as well as a manor house, Humphreys inherits the park and hedge maze constructed by his great-grandfather. At the centre of the maze is a column, at the top of which is a metal sphere bearing strange inscriptions. Abnormally, the sphere is burning hot to the touch, except when the owner of the manor touches it. However, the latter does have his share of misfortunes associated with the labyrinth and his suffering only comes to an end when he has had the maze destroyed. It is as if the ashes of his ancestor contained in the sphere had not grown cold, and that it was only after dealings with the realms of Darkness and their Prince, that the true hour of death had finally come.

The basic element in Grin's *Krysolov* (1924) and Weiss' *Dum o tisichi Patrech* (1929), is a huge building and the action seems more or less linked to the question of power. These two extremely good and enigmatic narratives leave an overwhelming impression of the nightmare and the endless search to discover its meaning. Virtually all the short stories by Lovecraft could be used to illustrate the labyrinthine aspect of the supernatural dimension. Two of them involve long descriptions of deliberately terrifying labyrinthine structures. Following in the footsteps of Pym, the narrator of 'At the mountains of madness' (1931) discovers, in the Antarctic, the fearsome stone labyrinth and the frightening megalopolis left by the Great Ancients who had probably come from another world. In 'In the walls of Eryx' (1935), the narrator dies on Venus, imprisoned in a labyrinth with completely transparent walls. In *Le Labyrinthe* (1949) by the Swiss writer Sandoz, we rediscover a very classical inspiration since the labyrinth of greenery harbours a creature which is half man and half toad, the true owner of the castle and the park. Robert Aickman's short story 'Bind you hair' (1964) (which has been translated into French under the title 'La nuit du labyrinthe'), has as its labyrinth a maze of low embankments, while in Ursula Le Guin's novel *The Tombs of Atuan* (1971), it is an ancient underground passage. In both works, it is the scene of terrifying and mysterious worship. The supernatural labyrinth supplies us with a glimpse of an alternative truth of the world.

The image of the labyrinth occasionally appears in more traditional, psychologically analytical novels – i.e. with a much smaller element of the 'irrational' – and it would probably be possible to identify a noticeable increase in its use during the inter-wars years when it was used much more to express a sense of confusion and loss than confidence and certainty. In Fitzgerald's *This side of Paradise* (1920), Amaury escapes from his tiny prison only to find himself in a 'great labyrinth'. Unlike the novels of the mystical or metaphysical quest, novels concerned with psychological wanderings placed the emphasis not so much on the search for a centre as for a way out. Even though the exit often fulfilled the role of a centre (i.e. by invalidating the labyrinth), the fact that one term had been replaced by another was extremely significant. In Alvaro's *L'uomo nel labirinto* (1926), where the man, lost in the city, is the victim of anguish, the way out simply consists of a return to a more natural and authentic way of life. It is sometimes possible to identify a certain complacency in the descriptions of psychological and moral complexities as well as a certain delight in the wanderings described. In *Le Voyageur sur la Terre* (1925), Julien Green denies having taken his reader 'through the labyrinth of these complicated emotions', whereas Mauriac, referring to seventeenth-century writers, said significantly: 'They do not take great pride in their inner labyrinth; they are not obsessed by it; they do not lose themselves in it, as is the modern passion' (*Vie de Racine*, 1928). This fashion for self-analysis and the attraction of deviation, marked the emphasis placed on individualism and egotism, at the same time as the erosion of the underlying and guiding principle of the world. In *Labyrinthe* (1924), even an extremely classical writer like Estaunié lingers over the description of the aberrations of a character who has become imprisoned in a tissue of lies. He hopes to find a 'way out' of the untenable situation in which he has imprisoned himself. But a belated reversion to truth is not enough to extricate himself from this maze in which he remains a prisoner, waiting to see 'the leaves turn green' once again. The psychological labyrinths were no longer entirely spiritual labyrinths, since they unfortunately left no room for grace.

The poetry of the same period, on the other hand, appears to have maintained the concept of the centre and the positive image of the labyrinth. But it is a very different centre from the one described by Comenius or Bunyan (which even Estaunié no longer presented as such). In search of the point of coincidence and cancellation of opposites through a system of analogy, the Surrealists recognized in the labyrinth a propitious image: 'labyrinths are not made for dogs' declared Eluard (who is familiar with the image) in *152 Proverbes mis au goût du jour en collaboration avec B. Péret* (1925). In *Le Paysan de Paris* (1926), Aragon advises the gardeners to increase the number of winding pathways, to indulge in 'a veritable labyrinthine extravaganza'. One of the group's most famous exhibitions – an international exhibition of Surrealism held in Paris in 1947 – was presented as an initiatory event. This was, of course, only an image, but André Breton valued this 'indication' at a time when 'poetry and art . . . are giving up the idea of preceding Man, required elsewhere, in the perilous labyrinth of the mind'. In his *Laberinto de Amor* (1936), Leopoldo Marechal, the heir to Spanish Baroque, pursued a search for the self which is also a search for the essence of Argentina. The writing of the enigma, knowledge achieved through the abyss, are at the heart of Michaux's poetic quest: in *Epreuves, Exorcismes* (1940–4), 'Labyrinthe' presents the labyrinth in terms of the image of the eternal cycle, of walking on the spot, as well as of the very order of reality. 'Contre' in *La Nuit Remue* (1934) leaves more room for optimism: 'In the darkness, we will see clearly, brothers/ In the labyrinth, we will find the straight path.' After losing his way along the winding pathways of time, Edwin Muir, lost in the various expanses of sea, land and air, seems to echo this feeling: 'Friend, I have lost the way/(. . .) The way is one/I must retrace the track' ('The way' in *The Labyrinth*, 1949). Although meaning is elusive, there *is* meaning – and it is the task of poetry to try to discover it.

Around the time of World War Two, there was a noticeable upsurge in the use of the theme of the labyrinth which anticipated the development of its structural aspect during the 1950s and 1960s. First of all, it was possible for the theme to be used as a metaphor for the collective adventure, an image which helped to present the human adventure within a historical context. Max Aub had already used the title *El laberinto magico* to evoke the Spanish Civil War in his trilogy (1940–2), to which he added a fourth novel in 1968. Paz's *El Laberinto de la soleded* (1950) is at one and the same time an analysis of the nature of being Mexican, a history of Mexico and a philosophy of this history. At the centre of the human condition, but even more so at the centre of the Mexican experience (individual as well as collective), lies solitude. Escaping from it is a long and difficult process, but it is only at the end of this labyrinth that Mexicans can finally communicate with other nations. Novels in which memories of war and totalitarianism attest to Kafka's decisive influence devote a great deal of space to wanderings in the labyrinth. Nossack's *Nekyia: Bericht eines Uberlebende* (1947), set in the deserted and nightmarish world of the post-Holocaust period, is a difficult attempt to remember the experience as well as an anxious search for someone to whom to tell it.

Kasack's *Die Stadt hinter dem Strom* (1947), also takes us into a post-Holocaust world in which the main character is appointed by the local authorities to the post of archivist and given the task of studying all the public and private documents of the town with a view to preserving those which might be of use to the community. While in the town archives, however, the character realizes that they in fact contain the entire history of humanity and he fails to see on which basis he can decide what should and should not be preserved. When the influence of Hermann Hesse, the German writer, began to supersede that of Kafka, the concept of an orientally inspired wisdom was introduced. Furthermore, in all existential literature – and particularly in the works of Sartre – the theme of a finding a 'way out' when confronted with the absurdity of the world is extremely persistent. The metaphor of the labyrinth is really only developed when the strangeness of the world can once more become the symbolic and secret route to adventure. In such cases, it is common for a 'real' labyrinth to be introduced into the fiction to reinforce the overall theme. In *Le labyrinthe ou le Jardin de Sir Arthur* (1946) by Vedrès, the labyrinth of greenery restored by the tycoon is both a duplication and intensification of the phantasmagorical dimension in which the action takes place. At the end of the story it is destroyed by fire. The labyrinth that Langlois has planned in Giono's *Un Roi sans Divertissement* (1947), represents his own personal mark, the trace that he will leave on this earth, before blowing out his brains. In *Labyrinthes* (1947), Guiges uses the image, through the discovery of Woman and the experience of the cosmic, to examine the secret of desire. The slot machine in Carrouges' *Portes Dauphines* (1954) transports the narrator into another dimension where a remarkable combination of futuristic visions and ancient secrets constitutes, under the aegis of the labyrinth, 'the path so long sought after'. The most representative of these 'novels of the labyrinth' is possibly Lawrence Durrell's *Cefalù* (1947); here, a travel agency offers, in addition to the crossing to Crete, a visit to the cave of Cefalù which, according to the agency, is the labyrinth of the Greek myth.

During the visit, a landslide leaves the seven tourists cut off from their guide in the darkness of the galleries. They will all be put to the test and will meet a fate which corresponds to their inner nature. This 'initiatory' scenario which lends itself so conveniently to the action is also a play upon what has actually happened: mystagogy of Hogarth the psychoanalyst, or mystification of Alexos the owner of the island? Durrell the novelist stands somewhere between the two. In *The Alexandria Quartet* (1957–60), he breaks with the deliberately schematic, anecdotal approach of *Cefalù* to present a complete picture of the reality of experience through the description of Alexandria, which is the centre of the world, the 'capital of memory', 'a harlot among cities'. To achieve this, the novel breaks up into four concurrent and complementary narratives. It becomes a labyrinth of mirrors, reflecting reality at the points at which the facets converge. The narrative no longer simply evokes the image of the labyrinth, it reproduces its structure and presents it as a personal experience: we have entered the age of the literary labyrinth.

From this point on, the labyrinth becomes one of the most deeply explored metaphors of the literary experience. A work may take on the characteristics of a labyrinth through various means, primarily through the use of language. Thus Beckett has written long texts in which the characters can be heard soliloquizing in what could appear to be interminable ramblings. In *Molloy* (1948), Molloy and then Moran recall numerous experiences of wandering, and their entire lives seem like the pitiful meanderings of hemiplegic tramps. The snatches of information which emerge from amidst pointless digressions, inconsequential associations and endless repetition, also constitute, in their own way, a labyrinth for the reader. However, the experience is not compared with that of the labyrinth because this is not a narrative in which the level of consciousness of the protagonists enables the metaphor to develop. Its confused and rambling speech falls short of such a well-constructed and cultural image. There is no reason for it to find a centre, or even an end. We are involved in it, as we are in language and the world – which are both finite and infinite. And yet not entirely, because speech is language used by a speaker and in this case it becomes increasingly impoverished and exhausted as the speaker degenerates and wears himself out. As long as he is speaking, however, we are with him and alive. So let us hope that the 'performance' lasts a little longer, for at the end of this wretched labyrinth of words, we face the imminent approach of death from the depths of silence.

In Blanchot's *L'attente L'oubli* (1962), which opens with the woman's question: 'Who is speaking, she said. Who is speaking?' the work seems determined to return to its source, using all possible means to reach it and making every effort to define as closely as possible the secret centre from which it originated, and which controlled its labyrinth. But precisely because it generates the movement, the centre cannot be reached, nor the origin defined, until the movement stops. The attempt to define it is at one and the same time the only effort worth making and completely pointless: 'The centre makes discovery and movement possible, and yet it is impossible to discover the centre' (1960). According to Blanchot, the literary work is doomed to express ad infinitum what motivates it to express itself. It is condemned to be tortured by the idea of the centre, condemned to the labyrinth of the unattainable, and to continual sacrifice so that a word may exist. Perec's *Un homme qui dort* (1967) is among the many texts noticeably influenced by Kafka. The voice, which addresses the reader in the second person singular, tells of the experience of suddenly breaking with everyday existence. One day, this former student stopped behaving in the way that was expected of him. He abandoned all his plans and gave up all types of organized social activities. He systematically chose to be insignificant and decided to restrict himself to the empty setting of his non-existent life. Like a cork bobbing about on the water, he drifted on the indifferent surface of the world and moving like a sleepwalker, he traipsed aimlessly and interminably through Paris. However, during the course of this very deliberate journey to the end of wandering, he proves unable to rid himself of Himself (or the Other). Like Bely's senator and Kafka's animal, he has taken the intellectual dimension with him. Soon the Parisian labyrinth of his imagination is filled with rats and the exits to madness and death are closing in . . . unless, while waiting for the rain to stop in the Place Clichy, you ('tu') decide that you have had enough of the isolation of the man in the crowd.

Another area in which literature puts itself to the test in terms of the labyrinth is that of the physical reality of the book itself. The importance of it in relation to the Holy Scriptures and in the use that was made of it in supernatural literature, i.e. as the book of magic spells which held the secret of ambiguous knowledge, is well known. Modern literature contributes its own fascinating examples to these familiar and prominent roles. In Borges' 'El jardin de senderos que se bifurcan' (1941), Ts'ui Pên, contrary to general belief, did not want to write a book or construct a labyrinth. The manuscript that he left is, in fact, the labyrinth of which he spoke. Instead of choosing one of the many possible ways of developing the narrative, Ts'ui Pên actually 'adopted them all simultaneously', thus creating various stories which proliferate, branch off, contradict one another and meet up again ad infinitum. Taken as a whole, this extensive and chaotic work is an enigma to which the answer is the word 'time', a word which, as should be the case, never appears in the text because Ts'ui Pên does not believe in a time which is uniform and absolute, but in an infinite series of time. Like Ts'ui Pên's manuscript, Borges' text extends into many books which are derived from it.

Perhaps it is possible to identify several types of labyrinth-novels. Some, like the works of Alain Robbe-Grillet, would fall into the category of the 'junctions and crossroads' novel. Thus, in *Dans le labyrinthe* (1959), a narrator appears who, from the opening lines, makes the reader brutally aware of the completely unrestricted situation in which he finds himself: 'Outside it is raining (. . .) Outside the sun is shining (. . .)'. Drawing his inspiration from the décor of the room in which he says he is, he appears, after choosing a version according to which it is snowing (or has snowed or is supposed to have snowed . . .) outside, to begin to invent the story of a soldier, lost in the town, who has to deliver a parcel to an unspecified person. In the room, one picture in particular serves as a springboard for the narrative, or rather narratives, since the narrator spends his time trying out several different versions. Two scenes (when the soldier meets a young boy or sits down in a café) recur five or six times with variations. There is obviously no definitive version. With the toing and froing between 'here' and 'outside', we experience the tension between interior and exterior, between subjective and objective (rather as in tales of enchantment and magic), but it above all develops and draws to our attention the space of the novel as a labyrinth of possibilities.

Humour plays a greater part in Barth's fictional work 'Lost in the funhouse' (1968), translated into French as 'Perdu dans le labyrinthe'. The narrator is thirteen and the narrative is both the story of his lack of sexual accomplishment during a family visit to the fair as well as of his lack of literary accomplishment in writing the story. The narrative constantly asks questions of itself, comments on itself, stops and deviates, until it reaches the envisaged dénouements, i.e. it either peters out telling itself stories in the darkness of the funhouse, or it has succeeded in constructing a truly astounding labyrinth which it controls from a huge central keyboard. In Calvino's *Se una notte d'inverno un viaggiatore* (1979), the experience recounted is that of a reader who begins to read several novels in succession. Each time, he is interrupted by an untoward event so that the first story is replaced by another which is in turn replaced by another, and so on. What is here being examined and illustrated by this 'branching' technique is the enjoyment of narrative based on the combination of what is revealed and concealed, what is offered and refused – but we are still in Borges' garden. We come close to it with the 'commentary', a book in which the text sets itself up, comments upon itself and opens out under our very eyes. This is one of the favourite exercises of Vladimir Nabokov, a great master of the labyrinth. In *Pale Fire* (1962), the poet dreams of producing a 'tissue of meaning', of finding 'some Daedalian link/a sort of corroborating structure within the system', while his publisher-commentator compares this wish with the image that people may have had of Aristotle correcting 'what had deviated', simplifying 'the Daedalian plan' and making 'a beautifully straight, single line out of all this complexity and confusion'. But this does not prevent the reader from losing his or her way in the extremely tortuous line formed by Shade's poem and the very fluent and extensive commentary of the amazing Kinbote.

Not content with giving his novel the title of the work apocryphally attributed to Herbert Quain by Borges, i.e. *The God of the Labyrinth* (1970), Colin Wilson makes the eighteenth-century libertine, whose memoirs the hero has to publish, a member of the mysterious Phoenix sect which was the subject of one of the most engimatic short stories by the Argentinian writer. It is not hard to imagine the interest of the protagonist – a writer who is both erudite and in the tradition of D. H. Lawrence or Miller – when he discovers that the members of this sect devote themselves to sexual practices as a 'magical mystery' which will enable them to come closer to the meaning of the world.

It might be possible to identify as 'books of Zeno' the novels which, like Butor's *Emploi du Temps* (1957), attempt to express the experiences of life but in which, as the time of the writing progresses, so the time of the adventure continues to pass, without the former ever being able to coincide with the latter. Another category could be the 'book of games' where the novel refers to a game closely associated with the labyrinth. In Cortazar's *Rayuela* (1963), superimposed on an exploration of Paris and then of Buenos Aires is the attempt to change the two cities into a single game of hopscotch, an adventure playground, a route between earth and heaven, the sphere of the novel. The reader also has a choice between two ways of reading the novel, i.e. two possible routes, from one chapter-square to another. The linear narrative therefore becomes a two-dimensional space, the upward route of the game, the realm of adventure in which communication would be restored. Perec's *La vie mode d'emploi* (1978) consists of a number of 'novels' which are like the pieces of a huge jigsaw puzzle and which enable the reader to build up a picture of a six-storey block of flats in Paris over a one hundred year period. But the pieces of the puzzle are in a certain disorder. The index of names and the table of stories told tend to encourage the reader to adopt a haphazard approach based on criteria other than the 'normal' succession of chapters. In Smautf's room, there is a traditional French print, bought in Bergen, which depicts a prize being awarded to a model pupil. An inscription gives the title, apparently unconnected with the scene depicted: *Laborynthus*. Was the prize a reward for a labyrinthine task?

On the basis of Queneau's 'Un conte a votre façon' (i.e. a story of your own), children's publications offer novels where readers choose their own adventure from a range of possibilities. In Packard's *Qui a tué Edouard Balaruc?* (1982), the reader can take the shortest route of fifteen pages or the longest, of one hundred and twenty-one. In Livingstone's *Deathtrap Dungeon* (1984) – translated into French as *Le Labyrinthe de la Mort* – the route is partly determined by the throw of a dice and, in spite of the 'hideous Creature' which lurks in the labyrinth, we leave literature to move into the realm of role play. It is also possible to categorize as 'garden books' works such as Dean's very Borgesian *Verborgene Gärten* (1982), in which everything is based on 'trompe-l'oeil' and the use of mirrors, or the alternate narratives of Dufour and Vignaux in *Jardins labyrinthiques* (1985). In the latter, however, rather than the structural device, we rediscover the theme of the garden of love and even, beyond that, the Greek myth.

There is, however, a final development of the theme of the book that it would be impossible not to mention, i.e. the theme of the library. From Petrarch to Baudelaire, via Montaigne, dreams on the theme of the library are nothing new. For Borges it is a veritable labyrinth leading to other labyrinths which are the books themselves. 'La biblioteca de Babel' (1941), which consists of 'an indefinite and perhaps infinite number of hexagonal galleries' linked by corridors, has existed for all eternity. On its shelves are the rows of books written using 'all the possible combinations of the twenty or so orthographic symbols' in all languages. Although the number of these combinations is extensive, it is not infinite. It is therefore difficult to imagine the library as limitless, but it is also difficult to imagine that the hexagons, the corridors and the staircases could disappear. Perhaps it is 'limitless and recurring', a labyrinth engendering other labyrinths? But a single book can also present the image of something that is both finite and infinite. For example, there is the great circular book with the continuous spine that mystics compare with God, or the absolute book, the total and perfect summary of all the others, and which the 'Biblioteca' necessarily contains because it is infinite. Alternatively, it may be enough to imagine a volume 'consisting of an infinite number of pages which are indefinitely thin'?

The fearsome library-labyrinth of *Il Nome della Rosa* (1980), whose former blind librarian, Jorge, came from Burgos, poses a problem. The only labyrinths known in the Middle Ages had a single passage, like those depicted on the tiling of French and Italian cathedrals. Since the first known drawing of a labyrinth with several passages dates from approximately the middle of the sixteenth century, it is extremely unlikely that the type of architecture imagined by Umberto Eco would have existed two hundred years earlier. This is further reinforced by the fact that he stresses that the Building in which the labyrinth is located is of a much earlier construction than that of the abbey, which could itself have already existed for several centuries. This Building 'possibly created for other purposes' is also somewhat reminiscent of the terrifying structures left by the Great Ancients in the works of Lovecraft. It is also worthy of note that the method of finding the way out, learnedly quoted by Guglielmo according to 'an ancient text' that he had once read, was in fact propounded by a nineteenth-century French mathematician. We begin to wonder whether we are perhaps being made fun of, or rather the idea is confirmed that the 'labyrinth-mania' which characterizes the modern age is here making fun of itself. This would not be in the least surprising insofar as the main function of this labyrinth, which is too much of a labyrinth to be genuine, appears to be to ensure the inaccessibility of the second book of Aristotle's *The Poetics* which has been discovered by Jorge. The former librarian (who has probably read Bakhtin) fears that if this study on comedy became generally known, laughter would be released. Man would be liberated from fear and the Law would be held up to ridicule. Once again, one of the Philosopher's works would bring uncertainty into the very heart of the book of books. Therefore, let the Library burn, let Babel fall into ruins, so that the Book may survive.

As a symbolic image which makes it possible to work out contradictory postulations simultaneously, the labyrinth falls within the province of mythical thought. It is interesting to see how literature, through this image and over a long period of time, has contributed to the development of this thought. Generally speaking, since the Classical age, the effort of modern thought has been presented as an attempt to free itself and break away from its mythical counterpart. This break has been a continual process: it remains incomplete. It was not made once and for all in the sixth century with ionic physics, nor in the sixteenth with Copernicus, despite the importance of the revolutions that these scientific discoveries entailed. It has been progressive. Nor is it certain that we are moving towards a definitive separation, nor indeed that the break has to be completed. The process is a complex one which may involve making leaps forward or taking steps backwards, although the latter are not necessarily regressive . . . Within the context of this analysis, Plato and the Cervantes of *Don Quixote* were well ahead of their time, while Calderón and Joyce represent extremely constructive reversals. The major periods that have been identified in terms of literature's appropriation of the theme of the labyrinth, correspond more or less to the breaks and re-orientations involved in the development of modern thought in relation to mythical thought. If it were necessary to identify the points at which the former most significantly diverged from the latter, we would consider that, in terms of the literary image of the labyrinth, this occurred during the Renaissance and the nineteenth century. During the Renaissance, the labyrinth ceased to be an external and hostile reality from which Man was only saved by magical or divine grace, and when the Renaissance poets imagined the labyrinth, although they undoubtedly had the Greek myth in mind, they no longer referred to it at every turn, as had previously been the case. They themselves replaced the monsters and heroes within the labyrinth, which they envisaged as a space in which they had to find their own way. During the nineteenth century, the conviction that there was necessarily a path leading to an end died out and, in the space left devoid of its sacred aura, the modern wanderings began. The knights of the Middle Ages meandered through forests under the watchful eye of God, whereas the modern seekers of meaning run the constant risk of indifferent and meaningless peregrinations. The collapse of the image of the centre is undoubtedly the reason for the prodigious development of the theme of the labyrinth. With the death of God, the knights left the forest and Man and humanity entered the labyrinth.

André Peyronie

Lilith

This myth has very distant origins in old Babylonia, where the ancient Semites had adopted the beliefs of their predecessors, the Sumerians, and is connected to the great creation myths. It is closely linked to the serpent through memories of a very ancient cult honouring a Great Mother Goddess, the cosmic power of the Eternal Feminine, also called the 'Great Serpent' and 'Dragon', who was worshipped under the names of Astarte, Istar or Ishtar, Mylitta, Innini or Innana.

Inscriptions discovered in the ruins of Babylon (the Library of Assurbanipal) have clarified the origins of Lilith, the sacred courtesan of Innana, who was sent by the latter to seduce men in the street and take them to the Goddess' temple, where sacred fertility rites took place. Lilith, who was called 'The Hand of Innana', was confused with the goddess she represented, who was herself sometimes called the 'Sacred Prostitute'.

Lilith's name is of Semitic and Indo-European origins. The Sumerian word 'lil', which is also a part of the name of Enlil, god of the atmosphere, means 'wind', 'air' and 'storm'. It was this burning wind which, according to popular belief, gave women in childbirth the fever, killing them and their children. Lilith was primitively considered as one of the great hostile forces of nature in a group of three demons, one of which, the Lilu, was male and the other two, the Lilitu and the Ardat Lili, female. The latter was the wife of the abductor of the light, or the female abductor of the light.

There is also a relationship between Lilith and the Sumerian words *lulti* (lasciviousness) and *lulu* (debauchery). Lilith uses her seduction (she is a beautiful, long-haired woman) and her (very animal) sensuality for destructive ends. It was probably during their captivity in Babylon that the Jews became acquainted with this demon who was active mainly at night, but the connection between the Hebrew word *lail* (night) and the name Lilith has been acknowledged to be unlikely. Lilith is however often represented with the features of a night bird, as one of the owl species.

Two other paths of research enable us to complete the description of Lilith with the potential links between her name and the Indo-European root *la* (to shout, to sing) on the one hand and on the other the Greek word λάω. The Sanskrit *lik* (to lick) is derived from *la*, as well as a large number of words related to the tongue and lips: *Lippe* (German), *lippe* (French), *labium* (Latin); Lilith eats children and her lips and mouth are always mentioned in later literary works. The word λάω, which is also related to the word 'light', as in *lux* (Latin), *luz* (Spanish), *Licht* (German), gives the idea of 'seeing with a piercing glance', 'seeing at night', 'being free of darkness'; some literary texts give a place to Lilith in a kind of strange initiatory search undertaken by the hero.

THE FOUNDING TEXTS

Lilith is mentioned in the Old Testament, *Isaiah* 34, 14, in an apocalyptic poem on the end of Idumea, which Yahweh's anger changed into a brasier of pitch and then into a desert that no one would ever pass through except the cormorant, the hedgehog, the owl and the crow, who would make their home in this place, and 'there shall the night hag alight, and find for herself a resting place' (*Revised Standard Version*). It is from the linking of this passage (the exile of Lilith) and the two versions of the creation of man and woman by Yahweh (*Genesis* 1 and 2) that the myth of Lilith was born in modern times: she was the first woman to be created and she uttered thc 'ineffable name', which gave her the wings with which she flew out of the Garden of Eden, where she left Adam, with whom she was incompatible. She was pursued by three angels, Sinoi, Sinsinoi and Samengeloff, who found her by the Red Sea and asked her in vain to return. Since that day, in answer to the three angels' threat (that she would see thousands of her children killed every day) and out of a desire for vengeance and jealousy of Eve, who was afterwards created to replace her – not like Adam from earth, as Lilith was, this being presented as the cause of their misunderstanding, but from one of Adam's ribs – Lilith returned to the world of human beings, the descendants of Adam and Eve, to do them harm.

The first known texts to mention her warn against the demon Lilith and offer spells and recipes to protect against her, particularly to keep her away from children and women in labour. These are *The Testament of Solomon* (around the third century), *The Talmud* (around the fifth century) in which there also appears a third class of winged demons with human shape, the 'Lilins', *The Alphabet of Ben Sira* (around the seventh century) which contains the most popular and naive version of the myth, *The Zohar* (around the thirteenth century), which gives the most occult version, and *The Kabbala* (around 1600), which portrays the union of Lilith and Sammael.

LILITH THE REBEL

Literature has mainly been concerned with Lilith the rebel who, in her assertion of her right to freedom and pleasure, to equality with men, brings about the downfall of both herself and those she meets. She is a sensual *femme fatale* who also aspires to power and supremacy. This is conveyed by a German play dated from 1565, *Jutta*, which explains the existence of Lilith in its account of the story of her granddaughter, Jutta or Johanna, the only woman known to have been pope. This story was reworked in the twentieth century by Lawrence Durrell in his novel *Pope Joan* and by Odile Ehret in a play performed at the Cartoucherie de Vincennes in Paris in 1983, *La Papesse ou la légende de la papesse Jeanne et de sa compagne Bartoléa*. At the same time Claude Pasteur also wrote a novel based on the story called *La Papesse* (1983). In 1667 in *Paradise Lost*, Milton alludes to Lilith as the 'snake witch'. She was a desperate heroine for the Romantics, described as a beautiful, sensual woman with long hair, who led others with her into a whirlwind of misfortune, disaster and death. Her hideous, bloodthirsty aspect was recalled by Victor Hugo, who combines her with Isis in *La Fin de Satan* (1886): 'La fille de Satan, la grande femme d'ombre/Cette Lilith qu'on nomme Isis au bord du Nil . . . /Je suis Lilith-Isis, l'âme noire du monde.'/('Satan's daughter, tall woman of shadow/That Lilith whom they call Isis on the banks of the Nile . . . /I am Lilith-Isis, the world's black soul'). He has her disappear when confronted by the angel of freedom.

In *Eden Bower* and *The House of Life* (1870–81), Dante Gabriel Rossetti makes Lilith a seductive siren, the eternal *femme fatale* with an irresistible and infernal charm who, in her mystery, arouses desire and a sense of adventure in men, thus leading them to their destruction. This was how she always appeared in modern and contemporary works of the late nineteenth and twentieth centuries. In Marc Chadourne's novel *Dieu créa d'abord Lilith* (1935), she sows ruin, death and an incurable despair before disappearing no one knows where, in despair herself and still a rebel: perhaps she is dead, perhaps not.

LILITH, LULU, LOLITA: COMPLEXITY OF THE MYTH

Wedekind's play *Lulu*, comprising two plays, *Earth Spirit* (1899) and *Pandora's Box* (1901), adapted for the screen by Pabst (1928), reworked in Berg's opera and performed in the complete adaptation by Pierre Jean Jouve (1983) at the Cartoucherie de Vincennes in 1985, provides a masterly and brilliant portrait of Lilith, revealing all her complexity and the principal themes of the myth. The surprising thing is that the woman who is presumed to have inspired Wedekind's play, Lou Andreas Salomé, was herself described by Freud as having the features and characteristics related to the Lilith myth.

In his 1892 play *Lilith*, Remy de Gourmont gives a cynically humorous and erotic account of the entire traditional creation story as described in the sacred Jewish texts, linked to a pessimistic vision of human life. And yet, despite this work's entertaining tone, it clearly shows that the myth of Lilith reflects the desperate human search for the origins and meaning of life.

This also emerges in George MacDonald's novel *Lilith* (1895), where the hero faced with Lilith is propelled down the dangerous path of a long and painful initiation, at the end of which he is left alone and uncertain.

Something similar happens to the hero of Nabokov's novel *Lolita* (1955), although the hero's initiation 'in reverse', which leads him to destructive madness and death, is presented in a quite different way. Imprisoned and awaiting his execution, it is to the glory of the 'Lilith' who has brought him to this, to remind himself of her and to escape the pain which her death gives him – Lolita dies in childbirth – that Humbert Humbert writes his story. Art is thus integrated here, like a shining sign, on the picture of the myth, through the brilliant writer Nabokov's wink, referring to his hero writing and asserting his freedom to transcend the national heritage at will.

Lilith's aspect as a devourer of children expanded to the size of the great destructive mother who swallows the human world whole in her great mouth of unconsciousness, violence and death. We can see this in the very title of the latest study to appear on the Lilith myth: *Lilith ou la Mère Obscure* by J. Bril (1981); and it is also this aspect of the myth that obsessively appears in Philippe Sollers' novel *Femmes* (1983).

PARALLELS

Some associations of Lilith with the Queen of Sheba recall her aspect of false luminosity. She satisfies the every wish of the man who lets himself be seduced by her charms and gifts, then sends him on a quest which isolates him from other people, down a path which runs against life. In 1932 the Austrian psychoanalyst Fritz Wittels invented a 'Lilith complex' (or neurosis, which is not unconnected to this).

The aim of the myth of Lilith is to keep men away from her by warning them of the danger she represents for them. However its main function is to warn women: she who does not keep Adam's law will be rejected, eternally unsatisfied and a source of misfortune. The end of Anatole France's short story in *Balthasar*, 'La Fille de Lilith', makes his heroine a feminine parallel of the 'Flying Dutchman', who aspires to Eve's destiny and the mortal condition in order to experience 'life' and 'pleasure'.

And yet, the myth's development from one text to the next and its repeated reappearances in modern times tend to draw our attention to this feminine figure – who also represents a vision of the human life and world, and the hierarchy that governs them – in a particular way: cast out from the society of human beings, Lilith wants to make herself known, negatively if necessary, through the harm she does them. The combining of Lilith and Isis, who is adored as the healing and redeeming Great Mother, and other related myths containing an ambivalence of benevolence and malevolence, remind us that her effects on human life depend largely upon the perspective from which people view her and the way they look at her. The fashion for tourist trips to the desert tells her story in its own way: some people are prepared to visit Lilith, if necessary in the place of her exile itself. It is sufficient that Israeli revolutionaries on the one hand and American women on the other have used the name Lilith as a journal title for its connotations of rebellion and freedom. If she is recognized and reintegrated into the human community and her talents and rights are respected, will she become a benevolent and protecting goddess, as was the case of Kishimojin, one of her sisters in India, daughter of the Dragon Goddess and a destroyer and stealer of children who, after the Buddha gave her back her son, became the goddess who helps at births. This at any rate is one optimistic way of looking at the future, alongside others that are less so. Whatever the case, Lilith always reminds us that the forces of death correspond to the forces of life and that everything is balanced – day and night, darkness and light, feminine and masculine – so that there can be no value judgement or domination by one aspect of the same whole without consequences that are deleterious to that same aspect. She also seeks to tell us that there is always something for the good of the whole to be found in any part that is cast out of creation and continues to gesture to us from a distance.

Brigitte Couchaux

Literary and Mythological Narratives

While it may seem difficult to define myth and literature succinctly, it is rather easier to go into the question of what they have in common, notably narrative. Therefore the question that will be considered here is the status of narrative both in myth and in literature; inevitably this limitation will result in viewing the question from a narrow perspective.

However, partial and narrow though this approach may be, it covers a larger field than might be thought, given that narrative is both protean and widely disseminated. Before we come to the points of convergence, similarity and divergence of narrative as found in myth and in literature, we should clarify some of the peculiarities of narrative found in both fields.

As the presence of narrative in myth is self-evident, all that is probably necessary is to repeat that most of the definitions of myth whether formulated by ethnologists, psychologists or literary critics emphasize its narrative aspect to such an extent that the most basic definition of myth seems to be: a story. On the other hand – to anticipate the conclusions reached in this essay – it is possible to demonstrate that narrative, concealed or otherwise, is also more frequently present in literature than is generally imagined. We will then try to ascertain where these two types of story hinge together, and perhaps speculate on how literary narrative can exploit mythical narrative, or be like it.

It has never been established that literature can dispense with story-telling, even in forms that are described as non-narrative, such as lyrical or descriptive passages. Narrative may well be ubiquitous in literary discourse, albeit in a latent form but still fulfilling a vital role. Analyzing some examples of underlying narrative gives some idea of its omnipresence. Thus lyrical texts – if we use Valéry's definition – are associated with giving expression to a feeling of exaltation or an outpouring of emotion and are equivalent, he says, to developing an exclamation; but it is harder than it would seem to remain on these peaks. The persons expressing themselves by the very fact of the exclamations they utter, present themselves as being invaded by the object of their feeling, be it love, or hate, etc., to such a point that they are temporarily bereft, if not of themselves, of their power to act: 'O lac . . .', 'Solitude, ô coeur d'homme . . .', 'Solitude et ténèbres au grand midi de l'homme . . .', 'O vive flamme d'amour . . .'. Each time, the persons speaking are deprived by their own amazement and their own outpourings, of their link with a verb. This effect is so clearly marked that the verbs which surge into this empty space (except when the invocation is resolved in dialogue and when the object of the exaltation develops a relationship with the speaker) take as their subject the *object* of the exaltation rather than the person enunciating it . . . What is expressed first of all is a suspension of the pronoun *I*, but soon everything is restored to normal, as if this absence of a link with action were not viable in literature for more than a fleeting moment . . . In other words, in order to speak, literature needs to recount.

Study of a text such as *Le Cantique Spirituel* by John of the Cross, which involves a passage from lyricism to mysticism, or to the lyrical expression of mysticism, provides a particularly significant example of these processes. Reading through it even quickly, it immediately becomes apparent that exaltation as such is extremely transient, while the author's recourse to lyrical poetry, and what is said in the theological commentary he gives of it, show a determination to make this exaltation *last* so that it can be communicated. In actual fact what takes up the poem in its entirety owes less to this exaltation than to the *story* of the quest which is superimposed on it. The verses cannot stay long at the culminating point; desire and love, like a ping-pong ball, are passed continually from one to the other of the partners in this divine love, the husband expressing his desire for his wife just as she expresses her desire for him. These poems of fulfilment, at a level beyond the clever and paradoxical reciprocity that they establish, are also poems of instability. At least from the literary point of view they tell the story of an unstable situation, of the throbbing of love. Ecstasy is depicted as the quest for ecstasy, so yet again, internal as the quest may be, narrative structuring is used.

In his poem 'Dévotion' from *Illuminations*, Rimbaud offers a partial theory of this idea, albeit expressed negatively and back to front. His invocatary poem chooses to use exaltation (as the possible and perhaps chimerical product of invocation) and the consecutiveness required for narrative to exclude one another: 'Mais plus *alors*' [No more '*thens*']. The nature of the object of this exaltation is immaterial; what *does* matter is that when this 'Dévotion' comes up against an adverb of time, an adverb which would reinstate temporality, chronology and the narrative possibilities those would imply, it rejects it, for fear of becoming pious, corrupt or at any rate devalued. Thus in theory two registers of discourse come up against one another – that of the *subject* of the devotion, a subject that is devout, devoted or dedicated to silence as a result of the desire for exaltation – and that of an organizational foothold in temporality and the world. On the one hand is the lyrical or mystical quest (even if it is specious) and on the other, the mental universe – here rejected – involving cautiousness, arrangement and installation.

Of course the 'then' is impossible to eradicate on a lasting basis; it threatens to come back in force, whence Rimbaud's backwards theory, which brings narrative in its train, and for all we know departure for Harrar. Writing without using narrative 'pointers' is simply not an option that can be sustained for any length of time, and the pieces of writing that set out most deliberately to be the opposite of anecdotal still inevitably end up using the props of narrative.

Description too is more closely allied to narrative than is evident, for description is always pregnant with a narrative yet to come . . . whether this is expressed or not. In the case of Balzac, for example, where future developments are woven in, narrative is expressed, but is perhaps not explicit in texts which set out to be as deliberately neutral in this respect as the haiku or 'La Connaissance de l'Est'. Thus we may wonder if the tension in these poems is derived from the fact that a setting is established for some metaphysical or human gesture, which we are then frustrated from experiencing. The failure of acts and events to materialize actually speaks as forcefully here as the acts and events themselves do elsewhere. A sense of unease comes from this deprivation, or perhaps just from the semblance of deprivation, and it seems that through its very absence, narrative may paradoxically assume an active function.

If narrative is fundamental therefore, and all literary texts tend towards narration, what distinction can convincingly be drawn between myth and literature – and what do they make of one another? Is there any difference between the proposition that Oedipus killed his father and married his mother, and the proposition that the well-known marchioness went out at five o'clock? This all depends on the way narration operates in the two fields of myth and literature.

The first point to make is that a different kind of response is expected to the two separate statements. But what if this response, which should differ in intensity, proves inadequate or incomplete, or even inappropriate? We know full well that a sentence can convey *everything*, simply by telling us that the marchioness went out at five o'clock. Moreover Proust in fact uses violence in depicting the final meeting between Swann and Madame de Guermantes. Even though she was only too eager to greet him appropriately when Swann – ill, and feeling that his end was near – came to pay his last respects, she nontheless took the time to go and change the black shoes she was wearing under her red dress . . . And as the way it is expressed is in keeping with the cruelty of the anecdote, the narrator devotes more time to describing Madame de Guermantes' dress than to describing Swann's emotional disarray, with a roundabout symbolism which nonetheless refers to human death.

However, the criterion of intensity is in fact essential when describing story in myth, though it is not sufficient in itself. This is because myth presents us with events on a large – one might even say a gross – scale. It depicts violent situations crudely, it expresses forcefully what is in itself forceful, it shows a liking for images and events with impact. Rather than being called a *crude story*, myth could be defined as the *crude story of what is in itself crude*.

Myth, however, is defined not solely in terms of the intensity of the scenes it evokes, but also by the organization it imposes on them, and one of the laws governing the privileged structuring of mythology is that of contrast.

Original scenes or images – forces, as Régis Boyer calls them – are always accompanied by contrasting scenes or images. Napoleon's glory is conjured up, but with it his love affairs and St Helena. When we talk of Joan of Arc, both her weakness and her strength are stressed, along with her belligerence and the stake. In the same way Oedipus is a king, then he is an outcast lamenting his exile; before his exclusion from Thebes he is a strong man, according to Sophocles 'the finest of mortals', yet weak too, wishing to be just and yet tainted. All myths, possibly, can be seen in terms of antithetical pairs – and it may be this fondness for contrast that ensures the natural link between myth and tragedy, especially as this link was spelt out at least partially in Aristotle's *Poetics* (par. 1453 b). Psychology, too, has been able to employ mythological themes as the double representation of desire perceived in its expansiveness and its precariousness. Life and death, gratified desire and unbearable intensity, repletion and want, satisfaction and frustration: in this double configuration of the opposite faces of desire the reason why so many myths seem to take the form of stories of crime and punishment can doubtless be found, provided we understand this as implying an existential or biological burden rather than as pointing a moral. And finally myth also tends to demonstrate graphically in terms of catastrophes the impossibility of being both mother and lover, son and husband, Antigone and Creon, an avenging wife and a happy mother.

However, myth is also defined by its outer form – how it tells a story, as well as by what it recounts. Another law is superimposed on the previous one, reinforcing it: what might be called the law of the shortest path and the straight line. We may wonder in fact if story in myth does not consist of a minimum narrative linking outsize images. It is constructed not just from powerful scenes, nor from powerful and contrasting scenes; but also seems to link these to one another by the most tenuous means imaginable. Narrative in the novel makes obvious use of a number of different registers covering probability, contingency, reference, logic or the conventional appearance of any one of these, or in the modern novel, of devices acknowledged to be arbitrary and set rules; mythological narrative on the other hand goes straight to the point. It does not clutter itself up with anything external to itself. It goes from one point to the next, and is characterized by a sort of violent brevity. Thus in the most striking cases, narrative may be reduced purely and simply to spelling out *consecutiveness*. The crude story mentioned earlier becomes a piling up of scenes. The only laws recognized are those of chronology and accumulation in chronology, to the point where the narrative proper ends up by being resolved in adverbs of time which serve to replace structuring: *and then, after that, next . . .*

Seen as a crude story that can be organized in accordance with a law depicting in sequence or taking the shortest path between, powerful and contrasting events, myth develops with so little consideration for its own evolution that we may wonder if it is not a kind of abstract narrative matrix, an algebraic equation transplanted into literature – Cocteau in fact interpreted myth as a sort of mathematics of the mind – or for Lévi-Strauss a permanent structure; he presents mythology as something capable of rising above historical time, time that has already elapsed (*Le Cru et le Cuit*, Plon, 1964). A narrative matrix, a permanent structure, even to quote Lévi-Strauss a victory over raw time – all this demonstrates a kind of narrative not amenable to anything that would prevent it from adhering to its own logic.

But what can be said about literary narrative in relation to what has just been established, given that we have already indicated above that it is protean, and even that the omnipresence of narrative in literature can be established only if this characteristic is accepted? Northrop Frye states that: 'Myth, then, is one extreme of literary design; naturalism is the other' (Frye, 1957: 136). This is so, but what takes place between these two poles?

There can be no question of defining literary narrative or narratives here – they could doubtless be diversified ad infinitum. We will simply pick out two recurrent characteristics, because of the way they can be further developed. Unlike mythical narrative, literary narrative permits digressions and accepts padding. The marchioness may be happy to go out at five o'clock and the narrative will at the same time gladly tell us the circumstances of, reasons for, effects of, in short all the details surrounding her outing. Considered thus, it might seem that the interplay between myth and literature could be thought of as a dance in which revelation and the desire to cover up, the raw presence of myth and the use of masks, what is latent and what is explicit move round each other like partners eternally changing places. Now that the peculiarities of the literary story and the mythological story have been stated, we come to the crucial question of how they meet, in collective thought and in works of literature, of their similarities and their differences, of their convergences and respective capacities to grasp or exclude one another – a question too large and perhaps too new to be dealt with here. Nevertheless, the study of some of the ways in which the two bodies represented by literary narrative and mythical narrative cut across one another will give us some idea of the scope of the question, and perhaps make it possible to shed some light on it.

However, the first of these analyses amounts virtually to a caution: we should not jump to the conclusion from what has already been said regarding the intensity of myth, its violent brevity and its vehemence on the one hand, and the digressions and padding happily accommodated in literature on the other, that literature is a *lesser phenomenon*. Any attempt to distinguish the two types of narrative using intensity as a criterion is inadequate. In theory at least, literature does not 'water down' myth. It has its own vehemence which owes nothing, or at least not its essence, to the intensity of the events it recounts, and far from degrading any mythical relevance or irrelevance, unless it be in anecdotal frivolity, this vehemence lies elsewhere. Its equilibrium is different. Its points of resistance are different. And it is vehement in a different way.

The reasons why this should be so are many and complex, but at least one can be named here as a vanishing point. Literary enterprise involves both the designation of what is happening around the narrative, in which process we have perhaps already been able to discern its tendency to digress, and the organization of the victory it has attained over language. It becomes impossible to talk about literature without referring to the fact that it is constituted as literature. The tension which in myth was partly derived from the nature of the events and their accumulation, is here replaced by a tension which comes from the confrontation between order and disorder, the order being contained in the discourse itself and the disorder in what it enunciates. The violence or vehemence of literary narrative is thus strictly literary, and comes from the discourse. Thus it would never be possible to trace it back to the violence it describes; it derives from the combat carried on in the discourse between light and dark, the discourse and its purport, the form and the organizing process that it carries out on the totality that perception offers.

This separation of myth and literature does not prevent them from being superimposed, or from overlaying one another. Myths such as Don Juan which are literary in origin serve to illlustrate this. However, we should be less concerned with the various literary guises that myth can don (a question already tackled many times), than with the intrusion of mythological segments into literature itself. A mythical story remains mythical and is recognizable as such beneath its literary trappings, although Claude Lévi-Strauss has claimed that anyone who talks about a myth creates another version of it. Nor does the use of myth have any effect on the specifically literary quality of the works in which it figures. It is possible for Sophocles to write plays of genius based on the Oedipus story while others chat about it. The more immediate question, however, is to know how literature can grasp the foreign body which myth represents for it, and use if for its own purposes. Ancient tragedy, and classical French tragedy too, rested on myth. Aristotle wrote his theory of tragedy on this basis: in many cases, tragedy displayed what myth was enunciating. Except for a few lapses which can be found even in *Oedipus Rex*, it can be transparent and crystalline in quality. When this happens, as it often does for the Greek myths which we know well only as tragedies, or for the great comedies based on Don Juan, literature serves as a vehicle for myth.

The situation can be reversed, however. Among those novels most closely associated with the suggestion of contingency and psychology and the mapping out of various social or moral codes, there are some points where the novel bursts through its own texture, giving way to a narrative discourse other than its own, consisting (as in myth) of events about which there is nothing to be said. Thus murder, rape, incest, and sometimes love, or the reunion of the two partners who make up a couple sometimes appear like meteors in texts, the guiding principle of which might have seemed different. To give just one example, Julien Sorel breaks free of an ambition that is very strongly anchored in a political and historical context to indulge via the sideways step of an attempted murder in amorous adventures that bear comparison with those in any story-book. Moreover, this example is all the more striking in Stendhal's work as the attempted murder and the love affairs that follow upon it are the vanishing point for the hero's destiny, and the author can do nothing about it. One narrative network has been superseded by another as a result of the recounting of events which in themselves represent a caesura or break, and this affects not only what is narrated but the narrative itself. Even so, the novel obviously has breaks that are integral to it, and its narrative as a whole will allow for the transgression of the limits of the type of narrative which defines it as being what it is. The work then forms a deposit round its own break, as a pearl oyster does round anything that wounds it.

Literary narrative can allow mythical narrative to appear through it or water myth down, as can be seen in many examples from Corneille's *Oedipe* – hardly read now – to Cocteau's version of Oedipus which has not lost its appeal, and it can also, by the very nature of its protean character, include fragments of 'crude stories' when it sees fit, detached from any explanatory, circumstantial accompanying detail. In every case these are vehement, often violent happenings involving the disruption of everyday life as it is recorded in the novel, while at the same time remaining internal to it. Every time they occur, these devices, which paradoxically signal an internal transgression, convey meaning, in the same way as they create form. From this point of view both literature and myth talk about man and depict him, and in the final analysis come together in enumerating events which say more in themselves than can be said about them. But we can be sure that literature turns to the brutal language of myth only so as to mimic from inside a departure from the codes which it regards as its own, and thus provide itself with an horizon.

There is one final significant aspect of the relationship between myth and literary narrative: it concerns the specific case of some forms of modernity that affect narrative. These narrative forms turn away from support logics or adventitious logics, from convention, from the use of a referent, from generally accepted probability or psychology, insofar as psychology really exists in the traditional novel. Even so it would be difficult to claim, as has sometimes been thought in the case of Robbe-Grillet for example, that they really break with narrative (we set out earlier to show that such an attempt could hardly be sustained); on the contrary, they raise it to a higher level, taking it to its extreme limits, renouncing not the story but an appearance of credibility in its trappings and what amount in the final analysis to presentational devices. Robbe-Grillet's novels, and many of René Char's poems such as 'Madeleine à la Veilleuse', could be analyzed along these lines. Once again novelty is about return and reunion. Desire for the mother, murder of the father, wandering and quest for the origin of oneself in one case, and in the other, rape, the powerlessness of the onlooker, and the victory of contemplation. In both texts the story as myth goes straight to the powerful scene which is at its foundation. To sum up, different though they may be, both only subscribe to the demands of myth, namely that it will admit only its own logic. Hence the effect of surprise, if not shock, engendered by both. Narrative here is laid bare, and what jars comes from the story as such. This is no doubt just an unexpected meeting, or perhaps an unexpected use of mimesis. This coinciding of myth and literature is not irrelevant, however, in that it widens the range of superimpositions that are possible between mythical story-telling and literary story-telling.

Among the convergences and divergences of myth and literature, or even among the possible uses of one by the other, there is a fertile field for research. The question of the relationships between mythical narrative and narrative in stories or tales could also be studied in the same way, with mythical narrative easily turning towards catastrophe because it denounces the ambivalence of desire and the difficulty of being, whereas the tale sets out to be more positively moral and encouraging by tending to reward diligence. Yet again there are the links between myth and melodrama, one internalizing the impossibility of desire while the other always assigns an external cause to it. Or again, for the list is endless, the links between myth, in its brutal reality as a crude story, and scandal which often replaces it in the nineteenth-century novel – a fundamental transgression as opposed to a social, conventional and psychological or moral transgression.

Literary narrative, for all its polymorphy, is just as amenable to analysis as mythical narrative, and even its meanders, such as its use of myth or the distance which it chooses to keep from it, are by their nature language, and consequently far from neutral, both as regards form and signification.

Colette Astier

Literature and Initiation

It is widely accepted that the work of art is universal and timeless, in other words that it constitutes an escape from the limitations of time and space, that it is the expression of a unity and totality whose example or equivalent is not to be found in reality and that it requires a freedom of creation and expression that are impossible to find outside the field of art. Less often accepted, however, is the nonetheless obvious fact that the work only has these qualities if the author has lived through the experience. In other words, one cannot explain the universal and timeless nature of the work of art, its unity, its totality and the liberty to which it bears witness (features one is not aware of but which are sensed in reading, hearing a piece of music or contemplating a work of the plastic arts), unless its author had not the imaginary representation but the feeling of universality, timelessness, unity, totality and absolute freedom, in other words unless that author was, if only for moments at a time, more than human.

The result of the concept that artistic creation is a lived experience of the process of metamorphosis is a belief in the possibility of the author's ontological transmutation; moreover, the work itself merely sets out the itinerary of its author's self-generation. Birth into a new way of being can only be ensured through initiation. And it is because the work reveals the process of initiation that it enables the reader, hearer or viewer to experience the poetic state they are hoping for, in other words to experience, at lesser cost and at a lower level, the sequence of apparent death, rebirth and metamorphosis of the self and of the world which are at last reconciled in one language.

The poetic experience is thus seen as a specific experience, which can be felt though the creation of a work, the siting of a passage from the 'profane' state to the 'true life', as the great contemporary writers all express it. Kafka, for example, wanted to reach 'true life', in which, he said, 'my face can at last age naturally with the progress of my work' (1965: letter of 3 January 1912). Elsewhere again he says, 'I can have happiness only if I succeed in raising the world to make it enter truth, purity, changelessness' (1965: letter of 25 September 1917). It is remarkable that we also find this sense of a different life and the words 'the true life' in Rilke's letters 'to a young poet' and in the work of Proust ('True life, life at last discovered and illuminated, thus the only life which is really lived, is literature', *Le Temps retrouvé*) and Breton (*Surrealist manifesto*).

This concept of poetic creation and its relationship to the author is the fruit of a development worth consideration in detail.

FROM MYTHICAL HERO TO ROMANTIC CHARACTER

Jung defined the mythical hero as an archetype of the self, an exemplary model, the ideal human type, a figure of the animus which incarnates the mana personality, whose drama unfolds according to the model of the return to the source, victory over the collective psyche and the conquest of immortality.

Otto Rank (1959) sees the usual itinerary of the character of the romantic work, who is a projection of the author's fantasies, in the triple thematic sequence (obscure birth, accomplishment of wondrous feats, affirmation of value and difference).

For Mircea Eliade (1954), the themes of epic narratives and romantic narratives do not change: the models passed down from the most distant past do not disappear. Ulysses' wanderings or the quest for the Holy Grail can be seen in nineteenth-century novels. All creations (a house, a child, a poem) have the cosmogony as a model (in other words regeneration – or reintegration – into original perfection). It is always an initiatory path that is in question: an individual return to the origins, a passage, a rebirth (Eliade, 1955 and 1959). For Eliade, indeed, literature is the expression of a rebellion against historical time and literary characters escape their conditions. Artistic creation is an effort to recreate language in order to make possible a passage from the verbal to the formal, access to sacredness, since what is at issue is to experience universality and timelessness.

Philippe Sellier (1970), Simone Vierne (1979) and Jean Biès (1979) have outlined a possible reading of the romantic text based on the (initiatory) cosmogonic myth. To read is to die to oneself and to the profane world in order to reach the sacred world of myths and symbols, whereas to write is to seek, through a false death, to be reborn immortal, to ensure that one's being will be permanent, to transcend the human condition which is to be destined for destruction.

According to these theorists there is no literary work that has no initiatory elements: the descent into hell (in *Hamlet* and the work of Bossuet, Baudelaire and Proust), the acquisition of powers, including that of metamorphosis (in *Tristan et Iseult* and the work of Ovid and Kafka), inspiration and ecstasy (in the work of Claudel, Romain Rolland, Breton, Rilke and Péguy) and the recreation of the world through the invention of a new language (in the work of Mallarmé). Poets, like the shaman, seek solitude, live on the fringes, practise an oneiric activity, use drugs, are subject to visions and believe themselves to be chosen.

Furthermore, the myth of the hero always uses the same structure, whether in mythological fiction, biblical narratives, the true novel, the detective novel, the western and even in political propaganda. The hero's itinerary (concealment, apotheosis, metamorphosis) can be found in the story of David and Goliath, of Hercules' labours, in the Passion of Jesus, in the life of Joan of Arc and in Pascal's meditations, in the work of the preromantics, the romantics and in that of the surrealists, in Karl Marx's Manicheanism and the Napoleonic epic, in Romain Rolland's novels and in Claudel's plays or in the poems of Saint-John Perse.

For René Girard, any really powerful work of art has an at least faintly initiatory effect insofar as it gives us a presentiment of violence and dread. To the rites of immobility which aim to keep things in their existing order, Girard contrasts rites of passage, whose aim is the acquisition of a new condition. The individual undertaking the passage, in other words isolation, is isolated, excluded, stands on the fringes of the community, is expelled. To this extent the passage is a fearful experience. Deprived of all status, individuals tend to become changed into their own monstrous double. This is how the ritual and mythical difference proper to ancient thinking is restored in the form of 'cultural' and 'aesthetic' difference.

FROM FICTIONAL CHARACTER TO WRITER

It is rather surprising to observe that the initiation of the mythical hero, reproduced in the itinerary of the character in a novel, can be revealed in the process of creation as it is described in writing by authors themselves. In the first stage, there is an impression of chaos, a state of absence and lack, loss of direction, distress, loss of self, separation, solitude, impersonality, dispersal; in the second stage, after a feeling of rebirth, there is a gathering together, coherence, autonomy, gaiety, ecstasy; lastly, in the final stage, there is a metamorphosis, recognizable in the discovery of unity.

It would seem that between the closed space of the work and its author a relationship of reciprocity is established: the work can reach the metamorphosis of language which makes it a new reality only if its author has experienced the initiatory experience by means of which that author has made the passage from one condition to another, thus arriving at the self-generation which was the motive force of the undertaking. Furthermore, writers cannot go through such an experience other than through constructing the work, an experience they undergo while the work is being created.

As a result, the true mythical character is no longer the character described by the work, but that work's author, in other words the individual who has in practice taken on the mythical condition of initiation.

Thus the role of the work and its characters is to provide the particular, privileged experience of the question, which meets with a greater or lesser degree of success with regard to totality, timelessness, universality and unity, which the reality of the world denies, but which language makes possible in a literary absolute, as they were made possible by faith in a transcendence which embodied them.

Through an initiatory itinerary (impersonalization, new birth, ontological transmutation) similar to that of the mythical hero (ordeals, revelation, apotheosis), the poet bears witness to our nostalgia for a solitary adventure which might constantly uphold the human need for freedom and love and through which writing might equal life, which would itself have been transformed.

THE TEXT: NARRATIVE OF THE CREATIVE EXPERIENCE

If we accept that literary creation is the way in which writers think they can break free of limitations and reach autonomous creation, the literary text, which allows them to do this, should lend itself to the revelation of a specific experience which guarantees a particular knowledge, ethics or salvation. This would then mean that the literary text is less what it recounts in more or less anecdotal form and more the experience of a particular attitude. Like that of the myth, this experience heralds the emergence of ineffable knowledge, and requires a slow and painful metamorphosis of state which makes it possible to recreate oneself, to transcend the human condition, to reach the uniqueness of an original language such that any writing born of this language appears as a founding text in a temporal dimension which has become reversible. If we add to these aspirations (which are those we should hope to discover in a work of art) the ordeals described by the writers themselves: dispersal before the gathering together, chaos before the coherence, alienation before autonomy, absence and lack before gaiety and overflowing, loss of direction and distress before ecstasy, loss of self before the revelation of the oneness of the world, breakdown and separation before harmony and communication, we have to agree that this is indeed a 'rite of passage' from the state of the common condition to that of an exemplary vocation.

Max Bilen

Lorelei

The world-famous legend of the Lorelei is a perfect though unusual example of successful literary fabrication, a piece of fiction that was confused from the start with authentic popular European myths. Even Nazi censorship did not dare touch it, leaving the ballad by the Jewish writer Heine in the textbooks, though cynically ascribing it to an 'unknown author'.

THE LOCATION

The legend is based on a tragic and picturesque spot in the Rhine valley, which also gave it its name: a slate rock, the 'Lürley' (from *Lür-*, a word of Celtic origin indicating the schistous nature of the rock, soon to be muddled in people's minds with *lauern* and *ley*, which meant rock in everyday Middle High German), near St Goar and downstream from Bacharach, towers 132 metres above the right bank of the river; it used to be one of the most dangerous stretches for boatmen. The danger, along with a loud, multiple echo that resonated through the caves in the rock, inevitably gave rise to a variety of popular legends, before the literary figure of the blonde fairy supplanted them at the beginning of the nineteenth century.

The 'Lurlaberg', 'Lurefels' or 'Lorleberg' had in fact enjoyed fame in a variety of guises for over five hundred years before it was taken over by the Lorelei. The Swabian poet Marner (d. *c.* 1270) declared that gnomes lived in the cracks, watching over the treasure of the Nibelungen buried there by Hagen. This is not mentioned in any other source, and writing around 1850 Wagner took care not to pinpoint the whereabouts of the submerged treasure to the vicinity of the accursed rock. The boatman in a song in the *Recueil de Colmar* (fourteenth–fifteenth century; cod. Germ. 4997, fol. 694) is content to talk to dwarves. Konrad Celtes, in a couplet from an elegy written in 1491 for his beloved Ursula of Mainz, associates the rapid swirling of the river and the echo of the rocks, which he says are inhabited by gods, according to local legend (*Quattuor libri Amorum, Elegia 13*, 11. 69–70). The *Bremer Druck* (1640) mentions only the echo, though attributing oracular powers to it, already vouched for in anonymous lines dating from the thirteenth century. Freher in *Originae Palestinae* (1612) again speaks of frightened creatures, gnomes and nymphs hidden inside the mountain, who cause the echo to reverberate. In this he was followed by later chroniclers of whom we will cite only the least obscure: Zeller (1632), Winkelmann (1637) and Gregorius (1715).

This tends to support the philological explanation according to which *Lur-*

can also refer to dwarves (*Luremus*), spying dwarves who are keeping a malevolent eye on passers-by (*lauern*) or a hole in the rock (from the Latin root *lausa, laura*). But however it may have fluctuated as to the nature of those dwelling in the reef, legend never placed the fatal figure of the Lorelei on it.

THE LORELEI MYTH

The Lorelei was the sole invention of Clemens Brentano, even if the theme's crystallization as a myth resulted from a collective fascination with it. The manner and speed of its dissemination can be explained mainly by the following external factors:

1 the traditional receptivity of the German population to legends woven around the Lurlaberg;

2 the highlighting of landscape in literature at the end of the eighteenth century, and more especially the praise of the Rhineland by the young Romantics centred on Heidelberg; they modelled themselves on Goethe's Rhine poems, while at the same time integrating more into their work the old background of the popular song (the *Volkslied*), as for example in the collection published by Brentano and Achim von Arnhim in 1804, *Des Knaben Wunderhorn*;

3 the invention of the steamboat and its introduction on the Rhine, soon to be accompanied by the introduction of railways, making it possible to undertake comfortable outings and cruises and strengthening the fashion for travel as a 'Riviera of the North';

4 the commercial exploitation of the ever-growing tide of tourists by producers of guidebooks, who were themselves tinged with Romanticism.

Brentano was at the point where these tendencies converged; he was born in 1778 on the right bank of the Rhine at Ehrenbreitstein, opposite Koblenz, and was familiar with all the legends conveyed by popular rumour regarding the site that he loved and knew well. His twenty-five verse ballad represents the Lorelei's birth certificate. It was first published in 1801 as a little song (*Liedchen*) in the second part of his long novel *Godwi*. It had been written a short time earlier on the occasion of a new cruise on the Rhine. In it we can simultaneously sense veneration for the past, the trace of the legendary echo that answers troubled knights, the memory evident in the first two verses of Queen Kriemhilde from the *Nibelungenlied*, and the influence of the author's favourite poems by Goethe: 'Der Fischer', 'Erlkönig' and 'Der König in Thule'; in these the eminently Brentanoesque themes of fatal love, perverted innocence and painful, disappointed fidelity are combined.

Lore is accused of witchcraft and condemned to live in retirement in a convent by the bishop, who is himself beguiled by her. Partly to escape from the men whom she attracts in spite of herself and partly to rid herself of life after being abandoned by her lover, she eludes the vigilance of the knights who are escorting her and throws herself from the top of the rocks into the waters of the Rhine on which she sees the boat carrying her beloved.

Brentano himself was the first victim of this theme of seduction, developing it in a variety of shapes and forms. A second version of the legend written shortly afterwards has the bishop as Lore's lover; his piety has led him to reject her, but his love is rekindled when he has to pass judgement on her. It is him she sees on the boat when she casts herself into the river, without realising that he has exchanged the cross for the sword, becoming a knight again and therefore free to dispose of his heart.

In *Rheinmärchen*, written ten years or so later in Berlin (written between 1810 and 1816, published in 1846), there are several important variations on the theme, some of which inspired subsequent versions, such as Loeben's. Lorelei has ceased to be a young woman in love from Bacharach and become an eternally young and beautiful fairy or water sprite. She lives in the rock with her seven daughters and has become the guardian of the treasure of the Nibelungen. She answers every cry she hears seven times over to demonstrate her vigilance. In 'Das Märchen vom Murmeltier' Frau Lurley is a good and beautiful water-elf who travels around the country accepting the hospitality of the spirits of the springs. In the story 'Die Ahnen von dem Müller Radlauf' she eventually marries a prince who becomes a miller, for love of her; she now stands out especially for her qualities as a wife and mother, going so far as to lull the children of Mainz to sleep with her songs. This inoffensive, kindly Lady Lurley no longer has anything in common with the unhappy lovelorn woman from Bacharach who is suspected of witchcraft. But the last story described is prefaced by a striking description which was to become a stereotype: the weeping Lorelei spends a long time combing her thick, blonde hair which glints in the light of the moon at the very top of the rock; some millers go past in a boat, mocking her, and immediately their boat is caught up in an eddy, founders and its occupants are drowned.

Despite constant elaborations Brentano never managed to give his creation a fixed and final profile. Of the hundreds of pages he devoted to her all that posterity would remember would be the two versions of the ballad 'Lore-lay' and a few separate images. However, the ballad in *Godwi* directly inspired two nobles with whom Brentano was friendly while in Heidelberg in 1807–8 finishing *Des Knaben Wunderhorn*, which he dedicated to Goethe: the Silesian baron Joseph von Eichendorff and the Saxon count Otto Heinrich von Loeben.

Eichendorff's 'Lied' dates from between 1808 and 1811 and it too first appeared in a long novel, *Ahnung und Gegenwart* (1815); it was then printed separately under the title 'Waldgespräch'. It is again because she had been betrayed in love that the Loreley becomes a demoniac creature; the nymph singing on her rock is heard by a knight who tries to reach her through a vast forest. She warns him of the danger, but to no avail. The novelty lies in the romantic setting of the fatal meeting, and in the change of location from the river to the forest, which in turn becomes a magic tomb. Eichendorff was never able to forget the great forests of his native land – according to him they were the only sources of poetry.

Loeben's poem, 'Lorelei, eine Sage vom Rhein', came a little later. Written between 1810 and 1820, it was published in 1821 in a small-format book, *Urania*. Loeben had lived in Berlin since 1809, frequenting the same literary and political circles as Kleist, Arnim and Brentano. He particularly developed the vision described in 'Die Ahnen von dem Müller Radlauf', and managed to integrate into his twenty-four lines the main traits of the figure that would become a myth: the golden gleam as the moon strikes the long blonde tresses of the betrayed sorceress, combing her hair above the Rhine, irresistibly sad, and wearing a string of pearls as an ornament. For the first time the power of her allure derives primarily from her voice and not from her eyes or her beauty. Loeben's poem is rather awkward and made no great impact on its readers, but this short, coherent version represented a challenge to a far more gifted poet – Heinrich Heine.

However, Heine's first knowledge of the myth was gained from travel guidebooks which were almost enough on their own to ensure the dissemination of the legend.

Two scholars of history and folklore had immediately recognized the commercial potential of exploiting the story in the travel books that were being snatched up by hordes of tourists avid for local colour. Niklas Vogt (1756–1836) was the first to introduce Brentano's theme, which he seems to have thought was derived from a genuine popular legend. Vogt, less scrupulous than the Grimm brothers, who carefully kept it out of their collections, was primarily concerned with providing young poets with the elements of future texts. First of all in 1811 he gave a summary of the first version of Brentano's ballad in a magazine, *Bildgalerie des Rheins*, then in 1817 he published it in its entirety in his *Rheinische Geschichten und Sagen*. He thus gave it enormous circulation, incomparably greater than provided by the very select number of readers of *Godwi*, which was in any case almost immediately disowned by the author himself. Vogt, who had been a professor at Mainz University, became a senator and an alderman in Frankfurt where he was a friend of the Brentano family. In his first brief *résumé* he cut out the bishop, making the girl herself decide to enter a convent; three suitors, her faithful admirers, cast themselves into the river on which she sees the lover who has spurned her; there is no mention of the echo.

Vogt's main disciple was Aloys Schreiber, the Professor of Aesthetics at Heidelberg University (the chair had originally been intended for Tieck, and was snatched from him by means of intrigue). This voluminous writer at first thought he had a vocation as a poet, then turned to publishing travel guidebooks, flooding the market with them until 1850 when his work was supplanted by the publications of Karl Baedeker, the son of an Essen printer who in 1836 had bought back the rights of the second edition of the *Guide* by J. A. Klein. In his *Handbuch für Reisende am Rhein*, first published in 1818, Schreiber embroidered on Brentano's story. The legend was never removed from the guidebook, which was almost immediately translated into French and English. Spice is added to the story by introducing not a bishop but the Count Palatinate's son, once again fatally attracted by the Lorelei. Enraged at the death of his son, the Count launches an expedition to capture the siren, dead or alive. Three knights manage to climb up to her rock but just as she is about to be cast into the river, the Lorelei smiles and calls on her father, the Rhine, to help her. He immediately sends two waves in the form of two white horses; the witch who is metamorphosed into a water sprite is not seen again, but her mocking voice still responds as an echo to the cries of the boatmen. This version borrows from a famous episode in Fouqué's *Undine*, published in 1816.

Thus in 1823 Heine had five different versions available to him. His 'Lore-Lei' is a condensation of all the elements of the definitive myth. The text gained acceptance, backed from 1837 by the haunting melody of Friedrich Silcher, which won the day over other settings by Schumann and Liszt.

Heine, twenty years younger than Arnim and Brentano whom he did not know personally, inherited the *Lied* into which they had breathed new life, but he was also heir to the intimism of the late Goethe of the *Westöstlicher Divan*, being the first to appreciate its implications. His main source of inspiration was Loeben's rather lacklustre poem: the situation, metre and length (five verses) follow his. From Schreiber, whose work he had read in several editions, he retained mainly the concept that the Lorelei derived her devilish power from her voice. His ballad, which is very musical, subjective and rigorously structured, has nothing in common with Brentano's except for the name of the heroine and its setting on the rock above the Rhine.

The episode is evoked as a dream from earlier times which haunts the memory and ends ironically by casting doubt on the reality of the myth. There is no intermediary, neither a bishop nor a Count Palatinate; centre stage, alone and resplendent, the fairy sings in the moonlight with her golden hair, her golden comb and her golden jewels; she casts her spell over a boatman, and his boat with no-one to steer it is smashed on the reefs. This great Romantic theme of fatal beauty runs through the poetry of the period, but by combining this harmonious vision with haunting music and the patina of a legendary past Heine beguiled the memory of all and gave the story the power to gain acceptance as a myth. Symbolically for him, the 'Lore-Lei' is an allegorical figure representing the Romantic Muse, seductive but to be dreaded precisely because of her song, leading people to forget the social realities of Germany which was in the throes of the industrial revolution.

Heine's poem, which was published in 1824, served as a point of departure or a point of direct or indirect reference for more than a hundred average or humdrum German-speaking writers, not all of whom have been catalogued: the most successful versions are by Karl Simrock (1837, 1840), Otto Ludwig (1838), Geibel (1834, 1846), Julius Wolff (1886) and Otto Roquette (1888).

It was the long poem by Julius Wolff which achieved the widest circulation: 46,000 copies were printed in 1898, and a new edition illustrated in colour came out in 1913. 'Major' writers, including Mörike in his poems and stories, Gottfried Keller in his novel *Der grüne Heinrich* (1854) and even Wagner, refrained from using the actual Lorelei myth, preferring the much wider and vaguer story of Undine.

It was in France that poets and intellectuals were quickest in appropriating and exploiting this German heritage, as if Heine, when he sought refuge in Paris in 1830, had brought the spirit of the legend with him. Inevitably the Rhine fairy beguiled the French Romantic movement, which was later in getting under way and delighted to find in Germanic mythology a store of exotic legends and a new source of grandiose, pathetic inspiration; and French Romantics were ready to quarrel with German nationalists to assert their rights to the political and legendary area represented by the Rhineland (e.g. the diatribe between Musset and Becker).

Famous travellers, succumbing to the fashion for travelling along the banks of the 'western Nile', acquired guidebooks and absorbed the most picturesque stories. Numerous French editions of Schreiber's work, which had been modestly translated in two minor editions in 1807 and 1813, got under way from 1826 on – by 1851 there were twenty of them. His story about the Count Palatinate was repeated in 1834 by *Landscape Français*; in 1838 baronne de Montavant (in *Les Bords du Rhin*) has the embracing lovers swallowed by the waters of the Rhine. In Nicolas Martin's version the enchantress 'casts herself into the river like Sappho' (*Souvenirs de Voyage at Tradition populaire* 1846). Schreiber's version of the story was repeated in the work of A. Poignant (*Le Rhin* 1855) and C.-P. Guinot, a man about town and a friend of Stendhal's (*Les Bords du Rhin*) as well as in the *Guide* by Joanne (1854). In the reign of Napoleon III Santines warned against the bewitching fairy in the name of religion and morality (*Mythologie du Rhin* 1861).

In 1846 A. Delrieu combined the three ballads by Brentano, Eichendorff and Heine, following the lines set out in Simrock's *Rheinsagen* (1836). These collections and two or three similar works by Karl Geib (1828, 1837, 1838) continued to be a prime source of inspiration for many German and foreign writers, including Apollinaire.

Whereas German guidebooks had turned to literary ballads for inspiration, the opposite happened in France where great literature drew inspiration from works with no literary merit, taking advantage of the fashion they had launched and the interest they had stirred up in the public.

In 1838 Alexandre Dumas took up the version found in Schreiber and *Landscape français* in a chivalrous tale, relating the fatal meeting between the water sprite and the count's son. In *Le Rhin* (1842; Ne Varietur edn, p. 180) Victor Hugo, no doubt better informed about Brentano's devices and all the more disappointed in his quest for the genuinely picturesque on the Rhine, speaks of the overworked, relatively recent legend combining the memory of

Echo (alluding to Vogt's version) with that of Hylas who was dragged into the river by sirens. Gérard de Nerval, an intimate friend of Heine's from 1838–9, on the other hand, was completely haunted and obsessed by the character of the Lorelei. His translation of *Intermezzo* and various lyrical collections contributed to revealing the intimist aspect of Heine's poetry; up until then he had been known primarily for his talents as a political pamphleteer. Admittedly the title of his work, *Loreley, souvenirs d'Allemagne* (1852), is deceptive, lumping together notes relating to different visits to Germany; nonetheless Nerval devotes two splendid pages to the Lorelei and throughout his work the image of the undine recurs in various guises, the fatal nixie 'who watches out for me and always draws me; yet I should distrust her deceptive grace, for her name means charm and lying'.

In 1897 Jean Lorrain published a slight tale in prose entitled *Loreley* (Librairie Borel), illustrated by the Swiss painter and engraver Edouard Guillaume with a double series of picturesque scenes alternating Romantic mediaeval inspiration and the sensuous exaltation of woman (of the type destined to flourish at the 1900 Universal Exhibition). Lorrain turns the Lorelei into a kind of truculent Salome whose free, intensified sensuality is unleashed against the crowd and the church. She is neither the lovelorn girl made desperate by faithlessness, as conceived by Brentano, nor the symbol of perfidious seduction, as in Heine's work; she is a lost woman who in the end prefers to die rather than go on living in a despicable world, which she nonetheless finally forgives.

The *Loreley* poems by F. Delacroix and Guillaume Apollinaire are both in verse and both faithfully transcribe Brentano's ballad, though the source is not acknowledged. The twenty-nine verses of Delacroix's poem (1843, Paris: Charpentier) make the mistake of transposing Brentano's simple, popular language into a grand, rhetorical style that destroys the delicate, suggestive charm of the *Lied.*

Apollinaire managed to avoid this danger and inspired his Lorelei with a personal passion, his love for Annie Playden, a young Englishwoman to whom he paid court while staying in the Rhineland near St Goar as tutor to a German countess. In the poem, written in 1902, the influences of the *genius loci* (it is part of a cycle of nine pieces entitled *Rhénanes*), his love, and literary memories of Brentano's and Heine's poems are combined. In a first draft he adopted the caricatured figure and sarcastic images of Heine's *Edith Schwanenhals*, a repudiated, ageing, degraded courtesan, then overcoming his anger as a rejected lover, he forgives the beautiful rebel and ends up by adopting the nostalgic tone of Brentano's ballad. It is because of her eyes, that 'wilful look' that many liked attributing to Annie, that his young girl is fatal to the men she meets, but to herself as well. In Apollinaire's version the Lorelei is less a victim of lovesickness than of narcissism, which impels her to gaze at her own reflection in the Rhine and bewitch herself. The poem is shorter than

Brentano's, better constructed and with a faster tempo, though the progression of the drama is based on the German model.

This poem was soon published and contributed greatly to Apollinaire's precocious fame in Paris, but nonetheless constituted the last great metamorphosis of the Lorelei in France. The legend effectively disappeared from literature along with the century that had witnessed its birth. Maurice Genevoix did attempt to revive it in his novel of the same name, but his heroine is bereft of any supernatural charm and seems very artificial and not at all convincing.

If the legend was particularly widely disseminated and successfully adapted in France, it also spread to other countries such as England, Scotland, the Scandinavian countries, Italy (especially thanks to Catalini's opera) and even the United States, where mention should be made of an excellent poem by Caroline M. Sawyer published in *The Female Poets of America* (an anthology edited by Rufus Wilmot Griswold, New York, 1873). The poem was even reintroduced into Germany in a translation by Adolf Strodtmann, who included it in his *Amerikanische Anthologie*. But in all these countries, and especially in Japan where it is also found, the legend has not taken hold of the popular imagination; it has remained the preserve of a public of well-educated connoisseurs, a cut flower. This may explain the absence of critical studies or even of any catalogue of the Lorelei's appearances in literature outside France and Germany.

Turning to the theme of the Lorelei seems – at least in the case of the 'great' writers who were inspired by it – to have been the province of young poets crossed in love, with a very romantic vision of their passion; in them we can recognize an innate desire to play the seducer along with a great uncertainty about their destiny and their vocation. In fact the Lorelei only ever seduces people who are adrift in their life, in the forest or on the water, and who lack the courage to close their eyes and block their ears, as Ulysses' sailors did. It seems that the Lorelei is basically a romantic, western avatar of a universal, timeless myth: that of the attraction and repulsion present whenever a choice has to be made, especially in the case of a commitment involving love. Lorelei as the *femme fatale* who has herself been hurt is an allegorical figure of the duality involved in choosing. The legend invented by Brentano was lucky enough to find not only a generation of poets unsure of themselves, but also a generation of enthusiastic readers, and to benefit from technical advances which spontaneously helped its dissemination.

There has not yet been any serious attempt to explain why the Lorelei myth fell from favour at the beginning of the twentieth century. Probably the technical and moral revolutions accelerated by the two World Wars are the prime culprits. With the advances in means of transport and in the cinematographic industry, the sources of exoticism and dreams have moved far away from the rock at Bacharach; the fairy perched on her rock has not managed to get away without losing her specific nature as a fair-haired *femme fatale* on the banks of the Rhine. The river itself, the eternal Father Rhine, is dying as a result of damming, pollution, radiation and canalization; it is no longer able to protect its sirens. Technical progress has ultimately gnawed away at the creature that it helped hatch. But the myth is also under internal attack as a result of changes in the image of woman in western societies, and her economic and legal emancipation. Today this wretched, over-flirtatious fairy resigned to wait in vain may seem very childish, sentimental and reified.

However, we should be careful not to be categorical about the death of the myth and its literary resurgence, at least in Germany where the legend is still very much alive in the collective consciousness of a people who are still torn and whose national identity was established just as Romanticism emerged, first and foremost in relation to the question of the frontier and mythology of the Rhine. The myth survives, preserved so far thanks to schools and school textbooks which still accord Heine's ballad a special place. But outside this sheltered environment the myth is now regarded more as a fetish from the past and a symbol of reactionary ideology. The former muse of the poets has become a favourite butt in the theatre world, especially in variety shows.

Karl Valentin (1882–1948), a talented cabaret artist, demystified Heine's vision in his 'Die Loreley'. After a presentation in which the fairy is relocated in her original romantic setting, couplets denounce the present-day imposture of this myth which conveys outmoded imagery: he makes his Loreley speak in a harsh language strewn with vulgar expressions and dialect terms. She says how bored she is crouched on top of her rock in every season, singing a stale tune; she speaks of her backache, of her sad fate as a virgin in spite of herself, and thinks only of swopping her legendary garb for more libertine trappings. Even her lover has ceased to please her; she insults him and threatens to throw her lyre at his head. She finally disappears at nightfall begging that they should at last switch off the tapes that keep blaring out from the boats of tourists.

Another poem, by Erich Kästner, a contemporary writer and song-writer, is along the same lines; he presents the Lorelei in her original setting which he relegates to the past, and pokes fun at the 'heroes' who still believe in German legends. The last of these heroes, a sportsman who is alone practising walking on his hands at the edge of the abyss suddenly thinks of Heine's Lorelei and plunges in, overcome by a mortal languor. Lorelei's seductive power now extends only to would-be suicides.

This grudging attitude is an upside-down proof of the amazing vitality of a myth which people cannot forget, and which crops up unprompted, even in the songs of certain singers whose names have become synonymous with scandal; thus in 1984 Nina Hagen sang a raucous, prophetic version of the Lorelei calling on future generations to tear themselves away from the seduction of drugs and blind consumption (on the record 'Angstios').

To sum up, the myth is submerged in a kind of lethargy from which it can be stirred only by goading it: to finish it off, or to revive it?

François Brisson

Louis XIV

When Louis XIV was born on 5 September 1638 there was no shortage of writers eager to celebrate the royal baby, calling him a young Mars or a new Alexander. There was nothing so very unusual about that: what prince was not hailed in such terms when he came into the world? And yet the birth of the child that would become Louis XIV was not a historical event quite like those others. From the start it carried the mark of the extraordinary, for it seemed like a real miracle: the long wait and the vow made by Anne of Austria, the prayers that had accumulated during the 'unfolding of five lustra of time' as the poet Colletet expressed it, made it stand out as exceptional, and writers such as Du Bois Hus exulted over the event as a true wonder:

> If his noble mother has taken twenty-three years to produce him, we may suppose that she has been working on some great miracle, that she has been preparing a piece of work intended for eternity, and that Anne in giving birth to an elder brother of the Church has performed a task more difficult than that of a Samuel.

Moreover, his birth came in answer to a very long wait on the part of the French people themselves, and old national dreams were immediately pinned onto the young prince. He was hailed as a Clovis who would bring prosperity to the Holy Monarchy of France, as the founder of the city of the Sun, the master of a monarchy centred on Jerusalem. Du Bois Hus presented him as a new *Sol justitiae*, promising Redemption. He was imagined embarking on a Crusade against the Turks, so long and ardently wished for by the devout who were opposed to Richelieu's policies. Finally, he was celebrated as a new Charlemagne destined to accede to the Empire. The imperial element which was to be such an important strand in the myth of Louis XIV was already present in 1638, for even then it matched the expectations of the French people.

Thus, well before he came to the forefront of the political arena, the character of the future king was weighted down by a great consensus: not only was his existence perceived as a wonder in itself, as a sort of historical and political miracle, the concrete realization of the dreams of a country. He was perceived as a necessity.

Thus the myth was approximately mapped out in 1638, but for it really to take shape the sketch had to become a picture, i.e. the different features of the rough outline had to be organized and the necessity that conferred life on it had to persist and develop, becoming more deeply embedded in the minds of the French people. The person of Louis XIV had to continue to be the favoured figure on which the expression of a collective drive, a striking, passionate vision, could be based.

The myth started to develop in 1660. History stepped in to serve it, lending credence to the miracle and suggesting that an exemplary reign was beginning. In 1658 the king was struck down by a very serious illness and his recovery took on something of the aspect of a resurrection. In 1660 Gaston d'Orléans died at a time when he might have seized power. Mazarin for his part suppressed the great dangers that were threatening the monarchy. The year 1660 marks a decisive turning point in the formation of the myth; the sovereign became more than a man and more than a king – a saviour destined to lead his country towards enlightenment. The aura was enhanced still further by his marriage to the Infanta Marie-Thérèse, for that put a seal on the end of war with Spain. Thus there was an extraordinary symbiosis between the elements which had struck people in 1638 and the facts of the 1660 period. Faced with their saviour king, people marvelled and detected the hand of Providence, remembering the miracle in 1638; it was this accumulation of events which very much opened up the way for the myth. Writers like Perrault extolled him with undisguised joy: 'of all the monarchs/The greatest that ever was,/Because he could step down/Shining with glory/From the fine chariot of victory/In order to embrace peace.'

Louis XIV was represented as the father of peace, the liberator of his people; the need for such a prodigious being, sent by God, was felt so strongly that everything seemed possible, through Louis XIV and by his agency. People's thoughts went back to the old national dreams expressed in 1638 which were now reinforced, with new life breathed into them. In 1660 in a little tableau entitled *Les Oracles du Ciel* an anonymous author imagined 'the king sitting on a throne [with] a captive Turk at his feet, [while] an Angel from Heaven presents him with a Cross intertwined with lilies'. In prophetic style Louis XIV was presented as the universal monarch whose 'Empire will extend over all the seas, and from the Rhine to the ends of the earth'; he was called 'the new Charlemagne'.

From 1660 to 1663 the portrait of the king was loaded with every potential; it was the meeting point of the humanist tradition which saw the sovereign as the father of the people, and those who supported the politics of prestige, for whom the ideal monarch was a rival to Alexander, a second Caesar. Precisely because, from that point on, the personality of Louis XIV became the incarnation of those two currents of opinion, it totally lost its 'individual, private and personal' character – a feature specific to the formation of myths, as Mircea Eliade demonstrates in *Mythes, Rêves et Mystères*.

From 1663, when the Petite Académie was founded, the myth took off with renewed vigour. From then on Louis XIV harnessed every form of expression current in his reign for his own propaganda. It would be impossible to exaggerate the importance of the Petite Académie, an institution truly dedicated to glorifying the king; it exercised absolute power in the domain of literature and the arts and included among its duties the striking of medals glorifying the main feats of his reign. Alongside it Colbert created quite a few other academies, each representing a link in the great network of concerted propaganda which the minister broadcast throughout Louis XIV's France. The Académie de Peinture et de Sculpture came into being in 1662; P. Goubert wrote concerning it, 'the Académie regulates the realm of Beauty for the glory of His Majesty'. In 1671 it was the turn of the Académie d'Architecture whose members were appointed by the king himself; the Gobelins workshops, the royal Académie des Sciences and the royal Académie de Musique should also be mentioned. As for the Académie française, it became an instrument of royal policy-making; in 1672, on the death of the Chancellor, Séguier, Louis XIV became its patron.

Henceforth, celebrating the king's accomplishments became a full-time job, a duty the imperatives of which were carefully fixed. Even newspapers like the *Gazette de France*, the *Mercure galant* and the *Journal des Savants* gave a warm welcome to royal propaganda. As was the case with Napoleon, the role of the press in the formation of the myth of Louis XIV was extremely important. Every political act, every campaign undertaken and every victory won were evoked as so many stages in the unfolding of the myth.

In 1663, in celebrating Louis XIV's personal assumption of power, C. Cotin drew this enthusiastic portrait of the king:

> What is the marvellous news which amazes the politicians? . . . This Atlas is not even looking for a Hercules to help him bear the burdens of State. . . . This is a cause for admiration among the wise, a most worthy topic for eloquence among the orators and the object of veneration by all Frenchmen.

In 1671, praising the monarch for abolishing duelling, a member of the Académie française lauded him as 'a famous Alcides' who had not hesitated to fight mercilessly 'Against the violent transports/Of hearts less brave than insolent'.

As the master of his kingdom Louis XIV was simultaneously Caesar, as he was called by writers including Corneille in *Othon* when he extolled Louis' great skill as a ruler, Neptune or Apollo, which was how Molière depicted him in *Les Amants magnifiques*. He was celebrated as bringing back the Golden Age, 'restoring beautiful Astraea to her original purity'. He was also Augustus, than whom he was judged even greater. There was already talk of the century of Louis XIV, and in 1674 Desmarets entitled one of his works *Le Triomphe de Louis et de son Siècle*. Whatever he did, it was seen as a miracle. We need cite only the Peace of Nijmegen in 1678; Charpentier, an academician, wrote about it in the following terms:

> Louis speaks and peace is made. . . . Everything has given way, everything has submitted to his invincible arms . . . . This manner of ending such a troublesome,

heated war has nothing at all in common with the ordinary course of possible events; supernatural, divine forces are at play.

In 1677 the *Mercure galant* declared: 'Everything he does is a miracle,/And everything he says is an oracle.'

The various components of the myth of Louis XIV do not constitute a long succession of virtues and feats presented serially, without order and structure. On the contrary, they are set in a context that is precisely concentrated, organized from the starting point of a few powerful elements the existence of which did not simply derive from the 'Pharaonic pride' of Louis XIV mentioned by W. Lavisse, but from a whole current of mental attitudes seeing prestige in battle as its ideal. The image of the invincible conqueror, the proud, eternal victor, that is preponderant in the myth of Louis XIV was not forged by the king alone; it matched a need of the time. In his book on *La Carrière de Jean Racine* R. Picard recalls how French public opinion at that time valued military triumphs above all else:

> In 1663–4 when the first royal gratuities were awarded Louis XIV's literary policy was so little understood that some people dared to express regret that those pensions had not gone to fighters, 'men of service', instead of uselessly putting money in the pockets of poets.

And Primi Visconti in his *Mémoires sur la Cour de Louis XIV* writes regarding the year 1678:

> In France only war honours are respected; those awarded for literature and any other profession are despised, and a man of quality who knows how to write is looked down on; I know that the d'Urfé family are ashamed that their forebear Honoré d'Urfé wrote the poem *Astrée*.

Thus when writers described their monarch as having 'carried arms as soon as he could walk', when they compared him to Caesar or Alexander, what they said was not hagiography, an example of rhetorical amplification, or stereotyped expressions handed down by tradition; it was in fact deeply meaningful, and to some extent history served only as a pretext for the manifestation of the collective psyche. As well as Le Brun's tapestry representing Alexander as a device for celebrating Louis XIV, we should remember the preface of Racine's play *Alexandre le Grand*:

> I foresee that while I recruit new strength Your Majesty Himself will be covered in completely new glory, that we will see Him . . . again completing the comparison that can be made between Him and Alexander, adding the title of conqueror to that of the wisest king on earth.

From the Flanders campaign in 1667 up until the War of the Spanish Succession in 1702 Louis XIV's destiny coincided so closely with this dream of military glory that the image of Louis XIV victorious leads us more fully than any other into what Albouy calls 'the domain of archetypes where legend is transformed into myth'. While Napoleon imposed on his contemporaries the images that constitute his golden myth, Louis XIV's personal involvement was less decisive. The king did of course opt for the current opinion that supported the politics of prestige, but he was also carried along by the force of that current.

The myth of Hercules was revived to serve this same stream of imagination; in 1672 in an *Ode pour le Roi* Abbé Genest claimed that his prince could be seen 'From the cradle/Like a new Hercules/Erecting trophies of serpents he had crushed'. As soon as he entered battle, everywhere and simultaneously, the same marvels occurred. The speed and effortlessness of his victories and the surrender of towns and fortresses were represented as taking place with so much ease that you might believe that he had only to wave a magic wand. For example, Martinet marvelled on the occasion of his crossing of the Rhine in 1672 and made the river speak in the following terms:

Who is this unconquered hero
To whom nothing is an obstacle?
I have seen Caesar triumph,
Behind his chariot I have seen
My captive hands bound.
But in bringing his laws to me
The Roman wrought less on my banks
Than the Frenchman has done.

In evocations such as these, who would recognize the historical ruler? History conveys a different message, indicating that the low level of the Rhine enabled the river to be forded almost the whole way across. Myth always affixes some star snatched out of the miraculous sky to the chariot of the victorious prince. Turning its back on reality, encomiastic literature recreates a sovereign covered in glory and painted in the colours of the imaginary: he is 'this other Jupiter', the 'invulnerable Achilles', this 'Caesar of Caesars', as Colletet put it in 1674. Novels, poetic works, tragedies, comedies, plays with ballet and operas, all literary genres glowingly orchestrated the myth of the great king.

Even heraldic devices were used as a mainspring for his fabulous prestige. In 1662 Louis XIV himself had chosen a device with the famous motto *Nec pluribus impar* and a huge sun lighting up the terrestrial globe as its emblem. In 1679 the enthusiasm with which Father Ménestrier commented on this device illustrates the extent to which it contributed to elevating the prince above the everyday world:

> What grander and more heroic effect could be wished for than the action of the sun lighting up the whole world and working incessantly to maintain everything? What could be chosen more worthy of a king who promised such great things as soon as he started governing his states on his own? . . . The idea is unique, and we will find nothing approaching it.

The evocation of the sun, like that of military prestige, is a line of force in the organization of the royal myth, perfectly reflecting moreover its evolution. Until 1665–7 the image of the sun referred as much to the idea of brilliance as that of temperance, as much to the prestige and glory of war as to gentleness and equity; at that time no one element dominated over another. Thus Father Le Moyne in his *Art de régner* has the sun address the king in these terms:

I have surrounded you with graces and charms
That can impose and conquer without arms.
I have marked your forehead with majestic traits,
With a glow which beams authority from afar,
And with a character in which the Great and the August,
The Strong and the Valiant are tempered by the Just.

After 1665 the sun of Louis XIV shone with a much more fearsome light; Louis XIV became a true god of light, in 1678 bringing down the dreaded Dutch Python – he was the great star that drained the marshlands of the United Provinces. At the time of the Revocation of the Edict of Nantes in 1685 he was, even more, a sun with a fixed light; he was the only fixed star with blinding rays. Up until 1702 the clouds could gather for all they were worth above the kingdom of France, the myth of the Sun King still continued to dazzle. Yet 1686 saw the formation of the League of Augsburg, 1689 the sack of the Palatinate, and 1701 the Great Alliance of The Hague. What did historical reality matter: in the mythical sky the sun of Louis XIV was bathed in perpetual light.

Moreover, after the Revocation of the Edict of Nantes there was new strength in the old dream of Louis XIV as the emperor of Christendom. The king of France had only to bombard Algiers three times, without exposing himself to any great risk, to be immediately vaunted as the most admirable defender of the Christian faith. In the minds of Catholics he had become 'this new Constantine, this new Theodosius, this new Marcian, this new Charlemagne', as he was hailed by Bossuet in the *Oraison funèbre de Michel Le Tellier*. And the preacher repeated to him 'what the thirty-six Fathers said in olden times at the Council of Chalcedon: By your agency heresy has ceased to exist: God alone has been able to work this wonder. King of heaven, guard the king of the earth'. The very succinct but very pertinent analysis made of the Revocation of the Edict of Nantes by B. de Jouvenal in his book *Du Pouvoir* shows how far the personality of Louis XIV was submerged in his own myth. Borne aloft into the domain of the ideal, the monarch proved incapable of lucidly analyzing reality, i.e. of understanding the mistake he was making with regard to France and to himself, or even of being egoistic, as de Jouvenal explains. Showing egoism would in fact have entailed both being conscious of the movement of history and considering himself as a private individual. Louis XIV no longer saw himself as he was or should be, but as the myth itself was making him: the great Catholic king whose duty it was to bring back into the fold all the sheep that had gone astray, the master of the world, the god of the earth, the representative of what Truchet, commenting on Bossuet, rightly calls 'a French and Christian dream', the dream of 'harmonious Christendom, France happy and holy'.

In this reworking of the character of Louis XIV through the imaginary, a cultural phenomenon came into play connected with the fact that the royal person was, in a kind of way, immediately part of the collective memory of the men of his day. Steeped in biblical typology and convinced that the events in the Old Testament foretold those in the New, Louis' contemporaries through a more or less explicit or conscious extrapolation saw deeds and men as recurring in an almost cyclical way, recent ones being prefigured by those of earlier times. Thus Louis XIV quite naturally became the reincarnation of Jason, Apollo, Hercules, David or Solomon, to quote only these names.

From 1702, with the advent of the War of the Spanish Succession, the myth of Louis XIV underwent a transformation. The king himself was attacked by doubts, as expressed on his deathbed: is he not reported to have then said, 'I loved war too much'? He carried on fighting in spite of himself, wanting to make peace but unable to do so. From 1704 to 1710 one military disaster followed another, and the 'French and Christian dream' collapsed. The prince whom people had come to think of as immortal was attacked by death, which pitilessly laid into those around him: between April 1711 and March 1712 his son the 'Grand Dauphin', his grandson the Duke of Burgundy, the Duchess of Burgundy and the eldest of his great-grandsons died. Yet the heroic myth of Louis XIV did not expire: it was transformed. In 1708 Mongin wrote, 'True heroes are heroes at all times. As their greatness resides in their soul and not in the fighting skills of their soldiers, they do not have to be always successful in order to be great.'

Faced with the inconstancy and fickleness of fortune, the unshakeable steadfastness of the French monarch commanded admiration. Stronger than everything, stronger than death, Louis XIV came face to face with the eternal. The author of a long poem on *Le Triomphe des Parques* declares:

> Only you, oh glorious monarch,
> Are capable of steadfastness . . .
> Triumphing over yourself is the great victory.
> Your virtues will bring you triumph over death,
> You will never die, and the voice of the oracle
> Seems to announce this miracle too,
> That Louis the God-Given with such a name must
> Not be made like us of earth and clay,
> But an outstanding being who through his essence
> Must be more than any other like omnipotence.

In the twilight of his life Louis XIV became the pattern of the Christian prince in all its purity, as those supporting humanist policies had called him in the wishes they expressed at the start of his reign. The myth then gathered around the current supporting the humanist ideal, no longer around that supporting the ideal of military glory; Mongin is careful not to confuse his king with 'those profane [conquerors] who owe their glory only to their ferocity, and whose whole merit lies in having successfully pursued ambition, injustice, and barbarous, usurping policies'. Louis XIV's prestige was of a different order: 'this immortal monarch whose undertakings have always been guided by religion and justice' belonged to the universe of grace.

Louis XIV died on 1 September 1715, but the myth of the Sun King did not expire with the man, and in the temple of eulogy that the Académie française represented it lingered on in the transfigured form found at the end of his reign. The fierce Hercules beloved of fortune from earlier days did not appeal to the Academicians as much as the new saintly Louis who had proudly withstood the blows that destiny rained down upon him. In an item that was read at the Académie in 1717 he was compared to those 'mountains topped by snow' which, despite being buffeted by the winds, raise their snow-capped heads above the clouds, preserving a deep calm. The royal star was no longer blinding as it had been at its zenith. Like Titus, the monarch who had passed on should be called the 'delight of the earth'.

In 1751 in *Le Siècle de Louis XIV* Voltaire went back to the myth of Louis as a second Augustus, the master of a century that would be remembered for ever. Just as it requires 'only one man to change sad Sparta into brilliant Athens', so according to him 'everything begins with Louis XIV', an exemplary prince who could make France overflow with genius, achievements in the arts and beauty. Disappointed by Louis XV's weakness, exasperated by the octogenarian Fleury, and irritated by what was not being done that could have been done, as he explained in a tract written in 1728, Voltaire, dreaming of unparalleled splendour for France, turned to a past which was more in line with his wishes, and so to a king whom he saw in his mythical dimension; even the image of Louis XIV as a conqueror was used to perfect the evocation.

After 1751 the myth of Louis XIV went through a period of relative eclipse; people became more interested in the Orleans branch of the family, and preferred to look back to Henri IV. The ultra-royalist policies reintroduced in 1815 were not conducive to a return to the myth of the Sun King: ultraist loyalties went back to earlier examples of the French monarchy, Henri IV and St Louis (Louis IX), feeling that Louis XIV's despotism had too much in common with that of Bonaparte or the Jacobins. The cry 'Vive Henri IV' went up, and people dreamt of restoring the mediaeval monarchy. After 1830 the legitimists (supporters of the elder branch of the Bourbons) celebrated the myth of a people's king, but that king was never Louis XIV. As Rémond wrote in his book *La Droite en France de la Première Restauration à la Ve* République, 'the Orleanist philosophy consummated its separation from theology; it became secular'; moreover 'attachment to Parliamentarianism is so strong that for Orleanists it has become a way of life, second nature'.

Neither the Bonapartism of the Second Empire nor the regime of moral order brought Louis XIV back to the fore.

Yet this long eclipse was not a death. Chateaubriand in *La Vie de Rancé* is certainly the best witness to this, for his reference to the myth, drawing a parallel between Napoleon and Louis XIV, highlights the way in which the figure of the monarch is rooted in his period:

> The eighteenth century tried to obliterate Louis XIV, but wore its hands out scraping away at his image. Napoleon has come and taken up residence beneath the dome of the Invalides, as if to ensure Louis's glory . . . . Bonaparte made his century; Louis was made by his: which will live longer, the handiwork of time or the handiwork of one man? At the tomb of Louis we hear genius of every kind speak; at the tomb of Napoleon we hear only the voice of Napoleon.

At the end of the nineteenth century and the beginning of the twentieth, with rationalism, the 'Action française' and writers like Maurras, Barrès, Gaxotte or Bertrand, the right wing went back to the myth of the great king. When Maurras for example dreamt of an ideal monarchy, his thoughts went less to 'the tutelary kingship of St Louis or the paternal administration of good King Henri', to use Rémond's words, than to the government of Louis XIV – once again envisaging him as the prestigious Sun King, surrounded by pomp and brilliance, encouraging genius in literature and the arts to flourish as his feet. In an over-simplified exaltation of him, Bertrand adapts the mythical vision of Louis XIV to suit his dearest wishes:

> Faced with all the consequences of Defeat I saw the abasement of my country in exaggerated terms . . . . All of a sudden I discovered in this poor humiliated land the figure that I so ardently desired for my country. [Louis XIV] was for me the glorious image of France.

Nowadays it is Versailles rather than Louis XIV that fascinates people and sets them dreaming, and the myth of the king has become the myth of the place. In a contribution published in 1985 in the book *Destins et Enjeux du XVIIe siècle* H. Himelfarb attests to this:

> Both in France and abroad the nostalgic idealization of Court ceremony, the 'sweetness of life', a great, solemn, harmonious and refined design springing full-blown from the magnificent ideas of Louis XIV and the painstaking ideas of Colbert, . . . that ecstatic dream is not dead, far from it, it survives in the most unexpected minds or social groups. . . . In short, without confining ourselves to its admirers of whom there are more than might be thought, . . . there is a fair-sized public ranging across every age group in the minds of whom this imaginary Versailles of bygone days has taken over from the cathedrals as they used to be portrayed, again as imaginary creations from a bygone age.

'Still outside history and reality', the myth of Versailles is again evoked by Himelfarb through a Baroque vision: 'Versailles is now perceived as a fabulous, many-coloured opera, irrational, choreographic and sensual, all the more beautiful because in it eroticism . . . seems to be tinged with physical death and political decadence.'

Thus today the imaginary has taken hold of this place, with its history – in fact extremely rich and complex – seemingly carried away by the tide of dreams and nostalgia which scientific knowledge has no power to stem.

The myth of Louis XIV, varied and protean as it is, has never been anything other than bright; it has never taken on the dark colours of the Napoleonic myth. Nonetheless, critics have not spared the Sun King. Starting with the arrest of Fouquet in 1661 they attacked him vigorously. The image of a conqueror prince who incessantly fanned war and burdened his subjects with taxes has been orchestrated by writers on more than one occasion: from 1672 shadows appeared, with more than one voice condemning the ambitions of a monarch eager for military glory. La Bruyère, Fénelon, Vauban and the exiled Protestants were also among those who brought charges against the king. But never at any time did a dark myth take shape. The portrait of the king was tempered for some people by a pardon, for others by resignation or a flash of admiration, or for others still by loyalty. After 1685 pamphlets and medals mostly emanating from the Netherlands and generally written by exiled Protestants made the most virulent criticisms, but they have more to do with satire and caricature than with myth; they stick too closely to events and are too specific and precise, never achieving the density of myth.

As time has elapsed, the detailed nature of the reproaches against him and the balance between fascination and hate have again made it impossible to talk of a dark myth relating to Louis XIV: neither Montesquieu, Saint-Simon or Michelet, to take some examples, has even suggested such a thing. And today, when G. Bonheur in *Henri IV* talks of the 'bashi-bazouk of Versailles', who 'will continue to occupy the place of honour in the international monsters' gallery as a promoter of genocide' he is talking in too narrow terms and without taking a sufficiently overall view in relation to the Revocation of the Edict of Nantes (to which he is referring) for his words to be more than satire.

As soon as Louis XIV came into the world and throughout the fifty-four years of his personal reign acolytes played what Guillou has called 'the majestic cadences [of the] humanist, Christian symphony' for him. With its roots deeply embedded in feudalism the idealized image of the sovereign immediately swept him away into a magical universe; rhetoric, in extolling him, borrowed 'its weapons from a very primitive emotion: the sense of thrill when confronted with the sacred and with light', as Starobinski expresses it.

With the strength of primitive beliefs and of ideologies that have been powerfully orchestrated, the myth of Louis XIV has come down through the centuries to be reborn, like the phoenix in whose colours the king was depicted by writers, into the kingdom of a Versailles which has not yet revealed its secrets to history.

Yet as Saint-Simon, whose visionary genius applied itself to penetrating the obscurity, wrote, 'Kings are men'. The Great King managed to be more than a man, an impressive figurehead, a crossroads of the living strengths of the civilization of his period and the strengths inherent in him; the spells that have led to the gateway into a dream world are not to be destroyed.

Nicole Ferrier-Caverivière

Mandrake

BOTANICAL DATA

The mandrake, or mandragora (Mandragora officinarum) is a Eurasian solanaceous plant with purplish flowers. Its forked root is long – up to 50 or 60 cm – white, and fleshy in appearance, vaguely reminiscent of the trunk and legs of a human body. This 'anthropomorphic' root came to be regarded as a kind of incomplete embryo which could be brought to life by the practice of magic.

Like deadly nightshade and henbane which are poisonous solanaceae, the mandrake root contains alkaloids. Its sedative properties have long been known to medical practitioners. In the eighteenth century it was applied externally as an analgesic; it has also been used in the past to induce anaethesia during operations, and aphrodisiac properties have been attributed to it. It is listed in the catalogue of medicinal herbs. Mandrake could therefore alleviate or even cure certain illnesses, and stimulate vitality.

MAGIC, DIVINE OR SATANIC PROPERTIES OF THE PLANT AND ITS MYTHICAL ORIGINS

The Greeks called the mandrake the plant of Circe, the sorceress, and in spite of its beneficent qualities it inspired reverence and fear. In his *Historia Naturalis* Pliny observes:

> People digging up the mandrake take care not to face the wind. They describe three circles round the plant with a sword, then they lift it from the earth, turning in the direction of the setting sun [. . .] The root of this plant, crushed with oil prepared from roses and wine, cures inflammation and pain in the eyes (XXV, 148).

This ritual method of harvesting, carried out in conditions of ceremonial purity which presuppose certain dangers, indicates that the plant is divine. It is not merely a question of collecting a botanical species but of obtaining a substance imbued with the sacred, a variant of the herb of eternal life. The magical and pharmaceutical value of the plant derives from the fact that it belongs to an archetype set apart from things secular. Like medicinal herbs, mandrake is believed to share the privilege of having been discovered 'at a cosmic and decisive moment on Mount Calvary', where it is supposed to have healed Christ's wounds. Thus the person digging it up is repeating a primordial act of healing.

The myth of the mandrake belongs with that branch of myths which describe the telluric birth of human beings at the beginning of time. According to Albert-Marie Schmidt it is the survival of the belief in 'the autochthonous (in the etymological sense of the word) human creature that grew from the seed laid down by divine rain . . . into a small telluric matrix' – a weak echo of the great cosmic sacred unions.

Thus in *De Natura Rerum* (Book V) Lucretius shows how:

> The young earth first of all produced grasses and small trees, only then creating human beings, but creating them in great number and a variety of species. [. . .] Matrices grew from roots in the earth and when they were fully formed, age liberated the newborn wishing to escape from the damp and struggling to reach the open air: nature then directed pores in the earth towards them, obliging the earth to dispense through them a sap that resembled milk.

Lucian inevitably poked fun at 'these first men grown like vegetables in the Attic soil'.

Pausanias (VII, 17) and Arnobius (*Adversus natione*, V, 5) tell how Zeus spilt his seed on to the earth when attempting to embrace the Great Mother, and from this incident the hermaphrodite Agdistis was supposedly born. In *Metamorphoses* (Book 15, 1.555 ff) Ovid pursues this ancient dream of humankind when he conjures up the appearance of Tages:

> The Tyrrhenian ploughman [. . .] saw the clump of earth in the middle of his field which had been shaped by destiny, move of its own accord [. . .] then metamorphose into the shape of a man and open its completely new mouth to foretell the future.

He also evokes Erichthonius, a 'child born without a mother' (Book 2, 1.553 ff). As his name indicates, Erichthonius is in fact born of the earth which served as his mother; when Athena had evaded Hephaestus' pursuit his sperm had spilt on the earth.

According to Barthélémy d'Herbelot, the Cabbalists' Adam engendered the first mandrake, a hybrid creature related to Tages, Erichthonius and Agdistis. After Adam had been driven out of the Garden of Eden, God, to punish him:

> did not allow him to meet [. . .] Eve whom he cherished most tenderly. When he was asleep with the face (of Eve) strongly imprinted on his imagination, he thought he was embracing her. This image of lovemaking produced the same effect in him as true possession might have provoked, so that when the fruitful seed of this first father of men fell on the earth a plant which took on human shape was formed from it (*Bibliothèque orientale*, 1777).

More often it was supposedly the blood of a god or of a primordial giant who had met a violent death that resulted in the appearance of plants similar to the mandrake. In an article called 'La Mandragore et les Mythes de la

Naissance Miraculeuse' Mircea Eliade quotes the myth of Gajomard, the original man in Iranian mythology who can be assimilated to Adam. When the spirits of evil brought about his death, 'a drop of sperm, came out of his loins and sank into the earth for forty years' before giving birth 'to a plant which was in turn transformed into a human couple'.

Christ on the Cross was supposedly the heir to these myths, which would explain the link between medicinal plants and Calvary. But Christian modesty, unable to accept such an indecent conclusion to the Passion of the Saviour, transposed it.

In the Middle Ages the hanged man whose last drops of seminal fluid – according to a legend already known to Avicenna (1037) – engendered the mandrake, the 'mannikin of the gibbet' as the Germans called it, would thus be the substitute for Christ crucified, who like him was 'killed by hanging him on a tree' as it is put in Acts v. 30. This would explain why the hanged man in Arnim's book *Isabella von Ägypten* is innocent and bears the sins of an accursed race. Some scholars who have studied the mandrake go so far as to assert that the water passed by the condemned man is the baptismal water that washes away sin.

Schmidt wrote:

> Seen in a strange gnostic light, the mandrake can be regarded as a reconstitution of the original Adam, the sum total of all the principles of health and peace of mind that flourished in Eden [. . .] It for ever predates the distinction between good and evil. Thus it is not inappropriate also to regard it as the development of a malleable clod taken from the holy store of clay, some of which God had used when modelling Adam.

Preserving the energy of nature as it was in the beginning, the mandrake can heal and ensure the fertility of which it is itself evidence since it is capable of obliterating the barrier that separates the human and plant kingdoms. However, its power can be used for evil. And from being a precious talisman, capable of realizing all the desires of the person possessing it, the mandrake – that 'imago dei' – can become the instrument of the tempter or the devil, which explains its ambiguous, demoniac aspect – the opposite face of its redemptive powers. The person who possesses it must sell it before his death for less than he paid for it, otherwise his soul will fall prey to the devil, as the story by La Motte Fouqué relates.

THE MANDRAKE IN LITERATURE

Machiavelli and La Fontaine

The great cosmic myth of the mandrake root first appeared in a debased form in the sixteenth and seventeenth centuries, in erotic literature – which only concerned itself with the aphrodisiac properties of the plant.

Machiavelli's famous comedy *Mandragola* features a young man who covets the favours of a young Florentine woman. Unfortunately the lady is married. As the couple have no child, the young man poses as a doctor and offers the following advice to the husband: 'Let me tell you that there is nothing better for making a woman pregnant than getting her to drink a potion made from a mandrake'. It is best to take it at night, he says, when 'the moon is in an auspicious phase', but he also points out the dangers to which the husband is exposing himself: 'The first man to come near a woman who has taken this potion will die without fail by the end of a week'. Thus it is necessary to find a substitute who 'spending the whole night at Lucrezia's side will attract all the venom upon himself'. Needless to say, this 'unfortunate' man is none other than the young seducer!

La Fontaine, inspired by Machiavelli, wrote a rather lewd tale in verse on the same theme; in it we again find the property of fecundity attributed to the mandrake. However, he tones down Machiavelli's somewhat frightening version in which the mandrake, associated with sex and death, was surrounded by an aura of black magic: 'This juice which has such unparalleled power/ Also has a very malign quality;/Almost always it proves fatal/To the first man to caress/The patient; and often people die of it.'

German Romanticism

It was during the nineteenth century, via German Romanticism, that the myth of the mandrake developed its full persuasive force, linked with people's intimate dreams, and was completely exploited in poetic terms by writers.

Ernst Theodor Amadeus Hoffmann, obsessed by the image of men as roots, in the story *Klein Zaches* (1819) drew a humorous portrait of Zinnober who was not a mandrake but looked just like one:

> What might well at first have been taken for a small, strangely gnarled stump was in fact a deformed little boy hardly two hands high [. . .] The head of this creature was sunk keep between his shoulders, a gourd-shaped excrescence took the place of his back and immediately below his chest hung little legs, as spindly as twigs of hazelnut; in short, the child looked like a big forked radish. Of his face [. . .] one could see [. . .] a long pointed nose springing straight out from a brush of black hair and tiny eyes with a black glint which, especially in conjunction with the shrivelled, old-mannish features of the face, seemed to suggest a small mandrake.

This deformed Tom Thumb, misshapen shrimp, this aged child Zinnober is just an ordinary 'freak' to whom a sympathetic fairy has granted the strange power of taking on the appearance and qualities of those around him. Balthazar, a student and a poet, is a victim of Zinnober's pranks since the woman he loves directs her love towards Zinnober, whom she sees in the guise of Balthazar. When the latter asks a magician, Prosper Alphanus, to free him from this spell, the wizard consults his catalogues listing all the mandrakes which he can summon to appear before him at will if they get up to any mischief. Zinnober's presumption in fact knows no bounds – he will usurp the highest offices if the magician does not discover his secret: all Zinnober's power resides in three fiery red hairs (hence his name of Zinnober, meaning cinnabar) which Balthazar pulls out on the day of his engagement. Once the spell has been broken, the general blindness disappears. This tale is a satire on the rationalist frame of mind which drives out poetry, viewing it as a 'venom which makes people completely unsuited to serving the cause of enlightenment'.

Another of Hoffmann's tales, *Die Königsbraut*, shows the king of the vegetables, Daucus Carota I, scheming to draw towards him the hand of young Anna, as elementary spirits aspire to union with human beings. When Anna pulls at the magnificent carrot top, rather than the groan of the mandrake she hears 'a discreet, joyous laugh' and to her amazement finds a superb golden ring fitted on to the carrot.

Daucus Carota looks like the root-man or the mandrake: he is small, with thin legs and a face that is out of proportion. Under the influence of a spell, Anna admires him and his aides-de-camp with their revealing names: 'Herr von Rettich [radish] from Pomerania, Signor di Broccoli from Italy, Prince Melon', etc. In the end Daucus Carota is vanquished by the magic of Anna's fiancé's poems, rather than the ineffectual, cabbalistic knowledge of her father. Once again he becomes 'a small, very small carrot' who 'plunged down into the earth where he disappeared without trace'. Hoffmann suggests that behind the mask of the most inoffensive vegetable may lurk a potential mandrake, perhaps thus expressing an ancestral fear.

More than any other writer, Achim von Arnim fully develops the myth of the mandrake in *Isabella von Ägypten* (1812). All the fantastic, dramatic legends relating to the mandrake can be found in that book, most potently expressed. Isabella, a gypsy girl known as Bella, lives at a time of persecution: her father, a kind of spiritual leader, has just been hanged for a theft he did not commit. She then feels that she had been entrusted with the destiny of saving her people, of guiding them towards the end of their troubles, as her father had done. For the gypsies believe they have been punished for turning away the Virgin and the baby Jesus when they came to seek refuge in Egypt.

The hanged man had let 'painful tears fall down on to the earth, thinking that he, the last male heir of his noble line, was being put to death in such a shameful way, for all that he was innocent'. For reasons of propriety the tears of the innocent victim replace the sperm of the hanged man which traditionally engendered the mandrake. Isabella consults her father's books of spells which are full of magic recipes: 'She fell upon a detailed recipe explaining how to get hold of mandrakes and telling how zealous, rapacious and unfailingly cunning they were in procuring money and everything that a heart attached to this base world could desire'. There are many difficulties involved in getting hold of the precious root. A young, innocent girl who is in love is required, with:

> the more than manly courage to go at night at the eleventh hour with a black dog to underneath the gibbet, to the place where the tears of the innocent hanged man have fallen on the grass; there she must carefully block her ears with cotton wool and grope around until she puts her hand on the root; then despite all the cries of the root, which is not a natural root but the child of the innocent tears of the hanged man, she must uncover its head, encircle it with a thin cord made of her own hair, harness this to the black dog and then run off so that the dog in its anxiety to follow her pulls up the root, and is then inevitably killed by an earth tremor accompanied by a flash of lightning.

Arnim scrupulously respects a secular tradition. It is on a Friday night that Bella discovers the mandrake: 'She explored what he [the dog] had found with her fingers; in her hands she had a small object of human shape, but its two legs were still rooted in the ground; it was the mysterious mandrake, the mannikin of the gibbet.' When she recovers from her faint, for in spite of her precautions she is shaken by the cry of the mandrake, beside the dead dog she finds 'a kind of human being, something like a rough living model from which the noble senses have not yet been released, a kind of chrysalis'.

Bella then acts towards the little incomplete creature like a mother with her child. Consulting her book of magic she learns that:

> she should first of all wash the mandrake; this she did; she should then sow millet on the rough surface of his head and when it grew forming a head of hair his other limbs would develop of their own accord; only at each spot where an eye should develop she must insert a juniper berry, and a rose-hip at the place where the mouth should form.

Bella cherishes the little shapeless monster that she has created, placing him in a cradle. He gets bigger and learns to speak, but his pranks soon show that his nature may be devilish. Cornelius Nepos, the name soon adopted by the mandrake whose pride is in inverse proportion to his size, shows great aptitude at discovering treasure, so much so that after numerous adventures in which he promotes Bella's rise in the world and her love affair with Archduke Charles, later to become Emperor Charles V, by whom she has a child and from whom she obtains the freedom of her people, he ends up as Minister of Finance. After Bella leaves he commits suicide and becomes the evil genius of Charles V:

> When he had been buried secretly Charles thought he was free of him – everyone thought he had been completely destroyed – but in his fury he had transformed himself into a demon and the Emperor was soon certain that unless he did strict penance he would never succeed in ridding himself of his intolerable presence.

The relationship between the mandrake and the original lump of clay from which man was supposedly fashioned is emphasized in this book by the love the mandrake feels for a Golem, a kind of animated clay statue, in Bella's image. But the Golem collapses into a heap of earth after a magic formula has been pronounced:

> When he found the coat of his beloved with a heap of common clay inside it, without understanding why, he started to love that earth as if it were the bride he had lost. [. . .] He again felt attracted by the clay which henceforth constituted the only treasure of his root's heart.

With all the possibilities of the marvellous and strange that it affords, the mandrake is intimately associated with German Romanticism. While Hoffmann's Zinnober and Arnim's Cornelius Nepos are the two most famous literary examples, the mandrake makes a fleeting appearance in many other tales. Thus in *Der Runenberg* (1793) by Ludwig Tieck, young Christian, a prey to melancholy, in the solitude of the forest at twilight,

> without thinking what he was doing [. . .] pulled out of the earth a root the head of which was level with the ground, when all of a sudden to his great terror he heard a low groan which spread through the earth in plaintive sounds and faded away in the distance.

For him it was the voice of the whole earth like some obscure organism and not just that of the root. 'The sound of that moan went straight through his heart and affected him as if he had inadvertently touched the wound of which the failing body of nature was about to die in pain.' A latent cosmic dimension is expressed in this image. The theme is echoed again at the end of the story: 'It was a plant that first taught me the misfortunes of the whole world.' At the beginning of the story the mandrake heralds the hero's misfortunes; hardly has he picked the root than a man appears who is going to lure him to the Runenberg with his tempting talk.

German tales also feature a different sort of mandrake, an 'imp shut up in a small glass bottle'. That is the image that appears in La Motte Fouqué's tale, and it was handed down from one writer to another. The tales of Hoffmann are full of mandrake-like apparitions: at the beginning of the *Der Goldene Topf* the student Anselmus stumbles against the basket of an old woman street-vendor who insults him with: 'Run, keep running, you limb of Satan, the crystal bottle for which you were meant is waiting for you!' There is the same mysterious crystal bottle at the beginning and end of the *Das öde Haus*.

This crystal container haunted by a latent presence would prove of interest to alchemists, wondering if artifice might not continue the work of nature and produce a semblance of humanity outside the female body. The mandrake in the bottle becomes the archetype of all possible experiments on the human embryo. Scholars give the name homonculus to these tiny creatures which have all the organs of a child but whose exceptional faculties – since they have been produced by the greatest of arts – make them akin to spirits.

The mandrake that can grant all its owner's desires is often simply designated by the word 'Spiritus', with no further explanation: 'Spiritus Familiaris' in Hoffmann's *Kreisleriana*, and 'Spiritus Papyri' living in an inkwell in *Simplicissimus* by Grimmelshausen.

French Romanticism

None of the works devoted to the mandrake by French Romantic writers achieves the symbolic depth of Arnim's or Tieck's writing, neither Nodier's *La Fée aux Miettes* (1832) nor Théophile Gautier's *Le Club des Hachichins* (1846).

In Nodier's work Michel is a young carpenter thirsting for the Absolute; he seeks salvation from the mandrake, which Nodier strips of its infernal horror, retaining only a perfect image of it. The mandrake is connected with the quest for immortality since it is capable of restoring the youth of the 'fée aux miettes', Michel's wife. In the asylum where Michel is confined, mandrakes are grown for therapeutic purposes. The sombre cry of the mandrake becomes a song to his ears. He looks for the unique plant that will save him. His initiatory quest takes him on to a higher level than that of man in the hierarchy of creatures. He is seen 'swinging for a moment at the top of the turrets of the Catholic church with a flower in his hand, singing so sweetly that people were not sure whether the songs came from the flower or from him'. Michel undergoes a sort of apotheosis: 'spirited away from his prison by Princess Mandragore [. . .] he married the Queen of Sheba and [. . .] he became emperor of the seven planets'. Nodier's irony – for in writing about the mandrake he regains the idea that it helps madmen to pursue their chimerical enterprises without suffering – deprives the myth of the power and conviction it had in Arnim's text.

In Théophile Gautier's book hashish causes Hoffmann's king of the vegetables, Daucus Carota, to appear in the narrator's dreams. He takes great delight in describing the monster, its legs in particular, 'made of the forked root of a black, rough mandrake full of knots and warts that seemed to have been freshly pulled as little deposits of earth were still sticking to its hair roots'. All the devilish energy of the character is in fact concentrated in these extraordinarily active legs, and he uses them to force his victims to obey him. But the horrible man-plant is only an hallucination born from a nightmare: it lies 'on the floor in the form of a double-rooted salsify' as soon as reality is re-established.

In *La Légende des siècles* Victor Hugo alluded to the mandrake when talking of Sixtus Malaspina, who smeared his weapons with its anaesthetic juice in order to kill his opponents.

Finally, in 1899, Jean Lorrain wrote a book entitled *La Mandragore* which dwelt only on the dark, repugnant and diabolic aspects of the plant. He dramatized the ceremonial pulling of 'the fearful root which grows amidst charnel-houses [. . .], and is obscene and hairy', and maintained that the plant was inhabited by the soul of a dead person.

THE TWENTIETH CENTURY IN FRANCE

The Surrealist Movement was responsible for restoring power to imaginary creations so it is not surprising to find the myth of the mandrake revived in *Onirocritique*, a dream story by Apollinaire. 'The islanders took me into their orchards so that I could pick fruit shaped like women. They dug up a transparent root and ate some. It was the size of a turnip.'

Jarry conjures up 'the Mandrake's lament' in *Les Minutes de Sable mémorial*:

> I am a plant and cannot creep like ivy, nor can I climb like ivy on to high pillars. the bottom of the earth is holding me by the feet. I am a dwarf at whom you as a man, my big brother, laugh – but I would like to have a bat's wings.

The plant promises wealth to anyone who will set it free.

> Gold sequins will cover your floors. All that touches me turns into gold. The eyes of the owl have often stared at me, and they will remain golden for ever [. . .] Come and set me free; the bottom of the earth is holding me by my feet.

The poem ends with the jeering of the freed mandrake, which has exchanged its freedom for that of the person liberating it: 'But his winning hand in a mocking wave blazes like a lighthouse, a gust of wind carries away his jeers. The bottom of the earth is holding ME by my feet.' An allusion is being made here to the popular etymology of the word 'mandragore' which in French is often debased into 'main de gloire' (winning hand), for it had the reputation of giving back twice as much as it had received.

In *Waiting for Godot* Samuel Beckett mentions the cry of the mandrake as it is pulled up, when one of his characters wonders if he should not put a rope round his neck, because he is so constricted by the boredom of existing.

The myth of the mandrake continues to appear in the work of present-day authors who have studied German literature. Giraudoux evokes the mandrake and its powers to confer immortality at the beginning of *Intermezzo*:

> Is what they say about mandrakes true?
> About constipation?
> No, about immortality . . . That children conceived on a mandrake by a hanged man become devilish creatures and never die?

The theme of the mandrake sets the tone in stories where a dream of consorting with creatures other than human is evoked, as in Giraudoux's *Ondine* which was adapted for the theatre from a tale by La Motte Fouqué.

The same cosmic impulse, of trying to suppress the barrier established by man between himself and the universe may perhaps explain the appearance of mandrakes in *Vendredi ou les Limbes du Pacifique* by Michel Tournier. The mandrakes are regarded by Robinson, the protagonist, as fruits of his love for Speranza, the island that had taken him in.

> That day he rushed to the pink combe and kneeling before one of those plants he very gently uncovered its root by scraping all round it with both hands. It really was true, his love for Speranza had not been sterile: the fleshy, white root, strangely forked, was undoubtedly in the shape of the body of a little girl. He trembled with emotion and tenderness as he put the mandrake back in its hole and drew the sand up round its stem, as one might tuck up a child in its bed.

The theme is reverted to later on: 'His daughters were there – the blessing of his union with Speranza – their scalloped skirts bending in the black grass . . .'

Michel Tournier reverts further than the mediaeval legends – on which he just touches – to the myth of Adam, the cabbalistic Adam quoted by Barthélémy d'Herbelot. On this unknown island where he is similar to the first man on earth, Robinson again discovers the mythical powers of his great ancestor and that mythical epoch when men, animals and plants were not really distinct from one another and could pass easily from one kingdom to another.

This nostalgia for universal unity among creatures is expressed through the myth of the mandrake, justifying the interest taken in it by Tournier, who investigates the great forgotten brotherhood between man and the elementary world, and restores its sacred dimension. The biblical quotation taken from the Song of Solomon which comes before Robinson's discovery, 'The mandrakes give forth fragrance', shows the plant in a favourable light and reminds us of the religious origins of the myth. We may note that in literature the mandrake engenders root-men, though in form it may be male or female. Here it is a feminine creature that appears, perhaps female because of its leaves which are compared to scalloped skirts. Although Tournier returns to the original myth, and re-experiences it intensely, the element of the fantastic plays a more discreet role in his work than in that of the German writers.

Thus the mandrake is a myth associated with our nostalgia for paradise lost; it seems to attest to the power of the earth at the beginning of time to create human beings directly, when it was fertilized by pagan gods or our great ancestors. Retaining divine powers from its origins, the mandrake with the passage of time has taken on the property of a talisman, but as with all sacred objects, its redeeming powers can be reversed and contribute to the downfall of anyone abusing them. The image of the innocent hanged man whose seed gave rise to the mandrake would thus appear to be the diluted, secularized image of Christ dying on the Cross whose blood made the earth fruitful, in a way similar to other more archaic myths. German literature has remained closest to this myth about origins and exploited it most extensively. French Romantics, to some extent in the grip of rationalism, attenuated the fantastic aspect of the myth by turning it into the obsession of a 'lunatic' or the dream of a hashish-smoker. Michel Tournier, remaining faithful to German literature in that respect, restores to the mandrake the persuasive force of a poetic myth.

Arlette Bouloumié

Medea

The fearsome sorceress Medea, daughter of Aeëtes, King of Colchis, and granddaughter of Helius, the Sun, took part in five mythical events which were written at different periods in Ancient Greek history. The first one involved her role in the quest for the Golden Fleece, which was owned by Aeëtes and kept in a sacred grove. Bewitched by Eros and Aphrodite, Medea helped Jason, leader of the Argonauts, to accomplish the trials imposed on him by her father. She produced a magic salve to prevent him from being burnt by fire-breathing bulls, advised him to throw the stone of Discord among the giants in the field of Ares, and gave him a herb which would cause the dragon guarding the Golden Fleece to fall asleep. To help the Argonauts escape, Medea either killed or helped Jason to kill her brother Absyrtus and scattered the pieces of his dismembered body.

In the second mythical sequence, set in Iolcus in Thessaly, Jason returned to his homeland, accompanied by Medea, to deliver the Golden Fleece to his Uncle Pelias. According to an early version of the myth, Jason and Medea lived in Iolcus on good terms with Pelias, and Medea rejuvenated Aeson (Jason's father), Jason and the Hyades (the nurses of Dionysus). In another version, which presented Pelias as a usurper who had killed Jason's parents, Medea helped the Argonaut to avenge them: the daughters of Pelias, acting on the advice of the sorceress who had 'transformed' and 'rejuvenated' an old ram by cutting it up into pieces and boiling it in a cauldron, did the same to their father. After the horrible death of the tyrant of Iolcus, Jason and Medea were banished by Pelias' son, Acastus.

The third major sequence, set in Corinth, is one of the most famous episodes in the myth and is presented as a mixture of traditions. Medea, who was worshipped as a goddess for having saved the city from famine, was associated with the cult of Hera. To reward Medea for having scorned the love of Zeus, Hera had promised to make her rival's sons immortal. During the ceremony, the children whom Medea had buried in the floor of the temple, died. Another tradition held the Corinthians responsible for the deaths of the children killed in the temple. Because a terrible plague descended on the land, an expiatory ritual was introduced which involved seven boys and seven girls spending a year in the temple, dressed in mourning. The death of her children provided a focal point for the presentation of Medea as a foreigner, abandoned by Jason who wanted to marry Glauce, the daughter of Creon, the tyrant of Corinth. Banished from the city, the sorceress took her revenge by sending a poisoned robe to her rival. The death of the children at the hands of the Corinthians was presented as the consequence of her action and the inhabitants of Corinth attributed the crime to Medea. (In the tragedy by Euripides (431 BC), Medea kills her own children and escapes in a chariot sent by her grandfather, Helius.)

In the fourth sequence, Medea cured the madness of Hercules in Thebes and, absolved of her past crimes, sought refuge at the court of Aegeus, King of Athens, who married her. When Theseus returned from Troezen, Medea tried to poison the hero or ordered him to confront the bull of Marathon. In this respect, there is a parallel between Theseus and Jason in Colchis at the time of the quest for the Golden Fleece. In the final sequence of the myth, Medea was driven from Athens and went either to Ephyra or to Colchis, where she returned with a son by Jason, Aegeus or an Asian prince. Medea restored the throne of Colchis to her father Aeëtes and, with her son Medus, helped to reconquer lands belonging to the kingdom of Colchis which later became Media.

The mythical events based on sorcery refer either to traditions associated with a particular locality, or legendary tales connected with great sea voyages. In this way, the nucleus of the Corinthian legend was grafted on to the story of the quest for treasure in far-off lands thought to be fraught with danger. The sorceress – keeper of the Golden Fleece which is the symbol of agricultural prosperity, fertility and royal authority – is associated with the dragon which is the manifestation of the infernal powers of which Medea holds the secret. Compared with Jason, who is seeking to establish royal ascendancy and introduce a reign of order, Medea is the image of chaos and the forces of evil. When she allies herself with Jason, she uses her sorcery to beneficial effect by throwing the stone of Discord among the armed giants, born from the dragon's teeth. Medea exercises her knowledge and power on the land ploughed by Jason, i.e. the field of Ares, god of war, which is opposed to the land of Demeter, goddess of the earth and fertility. Medea's superiority, asserted in a sphere of activity reserved for men, is reminiscent of the mythical image of Hera who was tempted to demonstrate her superiority over Zeus. The domination of Medea vis-à-vis the world of men was asserted in her practice of immortalization – when she tried to bring her children into the world again in the floor of the temple in Corinth, thus precluding the need for male semen – as well as in her use of the cauldron, which was exclusively a male preserve in the Greek pre-Classical era.

The sorcery incarnated by Medea and associated with 'metis' or ruse, is sometimes beneficial, as in the rejuvenation of Aeson, and sometimes used as an evil deception, as in the case of the deaths of Pelias, Creon and his daughter Glauce. It illustrates the ethical opposition underlying discursive thinking on mythology, i.e. the practice of sorcery for the purposes of good and evil. The soteriological nature of the myth is represented by the initiatory role of Medea – in relation to young heroes such as Jason in Colchis, in the blunt reference to the 'diasparagmós' or cutting up of Absyrtus and the 'boiling' of the ram and Pelias – which opens the way to the 'other dimension' and the realm of successful and unsuccessful metamorphoses. The infanticide, i.e. the failed attempt at immortality, is a distorted reminder of initiatory rites and crimes of passion, and becomes the polyvalent and 'barbarous' act which led to the 'offensive rumour' that has been associated with the name of Medea since classical times.

The parallels and oppositions which form the structure of the myth are incorporated into the two closely linked motifs of family relations and distorted or normal hospitality, since relatives are often hosts, as in the case of Aeëtes and Pelias. Another characteristic of the myth is the recurrent nature of the link which unites or opposes Medea to Jason and his male relatives, Aeson, Pelias and Creon, and Medea's confrontation with the authority of the tyrants Creon and Aegeus. These strained relations are resolved by the flight of the sorceress, who experiences a classic change of status, i.e. from princess she becomes a 'foreigner' or an exile. In respect of the final sequence, which appeared much later and in which Medea re-establishes normal family relations, the sorceress maintains a privileged relationship with the world of wandering and becomes a disconcerting figure who has come from 'elsewhere'. From the time of Euripides' tragedy, the opposition of 'barbarous/civilized' and 'foreigner/native inhabitant' – achieved indirectly via the presence of Aegeus, King of Athens, who agreed to receive Medea in Athens – were reinforced by the sorceress, who claimed responsibility for her exclusion and rejection by performing 'barbarous' and destructive acts. It is precisely the 'monstrous' nature of Medea at the level of these classic and fascinating paradoxes which explains the survival of the myth in literature to the present day.

Medea appears in fragments of epic poetry such as Eumelus' *Corinthian History* (eighth century BC), which refer to the sovereignty of the sorceress over Corinth, the death of her children as a result of the unsuccessful attempt to make them immortal and the discord which arose between Jason and his wife. Hesiod also refers to her in his *Theogony* (V, 992–1002), in which he describes how Jason carried off the heroine from Colchis, their arrival in Iolcus and the birth of Medus. In his IVth *Pythian Ode*, the poet Pindar provides the definitive image of Medea: endowed with the gift of prophecy, a foreigner skilled in the use of herbs ('pamphármakos xeína'), and the lover of Jason, she plays an important part in the quest for the Golden Fleece, is carried off from Colchis by Jason and later murders Pelias.

The Greek tragic authors dwelt on different aspects of the myth in tragedies of which only a few fragments have survived. Aeschylus describes Medea rejuvenating the Hyades in *Nurses* (i.e. of Dionysus). In *Women of Colchis*, Sophocles stresses the part played by the sorceress in helping Jason by offering him Prometheus' salve and killing Absyrtus, while in *Rootgatherers* (or *Pelias*), he refers to the death of Pelias following the gathering of the herbs for his rejuvenation. In *The Peliades*, another lost tragedy, Euripides emphasizes the evil and deceitful nature of the sorceress who beguiled the daughters of Pelias, the tyrant of Iolcus, with her words. According to the indications of a commentary, Medea also tried to poison Theseus in *Aegeus*, another tragedy by Euripides who in *Medea* (431 BC) gave the Colchian sorceress the characteristics of the criminal mother, probably following the example of a work by Neophron. Although Euripides' tragedy confers a new dimension on infanticide, it is, however, worthy of note that Medea bears the stigma of the tradition according to which the Corinthians were guilty of murdering children. It is significant that the heroine is afraid that the Corinthians will harm them and avenge the death of Creon and his daughter Glauce, killed by the poisoned robe that she sent to her rival as a wedding gift (l. 1240–1) and as a false sign of reconciliation after her divorce from Jason. This infanticide carried out by a 'barbarous' mother provided the poet with much greater tragic potential, since she was also the murderess of Absyrtus and Pelias. By refering to her bloody past, Euripides makes credible a murder which contravened all human and divine laws and also ensures the unity and coherence of the myth.

For Euripides, Medea is a humiliated woman, levelling recriminations at Jason and against the injustice of Creon who banished her from Corinth; she is a dangerous creature possessed by an inner 'demon'. He explores in *Medea* the psychology of a heroine who expresses herself passionately and is prey to her inner anguish, particularly in the famous monologue where, overcome by pity for her children and a burning desire for vengeance, she decides to kill her sons (l. 1078 et seq.). Euripides also situates his tragedy within the framework of a certain type of feminism – the position of the woman within the family home – as well as a political context – the intervention of Aegeus, King of Athens, offering Medea refuge. However, in contrast to the family drama, the dénouement of the tragedy (which was strongly criticised by Aristotle in *Poetics*, 1454 b 1), suddenly moves on to the level of the divine with the appearance of Medea in a chariot drawn by winged serpents, a gift from her grandfather Helius. Here lies a classic ambiguity. Is this in fact the true aspect of the foreigner who is transformed, in a surprising progression, from her role as a passionate wife and mother, to reveal her divine essence to Jason? Or was Euripides merely trying to respect the traditional and fantastical imagery 'in fine'? It is precisely these tensions and paradoxes that give Euripides' *Medea* a particular tragic depth.

By way of contrast, in Books III and IV of his epic poem *Argonautica* (third century BC), Apollonius of Rhodes develops the figure of Medea thus: as the young sorceress, priestess of Hecate in Colchis, who has been initiated into the powers of herbs and incantations and is endowed with a virginal modesty. Through his sophisticated descriptions of emotion, Apollonius evokes the anguish of an innocent young heroine, the victim of her ill-fated love for Jason, who betrays her homeland and family by delivering Absyrtus into an ambush at the hands of the Argonaut. In Latin literature, the lost tragedies of Ennius (*Medea in Corinth* and *Medea in Exile*, based on Euripides' *Medea* and *Aegeus* respectively), Pacuvius (*Medus* which refers to Medea's return to Colchis and her struggle to depose the usurper, Perses) and Accius (inspired by the work of Apollonius), provide evidence of the emergence of the myth during the second and first centuries BC.

During the period of the Empire, Virgil, referred to Medea, the infanticide, in his *Bucolics* (VIII l. 43–9), while in Book VII of the *Metamorphoses*, Ovid describes at length the 'magic herbs' used by Medea, a central figure in Greek and Oriental magic, in contrast to Circe the Roman sorceress. In *Heroides* XII, Ovid describes the suffering of Medea abandoned by Jason for Creusa, daughter of the tyrant of Corinth, the ingratitude of the Argonaut and the desire for vengeance on the part of the Colchian sorceress, who hopes that her epistle will bring back her unfaithful husband. In Seneca's tragedy *Medea*, the heroine is central to the quest of the Argonauts (which the Chorus of Corinthians considers to be a curse) and is compared to the sea monsters Scylla and the Sirens. With her magical incantations intended to poison the robe sent as a gift to her rival, she achieves a certain mythical temporality. Through the infanticide carried out in the presence of Jason in a paroxysm of violence, the sorceress annuls her current existence in the world of men, to reconquer her lost virginity and Colchian origins. Haunted by a desire for the absolute, a craving for destruction, and a desire to punish herself for the murder of Absyrtus, Seneca's Medea is no ordinary creature. Her monstrous grandeur represents an inverted form of the sublime and is linked to the moralistic treatises of the Stoics.

During the first century AD *The Argonautics* by Valerius Flaccus echoes Apollonius' epic poem and stresses the evil nature of Medea. In his poem *Medea* (fifth century), Dracontius presents the Colchian sorceress as a priestess of Diana, a figure very similar to Iphigenia among the Taurians. In medieval literature, from the twelfth to the fifteenth centuries, Medea makes episodic appearances in the *Romans de Troie*. Benoît de Sainte More, his German imitators Herbort de Fritzlar and Conrad de Würzbourg, the Fleming Jacques van Maerlant, the Italian Guido delle Colonna and the Englishman John Lydgate, all refer to Ovid to evoke the image of the princess abandoned by the knight she loves. There are references to Medea in Dante's *Inferno* (XVIII, l. 86–96), Garcia de Resende's anthologies of poetry from Spain and Portugal *Cancioneiro Geral*, *Los Infiernos de Amor* by the Spanish poet Santillana, the *Egloga Andres* by Francisco de Sà of Portugal and Boccaccio's *De Mulieribus claris*. She also appears in *Le Livre du preux et vaillant Jason* by Raoul Lefèvre, which tells of the foundation of the Order of the Golden Fleece in Burgundy in 1430.

At the beginning of the sixteenth century, the sorceress was linked to the allegorical tradition of the *Ovid moralisé* in which the rejuvenated Aeson symbolizes the repentance of the sinner and the spells of Medea are reminiscent of the influence of the preacher over his flock. In France, following Buchanan's *Médée*, a translation of Euripides' tragedy, La Peruse wrote a tragedy entitled *Médée* (1533), inspired by Euripides and Seneca. During the seventeenth century, *Medea esuele* (1602) by the Italian Zoppio centres upon the episode of the reconquering of Colchis by the sorceress and her son, Medo (Medus). In Spain, Calderón de la Barca produced an allegorical vision of the myth in the 'auto sacramental' *El Divino Jasón* (1634) in which Jason, with the 'celestial' Argonauts, becomes a Christlike figure who is contrasted to Medea and the world of idolatry. While Calderón compares the love of Jason and Medea in Colchis with that of Theseus and Ariadne, and Deïaneira and Heracles in *Los Tres Mayores Prodigios*, Lope de Vega's 'comedia' *El Vellocino de Oro*, echoes the origins of the conquest of the Golden Fleece and develops the jealousy of Fineo, rejected by Medea (here a huntress like Diana) in favour of Jason.

In 1635 Pierre Corneille, like Seneca, stressed the strange grandeur of the sorceress and reincorporated the figure into the supernatural context from whence it had originated. The terrible effects of vengeance shown through the deaths of Creusa and Creon on stage, after the most awful suffering, and the suicide of Jason after the killing of his children, are the reflections of Medea's 'ego' which she strongly confirms to her confidante Nérine. In fact, the only one of Corneille's scenes in which Medea's powers are put to beneficial use is when Jason's rival, Aegeus, who is in love with Creusa and imprisoned by Creon, is released by the magic wand of the Colchian sorceress. When referring to the divorce of the hero and heroine in Corinth in his 'comedia' *Los Encantos de Medea* (1645), the Spanish playwright Rojas Zorilla uses sorcery as a spectacular element which provides the catalyst for horror, by contrasting it to the humorous counterpoint of Jason's servant, Mosquete.

Corneille subsequently developed the adventures of Jason in Colchis and Absyrtus who was in love with Hypsipyle in *La Conquête de la Toison d'Or* (1659), which influenced the works of the Dutch writers Vos (1665) and Meijer (1666). Although the powers of the sorceress are used as an excuse, as they were by Rojas Zorilla, to produce dramatic scenic effects by the use of 'machines', Corneille stresses the fact that Medea's art is powerless against the soul. Her isolation in 'forsaken places' adds a new dimension to her character, which is expressed in elegiac verse form (Act IV, Scene 1). Far from being a plagiarism of the play by Pierre Corneille, the tragic opera by Marc-Antoine Charpentier (*Médée*, 1693) with a libretto by Thomas Corneille, presents the image of a more humane sorceress and introduces the figure of the Argonaut, Oronte (Orontes). An Argian prince who is in love with Creusa, he helps Creon in the imminent war against Thessaly which is the result of the murder of Pélie (Pelias) by the Medea. In his version of *Médée* (1694), Longpierre attempts to correct the excesses of the Cornelian model and recapture the atmosphere of Euripides' version of the play as well as certain elements used by Seneca, e.g. the monologue of the sorceress as she invokes divine vengeance in Act II. This 'tragedy of sensibility' was extremely successful during the eighteenth century, while Rousseau's tragic opera *La Toison d'Or*, written two years later, is an unoriginal reiteration of the dilemma of Jason, torn between Medea and Hypsipyle, and the death of the latter on learning the false news of Jason's death announced by her rival.

During the eighteenth century *Os Encantos de Medeia* (1735), a play written by the Portuguese dramatist Antonio José da Silva for the puppet theatre, presents a burlesque interweaving of the themes of the quest for the Golden Fleece and the rivalry between Medea and Creusa (here the niece of Aeëtes), as a result of the intervention of the buffoons Sacatrapo and Arpia. The English version of *Medea* (1761) by Glover explores a new approach to the myth. Medea kills her children in a fit of rage and, when her anger has subsided, confesses her crime. Jason significantly holds Creon responsible for the infanticide and the latter is killed by the Corinthians when he tries to seize the foreigner. There are echoes of Ovid in Sébastien Mercier's *Heroides* (*Médée à Jason*, 1773), while the structures of Euripides reappear in the dramatic version of *Medea* by the German poet Gotter and *Médée* by Clément (1779). The main interest of the last work, which was severely criticized by Diderot, lies in the idea of expiation at the end of the tragedy when the heroine commits suicide. In 1785, the German writer Soden extended the work by Gotter in his version of *Medea* (1785) by making his heroine a figure who, in accordance with the rules of Greek tragedy, was capable of arousing admiration and pity as well as being reminiscent of the image of the sorceress presented by Seneca (e.g. in Act IV she invokes the Furies and the infernal Spirits who pour the poisonous herbs intended for Creusa's veil into a cauldron). However, it was Klinger, one of the poets of the 'Sturm und Drang' Movement, who, in his first version of the drama (*Medea*, 1786), made the daughter of Aeëtes a creature of violence and passion. On the advice of her mother Hecate, 'the sombre inhabitant of Tartarus' (Act IV), Medea sacrifices her children and buries them in the temple of Pallas while the Eumenides seize Creon and Jason and throw them into the Underworld. In the later *Medea auf dem Kaucasos* (1790), Klinger offers a new vision of the destiny of the heroine who has repented of her past crimes. Medea renounces her magical powers and opposes the barbaric practice of human sacrifice introduced by the druids of the Caucasus Mountains. This civilizing and beneficial act brings about the downfall of the Colchian sorceress because, by using her sorcery to save Roxane, a young girl who is about to be sacrificed, Medea breaks her promise. The daughter of Aeëtes becomes a simple mortal, is condemned by the druids and commits suicide, the victim of fate and Nemesis.

Cherubini's famous opera (*Médée* 1797) with a libretto by Hoffmann, is inspired by Euripides and stresses the psychological tensions of the heroine who tries on several occasions to renounce her vengeance against Dirce (Creusa). The ambivalence of the sorceress endowed with a 'demoniacal' power assumes sacred proportions at the end of Act III when the fire – associated with the solar origins of the daughter of Aeëtes – which is burning Corinth (as in Seneca's version of *Medea*), is contrasted to the death of the heroine who is dragged to the shores of the Styx by the Eumenides. A poem by the Portuguese poet Barbosa de Bocage (*Medeia*, 'Cantata', 1799), portrays the criminal action of the Colchian sorceress as the victory of anger over the paradoxical forces of love, and it echoes the Senecan image of sorcery associated with the infernal divinities.

At the beginning of the nineteenth century, Mazoïer's *Thésée* (1801) retraces the failure of Medea in her attempt to seize power in Athens. Lamartine returns to Euripides as a basis for his outline of a tragedy entitled *Médée*, while the Italian Niccolini (*Medea*, 1830) softens the violence of the infanticide by interpreting it as a means of saving the children from being condemned by the Corinthians. In his famous trilogy *Das goldene Vlies*, which consists of *Der Gastfreund* (1818), *Die Argonauten* (1819) and *Medea* (1820), the Austrian dramatist Franz Grillparzer points to the coveted and unjustly obtained Golden Fleece as the embodiment of the evil forces of destiny, while Medea is seen as the victim of divine Nemesis. After unsuccessfully opposing the murder of Phrixus, the foreigner from Delphi and bringer of the Golden Fleece (*Der Gastfreund*), Medea, who has lived apart from her family since Aeëtes committed the crime, favours Jason's undertaking and accidentally causes the death of her brother Absyrtus (*Die Argonauten*). In Corinth, urged by her nurse Gora and spurred on by her jealousy of Creusa who has won the love of her children, the sorceress takes her terrible revenge. The Golden Fleece claimed by Creon is significantly restored to the shrine of Apollo in the final part of the trilogy, while Medea announces that she is placing her life in the hands of the priests of Delphi who will decide her fate (*Medea*).

Inspired by the work of Grillparzer, and particularly by the image of the emotional estrangement of the children in favour of Creusa, Legouvé's tragedy (*Médée*, 1854) presents new variations on the theme of maternal love held up to ridicule as well as a modern foothold for the myth which was considered to be 'the most terrible chapter in the story of seduction'. *Médée* (1855), a tragedy by Lucas, is a mixture of elements borrowed from the Classical authors in which the author compares the Colchian sorceress with Hypsipyle. The attempt to reinstate the myth in its entirety was once again evident in Morris' poem *The Life and Death of Jason* (1867), which was based on Apollonius; George Conrad of Prussia's tragedy *Medea* (1870) in which the heroine, fatally wounded in Athens by Aeëtes, is pardoned by Jason and his father; and the work by Lindsay called *Argo or the Quest for the Golden Fleece* (1876). In the same way, the Georgian poet Akaki Tsereteli tried to incorporate the figure of the sorceress into a trilogy of which only the first part has survived (*Media*, 1892) and which linked Jason's adventure in the Caucasus to the myth of Amiran-Prometheus. The 'barbaric' nature of the Colchian sorceress, a huntress who, according to an aesthetic concept inspired by the Parnassians, is likened to birds of prey by Simone Arnaud in her drama (*Medéia*, 1893), is also present in Catulle Mendès' tragedy (*Médée*, 1898) where the role of Medea was played by Sarah Bernhardt.

During the twentieth century the updating of the myth in *La Moderne Médée* (1901), a play by Duplessis which deals with the strained relations between a Frenchwoman and her German barrister husband, is subsequently presented via a certain exoticism. The Medea of the German dramatist Hans Henny Jahnn (1926) becomes a black princess whose eldest son, Jason's unfortunate rival, is tormented by the love that he has vowed to Creusa. The exiled Indochinese princess in *Asie* (1931), a drama by Lenormand, is a victim of the French protectorates and faces the xenophobia of the 'civilized races'. In *The Wingless Victory* (1936) by the American dramatist Maxwell Anderson, Oparre, who was born in Malaysia, is confronted with the puritanism and racism of the inhabitants of Salem in 1800.

Linked to the criticism of urban society, the modern avatars of Medea are presented as perverse adventuresses, e.g. the heroine of Léon Daudet's novel *Médée* (1935), who also refuse the civilization of city life, like Madrone Bothwell, the heroine of the poem *Solstice* (1935) by the American Robinson Jeffers, who takes refuge in a ranch near the Rocky Mountains. Parallel to these modern versions of the myth, there is a return to classical sources, illustrated by the Spanish playwright Miguel de Unamuno's adaptation of Seneca's *Medea* (1936), with the part of Medea performed by Marguerita Xirgu, reviewed by Antonin Artaud in the article 'Une Médée sans Feu' (Mexico, 1936). While Jean Anouilh contrasted the revolt of a Bohemian Medea with the ordered world represented by Jason in his famous 'black comedy' of 1946 (in much the same way as Elisabeth Porquerol in her drama *Jason*, 1942), Robinson Jeffers created a free adaptation of Euripides' tragedy with his version of *Medea* in 1946. Similarly, in contrast to *Medea Postbellica* (1947), a drama by the Austrian Csokor which is set in the Greek Balkans and evokes the ideological struggle of the partisans during World War Two, and the farce by Clot (*Médée et les Vieillards*, 1948) which is a grotesque representation of the rejuvenation of Aeson and Pelias, *La Lunga Notte di Medea* (1949), a drama by the Italian Corrado Alvaro, synthesizes classical tradition and modern references via a presentation of the sorceress as the victim of racial persecution in Corinth which will lead her to apply euthanasia to her children. In 1954, 'the explosive one-act tragedy' by the Spaniard José Bergamin, *Medea La Encantadora*, dispelled the cruelty of Seneca's tragedy in favour of the state of hallucination expressed by 'the mediumistic soul' of Medea. It is very different from the rather conservative version of the myth presented in the novel by Elena Soriano, *Medea 55*, which deals with the psychological tensions of a Spanish woman who, exiled during the civil war, becomes a famous actress in an imaginary Latin-American country. While Jean Vauthier adapts the world of Seneca in his tragedy *Medea* (1966), the play by the Finn, Willy Kyrklund (*Medea Från Mbongo*, 1967), uses anachronism and the grotesque to contrast the African world of Medea and the modern Greek environment of Jason. In *African Medea* (1968), the American Jim Magnuson places Medea's 'barbarism' within the context of the Portuguese colonization of Africa at the beginning of the nineteenth century, while Vergel's *Medea* (1971), based on the texts of Seneca and Miguel de Unamumo, associates it with the period of the Spanish conquistadors in Peru.

The myth, which was transformed into a magical and incantatory ceremony by Pasolini and Andreï Serban (*Medea*, 1972, based on the orginal texts of Seneca and Euripides), has more recently been further developed in the play by the Brazilian writer Paulo Pontes (*Gota d'Agua*, 1975) in which the story of Medea is transposed among the shanty towns of Brazil, and in the opera based on Euripides by Gavin Bryars and Robert Wilson, *Medea* (1984).

Duarte Mimoso-Ruiz

Medusa

Medusa's head, an apparently simple motif linked to the myth of Perseus, was freed through being severed and cut loose from its 'moorings' by the hero in the remote depths of the world. There is something paradoxical about the story since the monster was all the more indestructible because it had been killed. Indeed, the figure of Medusa is characterized by paradox, both in terms of the actual mythical stare, which turned men to stone, and in the interpretations that have been given to it. The fascination that she exerts arises from a combination of beauty and horror. Her head was used, in Ancient times, as an apotropaic mask – a sort of talisman which both killed and redeemed.

As well as being the very symbol of ambiguity, Medusa's head is also one of the most archaic mythical figures, perhaps an echo of the demon Humbaba who was decapitated by Gilgamesh. Everything implies that it is a 'representation' of the most meaningful aspect of the sacred. Insofar as it is the role of literature to assume responsibility for the sacred, each era, when confronted with the mystery of the 'origins', has re-examined Medusa's head with its mesmerizing stare as something which conceals the secret of the sacred.

THE OTHER AND THE MONSTER

If ambiguity is the hallmark of the sacred, the role of myths, as René Gerard purports in his *La Violence et le Sacré* (1972) is to generate differences and contrasts, to distinguish between the two faces of the sacred. Therefore, from the viewpoint of the oldest texts which are true to the spirit of the myth, Medusa is a representation of the Other by virtue of her absolute and terrifying difference. At first sight, her monstrous ugliness and her petrifying stare certainly bear this out.

In *La Mort dans les Yeux* (1985), Vernant demonstrates that, for the Greeks, Medusa represented the face of the warrior possessed by battle frenzy. In *The Shield of Heracles* (232–3), Hesiod describes the wide-open mouth, the fearsome hair and the Gorgons' shrill cries which conjure up her terrifying aspect. Thus Medusa's mask frequently appears within the context of a battle. It is present in the *Iliad* on the shields of Athena (V, 738) and Agamemnon (XI, 36), and also during the Renaissance, e.g. on Bellona's helmet described by Ronsard in the 'Ode à Michel de l'Hospital' (*Premier Livre des Odes*, 1560). The Gorgon also represents what cannot be represented, i.e. death, which it is impossible to see or to look at, like Hades itself. In Hesiod's *Theogony* (275 et seq.) and in the *Odyssey* (XI, 633–5), Medusa is the guardian of terrifying places, either the nocturnal borders of the world or the Underworld. She reappears in this role in Dante's *Divine Comedy* (*Inferno*, IX, 55–7) and Milton's *Paradise Lost* (II, 611). Guarding the doorway to the world of the dead, she prevents the living from entering.

In Christian symbolism, Medusa represents the dreaded enemy and death, and thus becomes an embodiment of the Devil. She appears in this guise in a passage in the *Book of Arthur* which belongs to the cycle of the Holy Grail (*Vulgate version of Arthurian romances*, Vol. VII, Washington, 1913). In fact, this is a female monster, the 'Ugly Semblance', who lives at the bottom of a river. She does not exercise her powers by turning people to stone, but by causing the waters to swallow them up. Similarly, a play by Calderón, which tells of the adventures of Andromeda and Perseus (*Fortunas de Andromeda y Perseo*), has the hero, a new incarnation of the Saviour, defeating Medusa who is the personification of Death and Sin.

At first glance, therefore, Medusa's head is very much a representation of the terrifying Other, of absolute negativity. She continues to fulfil this function in the twentieth-century trilogy by the Greek writer Pandelis Prevelakis, *The Ways of Creation*, which comprises *The Sun of Death* (Athens, 1959; Paris, 1965), *The Head of the Medusa* (Athens, 1963) and *The Bread of the Angels* (Athens, 1966). In the trilogy, the Gorgon represents both 'Nietzschian nihilism' and the foreign ideologies which threaten Hellenism. The hero sets out to free Greece once again from the monster, but he fails and realizes that there is no longer a single piece of untaited land in his country. Everything points to the fact that the malady specific to modern Greece, and the country's inability to accommodate change, have provoked this monstrous 'representation' of the Other. Medusa's head does indeed seem to be a mask which serves to justify her absolute and evil strangeness.

The fact that Medusa is a mask and that this mask hides a more human face, is borne out by the way in which her portrayal is developed from the pre-Classical era to the Hellenistic period. There is a dual transformation i.e. the disappearance of both facial quality and ugliness (see *Images de la Gorgone*, Bibliothèque Nationale, 1985). Beneath the mask lies what could be called Medusa's 'tragic beauty'.

THE MIRROR AND THE MASK

Many elements of the myth suggest, through its basic ambiguity, the tragic nature of Medusa. One of the most revealing of these is the gift from Athena to Asclepius of two drops of the Gorgon's blood, one of which has the power to cure and even resurrect, while the other is a deadly poison. Medusa's blood is therefore the epitome of the 'pharmakon', while she herself – as is shown by the apotropaic function of her mask – is a 'pharmakos'. As has been demonstrated by René Girard, the 'pharmakos' is the scapegoat whose sacrifice establishes the dual nature of the sacred and reinforces the separation of the monster and the god. However, it is for literature and the arts to reveal the close relationship between opposites and the 'innocence' of the victim. In this respect, the myth of Medusa is revealing. In his study *The mirror of Medusa* (1983), Tobin Siebers has identified the importance of two elements, i.e. the rivalry between Athena and the Gorgon, and the mirror motif.

According to Ovid (*Metamorphoses*, IV. 779ff), the reason for the dispute lay in Poseidon's rape of Medusa inside the temple of the virgin goddess. The goddess is supposed to have punished Medusa by transforming her face, which therefore made Medusa an innocent victim for the second time. However, another tradition, used by Mallarmé in *Les Dieux antiques* (1880), stressed a more personal rivalry: Medusa had boasted that she was more beautiful than Athena. Everything points to the face that the goddess found it necessary to set herself apart from her negative double in order to assert her 'own' identity. Common features are numerous. For example, snakes are the attribute of Athena, as illustrated by the famous statue of Phidias and indicated by certain Orphic poems which refer to her as 'la Serpentine'. Moreover, the hypnotic stare is one of the features of the goddess 'with blue-green eyes', whose bird is the owl, depicted with an unblinking gaze. Finally, because she has affixed Medusa's head to her shield, in battle or in anger she assumes the terrifying appearance of the monster. Thus, in the *Aeneid* (II, 171), she expresses her wrath by making flames shoot forth from her eyes. These observations are intended to show that Athena and Medusa are the two indissociable aspects of the same sacred power.

A similar claim could be made in respect of Perseus, who retains traces of his association with his monstrous double, Medusa. Using her decapitated head to turn his enemies to stone, he spreads death around him. And when he flies over Africa with his trophy in a bag, through some sort of negligence, drops of blood fall to earth and are changed into poisonous snakes which reduce Medusa's lethal power (Ovid, op. cit., IV. 618). Two famous paintings illustrate this close connection between the hero and the monster. Cellini's *Perseus* resembles the head he is holding in his hand (as demonstrated by Siebers) and Paul Klee's *L'esprit a combattu le mal* (1904) portrays a complete reversal of roles – Perseus is painted full face with a terrible countenance, while Medusa turns aside.

In this interplay of doubles, the theme of reflection is fundamental. It explains the process of victimization to which Medusa was subjected, and which falls within the province of the superstition of the 'evil eye'. The way to respond to the 'evil eye' is either to use a third eye – the one that Perseus threw at the Graiae – or to deflect the evil spell by using a mirror. Ovid, in particular, stressed the significance of the shield in which Perseus was able to see the Gorgon without being turned to stone, and which was given to him by Athena. Everything indicates that the mirror was the real weapon. It was interpreted thus by Calderón and Prevelakis, and also by Roger Caillois in *Méduse et Cie* (1960).

Ovid was responsible for establishing the link with Narcissus, a myth that he made famous. It seems that the same process of victimization is at work here. The individual is considered to have been the victim of his own reflection, which absolves the victimizer (Perseus, the group) from all blame. This association of the two myths (and also the intention of apportioning blame) appears in a passage in Desportes' *Amours d'Hyppolite* (1573) where the poet tells his lady that she is in danger of seeing herself changed 'into some hard rock' by her 'Medusa's eye'. Even more revealing is Gautier's story *Jettatura* (1857) in which the hero, accused of having the 'evil eye', eventually believes it to be true and watches the monstrous transformation of his face in the mirror: 'Imagine Medusa looking at her horrible, hypnotic face in the lurid reflection of the bronze shield.'

Medusa's head is both a mirror and a mask. It is the mirror of collective violence which leaves the Devil's mark on the individual, as well as being the image of death for those who look at it. Both these themes – violence rendered sacred and death by petrifaction – are found in *Das Gorgonenhaupt* (Berlin, 1972), a work by Walter Krüger about the nuclear threat.

However, when considered in terms of archetypal structures, Medusa's mask still retains its secret. What is the reason for the viperine hair, the wide-open mouth with the lolling tongue, and, in particular, why is Medusa female? What relationship is there between violence, holy terror and woman?

THE DISCONCERTING STRANGENESS OF THE FEMININE

Robert Graves (*Greek Myths*, 1958) believes that the myth of Perseus preserves the memory of the conflicts which occurred between men and women in the transition from a matriarchal to a patriarchal society. In fact the function of the Gorgon's mask was to keep men at a safe distance from the sacred ceremonies and mysteries reserved for women, i.e. those which celebrated the Triple Goddess, the Moon. Graves reminds us that the Orphic poems referred to the full moon as the 'Gorgon's head'. The mask was also worn by young maidens to ward off male lust. The episode of Perseus' victory over Medusa represents the end of female ascendancy and the taking over of the temples by men, who had become the masters of the divine which Medusa's head had concealed from them.

Although it may have become less intense, the battle of the sexes was not resolved. The feminine continued to remain a source of fear for men, and the association of women with Medusa evoked an aspect of the sex which was both fascinating and dangerous. Medusa often appeared in Renaissance poetry, e.g. Ronsard's *Second Livre des Amours* (S. 79, 1555), but the stare which turned men to stone was often only a conventional metaphor for the lover's 'coup de foudre'. The comparison took on a deeper meaning during the ninteenth century. Baudelaire's *Les Fleurs du Mal* (1857) and 'decadent' literature such as Lorrain's *M. de Phocas* (1901), provide illustrations of the dangerous fascination exerted by woman, with her deadly stare and mysterious hair. But it was Goethe's *Faust* Part I (1808) which supplied the real significance of this connection. During the 'Walpurgis night', Faust thinks he sees Margarita but Mephistopheles warns him that it is Medusa and explains that 'magic deludes every man into believing that he has found his beloved in her'.

This terrible woman, the paragon of all women, whom every man simultaneously fears and seeks and for whom Medusa is the mask, is in fact the mother, i.e. the great Goddess Mother whose rites were concealed by the Gorgon's face. Countless texts illustrate Medusa's affinity with the depths of the sea and the terrible power of nature, e.g. Hugo's *Les Travailleurs de la Mer* (1864), Lautrémont's *Chants de Maldoror* (1869) and Pierre Louÿs' *Aphrodite* (1896), but the most explicit example is probably the text written by Freud in 1922: *Das Medusenhaupt* – 'Medusa's Head'. He presents her as the supreme talisman who provides the image of castration – associated in the child's mind with the discovery of maternal sexuality – and its denial. The snakes are multiple phalluses and petrifaction represents the comforting erection.

From this point onwards, the myth of Perseus takes on a new psychological meaning. It tells of the exploit of the hero who, because he has conquered 'castrating' woman and armed himself with the talisman of Medusa's head (seen here in its comforting, phallic role), is able to conquer Andromeda, the terrifying virgin, and kill the sea monster which represents the evil aspect of woman. This motif is also found in the Christian legend of St George (Jacques de Voragine, *La Légende dorée*, 1264) as well as in the anthropological legends concerning the fear of the 'dentate vagina'. A 'sacred' man must perform the first sexual act with a woman.

Two texts illustrate this aspect of the myth. One is, the *Book of Arthur* (op. cit). in the passage devoted to the 'Ugly Semblance'. The monster occupies the lands of a maiden who not only asks the king for the assistance of a knight but also for a husband whom she describes as though he had always been intended for her. The task that he performs seems to have been the necessary requirement for his union with the Virgin. The story stresses the association of the monster with the element of water and, in particular, with the sea into which it has to be driven back. The second text is a short story by Döblin, *Der Ritter Blaubart* – the 'Knight with the Blue Beard' (1911). Because the hero has had mysterious and intimate relations with a primitive monster – a giant medusa – he is forced to either kill all the women he loves or allow them to be killed. However, one of them, because of her purity, confronts the monster in the secret chamber where it lurks. In this last example, the character seems to have been unable to free himself from the maternal influence and fear of the feminine.

Finally, this association of Medusa with castrating woman is very evident in a passage in *Chêne et Chien* (1952) by Queneau: 'Severed head, evil woman/ Medusa with her lolling tongue/So it was you who would have castrated me?' However, the myth reveals – and this seems to be obscured by the Freudian interpretation – that woman's 'castration' is a result of the violence imposed on her by the original hero. Woman only appears in the story divided by separative decapitation, casting off the feminine in the remote depths of the world. Cast down, the feminine remains unrecognized within its innermost recess and it is this 'ab-ject' void which maintains the theatre of the world and the logic of the talisman. In this theatre, woman occupies the two opposite extremes of evil (castration, sorcery) and their cure (the phallus, the Virgin), i.e. of the abyss and the Ideal. That is why, despite her terrifying power, she is fascinating. 'Fascinum' means 'charm' and 'evil spell', but also 'virile member'. Between the 'emptiness' and the Idol represented by the division of woman, yawns the gulf of male Desire. This persistent ambiguity can be found in the classification of the creature called the medusa. It owes its name to its resemblance to Medusa's head (Apollinaire, *Bestiaire*, 1920), but is included in the Acephelan category. Medusa keeps her secret behind the ambiguous mask. Although she is 'representable', she is never 'presentable' and even Perseus only sees her reflected in his shield. She is the hidden presence, absent from the world, which enables the scene to be played out. In his 'heroic comedy' *Le Naufrage de Méduse* (1986), Ristat shows Perseus searching for the Gorgons and meeting Hermes, the 'Guardian of Resemblances', who proves to the terrified hero that 'Medusa herself is only a shadow'.

However, the hero remains trapped in the interplay of images and the logic of the talisman, just as he remains fascinated by the Gorgon mask. Thus Medusa's head becomes, for the man who takes possession of it after severing it from the terrifying woman, and in accordance with the principle of the 'pharmakon', the complete opposite, i.e. the 'skeptron' – the sun.

'O MEDUSA, O SUN'

In the same way that there is a hidden similarity between Athena, Goddess of Wisdom, and Medusa, a similarity also exists between the sun, symbol of the Ideal, and the Gorgon's mask. Although they are both objects of desire, Athena and the sun are unapproachable and terrifying for those who come too close. This danger is illustrated by the Platonic myth of Phaedrus (247–8e) in which the downfall of souls is brought about by an overpowering desire to see the sun. Certain structural elements from the myth of Medusa also reappear in the myth of the Cave (*The Republic*, 514–7a), i.e. fascination, averted eyes, violence inflicted on the philosopher, etc.

In his poem (op. cit.), Queneau maintains that the sun, like the Gorgon, is fearsome and castrating: 'The sun: O monster, O Gorgon, O Medusa/O sun'. In this way, Medusa herself can become an incarnation of the Ideal, i.e. of Virtue (Du Bellay, *Epithalame*, 1559), of Beauty (Baudelaire, op. cit., 'La

Beauté') and of Truth (Kosmas Politis, *Eroica*, Athens, 1938). Surely the sun itself is the severed head that, like the head of St John the Baptist, only soars in the zenith: 'In triumphant flights/from that scythe' (Mallarmé, *Hérodiade*, 'Cantique de saint Jean', 1913). Whoever seeks Athena, finds Medusa's head. Whoever approaches too close to the sun discovers its castrating and castrated monstrousness (Bataille, *L'Anus Solaire*, 1931).

Although Nietzsche had embarked upon the destruction of all idols, he too, in this way, recognized the desire for death inherent in the desire for truth at any cost. The philosopher who wants to examine all things 'in depth', discovers the petrifying abyss. The destiny of the man whom Nietzsche refers to as 'the Don Juan of knowledge' will be paralyzed as if by Medusa, and will himself be 'changed into a guest of stone' (*Morgenröte* i.e. the Dawn of Day, 327, 1881). This is also the destiny of the 'lover of truth' who, in the *Dionysos Dithyramben* (1888) appears to be 'changed into a statue/into a sacred column'. Nietzsche, who was aware of the necessity 'for the philosopher' to live within the 'closed circuit of representation' (Derrida), to seek the truth even if he no longer believes in it, without ever being able to attain it, devised his own version of the 'truth', his Medusa's head, the Eternal Return: 'Great thought is like Medusa's head: all the world's features harden, a deadly, ice-cold battle' (Posthumous Fragments, Winter 1884–5).

All thinkers who reflect upon the nature of representation, as well as on thought which pursues the 'eidos' are in danger of confronting Medusa's head. Thus, Aristotle, in *The Politics* (VIII) differentiates between instructive and cathartic music which is associated with Bacchic trances, whose instrument is the flute and which should be avoided. To prove his point, he refers to the myth of Athena. When she played the flute, her face became so distorted that she abandoned the instrument. It was in fact she who had invented the flute to imitate an unknown sound, virtually unrepresentable, i.e. the hissing of the snakes on Medusa's head as she was decapitated (Pindar, *The Pythian Odes*, XII, 2–3). As she played, she noticed in a spring that her features were becoming distorted and assuming the appearance of the Gorgon's mask. This once more introduces the Narcissistic theme and the blurring of the difference between Athena and her rival, which here arises from tragic art. Therefore, in terms of philosophy, art should remain in the service of the 'eidos' by continuing to represent the image that arouses desire for the Object.

But it is also condemned if it presents the object in such an obvious manner that the remoteness of desire degenerates into dangerous enjoyment. This partly explains Tournier's condemnation of image and photography in *La Goutte d'Or* (1985). He explicitly links their power to Medusa's petrifying fascination and contrasts them with the art of writing which is the art of education and the route to wisdom 'par excellence'.

It would seem that the fear experienced at the sight of Medusa's head is the terror of discovering the secret behind the representation of the image. And it is precisely photography, more fascinating than any other image, which can reveal this secret. Roland Barthes endeavoured to discover it in *La Chambre Claire* (1980), beyond the fascinating and deadly power of photography, beyond the reassuring icon, in what he called 'the photographic ecstasy'.

THE POET AND MEDUSA AS MUSE

The cycle of the monster and the god, the Gorgon and the sun, and the 'emptiness' and the idol – this 'closed circuit' guarded by Medusa's head (by virtue of its ambiguity) – can be broken. The break need not necessarily be made by a Perseus, but by a man who is able to maintain dangerous and intimate relations with the terrifying monster, with the submerged feminine, without letting himself be deluded by the mask. Who, one may ask, can become 'the lover of the Furies' and not be misled by a snake (Nietzsche, *Posthumous Fragments*, January 1882)?

Aristotle provides the answer: the tragic, Dionysian artist. Thus Nietzsche invented Dionysian 'faith' to illustrate this possibility of life going beyond the logic of the talisman. And he linked Baubo, Medusa's goddess-head relative, with Dionysus ('Foreword', 4, *Die Fröhliche Wissenschaft*, i.e. The Gay Science, 1882). Baubo was the old woman who consoled Demeter after the abduction of Persephone, by showing her genitalia on which was drawn the laughing face of the child Iacchus. 'Iacchus' was the name given by the mystae to Dionysus in songs accompanied by the flute. The word should also be compared with 'choîros', the female genitalia. Demeter, Baubo and Dionysus are divinities which date back to before the historic 'decapitation' of woman in the history of metaphysics and representation. This is why, when Apollo placed an apotropaic Medusa's head in front of Dionysus, he was not frightened by a monstrous mask of himself (Nietzsche, 2, *Die Geburt der Tragödie* i.e. The Birth of Tragedy, 1871) (see DIONYSUS). The story of Baubo should be compared with the Japanese legend of Amenouzume's 'obscene' dance to entice the sun goddess Amaterasu from her cave (see Claudel, 'La délivrance d'Amaterasu' in *Connaissance de l'Est*, 1900–5).

Another god who seems to fulfil the role of Dionysus is Hermes, an ambiguous figure. Founder of the arts, he invented – in his own right – the flute and the lyre that he gave to Apollo. He also helped the Triple Muse (the Thriae, the Parcae and the Gorgons) to compose the arboricultural alphabet. It is Hermes whom Graves urges us to see behind the figure of Perseus in the scene with the Gorgons where, far from opposing them, Graves considers he was helping them. Thus, in *Le Naufrage de Méduse*, (op. cit.), when Perseus encounters Hermes (the god seeking 'the dual nature of everything'), he seems to be confronting the god who knows the 'truth' of his destiny.

Man, however, is imprisoned in the 'closed circuit of representation' and cannot enter the 'sacred way' opened by Dionysus without being continually confronted with Medusa's head which, for him, is fatal. But it is for the tragic artist, at the risk of his life and his sanity, to live in close contact with the monster. This is illustrated by one aspect of the myth. In 'L'Hippocrène' (*Second Livre des Poèmes*, 1573), a long poem devoted to the legend of Perseus, Baïf begins with an appeal for inspiration and writes: 'It is the Hippocrene that must flow through all its channels'. The Hippocrene was the spring which gushed forth when struck by Pegasus' hoof (the horse that was born from Medusa's severed neck) and is the place where the Muses gather. Therefore, the poet quenches his thirst with water that is like the very blood of Medusa, the true mother of the Muses (her name also means 'the Queen'). Nourished by this bloody 'pharmakon', his voice becomes the Gorgon's voice. He feels the distinctions blur within him and agrees to become the monster, Heauton Timoroumenos: 'I hear it in my voice – that shrillness/that poison in my blood!/I am the sinister glass in which/the Fury sees herself!' (Baudelaire, op. cit., 'l'Héautontimorouménos').

Having become the monster's accomplice, the poet advances into the appalling recesses of the world, where the word should lose its strength and eyes should be averted. Several 'works' bear witness to these often incredible attempts e.g. by Mallarmé, Artaud, Bataille and Michaux who wrote, 'I am in love with, I am at one with my death' ('Paix dans les brisements' in *L'Espace de dedans*, 1959) and also wrote us this 'Letter': 'We are watched in death's mirror. We are watched in the mirror of the insulted seal, of the blood which flows, of inspiration beheaded, in the clouded mirror of humiliation/we have returned to the sea-green springs' (op. cit., 'Epreuves, exorcismes', 1954).

But whoever arouses the tremendous violence of the sacred, condemns himself to a tragic destiny. The 'poète maudit', confronting the 'order of the world', found himself wearing Medusa's mask which marked him as the scapegoat of a society whch, after his death and according to the logic of rendering things sacred, made him a cult figure for our fascinated minds.

Camille Dumoulié

Melusina

In 1392, during the Hundred Years War, Jean d'Arras wrote 'the noble history of Lusignan' and of Melusina – the fairy who founded the lineage and the castle of Lusignan – for Jean, Duke de Berry, the brother of Charles V. Jean de Berry was Count of Poitou (he had spent nearly thirty years, from 1346 to 1373, fighting for the 'comté' against the English) and the owner of the fortress of Lusignan. In 1401, Coudrette wrote another romance about Melusina in verse (whereas the earlier version, which claimed to resemble a chronicle, was in prose), for the lords of Parthenay, Guillaume Larchevêque and his son Jean, who were related by marriage to the Lusignan family. The author of the second work seems to have drawn his inspiration from his predecessor.

A UNIVERSAL STRUCTURE

Melusina was not simply the product of Jean d'Arras' imagination. His work reproduces a universal folkloric theme that is in fact described as 'Melusinian', from the name of the figure who best illustrates it. It can be summarized as follows: a supernatural being falls in love with a human being, follows him into the world of mortals and marries him, after making him promise to respect one interdiction. The pact is broken and the supernatural being returns to the other world, leaving behind a line of descendants.

The earliest illustration of this structure appeared in a Vedic text with the story of the hero Pururavas and the nymph Urvasi. Urvasi gives herself to Pururavas, on condition that she never sees him naked. The Gandharvas, male spirits who want to bring the fairy back to the other world, cause the pact to be broken and the fairy disappears. In Greek and Roman mythology, although the roles of the two protagonists are reversed (as they are in the later mediaeval legend of the Knight of the Swan), the story of Eros and Psyche, like all the other versions of the tale of the Beauty and the Beast, is based on the same narrative outline.

The narrative has a tripartite structure. The first element is the meeting of the mortal and the fairy. Traditionally, the hero leaves his home alone or becomes separated from his companions during a hunting expedition, plunges deep into the forest and comes upon a clearing, often near water, where he discovers a lone and wonderfully beautiful woman who seems to be waiting for him . . . The second element is the pact. The unknown woman welcomes the hero's passionate declarations or declares her own love for him, agrees to marry him or offers herself as his wife, but sets one condition: he must vow to respect an interdiction, the transgression of which would end their life together. Subsequently, the marriage is celebrated; the couple experience wealth and happiness, and they have several children. Finally, it is time for the inevitable violation of the pact. An envious person (who fulfils the role of the aggressor in fairy tales) persuades the hero to go back on his promise, or the hero makes that decision himself. The human husband breaks the interdiction and thus reveals the supernatural nature of his wife. The fairy vanishes. The human husband loses his wife and the prosperity she had brought as a dowry, and occasionally even his own life. The children stay with their father: the fairy's lineage among mortals is thus assured.

The elements in this diachronic structure can be situated on either side of an integration (human society)/(other world) axis which demonstrates how deeply the tale has affected the human imagination. Contact with the fantastic alienates the mortal hero from his friends and family forever, for the attempt by the supernatural woman to integrate herself into the human world results in the hero's exclusion, i.e. his death or his disappearance into another world which is also the land of the dead. The hero must pay for the glory of his semi-divine lineage, with his life.

THE EMERGENCE OF A LEGEND

The story appears to have been introduced into the scholarly culture of the Middle Ages during the twelfth century, when there was an upsurge of folklore in literature. During this period, it in fact appeared on several occasions in Latin texts, i.e. in collections of anecdotes and legends compiled by 'folklorists' – before the term existed – such as Walter Map in the *De nugis curialium* (1189–93) and Gervase of Tilbury in the *Otia imperialia* (1209–14); as an edifying exemplum in the *Commentaire sur l'Apocalypse* by Geoffroi d'Auxerre (end of the twelfth century); and as a political weapon in the *De principis instructione* by Giraud de Barri (1217), which accused the Plantagenets of being descended from a diabolic Countess of Anjou. Walter Map, Gervase of Tilbury and Giraud de Barri all belonged to the same clerical milieu which was centred around the English court. The legends that they recorded were set in Wales, Normandy and Provence, and Geoffroi d'Auxerre, secretary to St Bernard, recounted a Sicilian and a Langrois legend. The Melusinian tales seem to have been scattered throughout the western mediaeval world, but as with most of the folk-tales, the fairy is never referred to by name.

In 1392, Jean d'Arras mentioned two sets of sources, i.e. written (the 'atteurs') and oral ('what was told and recounted by our forebears'). Among the 'atteurs', he mentions explicitly Gervase of Tilbury and the Provençal legend by Raymond de Château Rousset. In the latter, a knight on horseback meets a beautiful lady near a river. She agrees to marry him, on condition that he never sees her naked. One day, ignoring this condition, he goes into the room where the lady is bathing and sees her vanish into the water in the form of a serpent. However his children remain and the fairy's lineage has survived up to the storyteller's time. This is the most accurate prefiguration of the legend of Melusina, two centuries before the romance by Jean d'Arras.

MELUSINA AND LUSIGNAN

At the beginning of the fourteenth century, Pierre Bersuire (i.e. Pierre de Bressuire), prior of the Abbey of Saint-Eloi, continued the legend of Lusignan in his *Reductorium morale*: 'According to a story told in my homeland, the impregnable fortress of Lusignan was founded by a knight and his fairy spouse. The fairy is said to be the ancestor of many noblemen and people of rank, and the kings of Jerusalem and Cyprus as well as the Earls of the March and of Parthenay are apparently her descendants. (. . .) But the fairy, so they say, was seen naked by her husband and she changed into a serpent. Even today, the fairy is reputed to appear in the castle when a new master takes it over.'

Everything is there, except Melusina's name, which did not appear until the romance by Jean d'Arras. Did the name originate from a cult of the goddess Lucina, or of a Mater Luciniana who gave her name to the fairy, then the castle? The most probable explanation is that the name was invented during the fourteenth century from the name of the castle, to make the fairy the Mother of the Lusignan family.

THE ROMANCE BY JEAN D'ARRAS

Melusina was the daughter of the fairy Pressina and King Elinas of Albania, whose adventures exactly prefigured that of the couple who founded Lusignan, as does the magical adventure of Raimondin's father and the Lady of Forez. Two short 'Melusinian' tales thus foreshadow the main theme of the romance. One night, Raimondin is wandering in the forest of Colombiers after accidentally killing his powerful lord and uncle, the Count of Poitiers, during a boar hunt. At midnight, at the 'fontaine de Sé', he encounters three women. The most beautiful of the three offers to marry him and protect him if he swears never to try and see her on a Saturday. Raimondin takes the vow, marries her and enjoys good fortune, becoming increasingly successful. After the construction of Lusignan, which coincides with the birth of her first son, Melusina continues to give birth to a son and build a castle every year. The eldest of her ten sons conquers kingdoms and dukedoms, some of which (e.g. Cyprus and Armenia) had been or were still effectively governed by the Lusignan family at the time when Jean d'Arras was writing. The Duke de Berry and other readers of the romance thus encountered ideological knightly values and the glorification of lineage within the fairy tale.

Raimondin, the 'bachelor', the young nobleman with no wife and no kingdom, thus becomes Raimond, the powerful lord of Lusignan. However, an aggressor appears in the person of the hero's brother, the Comte de Forez, who urges Raimond to break the interdiction. One Saturday, the hero pierces a hole in the wall of the room which conceals Melusina and discovers her secret. She is bathing in a large tub and although the upper part of her body is that of a woman, the lower part ends in a serpent's tail. Raimond says nothing of his discovery and the fairy pretends not to know that he has broken the pact, but one of their sons, Geoffroi à la Grand Dent (Geoffrey with the Boar's Tusk), whose characteristics were based on those of a formidable thirteenth-century lord of Lusignan, sets fire to the Abbey of Maillezais and burns, not only his brother Fromont, but also the hundred monks who are inside. Then Raimond sees the fairy as nothing more than a demon and he publicly accuses Melusina, 'the deceitful serpent', of having been responsible for this crime. The fairy changes into a serpent, flies away from the castle of Mervent amid the cries of the assembled company and, swooping down upon the Poitou tower at the castle of Lusignan, disappears.

THE SURVIVAL OF THE LEGEND

The legend was Christianized from the Middle Ages onwards. In a Norman legend recorded by Walter Map during the twelfth century, the hero discovers that his wife leaves church before the end of mass and changes into a dragon in her bath. He causes her to disappear by having the priest sprinkle her with holy water. In the romances by Jean d'Arras and Coudrette, Melusina is a good Christian woman who nevertheless has some very disturbing characteristics. The very nature of her metamorphosis links her to the ambiguous symbolism of the serpent. Her children also share the partly animal nature of their mother and they each have one monstrous feature. Finally, because of her husband's infringement of the pact, Melusina is subjected to the punishment inflicted by her mother, the fairy Pressina. If Raimond had respected the interdiction, Melusina would have lived and died like a 'natural woman'. The hero's failure transforms her into a serpent until Judgement Day. Melusina is certainly the ancestor of Ondine. According to Paracelsus (1493–1541), 'the Melusinas are the daughters of kings, who are beyond redemption because of their sins. Satan carried them off and transformed them into spectres, evil spirits, into horrible ghosts and hideous monsters. It is believed that they live without rational souls in supernatural bodies, that they feed on the elements and that they will pass away with these at the Last Judgement, unless they marry a mortal man'.

Laurence Harf Lancner

Melusina in Literature From the Renaissance to the Present Day

Until recently the story of Melusina belonged to the oral literary tradition of western France. It appears in Chapter V of Noël du Fail's *Propos rustiques* (1548) where, together with stories about the werewolf, 'le cuir d'Asnette' and fairies, the tale of Melusina forms part of the repertoire of a village storyteller from the area around Rennes. Rabelais, who had already joyfully described Melusina in hell as a 'kitchen drudge wench' (*Pantagruel*, 1532, XXX), gives his own characteristic account of peasant beliefs from the areas with Melusinian connections in the *Quart Livre* (1552, XXXVIII) '. . . visit Lusignan, Parthenay, Vouant, Mervant and Ponzauges in Poictu. There you will find a Cloud of Witnesses, not of your Affidavit-Men of the right stamp, but Credible, time out of mind, that will take their Corporal Oath, on Rigome's Knuckle-bone, that Mellusine, their first Founder, or Foundress, which you please, was Woman from the Head to the Prick-purse, and thence downwards was a Serpentine Chitterling, or if you'll have it otherwise, a Chitterlingdiz'd Serpent'.

For his part, Brantôme records in his *Grand Capitaines françois* that, on the occasion of their respective visits to Lusignan, Charles V and Catherine de Medici were told 'several fantastic tales, which are very common in that area' about the origins of the castle, as well as Melusina's appearances and cries, which had been witnessed by several people.

The popularity of Melusina in oral literature and in the repertoire of nursery stories had an adverse effect on her literary career. In 1670 Monfaucon de Villars demonstrated this disrepute in the fourth 'Entretien' of *Le Comte de Gabalis ou Entretiens sur les Sciences occultes*. 'I think, sir, that you are going to tell me tales of Melusina,' says the sceptical interlocutor of Count Gabalis, to which Gabalis, unaware of the irony, replies that in actual fact, 'Nothing is more certain than that Melusina was a nymph.'

During the very period when fairy tales were fashionable in literature, the figure of Melusina inspired very few outstanding works. Nodot's *Histoire de Mélusine tirée des chroniques du Poitou, et qui sert d'Origine à l'ancienne Maison de Lusignan* (1698), which appeared a year later than Perrault's *Histoire ou Contes du Temps passé*, cannot be deemed to fall into this category. Although Nodot initially kept closely to the work of Jean d'Arras, he went on to devote a disproportionate amount of space to the story of the love affairs of Melusina's sons, recounted in the gallant style that was fashionable at the time.

The predilection of writers of the Romantic period for their national past and provincial traditions led some of them to take an interest in the fairy of the Lusignan family. Thus, in 1833, Edouard d'Anglemont devoted the third of his *Nouvelles Légendes françaises* in verse to Melusina. The poem, dedicated to Mme Récamier, retains many traditional features, such as the 'flying dragon' which brings Pressina's daughter to France and then carries her off again following Raimondin's indiscretion. But the end of the text, which relates how, when 'a person of her race' dies, Melusina returns, and from the top of the ramparts 'bids him a sorrowful farewell with piercing cries', seems to be a shadowy precursor of Gérard de Nerval.

The last hemistich of the sonnet *El Desdichado*, in which Nerval, after wondering whether he was 'Lusignan of Biron', evokes 'the fairy's cries', would alone be enough to assure Melusina's presence in Romantic poetry. A familiar reference in Nerval, Melusina appears twice more in the *Chansons et Légendes du Valois* and especially in the tale of *La Reine des Poissons*.

The Decadent and Symbolist period gave the figure of Melusina a new lease of life. Firstly, Jean Lorrain devoted a sonnet to her in the section entitled 'Le Pays des Fées' in his collection *La Forêt bleue* (1883), as being one of those supernatural women who haunted the imagination of the period. Melusina appears 'In oriental dress, with a Saracen headdress', a prefiguration of her metamorphosis: 'Already slender and slippery at the top of the tower, She sees the scales masking her naked arms with green And the serpent cold strikes at her inmost being.'

Nine years later, in the tale *Mélusine enchantée* (included in the section entitled 'Masques dans la tapisserie' in *Princesses d'Ivoire et d'Ivresse*), Jean Lorrain takes up the mediaeval theme of the 'proud kiss'. He describes the reverse metamorphosis of a Melusina who had been 'changed into a monstrous hydra' and who, in a magical natural setting, is returned to her female form by Lusignan's kiss.

This text has certain similarities with the long tale of *Prince Alberic and the Snake Lady*, which in 1905 was included in the collection entitled *Pope Jacynth and Other Fantastic Tales* by the English novelist and essayist Vernon Lee (the pseudonym of Violet Paget). The story is set in an Italian dukedom at the end of the seventeenth century and uses the Melusinian legend to illustrate the 'decadent' theme of the decline of a princely race. Alberic is the last descendant of the lineage and the grandson of the ruling duke. He has been greatly affected throughout his childhood by a tapestry which portrays the meeting, at the time of the crusades, between his ancestor, Alberic the Fair, and a snake lady. A wandering poet also tells him that the snake lady had reassumed her female form when she was kissed by the knight. The young Alberic is sent by his grandfather to live among country folk. Near a well, he discovers a grass snake which he eventually kisses, before falling into a swoon. Later, he refuses to marry out of loyalty to the snake and, when it is killed by the duke's dwarf, the young man falls prey to genuine or feigned madness and dies an untimely death. The story is constructed skilfully enough for the reader to enjoy imagining the existence of the guardian serpent, while being simultaneously aware that these are only the fantasies of a young prince who is the victim of loneliness.

In another vein, debates on woman's role within marriage and society led certain writers of that generation to re-use some of the Melusinian themes, although sometimes only implicitly. Conversely, Joséphin Péladan blatantly modernized this legendary character in his *Mélusine* (1895), which was the first novel in an unfinished series entitled 'Le Septénaire des Fées'. The two protagonists are Mary, a young American woman who is wealthy but crippled, and Lixus, a penniless poet who dreams of being granted happiness and wealth by the fairy Melusina. The dream becomes a reality when Mary's money fulfils the role of a magic wand which ensures the poet's material comfort as well providing him with easy access to a career in the theatre. The author of *Comment on devient fée*, has made a naive attempt to make his character's infirmity coincide with the Melusinian tradition. As a child, Mary's feet were severed by the wheel of a car, an accident for which her father was indirectly responsible. However, the young girl's desire to keep her deformity a secret becomes pointless after her lover, having spied on her as she was getting out of the bath, overcomes the revulsion that he could have felt at the sight of her stumps. There is nothing reminiscent of the tragic nature of the transgression in this novel which, ignoring the interdiction, rapidly assumes the dimension of a voluptuous daydream, accompanied by a defence of the position of the 'kept' artist.

The novel by Franz Hellens, *Mélusine ou la Robe de Saphir*, written in 1917–18, published in 1921 and revised in 1951, is a long way from observing the same anecdotal fidelity. It takes the form of a sequence of dreamlike tableaux, whose connection with the myth of Melusina is not immediately apparent. Melusina, the woman loved by the narrator, who appeared one day when he had been 'gazing at a wave for a long time', in fact seems to be more closely associated with birds than with snakes. Also, far from concealing her body from the gaze of men, she spends part of the novel entirely naked. These inversions of the basic elements of the myth are of the same order as the one involving another character, Nilrem, whose name is an inversion of Merlin (see MERLIN). There is, therefore, an underlying unity behind the apparent gratuitousness of the episodes. Franz Hellens' Melusina, a bird-woman associated with water, goes in search of the 'sapphire dress' which has been magically stolen from her. It is possible to recognize the central motif of the myth-tale of the swan-women, which is widely encountered from the island of Ushant to Korea and which presents a series of easily-definable structural inversions in terms of the myth of Melusina. Like Lusignan, however, the narrator sees Melusina vanish at the end of the story, after having witnessed the disappearance of an enigmatic cathedral of black stone, built by Nilrem in the desert.

Finally, André Breton used Melusina in *Arcane 17* (1947) to glorify 'everything which fell within the province of the female as opposed to the male system of the world'. Melusina 'after the cry', half-merging with the autumn landscape, embodies 'the whole of womankind and also woman as she is today, woman deprived of her human estate, as much a prisoner of her changing origins as you want her to be, but also, through these origins, in providential communication with the elemental forces of nature.' By interweaving Melusina's personal destiny with allusions to Nervalian and Romantic poetry, and with the history of the West at war, André Breton makes a reflection of these different levels of meaning, thus investing her with the greatest significance ever accorded to the fairy of Lusignan. Melusina, 'half reclaimed by her Panic existence (. . .) I believe that she alone can redeem these cruel times'. Melusina is the incarnation of the child-woman, who remains unaffected by the passing of time, and as such she is a prefiguration at one and the same time of Nerval's Balkis, Michelet's 'young sorceress', Bettina von Arnim, Gustave Moreau's 'la Fée au griffon' and the woman who was to become Elisa Breton. The Melusinian myth is cyclically completed and at the same time transcended. For after Melusina's first cry as she is reclaimed by her original form, André Breton imagines a 'second cry' and a reverse metamorphosis, which restores Melusina to her female form 'from head to toe'. She transcends herself and merges with Eve and with the woman portrayed on the seventeenth arcanum (the Star) of the Tarot cards.

Yves Vadé

Merlin

Merlin's literary career has long been dependent on that of Arthurian literature. However, his figure evokes so many different associations and exerts such charm that he has been able to exist outside the mediaeval context and to attain the status of a literary myth in his own right. He was first and foremost the prophet of the Briton revenge, founder of the Round Table and the initiator of knight errantry. Having been born of a devil and a virgin, he occupies a singular position between good and evil and between life and death (by his paradoxical survival in the 'prison of air' or in his tomb), and thus in modern times has been used to embody the enigma or history and evolution. Finally, Merlin was a magician, bringing about or undergoing the most diverse transformations, a mythical builder and engineer and sometimes a sorcerer who remains one of the most popular heroes of the magical imagination.

ORIGINS

The name and person of Merlin appear for the first time in the *Historia Regum Britanniae* (1136) and the *Vita Merlini* (circa 1148), two works written in Latin by the Welsh cleric Geoffrey of Monmouth.

It is unknown whether a figure by the name of Merlin (Myrddin, in Welsh) had actually existed previously. The very name Merlin could have been invented by Geoffrey, borrowing from the town of Kaermyrddin (known today as Carmarthen) for inspiration, or he may have taken advantage of the phonetic similarity between the place name and a 'Merlin(us)' belonging to the Armorican or a more widely continental tradition. However, Geoffrey of Monmouth did not start from nothing. In the middle of the twelfth century, Robert de Torigny, the librarian of the Abbaye du Bec, attested to the existence of two Merlins: a Merlin Ambrosius (Ambrosius Merlinus) and a Merlin Sylvester (Merlinus Sylvester), a claim which was taken up about thirty years later by Gerald of Wales. These two designations actually relate to two different traditions, both used by Geoffrey.

Merlin Ambrosius derives directly from a sixth-century figure called Ambrosius. According to Gildas (*De Excidio et conquestu Britanniae*, sixth century), he was the descendant of a Roman consular family. Nennius' *Historia Britonum* (circa 976) presents him as a fatherless child born as a result of his mother's sexual relations with an incubus, a tradition which was echoed in all subsequent texts. Nennius also supplied the model for the episode in which the child reveals to King Guorthigirn (Vortigern) the existence of two subterranean dragons which are causing his citadel to collapse. Discovered by the king's envoys to Kaermyrddin, the young Ambrosius interprets the battle between the two monsters as the prediction of the lengthy struggles between the Britons and the Saxons. When Geoffrey comes to narrate this scene, he clearly identifies Merlin with Ambrosius ('Merlinus, qui et Ambrosius dicebatur' HRB, Ch. 108).

Merlin Sylvester, who mainly features in the *Vita Merlini*, appears to be the heir to earlier and more specifically Celtic traditions, common to both Scotland and Ireland. They present a princely figure who is overcome by madness and flees into the forest where he lives in the wild and acquires supernatural powers. This happens in Scotland to Lailoken, whose story is told in a *Life of Saint Kentigern*. On the day of the Battle of Arderydd (which the *Annales Cambriae* situate in 573), Lailoken, the companion of King Rhydderch, is said to have heard a heavenly voice condemning him to a life in which his only contact is to be with wild animals. Various predictions are attributed to him, similar to those attributed to Merlin in the *Vita Merlini*. Apart from the name, most of Merlin Sylvester's characteristics are in fact present in this legend, which was possibly compiled as early as the eighth century. In Ireland, the legendary King Suibne, who went mad after the Battle of Moira and lived in the trees from which he eventually flew away, shared similar characteristics, as did the Armorican prophet Guinglaff, who appeared in a fifteenth-century rhymed work entitled *Dialogue entre le Roi Arthur et Guinglaff*.

Merlin's relationship to these 'wild men' becomes even clearer if we consider several Welsh poems which have been handed down under the name of Myrddin. Three of these – 'Afallenau' (The Apple Trees). 'Hoianau' (Greetings) and 'Ymddiddan Myrddin a Thaliesin' (The Dialogue of Merlin and Taliesin) – belong to the *Black Book of Carmarthen*, a Welsh manuscript from the end of the twelfth century. Although the prophetic passages cannot date from before the Norman invasion, certain verses – in which the bard talks to the trees and animals in the Caledonian forest (in particular to the young wild boar which keeps him company) and complains of his loneliness and his sorrows – could be the remnants of a poem written between 850 and 1005 and thus situating the earliest version of the legend of Merlin.

In spite of these obscure origins, it seems that even before the publication of the *Historia Regum Britanniae*, Merlin had aroused a keen interest among Geoffrey's entourage since, in response to various requests, including one from the Bishop of Lincoln, he decided to publish (circa 1134) a fragment of his still unfinished work, the *Prophetiae Merlini*. These Prophecies, inspired by the Sibylline books, the Apocalypse and the prophetic imagery of the Celtic and Germanic races, were supposed to have been translated from Breton. They transpose the events that took place in Great Britain from the Saxon invasion to the reign of Henry I, and then vaguely foretell the revenge of the Britons, before a series of cataclysms heralding the end of the world. The texts were extremely successful and were commentated and quoted as much as religious texts until the end of the Middle Ages. Alain de Lille, the 'universal Doctor' (circa 1128–1203), devoted a commentary of seven volumes to them. Merlin, who had become the major prophet of both the Welsh and the Scots, was even adopted in the fourteenth century by the English who, forgetting the originally anti-Saxon nature of the figure, 'always began their harangues with a prophecy by Merlin' (Mézeray, *Histoire de France*, 1685).

After the story of the two subterranean dragons (Ch. 106–8) and the text of the Prophecies (Ch. 112–8), the *Historia Regum Britanniae* attributes the construction of Stonehenge to Merlin, in memory of the Briton princes who had been treacherously massacred (Ch. 128–30). Finally, it records how the prophet had procured magic philtres for King Uther Pendragon which gave him the appearance of the husband of the Duchess Igerna, a stratagem which enabled the future King Arthur to be conceived (Ch. 137). Having performed this initial piece of magic, Merlin was presented both as a prophet and a sorcerer. According to one character, no one can compare with him 'either in foreseeing the future, or in carrying out ingenious stratagems' ('sive in futuris dicendis, sive in operationibus machinandis').

The *Vita Merlini*, in verse, completed Merlin's biography with adventures in a completely different register. It presents Merlin as both a sorcerer and the King of Demetia (South Wales), who loses his reason after a bloody battle and goes off to live in the woods like a wild animal. Only the sound of the zither is able to calm him. He is brought to the court of King Rhydderch, who has to put him in chains to keep him close at hand, and proves his gift of second sight during several 'divinatory' episodes. Before returning to the woods, he agrees to let his wife Guendoloena remarry, but he reappears on the day of the marriage, preceded by a herd of wild animals and mounted on a stag. He tears off the stag's antlers and uses them to deal a crushing blow to the new husband's head. The remainder of the text describes Merlin, in the care of his sister Ganieda, indulging in astronomical observations and making prophecies about Brittany. He is joined by his disciple, Thelgesin (who can be identified with the Welsh bard, Taliesin), who has returned from Armorica and they have lengthy discussions about nature. Finally, Merlin recovers his sanity after drinking water from a spring which has recently appeared, but he refuses to reign again and remains loyal to the forest.

Merlin in Arthurian Literature

From 1155 the Norman writer Wace transposed the *Historia Regum Britanniae* into French verse in his *Roman de Brut* for Eleanor of Aquitaine. He added the story of Arthur founding the Round Table, of which Merlin was to become the prophet and initiator in later romances.

It was in the work by Robert de Baron (d. circa 1210) that Merlin, who was hardly mentioned by Chrétien de Troyes, was given the role of the initiator of Grail knighthood. Although part of the original text of this verse work, which certainly included the three romances *Joseph d'Arimathie, Merlin* and *Perceval*, has been lost and may never have been finished, the surviving prose translation of *Merlin* seems to have remained faithful to Robert's poem. The beginning of the romance takes up the theme of the begetting of Merlin by an incubus, but incorporates it into an impressive theological perspective in which the demons want to create an Antichrist, also born of a virgin, in an attempt to regain their power which had been jeopardized by the Incarnation. A demon manages, with some difficulty, to take advantage of a chaste young girl who immediately confesses her sin and has the child baptized. Merlin inherits a complete knowledge of the past from his diabolic father. To balance this gift, God gives him the ability to know the future and he is therefore endowed with a universal knowledge. Merlin makes use of this from the first months of his life to save his mother from being burnt at the stake and then, at the age of seven, to reveal the usurper Vertigier the existence and significance of the two dragons hidden beneath the foundations of his tower. The red dragon (Vertigier) would be destroyed by the white dragon which represented the young princes Pendragon and Uther, the sons of King Constant. When Uther becomes king, Merlin, as his self-appointed adviser, enables him to win against the Saxons at the battle of Salisbury, during which Pendragon is killed. Merlin has the monument of Stonehenge built in his memory and from then on Uther reigns under the name of Uther Pendragon. At this point there is an important innovation, for Merlin is responsible for Uther Pendragon instituting the Grail Table, the 'third table' after that of Joseph of Arimathea, which was itself a copy of the one at the Last Supper. It is also because of Merlin (as in the work of Geoffrey of Monmouth) that Uther is able to father Arthur by his union with the Duchess Igerna, whom he marries shortly afterwards. Merlin has Arthur brought up in secret and, when the time is ripe, ensures his succession and coronation. He continues to act as his adviser which greatly benefits both the kingdom and Christendom.

According to the *Perceval* manuscripts of Modena and Didot (which were probably inspired, if not written, by Robert de Boron), Merlin had a peaceful, if enigmatic, end. After guiding Perceval in his quest and then announcing the end of the enchantments at the Grail castle, Merlin has a dwelling called 'esplumeor' (the meaning of which is unknown) built in the forest. He goes there to escape from time and withdraw from the public arena, but he holds himself in readiness to prophesy whatever God may ask him to reveal.

The two prose cycles compiled in France during the first half of the thirteenth century each trace the story in a different manner. In the *Suite-Vulgate*, incorporated into the great cycle of the *Lancelot-Graal* or *Vulgate* (circa 1215–30), Merlin plays the role of strategic adviser in the military campaigns which Arthur conducts against the barons who refuse to accept his authority, then against the Saxons, and finally against the Emperor of Rome. Through his mediation, Arthur marries Guinevere, King Leodegan's daughter, and becomes the ruler responsible for the Round Table. Most importantly, Merlin meets Vivien, daughter of a vavasor named Dionas, at the edge of a spring in the forest of Broceliande. The tales of battles are interwoven with a love intrigue, during which Merlin allows his magical knowledge to be wrested from him by Vivien. To keep Merlin for herself, Vivien eventually locks him in a 'prison of air' from whence the prophet, who has become invisible, is still able to make himself heard.

In the *Suite-Huth*, part of a cycle wrongly attributed to Robert de Boron (circa 1240), Merlin predicts the birth of Mordred and the problems that would be caused by Balin, the knight with two swords. It is he who strikes the 'Dolorous blow' which wounds King Pelleam and transforms his kingdom into a Waste Land. Merlin finds himself more involved in the adventures of knight errantry than in the earlier texts. His status as a sorcerer becomes more clearly defined, and he is seen as being able to control the wind, make the dragon on his banner breathe fire, command the gates of a town to open of their own accord, and prepare an enchanted bed which causes those who sleep on it to lose all sense and memory. The story ends with the unfortunate love affair between Merlin and Vivien which is reminiscent of that of Diana and Faunus. After casting a spell on Merlin, Vivien has him thrown into a tomb which is covered by a stone that no one can lift. In this tomb, Merlin utters one last cry which forms the subject of a separate story, the *Conte du Brait*.

Vivien was mentioned for the first time a little before the *Suite-Vulgate*. She in fact appears at the beginning of the original story of *Lancelot* as Niniane, a Briton sorceress who raises Lancelot in her sumptuous dwelling beneath the surface of a lake. Merlin is presented in an unfavourable light in this narrative which, while bearing witness to Merlin's popularity (he was 'so feared and so honoured by the Britons that everyone called him a holy prophet and the humble folk called him their god'), describes him as being 'with the nature of his deceitful and disloyal father', well-versed in 'all depraved knowledge'. The lady of the lake wisely rejects him and succeeds in imprisoning him 'in a vault within the perilous forest of Darnantes'.

The figure, whom Robert de Boron wanted to present as the prophet of Christian kinghthood, is not therefore free from an ambivalence which is possibly due to his heterogeneous origins, and which is in keeping with the myth of his half-diabolic, half-virginal conception. His ability to transform himself at will can also be seen as the reflection of the unstable and even contradictory nature of his composite character. This ability to assume different forms, which is probably also reminiscent of the powers hitherto ascribed to the druids, enables Merlin to appear now as a young man, now as an old man, often as a man of the woods, and even as a 'great antlered stag', as in the story of Grisandole which was included in the *Suite-Vulgate*.

Thus the story of Merlin, made up of successive contributions, was repeated, summarized and translated, completely or in part, in European literature until the end of the Middle Ages. By 1250, Robert's version of *Merlin* had been translated into Provençal. The figure appeared in numerous French romances written in verse during the thirteenth century, e.g. in *Fergus* (according to which he lives in a remote mountain), in *Le Chevalier aux Deux Epées*, in the *Roman du Hem*, in *Escanor*, in the *Roman de Silence* (which contains the Grisandole episode), and in particular in *Claris et Laris* which explains that Merlin's reclusion is the punishment of a sin for which he must atone until his death. In the prose version of *Tristan* (after 1240), Merlin takes in the motherless Tristan and entrusts him to a tutor (as he did Arthur, according to Robert de Boron). As a magician, he builds a marvellous vessel, the 'ship of joy', for the King of Northumberland. Outside the chivalric context, a tale in verse from the beginning of the twelfth century, 'Du Vilain qui devient riche et puis pauvre' (also known as the 'Dit de Merlin-Merlot'), confirms the supernatural status enjoyed by Merlin in the imagination of the 'humble folk'.

Described in one of Dante's sonnets as a 'buon incantatore', Merlin was extremely fashionable in Italy in connection with the thought of Joachim de Flore (circa 1132–1202). Among the work dubiously attributed to the latter, there is an *Exposito Sibyllae et Merlini*. The tradition of Merlin as a prophet was enriched by a thick volume of *Prophecies*, a mixture of political prophecies, sermons and fictitious events. The work was written in French in about 1276–9 by a Venetian, probably a Franciscan monk. At the beginning of the fourteenth century the Florentine Paolino Pieri combined the story of Merlin's youth with the Italian translation of part of the *Prophecies* in the *Storia di Merlino*. In 1480, the *Historia di Merlino* was published in Venice in six volumes, the majority of which also consisted of Merlin's prophecies.

In England, Robert's *Merlin* and the *Suite-Vulgate* were summarized in verse in an *Arthour and Merlin* between 1250 and 1300. Henry Lovelich gave another version in his *Merlin* (circa 1430). A translation in Middle English of the *Merlin-Vulgate* dates from the middle of the fifteenth century. Finally, Sir Thomas Malory (1408–71) divided the subject matter of Robert's *Merlin* among the first five books of his *Morte d'Arthur*. This work, written in Newgate prison where Malory spent the last twenty years of his life, published in 1485 and continually reprinted from then on, ensured Arthur's and Merlin's lasting fame in all English-speaking countries.

In Germany, *Merlin und Siefried de Ardemont* by Albrecht von Scharfenberg (thirteenth century, known via a version of 1478) summarizes Robert's *Merlin* with significant modifications (e.g. Pendragon and Uther became the prophet's sons). Other translations were published in Holland. In Spain, the cycle of the pseudo-Robert de Boron was translated in the fourteenth century by the friar Juan Vivas, while the *Baladro del sabio Merlin*, derived from the lost *Brait* (cry) *de Merlin*, was incorporated into the *Demanda del Sancto Grial* of which a Castilian version was published in Burgos in 1498 and another in Seville in 1535.

Merlin from the Rennaissance to Symbolism

From the end of the fifteenth century, the publishing industry took over both the story of Merlin and his *Prophecies*. An edition was published in Paris in 1498 by Antoine Vérard, and five other editions appeared in France alone between 1505 and 1535. Merlin also featured in several major works of the Renaissance, proof of the importance of his role in the culture of that period. Ariosto (1474–1533), combining the tradition of the prophet with that of the magician/builder (to whom the Italians attributed the construction of the arenas in Verona), introduced Merlin on three occasions in *Orlando furioso* i.e. in Canto III, where, from the depths of the tomb, he predicts for Bradamante the future greatness of the house of Este; in Canto XXVI, with the description of the prophetic sculptures decorating one of the four fountains that he was said to have created in France; and in Canto XXXIII, which describes the paintings that Merlin was said to have had executed to inform Pharamond of the vicissitudes that would be experienced in future French-Italian relations.

In a much more popular vein, *Les Grandes et inestimables Chronicques du grant et énorme géant Garguantua* (Lyon, 1532), Rabelais' primary source of inspiration, tells how Merlin created Grandgousier from the bones of a male whale crushed on an anvil and sprinkled with Lancelot's blood, and Galamelle from the bones of a female whale mixed with Guinevere's nail parings. Later, Merlin introduces the young Gargantua to the court of King Arthur, and gives him the benefit of his knowledge and his magic – which did not prevent Rabelais from treating the old magician in an extremely casual manner. In England, Edmund Spenser imagined that Merlin, having agreed to build a bronze wall around Carmarthen, called upon one thousand demons to complete it (*The Fairie Queene*, 1590–6). Finally Cervantes could not resist the opportunity of referring to the master of knight errantry in the second part of *Don Quixote* (1615) where Merlin appears in the cave of Montesinos (Ch. 12) and orders Sanchos to whip himself so as to disenchant Dulcinea (Ch. 35).

It was primarily Merlin the prophet who continued to exert a great deal of influence in Great Britain until the time of Shakespeare. Several collections of Prophecies were published during the first half of the sixteenth century. Among those interested in them were the occultist John Dee (1527–1608) and the playwright Thomas Heywood (circa 1570–1641) who devoted an erudite commentary to them entitled *The Life of Merlin surnamed Ambrosius; his Prophesies and predictions*. Shakespeare echoed these theories in a passage in King Lear (Act III. Scene 2, 11. 78–95) in which the Fool parodies Merlin's prophecies, in spite of the fact that the drama takes place before the latter was born. In 1644, William Lily published *The English Merlin revived; or, His prediction upon the affairs of the English Common Wealth and of all or most Kingdomes of Christendome this present Yeare 1644*. It should also be pointed out that, during the sixteenth century, a Welshman called Elis Gruffud had written a *Myrddin Wyllt* (Merlin the Wild) in Welsh, which restored the figure to his origins as an anti-Saxon prophet and man of the woods.

The only image of Merlin retained by the neoclassical period was that of a sorcerer who was represented by several stereotypes. In *La Grenouille et le Rat*, La Fontaine refers to him as the author of an expression which was probably famous at the time: 'Who aims to cheat a friend/Gets cheated in the end'. In *King Arthur* by Dryden (1631–1700), Merlin is nothing more than the sorcerer of a sort of fairy tale, as he is in the opera by Giffard (1736), based on the work. Merlin's name appears here and there in the tales from the *Cabinet des Fées*, as in the *Princesse printanière*, a story by Madame d'Aulnoy in which Printanière is destined to marry Merlin. *L'Ile de Merlin* by Gluck, performed in Vienna in 1758 and based on a minor Parisian work entitled *Le Monde renversé* (1717), reduced Merlin to the status of a good-natured sage who pacified rivals and gave his blessing to lovers.

In France, the figures of Arthurian literature were not restored to a semblance of life until the Comte de Tressan embarked upon his project, begun in 1775, of compiling a *Corps d'extraits des romans de chevalerie*. Furthermore, in the introduction to his *Roman de Merlin l'Enchanteur, Remis en bon français et dans un meilleur ordre* (1797), Martin-Sylvestre Boulard refers to the *Roman de Merlin*, published in 1498, as a virtually unknown work, in which it is possible to discover, despite some shocking flaws, 'a pure moral code, an extensive imagination and new ideas'.

Medieval texts were republished much more faithfully in Great Britain by Sir Walter Scott in 1802–3 and then by George Ellis in *Specimens of Early metrical Romances* (London, 1811). In Germany, Wieland paved the way (a text written by him on Merlin in 1777 inspired Ludwig Uhland to write the ballad of *Merlin the Wild*, 1829) for the erudite works of Friedrich von der Hagen and Walther Hofstätter (Altdeutsche Gedichte aus den Zeiten der Tafelrunde). Karl Lebrecht Immermann (1796–1840) used these texts, as well as a *Geschicte des Zauberers Merlin* written by Dorothea von Schlegel under the name of her husband Friedrich (1804), as the basis for *Merlin, eine Mythe*, a drama in three parts with a prologue and an epilogue, published in 1832. In the play, Merlin is the son of a demiurgical Satan and the virgin Candida. Brought up in England and initiated into the mystery of the Grail, he devotes himself, as the embodiment of all Gnostic myths, to the task of ensuring the success of salvational works. His love for Ninian, Guinevere's sister, who symbolizes communion with nature, leads him to imagine that he is the son of the Earth. However, Titurel accuses him of being the Antichrist and the drama ends with Merlin's madness. In the epilogue, Satan frees him from his madness, but Merlin refuses to dedicate himself to Satan, although this does not entitle him to benefit from divine redemption. According to the author, this ambitious work, that Geibel referred to as 'another *Faust*' was intended to illustrate the 'tragedy of contradiction' and the drama of a self-appointed redeemer.

In his poem 'Vivien' (1859) which in 1878 became 'Merlin and Vivien', Alfred Tennyson (1809–92) presented Merlin in a more directly moralizing manner. The poem, which belongs to the *Idylls of the King*, basically consists of a long dialogue between Merlin and Vivien in the forest of Broceliande. The 'gentle magician' is at first moved by the sorceress' coaxing, then exasperated by her lies and finally overcome by her laments. He then reveals the spell which she uses to conceal him from 'life and use and name and fame'.

In 1860, Edgar Quinet published the two volumes of his *Merlin l'Enchanteur*, a long allegorical epic in prose in which Merlin is represented as a universal genius, the incarnation of Western history and culture. All material prosperity, all technical inventions, all works of art are the result of his spells. Not content with having built St Mark, the Alhambra and the cathedrals, he covers the walls of Florence with portraits of Vivien. He even writes in advance the masterpieces of French literature in his tomb. This 'tomb' is in fact an immense underground kingdom which extends beneath the whole of Europe. To their great joy, Vivien and Merlin are imprisoned there until Merlin's demoniacal 'grandfather' reconciles himself with the Eternal. It is perhaps to be regretted that Quinet, carried away by fluency and possibly led astray by Ariosto's example, tempered the myth in this loosely written and ideologically inconsistent rhapsody.

At the same time, Hersart de La Villemarqué attempted to summarize the story of Merlin, whom he considered to be a 'Celtic Orpheus'. His *Myrdhin ou l'Enchanteur Merlin* (1862) divided the different aspects of the character between a mythological figure inherited from Antiquity, the legendary figure of the work by Nennius, the poetical hero of the *Vita Merlini*, a ficitional hero and the 'real' person remembered by the Britons. Edouard Schuré told the story of the initiation of this Celtic Orpheus in *Les Grande Légendes de France* (1892), in a fantastical narrative embellished with the explicit occult symbolism that was fashionable at the time. the success of Burne-Jones' painting *Merlin and Vivien* at the 1878 Exhibition, and the poem dedicated to 'Brocéliande' by Jean Lorrain in *La Forêt bleue* (1883) (in which he presented his own version of the theme already treated by Tennyson), both contributed to making Merlin a symbolist hero.

Merlin in Twentieth-century Literature

At the turn of the century, the myth of Merlin gained renewed poetical strength with the work of Guillaume Apollinaire (1880–1918). His poem *Merlin et la vieille femme*, which probably dates from 1899–1900, brings together the sorcerer and the ancient sorceress, Morgan le Fay, skilled in the art of illusion, as well as the figure of Memory, who was to give him an 'unfortunate and handsome' son. But it is above all in *L'Enchanteur pourrissant*

(1904–9) that Apollinaire brought the myth to life, by making Merlin's tomb the focal point of all the mysteries of life, love and death, and the forum of his own questions. While the sorcerer's body creates life from corruption, Vivien, the lady of the lake, rejects the carnal life and is revealed to be the source of death. This double paradox is illustrated by the procession 'in the deep, dark forest' of all the beings attracted by the sorcerer's body, i.e. snakes, druids, fays, various monsters, false kings, sorcerers and prophets, who have come to celebrate a strange 'funerary Christmas' and to bear witness in their own way to the 'different eternities of man and woman'. Directly inspired by mediaeval sources, the text (of which the original was illustrated by Derain), also experiments with new narrative techniques, closely associated with research into the pictorial avant-garde. It takes on the significance of the burial of Symbolism and, through the final pages of *Onirocritique* (added in 1909), of an opening up to what was to become Surrealism.

It is a modernistic Merlin who appears, under the inverted name of Nilrem, in the novel by Franz Hellens (1881–1972) *Mélusine ou la robe de saphir*, written in 1917–18, first published in 1921, and revised in 1951. Nilrem is an engineer, the architect of a cathedral of black stone in the desert, the builder of an artificial park in which mechanisms imitate natural phenomena, while he himself is a 'man of iron' with eyes 'as cold as steel'. At the end of the story, it is revealed that he is Merlin 'reduced to the role of an ordinary man' and in search of the sapphire which used to give him 'strength and subtlety'. As this sapphire has become Mélusine's dress, he strips her of it and disappears with it.

In *Les Chevaliers de la Table ronde*, a play by Jean Cocteau produced in 1937, Merlin is merely an impostor working for the devil. Helped by a young demon which he transforms at will by giving it the appearance of the other characters, he feeds off the life force of the land in which he is practising his sorcery, thereby rendering it infertile. Artus, who has made him his chaplain, and Guinevere and Lancelot, whose love he encourages, allow themselves to be imprisoned by his deceit. The arrival of Galahad causes the masks to be removed. He forces Merlin to leave Camelot and to free the land from the evil spell that he has cast over it. The author himself admits that Merlin's power here symbolizes the ascendancy of all types of drugs. The opposite meaning is found five years later in an image created by Aragon in a few lines of his poem *Brocéliande* (1942) where Merlin, imprisoned in an enchanted tree, represents all those held in thrall by the German occupation.

The sorcerer's ambivalence is also fundamental to Tankred Dorst's *Merlin* (1981), a drama consisting of a prologue and four parts which combines contemporary references with traditional elements and belongs to the tradition of Karl Immermann's *Merlin*. But the character – born as an adult, bearded man who immediately begins to read the newspaper and predicts Armstrong's landing on the moon and crematorium furnaces – no longer aspires to save the world. His father the Devil wants him to encourage human beings to commit evil acts freely, but he refuses, in order to devote himself, with few illusions, to the organization of the Round Table, a humanitarian and civilizing ideal. 'I would prefer to have nothing to do with you', he replies to Parsifal who asks him if he is God. However, he does claim to have set several men on the right road, the one which enables individuals to find themselves, although some, like Mordred, only discover their own wickedness. After many transformations and a number of episodes freely inspired by Arthurian literature, Merlin is still able to predict the discouraged Artus' victory over Mordred. He then allows himself to be imprisoned in the hawthorn bush, a victim of a love which is even more merciless than destiny.

Although Merlin lends himself to all types of anachronism, the mystery of his origins continues to remain a source of fascination. The devotees of Celtic lore endeavour to establish his roots more firmly than ever in ancestral traditions, either by means of erudite studies such as Jean Markale's *Merlin l'Enchanteur ou l'éternelle Quête magique* (1981), or pseudo-historical novels like the *Testament de Merlin* by Théodore Briant (1881–1956), published in 1975. The combination of the fictitious narrative and occult issues links this last work to the works of Schuré. Merlin is the son of a druidess and guardian of the mysteries of the Celtic religion, but he is moved by the Christian message and becomes 'the white druid of Broceliande' after Arthur's defeat at Salisbury. As the chief initiate, he initiates his disciple Adragante after bringing him back from the dead. As Vivien's lover, the death of the sorceress frees him from the magic spell, while as the new Orpheus, he is torn limb from limb by the druidesses at Morgan's instigation. Finally, as the new Christ, he reveals himself to Adragante in his heavenly form.

In a completely different vein, the poet Jacques Roubaud (b. 1932) has undertaken the considerable task of reverting to the texts as he rewrites the body of Arthurian literature. Merlin has been given his rightful place. Within the context of a cycle devoted to the *Graal Théâtre* by the Nouveau Théâtre National de Marseille, Florence Delay and Jacques Roubaud wrote a more 'piquant' version of *Merlin l'Enchanteur*, produced in 1979. On the other hand, the first volume of the *Graal Fiction* (1978) begins, in keeping with mediaeval tradition, with a summary of Merlin's story which is both faithful to the original and subtly ironic. In his consideration of the character of Blaise – confessor to Merlin's mother and most probably the sorcerer's father as well as the fictitious narrator of the adventures of the Round Table – Jacques Roubaud once again raises the issue of the textual origin of Merlin who is himself the source of the Arthurian text which is supposed to have been dictated to Blaise by the sorcerer-prophet. Merlin is not only the instigator of the Round Table, but also the mythical author of Arthurian literature.

Yves Vadé

Moses: Symbol of the Absolute and the Incomplete

'My servant Moses . . . With him will I speak mouth to mouth, even apparently, and not in dark speeches; and the similitude of the LORD shall he behold.'

Numbers XII, 8.

The figure of Moses is supremely valuable as an inexhaustible source of inspiration; more so than the various literary interpretations that exist of him. Every aspect of the story of Moses is enigmatic, despite the fact that it is written that God speaks with him plainly, 'mouth to mouth' and not in riddles or 'dark speeches'. The absolute nature of this statement has been endlessly modified by writers using different approaches. Their source, which is always evident in their work is in fact The Text itself; Borges (1) expressly describes the Bible as constituting an 'absolute text'.

Whereas additional (e.g. historical) sources exist for other biblical figures, in Moses' case the Bible is the sole source, and those parts of it that appeared much later in thc Koran. For this reason, well-meaning attempts by writers such as Freud to re-interpret the story of Moses are doomed to fail. In Freud's case, the interpretation was based on his own psychoanalytical ideology, and on occasions – as he himself admitted – it came into direct conflict with his own feelings (2). According to Freud, Moses was an Egyptian. The Bible, which remains our only source of reference, states that he belonged to the tribe of Levi both on his father's and his mother's side. However, the Freudian theme of Moses as an Egyptian who was murdered by the People of Israel, is certainly present in the Jewish tradition, but it has symbolic connotations which are at odds with Freud's apparent thesis. The relevant text is located in the *Zohar* (3) and refers to an Egyptian who is described as 'asher mareh' (i.e. who showed or revealed), a Hebrew term taken from the text quoted above in which God reveals Himself to Moses, and not in dark speeches. This ability to 'reveal' is at the heart of the myth, for it continually unfolds to reveal further aspects of human philosophical preoccupations.

In his work on the *Midrash*, Ariel Rathaus (4) defines the 'Midrash' and 'Targums', as 'creative' philology and historiography – a creative reading and 'ex novo' interpetation of the text. A less 'creative', more unambiguous approach can destroy the subtle arguments that place the meaning of the myth beyond more literal interpretation. For example, Freud insists on stressing that the name Moses – Moshe in Hebrew – is in fact an Egyptian name, and that Pharaoh's daughter could not have known Hebrew and could therefore not have invested it with the meaning so clearly indicated in the Bible, i.e. 'saved from the waters'. Freud is mistaken on both counts. Pharaoh's daughter would have known a few words of Hebrew since it was the language of her slaves, and would have been aware of their significance. Should the name have also been an Egyptian word, then she was demonstrating great subtlety in recording the Hebrew meaning of her rescue in her own language. Thus, the very choice of his name establishes the dual origin of the man who was to be the instrument of the exodus from Egypt, a great event which came to signify the liberation of all races from slavery (5). The enigma of Moses, what it tells us without ever truly revealing itself in entirety, is directly linked to the name of Moses.

As with all figures of this stature – or perhaps he is the *only* figure of this stature – Moses was carried along by events that he did not fully comprehend. Their significance was revealed to him gradually, above and beyond what he was capable of understanding. Moses 'kept the flock of Jethro his father-in-law', just as Jacob before him and David after him kept the flocks of their respective fathers-in-law and fathers. According to the *Midrash*, he was chosen for the compassion he showed towards the creatures in his care. Surely the man who carried a lamb dying of thirst to drink at a spring was destined to lead his people across the desert. The various episodes in Moses' life are recounted in the Bible, but their meaning is never made fully clear. This is evident in the account of the burning bush. While Moses 'kept the flock of Jethro his father-in-law, (. . .) the angel of the Lord appeared unto him in a flame of fire out of the midst of a bush: and he looked, and, behold, the bush burned with fire, and the bush was not consumed. And Moses said, I will turn aside, and see this great sight' (6). Just as Moses wanted to approach the mystery, the mystery inexorably approached Moses. It was in fact a dual approach. The Lord called to him out of the midst of the bush: 'Moses, Moses.' And Moses replied with that one word with which the story of Abraham, the first patriarch, had previously begun: '*Hineni*.' Here I am.

The bush burned and yet, miraculously was not consumed. Moses answered God and confirmed his presence in human terms. This is one of the enduring images of the myth, a potent source of literary inspiration. The bush, aflame but whole is an infinite source of light, in direct contrast to the phrase in the Book of Revelation (cited by Jung in his *Antwort auf Hiob*: 'Ardet, non lucet': it burns but sheds no light. Such a shadowy incandescence could only give rise to the catastrophes of the end of the world. And who could affirm their presence in the face of this melting pot, in which everything is likely to be consumed?

Moses' relationship to the burning bush is in fact a relationship to being. It is immediately after this episode that God defines Himself to Moses in the well-known phrase, 'Eieh asher Eieh.' An approximate meaning is I am that I am, but it is impossible to translate because, according to the sense of the

Semitic future – or incomplete – tenses, it signifies both essence and futurity in the true sense, being and posterity, the divine and the human (7). Indeed, the remainder of the text confirms that God defines Himself in terms of the initials of the unpronounceable Tetragrammaton, 'the God of Abraham, the God of Isaac, and the God of Jacob', sending Moses to deliver His People from Egypt. To do this He reveals Himself to Moses for the first time using His ineffable name, letters of the 'present' to which is attached the 'Yod' of the future (8). The Lord stresses that this is the first time He has revealed this aspect of His asbolute essence to a mortal (9). Thus there is a history of mankind which is linked to the manner in which he apprehends God's being, and it is through the manner in which He reveals Himself, that the Absolute Being influences the history of mankind.

This in turn affects literary history in that a poet, if he or she is *truly* a poet, stands at the crossroads of both being and posterity. Thus the Christian poet, Péguy, captures the progress and continuity of history in terms of revelation. This offers a possible explanation as to why comparisons have so often been made between Jews and poets. This is an example from Péguy's work:

> We have pretended to be merry pilgrims
> Even to enjoy travelling and be full of mirth,
> To have been through a hundred or more bailiwicks,
> And to be accustomed to being on the move . . .
>
> We have now reached the topmost terrace
> Where man stands naked before his God,
> Where no disguise, either of time or place,
> Can save us from your pursuit, O Lord. (10)

In his perception of the continuity of history Péguy unlike many Christians, does not dissociate Christ from history 'before Christ'. There is no BC and AD to distort the course of history as he sees it:

> Like the infant Moses on the shores of Egypt
> Like the infant Moses asleep among the reeds
> Lay the infant sleeping in that lowly crypt
> Under these paltry garlands, these sparse leaves
> Like Moses sleeping in the temples of Egypt
> Lay the infant sleeping concealed from Israel . . .

Péguy, who was both a Christian *and* a poet, compares two moments in mankind's spiritual history. And for those who aspire to be, or are, both Jew and poet, the red glow of the burning bush contains the entire history of mankind. And yet the bush was not consumed . . . In other words, no single moment summarizes its light. There is no division of history before and after Moses, as there is for Christians before and after Christ, only the undercurrent of a force which preceded the creation of the world. Moses is mysteriously linked to being, a combination of immanence and transcendence, and to the living springs of revelation. This may be why the manner of his death differed so greatly from that of Christ.

Moses lived out his 120 years weighed down by the most burdensome of tasks, subject to pressures from both God and His People and constantly trying to fulfil the role of mediator. We cannot tell whether he was a lonely man, for the type of solitude he experienced was that by the nineteenth-century French Romantic poet, Alfred de Vigny, in his poem *Moïse*. Vigny demonstrates the link between 'the poetic mission' of the Romantics and the Jewish mission – and the price exacted by each (11). In Moses' case, there was no blood – at least not his own – and he was beyond tears (12). But in a few words, Vigny conjures up a poignant image of Moses' solitude: 'You have caused me to grow old powerful and solitary. Let me die a mortal death.' His is the cry of a man to whom love appears to have been denied: '. . . And when I open my arms, they fall at my feet.'

Vigny's interpretation is both true and false – a contradiction which in Moses' case is intrinsic. He was indeed alone, and was expressly advised by his father-in-law Jethro (whose name is sometimes changed to Reuel, 'the Lord's shepherd') to choose able men to help him achieve his goal. And yet Moses had a family life with his brother Aaron, his sister Miriam and his wife Zipporah, who saved his life by reminding the Lord of the sign of the covenant (13) when God, in one of those moments of vexation and anger, had decided that he should die. Moses was alone in that it is never specifically stated, as it is in the case of other Biblical figures, that he 'knew' or loved a woman. He certainly took a wife, but there is a great deal of controversy as to whether Zipporah was the same Ethiopian woman who was strongly criticized by Moses' family or whether this was in fact a different Zipporah. He took a wife, but we do not know if he took the time to love her. The *Zohar* reproaches him for not having done so, basing its comments on the period during which he abandoned Zipporah for a time, but without conflict or bitterness, and later returned to her. It is possible that, in this respect, he represents the man who has too much on his mind (14). Moses was the most isolated and yet the *least* isolated of men, for the Lord was his constant companion and interlocutor. Most of the verses in the Book of Exodus begin with the phrase: 'And the Lord spake unto Moses . . .'

And there is also the – dual – episode of the gift of the Law, of this incandescent Presence which only Moses can confront, of God passing before him, revealing His glory and His goodness but, in order to do so, covering Moses with His hand (15). And Moses said: 'I beseech thee, shew me thy glory.' And God replied: 'I will make all my goodness (Kol Touvi) pass before thee,' but added: 'Thou canst not see my face, for, there shall no man see me, and live . . . there is a place by me, and thou shalt stand upon a rock: And it shall come to pass, while my glory passeth by, that I will put thee in a clift of the rock, and will cover thee with my hand . . .' It was when the

Lord had passed by that Moses could see Him, but not His face, although it is written elsewhere that He spoke to Moses 'mouth to mouth'. In this revelation which can never be fully achieved, this concealment which is never complete, is rooted the entire creativity of the human race, not just literary creativity, and indeed its very humanity.

The *Zohar* takes this relationship as the basis of the mystery of shadows and light. Moses only saw the shadows 'through a wall', in the same way that Bileam was only able to see the holy dimension through a wall (16) or, as he put it: 'Most dreams contain an element of reality'. The human condition is a dream through which an element of reality is revealed, and Moses was the man who came closest to the ultimate reality. The figure of Moses or – as Doryon describes him – 'the man Moses' (17) is, by his very stature, the synthesis of the relationship to Eternity which is inextricably associated with a history strongly dominated by Eternity (18). Edmond Jabès (19) sees 'the place where God revealed himself to Moses as an unattainable summit because it is the summit of the Name'. But according to Jabès, the Name (20) remains Moses' hopeless question to God. It was a question to which he had in fact already received the answer, but the answer merely repeated the question. 'God is the uplifting inspiration', the ineffable name or *absence of name*. Jabès defines the mystery adroitly: 'The infinite is a concealed root and . . . everything which germinates and produces shoots and blossoms is both nourished and inspired by it.'

Beyond the plentiful number of events in Moses' life, developed much more prolifically in the Commentary than in any other area of 'literature', there exists a boundary or point of access, a harshness which is dispelled by compassion, to the very mystery of death. After the plagues of Egypt, the departure from Egypt, the double gift of the Law, the episode of the golden calf – there exists this harshness which the *Zohar* considers to be directed against Moses (21). Yet it is linked to the name of Elohim, the origin of Creation. The Tetragrammaton is compassion. It is only in the distressing episode of the death of Moses that the two themes combine to formulate a question which will remain eternally unanswered, because it lies within an area which can never be defined.

Before undertaking his final task, to summarize for the People of Israel their imprescriptible duties and the foundations and conditions of their existence, Moses recalls that he beseeched the Lord to allow him to enter the promised land (22) but that 'the Lord was wroth with me for your sakes, and would not hear me: and the Lord said unto me, Let it suffice thee; speak no more unto me of this matter.' Moses would see the promised land from the top of Pisgah, but would not 'go over Jordan'. This is followed immediately by the verse concerning the instructions to be given to his successor, Joshua, and the laws and statutes that Moses must pass on to the People. The Lord has indeed adopted the children of Israel (23), he has 'brought [them] forth out of the iron furnace, even out of Egypt', but was angered because of the way they had behaved towards Moses. The Commentary has tried to find multiple reasons for this merciless decree issued against Moses, which is repeated in the text: 'The Lord was angry with me for your sakes, and sware that I should not go over Jordan . . . but I must die in this land . . . but ye shall go over and possess that good land', provided the covenant is kept and observed.

Moses did not fear death, but he did fear the particular death imposed upon him in that his task was not complete. The *Midrashim* (24) develop the story of Moses' plea, to the point of investing it with cosmic dimensions. God had previously sworn to Moses that the People of Israel would not perish but that Moses himself would not 'go over Jordan'. The two decrees were interdependent, and God could not go back on his word. However, Moses' plea shook the world 'like a sword which severs and cuts and does not stop, like the ineffable Name of the Lord that he had learned from His mouth'. And God was forced to close the gates of heaven and hell to Moses' plea, for it might destroy the order of the world. It was a close-fought argument and God had to beseech Moses who consented to die, but not by the hand of Samael, the angel of death. His soul was taken by the kiss of God and God Himself referred to Moses' soul as His 'daughter'.

This magnificent non-accomplishment of a human destiny was an experience shared (25) by Kafka, a prose poet whose own life was steeped in mystery, engima and non-accomplishment, that is to say, swept by the shadows which are the inevitable consequence of the quest for the Absolute . . . He wrote: 'The principle of the way through the desert . . . with a remnant of conscience . . . of what is in the process of being accomplished.'

That which is in the process of being accomplished therefore always lies beyond the remnant of conscience . . .

God's refusal to allow Moses to enter the land of Canaan when he had devoted his entire life and his 'intuition' [sic] to seeking it, 'can have only one meaning – to show human life as an imperfect moment. The extent of this imperfection is stressed by the fact that a life of this nature could last indefinitely without amounting to anything more that a moment. It was not because his life was too short that Moses did not enter Canaan, but because his was a human life.' (26)

In the same article, Kafta goes on to say that the mortal does not come to the end of his life, but with one hand pushes aside the despair caused by his destiny, while with the other he 'writes' [sic] what he sees beneath the debris, for he is able to see more and in a different manner from others. 'Dead during his lifetime', he is 'the authentic survivor'.

Whereas Jesus said: 'Thy will be done', Moses combated the divine decree with all his might and introduced the strength of mankind – which was both absolute *and* derisory – into the world in order to perfect creation. History had begun and time was recorded within an indefinable space.

Nobody knows the location of the tomb in which God Himself buried Moses' mortal remains. According to Rabbi Berechiah (27), it is 'Siman betoch Siman', the Sign within the sign itself. Alternatively, it is the sign within the absence of the Sign that we must be able to accept. The Muslims have a place known as 'Kever Moussa', the tomb of Moses, which it would be impossible for the Jews to recognize. The entire issue is linked to the reconstruction of the temple and to the achievements of history. Human destiny guarantees infinity by the fact that it is impossible to complete. Because of its very non-completion, it leaves future generations to complete a meaning which can never be completed within the space of a human lifetime. It has already been stated that Biblical figures (28) would be considered in this article less in terms of their multiple *literary* forms but rather for their value as a source of philosophical inspiration. In the final analysis, this source of 'literary' inspiration is in fact the inspiration of mankind. Thus Valéry was able to write: 'It has occurred to me to think that, if I were a philosopher, I would do my utmost to ensure that my philosophical thought was independent of all forms of knowledge that could be destroyed by a new experience.' (29)

By relinquishing the traditional approach to literary myth, this article has attempted to define the qualities that make Biblical figures a source of eternal inspiration.

E. Amado Lévy-Valensi

The Minotaur

Minos asked Poseidon to give a sign to prove to the Cretans that he was favoured by the gods. The god agreed, on condition that the bull that he would cause to rise from the sea, would subsequently be offered to him as a sacrifice. However, the animal was so beautiful that Minos could not bring himself to destroy it in this way. Poseidon was furious and decided to take his revenge by making Queen Pasiphae fall passionately in love with the white bull. Longing to be united with the animal, the queen enlisted the help of the ingenious Athenian, Daedalus, who was at the court of Minos. The artisan used his skill to create a heifer out of wood and leather. The queen concealed herself inside the heifer and the white bull, deceived by appearances, coupled with her. The fruit of this unnatural union was the Minotaur, also known as Asterion or Asterius, which had the head of a bull and the body of a man. Furious and ashamed, Minos had Daedalus construct a sort of huge palace-prison, the labyrinth, in which to keep the monster (see LABYRINTH). Every year (or every nine years), seven youths and seven maidens were fed to the Minotaur, a tribute imposed on the Athenians by Minos. One day, Theseus suggested that he join the group of youths and, with the help of the thread given to him by Ariadne, he found the Minotaur, killed it and emerged, triumphant, from the labyrinth.

The monstrous nature of the Minotaur derives from the way in which it was conceived. In this respect, the story of its origins is as important as its own story. Its life was in fact singularly devoid of incident. Imprisoned in the labyrinth, it was as if the tribute paid by the Athenians provided a periodic source of distraction and food. The story of the Minotaur is inextricably linked with that of the labyrinth – the maze that was constructed for the creature, that was doomed to disappear with it and in which it waited. Without knowing it, the Minotaur was waiting to be slain by Theseus. This was the only event of its life.

In Greek literature, the Minotaur only appears in relation to Theseus. For example, in *Hercules Furens* by Euripides, Theseus lists the gifts he has received from his fellow citizens for having killed the 'bull of Cnossos' (1326–7), while in his 'Encomium of Helen' (*Panegyric* X. 28), Isocrates stresses that Theseus defeated a 'monster which was half man, half bull', and Callimachus refers to a 'roaring monster' in his hymn to Delos (310). In each case, a circumlocution is used to refer to the Minotaur, partly because of the tradition of rhetoric, but also as if there were something shameful in naming it.

This impression is maintained in Latin literature, where the Minotaur is rarely described in connection with the adventures of Daedalus except in Virgil and Ovid. It mainly appears as the rather repulsive incarnation of Pasiphae's aberration. In the *Aeneid* (VI. 25–6) Virgil refers to the 'hybrid offspring, child of two breeds', 'a warning against wicked love', while in *Metamorphoses*, Ovid gives a similar description of 'the monstrous hybrid beast' which 'declared the queen's obscene adultery' (VIII. 155–6). Ovid again refers to the 'fruit of a mother's adulterous passion' in *Ars Amatoria* (II. 23) and then sums up the creature's basic 'otherness' as well as its fundamental relationship to us in that simple, famous line: 'semibovemque virum semivirumque bovem', 'a man who is half bull and a bull which is half man' (II. 24).

It is an accepted fact that during the Middle Ages scholars tried to interpret texts from Latin mythology in a symbolic manner in order to make them acceptable within a Christian context. This is noticeable in the glosses and commentaries which accompany the texts of Virgil and Ovid, but the temptation often goes much further. For example, in about 1300, an anonymous poet rewrote the *Metamorphoses* of the Latin poet in French. His *Ovid Moralisé* provides an allegorical interpretation of each episode, so that the Minotaur in its labyrinth becomes the angel who, out of pride, revolted against God and whom God was forced to imprison in the cage of Hell. After that, God created Man who, until his death, for a long time inevitably fell prey to 'the proud and hornéd beast/which dwells in the infernal cage' (VIII. 1451–2). But God is merciful and sent His son, Theseus-Jesus into the world to save humanity from the payment of this tribute.

In the secular works, the Minotaur only appears in relation to the other characters in the myth. For example, it has a place in the *Roman d'Athis et de Prophlias* among the various characters featured in the story of the labyrinth, but it is only in Dante's *Inferno* that it is given an original role and occupies a place in its own right. 'The infamy of Crete' is in fact, with the Centaurs, the guardian of the Circle of the Violent, the Seventh Circle (Canto XII. 1–48). The Minotaur is obviously an appropriate guardian for those being punished for the sin of bestiality. By implication, the Minotaur evokes the story of the labyrinth and we are reminded how it was conceived 'in the false heifer's side'. Also, those guilty of carnal sin who have not exercised the human potential for self-restraint, wander in Purgatory, calling the name of Pasiphae (XXVI. 40–2, 82–7). However, by including the Minotaur in his monsters' gallery, Dante has contributed to the creation of a particular type of image of the creature, i.e. there is a tendency to represent it as part of a mythical bestiary. It is sometimes even found in travel accounts, as for example during the thirteenth century, when it appears on Ebsdorf of Hereford's maps of the world. It can be seen in the 'East', near the mouth of the Oxus, with the tiger and the manticore, where it appears to lead the peaceful life of a monster, liberated from its myth and the complexities of its Greek and Cretan background.

During the Early Renaissance period of the fourteenth and fifteenth centuries, the Minotaur was reinstated in its original role. In Boccaccio's *Amorosa Visione* (1342), the narrator sees Theseus walking in the labyrinth 'towards the terrible Minotaur' (XXII. 6). The didactic Latin works by the author of the Decameron naturally include the Cretan episode in the adventures of Theseus. In the *De genealogiis deorum gentilium* (1347), which gives a symbolic interpretation of Classical mythology, the Minotaur is presented as the expression of the 'vice of bestiality' (IV. 10). In *De Casibus virorum illustrium* (1355), the slaying of the Minotaur earns Theseus 'eternal praise' (IX. X, 5). Chaucer's *Knight's Tale* (1387) describes Theseus astride his horse and carrying a pennant bearing the image of the Minotaur that he slew in Crete. The *Livre de Mutacion de Fortune* (circa 1410) by the French writer Christine de Pisan tells how Theseus was introduced into the Daedalian prison and acquitted himself so well that he killed the monster in the cage (1430).

At the height of the Renaissance, the 'loathsome half bull and half man' lies in wait in *Les Epîtres de l'Amant vert* (II. 159) by that great enthusiast of mythology, Jean Lemaire des Belges (1511). In England, it reappears in connection with the story of Pasiphae, in the tortuous prose of George Pettie in *A Petite Palace* (1576). It was only in Spain that the figure of the man-bull was given a more in-depth treatment in two poems of the mid-sixteenth century. One was the 'Romance de Teseo y el Minotauro' by Lorenzo de Sepúlveda, which reappeared as No. 460 in the *Romancero general* by Augustin Durán, and the other was 'La fábula del labarinto de Creta, y del Minotauro, y de Teseo' by Sebastián de Horozco, which reappeared in 1874 in his *Cancionero*. It should be pointed out, however, that the two poems are little more than paraphrases of Ovid. The monster is purely a means of highlighting the qualities of the hero and the language has little literary merit.

With the approach of the neoclassical period, in Shakespeare's *Henry VI* (1591), the Earl of Suffolk exhorts himself not to advance any further into the labyrinth of intrigues for 'There Minotaurs and ugly treasons lurk' (Part I, Act V, 188). However, the image which could have been further developed and expanded is limited to this one reference. The use of Minotaurs in the plural also suggests that the term continues to be associated as much with a general category of monsters as with the individual offspring of the Bull and Pasiphae. In the same way, the place occupied by the Minotaur in European theatre would never be more than a brief allusion made during references to the exploits of Theseus. The best example of this occurs in Racine's *Phèdre* (Act I, Scene I, 82) where Crete is described as 'smoking with the blood of the Minotaur'. The only development of the story of the Minotaur during this period was in a poem by Cancer y Velasco, *Fabula del Minotauro* (1651) which is undoubtedly the best work by the heir of Quevedo and Gongora. It combines a very strong degree of realism with astonishing metaphors.

During the nineteenth and twentieth centuries, the Minotaur once again became the representation of the monster. One of its most memorable characteristics is that it fed on human flesh. In France, it was frequently used as the 'bête noire' in political controversies: for A. it was the equivalent of imperial conscription. For J. Simon, it clearly represented the debauchery indulged in by the idle working classes, while for A. Barbier it symbolized the industrial society which devoured them. It stood for Villèle for Barthélémy and Méry, while according to one of Gautier's characters it was Robespierre, and for Souvarine in the twentieth century it was reincarnated in Stalin. Modern literature confirms it in this ogre's role. The novel by Mika Waltari, *Sinuhe Egyptilaïnen* (1945), contains a Cretan episode in which the Minotaur is the high priest, wearing the mask of the bull-God – a huge animal that feeds on human flesh and lives in a partly submerged cave. In modern novels of the fantastic such as *La Nuit du Minotaure* by M. Agapit (1965) and *Day of the Minotaur* by Burnett Swan (1966), it continues to be the incarnation of horror.

However, beyond this univocal meaning, Crete's source of shame began to appeal to the modern imagination in a variety of ways. Lord Byron made a passing reference to the myth, treating it with derisive humour. According to him, the entire Minotaur episode was an initiative on the part of Pasiphae to promote cattle breeding in order to increase the meat quota for the Cretan army with a view to making it more bloodthirsty! In France, the tone was more in keeping with bawdy vaudeville humour and the curious verb 'minotauriser' was invented, meaning to cuckold or deceive one's husband, rather as if the most significant and important person in the whole affair was in fact Minos. In this way, adultery came to be associated with an act of monstrosity and one is even left with the impression that, beneath the surface of the myth, there lies a more general feeling of a sort of animal guilt associated with sexuality, and with female sexuality in particular. Both Balzac and Baudelaire used the verb, but it was Swinburne who began to really question the nature of monstrosity via the legendary figure. In a dialogue in verse dedicated to Pasiphae, the pre-Raphaelite poet, using an image borrowed from Roman art, has Daedalus present the queen with the wooden heifer that he has constructed for her. In a totally new approach, Pasiphae tells him that she is waiting impatiently for the moment when, disguised as a heifer, she will slip beneath the bull. Nor does Swinburne present the lover of Hippolytus as guilty in his version of 'Phaedra', a dramatic poem of the same period (in *Poems and Ballads*, 1866). The victim of a cruel god, Phaedra wants to die, but she accepts her passion for Hippolytus without in any way trying to diminish or conceal it.

Standing like a look-out on the threshold of the next century, the *Minotaur* of the Victorian painter, Watts, seems to escape the intention of its creator and embody, not the Moloch of lust that was intended, but that touching animal anticipation of new developments. During the same period, Nietzsche's Minotaur represents another type of knowledge. In fact, the many references to the Greek myth of the labyrinth, scattered throughout his entire works, form a vast metaphor of knowledge. The labyrinth represents the reverse side of the world, the side that language, by imitating it, conceals. Within it lies the way leading to the discovery of original truth, an origin represented by the Minotaur-Dionysus. Basically, the way to knowledge leads down towards the Minotaur and not to safety by following the thread out of the labyrinth. Nietzsche asserts his 'particular interest' in the labyrinth and his desire 'to make the acquaintance of Mr Minotaur'. He advises those who hope to save themselves by using the thread, to hang themselves with it instead (ed. Kröner, Vol. XVI, p. 437). 'Sing me a song of the Labyrinth in which the hybrid bull was imprisoned', wrote Oscar Wilde at the end of the century in *The Sphinx* (1894), and from this it is possible to assess the amount of ground covered since Lord Byron.

Significantly, the character of Pasiphae opens up a new area of moral enquiry for the twentieth century. In the epilogue of *Prométhée mal enchaîné* (1899) Gide explains that, remembering the way in which Zeus visited Leda in the form of a swan, Pasiphae believed that her bull was also inhabited by a god. Because this was not in fact so, she gave birth to a calf. From then on, the contradictions of passion open the way for the ambivalence of sexuality. Echoing the story of Queen Pasiphae, the beautiful California, in the long narrative poem by Jeffers, *The Roan Stallion* (1925), gives herself to the horse-king which symbolizes pantheistic strength in contrast to the lethargy she sees around her. In *Pasiphaé*, the tragic poem by Henri de Montherlant (1938), the queen decides to fulfil her desire, not because she expects it to bring her happiness or pleasure, but because she considers it essential that she as queen should have the courage to perform an action that is censured by public opinion. The poem could be compared with the tragedy by Suarès, *Minos et Pasiphaé* (1913–38; published 1950): bearing the name Toro, the Minotaur is first of all the white bull and then its son, half man and half bull. The main interest of the play revolves around Pasiphae's all-consuming passion for this 'double' Toro and the jealousy of her daughters. From this it can be seen that, in the twentieth century, Pasiphae occupies a much more prominent position than has previously been allotted to her. To some extent, her myth has replaced that of Phaedra, who was still the subject of a work by d'Annunzio in 1909 and of Jeffers' *The Cretan Woman* (1954).

As for the Minotaur, it has ceased to be a repulsive figure and the first and possibly major discovery of the twentieth century in this respect, was that it was beautiful. The narrator in *Le Potomak* by Cocteau (1919 and 1939) refers to it as a 'pretty monster', while Fraigneau's 'Le point de vue du Minotaur' (1939) in *Cahiers du Sud* provides a very good illustration of this change of perspective. The Minotaur is handsome, it looks like Theseus and is perhaps in fact his reflection in the golden disk. It no longer kills its victims but overwhelms them in 'moving circumstances' and 'completes' them. After Theseus has caught up with it, it abandons the chase and allows itself to be taken for dead. There is much which leads us to believe that it was nothing other than the form assumed by Theseus when he entered the labyrinth. Similarly, in Gide's *Thésée* (1946), the narrator discovers that 'the monster was handsome'. In fact, since 1933 and the publication of the art review *Minotaure* by Skira, the Cretan monster has become a sort of symbol of the modern age, associated with the surrealist quest for 'tortuous beauty'. The front cover of the review has presented a series of representations of the monster by such artists as Picasso, Dali, Magritte and Rivera. Picasso undertook his amazing *Minotauromachy* (over 150 etchings in the 'Vollard Suite') to which he added various other pictures such as his *Minotaure et Jument devant une grotte* (1936). André Masson and Fabrizio Clerici have also dedicated extremely evocative works to the son of Pasiphae. It is possible to see an extension of this fascination in a very amusing play by Aymé, *Le Minotaure* (1967), in which a city dweller who misses country life, has a 'Minotaur' tractor installed in his sitting room. Some of his 'posh' friends misunderstand the reasons for the introduction of this decorative element and see it in terms of an aesthetic discovery of 'terrifying beauty'. Caught up in a general enthusiasm, the characters end up improvising a tragedy in Alexandrine verse on the theme of the Minotaur and Pasiphae in the best style of burlesque parody.

The Minotaur has also become the self-image that Theseus discovers as he descends into the labyrinth. In Yourcenar's *Qui n'a pas son Minotaure?* (1963), Theseus does not realize that he is in fact inside himself and that the familiar voices he hears are the expression of his various weaknesses and his overweening egoism. He is unable to recognize the Minotaur within himself with the result that, when the ordeal is over, he declares that the Minotaur was invisible and that he has no proof of the combat. In *Seduction of the Minotaur* by Anaïs Nin (1961), the narrator hopes to escape the labyrinth by leaving the United States. However, on arriving in Mexico, her childhood home, she realizes that instead of trying to escape it, she should explore it. She manages to overcome her fear of the Minotaur by discovering that it is the part of herself that she has refused to acknowledge. It will be noted that the figure of the Minotaur has by now become suffiently autonomous to represent the conquest of self by a woman as well as by a man.

The theme of personal identity sometimes assumes very complex historical and symbolic dimensions. In *Thésée* by Kazantzakis (1949), Minos I has created a world order by transforming the bull into the Minotaur, and it is now up to Theseus to fight the monster 'to allow the world to make a little more progress'. The combat frees the God imprisoned within the Beast and the doors of the labyrinth open to reveal Kouros, the Minotaur transformed into a man who is bigger, more handsome and more serene than Theseus. They depart together, leaving the old world behind them. In the short story by Borges, *La Casa de Asterion* (El Aleph, 1949), the ambiguity is taken to extremes. We are left wondering about the identity of the narrator who is describing his strange home as he waits for his 'redeemer'. Our suspicions that this is the labyrinth are gradually confirmed and the last sentence, in which Theseus takes over the narrative to tell Ariadne that the Minotaur offered virtually no resistance, puts paid to any doubts we may be entertaining. But it opens the way for even greater uncertainty. What does this redemption signify for Asterion, who had no idea that he was the Minotaur of the legend? What does the slaying of the Minotaur mean for Theseus, who had no idea that the creature which offered no resistance had possibly created 'the stars, the sun and the universe'? And lastly, what does the 'monstrous' experience of being imprisoned in the labyrinth of the text convey to us?

In the story by Borges, the Minotaur already appeared to offer no resistance to Theseus' fatal blow. In *Los Reyes* by Cortazar (1949), it is the victim of the despotic power of Minos as well as of another type of power represented by Theseus. When the latter catches up with it, the creature perceives that Ariadne has provided the thread in the hope that, when it has killed Theseus, the thread will enable it to escape from the labyrinth. Yet the Minotaur refuses to fight, because its freedom and fulfilment as a monster are inextricably linked with death. In a recent and successful novel by the Israeli writer, Binyamin Tammuz, *Minotaur* (1980, American translation 1982), the figure of the Minotaur is used to illustrate the complexities of history. The anonymous sender of passionate love letters to Théa is also a secret agent who eliminates the fiancé who is in his way. But the criminal is also a victim who is shot down in the café where he was finally about to meet Théa. As he dies, he remembers the etching (from the Vollard Suite by Picasso) which hung in his room as a child, and identifies with the destiny of the man with the bull's head towards whom a young woman is reaching down from an upper gallery, but is unable to touch him.

From a literary point of view, the Minotaur has experienced two major phases, one as the incarnation of horror and the other as illustrating the complexities of monstrosity. In the Greek and Latin Classical myth, the Minotaur was not the subject of an autonomous literary theme. It was either the monster slain by Theseus or conceived by Pasiphae. Its monstrosity left so little room for doubt that, during the Middle Ages, it sometimes appeared as a devil or a monster among many others, independently of its mythical background. During the Renaissance and neoclassical period, it was reinstated within the context of the Greek myth, but its role did not extend beyond that of providing a foil for Theseus. It was from the end of the nineteenth century onwards that the loathsome creature provided systematic food for thought rather than simply firing the imagination. The very particular circumstances of its conception, its monstrous nature, its relationship with the labyrinth and its slaying by Theseus became important points of reference as well as functional tools in the avant-garde mode of literary analysis. The shameful monster once more became the product of an unnatural love, but which this time had to be recognized and accepted. Through its association with desire, the hideous monster was found to be much less ugly than had originally been thought and was soon instrumental in developing the modern concept of beauty. When, in the very heart of the labyrinth and at the very moment of the confrontation, Theseus suddenly saw his own inverted image rise before him, represented by the Other, he had to acknowledge it and find a way of seeing it in a favourable light. It is impossible to destroy an image and impossible to kill the Minotaur. At the very most we can sacrifice it, in other words transform it, or else it 'completes' us. In conclusion, using a modern intellectual approach, the modern age has restored the monster to its former function of the pre-Hellenic era. It is, once again, a sacred monster.

André Peyronie

The Myth of Decadence

The myth of decadence can be considered from three different points of view, the metaphysical, the literary and the historical. These three viewpoints are distinct, but apply to the same underlying view of reality, which is primarily Western but also universal. The first relates to the roots of the myth, the second to its emergence in history, particularly during periods of crisis, and the third, to its expression in modernist European literature, in the form of the 'decadent imagination'.

The metaphysical approach makes it possible to talk in terms of cosmic cycles and ages of humankind. An example occurs in the *Vishnu Purana*, a mythical narrative that forms part of the story of cosmic Becoming and portrays the characteristics of the end of the present fourth cosmic cycle, the Kali-Yuga or dark age. Evola reproduces the most important passages in the 'Appendice sur l'âge obscur' at the end of his work *Révolte contre le Monde moderne*.

This description of Vishnu's role is linked to the *Kalki Purana*, which is somewhat reminiscent of the Christian apocalypse seen by John. This work first recalls the meaning of the four ages of the world, and then tells the apparently fictional story of Kalki, placing particular emphasis on the hero's fight against the demon embodying Kali Yuga. Kalki, who is Vishnu's last incarnation, reveals himself at the end of time: the god appears in the form of a warrior who travels the world on a white horse to help the just to survive the dark age, until the end of the present cosmic cycle. In fact, this is not an 'apocalyptic' text: Kalki appears to re-establish, in a very temporary way, a state of existence that was undermined as the fourth cosmic cycle unfolded. His attempts at restoration are short-lived and cannot halt the normal process of decline, for it is in no one's power – not even that of the gods – to alter the destiny of worlds.

This destiny manifests itself in human history, particularly in our own time, the end of the fourth cycle, whose accelerating pace can increasingly be felt.

The historical approach enables us to grasp the emergence of the myth in the course of the development of human civilization and has often been studied, notably in a recent work by Julien Freund called *La Décadence*. For the modern West, the historical paradigm of decadence is the myth of the fall of Athens and Rome, as Montesquieu realized in 1734. From the seventeenth century onwards, the Roman Empire was considered to be dead, as, for example, in the work of Saint-Evremond. The quarrel between the 'Ancients' and 'Moderns' made this fully apparent, aided by a sufficiently long historical perspective. La Bruyère expresses these feelings in a swan-song: 'Everything has been said . . .' Since that time, the end of Rome has continually haunted the Western imagination and the current of historical thought that nurtures the myth of decadence. For example, in England, at the end of the eighteenth century, Gibbon announced a new 'crisis of European awareness', at the dawn of Romanticism and of the 'European nihilism' condemned by Nietzsche.

In fact, the myth of decadence appeared in the West during successive and increasingly violent crisis. These were not only crises involving expansion, as has too often been thought on the basis of the smug illusion of universal expansion, particularly prevalent in the nineteenth century. They were also crises involving decline, which were imperceptible at first, but became increasingly apparent. These constitute the other facet of the ever more suicidal process of expansion, with its Promethean or Faustian nature. Thus, it can be argued that the Western myth of decadence corresponds to the period of a few centuries extending from the Renaissance to the current 'end of the Renaissance', to quote the title of a work by Julien Freund. After the end of the Middle Ages, the inhabitants of the West thought of themselves as being at the centre of the world. The modern humanist tendencies developed with the age of Enlightenment and triumphed with the growth of individualism, rationalism, universalism and scientific positivism. The result was 'the forgetting of Being' and the loss of 'tradition', in the sense in which René Guénon and Julius Evola understand the word.

Above all, it is clear that the myth of decadence is not an isolated myth: it belongs to modernist mythology. It is located within several highly complex networks of myths, linked to the idea of human time and the search for origins, development and metamorphosis. Thus the myth is connected to that of the Golden Age, the Fall, of paradise lost, of original humankind, of eternal recurrence, and so on. It is also linked to the very modern myths of the good savage and of exoticism; and can even, by constrast, be related to that of the barbarian, which became so widespread with the coming of Romanticism.

At the end of the twentieth century, in other words the end of both a century and a millenium, the myth of decadence is no longer a purely Western myth. It has taken on global dimensions, precisely reflecting the process of Westernization that has now reached every continent. The situation that this process has created is unprecedented in the known history of humankind and returns us to the theory of cosmic cycles mentioned above. It will doubtless give rise to new interpretations of the myth in the fields of art and literature, which we shall now examine in more detail.

An example of the literary myth of decadence – or 'decadism' or 'decadentism' to use the terms employed at the end of the nineteenth century – is provided by the legend, or mythical figure, of Heliogabalus, one of the 'mad emperors' who ruled Rome during its period of decline. In his work *Le Divine Héliogabale, César et Prêtre de Baal*, Roland Villeneuve recalls the little that is known about this adolescent emperor, whose contemporary relevance is quite clearly apparent 'at the time when the sciences known as occult, astrology and the so-called liberation from taboos on sexuality are exciting the imagination more than ever and leading minds astray'.

This extraordinary young ruler has always aroused strong passions: he has been greatly hated or admired because of his unorthodox life, which was as short as it was scandalous and is often presented in caricature. Thus, Lampride sees him as a monster who combines all the vices of his predecessors, such as Caligula and Nero. Leaving aside his debauchery and so-called orgies, he has chiefly been criticized for introducing an Eastern religion into Rome, that of Baal of Emesis, the Sun God of Syria. In fact, this adolescent, whose dissolute life has been condemned by history, was not a cruel prince; he was merely powerless to stop the growing disorder in the Empire.

Like the myth of decadence, the myth of Heliogabalus is a modern myth. Before the Romantic period the life of the young emperor seems to have been of interest only to the historians of ancient Rome (see Georges Duviquet 1903; preface by Remy de Gourmont). However, at the beginning of the nineteenth century, when history became 'the resurrection of the past', the life attributed to Heliogabalus provided material for colourful descriptions: the young emperor's 'erotic frenzies' and 'shadowy sensuality' coincide with the fantasies of de Sade, who actually mentioned him (see Chaussard 1802). When Chateaubriand describes Heliogabalus in his *Etudes historiques*, he seems fascinated by the romantic unleashing of passions and vices that accompanied this brief and tragic reign. Following the publication in Paris in 1836 of Samuel Bach's *Contes*, written by Théo de Ferrière, the figure of Heliogabalus was increasingly associated with a sense of decadence and became part of the literary tradition. He was at once the incarnation of the oriental despot and the Byronian poet. Gautier, who was one of the first to be fascinated by the decadence of Rome, speaks of Heliogabalus in his famous preface to *Mademoiselle de Maupin* and has him appear in the novel beside Caligula and Nero. He thus paves the 'Heliogabalic way' for Flaubert and Baudelaire, who Barbey d'Aurevilly regarded as an 'artificial Heliogabalus'.

In the 'fin de siècle' atmosphere of the late nineteenth century, the mythical figure of Heliogabalus appeared more and more frequently in French literature and in European literature in general, as the image of decadence in all its forms and in every domain was increasingly used to ambiguous effect. One could even speak of contemporary historical figures, such as the Comte de Montesquiou or Ludwig II of Bavaria, as being in the 'Heliogabalic' mould. We find Heliogabalus in the work of Verlaine (*Résignation*) while Mallarmé's Hérodiade has close affinities with him and des Esseintes makes mention of Elagabal in Joris-Karl Huysmans' *Against Nature*. The young emperor fascinated Octave Mirbeau, Maurice Barrès, Jean Lorrain and many minor French authors, such as Jean Lombard (*L'Agonie* 1901; with a preface by Octave Mirbeau). Outside France, the emperor's extraordinary figure was familiar to D'Annunzio (*Martyre de Saint Sébastien*) and Oscar Wilde. Meanwhile, Stefan

George made him the hero of his collection of poems called *Algabal*, dedicated to Ludwig II: he shows him intoxicated with beauty and youth, in his underworld realm gleaming with precious stones. More recently, Antonin Artaud continued the line of poets and novelists inspired by the extraordinary personality and tragic fate of this perverse adolescent emperor (Artaud 1934).

Thus the myth of the 'eccentric ephebe', a variation on the myth of decadence, continues to inspire poets in our era of crises and decline – but without ever becoming enslaved by the historical realities that surround us.

Claude Gerthoffert

The Myth of the Wandering Jew

The complex myth of the Wandering Jew combines disparate elements: the wandering is in relation to knowledge of heaven or destiny, is assimilated with the movement of human history itself or is linked to a punishment whose origins have been traced to the most ancient cosmic myths. This eternal traveller and supremely tragic figure is condemned to wander without rest until the Last Judgement; in him immortality on earth paradoxically appears as the most terrible punishment that can strike a human being, since it excludes him from all human affection and obliges him to watch everything around him die, disappear and be reborn. This drama leaves its imprint on the imagination because it covers the whole of human time and space. It is not therefore surprising that the traditional scenes bequeathed to us by the seventeenth century represent alternately the anxious restlessness of one who crosses seas and continents without ever stopping and the immobility of the venerable old man surrounded by citizens pressing him with questions. The contrast between these two situations shows the profound tension of the legend of the Wandering Jew at the pictorial level, for this narrative, to which episodes have been added in each period, to the point where the original pious legend has been profoundly transformed, is woven between two images of maximum rest and movement.

Human time is spatialized and dramatized via this foreigner's footsteps in a dynamic, repetitive structure manifested in the different attributes given to the hero: for the German poets, he became 'the eternal Jew', for the English, 'the Wandering Jew' and for the Spanish 'the Jew who is waiting for God', so no specific epithet can define his travels or their meaning. It is in the context of this oscillation that we must seek the fundamental core of a figure who stands at the crossroads of ethical and religious sensibilities and whose very flexibility perhaps explains his extraordinary literary vitality.

We can identify two great periods in the artistic development of the original scenario. The first, linked to a context of religious, political and social ferment, combines several traditions and encouraged the spread from East to West of a story contaminated by both biblical and profane legends and myths (the phoenix, Pages, Ogier the Dane, Sameri). At this time the hero's wandering acquired an allegorical meaning, insofar as it revealed a desire to explain the human condition. Then in the eighteenth century the earlier additions were used in art and the legend was weighted with diverse symbolism which changed the nature of the wanderings from allegorical to problematic, without abandoning the traditional source.

The first writers of the Romantic period gave the decisive impetus to the mythical potential of this magical story, which remains vital in the imagination today.

A RECENT PREHISTORY

Originally we find not a primitive legend but the diffuse image of a witness of the passion of Christ who, having survived the drama of Calvary, wanders all over the world. To the extent that an oral tradition can be reconstructed (Gaston Paris, *Le Juif Errant* 1881), the popular imagination seems to have worked on two disciples, John and Judas, and developed the divergent tradition of a survivor condemned either to wander for having slapped Christ in the face, or to wait, heralding by his waiting the final coming of the Lord at the end of time.

In the thirteenth century an English chronicle fixed these traditions: in his *Chronica Majora* (1259), Matthew Paris, a Benedictine monk of the Abbey of St Albans, records the words of an Armenian bishop who came to visit the abbey in 1258 and said that in the East there was a man called Cartaphilus who had been present at the Passion. He was supposed to have pushed Christ back on to the road to Calvary, shouting 'Go on! Go on!' and was thus in turn condemned to wait for Christ's coming until the end of time. Every hundred years he returned to the age he was when this incident occurred and could thus no longer lose his life, for he had lost his death. This character, who is an 'argument for the Christian faith', is primarily required by a theological discourse containing two essential motifs: the insult to God and an indefinite wait. This is the first stage of a story linked to the Crusades, which gives immortality on earth an edifying meaning of repentance and resignation.

The myth's prehistory is thus connected to the pilgrims' travellers' tales. Throughout north-western Europe the image of this figure was taken up by clerics and storytellers, who multiplied the number of names given to the hero. Morpurgo, in *Il Ebreo errante in Italia* (1891), records the words of Antonio di Francesco di Andrea, who said that he had met someone called Giovanni Buttadeo around 1450: could this be the man who 'struck' God, or the one who, for the Spanish of the same period, was 'waiting' for God, Juan de Espera en Dios? When questioned about his identity, the mysterious traveller did not reply; he thus acquired a truly magical prestige due to the compensatory gifts of his punishment: people were as interested in his longevity as they were in his curse. But while linked to the history of the Christian West, his message became increasingly composite as he was integrated into the history of the time.

A second stage was reached when the story reappeared in Germany at the time of the Reformation, at the end of the sixteenth century. An anonymous letter-writer states that in 1552 in a Hamburg church he saw an old man, of the Jewish race this time, a cobber by trade with a family, who said he was condemned to walk until the end of time under the new name of Ahsverus, to 'serve as a living witness against the Jews and the unbelievers'. This short tale, which was published in Leiden in 1602 and paraphrased throughout Europe, generated the popular poetry of the Laments and Ballads around its dark hero, singing of the accursed traveller's distress. The third stage in the legend's development is marked by the Brabantine Ballad of 1774, which renamed the Wandering Jew Isaac Laquedem and told of his passing through Brussels in moving verses: 'Est-il rien sur terre, / Qui soit plus surprenant / Que la grande misère / Du pauvre Juif errant?' ('Is there anything on earth more surprising than the great misfortune of the poor wandering Jew?'). During the seventeenth and eighteenth centuries there was a vogue for 'admirable stories' relating the hero's appearances more or less everywhere: dressed in a great coat and supplied with a few coins and a stick, the wandering Jew cannot stop more than three days, the period between Christ's Passion and the Resurrection; he speaks every language and knows the history of past centuries.

In 1668 Martin Dröscher distinguished two kinds of Wandering Jew in his *Dissertation théologique au sujet de deux témoins* and at this time up to twenty-two meanings attributed to his eternal wanderings were listed. The eighteenth century thus inherited a familiar but complex and disparate image. Nevertheless one can already make out two tendencies in the artistic treatment of the legend in Europe:

1 to the extent that the narrative covers the entire human history of the Christian era, it offers an all-inclusive structure which was given an epic dimension by the new philosophies of history;
2 in the Ballads the Wandering Jew expresses nostalgia, loneliness and insecurity which transform his didactic profile as a penitent chronicler and which were to be appropriated by early Romanticism, which abandoned the original aspects of punishment.

So here is a legendary hero who, enriched at the psychological and ideological levels, offers features conducive to the development of a specific myth insofar as he embodies certain fundamental questions: a man insults a God and is tragically condemned to wait or to walk until the end of time. Can the very nature of the sentence generate a dramatic narrative? What is the wrong he is expiating? The second version of the story already said that Ahasverus sinned through ignorance, but, whether through religious or racial antisemitism, the hero seems to incarnate absolute evil in himself. Lastly the fiction of the survivor is contrasted with real human history: the theological argument of the exemplary journey inspired by a transcendental revelation thus confronts the mobility of human history which the Wandering Jew constantly recalls through his gifts of longevity, ubiquity and omniscience; he was thus already linked to the Wild Hunter of German legend, or to the Flying Dutchman.

The fable of the Wanderineg Jew, who is valued for the human and theological duality of his story, is as fascinating as what he has to say: he is a part of both popular culture, in which there is identification with the condemned man, and learned culture. Indeed every author can see him as the representative of an ideology or a controversy.

A DECISIVE CHANGE IN THE IMAGE: THE LATE EIGHTEENTH CENTURY

The 'admirable stories' fragmented the legend into so-called historical episodes, so that the explanatory sense of the allegory was relegated to a secondary level, but the two elements that constitute the myth – the eternity of dead time and wandering linked to movement – each surface without excluding the other. At the end of the century of the Enlightenment several factors encouraged the development of the legend's meaning: the return to national legends advocated by Vico and Herder, the influence of the English gothic novel and the German poetry of *Sturm und Drang* all exalted the language of emotion and of the heart and individualized the character. The illuminist current, which prophesied a new syncretism, gave the survivor visionary power. In addition, the hero was provided with a mythical lineage by comparing him with Cain, the first fratricide. Rejected like the latter, the Wandering Jew also became subject to universalization through an internalization of the rebellion against an arbitrary power by the individual who is a prisoner to his own passions. Ahasverus' wanderings suggested to writers a dramatic canvas on which they could symbolize the condition of all human beings faced with space and time who, if they abandon themselves to their inner demons, can turn their curse into redemption.

During the nineteenth century, under the influence of post-Romantic nihilism and independent of historical Judaism, interest grew in the philosophical and religious problems set out in the myth. Thus the foreigner 'Cartaphilus', 'Ahasverus' or 'Isaac Laquedem' increasingly came to symbolize all marginal life, whether that of an individual or a group. There was a shift from a character incarnating a negative value in the drama of the Passion to the mythical ambiguity of a story which is a source of both fear and consolation because it suggests the rootlessness of humankind split between doubt and the thirst for life. It is thus with early Romanticism that three essential orientations in the symbolism of the 'New Ahasverus' appear, unveiling primordial images of vision, rebellion and salvation.

THE WANDERING JEW'S VISIONS

Many visionaries appeared at the end of the eighteenth century, including the Comte de Saint-Germain, which may partially explain the new powers attributed to the strange traveller. In the guise of the Mysterious Armenian of Schiller's *Der Geisterseher* (1786), the Wandering Jew incarnates the occult force of remorse, escaping all definition: 'He is in no way what he seems. He has worn the mask and costume of all states and all conditions'. The fantasy imagery of the ghost thus brings in a mysticism of horror which adds to the penitent's theological or moral didacticism the ambiguity of the phantom on whom an evil spell has been cast or who has come to right wrongs.

In Lewis' *The Monk* (1796), the episode of the nun of Lindenberg mentions the blood pact: a new sign appears on the Wandering Jew's forehead, that of the Fiery Cross, suggesting the mythical dualism of the damned soul who can yet be saved. In 1805 in *The Saragossa Manuscript*, Jan Potocki continues Cazotte's fairy tales and heralds Hoffmann's *Die Elixire des Teufels*. By means of the Wandering Jew, the plot of the novel goes back down the ages and the hero disturbs the rational order which has been so painfully acquired like a tenacious regret. So what does this kind of living dream reveal when he thus evokes the invisible in the magical or parodic mode? A certain number of personal preoccupations, illustrating the theme of the double, the ungraspable reflection of the self, which was dear to the German poets. But in parallel to the current that grew out of the English gothic novel, the hero personifies the Romantic feeling of the incompleteness of destiny. We see this in the case of Bonaventure in *The Nightwatchers* (1804) and later in that of the poet Amiel, who appropriates 'the instinct of the Wandering Jew' in his *Journal* (1865); collective fears concerning the future of nations are also reflected in the omniscient old man of the new chroniclers. In Alexandre Dumas père's unfinished novel *Isaac Laquedem* (1853), the hero enacts a kind of universal quest for the absolute which takes him on an initiatory journey to the centre of the earth.

Thus in his essence and in his journey, this 'devourer of time and space' (Mario Proth, *Les Vagabonds* 1859) makes dual human reality sacred; in the form of the journal, the epistolary novel or the chronicle he can restore the time of humiliated individuals like Croly's *Salathiel* (1926). His migrations certainly accustomed him to being the world's memory and thus there developed what were sometimes interminable narratives that fragmented the myth of the Wandering Jew into a collection of national emblems, such as H. A. O. Richard, *Der ewige Jude* (1785) and David Hoffmann's *Chronicles of Cartaphilus, the Wandering Jew* (1853–4).

The tendency to portray the hero reviewing history persisted in a trivial mode in the twentieth century. The decadent period created a companion for the Wandering Jew, Herodias or Salome, and the story *My First Two Thousand Years* (1928) provided a pretext for an indulgent erotic review penned by the writers Viereck and Eldridge.

Seen as the thread of human history, often placed in narratives between past and future, at the end of the nineteenth century this figure also took on the picturesque role of the questing hero, the terrifying preacher, a living exhortation of ungraspable time, as portrayed in Paul Féval's popular novel *La Fille du Juif Errant* (1878). In Meyrink's novel *Das grüne Gesicht* (1916) he seems, like the Golem, to incarnate the force of the spirit that guides human beings through historical catastrophes towards the truth: he bears on his forehead a mysterious sign which, unlike that of Lewis' damned hero, symbolizes a vision of truth and makes the First World War seem like a bad dream.

THE WANDERING JEW'S REBELLIONS

By questioning the origins of evil, Ahasverus also takes up part of Prometheus' challenge. Convinced in his despair, or demystifying it himself, the Romantic hero incarnates a myth of rebellion through the inversion of the legend's basic schema. Comparison with Cain makes him a rebel against the Father and gives him the elements necessary for a challenge to a vengeful god: a sinner accuses God by denying the validity of punishment and thus changes the theme of exemplary wandering into one of liberation. In this 'new Ahasverus', the human image is spiritualized to symbolize the progress of a soul who brings about his own salvation through his scepticism.

With its publication in 1786, the lyrical rhapsody of the poet Schubart, *Der ewige Jude* allusively challenges the Crucifixion; at the end of a series of frenetic tableaux, the Angel of Death arrives and promises Ahasver rest. Shelley knew this poem in 1809; he definitively inverts the elements of the legend in *The Wandering Jew's Soliloquy* (1812) and above all in his philosophical poem *Queen Mab* (1813). Like Prometheus, Ahasverus reinterprets the original scene and denounces 'divine injustice'. From this point of view, the cross on the damned man's forehead symbolizes the violence with which human beings are oppressed. The English poet thus prepares a canvas on which his whole century will elaborate: the phantom portrait of wandering human thought, for Mosen Ahasverus embodies the Angel of Doubt. In his poem *Ahasver* (1838) he contrasts this shadowy power with that of the luminous Christ in terms of a primordial antagonism on which, he says, the fate of humankind depends. For the Danish storyteller Andersen (*Ahasverus*, 1844) the hero is a modern sceptic who manifests the ambivalence of the punishment, since he incarnates the abstract notion of human progress. In Fischer's short poem *Der ewige Jude* (1854), the hero's struggle symbolizes that of humankind, long before the coming of Christ, a struggle which would have overturned heaven itself, if the hero had not converted at the end of the poem.

Thus the eternal wandering stages the original experience of a mythical conflict between Creator and creature and the rise of nihilist philosophies reinforces that structure. Richepin's Ahasverus in *Les Blasphèmes* (1884), who has no more limits or ties, laughs at a punishment which simply confirms him in his doubt and hatred; the allegorical dimension of the penitent is taken away in favour of a broader symbol, since the stranger merges with the 'uncountable proletarian' and sides with human beings and their despairs. The theme of the ever possible exchange between love and hate is strangely treated in the narrative of *Christus und Wanderer* (1918) by Palsen, when at the end of the dialogue Ahasverus dies on the cross while Christ sets off on the road. Ahasverus' atheism caught Trenck's attention in the epic poem which contrasts him with Don Juan, *Don Juan-Ahasver* (1930); for him the hero incarnates the sufferings of all the wanderers of the earth. But Pär Lagerkvist brings the most contemporary tone to the Wanderer's rebellion in *Ahasverus Död* (1960); the novelist presents an Ahasverus who, on his death-bed, having rejected God who was guilty of abandoning Christ, accepts the existence of something that we all vainly seek, and thus expresses one of the legend's mythical potentialities: the traveller is the man who can never find a satisfying explanation for his route.

Compared to other mythical rebellions such as those of Don Juan or Faust, the Wandering Jew, whether he is a central or secondary figure in these epic fragments, universalizes the image of human consciousness; by bringing the speech of a rebellious individual or group up to date, he reflects, with Sisyphus (Isi Collin, *Sisyphe et le Juif Errant* 1914), a mystery of the human being which is erected on the apparent failure of a revealed mystery.

This symbolism is however countered by the moralizing hero of satire and melodrama, similar to Goethe's incredulous chronicler in *Ewige Juden erstes Fetzen* (1774–5), who acts as an allegorical hold-all. The very excess of Romantic symbolism generated a demystificatory parody of the Wandering Jew's despair in the boulevard theatre of France. Writers are still using their irony on a characater who too fully embodies life's extreme aspects: youth and old age, joy and sorrow; thus F. Werfel's play *Jacobowsky und der Oberst*, published in Stockholm in 1944, was very successful on the New York stage in the same year.

THE SALVATION OF THE WANDERING JEW

The passive image of eternal wandering, profoundly changed as we have seen by the development of a myth of rebellion, was also updated under the influence of Romantic religious disquiet and, particularly in France, by the effects of the theories of Fourier and Saint-Simon. Popularized as the hero of a myth of salvation, Ahasverus synthesizes human history and a divine or messianic revelation within himself. In this new story the Wandering Jew redeems himself by making his suffering the impetus for inner progress or for the progress of nations, following the implicit structure of redemption myths: one rids oneself of evil and loads it onto someone else. In acquiring all the ignominious marks of the heirs of Cain and singing of the torments of a pointless journey, as in Schlegel's poem *Die Warnung* (1802), or in Béranger's song *Le Juif Errant* (1831), the legendary wreck of time became in this period the emblem of proscribed peoples, Jews or oppressed masses exposed to destitution. The hero was increasingly identified with contemporary Jewish figures, for example in Auerbach's *Spinoza* (1837), and for Constant in 1846 he also embodied the poor, those Wandering Jews of modern civilization. In that sense the success of Eugène Sue's serialized novel *Le Juif Errant* (1844–5) tells us much about the new popularity of this great shadow protecting humankind's forward march.

Often, for German poets such as Brentano and Görres, the Wandering Jew symbolizes the person who saves and mediates love, so that his wandering combines the motifs of forgiveness and marriage. He appears thus in drama, with Arnim's *Halle und Jerusalem* (1809–10) and in Grenier's religious epic *La Mort du Juif Errant* (1857). The eternal traveller, transformed into a figure of light, can herald the coming of new times and, through his own death, proclaim a spiritual victory over sin. Edgar Quinet's epic *Ahasverus* (1833) gives the character a messianic role which makes him choose life, since the theme of the journey crystallizes all the period's aspirations towards regeneration through and in time. Thus the totalizing structure of eternity on earth becomes the epic substance with which human time is made sacred: Ahasverus' different actions down the ages make present the link between the most varied symbols of salvation. In 1867 in *Les Quatre Incarnations du Christ*, the Belgian poet Van Hasselt heralded a social genesis in which all mythologies are synthesized in terms of an epic of human progress: in this dynamic orientation the 'new Ahasverus' can break his traveller's stick. History had condemned the Wandering Jew to live, history redeems him by making him die, for what dies with him is a past of human error and blindness, while on his forehead shine the promises of the universal future. The poetry of the eternal journey is a metaphor for a new conception of history: the religion of the future makes the time of error die with him, transfiguring human destiny. Here lies the legend's most obvious modernism, its most fragile modernism too, insofar as it does not seem to have survived the various contemporary examples of genocide.

The image of Ahasverus the eternal wanderer produced no mythical narratives of the highest order but a great number of secondary works. This has been seen as a weakness of the 'story' on the mythical level by some, such as the nineteenth-century commentator the Comte de Douhet who, in the *Dictionnaire des Légendes du Christianisme* (1855), noted the complexity and increasing strangeness of a character who has 'several incompatible stories'. In 1906 Theodor Kappstein in *Ahasver in der Weltpoesie* gave up the search for any unity to the Wandering Jew's odysseys. And yet this complexity itself bears witness to the poetic richness of the eternal journey, which, following the Sphinx, has taken on the weight of the human riddle. In his Romantic metamorphoses, the character of Ahasverus, a ghost-portrait of rebellion against an unchangeable order, mouthpiece and some would say portmanteau for mystical or humanitarian doctrines, impostor or superman, bears witness to the dominance of a didactic discourse which sometimes threatens the mysterious traveller's ambiguity. This may explain the difficulty writers have in transposing a religious legend into the poetic domain. In comparison to

Prometheus or Faust, Ahasverus is eclipsed. However the plenitude and finitude of human life is continually recognizable in the very diversity of his meanings. He is a figure of both wandering and conquest, staging Jacob's fight with the angel and that of human beings with Christ or with themselves. He is the mythical place of synthesis between past and future, between the Christian motifs of the wood or the road to the cross and the magical images inherited from Antiquity, who still, despite a relative artistic decline, expresses a human thirst for deliverance from sterile time, made poetic in images of flux and instability. At the same time, since the nineteenth century we have witnessed an apotheosis of the hero, who has changed from anti-saint into the prophet and reflection of humankind, and the demystification of a legend with too vast and empty a setting. That legend developed on the basis of what was said about him. From the nineteenth century onwards, it is he who tells his own fable, giving the answer of a man faced with the riddle of time. Whether his words are of life or of death, they can expose the conflicts that they imply. This indefinable man, the stranger we are to ourselves, who has been dechristianized by rationalist philosophies or transfigured by the religion of the future, has become for many the living discourse of humankind, constantly caught between nothingness and creation: his wanderings sum up individual or collective answers to the dramatic confrontation between mortal time and the thirst for eternity.

Marie-France Rouart

A Mythical Bestiary

It is not easy to define the limits of a mythical bestiary and, even once these have been established, not all the creatures included can be regarded as being of the same importance. This is all the more true in the present case, since there is the added complication of their treatment in literature.

First of all, the animal may form the actual subject of a myth (whether etiological or otherwise), of which the entire main theme is taken in literature. This may be done either in an 'emergent' manner or by making use of its 'flexibility' (Brunel), in other words, by restricting significant changes to the non-essential aspects of the story. In the latter case literature is able to 'rehabilitate' the animal by adopting a syntagmatic approach to the myth. This applies to the story of the Minotaur, for example, if we consider it as a mechanism involving a monster (half animal, half human), a periodic devourer of human flesh (youths and maidens) and a labyrinth (in Crete). This chain of components can be said to constitute the 'syntagma of the Minotaur', the peripheral elements of which could be excluded without any detrimental effect.

Again, if the monster can sometimes serve metonymically to recall the complete myth by its mere presence, it can also be used in literature purely as a syntagmatic element completely dissociated from the original sequence. In this case, there is a movement from the myth of the animal to the mythical animal, in other words, a movement from the myth, in the strictest sense of the word, to the archetype itself. In terms of the present example, the animal is no longer considered as a Minotaur in the context of the myth that bears its name, but evokes more general images that divert attention from the myth itself – in this case, towards the symbolism of the bull, the monster and even the labyrinth.

This leads on to a second type of example, that of the animal incorporated into a myth of which it is not the subject but in which it plays an active part (though it may also be the subject of another myth). In this case, the animal is used to embody an accumulation of mythical functions that vertically intercept the literary continuum. It is in this context that the bee appears as the nurse of Zeus, the companion of Apollo, the Tear of Ra, the messenger of the Gods, a desirable woman, etc.

Finally, in a third type of example, the animal occurs as the interpreter of esoteric mysteries or as the attribute of a god. Although it is not necessarily mythical, this does not mean that it is reduced simply to the status of a symbol. The reason why the goat can be considered as a mythical creature is not because it belongs to the retinue of Dionysus, but because its form sometimes adopted by the god and because, for example, it constitutes part of the monstrous composite figure of the satyr. It should be noted that this alone is not sufficient to secure the inclusion of the goat and the satyr in the present survey; it covers only those mythical creatures that have enjoyed a rich literary career.

As we shall see, the myth of the animal, the mythical animal and the mythical animal in literature are not necessarily equivalent ways of referring to the same thing. The mythical animal in literature may originate from either or both of the first two categories.

Finally, in compiling this very specific bestiary an effort has been made to identify the original myth or group of myths relating to each animal, before considering their adaptation in literature. For this reason, a number of mythical animals has been omitted, either because the original myths associated with them are obscure or untraceable, or because the literary use of the animal concerned has proved to amount only to irrelevant 'embellishment'.

THE ASS

The ass's ears bestowed on King Midas by Apollo symbolize his pursuit of the sensual rather than the spiritual. Meanwhile, this image is reiterated and extended by the figure of the Dionysian ass which creates an impression of lewdness and vulgarity verging on the absurd. However, the title *onos* (ass) reserved for followers of Dionysus who had attained a certain level of initiation, appears to identify the animal with an initiatory stage associated with a transient state of bestiality.

In *Convivio* (I. 7. 4), Dante stressed the first image of the animal, stating that: '. . . he who puts reason aside and employs only the senses, lives not as a man but as a beast: he lives as an Ass'. And later, La Fontaine developed this unflattering picture, emphasizing the ass's stupidity in 'The Donkey Loaded with Sponges' and 'The Donkey Who was Carrying Holy Relics', its egoism in 'The Donkey and the Little Dog' and 'The Old Man and the Donkey', and its hypocrisy in 'The Donkey Clothed in the Lion's Hide'. In contrast, the pseudo-Lucian's *Lucius or the Ass* and Apuleius's *The Golden Ass* showed the extent to which bestiality could be regarded as a stage in achieving a better understanding of spirituality. The two authors drew their inspiration from the same unidentified source, and in both stories Lucius has to eat roses in order to recover his original state. This enables him to move towards a better understanding of life, after having indulged in a monstrous form of love. Although Apuleius lays considerable emphasis on the unnatural union (X. 22), this is to provide a contrast with the appearance of the lovely moon goddess, who tells Lucius what the next stage in his adventure will be. His return to human form is signalled by the reappearance of a sense of modesty (XI. 14), safeguarded by a garland of mystical roses, and is the first step towards the worship of Isis.

Partly inspired by the classical story, Machiavelli produced his own version of *The Golden Ass, L'Asino d'Oro*, in which the poet, in the form of an ass, is able to venture on a sort of descent into the underworld that teaches him about the human condition. Shakespeare continued the tradition by making Titania fall in love with Bottom the Weaver, who had an ass's head, and even took up the motif of the crown of roses eaten by Lucius, although only to use it derisively: 'Titania: Come, sit thee down upon this flowery bed, While I . . . stick musk-roses in thy sleek smooth head . . .' (*A Midsummer Night's Dream* act IV. Scene 1).

The temporary madness that magically affects most of the characters in Shakespeare's play is linked not only to the Feast of Saint John and the moon, but also to the ass, which has the place of honour at the Feast of Fools, thereby reviving the animal's initiatory role.

It is probably this dual aspect of abandonment to the pleasures of the flesh and of victory over the powers of darkness that is stressed in Rimbaud's version of *Bottom*:

> Everything became a dark, burning pool. In the morning – the dawn of fiery June – I ran into the fields, an ass, braying and brandishing my grievance . . .

THE BEE

For the Hittites, the bee is the queen of the gods, for the Guarani, it is the mother of the gods, and for the Bushmen, it is the wife of the god of the dead. In addition, it is the Tear of Ra, the companion of Apollo and the nurse of Zeus and of the men of the Golden Age. It is the dispenser of a fundamental form of nourishment that is both primordial and initiatory, and that opens the way for the truth of the Word. This is stressed in Ecclesiastes (24. 19–20), Revelation (10. 8–10) and Ezekiel (3. 163), as well as in the *Rigveda* (4. 58), the *Atharvaveda* (8. 7) and the *Koran* (Sura XVI. 70–1). Eating this food gives a person 'a honeyed tongue', in other words, the ability to express purity and wisdom, which explains the connection made by Origen between honey and the manna referred to in Exodus (16. 31).

It was probably this sacred image that Saint-John Perse had in mind in four separate references to the bee. After introducing it for the first time in *Neiges* (III) in the form of 'the divine bee', he referred to 'the wild bee of the desert' in *Vents* (I. 3) and to 'the tiny bee of the desert' in *Chronique* (III), before remarking in *Chanté par celle qui fut là*: 'To the satirical tracts of History is added the bee of the desert'. It is not only the creature's miraculous ability to extract its essential and highly concentrated supply of food from an apparently sterile enivronment that is being evoked, but also the insect's role as an interpreter of esoteric mysteries. The same poet makes a mythical association between this function and the Word: 'the bee of language is on their brow' (*Vents* IV. 4). Meanwhile, in 'la Rose publique', Eluard creates a more extreme version of the image by inverting it: 'I have spoken of the "glue" of the desert and the desert is a bee' (*Bonne et mauvaise langue*).

The image of the bee seeking the flower was already used as a mythical metaphor for the search for the divine in the *Atharvaveda* (I. 34), and the same symbolism was employed by Hugo in *Quatre-Vingt-Treize* (III. chapter III): 'Nothing resembles the soul more closely than a bee which goes from flower to flower gathering honey, as the soul goes from star to star gathering light.' Meanwhile, Bonnefoy used the bee in a similar way, to clarify the perception of the divine:

> (. . . and all this sound
> of bees of impure and sweet eternity
> on the nearby meadow which is burning still.)
>
> ('L'Abeille, la Couleur', *Pierre écrite*.)

However, the pagan image of the bee that witnessed the love of Aphrodite and Anchises had an equally rich literary career. In an eclogue, Theocritus used it as a phallic symbol by establishing a daring association between the nectar-gathering bee and the sexual act: 'Would that I could become the bumblebee and enter your cavity through the ivy and ferns that envelop you.' The theme is echoed by Ronsard in *Amours de Marie* (II. 38). In Valéry's poem 'L'Abeille' (*Charmes*), the image of the sexual union desired by the beauty, or by the lover who watches her sleep, retains its ambiguity through the figure of the bee whose sting will arouse physical desire . . . or the sleeper herself.

Finally, there is the bee as a symbol of the erotic in the true sense of the word – the bee that bears Apollo's shrine of feathers and wax, whose sting is a reminder of divine power and whose honey a reminder of divine compassion. This is the aggressive bee of the Amorites (Deuteronomy 1. 44) and of Yahweh (Isaiah 7. 18). Meanwhile, the sting of the Bee-God reappeared in Dante's *Paradiso* (XXVIII and XXXIII) and in Verlaine's *Sagesse* (II, IV and V). In its role as initiator, the bee also plays an important part in 'Peuple du Ciel' (*Mondo et Autres Histoires*), a short story by Le Clézio in which a little girl, significantly named Petite Croix (Little Cross), is visited every day by bees. They settle on her and she talks to them, until one day she is stung and begins to experience an ineffable communion with heavenly light.

The bee's sting is a gift, which is all the more altruistic because the bee itself dies after inflicting it. This is what Bataille is referring to in his essay 'Erotisme' when he discusses the extraordinary link between love and death, illustrated even more graphically by the fate of the drone that dies after coupling with the queen. He maintains that, for a religious person facing temptation, the insect's coupling represents access to divine life through death itself, as well as moral death through abandonment to sexuality.

The altruistic aggressiveness of the insect is also represented in a nightmarish context. Thus the punishment that it inflicts assumes the proportions of a biblical scourge in Arthur Herzog's *The Swarm* featuring a glass technological marvel that is the antithesis of a real bee. This artificial creature does not offer an alternative and equally metaphysical form of wisdom, based on acceptance of a perfect match between the real and the imaginary that makes it possible to believe that we are guaranteed security in some overall 'plan' (compare Ernst Jünger).

THE BEETLE

The Egyptian *Book of the Dead*, the Chinese *Treatise of the Golden Flower* and later works on the hermetic arts, all connect the beetle with the moving or developing world, as well as with life after death and the passage from this world to the next. Associated with the course of the sun, the Zodiac (in which it sometimes replaces Scorpio), the lotus flower and the chemical symbol of Mercury, it is inevitably seen as the keeper of eternity (the ancient Jupiter-Scarabaeus referred to by Quinet in his *Création* and by Rilke in his *Neue Gedichte*) and as the Dispenser of Justice.

It is to this body of wisdom that Le Clézio is alluding when he refers to the Egyptian beetle of the god Khepera in *Mondo et autres Histoires*. Meanwhile in *Hazaran* the beetle teaches Petite Trèfle the answers that she must give to a stranger so that she can go with him to a fabulous land. Here, the role of guide of the dead has been transformed into the role of initiator into the ultimate mystery.

The funerary theme of the ancient beetle was used in a distorted form by Poe. The beetle in *The Gold Bug* represents a stylized death's head and, when passed through the eye socket of a human skull on the end of a piece of string, it indicates the whereabouts of the treasure. (The author has his tongue in his cheek, as the servant in the story is called . . . Jupiter.) The distortion of the beetle's mythical role lies in the fact that here it assists in the discovery of earthly treasure and not in the attainment of peace in the other world.

The theme of the beetle's ability to be extremely inflexible and even obstinately cruel in its administration of justice, first appeared in Aesop's Fables and later in those of La Fontaine. Both writers stress the inescapability of the beetle's vengeance, which renders vain all attempts by the eagle to reproduce ('The Eagle and the Beetle', II. VIII). Meanwhile Lautréamont portrays a beetle of truly monstrous proportions exacting a horrible punishment specially devised for the woman who has deceived it in love. She is reduced to a ball of flesh and is constantly rolled along like 'excremental matter'. Only the beetle – like Maldoror, and unlike the three other lovers, who were also transformed – seems to hold the secret of the Enigma. That is unless the beetle itself is the victim of the ultimate illusion and clings to its vengeance as if it were the only possible reason for living. If so, the automatic nature of its rebellion against the Female Magician (Eve?) reveals a desire to lay claim to a 'world down below' that turns out to be coherent after all (*Les Chants de Maldoror* V. 2).

This calls to mind another macabre metamorphosis that is at times 'beetle-like': that of Gregor in the short story by Kafka. The story describes another pointless rebellion, since the series of transformations that finally lead to dehydration and death do not release Gregor from his responsibilities but merely render him totally inadequate in relation to the world and its most elementary rules.

This 'terrible imagery of an ethic of lucidity' (Camus) is reinforced by Orwell's *Nineteen Eighty Four*, a futuristic story in which we witness the gradual (and metaphorical) transformation of the central character, Winston, into a beetle. Realization, rebellion and the final and complete acceptance of a truth other than the truth of logic are the three stages that the hero must pass through to be able to purge himself and become an empty human shell that society can fill with its own values so that it can function perfectly. Indeed, society functions so perfectly that it even denies the concept of death by incorporating each human cell that it creates in this way into the huge social body.

More recently, Lispector has also echoed this theme of the initiatory beetle, exploring it in a complementary and, at first sight, contradictory manner in *a Paixao sequndo G.H.* Here, the narrator is contemplating a cockroach that she has just tried to kill. When it is completely empty, and she has completely identified with it as a fragment of the pure present that she refers to as 'the Neutral' to the point of lifting part of its entrails to her mouth, she notices that the cockroach has turned into a beetle:

> The only destiny for which we are born is to serve the ritual [of life] . . . we should have put on ritual masks to make love. Beetles are born with the mask with which they will complete their destiny. We have lost our masks because of our original sin. I looked: the cockroach had turned into a beetle. It was nothing other than its own mask.
>
> (chapter 19)

Thus Man plays at being a beetle in an attempt to avert his destiny, to grasp the tragedy of it or to escape it by becoming part of a mechanism that is more vast than his own individual self.

It is probably this 'beetle complex' that gives rise to the frantic need to achieve a change of form and so gain control of a universe that is also portrayed in the works of Le Clézio:

> Then you reach the centre, the very depths of darkness. And you begin to vibrate, as if you had rasps and elytra and were emitting the sound that replaces sight.
>
> (*L'Inconnu sur la Terre*: 163)

This absurd monster, the beetle-cockroach, has featured prominently in two even more recent short stories, 'Le Cafard' ('The Cockroach') by Blagojevic and *Vouloir être insecte* by Amprimoz. In the first, without even killing an insect, a woman joins the insect world so that she can incorporate herself into its life in the way that G.H. does: 'I am the neutral body of a cockroach, with a life which ultimately does not escape me, because I can see it going on outside me' (*a Paixao sequndo G.H.*. chapter 8.). Meanwhile the second story expresses the same preoccupation with inner suicide as a response to the absurd: finding peace means losing one's identity in a continual changing of masks (*Vouloir être insecte*).

THE BULL

As a symbol of vital energy, reproductive power and the earthly revelation of a divine reality, in the Vedaic, Egyptian and Greek tradition the bull constitutes amongst other things a striking representation of the source of life-blood. The most significant illustration of this is furnished by the *taurobolium*, a rite introduced into Italy from Asia Minor at the beginning of the Christian era. During this ritual the warm blood of a bull that had just had its throat cut was poured over an initiate standing in a trench, to ensure his or her rebirth into eternal life.

In his *Aethiopica* (28–30), Heliodorus recalls that the bull was the royal animal sacrificed to the moon, just as the white horse was sacrificed to the sun; while Dante used its mythical power in developing a maxim on blindness (*Paradiso* XVI. 70–1).

It is mainly through its portrayal of bullfighting, which is represented as a form of communion with the forces of the earth and their mortal element, or as a sun festival (see Montherlant's *Les Bestiaires*), that modern literature has perpetuated many of the bull's mythological characteristics. The killing of the bull is depicted as a sort of 'bringing to life', a form of sexual union in which blood mingles with sperm, as in the case of Alain Borne's Mithraic bull:

> The white blood will mingle
> with the red blood of the creature
> of its death which died again this evening.
>
> (*Vive la mort*)

Meanwhile, Pierre Gamarra even echoes the Egyptian association of the bull with the Word and the bee, 'at the dazzling hour of the sword':

> Giant word, wise honey
> reason clothes your flight,
> A charger without a bridle, you become
> the durability of change.
>
> (*Taureau*)

In another instance, this time in the specifically mythological context of the abduction of Europa, Saint-John Perse associates the bull with the infinite fertility of the sea:

> Love is on the sea where the vineyards are greenest; and the gods run to the green grapes, and bulls with green eyes bearing on their backs the most beautiful girls of the earth.
>
> (*Amers*. strophe IX. VI. 2)

However, it is undoubtedly in its hybrid form as the Minotaur that the bull provided the richest source of literary inspiration.

Some authors such as Lucian, at the end of book II of his *True History*, merely evoke the monster's cruelty, while others, such as Dante (*Inferno* XII. 11–25), emphasize its violent bestiality. However, still other writers, and particularly contemporary ones, use the myth in a more profound way by adopting the systematic approach discussed in the introduction.

Thus, in *El Aleph*, Borges reworked the association of the bull and the Word by combining it with the myth of Daedalus, and so implied that we are all Minotaurs imprisoned within the labyrinth of meaning from which only God can free us. The labyrinth, which can be extended to mean the world (*La Casa de Asterion*), represents the maze of language in which Man wrestles with himself because he has not resolved the mystery of the animal nature that motivates him.

It is possible to come to terms with this particular aspect of the self and so achieve peace in the context of the senses. According to Camus:

> ... there exists in each of us a deep-seated instinct which is neither the instinct of destruction nor of creation. It is simply the instinct to avoid resembling anything.... Yes, let's agree to stone if we have to ... In order to be spared, we have to consent to the Minotaur.
>
> (*Le Minotaur*)

This is precisely the wish expressed later by de Sena:

> In Crete, with the Minotaur
> devoid of inspiration and life
> devoid of a homeland and a soul
> with nothing and no one
> ...
> I can drink my coffee in peace.
>
> (*In Crete with the Minotaur*)

Taming the monster no longer means controlling animal power, any more than it means silencing sexual passion. Instead, it involves reconciling the irreconcilable (mind and matter) in order to take refuge, exhausted but safe 'in the centre of the rebus' (Le Clézio).

THE CAT

From the Egyptian cat-goddess Bast, who was supposed to protect Ra from serpents, to the cat that, according to Islamic tradition was produced by the lion's sneeze in the ark, the cat's most striking feature is its associations with the 'other world'. These create the impression of a 'creature on the threshold', partly benign and partly evil, with which it is advisable to remain on good terms.

In *Romeo and Juliet* (III. 1), Tybalt asks meaningfully of Mercutio, 'What wouldst thou have with me?' to which the latter replies, 'Good king of cats, nothing but one of your nine lives'. Moreover, whenever the cat is endowed with human sentiments, whether as the Puss-in-Boots of the brothers Grimm or as his noble descendant, Hoffmann's 'Kate Murr', it is always disturbing in moral terms. As Kreisler remarks: 'Let them all look for their own fish heads and not rely on anyone else's skill: when they are really hungry, they'll soon manage!' This is the philosophy of the 'Kater Murr'.

The same hint of danger is apparent also in the feline's seductive nature – remember that Bast was a female cat! This aspect was stressed by La Fontaine in 'The Cat that Changed into a Woman' and was echoed by Baudelaire:

> When my fingers freely caress
> Your head and supple spine . . .
> My mistress comes to mind. Her gaze,
> Cold and deep as yours, my pet,
> Is like a stab of pain.
>
> (*Les Fleurs du Mal* XXXIV)

In the same vein, Verlaine exclaims:

> The other, too, turned on her charm
> And retracted her steel claw,
> But the devil was not deceived . . .
>
> ('Caprices' 1, *Poèmes saturniens*)

In Apollinaire's *Le Bestiaire*, the cat inspires the same elusive dream of security since possession of the cat-woman can have tragic consequences – one has only to think of the ending of *La Chatte* by Colette. Meanwhile, Bast herself is depicted from a Christian viewpoint in the work of Jean Follain, where she is killed just as Christ was crucified, and:

> Nearby, in a blue smock
> her unpolished medal on the close-fitting yoke
> the child, alone, seeks the millennium.
>
> (*Comme jamais*)

According to Baudelaire's *Les Fleurs du Mal* (LI and LXVI), cats with their 'mystical gaze' are 'familiar spirits' that flirt with the other world and embody the very mystery of existence. Perhaps Alice's cat, Kitty, has in fact been through the looking glass . . .

Baudelaire's 'couriers of Hell' ('Les Chats', *Les Fleurs du Mal*) can also be truly diabolic, just like the big black cat with the devil's tail encountered by Polichinelle in Feuillet's *Les Aventures de Polichinelle*. This is also true of the premonitory feline in *The Black Cat* by Poe, which encourages people to commit the most terrible crimes only subsequently to denounce them, as well as of Gascar's cat, which suggests the omnipresence of mystery and death.

THE CICADA

According to Socrates in Plato's *Phaedrus* (259), the cicada was born of Man and when it discovered the Muses, it began to sing like them and became so obsessed by what it was doing that it lost all need for sustenance.

This unambiguous myth is echoed by Quinet, who describes the insect as the 'patriarch of song'. However, this song of life, which is associated with the 'wonderful/joy/of peace/and the sun' (Apollinaire, *Aussi bien que les cigales*) and which is comparable with the song of the poet in providing the only possible form of victory over death (Miguel Torga, 'Cega-Rega', *Bichos*), can also become a song of self-negation, as it does for Valéry in *Le Cimetière marin*, where 'the brittle insect scrapes at the dry grit', and even a song of death.

In his famous fable about the creature, La Fontaine had already stressed the unavoidable outcome of the song, a celebration of day that inevitably leads to night, and this idea was echoed by Hugo:

> Their deep, raucous cry is heard intermittently in the darkness,
> Like the cry of cicadas in the evening.
>
> (*Les Contemplations* III XII)

For Saint-John Perse the comparison becomes a metaphor for mortality: 'Hear death living – its cry of a cicada' (*Amers*, strophe IX. V. 1). Meanwhile, Patrice Cauda regards the cry as a derisory and pathetic attempt at an incantation, and does not even give it a name:

> All summer long the cicada
> Seals its fate
> In an olive tree.
>
> (*Peut-étre*)

THE DOLPHIN

As in the mythology of Australia, New Zealand and the Amazon, in Greek mythology too, the dolphin is of human origin: indeed, Dionysus changed the pirates who kidnapped him into dolphins. Lucian of Samosata recalls this idea in his *Dialogues of the Sea* (IX. 8), where he presents an optimistic image of the dolphin as a virtuous creature – an image that is also found in Plutarch's *Moralia* (LVIII. 36) and that is fully supported by the story of the mythical dolphin that saved Arion and Enalus.

By the time that Aesop wrote 'The Monkey and the Dolphin', this stereotype was already well established:

> A dolphin caught sight of it and, thinking it to be a man, slipped beneath it, and bore it up and carried it to the shore.

La Fontaine presented his own particular version of this conventional view of the dolphin in book IV of his *Fables*, where the creature is portrayed as being kindly disposed only towards Man. This idea had already been expressed by Shakespeare in *A Midsummer Night's Dream* (act II. Scene 1) and was later echoed by Rilke in his poem 'The Dolphins' (*Neue Gedichte*), in which he refers to the constellation of that name and suggests that by evoking the dolphin, the navigator perhaps becomes the Navigator:

> . . . in his solitary danger
> [he] welcomed this new friend
> and, in his gratitude, imagined for it
> a universe: he considered it certain
> that it liked gardens, the gods and music
> and the deep silence of the sidereal year.
>
> (*Neue Gedichte*, part II)

For Odysseas Elytis in *Soleil premier* (XI), the appearance of three dolphins following a 'Holy Virgin of the Annunciation' who has become a siren results from an intense desire for dissolution in the great Mother, which would make possible the discovery of the secret of Being.

From this point of view, the novel by Nikos Athanassiadis, *Une Jeune Fille Nue*, represents a profound revival of the mythical tradition. Here, the dolphin is as erotic and sexually potent as it was in the myth in which it coupled with Amyon. On the shores of Lesbos, it seduces a young woman who was born in the sea during a shipwreck and who subsequently maintains sexual relations with the dolphin as well as with her human lover. This symbolizes her consuming desire to become a part of the Great Whole – a desire that is realized by her final metamorphosis into a dolphin:

> It is as if she had never left the sea. I even think I can feel the slender fin on her back (. . .). This must have been how the first myth came into being, the myth that taught Man that he is merely an illusion and that the only truth is the truth that exists in the imagination, in the images of dreams and in vertiginous visions.

If we reverse the sequence of the plot and the sex of the characters, the result is Sherman's *Brothers of the Sea*, which is probably inspired as much by the scientific discoveries of the last twenty years as by the sensual associations of the mythical animal. Meanwhile, in Szilard's science fiction story of human aspirations that are finally realized, *La Voix des Dauphins*, dolphins communicate with humans by means of a fully articulated language and use their wisdom to enable mankind to avoid a nuclear war. Similarly, in *Clickwhistle* by Watkins the dolphins are forced to take the offensive in order to destroy an atomic submarine and save humanity from complete obliteration. In a related vein, Merle uses two cheeky and talkative dolphins to cast as critical an eye over modern society as that of Montesquieu's Persans – and, in the process, these modern versions of the classical stereotype, Fa and Bi, also save humanity from a third world war. To all appearances, Verlomme has woven the same symbolic tapestry in his novel, *Mermère*, in which he examines, in a particularly sensitive manner, the relationship between the dolphin (*delphis*) and the womb (*delphos*) implied by the figure of Apollo Delphinius. Here, the dolphin seems to have achieved the impossible human quest and confirmed itself in the role of Mediator.

THE EAGLE

The eagle has been venerated since ancient Greek times as the emblem of kings and gods. It is the celestial, solar bird of Zeus, which unblinkingly confronts both the light of the sun and the light of knowledge. It is the bird of omen par excellence (*Iliad* XXIV. 308–21) and its face is also one of the four Faces of the Living Creatures on the divine chariot described in Ezekiel (1. 10) and in Revelation (4. 7–8). The tradition of the creature's power and wisdom inspired Dante's vision of earthly paradise, in which the imperial eagle speaks as one voice although formed of thousands of souls. The latter unite to demonstrate the perfect harmony between individual virtues within the sphere of Divine Justice (*Paradiso* XIX).

In the same way, the 'memorable fancy' described by Blake was probably influenced by the eagle's mythological image. The first chamber of a printing house in hell contained a dragon-man, while in the second was a viper and:

> In the third chamber was an Eagle with wings and feathers of air; he caused the inside of the cave to be infinite; around were numbers of Eagle-like men who built Palaces in the immense cliffs.
>
> ('A Memorable Fancy', *The Marriage of Heaven and Hell*)

As well as inspiring Dante and Blake, the angel with the eagle's face also provided inspiration for Saint-John Perse, who used it as an image of the spiritual quest:

> You whom I have seen reaching far beyond my haunch, like a watcher bent on the brim of the cliffs, you do not know, you have not seen your face of a peregrine eagle. Will the bird carved in your face pierce the mask of the lover?'
>
> (*Amers*, strophe IX. VI. 1)

However, the eagle also announces the three dreadful 'Catastrophes' sent by God (Revelation 8. 13) and can itself be invoked as an instrument of necessary cruelty. In *The Visions of the Daughters of Albion*, Oothoon exclaims:

> I call with holy voice! Kings of the sounding air
> Rend away this defiled bosom . . .
>
> (*Visions* 3. 7)

This is why the 'Aigle du casque' punished Tiphaine with a terrible death, calling upon the universe to witness the wickedness of the murderer:

> It put out his eyes; it crushed his teeth,
> And shattered his skull in its burning talons . . .
>
> (*La Légende des Siècles* XVII. IV)

Lautréamont went even further in his portrayal of the combat between the eagle and the dragon (*Les Chants de Maldoror* III. 3), in which the ferocious bird enters the monster's belly to tear out its heart. This reveals the sadism of Maldoror who, in another poem, uses a knife to disembowel a young girl whom he has just raped, as if she were a chicken.

The implacable nature of the bird, which has become a symbol of war, is apparent in Saint-John Perse's portrayal of it as the embodiment of the harsh light that challenges knowledge:

> The horsemen on the crest of the capes, battered by luminous eagles, and feeding on their spear-tips the pure disasters of sunshine . . . (*Anabase* VI)

This leads to the association of the eagle with pitiless barbs of steel and thorn:

> Oh, Handler of eagles by their angles, Feeder
> of women shrill in their iron plumes!
>
> (*Exil* III)

> It is snowing . . . on the hordes of black fir-trees entangled with barbed eagles like war trophies . . .
>
> (*Neiges* III)

The eagle that is the 'Warning of the god! Aversion of the god! . . . Eagle over the sleeper's head' (*Vents* V. 2) also symbolizes possession by the god (*Amers*, strophe III. 7) or metaphysical anguish (*Amers*, strophe IX. IV. 2).

The cliff on which the eagle dwells doubtless represents the way to redemption. For Hugo, this involves saving the 'words from below':

> Rise up, glide and mingle unrestrained,
> In the huge, wild vault of the eagles.
>
> (*Les Contemplations* XXXVI)

Meanwhile, for Saint-John Perse it represents the truth of being. For him the cliff becomes, in a sense, the flank of Prometheus, in an extraordinary vision that combines suffering, death and sexual and spiritual love:

> And who then has roused you again to violence, rearing on your wings, like the

> female eagle on its faggot of thorns, talon pressed against the flank of the Questioner? . . . O most powerful embattled briar backed against the rock, you hold higher than the sea your invective against death.
>
> (*Amers*, strophe IX. IV. 2)

THE FLY

The fly has always been an embodiment of diabolical forces and is the form assumed by Erynomus, the Persian demon of death and putrefaction who reappears in the Bible in the form of Beelzebub, 'Lord of the flies' (Matthew 12. 24 and Mark 3. 22).

According to Apuleius (*The Golden Ass* II. 22) witches disguise themselves as flies in order to attack men, while Shakespeare places the insect unequivocally in the realms of evil. In *Othello* (IV. 2) it is the symbol of moral degeneracy:

> Oh, ay; [as honest] as summer flies are in the shambles,
> That quicken even with blowing.

Meanwhile, in the mouths of Iago (*Othello* I. 1. 71) and Caliban (*The Tempest* I. 2. 339–40) it is an instrument of malediction; though Shakespeare also used flies to represent Man as the victim of a cruel destiny:

> As flies to wanton boys are we to gods,
> They kill us for their sport.
>
> (*King Lear* IV. 1)

The fly's dual role as an insect associated with death and hell is fully developed in Sartre's play *Les Mouches*. Jupiter, 'God of flies and death', introduces a persistent contrast first between white and red and then between red and black, colours which are used to represent tragedy and murder, as well as being those of the flies themselves:

> There are twelve of them on his eye, as if they were on a piece of bread and jam, and yet he keeps on smiling, he seems to like them sucking at his eyes. Incidentally, those 'peepers' of his are giving off a white discharge that looks like curdled milk.
>
> (*Les Mouches* I. 1)

To the blackness of the flies is added the red of the sexual pleasure inspired by the murder. Jupiter vividly conjures up the 'red feast' at which the fly, in this instance in the form of an old woman, derives sexual satisfaction from the murder of Agamemnon. The flies soon appear as the instrument of divine punishment – 'Sting, burrow and bore, avenging flies, dig deep into my flesh down to my filthy heart' (*Les Mouches* II. 2) – and as symbols of past and future crimes. As the embodiment of the Erinyes (the Furies), they are the inverted doubles of the bee, promising to make beautiful green honey from pus . . .

This opposition between the Christ-like bee and the evil fly was developed by Rimbaud in his famous sonnet *Voyelles*, in which he associates the fly with the colour of Saturn and with the letter A, as well as by Verlaine, who invested the serene figure of the bee with a divine meaning in *Sagesse* (II. IV. IV).

The image of the fly as an archetypal symbol of the hopelessness of death greatly influenced Baudelaire: 'Flies kept humming over the guts/from which a gleaming clot/of maggots poured . . .' ('Charogne' *Les Fleurs du Mal* XXIX). However, the fly is also a symbol of a psychological and spiritual struggle. Thus, in Hoffmann's *L'Enfant étrange* 'the melancholy king of the gnomes' who hesitates between the drone and 'the big fly with shining eyes' threatens the peace of the story's main characters.

This interior struggle can also assume a much more subtle dimension, when the fly challenges our perception of time, in a sort of 'imaginary present' at the very moment at which we are about to kill it:

> The world was flat and silent, and the fly remained in the same place. It was as if it had been there for years, in this room, in front of me, at that precise, peaceful moment. Never killed, forever . . .
>
> (Le Clézio, 'Assassinat d'une Mouche', *L'Extase matérielle*).

The result is a terrible lesson on 'the nature of happiness . . . the epitome of misunderstanding' (ibid.).

A squashed fly can also change its form: in Garcia Lorca's 'La Gallina', it becomes a god of poor-quality goods dressed in a flyskin; while in Béalu's *Mémoire de l'Ombre*, it becomes a cockroach, then a cockchafer and then a mouse. According to Béalu, there is conflict both within us and outside us, that results from a combination between mankind's basically aggressive nature and the inability of individuals to communicate with each other. As a result, the fly has even become part of the vocabulary of war denounced by Le Clézio (*La Guerre*, chapter 1). Spitz evokes this omnipresent threat in extremely apocalyptic terms: flies, spreading plague and cholera, control the destiny of the human race, in spite of the almost suicidal use of fire to get rid of the scourge. Nor is Golding's socio-political allegory, *Lord of the Flies*, free from this obsession with an image of original sin sanctioned by the authority of a cruel leader. On an imaginary island, dictatorship and *lebensraum* are a deadly dual necessity for this new generation of fly-children.

THE HORSE

In Greek mythology Poseidon transformed himself into a stallion to mate with Demeter, who had assumed the form of a mare, and the goddess subsequently gave birth to the wild horse Arion or, according to another version of the story, to two demons of death. Meanwhile, in another myth, Aphrodite urged on the mares of Glaucus as they devoured their master alive: a chthonic force had come into play, a force deriving from the underworld, and nothing was able to stop it. The unstoppable nature of this force is also illustrated in Revelation (6. 2–8) where the four horses of the Apocalypse appear in succession: the horses of war, one white, the other red; the black horse of famine; and the green (or pale, depending on the translation) horse of death.

This image of a deadly force emerging from the shadows is evoked later in 'L'Aigle du Casque':

> Thus during sleep, our soul filled with fear
> Sometimes escapes and feels behind it the breath
> Of some black horse of darkness and the night . . .

For Saint-John Perse, the horse may even become the guide of the dead:

> The horses running to the ossuary have passed by, with mouths yet freshened by the cool sages of the meadow.
>
> (*Chronique* II)

Alternatively, it may be an initiatory mount, as illustrated by the Kirghiz horse, Tchal-Kouirouk:

> It is at this point in your reverie that the thing occurred:
> the sudden flash of light, like a Crusader! – the Scarface on your path, athwart the road,
> like the Unknown One arisen from the ditch, who causes the Traveller's animal to rear.
>
> (*Vents* IV. 3)

In describing this journey always fraught with danger, the poet returns to the most ancient traditions, recalling '. . . the great master ceremonies when the blood of a black horse flows . . . Let us be gone! be gone! Cry of the living' (*Vents* I. 7).

As portrayed by Poe in *The Hungarian Myth*, the mount of Baron Metzengerstein becomes a fantastical creature and, like the horse of the Apocalypse, is associated with the red of hell. His account takes the form of an extraordinary tapestry in which the rider clings stubbornly to the nameless beast, a strange and powerful animal that carries him through the flames of his castle.

Red horses, this time representing anguish, reappear in an almost obsessive manner in the work of Joubert, where they are associated with blood, death and love:

> The red horses entered the chalky land
> the wasteland on which they graze by day,
> sleeping by night beneath the order of our walls
> and tired eyelids.
>
> (*Saison d'appel*)

> ——Horses of reverie, where are you taking
> My love dressed in red?
>
> (*Poèmes d'absence*)

Joubert is also haunted by 'their macabre gallop' (*Oniriques*) as well as by the image of time bearing us along in a tragic epic ('Parfois un cavalier', *Campagnes secrètes*). For Butor, this powerful force that cannot be harnessed (Michaux's *La Vie dans les Plis*), even raises questions about the nature of Being, and the result is a nightmarish vision:

> . . . on a horse whose bones were protruding like damp, blackened boughs of beech, partly visible through its loose flesh, with torn muscles and strips of skin flapping open and closed . . .
>
> (*La Modification*, chapter IV)

This probably explains why the horse encountered in a dream by the narrator in Valéry's *La Pythie* was neighing furiously.

However, the stallion is also the archetype of the sire, and this image too is evoked by Saint-John Perse, for whom the sea is associated with the domestic horse (*Amers*, strophe IX. V. 1) or, in its extensive purity, represents the omnipresence of sexual instinct:

> What whinnying of a white stallion has caused this tremor of a loving woman to course, with the breeze, over the robe of the waters?
>
> (*Amers*, strophe IX. VI. 2)

It is in the context of sexual passion that the centaur appears, the hybrid monster portrayed as half horse and half human. In preference to Chiron, the perfectly civilized centaur recalled by Swift's Houyhnhnms, writers have tended to focus their attention on Nessus, the wild and unrestrained centaur who, according to Jacob, had 'eyes which reflect his sexual desire and hind quarters which are more like a serpent's tail than the body of a horse'. This is the image of a centaur-Cecrops, always ready to mate.

In this context, Moacyr Scliar's *O Centauro no Jardim* provides an extremely significant revitalized portrayal of this mythical animal, describing the permanent struggle between the centaur's two opposing parts. While aspiring to be legendary, the hero of the story actually hesitates between complete abandonment to his animal nature – representing the appeasement of the senses and the obliteration of metaphysical doubt – and the outright rejection of a life, as it were, dictated by his hind quarters, which are a source of great shame. His love affair with a circus trainer does not fully consummate the animal side of his nature. The result is a lingering desire that he subsequently recognizes when it is expressed through an affair with a sphinx-woman at the clinic to which he returns in an attempt to rediscover his hybrid identity. The outcome envisaged in the last chapter suggests the possibility of a form of happiness founded entirely on abandonment to the basic instincts, in other words to the id. The centaur has won the struggle, particularly against Pegasus, the recurrent symbol of another type of happiness that is infinitely more spiritual, although disturbing and inaccessible. Pegasus had already captured the imagination of Louÿs:

... his virgin breast harnessed by neither man nor god
extended in untiring and mysterious flight.
... The poets mourning their lost cults
With joined hands still imagine
The white stallion soaring through forbidden skies.

(*Astarté*)

It is Pegasus who will raise Man to poetic heights, for he represents a creative force that must be controlled by the mind:

... my beautiful wild horse ...
do not stamp so loudly in the shadow of your stall:
a white and golden night is rising in the East.

(P. de la Tour du Pin, *Une Somme de Poésie*.)

THE MONSTER

It would take a whole volume to list the various forms of hybrid monsters that mythology has bequeathed to literature, but the best known of these is the dragon, which sometimes appears in the form of a sea monster and is usually winged.

Jason had to fight a dragon, as did Yahweh, who 'shall punish Leviathan ... that crooked Serpent; and he shall slay the dragon that is in the sea' (Isaiah 27. 1).

The dragon is usually associated with the forces of Evil, and in Revelation (12. 3 and 7) it actually becomes the incarnation of Satan, with seven heads representing the seven deadly sins. This is the source that inspired Dante's description in *Purgatorio* (XXXII) of the divine chariot changed by the dragon's sting into a seven-headed monster bearing Lust (which is also the symbolic significance of the diabolical wasp):

And then, meseemed, the earth 'twixt wheel and wheel
Gaped, and out came a dragon from below
And through the chariot's floor drove up his tail;
And as the wasp withdraws its sting, even so
He pulled away barbed tail and bits of floor,
And skimble-skamble off I saw him go.

(130–5)

Flaubert's depiction of the visions of Saint Antony makes use of the same type of imagery, since the seven deadly sins, lasciviously presented by the Queen of Sheba, are again associated with the monster:

Would you like the shield of Dgian-ben-Dgian, builder of the pyramids? ... It consists of seven Dragons' skins laid on top of each other, joined by diamond screws and tanned in parricide's bile.

(*La Tentation de saint Antoine*, II.)

Lautréamont's bitter scorn should be seen in the same context, when, in his description of the terrible combat between the eagle and the dragon, he deliberately inverts the usual symbolism of the West and makes the dragon represent defeated Hope (III. 3).

In his *Poèmes tragiques*, Leconte de Lisle used what was by this time the classic imagery of the Beast bearing the seal of Satan on its brow, an emblem countered by the seal of the Cross:

> And, with a yawn, each gaping maw
> Spewed forth onto the earth dense swirling pools
> Of men dressed in purple and in rags.
> . . . And each one had, impressed upon his brow, the awful image
> Of the two beams of a cross . . .

Indeed, in the *Poèmes barbares* the same writer had already given prominence to the dragon of Evil triumphing over Creation:

> And the dragon, standing on a solid rock,
> Delighted with his work, his crime complete,
> Cursed the dead universe and buried man,
> And said: – But for me, the Avank, who cannot die
> The fortunate are lying in eternal oblivion.

There is, therefore, no cause for surprise when the dragon of remorse, associated with formless night and pestilential water, fatally wounds the hero of Poe's *The Fall of the House of Usher.* The progressive appearance of the dragon in a novel read by one of the book's main characters, and its violent death accompanied by a horrible and powerful cry, are paralleled in the story itself by the appearance of the woman who was believed to be dead and who had been buried prematurely. Meanwhile, the house itself soon becomes closely associated with the monster: 'As Usher pointed, the vast antique panels slowly opened their heavy ebony jaws.'

Verlaine's monster is certainly related to the same nightmarish mythical vision, which is reinforced by the fact that it devours its human victims in a 'night devoid of stars and moon':

> Its flaccid skin was a dirty yellow, and for a long time
> I will not forget the horrible snout, like
> The trunk of a huge mammoth
> . . . its vast mouth, encircled by reddish whiskers
> . . .
> Like those of a gigantic lobster,
> And the slimy chin . . .

Somewhat less extreme is Michaux's Meidosem, which perhaps comes substantially closer to symbolizing our hopeless vigilance than does the image of the diabolical, deadly and destructive monster. 'Tortured', tense and anxious, it finds nothing of any importance to capture and is constantly keeping watch, 'its head studded with suckers' (*La Vie dans les Plis*).

The dragon can also be associated with forces that have merely to be controlled, and sometimes even with things that are only horrific because we have invested them with none of our own characteristics. Defeating the dragon can represent 'an essential moment in the eschatological drama' (Durand) or in the romantic drama, the mythical framework examined by Rilke:

> How can we forget the ancient myths from the beginning of the history of all races; the myths of dragons which at the eleventh hour change into princesses? Perhaps all the dragons in our lives are in fact princesses who are waiting for us to be noble and courageous. Perhaps all terrifying things are merely helpless things waiting for us to help them.
>
> (*Briefe an einen Jungen Dichter* VIII)

In this way, the dragon concealed within us can be perceived as representing the uncontrolled instincts of an animal nature that is essentially positive:

> Beautiful monsters of the night, quivering with shadows,
> You show a muzzle damp from beyond the skies,
> You approach me, and hold out your paw
> And then withdraw it as if suddenly mistrustful.
> And yet I welcome your shadowy gestures,
> My eyes penetrate the depths of your dark coats.
>
> (Jules Supervielle, *La Fable du Monde*)

Another hybrid monster that appears to have enjoyed great literary success is the Behemoth (Job 40. 15–23), which is related to the ox and the hippopotamus and endowed with immense strength. Meanwhile, the strange appearance of Heliodorus's camel-leopard inspired the same terrified panic (*Aethiopica* X. 27). This mythical figure was created by attaching one end of a long, spindly neck to the head of a camel with fearful eyes and the other to the misshapen body of a lion with a leopard's skin. It must surely have directly inspired Poe's Homo-Camelopard and Flaubert's Catoblepas . . .

The former appears in *Four Beasts in One* in the guise of King Antiochus Epiphanes, who is a quite fantastical creation and closely resembles Heliodorus's monster, to the point of having its protuberant eyes set in a human face. According to the narrator, this animal-like apparition, which arouses the joyful cruelty and stupidity of its admirers, owes its features to having massacred a thousand Jews. By an ironic paradox, it is only animals that are afraid of him and that are rendered aggressive by his appearance. It is they who want to put the king-camelopard to death.

Flaubert's Catoblepas is among the figures in the terrifying procession of monsters that appears in the dream of Saint Antony. This 'black buffalo with a hog's head which lolls on the ground and is attached to his shoulders by a narrow neck, long and flaccid like an emptied gut' has the deadly gaze of Medusa. Its companions include the Martichoras, 'a gigantic red lion with a human face, and three rows of teeth', and the griffin, 'a lion with a vulture's beak, and white wings, red paws and a blue neck'. The final vision is of the unicorn, which is preceded by a terrible menagerie in which the Tragelaphus, 'half stag and half ox', rubs shoulders with the Myrmecoleo, 'lion at the front, ant at the rear' and the Senad, 'a triple-headed bear which tears up its little ones with its tongue' . . . By this point, the Chimaera and the sphinx have already attempted an abominable coupling before the very eyes of the distraught saint (*La Tentation de saint Antoine*, VII), recalling the one that occurs at the end of Jorge de Séna's poem *La Dame à la Licorne*. In the poem, centaurs are treated as creations of the poetic imagination that are a fit topic only for drawing room conversations. The unicorn-poet, in the person of Gil, is brought back to reality by the sexual urges of the mistress of the house, thus establishing a link between poetic irrationality and uncontrolled animal passion.

THE SERPENT

It is impossible to list all the occurrences of the serpent even in the mythology of the western hemisphere. It is associated with formless existence, with the worm and the dragon, and is the embodiment of all that is hidden. It is the Egyptian Aton, the generator of all life, the Greek Ouroboros, the matrix of the Zodiac, and the plumed serpent that appears in most Amerindian mythology. At their birth, the twins Cassandra and Helenus were endowed with the power of prophecy by two serpents, just as serpents purified the ears of Melampus. The apparent contradiction between these positive associations of the serpent and the killing of Python by Apollo is purely superficial, as the death of Python opened the way for the establishment of the oracle at Delphi. Similarly, Dionysian madness, which drew its strength from *hubris*, can be considered as representing the therapeutic influence of the serpent, and as being intended to re-establish the balance associated with the serpent of the caduceus.

The serpent is therefore a particularly ambivalent mythical creature. However, in the Bible it is used only to convey an image of evil, in the form of the Seducer and Tempter – and also, more mundanely, as a divine means of punishing sinners (Numbers 21. 6). Its connection with evil and temptation is recalled by Dante in *Purgatorio* (XXXII. 32) with the words '[she] . . . that to the serpent gave ear', and is stressed by Flaubert in a terrible evocation of blasphemy. The python . . .

> passes slowly along the edge of the bread . . . , the Worshippers glue their mouths to its skin, grabbing from each other the bread that it has bitten

and cry out:

> It's you! it's you! . . . He had drunk you in the waves of baptism; but you left

> him in the Garden of Olives, and he felt all his weakness. Twisted round the arms of the Cross, up above his head, you slavered on the crown of thorns, you watched him die. For you are not Jesus, not you – you are the Word! you are the Christ!
>
> (*La Tentation de saint Antoine* IV)

For Blake, the serpent lives in hell and is worshipped there ('A Memorable Fancy' 3, *The Marriage of Heaven and Hell*). It is associated with poison and the terrible powers of formless existence (*The Book of Ahania* II. 3–5), and linked to the fatal nature of the Fall. Thus, Enitharmon gave birth to Orc, which was apparently evil, being condemned from birth by its unnatural carnal relationship with its mother:

> All day the worm lay on her bosom;
> All night within her womb,
> The worm lay till it grew to a serpent
> With dolorous hissing and poisons
> Round Enitharmon's loins folding.
>
> (*The First Book of Urizen* VI. 5)

This is reminiscent of the sadistic remark made by Maldoror to the python-Basilisk:

> Go and wash your immeasurable shame in the blood of a newborn baby.
>
> (*Les Chants de Maldoror* V. 4)

However, in Blake's poetry the serpent retains all its ambiguity (see 'The worm'). Meanwhile, Valéry presents it as a serious rival to God, in the same way as Hugo does the worm: although it is derided in *L'Ebauche d'un Serpent*, it is nevertheless seen as a possible initiatory figure revealing the way to divine perfection however great the hypocrisy that it may have demonstrated (*L'Insinuant*): '. . . the universe is but a flaw/In the Purity of Non-existence'. In *La Pythie*, where the Pythia 'utters her oracles in between kicks/From a tripod that is being strangled by a serpent', the animal appears as a combination of Apollo's Python and the Dionysian serpent. Her 'heaving breast/ Beneath the viperine ornaments' (verse 12) will receive 'divine gifts' (verse 15), the 'Honour of Men, Sacred LANGUAGE'. The serpent is a seducer but also a source of inspiration; it provides an image of damnation, whilst also representing the aspiration to redemption.

Perhaps for this reason, the serpent of flesh and sexuality that Titania encounters in the course of her amorous adventures (*A Midsummer Night's Dream* I. 1. 253–5) and that features in Hermia's significance-laden dreams during her night of love, has something of the terrifying and pitiful Geryon that Dante and Virgil encounter in hell (*Inferno* XVII. 1–15). The hypocrisy of all creation, underpinned by death, is reduced to lust. In this respect, the serpent has something of the cat about it, or more precisely of the female cat, a dangerous and perverse seductress whose gaze Baudelaire regarded as equivalent to the snake's forked tongue (see *Les Fleurs du Mal* XXIX and XXXIV: 'Le Serpent qui Danse' 5 and 'Le Chat' 3).

Finally, Saint-John Perse provides a unique re-evocation of many features of the primordial serpent, fully capturing the original bisexuality of the mythical creature and endowing it with a slight tinge of the fear inspired by Typhon:

> The Sea, moving, that makes its way on the gliding of its great errant muscles, the slimy Sea with the gliding motion of a pleura, and all running to the high flood of a sea, came towards us on its coils of a black python.
>
> (*Amers*: 'Invocation' 6)

THE SPIDER

While the myth of Arachne obviously emphasizes the act of spinning and creation, this theme is balanced by the theme of death, represented by the punishment inflicted on the young woman for having sought to compete with the gods. Many aspects of the myth are found in the mythologies of other cultures. For example, the Muisca of Colombia represents the spider as helping to transport the dead to Hell, the Aztecs regard it as the companion of the Master of Death, and the Ashanti maintain that it helped to create the world. Similarly, in Mali it is said to have created the stars, and in Borneo it is seen having created the first tree, which bore the ancestors of Man.

It is the particularly ambivalent nature of Arachne that is emphasized by Hugo and, later, by Odysseas Elytis. In the *Légende des Siècles*, the base creature despised by Athena, and represented here as being of satanic origin, is transformed by divine will into an extraordinary sun. This image of the redemption of matter is powerfully expressed in *To Axion Esti*:

> The insect of evil * memory in the earth
> Moved like sperm * in obscure wombs
> And just as the spider bites * suddenly it bit the ray
> of light and the banks shone * and the whole expanse of water.
>
> ('La Genèse' II. d.)

Hugo's 'Inconnu noir' in 'L'Epopée du Ver' (*La Légende des Siècles*) also insolently claimed to be the equal of the gods:

> Like the spider, I have made a web . . .
> The invisible black thread that I spin
> Would render dawn bereft and the great expanse a void
> If it were to reach up to God.
>
> ('L'Epopée du Ver' VIII)

For Lautréamont, the tarantula is an instrument of divine vengeance, the form assumed by the two brothers who have been deceived, and who will only cease to suck the juices from their victim at night when they receive an order 'from above' (*Les Chants de Maldoror* V. 7).

The Arachne who reappears in the guise of Clarimonde in Hans Heinz Ewer's short story, *Die Spinne*, is both derisive and deadly. Like the young woman in the original myth, the young man dies for having aspired to imitate the action of spinning, an art that is both divine and diabolical (in this context these are one and the same thing). His transgression drives him to hang himself, recalling the fate of his young Lydian counterpart.

The spider is also a metonym for divine power and celestial cruelty. It represents destiny, and, indeed, the Fates are also spinners. As Garcia Lorca exclaimed, we will all be eventually swallowed up by the heavens:

> The tiny banquet of the spider
> is alone enough to upset the balance of the entire universe.
>
> (*Poeta em Nueva-York* III)

The spider kills in order to achieve knowledge: after having killed herself for knowing too much, (compare Michaux's 'La Vie de l'Araignée royale' in *La Vie remue*) and after having put on mourning for her own fate, she loses all innocence and devours the male:

> . . . what mourning veil covers her hair
> of which the high-crossed comb recalls
> the emblem of the spider.'
>
> (Jean Joubert, *Les Familiers*)

This disturbing image recurs in the form of the terrifying young woman in Béalu's *L'Araignée d'Eau* who changes into a spider in order to 'suffocate (her lover) with her eight claws' in an endless headlong fall:

> Then there opened up around us pools of shadow crossed with rays of light, and I could hear a hideous face, pressed against my lips, announcing the reign of terror for all Eternity.

Perhaps the only remaining way to escape our destiny and achieve the peace described by Le Clézio is to take the place of the spider:

> We will live within the pattern, in the centre of the puzzle, at the very heart of the enigma, and then the whole problem will disappear of its own accord.
>
> (*L'Extase matérielle*)

THE WORM

Because of its shape, the worm is usually closely identified with the serpent, the main difference being that its connections with death are much more strongly expressed. It is always inextricably linked with dead bodies, while it is also from the worm that the phoenix, sometimes considered to be the image of Christ, is reborn. In part 3 of *Brasier*, which is based on Lesser's interpretation of the First Book of Kings (6. 7), Apollinaire states that the worm

Shamir helped to build the Temple, and, if so, its fellow creatures are made in our image, even though they devour us (Isaiah 14. 11).

The counterpart of the serpent of paradise is the hellish worm, as Dante emphasizes in his horrible vision of a six-legged worm coupling with one of the damned spirits in order to exchange its monstrous form (*Inferno* XXV. 46–78). It is against this form that Man rebels in Blake's *Tiriel* (8), while the virgin in the *Book of Thel* is told that she will bear a worm-child after the child of putrefaction (*Book of Thel* II).

The worm assumes a double temporal significance in the works of Hugo, where the infinity of destruction is opposed to the brevity of human life:

> And Cheops repeated: I am eternity . . .
> And the worm of the sepulchre sang.
>
> ('Les Sept Merveilles du monde', *La Légende des siècles* VII)

This is why the first thirty verses of *L'Epopée du Ver* represent the creature chewing incessantly. This is the black mass that it offers to the imminent cataclysm of which it will be the instigator. The Bible and the Koran are merely pathetic attempts to counter this monstrous worm, which controls the universal cycle and will destroy it when it chooses. Finally, the worm also represents the effort of the soul to free itself from matter, as well as the deep-seated doubt that it will be able to achieve this:

> Man feels both the purity of his soul and the baseness of his flesh,
> The earth worm's sting in the depths of darkness
> And the kiss of God.
>
> ('Au Bord de l'Infini', *Les Contemplations* VI. 2)

Baudelaire had already used the worm to illustrate the fact that action is irrevocable because it cannot be repeated. Man is a prisoner of time and is afflicted by remorse, which is rooted in metaphysical anguish:

> Who can destroy this old, this long Remorse,
> which fastens on our heart
> and fattens there like . . .
> . . . vermin on a corpse.
>
> ('L'Irréparable', *Les Fleurs du Mal*)

This stereotyped image had also been used by Shakespeare in *A Midsummer Night's Dream*, where Puck refers to the 'damned spirits' who 'already to their wormy beds are gone' (III. 2. 382–4).

Everything begins and ends with the worm:

> Your worm is your only emperor for diet: we fat all creatures else to
> fat us, and we fat ourselves for maggots: . . . that's the end.
>
> (*Hamlet* IV. 3)

The idea was reworked by Poe in his own particular way in *The Conqueror Worm* and reappeared in *Ligeia*:

And the angels sob at vermin fangs
In human gore imbued
... That the play is the tragedy 'Man'
And its hero the Conqueror Worm.

The worm may also be portrayed as an alternative form that Man can assume when he wishes to return to a basic, organic type of existence and so obtain a greater sense of security. Le Clézio describes just such a metamorphosis in one of Adam Pollo's fantasies in *Le Procès-verbal*:

> it moved its eyes forward ... carefully, cautiously, expecting a sort of electric shock that would contract its skin, throw its motor nerve cells into disarray and jar the segments of its body one against the other ... when it would be underground, contracted, gelatinous, yes, the one, the true, the obscure earth worm.

More recently, Boba Blagojevič depicted this regression in a more ambiguous manner. The description of an old man being eaten by worms and experiencing the slow process of his own putrefaction demonstrates that we are being simultaneously devoured and saved by our capacity for conscious thought:

> Where shall I begin? Thank you. Thank you. I am motionless. Cold. Nothing but skin and bone. But inside there are all sorts of things. The flesh is old and stinks accordingly ... lights, lungs. The important thing is that thought survives, a tiny thought, gnawing away in the darkness.
>
> (*Le Ver*)

Here, the worm represents the eternal presence of an order of time that does not progress and in which the One merges with the many:

> there were thirty two of them and they did not say 'us', these terrible thinking stumps which defied both death and the self! A single worm in thirty two people ... Who would have said, who would have believed that one day I would confront the enigma of death, and the way and the voices of immortality through the unworthy and profane flesh of a Worm?
>
> (Jacques Lacarrière, *Le Pays sous l'Ecorce* II)

Thus it is not surprising that even in a science fiction story such as Herbert's *Dune*, which is set on a planet mainly covered by desert, the main characters are giant worms anything up to twelve hundred feet long. These are the keepers of the 'spice', a substance that makes it possible to reach an incredibly advanced age, and all have the same name, Shai-Hulud, which means 'the old man of eternity'.

André Siganos

The Mythico-Poetic Attitude

The difficulty of defining a myth is equalled only by that of any attempt to define literature. Consequently, in the absence of any viable alternative approach the present study will attempt to establish a link between the two forms of expression in terms of their functions. However, here, the contrasts are more numerous than the similarities.

The narrative of a novel is more or less fictional, whereas the narrative of a myth demands to be accepted as true (Lévy-Brühl, Maurice Leenhart, Mauss, Eliade, Sellier); a poem is untranslatable, whereas a mythical narrative can be translated into any language (Lévi-Strauss); literary texts are structured in section, whereas a mythical narrative is a collection of symbols and can even be reduced to a permanent structure (Gusdorf, Lévi-Strauss); literary narratives refer to an historical moment, whereas mythical narratives presuppose a form of time that is reversible since reversibility is a feature of sacred time (Eliade); the individuality and rationality of literary narratives conflict with the collective and supernatural nature of mythical narratives (Sellier, Lévi-Strauss); a literary narrative leads logically towards a dialectical resolution of conflicts, while mythical narratives provide initiation into a radically altered state (Eliade) or mediate to establish a balance between two incompatible assertions (Lévi-Strauss); literary narratives are experienced privately, mythical narratives socially (Sellier); literary narratives fulfil a profane, socio-historical function, whereas mythical narratives serve a sacred, socio-religious purpose (M. M. Münch); literary narratives represent a relative form of truth, whereas mythical narratives convey absolute and eternal truths, since they are founding stories (Eliade); literary narratives give a partial psychological analysis of the hero, whereas mythical narratives reveal something mysterious and ineffable; the meaning of a literary narrative is more or less obvious, whereas that of a mythical narrative is hidden and requires exegesis; and, lastly, in contrast to the literary narrative, the mythical narrative often has an initiatory and transcendent character.

In the context of this comparison between literature and myth it is important to note that the word myth is usually associated with the word narrative. However, given that the mythical narrative is not portrayed as fiction, but demands belief in the truth of what is being said, we should perhaps talk in terms of a mythical 'attitude', since this stresses the subjective nature of myth.

People not only expect myths to provide them with an explanation of the world or a pattern for living in it; they also hope that mythical narratives will enable them to envisage a condition beyond the finite existence to which they themselves are subjected. Death, the confines of space and time, and the division and fragmentation of the world are everyday trials that prevent human beings from fulfilling the urge for independence that all have within them. The fundamental human sense of dissatisfaction has less to do with an actual lack of something than with a feeling of nostaliga for a state now unknown to mankind, but of which it has a strange intimation. No one has seen the infinite, no one knows what asbolute freedom would be, nor what the removal of the divisions of space and time would mean. Yet, since the dawn of time, people have maintained a belief in a state of existence completely different from their own and have sought to make this as real as their own world by means of mythical narratives and artistic production. Both the latter have always encouraged hopes that Man might be able to experience the infinite, absolute freedom, atemporality, universality and unity.

The mythico-poetic attitude can be defined as a mental or spiritual state that enables individuals – in this case poets or rather artists in general – to use their imaginations to achieve a metamorphosis of condition that allows them to free themselves from all controlling forces and to live in a time that has become reversible.

This state, which people would like to be permanent, eludes all efforts to represent it. It is a kind of enchantment familiar to us all, which lasts for an instant while we are reading a poem, listening to a piece of music or contemplating a work of art, 'forgetting ourselves' in them just as one may be lost in prayer or in the rapture of love. Things that took a long time to produce appear spontaneous, life and movement burst from what is fixed, unity is revealed in something fragmentary; and our feelings when we experience these phenomena seem to represent a form of completeness.

It is this attitude that gives the creator of a work of art the sense of revealing the ineffable, the secret, the hidden, of transcending the human condition, of returning to a primal language. In this language, the way in which the words, sounds or colours are put together seems to establish an order that is both closed and open, particular and universal, located in and outside time. In short, it is 'poetic', but also 'mythical': it is a rallying point, a place for interpersonal communication, a permanent meeting place for individuals and for groups of people.

Yet it is a common language: the objects depicted are familiar, the situations suggested are to be encountered every day. None the less, the message lies elsewhere, in a freedom from contingencies, in an absolute autonomy that the work has made possible. To read a poem, to listen to a piece of music or to contemplate a work of art is not to be offered an opportunity for escape: sometimes – indeed, more often than we might think – these works enable us to experience a sense of impossible freedom, the very freedom that was felt by the artist during their production. They create a realm in which we can join the artist, who broke free from all that is incidental by bending language to serve his or her artistic aim and had the clear sense of attaining timelessness. It is this extraordinary state of freedom, this rapture before a transformed universe that we should be able to discern in any work, through the situations, images, ideas and feelings that it suggests to us. Perhaps it is this vision that contains the secret of the mysterious sense of 'beauty' that we are all waiting to experience.

READING THE SECOND TEXT

Thus the creative experience engenders an attitude expressing the need that we all feel to become something 'other' than what we are, in other words to attain an unconfined state of autonomy, even if only for a few moments at a time. As a consequence, a work produced in this particular state is not a simple play of the imagination or the expression of a real emotion, but rather an account of the sort of existential experience that myths are felt to represent. Its aim is to initiate us into an awareness of the possibility of a change of condition. In other words, the qualities of universality, timelessness, unity and autonomy evoked by a poem are not merely the result of clever technique or skilful assembly, nor of unusual sensitivity or an exceptional faculty for representation; these qualities are primarily felt and experienced. Indeed, it is doubtless because they have been felt and experienced that they can be insinuated beneath the surface of the text and so communicated.

In fact, in a poetic text that epitomizes all the works by a given author, one generally encounters themes such as the revelation of the ineffable, the aspiration towards a transformed state of being, freedom from the bounds of time and space, and a hope of attaining autonomy that may even involve a desire for self-generation. These aspirations, which may be represented by metaphors or by specific situations, evoke a return to the origins, a descent into hell, a nostalgia for paradise, or the passage from one mode of being to another – all of which are mythical themes *par excellence.*

A poet is usually assumed to set out with the intention of producing a particular effect. Yet the actual testimony of writers suggests that during the creative process they feel that they are totally reinventing themselves and gaining access to a reality different from everyday reality, which they may call the 'poetic world' or a 'vision of the universe' or 'another life', or even 'real life'. In addition, it seems clear that the timelessness, universality, unity and so on of a work of art do not correspond in any way to imaginary representations and are not the result of the author's particular skill. Instead, they are emotional states that the author has actually experienced.

In Rimbaud's poem 'Aube' ('Dawn'), for example, beyond the metaphor of day breaking over a silently shifting world of shadow, the motifs of the sun, of return, of the giving of names, of unveiling and of awakening, clearly represent mythical themes related to a quest for the absolute – a return to our origins, a nostalgia for paradise, the passage (reversing the normal pattern) from a sacred to a profane state and the descent into hell. In the process, they also evoke an initiatory journey, as is apparent from the depersonalization represented by shadows and silences from the theme of a new birth, brought about by the appearance of the goddess, and from the image of the recreated world – recreated in the act of love and through the words in which the event is recounted.

In mythical texts, as in literary ones, metaphors have the power of metamorphosis. One could almost say that in a poem the images do not have a symbolic meaning: they are real, as they are in a myth. Indeed, the extent to which these images touch us is dependent on the extent to which they are able to communicate this 'reality'. However, the reality and credence that we accord them cannot be admitted: communion with a work of poetry remains a game, the source of a more or less fleeting pleasure. Even when the experience and aspirations behind them are the same, we seldom grant to poems the response that we accord to myths. Who would take Artaud literally when, in *A Table*, he invites people to leave their homes and strive after a surreal eternity, enduring appalling experiences (a descent into hell) to achieve this, and, at the same time, announces the possibility of inventing a new language and the discovery of a different world of reality opening out on to the nostalgic love of 'dreams that are true'? Artaud promises nothing less than the acquisition of autonomy by means of self-creation, liberation from the physical world and the destruction of the self.

In the sonnet by Mallarmé that begins with the famous words '*Le vierge, le vivace et le bel aujourd'hui*' ('The virgin, the undying and the fine today'), the poet's journey is represented as one involving ordeals and rites of passage:

1 His trials are represented by the impotence of the 'sterile winter'; by separation and rupture ('hard, forgotten lake'); by the anonymity of 'a' swan, and the alienation of the 'flights which have not fled' and of the 'plumage taken'; by nothingness ('boredom'); by the distress of 'hopelessness'; and by the solitude evoked by 'the frost' and the 'transparent glacier'.
2 The poet is subjected to these ordeals because he is seeking 'a region to live in' (nostalgia for paradise), which was not sung (in other words, experienced) when it should have been, because he was determined to 'deny space'. These ordeals thus demonstrate the need to recreate oneself and so transcend the human condition, in order to rediscover the primal, unique and fundamental language.
3 Lastly, the process involves the rejection of the world by one who was 'assigned to this place' because of his 'pure brilliance' and who, in 'pointless exile', compares the 'cold dream of contempt' with his own fate. In addition, there is a comparison between the fate of one who is now only a 'ghost' and 'white agony' and the 'horror of the ground'.

At this point, mention should be made of the image of the 'latent lord who could not become' – an image that Mallarmé uses to refer to Hamlet, to whose myth he remained faithful throughout his life.

As can be seen, the mythical themes – which are scattered through the poem and do not progress or develop in a dialectical way – evoke a journey involving segregation, revelation and metamorphosis. The stages are those that Mallarmé went through during his breakdown at Besançon, which he describes to Cazalis in the following words:

> My brain, invaded by Dreams, rejecting its external functions which no longer sought it [segregation], would have perished in its permanent insomnia, I implored the great Night, which granted my wish and spread its shadows [death and eternity, gestation periods]. The first phase of my life was finished. Awareness exhausted by shadows awakens slowly [awakening to a new birth, passage into light], making a new man [metamorphosis]. It will last for several years, during which I shall have to relive the life of humankind since its childhood becoming aware of itself [time made reversible and universalization of experience].

The value of this exploration of the mythical themes in one particular text is twofold: on the one hand, it shows us that the text in question centres on themes that recur constantly throughout the author's work; and, on the other, it reveals that the mythical attitude governing the production of that work was *experienced.*

There is, of course, nothing surprising in this, when we consider that poetry has always given expression to our inner yearning for infinity, transparency and timelessness – in other words, to our resistance to the finiteness of our existence, the opacity created by the multitude of people and things, and our confinement in time. It seems that when we become involved with art or literature, even by merely reading, we feel that this necessarily implies a change in our normal state, in other words, that the essential objective is to discover mythical elements in literary creation.

Though the extent to which one is affected depends on one's disposition and receptiveness, giving one's attention to a work of art always involves making a journey in the course of which one is reborn different, endowed with attributes that are foreign to one's so-called real state, for, freed of all restrictions, one is able to communicate with an anonymous 'other', who is absent but universal.

This subjective experience, which is lived out profoundly and with all its attendant risks by the poet, but felt fleetingly and almost unconsciously by the reader, is mirrored in the experience embodied by mythical narratives. For the insane desire to create oneself by one's own means, to become fundamentally different and to attain a state free of all spatial and temporal restrictions is apparent in the epic adventures of both poets and mythical heroes. These portray the same testing journey, and so make it possible for the person who reads or listens to the narrative to undertake that journey, to the extent that he or she believes in its existence.

Thus mythical cosmogonic narratives and poems have the same function:

they enable people to experience a state that it is impossible to experience. This state, represented figuratively by gods, heroes and poets, and attained through a particular initiatory experience, reflects the human aspiration towards freedom that underlies the desire for self-creation, for rebirth in one's chosen form.

In this way, beneath the surface of the text, there lies an account of an adventure that is experienced as a form of grace bringing salvation, and it is here that the real meaning of the text is to be found. Generally, religious themes and terms occur in profusion, as though they alone can express such an experience, as though they alone can communicate it.

What is strangest is to discover in a literary text the triple sequence of distancing, rapture and rebirth that characterizes mythical narratives. Today, such sequences refer to the 'journey' involved in the creation of a work of art. In this context, the word 'creation' carries all its possible connotations, since it relates not so much to the production of the work of art itself as to its author, who has become different, changed.

Max Bilen

Narcissus

The origins of the character and genesis of the myth remain unknown. In its first appearance in Ovid's *Metamorphoses* (III. 339–510), the legend of Narcissus is presented in a complete form, already containing a mythical meaning. Narcissus is the lovechild of Liriope (a river in Boeotia) and the River Cephissus. As soon as he was born his mother, who was uncommonly beautiful, wanted to know if he would have a long life. She asked Tiresias who told her he would, *if he did not know himself.*

The young and wild Narcissus, who was very handsome but very proud, remained untouched by love. During a hunt the nymph Echo fell in love with him; she pursued him passionately, without however telling him of her feelings, for she could never be the first to speak. Narcissus rejected her advances: 'Keep your arms from me / Be off! I'll die before I yield to you' (1986: 63). He had already scorned and rejected other nymphs. One of these pleaded with the goddess Nemesis to intervene and punish him for his coldness: 'So may he love – and never win his love!' (1986: 63). One day in the countryside Narcissus came to a limpid spring whose surface had never been disturbed by man or beast. It was surrounded by fresh, sweet grasses; he rested there for a few minutes and then leant over the water to quench his thirst. It was then that he saw his own image and immediately fell in love with it. 'He gazes at his eyes, twin constellations, / His hair worthy of Bacchus or Apollo, / His face so fine, his ivory neck, his cheeks / Smooth and the snowy pallor and the blush' (1986: 63). Without realizing it, he desired himself. Consumed by this inner fire, he forgot hunger and sleep and soon began to waste away. When he understood that he was in love with his own image and burning with love for himself, he longed only to die. After his death, the Naiads and Dryads wept as they prepared his funereal rites, but suddenly they noticed that his body had disappeared. In its place was a flower whose saffron-coloured centre was surrounded by white petals: the narcissus. The myth's original meaning is clear; it illustrates the power of Nemesis, who re-established universal justice. Narcissus was punished for having sought to escape the laws that apply to all, and for having refused to love anyone.

The myth surfaces here and there in the literature of the Middle Ages. The *Lai de Narcissus* (c. 1160–5), a short verse romance, draws directly on Ovid – like the later *Ovide moralisé* (early sixteenth century) – but emphasizes the motif of death from love. The nymph Echo becomes the princess Danaë; she expires of sorrow when she learns of the death of the handsome but indifferent Narcissus. Already the myth's meaning has evolved a little, since it is now showing the power of love. Thus Bernart de Ventadorn in *La Chanson de l'Alouette* is filled with hopeless love; the woman in whose eyes he saw himself one day feels nothing for him: 'Mirror, since I saw myself reflected in you, my deep sighs have been killing me; and I have lost myself, as the handsome Narcissus lost himself in the fountain'.

In the first part of *The Romance of the Rose*, written down by Guillaume de Lorris (1225–30), we see the poet entering the garden of Déduit and reaching a fountain. An inscription tells him that this is the place where Narcissus died. He then recalls the story: scorning the nymph Echo, Narcissus refused to love her and she called on heaven for vengeance; Narcissus fell in love with his own image, then was driven mad with despair. Fearfully, the poet then approaches the fountain in which everything is miraculously reflected; in it he sees two crystals and a rose bush. The allegory is transparent: those who lean over the 'perilous mirror' cannot fail to see the reflection of some object that will place them on the path of love. It is impossible to escape the traps set by the Fountain of Love.

In his elegy 'Le Narcisse pris d'Ovide' (*Le Bocage*, 1554), Ronsard is content to remain faithful to the legend as set out by the Latin poet and does not give the myth any new meanings. Cyrano de Bergerac, on the other hand, in his *Lettre sur l'ombre que faisaient les arbres dans l'eau* (1654), adds an original element although his allusion to Narcissus is brief. Lying by a river he sees 'the story of Narcissus renewed by the trees' and admires the trembling images of a poplar wood reflected in the water – an inverted world which makes him wonder about the nature of reality: is the reflection not just as real as the world?

It is not until the eighteenth century that the myth reappears. In a very fine but little-known poem called 'Narcisse ou l'île de Vénus' (1769), Malfilâtre sings of the dangers of self-love. Fleeing human vices, Love has departed from the Earth. To bring him back among the mortals, Venus creates an island on which thousands of adolescents live a life entirely devoted to love. But this paradise does not last, for self-love: *Qui, de l'Amour et rival et bourreau, Au fond des coeurs le cherche et l'assassine* (Who, being Love's rival and executioner, Seeks deep in hearts for him and murders him) appears there and ruins everything (Book 1).

Echo and Narcissus are destined to love each other, but Tiresias, who knows the fate that threatens the two young people, tries to separate them. When Venus presses him to explain his behaviour, he agrees, but Echo, who is hiding in a bush, overhears everything (Book 2). Tiresias recalls the disappointment of Juno, who was not given the golden apple, and his own story: Juno wants revenge on both Venus and Tiresias (Book 3). Narcissus, who loves Echo, prepares to fight the monsters that Juno may send against him, but then he looks at himself in an enchanted spring, falls in love with his image (which he thinks is that of a nymph) and forgets Echo. When he discovers that he is irredeemably in love with his own reflection, he abandons himself to death and metamorphoses into a flower. In turn the island's inhabitants come to look at themselves in the spring; they die victims to their scorn for real love (Book 4). Malfilâtre wanted to show the mortal danger of self-love: *Par qui chacun, devenu son idole, Et se compare et se préfère à tout* (Through which everyone becomes his own idol Comparing and preferring himself to all) and to paint the pleasures of real love in seductive colours. Narcissus is no longer guilty, but has become an innocent victim: Malfilâtre employs the myth to express a moral.

Rousseau's comedy *Narcisse ou l'amant de lui-même* (begun 1729; finished 1742 and first performed in 1752) only touches on the myth. Valère, who is engaged to Angélique, falls in love with a portrait in which he is depicted as a woman. 'Since he is attractive, is he so wrong to love himself?' says Angélique, acknowledging the possibility. His sister Lucinde, who loves Cléante, refuses to marry Angélique's brother Léandre until she understands that Léandre and Cléante are the same person. In gentle revenge for the portrait joke, Angélique has preserved Lucinde's misunderstanding. Everything turns out for the best when all the illusions are dispelled. These brilliant variations, in which Rousseau was criticizing a particular dandy, had profound resonance for him.

The myth of Narcissus became extremely significant at the end of the nineteenth century, when symbolism held sway. Gide's first published work *Le Traité du Narcisse* (1891, 1892), considerably updated its meaning. First, Gide depicts a worried and uncertain Narcissus consumed by boredom. Passionately longing to be able to look at himself, he goes in search of a mirror and stops 'on the banks of the river of time'. Wondrous apparitions pass before him, coming from the future and flowing away into the past: 'Why so many – and why the same? It must be because they are imperfect, as they keep beginning again . . .' Narcissus then dreams of Paradise, where everything would remain stable, in harmonious perfection. Here Gide introduces the myth of Adam. The primitive androgyne finally tires of looking at this enchanting vision of the forms of the world: he wants to see himself and dares to break a branch from the tree Ygdrasil. Then Adam splits; the harmony is destroyed and Man, henceforward incomplete, will never cease to look in vain for the lost paradise. Narcissus symbolizes the poet who wants to discover archetypes and essences behind imperfect appearances and the water represents the work of art: 'crystal – a partial paradise in which the Idea flowers again in its superior purity'. In contemplating the world's reflections, Narcissus finally sees his own image and falls in love with it. But he realizes that this love remains unattainable: 'One must not desire an image; a movement towards possessing it destroys it. He is alone. What can he do? Look.' Narcissus must not prefer himself to the world.

The same concept is to be found in the *Discours sur la mort de Narcisse ou l'impérieuse métamorphose* (1895) by Saint-Georges de Bouhélier. The author changes the legend to some extent: Narcissus admires his image so much that it turns him away from all women, for 'he finds himself so exquisite that he thinks it impossible to find anyone more beautiful'. But Bouhélier does not dwell on this part of the legend, for he considers it bland. He prefers to draw attention to Narcissus' final metamorphosis: the young man could not see and appreciate the splendours of nature, but turned away from them to confine himself to contemplation of his own being. Once he has metamorphosed into a golden flower, he regrets his mistake and longs to become first grass, then a pebble, then a spring, then a leaf. Like Narcissus, the poet should not lose sight of the fact that 'what he adores, firstly through Nature, remains only his Shadow . . . If, as an infatuated apostate, he leaves the Earth, [he] is punished for it'. Thus the poet must forget himself and look lovingly on nature: let him become dead to himself in order to be reborn in the flower of poetic work. This is the message of naturism, as advocated by Saint-Georges de Bouhélier.

The myth of Narcissus is a real 'poetic autobiography' for Valéry. In 1890 he wrote a sonnet on Narcissus in which the latter suffers from his unhappy love for himself: 'For I love myself! . . . Oh, ironic reflection of me.' The 1891 poem 'Narcisse parle', which he reworked after modifying it in the *Album de vers anciens*, develops the same theme. Narcissus vainly languishes for love of himself; he adores his body's reflection but weeps because he must remain alone. In *Charmes* (1926), the 'Fragments du Narcisse' give a greater coherence to the myth and introduce new meanings. Without the fountain, Narcissus would never have been able to admire his own image: nature is needed for self-awareness to dawn. At the same time, the self discovers that it is inexhaustible, but feels the limitations of the image which the fountain gives back to it. Valéry thus counters the myth's traditional meaning, which regards love for the self as a mistake. Indeed, lovers remain separated and strangers to each other, whereas Narcissus experiences the happiness of plenitude: *O mon bien souverain, cher corps, je n'ai que toi! Le plus beau des mortels ne peut chérir que soi* (Oh my sovereign wealth, dear body, I have only you! The most handsome of mortals can hold only himself dear.) One can love only oneself properly: *J'aime . . . J'aime! . . . Et qui donc peut aimer autre chose Que soi-même?* (I love . . . I love! And who can love anything other Than himself?)

However, Narcissus knows that the fusion of himself with his reflection, between the profound self and the ephemeral appearance, remains impossible. Night descends, death is close and a kiss breaks up the image; Narcissus must also disappear. Valéry's *Cantate du Narcisse* (1941), a libretto written to be set to music by Germaine Tailleferre, adds nothing new, but *L'Ange*, a prose poem of 1945, deepens the theme of the earlier poems. The angel sitting by a fountain looks at himself and, weeping, wonders at his sadness. He does not understand that the mystery of Being resists intelligence. For Valéry, the myth of Narcissus never ceases to represent the delicate relationship which temporarily unites consciousness and body, the self and its appearance.

Having shown the power of Nemesis, who punishes those who seek to escape the common lot, the myth of Narcissus depicted the imperious power of love. The generation that followed the Symbolists finally decoded in it, besides the indulgence of human beings towards themselves, 'the error of Narcissus' (in Louis Lavelle's apt words), who scorns the beauties of the universe and prefers to look at himself. In the myth they saw the conflict between identity and duality in human nature.

Yves-Alain Favre

Nietzsche, Disciple of Dionysus

As a destroyer of idols and denouncer of ideologies, Nietzsche took on the task of freeing human beings from their religious and metaphysical beliefs. Yet his lucid psychological insight obliged him to recognize the unavoidable fact that 'Man is a venerating animal'. Thus to suppress veneration, to take the divine out of the world, would be a deliberate act of nihilism that would amount to suppressing ourselves. As a consequence, Nietzsche proposed to complete the nihilistic process, in the simple hope that the old God's decline would announce the birth of a new faith: 'It is only after the death of religion that invention in the realm of the divine can once more proliferate.' When it is pitted against religion, the cult of reason and the hegemony of philosophical discourse, the myth once more becomes the speech of the future: the important thing is not so much to restore the old beliefs as to invent new possibilities for life and thought, which will give back to human beings a sense of the earth and the feeling of life's eternity. 'Such a faith', writes Nietzsche in *The Twilight of the Gods* (1888) 'is the highest of all possible faiths: I have baptized it with the name of Dionysus'.

DIONYSUS AND APOLLO

In *The Birth of Tragedy* (1872), Dionysus appears as one of the essential protagonists on Nietzsche's philosophical stage. His symbolism is a means of interpreting Greek culture and, more particularly, tragedy; but he can be understood only in relation to his solar antagonist, Apollo, the god of measure, appearance and dreams. The latter symbolizes the strictly Hellenic spirit confronted by the fearsome Dionysian power, which is sensed as foreign but, in fact, is buried in the furthest depths of the Greek soul. Dionysus is the god of music, which Nietzsche, following Schopenhauer, believes to be 'the true language of the universal', in that it emanates from the primal suffering heart of things and that it awakens nostalgia for the original One in the world of the Will. The Dionysian element thus provides human beings with a paradoxical experience: the horror felt by the individual faced with a primal lack of differentiation and the violence unleashed in the sacred celebration; and the 'delicious ecstasy' provoked by the breakdown of the principle of individual existence and the feeling of melting into the primitive One.

Tragedy is born of the reconciliation between these two 'artistic drives of nature', which are both contrary and complementary. It thus answers a metaphysical necessity implicit in the essence of the One which, 'as eternal suffering and contradiction', needs 'delicious appearance' as a consolation. Thus, it is always Dionysus who hides beneath the mask of the tragic hero. The god dismembered by the Titans represents the horrible reality of the world; but, due to the intervention of the Apollonian element (the images of the myth, discourse, etc.) which throws a 'veil' between the spectator and Dionysus, that reality appears transfigured. This gives rise to the pleasure of tragedy, the 'metaphysical consolation' that is made possible by the synthesis of the Apollonian and the Dionysian.

In *The Birth of Tragedy* and in subsequent works, Nietzsche expresses his basic intuition, but this remains hidden by the 'metaphysics of the artist' inherited from Schopenhauer and stamped with the influence of Hegel, as Nietzsche himself acknowledges in *Ecce Homo* (1888). Indeed, perhaps Greek tragedy itself was possible only because of a misunderstanding or occultation of Dionysian tragedy. Thus Nietzsche quickly abandoned Schopenhauerian vocabulary, the idea of a primal One and the dualist pairing of Dionysus and Apollo. He renounced the philosophy of tragedy to set off on the path of a tragic philosophy, the secret of which is held by Dionysus. The 'ambiguous god' comes to represent a world with neither origins nor end, a paradoxical image, liable to escape from conceptual categories and indeed from the confines of philosophy itself.

THE TRAGIC DIONYSIAN UNIVERSE

To defeat nihilism and metaphysics requires an affirmatory process of destruction. Dionysus thus not only acts as a standard-bearer in the war against the values of decadence but also represents a positive response to their collapse:

Dionysus against the philosophy of being. The philosophy of being is the sign of a declining will that rejects becoming and creates a rift between Man and 'the tragic economy' of life, implying suffering and a waste of effort. Conversely, what Nietzsche calls his 'Dionysian universe' must be viewed as a sea of forces in perpetual motion, a world that ceaselessly destroys and recreates itself, like Dionysus himself. Returning to the metaphors of Heraclitus, Nietzsche imagines the world as a 'divine game' beyond good and evil.

Dionysus against decadence. The victory of metaphysics is that of 'weakness'. This rejects life and war, the body and emotions, and, motivated by resentment, encloses existence in unhealthy 'systems of cruelties': morality, religions, states. Dionysus, who 'has the double nature of a wild, cruel demon and a benevolent and gentle ruler', provides the image of an economy of life that accepts the interplay of different elements, that accepts danger and the expending of effort. Dionysian cruelty is a source of exaltation and joy, an acceptance of the world of the 'will to power'.

'Dionysus against the crucified one.' This is Nietzsche's final formulation of his ideas. It occurs at the end of *Ecce Homo* and sums up his entire undertaking, which involves an attempt to replace a depressive representation of the divine

with an intensive one that constitutes a 'sanctification' of the world and of life. A fragment written in 1888 explains the meaning of the contrast between 'the two types: Dionysus and the crucified one': 'the "God on the cross" is a curse on life, an invitation to detach oneself from life. The dismemberment of Dionysus is a promise of access to life: he is eternally reborn and escapes destruction.' This divergence reflects the fundamental dichotomy between the Christian and the pagan: whereas paganism offers many different possibilities for making existence divine, monotheism reflects the death of the divine and the neglect of sacredness (compare *Thus Spoke Zarathustra* (1883–5), VI. 203). Finally, the Christian god is the god of sin and debt, whereas Dionysus, who created the world in an act of generous exertion, bears witness to the innocence of life.

DIONYSUS, THE SACRED PATH

Dionysus, the object of 'sacred faith', always remains apart from philosophy. His place is at the exorbitant centre of creation, which language must always skirt around. The superman, the great politician and Zarathustra himself belong to Nietzsche's philosophy and, to this extent, are only masks of 'Dionysus the philosopher'. No matter how positive the new evaluations of the world provided by Nietzsche's philosophy may be, they too must be subject to the law of Eternal Recurrence and be caught up in the Dionysian cycle of destruction and creation. Thus they cannot actually be truths, and in *The Dithyrambs of Dionysus* (1888–9), the god himself announces to the 'wise Zarathustra' that the latter must die and abandon himself to Dionysus as his mad truth. Understanding of the god's nature escapes Nietzsche the philosopher, but constitutes the secret of Nietzsche the 'disciple of Dionysus'. Lying beyond philosophical discourse and surpassing any possibility of conceptual expression, Dionysian 'truth' can only be suggested by metaphors, proper names or mythical images.

Eternal Recurrence is one of the god's revelations, which comes to Nietzsche in the form of an ecstatic experience, but whose deeper meaning remains hidden from him when he tries to express it (compare 'Eternal Recurrence'). Ariadne is another riddle in the philosophical text. As the interlocutor and lover of Dionysus, she gathers up his words and lets their echo play around the labyrinth of her ears ('Ariadne's lament'). She is thus a redoubled affirmation of the Dionysian world, through whom becoming takes on the character of eternity and for whom the Eternal Recurrence is a 'wedding ring'. However, she is also an image of life, a labyrinthine double of Dionysus, an interplay between appearance and itself, ungrounded and without hidden truth. Like life, she is wasteful and cruel through love. Gripped by her love for the god, she desires the hero's death: 'this is the last of my love for Theseus: "I cause his death" '. Lastly, she is a type of woman who has never been understood by Man, be he philosopher or hero. Dionysus's love for Ariadne expresses an essentially positive desire, free of all repression and exempt from the divisions on which Man's desire is based, including the clear-cut distinction between masculine and feminine.

These names and the mythical figures who bear them hide as much as they reveal and are as untrustworthy as they are seductive. Indeed, they refer to possibilities of existence that perhaps exceed the capacities of human beings, requiring a lucidity as dangerous as it is liberating. This is why Dionysus is a true god, a sacred figure who must remain an object of 'faith', keeping reason at bay. It is also why, when Nietzsche no longer kept a philosopher's distance and the philosophical myth combined with his personal myth, he was consumed by the uncontrollable violence of the sacred. At this point, as his last notes demonstrate, differences began to waver, Ariadne became Cosima, Dionysus was assimilated to the crucified one, and Nietzsche, identifying himself with Dionysus, abandoned himself to a last ecstatic experience with a sacrificial outcome demanding the annihilation of its subject.

Camille Dumoulié

Odysseus

> He holds out a palm calloused by tackle and tiller and his skin is engraved by heat, snow and the norwester.
> You would think he was trying to save us from the monstrous Cyclops,
> the Sirens with their song that carries forgetting, from Charybdis and from Scylla,
> All these monsters so strange they make us forget that he, Odysseus, was a man like us.
> That he joined battle in this world, with all his body and soul.
>
> (Georges Séféris, 'Reflections on a foreign line of verse', 1932)

These lines well illustrate the specificity of the myth of Odysseus: at every step of his literary destiny, the son of Laertes is offered to us with a force and presence which tend to remove him from the reverential aura enjoyed by, for example, Antigone and Oedipus, and give him the status of a person with whom it becomes possible to identify. Endowed with a remarkable flexibility which comes from the intelligence that he incarnates, Odysseus is a creature of resolved tensions, of contradictions overcome, but his ever-perceptible effort confers unforgettable human warmth upon him, whether we find him in the work of Dante, Shakespeare, Joyce or Kazantzakis. His actions are governed by the dialectic of the internal and the external, but it would be fruitless to look to him for some 'Odyssean scene' that would be analogous to the 'Oedipal scene'. Freud's couch could not hold a man who aspires to return to his bed of olive wood.

The very richness of Odysseus' deeds prevents us from giving any more than an outline here, which will begin with an examination of the essence that makes Odysseus what he is, his intelligence, and will move to a brief analysis of the contents of the myth. Finally, there will be a presentation of the major thematic developments suggested by the most important episodes of the story of the king of Ithaca, whether in the work of Homer or of others.

STUPIDITY IS NOT HIS STRENGTH, OR THE DOUBLE POSTULATION OF ODYSSEAN 'METIS'

It is in the *Iliad* and the *Odyssey* that we must first seek the elements of a subtle portrait of the components of Odysseus' character. All the later additions should not make us forget that they have something of the nature of 'apocrypha' in relation to Homer's Vulgate.

When he entitled his suggestive essay *Ulysse ou l'intelligence* (1946), Gabriel

Audisio went straight to the heart of the matter. Odysseus is the only one of Homer's heroes to be described in terms that define various nuances of intelligence carried to its height since, here too, it is only to him that adjectives beginning with *poly* are attributed. Let us take the three most important: *polymetis, polytropos* and *polymechanos. Metis* (which in divine form is the mother of Athena, by Zeus) is the ability rapidly to sum up a situation and the adaptation demanded by it. Detienne and Vernant (1978) have subtly analysed the entire register of this quality, which is characteristic as much of the artisan's inventiveness as of the detour required by some danger. The *tropoi* and *mechanai* are the 'engines' in the ancient sense of the word, which Odysseus' *metis*, quick to grasp reality, uses to overcome a difficulty either by unravelling it or by going round it. *Metis* is a detour, a step back, time to think. Odysseus never rushes headlong, like his companions, at the challenge with which hostile reality constantly confronts him. We should note another important term: *dolos*. In Homer's work this is partially a neutral word, or rather a word with positive and negative connotations: it can be a 'clever trick' or 'brainwave', or it may turn to 'dol', deception.

In Homer's work, Odysseus, favourite of Athene, the goddess of intelligence itself, is an eminently positive hero, stained only by a few innuendoes from jealous or irritated mockers. Odysseus is a hero who is both 'like others' and different from others. It is understood that he is a brave warrior (he is described as *ptolipothes*, town taker), but his *metis* sets him apart from the 'basic hero'. He is above all a man of difficult, complex situations where his intuition, accompanied by a gift for oratory recognized by all, works wonders. The speech on the danger of having many leaders and the way he takes a routed army in hand (*Iliad* II) were admired by Shakespeare and Gladstone. His concern to adapt to the person to whom he is speaking – the meaning given by the sophists to *polytropos* – marks him out as the perfect 'good offices man' for the representation to Achilles (*Iliad* IX). The pontificating Nestor himself looks insistently at him at this time, thus signifying the hope that all have placed in him.

The distance that *metis* takes in relation to reality is also coolheadedness and self control. *Compos sui*, Odysseus thus finds himself chosen for particularly dangerous commando missions. This is the case when (*Iliad* X) Diomedes insists on having Odysseus at his side in the episode when they capture Dolon, whose death is later falsely imputed to Odysseus, and for the theft of the Palladium. Whether confronting Ajax, the hero with the shield of seven bull skins, an allegory of his narrowness of mind, or the brutal and monstrous strength of Polyphemus the cyclops, Odysseus is always presented as the victorious champion of intelligence, which gives rise to a great deal of hostility against him.

Three examples illustrate both Odysseus' atypical aspects and the depth that his use of *metis* can reach. In *Iliad* III, the Trojan Antenor describes to

Helen the first mission, which inspired Giraudoux, sketching a parallel between Odysseus and Menelaus.

> When all were standing, Menelaus with his broad shoulders over-topped the whole company; but Odysseus was the more imposing of the two when both were seated. When their turn came to express their views in public, Menelaus spoke fluently, not at great length, but very clearly, being a man of few words who kept to the point, though he was the younger of the two. By contrast, when the nimble-witted Odysseus took the floor, he stood there with his head bent firmly down, glancing from under his brows, and he did not swing his staff either to front or back, but held it stiffly, as though he had never handled one before. You would have taken him for a sulky fellow and no better than a fool. But that great voice of his came booming from his chest, and the words poured from his lips like flakes of winter snow, there was no man alive who could compare with Odysseus. When we looked at him then, we were no longer misled by appearances.
>
> (Homer 1950: 69–70)

This exceptional attitude later gave much food for thought to the rhetors and sophists of the classical and hellenistic ages and in it we can already see Pascal's axiom: 'true eloquence thinks nothing of eloquence'.

Elsewhere a pause before speaking became the desire to stretch the possibilities of his intelligence to their fullest extent without resorting to the 'joker' of divine help, in the episode of Ino Leukothee's veil (*Odyssey* V). Alone on his raft, struck by a terrifying storm, Odysseus delays, without totally rejecting, the help that his *metis* considers as possibly 'some new snare that one of the immortals had set to catch him'.

> 'No,' he decided; 'I will not leave the boat at once, for I saw with my own eyes how far the land is where she promised me salvation. Instead I shall do what I myself think best. As long as the joints of my planks hold fast, I shall stay where I am and put up with the discomfort.
>
> (Homer 1946: 97)

Odysseus prefers a suffering he is fully aware of and requires him to use all his own resources to doubtful aid from heaven. His obstinacy here is similar to Don Juan's stubborn desire to confront the unknown. 'There is something I cannot understand here.' *Metis* is also the beginnings of a critical attitude.

The last facet of the self control which Odysseus has developed is suggested to us by the famous words, 'Patience, my heart!'. Thus 'he was able by such self-rebuke to quell all mutiny in his heart and steel it to endure' (Homer 1946: 304). Here Odysseus resists his desire for immediate vengeance on the unfaithful women. But that which is still only remarkable self control becomes a moral virtue when, after the massacre of the suitors, he forbids the faithful Eurycleia to rejoice at their deaths. If the punishment was just, all talking about it would be hubris, the supreme moral fault: 'Restrain yourself, old dame, and gloat in silence. I'll have no jubilation here. It is an impious thing to exult over the slain' (Homer 1946: 338).

In a passage full of humour and gentleness, qualities which belong to the world of the *Odyssey* (whereas that of the *Iliad* is full of Ares), Odysseus has just been deposited asleep on a beach in Ithaca by the Phaeacians. When he wakes up he does not know where he is. Athene approaches him in the form of a young shepherd and tells him that he is in Ithaca. Ulysses refuses to believe it and reels off one of the 'imaginary lives' he invents throughout the *Odyssey* and which act as shields against the unknown. But Athena reveals herself to him with jubilation. Her protégé is always the same! He cannot help lying. But, in this case, it is the trickster who is tricked, hence Athena's satisfaction. One line (*Odyssey* XIII. 332), which is the goddess' homage to her favourite, sums up the positive aspect of Odysseus' *metis* in three adjectives. 'That is why I cannot desert you in your misfortunes: you are so civilized, so intelligent, so self-possessed' (Homer 1946: 211). *Epetes* means 'civilized', 'polite'; *anchinoos* means 'whose intelligence gets the closest' to perceived reality, 'who catches on quickly'; and lastly *echephron* implies the 'lead in the brain' of those who know how to keep their distance.

It is this rare combination in one man that renders him dear to Athene, who appears here as Odysseus' big, divine twin sister. Furthermore, as Zeus' daughter she is related to him through his father's line, since Laertes is the son of Arkisios, who was Zeus' son.

Perhaps the word *epetes* places Odysseus completely apart from other mythological incarnations of intelligence, such as Prometheus, whose indisputable inventiveness does not let us forget that he is a Titan and thus separated from the very human beings he has so helped.

This is the positive aspect of Odysseus' *metis* and the character traits connected with it. Stendal ('fully nineteen years old' in 1802) plans to write a tragedy about Odysseus and notes: 'Odysseus has a most prudent nature which Homer gives him in his poems. He is never secretive, for that fault is debasing'. In so saying he nobly opted for an Odysseus who was irreproachable but mutilated in a no less important part of his character which constitutes the other side of the *metis* examined above. For Laertes' son is also that of Anticlea and her father was Autolycos, who was thus Odysseus' grandfather and gave him his name, linking him, according to the 'fatal' etymologies so beloved of the Greeks, to the verb *odysao*, meaning 'to be angry with', 'to be annoyed'. In taking his grandson on his knee and baptizing him with this name, Autolycos makes him in some sense a 'man of resentment'. This is only understandable when we know that Autolycos, who was descended from Hermes, was well known for his various frauds and tricks. Through this ancestry we go back to the pre-Homeric origins, no doubt pure folklore, of an Ur-Ulixes, linked to the universal theme of the crafty accomplice, the virtuoso deceiver of which Till Eulenspiegel gives us a fine and more recent example. In addition to this already fairly weighted inheritance through which

Hermes counters the benevolent influence of Athene, there is another version of Odysseus' birth, unknown to Homer but used by the Tragedians. According to this version, Autolycos gave the master bawd Sisyphus, who had stopped for the night at his house, the *jus primae noctis* with his daughter Anticlea, who then thus went off to Laertes ignorant of her misfortune, pregnant by the offices of that most disreputable of individuals. Later tradition developed the *odium* of Odysseus and did not fail to throw the description 'Sisyphus' bastard' at him, which has understandably sickened him.

But this inheritance is active and manifests itself through the same *metis* whose positive aspect we have seen. The negative version is most frequently an excess or distortion of the positive, when virtue turns to vice. We can counter the positive elements of his intelligence antithetically almost word for word. Skill becomes cunning or scheming, flexibility baseness and obsequiousness; reserve turns to hypocrisy, defiance to lies. The mocking smile becomes the hideous grin of the deceiver, satisfied that his plan has worked as he had planned. Politeness becomes pitiless, cruel cynicism. Odysseus' character turns from dual to duplicitous. Athena's protégé, the subtle son of Laertes, changes into Sisyphus' bastard, obeying the instincts of Hermes, the god of thieves.

The contrast is violent and forms the dynamism of the literary character of Odysseus. For, outside the work of Homer, who deliberately softens the other side of his *metis*, the fortune of the Odysseus myth rests on this constant tension in his characaster. He is this and that, and a reaction in one direction always leaves open the possibility that the attraction to its opposite is hatching within him. However this attitude is of course always within the scope of well-integrated personalities in control of their own complexity. To this aspect, which has been particularly suggestive to the creators of Odysseus, is added another, arising from a kind of conflict between Homer's Vulgate and the other traditions. Homer's account of the deeds of Odysseus is the obligatory reference work for any adaptation, transposition or indeed innovation of his myth. Often the creator is caught between Homer's Odysseus and the temptation to give him negative reactions. When it is fragmented, the *metis* risks breaking up, the tension is no longer bearable and such an avatar of Odysseus thus cannot accede to literary existence.

'NEITHER EXCESS OF HONOUR, NOR UNWORTHINESS': FORTUNES AND MISFORTUNES OF ULYSSES' LITERARY POSTERITY

After Homer, the various versifications (for their poetic worth is almost non-existent) of the Epic Cycle sought to denigrate Odysseus, whether deliberately or, more simply, by extending his biography to include all the great sweeps that either preceded or followed the Trojan War and that Homer had not described. *The Little Iliad, Cypriot Songs*, the *Aethiopid* and the *Telegony* were all precious references for the mythographers, whom they informed about the

'Palamede affair', in which Odysseus is said to have obtained the death of a man whom he presented as a traitor but whom, according to the same sources, Odysseus actually hated since he had forced him to leave Ithaca. They also informed them about the 'affair of Achilles' weapons' and the murder of Polyxenes and Astyanax. The *Telegony* depicts a sordid Ithaca where Odysseus finds a Penelope who has given in to her suitors, before dying from the arrows of Telegonos, the son whom he had had with Circe and who, after his death, marries Penelope, whereas Telemachus goes to marry Circe. This is a real soap opera; the sad thing is that some of these calumnies remain in great literature. Thus Pindar's Dorian violently attacks Odysseus the Ionian (fifth and seventh *Nemeans*) with a double accusation of cowardice and baseness. This theme is frequently taken up, illustrated particularly by the use of the bow, the 'weapon of cowards', made by Odysseus, and his acts 'committed in secret and profiting from the darkness', such as the capture of Dolon. In the fifth century, Odysseus became a greedy and libidinous character in the 'satyrical dramas'. But this is fair enough, he is not the only hero to have been ridiculed in this way.

The tragedy plays on the two facets of his *metis*, but while Sophocles tries to keep the balance, Euripides follows the tradition of *odium*. This *odium* was reinforced at that time by the dragooning of Odysseus by the Sophists and Cynics. As these two were not well thought of, Odysseus suffered the rejection to which they were subject. And it is no coincidence that Alcibiades was called *polytropos*. Odysseus was assimilated to a demagogue close to Cleon. What a fall! Although Plato drove Homer out of his city, he often refers to Odysseus with a certain sympathy tinged with condescension. Odysseus is the down-to-earth hero who did not want to see men go into battle on an empty stomach (the *Iliad* IX): he becomes the guarantor of a home-loving morality.

The Stoics' interest in Odysseus gave him back his inner dimension. He is *polytlas*, having experienced the trials of any human life. He is already the *homo viator* of the Christians. This philosophical component enables him to survive through contrary times.

For here is Rome with its Trojan legend and the *gens Julia*, through the intermediary of Augustus, imposes the version favourable to the vanquished. Yesterday's victors have moreover become the Graeculi of which Odysseus became the model. In the work of Roman writers of the classical period (first century BC to second century AD) a strange separation is observable between a negative literary Odysseus and a positive, philosophical Odysseus. This is the case with Seneca, whose *Troades* presents the treacherous and murderous Odysseus of Euripides, while the *Letters to Lucilius* make him a sage and model of temperance and equanimity. Ovid to his *Metamorphoses* (XIII) gives a very full account of the charges against Odysseus in relation to the *topos* of the dispute over Achilles' weapons, here expressed by Ajax, and the defence the accused makes for himself in a remarkable speech full of humour and subtlety, through which he of course wins his case.

From the second century AD a great number of allegorical works based on Homer were written, their most notorious representative being Heraclides of Pontus who never lets a word or gesture from Odysseus pass without weighing it down with a commentary, later taken up by the Church Fathers. Origen saw Odysseus on his ship as the symbol of Christ at the helm of the Church; Porphyrus and the Neoplatonists also recruited Odysseus, who had entirely lost his literary existence to become simply a pretext for interpretative digressions. Lastly, we shall give two examples which are contemporaneous but speak in the name of antagonistic gods. Saint Basil of Caesarea, in his discourse *On the Value of Greek Literature* made Odysseus cast naked on the shore his model for virtue. Nausicaa finds him and, far from having to blush at being seen naked, he inspires the princess with respect, for the poet has given him virtue as a coat. All the Phaeacians seek to imitate him and the poet tells us to cultivate the virtue that swims with the shipwrecked man and makes him appear more honourable in his nakedness than the honourable Phaeacians (V). At the same period, Julian the Apostate constantly refers to the *Odyssey* in his letters and discourses as a Church Father would refer to the Bible, prefacing his quotations with, 'for, as the poet said'.

Rome dominated the West and some centuries were unsympathetic to Odysseus, when only his truncated, negative image survived. He is a treacherous liar in Benoît de Sainte-Maure's *Story of Troilus* (twelfth century) and its Anglo-Saxon adaptations by Caxton and Lydgate (fifteenth century). However, there is one brief flash of light in the thirty lines of Book 26 of Dante's *Inferno*. In one sense it is not until Joyce that Ulysses again reaches such power. But the Renaissance missed the meeting we might have expected with Odysseus, despite the fact that his openness and flexibility made him a hero of the Renaissance type. For while the themes of the *Odyssey* may have inspired Le Primatice with the frescoes of the Ulysses Gallery in Fontainebleau, now lost, the sporadic mentions of his name by Du Bellay or Ronsard do not constitute a real use of the theme. Shakespeare alone proposed a truly remarkable and convincing Odysseus as a Renaissance man. The seventeenth century kept him in semi-oblivion or presented him powdered with winter weather. Towards the end of the century Pope and Dryden, translators and commentators of the *Odyssey*, were closer to Homer's Odysseus than was Fénélon, whose *Télémaque* is too full of politeness and good intentions not to provoke a degree of somnolence. Indeed, until the beginning of the eighteenth century Odysseus and Homer 'sleep sometimes'. Goethe abandoned a play on Odysseus and Nausicaa while Stendhal abandoned his tragedy on Odysseus' return.

The Romantic *Wanderlust* brought a fresh approach, letting in the wind of departure and the taste for sea spray which favoured Odysseus and washed away the cobwebs of centuries. In 1808 Charles Lamb's *The Adventures of Ulysses*, a work for children, gave the *Odyssey* back its freshness and liveliness as a tale, qualities which were to seduce the young James Joyce and underlay his attraction to Odysseus. From Tennyson (1833) to Moravia (1955) via

Pascoli (1904), Joyce (1922), Séféris (1935) and Kazantzakis (1938), the modern success of the myth of Odysseus is both varied and, usually, pertinent in its thematic choices.

The present outline was intended merely to indicate the changing fortunes of the 'brand image' of a character who is evidently the most contradictorily 'judged' of the mythical Greek heroes. Whether venerated or damned, he leaves no one indifferent. We shall now proceed to an examination of the various Odyssean themes, referring only to their use value for western writers and no longer respecting chronological order.

WHEN SOMEONE IS NEEDED, HE IS THE ONE: ULYSSES IN *PHILOCTETES*

Odysseus' very qualities as a political negotiator constantly place him in awkward situations: he is begged to accept a mission; he carries it out, usually successfully or, when he fails, it is because no one could have succeeded (as in the mission to Achilles, *Iliad* IX). When attempts are made to congratulate him, he rejects these signs of gratitude, sometimes brutally, as in the episode when Dolon is captured. And experience soon teaches him that the reason for his mission, the public good or reasons of state, has been forgotten and people are thinking only of how it was carried out. What he has done out of devotion to the general good is regarded as a crime. He thus finds himself at the centre of the old debate between integrity and practicality. 'Before' his words were 'of honey'; 'after', they are merely 'honeyed'.

A good example of Odysseus' unfortunate role as a man who always has to do the 'dirty work' to the advantage of the 'gaitered Acheans' is Sophocles' *Philoctetes* (*c.* 408 BC). The pestilential smell of his wound implied that Philoctetes should be left behind in Lemnos for the good of the army. But as an oracle had indicated that Troy would be taken only in his presence and with his bow and arrows, Odysseus is quickly despatched to achieve both ends. The candid Neoptolemus is to be the instrument of deception. He recoils at such dishonesty. Odysseus then turns to casuistry: 'For one brief hour of lying follow me. All time to come shall prove thy probity.' Neoptolemus again refuses, preferring 'to fail with honour [rather] than succeed by fraud.' (Sophocles 1957: 373) Odysseus goes one better: 'Mightier than deeds of puissance is the tongue', he says and goes on to say that there is no shame in lying 'if success depends upon a lie.' (Sophocles 1957: 375) What he is saying is that the ends justify the means. Throughout the play we feel that the bow must return to the Greeks and Philoctetes must also end his isolation. This is basically the mission to Achilles in another form, as the latter covertly threatened Odysseus by saying 'I loathe like Hell's Gates the man who thinks one thing and says another.' (Homer, 1950: 169)

Odysseus is convinced that he is the instrument of the general will and feels no personal animosity towards Philoctetes. The latter on the other hand keeps up an implacable criticism of Odysseus, whom he depicts to Neoptolemus in colours so dark that Achilles' son believes he is describing Thersites the abject troublemaker. Odysseus is certainly in no way hypocritical when he states that no one is more pious than he is. Did not Zeus himself acknowledge this in the first assembly of the gods (*Odyssey* I)? And in *Ajax* Sophocles gives us another facet of this Odysseus split between the responsibility he is asked to take on and the nobility of his soul. Ajax, siezed by madness and rendered suicidal by despair, makes Odysseus responsible for his death. Before he died, Odysseus had taken pity on the hero whom madness has rendered criminal and resisted the pressure of a cruel, cynical Athene, quite unlike the Athene of the *Odyssey*. Odysseus pleads Ajax' right to an honourable tomb before Agamemnon, who is opposed to it. In this play Odysseus has the part of a new Antigone. Speaking of Ajax he says to Agamemnon, who is surprised at his action: 'With me his worth outweighs his enmity' (Sophocles 1957: 113) and again, 'And who deserves my labour more than I?' (Sophocles 1957: 115), signifying the equality of all in the face of death and that Ajax' tomb is also his future grave.

Although Philoctetes' invective is not easily forgotten, Sophocles' Odysseus is a nuanced character overall. The unpleasant aspects of his missions are balanced by his awareness of being faithful to a duty imposed upon him.

Euripides seems to belong to the pro-Trojan camp at a time when the defeat of Athens made its inhabitants sympathetic to the vanquished. Thus in his work Odysseus is frankly antipathetic and seen almost exclusively from the point of view of his victims, of whom it is once more forgotten that they were singled out by the general will, Polyxena to satisfy the shade of Achilles and Astyanax so that Hector's line might be extinguished. It is hardly surprising that in *Hecuba* the old queen should call Odysseus 'an intoxicating seducer of crowds'. He is all the more odious because, to make him feel sorry for her, Hecuba describes how she kept silent to save his life during a mission to Troy. The queen's despair is understandable when, in *The Trojan Women*, fate alots her to Odysseus, 'that enemy of truth, that lawless viper'.

Before the Trojan murders Euripides' attention was focussed on Iphigeneia. Odysseus does not appear directly in *Iphigeneia at Aulis*, but the leaders, Agamemnon and Achilles, speak of him as 'Sisyphus' bastard'. Agamemnon fears his influence on the army and towards the end Achilles announces that Odysseus is at the head of the marching people. In *Iphigeneia in Tauris* Iphigeneia recalls that she was drawn to Aulis by Odysseus' lies. We should note the 'crowd' element, for it makes Odysseus a demagogue in the true sense of the word. This Odysseus is a sophist, a dangerous man. And we find him again in Seneca's *Troades*, which takes up Euripides' accusations unchanged.

Racine's Odysseus (*Iphigénie*, 1674) doubtless retains a little of this Machiavellian aspect. But Racine's skill as a dramatist is to have Odysseus criticize himself in the final scene for the pressure he earlier put on Agamemnon, while at the same time being the messenger of a happy end, all expressed in a few lines and with enough brilliance to obtain his absolution. This elegance in the 'sin admitted, sin pardoned' leads us towards Giraudoux. 'Yes, it is I, Madame, who long thought I had to strengthen your husband against her and against you . . . And who am come, since heaven is at last appeased, to repair all the hardship I have caused you'. (Act 5. Scene 6)

Aeneas describes Odysseus' blackness to Dido during his long narrative in book II of the *Aeneid.* But the very technique that Virgil uses implies a distance which prevents him from directly attributing to Odysseus the *odium* with which he is weighed down by Sinon. Indeed, by using an embedded narrative, it is the traitor Sinon who is given the task of describing the perfidy of the *pellax Ulixes*, but his hatred is all faked and his resentment against Odysseus has the sole aim of making the Trojans drop their guard and allow the horse inside their walls. And this tale is similar to Epimenides' sorites. For Sinon, who is here a kind of *alter ego* of Odysseus, is in fact working for the Danaeans when he drags Odysseus' name in the mud. The *odium* of Odysseus which is thus created appears as a very clever trick, with Sinon pushing his skill to the point of interrupting himself as though he could not go on with the account of horrors which, of course, arouse the anxious curiosity of the Trojans. Odysseus the *scelerum inventor* thus uses his discredit, through the deception of Sinon, one of his supposed victims 'promised for sacrifice', to perfect his decisive trick, the entry of the horse. So it is hard to state that Virgil's Odysseus is entirely negative, even though posterity may have perceived him as such, because of the distance implied by the subtle narrative mode he here employs.

All the unpleasant missions conferred upon Odysseus are spitefully listed by Ajax in his fight to obtain Achilles' weapons (Ovid, *Metamorphoses*, XIII). The importance of Odysseus' defence lies in the way in which he shows that all of his so-called crimes have served the general interest. This is the case with his trick to make Achilles reveal himself and thus leave for Troy when he was hidden at Lycomedes' home in Skyros. Dolon? He had to be killed after he had provided information necessary for the conduct of the war. Odysseus adds that he has supervised the material conditions and morale of the troops, which were neglected by the high command. He has done all the tasks that had to be done for the common good. This sums up the positive aspect of the myth. However we must analyse two interpretations which are more faithful to the spirit than to the letter, wherein their attraction lies.

Troilus and Cressida (1603) is one of the 'problem plays' in which Shakespeare seems to be questioning all values by displaying a world-weary cynicism. In a world where love, courage and received faith are violently and gratingly overturned, Odysseus appears as the only character apart from Troilus to retain his reason, sensitivity and integrity, while perfectly integrating certain elements of the Odysseus son of Autolycos. One long scene (Act I, Scene 3) presents the different facets of Odysseus the orator and negotiator, the

Odysseus of Book II of the *Iliad*, which was Shakespeare's source through Chapman's recent translation.

Odysseus starts with an analysis of the power relations between the Trojans and Greeks. The inferiority of the latter is explained by the general climate of insubordination among the troops. In a famous speech he then praises hierarchical authority (degree), a *topos* which he extends to the cosmic scale. It remains to him to propose a remedy to restore discipline. Odysseus skilfully cuts Agamemnon to the quick by reproducing a mimic portraying him as Patroclus facing Achilles in a very successful clown act which evokes Odysseus acting as a tramp at the end of the *Odyssey*. Odysseus' 'rich idea', which he expounds to Nestor, is to choose Ajax as the champion against Hector, which will inevitably exasperate the proud Achilles and bring him down a peg.

In his mission to Eacid, Odysseus uses another *topos*, the passing of time and the need for glory to restore it. Despite the extreme skill of his arguments, he does not manage to convince Achilles. But the context of this failure is that of the general climate of failure and lack of ideas chosen by Shakespeare. The force which breaks the door down like a ram wins out over intelligence, which has here become ineffective.

Odysseus shows his dignity by refusing Cressida's kiss, which all the other leaders have on the contrary avidly sought. He praises poor Troilus and remains sympathetically at his side when he witnesses Cressida giving herself to Diomedes almost before his very eyes (Act V. Scene 2). It is Odysseus' presence, his words of sympathy which are few but hit the right note, that prevent this cruel scene from sliding into vaudeville by adding a bit of the milk of human kindness which the play otherwise entirely lacks.

The Odysseus of *Troilus and Cressida*, a subtle politician and great orator of superior intelligence and a sensitivity which he has preserved in a world of treason and brutality, is undoubtedly the most perfect and coherent incarnation of the myth in its Renaissance form.

The Odysseus of Giraudoux' *The Trojan War Will Not Take Place* (1935) is on the contrary very hard to analyse, even more to define. He is protean, changing character with each person he speaks to (the *polytropos* of the Sophists) and, with the same one, here Hector, he demonstrates a disconcerting mixture of seriousness and impulse. Hector sums up this ambiguity when he asks, 'Is this Odysseus' cunning or his greatness?', in which the two components of his *metis* are combined.

Odysseus is present in two scenes (Act II. scenes 12 and 13) where he seems successively to incarnate four roles. First, during the account of the voyage of Paris and Helen, he deflates the lie constructed to save the peace with his ironic gibes. He is not fooled and he laughs at the expense of both the couple and the peace. His attitude is thus openly negative. After the intervention of Iris, the *dea ex machina*, Hector and Odysseus confront each other for the 'duet before the orchestra'. Odysseus changes completely, agreeing to act a short confession scene in which he defines himself to Hector as incarnating 'adult man', 'circumspection before gods, men and things' and 'the owl'. He goes no further with his confidences: he is a mature man who wants to warn Hector that his political vision is also that of the *Realpolitik* that Giraudoux had observed in those crucial years for Europe. This is the third aspect of Odysseus: a diplomat familiar with international conferences, an old traveller round the chancelleries who has certainly heard the analyses of Philippe Berthelot or Aristide Briand. His perspicacity is not restricted to political life: he has also 'understood everything' about Helen, and for a long time: she, the 'creator of destiny' is by her very 'narrowness' the most serious threat to peace.

In Odysseus' last change of character, he agrees to 'try peace' when faced with Hector's dejection and to use his eloquence to turn people's minds in his favour. In what Giraudoux calls the 'last rond de jambe', he justifies his change of heart in terms of basic human solidarity in love: Andromaque and Penelope 'flutter their eyelashes in the same way'.

This 'fast forward' analysis of Odysseus' successive changes of mind leads us to identify him as a Sophist taking pleasure in antilogies where he constructs or destroys with the same evident pleasure in the knowledge that he can make 'the strongest weak' or vice versa at will. One of Giraudoux's letters (1937) published by Body seems to confirm this negative view of the character: 'He has been seen as a model of wisdom and grandeur of spirit, but I thought I had made him far more fearsome than Demokos, that I had unmasked him'. However, this analysis may be a last pirouette, at a time when commentators on the play were seeing this last meeting between Hector and Odysseus as a fair fight.

'Penelope's fluttering eyelashes' now invite us to look at different moments in Odysseus' life, when he leaves history for his own story.

The Smoke of Ithaca

The *Odyssey* is certainly not the only *nostos*. Through the stories of Nestor and Menelaus (*Odyssey*. III-IV) one can glimpse what such 'returns' might represent in literature: adventure stories with many different episodes. Moreover Aristotle acknowledged in his *Poetics* that the *Odyssey* is complex because of its many episodes. But, he adds, it has one, simple plot (*drasis*): a man wants to go home and gets there after many ordeals. There is in Odysseus a 'strong desire to go home', a desire to live and a considered obstinacy in relation to a single goal which makes his *nostos* into a destiny whose singularity has understandably given rise to many allegorical commentaries. The gods themselves have to give way in the face of this inflexible will. Odysseus is a profoundly centripetal hero who thinks only of rediscovering himself through 'rocky Ithaca' or 'Penelope's bed'. He is the only mythological hero (apart from, to a lesser extent, Hector and Alcestis) in whom we see the notion 'of intimacy'. The *Odyssey* is simply a long 'outside', an expulsion of the self, until the reappropriation of the 'inside' represented by the return to Ithaca. This is the fundamental difference between Aeneas and Odysseus. Aeneas 'wanders for Rome', Odysseus for himself. The wedding with Lavinia is a messianic promise, while Odysseus' 'second honeymoon' is all for his own personal happiness. And yet it is the latter who has remained an 'open' myth, while Aeneas' destiny stays closed. From the outset the *Odyssey* clearly indicates that as far as possible Odysseus has long included his companions in his desire to return home. Homer calls him *philhetairos*: he thinks of his sailors, Ithacans like himself, who have shared with him the ten long years of the siege of Troy. Virgil (*Aeneid*. III) outlined the theme of these sailors who disappear during the adventures through Achaemenides, survivor of the massacre in Polyphemus' cave, who comes to warn Aeneas of the danger before being taken in by him. This poor soul describes the ill-fated Odysseus (*infelix Ulixes*) who, he says, 'proved true to himself' (Virgil 1956: 94) in inventing the trick that got his companions out. Let us mention for the purposes of memory only Giraudoux's *Elpénor*, which is a pleasant fantasy unrelated to the seriousness with which the theme can be treated.

It was Georges Séféris in 1935 who elaborated what can be called the 'elphenorism' of Odysseus' companions. These men are 'fools' (*nepioi*) insofar as they experience events but learn nothing from them. Experience is not enough, one must also incorporate what has been experienced, as Feste would say.

In 'Argonauts', so-called in ironic antiphrasis, for they will never win a fleece, the companions

> accept the night and the sun
> without changing in the midst of change.
> They were fine, whole days
> they sweated at the oars with lowered eyes
> . . . Their oars
> mark the place where they sleep on the shore.
>
> No one remembers them. Justice.

To each obstacle that Poseidon's hatred erects before him and his companions, Odysseus can both exploit his past experience and keep ever and intensely present his inner plan to return. He is mature and wise, they are scatterbrained. This is why Séféris justifies the oblivion into which they have fallen in terms of immanent justice. *Kleos*, or glory, is not just the result of lofty deeds, it is won by one's accountability to oneself. Odysseus has this 'moral' criterion as a reference point; for to him return means the happiness of being integrated once more into his highest self.

Ulysses' refusal

With his heart set on this constant call to return, Ulysses cannot give himself to those he meets by chance, he can only lend himself. This is doubtless true for a raid like the sacking of the town of the Cicones (*Odyssey*. IX), for even there Odysseus knows when to get away in time whereas his companions want to stay on and pillage everything. But tradition has rightly seen the fundamental aspects of his relations with others over his ten years of wandering in those he has with women. Confronted by the pre-eminence of the *mundus muliebris* in the *Odyssey*, Samuel Butler went so far as to claim that it was the work of a woman, Nausicaa. However T. E. Lawrence, who translated the poem, thought it was stamped with misogyny.

Odysseus' time with Circe has always set people dreaming. That luxurious brothel with its houri servants and refinements of exquisite sensuality somehow leave an uneasy feeling, like some *Island of Dr Moreau* where Odysseus was lucky enough to be able to resist the animality which was the sad and deserved fate of his companions.

Tyrannical Circe with her dangerous perfumes could not impose her law upon Odysseus because Hermes had given him the *moly* which acted as an antidote to the spell. Commentators soon interpreted this plant as reasoned intelligence dominating sensuality and bestiality. In *Love, the Greatest Enchantment*, a play of 1635, Caldéron elaborated on this conflict between flesh and spirit. He was sufficiently drawn to the theme to return to it later in an *auto*, *The Sorcery of Love*, in which the christianized combat becomes that between sin and faith.

Circe 'reveals' those who come near her and sends them away to something else, to somewhere else, if they are able to resist her spellbinding power. It is from her island that Dante's Odysseus leaves on his last voyage; it is from her island that he makes a return journey to the land of the dead.

Ezra Pound gave Circe an important place in his *Cantos*, going so far as to quote Greek words in the original and in transliteration, following his favourite method. She is a sensual being, the great prostitute, *cunni Cultrix*, but her bed, *eune*, is also a tomb and the 'little death' of orgasm refers to the great death. In Canto 47 Tiresias tells Odysseus that 'By molü art thou freed from the one bed that thou may'st return to another.'

In *The Thrush* (1947) Séféris placed an Odysseus 'who, when he arrives on Circe's island after so many ordeals, finds a house where luxury and softness await him. Of course he enjoys this good fortune. But the problem for him is that his real home is elsewhere. We shall give the name 'light' to this real home that he aspires to. This is the theme of *The Thrush*.'

It is not that he has shared the bed of

> a woman – eyelashes quivering, slim-waisted
> . . . [who] would glance impatiently

toward where they were frying fish: like a cat
that matters, it is that he got out of it and got away.

The second of Odysseus' women is the nymph Calypso. Her long relationship with him, lasting six or seven years, must have been satisfying before satiety and the boredom of Ogygia outside human time led Ulysses to remain alone on a rock, weeping for the smoke of his Ithaca. It is here that Odysseus saves himself: he refuses the immortality that the nymph so imprudently offers him. When he is on the point of dissolution, believing himself forgotten by all, this 'no' is redemptive. Henceforward the process of return is set in motion. The decision of the council of the gods (*Odyssey*. V) merely sanctions and rewards the inviolable will to return of Odysseus, who is like the gods but not one of them. It is because he chooses and accepts the condition of being perishable, like Penelope whose praises he skillfully sings to Calypso, that Odysseus has the right to a full life.

Although she is not an entirely ordinary woman, for the Phaeacians are a people partly untouched by human laws and constraints, the charming Nausicaa represents a real temptation to Odysseus, mastered as soon as it is felt. The seduction is doubtless reciprocal, but a tacit agreement holds at the level of a flirtation that which might otherwise, as he well knows, look like a greybeard setting his heart on a young girl. Hence their banter which, once the threat has been removed, gives Odysseus the freshness and joy of talking to a real woman rather than a witch or a nymph. Nausicaa is a sort of dress rehearsal for Odysseus' power of seduction before he uses it on the only woman who deserves it. Nausicaa caught the attention of many of the ancient writers, who often portrayed Odysseus leaving Ithaca again to go and marry her. Goethe sketched out an abandoned play on Odysseus and Nausicaa (1786), in which the latter, hopelessly in love with Odysseus, kills herself after his departure. But he was taking her for Charlotte.

In fact any literary interpretation which makes Odysseus' women 'devastating' and excessive fails to understand the reserve which, as we have seen, constitutes one of the fundamental components of Odysseus' *metis*. Thus Robert Graves, in his poem 'Odysseus', portrays Odysseus as a real sexual obsessive who eventually regards all the women he has 'had' with the same disgust, wife and whore, Penelope and Circe being one and the same.

Although it was natural that the 'dear masters' of nineteenth-century academic painting should represent *Odysseus and Calypso* (Böcklin 1882) or *Odysseus and Nausicaa* (theme of the 'historical landscape' competition of 1833 and 1845), the modern maîtres of Cinecittà have often reduced Odysseus to the image of a sailor on a spree, similar to Maciste, but a long way from the son of Laertes.

On this point Penelope should have the last word. When Odysseus tells her of all his experiences since leaving, she accepts and understands that his 'adventures' were not high jinks but the stages of a fate decreed by the gods.

The best proof that he loves her is that he has come back. And Molly (moly?) Bloom thinks the same way when Leopold heaves himself into her bed.

'Among the countless nations of the dead'

Odysseus is not the only hero to have gone down to hell, or rather, in his case, the gates of Hades. But when he is sent there by Circe, he wants to know what his personal fate will be. He wants to question Tiresias. The other dead, even those dear to him like his mother Anticlea, do not come until after the essential prophecy.

The catabasis or *nekyia* is situated at the very centre of the *Odyssey* (XI), and also at the heart of the central problem of the tales in Alcinous' palace. Independently of the content of Tiresias' prophecy, whose realization is deferred beyond the space of the *Odyssey*, Odysseus' journey to the land of the dead has given rise to poetic interpretations, such as Pound's *Cantos*, with Séféris doubtless the most Odyssean of contemporary poets.

Canto 1 is simply a translation of a Latin translation of book XI of the *Odyssey*. And Cantos 14 and 15 are almost entirely devoted to hell. Just as Circe sent Odysseus on to a different experience that she catalysed, so the catabasis is an initiatory act, a descent into wisdom and the secret of things. But this wisdom and vision have meaning only if there is a return to the land of the living. And this is why this 'experience of limits', which has value in principle only because of its unique character, is renewed in Pound's work in a sort of coming and going. The world of the living poses questions to that of the dead which catabasis resolves until new uncertainties appear.

In the *Pisan Cantos*, Odysseus appears with two epithets. As *outis*, 'noman', he has lost his identity. The catabasis gives him back the strength and wisdom of 'Odysseus'. He is then *polymetis*, identifying with Malatesta and Pound himself (Canto 9). One cannot fail to see a powerful Odyssean current in the reading of Pound's difficult work.

To return to *The Thrush*, Séféris describes a *nekyia* which is a cathartic ordeal before Odysseus gains access to the light. Elphenor, caught up in his sensuality, could not get beyond this stage and the poet Odysseus speaks only to the great dead, here Socrates and Antigone rather than Tiresias. Séféris' *nekyia* takes place by the sea and the dead resemble white lecythi slowly pouring into the abyss.

The distinction between Odysseus and Aeneas clearly appears in the episode whose framework Virgil nevertheless faithfully followed. At the centre of the Aeneid (book VI) Aeneas' visit to the Sibyl of Cumae leads to Anchises' prophecy of the glory of Rome, whose principal actors march past in a triumphal fresco. Aenas thinks only of his mission, Odysseus of his return.

The Sirens' song

These two-winged creatures with female torsos are given only a few lines in the story of Odysseus. But they have had their revenge in the ocean of commentaries and hypotheses to which their nature, that of their song and the place where they live have given rise. The dual form of the Greek reassuringly and clearly indicates that they are simply two death-dealing singers. Bérard did not fail to locate them, since there is no sea, reef or creek in the *Odyssey* that this enlightened topomanic has not identified. The case is thus clear: it was near the shore of Paestum that Odysseus exposed himself to their song, bound to the mast of his ship.

It is on Odysseus alone that we shall concentrate here. In antiquity all agreed that the episode of the Sirens was the illustration of an act of intellectual life: curiosity for Odysseus and the promise of 'more knowledge' from the Sirens, who know all that has already happened, although they do not seem to be able to predict the future. Cicero (*On Moral Obligation* V) devotes a page to this episode which becomes a praise of intellectual curiosity. But this is a rather flat explanation and the corpse-covered beach might lead us to assume that the risk Odysseus was running was truly deadly. It is to Blanchot (1982) that we owe the view of the Sirens' song as an 'experience of limits' to which we know, thanks to him, that the serious literary act must be linked.

Blanchot certainly reveals a certain condescension in relation to Odysseus, the 'Greek of the decadence', who egotistically gives himself the aesthetic pleasure of which he deprives his companions. But the following analysis is convincing. The relationship between Odysseus and the Sirens is that between reality and fiction, the story and the novel. Odysseus must resist the power of fiction if he is not to whiten his bones beside the earlier victims. It is a question of keeping one's distance from the imaginary, and it is the relationship between creator and work which is at the heart of the debate here, leading Blanchot to say that Homer has to melt into Odysseus as Melville does into Ahab:

> To hear the song of the Sirens is to turn from the Ulysses one was into Homer, but it is however only in Homer's narrative that the real meeting takes place, where Ulysses becomes the one who enters into a relation with the power of the elements and the voice of the abyss.

Ulysses defeats the Sirens by taking to extremes the creator's mastery of the imaginary world he shapes. The *Odyssey* offers us this fusion of Odysseus and Homer with the tales told at Alcinous' palace where the 'I' of Odysseus replaces that of Demodocus, the bard who was precisely singing Odysseus' *kleos*. Odysseus reveals himself, states his name and, through the story about and by himself, recreates his relation to himself. At the end of the stories, Odysseus has become fully himself again, ready to confront the perils of Ithaca. Homer can take up his song once more, the Sirens have been defeated by the giving of form to the story. Indeed, to be able to say 'I have heard the Sirens' song' implies that one has escaped it, and this is an experience which we can see as similar to 'literature as bullfighting', as seen by Michel Leiris.

Although it is a long way from the yawning depths of Blanchot's song, Jean Giono's *Naissance de l'Odyssée* (1930) nevertheless develops the theme of 'true lying', which here constitutes the character of Odysseus himself, who is otherwise insignificant, in a burlesque mode and with the express aim of degrading the myth. Odysseus seems in no hurry to return to Ithaca, aware that he has nothing to offer Penelope and his people that is not banal and far from glorious. He might thus be tempted to go on chasing serving girls in the 'dive' and not return at all did he not learn that his adventure with Circe has given rise to a tale that constantly gains new elements and has become a story of great deeds, 'Odysseus or the great journey', presenting him in a glowing light. Thus, from town to town and from feast to feast, at first stupefied, then embarrassed, Odysseus confronts this lie whose brilliant career soon poses an 'existential' dilemma for him: should he remain silent in the shadow of this false glory and allow himself to be definitively forgotten in favour of the 'myth of Odysseus', or can he adopt the false *kleos* and use it to return to Ithaca? Already in the *Odyssey* there is a very strange passage (*Odyssey*. XIV) in which we see old Eumaeus swallowing the imaginary tale Odysseus tells him hook, line and sinker, but rejecting the true part: 'It is when you come to Odysseus that you go wrong, to my way of thinking; you won't get me to believe that' (Homer 1946: 224).

Giono's Odysseus chooses to go with his myth and returns to Ithaca preceded by flattering renown. From then on the fiction governs his life, sometimes cruelly. When he has just arrived Odysseus strangles the magpie Gotton (a ridiculous substitute for Argos the dog) so that she will not betray him. By chance, events seem to coincide with the fiction. Thus the handsome Antinous, Penelope's lover, who becomes a nuisance to the perverse woman titillated as she is by Odysseus' new reputation as the 'lover of goddesses', is chased by the latter and falls over a cliff, breaking his neck. This allows Odysseus to attribute to himself a shortened version of the 'massacre of the suitors'.

At the end of the narrative the fiction's influence has become total. Odysseus manages his lie without hindrance, because he is the man that all have been waiting for. Thus when, after many years of real travels and experience of true adventures, Telemachus wants to tell his stories in his turn, no one believes him and the parasitic philosopher Kallimaquès puts him rudely in his place before asking Odysseus to be so kind as to recount an episode from his 'great journey', which is really true. The truth, says the philosopher, is like a tree that one aims stones at. Several must be thrown before one of them hits it. However the stone never knows that it has hit the truth and the narrative ends with the sight of Odysseus slopping water in a bowl in which corks are floating: he is 'rehearsing' a tempest which will soon decorate his 'true lying'.

Giono seems to have kept from the *Odyssey* only the 'imaginary lives' with which Odysseus decorates the stages of his recognition by other people. What is for Homer a temporary mask before a new step towards the truth is for Giono the very essence of an inauthentic life. This immersion in tall stories is a kind of abandonment to the Sirens' song. The 'narrative' is banished in favour of an imaginary story which degrades life, as witnessed by the death of the little serving girl who cannot bear the deleterious climate.

The great bow of divine Odysseus

Throughout the *Odyssey* the words 'Odysseus will return' are repeated and usually at once denied by another character. Odysseus is himself a party to this phrase, which not only constitutes a test but also has an almost sacred, 'apotropaic' value, intended to drive the suitors away. Words are not enough, however, and the royal palace is pillaged and seems to have lost its owner.

Edwin Muir (1889–1951) rendered this climate of abandonment very well in *The Return of Odysseus*. The palace doors swing in an ill wind, the locks have rusted. In an interior monologue Penelope wonders:

> . . . Odysseus, this is duty
> To do and undo, to keep a vacant gate
> Where order and right and peace and hope can enter.
> Oh will you ever return? Or are you dead,
> And this wrought emptiness my ultimate emptiness?
>
> She wove and unwove and wove and did not know
> That even then Odysseus on the long
> And winding road of the world was on his way.

The triumphant fanfares of Monteverdi's *Il Ritorno d'Ulisse nella sua Patria* (1641) allow us to forget that this return also soiled the palace floor with pools of blood while the unfaithful serving girls, 'thrushes lying in the sleep of death', are swinging from the beams. Odysseus has avenged himself, 'spattered with blood and filth like a lion' (Homer 1946: 342).

The real horror of the scene, softened by academic painting (official subject in 1812), does not however justify the distortion of *Odysseus' Bow* by the German playwright Hauptmann (1914), unfortunately followed by Kazantzakis in his *Odysseus* of 1928. The scene is in Eumaeus' hut and the play unfolds to the rhythm of the fits of insanity and despair of a manic-depressive Odysseus, whose madness may be real or faked, it is hard to say. Odysseus kills the suitors, few in number, but remains distraught. The self-control characteristic of the archetype is here entirely lacking. Hauptmann combines naturalism and the 'mad' philhellenism he contracted during a trip to Greece in a rather unconvincing way. The mixture is unhappy. Let us not discuss Kazantzakis' short work, as we shall turn our attention to his *Odyssey* below for other reasons.

The hero should not be abased beyond a certain point: one might think that Moravia's *Disprezzo* sought intelligently to show the rehabilitation of a Ulysses stained with infamy. 'A man loves his wife and is not loved by her.' This is the gist of the plot of *The Odyssey* which is the subject of a film 'in progress' whose screenwriter is going through a similar experience in his own life. The novel is thus structured in terms of a skilful counterpoint between the fiction of *The Odyssey* and the real couple, each level influencing the other, with the fiction preceding or following life. In this original interpretation of the myth Odysseus has lost Penelope's esteem by complacently accepting the presents given to him by the suitors who had not yet revealed themselves as such. During the war and his later wanderings, Odysseus realizes that he is constantly putting off his return, having in fact unconsciously desired the obstacles to it. When he finally understands the reason for Penelope's contempt, he returns to Ithaca and wins back his wife's esteem through the massacre of the suitors. Moravia makes an interesting distinction between Odysseus the civilized man, whose accommodating attitude is simply our modern 'understanding', and Penelope, who joins Medea among the 'barbarians' who do not accept any bending of conjugal ethics. Moravia's 'civilized man' may well come from the *epetes* of the *Odyssey* and this skilfully constructed novel sheds a subtle light on the theme of the suitors.

In his famous *Ulysses* (1833), Tennyson has the hero giving a kind of interior monologue, summing up his life before leaving again. He shows an affection tinged with condescension when describing Telemachus:

> Most blameless he is, centred in the sphere
> Of common duties, decent not to fail
> In offices of tenderness.

He could therefore leave him his sceptre and isle. 'He works his work, I mine.'

In this canonical succession the *Odyssey* has however left a trace of possible conflict between father and son. Telemachus bends the bow three times, but in vain and, the text says, 'the fourth time he put such pressure on the bow that he might well have strung it yet, if Odysseus had not put an end to his attempts with a shake of the head' (Homer, 1946: 319). Perhaps these are the vestiges of a primitive rite of royalty in the 'bow game'. In his *Odyssey* Kazantzakis superbly exploits this by adding to it the conflict between father and son which is thus superimposed over that between the reigning king and his heir. Odysseus is exultant when Telemachus rebels, for he sees the rebellion of his own blood in his son. And, in a confrontation that is brutal but yet full of gaiety, the two males, bull and bull-calf, compete in violence which is cathartic for both. Odysseus can set off again following his destiny, though not without having given way to a nihilist intoxication in sacking his own palace, which he leaves to Telemachus to whom he promises never to return. This is a fine staging of the 'murder of the father', checked by the affection which we sense between these two who fight through love, far more than in the haughty esteem of Tennysons' Victorian king for his Prince of Wales.

The olive tree bed

Odysseus has reconquered his *regia potestas* and has been acknowledged by all. Sulphur purifies the palace of the fumes of slaughter. He is on the threshold of the supreme recognition, the hope and expectation of which have sustained him through his years of ordeals. In the centripetal movement which governs the *Odyssey*, the most private and intimate thing is the bed whose secret is known only to him and to Penelope. And yet, displaying her own *metis*, Penelope briefly tests this Odysseus whom she knows to be her husband. In a cry, the most human and open in the whole of the *Odyssey*, Odysseus shows that any alteration of the bed would mean to him that he had been entirely stripped of his past and identity. For this bed is the stronghold of a love he experienced over twenty years before. To stop caring about it would mean turning him forever into the 'nobody' that he pretended to be and whom he would then become. But this cry saves him: everything is consummated and Athena is able to prolong the lovers' night of confessions. For Homer, as for Joyce who shows Bloom reintegrating Molly's bed to which he has returned at seven Eccles Street, Odysseus has nothing left to do but to be king, father and husband. Tiresias' prediction will be the concern of other bards.

Tiresias' prediction

'Death in his gentlest guise' will come to you *ex halos*, predicts Tiresias to Odysseus. The two words *ex halos* have given rise to many interpretations which are more than simply philology, for they locate Odysseus' destiny after his return in different ways. If they mean 'far from the sea', Odysseus, a country-dwelling king, will die peacefully in his palace. If they mean 'from the sea', he will die from an attack by either a sea monster or a man who has come ashore on Ithaca. The latter version was made official by Eugammon of Cyrene's *Telegony* (sixth century BC) mentioned above. We should add that the arrow fired by Telegonos, Odysseus' bastard, has a point made from the bone of a poisonous stingray, which confirms the latter sense of *ex halos* as meaning 'of marine origin'.

Happily for the success of the myth, the West has not found much satisfaction in this gruesome death and prefers to grant Odysseus a second life, all of his own this time, with no divine interventions. The prediction justifies his second departure, but the resulting voyage is a vocation, not a curse. And Bérard is lighthearted when he sees a joke in the prediction, which he has not surrounded with his fatal interpolations.

'As it pleased an Other'

Eliot saw Dante's Odysseus (Book 26 of the *Inferno*) as the most striking illustration of the 'effect of surprise' which Poe demanded of great poetry. For, at a time when St Thomas Aquinas had condemned *libido sciendi* and the various forms of *The Story of Troilus* were spreading the pro-Trojan version of the Trojan war, Dante presents the last voyage of a haughty Odysseus, hero of an intellectual quest, who takes his passion to its limits, even if the Christian god, the 'Other', breaks up his ship and his pre-Faustian dreams.

Odysseus is with Diomedes, in the eighth pit of the eighth Circle, with the perfidious councillors. They form a double flame in which 'they groan for the ambush of the horse which made the gate by which the noble seed of the Romans went forth'. This is the source of Odysseus' *odium*, clearly indicated by Virgil. But then a voice sounds from one of the flame's points. It is Odysseus, who acknowledges that no ties of affection 'could conquer in me the longing that I had to gain experience of the world'. He implores his companions to go and explore the uninhabited world. 'Consider your origin: you were not made to live as brutes, but to pursue virtue and knowledge'. This is followed by the voyage where the Equator is crossed before the Other swallows up the explorers: 'till the sea closed over us' (*Inferno* 26, 112–42).

Dante knew Odysseus through Latin sources. His recreation is all the more admirable for this and it can be said that there is no true 'vision' of his character between this Ulysses and that of Joyce, but only more or less skilful variations.

'To strive, to seek, to find and not to yield': Lord Tennyson's *Ulysses* (1833)

It is interesting to read this poem at the same time as *The Lotus-Eaters* and *Im Memoriam*, for which, as is well known, Tennyson was inspired by the death of a close friend: 'Oh rest ye, brother mariners, we will not wander more.'

It is to this fear of the apathy of nirvana and sorrow that the monologue of an Odysseus who is both world-weary and ready to attempt the 'last voyage' is addressed. The poem often has autobiographical tones and implies that not everything has been experienced, that there are still things to learn and even some glory to be won. Penelope, the 'aged wife', the kingdom whose subjects are true savages and Telemachus who has his eye on the throne and deserves it must all be left behind:

> I cannot rest from travel: I will drink
> Life to the lees . . .
> How dull it is to pause, to make an end,
> To rust unburnish'd, not to shine in use!

The line 'To follow knowledge like a sinking star' is doubtless from Dante.

The memories of a man who knows the 'cities of men' precedes a last call to the aging companions, whose willingness however remains intact, 'to strive . . . and not to yield'.

We can see the personal elements in this poem in which Tennyson exhorts himself to overcome a devastating sorrow. Nevertheless, this Odysseus combines most aspects of the centrifugal hero, in very modern terms but without really exploiting anything, as though we were dealing here with a life plan which might remain a dead letter. 'It may be,' says Odysseus, 'we shall touch the Happy Isles'. We are permitted to doubt it.

The search for a lost *Odyssey:* 'The last voyage' by Pascoli (1904)

In this poem from his collection *Convivial Poems*, Pascoli's originality lies in the way he combines Tiresias' prediction, which Odysseus fulfils with his oar transformed into a grain shovel, and the 'second voyage', which here appears as a funereal pilgrimage. Once he has carried out 'Tiresias' voyage', Odysseus grows old in gentle boredom with Penelope. He is waiting, but does not know what for. The tenth spring arrives: he decides to leave on 'the last voyage' with his old companions. They return to the places in his *Odyssey.* Nothing is left of all he once looked on with admiring eyes. Circe has disappeared, as have the Sirens. Everywhere he goes only cold ashes and the taste of death remain. And his last sailing takes him to Calypso's shore. His ship sinks in a tempest and he alone survives. He reaches the shore, where he dies. He has not seen Calypso again, but she comes to 'recover' (the etymological meaning of the Greek word) her former lover's body. This poem is not without *fin-de-siècle* nihilism, but it is stamped with a gentleness that brings its sadness close to true regret. And in Proustian tones of great beauty, Pascoli seems to be implying that we must imagine Odysseus happy when his body is recovered by Calypso.

'The hero without companions', as D'Annunzio depicts Odysseus in *Laus vitae*, is martial in tone. We shall not linger over this voyage which seems to lead to Fiume rather than beyond the Pillars of Hercules. Action, the tensing of the will, *andiamo:* these are grandiose, hollow tirades that our hero did not deserve.

'The Cretan gaze' or Odysseus' march towards himself. Kazantzakis' *Odyssey* (1938)

Kazantzakis' *Odyssey*, a vast fresco of more than 33,000 lines (more than the *Iliad* and *Odyssey* put together) could truly have been the 'modern sequel' that its creator saw in it, did it not suffer from excessive fidelity to the 'letter' of Homer's work, linked with the too-obvious presence of Kazantzakis' various philosophical leanings. This contradictory mix creates a tension which is moreover evinced by most of the Cretan novelist's heroes. 'Cretan' is how Paul Faure recently described Odysseus, referring to the 'imaginary biography' of book XIV of the *Odyssey*. Kazantzakis' Odysseus is also 'Cretan', but in a quite different sense, not like the deceitful son of Autolycos, but in terms of a particular set of ethics and vision of the world which implies the 'Cretan view' defined in *Report to Greco*.

This attitude, the result of the intense asceticism of those who have felt and then dominated their passions, no longer fears or dreads anything; it is 'beyond good and evil' – for he is Neitzschean at one point where human beings come 'to save' God (*Salvatores Dei*) and help his weakness with all the energy of full wisdom won with difficulty. This is the journey of Kazantzakis' Odysseus in the abstract, but with a plot and setting which follow Homer.

Having left Ithaca after his confrontation with Telemachus, Odysseus goes to Sparta, where he leaves Helen as a kind of stool pigeon for the Barbarians who are threatening to attack at any moment. In Egypt he becomes a rebel once more and leaves for the source of the Nile with a group of companions whom he has freed. Then, having climbed a mountain like Moses, he comes down with a 'law' for the new city that he is having built. But the city is hardly finished when it falls and Odysseus, alone once more, sets off towards his destiny. He has various, heavily symbolic encounters and then prepares for death, having become an ascetic stripped of everything. He meets it in the Antarctic, where it comes wearing his face. Among the icebergs, in a grandiose setting, Odysseus smiles fearlessly and hopelessly: he is free.

This appallingly schematic summary of so broad a fresco gives only fragments of the skeleton, leaving out what, in the Greek, is the luscious flesh of this work: the poetry, the splendour of the images, the inner passion that we feel burning in Odysseus, who in an instant can destroy what he has constructed. The spirit of Dante, whom Kazantzakis has translated, is present, but the awkward thing is this strange mixture of an Odysseus who is externally Homeric in style while being inwardly sustained by the philosophical contradictions of his creator. No doubt the philosophical daring of the Greek Kazantzakis could not go so far as to profane tradition by abandoning Homerisms that are as obsolete as Leconte De Lisle's translations, and in the same sense.

Brought up outside the harem, the Irish James Joyce has no such scruples and that is why his *Ulysses* is the second *Odyssey* that modernity had been waiting for since Dante marked out its trail.

A day in the life of Leopold Bloom, or *Ulysses* on the banks of the Liffey (1922)

'A decent man, *tout court* [that's all]' said Joyce, in French, of his Ulysses/Bloom. And Pound, a close friend of Joyce, saw in his hero an average, sensual man. He went so far as to describe *Ulysses* as the successful continuation of the project of *Bouvard et Pécuchet* in an accomplished form of the novelistic genre. The paradox is only apparent and is explained by reference to Plato. At the end of the *Republic* (X. 620–1), Er the Pamphylian describes metempsychosis. Souls are defined by their choice: Agamemnon wants to be an eagle and Ajax a lion. When Odysseus' turn comes to choose, he opts for 'the uneventful life of an ordinary man' (Plato 1974: 454), in other words of a decent man. And it is doubtless in this aspect that Joyce is most faithful to the spirit of the *Odyssey*, insofar as he was able to preserve all the mythical potential of the positive and negative versions of Odysseus by splitting them between Stephen Dedalus and Leopold Bloom, while giving him greater autonomy of action. To Stephen, 'the artist', the intellectual, the worrier, is given the centrifugal *metis* with a call to leave which becomes a real departure. To Bloom, 'the scientist' – though an amateur one – the down-to-earth realist, is given the centripetal *metis*, the one that, from Molly's, will bring him back to Molly's after his modest wanderings of 'Bloomsday', 16 June 1904. But Bloom is an anxious spirit, an autodidact who likes complicated books and learned words. His is an irenic temperament: he can calm café quarrels. He wants to be active in politics and pictures himself as the Mayor of Dublin, 'Sir Leopold Bloom'. More importantly, he is half Jewish and possessed by other names (Fleury and Virag, both meaning Bloom) and this 'jewgreek' has a deep longing for a distant place, Zion or even Tibet or the land of the Eskimos.

We can see here the traits of Odysseus, petty bourgeois in form, but faithful to the spirit. And it is certainly Joyce who best expressed the relationship between father and son which Homer had only sketched. The very structure of *Ulysses* respects that of the *Odyssey*, with three sections: the first three chapters of the 'Telemachy' devoted to Stephen, then twelve chapters of the 'Adventures of Ulysses/Bloom', with the meeting between Bloom and Stephen, then, after their separation, Bloom's return to 7 Eccles Street. In their 'parallactic' journey, to use the word dear to Bloom, they each experience symbolic events that appear ordinary and indeed trivial. And it is here that the patterns of correspondences established between the *Odyssey* and *Ulysses* by experts in the difficult art of 'Bloomology' are precious to us, since with investigation they reveal that the most successful of these modern transpositions of archetypal episodes are those using humour (the Sirens become barmaids who block their ears when Bloom speaks) or a strange poetry born of judiciously used anachronism (Circe becomes Madame Claude in a victorian opera hat; Elphenor is changed into poor Paddy Dignam whose funeral Bloom attends).

Just as he had done before in his self-portrait in *Stephen Dedalus* (1904), Joyce used his freedom as a creator to use the myth of Odysseus while expressing his own dual vision through Stephen and Bloom. But there are perhaps deeper reasons for the kinship between the *Odyssey* and *Ulysses*, each of them landmarks in our civilization. Odysseus, tossed between human beings and gods, between horror and sensuality, refinement and savagery, wants to keep his reason and the permanence of his being in the face of the world's mobility. The same principle of identity lies at the heart of *Ulysses*, in which Eliot saw the use of the myth as a framework giving form to the inconceivable pile of futilities which constitutes our universe. This is certainly the impression one gains by reading this *summa* in which Odysseus constantly recovers his identity, which is led astray right and left, just as Stephen remains faithful to his intellectual vocation by leaving. These two symbols of Odysseus meet, as though predestined for this fatherhood in spirit and, above the putrid fumes and vulgarity of Dublin, emblematic of the whole modern world, a moment of purity reveals the best Odyssean nostalgia. The fact that he chose not to isolate his *Odyssey* in some 'ivory Ithaca' – a reproach that could be addressed to Kazantzakis – was a powerful intuition on Joyce's part. Respecting the spirit of his time, he integrates the archetypical core into the most modern of narratives, in this case a real repertoire of different stylistic and narrative procedures.

Kazantzakis' Odysseus died with 'the Cretan smile' on his lips. Bloom is not going to die, but in the last two chapters of *Ulysses*, Joyce gives us first a *resumé*, in the form of a catechism of questions and answers about the past day and above all Bloom's meeting with Stephen. Then Bloom is weary, 'he has travelled' and dreams about the name 'Sinbad' before forgiving Molly her latest infidelity. Molly's monologue finishes with words of peace: 'Yes I said yes I will Yes'. This is doubtless a bourgeois serenity, but it should be taken as the Joycian form of 'peace in Ithaca'.

Although developments in the literary evolution of the Odysseus myth must always be related to Homer's original archetype with his double meaning of *metis*/deceitfulness, *metis*/analytic power and in his centrifugal and centripetal forms, we can today predict a fine future for this character/person whose extreme flexibility makes all identifications possible. It would be interesting to know, for example, what Michel Tournier would make of him, since he recently expressed his desire to write about Odysseus.

The relationship of the original to the personal myth is clearly indicated in these lines from Séféris' poem 'Reflections on a Foreign Line of Verse', mentioned above:

> He is the mighty Odysseus: he who proposed the wooden horse with which the Achaeans captured Troy.
> I imagine he's coming to tell me how I too may build a wooden horse to capture my own Tory.

And it is from Cavafis that we shall borrow the paradigmatic meaning of all existence contained in 'Le Voyage à Ithaque' (1911):

> Even if you find it poor, Ithaca has not deceived you.
> Wise as you have become after so many experiences,
> You have at last understood what the Ithacans mean.

Whether he is the subtle son of Laertes or the deceitful grandson of Autolycos, Odysseus will long continue to find bards seduced by his *kleos*.

Denis Kohler

Oedipus

The history of the relationship betwen the Oedipus myth and literature is probably unique. More than any other myth, that of Oedipus has been bound up with one poet's work, to the point where for generations of westerners, Oedipus was confused with Sophocles' *Oedipus the King* (*c.* 430 BC) or with *Oedipus at Colonus* (*c.* 406 BC) and the myth itself with the dramatic tragedy. However, it may be that for us, who have lost all traces of the myth outside Sophocles' crystallization of it, despite such exhaustive studies as that of Marie Delcourt (*Oedipe ou la légende de Conquérant*, 1944), the Oedipus myth is once again becoming separate from literature. Thus, even though until now we had no knowledge of it outside literature, the present age is once again making contact with a myth that has freed itself from books and entered our consciousness. It has rediscovered a non-literary and independent way of speaking about the myth of Oedipus; perhaps psychoanalysis has taken us back to the myth itself.

As is self-evident, these comings and goings between myth and literature are not without consequences for what happens to the myth in literature. Moreover, while it might be thought, following Kérényi (*Introduction to Oedipus*, 1971), that the history of Oedipus from his origins to the present day is that of a long degeneration, it may be that Oedipus' reappearance as a myth allows literature to reinvent its own discourse on the subject. Indeed, it would seem that the quality of Sophocles' tragedy weighed too heavily for anyone to free themselves from it sufficiently to be innovative, or at least to be innovative while remaining faithful to a subject which it was hard for them to grasp. On the other hand, now that Oedipus has been returned to our fantasies by psychoanalysis, abandoning the theatre and taking to the streets, it may perhaps be possible to restructure the myth's language, as demonstrated by Robbe-Grillet's novel *The Erasers*.

What are the major elements of Oedipus' destiny, as we read them in the work of Sophocles and in a more fragmentary way in that of his predecessors, in book IV of *The Iliad* and book XI of *The Odyssey* (*c.* 750 BC) and also in Aeschylus' *Seven Against Thebes* (525–456 BC), or in the allusions given in Euripides' *The Phoenician Women* (*c.* 407 BC)? In chronological order, the first of these episodes is the exposure of the baby. His parents, Laius and Jocasta, worried by the threat that he represents to them, abandon him outside the city. He is thus exposed to Mount Cithaeron (or, in a variation whose existence is reported by Marie Delcourt, put in a casket on the water like Moses). However, overcoming this ordeal, he is doubly marked; by weakness resulting from the wounds to his ankles, having been attached by the feet to a stick, and by the promise of his predestination and future royalty. In the second episode, Oedipus reaches adulthood and kills his father, Laius. Then, in the third episode, he defeats the Sphinx by solving the riddle she posed to young Thebans. This is in fact a definition of man, as its solution indicates, but its meaning, as recorded in a line by Aeschylus, which says that on Parthenope's shield the Sphinx is represented 'bearing a Cadmean beneath her', and in some iconographic representations, is probably more sexual. The fourth episode is the marriage to Jocasta: Oedipus arrives in Thebes, where the queen's hand is promised to anyone who can rid the city of the scourge of the Sphinx. Oedipus then marries his mother. For these two major crimes of parricide and incest, which are sometimes more or less attenuated in the earliest versions of the myth, Oedipus is punished, or, according to Sophocles and his descendants – in other words all of us – he punishes himself by blinding himself. Lastly comes the sixth episode, symmetrical with the preceding one, in which Oedipus is chosen by the gods, as portrayed in *Oedipus at Colonus*. We can also add to this Oedipus' heirs; his two sons Eteocles and Polynices, who are destined to die at each other's hands, and his two daughters, Ismene and Antigone, who are walled up alive by Creon for not agreeing to compromise with divine law where the burial of their brother was concerned. These are the most important elements in the patchwork formed by this biography before Sophocles tied it all together, along with the additional symbolic elements of Oedipus' royalty and lameness (analysed recently by, for example, Claude Lévi-Strauss, Jean-Pierre Vernant or Pierre Vidal-Naquet).

However, it is through its dramatization as tragedy that, to use Nietzsche's words in *The Birth of Tragedy* (1872), 'myth acquires its most profound content and most expressive form'. That which was scattered is gathered together; that which might have seemed a result of chance finds its own necessity, and the 'sublime' myth begins to 'vibrate in Sophoclean melodies'. In other words, thenceforward tragedy and poetry are superimposed on the myth of Oedipus.

For us, who have virtually no complete versions of the story of Oedipus that antedate Sophocles, it is rather difficult to contrast those of its elements that relate to the nature of the myth with those that belong to the tragedy. We can simply note that Sophocles' two tragedies cover the entire biography of Oedipus and that, while the playwright may have had to choose between different versions available to him, he was concerned to recall all their episodes. At the same time he crystallized the basic elements. He gave them a literary structure. He turned Oedipus' biography into a destiny. In other words, he interpreted it. Indeed, he doubly interpreted the earlier material, by giving it both form and meaning, and thus an intensity – a legacy that later generations of playwrights tempted by the subject were perhaps always to see as both fascinating and burdensome. It is also true that everything that writers, painters or musicians dreamed of achieving in their own work was already clearly written there: the plastic quality of the vision of the young man carefully thinking in front of the Sphinx, as Poussin represented him, or the greatness and authenticity in greatness that was to attract Stravinsky. Sophocles seemed to have said all there was to say with a blinding clarity which perhaps effectively blinded as much as it illuminated. At least in his work the legibility of the hero's destiny was allied to an indefinite potential for interpretations and projections. 'Oedipus has no depth', wrote Starobinski, 'because he is our depth itself' (*La Relation critique*, 1970).

All the elements of the legend now became clear. Oedipus' wanderings, for example, soon became a journey- and indeed an ambiguous one, as stated in Vidal-Naquet's recent analysis, 'Oedipus entre deux cités', according to which 'on the symbolic level (but the story throws necessary light on the symbol), Oedipus is both he who wanders and he who settles according to more or less ambiguous processes of integration or reintegration in Corinth, Thebes or Olympus' (Vernant and Vidal-Naquet 1986). In the same way, and no doubt following the myth, Sophocles' tragedy defined Oedipus' destiny by linking three poles of a triangular network which could be regarded as covering the entire field of experience: royalty, which represents not only political power but also all the qualities that can be assimilated to the independence won by the adult man; dependence and independence with regard to the oracle; and lastly dependence or independence in relation to the family. In addition, the poetic drama went straight to the essentials, and, ignoring all superfluous decorations or chatter in what Cocteau was to call 'the mathematical destruction of a mortal', it added to the legend only what was required to give it the quality of necessity or of a logic that was, if not rational, at least apparently rational. The law of destiny thus seemed more incontrovertible. Lastly, the poetic drama played characters off against each other as far as was possible, in other words to the point of catastrophe implied by the crossing of the boundaries, the three poles already mentioned of affectivity, piety and independence. Oedipus can no longer love Jocasta except by defiling the city and abandoning his adult independence. He can no longer regard himself as a conquering king and solver of riddles, unless by condemning himself and his love and seeing himself perjured in relation to the law of the gods. He can no longer respect divine law unless he abandons everything, as he effectively does at Colonus. Sophocles' two plays grasped the whole extent of desire in all its variegated manifestations: the desire to love; the desire for power and to be oneself; the desire to locate oneself in the order of things and of the gods, to make the relations between them clearer, and even more to contrast them with each other to be able to tell them apart; and also the desire for the impossible, for pleasure and a dizzy sense of unknowing. The tragedy was informed by the hesitation present in the myth but also crystallized it. Thus Sophocles' two plays were left to posterity as a weighty inheritance, which has been regarded as exemplary ever since Antiquity, as attested by Aristotle's *Poetics*.

But the model was disturbing by the very nature of the fact that it never ceased to be a model. The story had to be rediscovered without repetition. Sometimes the text or the context were strained in order to escape plagiarism. Sometimes the tone was shifted in order simply to produce something new. Whether in Platen, Gide, Cocteau, or indeed T. S. Eliot, inspiration drawn from Sophocles is accompanied by a rejection of Sophocles; we find the fascination of rejection. Thus there were modernized versions of Oedipus, which had shaken off, as Cocteau would say, the dust of the masterpiece: *La Machine infernale* (1934), Gide's *Oedipe* (1931), T. S. Eliot's *The Elder Statesman* (1959). Or else, on the contrary, writers and artists such as Corneille, and perhaps Poussin, sought to take from the ancient legacy and the subject it bequeathed only the idea of a tone and a nobility or, to put it another way, the correct or false idea of a form. This is to say that, unlike some other myths, such as that of Don Juan, whose constants and changeable elements have been highlighted by Jean Rousset, the Oedipus myth offered little that could be transformed.

But it also happened that an uncomprehended, misunderstood, or partially understood Oedipus – which all amount to the same thing – could no longer orientate the structures of a dramatic work. He could provide only a kind of ornamental motif or a disturbing central point of reference. Significant here is the example of *Passing Time* (1956), a novel by Michel Butor in which Oedipus is represented on old tapestries next to Theseus. Strangely enough, and even in Antiquity (with Seneca's *Oedipus* and probably that of Euripides, whose text is lost), the theatre soon broke with its tragic inheritance, unlike the theoretical commentaries to which it gave rise, whether those of Hölderlin, Hegel or Freud. The characters of the Oedipus story either become simple walk-on parts, as in the work of Corneille, Voltaire, Cocteau and perhaps even Seneca, or Oedipus ceases, as Hegel says, to be a 'sculpture and becomes a character'. As he becomes more individualized, he becomes more banal: (he turns into Lord Claverton in T. S. Eliot's work, lets himself be surrounded by familiarity in that of Tewfik el-Hakim, or in Gide's work is characterized by his unimportance). He may abandon his desire for knowledge, while the threatening truth advances from the distance, as in the work of Seneca, Voltaire, Cocteau, Henri Ghéon and certainly also that of Gide and Tewfik el-Hakim. Lastly, Oedipus' guilt may become too attenuated, as in the case of Corneille, and he may lose his initiative, his freedom and that which ensured both his quality and his wound, ceasing to be a tragic hero in Hölderlin's sense of the term. He is no longer defined by his inner agony, caused by the frontier between the possible and the impossible, the lawful and the illicit which he straddles; he is no longer ground down by what the poet calls 'the coupling of man and god'.

We should note too that Voltaire, Corneille and Ducis also ignore the potentially tragic import of the couple formed by Jocasta and Oedipus. This couple, who are to be separated rather than united, is of little interest to them. Thus Ducis cuts this part, while Corneille strangely wrote that 'love has no place in this subject, nor have women any role', and Voltaire, by contrast, overloaded the part of Jocasta by making her Philoctetes' lover. We thus have to wait until the arrival of psychoanalysis for the violence of the configuration to reappear. On the other hand, Sâr Péladan and Hofmannsthal – particularly the former (the German poet gives such sacred gravity to the relation between Oedipus and Jocasta that it becomes charged with anxiety) – both end their work at the moment of the hero's apotheosis when he enters Thebes (see Peladan 1903, Hofmannsthal 1905). Whatever the case, the relation between myth and tragedy, which was so close in the work of Sophocles that it could still provide a title for the recent studies by Vernant and Vidal-Naquet, was loosened. For whatever reasons, Oedipus ceased to be tragic.

And yet, in the place of the tragedy which was no longer felt, attempts were sometimes made to lend the subject tragic greatness. Oedipus had become a form. The singular return to Sophocles in the work of Ducis (1873), in Pasolini's film (1954), partially in Cocteau's work, where the legend undergoes a kind of mixing with Shakespeare's *Hamlet*, and certainly in that of Stravinsky, reflected a nostalgia for ancient ceremonial in all its grandeur and monumentality. The local colour of this grandeur, which was Hellenic in origin, mattered little: in it Stravinsky sought what he called the Tibetan side of his work, just as Henri Ghéon and T. S. Eliot (in *Oedipus* and *The Elder Statesman* respectively) were seeking a religious gravity not unconnected to some biblical memory. As for Corneille, Voltaire, Gide or Poussin, while they were sensitive to the specifically tragic quality of Sophocles' work, without wanting or being able to reformulate this in their own, what they sought in it was a subject in the ancient manner, in other words with an 'antique' grandeur and nobility.

However, in different circumstances and sometimes in the work of the same writers and artists, the impossibility of reproducing greatness was sometimes rather coyly mocked. In the work of Gide, Cocteau and Platen (1828) the appeal to greatness goes hand in hand with a parody of greatness. The tragedy is reworked in playful, amusing, comical ways; hence the joyful or grimacing transpositions, which are often incongruous and in which the archaism, sacrilege, and comic absurdity of such an integration of mythical narrative into daily life all have their place. 'My big baby' says Jocasta to Oedipus in *La Machine infernale*, and Platen's Sphinx demands proper distichs from her victims. According to Kérényi, however, she represents the 'most objective defence of Sophocles' *Oedipus the King* in its incomparable classicism, via a *reductio ad absurdum* which consists in resolutely following the path taken by Corneille following Seneca and taking it to the point of manifest absurdity'. This desire to distinguish oneself from one's source reflects both a concern with creating something new and, no doubt, a sense of the structural impossibility of the project.

We should however note the allegorical use that has been made of the Oedipus myth, probably in a more banal way to the extent that all myths lend themselves to such treatment. In his *Journal* Gide mentioned the 'combat of ideas' staged in his play. In Pasolini's film the ageing Oedipus, who plays the flute in front of a factory, having installed himself beneath a cathedral porch, becomes a kind of poet, or perhaps a prophet, of Marxism. In 1938, on the other hand, Ghéon's *Oedipe ou le crépuscule des dieux* reflected religious hope and anxiety about coming events. Sâr Péladan made Oedipus bear the weight of a glorious, accursed solitude, and Ducis gave this role to Polynices in his *Oedipus chez Admète* and *Oedipe à Colone*. The conflict so essential to the structure of the tragic model also lent itself to all kinds of debates. Corneille, Voltaire, Péladan, Gide, Ghéon and Eliot all seek to mark the boundaries of human power through the opposition of Tiresias and Oedipus. In Voltaire's work (1719), sometimes in Gide's and certainly in that of Tewfik el-Hakim (1958), who drew on Gide, this conflict could be read as one between political and religious authority: 'Let us trust only ourselves; let us see everything with our own eyes' (Voltaire, *Oedipe*, act IV, scene 5). Corneille, however, in 1659 and at a time when Jansenist theories were in conflict with those of the Jesuits, found matter in it for two purple passages on free will. The echoes of the defence that Oedipus put up against Creon in the ancient *Oedipus at Colonus* seemed to merge with the preoccupations of Port-Royal. Sâr Péladan's *Oedipe et le sphinx* seemed to suggest that the conflict between the human and the divine, sometimes manifested in the conflict between good and evil that is the supreme tragic conflict, could be resolved by divine generosity. In the same way Ghéon and Eliot saw the fable as an allegory of the triumph of grace over sin, and lastly as an image of possible forgiveness that was naturally reinforced by the memory of Oedipus in Colonus. As for the complex, lyrical work of Tewfik el-Hakim, this plays off against each other all the temptations of the desire to live: the temptations of happiness, of truth, of lying; the temptations of the gods and of human beings: 'Oedipus, the time of tranquillity is gone. Awaken from your happiness'.

And yet, over this relatively classical and unsurprising use of the Oedipus myth as an allegory, is superimposed another which is both more modern and more surreptitious. Just as in former times the mention of a hero's name was enough not only to recall ancient grandeur and classicism, but to avoid the necessity of a narrative and the articulation of a theme (as for example in Du Bellay's work '. . . Heureux qui comme Ulysse . . .' ['Happy the man who, like Odysseus . . .']), the simple mention of the names of Oedipus, Jocasta or the Sphinx are now enough to evoke Freud. In this way a psychoanalytic myth has been created, which can perhaps be interpreted as a myth of the myth. Lastly, we should recall that the narration of the story of Oedipus is itself subject to change. It is reshaped, as in the case of Platen or Péladan, or it is overloaded. Hence a proliferation of details, stories and sometimes of characters. The story itself is enriched in Seneca's *Oedipus*, which contains a famous scene of necromancy during which Oedipus calls up the shadow of his father, in Statius' *Thebaid* and in the *Roman de Thèbes*, where the titles of the chapters ('L'Exil de Polynice', 'L'Ambassade de Tydée', 'L'Episode de Montflore' or

'L'Arrivée du duc d'Athènes et la prise de la ville') show how much has been invented. Corneille was to invent a Dirce, whom he made the lover of Oedipus. Voltaire was to involve Philoctetes and Hercules, Sâr Péladan Prometheus and Hercules, Ducis the characters of Admetus and Alcestis, and Cocteau a ghost who owes much to that of Hamlet's father. Two episodes that are especially prized and developed, particularly in the *Roman de Thèbes* and some of the more modern works (including those by Péladan, Hoffmannsthal, Ghéon and Cocteau), are Oedipus' wedding celebrations and the fight with the Sphinx. Which is to say that these were two moments that Sophocles for his part preferred to leave out.

Lastly, in the most modern works, we can certainly observe a tendency to make the myth more ordinary. Not only is Oedipus variously portrayed as Lord Claverton or Wallas, but in *The Elder Statesman* the parricide is turned into a car accident and the incest into the breaking off of an engagement, while in Tewfil el-Hakim's work the Sphinx has become no more than a lion mythologized by political trickery. What we can glimpse in all this is the difficulty of writers in distinguishing themselves from Sophocles or, to put it another way, the difficulty of writing about Oedipus without repeating Sophocles. Perhaps this is the tribute that must be paid to a source which Aristotle had long ago asserted was the best tragedy of the time. It is also hardly surprising that a radical change was needed in our perception and understanding of the myth for the structures of the narrative to be changed, and it is probably no coincidence that the development of the social sciences and the birth of psychoanalysis were needed before the Oedipus story, which had so often been staged (not only in the theatre, but at the opera, with Zingarelli in 1799, Sir Charles Villier Standford in 1887, Ruggero Leoncavallo's *Oedipus Rex* in Chicago in 1920 and Stravinsky's *Oedipus Rex* in Paris in 1927), could provide the structure for a novel. For the first time in the myth's literary history, Robbe-Grillet's work had a different conception from that of a double variation on a form and a theme. In brief, his novel *The Erasers*, published in 1953, still occupies an entirely individual place in the long series of reworkings of the subject.

This is because Robbe-Grillet's starting point was impertinently to repudiate classical culture, by playing with tragedy – including that of Sophocles – as a genre, and probably also to repudiate that which is called modern, along with the social sciences, psychoanalysis and the detective novel. Thus he was obliged to be innovative. But perhaps he only managed this – and it matters little whether it was done unwillingly or not – by rediscovering what was lost. When the novel came out, it surprised people at first with its denials and derision. It was a rejection of stiff classicism and of Sophocles' structures, of the layered or folded time that the latter had preserved; a rejection of what this time expressed; a rejection of tragedy and even, apparently and in a way that was more provocative than real, a rejection of narrative. What remained of Oedipus in the novel, in the most obvious form at least, related to a play of allusions, innuendos and lastly of jokes. In it the exposure of the baby became a lacework motif, the Sphinx was represented by a chance encounter with rubbish in the canal, the murder of Dupont was a detective story that went wrong, and the incest became a vague and vaguely equivocal relationship between the hero and Dupont's ex-wife. Allusion, or multiple allusions, replace the narrative in the novel each time the story of Oedipus comes into play. All in all, the novel's references to the myth are artificial and ostensibly so. Even so, it may be that Robbe-Grillet's accord with the reasons for the existence and durability of the ancient story proved stronger than his disagreements, however well stated, and that he rewrote or reinvented the story of a contemporary Oedipus. In *The Erasers* Wallas is presented as an Oedipus without prowess or promise, who is deliberately returned to the common lot by a rather dull punishment. Rather than reaching Colonus, this Oedipus, who ceased to be a king in order to gain a salary, remains a prisoner of the waters of a strange aquarium in which fantasies spin round and where anything can happen because everything is gratuitous and pointless. For the parody did not get to the root of the signifying structures. Beyond tragedy, the novel connects with the myth, and beyond psychoanalysis it repeats the Oedipus complex. Sophocles had proposed a version that offered overt literary, philosophical and religious interpretations of the myth. Robbe-Grillet gives us an interpretation of the same order, albeit radically different. We thus move from a tragedy which exalted awareness to a novel of non-differentiation, of lifelessness and vacuousness – or more precisely a novel about the necessity, which is not perceived as tragic, that condemned human beings to impotence, crime and murder from the earliest versions of the myth. This break with a genre thus marks the rediscovery of the myth, at least of the undeveloped catastrophe as recounted by the myth. This is played out on two levels. On the one hand Oedipus, who has become Wallas, a man without qualities, project or will, becomes once more like the man of the myth, a pure representation of an inner compulsion that is bound to lead him to some bad end. On the other, the character who is no longer sufficiently strictly defined by the detective story plot in which he has a part becomes the empty centre towards which fantasies flow. In the end, he is present only in his unconscious, and, it might be said, in a return to the order of the repressed or to the Oedipus complex. Thus the break with tragedy made possible a new connection with psychoanalysis, beyond the narration of the myth and beyond the mockery of detective novels. Let us be clear on this point: Robbe-Grillet, though he does not mention it expressly, demonstrates the wandering implied by the Oedipus complex better than such poets as Cocteau or Hofmannsthal, who refer to psychoanalysis without touching what it puts at stake. He thus takes us from Oedipus to the Oedipus complex, and the inventiveness that this requires is considerable. Hence the return in this novel of lyricism, narrative, play and literature – and indeed of meaning, as one speaks of the return of the repressed – after they have all been placed in parentheses or perhaps on hold.

At least there is very little doubt that, in this almost fantastical evocation of relations between human beings, their unconscious and the world, the novelist rewrote a fateless myth of the modern Oedipus. He was to continue this in a possibly more systematic way in *Djinn* (1981), a modern version of *Oedipus in Colonus*, or in Cologne . . .

This panorama, though brief, would however be incomplete if it did not bring to light a certain number of theories relating either to Oedipus or to the Oedipus complex. It can be observed that at the same time as works concerning Oedipus reflected a loss and weakening in relation to the ancient source, the theoretical thinking which also started from the Greek model was constantly being enriched. Thus we have Hegel, Hölderlin, Nietzsche, all three of whom use Sophocles' work to define tragedy and whose thinking can be said to start from literature to return to it in the end. Psychoanalysis, on the other hand, despite its obvious kinship with tragedy and myth (further attested by Freud's famous letter of 15 October 1897 to Fliess), takes Oedipus out of literature. It even forces him to go down into the street and become an issue for everyone. But at the same time it grafts a therapeutic concern on to the mythological narrative. Oedipus thus seems to have ceased to belong to literary creation, in order to impart fertility to other discourses. The permanence of literature is not threatened, but speaking about Oedipus is no longer the preserve of writers. Through psychoanalysis, Oedipus has become a useful and common reference point for the most diverse thinking. Thus Oedipus, freed of the memory of the tragedy, from a certain classicism and from an idea of Greece, is more alive today than he has ever been since Sophocles.

But while, as Freud said, the Greek legend grasped a compulsion that everyone recognizes because everyone has felt it, it is notable that psychoanalysis has as its object of study the necessity and difficulty of loving and communicating. In this it may be followed by anthropology, with Lévi-Strauss' analysis (*Structural Anthropology*, 1958) of the Oedipus myth, and, even more recently, historical work, with Vernant's article taking up and continuing his thoughts about Oedipus' lameness. This certainly does not constitute a break either with Sophocles or with the myth, which encourages such thinking, but it does mean releasing its effectiveness and opening it up to the field of reality. This is doubtless the reason why so many modern writers have attached so much importance to the episode of the Sphinx. To the ambiguity of the narrative this episode adds the element of a riddle which the right answer cannot resolve, and this *mise en abyme*, which is all the more pressing because the terms of the question recall the very meaning of the name Oedipus and the metaphor of his journey, superimposes consciousness on the event. However, we cannot simply stop there, and, as Robbe-Grillet's *The Erasers* suggests, Oedipus apprehended outside literature can nevertheless return to it and change its language. One thing we can certainly say of these singular comings and goings is that we have not heard the last of them.

Colette Astier

The Ogre in Literature

The ogre is a familiar figure in folk tales from the African and European oral tradition. It appeared in the stories for children compiled from the oral tradition by Charles Perrault and Mme d'Aulnoy in the seventeenth century. These 'tales of Fairies and Ogres', as Perrault called them when he published his *Histoires ou contes du temps passé*, were also extremely popular with adults. The modern novel has revived and updated the myth of the ogre. Two novels which won the Prix Goncourt, Tournier's *Le Roi des aulnes* (1970) and Jacques Chessex's *L'Ogre* (1973), owe their success to this figure, which has not – as might have been expected – been relegated to the shelves of outdated children's myths. The publication of *L'Ogresse* (1977), a collection of tales transcribed from the Tunisian oral tradition by Nacer Khemir, illustrates the ogre's continued popularity.

A CONTROVERSIAL ETYMOLOGY

Bloch and Wartburg's *Dictionnaire étymologique de la langue française* states that the word appeared with its current meaning in 1300, and that it was probably a distortion of 'orc' from the Latin 'Orcus' – 'god of death' and 'hell' – who may have survived in popular belief and been incorporated into the legend of the ogre. This etymology is corroborated by the Italian 'orco' ('ogre'), the old Spanish 'huerco' ('hell', 'devil'), and by a passage from the life of Saint Eloi, who died in 659, and which alluded to a sermon in which the latter, condemning people who still believed in ancient pagan superstititions, mentioned Orcus, Neptune and Diana. It was Jacob Grimm who first linked the ogre with the Latin god Orcus. The ogre also appeared in the guise of 'Orque' in Richer's *L'Ovide bouffon* (1662) 'knowing by heart and word by word/Orcus, Tom Thumb, the Little Good Mouse, Donkey Skin and the fairy'.

The word 'ogre' is extremely rare in old French. Chrétien de Troyes used it several times but not in the sense of an anthropophagous monster. In a variant of *Lancelot*, the paladin who is on the trail of the knight who brought King Arthur's queen is given the following answer by the people he meets: 'A courageous and great knight/the King of the Ogres has captured him'. Elsewhere, ogres are described as the former inhabitants of the Kingdom of Logre. Lancelot discovers many men held prisoner in this kingdom who are unable to return to their country. According to Gaston Paris, this tale is a Celtic variant of the legend of Orpheus in which Lancelot descends into Hell to rescue his lady. Thus, the country of the Ogre or the Ogres is the Hell, from whence no one returns.

Dontenville discounts another etymology which suggests that the word 'ogre' is derived from Hungarian. 'At best, the much-dreaded Hungarian incursions into Gaul during the tenth century would have revived the old term and brought about the plural form of the noun.'

He connects the word 'ogre' with Gorgon and Gargantua, names which have been linked with the root 'garg' which means 'throat'. According to Dauzat, these words were more likely to be derived from an earlier, pre-Indo-European root, i.e. 'kar' or 'kal', 'gar' or 'gal', meaning 'stone'. This root is found in the names of all high places associated with the sun worship dedicated to Gargan-Gargantua, the Celtic sun.

The ogre, according to Dontenville, should be compared with 'Orcus of the underworld, who swallows the sun in the West'. 'He is the negative manifestation . . . of Gargan-Gargantua, the Celtic sun. He is the positive embodiment of the act of "swallowing" and of "eating", the father of all Gorgons living in the Western Gorgades.'

The link between the idea of devouring and swallowing and the shadows of death had been established. 'Darkness, the darkness of the earth and the tomb are represented by Orcus and the Ogre.'

Pieter Bruegel's painting *Dulle Griet* ('Mad Meg') and Jan Mandijn's *The Temptation of Saint Christopher* shared the same source of inspiration for their portrayal of hell as a gaping mouth, edged with teeth, in the middle of a gigantic head.

THE OGRE'S DOUBLES: THE DEVIL, THE WITCH, THE WOLF AND THE MONSTER

The origin of the word 'ogre', which links it to the darkness of the infernal (from 'infernus' meaning lower) regions of the underworld, proves that this figure is the folkloric double of the devil.

The term 'ogre' did not appear in print until Charles Perrault's tales were published in 1697. It was very quickly adopted by Mme d'Aulnoy, although it did not feature in the fairy tales by the Brothers Grimm, which only referred to the devil, i.e. 'teufel'. The *Okkerlo* by the Brothers Grimm was so untypical of the German tales that the authors did not include it in a new edition of the *Kinder und Hausmärchen* (*Grimm's Fairy Tales*), brought out at the end of the Napoleonic occupation. However, *The Devil with the Three Golden Hairs* clearly shows the close relationship between the ogre and the devil: 'I can smell warm young flesh' he says to his grandmother who is trying, like the ogre's wife in *Tom Thumb*, to conceal a child from him.

The witch is another of the ogre's doubles in another of Grimm's fairy tales, *Hansel and Gretel*. In the story, the parents, who are woodcutters, are driven by starvation to abandon their children in the forest. As in *Tom Thumb*,

Hansel lays a trail of white pebbles so they will be able to find their way back home. When there are no more pebbles, he uses crumbs which are eaten by the birds. The children meet a witch who lives in a little gingerbread house and who is in fact an ogress. Her animalistic sense of smell enables her to recognize the scent of human flesh. She intends to eat the children but fattens them up before preparing to cook them in her oven.

The ogre's final avatar is the wolf, Europe's wild animal *par excellence*, whose fearsome sharp-toothed jaws tear its prey to pieces. The wolf, like the ogre, is associated with the forest, solitude and hunger. The words of the wolf in *Little Red Riding Hood*, 'All the better to eat you with, my dear', could well be spoken by the ogre with his enormous, ravening teeth. Furthermore, an Italian version of Red Riding Hood describes an ogress whose tail betrays her animal nature. The wolf is associated, like the ogre, with funereal powers. Anubis, the Egyptian god who conducts souls to the land of the dead, appears in the form of a wild dog. In *The Eddas*, poems from Nordic mythology, two wolves, Sköll and Hali, sons of a giantess and the wolf Fenrir, hunt the sun and the moon, and are thus linked to the image of the ogre as the swallower of the sun.

The fact that the town of 'Ougernon' (the ancient name of Beaucaire, associated by Dontenville with the word 'ogre') was located in the region haunted by the Tarasque, enables a further comparison to be made between the ogre's voracity and that of the monsters which, according to legend, demanded their share of human flesh in the regions around Bordeaux, Tarascon and Poitiers. The Tarasque, an aquatic bull, is more like the dragon than the ogre, but the similarity should be stressed. In the modern novel *Le Roi des aulnes*, the ogre Tiffauges is also called 'Behemoth', after an aquatic monster from the Old Testament.

In Sweden, Scotland, Ireland, and Great Britain the ogre appears as a giant, while in Lithuania, Russia and Tartariya it takes the form of a seven-headed serpent.

THE AMBIGUOUS NATURE OF THE OGRE

These various avatars of the ogre in folklore and popular tales raise questions about its actual nature. Can it be evil and yet divine, animal and yet associated with supernatural powers, human although excluded from society by its cannibalism?

The Greek god Cronus (the Roman Saturn), made famous by Goya's painting *Saturn Devouring One of his Children*, is the symbol of the destruction of time. He is the divine prototype of the ogre. The infernal Orcus who devoured both the sun and mortals is depicted as a bearded, hairy giant in the funeral paintings of Etruscan tombs. The ogre is associated with those pagan deities who evoked death. Its representation as a giant is an indication of its supernatural origins. It is reminiscent of the Titans, the sons of the sky and the earth who, when the world was created, rebelled against the gods. The cannibalistic ogre seems to be 'the heir of those insolent giants, who scorned the heavenly beings who had reigned since before the flood'. 'I already existed a thousand years ago, a hundred thousand years ago', says the ogre in the *Roi des aulnes*, evoking its age-old origins. The similarity between the ogre and the Cyclops is often stressed. The Cyclopes were also anthropophagous giants, of which Polyphemus, who ate Odysseus' companions, is the best-known prototype. The ogre Ravagio and his wife Tourmentine in Mme d'Aulnoy's tale, *L'oranger et l'Abeille*, have only one 'squinting eye right in the middle of their forehead', while Camille Lacoste notes that in the North African stories, the ogre is often a cyclops. Although Geneviève Calame-Griaule considers that this characteristic is particularly Mediterranean and is not often found in black Africa, she does mention an ogress called 'Un Oeil' (One Eye) in a tale from Ngbaka. The ogre's similarity to the devil in the Germanic tales again reveals its supernatural quality.

It is possible that, despite its anthropomorphic form, the devouring ogre is a type of carnivorous, predatory animal.

The ogre's sense of smell, its weak eyesight (the theme of the blind ogress often recurs in fairy tales), its lack of intelligence (it is often deceived by Tom Thumb or the 'Mqides' in the Kabyle tales), the size of its teeth, its animal appetite, and the fact that it eats its prey raw, are all characteristics associated with the nature of wild animals (by virtue of the opposition of 'raw/cooked' and 'nature/culture' identified by Claude Lévi-Strauss). One small point often betrays its animal nature; e.g. Ravagio's and Tourmentine's long donkey's ears, or the tails of the Hausa ogres. The ogre is a monster, a hybrid creature which is related to the Minotaur (half man and half bull) which devoured young Athenians, the Sphinx (simultaneously woman, lion and bird of prey) which devoured young Thebans, and the mythical Cynocephali (men with dogs' heads). The latter often appeared in the writings of Pliny, Solinus and Saint Augustine, and later in Isidoro de Sevilla's *Etymologiarium* and Pierre d'Ailly's *Imago Mundi*, in the early years of the fifteenth century.

The ogre in the *Roi des aulnes* represents this animality within a modern context. It is a creature that is half man and half horse. Tiffauges' horse is called 'Barbe-Bleue' (Blue-Beard), which further stresses the analogy between the ogre and the gelding. It serves as a substitute for its master who proudly states: 'Blue-Beard . . . was merely an alter-ego', when he picks up the scent of a child and tracks it down. One of the ogre's physical characteristics is in fact its ability to assume the shape of an animal. In *Le Conte populaire français*, Paul Delarue refers to a Canadian version of Blue-Beard in which the lord changes into a giant horse when he is pursuing his victims.

Frank Lestringant raises the question of the ogre's nature when he writes: 'The wolf-man who hungers for human flesh is more of an animalistic monster than a cannibalistic human' . . . 'By his heinous crime, the ogre exceeds the limits of humanity'.

A third question therefore arises, i.e. could the ogre be a monstrous man who feeds on his fellow human beings through a perverse taste for human flesh? Could it be a depraved man, rejected by society because of the enormity of his crime? Is it a man possessed by the devil, a victim of lycanthropy?

Camille Lacoste quotes Frobenius, who believed that ogres 'were human beings who were socially maladjusted, and remained beyond the limits of civilization'.

The French language dictionaries *Littré* and *Robert* present the terms 'anthropophagy' and 'cannibalism' as synonyms. Jacques Geninasca suggests there is a distinction between the terms which, when applied to the ogre, accentuates the problem of its nature. He suggests that the term 'anthropophagy' applies to the consumption of human flesh, whatever the nature of the consumer, while 'cannibalism' either indicates anthropophagy when the consumer is human, or all consumption of flesh where a creature feeds on another of the same species.

The ogre, which is by definition anthropophagous, is only cannibalistic if it assumes a human form, in which case human flesh is forbidden. If it is not human, it is not breaking any taboo and is no different from the wolf in *Little Red Riding Hood.*

The reality of cannibalism in Europe, especially in times of famine and shortages, should not be overlooked. The myth of the ogre alludes to a terrible reality. Perrault's tales of *Tom Thumb*, and *Hansel and Gretel* by the brothers Grimm, deal with the parents' inability to feed their children in times when food was scarce. Children were in fact eaten during the great famines of the Middle Ages and the sieges of the sixteenth century. In *Les Tragiques*, Agrippa d'Aubigné describes a starving mother who kills and eats her child. In Perrault's tale, the ogre that kills and eats children could be seen as the double of the father and the objectification of his monstrous desire to eat his own children, just as the witch in *Hansel and Gretel* is the double of the mother who tries to abandon her children. The parents of Tom Thumb are certainly hungry for meat when, on their return, they find some money and immediately go to the butcher's. This parallel between the myth of the ogre and real acts of cannibalism offers an explanation as to why the coveted fresh meat is usually the flesh of children, who are obvious victims because of their vulnerability.

The tales often depict cruel mothers (or stepmothers) and fathers, who persecute their children so that they are forced to flee from their natural parents. According to Marthe Robert:

> The fairy tale, by allowing the indictment to show through its façade of official morality, is undoubtedly related to the ancient common heritage of myths and legends which was the depository for early Man's fear of existence. A sacred fear, no doubt, but which was not devoid of realism at a time when birth was still an uncertain and dangerous event.

Does the myth of the ogre express the 'cannibalistic impulses' of the parents, as distinct from the simple impulses of oral aggression, as discussed by the ethnopsychiatrist, Georges Devereux? The taboo which forbids the Mojavian mother to eat meat throughout the period following her confinement is, in his opinion, one of civilization's most unambiguous forms of defence against maternal cannibalistic impulses, which can be observed in the behaviour of certain animals where the eating of the placenta is sometimes followed by the eating of the umbilical cord and even of the new-born creature itself. These cannibalistic impulses are appeased by proxy in New Guinea, where the women of a certain tribe give their first-born child to the sows kept in a gully, while they adopt and breast-feed a piglet.

Even if metaphorical cannibalism is much more prevalent than actual cannibalism, it is useful to indicate the facts which reveal man's 'bestiality' and which are indirectly expressed by the myth of the ogre. By leaving the nature of the ogre in doubt, it becomes possible to eliminate and express the horror simultaneously.

The ogre is therefore a monster with supernatural powers, a magical creature which frequents and belongs to all kingdoms, without it ever being clear whether its nature is human, animal or divine. Its powers of metamorphosis makes it dangerous to try to define it too specifically, although it usually appears in the form of a giant who lives in the depths of the forest, is a great hunter and, as well as being extremely rich, possesses such magical objects as seven-league boots (this theme can be traced in the African tales), which enable him to move around with incredible speed. The myth of the ogre is a myth of abduction. If the ogre does not have boots, it has a steed, or is itself a horse which can travel at great speed. Finally, it often has a large bag or sack in which to carry its prey. This sack is possibly the avatar of the boat in which Charon transported dead souls. It should be noted that Hansel and Gretel have to cross a river when they return from the witch's house, as does the child who stole three golden hairs from the devil in Grimm's fairy tale. These images perpetuate the memory of the Styx, the reversed image of which is today represented by Saint Christopher, the kindly giant and ferryman who is the patron of fords and travellers.

THE AMBIVALENCE OF THE MYTH

The myth of the ogre, like any major myth, is in fact pulled in opposite directions, and it is because of these conflicting forces that the ogre is not a consistent figure.

The existence of a black ogre presupposes a white ogre, which is its alternative image. Etymology suggests that the ogre is the negative manifestation of Gargantua, the Celtic sun. Gargantua was a good ogre, although an insatiable glutton, resembling in that respect the ogre in Tom Thumb who has 'a whole spitted sheep for supper'. Like the ogre, Gargantua can go from mountain to mountain, without his progress being hindered by rivers. Although he is not wicked, he is nevertheless presented as a bogeyman, used to frighten the children at Saint-Chéron (Essonne): 'Beware of Gargantua who lives on the hill at Saint-Nicolas'.

The myth of the ogre is based on the opposition of 'life' and 'death'. A being who can mete out death can also save someone from death. In *Motif Index of Folk Literature*, Stith Thompson stresses that ogres can be rescuers and watchmen. This is the case with the wild man in Grimm's fairy tale, *Iron Hans*.

Le Roi des aulnes by Michel Tournier preserves the ambivalence of the myth. The hero Tiffauges initially compares himself to the King of the Alders, the Germanic ogre from Goethe's famous ballad, who carries children off to their death and later becomes Saint Christopher, the children's saviour. In *La Légende dorée*, Iacobus de Voragine recalls the fact that Saint Christopher used to be called the Outcast, that he was a terrible giant with an insatiable appetite and that he had initially entered the service of the devil. Saint Christopher is therefore a converted ogre. Marie Bonaparte explains this inversion of the myth in her study of the 'dog-headed' Saint Christopher at the Byzantine museum in Athens. In his role as ferryman, Saint Christopher is the double of Charon who, in Greek mythology, ferried the souls of the dead to the other side of the Styx. By dying, Christ transformed the meaning of death: 'The image of the cynocephalus subdued by Christ and transformed into the Christ-bearer, reverses his role and makes him a protector, a talisman against violence and death'. Saint Christopher protects travellers against sudden death, and this is because there is such a thing as a 'good death', which takes the form of a transformation and a reassuring transition. The ferryman's sack is therefore a reduced representation of Charon's vessel.

Saint Nicholas, venerated since the twelfth century for having saved some children that had been killed by a butcher and put into the salting tub, is another ambiguous figure in popular tradition. Catherine Lepagnol quotes the well-known popular song:

> 'There were three little children
> Who went gathering in the fields.

When Saint Nicholas arrived at the butcher's shop he was very hungry: he did not want to eat ham or veal, but preferred salted pork. The French for salted pork is 'petit salé', for which the entry in *Le Petit Robert* is: 'Salted flesh of a piglet; figurative and popular use: a small child, a kid'. Was Saint Nicholas, the patron saint of small children, an ogre? If the butcher in the popular song which describes the miracle of Saint Nicholas is reminiscent of the ogre in *Tom Thumb*, who eats piglets and small children indiscriminately, then Saint Nicholas is a very ambiguous rescuer, who seems to be using his miracles to atone for the crime that he was tempted to commit.

Saint Nicholas is the forerunner of Father Christmas, a popular figure associated with children who, on closer examination, is also ambiguous. He is, for example, traditionally accompanied by rather disturbing characters; bogeymen and ogres who punish naughty children and threaten to steal them and carry them off to distant lands. *Le Robert* suggests an etymology for the French word for 'bogeyman' or 'ogre' ('croque-mitaine') which is reminiscent of the image of the ogre: 'From the French verb "croquer" (to eat) and the French noun "mitaine" (glove) unless this is a derivative of the Dutch word "metjen" (little girl), which in German is "Mädchen" '. These lovers of human flesh are Father Christmas's doubles, and they clearly reveal an inherent ambivalence. Father Christmas, like the ogre, has boots and a sack. The illustrated book by Catherine Lepagnol, *Biographies du Père Noël*, presents numerous reproductions of drawings which play on the ambiguity of the ogre-Father Christmas, or Saint Nicholas-ogre. She even refers to a story, *Père Noël des Rats*, in which the ogre-cat, which is very similar to Raminagrobis, disguises itself as Father Christmas. In the Christmas story *La Fugue du Petit Poucet*, the novelist Michel Tournier plays on this ambiguity. The ogre gives his boots to little Peter, on Christmas Eve. The figure of Father Christmas can be seen behind the figure of the ogre which exerts such fascination on the child.

Furthermore, the attraction that the child feels for these figures may in fact arise from the mystery which surrounds them and even the fear that they inspire. This is demonstrated by Grimm's fairy tale about Frau Holle, a sorceress with huge teeth, who is simultaneously loved and feared by German children who await her arrival on Christmas Eve. In the German tale of the same name, the 'Pied Piper of Hamelin' is a 'large figure dressed in red' who leads the children away, as he did the rats, to an unknown destination, thus transporting them in both senses of the word. According to Pierre Péju in his work *La Petite fille dans la Forêt des Contes*: 'This tale is the imaginary realization of abduction fantasies, of those vague desires of being carried off, secretly nurtured by every child'.

The figure of the ogre is definitely mythical rather than legendary, and shares the ambivalence inspired by the sacred. Like all manifestations of the otherworld, it both attracts and repels. This attraction-repulsion, a power which is both evil and benign (the hero who braves the ogre often comes back a wealthy man), can still be identified in one North African tradition. During the festival of Achoura – a combination of Halloween, Christmas and Shrove-tide in which many pagan rites survive – a disturbing, masked figure appears, dressed in animal skins and with a long tail. This is 'the ogre of Achoura' in the Draa valley. It is the incarnation of ancestors, beings from the otherworld who have returned through the crack between the year which is drawing to a close and the year that is just beginning. It frightens women and children but is allowed to enter the houses, which are usually carefully locked and barred, because it ensures a time of plenty and fertility. This is reminiscent of the interpretation by Gaston Paris, according to which the ogre is the heir of the *rakshasas* in India, who were the souls of the dead (*Revue critique d'histoire et de littérature*, 1868, vol. II, pp. 5–6).

The myth of the ogre is based on yet another opposition, the opposition of 'love' and 'hate'.

In Grimm's fairy tale *Snow White*, the stepmother, jealous of the young girl's beauty, wants to eat her liver and lungs. She is not merely concerned with bringing about Snow White's death and taking revenge for the affront to her own beauty – hate is not the only motive for this mysterious act of appropriation of beauty. The desire for possession through the process of digestion indicates a desire for identification. The ogre that loves warm young flesh wants to appropriate the qualities of youth and to preserve its own immortality from this source of life. Among the superstitions surrounding the ogre, Stith Thompson draws attention to the belief in the curative and regenerative power of human flesh.

'I love meat, I love blood, I love flesh, it is the verb to love that is important. I am nothing but love. I love eating meat because I love animals,' says the ogre in the *Roi des aulnes*.

The religious nature of the sacrificial meal recurs when the ogre Tiffauges indulges in 'the pious and silent consumption of the remains of three little soldiers who have had their throats cut' (i.e. pigeons killed by drunken, ruffianly soldiers). In this instance, eating is an act of love, and the spitted pigeons foreshadow the children.

The ogre Tiffauges is fascinated by children. His hunger is not merely physical, he is hungry for youth and innocence.

The symbolic register of cannibalism is reminiscent of a Christian religious reference. In the sacrificial part of the mass, the bread is the body of Christ and the wine is his blood. Christ's invitation to the Eucharist assumes great metaphorical significance in the text of Saint John: 'Verily, verily, I say unto you, Except ye eat the flesh of the Son of man, and drink his blood, ye have no life in you. Whoso eateth my flesh, and drinketh my blood, hath eternal life . . . He that eateth my flesh, and drinketh my blood, dwelleth in me, and I in him'.

Nothing is said about the destruction of the body before it is eaten. Certain branches of the Christian Church forbid worshippers to chew the host. Others, like the sixteenth-century Protestants, refuse to acknowledge the symbolic significance of the consumption of the host and accuse the Catholic church of theophagy and omophagy.

These disputes highlight the ambiguity inherent in the act of eating. An important distinction should be made between swallowing and devouring. Gaston Bachelard, who has studied the Jonah complex, stresses that the cavity which ingests can be welcoming and even regenerative. If the digestive and the maternal functions of the stomach are combined, Jonah can be reborn. He becomes an image of resurrection. The text from the Gospel stresses that it is not only Christ who dwells in Christians but also Christians who dwell in Christ. It is a reversible relationship. Christians who take the host share in the purity and divinity of Christ. These examples of symbolic cannibalism demonstrate that the myth of the ogre is based on the opposition of 'love' and 'hate'.

THE METAPHORICAL DOMAIN OF IMAGINARY CANNIBALISM

The myth of the ogre in folk tales was possibly the result of an awful reality. The metaphorical domain of imaginary cannibalism is however infinitely more extensive.

The mythical image of Cronus devouring his children creates an initial shift in meaning, i.e. the ogre becomes the metaphor of the criminal father who kills his children to preserve his absolute authority.

In Tournier's *Gaspard, Melchior et Balthazar*, Herod converts Cronus' deed into reality by killing his own sons who want to usurp his power. Auguste's words on learning of the death of Herod's children, which were borrowed from Iacobus de Voragine and adopted by Tournier, revert to the alimentary image: 'At Herod's court, it is better to be a pig than a crown prince, because at least the prohibition on eating pork is respected there'. In this instance, eating means killing. The ogre Herod does not eat his children, he kills them.

L'Ogre by Jacques Chessex is another example of a shift in meaning. It is the hypertrophied image of the castrating father who, even when dead and reduced to ashes, continues to tyrannize his adult son. The latter believes he can see his huge shadow in the road, and he feels the weight of his father's disapproval in the same way that he felt crushed by his superiority, energy and authority as a child. This ghost swells in his imagination until it assumes the dimensions of the 'devouring' Ogre of the fountain in Bern. Paralysed and impotent, the hero is incapable of living and loving normally. Finally, he can stand it no longer and commits suicide.

The ogress may be a metaphor for the possessive mother who 'devours' her son, in the emotional sense, by loving him too much, by restoring him to the maternal breast, which is the most effective way of keeping him to herself and preventing him from marrying. Or else, she 'devours' him sexually, which becomes an imaginary representation of incest. The ogress stepmother who 'devours' the woman whom her son (e.g. Prince Charming in the *Sleeping Beauty*) has married, is a terrible mother who is over-possessive and jealous. Geneviève Calame-Griaule stresses the link between cannibalism and the refusal to accept marriage. She quotes a Bulu story from Cameroon in which the parents who eat their daughter are symbolically eating her fertility.

The myth of the ogre can describe a particular type of stifling relationship between parents and children. It can also apply to the destructive relationship between lovers. In this case, eating means loving as if the phrase 'warm young flesh' could have a double meaning, i.e. alimentary and sexual. Cannibalistic metaphors are often used to describe sexual attraction. 'She looks good enough to eat' and 'He devoured her with his eyes' are two commonly used phrases. In *La Pensée sauvage*, Lévi-Strauss points out that the French verb 'consommer' (i.e. consume/consummate) applies both to marriage and to a meal: 'All over the world human thought processes seem to perceive a basic analogy between the act of coupling and the act of eating, to such an extent that many languages use the same word to refer to both actions'. He continues: 'The sexual association and the alimentary association are immediately perceived in similar terms, even today. One has only to think of slang expressions such as 'faire frire' and 'passer à la casserole' [to screw] to realize that this is the case'. Furthermore, both areas – alimentary and sexual – are characterized by taboos.

The 'femme fatale' is an 'ogress'. Tournier uses the word to describe Sapho (in Daudet's novel), whose 'body, bruised by thousands of love affairs and thousands of broken relationships, closed like a trap on the young boy'.

The short story, 'Les Suaires de Véronique' (Veronica's shrouds) in *Coq de Bruyère*, presents another version of the ogress-femme fatale, a woman photographer who by the end of the story, quite literally, 'has the hide' of her naïve model. Although only the word 'witch' is mentioned, the cannibalistic motif is apparent. The amulet that the young man wears around his neck – a tiger's tooth, brought back from Bengal, which protects the wearer from being devoured – is stolen from him.

The ogre is also the metaphor of the seducer. The moral tale of *Little Red Riding Hood* written in verse – 'Wolves who speak honeyed words . . . are the most dangerous of all wolves' – evokes a particular type of human sexual behaviour which is reminiscent of Don Juan. In Matzneff's *L'Archimandrite*, the myth reappears with the cynical words spoken by a man who is attracted by very young girls: 'Thirteen years old is a good age: the bones are not yet formed, everything can be eaten'. In *Ariane et Barbe-Bleue* (1907), a 'musical tale' by Maurice Maeterlinck and Paul Dukas, Bluebeard – who has not killed his wives but keeps them imprisoned – appears to be a man who is very successful with women. Perrault's *Bluebeard* is an ogre in keeping with a typically Western, masculine fantasy. He is the representation of the violent husband who claims absolute authority over his subservient wife, whose personality he devours.

In the case of the ogre in the *Roi des aulnes* who is attracted by small boys, the cannibalistic image becomes the expression of a pre-genital sexuality. This 'cannibalistic tenderness' reveals the persistence of an early sexual phase, referred to as the 'oral' phase, during which sexual activity is still associated with eating food.

Although the myth of the ogre has developed considerably in the field of sexuality, it has also developed significantly in the field of politics. The new avatar of the ogre is the tyrant, the modern dictator. The rise of ideologies such as Stalinism and Nazism offers a possible explanation for the reappearance of the myth.

The horrifying poem about Stalin, written (November 1933) and quoted by Nadezhda Mandelstam in *Hope Against Hope*, was ultimately responsible for the author's death in a labour camp. It spontaneously adopts the cannibalistic metaphor. The 'Kremlin's mountaineer' is an ogre:

> His fingers are fat as grubs . . .
> His cockroach whiskers leer
> And his boot tops gleam . . .
> One by one forging his laws, to be flung
> Like horseshoes at the head, the eye or the groin
> And every killing is a treat
> For the broad-chested Ossete.

The animalistic image of devouring food expresses the enormity of his crime against humanity.

The success of the *Roi des aulnes* was due to the actualization of the myth of the ogre in terms of Nazism, the outright exploitation of Man by other men to the point of making fabric out of hair, and using human beings as laboratory animals. In one chapter Hitler, 'the ogre of Rastenburg', and Goering, 'the ogre of Rominten', are described at length. Tournier's originality lies in his simultaneous presentation of the other side of Nazism, i.e. its attempt to seduce German youth. The ogre disguises himself so as to be able to kill more effectively. The expression used by the royalists – 'the Corsican ogre' – to describe Napoleon is quoted by *Le Petit Robert* as an example of the metaphorical use of the word to mean a dictator, responsible for wars which consume young life.

Lévi-Strauss also used the image of the ogre to refer to the responsibility of Western civilization for the Indian genocide.

The character of *Dracula*, created by Bram Stoker (1897), is based on the historical figure of Vlad III 'the Impaler'. The use of metaphor transforms him into a vampire which sustains its immortality with its victims' blood, rather than their flesh, as in the case of the ogre.

Jarry's *Ubu Roi* is possibly the caricatured version of this ogre-dictator, a voracious swallower of people, who gulps down everything that appears before him. The thirty-three occurrences of the word 'merdre' (i.e. shit) could be interpreted as the reappearance of the myth of the ogre whose digestive, even anal, nature is always in evidence.

The bloodthirsty religions which carry out human sacrifices also used this image of the ogre. Flaubert described this 'cannibalistic' behaviour in *Salammbô* (1862) when he described the sacrifice of children to Moloch. 'A colossus' 'completely red like a giant covered in blood' represents the sun god. His open hands throw the children into his belly while the worshippers shout 'Eat, Lord!'

The Pope and the Roman Catholic Church were depicted as ogres in the Protestant pamphlets of the sixteenth century. The tortures suffered during the Inquisition, 'that cooking of the living' discussed by Montaigne, were horrific. The papal kitchen was supplied with:

> Boiled and roasted Christians, tortured
> Until they were reduced to ashes

The myth of the ogre thus attempts to convey the horror and fascination experienced by men when faced with individuals or ideologies which threaten to consume them.

The endurance of the myth of the ogre in such varied fields of human activity, its emergence in many popular expressions, and its presence in folkloric traditions, popular songs and stories from both the oral and literary traditions, demonstrate that, in spite of the taboo that surrounds it, the 'desire/repulsion experienced by human beings for the flesh of their fellows is an underlying, basic stimulus in Western mythical thought'.

If Perrault's ogres are presented as the brothers of the fairies who are etymologically associated with the Fata or Fates (which makes them the heirs of the Parcae), it is because they are also closely associated with the power of life and death. But whereas the powers of the fairy have developed in a benign direction, it is the malevolent side of the ogre which is predominant. If, like Gargantua, it is linked to a solar deity, it represents the destructive rather than the benign aspect of the sun. But the myth is highly ambivalent. The sexual imagery of the ogre as the seducer who attracts through the fear and fascination that he inspires simultaneously is as important as the political imagery of the diabolic ogre who is the incarnation of bloodthirsty tyrants.

Arlette Bouloumié

Orion

The author of the entry on 'Orion' in the *Real-Encyclopädie* refuses to credit any of the old etymologies (e.g. 'man of the mountains'), or indeed the new ones that have been suggested to explain a name which, according to him, is pre-Greek in origin. As far as the hero's genealogy is concerned, there are two conflicting traditions. The first, which is simple (from a fragment of Hesiod), makes Poseidon his father and Minos' daughter Euryale his mother. The other, more complex version gives him a foster father: according to a commentary by Servius on a line from *The Aeneid* (I.535), this adoptive father was King Oenopion; according to Ovid in book V of the *Fasti* (l. 493ff.), it was a poor farmer called Hyrieus, who lived in Boeotia. The stories told by Servius and Ovid agree on the fundamentals: an old man entertains three gods, Jupiter, Neptune and Mercury (other traditions replace Neptune with Mars or Mercury with Apollo). The host kills a bull in the gods' honour, is offered a reward for his hospitality and chooses the possibility of having a child without needing the participation of a woman. The three visitors urinate into the skin of the sacrificed bull and order the man to bury it in the ground for nine months. This results in the birth of Orion, whose name is related to heavenly urine. This version makes Orion the product of the four elements: the earth is his mother, while the male element is formed of fire (Jupiter), water (Neptune) and air (Mercury). Robert Graves is right to see it as 'something more than an ordinary comic tale'. We should note that the myth of Isaac's birth (Genesis 17) includes similar elements: a divine visitation by three men, the sacrifice of a calf and hospitality rewarded by a gift of fertility in old age.

Whether Orion is said to have been born at Tanagra (according to Korinne, sixth century BC), at Hyria or in Thebes, his country is almost always said to be Boeotia. Can a connection be established between the etymology that the Greeks gave to Boeotia and the role of the bull's skin? An interesting variation on the sacrifice and the role of urine is provided by Aristomachus (third century BC). According to him, it was Orion himself who sacrificed a bull, in reparation of a wrong he had caused to be done to a young man. The gods ordered him to drink the bull's urine and to cover himself in its skin: he then grew to gigantic size.

The genealogies all stress Orion's underworld origins. These are clearly manifested in the burial of the skin and also in the relation to Poseidon, the shatterer of rocks. When the latter is replaced by Ares, the lineage is of the same nature: both gods have violent giants as children.

Violence is characteristic of a great number of Orion's adventures. But the poets and mythographers always seek to find motives for and to excuse his hubris. Moreover, Orion experiences constant reversals in his fate, going from mutilation to cure, from catastrophe to salvation.

Orion has a wife, Side, whom he sends to the underworld himself, according to Apollodorus, because she wanted to compete with Hera. Conjugal violence is justified here by fear of the gods.

His aggressive strength has a beneficial aspect: he hunts dangerous animals. Homer shows him continuing his hunting activities in the underworld (*Odyssey* II.572). Like Heracles, of whom he sometimes appears as an avatar (both could be derived from Gilgamesh), he saves Chios from the wild beasts with which it was infested, hoping that this feat will win him the hand of Merope, daughter of Oenopion, the island's king. This is the version by Parthenos, a mythographer of the first century BC, who sought to excuse Orion for the crime of rape which he commits – Oenopion did not keep his promise. Other authors offer different excuses, such as Orion's drunkenness, or give him only the intention to rape.

A widespread tradition recounts both the punishment of Orion, who was blinded by Oenopion, and, above all, his healing: carrying Cedalion, the servant of Hephaestus, on his shoulders, he walks on the water towards the rising sun, whose rays cure him. Here we see the earliest prefiguration of St Christopher, with whom Orion shares giant size and the magical ability to cross the water.

In Orion's pursuit of the seven Pleiades and their mother Pleione we once more see the violent concupiscence already demonstrated by his relations with Merope. Sometimes Orion is the victim of an irrepressible desire, and sometimes he arouses it: according to Homer, Eos is responsible for carrying him off (*Odyssey* V.121). Ovid attributes this deed to Artemis, the goddess of Delos (*Fastes* V.537). The many different versions of the love between Orion and Artemis all have certain elements in common – concupiscence, pride, jealousy and murderous raving – these attitudes being attributed to one or other of the partners in the different cases. In all the versions the story ends with Orion's death, caused by either Artemis' arrows or the sting of a scorpion emerging from the earth in a reminder of the hero's underworld origins. The hunter's death is sometimes desired by his lover and sometimes presented as an accident of which she is either the clumsy instrument or the afflicted spectator.

But the reversible nature of the catastrophe, which can be observed in the mytheme of Orion's cured blindness, reappears in his death, when he and his dog are turned into a constellation.

Thus, while this story is the synthesis of many myths of different and doubtless prehellenic origins, it nevertheless has an attractive unity. Orion is an ambiguous hero, both the most pious (in Korinne's version) and the most impious of people, the most keenly devoted to the search for happiness and the most tragic victim of fate. It is an optimistic myth which constantly shows that misfortune – sterility, blindness, frustrated love or death – are inverted and become glorious triumphs. It is strange that having inspired so many Greek and Latin authors of epics, lyrics (Horace, *Odes* III.4.70ff), dithyrambs (a lost work of Pindar) and dramas (a satyr play by Sophocles was called *Cedalion*), this myth should have ceased for so long to be used in literary works and should then undergo a rebirth in twentieth-century literature.

From Antiquity to the present day painting has twice mediated the literary myth. In *De domo* Lucian describes a pictorial representation of Orion walking with Cedalion on his shoulders towards the rising sun. This scene is the subject of Poussin's canvas *Paysage avec Orion aveugle* (1658). Poussin's attention may have been drawn to Orion by the translation into French in 1627 of a study on mythology by Natale Conti (1551), which devoted five pages to Orion, giving a meteorological interpretation of the story of his birth. When, he says, the 'three gods come to join forces and faculties, substantial winds, rains and thunder are generated, which were long ago called Orion'. Poussin, who was also thinking of the autumnal season when the constellation of Orion appears, made it an allegory of rainy weather.

But Poussin's figure leaves the domain of allegory to give life to one of the most original novelistic achievements of our times, that of Claude Simon. For this writer, Orion is above all a man-landscape in whom the chaotic forces at work in the cosmos are incarnated. In *Conducting Bodies* (1971), Simon, giving new life to Poussin's silhouette by a reverie on the hero's underworld origins ('the muscled, rocky back of the giant bogged down in that clay'), generates landscapes and characters in the novel which constantly reflect one another: the Amazonian forest into which explorers blindly penetrate; the cloudy sky where the pilot finds it hard to make his way.

The myth of Orion illuminates three attitudes whose similarity is stressed by the novelist: sexual activity, war and artistic creation – although Simon is unwilling to accept the latter noun, preferring to speak of production.

Although for centuries the violent concupiscence manifested by the mythical hero was forgotten, it becomes a major theme in Simon's novels. The immense bodies of lovers, all mingled with wet earth and seashells, blindly grope after the illumination of pleasure; head-to-tail they slowly spin in the night in an endless fall, clamped together. The novelist makes us experience both the healing of their blindness and their transformation into constellations.

The warrior is also a mutilated and clumsy giant, linked to the earth by his activities. In *The Battle of Pharsalus* (1969), he is presented as a Goliath, or rather an Orion, who stumbled blindly.

Part of the text of the novel *Conducting Bodies* had already appeared in 1970 with the title *Orion aveugle*, in a collection published by Skira called *Les Sentiers de la création*. The introduction suggested that the giant's stumbling progress was also that of the writer 'gropingly discovering the world in and through writing', letting the words draw images to themselves as though by heliotropism. Simon does not, however, draw on the myth of Orion in too optimistic a way. He uses the hero and the constellation into which he is transformed in turn: when the giant recovers his sight at dawn, the constellation disappears. Thus the writer's work must always be begun anew, blindness is never definitively cured. The letter *O*, which is the initial of many of the protagonists of his novels (*The Battle of Pharsalus, The Georgics*), can refer both to the mythical hero and to the degree zero of his presence, the sign of his disappearance from the sky every morning.

While Poussin's painting acted as a relay in Simon's imagination, René Char's poetic imagination drew directly on the ancient forms of the myth. Whereas the former was drawn to the hero's sensuality, the latter is more attracted to the primitive aspect of the hunter of whom Homer sung; he sees him in dangerous close combat with the wild beasts. In *Placard pour un chemin des écoliers* (1936–7), his imagination works on the mytheme of Orion's birth. *Je distingue dans la corolle du soleil/Une jument/Je m'abreuve de son urine* ('In the corolla of the sun I see/A mare/I slake my thirst with her urine'). The discovery of the Lascaux cave paintings, which is the subject of *La Parole en archipel* (1959–60), leads him to exalt the hunter's passion. But it is in *Aromates chasseurs* (1976) that Orion appears with his mythical qualities: his gigantic size, his blindness and above all his ability to sing 'the morning songs of rebellion'. Like Claudel in *Le Soulier de satin*, Char is aware of his universal vocation: the constellation of Orion rises in each hemisphere in turn. He separates it from its hellenic roots to imagine an Iroquois Orion; he captures him 'escaped from an archipelago', 'painted with infinity and earthly thirst', a 'human meteor' in the ceaseless movement which makes him pass from one constellation to the next. Char's Orion is more a creature of the air than of the underworld. While he returns for a moment to the 'earth of loins', he is found at the next stage as the 'servant king' of the bees, taking the risk of bending his bow, despite his blindness.

While Simon and Char explicitly refer to the Orion myth, Patrick Grainville in his novel *La Diane rousse* (1978) confines himself to drawing inspiration from the hunter's adventures. The trio that he imagines of a narrator, a beloved woman (Hélianthe) and a bitch (Diane) is modelled on the trio of Orion, his dog and the goddess Artemis. The book has as its epigraph a phrase by Artaud: 'I want to adore the primitive life'. Like his mythical ancestor, whose drunkenness he shares at one point, Grainville's character suffers catastrophe after catastrophe: his dog is killed, he is blinded in a hunting accident, he loses Hélianthe. But for him too a tragic fate is reversed, becoming a glorious quest. His spiritual blindness is cured by memory and writing, through which he fully regains a Hélianthe who is open to the planetary forces: 'She was the tree up to the stars'. Questions of writing are present in the work of Grainville as they are in that of Simon, but in the former they find a more triumphant solution. 'This writing, day after day, files away my bars. Day will break under the pressure of memory.'

It might be asked why it is only in recent decades that the myth of Orion has regained its ability to give life to literary works. No doubt this is not unconnected with a certain fascination with eroticism, instinctive violence and primitive life, and with an awareness of what links us to animal life and to the elements, and which unites the hunter and his prey.

Marie Miguet

Orpheus

In the famous painting by Ingres Orpheus is shown in right profile on a rock, holding a lyre (*Orphée*, private collection, Montauban). It is hard to escape from this conventional image. At best we can try to outwit it: thus we have Orpheus as the conductor of the choir of Thebes, playing the violin, and performing a concerto that seems interminable to Eurydice, in the comic opea by Hector Crémieux and Jacques Offenbach, *Orphée aux Enfers* (two-act version 1858, four-act version 1874); or represented by the harp in Liszt's symphonic poem, *Orphée* (1853); or even playing a twelve-stringed guitar in Tennessee Williams's play *Orpheus Descending* (1957) – the guitar carries the signatures of the greatest American singers of the day, Bessie Smith and Woody Guthrie, and when Orpheus (alias Val Xavier) is arrested by the sheriff and his men, he fiercely forbids them to touch it. Orpheus is not only the figure of the musician; he is music's lover, and the lyre he holds in his hand is his mistress. Eurydice takes exception to this in Victor Ségalen's drama, *Orphée-roi* (1916): she detests her rival, the 'enchanted mistress', who possesses Orpheus and holds him in her spell. In *Orpheus Descending*, the guitar physically comes between Val and Lody when they first meet, and Carol dreams of eventually caressing Val in the same way that he caresses his instrument. The presence of this rival ought to inhibit the presence of any woman, which is why the original Orpheus in Greek mythology may have been *agamos* (without a wife). In a crucial article, Jacques Heurgon took care to remind us that 'there is no evidence of Eurydice's existence on the fifth-century vases, the Petelia tablets, the frescoes at Pompeii, or the paintings in the catacombs'.

For us, however, Eurydice has become as essential as the lyre. At the end of Gluck's opera (1762), Orpheus' famous song 'Que fara senza Euridice?' ('I have lost my Eurydice') expresses more than a situation of mourning. It expresses a necessity, which has become a necessity for us too. Orpheus and Eurydice are indissociable, yet dissociated: even Virgil in canto VI of the *Aeneid* describes Orpheus as a solitary figure advancing amidst the shades of the blessed ('Threicus longa cum ueste sacerdos'), and Rilke, in his first great Orphic poem, 'Orpheus, Eurydike, Hermes' (*Neue Gedichte*, 1907) imagines a Eurydice who is longing to return to death, where she had at last found her roots. This situation is no more astonishing than the separation of Tristan and Iseult, or that of Claudel's lovers, which was finally accepted. Human love is all the stronger and more poignant because it includes the scandal of separation, and if the myth brings some consolation, it is through the continuity of Orpheus' song, which in its appeal preserves at least the name of the beloved, if not her presence. 'Euridice, Euridice', Orpheus' repeated cry in Gluck's opera, could be used by Nerval as an epigraph for the second part of *Aurélia* (1853).

Orpheus' love for Eurydice may seem self-evident to us. Yet it survives the darkness of absence (in the first known versions), of the underworld (in the classical versions), and perhaps most importantly of desire. As Maurice Blanchot observed in *L'Entretien infini* (1969), we are dealing with 'separation which becomes attractive in itself', 'the interval which becomes perceptible', 'the absence which reverts to being a presence', night that becomes day. Orpheus is simultaneously 'le ténébreux' (a 'figure of darkness'; Nerval, 'El Desdichado' in *Les Chimères*) and a figure of light (Corot's Orpheus hailing the light, in the sketch for the large panel to the glory of day, intended for the Hôtel Demidoff, completed in July 1865 at Fontainebleau). This may seem surprising, since Pindar in the *Fourth Pythian Ode* says he is Apollo's son. But Apollo, the god of light, is also Loxias, the Oblique. Orpheus has a mysterious name, which has sometimes been connected with *ribhus*, Sanskrit for a poet or minstrel. At the beginning of the twentieth century, Salomon Reinach was more inclined to associate it with *orphnos*, a Greek adjective meaning obscure. He then linked Orpheus with the nocturnal Dionysus, and was tempted to regard him as a god of the underworld. In fact, for all that Nietzsche despised Orpheus, no doubt finding him too Apollonian, it seems certain that in this myth the two new gods, who are too often regarded by modern writers as antagonistic, should be considered in conjunction with one another. In book XI of Ovid's *Metamorphoses*, when Orpheus, after being torn to pieces by the Bacchantes, is no more than a head and a lyre borne on the waters of the River Hebrus, Phoebus-Apollo comes and repels a final onslaught from a serpent that fails to respect these sacred remains. But Dionysus (Lyaeus) also intervenes in favour of the Thracian poet, condemning the Bacchantes to stay in the forest and chaining them to the ground by twisting roots, and deciding to abandon this excessively barbaric country. Moreover, nothing could be less Apollonian than the first landscape in which Orpheus is located, the Rhodope Mountains (*Metamorphoses* X.11–12). These were to become the wild opening setting for *Orphée-roi* by Ségalen. But Orpheus can cast his spell on mountains, just as he can draw animals and trees to follow him: his procession is reminiscent of the famous procession of Dionysus. Like Dionysus Zagreus, he goes down into the underworld in search of someone he loves (Semele in Dionysus' case, Eurydice in Orpheus'; see under 'Eurydice' in Roscher's *Lexicon*). Like him he is torn to pieces: Dionysus as a victim of the Titans, who cook the pieces of his body in a cauldron; Ovid's Orpheus put to death by the Bacchantes after the *sparagmos* (rending and tearing) of the animals he charmed. Orpheus was to become like his god: the link had already been made by classical writers, especially by Diodorus Siculus. But which god? Apollo or Dionysus? The former upholds the master of the lyre, the latter 'the poet who celebrated the mysteries' (*Metamorphoses* XI.68). Modern writers sometimes push the assimilation to the point of confusion: in *Le Vice errant* Jean Lorrain dwells at length on a description of the frenzy of bodies which reaches a paroxysm at the feasts organized by Count Vladimir Noronsof, the new Nero: 'Like the Lupercalia, Bacchanalia or Orphic festivals with processions consisting of at least three hundred participants'. Admittedly Orphism, especially at this time, still obscured the figure of Orpheus himself. But the Orpheus myth on its own is obscure enough, for it is riddled with contradictions. The events in the story of which it offers an account were not present from the beginning, and the plot only became established at a late stage, from a collection of different traditions in which it is hard to sort out the authentic elements from those introduced by contamination.

ORPHEUS AND THE ARGONAUTS

Study of the first known text in which Orpheus features prominently means starting with an aspect of his deeds which has had a considerable posterity in literature: his presence among the Argonauts. At the same time we can visualize a modern image, the great unfinished canvas of *Les Argonautes* by Gustave Moreau, where Orpheus is seen sitting with his other companions around Jason, who is standing on the deck of a galley.

This first text, which dates from the sixth century BC, is the *Fourth Pythian Ode* by Pindar, exceptional for its length, its construction and especially for the considerable space allocated to the myth of the quest for the Golden Fleece. If we leave aside the stories relating to Iolkos and Jason's ancestry, and to Euphemus and the legend of the mythical foundation of Cyrene, we realize that the most memorable episodes in the expedition are dealt with mainly by means of allusion. Pindar names ten or so of Jason's companions. They are all demigods: Heracles, the Dioscuri, Euphemos, Periclymenus, Orpheus, Echion, Erytos, Zetes and Calais. So here Orpheus is the son of Apollo and not of Oeagrus, as another tradition would have it (his mother being Calliope). Orpheus' presence is essential for three reasons, which Pindar's text does not have the time to go into, though they are given in other long poems about the Argonauts; by Apollonius Rhodius, dating from the third century BC, by Valerius Flaccus in the first century BC, and the *Argonautica* of Orpheus in the fourth century BC, as well as in modern works inspired from them.

First of all the ship *Argo* had to be built, and it had to be tough and imposing. Orpheus, who had the magic power of drawing the trees of the forest to him by his songs, must also have had the power of getting them to sacrifice themselves in order to become building material for boats. Pierre Emmanuel remembered this in one of his *Hymnes orphiques* (1942), 'Orphée sur le navire Argo', in which the 'twisted oak' which 'tries in vain to get a grip on the fluid bones of the sea', 'wishes for the earth/whose tears and sorrow populate the sea'. This longing on the part of the tree is reflected in that of the sailors, who lament the country they have left behind to set off into the unknown.

In the course of their voyage they confront fearsome tests: the rocks-that-drive-together or Symplegades – Orpheus's song has the power to stay their murderous movement – and the Sirens, whose tempting voices try to lure human beings into the waves. The *epos* of the Argonauts here perceptibly echoes the *Odyssey*, with the same inescapable passage between Scylla and Charybdes, a variation on the Symplegades, and the Sirens. Following Circe's instructions, Odysseus got his men to tie him to the mast of his boat, so that he and he alone might enjoy the Sirens' incomparable music with impunity. Orpheus, by contrast, tries to dominate the voices of the sorceresses by the power of his *phorminx* (lyre). Only one of the sailors, Butes, is unable to resist their charm and leaps into the waves. Apollinaire may have remembered this in 'Lul de Faltenin', a poem in *Alcools* (1913), which must surely allude to Orpheus' period as an Argonaut.

When the expedition set out, King Pelias ordered a quest that was not confined to seeking the Golden Fleece. He invoked a dream, during which his ancestor Phrixus appeared to him, demanding that his soul should be brought back from Colchis where it had remained. This mission is clearly spelt out in the *Fourth Pythian Ode*, even if there is no account of how it was accomplished. Thus Orpheus the Argonaut was implicated in an adventure which this time repeated the Odyssean *nekuia* (visit to the underworld). Just as Circe instructed Odysseus, Medea, the Colchian king's daughter, instructs the hero on the trials he will be subjected to, guides him along the paths leading from one world to the other, and helps him through difficult straits (this is also the role of Siduri in *Gilgamesh*). But the hero in this case is Jason rather than Orpheus. Though Robert Graves in his mythological novel, *The Golden Fleece* (1944), speaks of the sons of Phrixus while neglecting the fate of Phrixus' soul, this matters little, since it is only too clear that the Golden Fleece is the metaphor for Phrixus' soul: it was just as dangerous to remove one from the shores of Colchis as the other. Like the dead man's soul, the fleece was a taboo that might not be touched – André Breton played on 'toison' (fleece) and 'poison' in his *Ode à Charles Fourier* (1947), where the Argonauts' expedition is an allegory for the Revolution, and Fourier is a new Orpheus.

ORPHEUS AND EURYDICE

The structure of the myth of Orpheus becomes clear provided this first, Argonaut episode is not omitted. For in many ways Orpheus' descent into the underworld in search of his lost Eurydice recommences and repeats the evocation of the dead man (or its emblematic representation, the taking of the fleece guarded by a chthonian monster). The folding back upon itself which is typical of the structure of myth is present here, though admittedly in this case it may be that the literary myth repeats the myth proper.

Eurydice's name does not in fact apear until relatively late, in a highly literary development of the myth, which has Orpheus married, Orpheus as a 'widower', 'inconsolable' Orpheus stepping in to take the place of the originally single Orpheus. Book IV of the *Georgics* has this double surprise in store for us, but this apparent 'Virgilian revolution' may well not be what it seems. Jacques Heurgon gives us a timely reminder that Virgil does not invent his stories: it is therefore probable that he did not come up with a completely innovatory plot in this book of the *Georgics*; 'He only deviated from the more or less official theme because a less well-known form of the legend had interested and emboldened him'. Phaedra in Plato's *Symposium* had already alluded reprovingly to Orpheus' descent into Hades in search of his wife. This written document must be linked with a crucial piece of archaeological evidence, the bas-relief of *Orpheus, Eurydice and Hermes*, dating from the time of Phidias (fifth century BC) but known to us only through three Roman copies.

There is no evidence of Orpheus' descent into the underworld from before the end of the sixth century BC. It was then that the most ancient monuments of Orphic literature were formed in the context of a huge undertaking to recast and codify religious traditions, sponsored in Athens by Pisistratus' sons.

The descent soon took on a secular rather than a mystical aspect, becoming a touching love story, a model brought to mind by Admetus in Euripides' *Alcestis* (438 BC), or even a pretext for a misconceived generalization ('Orpheus brought the dead out of Hades') in a formal speech by Isocrates, *Busiris* (*c.* 390 BC). Orpheus' wife is first referred to as Agriope (in *Leontion* by Hermesianax of Colophon, third century BC); the name Eurydice appears for the first time in the *Lament for Bion*, supposedly by Moschus: 'Your song will not go unrewarded; as Core once granted Orpheus the return of Eurydice in recompense for the sweet sounds of his lyre, so she will send you, Bion, back to your mountains'.

As we can see, this version suggests that Orpheus was ultimately successful. On the other hand, book IV of the *Georgics*, and a little later books X and XI of Ovid's *Metamorphoses*, suggest a sad outcome: the gods of the underworld allow Orpheus to return to the earth with Eurydice, but she has to walk behind him, and he is not allowed to turn back towards her or see her before they have both crossed the boundary separating the living and the dead.

At the very end, Orpheus proves unable to resist the temptation, and he loses Eurydice for a second time. Virgil's Eurydice protests, while Ovid's Eurydice, her arms outstretched towards Orpheus, sees it as a miracle of love that outweighs the total sum of their misfortunes.

The embargo on looking back has been interpreted in a number of ways. The most pedestrian version indicts Orpheus as a prey to his sensuality, and

Eurydice can be portrayed as a flirtatious, even irritating woman who, because of her insistent request (in Gluck's *Orfeo*), or through her quarrelsome nature (in Cocteau's play *Orphée*, 1927), carries a considerable share of the blame for the final catastrophe. Moreover, it is hardly a catastrophe if they are such an ill-assorted pair: in Anouilh's *Eurydice* (first staged in 1941), when Orpheus turns to look back at her, Eurydice announces that she has been Dulac's mistress. But it is more interesting to conceive of this embargo as a truly religious one. As Jacques Heurgon notes, the backward glance must originally have had some other meaning than the simple, loving look which inspired André Bellessort to lyrical couplets in *Virgile* (1920). Neither Orpheus nor Eurydice had the right to turn back towards the gods of the underworld. Servius in Virgil's *Eighth Bucolic* recalled that 'the divinities do not want to be seen' (*nolunt enim se videri numina*). The backward glance is sacrilegious, just as it is sacrilegious to break the silence. This was suggested by the author of the *Culex*, who was using Hellensitic sources. In a broader sense, Orpheus, like Don Juan, is prohibited from disturbing the silence of the dead. His call upsets Rilke's Eurydice: like Nietzsche Rilke opposes all looking back when it is neccssary to go forward, to say yes even to death, and to anticipate every farewell ('Sei allem Abschied voran', *Die Sonnette an Orpheus*, 1923, II).

The fact that the denouement of the story of Orpheus and Eurydice is left open partly explains the extraordinary literary posterity of what is really no more than an episode in the myth. The first theatrical version was by Angelo Poliziano: his *Fabula di Orfeo*, a 'commedia', 'egloga', 'festa', 'rappresentazione' or 'favola pastorale', was composed in Mantua in June 1480 'in two days, amidst a continual tumult, in the popular style' for a celebration by the Gonzaga family. The work was published, perhaps without the author's consent, a few months before his death in September 1494. Though very short (401 lines), it is in five acts: 'The Shepherds', 'The Nymphs', 'The Heroes', 'The Dead' and 'The Bacchantes'. They show respectively an evocation of the pastoral setting, Eurydice's original death when she is bitten by a snake, the descent into the underworld, Eurydice's second death, and the death of Orpheus. It is a tragic version. The pact imposes a limit on Orpheus' desires ('Therefore learn how to moderate the burning of your desires,' Pluto tells him, 'otherwise your Eurydice will immediately be taken from you'), but Orpheus at once sings out his joy and his victory, calls to Eurydice, turns back towards her and loses her. As Eurydice says, he has been the victim of his excessive love ('gran furore'), and the violence affecting them is none other than the violence of love.

By contrast Ottavio Rinuccini's libretto for *Euridice*, used for two exactly contemporaneous operas (1601) by Jacopo Peri and Giulio Caccini, moves towards a happy ending. The pronouncing of Eurydice's freedom, 'Trionfi oggi pietà', ends in smiling sweetness, 'Go, be happy and peaceful'. Orpheus and Eurydice set off towards a future bright with happiness, all the more intense for having been interrupted.

Is it possible to accept a second remission if Orpheus succumbs to the temptation to look back? Tisiphone formally opposes it at the end of act IV of Poliziano's tragedy. On the other hand, Gluck's librettist, Calzabigi, was tender-hearted and open to compassion. Amor, touched by Orpheus' lament, steps in to prevent him from killing himself, and allows the happy couple to be reunited: 'No longer doubt my power./I come to remove you from this frightful place;/Henceforth enjoy the favours of Amor'.

But where is the true resting place of Orpheus and Eurydice? Is it the life to which Cocteau restores them, both in his play and in his 1950 film; the 'household' that is their 'only paradise', the 'dirty water' to which they had to be returned? Or is it on the contrary in death, that 'other face of love' as Félicien Marceau describes it, writing about Anouilh's *Eurydice*? At the end of the poem *Orpheus en Eurydice* (1941) by Luc Indestege, one of the two lovers is cast on the side of death, the other on the side of life, whereas another Dutch writer, Hubert Lamp, finishes his novella *De Geliefden van Falun* (1964) based on the myth of Orpheus with these words:

> And yet what could separate us in this world? Time? Space? Death? We have loved each other for ever, we two are just the material manifestation of a love that was already ripe before we were born and which will live even if a day came to us . . . It is as solid as the world itself and cannot be destroyed by either time or eternity.

Victor Hugo in his rediscovered idylls in *Chansons des rues et des bois* and in that other idyll, the Orphée in the second series of *La Légende des siècles* (1877), also concluded on the same note, the immortality of love.

While Orpheus as an Argonaut was repeating the adventures of Odysseus, the disappearance of Eurydice is a repeat of the disappearance of Core/ Persephone when she was kidnapped by Hades. The parallel is suggested by Ovid in *Metamorphoses*, since Orpheus, to appease the gods of the underworld, reminds them of their own past history (X.26–9). But the analogy cannot be pushed too far. Orpheus shows cleverness, but perhaps *hubris* as well, in daring to make the comparison.

ORPHEUS AND THE BACCHANTES

After Eurydice has died for the second time and Orpheus has passed through the underworld, he seems much more fragile, and his power to charm is less reliable in its effect. The tragedy requires a scapegoat, and it turns out to be Orpheus himself. It would be marvellous to be able to observe in ancient literature this transition from lyric poetry to drama, but unfortunately the text of Aeschylus' tragedy *The Bassarides* has disappeared, and it is impossible to have a really clear idea of the trilogy it belonged to. It certainly presented the conflict between Orpheus and the Bacchantes of his native country of Thrace, and finished with his death.

There are, in fact, several ancient traditions regarding Orpheus' death: that he killed himself so as not to outlive Eurydice (Pausanias, *Guide to Greece* IX.30.6), that he was struck by a thunderbolt from Zeus for revealing the mysteries to men (Pausanias, IX.30.5; Diogenes Laertius), or that he was killed in a popular uprising (Strabo, *Geography* VI.18 – through contamination with the usual version of the death of Pythagoras). But the most widespread and persistent tradition is that of the murder of Orpheus by the Maenads of Thrace on Mount Pangaeum, either as a punishment wished on him by the gods (Plato, *Symposium*, VII.179c), or with Dionysus himself being forced to disown his devotees (Ovid, *Metamorphoses*).

Any attempt at reconstruction is fairly risky. According to Salomon Reinach, *The Bassarides* showed the bard of Thrace being torn to pieces by women dressed in fox's pelts (*bassaros* means fox in Greek), and Orpheus himself wearing a fox's pelt on his head and buskins made of fox skin on his feet. When this episode is translated into a more archaic, mystical language, it means that a sacred fox has been sacrificed and ritually eaten by women disguised as foxes. It may well be that this agrarian ceremony gives meaning to the Thracian version of the myth, but it seems far removed from the literary myth, which has developed more along the lines of seeing the situation in simple human terms. These include the mourning of the disconsolate husband which the women of Thrace in their jealousy find intolerable (Virgil, *Georgics*; Angelo Poliziano, *La Fabula di Orfeo*); the 'conversion' of Orpheus to the love of young boys (Ovid, *Metamorphoses*; Luciano Berio, *Orfeo II*, after Monteverdi, 1984, with the Bacchantes here as little boy hooligans); the jealousy of one of the Maenads, Aglaonice, who had previously had a liaison with Eurydice and cannot pardon Orpheus for taking her from her (Edouard Schuré, 'Orphée' in *Les Grands Initiés*, 1889, a book which Ségalen had in mind in act IV of *Orphée-roi*), and so on.

Apparently it is the power of Orpheus' singing and music that is called into question. In Ovid's poem, he does in fact succeed at first in deflecting the projectiles cast at him (the stones are entranced, and remain suspended in mid-air). But just as he succeeded in blocking the Sirens' song, so his song is blocked by the din made by the women of Cicones. The scene of violence is reproduced in Cocteau's film, but the Orphic charm does not operate. It is as if, after emerging from the underworld, Orpheus were pursued by the Furies he thought he had subdued, who are nothing more than relentless, bloodthirsty women. This would be a new fold in the myth, ensuring coherence between the second mytheme (Orpheus and Eurydice) and the third (Orpheus and the Bacchantes).

For a poet, and perhaps even more for a musician, there is something here that must be hard to accept. That is why Monteverdi felt he had to improve on the original denouement of his *Orfeo* (1607) – a bacchanalian orgy – by making Apollo appear *ex machina*. Orpheus has to make do with a Eurydice reduced to a beautiful picture ('sembianze belle') in the sun and the stars, but he himself will enjoy eternal life, immortality in the celestial regions. In Ovid's poem Phoebus-Apollo comes to the rescue of his son's remains, and we have the miracle of the head that sings or the lyre that plays of its own accord, a miracle that is renewed at the end of Ségalen's *Orphée-roi*, which was to serve as a libretto for Debussy.

> The Lyre rises gradually and soars over the abyss. And in this lightning rise, the Song grows stronger, and it is THE ORIGINAL VOICE OF ORPHEUS – dominating the heavy earth, the woods and rocks, the games, love-making and cries with its epiphany, and rising triumphantly – that reigns at the highest summit of the singing heavens.

So its passage through death has not blunted the power of the music. On the contrary, it has become more powerful, for 'Only he who already raised the lyre/ even among the shades/ can sense and proclaim/the infinite praise' (Rilke, *Die Sonnette an Orpheus*, I, sonnet 9).

Orpheus is taken as representing the perfection of all music or, to express it another way, absolute music. This gives him his supernatural power over animals, plants and even minerals – as well as over souls, since in the Middle Ages he becomes the Good Shepherd. That music, put to the test by the Sirens, reveals its greatest power when Orpheus descends into Hades, so much so that it gives the singer a confidence that may be excessive. There is still one final test, and this time Orpheus seems to emerge as the loser – the attack by the Maenads. Yet Orpheus' song in the midst of so much savagery, the music that survives the dead man, in fact constitutes the most important victory. And in *Orpheus* (1955) by the Hungarian poet Sandor Weöres the image of death begetting song is very beautiful: 'The funeral drum rolls, I dance in an everlasting round, a song fills the valley which my blood has fertilized, the trellis of death enlaces the secret of my eternal life.'

Pierre Brunel

Parsifal

Parsifal lies at the heart of the forest of myths which medieval literature lays before us; it represents the most perfect example, yet at the same time it is a striking exception. The myth of Parsifal is at the centre of the vast group of texts devoted to the quest for the Grail, and is thus part of the most original and crucial mythical edifice of the Middle Ages. Yet it also differs from the others in that it is remarkably autonomous and self-sufficient: the hero's trajectory does not demand a 'continuation' for his destiny to be accomplished, as is the case with Lancelot, who was followed by Galahad. Parsifal is also unique in that it can authoritatively claim to be a *genuine* literary myth, a myth derived from writing. Its originators, Chrétien de Troyes and Wolfram von Eschenbach, both claimed not to have invented it, attributing it to an earlier writer and book – almost certainly invented. The story of 'Perceval', free of any references, thus made its appearance as an original medieval myth.

From then on Parsifal became a beacon, a character incarnating an entire civilization through his exemplary story. First and foremost he constituted a counterpoint to Tristan, the other great mythical figure of the period, who came into being at the same time – the second half of the twelfth century. The two of them represent the most extreme positions that it is permissible to adopt vis-à-vis the two great forces on which the structure of society is based: the potency of love, associated with the court of love and divine power, and the temporal forces, operating at the court of the overlord, with which it interacts. Tristan and Parsifal both serve their apprenticeship in the medieval mode of existence following the thread of a tale of love and power, but the accent is not placed on the same values for both. In the case of Tristan, passion that transgresses the norms will end by failing to recognize the importance of temporal power, excluding it from the world which it inhabits. In Parsifal's case, the quest for the Grail (i.e. the conquest of power) allows in passing for the harmony of the world to be accomplished in marriage, the legitimate version of love. Thus, far from deliberately excluding any domain of human activity, Parsifal's path consists of a *progressive* advance towards the divine.

The myth of Parsifal lies at the roots of the 'apprenticeship novel': he starts off as a foolish, ignorant young man who abandons his mother, leaving her to die while he sets off to discover the world. To begin with he does not know his name, though he is of noble birth, and after this first revelation he has to pass through the successive stages of training. An elderly man, Gornemant, initiates him into practice of arms and courtly behaviour, which teaches that ladies should be protected. However, his meeting with his elected bride leaves him unfulfilled, and his desire to experience harmony in this world pushes him to accept the only conquest worthy of the highest ambition, the conquest of the Grail. This mysterious symbol, which was not originally Christian but which came to be portrayed in the texts as a holy chalice, leads him strangely enough to refuse at first to serve God, in order that he may accomplish his quest. A final apprenticeship, which teaches penitence and humility in Christ, is required of him so that he may have the right to rule over the Grail, by the side of Blanchefleur, the wife legitimately accorded him by the Christian faith.

Thus Parsifal is seen as reflecting the perfect image of medieval man. After succeeding in controlling the passions of the flesh and triumphing over the mysteries of a world of fable – which involves woods filled with wonders and unknown dangers – he moves on towards the divine conquest of the power destined to be his. This is the path through life of the Chosen, proceeding in brightness towards the world of excellence which is reserved for the pure. It would be impossible to imagine a more perfect antithesis to the Tristan myth, a tale of troubled waters in which transcendence is virtually unknown.

This almost Jansenistic austerity in the Parsifal myth, mixed with its marked fondness for the strange and wonderful, did not attract the interest of the neo-classical period, and we have to wait until the nineteenth century, which was more curious about the Middle Ages, for the figure of Parsifal to re-emerge, indissolubly associated with Wagner, a great evoker of myths.

The character of Parsifal had to be of considerable importance for Wagner deliberately to choose his story to crown his life's work. At the end of a long process of development, Wagner's syncretism finished with this ultimate confrontation with God, 'this unbearable hand-to-hand fight between man and the divine' as Julien Gracq expresses it. Boldly mixing old texts, which were Celtic in origin but overlaid with Christianity and Buddhist inspiration, Wagner refashioned Parsifal's progress according to his own ideas, making it purely initiatory. After emerging from his originally naïve state, the hero undergoes ritual tests. First of all he learns about the suffering of others: when Kundry reveals to him that his mother is dead, she causes him to go off into a deep swoon, already a symbolic death in this world; his meeting with the king of the Grail, Amfortas, leads to a repetition of this experience of compassion. His subsequent confrontation with womankind in the person of Kundry, an accursed creature, has nothing in common with the legitimate marriage to Blanchefleur. Quite the opposite, the temptress only serves to deepen his Christian compassion – as this is devoid of carnal contact it has something in it of the 'communion of the saints' – and to awaken the power of memory. Parsifal then remembers simultaneously the sufferings of Amfortas and of Christ and from then on he is the vessel of the Gospels, the living symbol of the church, which is memory. He is the Chosen One, who consecrates the new covenant between earth and heaven, achieved at the cost of a total renunciation of the world.

In the history of this myth we can see Wagner as representing both a peak and a dead end, in that his impulse towards the sacred completely upsets the balanced harmony of its progression. Thus, almost inevitably, new accounts of Parsifal's adventures were to emphasize the other pole of the story, knowledge of woman, at the risk of creating new imbalances and smashing the myth.

However, there is another, less frequented path, which takes Parsifal away from both religion and sex: the path of poetry. Provided the myth does not become the subject of a fragmented poem describing the failure of a quest, as in Jean-Louis Backès's work, there is a power in it which makes reality poetic. The fascination that the magic words Montsalvat, Grail and Brumbane exert on the modern reader appears to affect Parsifal himself, and he seems intoxicated by this language, which masks even from him the reality of his quest. In the end the naïve young poet who travels through Gracq's *Le Roi pêcheur*, bowed down under the weight of suffering – inflicted on him by a perverse Grail which burns him – renounces his mission. In order to exist outside time with all its disappointments, Parsifal's only option is to become a poetic object. Thus in Virginia Woolf's *The Waves*, 'Percival', who soon vanishes from the world of appearances, is transformed into myth, into a new Grail, the object of mankind's unavailing quest.

Such a metamorphosis is the only one that avoids profaning the myth. Almost the only possible way of forcing Parsifal to forget sacred love and choose human love in its stead is to resort to the devil. In Julien Gracq's book *Au Château d'Argol*, Parsifal – who has become Albert – has acquired knowledge but lost his innocence. Plunging into depravity, he believes he recognizes the Grail in a woman (Heide), and gradually changes into a demoniac figure, close to Wagner's 'foil', Klingsor. Like Wilde's Dorian Gray, he finally takes on the stigmata of decay and death.

Where Parsifal resists sensual temptation in other contexts, it is because he has become a figure of fun. Surrealism, in the person of Leonora Carrington (Gracq's novel already had Surrealist touches), treats him cavalierly. The story of *Le Cornet acoustique* tells of an upside-down apprenticeship, where the new Parsifal is an octogenarian who rediscovers physical youth. Wonders are again in evidence, but the author's departure from the original myth is all the greater here because the Grail reverts to being a pagan object: it ceases to be a sacred chalice and becomes the cup of Venus containing a regenerating liquid. The lesson, repeated in a different way by Italo Calvino in *Il cavaliere inesistente*, is this: the story of the Parsifal myth has ceased to be one of gradually increasing asceticism leading towards a sacred end (whatever that may be); nor is it like Tristan a 'beautiful story of love and death' – it is a story of love and *life*. The message of the myth in this case has been almost totally reversed.

However, it may not yet have finished revealing its secrets. We now have a Swiss writer, Jean Matter, at work. After undertaking to go back to the sources of the myth he presents the apprenticeship years of a Parsifal in the 'pays romand' – French-speaking Switzerland. This bold attempt sets out to show us the mythical hero in the guise of a young man of our own day for the first time. The novel is still incomplete, but we can already recognize the familiar tests or experiences (the mother's death, the torments of the sin of the flesh, the temptation of religion). It remains to be seen how it will prove possible to bring the story to a conclusion without resorting to the miraculous: can we imagine Parsifal without the Grail?

Pierre-François Kaempf

Phaedra

Phaedra was the daughter of Minos, ruler of Hades, and his wife Pasiphae, who later gave birth to the Minotaur as a result of her passion for the bull sent by Poseidon. On her mother's side, Phaedra was a descendant of the Sun and, according to Diodorus Siculus (IV.62), was given in marriage to Theseus, the Athenian hero, by Deucalion. In Troezen or Athens, where Theseus is said to have come to celebrate the mysteries, Phaedra met and fell in love with Hippolytus, the son of Theseus and an Amazon who, according to the different versions of the story, was called either Melanippe, Antiope or Hippolyte. The story of Phaedra properly speaking began with this passion, which she at first concealed and then confessed, either to her nurse or to Hippolytus himself during one of Theseus' absences. His return led to Phaedra's accusation against her stepson, her own suicide and the death of Hippolytus (whom his father had unwisely cursed) in combat with a sea monster sent by Poseidon. The basic scenario of the myth of Phaedra has been the subject of a succession of different treatments from Antiquity to the present day. The different versions of the myth or, more precisely, the variations on the theme, illustrate not only the relative rigidity of the narrative structure but also an ability to represent a wide range of different periods, points of view and outlooks through the use of slight variations, transpositions and allegorical interpretations. This has been made possible by all the latent and ambiguous elements contained within the original story, particularly in terms of the motivation of the characters and the explanation of events. Thus, Diodorus attributes the death of Hippolytus to causes which are psychological rather than supernatural, and Hippolytus, in an attempt to use his own story to console Egeria, who is mourning the death of Numa, cannot decide whether Phaedra accused him through fear that he would betray her secret or because she had been hurt by his refusal: 'Indiciine metus magis offensane repulsae' (Ovid, *Metamorphoses* XV).

From the outset, this version of the myth of Phaedra presents a number of original characteristics. On the one hand, it appears to follow the Greek, or more precisely the Attic, version of a universal mythical structure which has continued to exist in both folkloric tradition and literature. The story of the seductress, whether incestuous or not, who subsequently accuses the object of her desire, is found in India, China and Egypt (Anpu and Bata), and provides the framework for other legends in the western tradition: Joseph and Potiphar's wife (Genesis 39), Peleus and Hippolyte (Pindar), Stheneboea and Bellerophon (Homer, Euripides and Quinault). Furthermore, the myth of

Phaedra is the result of the coincidence of two legendary traditions, i.e. the son of the Amazon, which is chronologically earlier, and the daughter of Minos. Finally, the literary sources are basic and fundamental to the mythographical and archeological sources. From these obscure origins emerged Euripides' tragedy, which was probably the culmination of a development that has eluded us, as well as providing the *point de départ* for the myth of Phaedra as we know it.

OBSCURE ORIGINS

Although there is undoubtedly 'a sacred story, an event which took place in the legendary age of the beginning of time' (Mircea Eliade), its elements are too widely dispersed, diverse and delayed – for example, the reference in the *Odyssey* is a later addition – to speak of an early structure of the myth and its meaning.

However, disregarding any form of exact chronology, it is possible to observe a coincidence of locations and rituals, of local traditions and narrative elements, without there being any clear indication of the causal relationship which connects them. In other words, was the story a legitimization of ancient practices, or did the cult revive and reintroduce legends which already existed? For example, according to Pausanias (second century AD), there was still evidence in Troezen of the cult of Hippolytus, to whom young brides made an offering of their hair. Similarly, the site of the shrine of Aphrodite was associated with the place from which Phaedra watched her stepson's feats of horsemanship:

> Or let my eye piercing the glorious dust,
> Follow the wheeling chariot in the course!
>
> (Racine, *Phèdre*, I.3, which echoes Euripides, 228–31)

It was probably during the sixth century BC that the worship of Hippolytus moved from Troezen to Athens, where there was a myrtle whose leaves were said to have been torn to shreds with a hair-pin by Phaedra in her passion, and, according to Diodorus Siculus, it was Phaedra who had the temple of Aphrodite erected on the Acropolis. However, she tends to remain very much a secondary figure.

What does seem clearer is the aetiological function of the myth in terms of the names of the main characters. The etymology of these names provides a sort of generative core for the dramatic presentation of the myth, while its overtones echo within the metaphorical framework of Racine's play. 'Hippolytus', who has inherited the heroic stature of Theseus, the slayer of monsters, both frees and subdues horses, which are ultimately the cause of his death. This death inspired, from Euripides to Racine, among others, the great final narrative of Theramenes, Hippolytus' tutor. Phaedra (the name means 'brightness'), is a creature of light who is gradually inhabited by darkness. According to a legend from the region of Lokris (one of Hesiod's fragments), Theseus had a lover, Aegle, whose name is also associated with daylight.

This fragile network of significations illustrates the importance of the mediatory role of literature.

PHAEDRA IN TRAGEDY

Although the Greek tragedians were responsible for establishing Phaedra in the fields of literature and art, according to Jean Pommier 'their plays are in fact further from the original myth than the modern versions of Euripides' play'. In the case of Sophocles' *Phaedra* and Euripides' *Hippolytus Veiled* there are too few surviving fragments and references to give an accurate idea of the myth they were portraying. The figure of the impassioned lover probably appeared in the first version by Euripides and may have been in Seneca's mind when he wrote his own version of *Phaedra*. She is replaced in *Hippolytus Crowned* (428 BC) by a very different figure, who has very definite moral preoccupations, although, as the title suggests, she is not really the main character. The two human protagonists in the tragedy are used as the arena and the instruments in a conflict between Artemis, goddess of chastity, and Aphrodite, goddess of erotic love. In fact, the story of the myth has become the pretext for internal debate, and two essential characters appear and become fixed in their role, in terms both of the dramatic development and of the outcome of the tragedy. The nurse or confidante and the messenger or tutor were later represented by the Racinian characters Oenone and Theramenes. According to Paul Bénichou, subsequent versions were 'more constrained' because the myth of Phaedra is based on events which are difficult to avoid and are weighted down with a whole series of images and meanings. The mythical and transcendental environment created by the presence of two divinities, the aggression shown by Hippolytus towards Aphrodite (in the absence of *hubris*), and Phaedra's internal struggle, represent the essence of tragedy, the confrontation of the individual with him/herself and with the gods. Phaedra is seen as a wretched and unhappy figure (Plutarch, *Theseus*, 28) and Bénichou comments: 'If the story of the Temptress turned accuser represents the development of a youthful destiny, it is possible to say that the Hippolytus-Phaedra version depicts the failure of this destiny. It is this that makes it tragic rather than heroic.' Although the original myth incorporated social and marital codes expressed via incestuous desire and the rejection of temptation, from this point onwards the emphasis was placed on the moral responsibility of the individual and the way in which this was related to a form of transcendence. This was the point at which the myth of Phaedra was introduced into western culture. Artemis tells the dying Hippolytus that Phaedra's love for him will not be forgotten, and this was echoed by Ovid (*Fastes*, 745): 'Notus amor Phaedrae, nota est injuria Thesei' (i.e. Phaedra's passion and the wrong done to Theseus are well-known).

But this anxious debate on human freedom is expressed through a consideration of the use of language and words. At a time when discourse was dominating urban life, was the primary concern of philosophers and was encountering the first wave of sophistry, Euripides introduced an element of scepticism into the moral dilemma. He used language to conceal and betray internal truths, to reinforce the appearances of which Theseus is the unwitting victim, and to provoke death by revealing what should have been left unspoken. Seneca's tirades, like Racine's famous line, 'It is you who uttered the name', retained something of this idea, which focuses the tragedy around two central points of the dialogue, namely confession and imprecation. In the break caused by speech, tragedy reveals its relationship to time; because it is impossible to recapture speech and because, in passing from silence to speech, the point of no return has been reached, and history has been created. The characters therefore appear to be defined in terms of their relationship with language. For the nurse this is represented by the drama of finding release through speech; for Phaedra it is the fear of what may force her to be judged by others; for Hippolytus, aware of the stigmas and pitfalls contained in language, it is the vow of silence; while for Theseus it is the progression from revelation to atonement. In the end, however, the funeral oration and deification, and the solemnity and ceremony of the demonstrative style used by the messenger of Artemis, rehabilitate the hero and restore the disrupted order of language.

Encompassing confession, accusation, malediction, the episode involving the monster, the conflict between passion and chastity, desire and loyalty, the concept of heroic heredity and succession to the throne, and the antitheses of transgression and sin and of innocence and purity – all of which are expressed on theatrical, religious, moral, social and political levels – the myth of Phaedra reached the height of its career during the fifth century BC. As the archetype of the tormental soul, Phaedra inspired the tradition which began with Ovid's *Heroides* (first century AD). The author imagined a letter from Phaedra to Hippolytus in which the rhetoric used in the delineation of character and the *suasoria* (persuasive discourse) were successively developed in the form of a psychological analysis, a narrative, an appeal and a speech of justification, until the Belgian Jesuit, Hosschius, composed Hippolytus' reply to Phaedra, in Latin, at the beginning of the seventeenth century. Because of the great popularity enjoyed by the *Heroides* during the Renaissance and the neo-classical era, Racine's heroine was able to recall the vows, passion and hopes expressed in this reply.

INCIDENCE AND VARIATIONS

Although writers on mythology in the intervening period demonstrated that Euripides' version of the myth had in no way modified the traditional theme, the fact remains that his *Hippolytus* had become a major source of reference and that, rather than being misrepresented or completely rewritten, the myth was reworked in terms of changes of emphasis, modification of details and the relocation of events within a different context, which has tended to alter its meaning and impact. However, one feature that appears to dominate the many versions is that the character of Hippolytus becomes less prominent and is sometimes even weakened in favour of Phaedra. This is possibly due to the influence of Seneca, whose version provided the inspiration for Robert Garnier in 1585 and was paraphrased in 1591 by Jean Yeuvain, a Belgian from Mons. The title is often misleading. In 1640, Tristan l'Hermite dedicated an elegy to 'La Mort d'Hippolyte'. The Angevin, Pierre Guérin de la Pinelière, and Mathieu Bidar, a poet from Lille, both wrote versions of *Hippolyte*, in 1635 and 1675 respectively. But although he was represented as an admirer and lover, the chaste disciple of Artemis had lost some of his autonomy and rigour, and the myth generally speaking tailed off with *Phèdre et Hippolyte* (1677) by Nicolas Pradon, a contemporary and rival of Racine.

Independently of the various interpretations of Racine's *Phèdre*, which were sometimes so divergent that they constituted a new 'process of metamorphosis' (Francis) and ultimately acquired the status of reinterpretations of the myth, and independently also of the musical works by Rosingrave, Gluck and Lemoine, the music for Racine's *Phèdre* by Massenet and for d'Annunzio's *Fedra* by Honnegger and Pizzetti, four successive or concurrent phenomena have affected the myth. These are changes in emphasis, superimposition, actualization and thematization.

In spite of the relatively rigid narrative structure of the myth, the main events of which are established in advance and therefore constant, changes in emphasis occur, either in terms of the actual dramatic development or of the relationships between the characters, with more far-reaching effects on the organization and the actual meaning of the myth. For example, Seneca develops the conversation between Phaedra and Hippolytus, using the stage effect of the unsheathed sword, which will later be produced as evidence. He also replaces the accusation, made by the nurse or in a letter from Phaedra, with the accusation made by Phaedra in an encounter with Theseus, while Racine replaces it with Phaedra's silent evasion of Theseus' presence. The most significant modification is undoubtedly the one introduced by Gilbert in *Hippolyte ou le garçon insensible* (1646), in which Hippolytus is in love with Phaedra who is simply Theseus' fiancée. The story moves from a tragic to an elegiac register, possibly inspired by the love of Stratonice, Seleucus and Antiochus which had provided the background for five plays between 1642 and 1666. The Italian versions of Phaedra should be mentioned in connection with these changes of emphasis and variations on the theme. They range from Giuseppe Baroncini's *Tragoedia* (1552) to Paolo Bissaro's *Fedra incoronata* (1664), an opera written for the Bavarian court, via Zara's *Hippolito* (1558), Trapolini's *Thesida* (1576), Bozza's *Fedra* (1578), Giacobilli's *Hippolito* (1601), Santa Maria's *Hippolito* (1619) and Tesauro's *Hippolito* (1661), which is echoed by Racine in the confession scene and in Theramenes' story. The popularity of the subject, which held a strong fascination for the neo-classical consciousness, was a glorious phase in the myth's history which came to an end with Racine's play. After this, the myth made only spasmodic appearances: in England, Edmund Smith presented *Phaedra and Hippolytus* (1720) with a preface by Addison, while in 1866 Charles Swinburne composed a dramatic poem directly inspired by Seneca. In his *Fedra* (1909), based on an outline inspired by both Seneca and Racine, d'Annunzio expresses the triumph of passion over law and the sensual pleasure of despair, with Wagnerian overtones which are reminiscent of the death of Isolde. Miguel de Unamuno, Professor of Greek at Salamanca (*Fedra*, 1921), presents the opposition of reason and life which had inspired his book, *Del sentimiento trágico de la vida* (1912).

The ability to incorporate very different points of view and philosophies, which in turn represent specific outlooks and periods, into the relationships between its main characters, and its capacity for assuming new shades of meaning, through the use of suggestion, parallels and adaptations, makes the story of Phaedra a true myth. Seneca had already achieved this effect of 'superimposition' in his version of *Phaedra* (first century AD) by attributing to his characters such speeches as that praising the solitary life. He staged a confrontation between the Epicurean and Stoic philosophies and presented a moral analysis of a distraught conscience whose emotional development was marked by the scenes of confession. Robert Garnier followed his example, increased the number of moralizing speeches and phrases and echoed the accents of Virgil's Dido in Phaedra's passion. Without betraying his classical source, Racine succeeded in maintaining his character in an ambiguity which constitutes its very richness and, by means of discreet references, inspired new interpretations. As a 'tragedy of weakness and a drama of freedom' (Picard), *Phèdre* poses the problem of responsibility: 'but the evil which I would not do, that I do' (Saint Paul, Romans, 7: 15). 'Where can I hide?' (IV, 6): the similarity to the Old Testament text has made it possible to interpret Phèdre's tirade in terms of 'the anguish of damnation' (Pons). And from the phrase attributed to the great Arnauld ('a Christian without grace') to Chateaubriand ('the storms of a completely Christian conscience' in *Génie du christianisme*) and Claudel ('this innocent victim, a prey to ancient destinies'), the Christian interpretations are not simply an arbitrary extension of an interwoven biblical theme. They have a firm basis in Racine's culture and the polyvalency of his text. From the time that Philostratus represented the death of Hippolytus in one of his *Imagines*, iconographers were fascinated by the theme of the combat with the monster and made much of the analogy with Saint George's slaying of the dragon. In this way, the metaphor of the monster which runs throughout the Racinian text became more explicitly a metaphor of sin.

This is one of the possible processes of 'actualization'. In spite of the character clearly defined by Euripides, the figure of Phaedra reveals its mythical nature through this flexibility and adaptability to historical interpretations.

In this way, while keeping as close as possible to Seneca's version, even while paraphrasing the latter's apology of the solitary life, Robert Garnier is able to express the dream of a refuge against the misfortunes of time, in a play resonant with a gravity inspired by Christianity. Once again this raises the question, which has never really been resolved, of the Jansenist content of Racine's *Phèdre.* This does not mean that in 1678 the poet was transformed into a theologian, but rather that the moral preoccupations and the relentless lucidity of the character made it possible to produce a Jansenist or Augustinian interpretation of the play.

But although the mythological context may disappear and the names of the characters change, leaving only the framework of relationships and a myth which tends to degenerate into a simple 'literary theme', this does not preclude the possibility of there being other outstanding and valuable versions. In Barbey d'Aurevilly's *L'Ensorcelée* (1852), the analogy is explicitly suggested by references to Phaedra and by the use of quotations. In this story of a young woman who is passionately in love with an inaccessible individual, the Abbé de La Croix-Jugan is an avatar of Hippolytus, just as Jeanne de Feuardent is identified with Phaedra, and the novel makes skilful use of classical images. In Eugene O'Neill's *Desire under the Elms* (1923), a family tragedy set in New England, the return of Ephraim is highly reminiscent of that of Theseus. The myth of Phaedra has become no more than the distant allegory for an archetypal social or family situation. An excessive displacement has caused it to be weakened and lose its 'symbolic significance' (Cassirer). The character of Phaedra was undoubtedly too closely linked to a historical and geographical context, as well as to a group of characters, to be totally flexible in terms of the imaginative ideas inspired by a figure such as Proteus.

In the case of Phaedra, literature is not, at least according to the documentation at our disposal, 'the last murmurings of the dying structure' (Lévi-Strauss). On the contrary, it represents the stage during which the myth became truly structured, when a tale whose symbolic potential could only be developed within relatively restricted limits, was grafted onto 'a series of representations deeply rooted in the human consciousness' (Bénichou). Perhaps this combination of richness and constraint explains why the myth of Phaedra reached the height of its career during the neo-classical age.

Bernard Beugnot

Phoenix

The myth of the phoenix is hard to pin down. This mythological bird has either lent its powers to other animals in a real or fantastical bestiary (e.g. swan, eagle, salamander, griffin) or received some of its attributes from them. At the time when it featured in many texts and in an abundant iconography (between the first and seventh centuries AD), many religious and philosophical currents combined in its formation. In the Hellenistic period, and particularly during the Roman domination, Egyptian traditions concerning the *benou* and the Greco-Latin myth mingled in the intellectual circles of Alexandria, and Indian, Arab and Judaic myths may well have had an influence. This same milieu was later to see the christianization of the phoenix.

THE MEANING OF THE NAME

Apart from the magical bird, the Greek word *phoinix* also refers to three real elements, which were to become integrated into its story and iconography: the palm tree, the colour red and Phoenicia. Each of these elements was in turn interpreted by authors as the source of the others. For Pliny the Elder, the tree gave its name to the bird. Lactantius in his *Carmen de ave phoenice* (fourth century AD) thought that the word *phoinix* applied both to the bird's country of origin and the palm, its favourite tree. Ovid and Martial considered that the phoenix owed its name to Phoenicia, while for Isidore of Seville, the seventh-century Spanish bishop, it was named after the Greek word for the colour purple, *phoinos*.

Nineteenth-century egyptologists thought that etymology could form the basis for a thesis according to which the Greek phoenix was descended from the Egyptian bird, the *benou*, whose root 'ben' was said to have been pronounced as 'oin' and to have had the same origin as the Greek word. This thesis was later abandoned. In a recently decoded text in Linear B (*c.* 1200 BC), one finds the word *ponike*, doubtless of Phoenician origin, which is thought to refer to a griffin, the solar bird revered in Mycenaean civilization.

STAGES OF THE MYTH'S FORMATION BEFORE THE CHRISTIAN ERA

Between the eighth and first centuries BC, seven Greek and Latin writers spoke of the phoenix. The earliest, Hesiod (fragment 304), in a riddle which successively reveals the numbers 9, 4, 3, 9 and 10, makes the phoenix an animal of wondrous longevity, the link in the chain between real animals (crow, stag) and the nymphs, who are divine. The poet's numerical riddle could refer to a conception of the Great Year found in the work of the Babylonians. At the time of Hesiod the phoenix may have been linked to cyclical time and an idea of the eternal recurrence of the Golden Age.

In the sixth century BC Herodotus in his *Histories* (II.73) certainly located the Greek phoenix in Egypt. He tells the magical story of the patropherous bird: when its father dies, the young bird leaves Arabia, its country of origin, to carry his body, enclosed in an egg of myrrh, to the sanctuary at Heliopolis.

Aenesidemus, a sceptic of the first century BC, was the first to mention the phoenix alongside an animal of fire, the salamander, and to note its magical reproduction without sexual relations. Manilius, cited by Pliny, gives the bird's story its most miraculous developments: it lives for 540 years in Arabia (the number may reflect a periodicity dating back to Hesiod) and dies on a bed of spices. A worm is born from its remains and forms a new phoenix, which carries the remains of the old phoenix to the city of the sun in Panchaïa.

Each of these authors may have known other elaborations of the myth which the context does not require them to mention. But no document dating from before the birth of Christ indicates what was to become the myth's most popular aspect: the cremation of the phoenix. It has moreover been noted that Greek mythology did not often give a happy outcome to ordeals by fire.

The Greco-Latin tradition ties in with the Egyptian legend of the *benou*. The *benou* was a real bird whose body was inhabited by the sun god, Aten Ra (whom the texts say created himself). During his journey through the subterranean world between his setting and rising, the sun left the bird's body, which was the subject of embalming rites using aromatic herbs and spices. According to the Egyptians, the *benou* came out of the primordial hill from which the waters sprang. The Nile's flooding recalled this event and the *benou* was linked to the return of the floods.

THE FLOURISHING OF THE MYTH BETWEEN THE FIRST AND SEVENTH CENTURIES AD

Influenced perhaps by rites used in ceremonies for the funerals and apotheoses of the Roman emperors, the phoenix became associated with fire. The pyre of its death became the place of its resurrection. Between the first and seventh centuries AD, dozens of texts expressing different ideologies reproduced the myth. But although it was used to support different beliefs, its constitutive elements appear remarkably stable. Imagery won out over ideology.

Underlying ideologies and beliefs

Rome and the emperors made their mark on the story of the phoenix. In his *Epigrams* (V.7), Martial saw the phoenix as the glorification of the Roman

Empire of the first century and its potential for renewal. Neo-stoicism underlay the fourth-century poem by Claudian devoted to the phoenix, in which he celebrated a 'bird like the gods', which 'equals the stars'. In the second century Epicureanism was the inspiration for Celsus, who, in his praise of the patropherous bird's piety, seeks to demonstrate the excellence of animal nature and to dethrone humankind from its pretension to universal dominion over nature. At the same period Origen, in *Contra Celsum*, states that 'Nature has created a unique animal in order that it should generate admiration, not for the animal but for the one that created it'. This was because in the second century, with the first version of the *Physiologus*, the phoenix myth was often interpreted in a Christian light.

The elements of the myth

The texts that bring the literary myth of the phoenix to life often belong to the apocalyptic domain, to the literary genre of the sermon or to poetry. This myth is better suited to contemplation than to narrative: the story of the phoenix is quickly told.

The aromatic spices, which were mentioned in the pre-Christian era only by Herodotus and Manilius, later became an integral part of the myth. Ovid's narrative in the *Metamorphoses* (XV.391, 407), and those of Lactantius, Claudian or Sidonius Apollinaris (in book XXII of the *Carmina*, fifth century) all give great importance to these spices, and this is explained by the Biblical texts praising the perfumes of Lebanon and the memory of the Egyptian embalming rites. Cinnamon is often presented as the active agent of cremation.

The texts give two different versions of the phoenix's journey. Either they tell of the young phoenix that carries its father's remains to Egypt when the new age has already begun (Claudian), or else it is the old phoenix who, sensing that its death is near, leaves its country of origin (here the new age is about to begin). In its first edition, the Greek *Physiologus* tells of a journey in two stages: the bird first stops in Lebanon, where it fills its wings with spices, then it continues to Heliopolis. The motif of the journey is often complemented by that of an escort of birds accompanying their king, the phoenix.

The phoenix usually eats ethereal food: the rays of the sun, according to Claudian; manna and dew in pseudo-Baruch (second century), following a Jewish tradition, which gave the phoenix eschatological food that allowed it an early taste of the glory of the end of time. The place where the phoenix lived is described in terms recreating those of the Golden Age of the Latin poets or the Judeo-Christian paradise. The bird's favourite tree is the palm.

The phoenix reproduces without any form of sexual union, as there is only ever one living phoenix. The texts are uncertain on this point, sometimes speaking of asexuality and sometimes of bisexuality, presenting the bird as male or more rarely as female. The authors affected by Christian mysticism

(Lactantius, Zeno of Verona) make it a virgin creature whose earthly existence manifests the asexual afterlife promised by the Gospels.

The essential mytheme is that of the periodic death and rebirth of the phoenix. The texts offer two versions of the resurrection: either the bird is reborn from the decomposed remains of its predecessor (Tacitus, Clement of Rome), or from the latter's ashes. Claudian depicts the phoenix begging the sun to set it alight. Lactantius and other authors combine the two versions with a worm acting as a link in the chain between the ashes and the new phoenix. In texts inspired by Christianity, the process which leads to the resurrection lasts for three days so that the story of Christ can be read into it.

Rare elements bear witness to the survival of the original mythological traditions. Horapollo, an Egyptian writing in Greek in the fourth century, presents the phoenix's death as suicide: when the bird grows old it hurls itself against the ground and a young phoenix is born out of the blood from its wound. This is the only text that shows us the old phoenix coexisting with the young one; they then travel together to Heliopolis. The apocalypse of pseudo-Baruch presents a phoenix that does not die. It is an enormous bird, as big as nine mountains, which accompanies the sun on its course. Its mission is to spread its wings to protect creatures living on earth from the sun's rays. The eastern myth of a cosmogonic bird, which may have been a cock, doubtless left its traces in this text.

An original feature of the myth can be discerned in these different elements. There is neither crime nor punishment in the story of the phoenix. Nor are there any tests, unless we count the glorious death that leads to resurrection. All the elements combine to give the phoenix positive qualities: its uniqueness, beauty and special connection with the sun that is the source of life. It is easy to understand why it was so successful in literature, with few periods of eclipse.

FROM THE EARLY MIDDLE AGES TO THE BAROQUE PERIOD

The destiny of the phoenix as a literary myth has been a fortunate one. Up until the seventeenth century there were many who believed that the bird really existed. Proof of this is given in a work by René François that was published in Rouen in 1626, called *Essay des merveilles de nature et des plus nobles artifices*. No doubt this belief was held to differing degrees. Many authors link the fate of the phoenix to that of the silk worm. This is true of Montaigne who, in the chapter of his *Essays* called 'An Apology for Raymond Sebond', describes the two animals as obeying perfectly natural laws of metamorphosis. Montaigne demythifies the phoenix: it is a different bird and not the same one that is reborn. But Fabre, a late sixteenth-century alchemist, regards the silk worm and the phoenix as embodying a similar marvel: the new creature is both the same and different. In any case, the survival of a belief in the phoenix's reality encourages us to survey as a whole a very long period of literature lasting from the Early Middle Ages to the Baroque age. During this time, three kinds of texts assured the survival of the phoenix myth: allegorical works, hermetic and particularly alchemical texts, and the literature of love.

Allegorical texts

The best represented of these are texts reproducing a Christian allegory. A Saxon poem called *The Phoenix* (eighth century), certainly written by a disciple of Cynewulf, is a fine example. The first part is a paraphrase of Lactantius' text, stressing even more than did the Latin poet the theme of the *locus felix*. The second part gives the true meaning of Lactantius' poem: the resurrection of Christ and also of the believers who kept the faith. Each just soul is a phoenix. The misfortunes of sinning human beings who were forced to leave paradise after the fall are like the trial by fire that the phoenix has to undergo. God is the tree in which believers live. Praiseworthy deeds are the aromatic nest of the righteous.

In France the oldest text on the symbolism of the phoenix is that of Philippe de Thaon's *Bestiaire* (twelfth century). This author launches a descriptive tradition that interprets each aspect of the bird allegorically: its two wings represent the Old and New Testaments. Typological commentaries were also applied to the texts of pagan poets, as we see in the fourteenth century with *Ovide moralisé*. The author of this is as interested in Mary as he is in Christ, whom he calls 'the true phoenix'. Mary is the palm-tree on which the phoenix Christ builds his nest. But she is also the aromatic nest, 'the soft nest full of spices/full of sweetness, full of delight/ . . . where the true phoenix lies down'. The Christian allegory of the phoenix is also to be found in *La Sepmaine ou création du monde* (1578) by Du Bartas. Following the order of the Genesis story, Du Bartas recounts the creation of the birds on the fifth day. He takes up the ancient tradition according to which the phoenix is king of the birds. God first shapes this king, who is 'followed by an infinity of wings'. Above all, God creates the phoenix in his own image, this being rendered by the contrast between 'the heavenly phoenix' and 'the earthly phoenix'. The poet implicitly connects the bird's mythical bisexuality to that of the primitive Adam, which itself reflects divine bisexuality (in 1585 Jean-Edouard Du Monin, in his poem *Le Phénix*, explicitly recalls that the original Adam was both man and woman). For Du Bartas the creation of the phoenix anticipated the creation of human beings. His narrative ends with an exhortation: all must die 'in Adam/to be reborn in Christ'.

The philosophical, often neo-Platonic allegory is also to be found in sixteenth-century texts, for example in the Italian Giordano Bruno's *Heroic Frenzies* (1585). This author comments on an emblem representing a phoenix on a pyre from which thick smoke is rising. The latter hinders communication between the animal and the sun. This is the fate of the mind that is enflamed by the divine splendour of the sun but which can find only words that obscure the beloved star. This interpretation of the myth is less euphoric than the ones usually encountered.

Hermetic texts and alchemy

Few medieval alchemical treatises draw on the phoenix myth, which is on the other hand very active in the work of the authors of sixteenth- and seventeenth-century treatises: the German Michael Maier, Fabre and pseudo-Flamel. Developing as a fire myth in the Christian era, the phoenix answers the alchemists' search: they needed myths that expressed the reunification of opposites. In this myth such a reunification is suggested in three ways. The bisexuality of the magical bird reconciles masculine and feminine, sulphur and mercury. The synthesis of heaven and earth is also represented by the myth when the sun sets fire to the aromatic nest. Lastly, the bird can be seen as carrying out the reunion of body and spirit: it is incarnated through its nature as an animal, while its wings give it the properties of the spirit. Furthermore, the alchemists saw two ways to reach the Great Work: the way of humidity and the way of dryness. The two versions of the death of the phoenix provided them with potential illustrations, with decomposition representing humidity and cremation dryness. A text from the *Livre des figures hiéroglyphiques* (1612) by pseudo-Flamel uses the first version of myth of the death of the phoenix to describe the way of humidity. In his eyes the union of sulphur and mercury causes the putrefaction that must precede any generation. These elements are symbolized by the phoenix. At about the same time, the anonymous author of the *Psautier d'Hermophile* describes the way of dryness in a story that reworks the second version of the phoenix's death: 'The phoenix that is reborn from its own ashes is the salt of the Sages, and by this means their Mercury . . . it is the dry water, the ignited water and the universal Menses, or the spirit of the Universe'.

In *Die Chymische Hochzeit Christiani Rosenkreutz*, a work written in the early seventeenth century, Andreae describes a scene of funereal rites for kings which involves the phoenix and evokes the initiation of the Rosicrucians.

The eroticization of the phoenix

Love poems and romances gave the phoenix new life. This is a paradoxical rebirth for the myth if we recall the words of Lactantius, for whom death was the phoenix' only love. For a long time the mythical bird appeared as a stranger to sexuality, and for this reason it became emblematic of Christ. However, its beauty, as vaunted by a great number of texts and visual representations, encouraged its eroticization. In the Franco-Italian version of the *Jugement d'amour* (twelfth century), two sisters, Florence and Blancheflor, go to the court of the god of Love. The god's castle is surrounded by a paradisaical garden and guarded by a phoenix which asks a riddle. The sisters have to discover the bird's nature, a test in which only Blancheflor succeeds. The god receives the two sisters and offers them a dinner made of three roses and dew. The phoenix-sphinx, which we encounter once more in the *Fabiel du dieu d'amour* (preserved in a manuscript of 1285), makes passion into a sacred initiation. This sacred character does not appear in the *Bestiaire d'amour rimé* (fourteenth century), where the author in love is the phoenix, the lady is the nest full of spices, and the look of love corresponds to the beak which strikes fire from the stones. The name of the phoenix gives rise to the adventures which Chrétien de Troyes give his heroine Phénice in *Cligès* (second half of the twelfth century). A witch servant puts her to sleep with a magic potion, so that she seems to be dead and thus escapes the emperor's advances. Three doctors suspect that she is alive and subject her to burns. Finally the servant revives her in a romantic equivalent of the cremation and resurrection of the phoenix.

The Italian poet Petrarch's sonnets (fourteenth century) turn the woman he loves into a phoenix: the poet's heart is consumed by flames. Sonnet 321 speaks in elegaic tones of the flight of the phoenix-woman, who leaves the poet desolate before the deserted nest. The lover's recurring pain is signified by the constantly revived phoenix in poem 48 of Maurice Scève's *Délie* (1544). In contrast to these elegaic versions is the use made of the myth in French Baroque poetry. These poets use it as the happy counterpoint to myths of crime and punishment (e.g. Actaeon, Ixion). The phoenix brings an energy to this poetry which is not usually its fundamental feature. It is the myth of virile desire that is reborn after a period of detumescence: 'You are the Sun who gives me birth,/And I am the Phoenix who burns with love' wrote Desportes (1573), justifying in advance Freud's later commentaries on the myth in 'The Acquisition and Control of Fire' (1932).

In love poetry the phoenix is usually either the masculine or feminine partner. The elegy attributed to Shakespeare called 'The Phoenix and the Turtle' (1601) seems rather to have assimilated the phoenix to the couple in its indissoluble unity. The poem, which celebrates the funeral of two people mysteriously represented by the phoenix (treated as feminine) and the turtle, makes the beauty of their union everlasting. The pyre's flames erase the difference between man and woman, both of whom see themselves in the flame with the eye of the other. Like the phoenix, the couple have achieved the reunion of the same with the other. The fact that this text has been given an esoteric reading does not prevent us from seeing it firstly as a celebration of love.

FROM THE LATER SEVENTEENTH CENTURY TO THE PRESENT DAY

With the second half of the seventeenth century, the phoenix becomes a true literary myth. It is said that from Christian alchemy there arose a free-thinking alchemy. It may have been to this movement that Cyrano de Bergerac allied himself in his unfinished work *Les Etats et empires du soleil* (published posthumously in 1661). In it the myth gives life to a new literary genre, the philosophical tale, which tells of a utopian journey. In the middle of the account, when the narrator Dyrcano reaches the Empire of the Sun, he meets a phoenix who gives him a message in which we see the fundamental elements of the myth; periodic resurrection, reproduction without sexual relations, and the bird's uniqueness – at least in each world taken separately. This central element in the work illuminates and condenses the fundamental aspects of both the story and Cyrano's philosophy. In terms of the story, the airship coloured purple and gold is exposed to the sun, whose energy it absorbs, making it weightless. In terms of the philosophy, like Campanella whose tale guides Dyrcano, Cyrano believes that there is a burning soul within human beings that is in communication with the sun, the great soul of the world. The fiction of the journey simply makes his thinking concrete: after death the soul returns to its source, the sun, but during life the power of the imagination already makes for communication between the sparks contained in the individual and the world's soul.

While, like many myths, the phoenix was eclipsed in the positivist eighteenth century, the nineteenth century saw its rebirth. Erudite works prepared the ground for this new life. The nineteenth-century *Larousse* assimilates the phoenix to the bird of paradise. Apollinaire later owes to it his 'bird that makes its nest in the air' ('Cortège', *Alcools*, 1913). Creuzer and Guigniaut's work *Religions de l'antiquité* (1825–54) links the myth of the phoenix rising from the ashes to that of Heracles freeing himself of his mortality on the pyre to be reborn as a god. Henri de Régnier elaborates this comparison, which also set Apollinaire's imagination going. Many poems from the second half of the nineteenth century contain an implicit reverie about the phoenix. The first version of one of Mallarmé's sonnets, 'Ses purs ongles très haut dédiant leur onyx', was written in 1868 with the title 'Sonnet allegorique de lui-même'. The poet's imagination was moving in the direction of a certain autism which can be suggested by the phoenix myth. The solitary bird regenerates itself 'by itself', *per se*, as was constantly reiterated by the Latin texts and later by medieval authors. But Mallarmé for his part seems to have imagined combustion without resurrection: 'Maint rêve vespéral brûlé par le Phénix/Que ne recueille pas de cinéraire amphore' ('Many evening dreams burned by the Phoenix/Which are not gathered by any cinerary vase').

Mallarmé's myth of a poetic creation that is allegorical of itself gives way in the work of Henri de Régnier, in 'Cendres' and the sonnet that precedes it (*Episodes*, 1888), to a vision of cosmic renewal inspired explicitly by the story of Heracles on his pyre and implicitly by that of the phoenix.

In the twentieth century many poets have brought the phoenix myth back to life, giving it either an erotic meaning (Eluard, *Le Phénix*, 1951), or a mystical sense (Piere Emmanuel, *Sophia*, 1973). But the richest example is that of the poetic work of Apollinaire in the first half of the century. For him, and in a fairly traditional way, the phoenix primarily signifies love which is always reborn. This is expressed in the lines placed as an epigraph to the 'Chanson du mal aimé'. But the phoenix, which is confused with the peacock and the Great Pan, is also as big as the universe: 'Le ciel faisait la roue comme un phénix qui flambe/Paon lunaire rouant' ('The sky was rolling like a burning phoenix/A wheeling lunar peacock') (*Poèmes à Lou*, published posthumously, 1947). It could be psuedo-Baruch's cosmic bird that animates this line from 'Brasier': 'Et des oiseaux protègent de leurs ailes ma face et le soleil' ('And birds protect my face and the sun with their wings') (*Alcools*). But more profoundly, Apollinaire, who by his name makes himself a son of the sun, wanted to turn this myth into the divine privilege of poets to give birth to themselves through their own writing. Celebrating 'the phoenix, that pyre that engenders itself', he casts his biographical past, that of a son without a father, into the flames, to be reborn as a father to himself. We often move in his poems from a tragic fire (the image of burning hands is frequent) to a fire of apotheosis.

But the phoenix myth also fitted into an order that Apollinaire chose for the poems in *Alcools*. This has been shown by a critical study significantly called *Les Trajets du phénix*. Its author, Philippe Renaud, considers the poems that naturally belong together, such as 'Zone' and 'Vendémiaire' (the first and last poems of *Alcools*), or the 'Rhénanes', or the group of texts which includes the 'Rhénanes', from 'Brasier' to 'Fiançailles'. In each of these groups he sees a dark centre, a core of shadow formed, for example, by the end of 'Zone' and the beginning of 'Vendémiaire', or by 'La Loreley' for the 'Rhénanes'. This core contrasts with two sorts of burning at each end: the triumphant fire of the last lines of 'Fiançailles' regenerates that which had been thrown on the fire of the first lines of 'Brasier', 'Ce passé de têtes de morts' ('This past of death's heads').

In recent years the phoenix myth has sometimes been used to express a feminine or indeed feminist reverie. The woman thinks of herself as an Amazon: the modern derivative of the bird that is its own father is a woman who is her own mother, both of herself and by herself. The relation of mother and child is shown in the following passage taken from *Neutre* (1972) by Hélène Cixous, as the account of a parthenogenesis which can also be read as symbolic of the relationship between a writer and her text. Towards the end of the passage the author calls on the Nile, home of the phoenix, to give birth to new signifiers and things signified. In Latin *nil* is also the contraction of *nihil*, meaning nothing. This portrays the autistic recreation sometimes expressed by the phoenix myth:

> So I, the Subject, in unlimited, consanguine, material and creative relation with the object of its love . . . leaning all its faces at once over the unknown face of Itself, caress the beloved head still crowned with ashes. The text, seized with

> desire, with hilarity and resemblance, vaginas, laughs . . . and unfolds, Nil, neither one nor the other, nor Itself . . . but child of all: its mother is unlimited and this gives it pleasure.

For Monique Wittig, whose narratives *Les Guérillères* (1969) is in part both a poem and a parodic epic, the phoenix is indeed the Amazon, the single woman. This is what we are told in the introductory poem: 'chaleur intense mort et bonheur/dans les poitrines mamellées/les phénix les phénix les phénix/célibataires et dorés libres' ('intense heat death and happiness/in breasted chests/phoenixes phoenixes phoenixes/single and golden'). In an imaginary country there lives a race of arboreal women, who open their genitalia to the sun and soak up its rays. Two cremation scenes recall the myth. To honour their goddess who loves scents, they wear clothes made of sweet-smelling herbs next to their skin. At night they burn these clothes. The other cremation scene is a feminist manifesto: on a bonfire they make a pile of the tools of their enslavement, distaffs and washing machines. When the fire has died down, they collect the remains, cover them in blue and red paint and make them 'into grandiose grotesque compositions'. This ludic version demonstrates the myth's potential for renewal.

We should note the euphoric, positive nature of almost all the literary versions of the phoenix myth. Poetry and tales are its chosen forms, and it seems incompatible with dramatic expression. We have indicated its great ideological flexibility. It can reinforce greatly contrasting beliefs or philosophies; from Christian mysticism to the vitalist materialism of Cyrano, from the cult of virginity to the praise of Eros. The imagination feels free in a story which, since it often involves fire and almost always the sun, expresses an essential relation between human beings and the world. The mythical bird has the advantage of being a reflection of the human condition, but at a distance: it does not cause anxiety. When the phoenix is bisexual, its bisexuality does not appear dangerous or monstrous – as it does when a myth attributes it to human beings. Above all this myth is enchanting because it does not include the word 'end'.

Marie Miguet

From Primitive Myths to Literary Myths

It seems impossible to speak of 'literary myths' other than by misuse of the term or by external analogy, which to all intents and purposes empties the term of any precise content. Many specialists are of this opinion, including ethnologists and historians of religion.

FROM MISUSE TO VAGUENESS

Too many imprecise uses seem to justify Valéry's disdainful criticism: 'That which perishes from a little more precision is a myth' (*Variété, 2*: 251), as does familiar use of the word to refer to something unreal or false, 'that's a myth!' (cf. also Etiemble and the 'myth' of Rimbaud). A long line of rationalists, right down to Butlmann, willingly returned to the (late) Greek definition and paraphrased it: 'a lying discourse which can express truth [only] in images'.

Everyday language, and especially the Press, that great consumer of suggestive clichés, abuse the word too often, serving it up in all kinds of ways, from the 'personal myth' of a particular writer to the 'myth of the failure of myth' (Barthes, *Sur Racine*: 68).

Let us add to this a tradition which is well-rooted in France and which has long preserved the word 'myths' for a vast spectrum of fabulous narratives (about the gods, Heracles, the Atrides, and so on) from Greco-Roman mythology. Let us add the 'Platonic myth', for example the one in the *Republic* concerning the cave, which would be better described as an allegory (whereas the narrative about the transmigration of souls in the *Phaedrus* echoes an older, more authentic 'myth'). Until the eighteenth century (and often later still) 'the myths' that were known – and were opposed to Christian 'truths' – were those of Antiquity.

To confuse the issue completely, we have the systematic opposition of 'mythos' and 'logos' (to which Barthes returns once more), in which 'mythos' retains only the very vague meaning of 'what is told' (in Aristotle's *Poetics* it was the plot of a play, a well-constructed narrative), while Détienne notes (in *Le Temps de la réflexion* 1: 47–8) that before the 6th century 'mythos' and 'logos' were more or less interchangeable words.

'QUALIFIED' USES OF THE WORD

Any definition naturally implies methodological objections. The most certain starting point is to go back to the 'qualified' uses of the word in the work of specialists in a particular contemporary scientific language.

Thus for the ethnologist, the myth is 'a true story, which took place at the beginning of time and which serves as a model for human behaviour' (Mircea Eliade, *NNRF*, 1953: 441). The primitive myth 'encompasses', it is equally a narrative about origins and a religion, a knowledge, a practice, a justification for customs and so on. But it is different from other symbolic narratives, such as the profane tale, not only in its forms of expression and the particular conditions in which it is recited, but also in the different type of belief it demands: it is a more or less 'sacred' story.

In our modern world, as in the historical past, the sociologist and the political scientist refer to image-forces (for example Progress, the Race or the Machine) which can exert a collective fascination comparable to that of primitive myths. The myth is defined here as a 'collective belief of a dynamic, symbolic and global nature, taking the form of an image' (Janne, in *Cahiers Internationales de Sociologie*, 1962: 22). As for primitive peoples, the myth remains today an essential factor in social cohesion, encouraging the adherence of all to the same dynamic model.

A variation on the effectiveness of mythical images can be found in many clichés exploited by commercial advertisements: three palm trees under the sun and a line of waves on the sand is supposed to be enough to seduce potential clients of the Club Méditérranée (and others), reviving for them the old myth of the Blessed Isle, reduced to a simple cliché.

Many psychologists – notably (but not only) Jungians – use the word myth to refer to an image able to crystallize the energies of an individual or collective group by encouraging projections and transference on to a shared imperative or ideal. The phenomenon is more visible when the ideal proves inadmissible because it contradicts accepted values too directly: 'for myths to exist, there must be a belief which cannot openly assert itself, which feels a need to clothe itself in symbols that both mask and express it' (Sauvage, *Le Cas Don Juan*: 183; see also Rougemont, *L'Amour et l'Occident*). This is an excessive assertion, for myths can equally well express received values. Therefore we shall, more broadly, call 'myth' any image which can dynamically express an element or conflict in collective psychology.

AN ATTEMPT AT DEFINITION

Turning our attention to literature and starting from the qualified uses of the word, we shall use the term 'myth' for a symbolic narrative (or character involved in a narrative) which exerts a fascination (whether idealistic or repulsive), as well as a greater or lesser power to bring people in a large or small human community together by offering them the explanation for a situation or a call to action. The difference between the 'explanatory' myth and the 'normative' myth is little more than that between the implicit (any myth implies a certain concrete attitude) and the explicit; except that normative or dynamic myths seem more orientated towards a future to be realized, while other myths turn towards an order to be maintained. The word 'fascination' seems to us the best available equivalent for the effects traditionally attributed to the 'sacred' in a world which has become almost entirely secularized.

Our definition has some immediate consequences: a myth is not an individual's personal business, it is a group affair. In literary creation the myth has a role in the relationship of writers to their own time and audience: writers express their experience or beliefs through symbolic images, which may echo a myth that is already current and/or be recognized by their audience as expressing a fascinating image.

A myth cannot be identified with a single text. A literary text is not in itself a myth: it returns to and re-expresses mythical images and can itself acquire mythical value and fascination in such circumstances, for a particular audience at a particular time. In the same way it can lose this mythical value when the audience or circumstances change: Molière's *Don Juan* had lost all power of fascination until the twentieth century; Mozart's *Don Giovanni* acquired new mythical value when Hoffman interpreted it in his own way to the new Romantic audience of 1813.

Thus a simple literary 'theme' acquires the status of a myth when it expresses the mental constellation in which a social group recognizes itself (for example, the figure of Tristan in the twelfth century, for a small fringe of the courtly aristrocracy), and when it no longer fascinates the public it once more becomes a simple theme, to which writers return merely out of habit or literary tradition (Tristan in the fifteenth or sixteenth centuries). This is no doubt the case for most of the mythical images inherited from Antiquity which have become prestigious literary models throughout the West. They can occasionally regain their status as fascinating models; as did, for example, the great Roman stories in the time of Corneille, or in the language of the members of the Convention, or Antigone for the French Resistance, and so on. The vitality and contemporary relevance of a myth can be measured by its 'reception' and the various forms its reception takes.

The myth should be distinguished from the allegory, a far more demonstrative and calculated narrative form. Myths remain in the category of spontaneous creation – although today we know how to exploit methodically the old mythical images, such as the Blessed Isle in holiday posters; and there are many other, more dangerous clichés, which political discourse uses with fearsome efficiency.

Myths should also be distinguished from utopias (projections into an idealized future), from legends (which have a more or less historical basis or character), from secular tales, and so on. The vocabulary, however, is uncertain, even among specialists: thus for example, Mannheim uses the word 'utopia' to refer to what we would here understand by myth. Furthermore, it has happened more than once that a particular narrative form falls half way between myth and legend or between tale and utopia.

The very broad scope of our definition is confirmed by the easily observable continuity between one mythological level and another. In the past there was a continuity between Greek mythical representations or Biblical images and the literary themes they inspired (for example, Prometheus or Oedipus, David or the Creation). Today there is continuity between 'sociological' myths and literary images (Blessed Isle – the dream of a holiday – *Robinson Crusoe* or *Suzanne et le Pacifique*). This continuity between the 'sociological' myth and the literary myth stands out even more at the 'infra-literary' level (e.g. cartoons, science fiction, detective stories), where the fascination of myth is set to work in a more direct way.

ANALOGOUS VARIATIONS AROUND A DEFINITION

The shared definition should not obscure very important differentiations between types of myth. First of all, in moving from the oral to the written form – from what used to be listened to collectively (and was more or less sacred) to what is today read by individuals (more or less critically) – we enter a different world. Furthermore, form and the perfection of expression were already of importance in the oral lyric (that used by Pindar or the French troubadours), and increasingly so in written myths. The text entered the domain of aesthetics.

Primitive myths were linked to a ritual or to collective behaviour, whereas our modern mythical images have retained only a few traces of 'participation'; for example in a liturgy or in political rallies such as those of Nuremberg or the First of May. Where literature is concerned (apart from theatre and other shows), what remains of ritual participation?

In literature the 'fascination' exerted by a peculiar mythical figure reaches an audience which is limited (to what extent does this audience represent a human collectivity?) but measurable: for example by the number of times a work or a mythical theme is returned to in a particular period; by print runs; by the reactions of different sections of the public; by the different versions it gives rise to; by allusions to it which become commonplace and may even pass into the language, and so on. Thus between 1587 and 1599 the primitive 'Popular Narrative' of Faust ran to twenty-two editions, which reflects (and at the same time increases) the popularity of the character. Conversely, in Germany, when the Nazis came to power in 1933, people very quickly stopped writing *Fausts*, although the adjective 'faustian', a fairly recent derivation, was still used, at the cost of an ideological fuzziness which was skilfully exploited.

No particular literary style is peculiar to myths: great symbolic images, pairs of opposites, stereotyped phrases, repetitions and contrasts are all common to myths, tales, epics and other literary genres where the symbolic dominates. For myths are not characterized by formal sentence structures or narrative elements: their structure belongs to the organization of the phases and themes of the narrative as a whole, and most frequently it is of a dramatic type. Myths cannot be reduced to a simple symbolic theme: they are dynamic structures combining episodes, characters and situations in terms of a dialectic which is always original.

FROM PRIMITIVE MYTHS TO MODERN MYTHICAL IMAGES: A HISTORY

Primitive myths tended to be static; at the same time unavoidable and reassuring for people confronted by a universe in which they lived as though immersed. Already in Greek tragic drama, and more still in the Bible, the all-encompassing images begin to take on a new, dramatic and dynamic character; human freedom is involved, and we are no longer immersed in the myth but are offered free choice (or more or less free) between different forms of adherence to extremely heterogeneous mythical complexes.

In short, we have to give up the unambiguous concept of the myth and think more in terms of a kind of analogical history of myths, which could be schematized in the following way. Each primitive human group lived within an all-encompassing myth, which was both the image of the universe as a whole and the justification for the society and its rites: the gradual organization of mythologies acceptable to the greatest number corresponded to the formation of larger groups (e.g. city, people, empire). The great religions, and in the West particularly Judeo-Christianity, brought about a decisive renewal, and the vision that they introduced partly took over the place and function of primitive images. It retained certain of their elements (e.g. the Creation and the Flood), but radically changed their symbolic scope by annexing them to an overall vision which was entirely different from that of the earlier mythologies – to a universe of freedom evolving in a history orientated towards the future. Furthermore, centuries of theological thought gradually created a balance (which is always delicate) between symbolic images and abstract rationality. It is only by analogy that we can speak of biblical or Christian myths: here too, in reality, we are in a different world from that of earlier myths.

Later, in literature, the ancient themes of mythological orgins coexist with an all-encompassing Christian representation, which in turn gives rise to its own mythical images; for example Faust, Don Juan or Progress. In the nineteenth century romanticism renewed all the images (whether of ancient, Baroque or some other origin) and redefined them in relation to what we can call romantic religiosity, or *Weltanschauung*. Lastly, the twentieth century has been all the more able to combine these elements because it has (or at least its intellectuals have) become fully aware of the torrent of mythical inheritance. Thus from the single and all-encompassing myth of the primitive group, we have moved to the flood of shattered myths borne by modern culture. Mythical elements from everywhere have been, so to speak, successively deposited within us in a 'stratification' described by, for example, Bastide. They may return to emerge, one after the other, at the surface of the collective or individual consciousness.

Although literary myths no longer say all there is to say about human beings and life (a claim that has not been possible since the coming of the great religions), it is nevertheless easy to prove – at least concerning the most important of these myths – that they necessarily involve reference to a global vision, which provides them with a context and without which they would be inconceivable. Thus popular Lutheran religion is the context of the primitive myth of Faust (as popular catholicism is for Don Juan), where there is far more concern with judgement and condemnation than with evangelical forgiveness. Later, in the nineteenth century, the two characters acquired the context of a romantic vision. We can argue in a similar way in the case of the stories of Tristan, Prometheus, and doubtless many others which have not been analysed.

THE 'TRUTH' OF THE MYTH: WHAT DOES IT MEAN TO UNDERSTAND A MYTH?

Myths represent a finished and complex form of something we can call symbolic language (or significatory language, because in it human subjects really express themselves), as opposed to the language of objects, which is designatory, informational and utilitarian. Everything that gives meaning and value, everything that existing human beings say passes through this symbolic language, of which poetry and religious language are the privileged forms. Symbolic language is thus essential to existence, since, according to Novalis, 'man inhabits the earth poetically'. The primacy of 'symbolic forms' in human activity has been asserted by Cassirer, Durand and others, against Barthes, for whom it was only a 'secondary semiological system' (*Mythologies*: 111–5).

But for us moderns, it is impossible to stop at pure 'mythical thought' as our distant ancestors did. Today we have to put myths into a dialogue and symbiosis (both always difficult and full of conflict) with metaphysical or everyday rationality (as the great religions and poetic works have long been doing, each in their own way), with psychology (as in the works of James Joyce, Thomas Mann and many others), and so on. It is extremely dangerous to abandon entirely the critical monitoring of symbols by rationality, as some terrible political examples have proved. A return to primitive innocence, even that of symbols and literature, is an ultimately unhealthy dream.

The truth of myths is a symbolic truth: it offers, for the world, life and human relations, a meaning which can be neither imposed nor proved. I either enter it or I do not; myths either play on their power of fascination or else they do not touch me. Most of the myths which have come to us from the past or from other cultures (from the gods of Olympus to Chinese dragons) have value for us only as images or literary themes rich in poetic echoes: they no longer have anything vital to tell us about our lives today. Living myths fully represent what Détienne describes in phenomenological language (*Le Temps de la réflexion*, 1:41): 'the figures of transcendental imagination which open to presence'.

Insofar as a particular mythical figure appears alive and fascinating to a particular group, it is because it expresses some of that community's reasons for living, a way of understanding both the universe and its own situation in a given historical context. This function is very clear in the comings and goings of mythical images in politics, but also in those for which the epics of times gone by have been a vehicle (e.g. *La Chanson de Roland* in the eleventh century or the romance of *Tristan* in the twelfth) and in the various images reflecting romantic nostalgia and religiosity (Faust in the nineteenth century). No doubt what is valid for those myths most often taken up could be extended to less ample and more fleeting mythical images in the particular mental constellation of a certain group at a particular time.

Should we stop 'decoding' myths and translating them into an abstract formula, as, for example, Lévi-Strauss tried to do for Oedipus in *Structural Anthropology*? For to do this is to reduce myths to what they precisely are not, a pure conceptual logic. It would be better to try to formulate them at the existential level: they often come down to an imperative or a matter of choice (e.g. 'die and become!' or 'love longs for eternity and freedom and meets limitations'), which answer a specific urgent problem or a more or less permanent and multi-faceted question posed to humankind. For myths as for poems, beyond the decoding which is the aim of study, there remains listening: one must still enter into the images, experience them and verify (if possible, lucidly) what they help us (or do not help us) to live through.

ANALYSIS OF LITERARY MYTHS

In a society which has become secularized, literary production is one of the remaining privileged domains where myths can express themselves. But here more than elsewhere one must take account of the quality of the formal expression and of the authors' personalities, their introduction of transformations, their ability to project themselves into the narrative or to integrate into it a particular element of contemporary life. All these transformations could act on the oral recitation of the primitive myth, but in literary myths they are multiplied indefinitely, to the point of dismembering and sometimes almost completely obscuring the original dramatic shape. We must thus conclude, contrary to Lévi-Strauss' principle, that not all versions of a myth in literature have the same importance. Some, for example Goethe's *Faust*, are particularly admired, both for their formal sucess and for their mythical radiance, and may bring about decisive shifts in the meaning of the old structure.

We need to start with a kind of scale for the levels of interpretation of a work. First, what did the author mean to do with a version of a myth, to what extent and why it is innovatory? Second, what do the period and the collective mentality express through that author's intentions (or unconscious)? Lastly, how much of the myth's original schema comes through the 'updating' represented by the new text?

We can thus set out a model for a synthetic analysis of the myth in a literary text, which is similar to that of Durand (1979: 308):

1 Starting with the literary form: evaluate the more or less important place of the mythical image (open and omnipresent transportation, appearances beneath the surface of the text, simple series of symbolic allusions, and so on) and the more or less original literary means used.
2 Identify the echoes (and thus often the inflexions that modify the original mythical schema) coming from the historical and socio-cultural context.
3 The intentional or unconscious psychological development of the mythical figure or conflicts.
4 Thus, by gradually dissecting the text, the analysis will bring to light hidden symbolic-dramatic elements to be formulated, not as 'mythemes' of a linguistic type, but as antinomies and conflicts, to which the myth suggests the experience of solutions. A distinction should still be made here between marginal and more or less fortuitous symbolism (Faust growing younger) and the essential symbolic complexes, few in number (two or three), that we propose to call 'poles', since in themselves they already represent poles of contradictory tension (for Faust, the leap of desires towards the diabolical pact). The combination of these symbolic complexes constitutes the multi-faceted dynamic and symbolic structure which gives the myth in question its power and originality.

André Dabezies

Prometheus

Since the Romantic Movement, Prometheus has become the symbol *par excellence* in western culture of the rebellion in the field of metaphysics and religion, as well as the embodiment of the rejection of the absurdity of the human condition. Towards the middle of the twentieth century, expressions such as 'Promethean man' and 'Promethean humanism' were in current usage to describe attitudes which either destroyed or challenged traditional values. It should be pointed out, however, that this particular version of the theme is relatively recent and was only established after a long and tortuous development. During the course of an odyssey which has lasted for over two thousand years, the myth of Prometheus has proved extraordinarily flexible and has been the subject of many extremely varied and often contradictory interpretations.

Its origins remain obscure. According to Gaston Bachelard, myths were the product of pre-scientific thought which was anxious to produce an explanation for incomprehensible phenomena. They performed an aetiological function and provided reassurance by revealing a sort of pan-determinism within the universe. Very early on, they developed into more or less elaborate and complex accounts which were later combined into a close-knit network which formed the basis of the first theogonies. Viewed from this perspective, the story of Prometheus, which is indissociable from the question of the origin of fire, must be one of the oldest and most unviersal myths, since equivalent versions are found in Indian, Germanic, Celtic and Slav mythology (see Frazer's *Mythes sur l'origine du feu*, Paris, 1931). Becuase it was indispensable to the process of cooking food, fire appears to have been initially confused with the food itself in the 'ambrosian cycle' (Dumézil, *Le Festin d'immortalité*, Paris, 1924). It would therefore appear that the theft of fire originally represented an attempt by Man to rob the gods of the food which ensured their immortality, but the cult of the flame soon replaced the alimentary myth. Reinach maintained that, according to the earliest accounts, the perpetrator of the theft must have been an animal which assisted Man and which is remembered in the legends of Normandy and Brittany. He considered that the eagle which tears open Prometheus' side in the Greek version of the myth is an avatar of these animal worshipping traditions. During the next stage, the animal was replaced by a hero, who either 'invented' fire (an invention sometimes attributed to Phoroneus, a legendary king of Argos) or stole it from the gods.

The actual name of Prometheus has even inspired various speculations. Because of similarities with some of the stories contained in the Vedas, there have already been attempts, by Kühn and Müller for example, to establish a direct link. According to Diodorus Siculus, Prometheus was the inventor of the 'fire-stick' which produced a flame when rubbed. In Sanskrit, this stick was called *pramantha* from *manthani* meaning 'to rub', and he considered the Greek name Prometheus to be the result of the anthropomorphic personification of the action. Others, such as Frazer and Séchan, considered that the name should be related to the Indo-European root *man-dh*, which implies the idea of reflection, wisdom and forethought, an etymology which would take account of the symbolic opposition in Greek mythology of Prometheus (Forethought) and his brother Epimetheus (Afterthought). Duchemin pointed out some striking analogies with the Babylonian poem of the Creation and the myth of Atrahasis, which stemmed from a Sumerian tradition dating back to the third millennium BC. He suggested that the source of the myth lay in these stories from the Near East, which had subsequently been developed according to a specifically Greek tradition. The story of Prometheus eventually included the story of Pandora, the *fiancée fatale* sent by the gods to retrieve their stolen food and the harbinger of misfortune and death. However, these stories were most probably passed on by word of mouth before being presented in a structured written form. Homer was certainly familiar with the legend because he refers to Iapetus and the Titans; however, he does not mention Prometheus, who finally began to appear in literary works during the eighth century BC through the poems of Hesiod.

Hesiod produced two complementary versions of the myth. In the *Theogony* (I.507–616) he describes how, to resolve a quarrel between the gods and men, the latter were required to offer a sacrifice to Zeus. Prometheus, the son of the Titan Iapetus and the Oceanid Clymene, decided to deceive Zeus by dividing an ox into two parts and wrapping the best parts in the stomach and hide, while concealing the bones in rich-looking fat. By way of revenge, Zeus refused to give fire to men who were the protégés of the 'devious and wily' Prometheus. The latter responded by stealing the flame, a crime which involved a double punishment. Hephaestus fashioned the likeness of a woman and sent this 'beautiful plague' to torment men, while Prometheus was chained to a pillar, where his liver was devoured by an eagle only to be constantly renewed. This story was also close to the early traditions and developed the well-known theme of the 'cunning rascal' (the divine rogue of Indian mythology), as well as that of the *fiancée fatale*, associated with the 'ambrosian cycle'. As yet, fire had no symbolic value. In *Works and Days* (I.42–105), a moral and didactic poem, Hesiod included some additional information. The creature fasioned by Hephaestus is called Pandora (All Gifts). Endowed with 'beguiling speech, and a vile and deceitful nature', she brings with her a jar (*pithos*) containing all the evils, and is married by Epimetheus. The evils are released and plague humanity, with the exception of Hope (*elpis*), which is trapped under the lid. Hesiod's story therefore fulfils an aetiological function, i.e. it provides an explanation of the human condition and teaches respect of the gods: 'It is utterly impossible to escape the intrigues of Zeus'. But the story, with its still very obvious pre-classical substrata, has a somewhat negative conclusion. Prometheus, the misguided benefactor, is in fact responsible for the misery of the human condition, whose destiny is perceived in terms of decline and decadence, and no attempt is made to defend his rebellion. Hesiod's lesson is one of submission to divine will.

Three centuries later, between 467 and 458 BC, Aeschylus' *Prometheus Bound* (*Prometheus desmotes*) conferred an important religious and metaphysical significance on the myth. Aeschylus, a moral and religious man who was passionately devoted to the idea of the coincidence of justice and divine order, believed that moderation and harmony should be respected above all else. According to him, the greatest fault in both gods and 'transient beings' was hubris, an excess of ambition or pride which led to overreaching. In his tragedy, the first great masterpiece to be inspired by the theme, Prometheus is guilty of giving fire to men at a point when Zeus, who has recently become ruler of the gods, has decided to destroy them. The Titan, chained and nailed to one of the highest peaks in the Caucasus Mountains, is immediately presented as a martyr and the victim of an unjust power, a concept which does not appear in Hesiod's work. However, although the Oceanids who form the chorus pity him, they also reproach him for having 'exceeded his rights'. However generous his intentions, he has transgressed the divine law by his disobedience. Aeschylus' Prometheus is no longer the simple benefactor of the *Theogony*, and, in a long tirade, the author lists his gifts to humanity: he has delivered men from their obsession with death, has taught them hope and given them fire 'from which they will learn many skills' (11. 254, 441–68). The myth has been considerably extended and glorifies the progress and greatness of humanity, reflected in a Prometheus who is the founder of civilization, the arts and technology. Nor is the hero the defenceless victim described by Hesiod, because he possesses a secret which will enable him to bring about Zeus' downfall: Destiny has decreed that as a result of a union with the god, a mortal woman will one day bear a son who will be more powerful than his father. Zeus, through the intermediary of Hermes, 'messenger of the gods', demands to know the name of the woman. Prometheus scorns his threats and, drunk with pride, defies the heavens and demands an even worse punishment. The ending of the tragedy is cataclysmic. There is an earthquake, the mountains crumble and, amidst deafening noise, an abyss opens up. Prometheus, still chained, is crushed beneath the falling peaks of the Caucasus Mountains.

Prometheus Bound has presented scholars with a problem of authenticity. Zeus, who is here cruel, capricious and despotic, is not the god of *Agamemnon* and the *Suppliants*, while this rebellious Prometheus is not like Aeschylus' other heroes. Does this mean that the work has been wrongly attributed, or was it the result of a religious crisis on the part of Aeschylus? In fact, the problem ceases to exist if it is remembered that *Prometheus Bound* was to be followed, in accordance with the Greek tradition of the trilogy, by *Prometheus Unbound* (*Prometheus louomenos*) and even by *Prometheus the Firebearer* (*Prometheus pyrophoros*), which probably represented the beginning of a Promethean cult. *Prometheus Unbound* has disappeared, although its general outline is known. After a punishment lasting thirty thousand years, Zeus frees the Titan who, in return, tells him his secret. This gives us a better understanding of the existing tragedy, based on the poet's concept of justice and moderation. Zeus is a young god unable to use his power wisely. His first mistake is wanting to destroy humanity for no apparent reason. This is compounded by Prometheus, who disobeys Zeus instead of allowing Justice (which is superior even to the gods) to take its course. The *point de départ* is a conflict of rights, which is soon exacerbated, on both sides, by excess. Within a modern context, such a conflict would have no outcome, and this is in fact how it was seen by the Romantics. Christianity has accustomed us to envisage God *in esse*, perfect for alll eternity, whereas for Aeschylus, both gods and mortals develop and progress. They change with time and are envisaged *in fieri*. Zeus is young and 'a new master is always harsh', because he does not yet understand that it is necessary 'to suffer in order to understand'. The tyrant of *Prometheus Bound* is the Zeus of the beginning of the world, who has just replaced Chronos and defeated the Titans, in other words the Zeus of popular mythology. The Zeus of *Prometheus Unbound* was to be wiser and more mature, finally achieving perfection by the coincidence of his divine will and justice. This is why thirty thousand years are said to have elapsed between the first and second parts of the trilogy. An appeased Zeus frees Prometheus, who, with the passing of time and suffering, has also become wiser and makes peace with the ruler of Olympus.

The rebellion of Aeschylus' character should therefore be understood within its context. The work is not, as Nietzsche suggested in *Die Geburt der Tragödie* (The Birth of Tragedy), a 'hymn to impiety', and Prometheus is not, as de Lacretelle described him, 'the first Romantic'. The Titan is not rejecting the universal and divine order and his rebellion is against a Zeus who is only temporarily imperfect and not the essentially unjust divinity that the Romantics later claimed him to be. It is, however, possible to see how Aeschylus modified the myth by defining a new concept of the human condition, which, as a result of the benign actions of Prometheus, he saw in terms of progress rather than within the Hesiodic context of decline and nostalgia for the Golden Age. By reading between the lines, it is also possible to observe a development which was to catch the imagination of modern writers. By making men intelligent and giving them free will, Aeschylus' Prometheus does not incite them to rebel against the gods but presents such a rebellion as a possibility. Aeschylus' drama is not the tragedy of human rebellion against the arbitrary nature of the gods and metaphysical absolutes, but the story of the search for peace and harmony. The modern age, by ignoring this highly specific philosophical and religious context, was to interpret the lesson very differently.

During the classical era, the subject inspired other works by authors such as Epicharmus, Lucius Attius, Maecenas and Tiberianus. The fact that none of these has survived does not mean that the myth had disappeared. On the contrary, its popularity is borne out by a large number of texts, which cover a wide range of different versions and interpretations, in accordance with the structural organization of myths (Lévi-Strauss). Certain themes were extremely successful. These include: the theft of fire, accompanied by symbolic, allegorical or realistic explanations (Diodorus, Pliny and Euhemerus); the spectacular description of the punishment (Apollodorus, Seneca, Martial, Lucian, Valerius Flaccus, Quintus Smyrnaeus, Strabo and Philostratus), which is sometimes represented as a crucifixion (Lucian and Ausonius); and Prometheus as the inventor of the arts and sciences. An important variation presents the Titan as the creator of the human race and fire as the spiritual element which animates the creature of clay (Pausanias, Horace, Juvenal, Aesop, Menander). According to the allegorical realism of the euhemeristic interpretation, the creator of men was to become the inventor of statuary, (i.e. the artist), later understood in the sense of the inspired poet – a theme with very distant origins that was to be found in the works of Shaftesbury during the eighteenth century and in Herder and Goethe during the 'Sturm und Drang' movement. During the second century AD, the type of fervent faith practised by Aeschylus had long since been eroded and classical mythology, which had ceased to be taken seriously, was devoid of any truly religious content. This is borne out by Lucian of Samosata's *A Literary Prometheus* and *Prometheus or the Caucasus*, in which the religious content has been removed and the burlesque treatment of the myth expresses the rationalism and scepticism of the classical world.

From the fourth to the fifteenth century, there was a long twilight period during which Prometheus made only occasional appearances. Because western Europe was cut off from Greek culture at an early stage, the myth was only transmitted via works in Latin, with the result that Aeschylus' version remained unknown in these countries. Although Prometheus did not disappear completely, he was virtually absent from secular works and appeared mainly in the works of scholars and the Church Fathers, where he was used to fuel the controversy between Paganism and Christianity. The new faith used the euhemeristic interpretation to denounce in the myth a banal historical fact which had been embellished by poets and distorted by superstition. According to such writers as Clement of Alexandria, Eusebius of Caesarea, Cyprian and Lactantius, Prometheus was a famous figure of Antiquity, the inventor of statuary, who had been mistakenly deified by an ignorant nation and whom others (e.g. Saint Augustin, Adon de Vienne and Vincent de Beauvais) even considered to be a contemporary of Moses. After the Neoplatonist, Plotinus, writers such as Fulgentius preferred to develop the allegorical and philosophical interpretations, although the possibility remained of a simple assimilation, in the sense that the Greek myths were taken to be either the distorted expression of an original divine revelation or evidence that paganism had pillaged and reinterpreted Hebraic thought. In this way, Orpheus charming the animals represented the divine word attracting souls, and writers took pleasure in finding points of comparison between the lives of Heracles and Christ. A more sympathetic interpretation saw the pagan myths as an intuition, a veiled premonition of Christian truths. Although quite common, this type of assimilation did not include the myth of Prometheus, in which the potential for rebellion was difficult to assimilate. A phrase from Tertullian's *Adversus Marcionem* ('The real Prometheus is the omnipotent God tormented by suffering'), quoted by Stanley, the sixteenth-century publisher of Aeschylus, and misinterpreted by Edgar Quinet, was responsible for establishing the mistaken idea among critics that 'Christians throughout the Middle Ages saw Aeschylus' Prometheus as a prefiguration of Christ' (Lebel). In fact, the Christianization of the myth did not occur until the sixteenth century. Several references in texts written in the vernacular, such as Gower's *Mystère du Vieil Testament* and Molinet's *Roman de Dolopathos*, did nothing to dispel the misconception.

After being eclipsed for a long time by the Christian interpretation, the myth recaptured its earlier splendour with the first manifestations of the spirit of the Renaissance. Throughout this period, however, access to Aeschylus' work was mainly restricted to scholars, since, although the first Greek edition of *Prometheus Bound* appeared in 1518 and the first Latin translation in 1556, the first translation into French did not appear until 1770. The humanists therefore gained their knowledge of the myth via either the secondary classical authors or the many mythological dictionaries and compilations (Annius of Viterbo, Sardi, Iacopo da Bergamo, Gyraldi, Comes, Cartari, Estienne, Torrentinus, Calepinus), which were merely collections of the interpretations already outlined in classical literature or the writings of the Church Fathers. The only exception was Boccaccio's *Genealogia deorum gentilium* (1373) in which Prometheus symbolizes the scholar and becomes the champion of knowledge. Being chained to the Caucasus is no longer presented as a punishment but as the symbol of the mind chained to its search for knowledge, while the eagle represents the 'elevated considerations' which torment those who strive to achieve this in isolation. By revealing knowledge and culture to men, Prometheus frees them from their original condition and inspires them with the desire to seek fulfilment in terms of themselves and not as a function of some transcendental purpose. Here, he aspires to and is entitled to penetrate the secrets of nature.

Many Renaissance scholars echoed and developed this theme. For example, Pomponazzi (*De Fato*, 1520) rejected the concept of theocentrism in favour of ascribing to Prometheus the law of constant effort, and recognized the legitimacy of the search for rationalism, while Erasmus rejected the idea of a determinism which devalues the individual. In *De sapiente* (1510–11), Charles Bouelles used Prometheus to glorify the scholar who, by embracing the universe with his thought, assumes a function which is analogous to that of God.

Francis Bacon (*De sapiente veterum*, 1620) presented an allegorical interpretation of the myth in which he celebrated in Prometheus the *homo faber* and his power to influence nature, and in which fire symbolizes all technical and scientific progress. For Bacon, Prometheus is no longer Bouelles's aristocratic scholar of Neoplatonic thought. He is a man of science in the service of humanity, disdainful of metaphysics – which is considered a pointless exercise – and the founder of the experimental method. In Giordano Bruno's *Cabala del cavallo Pegaseo* (1585), Prometheus rebels against intellectual dogmatism and constraints and claims complete freedom. Marsilio Ficino (*Theologia platonica*) is alone in deploring the situation of the 'wretched Prometheus' who is perpetually imprisoned in his desire for self-improvement because of his status of a physical being condemned to imperfection. The Titan is the embodiment of the painful destiny of the individual who is unable to achieve fulfilment in the mortal world and remains a slave to tangible appearances.

Although it occurred frequently in philosophical analyses, the myth was also extensively used by poets, even though this was a primarily decorative use, combining the archaism of mythology and the dawn of lyricism (see Demerson's *La mythologie classique dans l'oeuvre lyrique de la Pléiade*, Geneva, 1972). The early allegorical interpretations reoccur, according to which Prometheus represents wisdom and forethought and the eagle symbolizes vanity and envy. The myth is generally used as a convenient form of comparison, selected from the arsenal of conventional images of humanistic culture. During the sixteenth century, it was also incorporated into romantic rhetoric, and Prometheus served the cause of Petrarchan lament and exaggerated suffering. Du Bellay and Sidney compare the ideal and inaccessible object of their love to the flame that the Titan attempted to steal. The image of Prometheus tortured by the eagle to represent the lover tortured by love soon became a commonplace in Ronsard and Jodelle, and Ronsard describes himself as 'having the passions of Prometheus'. For Ronsard, Scève, Donne, Southern, Du Bellay and Spenser, Pandora was the cruel mistress who left her lover with only vain hope. In fact, these images became so automatic that they lost their impact and powers of suggestion, although the frequency with which they were used does at least provide evidence of the vitality of the myth. It was particularly developed by philosophers, for whom Prometheus was the symbol of the human condition, the creative artist and the mind thirsting for knowledge and aspiring to comprehend the world.

The seventeenth century contributed very little that was new. In the academic field, the early euhemeristic (Vossius, Moya, Victoria, Thomassin, etc.) and allegorical (Ross) interpretations reappeared. The development of comparative mythology, based on the theory of the absolute authority of the Bible, saw Prometheus as the pagan misrepresentation of figures in the Scriptures. Thus he represented Magog for Bochart, Noah for Vossius and Galle, Japheth for Kirchner and Moses for Huet, while for Pfanner, Burton and Thomassin, the story of Pandora was the pagan version of original sin. Poetry did no more than repeat the clichés and *topoi* of the previous century (Vondel, Racine, Bracciolini, La Fontaine, Cowley and others) while in the field of philosophy, Thomas Hobbes condemned Prometheus in his *De cive* as being the instigator of political opposition and the founder of democracy. The seventeenth century primarily witnessed the return of the myth to the stage, already tentatively approached in Culmann's bourgeois allegory, *Ein schön weltlich Spiel von der schönen Pandora* (1544). Most theatrical presentations were a pretext for extravagant productions, with spectacular stage effects and scenery in which splendour was more important than meaning. In Thomas Campion's *The Lord's Masque* (1613), statues brought to life by Prometheus' fire perform a ballet at a royal wedding. In André Catulle's *Prometeus sive de origine scientiarum drama* (1613), the Titan, father of all knowledge, pays homage to the University of Louvain. In Bergamori's 'pastoral tale', *Prometeo liberato* (1683), performed in Bologna, Prometheus is freed by Heracles, and the transformation of the arid Caucasus Mountains into a pleasant garden is followed by a ball and refreshments! This was the beginning of the wealth of entertainments, pantomimes, ballets and animated tableaux of the eighteenth century.

However, a special place should be reserved for Calderón's *La Estatua de Prometeo* (1669). This was probably also an attempt to produce a 'complete' entertainment, similar to opera, with ballets, costumes, scenery, music and singing; but this particular work has a deeper meaning. It is an entertainment aimed at a cultivated audience in which Calderón used information provided by the Spanish writers on mythology, Victoria and Perez de Moya, both of whom had translated Boccaccio's *Genealogia deorum*, to produce an allegory in three days. Using the opposition previously illustrated by Hesiod, he presents Prometheus as the admirer of Minerva, goddess of reason, and Epimetheus as the servant of Pallas, the goddess of war. The play is based on one of the rules of Baroque theatre; that is, symmetry of situations and contrast achieved by the use of parallels and oppositions which establish the meaning. In the tradition of Boccaccio, Epimetheus represents natural man, subject to all animal weaknesses, Prometheus is the scholar, the intelligent, cultured being, while Pallas and Minerva symbolize the conflict between passion and reason. For Calderón, knowledge reinforced by morality justifies confidence in men and civilization: 'Whoever brings enlightenment to men, in fact brings them knowledge, and whoever brings learning, gives a voice to the clay and breathes life into the soul'. Calderón's play, which to a certain extent determined and systematized the main interpretations of the Renaissance, was the first major work devoted to the myth since Aeschylus.

With the Age of Enlightenment, Greek theatre became more widely known. The works of Aeschylus were translated into French (Brumoy, Lefranc de Pompignan, Du Theil), German (Goldhagen, Achtsnicht), English (Morell, Potter) and Italian (Cesarotti, Pasqualoni), although they remained unappreciated in the field of classical aesthetics. Dictionaries and manuals (e.g. Fontenelle, Banier, Newton, Hume, Lavaur, Neukirch, Tournemine) continued to be an important source of information for poets. A number of fairly unremarkable operas and entertainments continued the trend introduced during the previous century; for example Houdar de la Motte's *Prométhée* (1753), Meusnier de Querlon's *Les Hommes de Prométhée* (1748), Colardeau's *Prométhée* (1775) and Saint-Paterne's *Pandore* (1784). At most, the story of Pandora provided a basis for extremly conventional criticisms and satires of women, as well as gallant and insipid apologies of their powers (Parnell, Poisson, Poullain de Saint-Foix, Saint-Paterne, La Motte, Hagedorn, Schiebeler, Pepoli, Van Haren), while at the other end of the scale, the frequent appearances of the myth maintained its availability for more serious interpretations.

Curiously enough, the eighteenth century favoured a more pessimistic interpretation of the Promethean myth. Lesage's *La Boîte de Pandore* (1721) had already levelled accusations against a society corrupted by wealth and inequality, while in *Discours sur les Sciences et les Arts* (1750), Jean-Jacques Rousseau denounced Prometheus as the inventor of science and therefore as the perverter of Man's naturally good nature which had been distorted in a criminal process of socialization. In *Les Hommes* (1753), Poullain de Saint-Foix challenged the concept of the original goodness of Man, while an anonymous play, *Prometheus or the Rise of Moral Evil* (1775) saw the theft of fire – i.e. disobedience – as the source of all social evils, an opinion shared by Brumoy in his *La Boîte de Pandore* (1741). In Lefranc de Pompignan's *Prométhée* (1771), the Titan represents the disbeliever, the rationalist and freethinker; namely Voltaire and the Encyclopédistes, who were considered responsible for all types of disorders. In Tobler's *Der befreite Prometheus* (1792), Prometheus himself abjures and deplores the error of his ways and preaches humility and submission to divine will. In these works, the myth is used to challenge the progress of science, which gives men a false sense of self-confidence and distracts them from true values. Rousseau and the theologians were united in their protest against the spirit of the Enlightenment. Ironically, the version of Prometheus presented in these works is the negation of all Promethean effort, because his story no longer concludes with the rational reconciliation of reason and faith described by Calderón, but the unconditional surrender to a superior order.

The apologists of the theft of fire (i.e. the adherents of the Enlightenment) were to interpret the myth in a completely different way. The acceptance of Prometheus' act implied the criticism of Jupiter/Zeus as a representative of the Church and obscurantism. Prometheus is described in the 'Greek' article in the *Encyclopédie* as 'the daring genius of the human race', and Thomas Blackwell refers to him in his *Letters Concerning Mythology* in the same terms as Boccaccio – as the benevolent creator of a civilization, who 'transformed beasts into men'. After making a brief appearance as the rebel in Giordano Bruno's *Cabala del cavallo Pegaseo*, Prometheus became firmly established in this role in *Pandore* (1740). In this 'philosophical opera' by Voltaire, who in

1765 said he would have liked to see it 'performed in the presence of Bayle and Diderot', Prometheus the liberator rebels against Jupiter who is seen as the cause 'of moral and physical suffering'. The hero attacks the cruel and fearsome Jansenist God with whom Voltaire was obsessed. Taking up the fight against a 'jealous and omnipotent tyrant', against the 'Eternal persecutor,/ Creator of misfortune', he proclaims 'the eternal separation of earth and heaven', leaving men the three strengths that will free them from Jupiter: creative ability, love and hope. Within the context of the 'philosophical' struggle, this was the beginning of the Titanism of the Romantic Movement. The theme was echoed by Conz in *Prometheus und die Ozeaniden* (1793) and Falk in *Prometheus* (1803), while Wieland's *Pandora* (1779) attacked Rousseau's theories and confirmed his confidence in perfectibility.

The eighteenth century finally saw the development of an interpretation which was to enjoy a successful career and whose origins lay in the distant past. From the classical age onwards, euhemerism had defined Prometheus as a sculptor of statues. During the fifteenth century, Filipo Villani had used the myth to draw a parallel between artistic and divine creation, and during the sixteenth century Vida and Chapman had applied this parallel to the poet, an idea echoed by Shaftesbury in *Soliloquy or Advice to an author* (1710). While sculpture by its very nature has a model and works 'according to external forms', poetry can create a version of humanity which is completely independent of a specific model. It cannot therefore be classified as an imitation, since it is an authentic act of creation, while the poet, according to the famous phrase, is 'a second maker, a just Prometheus under Jove'. The artist of genius creates in the same way as God, producing the universe from nothingness. To this aesthetic concept, the young Goethe added the metaphysical concept of rebellion derived from the autonomy of the artist's creative act. The theme was clearly in the air, since the image of Prometheus reappeared in the works of Akenside, Young, Wieland, Court de Gébelin and Chenier; but it was the 'Sturm und Drang' and then the Romantic movements which gave it its final form. Thus far, Prometheus had been a creator *under* Jupiter. He would soon become a creator *in opposition to* him.

Prometheus (1773), an unfinished play by Goethe, is a complex work which combines several of the earlier themes. It presents Prometheus as a Boccaccian-type educator who rejects the myth of the 'natural state' and instructs men on their being and feelings, and teaches them love. He is also the founder and legislator of a just society, in which he rejects violence and conquest and allows only such wealth as is legitimized by right. Above all, Prometheus has become the poet of genius who, because his creations are based on an 'internal form', eliminates the transcendency of his philosophy of art and challenges all forms of imitation in the name of creative power. From this theory, which had already been dealt with by Shaftesbury, Goethe develops new conclusions. Prometheus throws doubt on the power of the gods who have become obsolete: 'The gods? I am not a god, and I believe I am equal to every one of them'. Creative talent frees the man of genius, but at the same time, the gods become hostile and make arbitrary and destructive demands because they want to limit creative power. Rejecting all forms of external law, Prometheus refuses to worship gods who are the product of his own faith and credulity. Thus, Goethe has reversed Shaftesbury's line of argument by progressing from an aesthetic to a metaphysical concept. Goethe's Prometheus is not the rebel who becomes an artist, but the artist who is inevitably a rebel, who relies upon his creative power to reject the traditional concept of divinity. It is this concept that the poet challenges in 'Prometheus' (1774), an ode written in the form of an impassioned declaration against a God who is either deaf, powerless or cruel, and who is in fact controlled by Destiny. Still relying on his creative power, Prometheus will manage without the god, children and madmen:

> Here I am, I mould men
> In my image,
> A race the same as me,
> To suffer and weep,
> Enjoy and experience pleasure,
> And to despise you,
> As I do!

It is possible to follow the development of thought from the fragment to the ode. Starting with Shaftesbury's concept of the creative poet, Goethe extols the role of the artist and, not finding in the gods anything that does not exist in human genius, criticizes them for allowing humanity to be ruled merely by Destiny, an indeterminate and impersonal power. He returned to the theme of Prometheus thirty years later in *Pandora* (1808), a play which was never finished and which was developed along very different lines. This time the poet used the opposition of the two brothers to represent two different attitudes to life. Prometheus is the creator, master of the 'effective', who symbolizes a positive and practical intelligence orientated entirely towards action. Epimetheus is the classic example of the 'ineffectual', the poet in love with Pandora, the beauty glimpsed only once. Here Goethe used the classical doublet to illustrate his own dichotomy in terms of the *vita activa* and *vita contemplativa* and to suggest, in his planned denouement, a harmonious union of Promethean effort and disinterested aspiration to beauty in a superior form of humanity. The Promethean tale of the Age of Genius, which had begun in an explosion of violence, was resolved calmly; but from then on rebellion was to constitute the essence of the myth of Prometheus.

The myth enjoyed an extraordinary popularity during the Romantic period, probably because certain traditional interpretations still persisted. For some writers, Prometheus continued to be the inventor of the arts and sciences (Ballanche, F. Schlegel, Browning), the creative artist (A. W. Schlegel, Balzac, Musset) and the symbol of misunderstood genius (Byron, Hugo). Although he even survived as the miscreant and sinner (Leopardi, Manzoni), a role which was questioned in Mary Shelley's *Frankenstein or the Modern Prometheus* (1818), he was more frequently used within the context of 'Titanism' (Cerny) to represent the rejection of an ethic of submission and blind faith in the name of freedom and responsibility. The debate on the origin of evil ended with the accusation of God as 'the creator of misfortune' as he appeared in Voltaire's *Pandore*, and with the rehabilitation of such great sinners as Satan and Cain, while Christ was seen as the victim of the omnipotent Jehovah. Prometheus in his role as rebel against Jupiter/Zeus was therefore to become one of the most popular figures of the Romantic movement.

The major work of the period was Shelley's five-act lyrical drama, *Prometheus Unbound* (1820), in which Prometheus represents a humanity responsible for the creation of suffering through its own weaknesses. This suffering, which is primarily metaphysical but also occurs in all its religious, social and political forms, is represented by Jupiter. Prometheus rebels against and defeats him but, because he does not know the meaning of hatred, merely throws him into the void. Prometheus-Humanity, with the help of Ione (Hope) and Panthea (Faith in Man), triumphs over evil and, thanks to the intervention of Demogorgon (representing force of circumstance, inspired by inner purification), restores the law of universal love. The poem expresses an optimistic confidence in the trinity of the Romantic Movement, namely the perfectibility of Man, knowledge and reason. Free of the influence of the useless gods, Shelley's Prometheus has confidence in a humanity capable of making its own way towards the achievement of goodness and justice.

On the whole, Romanticism made use of the themes introduced by Shelley. Prometheus became the champion in the struggle against tyranny and political despotism for writers such as Byron, Hugo, Hervey, Brereton and Reade, while for Monti, Wordsworth, Quinet, Hugo and Byron he represented the victorious Bonaparte, who was seen as the heir to the Revolution. He appeared primarily as the liberator from metaphysical suffering, especially in Edgar Quinet's *Prométhée* (1838), which aimed to present 'humanity saved and taken to the bosom of God under the guidance of the spirit of religion. Man, Man as a hero and Man as a god are the successive protagonists of the trilogy'. The work established the idea that religions are merely historical phenomena and therefore transitory stages in the development of humanity. The advent of a just divinity which destroyed the concept of God according to the ancient Law and the theme of the transient nature of religions reappeared in Pasquet's *Prometheus* (1828) and Grenier's *Prométhée délivré* (1857). Finally, for the majority of authors, the myth represented progress, knowledge and civilization. For example, in Hugo's *Les Mages* and *Les Contemplations*, Prometheus, the innovator of science and technology, rescues man, 'the plaything of monsters', from the arbitrary power of the gods and from blind Destiny. This Prometheus often suffers the fate of genius: unrecognized and misunderstood, he is persecuted by the authorities and by the Church, and jeered by the masses

(Hugo, Michelet). Freedom through progress is indissociable from attacks against an unjust and cruel divinity (Byron, Carducci), which has to be combated by reason and the development of knowledge (e.g. von Sallet, 1835; Blackie, 1857; von Feuchtersleben, 1829; des Essarts, 1835; Lodin de Lalaire, 1838; Defontenay, 1854). The theme is well illustrated by Louis Ménard in *Prométhée délivré* (1843), which proclaims the triumph of knowledge and the advent of universal love. In answer to the chorus, who ask which god they should worship from now on, Prometheus suggests the single ideal of faith in a humanity enlightened by knowledge: 'Time is now complete: Zeus is dead./ The ideal lies within you: that is the supreme god./I have given you the example of that divine pride:/Knowledge is the god whose church is my soul'.

The second half of the nineteenth century either developed or challenged the values established during the Romantic Movement. One group of works by such authors as Banville, Grandmougin, Schafheitlin, Giraud and Ackermann continued to make Prometheus the victim of an unjust god and alienating religions, while for Cornut, von Jagow, Dumas, Signoret and Kinon, scientism and positivism reinforced confidence in the power of knowledge to free the mind from fear and superstition. However, over the years, a second group of works revealed an increasing confusion, which was once again expressed via the character of Prometheus. While positivist agnosticism proved satisfactory from an intellectual point of view, the soul remained anxious. In works with such eloquent titles as *Prométhée repentant* (Goldberg, 1904) and *La Mort de Prométhée* (Delebecque, 1905), the Promethean quest in fact called Prometheus himself into question. Sometimes the tyrannical Jupiter proved to be just and peaceable, turning the Promethean rebellion into a vain and arrogant act (Saint-Yves, Bridges, Strada, Gilkin). In his *Prométheide* (1895), Péladan developed the theme of attaining maturity through suffering, the principle of true progress, and a number of texts began to present a repentant Prometheus, who was suffering from the absence of God. Others quite openly rejected all forms of tradition. Spitteler's *Prometheus* goes beyond the conflict between faith and knowledge and advocates a rigid Nietzschean individualism, while in *Prométhée mal enchaîné* (1899), Gide abandons the religious interpretation of the myth and points out that the story of Prometheus is in fact the story of the eagle; that is, his conscience, which is weighed down with taboos and interdictions. Gide's Prometheus rebels against dogma, tradition, social order and established principles with scant regard for either God – that incomprehensible being of which we are not obliged to take account – or a conformist morality which tries to impose him on our conscience. Finally, Elémir Bourges's *La Nef*, written between 1893 and 1922, is full of hesitations, doubt and questioning. This extensive and difficult work provides a synthesis for all the themes of the century, from the Romantic rebellion to nihilism, and concludes with the need for an unremitting and lucid search which defies all forms of illusory transcendency.

The twentieth century has scarcely added to the contribution of the nineteenth. Sometimes associated with historical events (e.g. the rise of Nazism in the works of Bertling and Schäfer), or used as a symbol of social protest (Aub), Prometheus has appeared as the master of matter and knowledge (Jouhandeau), the denigrator of the gods (Tardieu), the champion of humanism and freedom of thought (Las Vergnas), and even the apologist for a return to God inspired by the anguish of the modern age (Montagna, Brock, Burte, Garric). In 'Prométhée aux Enfers', one of the essays in *L'Eté* (1946), Albert Camus has placed Prometheus in the very centre of the dilemma of modern civilization: 'Prometheus is the hero who loved men enough to give them fire and freedom, technology and the arts, all at the same time. Today humanity only needs and values technology. It rebels through its machinery, and it considers art and what it postulates as an obstacle and a sign of servitude. What distinguishes Prometheus, on the other hand, is that he cannot separate machinery from art.' Once again, Prometheus found himself with the task of paving the way towards a problematic form of humanism.

Raymond Trousson

Psyche

All the versions of the love-story of Psyche and Cupid can be traced to a single, late source: these adventures were related for the first time in Apuleius' *The Golden Ass* (second century AD), in the context of an allegorical romance which was to be preserved in various forms in later adaptations. Apuleius' story is a typical allegorical fable, and the allegory is so transparent that the variants introduced down the centuries could alter only the details. Although unknown to us, the origin of the fable itself must clearly be sought in popular tales, for Apuleius' work already represents a secondary elaboration and probably restructuring of the compilation of several legends. However, we know that the allegorical figure of the Soul (*Psyche* in Greek) was widespread in Hellenistic culture, and had probably been so since the earliest times, in the form of a butterfly, or a girl with butterfly's wings. Her adventures with the god of love seem also to have long belonged to the oral culture of the Mediterranean.

While for the moderns the allegorical and philosophical worth of this fable is incontestable, Macrobius, who established a classification of myths in *Commentary on the Dream of Scipio* (fifth century), regarded Apuleius' fables as tales told by wet-nurses, entirely fictional and with no philosophical meaning. This should no doubt be taken as confirmation that this story dating from the end of Antiquity had the status of a 'tale'. It has nevertheless had repeated and regular success in modern literature, where it has been raised to the level of the Platonic myths.

Apuleius sets the story of Psyche in the middle of the story of Lucius, who is turned into a donkey because he is so inconstant. He can only return to his human form by eating roses consecrated to Isis, who, at the end of his misadventures, raises him to the dignity of the priesthood. The fable of Psyche's misadventures is told not to Lucius, who listens with great attention in his donkey's shape, but to Charity, the young bride who is carried off by brigands on her wedding day and whose jailer, an old woman, consoles her with this tale. In fact the tale could apply as much to Charity as to Lucius: it has been shown (see Carlier) that, at the initiatory level, its episodes correspond both to the stages of initiation into the cult of Isis and to episodes of the myth of Isis itself, as told by Plutarch (*Isis and Osiris*), while at the level of the romance and more schematically, they also herald the rescue of Charity, who is saved by her husband when her own attempt at flight has failed and she is ready to kill herself.

The structure of Apuleius' story gives the fable five movements in a complete cycle comprising: Psyche's election and transgression; the search for the lost god; and the final salvation after redemption through ordeals. The following resumé sets out this fundamental structure.

THE SECRET WEDDING OF CUPID AND PSYCHE

At the beginning of her story, Psyche, third daughter of an unnamed king, is adored by men as a goddess because of her exceptional beauty: she thus sins, albeit involuntarily, against Venus, whom she rivals. But at the same time, in the human world, she is the object of a taboo, because no one dares ask her hand in marriage, while her two sisters, who are no different from other human beings, are both married. The irritated Venus obliges her son to punish her rival. When he sees her, however, Cupid cannot resist her beauty either and decides to carry her off. He causes an oracle to state (ambiguously) that Psyche must be exposed in a desert and given to a monster. A funeral procession is formed, with great lamentations, but the sacrifice is only an act, because Zephyr carries Cupid's chosen one away and sets her down in an enchanted palace that has appeared in the desert. Psyche is alone in the Palace of Love, although she is surrounded by invisible servants and all kinds of wonders. It is there, in a secret place, that her marriage with the Invisible One is celebrated: her husband, whose identity she does not know, comes to her only at night and she is not allowed to see him (a similar element occurs in *Beauty and the Beast*, which then unfolds in a way that is different from but entirely consonant with the medieval theme of a mortal's marriage to a fairy; c.f. *Melusina*).

THE FALL

Despite her happiness, Psyche misses her family and gets her husband to allow her to see her sisters. Cupid then twice warns her against the dangers and temptations of these visits; but, despite his warnings, she allows her jealous sisters to convince her that her secret husband is certainly a snake who intends to kill her and that she must kill him first. When night comes she arms herself with a torch and a dagger and surprises her husband in his sleep. She recognizes Cupid by his quiver of arrows and his wings, and, in attempt to turn the dagger against herself, she drops some burning wax on the god's shoulder. The burn wakes Cupid, who flies off, and Psyche, who catches hold of him and is carried upwards, eventually falls back into the desert.

THE SEARCH FOR THE HIDDEN GOD

Guilty, desperate and banished by Love, Psyche wants to throw herself into a river, but the god Pan stops her and encourages her to do something to win her husband's forgiveness instead of abandoning herself to a dishonourable death. Psyche's first step towards redemption is to avenge herself against her sisters, whom she sends to their deaths by deceiving them as they had deceived her. After this first purification, she sets off to wander the earth in search of Cupid, who, weakened by his wound, remains a prisoner with his mother, Venus, throughout the period of Psyche's purificatory and initiatory ordeals. To prove her piety, Psyche asks for protection from Ceres and Juno, the two principal goddesses below Venus (the three goddesses, with their double Isis, are avatars of the primitive Great Goddess). But, despite their sympathy, the other goddesses are warned off by Venus and reject her. After many wanderings, the discouraged Psyche decides to abandon herself to Venus at a time when the latter has just enlisted the help of Mercury, who proclaims throughout the earth that Psyche is a fugitive slave. Once again Psyche thinks of killing herself, a recurring temptation which reappears with each ordeal like a leitmotiv, and it is with the sense that her search has failed that she arrives at Venus' temple.

THE ORDEALS

Before giving her a series of impossible tasks, Venus gives Psyche to her slaves Habit, Worry and Sadness, who put her through various humiliations and beat her. The Psyche has to undergo four tests, each representing a greater danger than the last, with additional difficulties. The first is to sort a pile of grain which fills a room in Venus' temple. Psyche is helped in this by ants, who sort the grain for her. For each test that Psyche cannot carry out on her own, an assistant comes to help her, each assistant being in some way connected to a god and also clearly linked to an element, for the four elements seem to act in solidarity with the captive god of love (from the Pythagorean point of view, Love is the cosmic principle of the unification of the elements, which forms Nature). Here the ants are linked on the one hand to Ceres and on the other to the element Earth.

The second test takes Psyche out of Venus' temple, from which she goes further and further in each successive test. She has to bring Venus wool from the golden fleece of certain ewes, which in fact kill people, although Psyche has not been told this. A reed tells Psyche of the danger and teaches her how to carry out her mission. Pan is invoked here through the plant associated with him, and also, as the reed is an aquatic plant, the element Water.

The dangers are increased with the third test: Psyche has to draw water from the source of the Styx, at the top of a very distant and inaccessible mountain. Psyche only gradually realizes what the true difficulties of this test are when she reaches the waterfall which is the spring itself and hears the waters shouting out to protect themselves from any approach. She is saved here by the intervention of an eagle, Jupiter's bird, who draws water in her place. The eagle represents the element Air.

Following the logic of initiation, the last test is a descent into the underworld. Psyche has to bring Venus a box containing Proserpina's make-up. This time she is fully aware of the dangers and decides to throw herself off the top of a tower. However, the tower starts to speak and tells her how to fulfil her mission and, above all, how to get back from the underworld. The tower is most probably linked to Juno (as Carlier believes), who was sometimes represented as a Great Goddess crowned with a tower. If we also link it to the element Fire (through the hermetic traditions, whose trace we see in the sixteenth card of the major arcana of tarot cards, which represents a tower struck by lightning), the initiation into the mysteries is complete and all the motifs in Apuleius' tale form a cosmic cycle. Through the elements that symbolically correspond to them, the series of tests involves the four fundamental gods who were already linked to Psyche's search (although Jupiter has not appeared yet, his intervention comes later, since it is he who makes possible Psyche's apotheosis). The order of tests itself organizes the four gods into pairs: in the first two tests Ceres and Pan symbolize the world of nature and in the latter two (which must thus be understood in ascending terms) Jupiter and Juno represent the heavenly world. We can also reconstruct the cosmic function of Psyche's helpers in terms of their species: the ants and the eagle represent two contrasting animal types, those that creep (attached to Earth) and those that fly (attached to Air); while the reed and the tower can be contrasted insofar as one belongs to nature as part of the vegetable order, while the other belongs to the super-terrestrial world, although it is harder to tell to what species the tower should be linked (we can see it either as the mineral order or, from a more radical, hermetic point of view, the human order, as an artificial product of the spirit, in keeping with the symbolism of the Tower of Babel). These symmetries seem to reflect the duality of Psyche's character, which is split between nature and spirituality.

THE REDEMPTION OF THE HEAVENLY MARRIAGE

Although Psyche is successful in her tests, she once more succumbs to her weakness: despite the advice of the tower, who warned her not to open Proserpina's box, she cannot restrain her curiosity and, as soon as she leaves the underworld, transgresses once more. Out of the open box comes a lethargic sleep, from which Psyche can be saved only by Cupid himself, who has at last been freed from his prison. Thus the last stage takes us back to the beginning and the god's original choice is confirmed by the repetitive structure of the story, as though all Psyche's tests and sins have been erased. This symbolic death at the end repeats the first symbolic death represented by the original sacrifice, and Psyche's two transgressions are superimposed, the first being followed by a fall and the second, on the contrary, followed by an apotheosis. Through the intercession of her divine husband, Jupiter grants immortality to Psyche, and her marriage to the god of love is celebrated in heaven. Their child Pleasure, who was conceived in secret, is born among the gods.

PRINCIPAL INTERPRETATIONS

The many similarities between Psyche's initiation and the Passion of Christ enabled the myth to be christianized almost immediately. In the sixth century Fulgentius, the first commentator on Apuleius (*Mythologiae* III.6), saw Psyche's parents as the Divine Principle united with Matter in their realm of the World, and her sisters as the Flesh and Free Will. Venus represented Libido and Cupid the duality of Desire, which is for good or evil. Psyche was not allowed to see Cupid in order to prevent her experiencing concupiscence (his negative aspect). In the fourteenth century Boccacio in *Genealogia deorum* analysed the two sisters as allegories of Vegetative Life and Sensory Life, Psyche herself being Intellectual Life, and saw their jealousy as the discord between sensuality and reason. In 1640 and 1655, Calderón wrote two *autos sacrementales* on the subject of Psyche and gave the three sisters, who to him represented the three ages of the world, the names Idolatry, Synagogue and Faith (or Grace). The story of Psyche thus retraced the symbolic history of Christianity. In the last years of the seventeenth century in France there were many attempts to give the myth a quietist interpretation.

Interpretations are perceptibly different depending on the value placed by the authors on Psyche's husband, in whom some see a universal erotic principle, others a Platonic symbol establishing the immortality of the soul (reflected in Lamartine's simplified reference to Psyche's story in his *Mort de Socrate*), and others still a spiritualist and mystical allegory. Adaptations generally follow Apuleius' narrative, the most noticeable variations usually involving the omission of some or all of the tests. The fable's peculiar status in relation to other myths remains the same, and its allegorical charge sometimes makes it hard to adapt from a profane point of view, theological discourse remaining dominant within it.

Some of the multitude of poetic or theatrical adaptations deserve attention. These are versions from the seventeenth century, when the fable was very much in favour (particularly for opera and court ballets) and, from the nineteenth century, an adaptation by a poet unknown today, Victor de Laprade.

Like Apuleius' original, the first important reworking of the fable was inserted into a long mythico-romantic poem in which the fable of Psyche takes up a whole book: this is Marino's *Adone* (1620). Marino follows Apuleius faithfully, stressing the relationship between Psyche and Adonis. For Marino the initiation is characterized by the active part taken by Psyche, and the myth is analysed as a person's entry into awareness (whereas in this poem Adonis appears as an essentially passive figure). The test of the descent into the underworld is only referred to, while the others are elaborated at length.

Besides the two religious *autos* mentioned above, Calderón also wrote a comedy on the subject of Psyche (*Ni Amor se libra de amor*, 1640), with clear differences from Apuleius' version. In this play the tests have been left out, and Calderón introduces suitors for Psyche's hand, who do not exist in Apuleius' work. The omission of all the tests is not unusual, although it is significant: Fulgentius' early exegesis, which accentuated the allegorical function of the myth as a whole, left out the details of the tests. The same unifying and schematic perspective is to be found in the work of Molière and Lamartine.

In 1669 La Fontaine in turn rewrote the story in a singular work, which is itself not an allegorical or mythical fiction, but a description of the gardens of Versailles. *Les Amours de Psyché et de Cupidon* appears here less as a myth than as an amusing, paroodical tale. The fantastical dimension is accentuated, while at the same time La Fontaine writes from a generally rationalizing and secularizing point of view: Psyche is implicitly compared to Orpheus, but the initiatory weight of her adventure is distorted by the added insertion of a second allegorical tale symbolizing the dangers of seeking to evade the power of love (the story of Myrtis and Megano). The structure of the tale here is even more complex than that of Apuleius, from which it omits nothing. On the contrary, it expands on the original work, making certain changes (notably to the order and content of the tests; and Diana, who is absent from all the other versions, is added to the series of Great Goddesses).

In 1671 a 'tragedy-ballet' for which the outline and a few scenes were written by Molière, the dialogues by Corneille, the interludes by Quinault and the music by Lully, used Calderón's structure (omission of the tests and introduction of suitors) in a version that was more tragic (stressing the role of Psyche's sisters) and moralistic (Psyche's revenge is indirect and becomes divine punishment). The original sin committed by Psyche, who differs from the rest of humankind, is also stressed, following the canons of tragedy, in which the crime of hubris sets the plot in motion: here Psyche, who rejects the human love of her suitors, is accused of pride by Venus. The general meaning of the myth is to reveal the power of love ('Is one wise/Not to love?'), but the Christian connotations are clearly stressed.

The rationalization of the myth, combined with its moralization, clearly poses a number of problems which critical minds did not fail to point out: thus Charles Perrault, who rejected allegories, regarded the tale as amoral, since Psyche's misfortunes are seen as the consequence of her desire to know the god of love (Preface to *Grisélidis*, 1695). One current of interpretation later regarded Psyche's transgression not as a crime but merely as the sign of her desire for knowledge. Independent of any theological content, Psyche then became the symbol of Philosophy (this was the thesis developed in 1908 by Bonilla in his study on the myth of Psyche).

Laprade's *Psyché* (1841) is the only example of the use of the myth which deliberately distances itself from the link to Apuleius, although it gives an exegesis of the latter's work. Laprade sees Psyche as a 'fundamental myth', retracing the entire history of humankind. His poem is divided into three books: the first is called 'L'Eden ou L'Age d'Or' and shows Psyche in the Garden of Love; after the fall begins 'La Vie Terrestre ou l'Expiation', the subject of book 2, in which the series of wanderings and tests is a passage through the Ages of Humankind, through all the stages of civilization and culture (Psyche in the hands of the Barbarians, Psyche as a slave, the Greece of orphism and the priests, the heroic times and Homer, the Greece of philosophy). At the end of her travels, Psyche is a 'queen' because she has knowledge, but her 'desire for the ideal' ultimately exhausts her, and she dies calling to her god. Book 3 is called 'l'Olympe ou le Ciel: Union de l'Ame humaine avec Dieu dans une autre vie'; for it is after Psyche's death that Laprade locates her triumph, which marks 'the end of the reign of Evil' inaugurated by her initial curiosity (Psyche is compared to Eve and Pandora). With this poem, which represents one of the last versions directly inspired by Apuleius, we have a syncretic synthesis of the different allegorical points of view. Later literary treatments of the vicissitudes of the soul were more abstract, and the fable of Psyche became primarily a symbol.

Françoise Graziani

Pyramus and Thisbe

The first known version of the legend of Pyramus and Thisbe was already a 'second hand' account, as it was first introduced into literature via the story told by one of the 'daughters of Minyas' in book IV of Ovid's *Metamorphoses.*

Set in Babylon, the subject of the legend is the encounter between the forces of love and fate. Pyramus and Thisbe have loved one another since childhood, in spite of the hostility between their parents. They have contact with each other through – but are at the same time separated by – the adjoining wall of their houses, which, according to de Viau, has become 'cracked out of pity'. The wall offers a 'chink' (Shakespeare) through which the lovers are able to communicate, and they agree to meet one night, outside the city walls, beneath a mulberry tree by a spring, near King Ninus' tomb. Arriving first at the rendezvous, Thisbe encounters a lioness and flees, leaving her veil behind. When Pyramus arrives, he finds her torn and bloodstained veil and, believing Thisbe to be dead, and blaming himself for her death, he kills himself. His blood spurts over the white berries of the mulberry tree, staining them black. Thisbe returns as her lover is breathing his last, and she in turn kills herself. In answer to her prayer, the lovers are united in a single tomb, and the dark fruit of the mulberry will henceforth bear witness to this double suicide.

THE ECLIPSING OF A MYTH

This particular story stands apart from the long list of myths in the *metamorphoses* in that it does not involve any divinities, and that it is not a 'metamorphosis' as such. It does not make use of a mythical subject but rather an external 'witness', which is only modified on the surface (i.e. in the colour of the fruit). The key to the reconstruction of its lost mythical function – of which traces still exist – can be found in the contiguity of the legend and other mythical narratives, and in the relationship between these and the Dionysian cult. This archaic function is indicated primarily by the fact that the legend is linked, by Ovid, to a number of Baylonian myths – Derceto, the original Mother Goddess, transformed into a fish, and her daughter Semiramis, the mythical founder of the great walled city, transformed into a dove, with both figures sometimes being identified with that of Ishtar-Astarte. Ovid tells how the three daughters of Minyas refused to worship Dionysus rather than Minerva, and, while weaving (a task forbidden by the Dionysian sabbath), told each other stories. The story of Pyramus came first, while the second recounted how Venus took her revenge on Apollo by making public his love for Mars, which she punished indirectly through Leucothea, the descendant of the Babylonian god Belus-Cronus, father of Ninus. The third story was that of Hermaphroditus and Salmacis, whose bodies were fused into one. The daughters of Minyas were subsequently punished by Dionysus, who changed them into birds of the night. It is obvious that the three stories – like the paralipses which introduce them – are of a similar type, and are actively opposed to the Dionysian cult. The latter is always presented in terms of rivalry with the cults of the Great Goddess (Astarte-Venus-Rhea-Ceres-Isis), while at the same time presenting certain affinities with them, particularly in connection with orgiastic rites. The worship of the eastern Great Goddess is characterized by adelphic hierogamies, as well as by the self-mutilation or the sacrifice of a priest-king.

A MESSIANIC SACRIFICE

It is possible to associate the legend of Pyramus and Thisbe with a hierogamy which was possibly incestuous becauase of the proximity of the two families, and, in terms of the final suicide, with certain initiatory sacrificial rites. This hypothesis appears acceptable if we consider the sequence of events in the legend which, from the time of Ovid onwards, were not modified in any way whatsoever but were persistently reproduced to the point of appearing superfluous. The various adaptations structured the legend extremely rigorously in a series of systematized mythical themes; namely the wall and its crack, the mulberry tree, the spring, Ninus' tomb, the lioness, the role played by the moon, the double suicide using the same dagger, the 'metamorphosis' of the mulberry tree, and the tomb in which the two bodies were united. The wall was usually seen as a symbol of separation, although in order to discover its mythical meaning, it would be more appropriate to see it as the symbol of Babylon (Babel, centre of the world), the sacred wall which surrounds the cosmos in most eastern religions. Within this perspective, it becomes the symbol of protection for the community, and the crack therefore signifies danger, in the form of the penetration of the forces of evil. According to Chantraine's *Dictionnaire etymologique*, the etymon of the Greek word *pyramos* is a synonym for the Latin word *hortus*, i.e. the wall surrounding a garden. The absence of the gods in Ovid's work is problematic. If the mythical themes which constitute the main scenario are reassembled, it will be seen that they can be linked together in a logical manner to form another story in which the hidden gods re-emerge. In these terms, the lioness should certainly be seen as the main attribute of the Great Goddess Ishtar who is assimilable to, among others, both Aphrodite and the Moon. The literary adaptations of the legend always stress the part played by the moon in Pyramus' misinterpretation of the situation, and in *A Midsummer Night's Dream* the Lion, Moonshine and the Wall are actual characters. The function of Ninus, the mythical spouse of Semiramis whose tomb plays a prophetic role in all versions, possibly becomes clearer if his name is associated with that of the Proto-Sumerian goddess of love, Ninni, subsequently identified with Ishtar and Semiramis herself. (In Ovid's work, his name appears in its genitive form, Nini, and is parodied in Shakespeare – who tends to distort names – as 'Ninny'.) For the Babylonians, the Great Goddess was also Fortune, who watches 'at the gates' of a city. The flight of Pyramus and Thisbe excludes them from the protection of the wall and delivers them into the hands of Fortune in the form of the lioness, which also represents both the Greek goddess Nemesis, the daughter of Justice (in the sense of retribution) and one of the principles of the Sumerian religion, the supreme force which issues divine decrees (the Fates). At this point, it is interesting to note that in his poem 'Les Filles de Minée', La Fontaine locates the meeting between Pyramus and Thisbe 'by the statues of Ceres', which seems to take account of this interpretation. The most important mythical theme in the story is undoubtedly that of the mulberry tree. This should be seen in terms of a sacred tree (in the East it is associated with the solar myths), which also seems to be associated with the Great Goddess when a dove flies above it. It should be remembered that it is only Ovid who sees it as a 'sign of mourning', which is a symbol intended to perpetuate the myth rather than being its determinant factor. Adapted to the Christian tradition, the mulberry tree, like all sacred trees, is compared with the Tree of Life and the Cross (it also appears in the Bible as a 'sign from God'; 2 Sam. 5:23–4). The fourteenth-century *Ovid moralisé* and Thomas Waley's *La Bible des poètes* (Poets' Bible; 1484) both see Pyramus as Christ and Thisbe as the human soul, whose mystical union is prevented by the sin of Adam (the wall). The crack symbolizes the mediation of the Prophets, while the lion is the Devil, the mulberry tree the Cross 'stained with Christ's blood', and the spring the baptismal font. Thisbe, the soul, cannot come first to this font 'if the son of God has not preceded her and is not waiting for her', and when she kills herself 'out of compassion', she becomes the Virgin Mary (whom the religious historians consider as another goddess-mother). This Christian allegory, which is the only truly mythical interpretation of the legend, constitutes the theme of the first theatrical adaptation of the subject: the *Moralité nouvelle de Pyrame et Thisbé* (1535).

CONFUSION, ILLUSION OR SUBTERFUGE?

For Ovid, the basic theme of the legend was the ultimate communion of Pyramus and Thisbe. The later adaptations echoed this theme of union in death and presented it in erotic terms, as an allegory of physical union. La Fontaine, who considered the episode of the daughters of Minyas as a story in its own right, reinstated the legend among a series of narratives based on the theme of the fatal misunderstanding and the dangers of love which 'like Bacchus . . . disturbs the reason'. In *A Midsummer Night's Dream*, the legend forms part of the performances given in honour of a royal marriage. It is also associated with the substitution of lovers, particularly Bottom, the character who plays Pyramus and who, having been transformed into a donkey, briefly becomes an object of love for Titania, Queen of the Fairies. (This reproduces the initiatory structure of Apuleius' *The Golden Ass* and identifies Titania with Isis.) Shakespeare's play is undoubtedly the richest and most complex version of the legend, in which the mythical symbols have been developed at several levels of intepretation. Furthermore, and with great irony, Shakespeare precedes the burlesque performance of the legend in the presence of the royal couple with a series of paralipses, including that of 'the thrice-three Muses mourning for the death of Learning'. The artisans who perform the play have no understanding of their roles and alter their meaning to such an extent that the spectators see both the legend and the actors as 'extravagant'. The poetic versions by Gongora (1618) and Marino (1620) are also parodies which develop the ambiguities of the legend via the ambiguities of language. For Gongora, the lovers are the victims of an illusion that makes them believe 'false testimonies' and they fall into a trap. Thisbe, drawn by the moans of the dying Pyramus, is compared to a bird caught in birdlime as it follows the cries of a decoy. Marino interprets the innocence of the extremely young lovers as naïvety, and the excess of their immature passion is seen as a form of hubris, a transgression of divine laws, although the gods are still not represented. What is more, Pyramus and Thisbe do not know how to interpret the signs, and are therefore duped by deceptive appearances. Within the same perspective, interpreting the misunderstanding as duplicity on the part of the gods, one of La Fontaine's daughters of Minyas says: 'The gods make their sport of human hope'.

Théophile de Viau's dramatized interpretation (1623) is clearly orientated towards a subterfuge (the guilt being entirely focused on the coalition of royal and parental authority), which interprets Fate as a truly tragic *tyche*, and the suicide as a sacrificial murder, situated entirely on a human level, but with the function of a ritual killing. Here, the stress is placed on the obstacles symbolized by the wall, which is the concretization of parental authority, and the lion, the concretization of royal authority (the king, who is in love with Thisbe, tries to have Pyramus killed). By their exclusion from within the city walls, the lovers fulfil the role of expiatory victims, whose martyrdom will facilitate the consolidation of the social group. Even in the simplified version of *Romeo and Juliet* – which makes use of the basic function rather than the themes of the myth – the sacrifice of the lovers has the effect of reconciling the previously antagonistic families.

Françoise Graziani

Revolution and Revolutionaries

MYTHS AND HISTORY

Any historian working on revolution must first eliminate the myths that distort the facts they are interpreting; for example, in the case of the French Revolution, Robespierre's dictatorship, the Jacobin clergy or the frog mask stuck to Marat's face. To historians myths are the rock from which they must extract the pure ore of the facts and processes they are studying.

Karl Marx, the theorist of revolution, also condemns myths, in which he sees the ideological weight of alienation, saying that 'the traditions of all the dead generations weigh very heavily on the minds of the living'. Revolutionary myths preserve a mist that conceals from those concerned (the agents of the current revolution) the meaning of their own actions. Marx describes how Camille Desmoulins, Danton, Robespierre, Saint-Just and Napoleon, the heroes and the mass parties of the first French Revolution, wore Roman costume and used Roman phraseology to carry out the task of their own period, which was the inauguration and establishment of modern bourgeois society.

This critique of the weight exerted by myths accompanies a profound and innovatory break in the philosophical conception of revolution. However, theorists of revolution were not finished with the question of myths: Gramsci re-examines George Sorel's declaration that myths should be judged as ways of acting on the present, and in Gramsci's eyes myths can have some effect only when embodied in a positive construction, such as a party manifesto. According to Gramsci, the collective will for national revolution could be recognized before Jacobinism, in Machiavelli's programme. Gramsci tells us that Machiavelli gave his conception imaginative and artistic form, in which the doctrinal and rational element was embodied in the *condottiere*, representing the symbol of the 'collective will' in a plastic and 'anthropomorphic' aspect. Thus, while the historian of revolutions should certainly be wary of the myths surrounding them, the debate on the role played by myths in periods of revolution remains open. These periods are fertile in myths, which they forge and bequeath to later generations.

Thus the myth of William Tell, the legendary hero of Swiss independence, fired the imaginations of people seeking freedom during the French Revolution. In 1804 Schiller used it as the basis of a play which had enormous influence among the young liberals of Germany. Then in 1829 – just before the European upheavals of 1830 – Rossini made it into an opera, with a libretto by Hippolythe Bis and de Jouy. William Tell's exemplary adventure seems to date from the beginning of the Swiss uprising against the House of Hapsburg in the fourteenth century: a popular song from the end of the fifteenth century and many chapels bear witness to the fact that enthusiasm for the hero goes back a long way. But perhaps the myth's origins lie even further back in the European past: it is accepted today that the legend of the apple is of Nordic origins.

The fate of English revolutionary myths was very different: they fell into oblivion, or left behind sinister examples. In the second half of the fourteenth century a long poem attributed to William Langland, *The Vision of William Concerning Piers the Plowman*, had a profound influence on public opinion, which was manifested during the Peasants' Revolt of 1381. The vehement mysticism it expresses also impregnated the revolutionary declarations of the Levellers and Saints in the seventeenth century: the intolerance which triumphed in the civil war did not provide an example to be recommended in the future. The French revolutionaries of the eighteenth century knew little of the history of the English revolutions: all they remembered was the regicide carried out against the 'man of blood', Charles Stuart. The notable exception was the figure of Cromwell, which was deeply engraved in the memory and imagination of posterity – a terrifying image! In the preface of his *Cromwell*, Victor Hugo meditates on the myth of the regicide who hesitates as he is about to mount the throne: 'History has never hidden a higher lesson beneath a higher drama'. This is the moment when the failure of the English revolution is in the balance. It is the moment when an inner revolution erupts in the mind of the hero – the moment chosen by the poet to proclaim the literary revolution of the nineteenth century. In Victor Hugo's book the political inheritance of the French Revolution and the Empire mould the myth of Cromwell.

MYTHS OF THE FRENCH REVOLUTION

The French revolutionaries of 1789 found mythical examples in the history of past centuries. During the trial of Louis XVI, we see orators recalling other heroic regicides. Robespierre enlists two seventeenth-century English republicans in his Montagnard minority: 'Hampden and Sydney were in the minority, for they died on the scaffold'. In fact, although John Hampden (1594–1643) rose up against the absolutism of Charles I, he died of a wound received at the Battle of Chalgrove Field. As for Algernon Sydney (1622–83), while he certainly was beheaded following a conspiracy, he refused to vote for the trial of Charles I, thus incurring Cromwell's hostility. It is even more remarkable to see how the members of the National Convention, impregnated with classical culture, invoked an entirely legendary Brutus. The circumstances and motives for his deed were never compared with the trial of the king. Sometimes a detail enables us to identify Caesar's adopted son, or the Brutus who drove out Tarquin and was one of the founders of the Roman republic. But most often all is so vague that we cannot tell which of the two is being referred to. Moreover, it matters little: Brutus' bust is called as witness because he embodies an ideal of heroic murder and republican virtue; his distance in Roman Antiquity reinforces his prestige and seems to guarantee his reality.

The Revolution of 1789 produced new myths as it unfolded. There was a sort of cult of the martyrs to freedom (Le Pelletier, Marat) and to more humble 'patriot saints', such as Perrine Dugué in deepest Brittany. In an entirely secular way, a complex process of constructing heroes immortalized the courage of very young soldiers like Bara and Viala, at least in the collective memory. They became symbolic characters embodying popular awareness of the grandeur of the struggle, with its thirst for sacrifice and glory. The last and by no means least manifestation of these myths was the legend of Napoleon: as long as defeat by the allied kings was not accepted, there were rumours that he could not be dead and would return again from Saint Helena.

The 'Thermidorian period' following Robespierre's overthrow saw the birth of the legend of Robespierre the monster. In his *Memoirs Illustrating the History of Jacobinism* (1797–9), Abbé Barruel interpreted the entire Revolution as an immense conspiracy against religion, whose working-class mainspring, the Jacobins, were, like the medieval heretics, inspired by the Devil. At the same time, royalist historians and memoir writers began to tell the 'golden legend' of the Vendée uprisings. The Terror produced a true myth, whose development is clearly shown by Jean-Pierre Faye: the number of those condemned to death in 'Year II' was exaggerated out of all proportion (it was small compared to the number of victims of the White Terror, or those shot in the Bloody Week); and historical facts concerning the causes and true instigators of the Terror (the Royalists, Brissotins and Dantonistes, before Robespierre and his friends) were obscured. Thus the Terror ceased to refer to a well-defined historical period, took on the appearance of a true myth – the Revolution devouring its children – and became the 'Medusa's head that haunts western history and political thinking'. We can still feel its effects through the more recent episodes of our history – the Commune, fascism and Stalinism. We find its traces in Latin America in Augusto Roa Bastos' work *I the Supreme*, in which a character called Francia is the incarnation of the dictatorship which was the fatal outcome of the principles of 1789.

Danton and Robespierre became mythical heroes for later generations, as we see in Georg Büchner's play *Danton's Death* (1835) and in Andrzej Wajda's film *Danton* (1983). Two conceptions of revolution confront each other in these two characters: Danton embodies the human heart with its thirst for freedom and its weaknesses; Robespierre represents implacable reason that demands perfection and sacrifice. The Robespierre of revolutionary legends in fact has two faces: most often we see the inhuman monster, but to his followers of 1848 he was the apostle of social revolution and the martyr of Thermidor.

The inheritance of 1789 bore fruit in the revolutionary myths of the nineteenth century. Flaubert points to its survival – in the form of useless copies – in *Sentimental Education*. However, to say that the nineteenth-century revolutionaries were playing parts they had learned in advance is to deny a real capacity for innovation in the social domain, as attested by the right to work proclaimed in 1848 and the experiences of the Paris Commune. It is hard to distinguish between myths and revolutionary traditions. However, experience allows us to classify as a revolutionary myth the power of example attributed by the Blanquists to the popular insurrection in Paris, supposedly the necessary and efficient spark that set the powder off. There is no finer image of the instinctive love of freedom and revolutionary spontaneity of the Paris people than Gavroche in *Les Misérables*. This child is not entirely the product of Hugo's imagination: more than one observer had seen him on the barricades, and, before Hugo's work, Delacroix had painted him in his great picture *Liberty Guiding the People* (1831). Gavroche incarnates the people of Paris – a childlike people, uneducated but free, anti-authoritarian and always ready to rebel. His death, as depicted by Hugo, is a scene particularly rich in myths: from the very refrain of his song, 'It's Voltaire's fault, it's Rousseau's fault', to his response to the bullets – one gun-burst, one verse, one gun-burst, one verse – to the fact that he falls several times, but always gets up again. This 'fairy child' is only temporarily cut down, and Hugo compares him to Antaeus, suggesting that he is in fact immortal. This is a living myth, rather than an isolated literary creation: the figures of Gavroche and Enjolras were seen again on the student barricades of May 1968.

The twentieth century has inherited moments and symbolic heroes from the French Revolution: we find them at the time of the Front Populaire (with Jean Renoir's *La Marseillaise*) or in the thought of Resistance intellectuals (Saint-Just in Camus' *The Rebel*).

REVOLUTIONARY MYTHS THROUGHOUT THE WORLD

Revolutionary myths are extremely diverse; and an additional difficulty springs from the fact that it is hard to distinguish social revolution from national uprisings for independence. This is demonstrated in the history of the nineteenth century, when the influence of the French Revolution abroad and the circulation of ideas throughout liberal Europe favoured the internationalism of the revolutionary current. The result is a certain contamination of revolutionary myths.

Throughout the world, where has Garibaldi not contributed to a struggle for emancipation? We find him in South America, Italy and France by turns; sometimes he is a merchant, usually a soldier and always an adventurer. His ubiquity and aptitude for getting out of the cells in which he is imprisoned greatly contribute to his legendary character. Who are his enemies? Dictators, the Pope and capitulation. All this was engraved on the imagination of the communards; in 1870 Garibaldi had just added another page to his epic by fighting with his volunteers in France for the 'universal Republic'.

Spanish literature of the early twentieth century reflects libertarian aspirations by embodying them in a character (for example Pio Baroja in *La Aurora roja* in 1904). But it was above all in Latin America that revolutionary myths flourished. The Mexican revolution of the early twentieth century inspired a literature of agrarian revolt (Mariano Azuela, *Tierra*; Lopez y Fuentes, *Vamonos con Pancho Villa*). The epic dimension of the Mexican revolution was incarnated in its war leaders, Zapata and Pancho Villa, who became legendary, for both their hardness and their bravery in the service of the people. These heroes of the desperate rebellion of the Latin American peasants inspired many cinematic works: Eisenstein's *Que viva Mexico* and Ben Hecht's *Viva Villa* around 1930; Elia Kazan's *Viva Zapata* in 1959.

In Russia the revolts that were bloodily quashed by the Tsars were not forgotten: they heralded the future, and the talent of poets and film-makers gave them a legendary dimension. This was the case of the revolt of the Decembrists (18325), celebrated by Pushkin in *Winter Morning* (1829). Through Eisenstein's film, the mutiny on the battleship Potemkin in the Odessa harbour symbolizes the revolutionary union of the Russian army and people.

It is impossible to consider the whole world's revolutionary myths. The Sonrhaï empire struggling against the Moroccan domination of the southern Sahara in the sixteenth century had its own myths: local tradition alone preserves their memory, and this must be true in many other parts of the world. The twentieth century has discovered some of these myths, as the interest of researchers grows keener and internationalism deeper.

The work of Alejo Carpentier seems to me typical of thinking that crosses space and time. In *The Rite of Spring* the Cuban writer builds his novel around three successive revolutions: the Soviet revolution of 1917, the Spanish revolution of 1936 and the Cuban revolution of 1956. This tendency is characteristic of the twentieth century, which also creates revolutionary myths.

In fact revolutionary myths always flourish in revolutionary times. May 1968 offers an example of the concentration and creation of new myths. The memory of the great French Revolution haunted the barricades; but at the same time the murdered Ernesto Che Guevara was attaining immortality, and the distant horizon of China was offering western minds the myths of the 'Great Steersman' and the 'Little Red Book' (see Jean-Luc Goddard's film *La Chinoise*).

Historical science is constructed by detaching itself further and further from myth. But, at the same time, we see new myths being born in history as it is lived and particularly in revolutionary situations. This is because the hope of one day creating a better world on earth is still alive, and the revolutionary myth is a bearer of hope. In Louis Aragon's words:

Un jour pourtant, un jour viendra couleur d'orange
Un jour de palme, un jour de feuillages au front.
Un jour d'épaules nues où les gens s'aimeront
Un jour comme un oiseau sur la plus haute branche.

But one day will come a day the colour of oranges,
A day of palms, a day of leafy crowns
A day of naked shoulders when people will love each other
A day like a bird on the highest branch.

Claire Gaspard

Salome

Originally Salome was not even named: she was described in the Gospels only as 'the daughter of Herodias'. Both Mark and Matthew, in explaining Herod Antipas' superstitious fears when he heard of Jesus' miracles, tell how he had had John the Baptist put to death. Herodias, Herod Antipas' sister-in-law and second wife, wanted to wreak vengeance on John, who had condemned her unlawful marriage. Her daughter 'danced, and pleased' Herod at his birthday banquet, then used the tetrarch's own incautious promises to trap him ('Whatever you ask me, I will give you, even half my kingdom'): on her mother's advice she asked for the head of John the Baptist on a platter. The dance (which must have been exhilarating, to judge from its consequences) and the platter (to avoid dirtying her hands, or to serve up a really novel dish at the banquet?) are the only acts originating from the girl: when the executioner brought in John's head, the girl took it to her mother, thus indicating who had really instigated the crime.

The historical existence of this fatal dance is suspect. Ther is no other case of a princess dancing alone at a banquet for men in the Old or New Testaments, and it is a highly improbable event in first-century AD Judaea. The historian Flavius Josephus (*Jewish Antiquities*) says nothing about the dance or the beheading, indicating only that John the Baptist was imprisoned and executed for purely political reasons. Therefore it would seem appropriate to regard the anecdote not as a factual report, but as a withering moral indictment of the dissolute court of Herod Antipas, aggravating the culpability of those who put the forerunner and herald of Jesus to death around 29 AD.

The Gospels had a famous model in the story of Lucius Flamininus (or Flaminius), a governor of Gaul. Cicero, Livy, Seneca the Elder and Plutarch all relate the story with a number of variations, Seneca even commenting that the theme was already very hackneyed. To please a courtesan he loved (or his favourite, depending on which version we go by), who had never seen a beheading, Flamininus had a condemned man put to death during a sumptuous banquet. Some writers add that the prisoner had offended the courtesan, that she and Flamininus took part in lewd dancing, and that the executioner brought the head to the banqueting table. This brought the wrath of Cato the Censor down on Flamininus, and resulted in his exclusion from the Senate in 184 BC. Most of the elements in the Gospels are there – except that in the Gospels the dance is directly linked to the beheading, and the crime is perpetrated by *two* women. Comparisons have also been drawn between the death of John the Baptist and that of Cicero, whose severed head was taken to Fulvia, who avenged herself on her enemy by piercing his tongue – a detail which the Fathers of the Church were to graft on to the story of John the Baptist.

The name Salome (meaning 'the Peaceful' or the 'Peace-maker' – it was also the name of the cruel sister of Herod the Great, and of one of the 'Holy Women') is given by Josephus, who tells us where the execution took place (Machaerus) and enlarges on the biography of the historical Salome. She was the daughter of Herodias and Herod Philip, the stepbrother of Herod Antipas, and married her uncle Philip; after being widowed she ended up as the queen of Lower Armenia, married to King Aristobulus; she bore three sons. She is depicted on a coin from Nicopolis, and this is the only true portrait of her. As for Herod and Herodias (by Josephus' account the latter had a lot in common with Lady Macbeth), they were exiled by Caligula to Lugdunum (Lyons, or according to a mediaeval tradition to Saint-Bertrand-de Comminges).

Be that as it may, the story of Salome as it is told in the Gospels – especially in Mark, who gives a more dramatic and subtle account than Matthew – established the fundamentals of a scene that was to have a prolific posterity: the superstitious fear of the tetrarch who feels an ambiguous admiration for John the Baptist; Herodias' hatred of the austere prophet; her daughter's spellbinding dance; the drunken, amorous promise made by Herod Antipas to the dancer; the request for the saint's head on a platter; Herod's qualms; and the handing over of the head to Herodias. There are episodes in the Old Testament that share some of the features of these Gospel accounts: the story of Elijah, Ahab and Jezebel (the same opposition betwen a prophet and a luxury-loving queen); that of Ahasuerus and Esther (the same promise prompted by love); and especially the story of Judith who seduced Holofernes and cut off his head – with the difference that she did the deed herself, with patriotism as her motive. But Salome's historically improbable dance, which is based on just three words (*saltavit et placuit*), makes all the difference: she silenced the voice crying in the wilderness. Even the historian Renan could not resist the all-too-thrilling story of the equivocal dancing-girl and the severed head.

While Herod (who in Mark's version has John put to death with great reluctance) and Herodias are given coherent characters in the Gospel, Herodias' daughter remains the incognita: her age, her motives, her reactions to the beheading are not mentioned, and the silence concerning them came to be filled in later centuries with some strange tales.

The Fathers of the Church – who called Salome Herodias, perhaps because they confused her with her mother, or following one possible translation of Mark – turned her into the epitome of 'woman as an instrument of the devil', and cited her as an example of the fatal consequences of lascivious dancing: an ecclesiastical council had forbidden dancing in sacred places. Their religious loathing added juicy details to the short account in the Gospels: Salome twisting her hips, uncovering her body, kicking her feet in the air, shaking her hair like a Bacchante. The Serpent was hidden in this luxuriously adorned woman, who was assimilated to the Synagogue that had put Christ to death; the Devil was leading the dance and advising Salome's mother. The two women were also compared to tigresses feeding on human flesh and drinking blood. A just punishment was meted out to them. From the fourth century, in accordance with the *poena talionis* (punishment to fit the crime), the dancer died with her head severed when the ice of a frozen river formed round her neck, while her mother and Herod were eaten alive by worms. Salome's shamelessness, the behaviour of a courtesan, is in stark opposition to John the Baptist's indomitable chastity. His personality as the greatest of saints, the last of the prophets, the first Christian martyr, a relation of Christ's and the person who foretold and baptized him, serves as a foil to heighten the heinousness of Salome's crime, making her the killer of God. But Salome has never played more than a very subsidiary role in the hagiography of John the Baptist: she is merely the means whereby he met his death.

From the early Middle Ages many legends were in their turn to embroider on the Gospel story, and more particularly to dream up exemplary punishments for Salome. They were linked with the popular rites celebrating the feasts of St John (24 June and 29 August), a saint with healing powers and the patron saint of many craft or trade guilds. As well as Salome's decapitation by ice, which can be found in Greek or Spanish legends and in Nicephorus Callistus's *Historia ecclesiastica*, she – or Herodias with whom she is so often confused – is killed by a deadly blast of air issuing from the mouth of the dead saint, or swallowed up by the earth (*Legenda aurea*). Germanic tales dating from the high Middle Ages feature Salome taking part in the 'wild chase' on the night of St John, when sinners who have to expiate their crimes for ever are dragged off into outer space. The twelfth-century poem *Reinardus Vulpes* was almost certainly the first version to portray Salome (called Pharaïldis) as being passionately in love with John the Baptist: when Herod has him killed she weeps copiously over the severed head, attempts to kiss it and is killed by the storm that issues from the saint's mouth. Seen as a 'wandering Jewess' participating in the hellish chase, the Goddess of Darkness, the organizer of night-time sabbaths, Salome-Herodias was put in the company of Holda, Diana, Abonde and Benzozia, becoming the Queen of the Witches with the bishops inveighing against her. In Italy, Germany and France she was confused with popular fairies, thereby demonstrating the survival of paganism: in these legends she was accorded supremacy over 'a third of the earth'.

All these traditions are reflected in the iconography of evangeliaries, tympanums, stained glass windows and baptisteries. In these Salome is sometimes depicted as a tumbler or acrobat with her feet in the air, as on the doorway of Rouen Cathedral, which may have inspired Flaubert. Flemish and Italian Renaissance pictures, which fascinated late nineteenth-century poets, endowed Salome with the same serene, luminous beauty as the Virgin, making her undeniably ambiguous.

From the thirteenth to the seventeenth centuries French, German and Italian mystery plays added the Devil and his demons or Death to the list of characters in the drama, and they finally led mother and daughter off to hell in a dance of death, which closely reflected Salome's second dance with the severed head. Then there were scholarly tragedies in Latin based on the character of John the Baptist, written for the purpose of edifying and teaching, sometimes with a clown included to introduce a comic note. From the end of the sixteenth century to the end of the eighteenth, many 'tragedies of St John' used the figure of the forerunner and herald of Christ for religious or political ends, in connection with the crises and movements of the day: John might, for example, represent Luther. *Baptistes*, a Latin version by the Scottish Calvinist Buchanan (published in 1577) which made a great impact in Europe, reflects on the rights and duties of a Prince; John was modelled on Thomas More and Salome played only a minor role. The obscuring of the figure of Salome or the watering down of the story may also have been due to considerations of artistic propriety: the German drama *Der Tod Johannes des Täufers* (Hudemann, 1770) cut out the dance, presenting Salome as the loving fiancée of Prince Philip. But the most memorable play is that by the Zurich theologian Leonard Meister (*Johannes der Vorläufer*, 1793), which contains two themes that herald the nineteenth-century treatments of Salome: Herodias attempting to seduce John, and Salome asking for his head to use it as a plaything.

Salome as a literary myth was really invented in the second half of the nineteenth century, though this new Salome of course drew on all the elements that tradition and literature had added to the biblical account. The figure of Salome was then cut free in a spectacular fashion from the religious story and iconography to evolve on its own, incarnating the archetype of the adored and execrated *femme fatale*, fascinating yet terrifying, a goddess of beauty and eroticism. Opposite her, John became a mere foil, a melodramatic adjunct. In the Italian play *Erodiade* by Silvio Pellico (1833) Salome is still just a little girl, and all the interest revolves round Herod and Herodias as a couple. But Heinrich Heine, a renegade Romantic who went back to the old Germanic legends in his epic poem *Atta Troll* (1841), makes Herodias-Salome his idol, a pale spectre taking part in a noisy, joyful 'doomed chase' in the Pyrenees, kissing John's severed head and tossing it in the air like a ball. Through a generalization that was soon to become stereotyped, she incarnated the principle of the 'Eternal Female', with all female psychology being resumed in her: 'Would a woman ever ask for the head of a man she did not love?' This mad, half-naked Herodiade demonstrates a nostalgia for the paganism of a dream world, and a desire to experience a new beauty, coming 'from heaven or hell, what does it matter', like that extolled by Baudelaire. *Atta Troll*, a blast against 'virtuous folly', bewildered the French public: when it was translated in 1847 all that poets retained from it was the highly imaginative evocation of Herodiade. It supplied the epigraph of a poem by Banville, and heralded a series of humorous versions of Salome, such as Gutzkow's (1869) or Laforgue's (1886); Laforgue was a great admirer of Heine.

Thus it was Heine who ushered in the character who became the ultimate *fin de siècle* myth, and a dominant collective obsession. All forms of art, literary, plastic, musical and theatrical, put themselves at her service, and journalists and chroniclers further fed her fame. In 1912 Maurice Krafft, who has often been quoted, claimed to have counted 2,789 poems in honour of Salome. Short stories and plays (but very few novels, interestingly enough; the story has more to do with dreams than narrative) made the dancing figure their dominant motif. The collective obsession was in fact reinforced by the fame of certain works, which in turn prompted others. Thus from 1870 Henri Régnault's painting of *Salomé* inspired poems by Banville or Charles Buet, as well as numerous articles, all hailing the 'true' Salome who had at last been revealed, a gypsy with a carnivorous smile on a yellow background waiting to be handed the saint's head. The tragic death of the painter at an early age increased the notoriety of his painting, which was still being talked about in 1912 – he had painted his own death in Salome. Throughout the second half of the nineteenth century so-called 'literary' painting and decadent or Symbolist writing were in continuous dialogue. The Salon displayed a good hundred paintings and sculptures of Salome between 1870 and 1914.

Gustave Moreau's two masterpieces (*Salomé dansant devant Hérode* in oil, and *L'Apparition* in water-colour) at the 1876 Salon (at the very time when Flaubert was writing *Hérodias*) made an exceptional impact. Moreau succeeded in endowing the dancing figure with a hieratic, sacred character, clothing her in a cascade of gems in line with his principles of 'beautiful inertia' and 'necessary richness'. Huysmans belatedly discovered the two pictures in his novel *A Rebours* (1884), celebrating them in such exalted terms that it marked an epoch; in his memorable lines Salome became 'the deity symbolizing indestructible lasciviousness, the goddess of immortal Hysteria'. Lorrain, Lahor, Montesquiou and André Godin were also inspired by Moreau's work in their poems written between 1885 and 1912. The same novel by Huysmans quoted the fragments of the uncompleted *Hérodiade* by Mallarmé, which the poet had worked on from 1864 until his death. Ignoring the 'archaic news snippet', Mallarmé made Herodias-Salome an untouchable, stonelike virgin 'with a diamond-clear gaze', close to the swan trapped in the ice in the famous sonnet. Singing of 'the horror of being a virgin', she awaits her bloody marriage with the saint, an impossible union between Genius and Beauty, which is an allegory for poetry. His version of *Hérodiade* was translated into English by G. Moore and A. Symons, who were also devotees of Salome.

We do not know whether Flaubert was inspired by Moreau, but his short store *Hérodias* (though he denied this) is one of the few attempts at an archaeological reconstruction of the theme, based on Josephus and Renan. His distinctive contribution lies in the unparalleled detail with which he describes Salome's dance, and in suggesting a fusion between the two women, with Salome rekindling the former erotic power of Herodias. The atmosphere of decadence embodied by Aulus Vitellius at a banquet worthy of Petronius is in contrast with the power of Iaokanann (John) and the compelling presence of his severed head – 'The head entered,' Flaubert wrote. At the end, in a symbolic dawn heralding the era of Christ triumphant, his disciples carry the saint's weighty head off towards Galilee.

In English literature Swinburne and O'Shaughnessy evoked Herodias and Salome among other sultry, imperious women from the past. In his dramatic poem *Herodias* (1867) J. C. Heywood charges the mother with the crime, exonerating Salome, whose love for John is pure. Milliet and Grémont used the same approach in the libretto for Massenet's opera *Hérodiade* (1881), as did J. de Pesquidoux, and Brunette and Jurion in tragedies in verse (1898 and 1899) – however, these are tainted by affectation.

Between the 'Gustave Moreau constellation' and the 'Oscar Wilde constellation' a stream of sonnets (by D'Annunzio, Lorrain, Lahor, Stuart Merrill, Louÿs, Samain and others) and miscellaneous poems described the dancing girl, traditionally decked with jewels. They often saved the saint's bleeding head for the 'fall' of the final line, in a somewhat facile effect. By way of contrast, Laforgue's version 'Moralité légendaire' (1886) was highly original: in it Salome does not dance, she declaims a hermetic text in the babble of one possessed by the Unconscious, in which incongruous, erotic appeals are hidden. Intended as a parody of Flaubert and written in an 'artistic' style laden with allusions and puns, this tale puts forward a none-too-critical denunciation of the quirks of decadence and the new woman – an aesthete and a blue stocking. It is reminiscent of Gutzkov's novella, *Die ewige Jüdin*, where John is a 'Communist' and Salome a flirt who is cited as a warning to heartless women. Laforgue's Salome was adapted by Ezra Pound in 1920. There is the same mood of irony in K. Hartmann-Plön's *Herodias*, in which a young man is dissuaded by the biblical story from marrying a heartless woman, and in P. Heyse's novel, *Merlin* (1892), where the beheading of John the Baptist is staged in a mental asylum – and the doctors have to interrupt the proceedings.

Wilde's *Salomé*, written in French (the language of naughty novels to Victorian England), is unquestionably the most famous version of all, thanks to the scandal provoked by Wilde's morals, Beardsley's venomous, sarcastic illustrations (1894) and above all Strauss's opera which is based on it (1905). Mario Praz deplores this state of affairs: 'The Salomes of Flaubert, Moreau, Laforgue and Mallarmé are known only to the literate and cultivated, but the Salome written by that brilliant charlatan Wilde is known to everyone.' It seems that Wilde originally intended to make a humorous contribution to the Salome craze. Trapped by his subject, however, he only succeeded in relaunching it more powerfully than ever, and exposing fully what had only been hinted at by his predecessors. Censorship prevented Sarah Bernhardt from staging his play in which Salome's erotic passion and the motif of necrophilia in the kissing of the severed head are so strikingly expressed; Strauss's 'wild' music further heightens the hysterical cry of the young woman. The unity of time, action and place, the concentration on the character of Salome, the language which oscillates between the strange stiltedness of a conversation manual and plagiarism from the Song of Solomon, and the possible mysticism of Salome, whom Wilde compares to St Teresa, combine to make this very disturbing play one of the most unforgettable celebrations of Herodias' daughter. In conjunction with Strauss's opera it inspired pictures and poems – and also caricatures by music-hall artists (one showed a 'Salome-Jaurès' procuring Briand's head in 1907, another in 1912 invented an 'Anti-Salomic League'). Wilde's play, which was translated all over the world (into German, Polish, Hungarian, Czech and even Yiddish, as well as other languages), spawned other writing. In J. Lauff's *Herodias* and M. Bruns's *Der Täufer* (1896) John is on the verge of succumbing to Salome's or Herodias' charms. Sudermann (*Johannes*, 1898) and the Polish writer Kasprowicz (*Uczta Herodiady*, 1905) revert to the motif of Salome's wild passion for the precursor of Jesus, describing her dancing with the bloody platter to avenge his refusal. Oscar Panizza who created as much scandal as Wilde with his *Liebeskonzil* (1895) depicted a Salome straight out of hell, the Devil's consort and mother of all-conquering Syphilis – which earned him a year in jail. At the turn of the century the Lithuanian poet Milosz, writing in French, formally expressed the latent sacrilege already hinted at by Heine: 'La vie d'un Sage ne vaut pas, ma Salomé,/ Ta danse d'Orient sauvage comme la chair . . .' ('The life of a wise man, dear Salome, is worth less than your Eastern dance, wild as the flesh . . .').

The figure of Salome was by then so well known that it had become commonplace. In paintings, any naked jewel-decked woman was called 'Salome'; in literature and on the stage every female dancer or wilful woman was more or less a Salome.

Apollinaire too celebrated Salome, firstly in a short story of ironic, familiar soberness inspired by the medieval legends, then in a poem where the crazed girl intersperses counting rhymes with cries of despair. Salome's jewellery had lost its lustre, and the dancing girl, as in Picasso's drawing (1905), had gradually lost her decadent finery. Just before 1914, R. de Souza spitefully refused his head to the woman he called 'the Eternal'. Loïe Fuller and Ida Rubinstein were still to dance in *La Tragédie de Salomé* to music by Florent Schmitt, and the first sirens of the cinema dressed up as Salome – and then the First World War came along, producing a distracted and very real dancer, Mata Hari, who was shot in the trenches at Vincennes.

Thus the *fin de siècle* Salome celebrated from the Romantic period to the dawn of Surrealism had – besides the inevitable platter – essential, easily recognizable attributes (jewels, veils, scents, lilies or lotuses, the black panther, the locust, the snake, darkness and the moon). She was always a very literary or a very pictorial creation, depending on a pre-existing text or representation, and the way in which stories and poems portrayed her was characteristic. She might be one of a litany of *femmes fatales* conjured up by wistful poets, leading a cohort of Eves, Helens, Semiramises, Cleopatras and other Judiths (Banville, D'Annunzio, Retté, Lorrain, Nechansky). Or again she might appear in a dream, lasciviously conjured up as entertainment for bachelor evenings (Samain, Fleischmann), in pictures by Luini or Moreau, or in imaginary paintings, the memory of which haunted the poet (Huysmans, Bein, Hartmann-Plön), in theatrical productions of the biblical episode, with theatre and reality coming together to bring things to a (bad) end (Lorrain, Heyse). Her story could also be used as an ironic moral illustration for a contemporary anecdote (Gutzkow). In the work of both Laforgue and Wilde the words evoking her, a pot-pourri of allusions and disguised quotations, establish the same distance between Salome and the public, as if to defuse the danger that she represents.

The way that Salome came into prominence during the decadent and Symbolist period – and Salome is more decadent than Symbolist, because of the bloodstained bad taste of her story and her dusky refinement, set against which John might well represent the Barbarian – can no doubt be explained by the fact that, more than any other woman, she concentrated in her person all the characteristics of the *femme fatale* as a dominating obsession of the time. The contemporary setting of certain stories (e.g. F. Zilcken, *Herodes*, 1902) was mainly aimed at illustrating the redoubtable permanence of the race of Salomes, from Mary Queen of Scots and Queen Christina of Sweden to the fashionable prostitutes of 1900. Some authors, such as Jean Lorrain, put Salome at the very centre of their oeuvre, under a variety of guises ranging from the exotic dancer to grotesque travesty. A 'phallic' woman and a castrator (even before Freud and Lou Andreas-Salome, the Decadents knew full well what it was all about), she became a focus for all the phantasms of a misogyny that was reactivated by the feminist movements. Laforgue's Salome is a blue-stocking who refuses to marry, but 'initiates herself' secretly; other Salomes embody the danger women represent with regard to syphilis (Huysmans, Panizza) or frightening virginity (Mallarmé). Not content with treating herself to a saint's head, she wades boldly in by displaying female desire, lascivious puberty, a woman's instincts that are controlled by the Unconscious. Unassuaged like Messalina, she keeps calling out (like Lewis Carroll's Queen of Hearts) 'Off with his head!' The biblical episode as perceived in the 1890s thus became the myth of the everlasting battle between man and woman, mind and flesh, the intellect and the irrational, thought and beauty. In it, love and death exchange their attributes. The orientalism then in vogue adorned Salome with all the seductiveness of sensual exoticism. As a Jewess she was denounced by anti-Semites (Lorrain, Buet), and contrasted with Joan of Arc or St Geneviève. Since her crime was a reminder of the collective wrongdoing which resulted in the beheading of a king, in a period of moral order Salome was characterized as the incendiary who set society alight and brought about bloodshed, the frontline female Freemason or anticlerical, and eventually a female spy working for the Enemy. But how equivocal those denunciations are, accompanied as they are by a delirious masochism which pushes poets – often men whose Christian name is John – to wish '*to lose their heads*' for her, and possess her by sacrificing themselves!

Finally, among all these *fin de siècle* avatars of Salome, very few are based on archaeological reconstruction or philosophical reflection. The figure of Salome is developed above all through associations of ideas, in the ambivalence and ambiguity of the world of dreams: she is both a virgin and a *cut-throat's* harlot; adored as a goddess and vilified as a whore; a hysterical little girl and an allegory of the epitome of Womanhood. The shape of the sibilant first letter of her name sums her up: it is the Art Nouveau curve and the snake symbolizing sin; her dance is the language of desire and a manifestation of terrifying beauty. She reduces to impotence, both artistic and sexual, poets who identify with the *beheaded* man or the jaded tyrant whose senses only she can arouse. If things are carried to their ultimate conclusion, she can become a representation of the supreme work of art to which the only possible response is death.

After the First World War Salome continued to crop up from time to time, as a psychoanalytical phantasm (*L'Age d'Homme* by M. Leiris) or a fleeting reference in a novel (*Un Beau Ténébreux* by J. Gracq), or in a short story with historical pretensions (R. Puaux). Robert Desnos stands alone, playing on the alliteration of the 'Nus nénés' (bare boobs) of Herodias' daughter. As there is a resemblance between the end of every century, ballet and cinema still occasionally conjure up this most famous of women dancers. The myth would lend itself very well to a feminine, and feminist treatment – not so far forthcoming. Women painters have evoked Salome, and some women poets have celebrated her, but without really departing from the traditional male, misogynous 'interpretation'. But in 1968 in the United States it seems that a militant Women's Libber, naked like Salome, presented a calf's head on a platter to the managing director of *Playboy* magazine.

Mireille Dottin

Satan

'The real, unrivalled, profoundest theme of the history of the world and of mankind, to which all others are subordinate, remains the conflict between unbelief and belief,' Goethe wrote as a footnote in his *West-östlicher Divan*. What could be more true? For many believers, for Pope Paul VI who spoke of the presence of a 'living, spiritual being that is perverted and corrupting', Satan could not possibly be reduced to a mythical, functional personification, the simple product of story-telling or projection. St Paul had already recognized him as really being an apostate angel who had become evil through jealousy of man, based on the concept of the sin he inspires and the temptation he suggests.

Satan was derived from the contact between Chaldean angelogony and Zoroastrianism after the period of Jewish captivity in Babylon. Up until then Satan had been a subordinate servant, but at this time he emerged as a rival God, a fierce adversary, a contradictor. Arising from an indeterminate supernatural principle, he thereafter took on the most varied forms in order to travel the world spreading doubt, blasphemy and news of the punishments in the world hereafter. This accounts for the fact that he appears fifty-three times in the New Testament, whereas the Old Testament mentions him almost only incidentally. His fate was already linked with that of Yahweh (some of whose unpleasant aspects he incarnated), and was to be even more closely linked with that of Christ, and consequently that of mankind, offered up to his insatiable covetousness. With the help of religious art, scholastic knowledge and literature, the figure of Satan took on in the course of time ever greater proportions, due to the fact that writers found a totally irresistible variety of themes and shades of meaning in describing his deadly qualities. Moreover, in their 'diabolical' desire to satisfy creative ambition, very few would hesitate to seek his collaboration, even his complicity. As the sole embodiment of Evil, he has ended up dealing on equal terms with a single God who incarnates all Good. And Michelet when he presented *La Sorcière* could exclaim:

> The Devil is a dogma, no more no less, that affects all other dogmas. Does contact with the defeated everlasting not imply contact with the victor? Doubting the feats of the former leads on to doubting the feats of the latter, the miracles which he performed with the specific purpose of combatting the Devil. The columns of heaven stand in the abyss. The foolhardy person who shakes their foundations in hell can cause cracks in paradise. People today keep saying *ad nauseam* that God is dead, but surely it seems that Satan has outlived him, stirring up so many wars, instances of genocide and holocausts?

Sartre was wont to say that hell is other people, referring to a phrase that Marlowe in *Doctor Faustus* put into Mephistopheles' mouth: 'Why this is hell, nor am I out of it'. It is a fact that the inversion of values, words and signs, the disorder reigning in people's minds, the anguish at the thought of a nuclear apocalypse and the ever-present arguments defending violence and eroticism that characterize our present-day society may lead a sincere believer to think that Evil is a person, enjoying an independent existence – an existence that is in some way necessary to justify the free choice human beings enjoy either to submit to Evil or reject it.

In attempting to stick as closely as possible to the development of a literary myth and adopting a resolutely rationalist stance, we will not examine the everyday, primarily eschatological consequences that result from the ontological reality of a devilish personality. Satan – who is referred to by such circumlocutions as the Tempter, Father of Lies, Prince of this World, Prince of Darkness, the archfiend, the Evil One, the serpent or Old Nick – is just an unfounded hypothesis, a metaphysical entity, 'a malign invention by men to justify their baseness' (Maxim Gorky). Seignobos commented that it would be impossible to reconcile his existence with the laws of all existing sciences. But that does not imply the radical elimination of the psychological impression whereby each and every one of us may conjure up or endure the presence of a mythical Satan, a projection of our desires or our fears. In *The Demon* by Lermontov, the demon of the title murmurs:

> I am the one you listened to in the darkness at midnight, the one whose thoughts whispered to your soul, the one whose sadness you vaguely divined, the one whose image you saw in your dreams; the one whose gaze kills hope, loved by nobody, the scourge of my earthly slaves, the king of knowledge and freedom, the enemy of heaven, the evil in nature.

Satan seen as an archetype engendered by our ancestral fear of outer darkness – in which, according to Dante, all hope abandons us – has become a kind of catalyst of phantasms, while at the same time being an ideal philosophical argument to explain the omnipresence of Evil. The myth of Satan thus takes shape as soon as creative thought and discourse get under way, conferring life on him and according him power. 'The Devil is a myth, therefore he exists and is always active,' was Denis de Rougemont's reply to sceptics. From that starting point the subjective, but amazingly malleable myth, which can adapt to the most varied socio-cultural contexts, takes on countless facets, especially in the realm of literature, reserving perpetual surprises for us. In contrast to some myths the inevitable (and so very trite!) denouement of which we know only too well, the myth involving the devil introduces a multitude of variants in a constantly shifting universe. He is legion, epitomizing plurality and metamorphosis. Hence the vortex of magical combinations involving evocations, spells, incubi, possession, pacts, sabbaths, lycanthropy and the whole arsenal of withcraft, rooted deep in the darkness of time. Hence also the feeling of metaphysical anguish experienced by everyone who believes in the existence of Satan, quite distinct from the pleasurable thrill of terror that reading tales of the fantastic is intended to induce.

THE DURABILITY OF A MEDIEVAL ARCHETYPE

We know what a determining influence the hallucinations and visions of monks had when it came to turning to Lucifer the bearer of light, the most beautiful of the angels, into a hairy, deformed monster, which in the course of time became an object of derision and ended up as 'Old Horny', a figure of fun. The accepted principle of physical deformity can be found in countless stories, even in the recent past. Henri Troyat in *Les Mains* describes 'a little, short waddling man with a roundish stomach' whose wife – who had been his manicurist – discovers without great surprise that he has cloven hoofs. Michel de Ghelderode claimed he had met Satan in London, with the same cloven hoofs but, as if to live up to expectation, adopting the familiar appearance of Mephistopheles as he appeared on the stage – 'dressed all in scarlet from the cock's feather on his hat to the points of his shoes', a fluent and distinguished conversationalist to boot, but looking older just the same. The Franco-Flemish Mystery plays (*Le Jeu d'Adam, Le Miracle de Théophile, Mariken Van Nymegen, Le Mystère de la Passion*, etc.), imbued with didacticism and wallowing in the supernatural, had previously emphasized the sordid, despicable aspects of Satan's behaviour to such an extent that they made him familiar to a huge public, who were always calling for his appearance on the stage. At least he and his little devils would create an ambience of jollity, which Rabelais described in the following terms:

> These devils were all decked out in the skins of wolves, calves and rams[. . .] girded round with great straps with large cowbells and little mule bells hanging from them, which made a horrible racket. Some held black sticks full of fuses in their hands, others carried long burning firebrands and at each crossroads they threw handfuls of powdered 'parasins' on them producing terrible flames and smoke.

In the absence of any works of real literary merit, spectacle and display thus kept enthusiastic crowds in suspense and gave the myth of Satan every appearance of reality. Eloy d'Amerval, a priest attached to the church of Béthune whose poem *La Grand Diablerie* appeared towards the end of the fifteenth century, gave him very short shrift:

> Satan, Satan, ne'er-do-well, swindler,
> Satan, foul, vile and stinking,
> Abominable creature,
> Enemy of human nature,
> Hypocrite and humbug
> From whom come the science and art

> Of every false fiction,
> Pretence and dissimulation;
> You great eater of crucifixes!

The inspiration in *Les Miracles* by Gautier de Coincy written between 1218 and 1227 is scarcely any more scintillating. Satan welcoming the deacon Théophile stipulates fairly baldly:

> But he cannot have my grace
> If he does not deny his faith,
> His God and Mary the Mother of God [. . .]
> And with no delay he must
> Give me good proof of it;
> For many Christians have greatly deceived me.

However, things were different in Italy, where poets worthy of the name magnified the *terribilità* of the Adversary. Dante, faithful to the Scriptures and to antiquity in his description of the *città dolente*, made the devil into a three-headed giant, whose six huge wings spread an icy wind over the River Cocytus, while Marino conjured up his darting glances from which flashes of lightning emanated (*Strage degli innocenti*) and Tasso celebrated the horrible majesty of his countenance: 'Orrida maestà nel fero aspetto/ Terrore accresce, e più superbo il rende'.

The monstrous character that haunted the dreams of Raoul Glaber in the dormitory at Cluny, and which appeared in sculpted form for centuries on cathedral tympanums and on the stage in the mystery plays, re-emerged hardly altered physically with the publication of Le Sage's novel *Le Diable boiteux* in 1707. We are told that he had:

> goat's legs, a long face, a pointed chin, a yellowish black complexion, and a very squashed nose; his eyes which seemed very small were like two burning coals, and above his excessively gaping mouth were two tufts of a red moustache and his two lips were like no other lips.

Basically this demon, whom the author calls Asmodée, is not so very wicked, showing his gratitude towards Don Cléophas, who has freed him from imprisonment in a bottle, by offering to show him the other side of the world – in other words the world as it really is. This theme was picked up by Alfred Le Poittevin in his *Promenade de Bélial*, in which Asmodée reveals himself as 'the Venus whom Lucretia invoked in that great poem you know'. Lucifer, Asmodeus, Belial, Venus – Satan has a marvellous way of confusing the issue and making us forget that he still is and always has been a murderer. In *the Monk* by Matthew Gregory Lewis (1797) he reverted to his 'classically' sinister looks when appearing to Prior Ambrosio: the prior, accused of rape, murder and witchcraft, has just fallen into the hands of the Inquisition:

> He showed himself in all the ugliness that had been his lot since his fall from heaven; his burnt limbs still bore the marks of the Almighty's thunderbolt; a

> swarthy complexion darkened his huge body; his hands and feet were armed with long claws; his eyes shone with a rage that would have struck terror into the bravest heart; on his great shoulders two enormous black wings were beating, and instead of hair he had living serpents that twisted round his forehead with dreadful hissings.

It is again a 'wild cannibal's gaze, contemplating the victim he is about to devour' that Satan turns on us in Frédéric Soulié's *Les Mémoires du Diable* and Gérard de Nerval's *La Sonate du Diable*. Nevertheless he will go to great lengths to hide the offputting aspects of his appearance. In spite of a permanent limp which Théophile Gautier stresses in *Albertus* (as lame as Byron, but no lamer'), he is capable of making himself completely attractive to us, if René Clément is to be believed: 'He makes his hard, red hair black and curly,/ Hiding his reddened skin with silk and fine cloth/ He can at will give himself a slender figure' (*Albert Love, ou l'Enfer*).

And, finally, he has no greater scruples about seducing us physically when the opportunity arises – in the guise of the ravishing Clarimonde in *La Morte amoureuse*, a she-demon and a vampire whom Gautier describes as 'Beelzebub in person', or of Biondetta, the ambivalent hero-heroine of Cazotte's *Le Diable amoureux* (1772). In this novel, which is a subtle analysis of the process of temptation, Satan, temporarily abandong any horrific characteristics, succeeds in winning the love of Alvare, a man 'hungry for new ideas', who would not be put off by the idea of a succubus:

> Let a little of this delightful flame that sets my veins on fire flow into yours; soften the sound of your voice if you can, a voice so well suited to inspiring love but which you use too much, so frightening my timid soul; then say to me, if you can, as tenderly as I feel towards you: my dear Beelzebub, I adore you.

And since, when it comes down to it, Satan is still Satan, Biondetta disappears after intercourse, transformed into a gigantic camel. As it happens, Alvare is far luckier than the lovers who hold incomparable beauties in their arms in the silence of the night, only to find beside them at daybreak the stinking carcass of some witch. Many *Histoires véritables* published in the sixteenth century mention this type of let-down. It might also happen that the devil would carry off men who were too sensual, as he nearly did in the case of *Thibaud de la Jacquière*, whose amorous adventures are recounted by Gérard de Nerval: 'I am not Orlandine, said the monster in a formidable voice, I am Beelzebub!'

To sum up, with the exception of Cazotte's *Le Diable amoureux*, Satan's appearances in literature up to the Romantic period are both terrifying and redoubtable, and it is hard to understand why so many people of every social condition should have tried to sign a pact involving love, money or power with him; all the more so as the conclusion of the contract was frequently accompanied by painful sexual relations and threats towards signatories who were not too careful about respecting the clauses. Here again the medieval fiction preserved an obvious perenniality: from the very famous and typical legend of the deacon Theophilus, saved on his deathbed by the intervention of Mary, to the case of the musician Leverkühn for whom 'art has now become impossible without the help of Satan and the infernal fire below the cauldron' (Thomas Mann, *Doktor Faustus*). Moreover, the universally accepted belief that an implicit pact might deliver up this person to Satan, with no reference to his or her own will, opened up a huge field to myth and fantasy. The detailed description of the signature of promissory notes by Dr Faust in the work of Marlowe and Goethe, by Rodolphe de Westerbourg in *Petit Pierre* by Spiess, Chamisso's *Peter Schlemihl*, Maturin's *Melmoth* and the wicked young people portrayed by Nodier and Mac Orlan in *Infernalia* and *Malice* alike has been succeeded by the simple but pervasive atmospheric diabolism of contemporary literature. 'The enemy of the human race is in our midst, recognizable only by the brilliance and devastating eloquence of his grey eyes,' André Breton wrote in this connection. The origin of this prestigious aura can be found in Oscar Wilde's *The Portrait of Dorian Gray*, or even more in the work of Honoré de Balzac. In *La Peau de Chagrin* Balzac excludes all considerations of salvation or damnation, leaving Raphaël with the choice of deciding his fate around Power and Will. The magic shagreen tells him, 'If you possess me you will possess everything. But your life will belong to me. God has willed it thus. Wish, and your wishes will be fulfilled, but regulate your wishes according to your life. It is there. With each wish I am diminished, as are your days. Do you want me?'

SATAN AS A ROMANTIC HERO

It might well have been thought that after the devil had been laughed to scorn by Piron, the 'Philosophes' and Voltaire as a figure described by the latter as the fruit of 'disgusting, horrible and absurd imaginings', the myth of Satan would vanish for ever from the minds of men. But any such idea would have failed to reckon with the crowd's passion for the weird and wonderful, reflected in the quick success gained by the Gothic novels and a return to medieval sources, fostered by Goethe, E. T. A. Hoffmann and Charles Nodier in particular, who strove to restore the malevolent aura of a character they accepted as real. Moreover, Anglomania was very much in fashion in France at the beginning of the nineteenth century, resulting in Milton's *Paradise Lost* being reread in a new light. In sharp contrast to the medieval mystery plays, Milton affirmed that Satan in his exile had lost none of his original beauty, and Byron hastened to confirm this, exclaiming: 'oh Heaven!/ Save *his* who made, what beauty and what power/ Was ever like to Satan's?' (*Heaven and Earth*, 11. 580–2). George Sand reaffirmed this, saying he was 'the most beautiful of the immortals after God, the saddest after Jesus, and the proudest of the proud' (*Consuelo*). Full of admiration for the tenacious spirit which Milton had ascribed to the Accursed One, Schiller spoke of a 'monster with majesty', and Chateaubriand regarded *Paradise Lost* as 'one of the most sublime and moving conceptions ever to issue from the brain of a poet' (*La Génie du Christianisme*). And finally Baudelaire commented in his *Journaux intimes* that 'the most perfect example of manly beauty is Satan – as described by Milton'.

If most of the Romantic authors were unanimous in restoring the glory of the Prince of Darkness which had been very much tarnished by the Encyclopedists, their ideas as to his behaviour varied widely. Some described him as a heroic insurgent, a blasphemous rebel; others portrayed him as a wretched creature trying to win the hearts of men, while others still had no hesitation in affirming that God would one day pardon him his terrible wrongdoing.

The first trend was represented by Lord Byron who, as Afred de Vigny put it, 'devoted his divine lute to hell' in both *Manfred* (1817) and *Cain* (1818), proudly rejecting any appeal to divine clemency. Polydore Bounin in his *Esquisses infernales* wrote rhymes in the same vein, if not with the same talent: 'Fine, I am content with your Eternity:/ You have it to punish me? – I have it to curse you!' And Alfred Le Poittevin anathematized God in the following words:

> You will then come down from your proud throne;
> A paltry few of the righteous will receive the crown
> For having kept your law;
> But trembling with rage and cherishing their crimes
> The rest of the human race, rolling in the abyss
> Will join me in cursing you!
>
> (*Satan*)

It would be easy to multiply the examples of poets vying to outdo one another, sometimes in a facile or even outrageous way, though this was raised to a theological level by Giacomo Leopardi and Charles Baudelaire, who posed the problem of the punishment of sin. 'Why, god of misery, have you put some semblance of pleasure in life?' Leopardi asks in his *Ad Arimane*. 'What kind of paradise is it that can be bought at the price of eternal salvation?' Baudelaire echoes him, in 'Le Poème du Haschisch'. Though his work stands outside the Romantic movement, Baudelaire, with exemplary sincerity, extols the consoler, the familiar healer of human anguish who 'on the pillow of evil [. . .] unhurriedly rocks our spellbound minds': Satan, who 'always does what he does well!' and to whom he addresses this prayer in *Les Fleurs du Mal* (120):

> Glory and praise to you, Satan, up high
> In the sky where you reigned, and down low
> In hell, where vanquished you dream in silence!
> Make sure that my soul one day beneath the Tree of Knowledge
> May rest near you, at the time when on your brow,
> Like a new Temple, its branches will spread.
>
> (*Les Litanies de Satan*)

When compared with the feverish tones of these poets for whom Satan is not a myth but a tangible reality (a daily reality for Baudelaire), the concept of redemption for the great Reprobate through the love he might feel for a mortal seems just a little mawkish, even if the couple of which he forms part is accursed. Writing about *Eloa* by Vigny, for example, Max Milner comments aptly that 'Lewis's Satan appears upright and naked. Vigny's lies limply on a bed of vapours and his robe contains "the hues of opal" '. *Eloa* started a movement advocating the redemption of Satan, an unhappy, sad and charming angel. He was portrayed in almost identical terms in Théophile Gautier's *Une Larme du Diable*, Lamartine's *Chute d'un Ange*, Leconte de Lisle's *Tristesse du Diable* and Béranger's *La Fille du Diable*. All these writers see our loves and sorrows as being intimately bound up with those of demons. 'We spirits and men should get on with one another; we go through the same sufferings,' Lucifer exclaims when talking to Cain, but in talking like that Byron forgets that Satan will always attempt to dupe mankind under the sweetish outer appearance of someone like Biondetta or Clarimonde. That is how the devil in Lermontov's *The Demon* operates, seducing then abandoning beautiful Tamara. Experiencing an 'ineffable emotion', a 'passion foreign to this earth', he tells her he wants to be reconciled with heaven, to believe in good, and promises her eternity for a moment of love. Before long evil has again gained the upper hand, and after Tamara's death 'the vanquished Devil cursed his crazy dreams and was once again haughty and alone as he had been before in the universe devoid of hope and love'. Thus Lermontov does not hold out the slightest prospect of any atonement.

In accordance with a concept once promulgated by Origen, some Romantic writers and poets affirmed that after an unspecified lapse of time the Creator would pardon Satan for his proud rebellion. Théophile Gautier, who did not feel the same respect towards Satan as a fair number of his contemporaries, put forward the figure of a hundred thousand years in *Une Larme du Diable*: a figure that is naturally open to discussion! In his *Hymne* Giosuè Carducci even went so far as to dare suggest that Satan was good, and Lautréamont put the following speech to Satan into the mouth of a cherubim:

> Oh Maldoror, has the day finally come when your abominable instincts will see the extinction of the flame of unwarrantable pride that is leading them to eternal damnation! So I will be first to relate this praiseworthy change to the phalanxes of cherubim, happy to welcome you back as one of their own. You know yourself and have not forgotten that there was a time when you held pride of place amongst us. Your name flew from mouth to mouth; now you are the subject of our solitary conversations. So come . . . come and make a lasting peace with your former master; he will receive you as a son who has gone astray, and pay no heed to the great heap of guilt you have accumulated in your heart, like a mountain of moose horns raised by the Indians.
>
> (*Les Chants de Maldoror*, chant 6).

Ths time it was not the physical love of someone like Eloa that would redeem Satan, but the infinite benevolence of Jesus, going and asking his Father to be merciful. 'Today it is Satan who comes, oh Redeemer!/ Judge of his sins by his consoler!' rhymes Alexandre Soumet, in his *Divine Epopée* (1841), and a few years later Alexis Jussieu reverted to the same theme in *Un Dernier Chant au Paradis perdu de Milton* (1856): 'Poor child, I loved you before your mad offence./ After your repentance I love you still more./ Your heart when it gave way was not criminal;/ The seizure that struck you was not eternal'.

As a brilliant inventor of myths Victor Hugo was to amplify this theme of salvation in his famous work, *La Fin de Satan*. Using the 'ubiquity of antinomy' he proved that it was impossible to dissociate good from evil, and conversely darkness from light. This long, unfinished, totally Manichaean series of apocalyptic, visionary poems lays emphasis on love, the very essence of the divine: 'The archangel comes back to life and the demon expires;/ And I wipe out the sinister night, and nothing remains of it./ Satan is dead; be born again, oh celestial Lucifer.'

These ideas, which smack of heresy, had already been expressed by Abbé Constant (who later wrote under the name Eliphas Lévi) in the second part of *La Mère de Dieu*, in which a celestial voice again proclaims the triumph of love which will save the world: 'Evil as it expires has given birth to light; Satan is dead and Lucifer has been delivered'. Even if he brought the wrath of a Church wedded to the past down on his head, the great Italian philosopher Giovanni Papini, like Origen, shared this conception of the future of Satan. Admittedly, to him Satan was in no way a myth, let alone a literary myth. Especially as the Accursed One had appeared to him, in the form of a tall pale man, worn out by debauchery:

> a deathly pale, elongated face, thin tight-closed lips, with a single deep crease running up between his eyebrows, he is respectably dressed in black and his hands are always smartly covered with gloves. His hair is hidden under a large silk beret which he never removes.

Would it be appropriate to talk of a hallucination? Or to place blind trust in what Papini says? – which does, after all, tie up with the words of Dostoyevsky and Ghelderode as regards the tangibility of such diabolical apparitions. Or should we repeat with Stanislas de Guaïta: 'Your only excuse, Satan, is that you do not exist'? Thus the conflict evoked by Goethe between belief and unbelief remains an eternal and insoluble problem.

EXTENSION OF THE MYTH TO THE HUMAN FIELD

Myth and reality are strangely intermingled in the portraits painted by some novelists based on characters whose historical existence is undeniable. Joris-Karl Huysmans in *Là-Bas* and Michel Tournier in *Le Roi des aulnes* drew inspiration from the tormented existence of the very devilish Gilles de Rays.

Jean-Paul Satre described the no less tragic existence of Goetz von Berlichingen in *Le Diable et le bon Dieu*, while Somerset Maugham based *The Magician* on Aleister Crowley. Nor should we forget Johann Faust, the great doctor of devilry the depths of whose soul have been plumbed by Marlowe, Klinger, Goethe, Lenau and Paul Valéry.

What is more, accepting or seeking the advice of what Denis de Rougemont described as the 'prompter of genius', a fair number of writers have deliberately set out to create, in a supremely satanic operation, heroes who are no less satanic. 'Characters in novels have souls,' Tolstoy commented, 'and it is no less than the truth to observe that malicious authors send them among us to tempt and destroy us.' Of course our minds turn immediately to the Marquis de Sade, whose work never mentions Satan directly, but is bathed in a sulphurous aura magnifying evil, sexual perversion and sacrilege, which writers including William Beckford, Matthew Gregory Lewis, C. Robert Maturin, Honoré de Balzac, Jean Lorrain and Georges Bataille were to relish. 'It is not the object of our libertine behaviour that arouses us, it is the idea of evil,' Sade affirmed. But lasciviousness does not necessarily mean cruelty, and we may be allowed to imagine that cruelty is sometimes uppermost at the purely cerebral level of pleasure taken in doing evil for evil's sake: *ad majorem Satanae gloriam*. Lautréamont's Archangel of Evil, Maldoro, the 'corsair with the golden hair', who regards humankind as being on a par with vermin, gives a marvellous definition of this state of mind when he proclaims:

> I use my genius for the purpose of painting the delights of cruelty! Delights that are not fleeting or artificial, but which began with man and will finish with him. Cannot genius ally itself with cruelty in the secret workings of Providence?

And why should that question not be asked?

Satan quite obviously inspires the *Schadenfreude* present in many of Hoffmann's tales, and has no hesitation when necessary in adopting the features of Dapertutto, the miracle doctor who buys simple Erasmus Spikker's reflection from him (*Die Abenteuer der Sylvester-Nacht*), Major O'Malley, a pander and purveyor of succubi (*Der Elementargeist*), and the sinister Coppeluis (*Der Sandmann*), who delights in upsetting the innocent games of the children whose eyes he dreams of snatching.

However, it would be impossible for Satan always to intervene in person, and he therefore sets about seeking out in every corner of the world the psychopaths best suited to serving his ends. Here writers join in wholeheartedly, for it is infinitely pleasanter and easier to depict vices rather than virtues, criminals and madmen rather than mystics and saints. But if this is the case, who holds their pens? Who other than Satan himself inspires them at times with such blackness, and forces them to linger over the spectacle of so many morbid delights? – Satan possessing them unbeknown to themselves, and causing to issue forth from their imaginations characters like Claude Frollo, Vautrin, Ivan Karamazov, Mr Hyde or Lafcadio, conforming so much to the mould that they in turn become mythical. Within this creative genre we must of course take account of the real talent of the story-tellers, fashion, and the 'atmospheric mood' of the time, as Sainte-Beuve put it, and, in the final analysis, there are very few literary mythical characters worthy of being remembered by posterity. If we may dare to put it that way, it is a question of knowing how to endow myth with some semblance of reality. Today Lord Byron's terrifying *Gaiour*, Baron Saturne, the clumsy amateur executioner in Villiers de l'Isle Adam's *Convive des dernières Fêtes*, or the ultra-Romantic Karl Moor, the hero in Schiller's *Die Räuber*, who is described by his fiancée as an adorable demon, are more inclined to make us smile because of the 'frenzied', even caricatured nature of their language and behaviour. The same is true of most of the protagonists (La Durand, Lady Clairwil, Saint-Fond, Minski, Prior Raphaël) Sade brings to life in *Juliette* and *Justine*, of the monsters Eugène Sue portrays in *Les Mystères de Paris* (La Chouette, the Stabber, the Schoolmaster), and of course of the dissolute monks who regularly crop up in Gothic novels. 'The Monk pushes reality straight out of the window, parading sorcerers, apparitions and spectres before me in the most natural way possible, making the supernatural a reality like any other,' Antonin Artaud commented with undisguised pleasure. There is no shortage of people like him, who enjoy experiencing a literary tingle in the spine and reading texts derived from unbridled fantasy. These include works written in a slightly different, but no less cruel – satanically cruel – vein such as the doctor's experiments in H. G. Wells's *The Island of Doctor Moreau*, or the coming into the world of Hans Heinz Ewer's *Alraune*, which Pierre Mac Orlan compared to the genesis of Dr Jekyll:

> The story of the little mandrake, created by the maleficent genius of man and set in the melancholy Rhineland, has similarities with that of Stevenson's Dr Jekyll who through his own will becomes Edward Hyde, a character representing absolute evil, just as the seductive Alraune represents the most extreme perversity.

On the other hand we find characters who are far more credible, albeit somewhat complicated, such as the heroes of Barbey d'Aurevilly's *Les Diaboliques*, the hysterical Clara in Octave Mirbeau's *Le Jardin des Supplices* and the painter Ethal, whose strange passion for watching death throes is described by Jean Lorrain:

> Oh, the cold, cruel sensuality of the English, the brutality of the race and their taste for blood, their instinct for oppression and their cowardice when confronted with weakness, how it all glowed in Ethal's eyes as he lingered with catlike delight over his account to me of the self-induced death throes of his little model.
>
> (*Monsieur de Phocas*)

Setting aside the suffering inflicted on the body, the systematic pursuit of Evil can also come in the form of the corruption of innocent souls: innocent, but nonetheless predisposed to fall into the traps set for them by Satan's henchmen. Thus the murky charm that emanates from Maldoror, or from the Caliph Vathek (*Vathek* by William Beckford), acts on the young people whose perdition they yearn for. Both physical inversion and an inversion of moral values can be found in the writings of Jean Genêt, by whom absolute evil is regarded as approximating to holiness. 'If they are not always handsome, men devoted to evil have manly virtues' – which according to Genêt only homosexuality can confer on them. Following in the wake of the proud Reverend Melmoth, who despises his fellow men while at the same time relishing tempting them, Vautrin (*La Comédie humaine* by Balzac), a many-faceted character, a rebel and a Frégoli of crime who pervades Balzac's work, symbolizes to perfection those hyper-virile creatures descended from Cain. A 'grandiose statue of evil and corruption', as Lucien de Rubempré describes him in his will (*Splendeurs et misères des courtisanes*, Balzac), Vautrin lives in others by proxy, but ends up by crushing those souls audacious or unfortunate enough to resist his indomitable will for power.

Finally, some of those who are committed to evil but believe firmly in the real presence of God in the Eucharist imagine they are in a position to cause suffering to God, simply by being priests. In this purely Catholic perspective, Joris-Karl Huysmans notes that 'the power of sadism, the attraction it offers, lies entirely in the forbidden enjoyment of transferring to Satan the homage and prayers due to God' (*A rebours*). Thus in *Justine* by Sade we find libertine clerics perched on the naked back of young Florette consuming 'the most awesome of our mysteries', while Juliette is sodomized by the Pope on the altar of St Peter's in Rome. For his part Canon Docre, a famous celebrant of black masses who feeds the consecrated host to white mice, pushes the furious zeal for sacrilege to the point of having 'the image of the Cross' tattooed on the soles of his feet 'so as to be able always to tread on the Saviour!'(*Là-bas* by Huysmans). Then, very close to the fearful Prior Ambrosio in *The Monk*, we have the fiery and passionate Montoni, who delights in the misfortunes of others (*The Mysteries of Udolpho* by Ann Radcliffe), and Father Schedoni, the 'superhuman' with the melancholy, livid face (*The Italian* by the same author). These, however, prefer carrying out bloody crimes to indulging in sacrilegious fantasies, as does Götz von Berlichingen, a peculiarly Romantic hero whose troopers in Sartre's *Le Diable et le bon Dieu* pillage sacristies, rape nuns and set fire to churches, but who learns finally that good is harder to accomplish than Evil. This idea is strangely contradicted, incidentally, by the remark made by the crucified Jesuit in *Le Soulier de satin* by Paul Claudel: 'It is really only evil that demands effort, since it is against reality'.

It is nonetheless certain that one could not do without the other and that a world in which evil (even mythical evil) did not exist would be inconceivable. It was this state of affairs that was humorously conjured up by Pierre Mac Orlan in *Le Nègre Léonard et Maître Jean Mullin*:

> Evil has disappeared from the earth. Few people have escaped this disaster, for as the balance between their faculties has been broken, a huge number of individuals of both sexes have died of goodness, like my maid. They became too good, all of a sudden, with no preparation, and the majority of them developed their feelings to an absurd extent, beyond what could be coped with naturally.

THE ASTONISHING VITALITY OF THE MYTH

Proverbs, exclamations and allusions made to the Devil in everyday speech make the permanence of the satanic myth obvious. Through fantasy, or in order to play games, quite a few contemporary authors, still attracted by the medieval archetype described above, have no compunction about presenting the Devil in his most recent guises. Following in the footsteps of Michel de Ghelderode and Henri Troyat who have already been mentioned, Abraham Merritt makes him intervene in person in *Sept pas vers Satan*; Robert Bloch leaves the field open to the pitiless fly symbolizing him (*Beelzebub*), and Isaac Bashevis Singer is continually evoking his henchmen, victims of the clever tricks reserved for them by Polish Jews (*Short Friday*). He again shows his trident and his forked tail in the stories recorded by Henri Pourrat, or arranged by Claude Seignolle (*Le Diable en sabots*), and he can be found in *Arrière-monde* by Pierre Gripari, *Le Faussaire* by Jean Blanzat and *Le Grand Nocturne* by Jean Ray – in the latter he amuses himself through intermediaries by upsetting our universe. The '*grande femme*' in *La Grande Femme: Récit à faire peur* by Pedro A. de Alarcón is none other than Satan, the 'living sarcasm' of the destiny of an engineer whom she pushes to suicide through harassing him. The Devil's appearance in a red leotard at the end of Jean Marsan's play *Le Noir te va si bien*, based on O'Hara, is somewhat ludicrous, but the monologue in Oscar Panizza's *Das Liebeskonzil*, act III, scene 2, adheres perfectly to the picture people had of Satan in the Middle Ages:

> Here you are, dog, on your own again, communing with yourself, abandoned and despised by all! Here you are, back from the audience, you sad thing, bereft both of ancestors and reputation! Yet again you have seen the gilded rooms of the upper classes, but you are and remain 'the' guttersnipe, 'the' nonentity, 'the' ne'er-do-well. Those at the top can do as they please, commonplace, despicable, mean actions: they are still noble and distinguished since everything takes place in the houses of the well-to-do! But whatever you do (even if you pushed your way through head first to the other side of the world), your actions will still be wicked, ignoble, ignominious!

More recently Paul Gilson was again inspired by Chamisso's famous story to exhibit Satan in *L'Homme qui a perdu son ombre* (1953). Sometimes the devil delegates his power to pretty succubi commissioned to tempt an ageing ecclesiastic (*The Wayward Saint*, a play by Paul Vincent Carroll), or to some lascivious incubus, ready, as in 'Péhor' in *Histoires magiques* by Remy de Gourmont, to lead an enthusiastic female recruited to solitary pleasures to perdition.

As a counterpart to this return to the classical sources of demonology, there are some fairly strange reminiscences of Romanticism. While Jean Genêt declares that handsome men 'all carry the signs of the power of darkness' (*Notre Dame des Fleurs*) and Georges Bataille in his *Histoire de l'oeil* brings the criminal exploits of the Gothic novels up to date, André Gide knowingly embarks on a dialogue with Satan, allowing himself to be 'possessed' as he exalts his own weaknesses: 'Now I no longer know the dark god I serve,' the title character in *L'Immoraliste* says. This same availability for sin and invasion by darkness is even more explicitly stated in the work of Marcel Jouhandeau, who says:

> There is a space within each of us which should not remain empty. If it does, we are at the mercy of the first person to come along, the Devil; and it is undoubtedly better for us if a tyrant or a scarecrow occupies us than to be left exposed to this licence which is the greatest misery, and the opposite of inner independence. We lose stature more through what we refuse than by what we welcome and subdue.

Did not Baudelaire for his part claim that there are 'in every man at all times two simultaneous postulations, one towards God, and the other towards Satan'? Finally Henry de Montherlant, sacrilegious in the style of Sade, Blake or Lautréamont, observed, in *Le Démon du bien* that:

> through all we know of God, through the words, feelings and actions that all religions have attributed to him over the centuries, we know that God is stupid. As the Devil is the antithesis of God, we might therefore infer that he is intelligent; and what is more he has given many proofs of it.

We can even assert without fear of contradiction that Satan has never multiplied these proofs as much as he has in the course of the twentieth century. Do not worldwide conflicts, massacres and genocides carry the mark of Satan, as well as the confusion of values, the disorder introduced into minds and morals by the permanent aggression of sex, violence and mendacious, degrading publicity? Satan, who knows how to adapt to every socio-cultural situation, even the most commonplace, has thus become *The Little Demon* in the hands of Fedor Sologub: a mediocre demon, moving in mediocre surroundings, cowardly, cruel and deriving pleasure only from besmirching other people:

> All that came to his knowledge was immediately transformed into mire and filth. All he saw in objects and people was their faults and those faults gladdened his heart [. . .] He laughed with joy when something was sullied in his presence [. . .] For him happiness consisted of doing nothing, of withdrawing from the world to think only of the satisfactions of his stomach.

The appearance of the devil Woland, with his lopsided face, deeply wrinkled forehead and pointed eyebrows, in *The Master and Margarita* by Mikhail

Bulgakov is no less wretched. He plays the role of a teacher of black magic who takes special delight in stopping clocks, predicting dire events and undressing women, whose clothes fall off while they are out on the street.

This extremely derisory attitude towards the human condition comes to a peak in the agonizing pages of Franz Kafka's *In the Penal Settlement.* There, in absolute silence, human beings reduced to the simple state of a cog in a machine are crushed without the slightest possibility of salvation or pardon. However, rather than this gigantic hell, worthy of the frescoes at Pisa or Albi, Satan now prefers some discreet, confined place where the expiation of sins takes the form of the permanent humiliation of individuals. Genêt in *Le Miracle de la rose* remarks:

> Infernal horror does not reside in a setting of unusual, boorish, inhuman, deliberate fantasy. It accepts the setting and manners of everyday life; only one or two details transform them (an object that is not in its place, or is upside down or that can be seen from the inside), take on the very meaning of this universe, symbolize it, so revealing that this setting and these manners are part of hell.

This leads on to *Huis Clos* by Jean-Paul Sartre, in which the sufferings inflicted on three damned individuals take on a deliberately mental character, symbolized by morbid jealousy, unrelenting hatred and self-disgust – which is so often cultivated by our contemporaries. This also leads us on to the words Satan hastens to address to a woman involved in an adulterous affair, who is brought straight down to the nether regions by the lift of a sordid hotel:

> If madam had seen what used to go in the old days, it was quite different. Nowadays there's nothing to be said against hell. We do all we can to avoid people noticing anything; on the contrary, people quite like it here . . . Now it is only the soul that suffers.
>
> (Pär Lagerkvist, *Tales of Cruelty*)

Thus Satan has become diluted in the air we breathe – and how pestilential it is! He has become the common man, an ordinary citizen, a moderate member of the middle classes, all the better to deceive us. 'I believed I could get the better of evil through moderation,' André Gide said; 'and on the contrary, it was through moderation that the Evil One took possession of me.' Appearing as self-effacingly as he could, and crippled with rheumatism, with the object of being as close as possible to us, even in illness, had Satan not already declared to Ivan Karamazov, astonished at such a meeting: '*Satanus sum et nihil humani a me alienum puto*' ('I am Satan and think nothing human alien from me')? Bereft of the tawdry finery with which he was decked in the medieval theatre and all the adjuncts dear to some of the Romantics, Satan no longer even needs to take the trouble to pretend that he does not exist. 'What am I called?' exclaims Méphistopheles in *Mon Faust* by Paul Valéry. 'I have no name. People can call me what they want. As I have told you, I am the Servant of the servants of themselves.' Behind this screen of everyday ordinariness, he listens to us, so claimed Léon Bloy, 'in a formidable silence' – which provokes thought. It is there that he stirs up the mad pride of man who, regarding himself as the kingpin of the world, exterminates his fellows, destroys his natural environment, juggles with nuclear weapons, and sows the seeds of the destruction of our species.

Needless to say, in such a context as this Satan again resorts to temptation, his favourite weapon. This takes the form of intellectual temptation for those who, like André Gide, turn willingly towards the 'irrational regions of the self' (Henri Massis) at the risk of perdition: 'And some days I feel within me such an invasion by evil that it already seems to me as if the wicked prince is setting about establishing Hell there' (*Journal des Faux Monnayeurs*). Erotic temptation appears in *L'Ennemi*, where Julien Green, whose obsessions confuse sensuality with mysticism, assimilates Pierre, the illegitimate brother, with the Seducer in person, who will eventually be murdered, then damned; and the temptation of violence occurs in *Brighton Rock* by Graham Greene, in which Pinkie, the solitary young gang leader, a repressed virgin, settles his problems through crime, destined as he was from infancy for hell. Viewing physical love as a bestial game, a repugnant hand-to-hand struggle, Pinkie can only think of dragging others down with him, especially his girlfriend: 'She was without sin, he knew that, while he was damned; they were made for one another'. In the final analysis the temptation to commit suicide is Satan's favourite resort – he is, after all, the epitome of negation – and he does it by sowing doubt and scepticism. Thus Antoine Roquentin, the pessimistic hero of Jean-Paul Sartre's *La Nausée*, though in his prime, does not know what to do with the 'huge absurdity' of his existence, and observes that 'things are just what they seem – and behind them . . . there is nothing'. Everyday despair likewise gives rise to the temptation of drugs; artificial paradises, a 'wretched miracle', reflected in the writings of Henri Michaux and *The Naked Lunch* by William Burroughs.

Haunted by the idea of mortiferous sin, inner emptiness and non-communication between human beings, Georges Bernanos drew a remarkable definition of this delight in nothingness which Satan inspires in *Sous le Soleil de Satan*, as well as in *Monsieur Ouine* or *Si j'étais vous*. Evil is as active 'as a beehive in April' in the village of Fenouille, where the mysterious Monsieur Ouine incarnates both a living person and a metaphysical entity. He is none other than Satan, undetectable in his disguise as a horse-dealer, bidet salesman and jolly fellow. Altering the night-time landscape to suit his whim, he literally catches Abbé Donissan, a simple, unimaginative, ultra-scrupulous man, in the palm of his hand: the Abbé feels 'burnt by the fire of hell in which all hope is consumed'. And without him even being aware of it, the sovereign of that hell is walking by his side, making him so tired he does not know whether he is coming or going, inciting him to rest on his shoulder and finally kissing him on the mouth to steal his breath from him:

> You have been kissed by a friend, the horse coper said tranquilly, pressing his lips to the back of his hand. In my turn I have filled you, the tabernacle of Jesus Christ, with me, you silly fool! There's nothing to be frightened of; I've kissed others besides you, many others. Do you want me to tell you? I kiss you all, waking and sleeping, dead or alive. That's the truth. My greatest pleasure is to be with you, little men-gods, strange, strange, such very strange creatures! To be frank with you I hardly ever leave you. In your darkest flesh you carry me, whose essence was light – in the innermost recesses of your entrails – me, Lucifer . . . I count you all. None of you escapes me. I would recognize every animal in my little flock by its smell.
>
> (*Sous le Soleil de Satan*)

Yet Donissan, a saint without knowing it, reacts in time, sending the horse dealer and the temptation to despair packing.

In Bernanos's work there can be no question that Satan relishes pursuing the pick of the souls with his hatred, but there would be no point in thinking that he therefore neglects the rest of his dark 'flock', whose perverse impulses he crystallizes: 'for the person attached to the universe of the flesh is himself Satan'. This same idea is also clearly expressed by Paul Valéry in verse in 'L'Ebauche d'un serpent': 'Whoever you are, am I not/That complaisance that dawns/In your soul when it loves itself?/At the root of this love I am/ The inimitable relish/That you find only in yourself.'

Even so, it is still true that self-love, as Luc Estang notes in *Cherchant qui dévorer*, can sometimes go wrong:

> to the point of thwarting the charity one owes oneself. If injured it poisons its own wound; if besmirched it will roll up into pus, and if shamed it will give way to the vertigo of total disgust. This attraction of the abyss is the worst temptation of pride! Does not Lucifer, less splendid than he dreamt of being, prefer the kingdom of darkness?

By gratifying man's worship of man, so relevant to the present-day world, Satan admittedly risks being forgotten himself, but at the same time causes God to be forgotten. As regards the Almighty, it does seem that he has been successful. More than ever the concept of a God who is both dreadful and kind asking us to account for ourselves at the Last Judgement appears outmoded, ludicrous and downright . . . mythical. Moreover his temples are ever more deserted in favour of Satan's. Not only does the latter have his churches, his sects and his sacrifices, but he also strives to inspire programmes on the media and to reign over show business: Satan Superstar steps forward onto the podium in stadiums and variety shows. In a world in which irrational impulses are ever more frequently at odds with the socialized self, the myth of Satan has regained astonishing vitality, and of course writing has not escaped this general trend. In 1950 Robert Kanters wrote prophetically: 'Whereas the reality of a personal God seems to be disappearing, the reality of a personification of evil is becoming more strongly established: in the literary sky, the sun of Satan shines brighter than the sun of truth.'

Roland Villeneuve

Saturn

The myth of Saturn would have been nothing more than the Roman version of the Greek myth of Cronus (see also '*Cronus*') if it had remained confined within the boundaries of imitative literature. It might even have been limited to the field of scholarly mythology, the offshoot of the compilations produced by Alexandrian scholars. This was the destiny reserved for it by Ennius' translation of Euhemerus' *Sacred Record.* By equating 'Saturnus' with Cronus, the 'father' of Latin poetry introduced this god of ancient Italy into the divine genealogies and dynastic conflicts of the ancient Greek gods, for which Euhemerus had proposed a rational explanation. Saturn was therefore incorporated into Latin literature in the form of a defeated god, exiled from heaven, who found refuge in Italy, where he reigned during the Golden Age.

In this dry and impoverished summary of the traditions of Hesiod and Plato, there is a sense of Euhemerus' prejudice against the gods and their great myths. The third-century BC philosopher maintained that the gods were merely ancient royal benefactors of humanity, who had been deified retrospectively by the collective imagination. This lacklustre theory would have been fatal for the myth of Saturn, if this god, whose name is associated with the myth of the Golden Age of Rome during the first century BC, had not had the benefit of a long history in his own right.

The true origins of Saturn are as much a mystery today as they were for the Romans who lived at the time of Cicero. He was undoubtedly a specifically Mediterranean divinity who assumed Sabine, Etruscan and Greek characteristics at different points in his history. It is possible that the memory of a god who ruled over the agricultural kingdom of Saturnia was inherited from the Sabines. Both his name (*sator*, i.e. sower, planter) and his fearsome aspect of an infernal deity (whose cult was associated with the cult of the dead) were certainly of Etruscan origin. Greek influence, evident from the fifth century BC, in the sculptural form given to this god almost wholly obscures his pre-classical nature as a *numen* of agriculture, who dominated the agricultural world and to whom a temple was dedicated in Rome in 497 BC. The ancient origins and significance of the god are conveyed in the most important agricultural festival of pre-classical Rome, the Saturnalia. The structure of these public celebrations was very similar to that of the Oriental New Year festival, an event which periodically revives the Golden Age. It was not a matter of chance that the reform of the Saturnalia in 217 BC, remodelled on the Greek *Cronia*, accentuated the resemblance between this festival of regeneration and its oriental prototypes. By presenting the public with the image of a divine banquet at which food was placed before the figures of the gods, the *lectisternium* was attempting to suggest the presence of the gods among mortals. The *convivium publicum* held after the sacrifice, dedicated the collective wealth in a public festival which made no distinction between rank and fortune. The fact that the festival was a public holiday for workers and slaves re-established the sacred *otium* of the Golden Age. Finally, the carnival procession led by the *Saturnalicius princeps* achieved the elusive unity of early times via the expression of public joy (*Io Saturnalia*).

The new Saturnalia assumed the aspect of a real-life myth. Under the protection of the gods, men lived happily, shielded from cares and toil, in their initial state of peace and prosperity. In their revised form of 217 BC, the Saturnalia became the most important Roman festival, because its content coincided with the collective unconscious. The festival was the first and most lasting encounter between Rome and the myth of the Golden Age.

Therefore, in terms of the development of a cult, Ennius' initiative and the reform of the Saturnalia during the third century BC were responsible for establishing the coincidence of myth and ritual in Rome. The explanation for this lies in Roman history. As a result of the dangers experienced by Italy due to Carthaginian pressure during the Second Punic War, it was important to strengthen and glorify national unity. To achieve this, the Senate created a religious event. One can only admire the wisdom of their choice – in using popular religion to create a collective sense of purpose; in choosing an ancient god with agricultural associations, whose dormant rituals were ready for a revival; in selecting those aspects of Greek tradition likely to fire the Roman imagination; and in drawing on the wealth of rustic festivals which, in both Greece and Italy, retained the ancient characteristics of rural life common to all Mediterranean countries. There was nothing surprising in the fact that, two centuries later, within the context of the civil wars, the Roman imagination once again accepted the *Saturnia regna* as the symbol of hope and regeneration.

The myth of Saturn assumes its final form in the works of Virgil where it is developed and completed as a political myth. The imminent return of the Golden Age is announced in the *Bucolics* (IV.6) in the expression *redeunt Saturnia regna*, as opposed to *tempus aureum*, the term chosen by Horace in *Epodes* (XVI.64). The famous eclogue describes, in sibylline terms, the three phases of the complete restoration of the Golden Age of Eden to the world. It is an extremely successful stylistic exercise and was responsible for the introduction of an authentic language of mythology into the Latin poetry of the first century BC. Greek and Oriental models probably contributed to making the essay a minor *chef d'oeuvre*. It presents the Golden Age as an era in which peace, justice and plenty reappear in a world freed from evil, and its main theme is that of a child destined to become the divine ruler who will eventually preside over universal joy. Virgil skilfully combines expressions from Hesiod, Pythagoras and Plato which ensure the continuity between the myths of Cronus and Saturn in this evocation of the new ruler of a regenerated world.

Developments in Rome in the decade during which the *Georgics* were written (39–29 BC) explain Virgil's more profound reflections on the potentiality of the *aureus Saturnus*. He could be presented as an ancient national god of agrarian origins, who could be opposed by a reunified Italy to the Hellenistic kingdoms, if the former were able to use him as the basis for her own essentially religious prophecy of universal domination. In the *Georgics*, Virgil deliberately associates the happiness of the Italian peasant with the way of life formerly established on earth by Saturn and in this way updates and romanizes the Golden Age (*Georgics* II.532–9). The spirit of the new *regnum*, which flourished on the idea that agricultural labour was sacred, established a perfect system of exchange between the gods, men and the land, an order which ensured the plenty, peace and justice of the Golden Age.

The sudden introduction of the mythical dimension into Roman history was consecrated in the *Aeneid*, where Virgil develops his ideas on the royalty of Latium, of which Saturn became the guarantor over the ages. *Saturnus rex* was not the founder of the Italic *regnum* because, when he arrived in Latium, he found Janus already there. Initially, the two gods assumed the function of civilizing kings, ruling over their subjects during the Golden Age. Virgil favoured Saturn in this role and incorporated him into a divine and royal genealogy, which extended over the centuries as far as Augustus. In this form, the Golden Age of Saturn became a founding myth, the prototype for the divine reign that Augustus, like Aeneas, was called upon to establish in order to ensure the moral and political regeneration of Rome. The expression *aurea saecula* (*Aeneid VIII* 324–5), more easily transposed during the first century BC, covers the archetypal triad of the Golden Age, the foundation of the perfect government based on the royal model: peace (*Aeneid* VIII.325), justice (*Aeneid* VII.202–4) and plenty.

The presence of the myth in history is celebrated by Horace's *Carmen saeculare* (Secular Hymn) written for the *Secular Games* in 17 BC. After this date, although there were echoes of the Golden Age of Rome in the works of all the Augustan poets, it is possible to observe the gradual decline of the *Saturnus rex*, evoked with nostalgia by Tibullus in *Elegies* I.3.35. The *aureum saeculum* of popular tradition (Tacitus, *Dialogue on Orators*, 12) made its last appearance in literature with Calpurnius Siculus, who placed his eulogy of the ideal ruler under the patronage of Virgil.

The last appearance of the *Saturni latialia regna* (*Bucolics* I.64) remains entirely faithful to Roman literary tradition as a whole. It confirms the political nature of the myth of Saturn, although its grandeur is lost in an excess of imperial propaganda.

Marie-Josette Bénéjam-Bontems

Scandinavian Myths

A nineteenth-century author observed that for us the North was always a subject of wonders. This view will be our starting point as we take this supreme opportunity of identifying a literary myth in its pure state, if one can call it that – in other words the North as a fantasy construction, born of our dreams and the things we lack, which a seriously documented view has not succeeded in revising, despite undeniable contact with reality.

For at least a millenium a few images of phosphorescent magic and a mass of received and apparently unassailable ideas have combined to construct an idea of the North to fit our fevered imagination; a Scandinavia, moreover, in which we insist on placing the Finns, the Laps, the Eskimos – and why not the Chukchi or the Tungus? – anyone who comes from a cold place. The Scandinavian myths, or rather myth, is still today, at the end of the twentieth century, a magnetic pole for our ignorance and expectations. Jules Verne chose to locate the entrance to the passage leading to the centre of the earth in the crater of Mount Hekla in Iceland. Ancient Greece situated the Hyperboreans at the edge of, if not outside, the world; and Pytheas could not fail to name his furthest port of call Ultima Thule. The North has certainly always been elsewhere and different: this is doubtless the prime reason for the fascination it exerts over us. It is, literally, the end of the physical and mental world. No matter how much we visit, study or demystify it, to us it will always be on the edge. This is why we cannot do without it.

It must be agreed that, because of its natural makeup, Scandinavia (in other words, let us repeat, Denmark, Sweden, Norway, Iceland and a few islands such as the Faroes) lays itself open to our mental ramblings. Leaving aside Denmark, which is more continental, and a good part of Sweden, a rather monotonous symphony of forests and lakes (although a whole body of films has ensured the popularity of these calm mirrors, where the landscape is effortlessly inverted before the eyes of some naturist naiad), the Norwegian or Icelandic fiords and the fjelds that they intersect, the glaciers and volcanoes of Iceland, the icy seas and the immense spaces, inhabited only by strange flora and fauna (elk, reindeer, eagle, ptarmigan, falcon) take us away from what we are used to. And even if the Nordkapp is an abrupt and desolate grey cliff, even if the farmers of the centre of Iceland are often truly Dantean of aspect, these settings are unforgettable, however melancholic they may often be.

First of all, as we have said, because they are born of the cold and shaped by it, and live in perpetual confrontation with it, ice, snow and even the 'furious whirlpools' of the Lofoten have a hard purity, which is lacking to the landscapes with which we are familiar.

Above all they have whiteness; and here is our introduction to the great, indisputable theme of light. It is perfectly true that, with the aid of the aurora borealis or the midnight sun, around Tromsø, Sundsvall or Akureyri and even in Helsingør (Elsinore), still haunted by the ghost of Hamlet, everything is transfigured, reality is doubled or magnified, it is elevated in a great leap to which we cannot fail to ascribe some mysterious, mystic or magical impulse. The Ancients used to say 'from the North comes the light'. It is there that alchemy has constantly located the seat of the Third Empire, or the Kingdom of the Dead, or the World of the Super-living.

Scandinavia is primarily a landscape, real or dreamed of, real *and* dreamed of. Its prestige here comes from the way that it coincides so well with our most fantastical desires. In it earth and sky are merged, it emphasizes with imposing force the great telluric, aquatic, aerien and indeed, if we are speaking of Iceland, phlogistic components, from which we have always (long before Bachelard's masterly analyses) known ourselves to be made. And it is not very important that the precise sciences teach us, for example, that Iceland is hardly a cold country, or that Denmark is little different from many more southerly coastal provinces: they are, by definition, part of our emotional septentrion. To remove them from it would make us blush.

Is it surprising, then, that a legendary, mythical and, once again, magical universe presides over our sense of Scandinavia? Indeed, is this whole landscape not peopled with dwarves, trolls and tomtes that we have tamed using Nils Holgersson's gander, the animal which has done more to fuel our myth in modern times than anything that can be said here? Let us take a random series of names which are as imperious as they are ill-understood: runes, Valkyries, sagas, Vikings. Whose imagination is not stirred by such things? It is absolutely pointless to try to explain that runes were no more or less magic than any other form of writing; that diachronically speaking the word Valkyrie encompasses half-a-dozen successive meanings, inspired as much by religion as by any occultism; that the sagas are simply historical romances in prose, though this is undoubtedly a remarkable thing given the date that they were written (thirteenth century); and that the Vikings are a hundred times more accurately described as particularly gifted traders, benefitting from the technical marvel that they took centuries to develop – their boat (which was never called *drakkar*) – than as invincible warriors (as a general rule, they were always beaten to a pulp in battles they fought on open ground) who came to punish the West for its sins, between the ninth and eleventh centuries. We are absolutely resolved to preserve a kind of sacred aura for them. Our daydreams need this dimension.

This is why in the field of literature, we regard the great Scandinavian writers – necessarily so in our view – as anguished, tortured souls, as incomprehensible to others as they are to themselves. It is completely untrue that the

Scandinavians, and particularly the Swedes, break all records for suicides; and it cannot be denied that Scandinavian literature includes great exponents of realism and naturalism, who are no less concerned to portray the external world without giving it occult dimensions than are writers of other latitudes. But in our eyes Swedenborg – whom very few people have actually bothered to read – Kierkegaard, Strindberg, Lagerkvist and many others tend always to be placed on the extreme edge of madness or esotericism, and Ingmar Bergman's films in no way contradict this impression.

The Scandinavians certainly have a way of looking at reality which does not bend to fit our analyses. They are particularly sensitive to the unexpressed, the ineffable, to people's secret aspects; they have an extreme respect for human complexity and are thus careful, usually unconsciously, not to violate what is secret with a formulaic rule. Doubtless this often gives us ambiguous works open to multiple interpretations. But this is no reason to place all Knut Hamson's heroes in the 'Mystery' category, or to regard all Ibsen's characters as shadowy and disturbing. To do so would be to force upon them romantic views which they would generally strongly reject.

It must be generally said that on occasion they have laid themselves open to this. For various historical and political reasons, which we cannot detail here, the Scandinavians themselves, particularly in the sixteenth century, gave credit to a number of legends which, as we might expect, found ready ears elsewhere. As early as the sixth century the historian Jordanes advanced his famous theory of Scandinavia as the 'womb of peoples', the 'headquarters of nations', to explain the unleashing on Europe of the Nordic peoples. The 'göticist' movement in Sweden, willingly orchestrated by the whole of Scandinavian Romanticism, made the same mistakes. This is where 'our' Viking comes from. He combined an invincibility, born of the hyperbolic pens of the horrified monks who wrote the chronicles in which his exploits were set out, with the prestige of the skilful masters of navigation – all of whom were superb romantics, each one a 'free man' who 'would always love the sea' – who perhaps discovered America (although they were not the first) and founded the Russian state (this aspect of their history is not in question, but strangely has made no impression on the West), and the dominance of the colonizers of Iceland, and parts of England, Ireland and Normandy. All in all, they could only have been supermen, come to regenerate the flabby West; hyper-energetic people – one need only look at Montesquieu and his scholarly physiological arguments – endowed with powers of organization and command which made them paragons. And what use is the knowledge that their chief asset was simply an astonishing capacity for responsible adaptation, in all the places that they settled, which ensured their complete assimilation in two or three generations? They have invincibly preserved their primacy as the ideal human type: masters of the poles – as Nansen and Amundsen indeed were – and the expression of an exemplary society. 'Proud children of the North', they are still recipients of an admiration which Chateaubriand could not stop himself displaying for the 'great white barbarians' and which makes their sagas (these do indeed reflect a quite remarkable talent for storytelling: the line has never died out, producing Hans Christian Andersen and Selma Lagerlöf on the way) into poetic, epic and, once again, magical masterpieces; all of which is the exact opposite of their real definition.

As ever, versions of the myth have complacently lingered over the Viking woman, whom the historian has difficulty distinguishing from her 'continental' sister. But she must have been exceptional if the myth is to be consistent. A documented study would easily show that, in a society whose structures clearly differed from ours, women enjoyed what would, at a similar period, seem to us to be privileges. But there is a yawning gulf between saying this and making them the model for our modern feminists. It is true that, aided by Ibsen's *A Doll's House*, a particular form of radical feminism currently holds sway in Scandinavia. However, we should need to know the precise ethnological, sociological, historical and political components which gave rise to this state of affairs. And this is what we refuse to do, so greatly does the splendour of the Valkyrie obscure lucid thought on this subject.

The same could be said of the current state of the myth of Scandinavia: these countries are seen as socialist paradises, only recently we used to speak at length about the 'example of Sweden'. Here too an undeniable social reality, whose roots are lost in the mists of time and which is bound up with geographical and historical imperatives, has produced a form of collective life in the North which social democracy and its ideals will prolong without much difficulty. But it is quite a different matter to see this as a phenomenon which can be exported wholesale and, in particular, to hold up as examples those who are actually the first to protest against it.

It matters little: our unconscious has no doubt decided to locate in the North a number of chimeras and utopias, which we know, in our clear-sighted moments, to be fallacious. This is because the images underlying our Scandinavian myths are too charming in the strongest sense of the word: they reflect our need to compensate, sometimes absurdly and often naïvely, but always magically.

Régis Boyer

Shaka the Zulu, a Bantu Myth

Shaka (1786–1828), the founder of the Zulu empire, was the driving force behind a massive upheaval in the ethnographical map of southern Africa in the first quarter of the nineteenth century. This involved two forms of population movement: the conglomeration of tribes in small independent communities; and the dispersal of peoples fleeing Shaka's domination.

The story of Shaka's rise to power and reign (1816–1828) has come down to us through the prose epic written in Sesotho by the schoolteacher Thomas Mofolo, based on tales from the oral tradition. This work, translated into German, French and, in 1949, English, belongs to the vast category of historical myths concerning the founding of a nation under the aegis of an outstanding personality.

BETWEEN LEGEND AND HISTORY

Shaka was born in Xhosa country (in what is now Natal), from the illicit union between Senza 'Ngakona, chief of the small Ifenilenja clan, who were vassals of the Abatetoas, and the young Nandi, and he suffered exile when his mother was repudiated as a result of the jealousy of his father's wives.

However, a witch-doctor predicted a glorious future for this 'bastard', and, supported by his loving mother, Shaka soon avenged his unjust fate, using his exceptional physical strength to assert himself. His first exploits date from his adolescence, when he killed a lion and then a hyena single-handed; but he was pursued by his jealous half-brothers and had to flee into the forest. Here, he was initiated into the occult powers by the seer and witch-doctor Issanoussi and underwent a decisive transformation that enabled him to prove himself as a warrior of great prowess in the service of Ding'iswayo, his father's sovereign and Chief of the Abatetoas, who took him under his protection. Having acquired a mastery of arms by fighting Zwide, an aggressive neighbour, Shaka turned his thoughts to marriage to Noliwé, Ding'iswayo's sister. However, his father's death distracted him from this plan. Instead, he fought and overcame his half-brother M'fokazana, who had been named as his father's successor, and established himself at the head of the clan of his birth. His prestige grew still further when Ding'iswayo fell victim to Zwide and died, and Shaka was recognized as sole chief of the Abatetoas. Shaka avenged his former master by forcing Zwide into exile, whereupon his people called on him to marry. However, Issanoussi the sorcerer sought to dissuade him with the vision of still greater glory, and Shaka acquiesced, even agreeing to sacrifice Noliwe to his ambition.

At this point, a new phase began in Shaka's life. Having built his capital, he completely reformed the institutions of the kingdom, presenting himself as the envoy of an all-powerful god. At Issanoussi's bidding, he chose a new name for his people: when he heard the sound of thunder, he cried out, 'Zulu! Amazulu!' ('the Sky! Clan of the Sky!'), after which he identified himself with the cloud, symbol of freedom (Mofolo 1981). His régime took the form of a military theocracy, based on strictly trained warriors, whom Shaka forbade even to marry.

At this point, Shaka sent his armies on many expeditions of conquest, considerably extending his empire to the north and south. After twelve years of his reign, around forty thousand villages were under his domination, as compared with an initial core of about forty. However, his campaigns were extremely destructive, as Shaka plundered the herds of conquered tribes and spared the lives of none but the young men, whom he took into his army. One particularly appalling episode, 'the massacre of the cowards', when Shaka had several of his regiments executed for having fled before the enemy or abandoned their weapons, marked the beginning of the excesses of a conqueror who could no longer control his lust for power. Some of his generals left him to establish their own kingdoms elsewhere and he was eventually completely discredited by the murder of his mother, who was accused of having spared the life of one of her children against his orders. The people began to murmur against the tyrant, and his half-brothers Di'ngana and Mahla'ngana exploited their discontent to organize his assassination.

A MYTHOCRITICAL APPROACH

In morphological terms, Mofolo's account retracing the stages both of the hero's training and of his slide into the tyranny that brought about his assassination, has a cyclical structure, to use the terminology first employed by Vladimir Propp and taken up by Denise Paulme (1976).

Starting from a situation of lack, Shaka's deprivation of his right of succession, the plot is organized around the quest for power, which is assimilated to a struggle against darkness and oblivion, the hostile forces represented by the bad father who rejected him and his enemy half-brothers. His aspiration towards sovereignty is thus linked to the theme of illegitimacy and to that of the persecuted child called to a great destiny, both constant and universal elements in heroic myths (Rank 1959).

The course of this quest, which is punctuated by ordeals, is played out entirely against a background of animistic beliefs and magic practices. The theme of qualifying tests develops in relation to the cult of the ancestors: at the site of his ritual ablutions (a river of dark waters), the adolescent Shaka receives the blessing of the 'Powers Below', through the agency of the 'Lord of the Deep Waters'. This spirit appears in the form of a monstrous snake, regarded as the envoy of the ancestors. Mafolo points out that 'water snakes are particularly revered in Xhosa country, and particularly those of the rivers'. Meanwhile, Paulme tells us that, 'In Africa, the snake is always a symbol of immortality: it is the avatar of an ancestor or a subterranean divinity, its image is always linked to that of Hell and the world of the dead'. This snake speaks to Shaka in the name of the ancestors, saying: 'You will be great, your domination will extend over nations and their princes . . .' Having mastered his fear at being confronted by the dragon symbolizing immortality, Shaka becomes an initiate. The theme of 'magical birth' in water (Rank 1959), a true rebirth, is clearly apparent in this sequence of events.

Various magic aids accompany the hero and assist his rise to power. From his childhood, Shaka is entrusted by his protective mother into the care of a female witch-doctor, who undertakes a number of different purification rites, instructs Shaka to carry out ritual ablutions at each last quarter of the moon, makes incisions, scrapes and scars on his body intended to ward off evil, and predicts a great destiny for him.

The exploits that Shaka performs to prove his worth are signs of the efficacy of the magic practices, which have strengthened his vital energy, raising him to a superior level of humanity. By killing a lion single-handed, he becomes the lion's equal; while by killing a hyena, which symbolizes cowardice, he banishes fear.

The diviner and witch-doctor Issanoussi, whom Shaka met by chance in the forest to which he had fled, then takes over, with his assistants Ndlebe and Malounga, who fight at the hero's side. Issanoussi acts as a 'supplier' for Shaka by concocting 'medicines' intended to ensure the invulnerability of the hero and his warriors. 'Among the ingredients from which these medicines were composed were lion heart, panther heart and some of the heart of a man who was known during his life for his extreme courage' (Mofolo 1981). Issanoussi also makes Shaka an assegai with a short shaft (evoking the theme of magical weapons), which the hero then uses to perform numerous warlike exploits, designed as tests of manhood, for example killing a madman who was terrorizing the Abatetoas and conquering the terrible Zwide. The repetition of the theme of the meeting with the witch-doctor, which appears each time that the hero runs into difficulties, indicates the importance of the character of Issanoussi, the essential agent of heroic metamorphosis.

The reversal of the original situation, in which what was previously lacking is attained, is marked by Shaka's enthronement. This is confirmed on his father's tomb, when the corpse speaks out to name him as the rightful successor. At the time of this 'epiphany', the hero receives both power, and the fiancée promised to him by Ding'iswayo in the role of substitute father.

The heroic myth that is completed in this way serves as a purification rite, warding off an unhappy fate. Meanwhile, it is also a rite involving collective compensation achieved through identification with the hero, who conquers the forces of his adversaries and so fulfills the unconscious desires for sovereignty, fame and immortality that all people carry within themselves.

The second part of Mofolo's tale represents a return to the original situation of lack through loss of power, the cause of decline being the instability of the hero, who uses his power destructively and oversteps his rights as a sovereign. A series of cruel and perverse acts mark the hero's decline into evil, starting with the murder of his pregnant fiancée Noliwé and culminating in matricide.

Unlike Soundjata, an entirely positive epic hero who triumphs over the sorcery embodied by his enemy Soumaoro, Shaka uses the sorcerer Issanoussi's occult skills to acquire limitless power, and the last stage of his initiation grants him the right to kill. In the myth of Shaka, the archetype of the hero who is 'bound', in the sense of bewitched, takes shape after the terrible 'blood pact'. In order to inoculate Shaka with 'blood medicine', Issanoussi demands the sacrifice of Noliwe, the person most dear to him. However, as the price for his promised fame Shaka is condemned to kill and massacre unceasingly:

'The medicine with which I inoculated you is the medicine of blood; so if you do not spill blood in abundance, it will turn against you, and it is you whom it will kill' (Mofolo 1981).

After the murder of Noliwe, Shaka experiences the appearance of fear and his decline into anxiety develops at the same time as his slide into evil. Both catamorphic symbols (dizziness and heaviness) and nyctomorphic ones (blindness, insomnia, nightmares, ghostly visions and hallucinations) accompany the hero's bloody madness (Mofolo 1981; and Durand 1969).

We are witnessing a true rite of magical possession: Mofolo describes Shaka as 'driven forward by an inner force unknown to him and which gave him no rest. His thoughts lost their lucidity . . . He was then seized by a frantic desire to see more death, and by his own hand; he was thirsty for blood, with an unquenchable thirst' (Mofolo 1981).

The theme of betrayal, involving the secession of several generals and Shaka's abandonment by his assistants Ndlebe and Malounga, prefigures the hero's ultimate loneliness before his murder, which is seen as the just punishment for his excesses.

The myth of Shaka can thus also be interpreted as an initiatory myth expressing the unease widespread in animistic societies concerning magical practices designed for the acquisition of power.

Transcribed by Mofolo in Sotho country, which suffered from Shaka's designs of conquest, the myth is also intended to provide an explanation for what the author calls the *lifaqanes*, or various calamities for which Shaka is made responsible. These were hardships in the form of incessant wars, deportations, famine, social decline and even cannibalism that the peoples pursued by Shaka's armies had to endure (Mofolo 1981).

LITERARY HISTORY OF THE SHAKA MYTH

After 1956, the version of the myth of Shaka recorded by Mofolo was constantly reused by African playwrights, with the dual aim of rehabilitating the heroes of the past and educating the inhabitants of the young nations that had arisen following independence. This produced a highly didactic form of theatre.

The myth's passage to the stage was accompanied by simplification and condensation of the events set out in the original narrative, while the speeches of the hero or his partisans were used as a vehicle for a nationalistic message. The plays were intended to serve as a reply to colonialist doctrines, in the tradition developed by black militants. They often took the form of a trial, in which the hero had to justify himself either to his detractors or before the tribunal of history (Senghor 1956; Badian 1961–72; Anta Ka 1972).

The author's personal identification with the hero is sometimes clearly apparent. Thus, in Senghor's *Chaka*, the poet endows the founder of the Zulu nation with his own ideal of universalist humanism; while in Badian's *La Mort de Chaka*, the writer projects onto the Zulu leader his own political aim of building a nation with highly centralized power in which interests of state must be the top priority for all citizens.

The old myth is thus updated to the detriment of traditional fantastical elements. Avoiding the problem of the relationship between power and magic, Senghor, Badian and also Nenekhaly Camara transform the sovereign's image by adopting a eulogizing stance and see in Shaka the exemplary prototype of the modern leader.

Using an arsenal of literary weapons ranging from poetry in the case of Senghor and rhetoric in the case of Badian to realism and modernism of language in that of Nenekhaly Camara, the authors glorify Shaka's unique role as a unifier of peoples. To justify the imposition of his power on to the scattered tribes of the Xhosa lands, they give him a brilliant intuition of the imminent danger of colonialization: 'Our land will soon be turned upside down. Something is going to happen. There will be storms, we shall have life without light, a life of torture and humiliation . . .' (Badian 1961).

In Senghor's work the hero's charisma is celebrated through various fleeting metaphors. The poem's two superb dramatic cantos evoke a solar image of a Shaka who is 'neither warrior nor butcher', a 'Zambesi mare running and kicking at the stars', a whole man, a poet and fine tactician with words as much as a man of action.

The constant resort to euphemism, whereby, for example, the murder of Noliwe is presented by Senghor, Camara and Anta Ka as a sacrifice to which she freely consents, or is simply omitted, as in the work of Badian, leads to a reversal of the myth theme developed by Mofolo. The hero's violent aggression is transmuted into a boldness that is well suited to the realization of a grand project of unification requiring the elimination of the weak and cowardly. As a man of desires and ideals in the work of Senghor, a clever tactician in that of Badian, and a responsible man of action and integrity in that of Camara, Shaka is absolved of all his crimes and saluted by his people as the worthy representative of an Africa undergoing revolution. The tradition is invoked only to illustrate collective identity, through songs of praise that assimilate Shaka to the lion or the elephant, symbols of strength and sovereignty.

While modernization seems to have gone hand in hand with the rehabilitation of the Zulu myth for nationalistic ends, there has, however, been conflict between two generations over the treatment of its resurrection.

The writers of the first decade of the period during which the African nations were granted independence produced eulogies in an updated epic style, in which the heroic myth of absolute greatness acted as a purification rite intended to give new confidence to the African peoples – a rite involving the rediscovery of roots in the collective memory, the aim of which was to preserve the cult of ancestral heroes, which had been obliterated by colonial history.

In contrast, the African writers of the following decade adopted a more critical approach to the Zulu hero. Thus their work exhibits a shift from a purely nationalistic form of drama to one involving reflections on the nature of power, which sometimes goes so far as to demystify Shaka and put tyranny on trial, as in the work of Djibril Tamsir Niane or Tchicaya U Tam'si.

In 1968, in a 'black African tragedy' on the baroque model, Abdou Anta Ka provided a synthetic vision of Shaka's life. Here, epic sequences celebrating a strategist worthy of a place in the 'Pyramid of Heroes' alternate with elements of parody illustrating the degradation of power in the hands of an 'Executioner-Prince' who prefigures the image of the black Macbeth created later by Tam'Si. As in the work of Niane, passages expressing the point of view of the people are used to convey the oppressive atmosphere of tyranny.

Leaving Shaka's exploits as a warrior and his resounding victories entirely to one side, Niane structures his play to form two antithetical tableaux. One represents the hero's unhappy childhood, with his compensatory dream of glory and recourse to occult powers, while the other portrays the image of an exhausted people, sick of having to endure the tyrant's excesses. The pathetic final theme of the hero's loneliness turns the play into a political tragedy: 'I wanted power. But my heart can no longer find rest. An assegai always dripping with blood, a terrified people, that is my glory . . . I am no longer loved' (Niane 1971).

This undermining of the heroic myth results from a re-examination of the legend recorded by Mofolo. Tam'si follows the same procedure, and his *Zulu* perfectly illustrates the psychological and fantastical components that make up a tragedy of ambition. These are enunciated in the prologue: 'He is damned . . . He's been bitten by the bug. That bright eye, that stiffness of the body, they're the signs that he's damned' (Tam'si 1977).

This highly original play breathes entirely new life into the myth. In an atmosphere of poetic mystery, it mingles the traditional themes of revelation and the magical weapons given to the hero with elements of modern psychology, plunging into Shaka's dream world and thereby revealing his secret desire for omnipotence.

Using ellipses, allusions and metaphors, Tam'Si creates a mystique of power, in which the theme of being bound predominates:

> SHAKA: It's as if I wasn't free . . . This dream binds me . . .
>
> (Tam'si 1977)

Given the secret title 'Spirit of Flesh', while his assistants Ndlebe and Malounga are respectively named 'Spirit of the Air' and 'Spirit of the Earth', Shaka feels that he has been entrusted with a mission to unify the earth by Umzikulu the Almighty. The dangers inherent in this undertaking are illustrated by two symbols: the bloodstain found on the magic shield, which represents a possible betrayal by his men; and the sea spray, an augury of foreign violence in the form of a threat of invasion.

Tam'si's Shaka sinks into mistrust, which leads him to betray his protector Ding'iswayo, to refuse to have any heirs and thus to murder his pregnant fiancée Noliwé. However, even this fails to save him, for the danger does not come from these quarters. Instead, it comes from his own mother, Nandi, whose horror at his excesses leads her to plot against her son, and, ultimately, from his half-brothers, who murder him with the help of white men brought by the sea.

Distancing himself from the elements of the original myth, Tam'si projects a personal fantasy into his drama, that of the 'treacherous mother' who punishes her son and causes his overblown dream to fail. The theme of 'bad blood', which is something of an obsession in Tam'si's poetry, derives from his personal mythology and replaces the collective mystique built up in the original myth around the 'blood pact', so that such magical beliefs are relegated to a secondary role. Having undergone this process of modernization, the old myth no longer reflects collective fears alone, but also mirrors deep-seated aspects of the poet's personality.

Nicole Goisbeault

Sirens in Antiquity

To anyone studying its content and forms of artistic expression in Antiquity, the myth of the Siren soon appears fearfully complex. The figure of the Siren is presented as an enigma: apart from her evolution through the centuries and in the work of different authors, which, though already considerable, is familiar to the mythographer, she undergoes a radical and definitive transformation, losing her original form as a bird-woman to become a fish-woman, a mermaid, the only form of Siren we know today.

Furthermore, the domains touched on by the myth are as different as they are fundamental in Greco-Roman civilization: the Sirens belong to the underworld of hell, the heavenly world of music and also to the marine world of sailors.

Lastly there are a great many representations of the myth, both iconographic and literary. No form of ancient iconography seems to have forgotten the Sirens, who are depicted on pottery and bas-reliefs, on cameos and mosaics, and so on. Literary representations can be divided into three broad types:

First the portrayal of the Sirens in a particular episode of their history. They may be 'characters' in poems or prose works, seeing their power thwarted by Odysseus' craftiness when, in the *Odyssey* (eighth century BC; XII.36–202), he manages to listen to their song, fatal to sailors, having filled his companions' ears with wax and had himself tightly bound to the mast of his ship. There is another failure for their nevertheless irresistible voices in relation to the Argonauts, who are saved from temptation by the music and song of Orpheus (Apollonius Rhodius, *The Voyage of Argos*, third century BC; IV.885–922). Then we find them with the features of sea-women and the legs of she-donkeys, transformed by Lucian's parodic writing, at the end of the fantastical journey of *The True History* (second century AD; II.6, 46). Lastly, in his *Metamorphoses* Ovid recounts the transformation of these lovely young girls into birds after the abduction of their companion Proserpina (first century BC/first century AD; V.551–63).

Second the Sirens are also to be found at the core of thought of a scientific or philosophical nature. In agreement with most traditions, Strabo (*Geography* I.2.12, V.4.7) located the Sirens in the Italian region of southern Sicily. Plato, in a text stamped with Pythagoreanism, uses the myth of Er to describe the structure of the universe: there is a Siren on each of the eight circles representing the planets, who turns with the spheres and sings in harmony with the three Moirai (*Republic* X.616–7; fourth century BC). Here the Sirens appear in a myth in the Platonic, positive meaning of the word – in other words the figurative representation of a reality that is hard to explain. Plutarch, taking up Plato's words, assimilates the Sirens to the nine Muses (*On the Creation of the Soul in the Timaeus* 1029c-e). For Cicero the Sirens offered knowledge and thus seduced the intellectual curiosity inherent in the human mind (*De finibus bonorum et malorum* V.49; first century BC).

Third the Sirens appear in the form of brief allusions, as elements in the comparison of different types of speech and song, from poetic work of quality – according to Pausanias (*Description of Greece* I.21; second century AD) Sophocles is said to have been designated by an oracle as 'the new Siren' – to debauched and Dionysian flute music, which was often associated with courtesans and the end of banquets (e.g. Plutarch, *Propos de table* V.706, VII.710). In the Christian tradition in particular, the dominant interpretation of the Sirens is as courtesans). Always plural in their adventures, the Sirens may appear here in the singular, for their name becomes almost a noun, the pure synonym of the song whose emblematic figure they are. They are one of those mythological examples that everyone knows and that tend to become fixed in a rhetorical 'topos', as, for example, in the Attic eloquence of the fourth century BC (Aeschines, 'Against Ctesiphon' 228 ff.).

Faced with such a profusion of meanings and such disparate representations, can we speak of a literary myth in relation to the Sirens? If we try to go beyond this first impression of diversity, we clearly see the outline of a literary hierarchy and a dynamic, organized around Homer's text, which is original both chronologically and in importance. However, Odysseus' adventure is only one episode in the Sirens' prolific history. The bas-reliefs on funerary monuments depict them more precisely as infernal divinities, a function directly portrayed in literature only in Helen's lament in Euripides' tragedy (*Helen* 164–79; fifth century BC). (The Sirens' presence at a song of mourning evokes other myths where metamorphosis into a bird is linked to a plaintive cry, such as those of Alcyone or Philomela. As those who conduct souls into the other world, the Sirens can also be linked to the Harpies, who are winged women, and to the Egyptian Sirens represented on sarcophagi as symbols of the soul leaving the body).

Other writers, particularly mythographers, mention the links between the Sirens and Persephone. This episode provides two explanations of the origins of their appearance: it was either requested from the gods by the Sirens themselves, so that they could go and look for their abducted companion and fill the whole world with their lament (Ovid); or it was a punishment inflicted on the Sirens by Demeter for not having watched over her daughter properly (Hyginus, *Myths* 141; first century AD). A third reason for their metamorphosis is given in a scholium to the *Odyssey* XII.39, according to which the Sirens were punished in this way by Aphrodite for having rejected love. Another episode mentioned is the competition between the Sirens and the Muses, which ends in the defeat of the former. The Muses are then said to have torn off the Sirens' wings and crowned themselves with them as trophies (Pausanias, *Description of Greece* X.34.3).

But the nature of Homer's text itself explains the weight of this particular episode. Homer's poems were to Greco-Roman Antiquity what the Bible is to our civilization – inspired texts to be meditated upon (most of the theoretical ideas discussed below are exegeses of Homer), imitated (Apollonius Rhodius) or indeed criticized (Lucian), but to which one could not fail to refer when speaking of the Sirens. Iconography was not immune to the influence of Homer's work, although it was affected to a lesser degree. 'Odysseus and the Sirens' was a favourite subject in representations of the myth. The most famous examples are probably the stamnos from Vulci (British Museum), which also portrays the Sirens' suicide after their failure to ensnare Odysseus, and the Tunis mosaic (Musée Alaoui).

The text on the Sirens occupies a privileged place in the general deference to Homer's poems. Neither Apollonius nor Lucian rewrote the whole of the *Odyssey*, and yet they followed Homer very closely in this particular episode. The richness of the original text, unequalled by its successors and at the same time potentially containing them all, is doubtless not unconnected to its success.

First, the text is rich in dramatic action, which gives depth to the myth by linking the Sirens to the figure of Circe the witch (it is she who advises Odysseus on how to survive the ordeal), to the monsters Scylla and Charybdis (encountered immediately after the Sirens and included in Circe's advice), and so on.

Above all it is rich in content. Homer's is probably the text that combines the greatest number of facets of the myth: traces of religious elements dating from before the eighth century BC and later lost; or elements which are still uncertain in the *Odyssey* and which are developed by Homer's successors. The bones littering the ground on the Sirens' island recalls their link to the world of the dead. The fantastical atmosphere surrounding the episode suggests the transcendent dimension of music and brings the hero into a supernatural world, which for him is where an initiatory trial takes place (the invisibility of the Sirens and the sudden dropping of the wind are doubtless connected to the myth's religious origins in cults linked to promontories, where the Sirens were supposed to calm the winds with their voices. This ancient status of the myth, of which only a few traces remain in Homer's work, is absent from later texts: the Sirens become the cause of tempests and shipwrecks, as in Apollonius Rhodius, for example). Odysseus' ordeal is far more clearly initiatory than other tests where the hero has to defeat monsters. Here he receives a message from them, and it is noteworthy that his companions are excluded from the ordeal. Of course Homer was clearly an inspired poet, and the Sirens become like an image of himself. Placed at the heart of *The Odyssey* they form one of the first and perhaps most subtle constructions of a *mise en abîme* in literature. For the song that they promise is an epic poem, the story of the Trojan War, a content which Homer alone mentions, in other words the subject of the *Iliad* and the *Odyssey* themselves. The Sirens are also Odysseus recounting his adventures (including the episode of the Sirens) to the Phaeacians, or the bard who sings the story of Odysseus, and lastly Homer himself creating the poem. While he creates a literary myth in the episode of the Sirens, more profoundly still Homer creates a true poetic myth, lacking neither the divine origins of song nor its initiatory power; nor the risk that it will merely be a false promise, finally bearing death, a dimension of the myth which Blanchot so well presents in *The Sirens' Song*.

This richness in Homer's text makes it the raw material, unrefined and close to the myth's magico-religious origins, from which posterity has sculpted many different figures of the Sirens, all of which remain indefinable. Scientists will never be able to dispel the mystery that floats around them (what 'reality of the Sirens' did Strabo prove by locating them geographically?), and imitators will find material with which to express their own sensibilities, giving the myth its new forms. Thus we see an increasing feminization of the Sirens, and indeed a sexualization of the myth. Femininity is discreetly present in Homer's work (in the links with Circe, consecrated by Lucian in a superimposition of the two figures, and a very obvious sexual symbolism in the hero's triumph), but is not primary in the process of temptation. The most ancient iconographic documents show the Sirens with bearded, possibly masculine heads. The sea also increasingly becomes the dominant element of the Sirens' microcosm, leading to the figure of the woman-fish. The sea was only one element of the microcosm depicted by Homer – sky/earth/sea – and it becomes the most important in alexandrine verse of a baroque sensibility, with its fountains, curving forms of fish and nymphs half rising from the water, and so on, as in Apollonios Rhodius and Ovid. The first documents on the transformation proper are two bas-reliefs contemporary with these authors, an Athenian bowl of the third or second century BC and a Roman lamp of the first century AD. Far from having the sterilizing effect of fixing the Sirens in a brief episode of their history, the dominance of Homer's text is open to the future and guarantees the myth its immortality.

Annie Lermant-Parès

Sisyphus

In dictionaries and literary texts alike, Sisyphus is first and foremost a name. At the beginning of a line by Baudelaire, the sibilant sound of the 's' is followed by the 'biting resonance' of the 'z', which 'is reminiscent of the sound of the castigatory whip or of an Erinyan insect', like the one heard by Roland Barthes in *Sarrasine*. We do in fact tend to associate the name with the idea of punishment. The concretization of this image, which is made even more tangible by the recurrent classical 'low relief' of Sisyphus bent beneath the weight of his stone, is not without a certain ambiguity, which is already present in the name.

THE MEANING OF THE NAME

Sisyphus is a Greek name which occurs in one of the books of the *Iliad* (VI.154), in a reference to a son of Aeolus, who was in turn the father of Glaucus and the grandfather of Bellerophon. It was Glaucus who revealed his identity to Diomedes as they were about to engage in mortal combat. He came from the region of Argolis – as did Sisyphus – and the city of Ephyra. 'Sisyphus' is also Socrates' interlocutor in the dialogue that Plato named after him, *Sisyphus: Or, Upon Taking Counsel.* He was a Thessalian from Pharsalus, but although the interlocutor is fictitious, the name was probably not chosen at random. In a dialogue which focuses on language, the name 'Sisyphus' is particularly symbolic.

In Greek, the name is in fact remarkable for the doubling of the 's' sound, without the variation of this voiced consonant which is possible in the French language. The name appears in Hesychius of Miletus' *Onomatologos* in the form of Sesephos, while Salomon Reinach points out that 'si-suphos' is 'an intensified form of the word "sophos" '. Sisyphus is therefore very wise, very knowledgeable, or rather very subtle. He is described in the line of the *Iliad* referred to above as 'that sharpest of all men' (*ho kerdistos genet'andron*), and in one of Horace's *Satires* (II.3, 1.21) as 'the artful Sisyphus' (*vafer Sisyphus*).

The glosses picked up on this characteristic. From the scholiast who explains the reference to Sisyphus' artifice in Aristophanes' *Acharneis* (1. 390), where the Chorus advises Dicaeopolis to *mechanai tou Sisyphou* ('expose your Sisyphean wiles'), we learn that, for the poets, Sisyphus was the archetype of the cunning and industrious man (*pansyrgos*), a veritable Panurge. In view of this, it is possible to understand how Odysseus was able to pass for a son, or at least a descendant, of Sisyphus (*Sisypheion sperma*), according to the expression used by Euripides in *Iphigeneia in Aulis* (1. 524). Sisyphus would therefore tend to be seen as a sort of super-Odysseus.

TOPONYMY

On the basis of the few indications given above, Sisyphus' dwelling-place appears to be divided between northern continental Greece and Ithaca. However, tradition tends to situate him in the city of Corinth, with which his name is usually linked. In the line quoted above, Horace associates his name with the bronze of Corinth which owed its characteristic colour to the fact that the white-hot metal was plunged into the Fountain of Peirene. In his *Thebaid* (II.380), Statius refers to the harbours of Corinth as the *Sisyphii portus*, while in Book VIII of his *Geography*, Strabo describes the site of Corinth, the famous city ruled by Sisyphus. He locates the Fountain of Peirene on the 'precipices of the Acrocorinth' and, a little below it, the impressive ruins of a temple or palace which, like Diodorus Siculus, he calls the 'Sisypheum'.

Because Ephyra was the ancient name of Corinth, the Homeric tradition can therefore be easily reconciled with later information. It is even possible to consider that it was the name of the most ancient part of the Acrocorinth, founded by Sisyphus.

In fact, 'constructed' would be a more appropriate term than 'founded', since it is here that the onomastic ('artifice') and toponymic aspects of the Sisyphus myth coincide. Modern tourists are still surprised by the Cyclopean blocks of marble which constitute the ruins of ancient Corinth, and of the Sisypheum in particular. As Salomon Reinach points out: 'in all countries where huge monuments have survived which, although of indeterminate date are certainly of ancient origin, legend (or rather myth, for this certainly involves a myth of foundation), adopts them and attributes their construction either to giants or to men endowed with magical powers or superior intelligence'. The ruins of the Mycenaean civilization were considered to be the work of the Cyclopes. On the frieze of the Theseum at Athens the Pelasgi are depicted juggling with large pieces of rock, an illustration of a legend which was, moreover, unknown and which 'explained' their ability to move extremely heavy materials. Sisyphus is said to have been one of the skilful architects admired by posterity. This is why, according to Salomon Reinach, he has been depicted as rolling a huge stone to the top of a mountain, which is supposed to be the Acrocorinth. We know from Pausanias (X.31.10) that the famous artist Polygnotus represented him in this way in his painting of Hell.

THE PUNISHMENT OF SISYPHUS

The parallel is both tempting and misleading, since it is difficult to make the link between Sisyphus as the architect of the Acrocorinth and the damned soul 'in torment' described in book XI of the *Odyssey* (ll. 593–600):

> wrestling double-handed with a giant stone. He would thrust with hands and feet, working it towards the crest of his ridge: but when he was almost at the top, it would twist back irresistibly and roll itself down again to the level [. . .] Once more he would push and heave at it, with sweat pouring down his limbs, and a dust cloud mantling higher than his head.

The passage fell prey to the mythoclasts, and Aristarchus had already condemned it. It seemed unlikely that Sisyphus would come to move his stone in the area prepared by Odysseus, according to Circe's instructions, for the evocation of the dead, although it is possible that evocation in the true sense of the word was replaced by vision. Nor did Aeneas penetrate any further into the depths of Tartarus, where damned souls expiated crimes punished by similar torments (e.g. the Lapiths also pushed a huge rock). However, Sisyphus was not among them or, at least, he is not mentioned by name.

Salomon Reinach, who finds the representation of Sisyphus' punishment just as absurd – as well as the punishments suffered by other damned souls in Homer's Hades and Virgil's Tartarus – has advanced the hypothesis that the myth has been distorted by the popular imagination. He suggests that there was a very early image of Sisyphus the architect rolling a huge stone towards the top of the Acrocorinth for the construction of the Sisypheum. Such an image would have been one of glorification, but when the distinction began to be made between the damned and the other souls in Hades, the image was reused with a very different meaning, that of punishment imposed for a crime.

Such a hypothesis is not entirely necessary. According to Greek representations of the world of the dead – as well as those of Dante's *Inferno* and popular belief – the dead are seen as continuing the main activity of their earthly existence. For example, Heracles, who was not damned, continued to practise archery (*Odyssey*, XI.601 ff.). Sisyphus as the bearer of stone can therefore easily continue to be seen in the same capacity after his death.

HIS CRIME

What crime did Sisyphus in fact commit? He is most likely to have been guilty of 'hubris'. He dared to carry, or have carried, stones of a greater weight than man is able to bear. Paradoxically, this is an idea that has been expressed more frequently by the 'Moderns' than by the 'Ancients'.

A few references in such Latin poets as Ovid and Horace, and the fables of Hyginus, have provided inspiration for various versions of an epic of which the basic and sometimes contradictory events have been preserved by the textbooks on mythology. Listed below are those elements recorded in François Noël's *Dictionnaire de la fable* (1801), which found in Homer what others may look for in vain:

1 He carried out various acts of brigandry throughout Attica and tortured to

death anyone who fell into his hands. Theseus, King of Athens, waged war against him and killed him in combat. The gods punished him in Tartarus for all the crimes he had committed on Earth.

2 He seduced Tyro, the niece of Salmoneus, King of Thessaly.

3 Sisyphus informed the distraught river god Asopus that Zeus had carried off his daughter Aegina, demanding in return that Asopus create a perpetual spring on top of the Acrocorinth. Asopus pursued Zeus, who escaped him by turning himself into a stone and ordered Hermes to carry Sisyphus off by force and take him to hell.

4 Sisyphus persuaded Hades to try on the handcuffs that the latter wanted to put on him. When the god put them on his wrists, Sisyphus locked them and kept him prisoner in his own house.

5 Knowing that death was approaching, Sisyphus instructed his wife not to bury his body. He wanted to test her love, hoping that she would ignore his instructions. However, she obeyed them to the letter and Sisyphus therefore asked Hades to allow him to return to earth in order to punish his wife and carry out his own burial. But having once more breathed the air of the mortal world, he did not want to return to the underworld. Hermes had to come and take him back by force and he was severely punished for breaking his promise to Hades.

INTERPRETATION

An examination of the different traditions reveals that the myth of Sisyphus has two focal points: innocence and guilt.

Sisyphus is not accused of any form of crime in the passage from the *Iliad* quoted above. Furthermore, in the *Apologia Sokratous* (The Apology of Socrates), the philosopher, who has been condemned to death, evokes those whom he will have the pleasure of meeting in the other world when he is 'freed from these men who claim to dispense justice':

> At what price would you not estimate a conference with Orpheus and Musaeus, Hesiod and Homer? I indeed should be willing to die often, if this be true. For to me the sojourn there would be admirable, when I should meet with Palamedes, and Ajax son of Telamon, and any other of the ancients who has died by an unjust sentence. The comparing my sufferings with theirs would, I think, be no unpleasing occupation. But the greatest pleasure would be to spend my time in questioning and examining the people there as I have done those here, and discovering who among them is wise, and who fancies himself to be so but is not. At what price, my judges, would not any one estimate the opportunity of questioning him who led that mighty army against Troy, or Odysseus, or Sisyphus, or ten thousand others, whom one might mention, both men and women? To converse and associate with them and to question them would be an inconceivable happiness.

However, Sisyphus was guilty of having tried to interfere with the activities of the gods, or of betraying their secret by believing that he would remain unpunished. Alternatively, he tried to outwit death and thus deserved to be treated in the same way as those guilty of fraud in Dante's *Inferno*. Or yet again, over-confident in his own strength and cunning and too attached to life, he believed himself to be above the human condition. Although he was generally recognized as intelligent, Sisyphus is considered to have sinned because he was too intelligent. But Socrates, confronted with human stupidity, preferred to converse with that kind of intelligence.

THE TEMPTATION OF ALLEGORY

As can be seen, the figure of Sisyphus lends itself to a wide range of interpretations and, as such, is a stimulating subject for modern thought. However, it has not managed to avoid the allegorical interpretation. In the second lesson of his *Philosophie der Mythologie*, Schelling – with whom this allegorical treatment was extremely unpopular – defines it as a concept 'which presupposes a doctrinal truth and meaning and which claims that a truth was, at least originally, implied'. The inconvenience as far as Schelling is concerned is that 'this concept sacrifices the appropriate meaning of the myth and invests it instead with a meaning which is entirely inappropriate'. In an attempt to propose an alternative meaning, the allegorical interpretation alters the meaning.

Given below are a few examples which apply to the case of Sisyphus:

1. In François Noël's *Dictionnaire de la fable* referred to above: 'The stone that he is made to roll continuously uphill is the symbol of an ambitious prince who turned ideas over in his mind for a long time but never carried them out'.

   There is no basis for this interpretation in the canonical texts, not even the later ones. It is rather based on a pun which is only made possible by the French language, i.e. *rouler un rocher* (to roll a stone) and *rouler des desseins* (to turn ideas over).
2. There is a reference to Sisyphus, not in the works of Jung, who does not appear to mention him, but in the introduction to *Metamorphoses de l'ame et ses symboles*, the French translation of Jung's *Symbole der Wandlung: Analyse des Vorspiels zu einer Schizophrenie* by Yves le Lay:

   > It was only belatedly and after a great deal of effort that man reached the stage of discursive reasoning which is expressed by words. Its spontaneous form is the image which is inaccessible and incommunicable to others, a mysterious rebus consisting of analogies which are often indecipherable because they are based on individual assumptions. Why, for example, should one person see life in terms of a cyclist riding a bicycle with great difficulty? Everyone is familiar with the image of Sisyphus' stone which represents disillusioned effort and which – contrary to Freud's claims in respect of numerous symbols – does not

involve a deliberate atempt at concealment. These are elementary forms of thought, those which occur to us spontaneously and which we encounter in the day-dreams in which we indulge, as well as in dreams, which it is impossible to consider as a product of our will.

SISYPHUS IN POETRY

For the poets, Sisyphus acts as a sort of foil. Hopelessly weighed down by the stone, and perhaps also by the earthly thoughts which prevented him from aspiring to the unknown, he is the anti-poet *par excellence.* At the very most, he became the patron of these craftsmen of words, who manipulated words and tropes in the same way that he bore heavy pieces of stone to the top of the Acrocorinth. According to Victor Hugo's preface to *Odes et Ballades* (1824), 'rhetors' and 'teachers' were 'poor, breathless Sisyphuses who are continually rolling their stone to the top of a hill'.

Baudelaire did not reject Sisyphus but rather kept him at a distance, or felt distant from him. We are familiar with his use of the myth in 'Le Cygne', which 'for [him] turns to allegory', i.e. enables him to write about himself. In 'Le Guignon' – sent to Théophile Gautier for *La Revue de Paris* between September 1851 and the beginning of January 1852, and published for the first time in *La Revue des deux mondes* on 1 June 1855 – he does not identify with Sisyphus, but points out the difference between the man who was able to bear the weight of his stone and modern man who is unable to bear that of his 'guignon' (misfortune):

Pour soulever un poids si lourd,
Sisyphe, il faudrait ton courage!
Bien qu'on ait du coeur à l'ouvrage,
L'Art est long et le Temps et court.

Flesh is willing, but the Soul requires
Sisyphean patience for its song.
Time, Hippocrates remarked, is short
and Art is long.

Throughout the poem, which is an outline of a moral portrait of the modern artist, there is a noticeable reluctance on Baudelaire's part to use the first person as a form of expression. He also makes a clear distinction between 'heart' (willingness) and 'courage' (Sisyphean patience). On the one hand, a simple surge of enthusiasm is doomed to failure and contrasts with the true heroism of Sisyphus, which is a new facet of his character. Sisyphus is not prepared to submit passively to the punishment meted out to him and raises the expiatory act to the level of a heroic deed. It is true that the damned soul has all eternity before him, even if it is to accomplish an action which must be perpetually repeated. The artist, on the other hand, feels pressurized and restricted by the constraints of time, which do not allow him to pursue his art to its conclusion. The consolation of the continued survival of Art is not enough for him. According to Paul Bénichou, 'the poet feels powerless to lift "the heavy weight" [*poids si lourd*] which impedes the creative act'.

Sisyphus is not mentioned in the three other stanzas of 'Le Guignon', but the thought of death which weighs heavily upon them is surely still the weight of the stone. The second quatrain evokes a funereal setting, using the effect of voiced and unvoiced consonants made possible by the French pronunciation of Sisyphus' name:

> Loin des sépultures célèbres,
> Vers un cimetière isolé,
> Mon coeur, comme un tambour voilé,
> Va battant des marches funèbres.
>
> No illustrious tombstones ornament
> the lonely churchyard where I often go
> to hear my heart, a muffled drum, parade
> incognito.

This is the solitude of great condemned souls such as Sisyphus. But it is above all the solitude of the artist who remains unrecognized. An anonymous death will mark the end of an existence which – 'parading incognito' – merely anticipates this death.

The contempt in which the artist is held by the general public may be due to their disregard for, or neglect of, an art which will possibly have more impact if it is left 'forgotten in the dust' and preserved for a brilliant exhumation:

> Maint joyau dort enseveli
> Dans les ténèbres et l'oubli,
> Bien loin des pioches et des sondes.
>
> Many a gem, the poet mourns, abides
> forgotten in the dust,
> unnoticed there.

But in its solitude it is possible for the work of art, like the artist, to fade away as a result of the gift of self which it is always ready to make and which nobody wants:

> Mainte fleur épanche à regret
> Son parfum doux comme un secret
> Dans les solitudes profondes.
>
> Many a rose regretfully confides
> The secret of its scent
> to empty air.

However, the poetry of René Char enables us to witness the identification of the artist with Sisyphus and, as a result, the latter's metamorphosis. Paying homage to Georges Braque on the occasion of his eightieth birthday, the poet describes him as 'a Sisyphus-bird' (*Recherche de la base et du sommet*, edn. de la Pléiade: 679). Miraculously freed from his burden, it seems that Sisyphus has achieved this freedom by becoming accustomed to its weight.

THE DELIVERANCE OF SISYPHUS

Curiously enough, the Romantics do not appear to have produced a Sisyphus reconciled, like Balzac's Melmoth, or a Sisyphus unbound, like Shelley's Prometheus. Sisyphus punished, the alternative Sisyphus, assumed another aspect and made use of another myth. This is the case, for example, in Mary Lafon's *Bertran de Born* (1839). Although the troubadour is in the same situation as Sisyphus, he able to move. He breaks out of the circle of his suffering and goes towards a real future:

> What a destiny! How fate had hounded him since his birth! [. . .] But his energy had never faltered in this constantly renewed and ill-fated struggle. Although this Sisyphus' stone had continued to rebound heavily against his chest, he had obstinately persisted in rolling it back up the mountain. He was bruised with the incurable wounds opened beneath his left breast by the bitter disappointment of great hopes, by unexpected disillusionment and by the ironic injustice of a blind destiny which, before your very eyes, unstintingly allows the unworthy to reap the reward of your sleepless nights, your receding forehead, and your soul withered by proud anguish. Bruised by these bleeding wounds, he continued to walk steadfastly towards the same goal.

It is precisely because he is able to walk that he is different from Sisyphus. Marked by fate, the hero is also touched by the wing of the future which makes him a prophet. He dreams of a free and great Aquitaine, and another author of that century, Laurens, is able to make him *Le Tyrtée du Moyen Age*.

Isi Collin's *Sisyphe et le Juif errant* (Sisyphus and the Wandering Jew, 1914) was a late Symbolist text which made it possible to achieve what Romanticism could not. The work presents the Wandering Jew, who arrives at twilight on a narrow mountain plateau, where he meets Sisyphus and the Faun whose music soothes suffering. The situation is the same as that of Prometheus in the Caucasus. The cry of rebellion of the 'unhappy Sisyphus' softens the heart of the Traveller who, until then, could not be moved to pity. He decides to give his cloak and staff to Sisyphus, who is momentarily attracted by the idea of rediscovering Earth and its inhabitants. But as the Wandering Jew paints the picture of past history, Sisyphus realizes that the gods of this earth have been good to him and that he loves the block of stone which has been moulded by his hands. Therefore, just as they are about to part company and exchange destinies, these two symbols of human suffering refuse to rid themselves of their curse – stagnation for one, and endless wandering for the other – and as night falls, they go their own separate ways, their hearts full of renewed hope. The dialogue is therefore the dramatization of a moral transformation of the two heroes, who come to reject any form of transcendence in order to be better able to bear the beauty and suffering of this world.

A text of this nature paves the way for Camus's Sisyphus, who is liberated insofar as he becomes reconciled to his fate and accepts it lucidly. The plan for the work dates from May 1936 and from a period when Camus was fascinated by the work of André Malraux, while still affected by the influence of his teacher and mentor Jean Grenier and his own philosophical reading, particularly of Kierkegaard and Nietzsche.

Suffering from ill-health and disillusioned by his political affiliations and personal relationships, Camus only resisted the temptation of suicide in order to ask himself the fundamental question of 'judging whether or not life is worth living'. According to Louis Faucon's notes to the Pléiade edition of the work, '*Le Mythe* [de Sisyphe] is constructed progressively on the theme of lucid defiance in the face of an unjust sentence, by the rejection of any form of supernatural assistance or posthumous revenge'. The work was finished in Oran in February 1941.

The choice of Sisyphus may have come from an observation made by Jean Grenier in his *Essai sur l'esprit d'orthodoxie* (Gallimard, 1932: 181):

> Whenever the myth of Prometheus is discussed, its outcome, which is the most important part, is always forgotten. And Sisyphus is never mentioned.

As Camus was finishing the work, between September 1940 and February 1941, he chose the story of Sisyphus' punishment as the title for the complete book.

The sources for the final chapter – which bears the same title as the book (i.e. *Le Mythe de Sisyphe*) – are modest: Commelin's *Nouvelle Mythologie grecque* (Garnier, 1909) and the *Grand Dictionnaire universel Larousse*. It is in fact possible to find most of what Camus has taken from the tradition of the myth in François Noël's *Dictionnaire de la fable*, which must have been freely plagiarized by his successors. A great deal is attributed to Homer in particular. Although it is true that the *Iliad* presents Sisyphus as 'the wisest and most prudent of mortals' (a phrase which Camus intensifies and expands), and that the *Odyssey* describes the inevitable descent of the stone, Homer does not explore the designs of the gods and makes no mention of the episode where Sisyphus put Death in chains. Camus was aware of the lesser traditions – Sisyphus the brigand, Sisyphus 'informing' on Jupiter, and Sisyphus returning to Earth and unable to tear himself away from its delights. But they provide him with the opportunity for the symbolism which is characteristic of his work – the non-contradiction of wisdom and brigandry (cf. Odysseus); the importance given to the healing power of water (cf. Prometheus in *L'Eté*); his ready indulgence in and enjoyment of the evocation of the delights of the Mediterranean landscape.

Camus chooses to make Sisyphus a character, and for him 'Sisyphus is the hero of the absurd'. He even creates in him a sort of trinity of the absurd, in the form of his contempt for the gods, his hatred of death and his passion for living. It is this last term that Camus stresses once again to the point of tripling its intensity: 'passions', 'passion for living' and 'passions of this earth'.

'We are told nothing of Sisyphus in Hell.' This is a strange statement because the *Odyssey* tells of nothing else. Camus revives Homer's description extremely successfully, as he turns from the contemplation of the stone to contemplate Sisyphus. He transfers the focus from the effort made by the body to the 'contorted face', and especially to Sisyphus' expression when the stone rolls back down the hill. It is this moment that interests him, and the expression on Sisyphus' face at this moment. He sees neither despair nor the satisfaction of pointless heroism, but a 'lucidity' which enables Sisyphus to rise above his destiny:

> Sisyphus, the proletarian god, powerless and rebellious, fully understands the wretchedness of his condition: it is of this that he thinks during the descent. The lucidity that was to be the cause of his torment, simultaneously confirms his victory. There is no destiny which cannot be overcome by contempt.

Attaching too much importance to the stone allows misfortune to triumph. Camus's Sisyphus accepts his stone, accepts the series of unconnected actions which stretches both behind and in front of him. 'We must imagine Sisyphus happy', and his happiness is born of his acceptance. Camus is here thinking not so much of the textbooks on mythology as of Nietzsche and his paradoxical remarks on the serenity of Oedipus in chapter 9 of his *Die Geburt der Tragödie* (1827; Eng. trans. as *The Birth of Tragedy*, in *Basic Writings of Nietzsche*, 1968), which gives rise to the comparison between Oedipus and Sisyphus, elevating the latter to the status of a tragic hero, while rising above the tragic. Sisyphus' acceptance is the equivalent of Nietzsche's '*amor fati*'. Camus had also noted in his *Carnets* the following phrase from the *Götzen-Dämmerung* (1889), translated into English as *Twilight of the Idols* in *The Portable Nietzsche*: 'The tragic artist is not a pessimist. He accepts all that is problematic and terrible'.

Sisyphus was therefore for Camus, as he was for Baudelaire, a potential representation of the artist, a superior (and for Baudelaire an ideal) artist who, like Camus, could say 'writing is my greatest joy' (*Carnets*: 77). But once the work was completed (i.e. the stone had rolled back down the hill), the expression of relief uttered as he realized he had finished *Le Mythe de Sisyphe* on 21 February 1941, and the feeling of freedom regained, were accompanied by the certainty that he would have to continue and begin all over again. Perhaps this is what Nietzsche meant by 'being equal to circumstances', when referring to Odysseus in *Morgenröte* (1881; Eng. trans. as *The Dawn of Day*, 1911). He also noted (306) that the Greeks knew that this required 'an aptitude for falsehood and for terrible and cunning retribution', i.e. not merely *sophia* but *se-sophia*.

Pierre Brunel

The Spinners

And it is also with cotton from Aleppo, with which we scarcely line our purses in Rouen, that the Syrian spinners weave the weft of the pastures; but spinning requires patience, and patience achieves everything.

Amsterdam *Mémoires du Baron de Tott sur les Turcs et les Tartares*, IV: 104 (1785)

Our human origins – the origins which, as soon as we try to explain them, make us feel that they are inexplicable – are always shrouded in silence and deep shadows. To distance himself from these origins, Man has continuously and painstakingly followed the paths of discovery and re-discovery because, to distinguish himself from the gods responsible for his existence, he has had to invent his own history. The history of humanity began with myths, and it is the myth of the Spinners in particular that still links us firmly to the most fertile and dynamic images in our collective imagination.

As the first images of divinity, the Spinners provide us with endless ways of interpreting the unfolding of every form of life within the framework established by birth and death. To comprehend all states of existence, to understand what links them to each other and what gives us, the human race, a sense of being connected to an earlier period, we are obliged to explore deeper levels of understanding, and so discover the periodic laws of temporal succession. It was in this context that these divinities, who were originally deities of heavenly waters, dispensed rain and dew, and it was the vision of natural substances as an interwoven fabric that provided the basis for the image of the goddesses as spinners. There are three goddesses, and the sacred nature of their number appears to reflect an association with winter, spring and summer, the only seasons recognized by ancient peoples. On a more temporal level, the concept of destiny, which Homer regarded as inescapable, was responsible for the development of the single figure of the Moira into the image of the three sisters. All such divinities from the Charities to the Horae, the Graces to the Parcae and the Norns, remind us that we are mortal and remain subject to the inevitability of death.

Thus, at the beginning of time, Woman worked and produced, and her first attributes were entirely related to the art of spinning. According to Paul Sébillot, 'it is in terms of spinning that the ancientness or the unlikelihood of a thing is expressed '. With its tendency to individualize and compartmentalize, Greek mythology stressed continuity of movement and successive circles of existence, and it represented these elements as the actions performed by the spinner.

The spinner was invested with the power of beginning and interrupting. In religious, spiritual and daily life, the Spinner or Spinners, as a single or triple image, impressed their female primacy upon the world, to the point of threatening the sovereignty and domination of Zeus himself. The human destiny that they span and controlled could only be influenced by the other gods.

In attempting to examine the nature of extent of the power of the Spinners, the present article will devote a considerable amount of attention to spinners' actions and implements, as well as to their symbolic significance. It will examine the link between the Spinners and time, and the reason for the Spinners' dependence upon each other. In addition, it will consider why the Spinners represent everyday womanhood, why they are the guardians of the divine fertility of the earth, and why they have the crucial task of watching over the cycles of day and life, and of enforcing the rigid laws governing our relationship with death – our individual deaths and death in general.

We do not know how beautiful, young or old, these divine Spinners are. Mythographers and poets alike are unable to tell us in what part of heaven they sat to spin their thread of natural flax. Whether they were goddesses from the outset, or were more recent personifications, they have become, first and foremost, an embodiment of Woman.

The Spinners evoke the image of the Triple Goddess, or are associated with the underworld or the moon. They are a holy or an ambiguous trinity, presiding over magical rites, deliveries and human births. But were they also women with desires? Was the association of the Spinners with desire responsible for the universal tradition according to which it is women who spin, weave and sew?

The present study of the myth of the Spinners will also take account of the new light thrown on the subject by modern psychoanalysis. In addition, by examining various aspects of spinning ranging from the emergence of its symbolic connotations to its status as an everyday domestic activity, it will also try to identify the element of femininity that affects the work and daily lives of men.

ACTIONS AND IMPLEMENTS

Among other artefacts related to primitive forms of craftsmanship, recent archaeological discoveries have included a perforated disk used as a spindle indicating that female members of ancient households were engaged in spinning and weaving well before 4000 BC. Indeed, for some, spinning must have provided their only means of subsistence. Thus, long before the period of pottery production, the spindle was among the many household articles employed solely by women. Its use proliferated throughout the regions bordering the Mediterranean, in the ancient cities of central and eastern Europe, in western Asia and throughout India. Consequently, its Indo-European origins appear to be clearly attested.

As in the case of other specialized crafts, it would be useful to define the technical parameters of early spinning and weaving. In *Le Fil du Temps, Ethnologie et Préhistoire* (1920–70), André Leroi-Gourhan provides information that enables us to reassess our historical perspective on the development of these techniques, and invites us to consider their symbolic and aesthetic value in a completely different light.

According to him, the actions and implements of the spinner-craftswoman as she is traditionally represented are a spatial extension of her body. Actions and implements combine to produce a concretization of space. Each engenders the other in the reciprocal relationship. In the myth, they are there from the very beginning, chosen elements that are described precisely and definitively. Their characteristics have been established for a long time, and the repeated circular movements are echoed in temporal terms. They are work-related elements that invalidate the fleeting and arbitrary nature of all other actions.

An attentive reading of *L'Homme et la Matière* raises new questions concerning possible interpretations of the significance of the female body as it works, spins, thinks, acquires, acts and creates.

FROM THE SPINDLE TO THE WHEEL

In more specific terms, the spinners' actions are precisely those that the body must adopt in order to make a particular product. The action of twisting the fibres produces a continuous thread that is fine and strong, and as long as possible. The spinner's main range of actions was originally limited, being deliberately confined to those primarily concerned with the preparation and twisting of the fibres. Three more specific actions were subsequently introduced into the process of making the thread. The first was 'teasing', which involved taking hold of a few strands from the mass of prepared fibres and using them to pull out the others. The second was 'twisting', which involved making the spindle revolve, so that it twisted the mass of fibres into a thread; while the third and final action was 'winding', which merely involved rolling the thread up.

The Fates or Moirae span flax, which has to be crushed so that it can be divided and then softened. Very early in the history of domestic life, the natural fibres then in use – flax, hemp and ramie – had to be retted, crushed and carded. This preparation work was followed by the action of spinning in the strict sense of the word, which required the use of specialized implements, described with great precision by Pliny. The spinning process produces both the qualities of a good thread and the faults of a bad thread.

At this point we should return to the division of the spinning process into three techniques, since this provides a link with the triple figure of the Moirae. The German tale of *The Three Spinners* by Grimm is a fine illustration of this motif. An idle young girl who does not want to spin is promised that, when she has spun all the flax that fills three rooms in the palace, she will marry the queen's eldest son. It takes her three days to realize the impossible nature of the task, at which point three women come to her aid:

> The first woman span the tow and turned the wheel, the second soaked the thread, while the third twisted it and pressed it on the table with her thumb, and each time she pressed it, a skein of the finest thread fell to the floor.

The three days and the three women appear to symbolize the triple unity of time, space and the body of the spinner. There are three temporal stages in producing thread, and the body has to accommodate this technical division through making three different movements or actions. It is the complementary nature of the temporal and spatial actions involved in spinning that gave the figure three its magical and religious significance in the myths of the Spinners. Three sequences and postures were required to achieve the state of completion, totality and perfection. The importance of the spinner's implements in popular ritual and tradition attests to their symbolic value in domestic life. They are responsible for establishing the image of spinning as an ancient female activity, and, indeed, the technology of spinning as a simple craft has scarcely developed since the description of Parcae given by Aristophanes.

Recent excavations at Gdansk in Poland have dispelled the traditionally held belief that all early spinning was carried out with a spindle. In fact, in *Die Entwicklung des Spinnens*, Horwitz identifies eight types of spinning, although the spindle was undoubtedly the first implement to be used by the spinner. By employing it, the spinner-craftswoman eliminated the need to twist the thread between her fingers or to roll it between her palm and her thigh. This appears to have partly freed the spinner's body from a sequence of functional actions and to have enabled her to develop the basis of the true circular movement associated with the craft. Thus, from the very outset, the spindle – the first mechanism to be involved – completely and unequivocally established the three operations that constitute the spinning process. Twisting the thread generally involved either allowing a spindle to hang freely at the end of the thread (in which case its rotation was slow and regular), or setting in motion a type of spindle that was fixed to the bottom of a bowl or to the ground. This spindle would spin on its point at great speed for a limited period, and before slowing down and then stopping.

With the invention of the wheel, spinning became a continuous and regular process, and the craft benefited in terms of savings in time and improvements in quality. Like thc spindle, the wheel also took numerous forms, with the number of cords driving it constituting the technical difference between the various types. The 'two-cord' spinning-wheel is the earliest model: one cord turns a flywheel, like a driving-wheel, while the other cord, which is also attached to the flywheel, operates the spindle. The thread is wound as a result of the difference in speed produced by a different rate of transmission. In technological terms, the development of the spinning-wheel provided the basis for changes and inventions that altered the course of human history, but did its introduction mean that the spinner required a new form of understanding so that she too could create a new type of instrumentation that would ensure the future of her craft? The wheel was the first element in a series of complex combinations of implements designed to satisfy the human desire for perfection. Thus, during the Renaissance, in his *Codex Atlantico*, Leonardo da Vinci suggested a process for spinning the most widely used textiles of the period.

According to a passage in the famous Brunswick-Lüneberg chronicle, the spinning-wheel was invented in 1530 by a stone mason and master sculptor from Wattenbüttel. The spinning-wheel was then developed into the treadle-wheel, and the device's introduction into Spain, Italy, Hungary and Poland was only slightly affected by the Industrial Revolution.

Without wishing to compare the life of objects with the life of human beings, the development of the wheel raises the subject of the spinner's creative desire. For example, did the relationship between the different types of wheels and their specific, localized distribution provide the basis for a social and cultural identity, and did women make a conscious decision to ensure that spinning remained their own particular domain?

'SPIN MY DISTAFF'

In Greek mythology, the safety of a city dedicated to the worship of the goddess Athena was guaranteed by the Palladium and, in addition to bearing her attributes as the goddess of war, this magical statue of Athena holds a distaff and a spindle. These symbolize the basis of city life, constituted by the domestic arts and manual dexterity, and also act as concrete metaphors for the passing of the days, for the end of the spinning process when the distaff is empty, for the inexorable passage of a finite period of time. The first representation of the distaff appears in the Spanish Ibrabanus manuscript (1023), but Paul Sébillot reminds us in *Légendes et Curiosités des Métiers* of the important role played by this precious object, at almost all periods of history, both in female initiation ceremonies and as an attribute of women in general. In Gaul, in the presence of the goddess Mehellenia, brides were given a distaff laden with flax, which they would spin for a short while. Similarly, at weddings in the Landes region of France, an old woman would carry a distaff and often stand between the bride and groom. Meanwhile, for a long time, spinning wheels and distaffs were the presents most commonly given to girls. In the story by Mme d'Aulnoy, German spinning-wheels and distaffs made of cedar wood were presented to the fairies who had helped the Princess Printanière. At other periods and in other regions (for example Britanny), lovers gave their sweetheart a carved distaff bearing symbols and mottoes, and inscribed with her name.

Finally, when a noblewoman who had lived a pious life devoted to domestic activities died, her distaff was the only object that was buried with her, as an item of personal property for the exclusive use of the departed soul. This was perhaps a manifestation of the belief, which has survived in nearly all nations since Neolithic times, that the dead have the same needs as the living.

In a technical context, the earliest form of distaff of which readily accessible examples still survive, is the 'heeled' type. When this was employed, the spinner passed the handle of the distaff through her belt and the rewinding was done using a spindle equipped with an upper hook.

As demonstrated by specimens of cloth in numerous museums – the best being in the Musée de Cluny with its collection of carved wooden distaffs – the main occupations of women over the centuries revolved around the production of thread. This represented a veritable act of female initiation, from which men were excluded. As they sat spinning in the evenings, out of sight of their menfolk, the spinners talked, told stories and sang. These practices were both disturbing and fascinating, and by the continual action of spinning, the spinner may have seemed to be able to enter another – perhaps sacred – dimension, supposed to exist beyond the secular world.

L'EVANGILE DES QUENOUILLES

In stories and legends, the stages in this process of initiation are marked by tests to which the heroine is subjected:

> The next day, she was sent into the fields. She was given tow, a distaff and a spindle so that she could spin while looking after her sheep. She went to fetch her wheel which was able to spin on its own, put the tow on the wheel and placed her distaff next to it, and the wheel began to spin while she looked after the sheep. In the evening, she wound the thread onto the spindle and took it home.
>
> (Type 31 B, version 4 in the *Catalogue Delarue*)

The heroine's success is associated with her acquisition of the magic wheel, for it is the wheel that enables her to meet the king's son. The version of the story of Cinderella from the Nivernais region of France portrays a heroine who 'worked diligently and, in the evening, brought home her seven spindles of thread . . .' – though she was fortunate enough to meet some fairies who relieved her of this wearisome task. In the story, the characters who carry out the spinning, serve primarily to illustrate the magical powers of the spinner and her implements, which are almost interchangeable. The combination or exchange of these powers always brings the spinner peace, happiness and love, while the initiatory nature of the spinners' work is further emphasized by the places and times at which it is carried out.

Although archaeologists and mythologists state that nothing is known of the time or place at which the Fates sat spinning, stories and legends favour the period from early evening to nightfall. The woman, alone or in the company of other women, sits spinning by the fireside, dreaming of some fortunate event that will befall her while she is looking after the flocks in the fields. Thus spinners, who have always adopted the same positions and postures when engaged in their work, acquired a reputation that endowed them with other roles and functions. For some, they became saints or sorceresses, while in the Dauphiné region of France, they were seen as debauched women or even prostitutes.

L'Evangile des Quenouilles related the habits and customs of spinners to a divine message, and the appearance of this idea in literature raises questions about the connections between such beliefs and revelations, and ultimately about the prophetic role of spinners. It remains to be seen how what is written here can be interpreted as the multiple echo of a voice from another dimension. For example, is it the voice of God, or the voice of the Spinners that predicts that, if a young woman hangs the thread that she has spun during the day outside her house, it will stop the young man who is to become her husband?

THE SPIDER'S WEB

The characteristics specific to the thread and to the start of the spinning process, are the same characteristics that set in motion the multiple powers possessed by Woman – by all women. They are responsible for initiating action, in the same way that the natural flax, which is received in a tangled, muddled skein, is frayed, untangled, twisted and wound. It is perhaps through considering the movements of straightening out and winding that form an integral part of the process of spinning that we are best able to understand how all spinning represents a task begun, a task whose unity is based on a process of interweaving. Particularly in stories, the thread provides both the link and the way, and the woman who creates the thread incorporates knots and joins into it. Again according to Paul Sébillot, the spinner is both woman and animal, she is the virgin and the spider, and possesses supernatural powers. She spins at night, so that the weather will be fine the next day, and the webs that she spins conceal sacred objects from view. 'Filasse de la Vierge Marie', 'filés-madame' and 'grippé' are all French magical terms that link the spinner, the fairy and the inventor of these earliest forms of movement. The thread has no beginning and no end. If it is broken by divine will, it can also be rejoined at the point at which it has been broken.

The thread achieves or makes it possible to achieve a connection between the most discordant of objects. It is the link between the abstract and the concrete, and the action of spinning engenders the one by way of the other in a single continuous, reciprocal movement. Noël du Fail reminds us of the traditions in some regions of France relating to penances undergone by certain fairies, whose presence was indicated by a thread lying on the ground near a spring. If a girl from the Lavedan region picked up and quickly wound in the thread, the fairy was freed and rewarded her with the power to use its magic wand.

The characteristic actions and movements of spinning are also trials of strength, imposed on women as if to mark their attainment of womanhood, during a period of emotional and sexual development. In spite of the apparent state of immobility and solitude in which it is carried out, spinning is a task that involves the whole of the woman's body, making it a body with desires. One evening, an old woman was spinning by the fireside, bored and unhappy in her solitude. Suddenly, two large feet fell from the fireplace. They were followed by a pair of legs and the remaining parts of a body that provided her with the companion that she longed for. This is a version of an old English legend that, like several others, is laden with sexual symbolism.

It is impossible to discuss the fertility and fecundity embodied by the spinner without thinking of the frequently used expression 'a woman in labour'. Spinning was the first form of production to establish a link between work and sexuality. This sexuality, which is intially felt only in a confused way, is subsequently formulated in both individual and universal terms and entitles us to represent the actual myth of the Spinners as a mythological place of origin. Indeed, it is a place of origin, a place that engenders other places specific to the female body: sexual organs that regenerate life and establish an immortality that transcends annihilation.

THE MOIRAE AND THE THREAD OF DESTINY

The spindle, the first implement or instrument of the spinner, symbolizes the law of the Eternal Return. According to Plato, the spindle of Necessity regulated the entire cosmos, maintaining an independent balance between life and death. In the course of developing from a single entity into what was conceived as a group of three beings, the Moirae established the female image of the world, representing periodicity, regeneration, transformation, separation and new life. It is this cycle – forming a uniform, circular movement – that unites the three Moirae and also engenders all the other movements involved in the process of spinning, as well as regenerating each individual movement in terms of its own precision and uniqueness. The Spinner-Goddesses had the power to initiate and bring to an end. The thread that they span and cut at will was invested with the same terrible power. In the very early history of the Greek religion, the places of worship dedicated to the Moirae in Athens, Sparta, Olympia and Thebes provided a link between the sacred and human dimensions.

The Moirae span human destiny with spindle and distaff, unmoved by the prayers of men and gods alike. These spinners were neither young and beautiful, nor old and ugly. They were the daughters of the night, the daughters of Themis and Zeus. They remained remote from Mount Olympus, unlike their mother, who was alone admitted to the world of the gods, and they alternated between being dependent upon Zeus and being in conflict with him. It is not known where or when they carried out their task, and thus the thread of destiny was born of mystery.

Until the final century of the Hellenistic period, the Spinners, like Isis, were known as the Triple Moon, and it was around this figure that the religious syncretism of Archaic Greece developed. Thus their myth represents the image of an untarnishable Unique. Like their sisters, the Parcae and the Horae, these unyielding women span destiny, clothed in their white gowns woven from linen thread.

Clotho (the spinning Fate) was the spinner in the true sense of the word, Lachesis (the apportioner of lots) measured the thread, while Atropos was the Fate that could not be avoided, and they intervened at will in individual lives. All three appeared throughout the early oral tradition, and went on to weave their immutable theme through stories and legends.

Their actions were translated into songs of the soil, into the figurative journeys of poetry, and into lyrical refrains. There are few works of art and literature whose basic structure does not imitate the movement of the little spinning-wheel. Meanwhile, in modern oral cultures, figures such as Laima and the Norns are extensions of the Moirae who are so essentially similar that it is often difficult for the non-specialist to distinguish between the Greek, Scandinavian and Slavonic motifs.

At this point, we should return to the image of the triad. According to Georges Dumézil, as well as representing the divine trinity, the number three is a universal symbol of the tripartite division of society into priests, warriors and producers. It is the golden number that lies behind the conception of the Fates as a group of three, which is the threefold embodiment of divine power. Their group recalls numerous other cultural and religious triads, such as the Christian Trinity, the trinity of 'Thunderbolt-Thunder-Lightning', or that of the supreme god in three persons – consisting, according to ancient Peruvian beliefs, of a father, who is the dispenser of justice, an elder son, and a younger son who is the adoptive father of humanity.

Since it first came into being, this ternary image of the Spinners has fascinated poets and philosophers alike. Homer portrays the goddesses in the *Iliad*, and Plotinus conceptualizes them in the *Enneads*. Their association with the number three, which can have benefic or malefic connotations, thus apparently helped to ensure the theme's success. As a consequence, the Spinners, who from earliest times were regarded as the Muses of literature, art and music, continue to fulfil this role in the modern art form of the cinema. In his *Essays on Applied Psychology*, Freud presents the image of the 'three caskets' as a reminder of the close ties between the Moirae, the Graces and the Horae, which he uses as a basis for interpreting the difficult choices that confront us. Meanwhile, many authors and historians have tried to define hypostatic situations by analogy with the physical attitudes and ritual actions of the goddesses. In this way, they have identified the more easily recognizable features that equip human life for its unique destiny: death.

The Moirae became the goddesses of law at a very early period, in the context of an order that existed long before the laws governing the destinies of Achilles and Hector. They differ from the other female figures who spin, in that they initiate all production, which represents the very essence of the reduction to all forms of duality in Man. The later characteristics that they have acquired – and that we have imposed on them – are merely assumptions on our part. Thus, they are called the Ciboria because of the idea that they claim to express. In his *Jeux rustiques*, Henri de Régnier wrote, 'Destiny has woven our days and our years', thereby personifying the universal constraint placed on each and every individual – that of knowing that their death is forecast in advance and in spite of them.

The spinner and her thread represent the most vivid archetypal figures in our imagination. Their images are revived by those of the good and bad fairies, because the fairies belong to the lineage of the Parcae. Indeed, Nicole Belmont sees them as the earliest active embodiments of the archaic figure of the Spinner.

PENELOPE AND THE THREAD OF PATIENCE

Spinning is a process involving continuous repetition of the same actions, and this has shaped the metaphors used to describe the inner – and infinite – labour of women: the dream of creation. By spinning, the spinner becomes all-powerful and ambiguous. In this connection, there is a clear distinction between the activities of spinning and weaving, even though weaving is sometimes merely the inevitable consequence of spinning. Weavers and needlewomen remained subordinate to spinners.

At night, Penelope unravelled, virtually thread by thread, the work that she had started to weave during the day. Her work was constantly being begun again, and when, at night, she unpicked the threads, her powers were those of an antithetical double of the spinner. The work to be completed was a shroud intended for old Laertes, a shroud for the body of Odysseus's father. The latter perhaps represented the body of her own father. In any case, it also represented the boundary between life and death for her husband, who had been absent for twenty years. Certainly, too, the shroud is a condensed representation of both shroud and bedsheet – the sheet on which both the dead and the living take their rest. Penelope's choice of this uniquely female task as a means of avoiding the unwelcome advances of her suitors, presents her in a very different light from the one in which she is usually seen as a symbol of conjugal fidelity. The task of weaving and spinning allowed her time to construct her own defences against men, husband and father. It gave her an opportunity to sublimate her fear of the return of a much older husband who would have forgotten the intimate conversations of their early life together.

If Penelope took Helen's defence, it was to weave appeals that would preserve the ambiguity of her attitude, that would divert attention from her desires. For she was still a woman who was prey to temptation and desires, and her suitors' fervour was a direct response to this. By her secret actions, concealed from their watchful gaze, she fixed in her heart the image of the only man she loved. As she worked, it was to him that she secretly addressed her reproaches, and against him that her mistrust was mainly directed. It would be easy for her husband to deceive her like any other man, by pretending to be someone else, and this was, in fact, the spinner's prediction of the future. Penelope would later tell Ulysses that he had no right to be angry with her because she had not recognized him at once. She had not forgotten his identity, but had rather reconstructed it. She claimed other rights and other considerations for her patience as a spinner and her resistance as a woman.

SPINNERS AND THE THREAD OF TIME

In the course of time, works have appeared featuring pastoral figures who are the handmaidens of the Spinner-Goddesses and whose beauty is invariably inaccessible. Artists have created doubles of the Moirae, and the backgrounds of water, vegetation and sky against which they carry out their task, do not affect their essential nature or weigh them down. Of all these works, Millet's *La Fileuse* (The Spinner, 1850–5; Boston, Museum of Fine Arts) is surely the most hieratic. A single figure dominates the painting. The spinner controls the wheel and the mass of white wool waiting to be spun and subordinates them to her own presence. The reason why we continue to be dazzled and haunted by the picture is because of the balanced harmony of its composition and the perfectly natural way in which this scene from rural life is reproduced. The figure of the spinner is at one with the slow revolution of the wheel as she leans forward to gather up the thread, in a movement that is both initial and complementary.

We are fascinated by the spinner whose body is at one with her movements and whose everyday and eternal nature complement each other in an even, unified pattern of light and shadow, veiled in solitude. In her eye we might catch a glimpse of the question – that still continues to be asked – of what path the thread will follow. Seamstresses, a shepherdess who sits knitting on a rock as her flock grazes around her, a child being taught to knit by her mother, a carder, another spinner from the Auvergne region: all provide the subjects of drawings and etchings in which Millet has tried to exhaust the theme of the spinner.

The theme of *Gretchen am Spinnrade* is completely different. It is a reflection of anxiety and illusion in which the words of the spinner are exalted in a magnificent monologue revealing an inner miracle. Schubert's skill at polishing and refining his musical compositions has resulted in one of his most beautiful lieder, the effect of which is reinforced by the simulated whirring of the spinning wheel. The voice that accompanies the progress of the thread gradually rises, in anguish and despair, to become a deeply moving and shameless cry of love. It is as if the spinner has become transfixed in her distress. The concluding passage evokes a state of total desolation, before she brings her youthful suffering to an end almost in a whisper, representing an inner peace, the calm of rediscovering words after a period of torment. One of the most celebrated performances of the work is that by Elizabeth Schwarzkopf, with piano accompaniment by Edwin Fischer. Once again, for Gretchen and for the singer, it is when she is spinning that she has the time to think about her suffering. This is the time of words, words that have the power to heal.

The period of time involved can be short or long. It can be a time of silence or a time filled with cries. It is a time for fulfilling a function that is always the same and unique. Women have spun since the beginning of time, so that their language was the product of this early time of spinning and represented a multiplicity of voices born in the mind of a woman whose hands were never still. Early language meant mythos and logos, and speaking meant defining oneself. Meanwhile, spinning represented the persistent domestic tasks and daily obligations, in all their repetitious and monotonous detail, that establish Woman's association with origins and make her the only substantial mother. It is she who gives us life, a concept of order, she whom we imitate and from whom we learn speech. She is the first scene in the performance of life. However, in spite of its attraction and its immutable nature, this revelation leaves us confronted by the same obscurities and prey to the same unsatisfied curiosity as before.

THE THREAD OF DESIRE

From this point on, as we disentangle the image of the spinner, which underlies every aspect of our imaginations, from the elements that obscure it, we discover an emphasis on things eternal. The mythical spinner both is and creates these things. She and the things are one and the same – the first objects of desire. From the outset, the myth of the Spinners presents Woman as both desiring and desired. Her body, 'in labour', as it bends over its work, is both what causes desire and what attracts desire – the second element arising as a result of the first. On closer examination, what one might call the morphological context of the stories and legends, involves interchanges between the spinner, her actions and her attributes that produce new configurations. New images of desire appear, and the image of Man, which is both complementary and necessary, is experienced before actually being formulated. More than the act of spinning itself, it is the agents and products of spinning that create this desire – the initial functional state of the producer, along with an earlier link between the pursuit and the satisfaction of desire.

– Spin a very fine thread, wife, spin it very long.
– . . . Here is my flax, but I have no fiancée to whom I can give it to spin.

Here, the figurative nature of the spinner's action portrayed in versions seven and twenty-five of the story of *La Chatte Blanche* is expanded either by a standard, archetypal repetition or by virtue of a hidden meaning that is made only too obvious by omission. Thus less emphasis is placed on the actual figure of the spinner than on the spinner as a woman. The semantics of the narrative forms used, and the new textual function of the narrative are combined and intensified by means of an echo representing the couple, the woman who spins and the man to be loved, and who is loved.

What was previously represented as a secret hope, by means of the continuous turning action and resigned attitude of the spinner-heroine, is suddenly converted into the embraces of which she dreamed. The man arrives, and readily affirms that the woman produces an active, creative, voluptuous and fertile thread.

– Once upon a time, there was a poor widow who had three daughters. All they had to live on was the produce from a kitchen garden where they grew cabbages. One day the eldest daughter said to her mother: today I will go and spin my distaff in the kitchen garden, and I will stop the horse eating the cabbages.
– Very well, said her mother. The girl went out, the horse approached and she took her distaff and struck the horse with it. The distaff remained attached to the horse, and her hand to the distaff. The horse fled to a green hill.

The very scheme of the story of *La Veuve et ses trois Filles* formulates the context of the desires of Woman as a spinner. It represents the realization of a girlhood dream. After the mother's acceptance that her daughter has in turn become a woman, the latter reveals her unconscious desires, and carries them out in the form of ritualized games – catching and allowing herself to be caught, seducing and being seduced. This is the universal story of the female dream, which moves from idealization to realization. It is the story of the ever-present wound of love, from the moment at which it is inflicted until it is converted into a scar, impressed like a seal. In the story, it is the youngest of the spinner-daughters who finds love. Benefiting from her sisters' experience of death, she creates her own ideal suitor. Though the act of spinning is never even performed, it is the woman present in every spinner and the implement or weapon that she uses that give their meaning to these familiar figures. There is a shift in the semantic significance of the act of spinning, which is displaced within the text, and this displacement is punctuated by the various stages in the development of the spinner's desire. It was perhaps when it was transposed into written form that the story abandoned a divine image of Woman in favour of a more human one. The sacred horse turns into a handsome young man when it is decapitated by the spinner, an act carried out with the magical distaff. Thus the new spinner spins the thread of enchantment, the thread that will unite separated bodies – the bodies of male and female. However, the union is not eternal and must constantly be renewed.

The action of spinning and the thread that is spun are firmly associated in the depths of our minds. Their dual movements – repeated, cyclic and rhythmic – perform the unique function of encircling the sacral womb.

According to Pliny the Elder, spinning flax was also an honourable occupation for men. Does this mean that male cultural creativity benefits from a constant link to the entrancing power of some female point of reference? Might mens' writing also be based on the ambivalent and ever-open division in the female nature?

Since the time of the divine Spinners, women have been represented by the entire length of the thread – the thread of desire, the same thread that they hold in one hand, while winding and coiling it around the symbols that they hold in the other. Penelope was Helen's accomplice, just as Anticleia was Penelope's. The linear nature of the thread and its convolutions create the weft of this womens' work, woven by the endless regularity and continuity of movement.

WHEN THE THREAD BECOMES A BODY

Ariadne was another representation of the Spinner-Goddesses. She gave the precious gift of a ball of thread to a man with whom she fell passionately in love as soon as she saw him. By unwinding the thread he was able to find his way back to her. Together they escaped from the hell of repetition. She saved him from the Minotaur, but he abandoned her and she died of grief. Ariadne's magic thread deserves to be examined more closely. It was the thread that provided Theseus with both the power and means of staying alive: virtually constituting the gift of immortality, it represented desire, protection and preservation. In return for it, Ariadne wanted Theseus to give her eternal love, an indestructible bond that would unite their two beings – but this bond was so strong that it ultimately prevented their union. 'When the bloodstained Theseus emerged from the labyrinth, Ariadne took him in her arms in a passionate embrace.' There is no need to explain the underlying image of the thread. It was because they were attached to each other by the thread that he returned to her. In this inverted representation of childbirth, Aridane physically experienced the entire mortal combat between the monster and the man she loved. She was also in physical contact with the doorway of the cave in the mountain, and the woman and mother within her directed the entire rescue operation by means of the thread. It is easy to understand why it is not clearly stated whether the courageous hero killed the Minotaur with his sword or strangled it barehanded. We are left free to imagine the thread as a magic weapon, so that the valiant warrior cannot be perceived as a murderer. He was not carrying out a murder that he had consciously decided to commit, but was merely acting as an agent. At the end of Ariadne's thread, Theseus was a toy that she had recreated and whose movements she controlled. The thread allowed Ariadne to re-enact her childhood memories, since Theseus involuntarily mimicked the movements of the dolls with articulated joints invented by Daedalus that had fascinated both her and her mother, Pasiphae. Thus Ariadne pulled the strings of Theseus's destiny as he fought the Minotaur, just as she had used to pull the strings of her puppets to make them dance. The thread both ties and ties up. It was the instrument of Daedalus's genius, and as well as being used on many occasions to construct, tie and consolidate, it was also used to prevent death, to kill and to animate the human body through a power to create movement that destined it to control time and space. Finally, after fleeing to the city of Camicus to escape the wrath of Minos, Daedalus also made puppets for the daughters of King Cocalus. The thread is associated with all Daedalus's inventions, while it also saved his life when he solved the riddle of the 'thread and the snail shell' set for him by his pursuer. In Greek, Ariadne's name meant 'Very Holy'. She was the 'Moon Goddess', the 'Most Worthy', the 'Omnipresent', in whose honour initiatory and ritual dances were performed, dances in which thread was wound, unwound and intertwined. In this capacity, Ariadne must have taught Theseus other things. On the island of Delos, before a statue that Ariadne had had erected to Aphrodite, Theseus performed a very complicated, circular dance. This apparently evoked the winding passages of the labyrinth, the twists and turns of the divine thread, and possibly the single combat that had saved his life. Alternatively, it may have represented the undulations, curves, waves and meanders of Ariadne's body – the thread unwound from the female body in a succession of waves that moves the male body to both happiness and suffering. This thread for an imaginary body coils in all directions, rolling up time, and extending space, until the process culminates in suicide by hanging, or suicide by being precipitated into the void.

According to one version of the myth, when Ariadne was abandoned on the island of Dia, she hanged herself through fear of Artemis, while Theseus was treacherously pushed over a cliff by Lycomedes.

THE THREAD OF VOYAGE

The island of Ogygia which, according to Homer, was the 'centre of the sea', was also the home of Calypso, 'the one who conceals', and like Circe and Penelope, she too was a spinner. In this unique and favoured setting, she sat by her hearth with her serving maids, and used her golden shuttle to weave cloth of the finest quality. She, too, produced magical threads intended to act as bonds uniting her and Odysseus for ever as man and wife, as well as to make Odysseus immortal. However, Hermes, the messenger of Zeus, was sent to order her to free Odysseus, and so the spinner had to abandon her desires. Calypso converted the thread of desire into the thread of voyage.

Although she renounced her claims on Odysseus and allowed him to leave, this was not until she had lovingly prepared threads with which to weave the sails of his ship. Made of animal and vegetable fibres, they would have to withstand the onslaught of the elements for a long period, but the sublimated power of the woman would compete with the power of the forces of nature. Marcel Bréal presents Calypso as 'the veiler', the nymph or goddess who envelops herself and others in mist. In this central point of the cosmos where she lives she hides both herself and others. As the inverted image of the spider, she remains at the centre of her web and, although she draws the man that she loves into it, this is not with the intention of devouring him. This 'centre of the sea' could be seen as the setting for a re-enactment of the first stage of symbiosis. In giving up her lover, the woman-nymph allows him to leave attached to the end of the most supple, most enduring thread, which will take him to his journey's end and to the discovery of new truths. The magnificent fabric produced by Calypso's threads is reminiscent of the fabric produced with byssus. This very fine flax, forming bundles of silken strands, is described in the Book of Esther as a raw material of great luxury, while the writer of Revelation twice calls down misfortune upon the 'city clothed in flax'. Calypso's thread is steeped in luxury and lust, like the secretions that bivalve molluscs use to form the threads that bind them together and hold them in place.

At this point, the secret meaning of the thread shared by Calypso and Odysseus emerges, and the latter seems also to be invited to reconstruct the thread of his wanderings. The thread of the voyage enables Odysseus to overcome his final trial without his eyes being clouded by death.

THE THREAD OF THE DREAM

By referring to Garbo as the 'Goddess' of the silver screen, cinema critics have sought to encapsulate her fundamental quality as woman and actress, and this alone would be sufficient to establish her as the modern avatar of the divine Spinners. Like the figure of the archaic Spinner, she is seated hieratically in the depths of time. Simultaneously accessible and inaccessible, she remains sculpted in the eternity of her various roles, deliberately protected from all possibility of transformation. In the film *Queen Christina*, which is generally agreed to be the actress's most biographical film, Garbo turns the seduction of the character that she portrays into a performance that works to her own advantage. After the one wonderful night spent with her chance lover, the Spanish ambassador, she awakes before him and realizes that this was her first night of love. Then, as if she has become a multiple being, she gazes at or touches all the objects in that hallowed room. She is dazzled by the manifestations of her own femininity, born of obscurity, that have come together in that room, for her and within her, far removed from her royal obligations. As an inset in the film, she imagines herself, a happy woman, spinning peacefully by the fireside. This image, which occurs halfway through the story, effectively leads to the metamorphosis of the queen. Decisive both as a woman and as a lover, she converts her deepening melancholy into physical strength, fighting for the man she loves until he is unjustly killed and her desire for exile is realized.

The identification of Garbo with the spinner of times gone by, who is free only to love, marks the beginning of her search for a world of personal happiness. When, at the end of the film, she boards her own specially equipped ship, she does so evidently with a sense of pain, but also in the certain knowledge that she will pursue and ultimately find fulfilment in the new direction that her life has taken. At the point at which the threads of her life as a queen and of her lover's destiny are broken, another thread is joined on which is made of both solitude and hope. This should be seen in terms of the symbol of the knot incorporated into the thread of fate. In this instance, the thread of the dream contains a knot that seals together love, life and death. Although the knot marks the end of individual destiny, it also leads to an overwhelming desire to continue. The 'knots' in the life of Queen Christina obstruct the plans of her court and, as in the Middle Ages, prevent the marriage between the two lovers.

On screen, Greta Garbo presents a strange image, which, like the body of the early Spinner, is either a state of absolute physical being or the exact opposite, a body that can neither be attained nor renounced. When she had exhausted the potential of the cinema as a vehicle for her artistic fantasies, Garbo withdrew to her own fragile, rebellious and dependable reality, having ensured that there was absolutely no possibility of ever being imitated.

THE IMPLICIT THREAD

The theme of the Spinners inevitably revives fantasies about the female body. We return to our origins. We begin again and repeat with our own body the action that will facilitate its reintegration into an ambivalent system of death and preservation – a process that must constantly be renewed.

In the process of reading and writing, the body seems to create solid threads, and this image inspires a strong desire to combine the past and the present, thereby producing a synthesis of linear and circular time. Such necessary, structuring inspiration enables us to appropriate time from the beginning, which for us is our own time. The time of the original female act – the time of spinning – has no masculine equivalent. It is the time of annunciation and revelation, the time of fertility and its double.

The body in the posture of reading and writing reflects the mythical theme of the Spinners and is itself a representation of the miraculous thread being spun. When a man or woman traces signs and reads them, his or her being is in a state of regeneration and becomes the 'sealed document-thread-manuscript'. The inscriptions – which may be threads of words or names, or our traces and marks of absence – are the expression of original interdictions.

The state of having to say or write what one is alone in having to say or write, is a state of nothingness from which one has to create something with the assistance of the thread and the word. It is in this way that we learn to evoke, in our mind's eye, the image of the 'other', in an attempt to identify the space in which our own words are deployed. The word is wound, as if around the roller of the loom, thread by thread, misrepresented and embellished. It is from these labyrinths, these initiatory structures, that we draw our images of the writer, which are based on the image of one of the Moirae.

Our writing is drawn from our pantheons, for writing involves the introduction of myth into literature and so is a reflection. It reflects the activities of the gods and is perpetuated by association. This process of writing-spinning enables us to move around within the unique and symbolic field encompassing all forms of evocation and notation, without ever indicating whether we are accompanied by Atropos, Clotho or Lachesis.

THE THREAD OF CONTINUITY

In literature, the spinner and her thread are both an echo of earlier sources and an image of the future. The thread, in the sense of some sort of link or agent, has undoubtedly existed since the beginning of time, in various forms, uniting all types of materials. In the tropical forests of Africa and the West Indies, the strands of vegetation hanging from the foliage are used by female healers to bind both green and dead wood – both sticks for lighting fires and sticks for preparing ancient remedies. The pads that the women traditionally place on their heads to carry these heavy loads, are made of coils of the same fibres, which have been trimmed, cut into equal lengths and wound around their left hand.

In Guadeloupe, the old women who work in the sugar-cane fields and on the plantations, traditionally kept the first pad that they had made for a considerable time, rather as if it was a fetish or a sacred object. Meanwhile, young girls use these threads of vegetation for skipping, and to plait bridal crowns, which they decorate with flowers for use in rites of passage. Finally, when a small boy is ill with whooping-cough, his mother makes him wear a necklace and bracelets of red thread. The thread, which may be cosmic, malefic, protective or initiatory, is the thread of history, which also links different worlds and different states – the worlds of the visible and the invisible, the states of offering and receiving a sacrifice. The thread of vegetation engenders the bond, the cord, the plait and the liana, and makes us aware of space in physical terms. Its curving line, and the vibrant movements that bring it to life, make it the symbol of love and duality, as it winds around the tree. It was the huge, swirling coils of these climbing plants that gave

Man the beautiful, circular, open movement that emerges from the original point of the spiral.

Even in prehistoric times, crude woven palisades made of vegetable fibres were used to delimit the territories of individuals and communities. They parallel our modern networks of interwoven mesh and wire, designed to contain and enclose, to break up the vast expanse of the earth's surface, dividing it into interiors and exteriors.

In all civilizations throughout the ages, man-made constructions will always be related to these early structures, and they will attain perfection only when they include a main thread that makes it possible to pass from the inside to the outside. The images of retreat, refuge, enclosure and intimacy produced by our imaginations lead us to the most complex forms of these constructions – nets. These fearful weapons represent what impedes us both in our inner and external lives: the mesh of our life in general, which it is so difficult and painful to disentangle, unknot and untie.

The thread has made what amounts to a second and independent entry into literature involving the myth of the Spinners. The numerous expressions using the word 'thread' that are woven into the French language, for example, not only relate to the actual images of the Spinners themselves, but establish a firm connection between the thread, speech and writing.

The French expression 'de fil en aiguille' (i.e. one thing leads to another), which was used as early as the *Roman de la Rose*, and which refers to needlework since it literally means 'from the thread to the needle', is used at a point in a narrative where the story is interrupted, either because of a gap in the narrator's memory or because of some secret that must be concealed by language. In employing it as an unobtrusive way of indicating such an intended or unconscious break, the narrator alludes to the fragility of the thread of speech itself. However, on analogy with the threading process, the expression also allows the establishment of certain points in the narrative at which language is condensed. It is an image that condenses time and action, the movements made at a particular moment by the hands, the first hands, – the mother's hands, which create, at first hand, what will not be undone. The use of the expression 'de fil en aiguille', in a context in which a speaker has replaced the reader, involves recalling the very first image in one's entire history, that of the active hands of one's mother. The narrator employs this image as a point of reference to rejoin the thread of what he or she was saying and so continue recounting and narrating in a more rapid and meaningful way. In the process, a traditional adverbial expression, which is fixed and invariable, becomes the creation solely of the person who uses it, perhaps in an attempt to appropriate the text of his or her narrative. It ensures that the narrator emerges from his or her own narrative as a being with a real existence. It represents the point at which it becomes clear to the reader that he or she cannot continue the thread of that particular narrative alone: the action to which it alludes is not repeated and so does not occur, except to the extent that the reader can only visualize it or recollect it. Thus the expression 'de fil en aiguille' is a unique linguistic image. It is the representation of the thread and its silence, the silence of a condemnation that is never pronounced – of being the person who recounts and never the person who does or redoes. The meeting of the male thread and the female needle is the link between Man and Woman, and constitutes the response of the former, who is the link between the mother and child. It is the heavenly meeting between the Weaver and the Herdsman, the equinoctial point, the balance. In a philosophical context, it represents the union and complementarity between Yin and Yang.

Myth and tradition also associate ploughing with the task of spinning – the earliest of our memories. Ploughing along the thread of the furrows was an act of creation, so that for a long time wool was a symbol of the land and of ploughed fields. In the *Cave of the Nymphs*, Porphyry suggested that spinning was the most suitable task for souls that had descended in the scale of regeneration.

THE THREAD OF THE VOICE

The expression 'a thread-like voice' invites another approach to the symbolism of the thread, focusing on the thread spun by the voice itself. It is a representation of what emerges from the darkness within us. It constitutes the most powerful autobiographical evidence available to those who dare to look within themselves. We are continuously defined by our vocal expressions rather than our visual ones, and the voice, the thread-like voice, is the most perfect self-portrait of the inner self. To describe ourselves completely through speech to others, and to teach them to do the same, we would have to start the songs of the self with incantations of self.

Jean-Jacques Rousseau gave us some important lessons when he spoke of the 'gentle, thread-like voice' of his Aunt Suson: 'Apart from the time I spent reading or writing at my father's side, or when "Mamie" took me for walks, I was always in the company of my aunt, watching her embroider, listening to her sing, either sitting or standing next to her, and I was happy.' According to Nietzsche, if lyric poets and artists continue to say 'I', 'it is because they are constantly unburdening onto us the entire chromatic range of their passions and desires'. The voice is our voice, which winds the thread of our history into a skein. The voice itself – the magical distaff of time – constantly calls upon us to record in writing the cries and murmurs, the shouts and roars of pain and anger. The voice unwinds and is the hallmark of communication with the self and with listeners-readers, who, on hearing it, unerringly recognize the voice of the author. The voice – an echo of our origins – spins the basic innocence of the self from eternal silence.

To pick up the thread of the 'gentle, thread-like voice' of the *Confessions*, in this work, the philosopher and educationalist points out that the voice, like the thread, is the ambivalent representation of both past and present. It is in the *Confessions*, more than anywhere else, that we encounter the fine thread of the beloved voice, the very essence of the voice, a thread that brings things into existence like a divine creator and that assumes forever the burden of sighs and groans. For Rousseau, the thread-like voice runs through life – through 'the thread of time' – concealed in voices. It is the fibre that holds together the words, phrases and pauses and consolidates them into a fabric of sounds that has meaning. It is like a river-bed that, without being aware that it is being carved out by omissions and absences and failures to record events, reproduces the ancient sound of the spools. The gentle voice of Aunt Suson, although thread-like, continues to sing; and, as the author writes, she never tires of telling him 'how great a number of airs and songs' she sings. It is the voice of old age and death, which gathers together the visible and the readable. It is not longer audible, unless it is contained in writing, like a thread that reproduces our voice and that we follow.

There is also a network of voices. This is the domain of popular songs, airs that people in all nations sing together on the occasion of births and deaths. It is the musical reflection of the world, a constant flow fed throughout the ages by the tributaries of dreams and poetry.

'What more appropriate way of expressing a tenderness which earnestly wants to imitate music.' For us, the thread-like voice traces and retraces; and, like the thread, its task will inevitably remain unfinished.

Incessantly spinning to calm their inner passions – by day, in the fields and in the evening, in the humble dwellings of bygone eras – women disturbed men, as they did the Church and society in general. Their secret thoughts, whether profane or sacred, were formed while they were spinning, and were directed towards the acquisition of a different role and a different social status. The spinners thought, and their thoughts were formulated 'à contre fil' – to use a French expression equivalent to our 'against the grain', but literally meaning 'against the thread'. Although, according to Georges Bernanos, Joan of Arc was a 'relapse and saint', it was protected by her spinning that she learned to be 'a lamb in terms of humility' and 'a lion in terms of strength'.

Charles Péguy's *Le Mystère de la Charité de Jeanne d'Arc* opens in the familiar setting in which the heroine, Jeanette, spins every morning while looking after her sheep. This is a traditional image from the depths of our memories. As the work continues, its plot is developed by the revelation of the shepherdess's beliefs, which she expresses to her friend Hauviette, and to Mme Gervaise, who accuses her of blasphemy. However, as the curtain falls, following her remark 'Orléans, you are in the land of the Loire', Jeannette has resumed her spinning.

In Régine Pernoud's book *Christine de Pisan*, the poetess is also presented as acting 'à contre fil' (against the grain). The author records that she did not like spinning and reproached her mother for wanting her to work with flax. Thus Christine defied her mother's wishes and took on her father's 'extraordinary appetite for learning':

> the knowledge that is obtained
> at the fountain of great worth.

Hugues Liborel

Sundiata

During the eleventh century, the kingdom of Ghana (or Wagadou), the most ancient of the Sudanese states, fell to the conquering drive of the Almoravides, who were trying to impose Islam on the populations of black Africa. Ruled by the Cisse, of the Sarakolle people, Ghana had been at its most powerful in the tenth century. Its riches came chiefly from several gold seams (notably Bambouk). In the thirteenth century Ghana was superceded by Mali, which had grown out of the small Mandigo kingdom founded by the Keita dynasty, under the aegis of Sundiata, the conquering and unifying hero of a vast empire stretching from the Niger (Djenne) to the lower Gambia in the west.

Mali reached the height of its power in the fourteenth century in the reign of Kankan Mussa, whose famous journey to Mecca was recorded in detail by the Arab historian Ibn Khaldun. But the oral tradition of the Sudanese chroniclers known as *Belen-Tigui* or 'masters of speech', presents Sundiata as the true founder of the Malian empire. The traditional epic celebrates the birth and rise of the hero, who succeeds in re-establishing the legitimate rule of the Keita and in extending their sovereignty. For at the beginning of the thirteenth century, the king of Soso had seized Ghana (1203) and imposed his rule on the Mandingo people. The story is thus one of many heroic myths glorifying the civilizing activity of great historical figures, who have now become legendary.

In 1960 the African historian Djibril Tamsir Niane gave us a version of the Sundiata myth, which he turned into a novel called *Soudiata ou l'Epopée mandigue.* To lend authenticity to his story, the author leaves the narration to the sorcerer-musician Mamadou Kouyate from Siguiri (Guinea), whose ancestors served the Keita princes of the Mandingo.

THE MYTHICAL STORY

In Niani, the Mandingos' first capital, on the river Sankarani, king Nare Maghan Kon Fatta, future father of Sundiata, had already been reigning for a long time when he received the visit of an unknown hunter. This man practised divination using cowrie shells and predicted the birth of a child destined to become 'the seventh star, the seventh conqueror of the earth', more powerful than Djoulou Kara Naini (Alexander the Great). For this to happen, the king had to take as his second wife an ugly, hunchbacked woman who would be presented to him by two young hunters.

Some time later, the prediction came true and the king married Sogolon the hunchback, who came from the Do country. Sundiata was born (in 1205) on a stormy day. He had a difficult childhood due to physical infirmity: at the age of three he could not walk, he was ugly and very greedy. This greatly pleased the king's first wife Sasuma Berete, as she wanted to see her own son reign. The king was disappointed and withdrew his attentions from Sasuma, taking a third wife by whom he also had a son, then, on the advice of a blind blacksmith and seer, who confirmed Sundiata's destiny to him, he once more bestowed his favours upon Sogolon. Before he died, he spoke to the then seven year-old Sundiata as to his successor and put the sorcerer-musician Bella Fasseke into his service. However, following some intrigues set in motion by the first wife, the Council of Elders did not respect Nare Maghan's wishes and named his eldest son Dankaran Tuman as his successor. The queen-mother, Sasuma Berete, who had become all-powerful in the Council of Regency, took pleasure in teasing and persecuting Sogolon, mother of a sickly child. One day, when she had humiliated her about some baobab leaves, Sogolon went trembling to her son. It was then that the miracle occurred: to avenge his mother, Sundiata vowed to bring her not just the few baobab leaves she needed for cooking, but the whole tree. He sent his sorcerer to the smith for an enormous iron bar. The master smith was a seer who knew that the great day had come and placed before the sickly boy the famous iron bar 'forged', says the legend, 'in seven years, by seventy-seven smiths', which Sundiata used to help him in his effort to stand. Then, suddenly cured, he let go of it and walked over to a young baobab tree, which he uprooted and brought to his mother. This was the feat destined to reveal the superhuman nature of Sogolon's son.

After this first exploit, Sundiata showed himself to be very good with the bow and arrow: he hunted with his young brother Manding-Bory, whom he loved very much, and his sorcerer, who instructed him in the secrets of his origins. Thus he knew that his mother Sogolon was the double of the terrible buffalo that had long ravaged the Do country and that the lion was the protector of his paternal clan. At the age of ten, now physically very strong and highly authoritative, Sundiata listened enthralled to the story of the great exploits of Djoulou Kara Naïni. However, his popularity had only increased the jealousy of the queen-mother, who instructed nine witches to kill him. The witches were defeated by Sundiata's great goodness and could do nothing to him. Nevertheless, as a precaution, Sogolon decided to take her children away, and this became seven years of exile. Sundiata agreed to this plan to save his younger brother, who had no occult powers, but he left uttering threats against king Dankaran Tuman, who meanwhile had overstepped his rights by taking away his personal sorcerer, Balla Fasseke, and sending him as ambassador to the powerful king of Soso, Sumaoro Kante. Sundiata swore he would return to the Mandingo to erase this insult.

In exile Sundiata matured, finished his training and performed his tests. He knew no fear and challenged and defeated the king-sorcerer Mansa

Konkon at the game of Wori; on the road to Wagadou (the Mandingo name for old Ghana), he learned from merchants' stories all about Sumaoro, the cruel king. Most important of all, at the court of King Tounkara of Mema, came his first experience of battle. At the age of fifteen he accompanied the king on his military campaigns, where he astounded the army with his ardour in the charge, his great physical prowess and his moral strength. Three years later the heirless king named him his viceroy. But Sogolon reminded her son that his true destiny lay in the Mandingo lands, where he had a mission to fulfill.

During the reign of Dankaran Tuman, the Mandingo had fallen under the domination of Sumaoro Kante, the great sorcerer, whose many fetishes made him invulnerable and who could, according to legend, 'throw death on to whomever he chose'. He was descended from the first smiths who had tamed fire and taught men how to work iron. He had destroyed Niani and Dankaran Tuman had fled; the Mandingo people were thus waiting for a saviour. It was then that they remembered Sundiata who, according to the seers, was the only one who could return freedom and dignity to the Mandingo. A delegation of important people set off to find Sundiata, which took them two months. They greeted him as the true king of the Mandingo, 'the giant who will strike down the giant Sumaoro'.

Sundiata, who had just buried his mother, accepted his mission. His protector, the king of Mema, helped him to gather an army and he took the road to Wagadou, whose king gave him half his cavalry, then went on to Tabon, where he had once stayed, and found a childhood friend, Fran Kamara. He made a detour around the kingdom of Soso; his plan was to destroy its capital, Soso, before returning in triumph to Niani. After an early victory over Sumaoro's son at Tabon, Sundiata fought the king of Soso directly at Wagueboria, in Boure, using his usual tactic of arranging his troops in a square. But neither Sundiata's lance nor his arrows could kill Sumaoro, who had been rendered invulnerable by his protecting spirits. Sundiata was worried; he consulted the seers and made sacrifices. The secret of the sorcerer king's invulnerability was revealed to him by his half-sister Nana Triban. She had been married against her will to the cruel Sumaoro and had become his favourite, so she knew about Sumaoro's magic chamber and told Sundiata that only an arrow with the spur of a white cock could overcome his power.

It was at the battle of Kirina (1235), still famous today, that Sundiata finally defeated Sumaoro, firing the fatal arrow at him. He followed his enemy for a night and a day; according to the legend, Sumaoro disappeared into the Koulikoro cave which leads to the Niger river and was never seen again. In another version which is popular in Siguiri (Guinea), Sumaoro called on his protecting spirits one last time and was turned to stone on Mount Koulikoro.

Sundiata kept his promise to take Soso and its three ramparts in one morning: the city was entirely razed to the ground, with the destruction of Sumaoro's seven-storey tower containing the magic chamber and all its fetishes marking the end of the occult power of the terrorist sovereign. After this Sundiata continued his glorious march on Kita, where he defeated the powerful Kita Mansa, who had refused to submit to him. However, he spared the inhabitants (Kamara people, who became his allies), sacrificed to the mountain spirits and drank the water of the magic pool which had given Kita Mansa his power. He thus became the chosen one of the mountain spirits and stayed at Kita before going back to Do, his mother's country, where he sacrificed a white cock on the buffalo's burial mound. A whirlwind told him that the time had come to return to the Mandingo, so he went down the river valley, saluted by the twelve kings of the 'light savannah country', who proclaimed him Emperor. After a great feast, Sundiata gave each king back his respective lance and kingdom, thus setting the seal on the friendship between their peoples. He was welcomed as a saviour at Niani and undertook the rebuilding of the city of his fathers, making his young brother Manding Bory governor of the conquered lands. After this, he ruled wisely, calling a meeting of the kings and important people of his Empire every year and bringing about a time of peace and prosperity for his country, based on the development of agriculture. His death is shrouded in mystery: some say he drowned in the river Sankarani in 1255, but in another version he was accidentally killed by an arrow during a celebration.

IMPLICATIONS OF THE MYTH

The myth presents a hero who is entirely positive in qualities and deeds. It shows a model on two levels: Sundiata is both a dispenser of justice and a civilizing hero. On the individual level, he is an infant prodigy who avenges the humiliations inflicted on his mother because of his sickliness: at the age of seven he comes to his first epiphany when he single-handedly uproots a baobab tree as a symbol of his wondrous strength.

On the collective level, he is identified with the fate of the Mandingo: at the age of thirty he comes to his second eiphany by triumphing over Sumaoro, liberating the Mandingo and the neighbouring kingdoms from the sorcerer king, whose magic chamber was papered with human skin and decorated with the nine heads of vanquished kings.

The duel between Sundiata and Sumaoro thus has the symbolic meaning of a struggle between the forces of Good and Evil, light and darkness, the occult powers of the day (benevolent magic) and those of the night (sorcery).

In relation to Africa beliefs, he is the one against whom spells were useless, both when Queen Sasuma's jealousy and ill-will made her send sorcerers to kill him as a child, and when Sumaoro's instinct for power made him set his fetishes against the superior battle skills of 'Sogolon's son'.

Sundiata's life is exemplary, symbolizing the transition of African states as they became islamicized and moved towards a new type of power in which intimidation through sorcery was replaced by the triumph of truly human qualities. The destruction of Soso and of Sumaoro's fetishes is the symbol of the progress of civilization and after Sundiata Mali enjoyed the height of its power under islamicized rulers. The myth thus fully illustrates the period of transition through which Sundiata lives, in which black African civilizations hesitated between adopting the Muslim religion and remaining attached to animist values. According to Ibn Batouta, Sundiata converted to Islam. In the myth recorded by Djibril Tamsir Niane, Sundiata left Mema 'dressed in the Muslim style', but it was in the dress of the 'hunter king' endowed with magic power capable of defeating that of Sumaoro that he faced his main enemy. In this the myth is the expression of the search for a fusion of authentically black African values with the new ones introduced by the foreign islamic civilization. The myth condemns the practices of sorcery through the character of Sumaoro, the evil spirit, Sundiata's true malevolent 'double', but in Sundiata, 'son of Sogolon', who is protected by the spirits of the savannah, it sanctifies the authentic representative of a positive animism, directed towards legitimate aims and noble action. Sundiata is the man endowed by his mother with magic powers, for he is the 'Na' Kamma', the man with a mission to fulfill, the man whom the seers foretold would liberate the Mandigo.

The heroic myth should be interpreted with reference to totemic institutions: each clan has a corresponding guardian animal, recalling the ancient alliance between the founding ancestor and a particular natural force. Thus Sundiata is the 'son of the buffalo' through his mother Sogolon and the 'son of the lion' through his father, and he has the attributes of these spirits: the strength of the buffalo and the majesty of the lion. In Sundiata the traditionalist sorcerer-musicians celebrate the incarnation of the spirit of the savannah lands itself. He is the hunter king armed with bow and arrow, whereas Sumaoro, who is descended from the smiths, is linked to fire, the most fearsome and destructive element. The legend states that a hero with magic powers was required to defeat him and, before the decisive battle of Kirina, Sundiata and Sumaoro talk to each other in the manner of sorcerer kings, through the intermediaries of their respective owls.

The hero's path is marked out by the presages and predictions of seers, hunters or smiths, men in direct contact with the forces of nature. In this the myth entirely fits into the framework of animist tradition. The birth of the hero itself is adorned with a full complement of African marvels: although it is the dry season, the sky suddenly darkens, thunder rumbles and rain falls and suddenly ceases, to salute Sundiata's birth. This participation of heavenly forces bears witness to his superhuman nature.

In addition, Sundiata's destiny is predetermined by that of Alexander the Great, the model who is constantly present in the hero's mind and who acts as a catalyst for him, affirming the messianic dimension of his undertaking. In their turn, later conquerors and rulers of the western Sudan (notably Samory, in the nineteenth century, who regarded himself as Sundiata's reincarnation), and even leaders of the modern states (for example Sekou

Toure) have seen Sundiata as a model to imitate, in the unifying role that he played in his own time.

LITERARY INTERPRETATIONS OF THE MYTH

One of the things Djibril Tamsir Niane was reproached with was that in his tale he did not render the rhythm of the traditional epic, dictated by its musical accompaniment. In Mali a translation of the primitive epic with songs, entitled *Kala Jata*, was made by Massa Maghan Diabate in 1970 and published by Présence Africaine (*Janjon et autres chants populaires du Mali*, 1971).

Although the Sundiata myth did not share the same literary destiny as that of Shaka, it has been staged several times. In black Africa the most accomplished form of dramatic art, that is to say dialogue, is for the most part the result of cultural integration with the West. Thus, in colonial times, the myth was staged by the students of the William-Ponty school in Senegal, with the title *La Ruse de Diégué*. This play used dialogue, songs, music and dance to dramatize one of the epic tale's most important episodes: in order to defeat king Sumanguru (Sumaoro), Sundiata's sister reveals to him the secret of the king of Soso's invulnerability. The play was strictly commemorative in intentions and remained faithful to tradition by presenting sorcerer-musicians who embelished their speeches with numerous proverbs.

In the context of the development of nationalist theatre in Africa after 1960, the aim of which was to revalue African history and to celebrate the heroes of the past, some African playwrights returned to Niane's text. In its adaptation for the stage, the mythical tale was simplified and condensed. Attention was concentrated around the most spectacular events of the hero's life: the hunter's prediction, the birth and healing of Sundiata or the reconquest of Mandigo. Thus Sory Konake's play of 1971, entitled *Le Grand destin de Soundjata* ends with the heroic epiphany of the Kirina victory. The whole is presented as a wake held by the sorcerer-musician Djeli Madi and it has an intermediate structure, somewhere between the traditional tale and a theatrical text.

More recently, in an edifying drama, Laurent Gbagbo avoided elements relating to the hero's birth and training, concentrating the action on the struggle to reconquer the throne of Mandigo and posing the problem of the legitimacy of power. This play, called *Soundjata, le Lion du Manding*, published in 1979, is structured in three acts: 'the plot', which distanced Sundiata from the throne, 'exile' and 'the triumphant return'. The argument thus conveyed glorifies in Sundiata not so much the man protected by the gods as the ruler acclaimed by the people and traditional marvels are eclipsed in favour of a political 'lesson'. Following a general tendency in modern black African theatre, the old myth is updated for didactic ends.

In 1978 *Le Maître de la parole, Kouma Lafôlô Kouma* appeared. This is a version of the myth collected in 1963 by Camara Laye in the Kouroussa region (Guinea), from the *Belen-Tigui* Babou Conde, whose ancestor was the personal sorcerer-musician to Sundiata's younger brother Manding-Bory.

The story describes the marvellous elements linked to Sundiata's birth in a most detailed way and in relation to totemic institutions. In particular, the theme of heroic predestination provides an opportunity to go back to the story of the buffalo of Do, and Sundiata's destiny is seen as set by his three powerful totems: buffalo and panther through his mother, lion through his father. The miraculous cure of the sickly child is portrayed as resulting from the combined efforts of these three powers. After this, the young warrior's exploits prove him to be 'agile like the panther, noble like the lion and fiery like the buffalo in the charge'.

Lastly, although in Sundiata the story celebrates above all the 'hunter king' who is in direct contact with the most powerful forces of nature, the myth's end presents him wearing a white jellaba and thanking Allah for granting him victory against Sumaoro. The final image of the hero shows him as the man who brought about the peaceful coexistence of Islam and animism, the initiator of the synthesis of two civilisations that have been brought into contact and are destined to penetrate and mutually influence each other.

Nicole Goisbeault

Tahiti

Travellers' tales, ships' logs and works of fiction have all treated Tahiti as special. A great many people have fallen in love with the islands: navigators, adventurers, sailors and ship's doctors have felt the need to explain to their contemporaries, relations, friends and readers what Tahiti was, or at least what the island meant to them. Because of this, novels, personal accounts, poems, descriptions and mission reports relating to Tahiti generally convey such a strong emotional and suggestive power that it has finally given rise to a genuine myth. It is therefore interesting to observe how this 'myth of Tahiti', both literary and sociological, came into being in the eighteenth century, gained its full force in the nineteenth and, in the course of the twentieth, acquired components and meanings that are sometimes contradictory and unexpected. It is not an arbitrary decision to study the Tahitian myth, and the way it has been perceived by the public, chronologically. Such an approach is essential, for there has been a profound evolution in people's perception of the island, and more particularly in its interest in the context of a leisured civilization, from the time of the 'founding fathers', with their paradisiacal image of Tahiti, to the tourist leaflets and posters of today. At the same time, it is because the 'image' of Tahiti (as a myth, an exotic dream, a tourist creation) take us into the domain of a configuration or vision of reality in which the imaginary, writing and the archetypes of the western psyche intervene, that it is legitimate to consider several constituents of the Tahitian myth, from the eighteenth to the twentieth century, through literature.

THE FOUNDING FATHERS OF THE TAHITIAN MYTH

The existence of an island that is a haven of peace, a source of happiness and joy, a veritable paradise providing relaxation, rest, enjoyment and voluptuous pleasure is a constant idea throughout western literature. We only have to think of the islands celebrated in Greek poetry or the island of love in Canto X of *The Lusiads* which welcome Vasco da Gama and his sailors.

In the seventeenth and eighteenth centuries treatises on geography and accounts of voyages picturing the beauty of far-off islands and the moral purity of their inhabitants abounded. The island of the good savage was not an eighteenth-century invention: it cropped up frequently in the imagination and literature of preceding centuries. Thus when Wallis, in June 1767, then Bougainville a few months later (4 April 1768) and finally Captain Cook (10 April 1769) in turn landed on Tahiti, they had a feeling of *déjà vu*, and were certain that they had discovered the island of the Golden Age, beloved of the ancients. From that point of view, literature had in a way anticipated objective knowledge of Tahiti, the regenerated archetype of the paradisiacal island.

Of the twelve chapters in *Account of the Voyages [. . .] of Captain Wallis* (1773) five relate to Otahiti, which he named St George's Island. He and his crew stayed there just over a month (24 June – 27 July 1767). The beauty of the landscape, the warm welcome of the women who made themselves freely available (before later selling their charms in return for nails, instruments and tools), and the queen's tears when the *Swallow* weighed anchor were the high points of a stop that Wallis did not regard as decisive. Chapter 8, 'A more detailed description of the inhabitants of Otahiti, the domestic life, morals and customs of these islanders', which provides the first ethnographical approach to Tahitian customs, is only superficial since Wallis either did not make the effort or did not have the time to go into the morals or the cosmological, religious and political ideas of the Tahitians in depth.

Bougainville is immediately different in his approach. For Wallis it had been a port of call, a pleasant encounter. Bougainville fell in love, and was subjugated by its charms. His sixteen-chapter long *Voyage autour du Monde* gives pride of place to Tahiti (chapters 8–10) where he had arrived on 4 April 1768. A quick literary study of these chapters shows that time stopped, chronology became blurred. Bougainville, thoroughly versed in Homer and Virgil, was more receptive than Wallis to the beauty of the area. He quite naturally drew many parallels between Tahiti and the Golden Age, especially in chapter 9:

> I went several times as the second or third of a party to walk in the interior. I felt I had been transported into the Garden of Eden: we went over a grassy plain covered with fine fruit trees and intersected by little rivers which preserve a delightful coolness without any of the unpleasant effects of damp. A large population enjoy the treasures which nature dispenses so generously to them. We found groups of men and women sitting in the shade in the orchards; everyone greeted us in a friendly manner; people we met on the paths stood aside to let us pass; everywhere we encountered hospitality, rest, a quiet joy and every appearance of happiness.

Bougainville and those travelling with him were convinced they had revealed a 'New Cythera' to the world. But his enthusiasm did not prevent him from gaining a better understanding than Wallis of the customs of the Tahitians (chapter 10), analysing their political, social and religious system and even discreetly mentioning the ritual of human sacrifice that was practised by the natives. Eager to learn the language and customs of the people, the French navigator took on board the *Étoile* a young man called Aotourou whose presence served to preserve the vitality and 'image' of the Tahitian paradise as a live experience as well as a written account.

The reactions of Captain Cook were more complex. When he first put in at Tahiti on 10 April 1769 he met the aged Owhaw and Queen Oberea who had by then recovered from Wallis' departure. He responded to the landscape and dwellings of the people, nor was he indifferent to the charms and attentions of the Tahitian women. Chapter 17, 'A detailed description of the Island of Otahiti, its products and its inhabitants. Clothes, dwellings, food, domestic life and amusements of these islanders', contains valuable information, for Cook chose to stress those characteristics that he regarded as barbarous: the sexual morals, human sacrifices and ritual deaths. On his second visit in August 1772, when he witnessed political rivalries and internal strife, he formed an unfavourable opinion of the place. For Cook as for Voltaire (*Les Oreilles du Comte de Chesterfield*, 1775) there was no such thing as the 'good savage'! As Bougainville had done, he took on board a Tahitian called Omaï who even appeared in London drawing-rooms. The account of his third call (August 1777) describes the return of Omaï and sacrificial practices.

Important differences can be noted between the three accounts by the first sailors to visit the island. Wallis, the most neutral in tone, was not seduced by the shores of the Pacific. Bougainville, the most enthusiastic, extolled Tahiti, and was the only one to achieve a poetic style when writing about the New Cythera. As for Cook, though he enjoyed the Tahitian paradise, he was primarily critical, never abandoning the standpoint of a civilized, superior man faced with savages. Thus the fact that the island lost in the middle of the Pacific became synonymous with an Eden inhabited by good savages is due to Bougainville. In his *Supplément du voyage autour du monde de Bougainville* (1774), Diderot made it easier to criticize Europe and western prejudices systematically, at the same time enhancing the image of Tahiti as a 'model' where the state of nature had been preserved. Orou, the hero and Diderot's mouthpiece, enjoys denouncing the 'strange precepts' of old Europe which are 'opposed to nature' and 'contrary to reason'. Such a contribution was valuable in that it caused living experience – which Bougainville had felt was so close to literature – to be annexed again by literature, so amplifying the power of illusion and the attraction. Perhaps the triumph of the islands of love, New Cythera, had also to go hand in hand with the triumph of reason, and it was because Diderot made use of the facts provided by Bougainville, because he made this island dedicated to Venus into a kingdom where reason reigned, that the myth of Tahiti more easily found its way into the eighteenth-century western mentality. It served as a vehicle for the meeting, so much desired by all thinkers, with a civilisation that was more natural, closer to our origins. Tahiti is very much a realisation of what Mircea Eliade has called the 'nostalgia for our origins'.

It took only three travellers to crystallize an image of Tahiti in which the rebirth of the literary theme of the Island of Enchantment was inevitably outlined. The paradox lies in the fact that Diderot working in his study should have enriched this 'image' by attributing to Tahiti both a philosophical status and an undeniable cultural brilliance. By the Age of Enlightenment Tahiti was perceived as another possible form of civilization, or, more accurately, as representing the initial state of human affairs.

THE TAHITIAN MYTH IN THE NINETEENTH CENTURY

In the nineteenth century, the literary, scientific and economical output devoted to the Tahitian archipelago was very rich and extremely varied. Everyone felt obliged to have their say about the Tahitians, or to compose a poem on the inexhaustibly popular theme of the beautiful, tender *vahine* abandoned by the European traveller. As well as being the object of dreams, exciting curiosity and arousing the desire to go there, Tahiti was also a political stake being disputed by France and Great Britain. But outside and beyond the conquering, anarchic colonialism that set the sons of Albion and the descendants of Joan of Arc against one another, the career of the myth of Tahiti carried on, though it was already being questioned or contested by clear-minded thinkers who discreetly or explosively pointed out its illusions, limits and lies, even its imminent collapse.

Tahiti's strategic interest and the desire to create a colony there were briefly explained by Max Radiguet, secretary to Dupetit-Thouars (later Admiral Dupetit-Thouars). These were the real reasons behind the muted opposition and disguised, then official hostility between the famous Pritchard, a missionary and agent of England, and France. The editor's introduction to Pritchard's book, *The Missionary's Reward, or the Success of the Gospel in the Pacific*, extolled the work of the British churchmen. Pritchard very skilfully demonstrates the benefits brought by the Gospel, after making a severe indictment of Tahitian morals, denouncing the wretched condition of the women and, like Cook, stressing the practices of infanticide and ritual sacrifice. His rival, Dupetit-Thouars, stigmatized the action of the missionaries, of Pritchard in particular, accusing him of diverting religious zeal for political ends so as to control Queen Pomaré and use her as a tool to practise real tyranny, leading to the destruction of Tahitian customs, beliefs and structures. The echo of Pritchard's tactics and their disastrous consequences (loss of identity as a people, destruction of the communal way of life), which were again found at the beginning of the twentieth century in Ségalen's novel *Les Immémmoriaux*, does to some extent justify Dupetit-Thouars's point of view when he took against Pritchard and accused Great Britain of being responsible for depopulating the archipelago. After several months of struggles for influence, plots and bloodshed (for instance the night-time attack on Moerenhout, then the United States representative), Dupetit-Thouars landed on the island, deposed the queen and started to occupy it (6 November 1843). Though he was disowned by Guizot, Dupetit-Thouars had through his military intervention finally supplanted England and conquered Tahiti in the name of France, and 'civilization'. However, let there be no mistake: both Pritchard and the man who defeated him used civilization and its benefits in an argument to justify their colonial zeal. In fact Melville some forty years later could quite easily denounce 'this act of piracy' perpetrated by the French!

In the years prior to this coup, in 'La Fille d'O-Taiti', a poem in *Odes* which is now quite forgotten, Victor Hugo turned to a fashionable theme which was to be widely exploited, that of the Tahitian girl left behind:

> 'Why leave our island? In your foreign isle,
> Are the skies more lovely? Have people less sorrows?
> Will your family when you die cry for their brother?
> Will they cover your bones with the funerary plane tree
> Whose flowers are not picked?
> [. . .]
>
> If the humble banana tree welcomes your coming,
> If ever you loved me, do not reject me.
> Do not go away without me to your unknown island,
> For fear that my young soul, wandering in the clouds,
> May set out alone to follow your steps!'
>
> When the morning gilded the departing sails,
> They sought her in vain beneath her light dome;
> She was seen no more in the woods, on the shores;
> Yet the sweet virgin who spoke these plaintive words
> Was not with the foreigner.

The above lines do of course anticipate the accents of Loti's *Le Mariage de Loti* which enjoyed a resounding success as soon as it appeared, first as a serial (1880) then as a book (1882). Madame Butterfly set in Tahiti! The prestige of this story won Loti membership of the French Académie, in rivalry with Zola than whom he gained more votes.

Following the good advice of his friend Jousselin (known as Plumkett), Loti had agreed to his novel being published in *La Nouvelle Revue*, which had just been launched by J. Adam. The magazine changed the title proposed by the author, *Rarahu*, to *Le Mariage de Loti*. The novelist, whose knowledge of Tahiti was limited to two short stays, explained in a letter to his friend Plumkett:

> They are really old notes that I have put together, a real young man's book: [. . .] the basis of the story is not true; I have combined several real people to make one character, Rarahu, and it seems to me that it is a fairly faithful study of a young Maori woman. Everything relating to Taïmaha is strictly true (letter dated 24 February, 1879).

Le Mariage de Loti, with its disconnected, almost impressionist side, shades in the 'image' of Tahiti, the land of delights, the New Cythera. But there is one new characteristic, exoticism. Whereas the first navigators had not paid homage to the exotic, in his descriptions Julien Viaud – who had been given the poetic name 'Loti', which refers to a Tahitian flower, by Pomaré's servant women – cultivated the exotic colour and charm of the delightful shores 'eternally caressed by balmy breezes'. From this point of view the novel combines a setting from the beginning of the world with a 'map of gentleness', with the paths full of scents, flowers, songs, waterfalls and trees with a thousand colours.

Gauguin – it is inevitable that his name should crop up – was in thrall to the Tahitian myth before bringing it to life. If he wished to 'approach the longed-for land', he was not taken in by his own illusion. Just as Melville abandoned Fagaway in *Typee, a narrative of the Manquesas Islands*, the painter left Tehamana in tears. More than other people he responded to the light, the colours and the Tahitian legends. He contributed one essential element to the myth: the conviction that the European must shed his 'old stock of civilized ways' (*Noa Noa*) in order to get to know a different form of life, to drink at the Fountain of Youth of the southern seas. In spite of the disappointments and petty annoyances of his sojourns in Tahiti and the Marquesas Islands, his paintings constantly glorify the myth of Tahiti as being synonymous with Eden. And it is no accident that adventurers, sailors and writers have made many pilgrimages to Tahiti and the Marquesas to trace his footsteps.

Running parallel with the unfolding of the main image of Tahiti in the western consciousness, we can observe the development of a critical trend, the result of more objective observation of what was going on in these Pacific islands. Colonization was not directly questioned; nonetheless it is clear that people with an increasingly serious turn of mind, disciples of the philosophers or witnesses of events, had begun to question the validity of the Europeans' civilizing impact.

Chateaubriand, in a couple of short paragraphs in the preface to his *Voyage en Amérique*, deplored the spreading of the Gospel and its consequences in these terms:

> Otahiti has lost its dances, its choirs, its voluptuous customs. The beautiful women of the new Cythera, perhaps vaunted too highly by Bougainville, are now puritans sitting below their breadfruit trees and elegant palm trees going to services, reading the Scriptures with Methodist missionaries, debating earnestly from morning to evening, and expiating in great boredom for the excessive gaiety of their mothers. Bibles and ascetic works are being printed in Otahiti.

Moerenhout, a high-class adventurer and the United States consul in Tahiti, who later worked for France (he was French consul in Monterey in 1846 and in Los Angeles in 1853), stigmatized the actions of his enemy Pritchard, and in his *Voyages aux îles du Grand Océan [. . .]* willingly emphasized the decadence of the Tahitian myth: corruption and prostitution had replaced goodness, generosity and wisdom. When he wrote *Les Derniers Sauvages. Souvenirs de l'occupation française aux îles Marquises (1842–1859)*, Dupetit-Thouars's secretary Max Radiguet also showed up the wrongdoings of Europe in the Marquesas Islands, implying that there was a risk of the same thing happening in Tahiti. Reverting to the myth of the paradisiacal islands, he went on:

> After travelling through the islands of the group where our supremacy now holds sway we were able to recognize that half a century had not noticeably dated the stories of Bougainville, Cook and Mariner. Nonetheless, since the time of these navigators civilization had frequently touched the Polynesian shores, but civilization in its most deplorable form, bringing its imperfections, abuses and vices rather than its knowledge, arts and virtues. Thus the island savage has not changed very much. He has only perfected through contact with a few coarse sailors the bad side of his nature. [. . .] If death for its part continues its ravages in the Marquesas Islands, some of them will before long be depopulated. Perhaps the navigator when confronted with these deserted shores will then look back with interest to the days when their inhabitants lived ignorant and uncouth no doubt, but peaceful, happy and perhaps less savage at heart than a fair number of civilized people.

Melville had the same thoughts in mind when he accused westerners of ruining the traditions of Maori civilization in *Omoo, a narrative of Adventures in the South Seas* (1847).

Condemnations such as these tell us how the myth had been degraded. The state of nature and the golden age of Tahiti were just an image, an illusion cruelly belied by reality. Instead of a New Cythera, a land of delight where Love and Reason reigned, Tahiti then became confused in the world of the imagination with iniquitous Babylon!

Overall the few texts cited give some idea of the extreme vitality of the Tahitian myth throughout the nineteenth century. The South Sea Islands exercised a powerful fascination, and aroused infatuation. We only have to look at the 'tempting', not to say 'come-hitherish' illustrations in travel stories or geographical works dealing with the sunlit archipelago, and the islands of the Pacific in general. For the myth of Tahiti to survive in the twentieth century, perhaps it had to show a new face. It could be assumed that alongside the Tahitian imagery that was fashionable in the nineteenth century, other images, conveyed by tourism and advertising, would come into being.

THE MODERN FACES OF THE TAHITIAN MYTH

It is easy to see that the image of Tahiti in the twentieth century has been exploited by tourism and advertising. While there is no doubt that criticism of the westernization of the Polynesian islands still continues, we can observe a strange renaissance of the original myth, that of a New Cythera, but largely for economic ends. The island of Wallis, Bougainville, Loti and Melville plays an archetypal role, but it also and primarily constitutes a market from which the maximum profit must be extracted.

With the help of detailed documentation and driven by a lively desire to record what he had seen, Victor Ségalen in *Les Immémoriaux* (1907), dedicated 'to the Maoris of forgotten times', continued to arraign Europe, and the Christian religion in particular. Using the excesses committed by Pritchard and the missionaries as his background, he demonstrates how Christianity has been responsible for annihilating indigenous traditions. The hero Térii, at first resistant to the missionaries' teaching ('Térii wondered gloomily if the land of Tahiti had not changed its inhabitants and sky at the same time as its gods and priests!'), is brought to change his faith. Christened Iakoba (Jacob), he rejects Paofaï who had initiated him and who still serves the Tahitian gods. In a supreme irony Iakoba, in order to finish building the prayer *faré* (church), sells Eréna to sailors who have called in to port. And the novel ends with Eréna coming back with two sturdy sailors on either side of her carrying bags of nails! Giraudoux wrote his *Supplément au Voyage de Cook* (performed in 1935) in a lighter vein; he pokes fun at Mr Banks who has been anxious to inculcate the concepts of work, propriety and morality into the savages. In the final scene, the chief Outourou addresses his subjects thus:

> Mr Banks's magnificent work is coming to an end. Men and women alike, you will be able to welcome our guests tomorrow as they are welcomed in their own towns [. . .] and I will repeat my instructions. All young men and friends who are in their prime, do not forget that you are workers, and all of you must have your spades with you – fan yourselves with your spades, protect yourselves from the sun with your spades, dance the spade dance, and when you sleep, sleep the sleep of the spade. And whatever you do don't use them, they have to be handed back when they go. As for you, children and old people, make sure you don't ask the sailors for their buttons and their spectacles. There is an English method for getting hold of them called theft. And as for the women and girls, insted of quietly waiting for our guests in your festive clothes, run up to the sailors asking them to give you a child, as Mr Banks demands, and as soon as they appear discard anything inflammable, I mean your clothes, for according to Mr Banks women are burnt when Europeans look at them; then drag them off, sated with palm wine, into the darkness of your huts where our thieves can discreetly relieve them of their knives and tobacco pouches at their leisure. These are the lessons that clever Mr Banks has managed to convey to us within two hours. Show yourselves worthy of him (Scene XI).

The civilized man's message is completely deformed, perverted and diverted from its end purpose! In *Touriste de Bananes ou Les Dimanches de Tahiti* (1938) G. Simenon less humourously set about reducing the compass of the myth of Tahiti by developing a detective story plot which draws the reader into the seamy side of the island. On the whole he contributed to uncovering what lies behind the setting, exposing one of the far from paradisiacal faces of the island in his book.

In the inter-war period two phenomena reinforced the rebirth of the tendency to regard Tahiti as a New Cythera. First of all the cinema revealed unforgettable scenery to its viewers. Méliès had already paid homage in the studio to exotic dreams (*Ballade des Mers du Sud*, *Histoire de l'Antique Tahiti*). In 1923 the film *Moana* was shot in Samoa by Flaherty, and in 1931 Flaherty and Murnau together made *Tabu* in Bora Bora. Finally in 1935 Tahiti was used as the setting for *Mutiny on the Bounty* with Charles Laughton and Clark Gable. Secondly, luxury tourism in the 1930s made Tahiti an essential port of call for liners. In his book *Nelle Isole della felicità* (1934) Gino Nibbi describes lucidly and brilliantly the reactions and behaviour of these rich Europeans and Americans playing at acting out the lives of characters in *Le Mariage de Loti*. When the moment came to leave the island, the inevitable 'Farewell to Tahiti' was a bravura display in which the ridiculous conveyed the myth of New Cythera and its faithful, while at the same time mocking it: 'Coming from San Francisco (or from Frisco as they all say) the steamer had set down that same morning forty sufferers from infinity-sickness, not to mention any other kind of sickness.'

From the 1930s, thanks to luxury tourism and the cinema, Tahiti as a 'label' and the 'branded image' of the island of enchantment seemed to take off once more. During the following decades the Tahiti label continued to flourish. Around 1950 a large number of books and tourist guides by Darnois, Putigny, Villaret and T'Sertsevens (1950, 1951, 1958) attest to this. Tourist literature, travel agencies and publicity leaflets deliberately used the image of an island that is a refuge and a haven of peace where 'There is only order and beauty,/Luxury, calm and voluptuousness'. The Blue Guides (one by G. Kling in 1971) and P.-E. Victor's guide (1966) to a certain extent kept in existence the image of Tahiti as the ultimate Cythera which neither war nor civilization could destroy. At the same time this 'tourist' literature was aimed at urging the public to visit a place which might not exist tomorrow. Leave for Tahiti now, just as you should set off for Venice! But as the original myth of Tahiti was still extant, and moreover in the twentieth century was seen in association with the four S's (Sun, Sea, Sand and Sex), guidebooks and picture books devoted to Bougainville's island erased anything referring to an unpleasant reality. As the myth was lucrative, people made efforts to make it last, embellish it and avoid internal stresses within it that might risk ruining it.

For the last fifteen years or so we have witnessed a complex and revealing phenomenon in this respect. Tahiti, for reasons connected with geography, economy, fashion and advertising, is no longer the only paradise that is disappearing. Admittedly there are still captains who are enjoying a golden retirement on the blessed island, and there is still a sizeable tide of tourists following in the footsteps of Gauguin and Loti, but there is increasing competition from other paradise islands: Hawaii, the Bahamas, the Seychelles, the West Indies, the Maldives . . . Well for some travellers, and this is the legacy of the myth skilfully maintained by advertising, the image of all these exotic, erotic paradises is inextricably associated with the image of Tahiti: this is due to the power of the myth of New Cythera and the audio-visual media, which were aware of all there was to gain from the Tahiti label in the field of tourism and other forms of the economy.

So what does it matter if France is carrying out its nuclear test programme in Polynesia, or if the dances of the *vahines* are now no more than a typical product to satisfy the tourist. The myth is becoming perennial, engendering its own sap, secreting its spells, perhaps because it relates the geographical reality of Tahiti with the reality of the imaginary world and the collective unconscious.

Tourists have not changed the myth of Tahiti, they have made use of it, subtly yet radically removing its contradictions and tensions so as to leave it with only a totally positive message. In fact Tahit functions as a master image. Even mass tourism has not destroyed the Tahitian dream: it has put it within reach of a larger number of people. At first at least this phenomenon did not harm the survival of one tradition: of travellers and writers making the Pacific Islands a virtually official port of call for their inner fulfilment and as a source of inspiration. Jack London and Somerset Maugham, following in the footsteps of Melville and Robert Louis Stevenson, brought back from the South Seas experiences and stories that were sometimes decisive, with the mythology of the peoples encountered benefiting that of the narrator. Later the affirmation that Tahiti meant liberation, the 'gospel of the sun', slowly faded for clear-minded writers who knew, like Gerbault, that 'the islands of beauty' were 'a paradise that is dying'. Today virtually nothing is written about Tahiti – the Blue Guide and tourism have dried up the inspiration of genuine travel writers. And where the island still continues to be a source of creativity, this is due to what it represents and its history, as in Robert Merle's novel *L'Île* (1962).

In the twentieth century, alongside writers and navigators who have magnified or denounced the illusions of Tahiti, thereby treading the same paths as their predecessors, we may observe a special development of the master image of the paradise island in the context of the world of leisure. The myth exploited in this way has been limited, seeming now to offer only a single facet. And paradoxically one of the merits of the Tahitian movement for self-rule is that it reminds us how artificial the paradise in which the Tahitians are living is, to what extent it generates illusions and dreams.

Influenced by the 'founding fathers' of the myth of Tahiti, writers, navigators, artists and tourists have taken pleasure in visiting and celebrating the New Cythera. The power of such a myth on the world of the imagination, the unconscious, the libido, advertising and the economy has turned Bougainville's island into a picture of Eden. From Wallis to Victor, from Gauguin to Gerbault, even denunciation of the island's delights has bolstered up its 'image'. It is clear, however, that rather than being threatened by the development of literary criticism as a component – such an important one at the beginning of the twentieth century – the myth of Tahiti has survived, becoming stronger thanks to the techniques of clever advertising which has transformed the literary and sociological myth of the eighteenth century into a very lucrative economic myth. Thus the singer Carlos, vaunting the merits of 'Oasis' fruit juice, is not transported to an arid desert: instead he is a jovial captain coming to land on the enchanting shores of an island covered with coconut palms. Yet it is both disturbing and reassuring to find examples of the pursuit of the myth of Tahiti in its original aspect. When Jacques Brel, tired and ill, retired from the stage and escaped, he set off for Tahiti and the Marquesas where, he sang, 'Groans are out of place' . . . When P.-E. Victor tired of the lonely icy wastes, he chose to go and live with his family in an enchanting Pacific island . . . We must therefore accept, with examples such as these, that for all its contradictions the myth is tenacious and hardy, and that Tahiti will still continue to incarnate that desire for escape, that eternal 'need for elsewhere' that is so deeply rooted in men's hearts: 'Tahiti, or an invitation to travel'.

James Dauphiné

Tales and Myths

La voix sonne – ou se tait – au coeur – au choeur – du drame
(The voice sounds – or is silent – at the heart
– in the chorus – of the drama)
(Zumthor 1983)

Human history is written in the fallow fields of silence. It is a tissue of murmuring words and specific gestures that the teller organizes into unique tales. A horse's shoe strikes the area of ground all sprinkled with toasted barley flour where the listeners are gathered. A golden dust rises between us and the dream. The hero has passed, he has left his trace in the sand of our memories, where it will long outlive him.

Myth or tale? It may seem pointless to seek to divide up the territory of the imagination in this way, and, indeed, it remains inappropriate to try to tie down stories that take their shifting fluidity from human speech. The approach adopted here will thus involve an attempt, not so much to define tales and myths by enclosing them in unambiguous definitions, as to show how these two terms have a living relationship with each other. This necessitates discovering the circumstances in which the relationship manifests itself and the ways in which it has been shaped through history. It is as hard a task as that of the goldsmith in the story who was obliged by a woman's whim to work drops of water. Ambiguous, equivocal and sometimes contradictory, myths and tales subvert the theoretical frameworks that seek to determine their relationship.

SPEECH

'When one makes a tale, it is for someone who is listening to it', wrote Diderot in the preface to *Ceci n'est pas un conte* in 1773. Whilst in traditional societies adults and children alike often gather to hear tales that were not composed specifically for either age group, in our everyday lives tales are generally perceived as a medium of communication between adult narrators and children who are sucking their thumbs and on the verge of sleep and yet eager for one last delicious scare. But whatever the cultural framework in which transference takes place and whatever the expectations involved, the tales themselves remain inseparable from body and voice, from intonation and rhythm, mimicry and expressions, and the gestures that are an extension and sometimes an anticipation of speech. Tales are woven of the laughter, whispers and exclamations of an audience that can comment on, interrupt or alter the story at any time and who seek to ensure that it conforms to a pattern that they already know. In this shared speech, silences acquire a particular significance: they are mirrors in which the teller glimpses the power of words in the inverted image reflected by the listeners and by the way in which they listen.

We can sense the fragility of this transmission from mouth to ear, of this 'hearsay'. We can also sense the difficulties inherent in the transcription of an oral text; while seeking to fix it and record it in lasting form, the transcriber risks freezing and destroying it.

The fact that myths – and primarily ancient Greek myths – have come down to us in written form should not be allowed to hide their oral and indeed incantatory nature. To master myths, it is not enough to know them, one must also know how to recite them. The term 'recitation', used by Mircea Eliade, does not mean repetition; it is the ritualized incarnation in a voice and a body of a tale borrowed from the collective memory that is regenerated at the moment of narration. There is no element either of overuse or of usurpation in this new and yet familiar creation. Indeed, it is through this new act of creation that the listeners can fully enter into the events related, that they can leave the sphere of everyday experience to penetrate the other world, that they can escape profane, relative and mortal time to enter the eternal.

For, although both myths and tales are presented as retrospective narratives, echoes of memorable events that touch us through the stories themselves, the past that they portray is not of the same kind. The unspecific past of the magical tale (where 'once upon a time' functions as a textual signal placing us at the heart of the story), stands in contrast to mythical time (*in illo tempore*), the time of genesis and creation, which is radically separate from our own time. Mythical time is not part of history.

EARLIER VOICES

Like myths, tales emanate from the collective memory and are recounted by a great anonymous speaker whose characteristics are vague. Like myths, they are part of a tradition. It is from this tradition that the storyteller draws, if not the motifs of the story, then at least the framework that gives them order, meaning and a direction. The concept of the typical tale, defined by Aarne and Thompson as an organization of motifs that is sufficiently stable to be repeated in different stories, is primarily useful as a tool for classifying tales. However, despite its abstraction, it also helps us to grasp a fundamental truth about the oral tradition, which is that the teller's freedom is supervised. The art of improvisation, which turns a gifted story-teller into a true creator, an artist in the full sense, has to operate within strict confines. Tellers are not prisoners of the model set for them by the oral tradition. They make it their own. Just as a musician who is careful to remain faithful to a score may still experience the dizzy excitement of a unique moment during a performance, so the story-teller tries to act as a resonance chamber for anonymous speech, arising from a distant elsewhere and buried in our memory, that is already known but that surfaces at the moment of its narration like something new. Using Lévi-Strauss's words, one can argue that like myths, tales are defined only by the sum of their variations. Only a comparative analysis of all recorded versions of a tale can enable us to grasp its multicoloured kaleidoscopic pattern and perhaps also to explore the changes that it has undergone in the course of time. This journey of discovery will not be without surprises. To take the example of one of the best-known tales in the European repertoire, in the oral tradition, the story of Little Red Ridinghood can vary astoundingly from the version made famous by Perrault in 1697. Here, she loses her hood but gains a coat of iron, takes strange paths strewn with needles and pins, eats the flesh and drinks the blood of her grandmother and happily performs a strip-tease for the wolf before escaping by means of a scatalogical trick when all is almost lost. Detailed study of existing variations of the tale clearly reveals that the motifs – which undergo permutations from one version to the next – are neither accidental nor arbitrary and that, as Lévi-Strauss has remarked, in tales as in myths, 'even substitutions are constrained by laws'.

Evidently, there are many points of convergence between myths and tales. Thus both can be defined as oral narratives of a retrospective nature to which the collective tradition gives a relative stability, and which accidents of memory and variations in human speech render shifting and changeable. Indeed, the similarities between the two genres are so great that they suggest an analysis of their relationship in terms of kinship.

A FAMILY AFFAIR?

For the brothers Grimm, myths certainly represented the bedrock of the most ancient poetry because of their way of interpreting 'supersensible things'. They believed that tales preserved the fragments or debris of myths in an elliptical and deliberately allusive form. In this context, it is worth quoting from the postface of the 1850 edition of their work: 'These mythical elements resemble the little pieces of a shattered gemstone which have been scattered over ground covered in grass and flowers and which only the most penetrating eyes can discover.' Perhaps the grass and flowers are the narrative element, the action of the tale; while diverting our attention, these obliterate the secret meanings, the real issues that underlie the narrative. Thus it has been said that, for the brothers Grimm, tales were myths rendered profane – myths that had fallen to earth from heaven. According to Albert Wesselski, tales are the children of myths, which the latter engendered as they were dying, or after their death. One objection that can be raised to this theory of posthumous birth is that tales and myths can co-exist perfectly well in some societies and so are not mutually exclusive. Lévi-Strauss's analyses are absolutely explicit on this point.

Whilst preserving the theory that one genre is descended from the other, Wilhelm Wundt strangely inverts the two terms in Wesselski's proposition. For him, the tale precedes, heralds and anticipates the myth. According to him, *Urmärchen* are explanatory narratives, lying between mythology and history, from which legends, myths and all other kinds of narratives are constructed, though it is true that he applies the ambiguous term *Mythenmärchen* (myth-tales) to these *Urmärchen*, thereby linking the two genres.

Strangely, Vladimir Propp later revived this term 'mythical tales', suggesting that it should be re-instated, at least for fairy stories. Although his prime aim in *The Morphology of the Folktale* (1928) was to demonstrate the formal homogeneity of all tales by using a narrative analysis that was entirely new at the time, he also came to the conclusion that tales and myths were indistinguishable from a morphological point of view.

For Propp, the distinction between the two genres lay not in their form but in their social function. While he defined as myths narratives carrying religious truths that were accepted and recognized by all members of a society, he regarded tales as arising from a fault whereby this harmony was threatened. Their existence indicated that cracks had appeared in the myths, in the rites that inspired or echoed them and in the belief that people had in them.

This view does not necessarily imply kinship between one genre and the other. Tales may certainly borrow and transpose certain motifs taken from myths that still survive. However, they may also be alone in preserving the traces of rites that have fallen into disuse, and thus appear more ancient than the myths themselves. Because they form an integral part of society whose evolution Propp presents as inevitable, tales retain the traces of successive epochs 'like a landscape in which the most ancient strata rise to the surface beside the most recent, as they do in a geological fold'. This fine comparison, used by Jean-Claude Schmitt and Daniel Fabre, illustrates the difficulties inherent in the exploration of what could be called the tale's 'stratification'. It was certainly this sort of exploration that Propp was undertaking in *Les Racines historiques du Conte merveilleux*, when he sought to uncover the complex transformations that tales may undergo.

LOST CLARITY

Lévi-Strauss posits the relationship between myth and tale not in historical terms but in logical ones: the two genres are not affiliated to each other but complement each other and can co-exist like two ends of a spectrum that includes hybrid narratives and 'intermediate forms'. The difference between them is thus not of nature but of degree. For, in terms of their structure, they present such considerable similarities that the same tools can be used in their analysis. In any given society, they unendingly rework the same material, articulate the same motifs and reuse the same sequences. However, they do so on a different scale. For the 'cosmological, metaphysical or natural conflicts' that form the basis of the mythical narrative, tales substitute 'local, social or moral conflicts' in an almost mimetic way. Thus, in the mirror of the tale, we can see, like a veiled reflection, 'a weakened transposition of themes whose amplified manifestation is the preserve of myths'. The tale's cohesion and its appropriateness to the context in which it is passed on are compromised or at least threatened as a result, because in its case the narrative logic, the imprint of the sacred and the hold of society are weaker than in the case of a myth. The elements of the tale are fluid and malleable, and this relative looseness favours the tale's appropriation by other forms of expression, including literature.

Conversely, does the strength of myths lie, as Eliade suggests, in the fact that they enable the world to be understood as a consistent and perfectly intelligible cosmos? By placing us from the outset in the time of creation, of the primordial event, by evoking a 'primal thought', by bringing exemplary deeds into the present, myths provide models for every aspect of human behaviour. Their symbolic language constantly awakens us to an awareness of the divine and permits us to contemplate the universe in all its transparency with opened eyes.

While tales take up and extend the initiatory scenarios that are at work in myths, Eliade is categorical that they do so at a different level. This is not because they belong to a world devoid of any trace of the sacred (gods still pace the lands of the tale, even if they are only rather threadbare figures), but because in tales the initiatory function of the narrative has often ceased to be perceptible. After all, did the tale not degenerate into the fairy story when traditional rites declined and people began to recount with impunity things that had formerly been jealously guarded secrets? While an initiatory element persists at the level of the imagination, it is presented in a diffuse fashion, under the cloak of fiction and in the misleading guise of entertainment. Our inattentive minds, our banal modern consciousness, can no longer perceive it in all its colours.

LIKE AN INTANGIBLE WISP OF SMOKE

In the transition from myths to tales the transparency that Eliade described as primal has been lost. This gradual process of obfuscation has led researchers to open up new areas of investigation using a multidisciplinary approach based increasingly on detailed case studies. For too long abstract definitions of the tale, the myth and the relationship between the two genres anticipated examination of pretextual material, which actually supported previous assumptions rather than subverting existing categories. An important illustration of the recent approach is provided by the work of Nicole Belmont, who has revealed the existence of a mythical pattern, which tales take up and transform. Thus the many versions of tale type 313 provide a kind of symmetrical and inverted reflection of the Orpheus myth, and these associations seem to endow the tale with renewed meaning. Orpheus's descent into the underworld in search of his lost wife – that part of himself for which he cannot mourn – has certain parallels with the perilous quest that takes the hero of type 313 into the other world – not to hell, but to the home of the devil – to find a wife and hence to find himself. However, there are many divergences between the two narratives. While Orpheus loses his beloved because he turns to look at her – she dissolves into the shadows 'like an intangible wisp of smoke' – the hero of type 313 succeeds in carrying off the devil's daughter only by constantly looking round, at her request, to watch the black cloud signifying the threat posed by her hostile father's pursuit. While Orpheus preserves the memory of his vanished wife by withdrawing to the frozen wastes of Thrace, the tale's hero is keen to forget his love by making conquests in his own country. While Orpheus dies, torn to pieces by the Bacchantes, the boy in the tale owes the entire success of his quest to the sacrifice of the girl, who asks to be killed, dissected and boiled so that he can make a ladder from her bleached bones. The water of death that bears away Orpheus's head, still calling to Eurydice, contrasts with the theme of the water of life that first strips the girl of her flesh and then resuscitates her. Thus the fairy story reproduces the myth in a disguised form – which may have been developed for historical reasons, to protect it against the censures of the Church by disguising it as fiction. Today the reappearance of the mythical pattern confers an eschatological dimension on type 313 that had previously been lost from sight. Belmont concludes that tales and myths function in relation to each other, like the two texts in a palimpsest.

UNGRASPABLE GENRES

Whatever the divergences between the various approaches discussed above, they are all based on the same implicit hypothesis that tales and myths are autonomous genres. However, this autonomy appears very fragile once the two genres enter literature; and we can then clearly grasp their amazing ability to infiltrate other forms of expression.

Where tales are concerned, this point has been strongly emphasized by Lévi-Strauss in relation to societies such as our own, in which myths have disappeared and tales alone survive. The initial balance is broken and, 'like a satellite without a planet, the tale tends to leave its orbit and to be diverted by other poles of attraction'. The force of attraction first operates between the tales themselves, which may conglomerate, enmesh their motifs and combine their sequences. These groupings, which somewhat upset the rigour of the Aarne-Thompson classification pattern, have often been regarded as involving a process of contamination. According to Henri Pourrat, episodes become tacked on to each other and merge, giving rise to almost innumerable hybrids. In fact, such unions often bear witness to deliberate affinities between certain typical tales. Little is known of the principles underlying these, but the Hungarian school is seeking to uncover them.

The tale's entry into literature creates other relationships involving the structure of the work into which it is integrated. Sometimes, as, for example, in *The Decameron*, the setting involves a story-telling culture in which many narrators take turns to recount their tales. At other times, the structure is that of a tale within a tale, a *mise en abîme*, composed of stories that nest into each other like Russian dolls: the nest of stories comes apart to reveal other stories, so that, for example, Scheherazade's first night leads to a thousand and one nights of tales. As Tzvetan Todorov has clearly shown, the complexity of this literary form derives from the fact that each 'narrative person' reveals and hides a new narrator: the new narrators derive their existence and the authority of their speech from their immediate predecessors.

Thus, in the *Saragossa Manuscript (Alvadoro III)*:

Alfonso tells how
  Alvadoro tells how
    Don Lope tells how
      Busqueros tells how
        Frasquetta tells how . . .

This approach was used in the context of the novel by Selma Lagerlöf, who made a multicoloured mosaic like the patchwork landscape seen by wild geese out of the vast tissue of tales gathered or experienced by Nils during his travels. These were passed over to the narrator, who tries to recount the wonderful journey. The narrative organization of Pourrat's *Gaspard des Montagnes* is even more complex: the dimensions of the main tale expand to encompass a whole universe and give the novel its framework, while other tales are embedded in it, which the narrative orders into evening sessions and pauses, as in the oral tradition. The book thus measures itself against the ell of story-telling, which brings from the shadows 'the story of a hundred stories'.

Tales, then, do not create barricades around themselves to preserve a proud solitude: they have complex relations with legends, short stories and novels. Their shifting boundaries delineate a multiform territory, which researchers are doing their best to map.

Are the boundaries of myth more rigid, and is its area more clearly defined? This is far from being so, not only because the powerful framework that unites myths ensures that each myth developed by any given ethnic group is linked to all the others (Lévi-Strauss wrote that the earth of mythology is round), but also because of the genre's infinite plasticity. It is a malleable and multiform genre, which has been appropriated in turn by epic, by lyric poetry, by tragedy and by the philosophical dialogue; it is a hardy plant that seems able to tolerate so many transplantations when it enters literature that it becomes difficult and indeed perilous to try to isolate it.

If we accept that the term 'myth' refers first and foremost to the Greek tradition, we must follow Eliade in recognizing that Greek myths have come down to us in the form of 'literary and artistic documents, and not as sources or expressions of a religious experience closely bound to a ritual'. The process whereby a myth comes to be written down is governed by complex laws, for the flexibility of the genre allows it to flow into different forms without being imprisoned within them. Thus when myths are incorporated in Plato's dialogues, this involves processes of embedding exactly comparable to those used in connection with tales. In this embedding technique, examined by André Philip, the narrator becomes many different characters who echo narratives told to them by others. Thus, in *Timaeus* (20d–21d), Critias claims to be telling a story told to him by his grandfather, who heard it from the mouth of Solon, who himself brought it back from Egypt after a conversation with a priest at Sais. Each of these fictional narrators is both the holder and transmitter of a narrative that is propagated by ricocheting from one to the other and that undergoes constant changes in the process. The durability of myth seems here to be dependent on a string of human voices, and this even affects the way in which it is written down. Is not the same true of its oral transmission? As a result of the work by Jean-Pierre Vernant, myths have come to be seen as 'hold-alls', dustbins full of residual utterances, collections of 'hearsay', echo chambers resounding – sometimes implicitly – with other people's words. Are not myths always quotations?

THE GLASS BEAD GAME

Should we follow Jan de Vries in contrasting the rigour and the serious aspect of myths with the game of fiction at work in the tale? This distinction, which is often made, merits investigation, for it tends to present the tale as a *Spielform*, a playful variant of the myth. The stylization of the narrative, the perfection of the smooth and self-contained chain of events, the lack of any depth of character and the transparency of the universe that it presents have even led Max Lüthi to define the tale as a 'glass bead game' – a reference to the novel by Herman Hesse. Similarly, Georges Jean speaks of the tale's 'Meccano-like' quality, while André Jolles talks of a 'perfectly oiled dream machine, in which the tragic is both presented and removed'.

The playful dimension is again evident, although only implicitly, in the rather stiff definitions given by dictionaries, which tend to see the tale simply as something used by women and small children to pass the time: hence the references to old wives' tales, servants' tales, nannies' tales, Mother Goose tales, storks' tales, tall stories and so on. It is vital to beware of this simplistic and deprecatory approach, which suggest that texts whose deeper significance is no longer apparent belong in the category of games and recreation. In traditional societies, tales had other functions. They fitted into the temporal dimension that historians since Fernand Braudel have called *la longue durée*, the long time, and preserved a memory, in the same way as Indonesian shadow theatre, in which it is the ancestors, the shadows of the past, who speak through the story-teller's mouth. This emphasis on a protective inheritance also gives the tale a moral function. In cautionary tales, this takes the form of a warning conveyed through a scenario condemning behaviour regarded as reprehensible. Lastly, it is not only myths that have an aetiological dimension; this also occurs particularly frequently in animal tales, which the folklorists of the nineteenth century called 'Whys'. These poetic fictions, which explain currently observable facts, serve to fill a gap or crack, by resolving an inconsistency in the world as we perceive it. They also provide simple answers to the questions that children ask of themselves and of adults: why do nightingales sing only at night, why do cats and dogs fight, why do bears have no tails?

So, far from having a simply ludic function, tales perform necessary gnomic and heuristic functions. The play of fiction follows laws and its progress is charted by reference points that often mark the stages of an initiatory journey. The importance of symbolic elements in the narrative should not be underrated even when they are presented in the form of entertainment or lies. When, in the oral tradition, the wolf asks Little Red Ridinghood to choose between two paths – that of the needles and that of the pins – along which to race him, he is proposing both a competition and a riddle, a double game. However, the question that this hairy sphinx asks at the crossroads of life also sounds like a threat: not knowing the right answer can lead to death.

It is not surprising, then, that some ethnic groups establish a kind of continuity between tales and myths, giving tales an introductory role. Geneviève Calame-Griaule has shown how the Dogon use tales as a first stage in inculcating the knowledge of myths, for which they act as a kind of 'translation into a more easily accessible language'. The close relationship between myths and tales and the common function performed by both are thus clearly in evidence.

SPEECH IN CHIAROSCURO

This shows how tenuous is the distinction so often made between tales, which are presented as games of the imagination, and myths, which many commentators regard as serious representations of sacred ideas, solemn and sometimes oracular expressions of incontrovertible truths. Returning to an ancient Greek context, and the evidence of the works of Plato, whose authority is undisputed, it is quite clear that the latter's dialogues contain what must be called a ludic element. This takes the form of a dialectical game, in which each participant is free to use myths as weapons, striking a rhetorical 'blow' in a struggle in which every discussion is presented as an *agon* (*contest*) involving what André Philip would call the staging of a minutely regulated confrontation. It is a clever game, in which surprises are always possible, although nothing is left to chance. It is a play of light and shadow too, for myths always involve revelation and concealment, they are both naive and complex, transparent and enigmatic, offering the possibility of multiple interpretations of their meaning and their peripheral meaning. Furthermore, the strategic position of myths in Plato's dialogues places them on the edges of the text: as André Philip stresses, they often occur in the prologue or epilogue and sometimes also appear at certain decisive moments in the confrontation.

André Jolles saw myths as a completely closed form: one asks the stars a question and the stars reply. If myths deceive us, this is because they always provide room for silence between question and answer: it is only a tiny step from *mythos* to *mutus*. Myths overstep the boundaries in which one would like to contain them. Like the Spirit floating above the waters at the moment of creation, they wander.

WHAT THE BIRD SAYS

Alan Dundes is inclined to see the significance of tales as individual and that of myths as collective. However, the first part of this proposition seems to have been undermined by certain recent studies. Far from performing the merely aesthetic function far too often emphasized today, tales were used in traditional communities as the preferred means of passing on memories, moral principles or training, as we have seen above. This means that even if the hero's story takes the form of a solitary quest, it greatly overlaps the framework of an individual adventure and weaves different connections between the listeners. While the story of Little Red Ridinghood seems to use women's gestures and tools as a technical code based on lacemaking, to talk about the destiny of girls, the initiatory journey that it portrays also fits into a collective setting, for example that of the Burgundian circles called *écraignes* where women gathered together to sew, embroider or weave both cloth and words, tying the material thread to the thread of speech in a special area free of all control. In the same way, according to Fabre's illuminating analysis of the subject, the theme of birds in the springtime, which features in many typical tales, seems closely linked to masculine rites of passage. For mastery of the language of birds signifies the acquisition of a double skill, both linguistic and erotic – the taming of both body and metaphor. This seeking after language and what lies on the other side of language is universal, even though the paths of initiation vary from one culture to another: it underlies a network of meanings that concern all boys without exception.

While it is true that myths constitute a 'language of the world' that people try to decode to organize it into narratives, into the great silent book, is this myth's distinguishing characteristic? Evguéni Mélétinski asserts that 'in myths the lacks are cosmic lacks'. This is no doubt correct; but when, in tale type 302, the hero goes off in search of the body without a soul, hidden beneath the waves or between heaven and earth, far from the egg palpitating with the life that left it, or when, in tale type 425, the young woman seeking her vanished husband questions the wind, the moon and the stars after filling a vase with her tears, or when, in tale type 720, the bones of the son murdered by his mother and eaten by his father rise up into the sky and assume the form of a bird to sing a song of truth for all the world to hear, can we say that the lacks are not cosmic and that the wording of the tale is not intended to give expression to the voices of the universe? 'I am no tree, but I am full of leaves', said the book.

Thus tales and myths foil all our attempts to lock them into logical categories because their richness and complexity frighten us. The boundary between their territories remains indistinct – or rather, like a shadow, it constantly changes. However, the very resistance put up by myths and tales to all efforts to define them is proof in itself of their vitality. The infinite possibilities that they present for playing games and setting tales within tales, for pastiche, parody and palimpsest; the special relationship that they have with the imagination; their plasticity, their slipperiness, and their capacity for variation, which often allows us to forget the durability of their underlying structures – all these things make them into protean genres that excite creativity, that bring about metamorphoses, that offer freedom and subversion and that, in the openness of literary creation, become renegade forms of expression.

Bernadette Bricout

The Temptation of St Anthony

Near the beginning of the Christian era, Anthony was a recluse living in the desert in Egypt. He sought God in the absoluteness of renunciation of the world. But the world would not leave him alone, the 'Adversary' persecuted him, sending demons to attack him and visions to seduce him. Anthony successfully overcame attack by temptation, from the age of twenty until his death aged about 105 (in 356). Very quickly, probably within ten years following his death, his story was written down. The author of *The Life of St Anthony* is anonymous, but he knew the hermit, though there is nothing to substantiate the traditional attribution of the work to Athanasias, the Archbishop of Alexandria. There survive 160 manuscripts of the life in Greek alone, and there are others in Latin, Coptic, Armenian, Syriac, Arab, Ethiopian and Georgian, indicating how successful the work was. At this stage no myth had been formed. The original text is a long, chronologically arranged account reporting events and quoting speeches. It had just one aim: to offer the faithful an exemplary figure who could be their 'mirror of life'. Used for many centuries as a charter for Christian monasticism, the *Life* was destined to be transformed into a legend. In the *Legenda Aurea* four pages are devoted to St Anthony. Points of reference are scarce, each example being introduced with the formula 'One day . . .', and the account proceeds by juxtaposition and accumulation. Instead of a story we have a situation full of clearcut oppositions, intense because of the repetitive nature and contracted length.

The essential element in the elaboration of the myth was the vision, not only because the visionary is someone out of the common run, but because visions imply something that can be represented – at the cost of projecting outside into the tangible world the kind of mental theatre that took place within the hermit. Representation had two possible outlets, the stage and the picture.

Like his distant cousin Dr Faust, St Anthony was in the repertory of the puppet theatre. In about 1825 Gustave Flaubert as a child applauded the saint and his pig at Saint-Romain fair in Rouen. There is evidence of similar shows right up to the present day. The puppets can be linked to a whole popular vein in the cult of St Anthony. In the Middle Ages he was invoked with the help of pious images for 'visible' illnesses, those that leave a mark on the body: various types of plague, St Anthony's fire (erysipelas, or gangrenous ergotism – modern medicine is not sure which). In iconography this cult has its coded language. There is a plague victim in one corner, and a brazier on the horizon; and from the fifteenth century, St Anthony's faithful companion, the pig wearing a little bell. This emblematic animal is generally regarded as the devourer of rubbish, a physical representation of the spiritual combat by means of which the saint, who is himself almost always marked with the symbolic tau cross, purifies the world of its sins.

There was a proliferation of iconography. On the one hand, there are countless pictures of St Anthony: a recently published book of reproductions gives some idea how many. Everyone knows the great painters working *c.* 1500: Grünewald, who included a 'Temptation of St Anthony' in his famous Issenheim retable; Bosch, whose treatments of the subject are scattered across museums in Lisbon, Madrid and Venice; or Lucas van Leyden and Brueghel. Callot's engravings were distributed widely. But 'Temptations' by Veronese, Tiepolo, Watteau, Fantin-Latour, Odilon Redon and, nearer our own time, Salvador Dali, Paul Delvaux or Max Ernst are less well known. On the other hand, there is a proliferation of iconography within the pictures: the saint himself occupies relatively little space, withdrawn with lowered eyes, or viewed from behind, sometimes barely discernible, almost drowning amidst the unfolding visions. The artists' flights of imagination seem to be in inverse proportion to the relative reticence of the original text. *The Life of St Anthony* tells us that the Adversary went 'as far as to appear to him even in the form of a woman'. How much lascivious nakedness that laconic phrase has given rise to! Again the *Life* tells us that the anchorite spent his final fifty years not in the deserts of Thebaid, but in a humble 'inner desert'. That does not prevent painters from depicting him in huge Apocalyptic landscapes! However, by turning *The Life of St Anthony* into a spectacle, all the painters are doing is developing its hidden potential, without betraying the religious aims of the text. People such as Matthias Grünewald or Hieronymus Bosch were religiously motivated. The Issenheim altar was commissioned by an Antonine monastery. All the swarming horrors that the painters show us, the catastrophes in the far distance and the fantastic anatomies in grotesque, threatening postures in the foreground, while they admittedly attest to a dark vision of the world, are not based on any permissiveness towards instinct-driven abandon. They thought of their pictures in the same way as they thought of epidemics of the plague. They worked on the bodies because they had to give a body to the invisible powers of evil. According to that logic (and nobody in our own day had understood it better than Antonin Artaud), the extreme of purification is the counterpart of the extreme of materialization.

The two outlets of representation – the stage and pictures – were in communication. They fused in a theatrical style of painting. If the dogmas that once justified it have no sway over us, we nonetheless feel their metaphysical vibrations. This journey through the works of great painters was necessary to allow Anthony's destiny to go beyond hagiography and express all the ambiguity of existence-in-this-world. Conveying ideas by means of images, the pictorial discourse intensified the effects, and heightened the oppositions. What is more, in the case of temptation, the idea being aimed at is the opposite of the image shown: God is signified by pandemonium, solitude by the crowd, chastity by lewdness, spiritual struggle by the seething of matter. This repressed aspect of the representation, what the picture does not say, contributes to the uneasiness it provokes.

In 1845 a romantic young traveller stood in front a 'Temptation' by Brueghel in Genoa:

> This picture at first seems confused, then it becomes strange for most people, funny for some, and something more for others; for me it wiped out everything else in the gallery where it is, already I can no longer remember the rest.

This overwhelming encounter between Flaubert and a 'primitive' artist was to lead to a text, *La Tentation de saint Antoine*. It is more than a text, it is an adventure: Flaubert was to write three versions (1849, 1856, 1874), publishing only the final one. He was to say: 'It is my whole life's work.'

The literary myth began with Flaubert. First of all it must be stressed that the writer used the tradition in its entirety. The theatricality of his *Tentation* is undeniable, even if he never imagined that his work, a kind of prose poem with dialogue, could ever be staged. The first version with its allegories and diableries refers back to the medieval Mystery play and puppet theatre. (The second version is an abridgement of the first.) The whole beginning of the third version is lifted from *The Life of St Anthony*. As for the monsters, they are partly derived from Brueghel and Callot. We should of course remember that, if Flaubert felt challenged by the figure of the anchorite, it was because he was himself a great visualizer, and in his way a recluse. (Subsequently critics in their turn, from Valéry to Barthes and Sartre, fabricated a myth: Flaubert the hermit of Croisset, a martyr to writing, saved thanks to the doctrine that 'the loser wins'.)

Thus here we have a text located at the point where a tradition, a personal story and modernity intersect. It was by integrating the up-to-date scientific ideas of the nineteenth century into his approach that Flaubert transformed the myth and made it a fascinating literary creation. First of all the character of St Anthony is internalized, reframed in psychological terms. By crediting his character with his own psychosomatic experiences, in the third version especially, the author turns him into a great sufferer from hallucinations with whom the end of the nineteenth century, obsessed with neurosis, would identify. More than ever the visionary is subordinate to his visions. Painters had already represented Temptation on a worldwide scale. Flaubert took the extreme step of removing the limits of space and time. In the words of Michel Foucault (1967):

> In the space of that Egyptian night haunted by the oriental past, the whole culture of Europe unfolds: the Middle Ages with its theology, the Renaissance with its erudition, the modern age with its scientific knowledge of the world and living creatures.

It is the Devil, in the guise of a romantic Archangel, who 'comes forward to introduce western knowledge'!

The distortion is obvious. While *The Life of St Anthony* supported the Christian faith by exalting the saint, *La Tentation de saint Antoine* makes Christianity relative and exalts the visions. There are swarms of ever more varied tempting figures. There are the Queen of Sheba and Buddha, the great heretical leaders and Nebuchadnezzar, monsters from the bestiaries, and all the gods of the Orient and Greece. Each image steps to the front of the stage for an instant, utters a speech brilliantly illuminating the myth to which it relates, and then fades to make way for the next image. The literary myth thus seems like a second-stage myth, for it incorporates primary myths, some of which are quoted directly, while others are presented through an intermediary. For example, the pig is present in the first two versions: no longer the pig with bells of medieval tradition, it is a double of Anthony and one of the figures on which the myth of metamorphosis is centred. A second example: in setting up a dialogue between the Sphinx and the chimera Flaubert crosses two different mythical traditions, and provides textual backing for a new myth, which was seized upon by the decadent movement. It involves condensation, dislocation, and a reversal of values . . . The analogy with the workings of the unconscious is striking. *La Tentation de saint Antoine* is as much about desire as about knowledge, about the desire for knowledge and knowledge about desire. Flaubert links up with the archaic equivalence between 'knowing' and 'seeing'. As a visionary, a seer and a voyeur, Anthony is on the look-out for the elusive scene showing our origins. Fragmented, distorted and lost, the myths wind through the text in a constantly renewed quest.

But to gain access to ancient knowledge, Flaubert used the science of his century. He had read Creuzer, Matter, Maury – a whole library. His *Tentation* is a book of books: not a sum total of them (though the Bible is a model), but a patchwork or collage. Scholarly or religious quotations are chosen for their figurative power, taken out of the context in which they made sense, and systematically altered. In the third version Buddha says, 'I too have done amazing things – eating just a single grain of rice in a day, and grains of rice then were no bigger than they are now.' Here we are getting to the crux of the break between tradition and the literary myth. By reinscribing the myth in the context of the written word, by placing his *Tentation* in the spaces between a huge intertext, Flaubert makes representation problematical. The two areas where the myth had developed – the stage and pictures – were affected by it. The stage tilts towards the 'other stage', and the fantastic towards the unrepresentable phantasmic. In the field of pictures, it is the same as with the written word. Nothing is really put on show, for nothing can be. There are only textual effects which hold the meaning suspended between hallucination and irony.

Whether it is regarded as sulphurous or boring, this work is the least well known of Flaubert's writings. Yet Baudelaire had some inkling of its importance as early as 1857, hailing it as the 'secret chamber of his mind' (Baudelaire 1868). The literary myth spurted a few flames in the 1880–90 decade. Thus in *À rebours* (Huysmans 1884) Des Esseintes goes into raptures over the dialogue between the Sphinx and the chimera. Strangely enough, when transferred into Huysmans' text the passage by Flaubert is given a more theatrical dimension, since the words exchanged by the two monsters are spoken by a woman ventriloquist – also a monster, in her way. The myth's links with literature are fragile, and at any moment it may revert to theatre or painting. When Huysmans again spoke about Flaubert's *Tentation* in an article of art criticism (1889), it was from the point of view of Odilon Redon's lithographs. Redon did not illustrate Flaubert, he invented monsters in accordance with the master's scientific principles: Huysmans in fact conjectured that Redon might have looked at microscope slides for new forms.

Elsewhere it was parody time. A novella by Maupassant, *Saint-Antoine* (1883), relates a sinister war story: how a Norman peasant nicknamed 'Saint-Antoine' set about subjugating a Prussian soldier, his 'pig', eventually murdering him, or one might even say 'digesting' him. It is really winking at the myth rather than treating it seriously, but it may be noted that Maupassant's story serves as a vehicle for physical phantasms that were not unknown to Flaubert. At a more cerebral level, Anatole France remembered Anthony when creating his character Paphnuce. *Thaïs* (1889) is 'a *Tentation de saint Antoine* written from the standpoint and with the pen of *Candide*', as Gustave Kahn put it. Parodies continued to crop up until the 1920s: at the Moulin Rouge a Queen of Sheba appeared in a 'Temptation' arranged for the Gertrude Hoffmann Girls!

Outside France it was mainly in German-speaking countries that Flaubert's work was appreciated most, for its symbolism, existential overtones and disturbing strangeness. Kafka was familiar with it, as was Freud. It inspired one of Freud's pupils, Theodor Reik, to write one of the very first attempts at literary psychoanalysis (1912). From time to time a twentieth-century visionary gets hold of Flaubert's text, confirming its modernity. Maurice Béjart, who produced a stage version with Jean-Louis Barrault, took it in the direction of Theatre of Cruelty. Salvador Dali, who painted the most disturbing contemporary version of the Temptation, re-establishes an ambiguous mysticism by means of a perverted form of the wonderful. Nonetheless, St Anthony has not enjoyed the same success as Faust, with whom he has so many affinities. In constructing the literary myth Flaubert may simultaneously have exhausted it. To start a new life perhaps the myth should yet again change its medium, leaving the canvas, the boards and the page to transfer to the screen. St Anthony's temptations are still awaiting their Fellini.

Jeanne Bem

Theseus

Following the visit of Aegeus to the court of King Pittheus at Troezen, Aethra, one of the king's daughters, gave birth to a son whose father was either Aegeus or the god Poseidon. When the boy, Theseus, was sixteen, his mother told him of the circumstances of his birth and took him to the rock under which Aegeus had placed a sword and a pair of sandals as a test of his identity. When he had lifted the rock and taken these tokens of proof, Theseus decided to go to Athens to claim the recognition of Aegeus. Ignoring his mother and grandfather, who advised him to make the journey by sea, he went via the isthmus which at the time was inhabited by brigands and outlaws. He killed Periphetes and kept his club, and subjected Sinis to the same fate that the latter used to reserve for travellers. He killed the Crommyonian sow, and Sciron who forced travellers to wash his feet and then kicked them into the sea, as well as Cercyon the fighter, and finally Procrustes who either 'stretched' or 'shortened' travellers so that they were the right size for his bed. Medea, who had won the confidence of Aegeus in Athens, guessed Theseus' identity and tried to kill him by preparing a poisoned goblet for a banquet to which she made sure he was invited. But, as Theseus drew his sword, Aegeus recognized it and knocked over the goblet. According to another version of the story, Medea sent him to fight the monstrous bull of Marathon, but Theseus captured it and, as he drew his sword to offer it as a sacrifice, Aegeus realized who he was.

Once had had been officially recognized by his father, Theseus then had to dispose of the fifty sons of Pallas, his cousins, who contested his right to the throne, as well as killing the bull of Marathon. Then, as the tribute of seven youths and seven maidens, paid every nine years, was due to leave for Crete to be delivered to the Minotaur, Theseus volunteered to go with them (or was chosen by Minos). He promised that, if he killed the Minotaur, he would hoist white sails on his ship on his return. On the island of Crete, Ariadne fell in love with him and provided the ball of thread (or a luminous crown) which would enable him to find his way through the Labyrinth, the home of the Minotaur. Theseus killed the monster and kept his promise to take Ariadne away with him. However, he later abandoned her as she slept on the island of Naxos, either because he was in love with another woman or at the request of Dionysus, who had seen and fallen in love with Ariadne himself. On the island of Delos, he dedicated a statue to Aphrodite and led a dance which imitated the winding passages of the Labyrinth. As he came within sight of the shores of Attica, he forgot his promise to hoist the white sails on his ship, probably because of his grief over the loss of Ariadne. Aegeus, who was awaiting his return, threw himself in despair into the sea which still bears his name today.

As king, Theseus united the towns of Attica around Athens, established the festival of the Panathenae, introduced a general democratic structure, granted his protection to Oedipus who had sought refuge at Colonus and, as a gesture of defiance to Creon, ensured that the heroes who had fallen at Thebes were buried. Then, because of an affair with their queen, Antiope, he had to defend Athens against the Amazons who, according to some sources, had invaded Attica on the day of his marriage to Phaedra. With his friend Pirithous, he joined the Lapiths in their fight against the Centaurs, carried off the still very desirable Helen, and went down into the Underworld to win Persephone for Pirithous. Hades cordially invited them to sit on a chair from which they were then unable to rise. Pirithous would remain there for eternity while Theseus was rescued by Hercules. During his absence, Helen's brothers, Castor and Pollux, invaded Attica and placed Menestheus on the throne. It was during this period that Phaedra fell in love with Hippolytus, the son of Theseus and Antiope, Queen of the Amazons. Because he did not return her love, when Theseus returned she accused him of having tried to force his attentions on her and Theseus, deceived, brought about the death of his own son. Overwhelmed with grief, and abandoning all hope of recovering his throne, Theseus sought refuge on the island of Scyrus at the court of King Lycomedes who killed him by pushing him from the top of a cliff. At Marathon, the Greek army witnessed the amazing sight of the ghost of a hero leading them into battle. They realized it was Theseus and his remains were taken back to Athens from Scyrus.

As the tenth mythical king of Athens, said to have lived a generation before the siege of Troy, and a sort of second father of the homeland after Cecrops because of the communality and institutions that he established, Theseus was worshipped as a national hero throughout the Greek state, from the time of the Median wars. A huge temple was built and dedicated to him, numerous statues were erected and the feasts held in his honour in the Oschophoria were revived. Mythologists have tried to explain how the legend was constructed in successive layers, from its earliest origins (which include the question of his birth, the episode of the Labyrinth, and the battle against the Centaurs . . .) to the later additions which have not been described here because they are not directly related to the legend of Theseus (where he is seen, for example, taking part in the expedition of the Argonauts or the Calydonian boar hunt). Among other points of interest, this historical perspective brings to the fore the competition between the heroic cycle of the Athenian who is most probably the son of Poseidon, and the much longer cycle of the pan-Hellenic hero, Heracles, son of Zeus. The literature that provides a retrospective and synchronic account of the story of Theseus selects one or other of the hero's adventures, as the case may be. However, five typical roles, which are very unequally represented, emerge from the myth. Theseus is first and foremost the slayer of brigands and monsters, and the instigator of various exploits. Among the ordeals that he has to overcome, those of the Labyrinth and the Minotaur appear to occupy a prominent position. He has always been the friend of Pirithous, but he is associated with a number of women: Ariadne, Phaedra, Antiope, Helen. . . . Finally, he always appears as the respected ruler of Athens. While the myth's diversity provides a rich source of archetypal motifs, it is also responsible for a certain fragmentation of the heroic figure.

In Greek literature, the story of Theseus has never reached real epic proportions. It is probable that the earliest part of the legend (i.e. Theseus as the slayer of the Minotaur, the lover of Ariadne and the friend of Pirithous with whom he went down into the Underworld) was sung in Attica by poets before the time of the Trojan cycle, although these songs have not survived. In the *Iliad*, Theseus is included in the list of heroes that old Nestor once knew (I. 265–7), while in the *Odyssey*, a terrified Ulysses flees just before he is able to meet Theseus and Pirithous in the underworld (XI. 322–4 and 631). A *Theseid* (or even several) probably existed during the sixth century, which used more recent episodes of the legend (e.g. his childhood at Troezen, his victory over the brigands, his fight against the Amazons, etc.) and placed Theseus at the centre of the action, but Aristotle and Plutarch considered this a very mediocre epic. However, fragments of a work by Callimachus of Alexandria have survived. *Hecale* was a minor epic inspired by the legend (used later by Plutarch) according to which, on the eve of his combat with the bull of Marathon, Theseus was welcomed into the home of old Hecale. From the fragments and snatches of quotations available, it is possible to observe a sort of meeting on an equal footing between the two characters, a very worthy, humble old woman who is confronting death and a brilliant young hero on the verge of glory. The scenario is captivating, but the epic aspirations are lost in the Alexandrian preoccupation with detail.

However, from the fifth to the third century, logographers such as Hellanicus, Pherecydes, Demon and Polichorus were responsible for the continuation and transmission of the legend, although only fragments of their writings have survived. At the same time, historians, orators and philosophers contributed to the development of a flattering image of Theseus. In his *History of the Peloponnesian War* (II. 15. 1–21), Thucydides has no hesitation in presenting him as a historical king who 'combined power with intelligence' and was responsible for grouping the institutions of the regional cities around the councils and prytanea of Athens, introducing taxes for everyone, in short, for setting up the social institutions which became the focal point of the Athenian national festival. In his *Encomium of Helen*, Isocrates began by describing how Theseus was so captivated by the beauty of Helen, who had still not reached the age of puberty, that he abducted her. He then suddenly decided that the best way to sing the young girl's praises was to show that her admirers were no ordinary men and launched into a long eulogy of Theseus (23–37). It is the most complete description of his heroic exploits which has survived in Greek classical literature. Because it was so important for the political thinkers of the classical age to present a consistently strong image of Theseus, Plato (*Republic* III. 391c) preferred to deny rather than justify the shocking episodes of the abduction of Helen and Persephone, and declared that it would be wrong to think that Theseus and Pirithous would have attempted such criminal actions. Much later, Plutarch made no mention of the delicate matter of the descent into the Underworld.

The image of Theseus as an exemplary king was also confirmed and stressed in Greek classical theatre although this is another area in which the subsequent fate of the manuscripts has not favoured his myth. In his *Eleusinians*, Aeschylus celebrated his intervention in favour of the Argians, Sophocles probably gave him an important role in *Aegeus* and *Phaedra*, while it appears that Euripides wrote a trilogy, *Aegeus, Theseus* and *Hippolytus Veiled*, and possibly also *Pirithous*. It would be reasonable to suppose that the episode of the Labyrinth occupied an important place in the second part of the trilogy. As well as a few surviving fragments, there is also a second version of Hippolytus, *Hippolytus the Crown-bearer* (428 BC), in which Theseus is confronted with the dying Hippolytus who forgives him for having been the indirect cause of his death. Thus the King of Athens discovers the generosity of his son and achieves lucidity in terms of himself and those closest to him, but at the price of eternal remorse. Tragic misunderstanding is a cruel means of attaining knowledge. In this instance, it illustrates how passion distorts reason (all are the victims of Aphrodite) and shows that the truly important values are learnt through suffering. Theseus also appears in two other plays by Euripides. In the *Suppliants* (424–1 BC), he represents the ideal ruler in a somewhat conventional manner and has been described as a sort of Pericles. But at the same time, his character, which is a combination of the wise ruler and the 'fighting' dispenser of justice, constitutes the main interest of the play. In *Hercules Furens* (421–16 BC), Theseus adds the role of the exemplary friend to the repertoire of the generous hero that Europides was building up to his glory. Finally, in Sophocles' admirable *Oedipus Coloneus* (406 BC), he generously welcomes Oedipus who has been rejected everywhere else and is looking for somewhere to die. By receiving Oedipus, Theseus places himself above the level of human dispute, perceiving the inhumanity of the King of Thebes as inevitable. As a result, he is placed on an equal footing with the gods and when, at the end of the play, Oedipus enters the sacred wood, he symbolically accompanies him across this supposed threshold of immortality. Although the character of Theseus is not particularly well developed, this does not detract from the nobility of the figure. His greatness overshadows the fairly abstract portrayal of his character and makes the King of Athens a worthy host for Oedipus.

The lyric poets were not particularly interested in Theseus. According to Pausanias (I. 41. 5 and I. 2. 1), Pindar mentioned the descent into the

Underworld and the war with the Amazons and both Alcman and Stesichorus described the abduction of Helen (I. 41. 4. and II. 22. 6). It is also possible that Sappho and Simonides glorified the Cretan episode, but all that remains is a fragment by the former (144) and a reference to the latter by Plutarch (*Theseus* 17. 5). The only poems dedicated to the myth of Theseus are the dithyrambs XVII and XVIII (in Teubner) by Bacchylides, a contemporary of Pindar. In the first, Theseus takes up the challenge issued by Minos to find a golden ring that he has thrown into the sea. As he dives in, he meets the Nereids and Amphitrite, i.e. he is received by women and his father's wife, and re-emerges dry and covered with divine gifts. Behind the rather indulgent evocation, the myth confirms a hidden presence. The 'sacred depths' which receive him are female and almost maternal in nature and the entire passage is bathed in the fluid imagery of a mystic union with the sea. This is one of the rare occasions in Greek literature when the legend is presented in poetic form.

Although the legend of Theseus was no longer of any national value in Latin literature, it was known to educated Romans during the reign of Caesar. To illustrate the fact that it was possible to have two homelands – one's native town and the 'federal capital' – Cicero used the example of Theseus who established the communality of small states within a larger one (*De legibus* II. 5), while Propertius referred to the road from Piraeus to Athens as 'Theseus' route' in *Elegies* III. 21. 24. However, the figure of Theseus in Latin literature did not achieve the dimension accorded to him by the Greeks.

Theseus was not often represented as an epic hero. At the beginning of Book V of the *Aeneid*, where the myth of the Labyrinth is evoked by suggestion, he is only referred to indirectly. Although he makes three further appearances in the Book, these are brief and primarily relate to his descent into the Underworld: Aeneas refers to Theseus and Hercules in his address to the Sibyl (123–4); Charon, the ferryman, deplores having taken him across the Styx with Hercules and Pirithous (392–4); and, in two suspect lines (which contradict the previous references as they seem to ignore the intervention of Heracles), it is Theseus who remains eternally seated in Hades (617–8). In Statius' *Thebaid* (90 AD), there is more than an incidental reference. As King of Athens, he once more assumes his role of dispenser of justice and, at the request of the widows of the Argians whom Creon will not allow to be buried, he goes to Thebes and obtains redress (XII. 519–809). The epic concludes with this action but, even so, the role of Theseus is not central and, although it does not deserve the disrepute into which it has fallen (after enjoying an exaggerated prestige), its main interest lies in the fratricidal struggle between Eteocles and Polyneices. Nor do we know anything of the *Theseid* by a certain Cordus with whom Juvenal declares his exasperation in the opening of his *Satires* (I. 2). As a result, Theseus' unsuccessful epic career – from a secondary role to a lost or failed epic (or both) – is confirmed.

Similarly, lyrically inspired Latin poetry reduced the hero and slayer of monsters to a mere shadow, Ariadne's lover disappearing in the distance. On a length of cloth intended to cover the marriage bed in Catullus' *Marriage of Thetis and Peleus*, a tearful Ariadne eternally watches the ship of the young Greek hero as it sails away. A fairly long digression (75–123) recalls the episode of the Labyrinth but, above all, Ariadne's complaint presents Theseus as the embodiment of 'perfidy', the betrayer of her love and breaker of promises as she refers to him as '*fallax*' and '*inmemor*'. Similarly, the tenth letter of Ovid's *Heroides*, written by Ariadne to Theseus, describes her despair and suffering.

Theseus' role in tragedy is equally limited and seems even less important in the two plays by Seneca than in the play by Euripides. In *Hercules Furens*, Theseus and Hercules return from Hades, and the value of the play lies mainly in the description of what the two heroes have witnessed in the kingdom of shadows. In *Phaedra*, the shift of emphasis begun by Euripides (and completed by the French writers of the Classic period) became more pronounced so that, in terms of the theatre, Theseus fulfilled a secondary role in the story of Phaedra.

Later Greek texts complete the general perspective. Perhaps it was because Theseus was tending to disappear from Latin literature in favour of Ariadne and Daedalus that, at the end of the first and the beginning of the second century AD, Plutarch dedicated one of the first of his *De Viribus Illustrium* (Parallel Lives) to him, in which he compares him with Romulus. In any event, there is no doubt that, as well as relocating the story of the labyrinth within the Greek heroic perspective, the very complete account of the life of Theseus would also remedy a deficiency. Although at the time there were still a great many texts in circulation written by Greek logographers of the fifth and third centuries BC, these were no longer of any great literary or historical value. Plutarch was familiar with them and refers to them with great accuracy. His extensive knowledge, exemplary critical mind and mastery of narrative were undoubtedly the basis of a great success. Although Theseus may not always have found a poet to do him justice, he did at least find a biographer. For those interested, Pausanias suggested a number of other interesting versions of the myth in his *Description of Greece* (second century BC).

Since Ovid and Virgil were the most widely read Latin authors during the Middle Ages, it is hardly surprising that the period was still familiar with the myth of Theseus. In the glosses and commentaries added to Latin texts by scholars, a Christian interpretation of the story of the Labyrinth was developed. Thus, an eleventh-century manuscript from Freising Cathedral (a commentary on the *Aeneid* by Servius), contains an anonymous poem in Latin which is actually arranged in the form of a circular labyrinth and encloses in its centre an image which is probably that of the Minotaur. As far as it is possible to make out, the poem (which is partially obliterated) tells us that the world is a labyrinth controlled by the 'zabulus', the Devil-Minotaur, which keeps the citizens of the world prisoner in order to devour them, until Theseus-Christ manages to find him with the divine help of Ariadne. Thus a Christian interpretation of the myth was developed in the margins of these manuscripts and was given free rein, particularly in the commentaries on Ovid which tended, among other things, to make him acceptable from both a moral and religious point of view. This tendency was developed to the full in the anonymous *Ovid Moralisé* which in *c.* 1300 rewrote the Latin poet's *Metamorphoses* in 72,000 lines of French verse. It presents the Minotaur as the fallen angel, imprisoned by God in the infernal cage, and devouring men on their death until God sends his son, Theseus, into the world to deliver humanity from this terrible fate. The sleeping Ariadne represents blind Judaism, which is both stupid and wicked because it complains wrongly of having been abandoned, while Phaedra represents 'gentilise' (i.e. compassion) (VIII. 1513) and provides the basis for the founding of God's Church. But this type of global intepretation of the myth was only found in academic and primarily Latin literature.

In secular literature, Theseus, like other mythical figures, became almost completely dissociated from his traditional myth. In the French 'romans', he appeared as the 'Duke of Athens', from the Latin 'dux' which originally meant the leader of an army. During the twelfth century, he is the noble horseman of the *Roman de Thèbes* (l. 10291). In the prose *Roman de Troie*, he arrives with other princes in the ships of Thalamon Ayas (75), kills the Trojan, Ordinel, and saves the wounded King Thoas (106). He and his friend Pirithous descend into Hades in defiance of its ruler and to 'steal and abduct' his wife (*Roman d'Eneas*, *c.* 1160, l. 2528). He appears again with Pirithous, who has become his son, as well as with the other figures of the myth in an extensive novel attributed to Alexandre de Bernay, *Le Roman d'Athis et de Prophilias*, in which he actively helps the two protagonists against Télamon, their common enemy. During the thirteenth century, in the *Roman de la Rose* (Jean de Meun's continuation, from 1270), he is referred to in passing as being so fond of his friend Pirithous the he went to find him in Hades (8145–55). For Dante, the figure appears to be mainly associated with the most mythical aspects of his story. He is described in the *Inferno* (IX. 53–4 and XII. 17–20) in terms of his descent into Hades and his victory over the Minotaur and in *Purgatorio* (XXIV. 121–3) in terms of his fight against the Centaurs.

With the beginning of the Renaissance during the fourteenth and fifteenth centuries, Theseus was only partially reunited with his traditional exploits. Thus, although he is indeed one of the protagonists of Boccaccio's *Teseida* (1339–40), it would be wrong to see this as the work which 'fills the gap' in Theseus' epic career. Although it certainly has the atmosphere of Greek and Latin mythology, with Mars and Venus playing their part, little remains of the original Legend of Theseus. With the exception of the battles with the Centaurs and Creon, the rest is modern fabrication, and the general register of this long poem is fantastic rather than epic. Theseus is presented as being just and wise, with the wisdom of the perfect knight, but his new role as the judge of lovers' quarrels takes him even further from the grandeur of the myth. He appears again in connection with the theme of love in the first of Petrarch's *Trionfi* (1352), walking between Ariadne and Phaedra in the lovers' procession, and is mentioned in the debate on love in Guillaume de Machaut's *Jugement du roi de Navarre* (*c.* 1350). In a similar vein, Chaucer, who used Boccaccio's *Teseida* as the basis for his 'Knight's Tale', the first of his *Canterbury Tales* (1387), evokes the battles with the Centaurs and Creon in only a few lines, while the section devoted to lovers' quarrels and the debate on love (i.e. whether is it better to be like Arcite, who is free but far away from the object of his love or, like Palamon, close at hand and yet a prisoner) is greater than in Boccaccio's epic. It is in this perspective that the story of Theseus was evoked on several occasions by Christine de Pisan (e.g. in the *Livre de Mutacion de Fortune*, *c.* 1410, l. 13357–456). As the Renaissance flourished, Theseus tended to resume his original role as a slayer of monsters. During the lavish festivals held at the beginning of the sixteenth century, he was sometimes represented, like Heracles, as the 'conqueror of monsters'. In Spain, during the second half of the sixteenth century, Lorenzo de Sepúlveda dedicated a 'romance' to his victory over the Minotaur (No. 460 in Agustin Durán's *Romancero general*) and Sebastian de Horozco produced his version of 'La fábula del laberinto de Creta, y del Minotauro, y de Teseo' which reappeared in 1874 with the publication of his *Cancionero*. Relying very heavily on Ovid for their inspiration and virtually devoid of any poetic value, the two texts mainly serve to confirm the survival of the heroic figure. He appears in some of Amadis Jamyn's occasional poems as the ideal hero with whom the prince is compared in an attempt to flatter him. It is also sometimes possible to observe the beginnings of the use of the story in literature. In the field of love poetry, this is an extension of the autonomous theme of the labyrinth of love first developed by Boccaccio and Petrarch and later by the poets of the Pléiade. Sometimes the lover complains of being imprisoned like Theseus in the labyrinth without the thread ('filet') which would enable him to escape, as for example in Ronsard's *Amours de Cassandre*, I. 168 (1552) and Jean de Boyssières's P.O.A., 101 (1578). Less frequently, he congratulates himself on having found the thread, e.g. La Roque in *Les Muses ralliées* (1599): 'Inconstancy is rewarded with inconstancy'. But although rich in possibilities, the parallel was not fully exploited.

During the seventeenth and eighteenth centuries, Theseus mainly appeared in the theatre and its extension, opera. In some instances only a theoretical connection with the traditional story was maintained, while in others a particular aspect of the story was persistently repeated. However, the article on Theseus in Champré's *Dictionnaire abrégé de la Fable* (1727) is primarily the story of a 'womanizer' and the complications that this introduces into his life. In theatre and opera Theseus was primarily the husband deceived by Phaedra or the inconstant lover of Ariadne, which obviously did not entitle him to play the leading role.

During the second half of the sixteenth century, the story of Phaedra and Hippolytus began to reappear for the first time on stage since Seneca's version with Zara's *Hippolito* (1558), Trapolini's *Thesida* (1567) and Garnier's *Hippolyte* (1573). The role of Theseus was fairly secondary in these versions, as was the case in the numerous tragedies that appeared during the seventeenth century: *Hippolyte* by la Pinelière in 1635, Gilbert in 1647 and Bidar in 1675, and *Phèdre et Hippolyte* by Pradon in 1677. However in Racine's *Phèdre* (1677), the numerous references to the legend of Theseus (e.g. the slaying of monsters, his armorous adventures, the descent into the underworld, etc.) provide one of the mythical backcloths against which the drama unfolds, while the character of Theseus is clearly the mainspring of the action via his absence, the false news of his death, his return, the error into which he allows himself to be led, etc. But he is the involuntary cause of events and in no way controls the action. The nobility of his royal status and his final suffering are unable to conceal the fact that, in his role as a husband and father, he is significantly absent from the play.

The role of Theseus is undoubtedly more important when the story is centred around the figure of Ariadne, as is the case in *Theseus ende Ariadne* (1601) by Pieter Corneliszoon Hooft, a Dutch playwright who is extremely representative of the Classic period, and in *Ariadne* (1628) by Ivan Gundulic, the great poet of Ragusa. In Lope de Vega's tragi-comedy, *El laberinto de Creta* (1621), Ariadne gives Theseus a golden thread, three pieces of poisoned bread (to put the Minotaur to sleep) and a club. In return the 'Duke of Athens' promises to take the two sisters away with him and to marry Ariadne, but he betrays her for Phaedra. Significantly, in *Los tres mayores prodigios* (1636) by Calderón de la Barca, he cannot choose between the two women and brings them both back from his European expedition. The theme of the lover torn between the two sisters is very revealing in terms of the representations of Theseus during this period. It is central to *Arianna abandonata* (1641), an opera by Bonacossi, and reaches its peak in Thomas Corneille's play, *Ariane* (1672), where Oenarus, King of Naxos, is in love with Ariadne who is in love with Theseus who is in love with Phaedra. When Ariadne discovers that Theseus secretly adores another woman, she unburdens her despair and her plans for vengeance to her confidante who is in fact her sister Phaedra. In this world of proprieties and noble sentiments, Theseus and Phaedra are ill at ease in the situation they have created. The 'fiancé' is torn between his love and his concern for honour and tries to soften the blow that his betrayal will cause before he leaves. In spite of the fact that its elegance is a little contrived, Corneille's tragedy remains the most readable of an entire series of plays on the theme of Ariadne abandoned by Theseus on the island of Naxos and subsequently consoled, or not, by Bacchus. In fact, during the seventeenth and eighteenth centuries, it is possible to count several dozen plays and operas on this dual theme.

Other aspects of the legend have been more happily evoked. In Shakespeare's *A Midsummer Night's Dream* (1595–1600), Theseus is about to marry Hippolyta, Queen of the Amazons. He has retained his title of the 'Duke of Athens' from the Middle Ages as well as a feudal taste for hunting and war, but he is also gallant and reference is made to his past romantic conquests. Although his role in the play is primarily that of a prince and judge, he is also a thoughtful and cultured man of the Renaissance who enables the world order to be re-established. His serene sovereignty adds the weight of generous humanity to this phantasmagoria, and the play provides a link between the fantastical quality of the old novels of chivalry and European theatre of the Classic period. In France, reference was sometimes made to the combat with the Pallantids (Pradon, La Fosse) and to the descent into Hades (Hardy, La Pinelière), but one theme is more persistent than others, i.e. the acknowledgement of Theseus by his father, Aegeus. In Puget de la Serre's *Thésée ou le Prince reconnu* (1644), Theseus is a dutiful son and, in spite of the initial misunderstanding with Antiope, an exemplary lover. In the libretto for the opera, *Thésée* (1657), written by Quinault for Lully, Medea is in love with Theseus, as she was in La Serre's version, but this time Theseus and Aegeus are in love with the same woman. La Fosse's tragedy, *Thésée* (1700), is a much richer version. To the rivalry between Medea and Theseus as to who has greater influence over Aegeus, are added the themes of the enmity between the brothers, Aegeus and Pallantes, of the inequality of fortunes, and especially of the shepherd's son, Sthelenus (Theseus), who takes such great care to conceal his origins that it is impossible to recognize him as the king's son. Also worthy of mention is the *Thésée* written by Mazoyer, performed in 1800 at the Théâtre Français, not with a view to disturbing the well-deserved respite enjoyed by the play, but rather to illustrate the persistence of the theme. All these tragedies attribute an important role to Medea, on whose myth we are encroaching in this instance.

But the central issue of these plays is more important than the problem of the bad mother. It concerns the recognition by the king-father, provided that he recognizes the sword in the hands of his son in time. Associated with the problem of identity, this desire for recognition has echoes at both an individual and collective level. As well as producing interesting variations on the theme of the story of the family, it also raises questions of legitimacy and power. A fine painting by Poussin is entitled *Thésée découvrant l'épée de son père* (Theseus Discovering his Father's Sword). In Pierre Corneille's *Oedipe* (1659), Theseus escapes his traditional romantic destiny because he is in love with Dircé, the sister of Oedipus and, somewhat unexpectedly, the daughter of Jocaste and Laïus. His refusal to believe in oracles could have made the character the champion of free will and the play a tragedy of responsibility. But to save Dircé, Theseus prefers to convince people that he is in fact the son of

Laïus . . . the son who was abandoned on Mount Cithaeron. The play also remains firmly academic and chivalrous. Towards the end of the eighteenth century, a stronger image of Theseus was sometimes depicted. In Canova's very beautiful statue, *Theseus triumphant* (1781), he has defeated the Minotaur and appears supremely free and serene. The forty or so lines of 'L'Aveugle' (*Bucoliques*, *c.* 1786), in which Chénier evokes Theseus' combat against the Centaurs, revive the violence of the epic and, without ironic intent, are spoken by Homer. This piece of gallantry belongs among those rare and brilliant fragments which appear to be the fate of the legend of Theseus. In Friedrich Leopold de Stolberg's pre-Romantic drama, *Theseus* (1787), the hero is a sort of champion of freedom. Later, in his *German Constitution*, Hegel demanded that a new Theseus should rise up to unite the country.

During the nineteenth century, although Theseus was seen as the prototype of the inconstant lover in contemporary culture, was featured in several operas which evoked the abandonment of Ariadne and was widely represented in the sculpture of the Romantic period, he was virtually absent from the literary scene. Towards the end of the century, there were obvious signs of a revival of interest, with John Ruskin's *Fors Clavigera*, a series of ninety-six letters written between 1871 and 1884 to the working-men of Great Britain under the aegis of Fortune, the key-bearer. In Letter 23, he invites the people of England to re-appropriate the myth of Theseus, not by going to see the statues of the British Museum, but by realizing that the story of the Labyrinth is not so very different from the story of 'the House that Jack built'. It was therefore through the mystical combat between Theseus and the Minotaur that we would learn what the Greeks understood of the most terrible and mysterious aspects of the relationship between men and inferior beings. As the destroyer of animal impulses, the hero represents the human potential that the works of Ruskin were trying to develop and which is summarized by the words 'Gentleness and Justice'. But it was not until the twentieth century, with the 'return to the myth', that Theseus and the story of the labyrinth became the focal point of a complex and sustained examination. In August-September 1939, a special issue of the French literary review *Cahiers du Sud* was published. It was devoted to Greek myths and, curiously enough, half of it was concerned with story of the Labyrinth. This could well be considered as a sign of the times.

In Marina Cvetaeva's *Ariadne* (1924), the issue of freedom is explored through the figure of Theseus. While the people demand that Aegeus should make Theseus take part in the drawing of lots, the latter prefers to go as 'a supernumerary' without relying on chance. He hopes that, by presenting himself unarmed before Minos, the latter will spare the young Athenians. He therefore initially appears as someone who confirms his freedom of choice, against the general will, independently of destiny and in defiance of the gods. But having appeared to shape his own destiny, he subsequently allows himself to be manipulated by the jealousy of the gods. He suddenly accepts the 'thread and the sword', kills the Minotaur and then betrays Ariadne. Tempted by glory, he breaks his promise. Similarly, on the island of Naxos, he abandons Ariadne at the request of Bacchus, trading off human love against a divine whim. It is a well-known fact that the gods render those they want to destroy insane. In his emotion, Theseus forgets to hoist the white sail and, as a symbol of Aphrodite's vengeance, the body of Aegeus is brought before him 'swathed in seaweed'. The tone of Gide's *Thésée* (1946) is completely different. It is a lighthearted and humorous story with which the hero intends to instruct his son, Hippolytus. The descriptions of the labours of Theseus and the various characters involved make it possible to examine most of Gide's themes. Freedom is one of the central issues and the story of the Labyrinth provides the most complete definition. Daedalus is quite certain that Theseus' only chance of success is to attach himself to Ariadne's thread and to maintain throughout the incident 'an unshakeable determination to return'. But it is also essential to know how to free oneself from the thread. According to Pirithous, one should 'carry on regardless', a piece of advice twice echoed by Daedalus and which Theseus applies in his own case. Gide's version of the life of the Athenian hero is an excellent example of this ambiguous and essential exercise of freedom.

Who is the Minotaur and what does Theseus do when he kills it? Is it possible to become oneself by eliminating or recognizing the monster? The central episode of the story of Theseus places us within a dialectic of 'other' and 'same', and it is easy to understand that it is a powerful evocation of the issue of identity. Nizan's short story 'Histoire de Thésée' (1934), raises the same type of questions as to the true nature of the hero. Theseus descends into the Labyrinth with Ariadne and kills the sleeping Minotaur. On their return, the exploits is celebrated and embellished by the self-satisfied hero. Theseus deals a blow to the smiling Ariadne and takes advantage of the situation to return to Athens in glory. Is the hero not a false hero (and a true story-teller)? The plays by Jünger (*Der Verkleidete Theseus* 1934), Bacmeister (*Theseus* 1940) and Neveux (*Le Voyage de Thésée* 1943) also focus on this question of the nature of the hero. In Neveux's play, he renounces personal happiness and it is this victory over himself which is the real victory over the Minotaur. In Yourcenar's 'sacred entertainment', *Qui n'a pas son Minotaure?* (1963), Theseus, on the deck of the ship which is carrying the fourteen victims to Crete, devises a plan to turn the mission with which he has been entrusted to his own advantage and glory. As he cannot destroy his victims like the Minotaur, he decides to save them. However, when he arrives in Crete he allows himself to be seduced by Phaedra and the hostages are led to their death as he sleeps. By enabling him to enter the labyrinth, Ariadne offers him a second chance to save them. But once inside the labyrinth, Theseus is unable to recognize the voices which pursue him and which are in fact his own inner voices reminding him of his own weakness and guilt. He is unable to become the hero that we expected and chooses Phaedra and the easy option. 'Qui n'a pas son Minotaure?' We all have our own Minotaur. We all have the god and the monster within us. We all have a choice.

Sometimes the central issue shifts in terms of historical perspective. In 'Ariane' (*Cahiers du Sud* 1939), Talodoire and Fuzellier imagined Theseus arriving in Crete, under an assumed name, to kill the Minotaur. During a conversation with Minos (the only published extract), Theseus is astonished to realize that Minos has discovered his true identity and that he is in fact prepared to help him because, above and beyond any personal affiliations, they are both in a position of power. Nikos Kasantzakis' tragedy, *Thésée* (1949), appears to deal with the same issue, but it is also one of the few attempts to reinvest the legend of Theseus with the significance of the original myth. Guided by Ariadne, Theseus descends into the Labyrinth. Put to the test, he proves to be a worthy successor of Minos. As Ariadne, furious at being deserted, tries to persuade the latter to kill him, the doors of the Labyrinth open to reveal Kouros, the freed Minotaur, who is taller, more handsome and more serene than Theseus and the two men finally leave together. The play places us in a time spiral in which each new spiral involves a painful detachment from the last. Just as Theseus has replaced Minos, he will be succeeded by Kouros and many other heroes, until the last in the line, i.e. fire.

One of the major issues in Butor's *L'Emploi du Temps* (1956), as in the works of Gide and Yourcenar, is the question of artistic creation. But the character of Theseus is merely a hypothesis on work by the narrator and the theme of artistic creation is very closely involved with the problem of writing. In the city where it is so easy to lose one's way, the account of what has happened is, for the narrator, the main thread in the true sense of the word. But will this thread be the antidote to the Labyrinth that the narrator wanted it to be, i.e. the thread which will destroy the labyrinth of the town? In other words, will writing produce the Work of Art which will make it possible to impose order on the world? The question remains unanswered. The time at which the story is written will never coincide with the time of the actual incident. The labyrinth of words, which one may conceivably think will neutralize the labyrinth of the world when they both coincide, ultimately remains asymptotic to it. It is true that what has not been attained is to do with what happened on 29th February. In *Thésée ou la puissance du spectre* (1981), Thomas Stern endows the Minotaur with the power of speech and then skilfully evokes the image of Theseus to consider how the myth is linked to modern speech. In a similar manner, in an account of a consideration of the meaning of the myth of the Labyrinth which is rooted in his biography and expressed in several of his works, Friedrich Dürrenmatt concludes that 'whoever undertakes to represent the labyrinth should enter it freely, and therefore become Theseus' (*Stoffe* 1981).

The story of Theseus was finally revived in 'historical novels' which are less ambitious from a literary point of view but which testify to the insistent topicality in terms of the character of Theseus. Thus in the extensive narrative portrait painted by Mary Renault in *The King Must Die* (1958) and *The Bull from the Sea* (1962), Theseus tells his story in the first person, from his childhood at Troezen to his return to Crete, and from there to his suicide on the island of Scyrus. In most of the episodes he appears as the lively and enterprising hero of the traditional myth. Similarly, his role in Daniel Kircher's *La Colère des Dieux* (1980) suggests that, based on a varied story, the myth of Theseus is far from being exhausted in the field of literature.

We have therefore seen that Theseus occupies a place in Greek tragedy where he is presented as a reasonable ruler, extremely aware of his religious duties, charitable but firm. Theseus the king, friend of Oedipus and Heracles, has a certain grandeur, but he is a far cry from the lively, enterprising and many-faceted character generally described by the legend. Latin lyric poetry presented the hero as the slayer of monsters, almost a minor character. He is the shadowy figure of the lover eternally abandoning Ariadne, and Seneca's tragedy further reduced the role allotted to him by Greek theatre. However, in second-century Greece, he found a brilliant biographer in Plutarch. During the Middle Ages, Theseus, the king, was noticeably younger and became the dashing 'Duke of Athens', but his participation remained limited and his association with Christ occurred only in religious and academic literature. During the seventeenth and eighteenth centuries, his presence was undoubtedly more remarkable in terms of quantity than quality. Although he made frequent appearances, it was in fact as if Theseus were absent from his own story. His exploits and heroic deeds had become merely a traditional aura which bore no relationship to the royal character of the theatre. His story is rich in dramatic situations, but his function was for the most part reduced to providing a foil for Ariadne and Phaedra. With the updating of the myth of the Labyrinth, the situation developed noticeably during the twentieth century when Theseus is found at the centre of an intense debate on the nature of space, being and destiny. But even here there is a tendency for the centre of gravity of the issue to shift towards the Other (the Minotaur), the Initiator (Ariadne) or the Creator of the Labyrinth (Daedalus). So even during the twentieth century, the literary fortunes of Theseus are not entirely satisfactory and we are left with the impression that he does not quite coincide with the great role for which he was intended. Perhaps we should conclude that history is hard where epic heroes are concerned and that problematic literature has little use for the man who went, conquered and returned. He could have gone a little deeper into the Labyrinth! But the fact remains that he returned. However, he has never ceased to be represented in one role or another, and we now tend to meet him in all sorts of places. He undoubtedly enjoys the fortune of those who are responsible for bringing about events and the future of those who take risks.

André Peyronie

Tristan

What is known as the myth of Tristan poses a problem peculiar to it, in the form of its traditional name. We are actually here dealing with a mythic experience that involves two people: no Tristan without Iseult (or Isolde), any more than there is Iseult without Tristan. As Marie de France puts it in 'Le lai du Chèvrefeuille': 'My dear love, so is it of us/Neither you without me, nor me without you.'

In fact the myth even involves three people, since the dynamics of the drama depend on a third force, in the form of Mark. But Mark is there only to provoke the dilemma. As Pierre Gallais in *Genèse du Roman occidental: essais sur Tristan et Iseut et son modèle persan* (1974) observes, 'Mark exists only as Iseult's husband'. The other two are thus subsumed in the character of the lover, and the meaning of the myth is crystallized in the name Tristan.

ONOMASTICS

Dictionaries and scholarly works (H. Zinner, F. Lot, J. Loth) trace the name Tristan back to the Pictish man's name 'Drustan', which occurs in the lists of names of kings in the Scottish Borders area from the sixth to the eighth century. The form 'Drystan' is found in the triads of the Welsh *Red Book of Hergest* in which the hero features among the three 'masters of the machines', the three swineherds and the three lovers from the British Isle, and elsewhere.

In the same texts, some of the material in which dates back to the ninth and tenth centuries, the names 'Essylt' and 'March' also occur. In addition *La Vie de Paul Aurélien*, written in Brittany in the ninth century, mentions a King Mark supposedly visited by the holy bishop in the sixth century. Much has also been made of the Breton legend which ascribes the ears of a horse to Mark. As for 'Essylt', René Louis (*Tristan et Iseult*, 1972) thinks the name is derived from the Germanic 'Ischild' (*-hildis*, becoming *-eut* or *-eult* in Old French), which would tend to bear out the attribution to the Germanic root *ieg* ('ice' in English) of the form 'Isolde' (literally 'ice rule', according to Joseph Shipley in his *Origine des mots anglais: dictionnaire raisonné des racines indo-européennes*, 1984). Of the various modern forms 'Iseult' seems to be the most widely used in English, 'Iseut' in French.

The contribution of French is to be noted specifically in the adoption of the form 'Tristan'. Once it had been accepted the very root of the word (*tristis*, *triste*, meaning 'sad') added an association which poets promptly seized on. The analogy even passed into the everyday French language since 'chanter de Tristan', according to the *Dictionnaire de l'ancienne langue francaise du IXe au XVe siècle* (F. Godefroy), meant 'to be sad'. The anagram 'Tantris' used by the hero when he wanted to conceal his identity served as a *nom de guerre.*

TOPONYMY

Tradition locates Tristan's native country, Lyonesse (or Lyones), sometimes in the vicinity of Edinburgh, sometimes on the borders of the ancient kingdom of Cornwall. The important thing is the role played by the sea in the hero's destiny, conveying him from one shore of the Celtic world to another, between Cornwall, Ireland and Brittany.

Archaeological excavations undertaken near Castle Dor and Fowey in south-west Cornwall and research in the archives have enabled some of the sites mentioned in the mediaeval texts to be rediscovered. Thus Lancien, a manor mentioned in the Exeter *Domesday Book* in 1086 and one of the palaces attributed to King Mark by Béroul in the twelfth century, has been located. Documents relating to St Samson tell of the foundation by the saint of a church and monastery near Fowey, before he left for Brittany in 625. And in Béroul's *Tristan* the monks and abbot of that church are there on Iseut's return. Currently work is being enthusiastically pursued around a stele dating from the sixth century found near Castle Dor. Its inscription, now partly worn away but transcribed in 1538 by John Leland, Henry VIII's archaeologist, would suggest that it is nothing less than the tombstone of Tristan and Iseult.

Cornish sites in particular often feature in treatments of the myth, even recent ones. Thomas Hardy set *The Famous Tragedy of the Queen of Cornwall* (1916–23) in the fortress of Tintagel, even going to the length of reconstructing the plan. In *Castle Dor* (1962), a novel by Arthur Quiller-Couch and Daphne Du Maurier, the suggestive power of the locality leads ordinary human beings, as if by osmosis, to reincarnate the famous actors in the drama.

THE NARRATIVE TRADITION

As research into the subject now stands, the question of the origins of the myth of Tristan is still far from settled. The debate between adherents of Celtic, Persian and Arab sources continues. To similarities with these traditions noted by scholars, we must add mythemes borrowed from classical antiquity (Morhaunt, the Minotaur and the legend of Theseus, the myths of Perseus and Peleus) and from folklore (the dragon, the golden hair). Attempts have been made to reconcile these various contributions and work out a theory as to how the myth was transmitted. Writing recently Pierre Gallais declared:

> *Tristan* is the result of synthesis. He too was born from the contact between several 'folklores' – three at least: Arab (which had popularized the Persian romance of Gurganai [*Wis et Ramain*]), Celtic (in which *aitheda* [stories involving

abductions] had likewise been made popular) and French (both southern and northern), which had itself long been infiltrated by Celtic and oriental contributions.

In any event, from the time when the great Tristan poems of the twelfth century were composed up until modern treatments, the same structural pattern recurs from one version to the next, and we are struck by the constancy of the narrative schema. Poems, novels, plays, complete texts and fragments, icons, musical and cinematic versions all repeat with remarkable faithfulness not onlly the main episodes of the story of the lovers, but even stick to the functions assigned to the main agents.

Considered as a whole the saga of Tristan takes the form of a double quest of which the main stages are as follows:

1a Tragedy is already present when the hero comes into the world as the son of Rivalen, King of Lyonesse, and nephew of King Mark of Cornwall, as the child's mother Blanchefleur loses her life in giving birth to him.
1b Singled out as someone special by his orphanhood and the possession of exceptional gifts (as a fighter, hunter, athlete, musician and poet), Tristan at first seems destined to carry out 'feats' of liberation. Like David, he kills an oppressive giant (Morhaunt of Ireland, who has come to claim his tribute) and so liberates his adopted country (the kingdom of Cornwall) from terror and subjection. A second victory, this time over a dragon, brings another people (the people of Ireland) similar relief. Like St George or Perseus, Tristan at the same time delivers a young girl who is under threat (Iseult the Fair, an Irish princess, about to be sacrificed in marriage to the unprepossessing impostor who claims to have overcome the monster).
1c On each occasion Tristan nearly dies and only survives thanks to the healing gifts of Iseult, the woman he has in fact come to win, but for another man (his uncle). Here again he accomplishes his task successfully. The hero emerges from this first successful quest, in an aura of purity, as a second Galahad.
2 The myth then becomes more human. At the very moment when Tristan of his own free will places the triple interdict of marriage, loyalty as a vassal and the 'filial' affection tying him to his uncle between Iseult and himself, destiny or nature attaches the two young people together in an indissoluble bond. On the vessel taking them back to Mark they are thirsty, and drinking from the same magic cup they imbibe love, and death, and life.
3 At the court of Cornwall, the couple becomes a threesome. From that point the quest is renewed, a selfish quest this time, clandestine and totally absorbing, with union with the Other as its sole objective. All the hero's gifts are devoted to it, and to allaying suspicion and avoiding traps (the most popular episode: the meeting at the fountain with the king looking on, so subtly transposed to the modern period in the film *L'Eternel retour*). Finally the queen

and her lover are caught *in flagrante delicto* and the two narrowly escape being put to death, but are banished from society.
4 A short interlude in the form of exile unites the lovers in the enchanted circle of shared solitude (life in the forest). The king finds them, social order is re-established, and they are again separated.
5 Though the triumph of order has not extinguished their passion, it re-establishes and even strengthens the interdict, since Tristan in turn marries, without love (Iseult with the White Hands). The chalice has been drained to the dregs. A long journey towards exhaustion, punctuated by the hero's 'returns', braving everything, even madness, to spend a few moments within reach of the Other.
6 The end is a double death from love: how, when and where varies from one version to another. This is the most beautiful version (*Tristan* by Thomas): returning wounded and exhausted to the wife he does not love in Brittany, Tristan is near to death. He sends for Queen Iseult. She hastens to answer his call, but Tristan's wife, motivated by jealousy, tells him she has not come (the episode of the white or the black sail). Iseult the Fair arrives too late. Then she in turn dies at the side of the dead hero. The trial through the martyrdom of separation has come to an end. The second quest is finished.
7 Some early texts (Eilhart von Oberge) and even some modern ones complete the ultimate meaning of the myth by having intertwining trees grow over the lovers' tombs.

Countless later versions followed the formula established in the twelfth and thirteenth centuries, concentrating mainly on one of four aspects. Some – the majority, even among the most recent – are archaically presented. Especially in French literature, some purport to be palimpsests of a master text which, however, nobody has ever seen. Others transpose the characters and vicissitudes into a modern setting, so suggesting intriguing equivalences, which the reader then has the pleasure of decoding. Last of all, some less usual versions weave the elements of the Tristan story – its motifs, episodes or agents – into the texture of another story, which is then enriched by the myth's profound echo.

THE POLARITY OF HOW THE MYTH IS PERCEIVED

How have the various versions of Tristan been understood? We find that there are two poles: some see only a simple story of adultery, while others see the fullness of human love.

Chrétien de Troyes, who saw only madness, 'which I feel ashamed to recount' put a denunciation of the 'vilénie' of Iseut la Blonde in the mouth of another woman, Fénice, the heroine of *Cligès*: 'For her body had two owners/While her heart belonged entirely to one/And she acted thus throughout her life/Never refusing the two of them./That love was unreasonable'

(l. 3153–7). It must be said that the premise put forward in l. 3163 that 'He who has the heart has the body too' is of no help in the circumstances, for as far as Mark was concerned Iseult was not free to choose.

In the fifth canto of the *Inferno*, Dante was even more censorious, relegating Tristan (with no mention of Iseult) into the Second Circle, along with Paris and Helen, Semiramis, Alexander and 'all those who sin through the flesh', 'those who make reason the slave of their appetites'.

In the fourteenth century the English poet John Gower in a ballad written in French mocked Tristan and Lancelot for their 'besottedness'. It was also Gower who 'from the story of the love philtre draws the completely unexpected conclusion that one should be careful not to drink too much'. It has to be admitted that the actual popularity of the 'herb-flavoured wine' was tempered by a certain condescension among those like Thibaut de Champagne who thought they could love better without having to resort to the brew 'which poisoned Tristan'.

Let us now turn to Sir Walter Scott. In a letter written in 1803 he granted that probably Sir Tristram really had existed, and resumed his fate thus:

> . . . to my way of thinking, a person of that name really did swallow a dose of cantharides powder intended to stimulate the prowess of his uncle, the princeling of Cornwall, and he of course embarked on an affair with his aunt . . .

Still closer to our own day, a German dramatist, Georg Kaiser, gave his play – not a comedy – the explicit title *König Hahnrei* [King Cuckold] (1913).

By way of contrast, when Lépold Sudre collected 'allusions to the Tristan legend in mediaeval literature' in 1886, he regarded Gower's attitude, mentioned above, as exceptional. The many examples listed show that the love story of Tristan and Iseult was so much admired that it was used as a common yardstick by Provençal and French writers of love poetry, as well as those of other nationalities. At a very early stage fragments of the legend were inserted in semi-didactic texts such as the *Donnei des amants*, or the *Roman de la Poire* by Messire Thibaut, a 'slotting-in' technique still valid in our own day, used for example by the English novelist Charles Morgan in *Sparkenbroke* (1936). In the *Roman de l'Escoufle* (c. 1200) Jean Renart goes so far as to adorn a precious cup which he describes lovingly with episodes resuming the story; his hero intends the cup for the high altar at Saint-Sépulcre.

Here adultery gives way to the greatness of an exemplary attachment, with all the joys and pains it entails. The Icelandic ballad on the death of Tristan, composed in the second half of the fifteenth century, reminds us that in the case of these two 'honourable people' it is a question of the triumph of love. Four hundred years later the inhabitants of the Faroe Islands were still singing about the lovers who had died of a broken heart: 'I promise you they did. Today things like that don't happen to people any more.'

So this is the other side, the 'beautiful tale of love and death' (J. Bédier), the 'marvellous story' (A. Mary and a hundred others), the myth of total, overwhelming love. In the chapter dealing with 'themes of exaltation' in his *Essai sur L'Amour humain* (1948) Jean Guitton asserts:

> Three great themes in history have expressed love: the Platonic theme, the theme of Solomon and the theme of Tristan. Each of these corresponds to a civilization: Greek, Hebrew and modern. They now represent the three harmonics of love among human beings.

EXEGESES

A heroic myth

If we consider the collected body of work relating to Tristan, we find that, from whatever pole it is perceived, the myth of Tristan is first and foremost the myth of a hero. There are a number of elements present from the universal heroic schema described by Marie-Louise von Franz in *L'Homme et ses symboles* (Carl G. Jung, 1964). The tutelary presence of an adoptive father protects the vulnerable childhood of the hero, who develops into a superman. All those who have treated the myth of Tristan agree in recognizing that he was unusually strong and precocious. For him, as for El Cid, 'valour does not wait for the fullness of years'. Thus he brings his struggle against the powers of evil to a successful conclusion. But it is not just a question of muscle power: he is also intelligent and brave. As if that were not enough, all these virtues are further enhanced by good looks. The hero's climb is rapid, and inevitably kindles the envy of those who are less favoured, especially as Tristan is also incorruptible.

A civilizing myth

This superman was also seen as a hero with a civilizing influence. Tristan refines and educates the barbarians of Cornwall. His ingenuity causes him to be portrayed even in the early texts as an inventor of machines (a 'bow-that-does-not-fail', automata in the image of Iseult and her attendant). He perfects new techniques for safety (the silent pursuit of the dog Husdent in the forest) or communication (telegraph wood chippings, the stick message in the 'Lai du chèvrefeuille').

The myth of the artist

In addition to being a heroic myth and a civilizing myth, the myth of Tristan is also a myth about an artist. Tristan is a protean character, a born actor who can disguise himself beyond recognition, play parts and speak other languages, even the language of the birds. As an example of this we may quote the delightfully sweet imitation of a nightingale's song in the silence of the night which reduces the queen, trapped in her husband's arms, to tears (*Donnei des amants*). As a musician and a poet Tristan teaches Iseult to interpret and compose lyric songs in which both pour out their joy and their sorrow. You might say he was Theseus, Ulysses and Orpheus all rolled into one.

It is striking what a synthesis this full-length portrait of the male ideal is. In the language of the seventeenth century he would have been 'the most perfect of men'. This excess of perfection did not escape some iconoclasts; like John Erskine (*Tristan and Isolde: Restoring Palamede* 1932) they demythified their hero, reducing him to an expression of machismo, and sometimes transposing his virtues onto his rival. Remarkably enough, the love between the couple survives this debunking.

The myth of the couple

This male ideal is in fact matched by an ideal female counterpart. Iseult too has good looks, courage of a certain kind and above all the gift of healing the wounds suffered by the hero. She alone can restore him to life. There is no need to know any more.

It has to be conceded, as Françoise Barteau has said, that sometimes 'Iseult the Fair ends up by seeming paradoxically abstract to us, as if she were a principle or an allegory' (*Les Romans de Tristan et d'Iseut: introduction à une lecture plurielle* 1972). But in contemporary treatments of the myth, where authors have managed to make Iseult less diaphanous and in some measure to reverse the roles, it may be observed that this does not affect the final outcome. In fact what we are given to understand, one of the constants of the myth, is that Tristan and Iseult were exactly made for one another.

And it is the ultimate function of the magic potion to express the ineluctable nature of this complementariness, another constant. In the double nature of the 'lovendrin' or love potion, alternately an 'elixir of life' and happiness and a 'poison', the agent of destruction and death, Pierre Ponsoye discerned the image of 'two apparently opposing forces that are in reality complementary, intended to reach equilibrium' in the fulfilment of love, and hence of the innermost Self of the lovers (*Qualités anagogiques de la littérature* 1971).

Authors such as the writer of *La Folie Tristan de Berne* who linger over the composition of the philtre which was perhaps 'badly mixed' only remind us, in such a way as to underline the miracle still more, of the atavistic anguish of man haunted by his incompleteness: an anguish that Mark and the other Iseult who are not well loved are forced to experience.

To quote Françoise Barteau again, 'Iseult more than Tristan is the soul of the couple'. Yet, if the soul is a vital principle, in the case of this couple it cannot belong to one partner rather than to the other. Their soul is in fact their coming together, a miracle of reciprocal integration expressed in an ecstatic duet in Act II of Wagner's version:

> '*Tristan*: You Tristan, I Isolde, no longer Tristan!
> *Isolde*: You Isolde, I Tristan, no longer Isolde!'

Thus the myth of Tristan is a myth of the couple, 'Thee and Me, Thine and Mine, joined for ever in sublime happiness' (Thomas Mann, *Tristan* 1903), a single consciousness welded into the universal principle.

A myth about marginalization

From the time when the Other is discovered, the quest for the togetherness of the couple thus constitutes the only opportunity for the Self. Since the mythical hero serves as an example, or as Mircea Eliade (*Aspects du mythe* 1963) puts it 'a paradigm for every meaningful human action', the subversive side of the myth of Tristan could not pass unnoticed by his exegetists.

In fact this couple is sufficient unto itself. Finally free to live in the forest they have nothing left to wish for. Gottfried von Strassburg describes them thus: 'There was the Man beside the Woman,/There too was the Woman beside the Man,/What more could they wish for!' (l. 16,904–6).

So it is easy to see in this sufficiency 'an anarchic burgeoning' of the Self (Françoise Barteau). And this was the reproach Denis de Rougemont levelled at the lovers in 1938 in the name of social morality. (He later went back on his famous aphorisms, incidentally.) 'Tristan does not love Iseult, he loves love itself.' Or again, Tristan was 'the myth of a love that despises commitment in social relationships'. Finally, 'we draw back in horror at the idea of Iseult becoming Mrs Tristan!'

There has been a lot of emphasis on the 'rebirth' of the couple, each sacrificing his or her social role to preserve the flame of passion, as well as on the clandestine nature of their existence as a couple; even on the hero's decline, reduced to various roles as an outcast (a leper, a madman, etc.) and condemned to a wandering life. Such a human mess could only be reprehensible, in the eyes of society.

The spellbound hero and heroine created by Wagner's genius, and those of D'Annunzio (*Il Trionfo della Morte* 1894) and in *Tristan* by Thomas Mann, have also been reproached with abandoning themselves to an infatuation with death. In this condemnatory reading of the myth, which was fairly widespread for a time, Herbert Marcuse perceives a defence mechanism by society against the destructive power of Eros.

> It is no accident that great western literature celebrates only 'unhappy love', nor that the myth of Tristan has become the exemplary expression of it. The morbid romanticism of the myth is *realistic* in the true sense of the word (*Eros and Civilisation*, 1955).

Tristan and Iseult, originally destined for the light, are led to flee it and seek darkness. However, recognition of what Jean-Charles Payen calls the 'nocturnal' face of the myth may lead to another interpretation. At the end of this journey through the night, some people have seen another light dawning.

A myth about transcendence

When Marie-Louise von Franz analyzed the difference between the heroic myth and the initiation rite, she pointed out that in the latter the novice must abandon all ambition and all desire before submitting to the test, and do so 'without hope of success'. In fact he must 'be ready to die'. This is true of our protagonists. And the will to go beyond oneself should not be confused with a morbid desire for death. As Henri Lichtenberger said in *Wagner, poète et penseur* (1898), 'love leads to death . . . but not to perdition . . . and leads on to the peace of nirvana'.

Pierre Emmanuel, in his turn, in the preface he wrote for *La Femme essentielle* (1980) by Pierre Solié, presents mythical experience 'taken to its conclusion' as 'the supreme accomplishment of a destiny'. But it turns out to be 'a difficult incarnation'. For the poet, in fact, 'the true dimension of the quest is not given by a return to health free of suffering, but by the painful conquest of Wisdom, because that suffering *makes Sense*'. In his 'Orphic' book Solié devotes a whole section in the chapter on the quest for love by lunar heroes to the 'Passion of Tristan and Iseult'. In it, as in the Babylonian epic of Marduk, the author sees a *metanoïa*, i.e. as he explains it himself, 'a metamorphosis by means of/and into the spiritual'. Then, adopting the opposite stance from Rougemont, he adds:

> It is not a struggle between courtly chivalry and feudal right, nor a Cathar vision of love, nor a tantric allusion. Nor yet love of love, and still less love of death, but yet again the original first constituent experience of *homo* and of Passion which every lunar hero – which is to say every man – has to undergo at some points of his life.

Michel Cazenove even claims that the myth of Tristan 'is finding its true grandeur only now', and that it is in 'the subversion by the soul of so many of the structures of our collective consciousness, and so many of our traditional masculine values' that 'the real *practical* compass' of this 'mystique of Life' should be discerned (*La subversion de l'âme: mythanalyse de l'histoire de Tristan et Iseut* 1981).

Thus the myth of Tristan is an initiatory myth, the successful resolution of which leads to a rebirth. Iseult plays the role of guide, so often reserved to a female character in rites of passage, according to Carl Jung. In this esoteric interpretation, the story of Tristan and Iseult no longer appears just as a myth about the fullness of human love, but as a myth about ontological fulfilment in which the flesh, finally replete, receives spiritual life from the beloved.

In this case everything depends on discovering the Other, the sole epipsychidion. However, there is another possible interpretation.

A myth of individuation

Already by 1973, when writing the preference to the Folio edition of *Tristan* by André Mary, Denis de Rougemont had conceded that Tristan and Iseult drank 'love', 'a love which is addressed to the immortal part which only it can divine, or arouse in the other: the part of the Angel'. But, he adds, 'one has to believe in angels to believe in it'. He was suggesting that the 'last secret' of the myth might perhaps be discovered in 'the angelology of ancient Iran'. According to this mystic view, three days after death the soul of each individual meets its celestial Self, in the form of a female angel for the elect, or of a monster for those who are damned. Thus 'the seeming narcissism of Tristan would here find its spiritual interpretation'.

What is more, given the presence in the texts of symbiotic androgynous symbols (honeysuckle and hazel in Marie de France, the intertwining trees on the lovers' tombs, or the single bramble in *Le Roman de Tristan en prose*), given the catalytic function of Iseult and the abstract character we have already recognized in her, we are justified in wondering whether Tristan and Iseult might not be one and the same person. The myth of Tristan would then be that of the resolution through initiatory death of human dualism into a single, finally unified being: a myth of the reconciliation of 'the Man and the Woman that God made *one* in his image' and which each of us carries within ourselves.

A cosmic myth

In 1821 in his preface to the von Groote edition of Gottfried von Strassburg's *Tristan*, Franz J. Mone saw Tristan as a solar hero. The idea was referred to again in 1847 by Hermann Kurtz, who compared Tristan and Siegfried and thought both were derived from the Osiris myth brought by expatriate Phoenicians to areas inhabited by the Celts. In 1869, in a paper published by the Société Asiatique, Edward Tyrell Leith attributed an Aryan origin to the myth, seeing Tristan as a deification of the spring Sun, with Mark as Winter, and Iseult as the Earth Goddess. The magic drink became the spring rain that made the Earth fecund. 'Finally sad winter returns and, as Mark, reasserts its power over the poor Queen; while the Sun-God, wounded, dies, or wanders in other countries and seeks another wife.'

The cosmic interpretation of the myth again found favour in the twentieth century. Jean Markale in *L'Epopée celtique d'Irlande* (1971) and *La Femme celte* (1982) demonstrates that Iseult shares with her 'archetype' Grainné (the word *grein* means sun) her quality as a solar power and her function as an initiator. Seen from this standpoint, Tristan is a lunar character.

Recently the importance of the solstice in Béroul's *Tristan* has been demonstrated; the crisis of the lovers' repentance in the forest the day after the feast of St John the Baptist is 'the figuration in microcosm of the macrocosmic upheaval of the solstice'. This line of interpretation, which notes the synchronism of spiritual evolution with the influence of the stars, also opens up the way to a theological reading of the myth of Tristan.

A Christian myth

A careful reading of the early versions reveals the immanence of God in this story which is thought of as pagan and erotic. The lovers constantly call on the Lord as their witness and beseech him, seldom in vain. He 'works' for these adulterers at the times when they seem to deserve it least. The author of *La Folie Tristan de Berne* confidently declares, when the king discovers the lovers asleep in the forest, separated by Tristan's unsheathed sword, that 'God indeed did what he wanted'.

This Christian content in the myth is obvious for Wolfgang Golther in the presence, in Gottfried's version particularly, of a 'concept of an extreme seriousness', symbolized by the placing together on the lovers' tomb of the rosebush and the vine, indicating that in the name of Christ's love 'before the throne of God, Tristan and Iseult are absolved of all blame' (*Tristan et Iseut dans les poèmes du Moyen Age et de l'époque moderne* 1907). In a study on 'the development of the tale of Tristan and Iseult in the theatre' Edward Savage demonstrates that the changes made to the myth from the thirteenth century were aimed at Christianizing it (*Le Rosier et la Vigne* 1961). It is not therefore surprising to note that the couple have been integrated into religious iconography, for example on the floor of Chertsey Abbey.

But with the rise of middle-class values the myth for a time ceased to be amenable to a mystic interpretation. To be convinced of this, one only has to read the prosaic, dogmatic rendering by the Lutheran Hans Sachs in 1553: it is a tragedy in seven acts with twenty-three characters recounting the 'passionate love of Sir Tristan and the beautiful Queen Iseult'. We hear the latter baldly stating after she has drunk the philtre that there is something 'wrong' with her. Afer three centuries of disintegration it took the visionary genius of Wagner and Swinburne to restore the myth's value as a spiritual odyssey to it.

À propos of the initiatory experiences, including Tristan's, recounted by Pierre Solié in *La Femme essentielle*, Pierre Emmanuel had already observed that there was 'still one stage to pass through', 'for the redemption is not yet complete, the anima still remains in hell'. The most recent exegetists of the myth have passed through this stage. In his article on 'Tristan's solstice' Philippe Walter sees in the story of the lovers 'the illustration of the tribulations of human development unceasingly guided by God'.

Only recently Jacques Ribart, taking the results of the cosmic, transcendental interpretations as read, added a resolutely Christian perspective to them. The philtre 'is nothing other than the expression in romance or novel form of original sin'. Thus Tristan and Iseult, like Adam and Eve, incarnate fallen humanity which is nonetheless aware. Their former innocence will be regained at the cost of suffering and in the Hereafter. This is really what Paul Claudel had already implied in *Partage de Midi* with the ecstatic end of Ysé and Mésa, the prelude to the final metamorphosis of 'man into the splendour of August, the conquering Spirit into the transfiguration of Midday!'

The many and varied modern treatments are evidence of the vitality of the myth. The conjunction of Tristan and Iseult still exercises its strange magic even today. To the man of clay, stuck in routine and isolation, the myth of Tristan offers the ultimate temptation of exaltation shared with another self: the perfect synchronization of two beings, each the country of the other, breathing, living and dying in unison, it is 'sublime love' (Benjamin Péret). Because of this, it touches us in our innermost being.

Jacqueline Schaefer

Twins: Quadratures and Syzygies

THE SEDUCTIVE ATTRACTION OF TWINS

The literary myth of twins is close to that of the double, which it reinforces, while encasing it in a strictly familial setting. It is also related to the androgyne myth, giving an inverted image of it in the case of twins of different sexes. However, within this grouping of myths it derives the strength of its particular attraction for the imagination from the genetic element that it implies. For twins lead us to the physical centre of personality and to a mental territory where the constraining power exerted by taboos is at its strongest. Twins also represent another mystery as challenging to the unschooled as it is to those trained in the increasingly complex field of science, for does not the marvel of perfect similarity and double birth preserve intact the 'paradox' emphasized by René Zazzo? Twins may be identical in appearance, but they are not so intellectually or emotionally. This psychological fact, which receives graphic confirmation from contemporary novelists (notably Michel Tournier) underlies the use of the duplicate figures of twins to create comic or fantastical effects and sophisticated novelistic scenarios. The element of duplication, which can be interpreted as a split when looked at from another angle, is a challenge to a view of humanity based on the concept of the unity of the individual and, as such, it carries a hint of transgression in the modern unconscious. It arouses the particular sort of jubilation produced by the sight of a crack in the representation of a character. Indeed, the image of twins is often a 'literary device' apparently designed to give rise to the 'pleasure of the text' referred to by Roland Barthes: it is highly 'erotic' because, like the text, it plays on 'intermittence' and involves appearance and disappearance, alluding to the hole in meaning at the core of the person. It provides an illusion of temporary neutrality, which produces a giddy void and thus an appeal to curiosity. Sometimes it reinforces the 'density of the flesh'; it is, as Michel Tournier says, an 'inaccessible absolute'.

Marcel Aymé saw this clearly in *Les Jumeaux du diable* (1928) when he portrayed two men 'made in Hell' by Satan who were 'identical in appearance and in soul', of the same age, with 'the same name and the same memories'. The play of difference, that 'indefinable alertness, I might almost say spirituality', as one of the twins in the book puts it, is the motor force behind the plot and the fundamental cause of the enchantment aroused by real twinhood, which seems a scandalous affront to logic. The Devil's twins are plunged into a world of time and love affairs that might be expected to tear them away from the fantasy of alienating duplication ('I see you as two prints of the same photograph!' exclaims the captain), but they are pursued by the Satanic fate that governed their birth. Louis pushes Norbert into the sea 'where it is sweet', then joins him, thinking of the closeness of their skeletons, which will be 'identical for a while'.

This use of heavy symbolism reflects the anxiety of a culture haunted by the destructive principle of Repetition. It is also related to the obsessional search for differences, which, from Plato's *Sophist* to the works of Nietzsche and Gilles Deleuze, has been presented as the necesssary survival strategy for societies that are a prey to stifling narcissism. In this sense, Uncle Alexandre, the hero of the rubbish dump in *Gemini*, provides a masterly example of the death drive that the twins Paul and Jean both carry within them and must exorcize in the world created by Tournier's novel. In this sense too, René Zazzo's book *Les Jumeaux, le couple et la personne* also illustrates the system behind the myth and well reflects what Claude Lévi-Strauss, in his analysis of the Oedipus myth, calls the overvaluation of kinship relations. The use of twins as a sort of laboratory in which the constitution of the human being can be observed merely represents the ultimate rationalization of this approach.

However, other cultures, less centred on the notion of the individual, use the image of twins to concentrate, not on withdrawal into similarity, but on its opposite, on the benefits to be gained from the multiplication of identical beings. This represents the perspective of the clan, which undervales the relationship of the couple. Here, the fantasy imagery of twinhood is governed by a euphoric vision of original fertility, symbolized by a double birth. This provides the context for the similarity of, for example, the descendants of the twins Hunaphu and Ixbalamque, the founding heroes in *Popol-Vuh*. Likewise it establishes the particular tone of Gabriel Garcia Marquez's novel *One Hundred Years of Solitude*, in which the twin Aureliano Segundo is the comic embodiment of extraordinary prosperity: the domestic animals on his farms multiply in an astonishing way, 'his mares would bear triplets, his hens laid twice a day' (1970: 158). Aureliano is suspected of 'black magic', but ascribes his luck to his concubine; he has a vitality and colossal strength inherited from his grandfathers and also an irresistible charm. This charm is primarily based on strangeness and on games played by twins. Indeed, during their childhood, the twins in Gabriel Garcia Marquez's book often use their complementarity to do a little act: 'so precise was their co-ordination,' says the narrator, 'that they did not look like two brothers sitting opposite each other but like a trick with mirrors' (1970: 145).

Though they prosper through their imitation of 'two synchronized machines' (1970: 152), the twins are constantly threatened by the abstract nature of this artificial logic. Understandably, in Marquez's mind, they inspire the vision of a whole literary domain of chance and surprises. Thus the heroes gradually lose control of the narration and are carried away in the whirlwind of epic. Merged with the group but still retaining the privileged status conferred by their birth, they remain as a necessary reminder of the time of origins. Ultimately, they have the substance only of an ethnographic concept, and serve to evoke an intermediate time, halfway between historical time and the eternity of myth.

However, the seductive attraction of twins does not result from the power of illusion alone. Other factors, which vary from period to period, have helped to shape the literary manifestations of the myth. These certainly include the influence of 'primitive imagery', but also include scientific developments and the appeal of certain exceptional works that have given persuasive portrayals of representative and coherent aspects of twinhood. All these factors should be considered in a brief study of the myth's development.

THE FUTURE OF A PARADOX

From duplication to differentiation

If naming is indeed a simple form of narrative, as it is in oral cultures, the association between twins seems particularly conducive to a kind of doubling of names designed to express the sameness of two people who are nevertheless different. Thus a difference of one letter or a few letters attached to a stable stem is sufficient to establish the difference between two identities. This seems to apply to the names Florus (or Flaurus) and Laurus. According to Rendel Harris, these refer to the laurels held by Leda, who is shown surrounded by twins in a scene painted on a vase from Vulci; while they later became the names of saints in places of worship that were once dedicated to twin powers. George Dumézil views the names of the Vandal gods Raos and Raptos in a similar light. Their etymological roots lie in the words *rauzaz* and *raftaz* ('reed' and 'beam') while the emblematic representation of the deities is modelled on *dokanas*, conjoined beams symbolizing the emotional unity of twins. In this way, echoing effects or verbal analogies can be used to suggest functions or qualities common to twins.

Thus the names Castor (from the Greek meaning 'the resplendent') and Pollux both indicate astral and luminous origins. A slightly different approach involves the use of devices such as inflections of the stem (Romulus, Remus, Set, Cham), homophonous endings (for example, Einbett, Warbett, Villbett, Heracles, Iphicles), or the sort of word plays or metatheses inspired by the saintly triplets of the calendar. It is apposite here to recall the understandable astonishment felt by the character in Gogol's *The Overcoat* when, before naming his son Akaky Akakievich, he is confronted by the fearsome names 'Mokkia, Sossia and Khozdazat' and then 'Trifily, Dula and Varakhassy' and who, as the narrator humorously confesses, would have preferred 'Varadat or Varukh' (Gogol 1956). The blurring of identities represented by twins is thus expressed through a search for homophony designed to reflect an equivalence of meaning: the notion of twinning or pairing conveyed by the grammatical dual (in Latin 'Augg' means 'the two Augusti') is the ancient manifestation of this. It is based on a psychology of indistinction in which, as Piaget has remarked, duality precedes unity. In contrast, the desire to denote difference leads to a hierarchical organization based on a more complex form of logic. Here, one should recall Roman Jakobson's famous comments on the names of the twins Jeanne and Marguerite in the *Essais de Linguistique générale*: taken as a whole, the antitheses between the phonemes ('J' opposed to 'M', 'a' developed into 'a, i') lead the distinguished linguist to stress the system effect projected by the 'configuration of symbolizers' onto the configuration of what is 'symbolized'.

However, the second configuration is governed by a dynamic involving splitting. In stories about twins, this extends to the pattern of actual relations between the twins, giving rise to a generalized emphasis on symmetry and on the harmony embodied by even numbers. Thus, in the first version of the Greek legend, Helen is born from an egg laid by Nemesis, who turned into a goose to achieve sexual union with Zeus. Soon afterwards she appears with the Dioscuri: consequently, as Chapouthier has demonstrated, a vase painting depicts the egg being given to the family of Tyndareus for safe keeping. Later, a change of roles means that Zeus turns into a swan to impregnate Leda, the mother of the Tyndaridae. In another representation of Helen's birth, the twin Dioscuri are shown next to her, as though springing from the same shell. The power of twinhood then results in the splitting of the egg into two symmetrical eggs. Later, in a highly 'logical' way, Clytemnestra is introduced into the legend to share the second egg with Castor: the couple of Pollux and Helen, who were fathered by the god, is then contrasted with the human couple of Castor and Clytemnestra. The inclusion of Clytemnestra necessarily completes the quartet.

RETROACTIVE EFFECTS OF TWINHOOD

In the same way, as the present writer has shown in *Mythe et Littérature sous le Signe des Jumeaux*, in Plautus's *Amphitryon* the contagious properties of twinhood had a systematic effect not only on Jupiter and Mercury, who were forced to turn into Amphitryon and Sosia, but also the actual plot of the play and even on the objects in it. Thus Sosia himself cries: 'You have spawned another Amphitryon; I have spawned another Sosia; now if the bowl has spawned another bowl, we've all doubled' (1925: 83).

The entertainment given at the feast to commemorate the birth of Heracles and his human twin Iphicles has a retroactive effect on the work itself, which seems to be taken over by a sort of 'twin mania' and sprouts parallel elements at will. Conversely, the opposition between the divine character and his human double is firmly established by a series of antitheses: similarity is the starting point ('two drops of milk') in illustrating the role of the logical constraints that govern non-scientific reasoning.

It is such reasoning that gives order to the universe of Shakespearian drama. The playwright's use of Latin authors took on a particular significance with the birth of the twins Hamnet and Judith to Ann Hathaway in 1585. Thus *The Comedy of Errors* (1590–2?), which was inspired by Plautus's *The Two Menaechmi*, was constructed around the theme of the formation, opposition and reunion of contrasted couples. In this early work, Aegeon's wife Aemilia becomes 'a joyful mother of two goodly sons; and, which was strange, the one so like the other as could not be distinguish'd but by names'. Aemilia is justifiably proud of the miraculous similarity between her children and is keen to put to sea to show them to her parents. However, a storm during the voyage causes the family to become separated: one of the twins remains with the father, the other with the mother. This provides the play's central theme, and one that was to reappear in some later Shakespearian works: that of the search for the lost twin, combined with the search for family unity. This theme only appears at the end of the play, in its dramatic dénouement. In contrast, Michel Tournier later placed it at the forefront of the novel that takes his twin characters on a world tour that is also a double of that of Phileas Fogg and Passepartout. Shakespeare's entire play takes place in Ephesus: indeed, it is in the closed world of a city that twinhood is most likely to give rise to delusions. The arrival of Antipholus of Syracuse, the identical twin of Antipholus of Ephesus, enables the use of the dramatic device of ubiquity: a twin who is the exact double of his brother can apparently be in two different places at the same time. The city becomes a place of dangerous enchantment, of evil spells by which the characters themselves become bewitched. The same form of delusion is at work in the strange world of Venice portrayed in Goldoni's *Venetian Twins*: the twin brothers in both plays are caught up despite themselves in the romantic to-ings and fro-ings made possible by their physical resemblances; and this emotional instability is ultimately extended to the city itself and to the values that it represents. Nonetheless, the Shakespearian world is solidly anchored in reality, despite these passing fluctuations. Its solidity is primarily that of the family, since the two women who are loved by the twins are themselves sisters. The ordeal – in other words, the test of indistinction – is thus confined to a particular moment: the family is soon reunited in the temple of Diana, the twin sister of Apollo. In one of the sanctuaries of twins, where the mother has taken refuge and became an abbess, all find their rightful partners – even the servants, the Dromios, who are themselves separated twins, achieve contentment.

GLORY AND DECADENCE

Clearly, the play reflects a well-oriented use of myth: the entire plot involves the expulsion of the 'bad spirit of twinhood', recalling a ritual performed for the same purpose by the Irigwe Indians, described by Sangree. The crucial point here is that one of the twins bears within him an inhuman element that must be removed. Shakespeare's text makes this absolutely clear: one of the two brothers is the other's Genius. Thus, in choosing Ephesus, and specifically the temple of Diana, as the place where the family of twins is reunited, the playwright was making a symbolic allusion to one of the rites of exorcism that enable Culture to transcend Nature. Motherhood, transformed by priesthood, sanctifies the symmetrical happiness of parents and children. It is no surprise that the *Comedy* ends with 'a gossip's feast' held at Christmas, stressing the supreme civilizing functions of this dénouement. In *Twelfth Night*, a play written for the twelfth night of the Christmas festivities, a similar plot involves the same symmetry between a parental couple and a pair of twins – in this case Viola and Sebastian – and after a comparable period of trials and uncertainties, the latter marry Orsino, Duke of Illyria, and the Countess Olivia respectively. Clearly, in Shakespeare's work, the hierarchy of the family soon matches the political hierarchy.

This limited aspect of Shakespeare's work has been stressed because it clearly reveals the extent to which the playwright exploited the miraculous aura that accompanies the birth of twins. This enabled him to develop an acute sense of all the myth's literary manifestations and a particularly subtle sensitivity to the interplay of relationships created by complementary and contrasting characters. It should also be noted that the final quartet comes together after the resolution of a quarrel and the subversion of the 'odds', as Puck says in *A Midsummer Night's Dream*. Conversely, it would be interesting to show how tragedy involves the impossibility of such an outcome and concludes with the figure three (the number of witches in *Macbeth* and of the Fates). The dissemination of twins throughout Shakespeare's work – a development that the present writer has sought to trace in *Mythe et Littérature* – clearly made his drama an effective vehicle for introducing the myth into Western culture.

In this context, Shakespeare's direct heir was Edgar Allan Poe, who saw his name as a doublet of 'poe-t', and identified with William Wilson, the emulator of the 'Great Will' of world literature. However, the works of the Romantics and the first works tinged with narcissism of the Decadent movement transformed Shakespeare's Christmases and Easters of twins into an apocalypse: Usher and his sister Madeline are certainly 'twins', as the narrator brutally reveals, but this *coup-de-théatre* marks a collapse into madness and the 'fall of the house'. The atmosphere of love and incestuous imprisonment becomes increasingly obsessive – so much so, that Poe's entire work is simply a histrionic inversion of Shakespeare's optimistic universe. *The Purloined Letter* is the true converse of *Troilus and Cressida*, and Poe is the 'triumphant' secret rival of his great predecessor.

A new direction was given to the use of the myth by Elémir Bourges's *Crépuscule des Dieux* (1884). Here, the twins Hans Ulrich and Christiane, who are based on Poe's characters and on their Wagnerian counterparts Siegfried and Sieglinde, actually consummate their incestuous desires and then kill themselves. In 1905, Thomas Mann transferred elements of this theme to a Germany setting with his representation of the Jewish twins Sieglinde and Siegmund Aarenhold. They, however, have no misgivings about enjoying their physical similarity. Indeed, *The Blood of the Walsungs* portrays a narcissistic love that merely represents an extreme racism rejecting all forms of difference. Paradoxically, through their actions, these characters – 'two orchids in a vase' – who are children of the rich bourgeoisie, ensure the failure of the 'assimilation' that their father intended when he gave them their first names. At the same time, by superimposing the story of their tragic passion on that of Wagner's opera, Mann emphasizes the characters' involuntary identification with their mythical ersatz doubles: blond actors of aryan race. In *The Man Without Qualities* by Musil (1930), the obsession resurfaces in the form of the imaginary twinhood invented by Ulrich and Agatha, which as Zazzo has clearly pointed out, establishes a 'utopia of twins'. It is evident here how Wagner's relaunching of the myth became associated with the sentiments of Decadence, so that twins were presented as witnesses to the fall of the West, portrayed in a theatrical setting. At the high point of their journey, the literary twins who founded civilization have become no more than extras. In Germany, a last grating memory of this caricature appears in the figures of Castor and Pollack in Fred Uhlman's *Old Friend* (1971).

TOWARDS THE NEW PSYCHOLOGY

After 1869, scientific views changed the literary approach to twins. In his famous twins method, Darwin's cousin Sir F. Galton states that the differences apparent in a pair of twins are due to chance events that occur during their development and that upset the laws of heredity. This theory was contested by William James in the heat of the spiritualist reaction and in his efforts to champion human freedom against the theories of determinism.

Various works appeared at this crossroads. Some were grotesque, such as Mark Twain's *Those Extraordinary Twins* (1869) with its fairground humour and the short comic piece of 1894 *Pudd'nhead Wilson*, an amusing metamorphosis of Poe's *William Wilson*. *The Prince and the Pauper*, written in 1882, reflects a similiar approach to the theme, just as *The Strange Case of Doctor Jekyll and Mr Hyde* by Robert Louis Stevenson (1885) presents a hero torn apart by the 'perpetual struggle' between twins with diametrically opposed natures. In a more reserved vein, William James's philosophy and the work of his brother Henry are designed to transcend the 'sickness of twinhood' with which they were afflicted and for which George Sand's *La Petite Fadette*, inspired by a story by Jules Janin, provided them with a literary model. With the help of Shakespeare's plays, but also drawing on examples of twins scattered through Poe's stories and in tales collected by his friend Andrew Lang, Henry James was particularly successful – from *Roderick Hudson* in 1875 to *The Ambassadors* of 1903 – in giving a splendidly discreet portrayal of the fantasy world of twinhood. As the present writer has shown in *Henry James, une écriture énigmatique*, Henry James consciously accomplished a tour de force similar to that observed by Marc Soriano in the work of Charles Perrault: the 'detour' by way of twins that explains the ambiguities of *Riquet à la Huppe* and led Soriano to the core of the storyteller's textual problems shapes the entire output of the American writer. Here, the Dioscouri are not so much representatives of a new form of literary health as 'ambassadors' of cultural renewal on an international scale.

Later reappearances of the theme regularly accompany the re-emergence of determinist ideas. Thus it is the diffusion Mendel's theories that ultimately underlie André Maurois' story of the *Fattupuffs and Thinifers* (1930), which plunges readers into a fantastical world entered by way of the Twin Rock of Fontainebleu. The people in this world are strictly divided into two antithetical categories of individuals, and the heroes must negotiate the contradictions that these represent in order to reach maturity. In the same spirit, Aldous Huxley's dystopian work *Brave New World* (1932), which is characterized by humour based on parody and hyperbole, takes halluncinatory twinhood to absurd extremes with its ninety-six identical twins working ninety-six electric machines. Once again, twins act as catalysts in the development of the social malaise and uniformity brought about by inhuman science. Their future is thus established: they are placed at the outposts of changing societies and subjected to the running fire of heredity, whether natural or artificial. Consequently, if they are not actually dolls or robots, they are at least almost fetishes. Decisive action by psychologists was needed to break this enchanted circle and make them the refined champions of an unheard-of freedom.

THE MODERN SYNTHESIS: ASTRAL PERSONALISM

Twins constitute a cell embodying the main aspects of a period or culture, and initially, in cosmogonic myths, their double birth represented the major opposition between masculine and feminine and between the divine and the human. Subsequently, in the context of founding rituals, the descent of these celestial creatures to the level of everyday humankind was portrayed in terms of conflicts between eponymous twins. In these, civilization was established either through the elimination of the weaker of the two (Abel, Remus and so on) or through sending the gods back to the heavens (Plautus). Next, through the medium of Platonism, aristocractic government contributed to the vision of twinhood as a balance achieved through identity (*Ami and Amile*) – an idea that prevailed in the Middle Ages. However, the birth of bourgeois society, forming the background to the works of Shakespeare, revived the theme of a quartet of twins (two couples of identical twins of different sexes) in which the temporary indecision of the androgyne (Ganymede in *As You Like It*) gives way to the union of complementary characters in a perfect hierarchy. Subsequently, the 'decadent Europe' of the late nineteenth century foundered on the treacherous shoals of sexual indecision and incest between twins of different genders. However, a return to Platonic and astral imagery is apparent later in Ulrich and Agatha's dialogue on the moon in *The Man Without Qualities*, and this search for liberated relationships finally culminated in Michel Tournier's *Gemini* (1975). Here, an uneasy search for the 'unfolded soul' and the separation of identical twins leads to a revelation of triumphant homosexuality and perfect communion with the universe. The twins' adventure makes 'meteorological time' coincide with that of the conventional calender and is portrayed as the manifesto of a complete sensualism that divests itself of human limitations in the confusion of natural rhythms. This hedonism is reflected in a specific variety of fantastic imagery featuring the compensations sought by an 'odd' twin. Thus everything reminds Tournier's hero of his identical brother, whom he sees as scattered through the world like a meteorite that melts in a burst of flames on contact with the atmosphere. His reserve results in a new form of solipsism based on the terror inspired by Otherness: in *Gemini* the 'generalized twinhood' that appears in Japan at the high point of the international journey is in fact only an impoverished type of twinhood based on lack of distinction. Nonetheless, the work expresses a flamboyant cosmopolitanism and neo-romanticism, combining an analysis of myth and the practical use of myth. Tournier discussed this approach at length in *The Wind Spirit* (1977) and in an interview with Zazzo recorded in *Le Paradoxe des jumeaux*.

Many writers of modern novels on twinhood implicitly follow the approach adopted in Zazzo's book and in the work of Jacques Lacan on the 'mirror phase'. Indeed, even when this is not so, as in the case of Kawabata's *Kyoto* (1970) or Bruce Chatwin's *On the Black Hill* (1984), which deal with the theme in a more prosaic and 'sedentary' way, or in the case of *La Mémoire double* by I. and G. Bogdanov (1985), where the magic created by the couple provides an opportunity for surprising anthropological insights, the writing always represents a profession of faith in a demanding humanism befitting the ambiguous twins who are its standard-bearers.

In any case, with *Gemini* the literary journey of the myth has certainly come full circle: deprived of their superhuman nature since their descent from the flies of the Shakespearian theatre, twins are today returning to heaven in a context of criticism and existential ecstasy that constitutes the mundane manifestation of their nostalgia for the divine.

Jean Perrot

The Unicorn

The myth of the unicorn is primarily represented by 'La Dame à la Licorne', an image was popularized iconographically, particularly by that late representation, the result of a long process of evolution, the tapestry in the Cluny Museum collection. It is also the story of the capture of an elusive and inaccessible wild animal which is timid rather than fierce, and which can only be pacified by a young maiden. Since it is reduced to this single event, the legend is surprisingly devoid of incident. However, it does have extremely strong powers of suggestion due to the ambiguities that it has contained from the outset; these increase in proportion to the number of literary and artistic adaptations as well as equivalent versions in heraldry, alchemy and occultism. A changing and symbolic tale, often far-removed from the original image, has been woven around the unicorn. The common factor in its development is found in the chapter devoted to this (and many other animals) in the *Bestiaires du Moyen Age*, where the hunting of the unicorn is used to support a Christological interpretation, and the myth seems merely to serve as a vehicle for a more profound meaning. In other words, it provides an agreeable form of presentation for a deeper significance which constitutes its true function. There was a brief stable period occurring on the literary fringes during which the creature was associated with encyclopaedic texts and characterized by the ideological and formal influence of the Biblical interpretation. The appearance in literature of the unicorn as a metaphor for the snares of love and then as a familiar spirit, the antithesis and the complement of the lion, is a reinterpretation of the early theme, which was purely religious.

The myth of the unicorn provides a point of convergence for traditions which are often ancient. Before the typically fifteenth-century image of the graceful white filly with the long twisted horn had become firmly established, descriptions tended either towards the monstrous, in which the unicorn, like the griffin, the basilisk and the dragon, was a synthesis of different animals, or towards a more stylized approach, in which the only detail retained was the single horn in the centre of the forehead, sufficient indication of its strangeness. Three types of description can be identified within the body of mediaeval literature. Encyclopaedists and travellers preferred the hybrid version which combined the horse's body, the stag's head and the sow's tail (see *L'Image du Monde* by Gossuin de Metz). In line with the Alexandrian *Physiologus*, the *Bestiaires* tended to stress the creature's small size, equal to that of a stag or a goat, and its horn. Finally, the moralistic tales, which considered it to be an incarnation of death, described it in terms of 'a creature with a hideous body and head' (*Dit de l'unicorne et du serpent*). The image of a white creature of average size retaining some of the features of a goat (the unicorn in the Cluny Museum has a goat's head and beard) has tended to persist until modern times, together with a strong tendency to associate it with the horse. These different forms are explained by the dominance of the anecdote of capture which does not require excessive size and strength and by the iconographic motif, in Italy, Germany (Dürer) and France (Jean Colombe in the *Heures de Chantilly*), of the unicorn being ridden,

The very different representations which occurred during the Middle Ages were the result of the complex origins of the creature. The unicorn was part of a rich legacy of legends from the East. It is described in the *Atharvaveda* as a creature of destruction, and is incorporated into Chinese political mythology as a favourable omen presaging a worthy emperor. The kylin occupies a prominent place in the story of Confucius, while the Ancients included the unicorn among the many wonders of India and Ethiopia, two countries which embodied the exotic dreams of the West. Accounts passed on or compiled by such historical figures as Ctesias, a Greek physician of the fourth century BC, and authors of the late Classical period such as Aelian and Cosmas, established the image of a composite monster, described as a 'monoceros' and a 'wild ass', which was strong and invincible and whose horn was the ultimate antidote to all forms of poison. This image was preserved during the Middle Ages by authors such as Isidoro de Sevilla, Raban Maur, Albert le Grand and Barthélémy. Until the sixteenth century, travellers such as Bernard de Breydenbach continued to look for the monster and sometimes, as in the case of Marco Polo, found it in the form of the Sumatran rhinoceros, 'an ugly and repulsive creature to behold' (Chapter CLXVII). The most vivid element of the tradition was the horn which was a royal gift and the object of a flourishing trade (its value was eleven times that of gold), as well as providing the 'point de départ' for the criticism undertaken by Ambroise Paré in his *Discours de la Licorne*.

The literary myth of the unicorn has developed against a background of both fact and legend. Its origins can be pinpointed with accuracy. The *Bible* refers to the powerful and untameable unicorn, while the *Physiologus* includes it in its catalogue of fantastical creatures whose appearance and behaviour refers, via the circuitous routes of a mainly typological and moralistic allegorical interpretation, to the Christian virtues and vices, to Christ and the devil, to the Story of Salvation. It was in this work, from the second century AD, that the story began to take shape; there are no sources of reference prior to this. Because of mediaeval respect for the original source, its structure was reproduced without variation in the *Bestiaires*, translations into the vernacular which spread throughout Europe from the second half of the twelfth century. There were five texts in the 'langue d'oïl' (i.e. northern French) – those of Phillippe de Thaon (1119–35), Pierre de Beauvais (1175–1217), Gervaise (beginning of the thirteenth century), Guillaume le Clerc (*idem*) and the anonymous text of Cambrai – which maintained a constant structure. The unicorn had a single horn in the centre of its forehead. It was a solitary creature which lived in mountainous areas and was impossible to hunt. Its 'feriocity' was such that it even attacked elephants which were its deadly enemy, and could only be captured by a young maiden who stood in its path. When the creature saw her and came to lie 'on her breast', the hunters would take advantage of the opportunity to bind it and take it to the king's palace. To these various different 'elements', the Biblical interpretation added the dogma of the unity of the Trinity (the horn), and particularly the destiny of Christ, incarnate (the bosom of the maiden), captured by treachery and taken before Pilate. But the story as a source of allegorical interpretation is less rich than its ambiguities, although it did give rise to developments in the field of iconography, especially in the Germanic countries, during the fifteenth century. The Virgin in the *Hortus Conclusus* takes the unicorn-Christ onto her knee as the creature is being pursued by four dogs, designated by their banderoles as Compassion, Peace, Justice and Truth.

The image of the *Bestiaires* also has erotic connotations which, although usually discreet, are quite explicit in the *Physiologus* and the version by Philippe de Thaon. In the latter, the first in the Romance language, the maiden takes: 'Her breast from her bodice/And by its scent/The monoceros (unicorn) smells it./It comes to the maiden/And kisses her breast/And falls asleep on her bosom' (V, 403–9).

The virginity which arouses desire also destroys it. The fatal sleep, love's 'temporary death', is also the metaphor for death to the world i.e. desire (see the myth of Tristan). Love and death, a joining of opposites (the theologian Alain de Lille explains that the warmth of the unicorn, i.e. desire, is attracted by the coldness of virginity), strength conquered by weakness, the disturbing power of chastity, the seduction of the inaccessible, the snare of desire in which the male is dominated by the female: there is a long list of implications providing a rich source of inspiration for subsequent interpretations of the myth.

During the thirteenth century, the untameable animal which abandoned its strength and ferocity on the bosom of the maiden became the symbol of the Lover 'captured' by his Lady, of the courtly poet who chose the suffering and martyrdom of 'fin amor' (idealized love), of the vassal who fearfully awaited a gesture of acknowledgement from his lady, i.e. the satisfaction of a desire which is destroyed once it has been satisfied. Although this theme was taken directly from the *Bestiaires*, there is, however, one text which provides a transition. Richard de Fournival's *Bestiaire d'Amour* replaces the religious interpretations with courtly symbolism. Love leads the chase and pride is punished. Sleep is unambiguously associated with death, with the abandonment of self, annihilation in and through desire: 'I fell asleep and am dying such a death as belongs to Love, it is despair with no hope of clemency'.

A famous poem by Thibaut de Champagne echoes the image in a less dramatic manner: 'I am like the unicorn . . .' The destiny of the animal is compared with a 'prison of love', with this mysterious and relentless power of seduction, of the look that ensnares. German lyric poets (*Minnesänger*) such as Burckart von Hohenfels, Konrad von Würzburg and Hugo von Langenstein, and Italian poets such as Guido Cavalcanti, Stefano Protonotario and Chiaro Davanzati, contributed to the popularity of this image, which only retains a few elements of the original myth (ferocity symbolizing pride, the capture and deathly sleep), by eliminating the motif of virginity. As well as this reduced and revised version, there was also an even more basic form of the myth which stressed only the ferocity of the animal and according to which the unicorn, a symbol of Death, pursued a man who sought refuge in a tree. It was based on the oriental tradition (the Indian *Pañcatantra*) transmitted via the *Roman des Sept Sages*, the *Roman de Barlaam at Josaphat* and the *Parabole de l'Unicorne et du Serpent.*

During the fourteenth and fifteenth centuries, the myth was transformed and the episode of the capture no longer formed the focal point. There was a reduction and a change of emphasis in terms of the opposition of the animal strength of desire and of chastity, of the unicorn and the lady. The unicorn was directly associated with the lady in the role of companion and became the symbol of timid and inaccessible femininity. The male element was transferred to the lion which became the symbol of the knight and male desire. The association of the two creatures, which from then on was common in both heraldry (the Scottish coat of arms) and alchemy (where both male and female represent mercury and the lion is also the alchemist while the unicorn is his companion), appears in two texts, *Les Echecs amoureux* and the *Roman de la Dame à la Licorne et du Chevalier au Lion*, as well as in the Cluny tapestry. In the first of the two texts, the lady's knights are given the emblems of the hare (passive resistance by flight and fear), and the unicorn (active modesty and uncompromising chastity), while those of the knight bear the symbols of the lion and Orpheus. In the second text, Love offers a unicorn to the lady, for her perfection, while the knight's bravery wins him the friendship of the lion which follows him into combat. The Cluny tapestry offers similar possibilities for interpretation which have been developed, in particular, by Bernard d'Astorg in his novel and essay, *Le Mythe de la Dame à la Licorne* (1963), in which the female character, the virgin and the seductress, Mary and Eve, the young girl and the woman, is continuously placed between the two emblems bearing the coats of arms.

With these literary monuments, the myth of the unicorn reached the high point of its career. From then on it appeared much more intermittently and was ofted reduced to allusions. Manneristic iconography appropriated the ambiguous creature and turned it into a theme of inversion – see *Labyrinthe de l'Art fantastique* (1967) by Hocke. It became the example *par excellence* of the unorthodox and eccentric belief denounced by Ambroise Paré (op. cit.) and Athanasius Kircher in *Chinae Monumentis* (1667). The narrative and symbolic richness of the medieval myth are only found in revivals directly inspired by the past. Cocteau gave a new interpretation of the Cluny tapestry with his ballet, *La dame à la Licorne* (Munich, 1953), with choreography by Rosen and music by Chailley. The knight appears, galloping on a lion, while the unicorn accompanies a maiden who is the only person who can feed it. One day, when the young maiden shows the creature its reflection in a mirror, it sees the image of the knight. The unicorn dies as a result of this contact with violence and the imperfection of the world, leaving the maiden alone with her grief. The author has preserved the values of purity and chastity associated with the unicorn during the fifteenth century and opposed to the aggressive nature of the lion. Tennessee Williams used an identical although much less direct type of symbolism in *The Glass Menagerie* where the heroine, Laura, breaks the unicorn, the most precious item in her collection of glass figurines.

Although the unicorn has continued to survive in the literary memory, it has been detached from its myth and remains purely an example of the inaccessible, the fantastical and even the fabulous. Among the occasional references in the works of writers such as Spenser, Shakespeare, Cervantes, d'Urfé and La Fontaine, it is possible to encounter precise and even accurate examples. Fragments of the mediaeval tales re-emerge in Voltaire's *Princesse de Babylone* where Formosante has to marry the king who successfully completes a series of tests. Among the contestants is an unknown knight, mounted on a unicorn, who defeats a terrible lion in the arena. We are told that he comes from the land of the Gangarides whose fearsome armies put all their enemies to flight, even those who ride elephants,thanks to their unicorns. It is also the unicorn which enables the mysterious prince and his beautiful princess to travel throughout the world. In spite of many surviving elements of the tradition (lion, elephants, ferocity, India), the unicorn does not appear in its conventional role, but rather forms part of the exotic bric-a-brac, as does the phoenix in the novel. It is used in a similar manner by Hoffman in *Klein Zaches* as the familiar spirit of the magician Prosper Alpanus who deals in metamorphoses and enchantment and travels in a conch drawn by unicorns. German literature from the Baroque period (Gryphius and Weckherlin) to the eighteenth century (Wieland) maintains a certain fascination for this legendary creature. With Wolfram von Eschenbach's *Parzival*, the unicorn became associated with the realm of the occult, since its horn was adorned with a carbuncle, the stone of light.

Although the association with woman and love had disappeared, the aura of mystery still survived from the forgotten myth of the creature which was inaccessible to mortals. Two poets took advantage of the mixture of scepticism and attraction aroused by the mention of the unicorn. In both *Neue Gedichte* and *Sonette an Orpheus*, Rilke used the ambiguity of the 'creature that does not exist' ('dad Tier, das es nicht gibt'). 'It certainly did not exist. And yet, because they loved it, it became a real animal'. Garcia Lorca evokes it in

Chansons de Luna ('a grey and green unicorn, trembling and ecstatic') and in the *Poema del Cante Jondo*: 'Along the alleyway come/Strange unicorns/From which countryside/From which mythical wood?/Closer/They look like astronomers.'

As in the works of Rilke, the unicorn is infinite in time and space. But such considerations can also be treated ironically, as they are by Thurber, the author of *Fabeln für Zeitgenossen*. In the 'Unicorn in the Garden', a man sees a unicorn with a golden horn appear and eat a rose in his garden. Fascinated, he offers it a lily. His wife, amazed and concerned, wants to have him taken into a mental hospital, but the tables are turned and it is she who is taken away.

With W. B. Yeats, the mystery re-assumes divine dimensions. In *The Unicorn from the Stars*, before completing his great work, the Irish wheelwright, Martin Hearne, has a vision of shining young men riding unicorns, who destroy the world and trample vines underfoot. The play tells the story of the search for the meaning of the dream. The unicorn is revealed as the symbol of the spiritual and the supernatural, destined to destroy all human imperfection. But literary undertakings of this type, like that of Cocteau, are few and far between. Most contemporary authors who refer to the unicorn are simply making use of the evocative power of its name, particularly in titles. But they are only doing so in order to create a dreamlike atmosphere, and to take advantage of the significance still associated with the name when describing an idealized female character who is either inaccessible and reserved, as in Herbart's *La Licorne* (1964), where the resigned and distant Juliette is one of a group of children who play in a huge and dilapidated house, or disconcerting, as in Walser's *Das Einhorn* (1966). Perhaps it is children's literature which remains closest to the mediaeval receptiveness to the fantastical, as for example Hahn's *The Unicorn who Wanted to be Seen* (New York, 1968) and Mankowitz's *L'Enfant et la Licorne*.

Armand Strubel

Utopia and Myth

To the extent that Utopia converges with myth, it is primarily in the sense current today that sees myth as an idealized representation of a state of humankind, either in the past or in a fictional future. Moreover, before referring to the term 'utopia', many dictionaries use or cite the famous definition given by Sorel in the introduction to his *Reflexions sur la violence*: 'Our present-day myths lead men to prepare for a battle'.

The study of the relationship between myth and utopia should in practice be kept separate from belated ideological interpretations, in order to measure fully the literary specificity of the utopian genre and the complex relationship which links it to a particular mythical structure, while maintaining the distinction between them.

To redefine utopia we need only question the creator of this neologism, Thomas More, author of the famous work published in 1516 with the Latin title *De Optimo reipublicae statu deque nova insula Utopia*. This title-cum-manifesto allows us to recall the elements that constitute what we can regard as the literary utopia's founding text: 'Utopia' refers to an island space remarkable for its newness – 'new island' – which is intended to illustrate the best way of organizing society – 'the best constitution for a republic' – in other words a political space in the full sense of the words, according to their Platonic meaning. The reference to Plato comes in the second line of the six-line Latin stanza placed on one of the first pages of the original Latin edition and ironically attributed to Anemolius, supposed poet laureate, whose name in Greek means 'empty as the wind', in accord with the negative onomastics of Utopia:

Utopia priscis dicta ob infrequentiam *Nunc Civitatis aemula Platonicae* *Fortasse victrix (name quod) illa literis* *Deliniavit, hoc ego una praestiti* *Viris et opibus, optimisque legibus)* *Eutopia merito sum vocando nomine*	'The Ancients called me Utopia or Nowhere because of my isolation. At present, however, I am a rival of Plato's republic, perhaps even a victor over it. The reason is that what he has delineated in words I alone have exhibited in men and resources and laws of surpassing excellence. Deservedly I ought to be called by the name of Eutopia or Happy Land (1965: 21)

This apparent poetic fantasy reveals many lines of thought. To begin with, while the Greek etymon of 'U-topia' literally refers to a 'non-place', its historical rather than philological origins provide the reasons for its paradoxical location: the unplaceable nature of the place merely signifies isolation in relation to human ignorance: the translation of the Latin word *infrequentiam* by 'isolation' emphasizes the particular insularity of this space, 'isolated' meaning in the first place 'isolated like an island'. From the outset More's utopian model is defined in terms of an ante-historical origin; the Latin expression refers to human beings of the earliest ages. One might therefore be justified in searching for a possible link between myth and utopia, since the question of mythical origins exists in the paradigm as defined by the genre's initiator, at least in its positive version, which significantly brings together 'u-topia' and 'eu-topia', in other words the ideal place.

Thomas More's *Utopia* is the true paradigm of the classical utopia, marking the official birth, in 1516, of a literary genre: Raymont Trousson in his work devoted to the 'literary history of utopian thinking' and published with the title *Voyages aux pays de nulle part*, placed it at the top of his chronological bibliography of texts referred to, although the first chapter of his study discusses 'ancient origins and the Judeo-Christian tradition', not forgetting the obligatory reference to Plato. From a historical point of view, More's *Utopia* represents the other side of the English society of the time, as is demonstrated by the debate in the first book on the socio-economic crisis resulting from the system of 'enclosures'; as a counterpoint to this, the second book presents a model republic without crisis, backed up by a minute description of the political, economic and social regime, stressing the importance of symbiosis between urban society and rural life, balance within institutions and harmony between work and leisure. The absence of crises gives the model an a-historical character and the truly 'eutopian' stability of the ideal city takes away any temporal dynamic. These aspects characterize many classical utopias with their changeless existence, which renders them similar to mythical representations of the ideal city. While More's *Utopia* defines a new mode of literary representation and thus opens the way to the classical 'eutopia', it nevertheless retains the imprint of the ancient myth of Atlantis, which is associated with the Platonic debate about the ideal city in the narrative sketched out in the *Timaeus* and reworked in the *Critias*, where the Athenian city and that of the Atlanteans are at war. The city of the Atlanteans displays its mythical origins in the version in the *Critias*: Poseidon is said to be the founder of this immense island and to have raised its fortifications, which the rulers of Atlantis, all descended from the god and his son Atlas, have completed, notably by digging a canal to the sea. In a parallel way More's Utopia refers to a mythical past in which Utopus, the eponymous ruler, undertook works which in many ways resemble the founding of Atlantis. But, unlike Plato's Atlantis, which remains entirely orientated towards its mythical founding – the presence of a temple to the sea god in the middle of the island bears witness to this nostalgia for the time of its origins – More's *Utopia*, while including the archaic cult of Mithras – a god to whom bulls were traditionally sacrificed, as they were to Poseidon – opens its religious life up to Christianity. This detail discreetly emphasizes the passing of the cyclical conception of the mythical cult and a new conception of time, made possible by the Christian doctrine of salvation. Thus the classical utopia connects with the ancient myth, but remains separate from it.

The paradigm defined by More's *Utopia* enables us to make several distinctions: whereas the myth of Atlantis remains enclosed in circular time, as is demonstrated by its catastrophic entry into history when its final sinking ends all possibility of change, the classical utopia is located in a kind of continuous present, a sign of the completed state of a positive development on to which a compensatory fiction of insufficient historical reality is grafted. Although More's *Utopia*, like Tommaso Campanella's *City of the Sun* a century later, is encumbered by the memory of the mythical Atlantis, in it we can already sense an effort to escape the myth's retrospective clutches and to project the model of the ideal city into a para-historical time. Going further than *The City of the Sun*, Bacon's *New Atlantis* (1627) successfully installs a prospective utopian model by asserting the importance of progress, improvement of living conditions being seen as linked to scientific and technical developments. In it Solomon's House is a kind of Academy of Science and replaces in a clearly progressionist way the Temple of Hoh the metaphysician created by Campanella in the centre of the ideal city. Whereas the permanence of the solar cult still bound the classical utopia to a mythical space, the appearance of the new cult of science heralds the modern, rational and technical utopia. Furthermore the opening of *The New Atlantis* to time is reinforced by a remarkable opening up to space, since the mythical island expands to the size of a true continent. This precursor of the modern utopia definitively orientated towards the future and spatial expansion differs from the classical utopia whose initial schema was still drawn from the mythical microcosm of the ideal city, an island city whose spatial insularity seems to have kept it outside time.

It is no coincidence that the utopia genre developed after the discovery of the New World, since this new geographical horizon made possible the reactivation of a mythical storehouse, giving it scientific validity and a prospective dimension: the mythical geography of the Happy Islands, linked to the suspended time of the Golden Age, was suddenly brought up to date with the scientific proof of a land which had suddenly emerged from an ocean of ignorance. This real discovery continually influenced the utopian imagination, which was concerned to locate its fiction in relation to possibility and not merely to nostalgia for a mythical time and place which had disappeared forever. Thus More rests his fiction on the tale of a supposed companion of Amerigo Vespucci and Campanella imagines a dialogue with a Genoan captain, one of Columbus' former pilots, who is supposed to have discovered the City of the Sun near Ceylon. Bacon meanwhile rearranges the Platonic myth by identifying the Great Atlantis (from which the New Atlantis arises) with

America, which was rediscovered by the great navigators long after the terrible cataclysm that isolated it from the world. Plato's version is skilfully transformed, precisely to lend plausibility to the fate of the forgotten continent beyond the final catastrophe and thus to allow the myth of Atlantis to survive on the margins of a history which had until then negated it. For the location of utopias must remain a paradox in space as in time: in their ceaseless drift, from the Renaissance to the Enlightenment, they often fitted with the discovery of the New World, functioning as imitations of travellers' tales. Added to this was the influence of the Judeo-Christian doctrine of salvation, insofar as Columbus' deed was supposed to represent that of the redeemer, following an assimilation systematically exploited by colonialist ideology. The lost paradise was said to have been rediscovered in America, which explains the naturalist and regressive tendency of some utopias which saw the New World as the sign of a possible return to a new Eden predating the Fall. However this primitive myth, in which the biblical Eden echoed the ancient Arcadia in the way that nostalgia for an archaic Golden Age reflects the fear of collapse, was soon countered by utopia as such, with its prospective vision of a civilized and organized micro-society, where poetic nostalgia gives way to political projects. In relation to the New World, utopia is to myth what the jesuit 'reductions' are to the myth of the 'good savage': a contradiction in terms, in other words a total inversion of natural meaning, which is truly mythical, by the process of acculturation; for, whether written or put into practice, utopia demands different values. The poetic, naturalist and regressive vision of myth contrasts with the political, culturalist and prospective vision of the place that is called utopian. The American Eldorado is located at the point where these visions intersect.

Reactivating the myth of the Happy Islands whose golden flowers are described by Pindar in his *Isthmian Odes* (like the golden apples of the garden of the Hesperides, significantly located in the extreme West, where the daughters of the gods are said to guard the miraculous fruit offered by the Earth to Hera to celebrate her marriage to Zeus), the American Eldorado illustrates the relations that utopia can maintain with myth. The search for the land of gold, with its underlying solar symbolism of a westward course, is an element in the transposition of a mythical geography on to the unexplored lands of South America by the Spanish conquerors led by Francisco de Orellana. As they went on, these men, who were true prospectors, literally projected before them the ancient myth, which had become a mirage, of a fabulous land overflowing with gold. It is in Voltaire's famous version of Eldorado that the poetic, naturalist and regressive vision of the myth encounters the political vision, in the full meaning of the words, of utopia. Despite being on a continent, the place is clearly insular, as is indicated by the wanderings of the two travellers, Candide and Cacambo, who are carried along by water for a day, until they reach the natural fortifications of the Cordillera, recalling the ramparts of the classical utopia. The presentation of the city has elements of both poetic fantasy and the rationality of the Enlightenment, represented by the gallery of the Palace of the Sciences, whose instruments for the study of physics and mathematics contrast with fountains of rose water and sugar cane liqueurs! Their departure using a machine developed by the city's engineers, before the so-called 'red sheep' took over, illustrates this strange encounter between mythical naturalism and the technical project of Enlightenment utopia. Voltaire's Eldorado uses the New World as the location for a utopia which is primarily characterized by its geographical distance, retaining from the regressive myth of the ideal city the aspect of an independent structure cut off from the outside, its spatial insularity undermining temporal insularity. In this critical utopia, mythical geography exploits the guarantee of the historical reality of the New World, without managing to go beyond the contradiction between primitivist naturalism (Edenic overabundance belonging to the myth of the Garden of the World) and an institutional project requiring an advanced state of civilization (scientific and technical innovations lauded by the Enlightenment). Indeed Voltaire's Eldorado reproduces the schema used by Garcilaso de la Vega to describe the Inca empire. Between myth and utopia one sometimes finds history.

From Cyrano de Bergerac's *L'Autre Monde* (1657), open to the imaginary empires of the Sun and Moon, to the Eldorado of Voltaire's *Candide* (1759), via Swift's *Gulliver's Travels* (1726), and whether it is the New World or new worlds that are being portrayed, utopia primarily employs displacement in space to give reality to its other world, to make up for a historical reality which is seen as insufficient. It is not until *L'An 2440. Rêve s'il n'en fut jamais* (1771) by Sébastien Mercier that utopia asserts its difference not in space but in time. Mercier may have had a few little-known precursors but he wins his right to posterity through his exploitation of a new utopian dimension: *L'An 2440* describes a utopia in time, in other words, and before its time, a 'uchronia' as Charles Renouvier, inventor of this neologism a century later, officially called it *Uchronie* [Utopia in history], an apocryphal historical outline of the development of European civilization as it has not been, as it could have been, 1876. While the ideal city of the classical utopia retains a reference to the mythical time of its foundation, real time being merely the dimension of forgetting, degradation and catastrophe – More and Campanella are haunted by the memory of Atlantis – Mericer's 'uchronia' no longer locates his ideal city in an elsewhere in mythical geography, since it is Paris in the twenty-fifth century. This anticipation of possible historical transformations in a well-known place takes utopia away from the spatial level which had rooted it in regressive mythology and projects it into the future. Mercier's *L'An 2440* clearly rejects the geographical isolation of most classical utopias, the better to stress the possible link between the contemporary world and that imagined in a more or less fixed future. Mercier places Leibniz' words, 'Present time bears the future within it' as an epigraph to his work. As to the device of revelation through a dream, this was to be exploited in the numerous uchronias which have dotted literary history since then, notably *Looking Backward 2000–1887* (1888) by the American journalist Edward Bellamy, who imagines Boston at the dawn of the twenty-first century, or *When the Sleeper Wakes* (1899) by the celebrated English utopian H. G. Wells, which represents London in the twenty-second century, covered by an enormous transparent dome. The modern utopia was born as a result of this detour through 'uchronia', which ended the regressive tendency of classical utopia and overturned mythological archaism, imagining the supposedly ideal city in the context of historical development and stressing the profound ambivalence of the now threatened 'eutopia'.

While there is a clear distinction between the regressive time of myth and this new time of utopia which turns into a 'uchronia', one current still preserved the ancient spatial symbolism in a reaction against the ever more industrialized world of the nineteenth century. The integration of utopia into the myth of a pastoral Arcadia underlies the experiment of Brook Farm for example, described by Hawthorne in *The Blithedale Romance* (1852). This utopian sketch also illustrates the link can be established between written utopias and those put into practice, in a modern America still seen as the New World of yesteryear, using a paradisaical symbolism that rejected the emergence of urban, industrial reality. Even when this reality was perceived, the myth of the ideal city was strangely reactivated by the desire to put the utopia in parentheses, in other words to turn it into a micro-society sheltered from history on the biblical model of the New Jerusalem, as condemned by Marx in the form of Cabet's Icarie. Like myth, utopia is not simply a written phenomenon, it can also be practised as the object of a group's collective faith and considered real beyond the experience of failure. After writing *Le Voyage en Icarie* (1839) and following the example of the British socialist Robert Owen, founder of New Harmony in Indiana ten years earlier in 1825 – the plan was first presented in 1817 and the attempt ended in failure in 1827 – Étienne Cabet simiarly tried to put his written utopia into practice on the lands of a former Mormon colony in Texas, with the help of five hundred volunteers. Despite difficulties, this utopia managed to keep going until the end of the century. Jules Verne, in *Les Cinq cents millions de la Begum* (1879), openly drew on the Icarian model, but took from the manuscript of the former Communard Pascal Grousset the idea of the contrast between an industrial town, the work of a German scientist, and a model city, the work of a French doctor, in the north-east of the United States. The transposition of the 1870 Franco-Prussian war is explicit and seems to follow the path of 'uchronia' defined some years earlier by Renouvier. It is chiefly interesting for the somewhat Manichean contrast between the 'eutopia' of France-Ville, informed by the archetype of the town as womb and a product of poetic, naturalist and regressive reverie in which utopia is reunited with myth, and the 'counter-utopia' of the City of Steel, a caricature of a highly organized factory town centred on a steel-making complex in the manner of Krupp, where political order is synonymous with totalitarian organization. Just as the myth engenders its counter-myth through an inversion of the values of the original structure – the myth of the ideal city is countered by the myth of the accursed city – so classical utopia, long confined to the positive model of the 'eutopia', was no stranger to the constitution of the counter-model which ultimately came to dominate, under the various appelations of 'counter-utopia', 'anti-utopia', 'dystopia' or indeed 'cacotopia'! We should note that Plato's Atlantis already functioned on this model through a contrast with the Athenian city, indicating the profound ambivalence of the model city.

The recent history of utopias shows a tendency towards the death of classical 'eutopias', avatars of the myth of the ideal city projected into a more or less distant time, in favour of the counter-model which springs from a total inversion of the values of the orginal structure and reactivates the counter-myth of the accursed city. While 'eutopias' survived in the nineteenth century, born on messianist currents and still identifying the elsewhere of the American continents with the Promised Land of prophecy, the failure of their practical applications, the saturation of space and growing anxiety of human beings in the twentieth century, haunted by the thought of the last millenium, have resulted in the marginalization of positive models reproducing the old ideal of the perfect city, yesteryear's imaginary voyages being now appropriated by science fiction. The occupation of habitable areas and the displacement of *terrae incognitae* from earthly to cosmic space have transported utopia into interstellar regions. The relativism of the new space-time leads to 'uchronias' being imagined on much grander scales than the one timidly envisaged by Mercier in *L'An 2440*. Furthermore, in the context of a topic of the literary utopia, 'eutopia' should be replaced by 'dystopia', reworking the ancient apocalyptic eschatology at the dawn of the second millenium, while indicating the powerful historical dynamic of representations disconnected from mythical time. 'The modern utopia must be not static but kinetic' says H. G. Wells in *A Modern Utopia* (1905: 16), at the very time when the definition of a new space-time was rendering obsolete the fixed representations of classical utopias, which had long been suspended in the immobile time of the ideal city, supposedly sheltered from history in the closure of its mythical space time and which could encounter that history only in a catastrophic manner.

The era of the modern 'counter-utopia', obsessed with a civilization of totalitarian transparency, extreme technicality and the 'massification' of urban crowds, begins with Eugene Zamiatin's *We* of 1920, which represents a thirtieth-century city covered by a gigantic translucid dome, just as H. G. Wells imagined the London of the twenty-second century. Zamiatin creates a caricatured projection of the totalitarian political model whose seeds were already present in some of the classical utopias. The old biblical myth of the accursed city is brought up to date in a technical civilization which rejects the old poetic, naturalist and regressive vision of the world, other than in terms of political and scientific ecology prophecying some nuclear apocalypse on the threshold of the third millenium, or else a return to nature. The scientific aspect of the anti-utopia presented in *Brave New World* (1932) is paralleled by the political aspect of *Nineteen Eighty-Four* (1949) by George Orwell, emulator of Aldous Huxley. Rejecting the increasingly lengthy time-scales that had become usual since Mercier's work, Orwell's counter-utopia uses an almost contemporary elsewhere, whose dated horizon suggests a historical threat, although its chronological precision may give the reader (or spectator) the illusion that this utopia will ultimately return to a past soon to become mythical.

It is no coincidence that a gigantic city somewhere in America should provide the setting for Ray Bradbury's prospective vision in the famous novel whose title, *Fahrenheit 451* (1953), indicates the temperature at which a book bursts into flames and is consumed. America, long the miraculously preserved continent seen as the location predestined for all utopias until the last century, is the very place where the end of positive and culturalist utopias is portrayed. Duhamel had already predicted this in his *Scenes de la vie future* (1930). Bradbury's counter-utopia proclaims the impossibility of all culturalist and humanist utopias in a world in which books are no longer consumed by their readers but by flames. Only human books, the last depositories of culture and knowledge, exiled outside the immense American city in an unspecified future, refugees in what remains of nature, seem to represent the margin through which human memory can retain something of the old myth of what human beings might be outside the destructive time of the totalitarian city.

Patrick Hubner

Virile Women

This subject is rich and confused and is often approached with a lack of calm; it can easily inspire polemic, vulgarity or ambiguity. The myth of virile women occurs in many cultures and has all kinds of different meanings. However, though such exclusivity clearly has risks and may attract accusations of abuse the present study considers the theme only in terms of the two figures that seem best to encapsulate the issues involved: the Amazons and the Valkyries. Both have the added advantage of being directly mythical.

The myth of virile women may have a basis in historical reality. According to the Greeks and, later, to Tacitus there once existed on the edges of the known world one or many peoples of warrior women whose presence went back to the earliest times; and this idea was echoed as late as the thirteenth century by the Icelandic sagas. Following Herodotus, Plutarch regarded the Amazons as distant ancestors of the Sarmatians, while Tacitus knew of a people called the Sitones, who took their orders from a woman. Their territory was said to be by the Black Sea, but it is hard to know whether these writers were not actually trying to represent some vague memory of the ancient and universally observed cult of the Mother Goddess: superficial reading or incomplete information can easily turn matriarchy into government by women!

Starting from the image offered by the Greeks, the present article focuses on three aspects of the myth that extend the origins of our collective unconscious right up to the present day.

For the Greeks, the Amazons were primarily 'barbarians', in the sense in which they used that word: they were unaware of the pre-eminent status of the *polis* as a social and political institution and, in addition, they broke the laws. They were thus unaware of navigation (Herodotus) and the cultivation of cereals (Diodorus Siculus). Aeschylus described them as flesh-eaters and almost all commentators regarded them as warriors, who fought on horseback using bows and arrows. To do this more easily they burnt off their right breasts, hence their name, a-mazon, meaning without a breast. Apollodorus notes that Heracles tore off the Amazon queen's belt (*zóster*), the symbol (*sumbolon*) of her great skill at arms. The myth according to which these fearsome creatures were the bellicose daughters of Ares, enemies of men and marriage, portrays them in a similar light. Much the same picture is presented by those complex figures the Valkyries, the 'virgins with shields' (*skjaldmeyjar*), according to the theory that they are later manifestations of cruel sacrificing priestesses serving a fierce goddess of war (an interpretation supported by one of the motifs that decorate the famous Gundestrup cauldron). They too embody the martial virtues that are usually the preserve of men. The popular imagination was so struck by them that it instinctively gave them the supernatural attributes of wings, and connected them to Odin, though this certainly represents a development of the way in which they were originally depicted. The rather fraught prestige of these creatures who transgress our sexual categories has never faded, to the extent that Woman has always been felt to be the Other, the holder of powers that, normally, are not supposed to belong to her.

In other words, as the Greeks observed, they are women-men, *antianeirai*, as Homer puts it (*Iliad* VI. 186). Homer is apparently playing on the double sense of the prefix 'anti', to imply that they are both the equals and the enemies of men. Indeed, any young warrior keen to prove himself must lead a campaign against them. In a parallel way, the Germanic texts, and particularly those concerning the heroic cycle of Sigurdr-Siegfried, portray Valkyries (such as Brünnhilde) accomplishing all the deeds of which the hero himself is capable and even ridiculing him (in the *Nibelungenlied*). Meanwhile the Icelandic sagas present a similar vision. It is true that, with conscious or unconscious irony, both the Greeks and Scandinavians often imply that engaging in this type of activity is not without its difficulties for the women involved: for in trying to act like men, women often fail and, in the face of peril, revert to their natural behaviour. Their tragic tears and vociferous curses then seem to be as effective a weapon as any javelin, albeit different in a way!

Nevertheless, an aggressive and voluble strain of feminism, which is coincidentally, particularly active at the present in the Anglo-Saxon and Scandinavian countries, seeks to establish total equality between the sexes, without admitting any distinctions. Meanwhile, recent biological discoveries that challenge immemorial traditions concerning conception and motherhood are also leading in the same direction.

In fact, it is the aggressive aspect of the myth, that has always attracted the greatest attention centring on the concept of women-men. On first analysis this seems to mean women who are 'anti-men', who seek to eliminate the male or reduce him to an inoffensive and indeed subordinate state. Freudian psychoanalysis with its famous castration complex that, apparently, explains so many literary works, has been liberally employed in this context. However, it has merely succeeded rediscovering the old motif of the female praying mantis who devours the male after she has gratified her sexual impulses; or that of insect societies, such as those of bees or ants, where, after performing their indispensable part in copulation, the males take on all their allotted tasks in the most perfect order, or in an ideally peaceful state. (It is noticeable that feminist movements and pacificist movements often go together). In one sense, this explains why the Valkyrie kills her adversary on the battlefield. Is it a coincidence that the playwright who perhaps gives the most extreme portrayal of this irrepressible hatred between the sexes, in which Woman is always 'the stronger' (the title of one of his plays), is the Swede August Strindberg? For there are no accounts of the Amazons fighting against each other, or other peoples of women. Their pugnacity is always directed against men; and this is why they reject marriage, which they see as inevitably entailing subservience. For a Valkyrie, marrying a man is a form of sheer torture inflicted as a punishment by Odin.

The Greeks, again, concluded that the Amazon represents Woman as an expression of animality. According to Herodotus, it is because of this aspect of her nature that she kills men. But Herodotus clearly sees that there are two ways of annihilating or killing the male: this can certainly be done with the sword, but it can also be achieved by seduction, which implies subjection. And here the woman-man turns into the man's woman, the *philandros* to whom Plutarch was to refer later. From Medea or Phaedra to Nana, from Cybele or Freyja to the femme fatale of our modern novels, this theme has never been eclipsed even for a moment. Sometimes it is expressed directly, in the form just described. At others, it takes on the opposite guise and is expressed through the image of the virgin woman, ideally pure and rejecting any 'taint': seen in this light, her 'sanctity' comes from the truly exceptional and admirable nature of her rejection of men. Here we can certainly see the figure of the Valkyrie. She kills men – though as Odin's messenger, it is true, and as executrix of his decrees – but at the same time she is also a seductress: no one can resist her literally magic charms. The names that she bears often bear eloquent testimony to this aspect of her nature: she is the one who binds in chains (Herfjötur), who, whether in the heat of battle or elsewhere, puts the fatal thong around her victim's neck (Hladgunnr), or who, recalling Circe, turns him into a pig, as in a poem from the *Edda* (*Hyndluljoth*).

The final possible interpretation of the significance of the Amazon derives from the earlier one. Here, the Amazons represent what may be seen as a kind of ideal for an adversarial attitude to relations between the sexes: they are women-without-men, in other words, women who have found a way of dispensing with such inconvenient partners. An ancient Hittite story described how the queen of Kanes exposed her thirty sons on the river and only kept and brought up her thirty daughters. Strabo too claimed to have heard of a society without men: once a year its women mated with men from neighbouring peoples; they then kept only the female offspring of this union; any boys were sacrificed. Strabo states that these sexual encounters took place 'at random and in the dark'. It is also worth noting that if a Valkyrie agrees to bear a child, she automatically loses her status and becomes, as it were, a mere woman, a servant of the chosen warriors of Valhöll (Valhalla) and mother of princes. It seems that the untouchable swan-woman and the helmet-wearing virgin are incompatible with the 'beer mistress' (Ölrün). Here again, the image of the woman who wishes to do without men, except when it comes to perpetuating the species, has strange echoes today that would attest to the vitality of the myth were it in any doubt. In any case, it is clearly the idea of the necessary complementarity of the sexes that is being rejected. Is this a question of pride? Perhaps, although many cultures have resolved this primal antagonism by dominating it. A more fundamental issue seems, in fact, to be involved. There have been few perfectly satisfying mythical solutions to the dream of totality, of unity, that humankind has been pursuing obscurely for as long as it has existed.

Régis Boyer

Witches

A myth is a gash in time, in history, and each period focuses on one of its shifting aspects. According to Jauss (1982) it thus reflects an 'horizon of expectation', defined by the social fear of a particular present. The mythical material is thus stirred and restirred, as Claude Lévi-Strauss (1964, 1968) has shown, with its various facets sometimes illuminated, sometimes hidden in shadow.

If the witch and her many representations now appears as an archetype of our culture, present in literature, painting and opera, it is because she was originally alive. Human beings who were suspect or persecuted, witches belong to the sphere of speech. Expert in the art of incantations and magic formulas, the witch was born as the beautiful pagan Sybil or Cassandra, and died at a Christian stake, condemned by the words that were her secret weapon. The witch, a person gifted with speech, inhabits the speech of others, be they storytellers or inquisitors.

If, insofar as it is formulated speech, myth is discourse in the domain of the *muthos*, which Vernant (1980) contrasts with the *logos* of written discourse, then the character of the witch, borne by the tales of the oral tradition, made present and reanimated by the words of storytellers and the accusatory speech of inquisitors, can clearly be seen as a founding element in the elaboration of myths.

We can recognize here, following Mircea Eliade (1963), that the essential function of the character of the witch is to establish the myth. Far beyond history, the witch is part of a long-term process and it is her permanence in our minds which gives her existence and makes her perennial.

Thus, crouching in the shadow of our fearful nights, the witch haunts, seduces and amuses us.

If we look back along the myth, reading literary texts and listening to our oral traditions that preceded them, the strata of yesterday communicate to us today. Who is the witch? What are her attributes and what makes her contemporary? So many trials lead us to the archaeology of the character, making us understand the avatars of the myth in its irreversible process of change.

WHO IS SHE?

The happy era

'In the beginning woman is all' (Michelet 1958). It is hard today to imagine that the witch was once anchored in reality as a positive character, cause of harmony rather than catastrophes.

The happy era goes back to pagan times, the founding time of the myth, now erased and forgotten. She was then granddaughter to the Mother Goddess, queen of the Babylonian heaven, cousin to Isis in Egypt, to Ishtar in Assyria, to Innanna for the Sumerians and Astarte for the Phoenicians. She was also related to Venus/Aphrodite, goddess of Love, the true creative power, and to Circe, who presided over metamorphoses, or Cassandra, the incomparable Seer. She was without doubt woman, her young sexual body destined for pleasure and motherhood. Her power was total. She presided over life, death and harvest, leading the elements and men in matriarchal societies. The patriarchal societies that followed made her pay for this plenitude dearly; they were the ones that gendered her name in the feminine, clearly distinguishing wizard from witch when they thought the time was right.

For the wizard does not belong to the myth; he does not have the same emblematic force, his power is not the same, he represents a distant derivative of womanly knowledge. For, while man is sometimes the devil, it is all of sorcery that became woman in the witch. On this point Jules Michelet (1958) records what Sprenger was saying before 1500: 'We must speak of the heresy of witches and not of wizards, the latter are of little concern!' And another, in the reign of Louis XIII of France, said, 'For one wizard, ten thousand witches.'

The positive figure with a balanced, sexual body gradually cracked and shattered, changing into negative values under the pressure of men and religions, and few texts allow us to glimpse the myth's golden age. However, the diversity and richness of the witch apparent in pagan rites appear in one of the earliest written tales, Apuleius' *The Golden Ass*, which dates from the second century AD.

This text retains the ambivalence of the character of the witch through various feminine representations, each of which crystallizes a function and a power of the former Mother Goddess.

Thus Psyche and Fotis are at once both tender, innocent and perverse damsels who, to bring about the initiation of Lucius, naturally know how to 'season a dish and a bed pleasantly and to make them dance voluptuously.' There were vestal virgins skilled at cooking and they alone could extinguish the fires they lit. Adulated, glorified, preparing for the final coming of the goddess Isis, laden with all the virtues, they represent the positive side which was immediately balanced by other feminine figures (inspired by the patriarchal societies): the already old Meroe, queen of the tavern, and Panthia the All-Powerful. Here we also find Pamphile, who lived outside the religious bounds of the town and performed all kinds of sepulcral incantations. What these figures lacked in beauty, they made up in knowledge and skills. These are the first cracks, the first breaks in the polished surface of the founding myth. The woman who had everything (beauty, knowledge and power) now only has a fragment, one attribute taken from the disturbing completeness. To express them all she has to split into many female figures, who shatter her power.

Compared with the feminine principle in its totality, as it appeared in the pagan rites, the witches of *The Golden Ass* reveal to the hero the hidden, underworld face of the Great Mother, incarnated in the story by Isis. The initiatory story was in fact seen by Jung and his followers as an attempt to rehabilitate the feminine archetype.

Originating in paganism and following the feminine path of totality and deviance, the witch gradually became the other face of the fairy, crystallizing negative powers and preserving the imprint of her knowledge and powers.

The times of despair

'How long have there been witches? I say without hesitation, since the times of despair' (Michelet 1958). The most violent view of the myth of witches remains that of the Catholic church and the judges who imputed to them the most absurd fears and the most avowed madness. For nearly three centuries witches, assimilated to heretics, were hunted, tortured and burned alive. It took the Catholic church several centuries to silence and then to eliminate reappearances of the ancient pagan rites still present in the villages of Europe.

In 785, the Synod of Paderbor proclaimed that, 'Anyone who, deceived by the Devil, believes, like the pagans, that someone can be a witch and burns them for this reason shall be punished by death'. This proclamation remained valid under Charlemagne. In the ninth century, the witch was described as a 'pure illusion' (canon episcopi of Ancyre).

The growth of heretical sects, however, in the thirteenth century led the church to integrate ideas of sorcery and heresy. In 1227 the papal bull of Gregory IX became 'the core of the future inquisition' (Jones 1971). Then, the witch epidemic which spread throughout Europe for nearly three centuries was finally unleashed by two important events. In 1484 Sprenger and Institoris published the *Malleus Maleficarum*, in which questions of witchcraft were debated in the finest detail (flight, Sabbats, etc.) and which formed the basis of a sophistry that ensured for its victims horrible tortures and death.

For what was witchcraft condemned? The witches who were burned, called the Devil's fiancées, were often young and beautiful, denounced by a neighbour, a concupiscent man or an abandoned woman. Sometimes they had only to be redheaded or widowed, living without a man and thus destabilizing the precarious order of a village ravaged by famine and oppressed by political and ecclesiastical authority.

The witch in time became an incarnation of evil, ugliness and parallel practices and powers, which were to become established in literary history, from Lilith to the romantic witches of Victor Hugo and Lamartine. Associated with night, the Devil and disturbing places, the three sisters who are witches in *Macbeth* 'can look into the seeds of time'. It is they who govern the action in this play, declaiming 'Fair is foul and foul is fair' before they disappear, as though establishing a demonic reversal of values in the name of which they will work for the greatest evil.

In this period of despair, and particularly in the sixteenth and seventeenth centuries, there was great sexual repression, in relation to which Muchembled (1979) reminds us of 'the old mistrust of the men of the Church for the daughters of Eve', who were responsible for original sin. The Church and judges established a link between the female sex and death.

The figure of the Devil did not belong to the myth of the witch. It was painfully grafted onto it, making the witch into the opposite of the Virgin Mary: the sexless woman-mother was contrasted with the body and pleasure of the sexed woman who both attracts and repels men.

The witch, now grown old, returned to folklore and to the village to look for traces of herself, for the old practices.

Village knowledge

The times of despair were not enough to erase the image of the witch. With a mixture of respect and fear, every region and every village observed and sought out the silent and solitary old woman who carried faggots, gathered plants, healed bodies and unsettled minds. The witch became real again and it was as 'Mother Nature' that she remained in the village. Healer and midwife, in times of peace her 'medical functions were acknowledged' and sought. Michelet (1958) stresses that 'for a thousand years the sole doctor to the people was the witch'. Over time she managed to preserve her herbal medicine secrets. Her role was traditional, with her parallel folk knowledge all the more marginal for being feminine.

She was to be found apart from others, in remote, wild places, on the bounds of inhabited areas, between Earth, Heaven and Water. She was always on the margins. In *Les Cahiers de Fontenay* (1978) Nicole Chaquin clearly shows the correlations between the characteristic instability pervading the power of witches and that of the places in which they lived. Her study reminds us that impermanence, mobility and temporariness are all signs of demonic presence. Moreover Pierre de Lancre (1612) writes:

> And to show particularly that the situation of the place is partly the cause of the great number of witches, it should be known that it is a mountainous country, the edge of kingdoms . . . the mixture of three languages . . . the interlocking of two dioceses. All these various things give Satan marvellous ease for holding his assemblies and Sabbats in these places, since moreover it is a sea coast which makes the people rustic, coarse and poorly policed . . .

Places traditionally linked to witchcraft were mainly, as Chaquin indicates, 'places outside the enclosed area of society: forests, mountains, the banks of lakes' and particularly the island described by Lancre as a place of walks, dances and inconstancy. Indeed the island evokes the ambivalence and shifting nature of the location, but it is also an enclosed, narcissistic space, symbolically linked to the feminine because it is surrounded by water. It is a place of differences and of passage, an inner space which the witch controls.

The witch lives in a cave or a corner of the forest, in a poor, ill-lit and dirty house which no one enters. Thus her place of privacy and secrets is protected. Outside, she is mistress of more open domains, the heath of Macbeth's witches, the cliffs of Babe Ozouf in Didier Decoin's novel (1984); she is also to be found on the tops of mountains.

The witch likes free spaces; in them she describes her circle, she commands wind, water and fire and talks with the earth, sea and sky. Her power of unity is born of her conversation with places and complicity with the elements and also of her role as mediator between the land of the living and that of the dead. The damp places that the witch particularly likes are traditionally areas that people pass through. As for the relationship, the alliance between the witch and the moon, this recalls the fact that in some Gnostic or Neoplatonic traditions the moon is the place where the souls of the dead transmigrate.

Her initiatory role and task as a 'ferrier' are comparable to that of the storyteller, the 'woman who helps' according to Yvonne Verdier (1979), or simply to that of the grandmother, who passes on ancient recipes, practices and skills as well as teaching tales, rhymes and legends on winter nights.

Folk practices and tales reveal the remains of the myth which are specific to the function of the village witch.

According to the tale type 402 in Aarne and Thompson's classification (1973), called *The Love of Three Oranges* (as in *The Search for the Vanished Husband*, tale type 425), she is the ferrier, the intiator of girls. In *Cupid and Psyche* and *Beauty and the Beast*, her role is more that of a mediator. The witch speaks to girls of love, reveals secrets to barren women and performs abortions for anonymous women who are pointed out to her.

But when her skill is reinforced with power, the witch's power inverts the religious, political and moral values of official knowledge: the farce, lies and humorous tales of the oral tradition are all examples demonstrating the need for inversion contained within popular culture. The work of Rabelais (as analysed by Mikhail Bakhtin 1984), carnival figures and Claude Gaignebet's research (1974) into the obsence folklore of children all fit into this tradition.

Thus witchcraft and the witch who says the mass backwards and, as Michelet (1958) put it, offers the three sacraments of baptism, priesthood and marriage backwards clearly have a role in the pagan and political disrespect found in any popular culture. It is not surprising that the witch of *The Golden Ass* has the power to lower the sky, to hold the earth in suspense, to turn springs to stone and to dissolve mountains. She has the ability to halt the play of opposites in nature and to invert others. 'Through the circle of motifs relating to the other side of the face and to the replacement of the high by the low, the witch is linked to death and to hell' (according to Bakhtine and Gaignebet).

But when the 'village is saturated with fears' to use Muchembled's words (1979), it turns against the witch, even the witch without a devil, without demons. The peasant who drives her out does not do so for the same reasons as the magistrates and members of the élite. Indeed in peasant societies, as Muchembled reminds us, 'the most fundamental worries concern not the Devil but more immediate and frequently occuring phenomena, chains of multiple misfortunes in the fabric of their daily lives'. When sickness, famine and destitution strike at the village gates, the witch becomes the other, the woman, the neighbour, the parent, the one who still has something when no one has anything, the one who is spared.

The witch then becomes the core, the centre of all that cannot be understood or accepted. She attracts suffering, fear and hatred; she is no longer a living being who belongs to a community but the expression and cause of the misfortune that has befallen everybody. Fear drains away all logic and reason, retaining only drama. The witch who is feared as a principle of disorder is also a woman who goes about and disturbs the established order. As much as her anchor point outside the socialized space, the villagers and inquisitors fear her omnipresence, her capacity to be everywhere. Having met her at the end of a field or seen her in a nightmare during a troubled sleep, they endow her with the gift of ubiquity and everlastingness.

In the course of her journey the witch ages from the timeless young woman who was burned to the menopausal woman who is consulted in the village. She regains not only the practices of a feminine knowledge that has become taboo, but also the mysterious power linked to the 'spoken' and the 'unspoken'.

TACITURNITY, SILENCE AND RESISTANCE

Indeed the witch and her accompanying myth make her speech into a ritual act. This applies to the words uttered by the witch herself, from public incantations to the words murmured to another woman in the village, passing on the secret legacy of ancestral practices, and the spoken threat which turns words into killers, as Jeanne Favret-Saada attests today:

> If anyone can be caught by spells, the precise question is not one of knowing whether or not the spells are objectively true or false but whether it is true that words can kill. And this is proved every day by psychoanalysts in the private speech of their patients. In witchcraft the private vows of death are in addition upheld by the authority of a collective discourse, which has been effective over several generations. This is why it is in no way irrational and even less stupid to believe in spells.

The witch, or rather witchcraft, still reappears here and there in some regions nowadays. Jeanne Favret-Saada had encountered witchcraft in the Department of Mayenne in the Loire valley. Behind words apparently devoid of meaning the spell is cast, without any identifiable ritual or incantations. Anodyne words, gestures and displacements still make animals and human beings ill or can kill them.

This ethnological recognition of the practices of witchcraft was long impossible to sustain in scientific circles. What was then said about witches by judges, inquisitors or the doctors who took over from them merely contributed to establishing the evil spell of taciturnity and then the silence of witches.

In the period of the witch-hunts, the evil spell of taciturnity was the tangible proof that witchcraft was being exercised. This reluctance to speak was a gift of the devil which Pierre de Lancre (1612) describes as follows:

> In order never to confess the secret of the school, a paste of black millet is made at the Sabbat, with the powdered liver of some unbaptised child which is then dried; then mixing this powder with the paste, it has this power of taciturnity; so that whoever eats it never confesses.

Thus witches cannot confess their crimes, the spell stifles them and marks them out as guilty. But what is it that they want to make women say, which cannot be heard or understood and which becomes her strength, the last bastion of her specific culture and identity? What has she to confess other than her own existence, her different reality?

The judge, men in general and the authorities will tolerate only one form of speech. The other, that symbolized by the witch and which relates to popular and furthermore feminine knowledge, must be stifled, the witch must be reduced to silence. She is thus dispossessed of her own speech: 'In the witch who has been physically broken and reduced to silence, the world of disorder and shadows has been defeated,' says Chaquin (1978).

This taciturnity can be interpreted as the sign of a clash of two cultures. We are certainly dealing here with the struggle between two forms of speech that are each invested with power: popular culture, that of the witch, and the scientific culture that belongs to the judges and, after them, the doctors. The speech of women who escape the established order turns from heretical to hysterical, that of madwomen who must be bound. The incommunicability crystallized by the figure of the witch becomes not only the social Other but also the sexual Other. It is thus no coincidence that the witch and all the resistance that she brings with her have come down to us.

Again, what emerges from the functions attributed to witches is that human passions have a fundamental role in any phenomenon of witchcraft. Village fears and pressures create the witch. Thus, marginal and marginalized, she continues to exist.

THE CONTEMPORANEITY OF WITCHES

What have witches become in our contemporary world? What is left of the myth? Should we see the myth's avatars or remains, or the other forms of its expression, illuminated as different readings or as a simple reappropriation of the symbolic values that it bore? Today the witch and her symbolic universe principally invest three domains of our world: psychoanalysis, feminism and advertising. Is this a corruption or a new anchor point allowing the myth to transcend other times, to nourish future societies?

SYMBOLS AND PSYCHOANALYSIS

Psychoanalysis illuminates the unconscious foundations of the myth of the witch. In *On the Nightmare* (1971) Ernest Jones studies the connections between witches and succubi, incubi, vampires, werewolves and the Devil. He interprets them as the projection of repressed and unconscious sexual material dominated by incestuous desires associated with infantile (sadistic) forms of sexuality. Jones stresses the importance of dream experiences in belief in such persecutors, who share a few broad characteristics such as nocturnal movements, flight and the ability to turn into animals. These specific functions are based on precise attributes which have retained their symbolic value to the present day.

No witch is without a broomstick to take her through the air to the Sabbat: having anointed herself with a mysterious ointment, the witch straddles her broomstick, utters the magic words and flies off. Margaret Murray (1970) tells us that the first mention of a broomstick as a 'means of locomotion' appears in 1453 during a trial. However, the assimilation of woman to broomstick dates from far earlier, for this object symbolizes woman's domestic role. It thus first appears as an ordinary object used by women every day. Its substance and use give it no particular value other than that of belonging to a strictly feminine environment. From this point of view Margaret Murray reminds us that, primitively, the broomstick used for domestic or magic purposes consisted of a stick of broom ending in a tuft of leaves. She says that broom figures in so many proverbs and superstitions that its magical nature is indisputable and broom is indeed associated with the gift and destruction of fertility.

From this point of view, René Alleau in an article entitled 'De la sorcellerie antique au Sabbat médiéval' (1965), puts forward an interpretation which is upstream of the myth, at the time when witches were 'rainmakers'.

> Until recent times widows would be made to sweep the bottom of a dried up lake to the sound of a drum so that heaven, seeing the dust rising above a place that was usually covered in water, would understand its error and put it right with abundant rains.

This originally pagan practice also explains the drift towards believing in the disappearance, the flight of witches, who:

> places at the centre of these whirlwinds, became invisible. They seemed to those watching to merge with the thick clouds and to fly like them on the wings of the wind. When their social role was forgotten the tool of their trade, the broom, became the sign of their magic power.

The broomstick linked to flight and ointments also has a phallic meaning which cannot be sidestepped and which the act of straddling merely confirms. This interpretation of the broomstick appears in pagan rites as the intermediary of fertility between earth (woman) and heaven (rain), but it is also a tool, the symbol of women's access to the expression of sexuality, pleasure and a liberation rendered by the metaphor of flight. This path is analogous to Erica Jong's (1982) idea that for witches the broomstick symbolizes 'the transmutation of the tool of their subjection into a tool of liberation'.

The witch has other allies, notably in the world of the living, who act as her accomplices and intermediaries. Most frequently it is an animal, but sometimes a human being, who becomes her messenger, her signature, the more so since it can appear where the witch cannot go. Margaret Murray (1970) distinguishes between two sorts of familiar: the domestic and the divinatory. The domestic familiar was a small animal that lived with the witch: it might have been a dog, cat, rat, mole or mouse that the witch trained to carry out magical operations and return to her. She kept it in a state of dependency and delegated some of her powers to it by regularly feeding it a few drops of her blood. These animals had names. The divinatory familiar was more impressive. Margaret Murray mentions a horse, stag, crow or wood-pigeon whose role was that of prophetic mediator from whom the witch obtained her predictions. One often finds the snake and the cat in the witch's bestiary. We should also note that the favoured colour for these familiars was black.

The connection between the world of the witch and the animal kingdom relates to the privileged relation she has to Nature and leads us to one of her most spectacular powers: that of metamorphosis.

Insofar as they are demons, witches originated in and are related to the instability of places and powers; in the same way they are able to acquire instability of form. The poet Ronsard, in the hymn 'Les Daimons' (1963 edition), lists the possible changes of shape open to demons with 'skillful bodies', who can change themselves 'into whatever they please': objects, people and particularly 'often they are seen turning into beasts that are cut in half, one having only the head, another only the eyes, another only the arms. And the other has the feet that are all hairy'. Witches have been seen turning into trout, foxes, donkeys, weasels, snakes, owls, wolves, mermaids or flea-ridden nanny-goats.

This power to change shape places witches firmly in a world of wanderings, in the category of the indefinable, linking them to the theme of passage, from one physical state to a new shape and from one place to another. All remains shifting, ungraspable, intangible; the witch escapes all structures, she expresses every ambivalence and that is why she is frightening.

Even when they are sitting by the fire, stirring some mysterious brew, witches once again corrupt the usually reassuring use of a household utensil, which becomes one of their principal magical accessories. The cauldron serves to prepare potions and philtres made of plants like mandragora, monkshood, hemlock and belladonna. Almost all these herbs have a dual function: in a strong dose they are deadly poisons, but used in small quantities they make excellent love potions. The witch did not use the cauldron only in her lair, at the Sabbat the meal for the feast was cooked in it.

Margaret Murray (1970) sees a religious and again pagan origin to this object and the ceremonial surrounding it. She tells us how the preparation was boiled in the presence of the Devil and all the wizards, while prayers and charms were recited. Then, when the operation was finished, the cauldron was upturned and its contents flowed out onto the ground or else the liquid was shared out among the faithful who smeared it on their chosen places. In the times when witches were the priestesses of a cult which was itself at its height, they blessed the harvests with the sacred product as priests do today with holy water.

In a less serene world, the witch and her cauldron were associated with cannibalism and Baba Yaga, the Slav ogress who travels in a flying cauldron and carries off and eats little children, has come down to us. In her article 'Le Maléfice de taciturnité', Chaquin (1978) reveals that witches do not eat raw flesh, they eat it cooked, boiled as long as possible. Being neither carnivores nor drinkers of blood, witches prepare a soup which is easy to drink from the bodies of children that have not been baptised. 'With the solid elements we make an ointment that has the power to help us in our movements and pleasures.'

All culinary symbolism is linked to woman. Through its shape and function the cauldron once again invokes feminine skills. It is equivalent to the African calabash and contains the same symbolic elements. The witches' cauldron, which has become the emblem of a negative womb and of cannibalism, is today seen as a fantasy of transgression. The object assists the expression of taboos and, the more common it is, the more anodyne it seems, the more violent the transgression will be. We must agree with Chaquin (1978) that 'in the Sabbat cauldron it is society and the cosmos which are symbolically destined for dissolution, for liquefaction'.

The analogy between the infernal cook and the devouring mother is easily established and has been analysed by Denise Paulme (1976) in African culture. In the unconscious and in fantasy the witch is the terrible mother who reinforces sexual prohibition. Sigmund Freud (1923) and Melanie Klein link this to an aggravation of the Oedipus complex, which enables us to recall the etymological system of Mater-Matrix-Materia.

In her analysis of the unconsious process of projection and introjection, Klein indicates to what extent the sadism of any infant generates anxiety and enables us to understand how these destructive drives are a threat to the 'ego'. During the earliest months of his existence, she says, newborns direct their sadistic tendencies not only against the mother's breast but also against the inside of their own bodies: they want to empty them, to devour their contents and to destroy them by all the means that sadism offers. Thus babies project their own aggression and turn it against themselves, which makes them frightened of all the fears, all the evils that they had destined for the mother.

Indeed, for psychoanalysis, the witch is a projection of negative feelings that children feel in relation to their mother in the sadistic (oral, urethral and anal) phases of their development:

> The fact that the witch is the old woman who attacks the nipple (of both humans and animals) shows that she incarnates the child's aggression towards the mother's body. This aggression is seen in the light of the law of an eye for an eye, in other words it is turned against the self.

The author of these words, Géza Roheim (1974), mentions a great number of tales of witches taken from European folklore in which the tight correlation between the witch and the breast, milk (sucked) blood, urine, faeces and the phallus clearly appears. If for Roheim the witch is defined as a 'phallic mother', this is because the penis can be assimilated to the breast in the oral phase. Indeed Berglu and Eidelberg note that there is a certain irony in the fact that the mother of the oral phase is imagined not as a mother with a breast but as a mother with a phallus. What Roheim sees in the witch is not just the child's oral aggression, but also the masculine nature of the maternal symbol (recalling the phallic attributes of the witch: broomstick, horn and so on) and the egotism that the child attributes to its mother. This is why, 'if it does not rain, if there is no milk, or in a general way if there is any frustration, the responsibility for it falls on the witches, the mothers'.

But her reality as a bad mother is softened in the tradition of French tales into the mother-in-law who is jealous of the incestuous, hidden or substituted fiancée. And in today's children's literature, the witch is a puppet figure who generates only laughter.

CHILDREN'S LITERATURE: LAUGHING AT FEAR

The witch's passage into literature could not have left her myth intact. This myth was gradually fixed in the structure of the written narrative and was relegated to the level of the magical, of the purest fable. The 'witch' character thus portrayed is stripped of her mystery, her sgguestive power and her reality. Vernant (1980) says:

> From this point of view all that gave speech its impact and its capacity to act on others is now brought down to the rank of 'Muthos', the fabulous, the magical; it seems that discourse could gain reality and intelligibility only by at the same time losing its amusing, moving and dramatic aspects.

Writing about and describing witches (from Perrault's tales to today's children's literature) still means giving them a public audience and a far greater influence than that of the primitive storytelling circle. In order to be understood by a broad and diverse audience of readers, the figure of the witch has had to take on more stable characteristics which can easily be decoded and which are thus reductive.

In becoming a character, taking on a persona (the Latin word for mask), the witch, like actors in the theatre, has to adopt fixed characteristics and set behaviours that the readers can predict. She then becomes a senile and grimacing character with precise attributes that are however devoid of all meaning (broomstick, crook, owl, pointed hat and wart on the nose).

If, as Thierry Maertens (1978) indicates, the wearing of a mask in primitive societies remains an essentially masculine privilege, the witch, the persecuted feminine principle, thus finds a way to reappropriate the Other to herself and to exist behind a fixed grimace, as though this might enable her to see the Other without being recognized.

Thus witches' masks might humorously or aggressively simulate the chinks in history or in the social discourse which brought them into being. According to Maertens, 'the mask springs from the void which separates subject from object', or in one sense the other from the Other. In so doing it thus answers a need for mediation.

So written texts and literary works gradually fix the traits of a caricature, as though the outrageous nature of psychic and physical characteristics could make up for the myth's loss of density. The traits grow sharper in a simplistic and morbid schematization which pictorial representations then reinforce. One example among many is provided Goya's series of etchings, the 'caprices', half of which represent toothless, hideous and diabolical old women.

There is one literary domain in which the disembodiment of the myth of the witch is now established, and that is children's literature. The character of the witch has thus gradually slipped from reality into the realm of the imagination, surviving through the force of the symbols which characterize her. Authors and illustrators of children's colouring books most frequently serve up a stereotyped or bloodless character who is resolutely simplistic. And many witch characters must be combined in an attempt to rediscover the complete form of the primitive myth. This is what François Ruy-Vidal, designer of childrens' books, tried to do in his last tale, *Sorcières!* (1985).

But, in most cases, we are a long way from the traditional witches with their terrifying features as in 'Hansel and Gretel' illustrated by Zwerger in the 1979 Duculot edition of *Grimm's Fairy Tales*. For the complete clothing of the perfect witch included a cape and a belt of puffballs with a purse containing 'charms and amulets'. The witch wore fur-lined catskin gloves and long, pointed shoes on her feet. To complete the portrait we should add the garter 'of green leather, lined with blue silk', one or several silver buckles and a crown, a thin band of silver with a silver crescent moon at the front, in Erica Jong's (1982) description. A few small personal objects completed her adornment: the wand (which takes us back to the fairy), the double-edged dagger, the knife with a white handle, the magic rope that the witch wore around her waist and the chalice or horn to drink from at sacrifices.

Modern witches, like Held's Clapiclote (1978), with moustache and trousers, look quite different. Colin Hawkins' *Witches* (1985) or those of the 'Rue Mouffletard' imagined by Gripari (1980) use humour to lessen the anxiety they could generate. This tradition, which is very much alive in the United States, has been established as a ritual at the feast of Halloween: on the night before All Souls Day, children dress up as witches to receive presents!

We also see the witch, adorned with warts on her nose, one tooth, a hump on her back and a rather stubborn bun, portrayed in a jovial light in Claude Lapointe's mischievous images.

Advances in photoengraving and the imagination of contemporary illustrators have brought a bit of colour and fantasy to the traditional picture. However, in texts themselves the character tends towards uniformity. As if representing the Unnamable, most witches in contemporary stories (Pierre Gripari's *La Sorcière et le Commissaire* 1981) have no names. But in the image of their ancestors (Medea, Circe), they retain the power to change their shape.

So broomsticks turn into vacuum cleaners or alchemists' retorts, while incantations give way to a vernacular language based on sayings and proverbs, backed up by ordinary common sense. This is particularly apparent in *Le Chat de Simulombula* by Jacqueline Held (1978). Very often in contemporary children's stories the character of the witch acts as a counterpoint, an interlocutor for a 'modern' character. Challenges and verbal provocation make witches into characters who are manipulated like puppets, serving as mouthpieces and foils for authors themselves and their fantasies. Thus authors may portray themselves, like 'Monsieur Pierre', who is Gripari himself, in *La Sorcière du placard aux balais* (1980). It may be that the witch in turn has a kind of revenge and exorcizes the underlying misogyny of these tales.

To find the original myth in literature written for children, one has to go beyond the images and probe the text. Thus Robinson in his cave, as Michel Tournier (1971) imagines him, submits to a kind of regression into the maternal womb, a salutary burial from which he is reborn with new strength. This is a pertinent example of the reappropriation of the myth, which contrasts with many works that portray witches to moralistic ends. In the latter case witches become good or have their powers reduced, as in *Le Château des enfants volés* by Maria Gripe (1975) or in *La Délicieuse petite sorcière* by Preussler (1978).

Fear must be laughed at or tamed; such is precisely the aim of this kind of children's literature, and of some films more or less intended for children, like the American television series *Bewitched.*

For older people, the witch remains an exotic and extraordinary renegade. Books of the kidn where 'you are the hero' have unconsciously or naturally rediscovered the function of the mediating witch who, from one paragraph to the next, propels a recalcitrant reader acught up in the role-play along the labyrinthine paths of her imaginary kingdom (for example, *Caverns of the Snow Witch*, Livingstone 1984).

The real witches of the twentieth century do not appear in play, humour and desertion to the other side, for they are still hidden beneath the rags of the traditional witch.

FEMINISM – THE WITCH ON A BANNER

The witch, figure of rebellion, martyred woman and storyteller's character, has carried her smell of sulphur and her drive against authority down to the present day. The new dawn of feminism in the 1970s naturally adopted the witch as a symbol. Who better to symbolize a form of speech, a rebellion and women's bodies freed from masculine tyranny?

Women's desire to write, to speak and to experience their bodies in relation to sexual difference, their demands for social change and political rights and also the somewhat ironic and suspicious way that men looked at these rebellions all tie in with the practices of witches.

Marguerite Duras gives the following words to her Stranger:

> Stranger: A thousand years ago round here, in these forests on the Atlantic coast . . . There were women. [. . .] their husbands were away, almost always fighting the Lord's war, the Crusade, and the women sometimes stayed for months in their shacks, waiting for them alone in the middle of the forest.
>
> And that was how they came to start talking to the trees, to the sea, to the forest creatures . . .
>
> Vera Baxter (*Off. Pause, remembers*): Were they burnt . . . ?
>
> Stranger: That's right, yes (*pause*). One of them was called Vera Baxter.

The journal *Sorcières* (Witches) devoted its issues to themes of feminist struggle which also had universal scope and were vehicles for a mythology of the feminine: 'Blood – Smells', 'Enclosures', 'Food'. In the editorial of the first issue Xavière Gauthier explains:

> Why Witches? Because they dance. They dance in the light of the full moon. Lunar, lunatic women, struck – they say – with periodic madness . . . Because they sing. Can I hear them like that?
>
> Listening to a different form of speech. [. . .]
>
> . . . Because they live. Because they are in direct contact with life and their bodies, with the life of nature, with the life ofother people's bodies . . .
>
> . . . because of their sexual pleasure. We've been taught to believe that women were frigid, prudish and chaste.

The image of the witch is thus given new value, she has rediscovered her matriarchal power, her past as a complete woman and her present as an untamed one. Whether she fascinates and charms men or causes a castrating fear in them, she becomes the banner carried by women's voices.

THE ADVERTISERS' WINK

A few years ago the contemporary imagination, and particularly that aroused by advertising, drew on the myth of the witch. There was a poster that read: 'My Renault 5 is a witch'. The picture showed a Renault 5 apparently flying on a magic broomstick which was suggested, stylized with a single line. It was an amiable poster that played a game of collusion, identifying the car at first glance with a woman who could be described as seductive, young, dynamic and magical, in the sense of capable of anything! On the basis of this reading, it would seem that the advertisers were exploiting a parallelism: my Renault 5 is a witch equals my woman is a witch. Here the car is certainly a woman and her main feature is that she is different from the others, be they cars or women. The image and words are invested with erotic innuendos arising from the sensual and sexual nature of witches. And as we should not forget the real function of the object, which also has to tantalize on the commercial level: travel, transport, speed, performance and new places are suggested by the broomstick that goes further and for longer!

The temporal nature of the poster is also important: its composition, which links the modern object to mythology, connects past to present and by this juxtaposition also assures the present of a promising past.

This advertisement was a success, doubtless because, while remaining consistent in relation to its aim and commercial design, it was able to appeal to reflexes and cultural references in the collective unconscious by unveiling and recalling a mythical element.

In *Mythologies* Roland Barthes (1973) similarly analyses another advertisement for a car which also has an evocative name: the Citroën DS, *déesse* or 'goddess'. This car 'has all the features . . . of one of those objects from another universe which have supplied fuel for the neomania of the eighteenth century and that of our own science-fiction: the *Déesse* is first and foremost a new *Nautilus*'.

Should the object be expanded to fit the myth or the latter reduced to the size and function of the everyday object? Should we regard this fragmented illumination as a reappropriation, a corruption of the myth or, more optimistically, as its simple integration into our time, allowing it to shine a little and to last?

The witch in literary practice perfectly illustrates the avatars of the myth.

Established, made sacred with the rank of a goddess or reviled as a satanic being, she combines all extremes. Gradually she has become disembodied through her entry into literature and has acquired the fixed features of a mask.

It would seem that the collusion of Celtic and western mythology with the jolts of history shattered the myth into tiny pieces and tried to replace it with a Judeo-Christian religious system, which, it was believed, was sufficient unto itself. But certain beliefs and practices were able to slip into the cracks, a fragmented folklore and pieces of mythical material which educated culture refused to allow more complete and adult expression.

Lydia Gaborit
Yveline Guesdon
Myriam Boutrolle-Caporal

Zoroaster

It would seem that for us Zoroaster is a Greek name – ΖΩΡΟΑΣΤΡΗΣ – referring to Zarathustra, a figure of ancient Iran. The earliest references to Zoroaster come down to us from the first Greek historians of Asia. Foremost among them is Xanthus the Lydian, author of the *Lydiaka*, who was writing in the fifth century BC, before Herodotus. It is not surprising that he should have been interested in the legendary founder of Mazdaism. Already, in his time, magi who had emigrated from the East – or Magusians – had lit their pyre in Lydia. Anaïtis, the Persian Artemis, had a temple at Hyjaipa and another at Hierocaesarea, which was supposed to have been founded by Cyrus (Pausanias, *Description of Greece* V. 27. 5; Tacitus, *The Annals of Imperial Rome* III. 62).

In Sardis, Ephesus and Dascylium remains of sanctuaries and Mazdaic cults have been found (Cumont 1929: 135 and 275 n. 29). Iranian penetration thus extended some way into the West of Anatolia, which enabled a Lydian like Xanthus to gather information on the religion of the new masters of Asia.

It was probably he who introduced the name ΖΩΡΟΑΣΤΡΗΣ (Zoroaster) into Greek literature. This transcription is the hellenized form of the Avestan Zarathustra, via a form in Western Iranian, Zarahustra (Bartholomae 1. 93. 264 (8), followed by Williams Jackson (1899: 13, n. 1)). As the second part of the name seems to contain the word 'aster' or star, strange etymologies have been devised, related to the fact that the prophet has been regarded as an astrologer. Sometimes Zoroaster is translated by the word 'star gazer' (Dino, *Histoires* V; Hemodorus, quoted by Diogenes Laertius, *Lives and Opinions of the Eminent Philosophers*, preface 2, P), sometimes he is broken down into 'Zoroaster', 'the pure star' (Clement of Rome, *Homilies* IX. 4f. in vol II. col 244). The form ΖΑΘΡΑVΣΤΗΣ which we find in the work of Diodorus of Sicily (1. 94. 2) recalls the Avestan form of the name of the prophet, Zarathushtra.

In Ancient Iran, Zoroaster was called 'Zarathushtra' or 'Zarathushtra Spitama', 'Spitama Zarathushtra' or simply 'Spitama'. The latter term designates a Median family founded by an ancestor, a hero with the same name as the clan. The origin of the patronym seems to have been the fact that the Avestan 'Spit', meaning 'white being' is the same as the Sanskrit S' Vit and it probably means 'descendant of White'. The origin of the name Zarathushtra is more obscure and disputed. One point does however seem to be agreed: 'Ushtra', the second term of the word, means a camel. But the exact nature of the composite and its real meaning elude analysis. The most frequently advanced interpretation is 'he whose camel is old' ('zar' meaning 'to be old') or 'the old camel' (Williams Jackson 1899: 14 and 147–9). Along with the chronology and toponomy, this uncertainty about the meaning of the name itself is one of the obscure elements in the original, collective and anonymous narrative which founds the myth of Zoroaster.

His biography adds to the uncertainties. Although it is generally accepted that he lived between the second half of the seventh century BC and the middle of the sixth, the dating of his life is often fanciful.

According to Pliny the Elder, who draws on information taken from Aristotle, Eudoxus and Hermippus, Zoroaster lived 6,000 years before Plato's death (*Natural History* VII. 15. XXX. 2. 1). For others such as Diodorus of Sicily, Justinus, Arnobius, Eusebius, Orosius and Suidas, the name Zoroaster was that of one of the Bactrian kings, defeated by King Ninus of the Assyrians (Williams Jackson 1899: 154–7 and 242 onwards). Yet others, representing the eastern tradition based on the Pahlvi book *Bundahishn*, confirmed by Albīrunī and Masudī, consider that Zoroaster lived between 660 and 583 BC.

Tradition has it that Zoroaster converted king Vishtaspa to his religion. This gave rise to another legend which links this ruler with Hystaspes, father of Darius (Ammianus Marcellinus, *Rerum gestarum libri qui supersunt, Histoires res gestae* XXIII. 6. 32–4). This would mean that the prophet lived long enough to be a contemporary of both Semiramis (*c.* 800 BC) and Hystaspes (*c.* 550 BC).

His birthplace is no easier to identify. Was it Media? Bactria? The border between Iraq and Afghanistan? This question has given rise to many disputes (Christensen in Müller, 1933: 212 onwards) and the uncertainty of the Eastern tradition is reflected in Greek literature. The confusion is particularly apparent in the work of Pliny (XXX. 3 and 8), who successively refers to a Persian Zoroaster, the Median Zaratus and a second Zoroaster from Proconnesus, a little earlier than Ostanes. He was most commonly believed to have been Persian: '*Magice orta in Perside a Zoroastre, ut inter auctores convenit*' (Pliny XXX. 3 and 8, after Hermippus). Among these 'authors' we should mention Clement of Alexandria, (*Stromata* I. 15. 69. 6); Origen, (*Contra Celsum* I. 16); the writer of the *Anonymous Prolegomena to Platonic Philosophy* and Porphyry (*De Antro nympharum* 5).

Sometimes he is said to be Median (Pliny; Clement of Alexandria 1. 21. 133. 2) or, reconciling all the possibilities, 'Perso-median' (Suidas, *Antisthenes* I. 159–61) or else he is naturalized Greek (Plato, *Alcibiades* I. 122a). A tradition said to come from Ctesias places him on the throne of Bactria (Arnobius, *Adversus Nationes* 15. 152). One writer portrays him as descended from invaders from a vague 'continent situated beyond the great sea', perhaps a new Atlantis (Plato, *Alcibiades* I. 122a). More serious is the indication given by Hecate of Abdera in the work of Diodorus, according to whom Zathraustes lived in Ariadne, in other words a country near the land of the Bactrians (1. 94. 2). This would then be the location of Airyana – Vaya h (Airan Vej) where, according to Iranian tradition, Zoroaster was born (*Bundahishn* XX. 32).

Nowhere do the Greek and Latin authors mention Zorosater's family, nor do they give his parents' names. For we cannot regard as true the assertion that he was the son of Ormuzd (Plato, *Acibiades*; Agathias, *The Royalty of Justinian* II. 24), or that he descended from the highest sphere of the heavens through the fires of the ether: '*per igneam zonam*' (Hermippus in Arnobius I. 42). However, here we have a very distinct echo of a doctrine characteristic of Mazdaism. Although, in his flesh, Zoroaster was the son of mortals, his mind was of heavenly origins. A lost nask from the *Zend-Avesta* recounted how the Hvareno, which sat in the eternal light near Ahura Mazda, came through the heavens to earth and, uniting with Zarathustra's mother, remained within her from her birth until she was fifteen years old, when she bore the prophet (Williams Jackson 1899: 24). Only a superior and unique man could come from this theogynic combination. Pliny takes up the Mazdaic legend according to which, alone among mortals, Zoroaster laughed the day he was born, thus giving extraordinary proof of his precocity, and he adds a thing unmentioned in the Pahlvi books, that the child's brain palpitated so strongly that it pushed off any hand placed upon it: '*Ut impositam repelleret manum*' (Pliny VII. 72). Eastern 'palmomancy' interpreted this astounding phenomenon as a presage of the Iranian sage's future knowledge. Among the wonders that marked the day of his birth, the Pahlvi books also mention his sonorous laugh which frightened the midwives (*Dînkart*, first half of the ninth century, in West, 1897: 35, 41, 123, 142) and Eastern literature preserved the memory of this (Williams Jackson, 1899: 27. n. 5). Pliny's assertion is thus part of a well-established tradition.

Before Zoroaster began teaching, the Greek writers show him as having a long period of retreat. At the age of seven he is said to have started to observe silence (*Scholiast on The Alcibiades* I, Plato, 121e) and for thirty years he is said to have lived in retreat, abstaining from eating any animal products (Pliny XI. 242). Dio Chrysostomos adds that he withdrew from other people out of love of justice and wisdom and went to a mountain (*Oratio* XXXVI). According to Porphyry he made sacred to the cult a flowery cave in the mountains of Persia, watered by springs, which became the model for Mithraic 'spelaca' (*De Antro nympharum* 5). These are the rare elements provided by the classical authors on the origins of Zoroaster's mission, in which we can see some Mazdaic traits. Herodotus records that the Magi used to sacrifice on the highest peaks (*History* I. 131) and other texts describe sacred caves where they chose to live (Pseudo-John Chrysostom, *Opus imperfectum in Matthaeum*; Synesius of Cyrene, *Patrologia graeca* LV).

If we take the Greco-Roman tradition as a whole, we can see a clear discord with the Mazdaic sources, which do not mention the story of Zoroaster's retreat, in which he adopted the austerities of an anchorite (Williams Jackson 1899: 32). Mazdaism does not preach renunciation. Neither the precepts of its morality nor its conception of its founder are inspired by asceticism: it accords Zoroaster three wives and many descendants (Williams Jackson 1899: 20).

The explanation for this divergence would seem to be provided by a passage from Ammianus Marcellinus. According to him Zoroaster, wanting to penetrate the secrets of India, installed himself in a wooded region where he received visits from the Brahmans who taught him knowledge of the system of the world and the pure rites of religion (XXIII. 6. 32–6). The Greek author, whom the Latin historian follows, claimed thus to establish a relationship between Zoroaster and the Indian clergy. This makes clear the transformation undergone by the figure of the master of the Magi. He became the hero of the legend of Buddha, who left his father's palace at the age of twenty-nine and wandered in the woods for seven years, shunning human society, until the moment that he received enlightenment, which freed him of desire and suffering (Oldenberg 1920: 121 onwards).

It is likely that the Greek writer who brought about the metamorphosis of Zoroaster was a Pythagorean. By making the founder of the Magi's religion into an anchorite given to silence and vegetarianism, he made the sage who was supposed to have instructed Pythagoras the first author of the rules of mutism and abstinence imposed on members of the sect by Pythagoras' disciples. When he left his isolation, the prophet received his revelations from heaven (Plutarch, *Vita Numae* e. 4. 10). The idea that heaven first revealed the divine things of the universe to kings and priests was an idea frequently expressed by the Greeks. Zoroaster was one of the privileged: we are assured that he learned all his wisdom from the Spirit of Good (Plato, *Alcibiades* I. 121e) and that, as king of Bactria, he knew the principles of the world (Justinus, *Historiae Philippicae* I. 7–10).

More tenuous is an indication given by Diodorus, according to which the Spirit of Good gave Zoroaster the laws he then promulgated (I. 94, 2). According to the Mazdaic sources, Zoroaster began to preach at the age of thirty (Williams Jackson 1899: 36); ten years later, he went to the court of king Vistastaspa, proved his divine mission to him by miracles, and thus brought about his conversion. Knowledge of a similar legend in the West is demonstrated in the work of Plato's scholiast (*Alcibiades* 121e) and of Dio Chrysostomos (*Oratio* XXXVI. 40). In the first case Zoroaster is philosophy teacher to king Hystaspe (Vistaspa) and in the second it is he who, having gone through a rain of fire, taught the Magi the true religion. There is a clear similarity of effect here between the fire which pours from the mountain-top, from which the prophet emerges unharmed, and the burning river which, according to Iranian belief, will flow at the end of the world and which the just will cross without feeling the burning suffered by the impious.

Thus the character of Zoroaster becomes polysemous: he is both a mythical being whose historical existence is said to have been millions of years ago, and the founder of a philosophical school in Babylon, Mazdaism, which

Pythagoras is said to have attended (Lévy 1927: 20). After Cyrus' conquest of Babylonia (539 BC), the Mazdaic cult was introduced to Babylon. Relations were necessarily established between the Magi and the 'Chaldeans'. The Babylon conquered by the Persians was the most brilliant scientific centre in the world. It was inevitable that Mazdaism should be strongly affected by the rise of its prestigious science. This was a meeting of two civilizations, two religions, one of which, that of the invaders, was influenced by the other. It is therefore not surprising that Zoroaster was regarded as a Chaldean (Porphyry, *Vita Pythagorae* 12; Lydus, *De mensibus* II. 4) and Babylon as his country of adoption (Lucian, *Menippus Sive Necyomantia* 6), or even that he should have been turned into an Assyrian (Clement of Alexandria). It is sometimes asserted that he drew part of his wisdom 'from the arcana of the Chaldeans' (Ammianus Marcellinus). Others present him as not the disciple of the Chaldeans, but their master and the inventor of astrology (Bidez 1935: 70).

It would not be right to see these different traditions as simply the products of the imagination of ignorant Greeks. It was doubtless the Magi of Mesopotamia and Anatolia who first transformed the reformer of Mazdaism into a 'Chaldean' prophet, revealer of the mysteries of the starry heavens.

The Greeks gave the new name ΖΩΡΟΑΣΤΡΗΣ to the character who had been thus transformed. Next to it, we find the Avestan name Zarathustra, Zaratust in Pahlvi and Zaradust or Zardust in Syriac. The fluidity of vowels in Semitic tongues must also have given the pronunciations Zaradost, Zaradast and Zaradest. The group of the two final consonants was unpronouncable to a Greek tongue so the 't' was dropped and the 'sh' sound of 'Š' became a sibilant 'S'. In the old form of the name, the Iranian ť is preserved and Zaratôst or Zaratǎst becoms Zaratos (Plato's scholiast, *Politeia, The Republic,* 600B; Porphyry; Pliny writes 'Zaratum').

The Babylonian Zaratas had taken on so different a character from that of the real Persian Zoroaster that some ancient authors, such as Pliny, Porphyry and Clement of Alexandria, thought they were two different prophets. Some modern authors have followed them in this and sought thus to explain the contradictory elements of a very muddled tradition (Windischmann 1863: 263 and Bousset's peremptory refutation 1907: 34). Only the historian Agathias, who has given us a long exposé of Persian beliefs, asserts that Zoroaster and Zarades are two names for one and the same person (*The Reign of Justinian* II. 24). We should thus classify as a legend the narrative according to which Pythagoras went to Babylon to discuss philosophy with Zoroaster-Zaratas, since the Babylonian Zaratas never existed. However, the legend proves that the mythical character had entered history in the fourth century BC. Through their contact with the Magusians of Anatolia and Syria, the Greeks had learned of the merits of the sage said to be their founder. It was to this mythical person, the magician and astrologer, and not to the real Mazdaic Zoroaster – Zarathustra – that Greek writings circulating in his name were attributed.

This great moral figure, who had become the master of the Magi and Chaldeans in Mesopotamia, came to the attention of the Jews, who had numerous colonies in that country. They claimed Zoroaster as one of their own. Since they had regarded Abraham as the inventor of astrology (Bouché-Leclerc, *Astrologie grecque* 578, n. 1), the Haggadah portrays him initiating Zoroaster himself into the mysteries of his art (Bin Gorian 1935: 219). More often, however, Zoroaster was introduced into the biblical tradition by assimilation with some character from the Old Testament (Bousset 1907: 369–78 on Nimrod-Zoroaster; 381–2 on Seth-Zoroaster). The combining of Balaam with the Iranian prophet is no less interesting. According to Scripture, this seer and magician was living in Mesopotamia when he was called by the king of Moab to curse the Israelites, but, compelled by the divine will, he blessed them and, in his prayer, uttered words translated by the Vulgate as 'Orietur stella ex Jacob et consurget virga de Israel' ['A star shall come forth out of Jacob, and a sceptre shall rise out of Israel'] *Numbers* 24: 17), in which the Jews were quick to see a messianic prophecy. The very similar predictions of the two Magi about the coming of a Saviour who would establish justice and happiness on earth made it easy to confuse one with the other. The Mazdaic apocalypse strongly influenced Israel's messianism, so that it is probable that the equation of Balaam with Zoroaster predates our own age. But we cannot exclude the possibility that it was devised with the idea of making Zoroaster announce the birth of Jesus (Bidez I, 48–9). When the star appeared the terrified Persians nevertheless recognized that it was the one foretold by Balaam, and their king prepared splendid offerings which he sent in the hands of the Magi, worshippers of fire, who were led by the star to Bethlehem (Wright 1866a: 117 and 1866b: 150).

Zoroaster still had to be turned into a prophet of Christianity and made a precursor of the new faith. This metamorphosis of the founder of Mazdaism was brought about by Matthew's narrative of the Magi (2:1–11) who having 'seen his star in the East', came to worship the divine child in Bethlehem (see 'I Magi a Betlemme e une predizione di Zoroastro', in *Sacra Scriptura Antiquitatibus Orientalius illustrata*, 3, Rome, 1933).

This very favourable conception that the Christian authors had of Zoroaster is contrasted by another, which sees him as an enemy. He was the legislator of a rival religion to Christianity which persecuted the Church under the Sassanids (Theodore of Mopsuestia, *Magic in Persia*, Photius, *Biblioteca*, cod. 81: 63).

Now he becomes the creator of magic, said to know all the mysteries of sorcery. To his knowledge of the diabolic arts he adds that of astrology, the science of lies. A malevolent magician and fake seer, such is the image of Zoroaster bequeathed to the Middle Ages by Christian antiquity. It was to be passed down from book to book to the eighteenth century.

Although the eighteenth century echoed this rich and contradictory tradition it had inherited, it set about rectifying it while making it serve its own ends. Three expositions of the Zoroastrian religion, by Herbelot (*Bibliothèque orientale ou Dictionnaire universel*... 1697), Hyde (*Historia religionis Veterum Persarum* 1700) and Chardin (*Voyages en Perse et autres lieux de l'Orient* 1711), summed up knowledge at the dawn of the century. For the traveller and founder of oriental studies in France, Zoroaster, 'founder of the sect of Magi', was an 'impostor'; according to the Oxford scholar, he was a true 'prophet', author of the 'Zendavastan', or *Zend Avesta*. These two images of the Zoroastrian religion and its creator circulated among the 'scholars' for more than half a century. Everything about them still contributed to discrediting Zoroastrianism as a religion and lowering Zoroaster in relation to Jesus. But arguments and explanatory essays of an historical, a geographical, climatic, sociological or political nature came to replace anathema and insult. The article on 'Zoroastre' in Bayle's *Dictionnaire historique et critique* provides remarkable proof of this. More clearly, Beausobre maintains that the intentions of this 'so famous impostor' were not so bad 'since he banished simulacra and brought the Peoples of Idolatry back to the worship of a single God and made it his task to regulate customs' (*Histoire critique de Manichée et du manichéisme*, Amsterdam, 1734, I, 1, 6: 316).

In closely examining Zoroastrian thought, Beausobre not only rehabilitates Zoroaster, he also helps define the image of the real 'Legislator' and 'Philosopher' of the Persians which had been outlined in Hyde's work. The philosophers of the Enlightenment recognized this 'Magus' as a defender of their own ideas: through his doctrine, he represented the most ancient response to the problem of Evil and the purity of his morality makes him one of the pillars of civilization. This being so, the myth of Zoroaster gained a new dimension. The philosophers' attitude in relation to the *Zend Avesta*, published by Anquetil-Duperron in 1771, was motivated by the assertion that all founders of religions bear within themselves an element of essential truth (Votaire, 'Essai sur les moeurs et l'esprit des nations', 1756, *Oeuvres complètes*, XIX, 521; 'Le Philosophe ignorant', 1766, XXVI, 86; 'Les Guèbres', 1769, VI, 481; 'Questions sur l'Encyclopédie', 1771, article on 'Zoroastre', XX, 616–9). Zoroaster was now seen less as a 'Magus' than as a 'Sage'. That was how he appeared in novels (Ramsay's *Les Voyages de Cyrus; Zoroastre, histoire traduite du chaldéen* by the chevalier de Mehegan, 1751); in opera libretti – after the Zoroaster of Scarlatti and Le Brun, those of Rameau (1749) and Mozart (1791), which lays more stress on Sarastro's role as the guardian of Enlightenment and Freedom. Goethe's libretto, called *Sarastro* (1794), remained unfinished; in philosophical and poetical writings: Rousseau shows 'the great Zerdust [who] saw thc infancy of the world' proving the dignity and force of human beings in the face of darkness (*Lettre à Christophe de Beaumont*, 1763); Sylvain Bailly makes him the earthly representative of a 'God who rewards virtue' (*Lettres sur l'origine des sciences et sur celles des peuples de l'Asie adressées à M. de Voltaire*, 1777); Florian saw him as the author of the *Zend Avesta* which was to be 'the rule of nations' (*Numa Pompilius, second roi de Rome*, 1786); Pastoret sees him as an exceptional person guided in all things by a God (*Zoroastre, Confucius et Mahomet comparés comme sectaires, législateurs et moralistes; avec le tableau de leurs dogmes, de leurs lois et de leur morale*, 1787). Thus Zoroaster appears as one of the sages who mark the history of humankind. He was a philosopher who knew all the sciences. As a lawgiver, 'according to the Zend books [he was] in contact with the Supreme Being and thus master of good and evil' (Anquetil-Duperron, *Le Zend-Avesta . . . suivi de la vie de Zoroaster*, 1771). As a prophet he was called to serve as an intermediary between God and human beings.

We find these images of Zoroaster – whose brilliance tended to attenuate the divinity of the Christian religion – once more in the early nineteenth century, collected by François Noël (*Dictionnaire de la fable ou mythologie grecque* 1810, 'Zoroastre' entry). This author draws on Delacroix' article, but stresses the gift of prophecy of the man who, 'according to the Gaures . . . will one day be the light of the world'. But the life of 'these great men' is full of 'fables'. For Collin de Plancy he was only 'the first and most ancient of magicians' who, if the cabbalists are to be believed, was 'son of Vesta, Noah's wife' (*Le Dictionnaire infernal*, 'Zoroastre' entry, 1825). This would explain his particular connections with fire. Victor Hugo's manuscript collection called *Feuilles paginées* (B.N., n.a.f., 13425), which draws on de Plancy's work, presents Zoroaster prefiguring one of the 'Magi' of the poem in the *Contemplations* (1855–6). He is one of those who seek both to illuminate the great dark fact of creation and to work towards the transfiguration of the Titan people and the pardon of Satan (Hugo, 1891, Fragments 120, 225, 162 in Journet-Robert (ed.) 1969). Like Prometheus, Orpheus, Manu, Pythagoras, Homer or Buddha, he belongs to the brilliant constellation of those who are subordinate to Jesus Christ but dispel the shadows (*William Shakespeare*, 1862). Nietzsche expands on the myth and, characterizing the world that matters to us (1968a, 616) as a will to power and the eternal recurrence of the same, sets the abolition of the world truth and world appearance at midday, the time of the shortest shadow, so that humankind can be at its zenith: 'Incipit Zarathustra' (1968b). Zarathustra has become more than the romantic Magus, he is the new Messiah, 'he who loves men' (Barrault 1974: 2), he who has come to teach them 'the Superman' through suffering (Barrault 1974: 3). Zarathustra is an image of the 'new philosopher', of Nietzsche himself, whose mission is to inspire human beings with what is already in his eyes their most proper aspiration: the unconditional domination of what is. This is the meaning of the 'Credo' of Richard Strauss' orchestral composition *Also Sprach Zarathustra* (1895), a 'Credo' which does not grant the philosopher the relief he seeks.

Olivier-H. Bonnerot

Further Reading

Aarne, A. and Thompson, S. (1973) *The Type of the Folktale*, Helsinki: Academia Scientiarum Fennica.
Abastado, C. (1979) *Mythes et rituels de l'écriture*, Paris: Complexe.
Adel, K. (1971) *Die Faust-Dichtung in Österreich*, Vienna.
Agel, H. (1985) *Le visage du Christ à l'écran*, Desclée.
Akimoto, K. (ed.) (1958) Fudoki, NKBT 2, Tôkyô: Iwanami Shoten.
Albouy, P. (1969) *Mythes et mythologies dans la littérature français*, Paris: Colin.
Alcock, L. (1973) *Arthur's Britain. History and Archeology, A.D. 367–634*, Baltimore: Penguin Books.
Allen, D. C. (1949) 'The Legend of Noah', *University of Illinois Study in Language and Literature*, vol. 33, University of Illinois Press.
Amandry, Pierre (1950) *La Mantique apollinienne à Delphes*, Paris.
Ambacher, M. (1967) *Cosmologie et philosophie*, Paris: Aubier-Montagne.
Amodido, E. (1930) *Da Euripede a d'Annunzio: Fedra e Hippolito nella tragedia classica et nella moderna*, Milan.
Anderson, G. K. (1965) *The Legend of the Wandering Jew*, Providence: Brown.
d'Anglemont E. (1833) *Nouvelles Légendes françaises*, Paris: Mame-Delaunay.
Anta Ka, A. (1972) *Les Amazoulous*, Paris: Présence Africaine.
Anzieu, D. (1966) 'Oedipe avant le complexe', in *les Temps Modernes*, January.
Aoki, K. (ed.) (1982) *Kojiki*, NST 1, Tôkyô, Iwanami Shoten.
Arenberg, C.-R. (1979) *The double as an initiation rite, a Study of Chamisso, Hoffmann, Poe and Dostoevsky*, Washington.
Arendt, H. (1951) *The Origins of Totalitarianism*, New York: Harcourt & Brace.
Aristotle (1987) *The Poetics of Aristotle*, trans. S. Halliwell, London: Duckworth.
Aron, R. (1964) *Histoire de Dieu. Le Dieu des origines*, Paris: Perrin.
Artaud, A. (1934) *Héliogabale ou l'Anarchiste couronné*, Paris.
Assoun, P.-L. (1983) *Freud et la Femme*, Paris, Calmann-Lévy.
d'Astorg, B. (1963) *Le myth de la Dame à la Licorne*, Paris: Editions du Seuil.
Asturias, M. A. (1965) *Clairvigilia primaveral*, Buenos Aires: Losada.
Auget, R. (1977) *La Légende du Juif Errant*, Paris: Payot.
d'Aulnoy, Mme. (1956) *Les Contes de fées*, Paris: Mercure de France, vol. I, p. 180.
Aymé, Marcel (1967) *Le Minotaure*, Paris: Gallimard.
Ayrton, M. (1968) *The Maze-Maker*, London: Solitaire Books.

Ba, A. H. (1969 and 1974) *Kaïdara, récit iniatique Peul*, Paris: Julliard and Paris: A. Colin.
—— (1974) *Laaytere Koodal ou l'Eclat de la Grande Etoile*, Paris: A. Colin.
Ba, A. H. and Dieterlen, G. (1961) 'Koumen, texte initiatique des pasteurs peuls', *Cahiers de l'Homme*, Paris: Mouton.
—— (1961) *Koumen*, Paris-The Hague: Mouton.
Bachelard, G. (1942) *L'Eau et les rêves*, Paris: Corti.
Bachelard, G. (1942) *L'Eau et les rêves: Essai sur l'imagination de la matière*, Paris: José Corti.
—— (1948) *La Terre et les rêveries du repos*, Paris: Corti.

—— (1988) *Air and Dreams: an essay on the imagination of movement*, E. R. Farrell and C. F. Farrell trans., Dallas: Dallas Institute of Humanities and Culture.
Backès, J.-L. (1983) *Fragments pour un Perceval*, Paris, les 4 Fils.
—— (1984) *Le Mythe d'Hélène*, Clermont-Ferrand: Adosa (Bibliothèque de littérature générale et comparée).
Badian, S. (1961–1972) *La Mort de Chaka*, Paris: Présence Africaine.
Bailly, J. S. (1777) *Lettres sur l'origine des sciences et sur celle des peuples de l'Asie adressées à M. de Voltaire*, London: M. Elmesly and Paris: Les Frères Debure.
—— (1779) *Lettres sur l'Atlantide de Platon*, Paris.
Bainville, J. (1935) *Les Dictateurs*, Paris: Denoël & Steel.
Bakhtin, M. M. (1984) *Rabelais and his World*, trans. H. Iswolsky, Bloomington, Indiana: Indiana University Press.
Balandier, G. (1965) *La Vie quotidienne au royaume du Kongo du xvi*[e] *au xciii*[e] *siècle*, Paris: Hachette.
Banerji, T. (1975) *Râdhâ au Lotus et autres nouvelles* trans. F. Bhattacharya, Paris: Gallimard, Collection 'Connaissance de l'Orient'.
Barber, R. (1972) *The Figure of Arthur*, London: Longman.
Barberis, P. (1970) 'Napoléon, Structure et signification d'un mythe littéraire' in *Revue d'histoire littéraire de la France*, Sept.-Dec., pp. 1031–58.
Barbier de Meynard, C. A. C. (1861) *Dictionnaire géographique, historique et littéraire de la Perse et des contrées adjacentes*, Paris: Imprimerie Impériale.
Bardon, F. (1963) *Diane de Poitiers et le Mythe de Diane*, Paris: P.U.F.
Barnes, H. E. (1960) *Hippolytus in Drama and Myth*, Nebraska: University of Nebraska Press.
Barruel, Abbé (1797–8) *Memoirs, Illustrating the History of Jacobinism*, trans. R. Clifford, London: T. Burton.
Barthes, R. (1957) *Mythologies*, Paris: Seuil, 'Points'.
—— (1973) *Mythologies*, trans. A. Lavers, London: Granada.
Bastide, R. (1960) 'Mythes et utopies' in *Cahiers internationaux de sociologie* 28.
Bastrusaitis, J. (1967) *Essai sur la légende d'un mythe, la quête d'Isis; introduction à l'égyptomanie*, Paris: Olivier Perrin.
Baudouin, C. (1952) *Le Triomphe du héros*, Paris: Plon.
—— (1972) *Psychanalyse de Victor Hugo*, Paris: A. Colin.
Bayle, P. (1734) *Dictionnaire historique et critique*, Amsterdam: Compagnie des Libraires.
Beauchesne (1983) 'Job et le silence de Dieu', *Concilium*, 189.
Beausobre, I. de (1734) *Histoire critique de Manichée et du Manichéisme*, Amsterdam: J. P. Bernard.
Beck, C. A. (1981) *Waters on the Earth – The Flood in Modern Drama*, Ann Arbor, Michigan: University Microfilms International, 1982.
Béguin, A. (1939) *L'Ame romantique et le Rêve*, Paris: José Corti.
Belbir, N. (ed. and trans.) (1979) *Chants mystiques de Mîrâbâî*, Paris: Les Belles Lettres.
Bellamy, E. (1982) *Looking Backward 2000–1887*, Harmondsworth: Penguin.
Belmond, N. (1973) *Mythes et croyances dans l'Ancienne France*, Paris: Flammarion.
Belmont, N. (1985) 'Orphée dans le miroir du conte merveilleux', *L'Homme* 93, 25: 59–82.
Benesch, K. (1977) *Rätsel der Vergangenheit*, Berlin: Verlagsgruppe Bertelsmann.
Bénichou, P. (1967) 'Hippolyte requis d'amour et calomnié', in *L'écrivain et ses travaux*, Paris: José Corti, 237–323.
Benveniste, E. (1960) 'Le Dieu Ohrmazd et le démon Albasti' in *Journal asaitique*, 248.
Berg, A. (1964) *Lulu: Oper nach Frank Wedekind Tragödien Erdgeist und Büchse der Pandora*, Vienna: Universal Edition.

Bergerac, C. de (1923) *Voyages to the Moon and the Sun*, trans. R. Aldington, London: Routledge.
Berveiller, M. (1961) *Eternel Don Juan*, Paris: Hachette.
Beugnot, B. (1985) 'La figure de Mécénas' in *L'Age d'or du mécénat 1598–1661*, pub. by CNRS, Paris, pp. 285–93.
Beutler, E. (1942) 'Der König in Thule und die Dichtungen von der Loreley' in *Essays um Goethe* Sammlung Dietrich, vol. 101.
Bévotte, G. G. de (1906–11) *La Légende de Don Juan*, Paris: Hachette.
Bianquis, G. (1935; new edn 1955) *Faust à travers quatre siècles*, Paris.
Biardeau, M. (1981) *L'Hindouisme. Anthropologie d'une civilisation*, Paris: Flammarion, Collections 'Champs'.
Bickel, E. (1921) 'Gyges und sein Ring. Zum Begriff Novelle und zu Hebbels tragischer Kunst' in *Neue Jahrbücher für das Klassische Altertum*, Leipzig.
Bidez, J. and Cumont, F. (1938) *Les Mages hellenisés: Zoroastre, Ostanes et Hystaspe d'après la tradition grecque*, Paris: Geuthner.
Biès, J. (1979) 'Chamanisme et littérature' in *L'Herne* 33: 330.
Bilen, M. (1977) *Ecriture et initiation*, Paris: Honoré Champion.
Birkhan, H. (1976) 'Laborintus – labor intus. Zum Symbolvert des Labyrinths im Mittelalter', *Festschrift für Richard Pittioni*, Vienna: Archaelogia Austriaca, Beiheft 13.
Bloch, E. (1986) *Natural Law and Human Dignity*, trans. D. J. Schmidt, Cambridge Massachusetts: Massachusetts Insititute of Technology Press.
Bloch, M. (1961) *Les Rois thaumaturges, étude sur le caractère surnaturel attribué à la puissance royale particulièrement en France et en Angleterre*, Paris: A. Colin.
Bloch, O & Wartburg, W. von (1964) *Dictionnaire étymologique de la langue français*, Paris: PUF, p. 442.
Bloch, R. (1980) *Recherches sur les Religions de l'Antiquité classique*, Paris: Droz.
Blotner, J. (1966) *The Modern American Political Novel 1900–1960*, Austin-London: University of Texas Press.
Bochet, M. (1988) *Présence de Job dans le théâtre d'après-guerre II en France*, Berne: Peter Lang.
Bohrer, K. H. (1983) *Mythos und Moderne*, HRSG: Suhrkamp.
Boissier, G. (1879) 'Les Origines du roman grec', in *Revue des deux mondes*, Paris.
Bonaparte, M. (1952) *Psychanalyse et Biologie*, Paris: PUF, p. 124.
Bonardel, F. (1985) *L'Hermétisme*, Paris: P.U.F.
Bonilla y San Martin, A. (1908) *El mito de Psyquis, un cuente de ninos, une tradición simbolica y un estudio sobra el problema fundamental de la filosofia*, Barcelona.
Bonnefoy, Y. (1981) *Dictionnaires des mythologies*, Paris: Flammarion.
Borges, Jorge-Luis (1949) 'La Casa de Asterion' in *El Aleph*, Buenos Aires: Emece Editores (1962). 'La Demeure d'Asterion' in *L'Aleph*, Paris: Gallimard (1967).
Borie, M. (1981) *Mythe et théâtre d'aujourd'hui: une quête impossible?*, Nizet.
de Boron, R. (1980) *Merlin*, Geneva: Droz.
Bouche-Leclercq, A. (1899) *Astrologie grecque*, Paris: E. Leroux.
Bourges, E. (1987) *Le Crépuscule des dieux*, Saint-Cyr-sur-Loire: Christian Pirot.
Bourlet, M. (1983) 'Dionysos, le même et l'autre' in *Nouvelle revue d'ethnopsychiatrie*, Grenoble: La Pensée Sauvage.
Bourricaud, F. (1961) *Esquisse d'une théorie de l'autorité*, Paris: Plon.
Bousquet, J. (1964) *Les thèmes de rêve dans la littérature romantique*, Paris: Didier.
Bousset, W. (1907) *Hauptprobleme der Gnosis*, Göttingen.
Bowman, F. P. (1973) *Le Christ romantique*, Geneva: Droz.
Boyer, R. (1981) *Yggdrasill. La Religion des Anciens Scandinaves*, Paris: Payot.
—— (1986) *Le Mythe viking dans les Letrres français*, Paris: Porteglaive.

Boyer, R. and Lot-Flack, E. (1974) *Les Religions de l'Europe du Nord*, Paris: Fayard.
Bradbury, R. (1954) *Fahrenheit 451*, London: Hart-Davis MacGibbon.
Braun, R. and Richer, J. (1978) *L'Empereur Julien. De l'histoire à la lègende (331–1715)*, Paris: Les Belles Lettres.
Breton, A. (1947) *Arcane 17*, Paris: Sagittaire.
Breuer, J. and Freud, S. (1974) *Studies in Hysteria*, trans. J. and A. Strachey, Harmondsworth: Penguin.
Bricout, B. (1982) 'Les deux chemins du Petit Chaperon Rouge', *Frontières du conte*, Paris: Centre National de la Recherche Scientifique.
Brieger, A. (1934) *Kain und Abel in der deutschen Dichtung*, Berlin.
Brill, J. (1981) *Lilith ou la mère obscure*, Paris: Payot.
Brincourt, A. (1935) *Satan et la Poésie*, Paris: Bernard Grasset.
Brion, M. (1968) *L'Art fantastique*, Marabout université, pp. 178–9.
Brisson, L. (1982) *Platon, les mots et les mythes*, Paris: Maspero.
Broch, H. (1966) 'L'Héritage mythique de la littérature' in *Littérature et connaissance*, Paris: Gallimard.
Brooks-Davies, D. (1983) *The Mercurian Monarch. Magical Politics from Spenser to Pope*, Manchester: Manchester University Press.
Bruhl, A. (1953) *Liber Pater. Origine et expansion du culte dionysiaque à Rome et dans le monde romain*, Paris: de Boccard.
Brun, J. (1976) *Les Vagabonds de l'Occident*, Paris: Desclée.
Brunel, P. (1974) *Le Mythe de la métamorphose*, Paris: A. Colin.
—— (1982) *Théâtre et cruauté ou Dionysos profané*, Paris: Klincksieck.
—— (1983) 'Borges et l'autre' in *L'autoportrait*, Paris: PUF 2.
—— (1986) 'Le Tombeau de Sisyphe' in *Territoires de l'Imaginaire*, Paris: éditions du Seuil.
Burdeau, G. (1977) 'Mythologies du pouvoir', *Projet*, 120, December, 1161–72.
Butler, E. M. (1952) *The Fortunes of Faust*, Cambridge.
Butor, M. (1956) *Passing Time*, S. Stewart trans., New York: Simon and Schuster.
Büchner, G. (1988) *Danton's Death: Leonce and Lena; Woyzeck*, V. Price trans., Oxford: Oxford University Press.

Cabet, E. (1970) 'Voyage en Icarie' in *Oeuvres* 1, Paris: Anthropos.
Caillois, R. (1938) *Le Mythe et l'homme*, Paris: Gallimard.
—— (1951) 'Le pouvoir charismatique: Adolf Hitler comme idole', in *Quatre essais de sociologie contemporaine*, Paris: Perrin.
—— (1960) *Méduse et Cie*, Paris: Gallimard.
—— (1963) *L'Homme et le sacré*, Paris: Gallimard.
Calame-Griaule, G. (1970) 'Pour une étude éthno-linguistique des littératures orales africaines', *Langages* 18: 22–47.
Campanella, T. (1981) *The City of the Sun*, trans. A. M. Elliott and R. Millner, London: Journeyman.
Campbell, J. (1988) *The Hero with A Thousand Faces*, London: Paladin.
Camus, A. (1942) *Le Mythe de Sisyphe*, Paris: Gallimard.
Cartari, V. (1556) 'Giove' in *Imagini degli dei degli antichi*, Venice.
Carter, A. E. (1958) *The Idea of Decadence in French Literature, 1830–1900*, Toronto: Toronto University Press and London: Oxford University Press.
Cassirer, E. (1972) *La Philosophie des formes symboliques Vol II: La Pensée mythique*, Paris: Minuit.
Cendrars, B. (1947 and 1972) *Anthologie nègre*, Paris: Buchet-Chastel and Paris: Livre de Poche.

Cerny, V. (1935) *Essai sur le titanisme dans la poésie occidentale entre 1885 et 1850*, Prague: Orlis.
de Certeau, M. (1970) *La Possession de Loudun*, Paris.
Chalon, L. (1976) *L'histoire et l'épopée castillane du Moyen Age*, Paris: H. Champion.
Champagne, T. de (1925) *Oeuvres Poétiques, (Société des Anciens Textes Français)*.
Chapouthier, M. (1935) *Les Dioscures au service d'une déesse*, Paris: de Boccard.
Chaquin, N. (1978) 'La Sorcière et le pouvoir – Essai sur les composantes imaginaires et juridiques de la figure de la sorcière' and 'Le Maléfice de taciturnité, esquisse d'une étude de mythe de la sorcière' in *Les Cahiers de Fontenay* 9–10.
Chardin, J. (1811) *Voyages en Perse et autres lieux de l'Orient*, Paris: Langlès.
Chatelet, F. (1981) *Les Idéologies*, Verviers: Marabout.
Chatelet, F. and Pisier-Kouchner, E. (1981) *Les Conceptions politiques du XXe siècle*, Paris: Presses Universitaires de France.
Chaunu, P. (1981) *Histoire et décadence*, Paris.
Chaussard (1802) *Héliogabale ou Esquisse morale de la dissolution romaine sous les empereurs*, Paris.
Chenu, B. (1984) *Le Christ noir américain*, Paris: Desclée.
Christensen, A. (1928) 'Etudes sur le zoroastrisme de la Perse antique' in *Kgl. Danske Videnskab Selskab. – Hist. fil. Meddel.* 15:2.
—— (1933) 'Die Iranien' in I. Müller (ed.) *Handbuch* 3, Munich.
Claudel, P. (1946) *Le Livre de Job*, Paris: Plon.
Cohn, N. (1976) *Europe's Inner Demons*, St. Albans: Paladin.
Collin de Plancy (1825) *Dictionnaire infernal*, 4 vols, 2nd edn, Paris.
Conte A. (1984) *Les Dictateurs du XXe siècle*, Paris: Laffont.
Contenauu, G. (1941) *Le Déluge babylonien, Ishtar aux enfers, La Tour de Babel*, Paris: Payot.
Corbin, H. (1961) *Terre céleste et corps de réssurection: de l'Iran mazdéen à l'Iran schîite*, Paris: Buchet-Chastel.
Cornevin, R. and Cornevin, M. (1970) *Histoire de L'Afrique des origines à la seconde guerre mondiale*, Paris: Payot.
Couffignal, R. (1970) *Aux premiers jours du monde, la paraphrase poétique de la Genèse de Hugo à Supervielle*, Minard.
—— (1976) *L'Oeuvre d'Abraham, le récit de la Genèse et sa fortune littéraire*, Publications de l'Université de Toulouse-Le Mirail.
—— (1980) *Le drame de l'Eden, le récit de la Genèse et sa fortune littéraire*, Publications de l'Université de Toulouse-Le Mirail.
Courtet de Lisle, V. (1836) *La Science politique fondée sur la science de l'homme ou Etude des races humaines sous le rapport philosophique, historique et social*, Paris: Arthus Bertrand.
Cumont, F. (1929) *Les Religions orientales dans le paganisme romain*, Paris: Geuthner.
Cyrano de Bergerac, S. (1923) *Voyages to the Sun and Moon*, trans. R. Aldington, London: Routledge.

Dabezies, A. (1967) *Visages de Faust au XXe siècle. Littérature, idéologie et mythe*, Paris.
—— (1972) *Le mythe de Faust*, Paris.
—— (ed.) (1987) *Visages de Jésus-Christ dans la littérature français*, texts dating from the Middle Ages to the twentieth century, 2 vols, Paris: Desclée.
Daffner, H. (1912) *Salome, ihre Gestalt in Geschichte und Kunst*, Munich: H. Schmidt.
Dammann, E. (1964–78) *Les Religions de l'Afrique*, Paris: Payot.
Dardel, E. (1954) 'Le Mythique' in *Diogène* 7.
Darmon, P. (1981) *Mythologie de la Femme dans l'Ancienne France*, Paris: éditions du Seuil.

Dauzat, A. (1946) *La Toponymie français*, Paris: Payot, p. 68.
Davidson, H. R. E. (1964) *Gods and Myths of Northern Europe*, Harmondsworth: Penguin.
De Vries, A. (1974) *Dictionary of Symbols and Imagery*, Amsterdam and London: North-Holland Publishing Company.
Decaudin, M. (1967) 'Un Mythe fin de siècle, Salomé' in *Comparative Literature Studies*, IV.
Dédeyan, C. (1954–67) *Le thème de Faust dans la littérature européenne*, 6 vol., Paris.
Defradas, Jean (1954) *Les Thèmes de la Propagande delphique*, Paris.
Delange, J. (1967) *Arts et peuples de l'Afrique noire*, Paris: Gallimard.
Delarue, P. and Tenèze, M. L. (1976) *Le Conte populaire français Vol 1*, Paris: G.P. Maisonneuve et Larose.
—— (1977) *Le Conte populaire français Vol II*, Paris: Maisonneuve et Larose.
Delcourt, Marie (1955; 2nd ed, 1981) *L'Oracle de Delphes*, Paris.
Deleury, G. (1985) 'L'Inde en fête' and 'Rites et Mythes de l'Inde' in *Mythes et Croyances du monde entier*, vol. IV, *Les Mondes asiatiques*, pp. 72–102 and pp. 103–40, Paris: Lidis-Brépol.
Deleuze, G. (1983) *Nietzsche and Philosophy*, trans. H. Tomlinson, London: Athlone.
Delmas, C. (1985) 'Andromède et les Monstres', *Cahiers de littérature du XVIIe siècle*, Toulouse, 167–73.
Demerson, G. (1972) *La Mythologie classique dans l'Oeuvre lyrique de la Pléiade*, Geneva.
Demichel, F. and Demichel, A. (1973) *Les Dictatures européennes*, Paris: Presses Universitaires de France.
Derche, R. (1962) *Quatres mythes poétiques*, Paris: S.E.D.E.S.
Deschamps, H. (1970) *Histoire générale de l'Afrique noire*, Paris: Presses Universitaires de France.
Détienne, M. (1977) *The Gardens of Adonis: Spices in Greek Mythology*, trans. J. Lloyd, Hassocks: Harvester.
—— (1979) *Dionysus slain*, trans. M. Muellner and C. Muellner, Baltimore: John Hopkins University Press.
—— (1989) *Dionysus at Large*, trans. A. Goldhammer, Cambridge Massachussetts: Harvard University Press.
Devereux, G. (1970) 'Les pulsions cannibaliques des parents' in *Essais d'ethno-psychiatrie généale*, Gallimard, Ch. 5, pp. 143–61.
—— (1982) *Femme et Mythe*, Paris: Flammarion.
Dramani-Issifou, Z. (1982) *L'Afrique noire dans les relations internationales au XVIe siècle*, Khartala.
Diény, J.-P. (1987) *Le Symbolisme du dragon dans la Chine antique*, Paris: Bibliothèque de l'Insititut des Hautes Etudes Chinoises, Vol. XXVII.
Diet, E. (1972) *Nietzsche et les métamorphoses du divin*, Paris: Cerf.
Dieterlen, G. (1955) 'Mythe et organisation sociale au Soudan français', *Journal de la Société des Africanistes*, 25: 39–76.
Dietrich, B. C. (1974) *The Origins of Greek Religion*, Berlin and New York: De Gruyter.
Dilthey, W. (1946) *Théorie des conceptions du monde*, Paris: Presses Universitaires de France.
Dodds, E. R. (1951) *The Greeks and the Irrational*, Berkeley: University of California Press.
Donneau de Visé, Jean (1672) *Le Mariage de Bacchus et d'Ariane*, Paris: Le Monnier.
Donnelly, I. (1882) *Atlantis, the Antediluvial World*, New York.
Dontenville, H. (1948) *La Mythologie française*, Paris: Payot.
Doyon, R.-L. (1943) *Le Christ aux romans, bibliographie anecdotique*, La connaissance.

Dronke, P. (1974) *Fabula Exploratio into the Uses of Myth in Medieval Platonism*, Leiden and Cologne: E. J. Brill.
Duby, G. and Duby, A. (1973) Les Procès de Jeanne d'Arc, Paris: Archives.
Duby, G. and Wallon, A. (1975) *Histoire de la France rurale* 2, Paris: Le Seuil.
Duchemin, J. (1974) *Prométhée. Le mythe et ses origines*, Paris.
Duchemin, J. (1983) (Mélanges), *Visages du Destin dans les Mythologies*. Studies and dissertations. Proceedings of the symposium held in Chantilly on 1st–2nd May 1980. Paris: Les Belles Lettres.
Duchesne-Guillemin, J. (1948) *Zoroastre, étude critique avec une traduction commentée des Gatha*, Paris: Maisonneuve.
—— (1958) *The Western Response to Zoroaster*, Oxford: Oxford University Press.
—— (1962) *La Religion de l'Iran ancien*, Paris: Presses Universitaires de France.
Dugas, C. (1944) 'Le Premier Crime de Médée' in *Revue des Etudes Anciennes*, Vol. XLVI: 5–11.
Dumézil, G. (1944) *Naissance de Rome*, Paris: Gallimard.
—— (1966) *La Religion romaine archaïque*, Paris: Payot.
—— (1968–73) *Mythe et épopéé* Paris: Gallimard.
—— (1970) *Du mythe au roman*, Paris: Presses Universitaires de France.
—— (1977) *Les Dieux souverains des Indo-Européens*, Paris: Gallimard.
—— (1970) *La Nostalge des origines*, Paris: Gallimard.
—— (1975) *Traité d'histoire des religions*, Paris: Payot.
—— (1982) *Apollon sonore et autres essais: vingt cinq esquisses de mythologie*, Paris: Gallimard.
Dundes, A. (1964) 'The Morphology of North American Indian Folktales', in *Folklore Fellows Communication*, 81:195.
Duquoc, C. (1973) *Jésus, homme libre*, Cerf.
de Duran, Fray D. (1967) *Historia de las Indias de Nueve España e Islas de la Tierra Firme*, Mexico: Porrúa.
Durand, G. (1969) *Les Structures anthropologiques de l'imaginaire*, Paris: Bordas.
—— (1979) *Figures mythiques et visages de l'oeuvre*, Paris: Berg International.
—— (1985) 'Permanence et dérivations dy myth de Mercure' in *Actes del Colloqui International.*
Duverger, M. (1961) *De la Dictature*, Paris: Julliard.
Duviquet, G. (1903) *Héliogobale raconté par les historiens grecs et latins*, Paris.

Eckhardt, A. (1943) *De Sicambria à Sans Souci*, Paris: PUF.
Edelmann, R. (1968) *Ahasverus, The Wandering Jew, origin and background*, Jerusalem: World Union of Jewish Studies.
Ehrenzeller-Favre, R. (1948) *Loreley, Entstehung und Wandlung einer Sage*, dissertation, Zurich: Flensburg.
Ehret, O. (1982) *La Papesse ou la légende de la papesse Jeanne et de sa compagne Bartoléa*, Paris: Limage Théâtre.
Eigeldinger, M. (1973) 'Le myth d'Icare dans la poésie français du XVIe siècle' in *Cahiers de l'Association internationale des Etudes françaises*, Paris: Les Belles Lettres.
Eigeldinger, M. (1983) 'Structures mythiques d'*Arcane XVVII*', *Lumières du mythe*, Paris: Presses Universitaires de France.
Einhorn, J.-W. (1976) *Spiritualis Unicornis. Das Einhorn als Bedeutungsträger in Literatur und kunst des Mittelalters*, Munich: Finck.
Eliade, M. (1940–2) 'La Mandragore et les mythes de la Naissance Miraculeuse', *Zalmoxis*.
—— (1952) *Images et Symboles. Essais sur le symbolisme magico-religieux*, Paris: Gallimard.
—— (1954) *The History of Religion*, Chicago: Chicago University Press.

—— (1955) 'Genèse des littératures' in *Histoire des littératures*, Paris: Gallimard.
—— (1959) 'Les Thèmes initiatiques dans les grandes religions' in *La Nouvelle Revue Français* 75 and 76.
—— (1956) *Forgerons et Alchimistes*, Paris: Flammarion.
—— (1957) *Mythes, rêves et mystères*, Paris: Gallimard.
—— (1958) 'Prestiges du mythe cosmogonique' in *Diogène* 23.
—— (1961) *Images and Symbols*, P. Mairet trans., Kansas City: Sheed Andrews and McMeel.
—— (1963) *Aspects du mythe*, Paris: Gallimard.
—— (1969) 'Paradise and utopia' in *The Quest. History and Meaning in Religion*, Chicago: University of Chicago Press.
—— (1974) *Traité d'histoire des religions.*
—— (1978) *La Nostalgie des origines*, Paris: Gallimard.
—— (1985) *Cahier de l'Herne*, Paris: Livre de Poche.
—— (1965) *Le Sacré et le profane*, Paris: Gallimard, Collection 'Idées'.
—— (1988) *The Myth of the Eternal Return, or, Cosmos and History*, trans. W. R. Trask, London: Routledge.
Ellenstein, J. (1976) *Histoire du phénomène stalinien*, Paris: Grasset.
Enderlé, M. (1980) *Recherches sur la représentation dans l'art de la figure de Judith*, in Papers from the XVIth Conference of the Société Française de Littérature Générale et Comparée, Montpellier: Université Paul Valéry.
Endert, J. von (1865) *Die Prometheussage im Lichte der Offenbarung betrachtet*, Köln.
Endrei, W. (1968) *L'evolution des techniques du filage et du tissage du Moyen Age à la révolution industrielle*, Paris: Mouton & Cie, The Hague.
de Epalza, M. & Guellouz, S. (1983) *Le Cid, personnage historique et littéraire*, Paris: Maisonneuve et Larose.
Esnoul, A. M. (ed.) (1972) *L'hindouisme. Textes et Traditions sacrées*, Paris: Fayard/ Denoël.
Esslin, M. (1980) *The Theatre of the Absurd*, London: Penguin.
Evans-Pritchard, L.-E. (1971) *La femme dans les sociétés primitives et autres assais d'anthropologie sociale*, Paris: P.U.F.

Fabre, D. (1983) 'Myth de la Nouvelle Histoire', *Les Encyclopédies du Savoir Moderne*, Paris: CEPL: 430–7.
Fadipe, N. A. (1970) *The Sociology of the Yoruba*, Ibadan: Ibadan University Press.
Faisant, C. (1978) *L'Empereur Julien, De l'histoire à la légende*, Paris: 'Les Belles Lettres'.
Faivre, A. (1978) 'Les Contes de Grimm, mythe et initiation', *Cahiers de Recherche sur l'imaginaire 10–11*, Paris: Circe.
—— (1986) *Accès de l'Esotérisme occidental*, Paris: Gallimard, 'Bibliothèque des Sciences Humaines' series.
Fasce, S. (1977) *Eros, la figura e il culto*, Universitá di Genova.
Faurie, M.-J. (1966) *Le modernisme hispano-américain et ses sources françaises*, Paris: Centre de recherches de l'Institut d'études hispaniques.
Favret-Saada, J. (1980) *Deadly Words: Witchcraft in the bocage*, trans. C. Cullen, Cambridge: Cambridge University Press.
—— (1971) 'Le Malheur biologique et sa répétition' in *Annales ESC*, 26a, 34: 873–88.
—— (1971) 'Sorcières et lumières' in *Critique*, 27: 351–76.
Faye, J. P. (1982) *Dictionnaire politique portatif en cinq mots*, Paris: Gallimard.
Fernandez-Bravo, N. (1980) 'Figures et anamorphoses dans *Le Golem* de Gustave Meryrink', *Recherches germaniques*, Strasbourg: Université des Sciences Humaines de Strasbourg 10.

Ferrier-Caverivière, N. (1981) *L'Image de Louis XIV dans la littérature français de 1660 à 1715*, Paris: PUF.
—— (1985) *Le Grand Roi à l'aube des Lumières, 1715–1751*, Paris: PUF.
Festugière, A.-J. (1981) *La Révélation d'Hermès Trismégiste*, Paris: Les Belles Lettres.
Fraisse, S. (1974) *Le Mythe d'Antigone*, Paris: A. Colin.
Francis, C. (1967) *Les métamorphoses de Phèdre*, Quebec: Editions du Pélican.
Frank, Hankins H. (1935) *La Race dans la civilisation. Critique de la doctrine nordique*, Paris: Payot.
Fränkel, J. (1910) *Wandlungen des Prometheus*, Bern.
Frappier, J. (1959) 'Variations sur le thème du miroir de B. de Ventadour à M. Scève' in *Cahiers de l'Association internationale des études françaises* 11.
Frappier, J. (1979) *Chrétien de Troyes et le mythe du Graal*, Paris.
Frazer, J. G. (1920) *Les Origines magiques de la royauté*, trans. P. Hyacinthe, Paris: Paul Geuthner.
—— (1966) *The Golden Bough. A Study in Magic and Religion*, New York: Macmillan.
Frenzel, E. (1962) *Stoffe der Weltliteratur*, Stuttgart.
Frenzel, E. (1963) *Motiv des Weltliteratur*, Stuttgart: Kröner.
Freud, S. (1913) 'Das Unheimliche' *Psychologische Schriften Freud-Studienausgabe*, Fischer, vol. IV.
Freud, S. (1923) 'A Seventeenth-Century Demonological Neurosis', in *The Standard Edition of the Complete Psychological Works of Sigmund Freud* 19, trans. J. Strachey, London: Hogarth Press and the Institute of Psycho-Analysis and New York: Basic Books.
Freud, S. (1953–74) *The Standard Edition of the Complete Psychological Works of Sigmund Freud*, trans. J. Strachey, London: Hogarth Press and the Institut of Psycho-Analysis.
Freund, J. (1984) *La Décadence*, Paris.
von Fritz, K. (1962) *Antike und moderne Tragödie*, Berlin: de Gruyter.
Frontisi-Ducroux, F. (1975) *Dédale, mythologie de l'artisan en Grèce ancienne*, Paris: Maspéro.
Frye, N. (1970) 'Varieties of literary utopias', in *The Stubborn Structure. Essays on Criticism and Society*, Ithaca: Cornell University Press.
—— (1971) 'Littérature et mythe' in *Poétique* 8.

Gaer, J. (1961) *The Legend of the Wandering Jew*, New York: New American Library.
Gaignebet, C. (1974) *Le Folklore Obscène des enfants*, Paris: Maisonneuve et Larose.
Gaignebet, C. and Florentin, M. C. (1974) *Le Carnaval*, Paris: Payot.
Gallais, P. (1973) *Perceval et l'initiation*, Paris.
Galton, H. (1869) *Hereditary Genius*, London: Macmillan.
Gamov, G. (1956) *La Création de l'univers*, Paris: Dunod.
Gardair, J.-M. (1972) *Pirandello. Fantasmes et logique du double*, Larousse.
Gatz, B. (1967) *Weltalter Goldene Zeit und Sinnverwandle*, Hildesheim: Spudasmata.
Geninasca, J. (1972) 'Conte populaire et identité du cannibalisme' in *Nouvelle Revue de psychanalyse*, No. 6, Paris: Gallimard.
Gérard, A. (1970) *La Révolution français, mythes et interprétations*, Paris: Flammarion.
Germain, J. (1897) *La chasse ä la licorne et l'Immaculée Conception*, Nancy.
Ghéon, H. (1966) *Oedipe ou le crépuscule des dieux*, Paris: Gallimard.
Gielen, J. J. (1931) *De wanderlande Jood in volkskunde en letterkunde*, Amsterdam.
Gillet, J. (1931) 'Traces of the Wandering Jew in Spain', in *Romantic Review* 22.
Gilroy, J. P. (ed.) (1982) 'The theme of Christ in Francophone Caribbean Literature' in *Francophone Literature in the New World*, University of Denver Press.
Girard, R. (1969) 'Symétrie et dissymétrie dans le mythe d'Oedipe' in *Critique*, 34.

—— (1977) *Violence and the sacred*, trans. P. Gregory, Baltimore: Johns Hopkins University Press.
—— (1977) *Violence and the Sacred*, trans. P. Gregory, Baltimore: Johns Hopkins University Press.
—— (1978) *Des choses cachées depuis la fondation du monde*, Paris: Grasset.
—— (1982) *Le Bouc émissaire*, Paris: Grasset.
—— (1985) *La Route antique des hommes pervers*, Paris: Grasset.
Glasenapp, H. de (1963) *Les Littératures de l'Inde*, Paris: Payot.
Gnoli, G. (1980) *Zoroaster's Time and Homeland. A Study on the Origins of Mazdeism and Related Problems*, Naples: Asmali Istituto Orientale.
Gobineau, A. de (1983) *Essai sur l'inégalité des races humaines* in *Oeuvres* vol.I, Paris, N. R. F., Bibliothèque de la Pléiade.
Goblot, J.-J. (1967) 'Le mythe de Prométhée dans la littérature et la pensée moderne', in *La Pensée*, April: 72–82.
Gould, K. L. (1979) *Claude Simon's Mythic Muse*, Columbia: French Literature Publications.
Gracq, J. (1948) *Au Château d'Argol*, Paris: José Corti.
Graf, A. (1880) *Prometeo nella poesia*, Torino.
Gramsci, A. (1983) *The Modern Prince and Other Writings*, trans. L. Marks, New York: International Publishers.
Grant, M. (1926) *Le Déclin de la grande race*, Paris: Payot.
Grassin, J-M. (ed.) (1979 and 1980) 'Mythe et littérature africaine', *L'Afrique Littéraire et Artistique*: 54–55.
Grassin, J.-M. (1973) 'Le mythe littéraire de Thomas Becket à l'époque moderne' in *Thomas Becket*, papers from the international symposium at Sédières, 19–24 August.
Graziani, F. (1984) 'La Fontaine lecteur de Marino: *Les Amours de Psyché*, oeuvre hybride' in *Revue de Littérature Comparée* No. 4.
Green, A. (1969) '*Iphigénie en Aulide.* L'économie du sacrifice', in *Un Oeil en trop*, Paris: Editions de Minuit.
Greimas, A. J. (1966) 'Eléments pour une interprétation du récit mythique' in *Communications* 8.
Grillet, C. (1935) *Le Diable dans la littérature au XIX*[e] *siècle*, Lyons, Paris: Emmanuel Vitte.
Grimal, P. (1951) 'Orcus' in *Dictionnaire de la mythologie grecque et romaine*, Paris: PUF, p. 329.
—— (1963) *Mythologies de la Méditerranée au Gange*, Paris: Larousse.
—— (1963) *Mythologies des steppes, des forêts et des îles*, Paris: Larousse.
—— (1969) *Dictionnaire de la mythologie grecque et romaine*, Paris: Les Belles Lettres.
—— (1978) *Le Lyrisme à Rome*, Paris: Presses Universitaires de France.
—— (1986) *Dictionnaire de la mythologie*, Paris: Presses Universitaires de France.
Gripari, P. (1978) *Pirlipipi, deux sirops, une sorcière*, Paris: Grasset.
—— (1980) *La Sorcière de la rue Mouffetard et autres contes de la rue Broca*, Paris: Gallimard.
—— (1981) *La Sorcière et le Commissaire*, Paris: Grasset.
Gripe, M. (1975) *Le Château des enfants volés*, Paris: Amitié.
Gross, T. (1971) *The Heroic Ideal in American Literature*, London: Macmillan.
Guarini, G.-B. (1971) *Il Pastor Fido* in *Opere* ed. M. Guglielminetti, Torino: UTET.
Guillet, J. (1963) *Jésus-Christ hier et aujord'hui*, Paris: Desclée.
Guillou, E. (1965) *Versailles, le palais du soleil*, Paris: Plon.
Guittard, C. (1976) *Recherches sur la nature de Saturne des origines à la réforme de 217 avant Jésus-Christ*, Paris.
Gusdorf, G. (1953) *Mythe et métaphysique*, Paris: Flammarion.

Gutschmid, A. von (1894) *Kleine Schriften*, vol. V, Leipzig: Trubner.
Güterbock, H.-G. (1946) *Kumarbi Mythem vom Churristischen Kronos*, New York.

Hansen, C. (1970) *Witchcraft at Salem*, London: Hutchinson.
Harris, R. (1906) *The Cult of the Heavenly Twins*, Cambridge: Cambridge University Press.
Hatherly, A. (1980) 'Laberintos Portugueses dos seculos XVII XVIII', *Colloquio Artes*, 45, June.
Haubrichs, W. (1980) 'Error inextricabilis, Form und Funktion der Labyrinthabbildung in Mittelalterlichen Hanschriften', *Text und Bild*, Wiesbaden: Dr. Ludwig Reichert Verlag.
Hausen, A. (1972) *Hiob in der französischen Literatur*, Berne: Herbert Lang.
Hautecoeur, L. (1953) *Louis XIV roi-soleil*, Paris.
—— (1954) *Mystique et architecture, symbolisme du cercle et de la coupole*, Paris: Picard.
Hawkins, C. (1985) *Witches*, London: Armada.
Heidegger, M. (1959) *An Introduction to Metaphysics*, trans. R. Manheim, New Haven: Yale University Press.
Held, J. (1978) *Le Chat de Simulombula*, Paris: Gallimard.
Hellens, F. (1951) *Mélusine ou la robe de saphir*, Paris: Gallimard.
Hennequin, J. (1977) *Henri IV dans ses oraisons funèbres ou la naissance d'une légende*, Klincksieck.
Henning, H. (1966–76) *Faust-Bibliographie*, 5 vols, Berlin.
Heusch, L. de (1966) 'Vers une mytho-logique?' in *Critique*: 219–20.
—— (1977) 'Mythologie et littérature' in *L'Homme* 17: 2–3.
Himelfarb, H. (1985) 'Versailles en notre temps' in *Destins et enjeux du XVIIe siècle*, Paris: PUF, pp. 139–51.
Hoffmann, E. T. A. (1961) *Die Elixiere des Teufels*, Munich: Winkler.
Hollander, J. (1981) *The figura of Echo: a mode of allusion in Milton and after*, Berkeley: University of California Press.
Hook, S. (1943) *The Hero in History*, New York.
Hooke, S. H. (1963) *Middle Eastern Mythology*, Harmondsworth: Penguin.
Huang, G. W., Tang, R. and Tung, J. (1977) 'Chinese Mythology': A Bibliography', *Chinese Librarians' Association Newsletter*, III, 4 December.
Hubaux, J. and Leroy, M. (1939) *Le Mythe du phénix dans les littératures grecque et latine*, Liège and Paris.
Huhn, L.-K. (1961) *The Unicorn who Wanted to be Seen*, New York/London.
Hyde, T. (1700) *History of the Religion of the Ancient Persians*, Oxford: Sheldon.

Imbelloni, J. and Vivante, A. (1942) *Le Livre des Atlantides*, Paris: Payot.
Inaoka, K. (ed.), (1982) *Nihon shinwa hikkei*, Bessatsu Kokubungaku No. 16, Tôkyô: Gakutôsha.
Iqbal, M. (1980) *La Métaphysique en Perse*, Paris: Sindbad.
Itô, S (and Obayashi, T.) (ed.), (1977) *Nihon shinwa kenkyû*, Tôkyô: Gakuseisha, (3 vols).

Jahn, J. (1961) *Muntu: An Outline of the New African Culture*, trans. Marjorie Grene, New York: Grove.
James, E. O. (1960) *Mythes et rites dans le proche-Orient ancien*, Paris: Payot.
Jauss, H.-R. (1978) 'De l'Iphigénie de Racine à celle de Goethe' in *Pour une esthétique de la réception*, Paris: Gallimard.
Jauss, H. R. (1982) *Toward an Aesthetic of Reception*, trans. T. Bahti, Minneapolis: University of Minnesota Press.

Jayadeva (1904) *Le Gîta Govinda*, trans. Gaston Courtillier, Paris: Ernest Leroux.
Jean, G. (1980) *Le Pouvoir des contes*, Paris: Casterman.
Jean, R. (1976) *La Fontaine obscure*, Paris: Le Seuil.
Jeanmaire, H. (1970) *Dionysos, histoire du culte de Bacchus*, Paris: Payot.
Jenkins, E. (1975) *The Myth of King Arthur*, London: Joseph.
Johnston, H. (1966) *A Selection of Hausa Stories*, Oxford: Clarendon Press, p. 53.
Jolles, A. (1930) *Einfache Formen*, Tübingen: Niemeyer.
Joly, A. (1936) 'Le Roi-Soliel, histoire d'une image' in *Revue de l'Histoire de Versailles*, Oct.-Dec.: 213–35.
Jones, E. (1949) *Hamlet and Oedipus*, London: Gollancz.
—— (1971) *On the Nightmare*, New York: Liveright.
Jong, E. (1982) *Witches*, London: Granada.
Joukovsky, F. (1969) Poésie et Mythologie au XVIe siècle. Quelques Mythes de l'Inspiration, Paris.
Jouve, P. J. (1983) *Lulu*, Paris: L'Age d'Homme.
Jullian, P. (1969) *Esthètes et magiciens*, Paris.
Jung, C. G. (1953–71) *Collected Works*, London: Routledge and Kegan Paul.
Jung, M. R. (1971) *Etudes sur le poème allégorique en France au Moyen-Age*, Berne: Franck.

Kahn, L. (1978) *Hermès passe, ou les ambiguïtés de la communication*, Paris: Maspéro.
Kakr, S. (1978) *The Inner World: a Psycho-Analytic Study of Childhood and Society in India*, Oxford: Oxford University Press.
Kanda, H. (1959) *Kojiki no kôzô*, Tôkyô: Meiji Shoin.
Kandinsky, W. (1969) *Du spirituel dans l'art*, Paris: Denoël/Gonthier.
Kappstein, T. (1906) *Ahasver in der Weltpoesie*, Berlin.
Kapschutschenko, L. (1982) *El laberinto en la narrativa hispano americana comtemporánea*, London: Tamesis Books.
Kaufmann, W. A. (1968) *Nietzsche, Philosopher, Psychologist, Antichrist*, New York: Vintage Books.
Kazantzakis, Nikos (1953) 'Mélissa' and 'Thésée' in *Tragédies grecques*, trans. Ch. Guillemeau, Monaco-ville: Editions du Rocher.
Keller, L. (1966) *Piranese et les romantiques français, le mythe des escaliers en spirale*, Paris: José Corti.
Keppler, C.-F. (1972) *The literature of the second self*, Tucson, University of Arizona Press.
Kereniy, K. (1976) *Dionysos, Archetypal Image of Indestructible Life*, trans. R. Manheim, London: Routledge and Kegan Paul.
Kerenyi, K. (1963) *Medea, Vorwort*, Munich: Langen Müller.
Kerenyi, K. (1976) *Hermes Guide of Souls (The Mythologem of the Masculine Source of Life)*, trans. Murray Stein, Zurich: Spring Publications.
Kern, H. (1981) *Labirinti*, Milano: Feltrinelli.
Khemir, N. (1977) *L'Ogresse*, Paris: Maspéro.
Ki-Zerbo, J. (1972) *Histoire de l'Afrique noire*, Paris: Présence Africaine.
Kierkegaard, S. (1987) *Either/or*, trans. H. V. Hong and E. H. Hong, Princeton New Jersey: Princeton University Press.
Killen, A. M. (1925) 'L'évolution de la légende du Juif Errant', in *Revue de Littérature Comparée* 5.
—— (1932) 'La Légende de Lilith et quelques interprétations modernes de cette figure légendaire', in *Revue de Littérature Comparée.*
Kimbembo, D. (1964) *Fétichisme et croyances de l'au-delà les Bakongo du Congo-Brazzaville*, Collège Saint-Pierre Apôtre de Rome.

Klein, M. (1964) *Contributions to Psychoanalysis 1921–45*, New York: McGraw-Hill.
—— (1989) *The Psychoanalysis of Children*, A. Strachey trans., London: Virago.
Klemm, G. (1842–53) *Allgemeine Kulturgeschichte der Menschhheit*, Leipzig.
Klossowski, P. (1969) *Nietzsche et le cercle vicieux*, Paris: Mercure de France.
Knecht, E. (1977) *Le Mythe du Juif Errant*, Grenoble: Presses Universitaires de France.
Kofman, S. (1979) 'Baubo. Perversion théologique et Fétichisme' in *Nietzsche et la scène philosophique* 10/18.
Kofman, S. (1980) *L'Enigme de la femme*, Paris: Galilée.
Kônoshi, T. (1983) *Kojiki no tassei*, Tôkyô: Tôkyô Daigaku Shuppan.
Kôza nihon no shinwa (1976–8) Tôkyô: Yûseidô, (12 vols).
Krappe, A. H. (1930) *Mythologie universelle*, Paris: Payot.
—— (1952) *La Génèse des mythes*, Paris: Payot.
Krauss, W. (1930) 'Da Doppelgängermotiv', in 'Romantik, Studien zum Idealismus', *Germanische Studien*, 99, Berlin.
Kretzulesco, E. (1976) *Les Jardins du Songe* (on the *Dream of Poliphilo*), Rome/Paris.
Kreutz, C. (1963) *Das Prometheussymbol in der Dichtung der englischen Romantik*, Göttingen.
Kurano, K. (1973–80) *Kojiki zenchûshaku*, Tôkyô: Sanseidô, (7 vols).
Kuschel, K.-J. (1978) *Jesus in der deutsch-sprachigen Gegenwarts-Literatur*, Benzinger V.

Lacan, J. (1966) *Ecrits* 1, Paris: Le Seuil.
—— (1971) *Ecrits* 2, Paris: Le Seuil.
—— (1977) *Ecrits: A Selection*, trans. A. Sheridan, London: Tavistock and New York: Norton.
Lacoste, C. (1965) *Traduction des légendes et des contes merveilleux de la grande Kabylie*, Paris: Geuthner, Vol. I., p. 136.
Lacoste, C. (1970) *Le Conte kabyle. Etude ethnologique*, Maspéro, p. 82.
—— (1972) 'Les Hommes sauvages à travers quelques récits maghrébins'; presented at the 1st 'Congrès d'Etudes des cultures méditerranéennes d'influence arabo-berbères', Malta.
de Lacroix, J. F. (1770) *Dictionnaire historique des cultes religieux établis dans le monde depuis son origine jusqu'à présent*, Paris: Vincent.
Lambert, J.-C. (1983) 'Le labyrinthe des labyrinthes' in ed. F. de Ranchin *Labyrinthes*, Paris: Hatier.
de Lancre, P. (1612) *Tableau de l'inconstance des mauvais anges et démons*, Paris.
Lanoë-Villène, G. (1937) *Le Livre des symboles*, Vol. VI, 'Symbolique de voyage de Ulysse', Paris: Librairie Générale, 140, bd. St-Germain.
Lapierre, J. W. (1968) *Essai sur le fondement du pouvoir politique*, Gap: Orphrys.
Laplanche, J. (1969) *Hölderlin et la question du père*, Paris: Presses Universitaires de France.
Lasserre, F. (1946) *La Figure d'Eros dans la poésie grècque*, Lausanne: Imprimeries réunies.
Laude, J. (1964) *Les Arts de l'Afrique noire*, Paris: Gle Fse.
Laurens, G. (1973) 'Salomé et l'Agonie romantique' in *Recherches en Sciences des Textes*, Grenoble: Grenoble University Press.
Laurent, D. (1971) 'La gwerz de Skolan et la légende de Merlin' in *Ethnologie français*, new series, No. 3–4, Paris.
Lawler, J. R. (1978) *René Char, The Myth and the Poem*, Princeton: Princeton University Press.
Le Corsu, F. (1977) *Isis, mythe et mystères*, Paris: Les Belles Lettres.
Le Maître, H. (1946) *Essais sur le mythe de Psyché dans la littérature française, des origines à 1890*, Paris.

Le Rider, P. (1978) *Le Chevalier dans 'le Conte du Graal' de Chrétien de Troyes*, Paris.
Leclerc, A. (1975) *Parole de femme*, Paris: Grasset.
Lee, R. W. (1967) *Ut pictura poesis: the humanistic theory of painting*, New York.
Leenhardt, M. (1979) *Do Komo: person and myth in the Melanesian world*, trans. B. M. Gulati, Chicago: Chicago University Press.
Lemaître, S. (19565) *Textes mystiques d'Orient et d'Occident*, Paris: Plon.
Leon-Portilla, M. (1974) *Los antiguos mexicanos*, Mexico: Fondo de Cultura Económica.
Lepage, F. (1980) *Les Jumeaux*, Paris: Laffont.
Lepagnol, C. (1979) *Biographies du Père Noël*, Paris: Hachette.
Leroi-Gourhan, A. (1943; 1971) *L'Homme et la Matière*, Paris: Albin Michel.
—— (1965) *Le Geste et la Parole*, Paris: Albin Michel.
Leroy-Ladurie, E. (1983) *La Sorcière de Jasmin*, Paris: Le Seuil.
Lestringant, F. (1985) 'Rage, fureur, folie cannibales: le Scythe et le Brésilien' in *La Folie et le Corps*, Presse de l'Ecole Normale Supérieure, p. 80.
Lévêque, J. (1970) *Job et son Dieu*, Gabalda.
—— (presentation) *Cahiers Evangile*, no. 53, Paris: Cerf.
Lévi-Strauss, C. (1964) *Le Cru et le Cuit*, Paris: Plon.
—— (1966) *The Savage Mind*, London: Weidenfeld and Nicholson.
—— (1968) 'Du mythe au roman', in *L'Origine desmanières de table*, Paris: Plon.
—— (1968) *Structural Anthropology*, trans. C. Jacobson and B. G. Schoepf, London: Allen Lane.
Levinas, Emmanuel (1961) *Totalité et Infini*, The Hague.
—— (1982) *L'Au-delä du Verset*, Paris: Minuit.
Leyssère, M. and Valière, M. (1984) *Les jours d'Angles*, France: Editions Christine Bonneton.
Loewenstein, J. (1984) *Responsive Readings: versions of Echo in pastoral, epic and the Johnsonian Masque*, New Haven-London, Yale University Press.
Loomis, R. S. (1956) *Wales and the Arthurian Legend*, Cardiff: University of Wales Press.
Loomis, R. S. ed. (1959) *Arthurian Literature in the Middle Ages. A Collaborative History*, Oxford: Clarendon Press.
Lopez-Pedraza, R. (1st ed., 1977) *Hermes and his Children*, University of Dallas: Spring Publications.
—— (1980) *Hermès et ses enfants dans la psychothérapie*, Paris: Imago.
Loth, J. (1979) *Les Mabinogion. Contes bardiques gallois*, reprinted Paris: Presses d'aujourd'hui.
Lu Xun (1961) *Old Tales Retold*, Peking: Foreign Language Press.
Lulle, R. (1965) *Le Livre des Bêtes*, ed. A. Lllinares, Paris: Klincksieck.
Luxun (1989) *La Véridique Histoire d'A Q*, trans. Michelle Loi, Paris: Le Livre de poche.
Lüthi, M. (1976) *Once Upon a Time. On the Nature of Fairy Tales*, Bloomington: Indiana University Press.

Macchia, G. (1966) *Vita avventure e morte di Don Giovanni*, Bari.
Macé, F. (1976) 'Origine de la mort et voyage dans l'au-delà selon trois séquences mythiques du *Kojiki* at du *Nihonshoki*' in *Cahier d'etudes et de documents sur les religions du Japon*, Paris: E.P.H.E., Section V.
Maertens, J. T. (1978) *Ritologiques* 3, *Le Masque et le miroir*, Paris: Aubier.
Maier, M. (1984) *Chansons intellectuelles sur la résurrection du phénix*, Paris: Bailly.
Maiorana, M. T. (1958) *Rubén, Darío et le mythe du Centaure*, Toulouse: L'Amitié Guérinienne.
Mandrou, R. (1968) *Magistrats et corciers en France au XVII*[e] *siècle*, Paris: Plon.

Maquet, J. (1962) *Afrique: Les Civilisations noires*, Paris: Horizons de France.
Marañon, G. (1957) *Don Juan et le donjuanisme*, Paris: Gallimard.
Marin, L. (1984) *Utopics: Spatial Play*, trans. R. A. Vollrath, Atlantic Highlands, New Jersey: Humanities Press.
Markale, J. (1976) *Le roi Arthur et la société celtique*, Paris: Payot.
Markale, J. (1981) *Merlin l'Enchanteur ou l'éternelle quête magique*, Paris: Editions Retz.
Marot, P. (1958) 'De la réhabilitation à la glorification de Jeanne d'Arc', in *Mémorial du Ve centenaire de la réhabilitation de Jeanne d'Arc*, Paris.
Martin, G. (1979) '*Mío Cid el Bataillador*, vers une lecture sociocritique du *Cantar de mío Cid*' in *Imprévue*, Université de Montpellier III, No. 1–2, pp. 27–91.
—— (1983) 'Les Juges de Castille' in *Imprévue*, Université de Montpellier III, No. 2, pp. 63–97.
Martin, H. M. (1925–6 'Corneille's *Andromède* and Calderón's *Las Fortunas de Perseo'*, *Modern Philogy*, 23: 407–15.
—— (1931) 'The Perseus Myth in Lope and Caldéron, *PMLA*, 46: 450–60.
Martin, T. H. (1841) 'Dissertation sur l'Atlantide' in *Etudes sur le Timée de Platon*, Paris: Vrin.
Marx, J. (1952) *La Légende arthurienne et le Graal*, Paris: Slatkine Reprints.
—— (1965) *Nouvelles recherches sur la littérature arthurienne*, Paris: Klincksieck.
Mathewson, R. (1975) *The Positive Hero in Russian Literarture*, Stanford: Stanford University Press.
Mathière, C. (1985) *Imaginaire et mystique. La dramaturgie de Gustav Meyrink*, Paris: Minard.
Mathieu-Castellani, G. (1981) *Mythes de l'éros baroque*, Paris: Presses Universitaires de France.
Mathieu, R. (1983) *Etude sur la mythologie et l'ethnologie de la Chine ancienne*, Paris: Institut des Hautes Etudes Chinoises.
Matsumae, T. (1970) *Nihon shinwa no keisei*, Tôkyô: Hanawa Shobô.
Matsumoto, N. (1956) *Nihon no shinwa*, Tôkyô: Shibundô.
—— (ed.) (1971) *Ronshû Nihon nunka no kigen 3. Minzokugka 1*, Tôkyô: Heibonsha.
Matsumura, T. (1954–8) *Nihon shinwa no kenkyû*, Tôkyô: Baifûkan, (4 vols).
Matthews, W.-H. (1922) Mazes and Labyrinths, London: Green and Co.
Matthey, H. (1915) *Essai sur le Merveilleux dans la littérature française, depuis 1800*, Paris: Payot.
Maturin, C. R. (1977) *Melmoth the Wanderer: a tale*, Harmondsworth: Penguin.
Maurin, M. (1972) *Henri de Régnier, le labyrinthe et le double*, Montreal: les Presses de l'Université de Montréal.
Mayer, S. (1975) *Der Golem. Die literarische Rezeption eines Stoffes.*
Mbiti, J. (1974) *Religions et philophie africaines*, Yaoundé: Cle.
Migne, J. P. (1844–6) *Patrologie grecque*, Paris: Migne.
Méla, C. (1984) *Le Reine et le Graal*, Paris.
Mélétinski, E. (1970) 'L'Etude structurale et typologique du conte' in V. Propp, *La Morphologie du conte*, Paris: Le Seuil.
Menendez Pidal, R. (1929) *La España del Cid*, Espana: Calpe.
Menozzi, D. (1983) *Les interprétations politiques de Jésus, de l'Ancien Régime à la Révolution*, Paris: Cerf.
Mercier, L. S. (1970) *L'An 2440, rêve s'il en fut jamais*, Bordeaux: Ducros.
Merquior, J. G. (1970) 'Analyse structurale des mythes et analyse des oeuvres d'art', in *Revue d'Esthétique* 3–4.
Metraux, A. (1958) *Le Vaudou haïtien*, Paris: Gallimard.
Métraux, A. (1967) *Religions et magies indiennes d'Amerique du Sud*, Paris: Gallimard.
—— (1964) *Mythology of All Races*, New York: Cooper Square Publishers.

Meyer-Matheis, V. (1974) *Die Vorstellung eines alter ego in Volkserzählungen* (dissertation), Freiburg im Breisgau.
Micha, A. (1976) *De la chanson de geste au roman*, Geneva: Droz.
—— (1980) *Etude sur le 'Merlin' de Robert de Boron*, Geneva: Droz.
Michel-Jones, F. (1978) *Retour aux Dogons*, Paris: Sycomore.
Michelet, J. (1958) *Stanism and Witchcraft*, trans. A. R. Allinson, London: Arco.
Miguet-Ollagnier, M. (1982) *La Mythologie de Marcel Proust*, Paris: Les Belles Lettres.
Milner, M. (1971) *Le Diable dans la littérature française de Cazotte à Baudelaire, 1772–1861*, 2 vols, Paris: José Corti.
Mimoso-Ruiz, D. (1982) *Médée Antique et Moderne, Aspects rituels et socio-politiques d'un Mythe*, Paris: Ophrys.
Minder, R. (1977) 'La Loreley et le bateau à vapeur, métamorphose d'un mythe' in *Revue d'Allemagne*: 619–29.
Mishina, A. (1970) *Nihon shinwa ron*, Tôkyô: Heibonsha.
—— (1972) *Nissen shinwa no kenkyû*, Tôkyô: Heibonsha.
Mofolo, T. (1981) Chaka the Zulu, trans. from Sesutu, London: Heinemann.
Mole, M. (1963a) *Culte, mythe et cosmologie dans l'Iran ancien*, Paris: Presses Universitaires de France.
—— (1963b) *Le Problème zoroastrien et la tradition mazdéenne*, Paris: Presses Universitaires de France.
—— (1967) *La Légende de Zoroastre selon les textes pehlvis*, Paris: Presses Universitaires de France.
Montaigne, M. de (1958) *The Complete Essays of Montaigne*, trans. D. M. Frame, Stanford: Stanford University Press.
More, T. (1965) 'Utopia' in *The Complete Works of Thomas More* 4, New Haven and London: Yale University Press.
Morpurgo, S. (1891) *L'Ebreo errante in Italia*, Florence.
Moyano, D. (1984) *Libro de navios y borrascas*, Gijón: Noega.
Mucchielli, R. (1960) *Le Mythe de la cité idéale*, Paris: Presses Universitaires de France.
Muchembled, R. (1978) *Culture populaire et culture des élites dans la France moderne XVe – XVIIIe*, Paris: Flammarion.
—— (1979) *La Sorcière au village (XVe-XVIIIe siècle*, Paris: Gallimard-Julliard.
Muchembled, R., Dupont-Bouchat, M. S. and Frozhoff, W. (1978) *Prophètes et sorciers dans les Pays-Bas (XVe-XVIIIe siècle)*, Paris: Hachette.
Mullahy, P. (1948) *Oedipus: myth and complex*, New York: Hermitage Press.
Munitz, M. K. (ed.) (1957) *Theories of the Universe*, Glencoe: Free Press.
Murray, M. (1970) *The God of the Witches*, London: Oxford University Press.
Musschoot, A.-M. (1972) *Het Judith-Thema in de nederlandse letterkunde*, Ghent: Koninklijke Academie voor Nederlandse Taal-en Letterkunde.
Müller, H. P. (1978) *Das Hiobproblem*, Darmstadt.
Myoshi, M. (1969) *The divided self*, London: New York University Press.

Naïs, H. (1961) *Les Animaux dans la poésie français de la Renaissance*, Paris: Didier.
Nakanishi, S. (1985) *Kojiki o yomu*, Tôkyô: Kadokawa Shoten, (4 vols).
Ndaw, A. (1983) *La Pensée africaine. Recherches sur les fondements de la pensée négro-africaine*, Dakar-Abidjan: N.E.A.
Nebel, G. (1951) *Weltangst und Götterzorn. Eine Deutung der griechischen Tragödie*, Stuttgart: Ernst Klett.
Neher, A. (1970) 'Du Silence biblique au silence d'Auschwitz' in *L'Exil de la parole*, Paris: Le Seuil.
—— (1979) *Ils ont refait leur âme*, Stock.
Nemo, P. (1978) *Job et l'excès du mal*, Paris: Grasset.

Nenekhaly-Camara, C. (1970) *Amazoulou*, Paris: P. J. Oswald.
Newton, W. (1939) *Le thème de Phèdre et d'Hippolyte dans la littérature française*, Paris: Droz.
Niane, D. T. (1971) *Chaka*, Paris: P. J. Oswald.
Nodot, F. (1698) *Histoire de Mélusine, tirée des chroniques de Poitou, et qui sert d'origine à l'ancienne maison de Lusignan*, Paris.
Noël, F. (1801) *Dictionnaire de la Fable*, Le Normant.
Novarra, A. (1983) *Les Idèes romaines sur le progrès d'après les écrivains de la République*, Paris: Les Belles Lettres.
Nutt, A. (1888) *Studies on the Lwegend of the Holy Grail*, London.

Obayashi, T. (1973) *Nihon shinwa no kigen*, Tôkyô: Kadokawa Shoten.
—— (1973) *Inasaku no shinwa*, Tôkyô: Kôbundô.
—— (1975) *Nihon shinwa no kôzô*, Tôkyô: Kôbundô.
—— (1984) *Higashi ajia no ôkenshinwa*, Tôkyô: Kôbundô.

Palmer, P. M. and More, R. P. (1936; new edn 1966) *The Sources of the Faust Tradition*, New York.
Panofsky, (1967) *Essais d'iconologie*, Paris: Gallimard.
—— (1983) *Idea*, Paris: Gallimard.
Panofsky, D. and Panofsky E. (1956) *Pandora's Box. The changing aspects of a mythical symbol*, London.
Panofsky, E. (1962) *Studies in iconology*, London: Harper.
Paques, V. (1974) *Les Peuples de l'Afrique*, Paris: Bordas.
Paré, A. (1840) 'Discours de la Mumie, des Venins, de la Licorne, de la peste', in *Oeuvres Complètes*, ed. J.-F. Malcaigne, Paris (Geneva: Slatkine Reprints).
Parrinder, E. G. (1942) *West African Religion: a study of the beliefs and practices of the Akans, Ewe, Yoruba, Ibo and kindred peoples*, London: Epworth.
Pasteur, C. (1983) *La Papesse*, Paris: Oliver Orban.
de Pastoret, C. E. (1787) *Zorostre, Confucius et Mahomet comparés comme sectaires, législateurs et moralistes*, Paris: Buisson.
Paulme, D. (1976) *La Mère dévorante – Essai sur la morphologie des contes africains*, Paris: Gallimard.
Pautrat, B. (1971) *Versions du soleil. Figures et système de Nietzsche*, Paris: Le Seuil.
Pautrat, B. (1973) 'Nietzsche médusé', in *Nietzsche aujourd'hui?* Paris: Union Générale d'Edition.
Payen, J.-C. (1964) 'L'art du récit dans le *Merlin*, le *Didot-Perceval* et le *Perlesvaus*' in *Romance Philology*, 17.
Peladan, J. (1895) *Mélusine*, Paris: Ollendorff (Diathèses de décadence).
Pepin, J. (1976) *Mythe et allégorie*, Paris.
Pernoud, R. (1953) *Vie et mort de Jeanne d'Arc*, Paris: Hatchett.
—— (1962) *Jeanne d'Arc par elle-même et par ses témoins*, Editions du Seuil.
—— (1981) *Jeanne d'Arc*, Paris: P.U.F.
Perrault, C. (1697) *Histoires ou contes du temps passé*, Paris: Gallimard.
Perrault, C. (1969) *Perrault's Fairy Tales*, trans. A. E. Johnson, New York: Dover.
Perret, J. (1983) *Daphnis pâtre et héros: perspectives sur un Age d'or*, Paris: R. E. L.
Perrot, J. (1976) *Mythe et littérature*, Paris: Presses Universitaires de France.
Perroud, F. (1935) *Les Mythes hitlériens*, Lyons: Bosc.
Philonenko, M. (introduction and translation) (1968) *Le Testament de Job, Semitica XVIIIe*, Paris: Maisonneuve.

Pierrot, J. (1981) *The Decadent Imagination*, trans. D. Coltman, Chicago: Chicago University Press.
Pococke, E. (1649–50) Specimen historiae Arabum primis et postremis, Oxford.
Poirier, J. (ed) (1968) *Ethnologie générale*, Paris: Gallimard.
Poliakov, L. (1968) *The History of Antisemitism* 3, trans. M. Kochan, London: Routledge and Kegan Paul.
—— (1971) *Le Mythe aryen*, Paris: Calmann-Lévy.
Pommier, J. (1954) 'Histoire littéraire d'un couple tragique' in *Aspects de Racine*, Paris: Nizet.
Potocki, J. (1960) *The Saragossa Manuscript*, trans. E. Abbot, London: Cassell.
Praz, M. (1966) *La Carne, la Morte e il Diavolo nella Letteratura romantica*, Florence: G.-S. Sansoni.
—— (1971) *La Chair, la mort et le Diable; le Romantisme noir*, Paris: Denoël.
Prémont, L. (1964) *Le mythe de Prométhée dans la littérature française contemporaine*, Quebec.
Propp, V. (1968) *The Morphology of the Folktale*, trans. L. Scott, Austin: University of Texas Press.
—— (1983) *Le Racines historiques du conte merveilleux*, Paris: Gallimard.
—— (1984) *Theory and History of Folklore*, trans. A. Y. Martin and R. P. Martin, Manchester: Manchester University Press.
Purdie, E. (1927) *The story of Judith in German and English literature*, Paris: Champion.
Pury, R. de (1958) *Job ou l'homme révolté*, Geneva: Labor et Fides.

Quicherat, J. (1841–9) *Procés de condamnation et de réhabilitation de Jeanne d'Arc* (5 vols.), Paris: Société de l'Histoire de France.

Rabate, M.-R. (1970) 'Les Jeux de l'Achoura dans la vallée du Draa' in *Objets et Monde*, 4: 247.
Raggio, O. (1958) 'The myth of Prometheus. Its survival and metamorphoses up to the Eighteenth century' in *Journal of the Warburg and Courtauld Institutes*, XXI: 44–62.
Rameau, J. P. and de Cahusac, L. (1749) *Zoroastre*, Paris: Delormel et fils.
Ramsay, A. M. (1727) *Les Voyages de Cyrus*, Paris: F. G. Quillau et fils.
Rank, O. (1919) 'Der Doppelgänger' in *Psycho-analytische Beiträge zur Mythenforschung*, Leipzig, Vienna: Internatioler Psychoanalytischer Verlag.
—— (1925) *Der Doppelgänger, Psychoanalytische Studie*, Internationaler Psychoalytischer Verlag.
—— (1959) *The Myth of the Birth of the Hero and Other Writings*, New York: Random House.
—— (1973) *Don Juan et le double* Paris: Payot.
Régeard, P. (1980) *Jésus a tant de visages*, Centurion.
Regnard, A. (1890) *Aryens et Sémites*, Paris: Dentu.
Reinach, S. (1905) *Cultes, mythes et religions*, Paris: Leroux.
—— (1928) 'Sisyphe aux enfers et quelques données' in *Cultes, Mythes et Religions*, Vol. II, Ernest Leroux.
Reinhardt, K. (1948) 'Gyges und sein Ring' in *Von Werken und Formen*, Godesberg: Verlag Helmut Kupper.
Reiss, E. and L., and Taylor, B. (1984) *Arthurian Legend and Literature: An Annotated Bibliography*, Vol. I, *Middle Ages*, Vol. II, *Renaissance to the Present* London: Garland.
Renaud, P. (1983) *Les Trajets du phénix*, Paris: Minard.
Renault, P. (1968) 'La figure de Thésée dans le théâtre du XVIIe siècle' in *Revue des Sciences Humaines*, Part 138, April-June.

—— (1970) 'La figure de Thésée dans le théâtre du XVIIe siècle' in *Zeitschrift für französische Sprache und Literatur*, Band LXXX, Heft 1, February.
—— (1981) 'Le Mythe de Thésée' in *Mythes, Images, Représentations.* Actes du XIVe congrès de la Société française de Littérature générale et comparée Univeristé de Lomoges: Trames.
Renou, L. and Filliozat, J. (1947, 1953) *L'Inde classique. Manuel des études indiennes*, vol. I, Paris: Payot, vol. II, Hanoi: Ecole Française d'Extrême-Orient.
Rezler, A. (1981) *Mythes politiques modernes*, Paris: Presses Universitaires de France.
Ribard, J. (1984) *Le Moyen Age, Littérature et symbolisme*, Paris: Champion.
Richer, J. (1970) *Nerval. Expérience et création*, Paris: Hachette.
—— (1984) *Iconologie et tradition, symboles cosmikques dans l'art chrétien*, Paris: G. Trédaniel.
Ricoeur, P. (1969) *Le Conflit des interprétations*, Paris: Le Seuil.
—— (1969) *The Symbolism of Evil*, trans. E. Buchanan, Boston: Deacon Press.
Robbe-Grillet, A. (1966) *The Erasers*, trans. R. Howard, London: Calder.
Robert, M. (1966) *The Psychoanalytic Revolution: Sigmund Freud's Life and Achievement*, trans. K. Morgan, London: Allen and Unwin.
—— (1977) *Roman des origines et origine du roman*, Paris: Gallimard.
—— (1980) *Origins of the Novel*, trans. S. Rabinovitch, Brighton: Harvester.
Rogers, R. (1970) *A psychoanalytic study of the double in literature*, Detroit: Wayne State University Press.
Rohde, E. (1925) *Psyche: the Cult of Souls and Belief in Immortality among the Greeks*, London: Kegan Paul, Trench, Treubner.
Roheim, G. (1974) *La Panique des dieux*, Paris: Payot.
de Romilly, J. (1970) *La Tragédie grecque*, Paris: Presses Universitaires de France.
Ronzeaud, P. (1982) *L'Utopie hermaphrodite, La Terre Australe connue de Gabriel de Foigny (1676)*, Marseilles: C. M. R.
Roscher, W. H. (1902–9) *Ausfürliches Lexikon der grieschischen und römischen Mythologie*, Vol. III, col. 2220–32.
Rosenfeld, B. (1934) *Die Golemsage und ihre Verwertung in der deutschen Literatur*, Breslau: Verlag Dr. Hans Priebatsch.
Rouart, M. F. (1988) *Le Mythe du Juif Errant dans les littératures européennes du xixe siècle*, Paris: José Corti.
Rougemont, D. de (1956) *L'Amour et l'Occident*, Paris: José Corti.
Rougemont, D. de (1956) *L'Amour et l'Occident*, Paris: U. G. E. 10 × 18 collection.
Rousseau, H. (1961) 'Les métamorphoses de Pandore' in *Revue des Sciences Humaines*, CIII: 323–33.
Rousseau, J. J. (1969) 'Lettre à Christophe de Beaumont' in *Oeuvres Complètes* 4, Paris: Gallimard.
Roux, Goerges (1976) *Delphes, son Oracle et ses Dieux*, Paris.
Rudhart, J. (1971) *Le Thème de l'eau primordiale dans la mythologie grecque, Bern: Francke.*
Rudwin, M. (1931) *The Devil in Legend and Literature*, Chicago and London: Open Court.
Ruy-Vidal, F. (1985) *Sorcières!*, Paris: Berger-Levrault.
Ruyer, R. (1950) *L'Utopie et les utopies*, Paris: Presses Universitaires de France.
Rühle, J. (1969) *Literature and Revolution*, London: Pall Mall Press.

Sabais, H. (1971) *Des Dieux, des Empereurs, des Dictateurs*, Paris: Castermann.
de Sahagun, B. (1975) *Historia general de las cosas de Nueva España*, Mexico: Porrúa.
Saintyves, P. (1923) *Les contes de Perrault*, Paris: Librairie crit., p. 299.
Santarcangeli, P. (1967) *Il libro dei labirinti, storia di un mito e di un simbolo*, Florence: Vallechi Editore.

—— (1974) *Le livre des labyrinthes, histoire d'un mythe et d'un symbole*, Paris: Gallimard.
Sauvage, M. (1953) *Le Cas Don Juan*, Paris: Seuil.
Sauvy, A. (1971) *Mythologies de notre temps*, Paris: Payto.
Schaeffer, G. (1967) *Le Voyage en Orient de Nerval*, Neuchâtel: La Baconnière.
Schmidt, A. (1927) *Das Volksbuch vom Ewigen Juden*, Danzig.
Schmidtbonn, W. (1928) *Der Doppelgänger*, Berlin: Duetsche Buchgemeinschaft.
Schmitt von Mühlenfels, F. (1972) *Pyramus und Thisbe: receptionstypen eines Ovidischen Stoffes in Literatur, Kunst und Musik*, Heidelberg.
Scholem, G. (1977) 'Die Vorstellung vom Golem in ihren tellurischen und magischen Beziehungen' in *Zur Kabbala und ihrer Symbolik*, Zurich: Suhrkamp.
Schrader, L. (1958) *Panurge und Hermes. Zum Urpsrung eines Charakters bei Rabelais*, Romanisches Seminar der Universität Bonn, Bonn (R. F. A.)
Schuhl, P.-M. (1968) *La fabulation platonicienne*, Paris: Vrin.
Schwab, R. (1950) *La Renaissance orientale*, Paris: Payot.
Schwerte, H. (1962) *Faust und das Faustische*, Stuttgart.
Sebeck, T. A. (ed.) (1965) *Myth. A Symposium* Bloomington: Indiana University Press.
Séchan, L. (1877–1919) 'Thésée' in *Dictionnaire des Antiquités*, Paris: Hachette.
—— (1927) 'La Légende de Médée' in *Revue des Etudes grecques*, Vol. XL: 234–310.
—— (1931) 'Le Sacrifice d'Iphigénie' in *Revue des Etudes Grecques:* 368–426.
Séchan, L. and Lévêque, P. (1966) *Les Grandes Divinités de la Grèce*, Paris.
Seche, A. (1924) *Le Dictateur*, Paris: Bossa.
Secundus, R. (1905–7) *Stoffgeschichte der Salome-Dichtungen*, Leipzig: O. Wigand.
Sellier, M. (1974) *L'image du Christ dans les recueils de morceaux choisis de l'enseignement secondaire läque de 1870 à 1914*, thesis, Aix-en-Provence.
Sellier, P. (1964) *Regards sur Jésus-Christ, textes français 1450–1960*, Paris: Cerf.
—— (1970) *Le Mythe de l'héros*, Paris: Bordas.
—— (1977) 'Récits mythiques et productions littéraires' in *Trames, Mythes, Images, Représentations*, Papers from the Conference on General and Comparative Literature, Limoges.
—— (1984) 'Qu'est-ce qu'un mythe littéraire?' in *Littérature*, no. 55, October, pp. 112–26.
Senghor, L. S. (1956) *Theiopiques*, Paris: Seghers.
—— (1964 and 1973) *Poèmes*, Paris: Le Seuil.
Sergent, B. (1986) *Homosexuality in Greek Myth*, trans. A. Goldhammer, Boston: Beacon Press.
Sesboué, B. (1977) *Jésus-Christ à l'image des hommes, brève enquête sur les déformations du visage de Jésus dans l'Eglise et dans la société*, Paris: Desclée.
Seznec, J. (1980) *La Survivance des deiux antiques*, Paris.
Shepard, O. (1930) *Loer of the Unicorn*, Boston.
Shils, Edward (1958) 'The concentration and the dispersion of charisma' in *World Politics*, XI, October: 1–19.
Shirt, D. J. (1980) *The Old French Tristan Poems: a Bibliographical Guide*, London: Grant and Cutler.
Siebers, T. (1983) *The mirror of Medusa*, University of California.
Sikelianos, A. (1986) *Dédale en Crete*, ed. and trans. R. Jaquin, Montpellier: Université Paul Valéry, G. I. T. A.
Simoni-Abbat, M. (1976) *Les Aztèques*, Paris.
Singer, A.-E. (1954) *A Bibliography of the Don Juan Theme. Versions and Criticism*, in *West Virginia University Bulletin*.
Sirk, G. S. (1970) *Myth, its meaning and functions in ancient and other cultures*, Cambridge: Cambridge University Press.
Sironneau, J.-P. (1982) *Sécularisation et Religions politiques*, Paris: Mouton.

Smeed, J. W. (1975) *Faust in Literature*, Oxford.
Smith, K. F. (1902) 'The Tale of Gyges and the King of Lydia' in *American Journal of Philology*, vol. XXIII.
—— (1920) 'The literary tradition of Gyges and Candaules' in *American Journal of Philology*, vol. XLI.
Smith, P. (1973) 'La Nature du mythe', in *Diogène* 82.
Soboul, A. (1988) *Understanding the French Revolution*, New York: International Publishers.
Soeffner, H. G. (1974) *Der geplante Mythos. Untersuchengen zur Struktur und Wirkungsbedingung der Utopie*, Hamburg: Helmut Buske.
Soriano, M. (1968) *Les Contes de Perrault, culture savante et traditions populaires*, Paris: Gallimard.
Sprague de Camp, L. (1954) *Lost Continents, The Atlantis Theme in History, Science and Literature*, New York: Gnome.
Stanley, T. (1690) *Histoire de la philosophie orientale*, Amsterdam.
Starobinski, J. (1961) *L'Oeil vivant*, Paris: Gallimard.
—— (1970) *La Relation critique*, Paris: Gallimard.
Stefos, Anastase (1975) *Apollon dans Pindare*, Athens.
Stegmann, A. (1962) 'Les metamorphoses de Phèdre in *Actes du 1er colloque international racinien*, Uzès: 43–52.
Steiner, G. (1986) *Antigones*, Oxford: Clarendon.
Stocker, A. (1946) *Le double. L'homme á la rencontre de soi-même*, Geneva.
Stone, M. (1978) *When God was a Woman*, New York: Harcourt Brace Jovanovich.
Strade, B. (1894) 'Das Kainzeichen' in *Zeitschrift für A. Test. Wissenschaft*, pp. 250–318.
Suarès, André (1950) *Minos et Pasiphaé*, Paris: La Table Ronde.
Sue, E. (1983) *Le Juif Errant*, Paris: Laffont.
Suite-Huth du Merlin, (1886) ed. G. Paris & J. Ulrich, Paris: Société des anciens textes français.
Suite-Vulgate du Merlin (1908) ed. O. Sommer, *The Vulgate Version of the Arthurian Romances, 2, Lestoire de Merlin*, Washington.
Swart, K. W. (1964) *The Sense of Decadence in Nineteenth-Century France*, The Hague: Martinus Nijhoff.

Tardieu, M. (1974) *Trois mythes gnostiques*, Etudes Augustiniennes.
Tauxier, L. (1937) *Moeurs et coutoumes des Peul*, Paris: Payot.
Tchiedel, H. J. (1969) *Phaedra und Hippolytos. Variationen eines tragischen Konfliktes*, Erlangen.
Tempels, P. (1959–69) *Bantu Philosophy*, Paris: Présence Africaine.
Tenèze, M. L. (1970) 'Du conte merveilleux comme genre', *Arts et Traditions Populaires* 18: 11–65.
Testa, D. (1962) *The Pyramus and Thisbe theme in 16th and 17th Spanish Poetry*, Michigan: University of Michigan.
Theens, K. (ed.) (1967–80) *Faust-Blätter*, nos. 1–38, Stuttgart.
Thomas, L. V. and Luneau, R. (1975) *La Terre africaine et les religions*, Paris: Larousse-Université.
Todorov, T. (1980) *The Poetics of Prose*, trans. R. Howard, Oxford: Blackwell.
Tournier, M. (1970) *Le Roi des Aulnes*, Paris: Gallimard.
—— (1984) *Friday or the Other Island*, trans. N. Denny, Harmondsworth: Penguin.
—— (1989) *Gemini*, trans. A. Carter, London: Mandarin.
—— (1989) *The Wind Spirit: an Autobiography*, trans. A. Goldhammer, London: Collins.
Träger, C. (1961) 'Prometheus-unmittelbare und mittelbare Produktion der Geschichte' in *Festgabe für W. Krauss*, Berlin: 187–225.

Tresch, M. (1909) *Prométhée et sa race: Satan, Caïn et Faust dans la poésie*, Luxemburg.
Trousson, R. (1964) *Le thème de Prométhée dans la littérature européenne*, 2 vols, Geneva.
Trousson, R. (1975) *Voyages aux pays de nulle part. Histoire littéraire de la pensée utopique*, Brussels: Université de Bruxelles.
—— (1981) *Thèmes et mythes, questions de méthode*, Brussels: Université de Bruxelles.
Tulard, J. (1971) *Le Mythe de Napoléon*, Paris: A. Colin.
Tunner, E. (1976) 'L'imagination et le sentiment religieux chez Clemens Brentano', thesis presented at Paris X, 10 April.
Turcan, R. (1961) 'L'Oeuf orphique et les quatre éléments', in *Revue de l'Histoire des Religions* 160: 11–23.
Tuveson, E. L. (1982) *The Avatars of Thrice Great Hermes: An Approach to Romanticism*, Lewisburg: Bucknelle University Press.
Tuzet, Hélène (1987) *Mort et Résurrection d'Adonis*, Paris: José Corti.
Tymms, R. (1949) *Doubles in Literary Psychology*, Cambridge.

U Tam'Si, T. (1977) *Le Zulu*, Paris: Nubia.

Vadé, Y. (1980) 'Merlin dans la littérature moderne: lecture littéraire et lecture anthropologique', in *Lecteurs et lectures*, Université de Nantes (*Textes et Langages*, IV).
—— (1982) 'Orphée et Merlin entre le mythe et la littérature' in *Objets et Mondes, Revue du Musée de l'Homme*, Vol. 22, Paris.
Valadier, P. (1979) *Jésus-Christ ou Dionysus*, Paris: Desclée.
Van Gennep, A. (1977) *The Rites of Passage*, trans. M. B. Vizedom and G. L. Caffee, London: Routledge and Kegan Paul.
—— (1980) *Coutumes et croynces populaires en France*, Paris: Le Chemin Vert.
Van Hasselt, A. (1867) *Les Quatre incarnations du Christ*, Brussels.
Varenne, J. (1975) *Zarathustra et la tradition mazdéenne*, Paris: Le Seuil.
—— (trans.) (1967) *Mythes et Légendes extraits des Brâhamana*, Paris: Gallimard.
—— (ed.) (1967) *Le Veda. Premier livre sacré de l'Inde*, Paris: Editions Planète, Collection 'Trèsors spirituels de l'humanité'.
—— (ed.) (1975) *Célébration de la Grande Déesse (Devî Mâhâtmya)*, Paris: Les Belles Lettres.
Verdier, Y. (1979) *Façons de dire, façons de faire*, Paris: Gallimard.
Vernant, J.-P. (1962) *Les origines de la pensée grecque*, Paris.
—— (1960) 'Le mythe hésiodique des âges; in *Revue d'Histoire des Religions*.
Vernant, J. P. (1980) *Myth and Society in Ancient Greece*, trans. J. Lloyd, Brighton: Harvester.
Vernant, J.-P. (1985) *La mort dans les yeux*, Paris: Hachette.
Vernant, J. P. and Vidal-Naquet, P. (1981) *Tragedy and Myth in Ancient Greece*, trans. J. Lloyd, Brighton: Harvester.
Vidal Naquet, P. (1960) 'Temps des Dieux et Temps des Hommes', in *Revue d'Histoire des Religions*, 157.
—— (1964) 'Athènes et Atlantide' in *Revue des Etudes Grecques* 27: 364–5.
—— (1982) 'Hérodote et l'Atlantide: entre les Grecs et les Juifs. Reflexions sur l'historiographie du siècle des Lumières' in *Quaderni di Storia* 16.
Vierne, S. (1973) *Rite, roman, initiation*, Grenoble: Presses Universitaires de Grenoble.
—— (1972) 'Le Voyage initiatique' in *Romantisme* 4.
—— (1979) 'La littérature sous la lumière des mythes' in *L'Herne* 3: 351.
Villeneuve, R. (1984) *Le Divin Héliogobale*, Paris.
Vivier, R. (1962) *Frères du Ciel. Quelques aventures poétiques d'Icare et Phaéton*, Brussels: la Renaissance du livre.

Voelker, K. (1971) *Künstliche Menschen. Dichtungen und Dokumente über Golems, Homunculi, Androïden und lebende Statuen*, Munich: Hanser.
Von Franz, M. L. (1978) *Interprétation d'un conte, l'Âne d'or*, Paris: La Fontaine de Pierre.
—— (1979) *La Femme dans les contes de fée*, Paris: La Fontaine de Pierre.
de Voragine, I. (1967) *La Légende dorée*, Paris: Garnier-Flammarion.
Vovelle, M. (1985) *La Mentalité révolutionnaire*, Paris: Editions Sociales.
Vries, J. de (1961) *Forschungsgeschichte der Mythologie*, Friburg/München: Karl Albert Verlag.
Vuillemin, A. (1986) *La Figure du dictateur ou le dieu truqué dans les romans français et anglais de 1918 à 1984*, Paris: Université de Paris, Sorbonne.

Wace (1938–40) *Roman de Brut*, ed. I. Arnold, Paris: Société des anciens textes français (2 vols).
Walcot, P. (1966) *Hesoid and the Near East*, Cardiff.
Walzel, O. (1932) *Das Prometheussymbol von Shaftesbury zu Goethe*, Leipzig.
Ward, A. G. ed. (1970) *The Quest for Theseus*, London: Pall Mall Press.
Weber, M. (1959) *Le Savant et le Politique*, Paris: Plon.
Wedekind, F. (1972) *The Lulu Plays and Other Sex Tragedies*, trans. S. Spender, London: Calder and Boyars.
Weil, R. (1959) 'L'Archéologie de Platon' in *Etudes et Commentaires* 32, Paris: Klincksieck.
Wenkauf, M. (1970) 'The God Figure in Dystopian', *Riverside Quarterly*, 4, Fiction: 266–71.
Weinrich, H. (1970) 'Structures narratives du mythe', in *Poétique* 1.
Weinstein, L. (1959) *The Metamorphoses of Don Juan*, Stanford.
Weintraub, S. (1968) *The Last Great Cause. The Intellectuals and the Spanish Civil War*, New York: Weybright & Falley.
Werner, E. T. C. (1961) *A Dictionary of Chinese Mythology*, New York, The Julian Press.
West, E. W. (1897) 'Pahlavi Texts V' in *Sacred Books of the East* 42, Oxford: Oxford University Press.
Westermann, C. (1971) *Genesis. Biblischer Kommentar*, 1: 5–6, Neukirchen.
Wilamowitz-Möllendorf, U. Von (1880) 'Excurse zu Euripides Medeia' in *Hermès*, XV: 481–523.
Wille, W. (1930) *Studien zur Dekadenze in Romanen um die Jahrundertwende*, Greifswald.
William, C. A. S. (1931) *Outlines of Chinese Symbolism*, Peiping: Customs College Press.
Williams Jackson, A. V. (1899) *Zoroaster, the Prophet of Ancient Iran*, New York: Columbia University Press.
Wind, E. (1967) *Pagan Mysteries in the Renaissance*, London: Peregrine Brooks.
Windischmann, F. (1863) *Etudes zoroastriennes*, Berlin: F. Dümmler.

Yates, F. A. (1964) *Giordano Bruno and the Hermetic Tradition*, London: Routledge and Kegan Paul.
Yourcenar, M. (1957; 1983) 'Sur quelques thèmes érotiques et mystiques de la Gita Govinda' in *Cahiers du Sud* 342, September: 218–28.
—— (1971) 'Aspects d'une légende et histoire d'une pièce' in *Théâtre II*, Paris: Gallimard.
—— (1981) *Fires*, trans. D. Katz, Henley-on-Thames: Aidan Ellis.

Zagona, H.-G. (1960) *The Legend of Salome and the Principle of Art for Art's Sake*, Geneva: Droz.
Zahan, D. (1970) *Religion, spiritualité et pensée africaines*, Paris: Payot.
Zazzo, R. (1960) *Les Jumeaux, le couple et la personne*, Paris: Presses Universitaires de France.
—— (1984) *Le Paradoxe des jumeaux*, Paris: Laurence Pernoud Stock.
Zilliacus, E. (1901) *Die Sage von Gyges und Kandaules bei einigen modernen Dichtern*, Helsingfors.
Zimmer, H. (1951) *Mythes et symboles dans l'art et la civilastion de l'Inde*, Paris: Payot.
—— (1972) 'Quatre épisodes du roman de la déesse' in *Le Roi et le Cadavre*, pp. 127–97, Paris: Fayard.
Ziolkowski, T. (1972) *Fictional Transfigurations of Jesus*, Princeton: Princeton University Press.
Zumthor, P. (1943) *Merlin le prophète, un thème de la littérature polémique, de l'historiographie et des romans*, Lausanne: Payot.
—— (1956) 'Merlin dans le *Lancelot-Graal*' in *Les Romans du Graal auz douzième et treizième siècles*, Paris: Ed. du C.N.R.S.
Zumthor, P. (1983) *Introduction à la poésie orale*, Paris: Le Seuil.

Index